Frommer's®
France

Our France

by Darwin Porter & Danforth Prince

STILL IN HIGH SCHOOL, WE LANDED IN PARIS, CHECKED INTO A HOTEL near Place Clichy, and headed at once to the Seine for a stroll. Our first image was of a father peddling a bike along the river, his young son hugging his waist to keep from falling off. Tied on were two long loaves of freshly baked French bread. It was at that moment that we fell in love with France. And it was there in the fading sun of a Parisian afternoon that we decided that the key to unlocking the French heart was through food—and not just bread.

Of course, you must not be faint of heart. In a 17th-century farmhouse near the border with Catalonia, we dined on a platter of *cargolade,* an assortment of pork sausages, fat escargots, lamb kidneys, and blood sausage grilled over an open fire. In the heart of Gascony a local mayor invited us to enjoy a dinner prepared by his wife—a platter of goose hearts. In Auvergne, we dined with the owner of a stone-built B&B on fresh bread and Cantal, the hard, strong cheese she made from a cow she'd milked by hand.

Our journeys over the years reached celestial levels in sheer kilometers. But it was more than cuisine that drew us. France unfolded, from the Basque country beaches to the icy lakes of the Alps. These days, France is undergoing rapid change. But much that is authentically French still waits to be discovered. See it before it disappears.

© Doug Scott/AGE Fotostock

BURGUNDY WINE HARVEST (left) In the heart of France, the former rich and powerful Duchy of Burgundy creates world-renowned wine from grapes harvested here in the celebrated Côte de Beaune district. A nearly unbroken array of vineyards stretches from Dijon to Santenay, with golden red soil providing the planet's most succulent grapes. The typical autumnal baskets depicted have been in use for centuries, harvesting the tender grapes.

MONT ST-MICHEL (above) Often engulfed by the sea and shrouded in mist, Mont St-Michel—one of the greatest attractions in all of France—is totally ignored by the black-faced, long-horned Norman sheep grazing on the salty grass in the foreground. A causeway provides a fragile link to the mainland, leading to this grand abbey that grew out of a modest 8th-century oratory to become the greatest Benedictine monastery of the Middle Ages. The great center of medieval learning reached its lowest point after the French Revolution, when it was turned into a political prison.

First page: top, © Art Kowalsky/Alamy; bottom, © Chris Cheadle/AGE Fotostock

© Andrew McKim/Masterfile

GIVERNY (left) In the little town of Giverny in the Ile de France, the Impressionist painter Claude Monet (1840–1926) discovered an idyllic pink house enveloped by beautiful flower gardens, where he set about to paint for the next 4 decades. When Monet died, he left the house and gardens to his son, Michel, who allowed the gardens to become a jungle overrun with river rats.

LES DEUX MAGOTS (below) Once Les Deux Magots, the most famous cafe on the Left Bank in Paris, announced itself as "the rendezvous of the intellectual elite," its success was assured. In the long ago and far away, you could see Mr. Sartre and Madame Simone de Beauvoir passionately perusing *Le Monde* at a sidewalk table here. In time they vacated their seats to American refugees from the Red States who come to gawk at *faux* painters and not-quite poets, some of whom still quaintly wear berets.

© Bob Krist/eStock Photo

© Doug Scott/AGE Fotostock

MARSEILLE'S OLD HARBOR (above) With its fishing boats in dock and its pastel-hued narrow houses in the background, Marseille's Vieux Port was the "Gateway to the West" in the 1st-century B.C. for most of the trade from the Far East. The fish market here is still the most famous in France, and from its daily catch chefs concoct the city's fabled fish stew, bouillabaisse.

THE FRENCH ALPS (right) The French Alps exist for worldly pleasures, including the greatest skiing at such chic resorts as Megève from mid-December to mid-April. But summer is also a special delight, as shown here. Picture 500km (311 miles) of marked trails across rock-studded hills ablaze with wildflowers such as the green-winged orchid. At every turn along the trail, there are snow-covered and craggy alpine peaks in the background, usually under a cloud cover as thick as buttermilk.

© Art Kowalsky/Alamy

ART & ARCHITECTURE France holds a dazzling display of great art and architecture. The greatest collection of medieval stained glass found anywhere in the world is in the city of Chartres in its **CATHEDRALE DE NOTRE-DAME (top left).** The stained glass, mostly from the 13th century, gave the world a new color—Chartres blue. Hoping to ease the pain of his arthritis in the warm, dry climate of the French Riviera, the great Pierre Auguste Renoir journeyed to Cagnes-sur-Mer where his rustic studio at **MAISON LES COLETTES (lower left)** still appears as it did on the day he died in 1919. The **GALERIE DES GLACES (HALL OF MIRRORS) (top right)** at Versailles was such an outrageous architectural extravagance that cynics later claimed it brought on the French Revolution. In Caen, hometown of William the Conqueror, the monumental **ABBAYE AUX HOMMES (bottom right)** was launched in 1066 and almost completed 20 years later at the time of his death.

© Carl Purcell/Alamy

GRAND CASINO AT MONTE CARLO (left) On the French Riviera, hopefuls still flock to "break the bank at Monte Carlo," in the chic Principality of Monaco. Formally dressed adventurers are seen in one of the Grand Casino's *Salon Privés*—reserved for big spenders—following in the tradition blazed by Russian grand dukes, British lords, and even the fabled actress Sarah Bernhardt, who lost her last 100,000 francs at these tables.

PONT DU GARD (below) In the city of Nîmes, a major crossroads in the ancient world and a once-flourishing Roman colony, you encounter the past at every turn. The Romans considered this bridge, the Pont du Gard, a crowning glory of their architectural legacy. Lying 23km (14 miles) northeast of the city of Nîmes, the three-tiered, 2,000-year-old bridge spans the River Gard and rises 480m (1,574 ft.), the highest bridge ever constructed by the Romans. Roman engineering genius and slave labor led to the moving of mammoth stones, some weighing as much as 6 tons.

© David Buffington/AGE Fotostock

CHATEAU DE CHENONCEAU (above) Catherine de' Medici, wife of Henri II (1519–59), and his lifelong mistress, Diane de Poitiers—the *dames de Chenonceau*—are forever linked to the Loire Valley's romantic pleasure palace, the Château de Chenonceau. With its five-arched *galerie de bal,* like a bridge, spanning the River Cher, the château is reflected in the languid waters, with its pepperpot towers, chimneys, turrets, dormers, and elegant beauty.

THE FRENCH RIVIERA (right) In 1895 Queen Victoria joined the parade of *promeneurs* strolling along the curving beach of Nice, the largest resort on the French Riviera. Her Majesty, with her steely reserve, didn't shuck her elaborate clothing and run stark, raving nude toward the placid waters. Such a scene would be more typical of what you'd see today, as all summer long sun worshippers flock to these pebbled sands in search of "sun, sand, and sex," or so rumor has it.

Paris's Best Museums & Galleries
pl. du Gal Koenig
Palais des Congrès
av. Charles de Gaulle
bd. Pereire
av. des Termes
St-Ferdinand
BOIS DE BOULOGNE
bd. de l'Amiral Bruix
av. de Malakoff
av. de la Gr. Armée
Salle Wagram
pl. des Ternes
avenue de Wagram
Salle Pleyel
rue du Faubourg St-Honoré
bd. de Courcelles
PARC MONCEAU
bd. Malesherbes
Conservatoire de Musique
rue de Constantinople
rue de Rome
bd. des Batignoles
St-Augustin
pl. St-Augustin
Gare St-Lazare
bd. Haussmann
place Charles de Gaulle
Arc de Triomphe
av. de Friedland
avenue Foch
av. Bugeaud
avenue Victor Hugo
pl. Victor Hugo
rue Lauriston
avenue Kléber
Centre de Conférences Internationales
avenue Marceau
avenue Raymond Poincaré
rue des Belles Feuilles
rue Bissière
av. d'Iéna
avenue des Champs-Elysées
Rond Point des Champs-Elysées
av. F. D. Roosevelt
Théâtre Marigny
Palais de l'Elysée
pl. de la Madeleine
La Madeleine
av. Montaigne
rue François 1er
rue J. Goujon
place de l'Alma
av. W. Churchill
place de la Concorde
JARDIN D
rue de Longchamp
avenue du Président Wilson
cours Albert 1er
cours la Reine
place du Trocadéro et du 11 Novembre
Seine
pont de l'Alma
pont des Invalides
pont Alex. III
pont de la Concorde
pont de Solferino
JARDINS DU TROCADÉRO
avenue de New York
passerelle Debilly
quai d'Orsay
Aerogare des Invalides
Egouts
quai Anatole France
rue de l'Université
Musée d'Orsay
rue de la Tour
av. Paul Doumer
pont d'Iéna
quai Branly
avenue de la Bourdonnaise
rue St-Dominique
av. du M. Gallieni
rue de Passy
av. Gustave Eiffel
CHAMP DE MARS
av. Joseph Bouvard
avenue de Suffren
av. Charles Risler
bd. de la Tour Maubourg
Ste-Clotilde
rue de Bourgogne
bd. St-Germain
Hôtel des Invalides
bd. des Invalides
rue de Varenne
avenue de Tourville
rue du Bac
av. du Président Kennedy
pont de Bir Hakeim
Allée des Cygnes
rue de la Federation
place Joffre
av. de La Motte Picquet
Ecole Militaire
av. de Lowendal
av. de Ségur
av. de Breteuil
St-François Xavier
rue de Babylone
rue Vaneau
bd. de Grenelle
place de Brazzaville
St-Léon
pont de Grenelle
rue Fondary
rue du Théâtre
U.N.E.S.C.O.
rue Linois
rue Fremicourt
bd. Garibaldi
place de Breteuil
rue de Sevres
rue du Cherche Midi
avenue Émile Zola
rue des Entrepreneurs
Imprimerie Nationale
rue de la Crix Nivert
bd. du Montparnasse
rue de Vaugirard
place Henry Queuille
MONTPARNASSE
place du 18 Juin 1940
Institut Pasteur
bd. Pasteur
Tour Montparnasse
Gare Montparnasse
bd. Edgar
rue Lecourbe
r. de Vaugirard
rue du Dr. Roux
avenue du Maine
CIMETIÈ
rue Dutot
Objets Trouvés
rue Brancion
rue d'Alésia
Centre Pompidou 5
Musée de Cluny 8
Musée de la Carnavalet 7
Musée d'Orsay 9
Musée des Arts Decoratifs 3
Musée du Louvre 4
Musée Guimet 1
Musée Picasso 6
Musée Rodin 10
Petit Palais 2

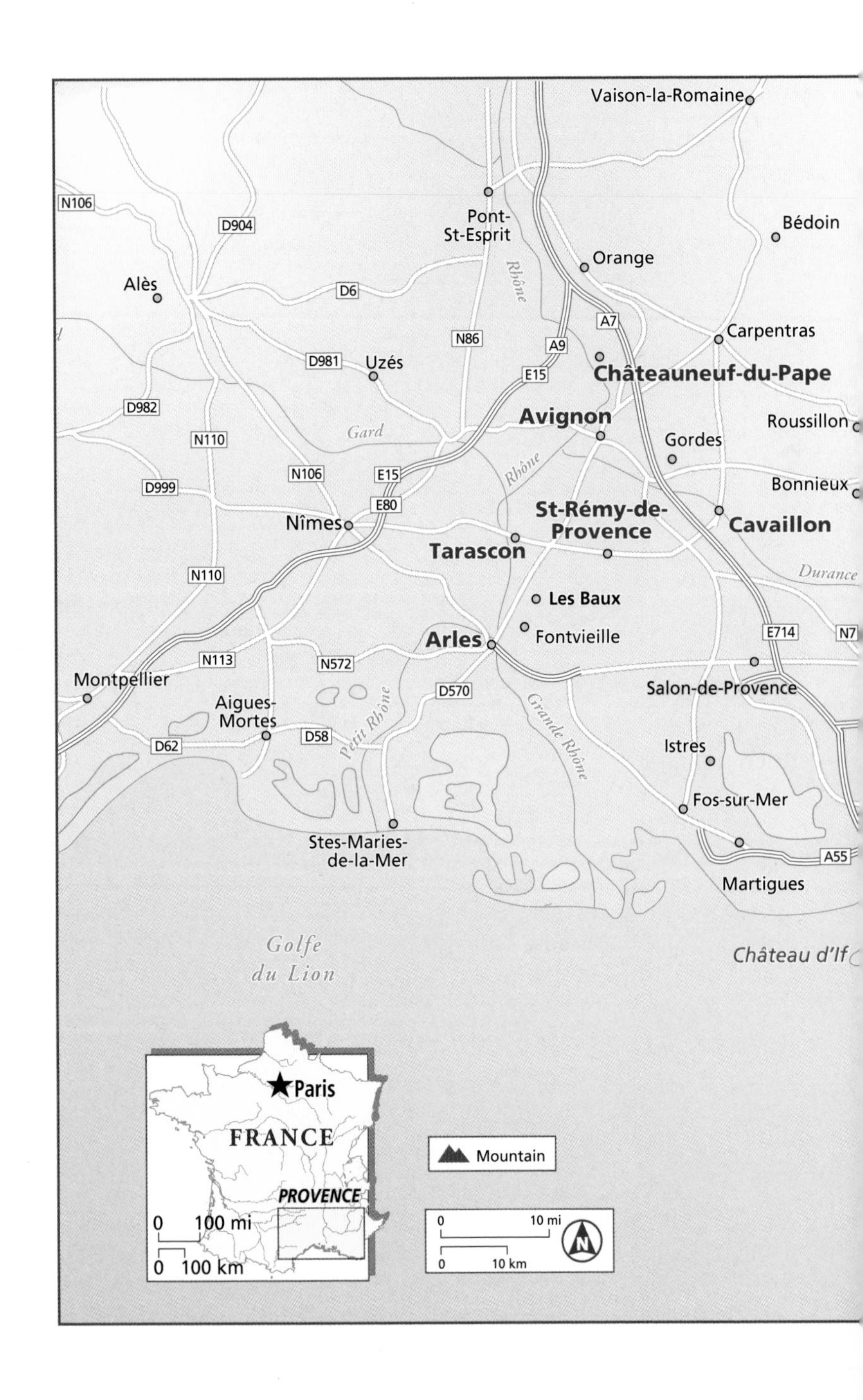
Vaison-la-Romaine
N106
D904
Pont-
St-Esprit
Bédoin
Orange
Rhône
Alès
D6
A7
Carpentras
N86
A9
D981
Uzés
E15
Châteauneuf-du-Pape
D982
Avignon
Roussillon
Gard
N110
Gordes
Rhône
N106
E15
Bonnieux
D999
E80
St-Rémy-de-
Provence
Cavaillon
Nîmes
Tarascon
N110
Durance
Les Baux
Fontvieille
Arles
E714
N7
N113
N572
Montpellier
D570
Salon-de-Provence
Aigues-
Mortes
Petit Rhône
Grande Rhône
D62
D58
Istres
Fos-sur-Mer
Stes-Maries-
de-la-Mer
A55
Martigues
Golfe
du Lion
Château d'If
Paris
FRANCE
PROVENCE
0 100 mi
0 100 km
Mountain
0 10 mi
0 10 km
N

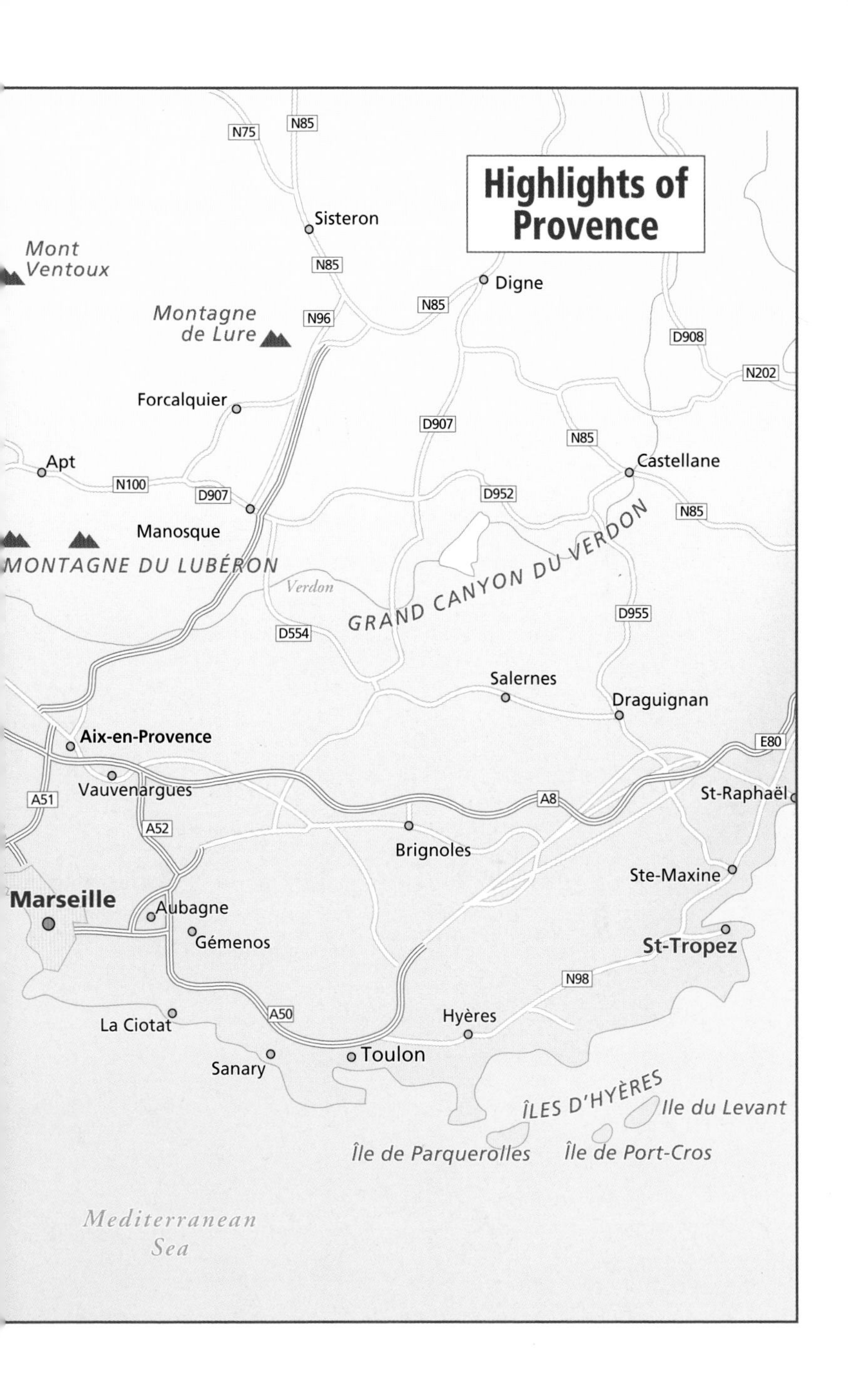

Highlights of Provence
N75
N85
Sisteron
Mont Ventoux
N85
Digne
Montagne de Lure
N96
N85
D908
N202
Forcalquier
D907
N85
Apt
N100
D907
Castellane
D952
N85
Manosque
MONTAGNE DU LUBÉRON
GRAND CANYON DU VERDON
Verdon
D955
D554
Salernes
Draguignan
Aix-en-Provence
E80
Vauvenargues
A8
St-Raphaël
A51
A52
Brignoles
Ste-Maxine
Marseille
Aubagne
Gémenos
St-Tropez
N98
A50
La Ciotat
Hyères
Sanary
Toulon
ÎLES D'HYÈRES
Ile du Levant
Île de Parquerolles
Île de Port-Cros
Mediterranean Sea

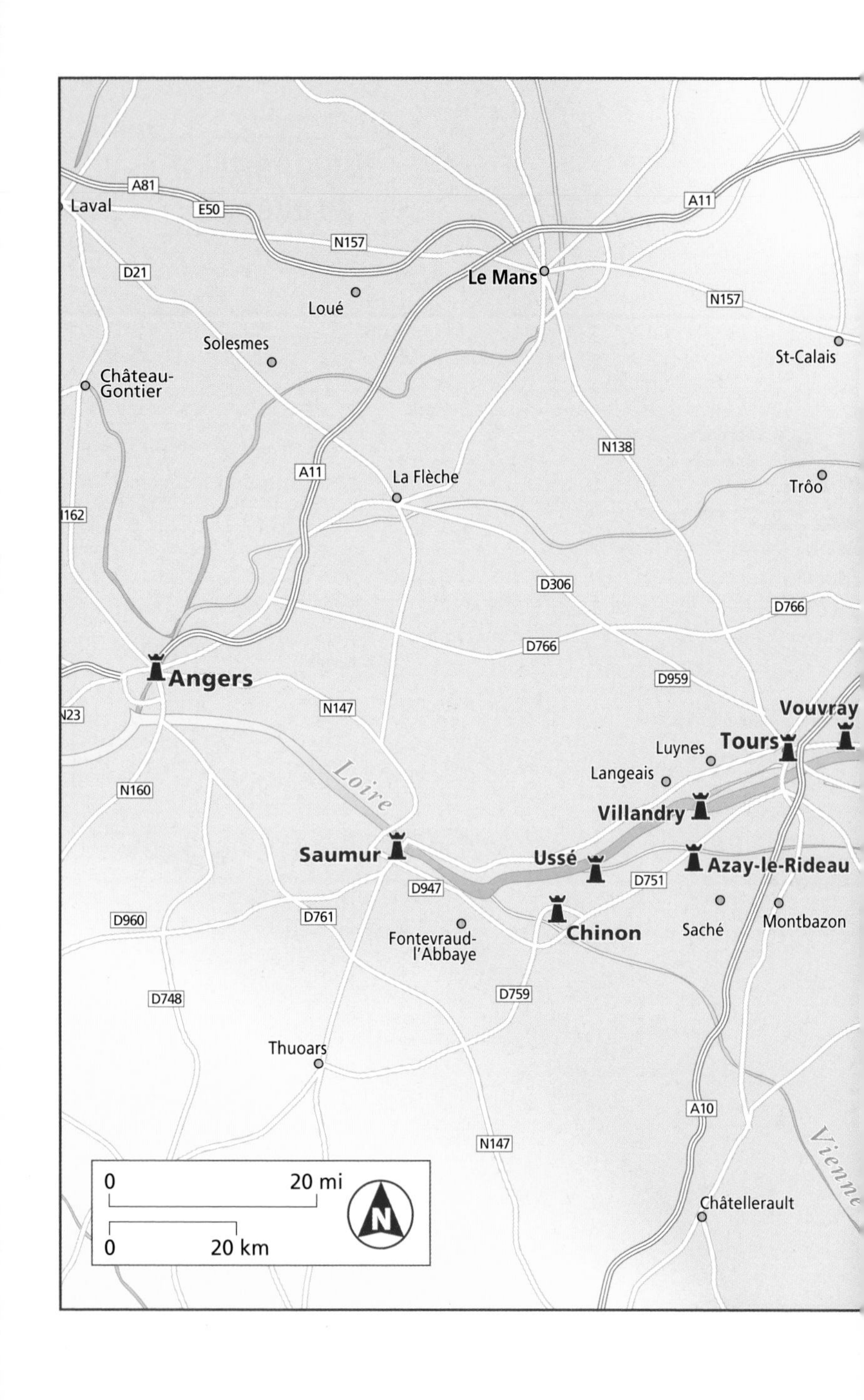

A81
Laval
E50
N157
A11
D21
Le Mans
Loué
N157
Solesmes
St-Calais
Château-
Gontier
N138
A11
La Flèche
Trôo
162
D306
D766
D766
Angers
D959
N147
Vouvray
N23
Tours
Luynes
Langeais
N160
Loire
Villandry
Saumur
Ussé
Azay-le-Rideau
D947
D751
D960
D761
Chinon
Saché
Montbazon
Fontevraud-
l'Abbaye
D748
D759
Thuoars
A10
N147
Vienne
0
20 mi
0
20 km
N
Châtellerault

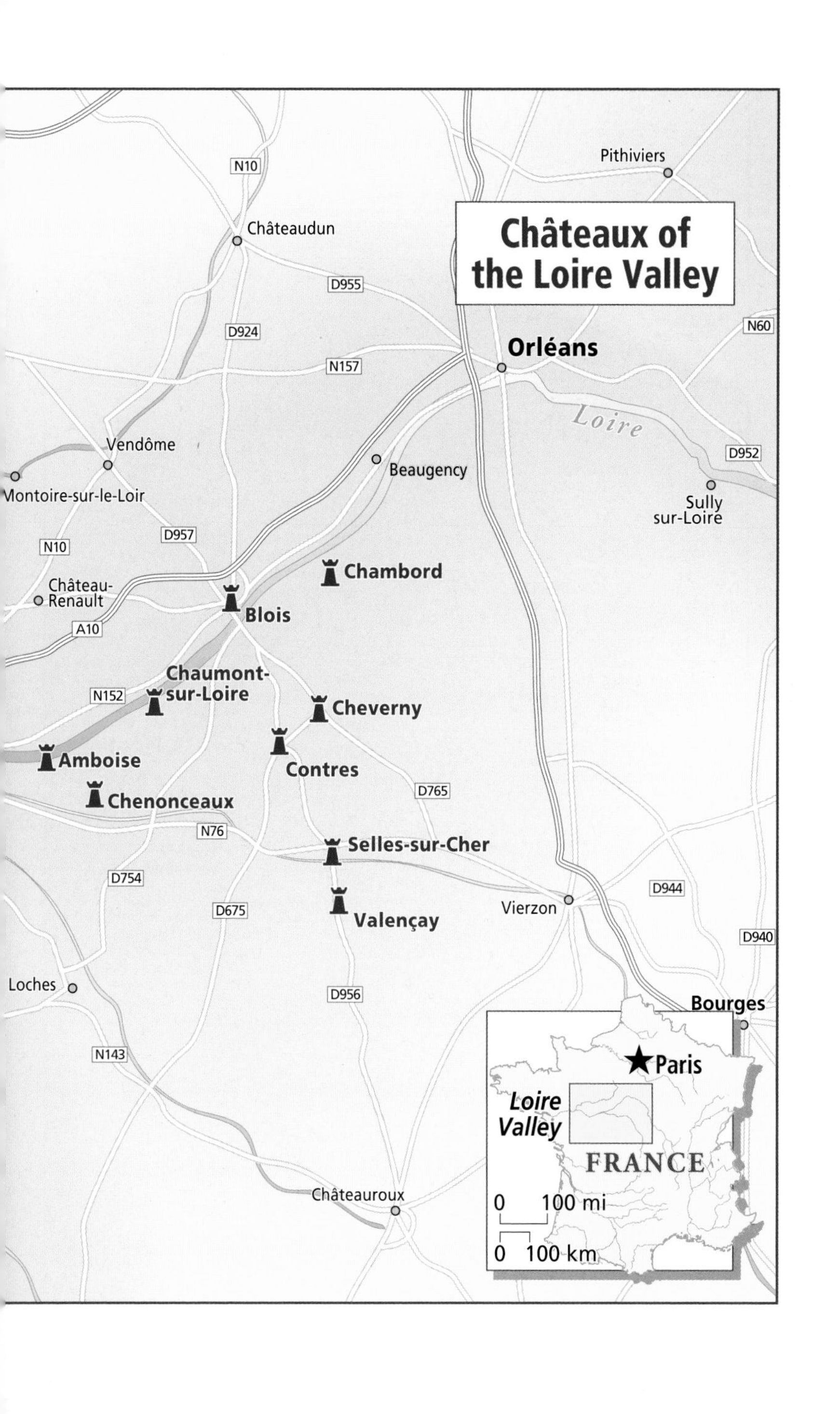

Châteaux of the Loire Valley
Pithiviers
N10
Châteaudun
D955
D924
N60
Orléans
N157
Loire
Vendôme
Beaugency
D952
Montoire-sur-le-Loir
Sully
sur-Loire
D957
N10
Chambord
Château-
Renault
Blois
A10
Chaumont-
sur-Loire
N152
Cheverny
Amboise
Contres
D765
Chenonceaux
N76
Selles-sur-Cher
D754
D944
D675
Vierzon
Valençay
D940
Loches
D956
Bourges
N143
Paris
Loire
Valley
FRANCE
Châteauroux
0 100 mi
0 100 km

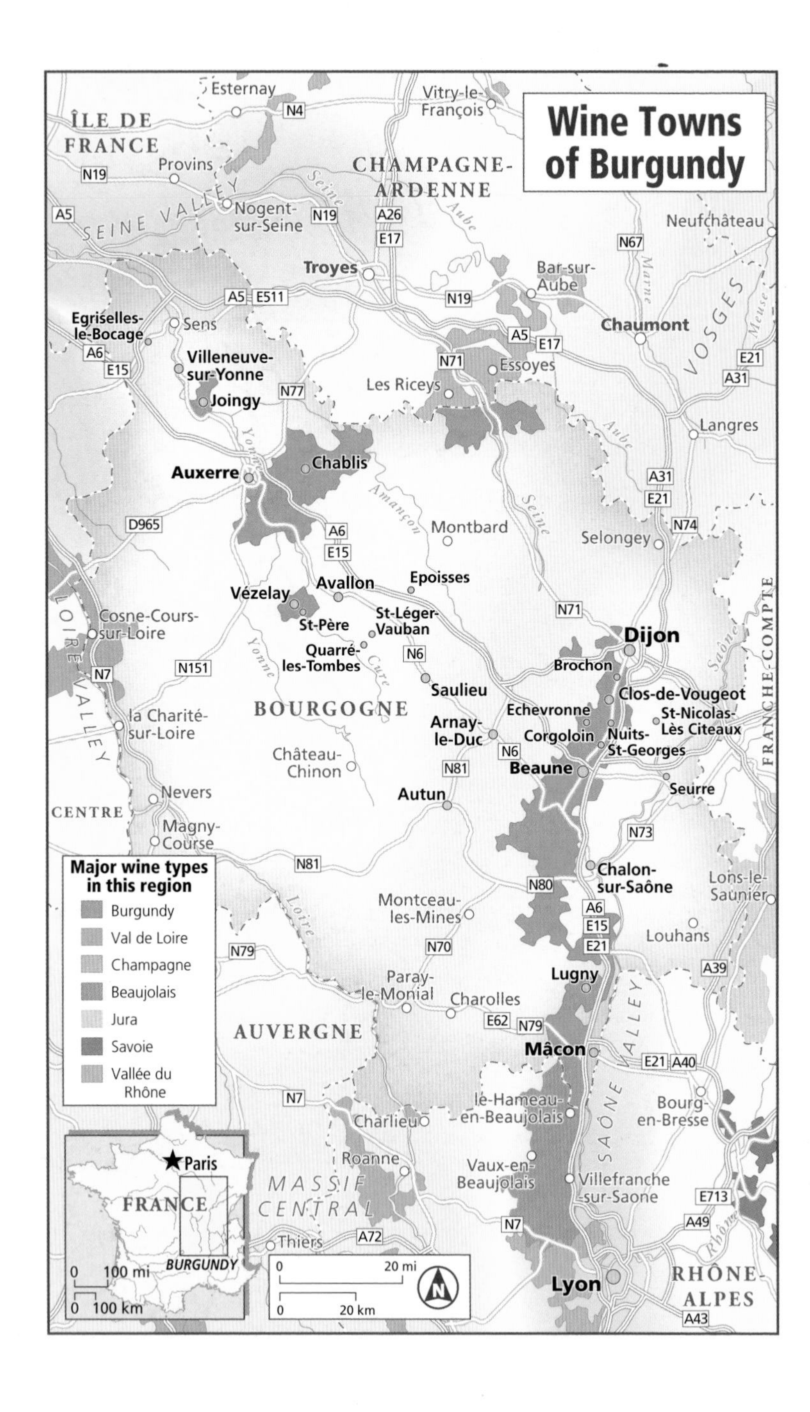

Wine Towns of Burgundy
ÎLE DE FRANCE
CHAMPAGNE-ARDENNE
SEINE VALLEY
LOIRE VALLEY
BOURGOGNE
CENTRE
AUVERGNE
MASSIF CENTRAL
VOSGES
FRANCHE-COMPTE
RHÔNE-ALPES
SAÔNE VALLEY
Esternay
Vitry-le-François
Provins
Nogent-sur-Seine
Neufchâteau
Troyes
Bar-sur-Aube
Chaumont
Egriselles-le-Bocage
Sens
Villeneuve-sur-Yonne
Joingy
Essoyes
Les Riceys
Langres
Auxerre
Chablis
Montbard
Selongey
Epoisses
Vézelay
Avallon
St-Père
St-Léger-Vauban
Quarré-les-Tombes
Cosne-Cours-sur-Loire
Dijon
Brochon
Clos-de-Vougeot
Saulieu
Echevronne
St-Nicolas-Lès Citeaux
Arnay-le-Duc
Corgoloin
Nuits-St-Georges
la Charité-sur-Loire
Château-Chinon
Beaune
Seurre
Nevers
Autun
Magny-Course
Chalon-sur-Saône
Lons-le-Saunier
Montceau-les-Mines
Louhans
Lugny
Paray-le-Monial
Charolles
Mâcon
le-Hameau-en-Beaujolais
Bourg-en-Bresse
Charlieu
Roanne
Vaux-en-Beaujolais
Villefranche-sur-Saone
Thiers
Lyon
Seine
Aube
Marne
Meuse
Yonne
Armançon
Cure
Saône
Loire
Rhône
N4
N19
A5
A26
E17
N67
E511
A6
E15
N71
N77
E21
A31
D965
N74
N6
N151
N7
N81
N73
N80
N79
N70
E62
A40
E713
A49
A72
A43
A39
Major wine types in this region
Burgundy
Val de Loire
Champagne
Beaujolais
Jura
Savoie
Vallée du Rhône
Paris
FRANCE
BURGUNDY
0 100 mi
0 100 km
0 20 mi
0 20 km
N

Frommer's®

France 2008

by Darwin Porter & Danforth Prince

Here's what the critics say about Frommer's:

"Amazingly easy to use. Very portable, very complete."

—Booklist

"Detailed, accurate, and easy-to-read information for all price ranges."

—Glamour Magazine

"Hotel information is close to encyclopedic."

—Des Moines Sunday Register

"Frommer's Guides have a way of giving you a real feel for a place."

—Knight Ridder Newspapers

BICENTENNIAL 1807 WILEY 2007 BICENTENNIAL

Wiley Publishing, Inc.

Published by:

Wiley Publishing, Inc.

111 River St.
Hoboken, NJ 07030-5774

ISBN: 978-0-470-13824-3

Editor: Anuja Madar
Production Editor: Michael Brumitt
Cartographer: Tim Lohnes
Photo Editor: Richard Fox
Anniversary Logo Design: Richard Pacifico
Production by Wiley Indianapolis Composition Services

Front cover photo: Provence: Woman in lavender field
Back cover photo: Loire Valley: Chateau Sully reflected in water

For information on our other products and services or to obtain technical support, please contact our Customer Care Department within the U.S. at 800/762-2974, outside the U.S. at 317/572-3993 or fax 317/572-4002.

Wiley also publishes its books in a variety of electronic formats. Some content that appears in print may not be available in electronic formats.

Manufactured in the United States of America

5 4 3 2 1

Contents

List of Maps ix

What's New in France 1

1 The Best of France 4

1 The Best Travel Experiences 4
2 The Best Romantic Escapes 5
3 The Best Driving Tours 6
4 The Best Châteaux & Palaces 7
5 The Best Museums 7
6 The Best Cathedrals 8
7 The Best Vineyards & Wineries 9
8 The Best Luxury Hotels 10
9 The Best Affordable Hotels 11
10 The Best Historic Places to Stay 12
11 The Best Upscale Restaurants 13
12 The Best Affordable Restaurants 14

2 A Traveler's Guide to France's Art & Architecture 15

1 Art 101 15
2 Architecture 101 20

3 Planning Your Trip to France 27

1 The Regions in Brief 27
2 Visitor Information & Maps 32
3 Entry Requirements 33
4 When to Go 34
France Calendar of Events 35
5 Getting There 39
Getting through the Airport 40
Under the Channel 44
6 General Travel Resources 44
The Euro 46
7 Specialized Travel Resources 50
8 Sustainable Tourism/Ecotourism 53
Frommers.com: The Complete Travel Resource 53
9 Staying Connected 54
Online Traveler's Toolbox 55
10 Packages for the Independent Traveler 56
Ask Before You Go 56
11 Escorted General-Interest Tours 57
12 Special-Interest Trips 57
13 Getting Around France 59
14 Tips on Accommodations 63
15 Tips on Dining 67
Fast Facts: France 68

4 Suggested Itineraries in France 76

1 France in 1 Week 76
2 France in 2 Weeks 79
3 France for Families 81
4 A Wine Lover's Tour of Burgundy ...83

5 Settling into Paris 87

1 Orientation 87
The Arrondissements in Brief 92
2 Getting Around 95
Discount Transit Passes 96
Fast Facts: Paris 97
3 Where to Stay 99
4 Where to Dine 118
5 The Top Cafes 142

6 Exploring Paris 144

1 The Top Attractions 146
2 Musée de Louvre/Les Halles: The 1st Arrondissement (Right Bank) 156
3 Le Marais: The 3rd Arrondissement (Right Bank) 158
4 Where Paris Was Born: Ile de la Cité & the 4th Arrondissement 160
5 The Champs-Elysées, Paris's Grand Promenade: The 8th Arrondissement (Right Bank) 160
Where Royal Heads Rolled 161
6 Montmartre: The 18th Arrondissement (Right Bank) 162
7 La Villette: The 19th Arrondissement (Right Bank) 163
8 The Latin Quarter: The 5th Arrondissement (Left Bank) 163
9 St-Germain-des-Prés: The 6th Arrondissement (Left Bank) 165
10 The Eiffel Tower/Musée d'Orsay: The 7th Arrondissement (Left Bank) 166
11 Montparnasse: The 14th Arrondissement (Left Bank) 167
12 Parks, Gardens & Cemeteries 168
Royal Remains at St-Denis 170
13 Paris Underground 171
14 Shopping 173
15 Paris After Dark 181
After-Dark Diversions: Dives, Drag, & More 188

7 Side Trips from Paris: Versailles, Chartres & the Best of the Ile de France 192

1 Versailles 192
A Return to Faded Glory 194
2 The Glorious Cathedral of Chartres 199
To Taste a Madeleine 202
3 Barbizon: The School of Rousseau 205
4 Fontainebleau: Refuge of Kings 207
5 Vaux-le-Vicomte: Life before Versailles 210
6 Disneyland Paris 211
For Those with Another Day: Walt Disney Studios 213
7 The Remarkable Zoo of Château de Thoiry 216
8 Giverny: In the Footsteps of Monet 217
9 Chantilly: A Day at the Races 219
10 Senlis 222
11 Compiègne 224

8 The Loire Valley 227

1 Orléans 227
Biking Your Way through the Loire 228
2 Châteaudun 232
3 Beaugency 233
4 Chambord 235
5 Blois 236
6 Cheverny 239
7 Valençay 240
8 Chaumont-sur-Loire 241
9 Amboise 242
10 Chenonceaux 246
11 Tours 248
Fun-Filled Ways to Get Around 250
12 Loches 255
13 Villandry 256
14 Langeais 257
15 Azay-le-Rideau 258
16 Chinon 260
In Pursuit of the Grape 261
17 Ussé 264
18 Fontevraud-l'Abbaye 264
19 Saumur 265
20 Angers 268

9 Normandy & Mont-St-Michel 272

1 Rouen 272
A Drive along the Route des Abbayes 276
2 Honfleur 282
3 Deauville 285
4 Trouville 289
5 Caen 291
An Excursion to the Forbes Château 292
6 Bayeux 296
7 The D-Day Beaches 298
8 Mont-St-Michel 301

10 Brittany 305

1 St-Malo 305
2 Dinard 310
An Idyll on an Ile 313
3 Dinan 314
4 Quimper 317
5 Concarneau 320
6 Pont-Aven 321
7 Carnac 323
The Wild, Wild Coast 325
8 La Baule 326
9 Nantes 328

11 The Champagne Country 334

1 La Ferté-sous-Jouarre 334
2 Château-Thierry 336
3 Condé-en-Brie 337
4 Reims 338
5 Side Trips from Reims: Laon & Amiens 345
6 Epernay 351

12 Alsace-Lorraine 354

1 Strasbourg .354
2 La Route du Vin (Wine Road) .365
3 Colmar .372
4 La Route des Crêtes .377
5 Nancy .378
6 Domrémy-la-Pucelle .383
7 Verdun .383

13 Burgundy 386

1 Auxerre .386
2 Vézelay .389
3 Avallon .391
4 Autun .392
5 Beaune .394
6 Dijon .398
Side Trips from Dijon .402
7 Saulieu .405

14 The Rhône Valley 406

1 Lyon .406
Beaucoup Bocuse .418
2 The Beaujolais Country .419
3 Roanne .421
4 Pérouges .423
5 Bourg-en-Bresse .424
6 Vienne .425
7 Valence .428
8 The Ardèche .429
The Grand Canyon of France .429

15 The French Alps 432

1 Evian-les-Bains .432
2 Annecy .435
3 Talloires .439
4 Aix-les-Bains .441
5 Grenoble .443
6 Courchevel 1850 .447
7 Megève .451
8 Chamonix–Mont Blanc .455
9 Val d'Isère .459

16 Provence: In the Footsteps of Cézanne & van Gogh 464

1 Orange .464
Shopping for Brocante *in Provence* .467
2 Avignon .468
3 St-Rémy-de-Provence .477
4 Arles .480
5 Les Baux .487
6 Aix-en-Provence .490
7 Marseille .497
8 Toulon .508
9 Iles d'Hyères .510

17 The French Riviera 513

1 St-Tropez 513
2 La Napoule–Plage 522
3 Cannes 524
Seeing Cannes from a Petit Train 529
4 Mougins 537
5 Grasse 539
6 Biot 541
7 Golfe-Juan & Vallauris 543
8 Juan-les-Pins 546
9 Antibes & Cap d'Antibes 549
10 Cagnes-sur-Mer 552
11 St-Paul-de-Vence 555
12 Vence 558
13 Nice 562
14 Villefranche-sur-Mer 577
15 St-Jean-Cap-Ferrat 578
16 Beaulieu-sur-Mer 581
17 Eze & La Turbie 584
18 Monaco 586
19 Roquebrune–Cap-Martin 597

18 Languedoc-Roussillon 601

1 Nîmes 601
2 Aigues-Mortes 608
France's Cowboy Country: The Camargue 609
3 Montpellier 611
4 Narbonne 615
5 Collioure 618
6 Perpignan 620
7 Carcassonne 624
8 Castres 629
9 Albi 630
10 Cordes-sur-Ciel 633
11 Toulouse 634

19 The Basque Country 644

1 Lourdes 644
2 Pau 649
3 Bayonne 653
4 Biarritz 656
5 St-Jean-de-Luz 661

20 Bordeaux & the Atlantic Coast 665

1 Poitiers 665
2 La Rochelle 669
Sailing the Ports of La Rochelle 673
3 Cognac 674
4 Angoulême 676
5 Bordeaux 679
6 The Wine Country 687

21 The Dordogne & Périgord: Land of Prehistoric Caves, Truffles & Fine Wine 692

1 Périgueux 692
Biking through the Dordogne 695
2 Lascaux (Montignac) 696
3 Les Eyzies-de-Tayac 698
4 Rocamadour 701
5 Cahors 704
6 Montauban 706

22 The Massif Central 709

1 Bourges 709
2 Nohant/La Châtre 713
3 Vichy 714
4 Clermont-Ferrand 717
5 Aubusson 721
6 Limoges 723
7 Le Puy-en-Velay 726

Appendix: Useful Terms & Phrases 729

1 Basic French Vocabulary & Phrases 729
2 Food & Menu 732

Index 737

List of Maps

France 28
France in 1 Week 77
France in 2 Weeks 80
France for Families 82
A Wine Lover's Tour of Burgundy 85
Paris Arrondissements 88
Where to Stay on the Right Bank 100
Where to Stay on the Left Bank 112
Where to Dine on the Right Bank 120
Where to Dine on the Left Bank 136
Top Paris Attractions 148
The Louvre 152
Notre-Dame de Paris 154
Paris & the Ile de France 193
Versailles 195
Notre-Dame de Chartres 201
The Loire Valley 229
Orléans 231
Tours 249
Normandy 273
Rouen 275
Mont-St-Michel 303
Brittany 307
Nantes 329
Champagne 335
Reims 339
Alsace-Lorraine 355
Strasbourg 357
Nancy 379
Burgundy 387
Dijon 399
The Rhône Valley 407
Lyon 409
The French Alps 433
Provence 465
Avignon 469
Palais des Papes 472
Arles 481
Aix-en-Provence 491
Marseille 499
The French Riviera 515
St-Tropez 517
Cannes 526
Nice 563
Monaco 589
Languedoc-Roussillon 603
Nîmes 605
Toulouse 635
The Basque Country 645
Bordeaux & the Atlantic Coast 667
Bordeaux 681
The Dordogne & Périgord 693
The Massif Central 711

An Invitation to the Reader

In researching this book, we discovered many wonderful places—hotels, restaurants, shops, and more. We're sure you'll find others. Please tell us about them, so we can share the information with your fellow travelers in upcoming editions. If you were disappointed with a recommendation, we'd love to know that, too. Please write to:

Frommer's France 2008
Wiley Publishing, Inc. • 111 River St. • Hoboken, NJ 07030-5774

An Additional Note

Please be advised that travel information is subject to change at any time—and this is especially true of prices. We therefore suggest that you write or call ahead for confirmation when making your travel plans. The authors, editors, and publisher cannot be held responsible for the experiences of readers while traveling. Your safety is important to us, however, so we encourage you to stay alert and be aware of your surroundings. Keep a close eye on cameras, purses, and wallets, all favorite targets of thieves and pickpockets.

About the Authors

A team of veteran travel writers, **Darwin Porter** and **Danforth Prince** have produced numerous titles for Frommer's, including best-selling guides to Italy, France, the Caribbean, England, and Germany. Porter, a former bureau chief of *The Miami Herald,* is also a Hollywood biographer, providing inside looks at the private lives of such stars as Humphrey Bogart, Katherine Hepburn, and aviator Howard Hughes. His latest bio is *Brando Unzipped.* Formerly of the Paris bureau of *The New York Times,* Prince is also president of Blood Moon Productions and other media-related firms.

Frommer's Star Ratings, Icons & Abbreviations

Every hotel, restaurant, and attraction listing in this guide has been ranked for quality, value, service, amenities, and special features using a **star-rating system.** In country, state, and regional guides, we also rate towns and regions to help you narrow down your choices and budget your time accordingly. Hotels and restaurants are rated on a scale of zero (recommended) to three stars (exceptional). Attractions, shopping, nightlife, towns, and regions are rated according to the following scale: zero stars (recommended), one star (highly recommended), two stars (very highly recommended), and three stars (must-see).

In addition to the star-rating system, we also use **seven feature icons** that point you to the great deals, in-the-know advice, and unique experiences that separate travelers from tourists. Throughout the book, look for:

Finds	Special finds—those places only insiders know about
Fun Fact	Fun facts—details that make travelers more informed and their trips more fun
Kids	Best bets for kids and advice for the whole family
Moments	Special moments—those experiences that memories are made of
Overrated	Places or experiences not worth your time or money
Tips	Insider tips—great ways to save time and money
Value	Great values—where to get the best deals

The following **abbreviations** are used for credit cards:

AE American Express	DISC Discover	V Visa
DC Diners Club	MC MasterCard	

Frommers.com

Now that you have this guidebook to help you plan a great trip, visit our website at **www.frommers.com** for additional travel information on more than 3,600 destinations. We update features regularly to give you instant access to the most current trip-planning information available. At Frommers.com, you'll find scoops on the best airfares, lodging rates, and car rental bargains. You can even book your travel online through our reliable travel booking partners. Other popular features include:

- Online updates of our most popular guidebooks
- Vacation sweepstakes and contest giveaways
- Newsletters highlighting the hottest travel trends
- Online travel message boards with featured travel discussions

What's New in France

France held its spot as the number-one tourist destination in the world this past year, with 78 million foreign tourists reported in 2006. Visitors are intrigued by France's glorious past as well as its cutting-edge cuisine, style, and fashion. In this chapter, we preview some of the latest developments in an ever-changing land. Note that because of a sour economy, there have been few new hotels, grand restaurants, and fabulous resorts opening. In fact, some upmarket choices have closed down because of lack of business. Don't despair, however, as most of the old favorites are still going strong for returning visitors to enjoy once again—or for new arrivals to discover for the first time.

PARIS ACCOMMODATIONS The hotel getting all the press is the provocatively named **Hotel Amour,** 8 rue de Navarin, 9e (✆ **01-48-78-31-80;** www.hotelamour.com). It's centrally located just off the rue des Martyrs, currently the hippest street in Paris. Starlets and bright young things check in here. Walk up the steps to the bedrooms (there's no elevator), where the beds are incredibly comfortable (they come from the same company that supplies the Ritz). Expect to encounter an oddball charm. Comfort food, including *steak frites,* is served on-site.

The film *Amélie* made the Goutte d'Or neighborhood of Montmartre world famous, and thousands continue to flock to this up-and-coming sector because of it. **Kube Rooms & Bars,** 1–5 Passage Ruelle, 18e (✆ **01-42-05-20-00;** www.kubehotel.com), opened as a result of the area's popularity, but is not your average overnight stay. The cube-inspired hotel boasts a reception area that was inspired by the architecturally controversial glass box in front of the Louvre. Rectangular beds are lit from below and appear to be levitated. Expect shag-covered sofas and faux fur throws. The Ice Kube Bar is made with—you guessed it—ice. Instead of room keys, guests are electronically fingerprinted.

PARIS ATTRACTIONS After a $46-million renovation, the **Musée des Arts Décoratifs** has reopened in a wing of the Louvre, 107 rue de Rivoli, 1er (✆ **01-44-55-57-50**), which is attracting thousands of new visitors after the release of *The Da Vinci Code.* The new museum is a dollhouse on a grand scale, where each room offers up treasures—Napoleon's golden throne, fashion designer Jeanne Lanvin's purple boudoir, and the velvet-draped bed of a 19th-century courtesan. "The Splendor of the Courtesan's Room" was the first abode of Valtesse de La Bigne, an inspiration for Emile Zola's *Nana* about a prostitute who captivated Parisian high society.

In the shadow of the Eiffel Tower, the museum getting all the press is Jean Nouvel's sweeping **Musée du Quai Branly,** 37 quai Branly, 7e (✆ **01-56-61-70-00**). With an exterior wall covered with 150 exotic plant species, it is devoted to the art of Africa, the Americas, the South

Pacific, and Asia. In all, nearly 300,000 tribal artifacts are on parade in this $256-million project. During its decade-long construction, there were many scandals, such as when the museum's curator discovered that the terra-cotta figurines from Nigeria were stolen. Galleries stand on sculpted pillars that evoke totems. Nouvel said he wanted to "create something unique, poetic, and disturbing."

The long-closed **Musée de l'Orangerie,** Jardin des Tuileries, 1er (✆ **01-44-77-80-07**), reopened its doors. The museum's 19th- and 20th-century works were relocated underground. Claude Monet's celebrated *Nymphéas* are displayed as the artist intended them to be—lit by sunlight. The spacious oval-shaped galleries evoke the garden ponds at the artist's Giverny estate. Over the years we've come here many times just to gaze upon Marie Laurencin's *Portrait of Mademoiselle Chanel* in 1923.

It's had a number of roles in its long life, but today the newly reopened **Jeu de Paume,** 1 Place de la Concorde, 8e (✆ **01-47-03-12-50**), is devoted to photography and video, exploring a world of images. It presents ever-changing exhibitions, many of them daringly avant-garde, and is one of the finest museums of its type in the world.

THE LOIRE VALLEY In the ancient city of Saumur, in France's château country, **Les Terrasses de Saumur,** 2 rue des Lilas, St-Hilaire-St-Florent (✆ **02-41-67-28-48**), is a recently built hotel that is also one of the best bargains in the area. The best of its accommodations have private balconies overlooking the Loire Valley. Its best feature is a large outdoor swimming pool, and it also enjoys a parklike setting.

NORMANDY Sixty-three years after D-day, the **Normandy American Cemetery** (✆ **02-31-51-32-00;** www.abmc.gov) opened a $30 million visitor center earlier this year, dedicated to educating the more than 1 million annual visitors through photo and film exhibits, artifacts, interactive displays, and personal stories. The center is open year-round 9am to 6pm (closed Dec. 25 and Jan. 1), and admission is free.

In the ancient city of Caen, the closing of Le Dauphin shocked gourmets, many of whom drove here from Paris to dine. It's not in the same league, but **Le Carlotta,** 16 quai Vendeuvre (✆ **02-31-86-68-99**), has filled in the gastronomic gap. With the renewed attention focused on this restaurant serving fresh seafood and French specialties, the menu has been remarkably upgraded in the past few months. Even the braised oxtail now comes with truffles.

ALSACE-LORRAINE Call **Chez Hansi,** 23 rue des Marchands (✆ **03-89-41-37-84**), so old it's new again. In the autumn of 2006, the gourmet press of France seemed to discover this place for the first time. Perhaps tiring of the more experimental versions of nouvelle cuisine, many residents of Eastern France are turning to the food of their childhood. In this district of France, and at Chez Hansi, that means heaping platters of sauerkraut, foie gras, and onion tarts. The women on the staff are clad in dirndls.

THE ARDECHE In the northern Ardèche—a land of hamlets, vineyards, shepherding, and hill trekking—Lamastre has long been considered the most evocative village. The **Château d'Urbilhac,** route De Vernoux-en-Vivarois (✆ **04-75-06-42-11;** www.chateaudurbilhac.fr), has been altered from its former days of upmarket glory and is now a more family-friendly and democratically priced retreat. Its high-ceilinged rooms (often furnished with antiques) and spectacular pool overlooking the valley of the River Doux are still intact, attracting visitors from all over the world.

PROVENCE In ancient Arles, known for its Roman ruins, **Hotel de l'Amphitheatre,** 5–7 rue Diderot (✆ **04-90-96-10-30;** www.hotelamphitheatre.fr), completed a 2-year renovation program in 2007 and is now one of the most recommendable oases in town for the frugal traveler. The antique atmosphere of the building, dating from the 17th century, has been retained. Bright fabrics, new furniture, and modern fittings have made this once-tired address fresh and new again.

The big news coming out of Marseille is the restoration of **Hôtel Le Corbusier,** La Cité Radieuse, 280 bd. Michelet (✆ **04-91-16-78-00;** www.hotellecorbusier.com). The original building was designed in 1952, by Le Corbusier himself, 2km (1¼ miles) south of Marseille. A husband-and-wife team spent a ton of money returning the hotel to its original condition, with the kind of spartan, functional design that Le Corbusier intended. Even so, this is not an address for everyone, but a curiosity for architectural buffs. A restaurant has opened on-site called The Architect's Stomach.

THE FRENCH RIVIERA In the chic resort of the Côte d'Azur, St-Tropez, two ex-pat Brits, John and Pauline Larkin, have opened a boutique hotel of charm and grace: **Pastis Hotel-St-Tropez,** 61 av. du Général Leclerc (✆ **04-98-12-56-60;** www.pastis-st-tropez.com). A portside Provençal house has been renovated and transformed into this intimate enclave of comfort, with an eclectic decor that includes everything from framed albums of the Sex Pistols to Chinese armoires.

LANGUEDOC In the city of Toulouse, **St-Claire Hotel,** 29 place Nicolas Bachelier (✆ **05-34-40-58-88**), is a government-rated two-star hotel that has undergone a complete renovation. Today it is one of the best value hotels of Toulouse, lying in the heart of the city. The hotel offers personalized service, provides a high level of comfort, is decorated in a homelike way, and is immaculately kept.

THE ATLANTIC COAST In the city of Poitiers, **Le Grand Hotel,** 28 rue Carnot (✆ **05-49-60-90-60**), has been restored and has emerged as the finest hotel address in town. Though modernized, it has maintained its 1920s Art Deco architectural style. The location is in the heart of Poitiers near the Théâtre National de Poitiers.

1 The Best of France

France presents visitors with an embarrassment of riches—you may find yourself bewildered by all the choices. We've tried to make the task easier by compiling a list of our favorite experiences and discoveries. In the following pages, you'll find the kind of candid advice we'd give our closest friends.

1 The Best Travel Experiences

- **Hunting for Antiques:** The 18th- and 19th-century French aesthetic was gloriously different from that of England and North America, and many objects bear designs with mythological references to the French experience. France has some 13,000-plus antiques shops throughout the country. Stop where you see the sign ANTIQUAIRE or BROCANTE.
- **Dining Out:** The art of dining is serious business in France. Food is as cerebral as it is sensual. Even casual bistros with affordable menus are likely to offer fresh seasonal ingredients in time-tested recipes that may add up to a memorable meal. For our favorite restaurants in France, see "The Best Upscale Restaurants" and "The Best Affordable Restaurants," later in this chapter.
- **Biking in the Countryside:** The country that invented La Tour de France offers thousands of options for bike trips. For a modest charge, trains in France will carry your bicycle to any point. **Euro-Bike & Walking Tours** of DeKalb, Illinois (© **800/321-6060;** www.eurobike.com) offers some of the best excursions, including walking and cycling tours of areas such as Provence, Burgundy, and the Loire Valley. See chapter 3.
- **Shopping in Parisian Boutiques:** The French guard their image as Europe's most stylish people. The citadels of Right Bank chic lie on rue du Faubourg St-Honoré and its extension, rue St-Honoré. The most glamorous shops are along these streets, stretching between the Palais Royal to the east and the Palais de l'Elysée to the west. Follow in the footsteps of Coco Chanel, Yves Saint Laurent, and Karl Lagerfeld on the shopper's tour of a lifetime. See chapter 6.
- **Exploring the Loire Valley:** An excursion to the châteaux dotting the valley's rich fields and forests will familiarize you with the French Renaissance's architectural aesthetics and with the intrigues of the kings and their courts. Nothing conjures up the aristocratic *ancien régime* better than a tour of these landmarks. See chapter 8.
- **Paying Tribute to Fallen Heroes on Normandy's D-Day Beaches:** On June 6, 1944, the largest armada ever assembled departed on rough seas and in dense fog from England. For

about a week, the future of the civilized world hung in a bloody and brutal balance between the Nazi and Allied armies. Today you'll find only the sticky sands and wind-torn, gray-green seas of a rather chilly beach. But even if you haven't seen *Saving Private Ryan* or *The Longest Day*, you can picture the struggles of determined soldiers who paid a terrible price to establish a bulkhead on the Continent. See "The D-Day Beaches" in chapter 9.

- **Climbing to the Heights of Mont-St-Michel:** Straddling the tidal flats between Normandy and Brittany, this Gothic marvel is the most spectacular fortress in northern Europe. Said to be protected by the archangel Michael, most of it stands as it did during the 1200s. See "Mont-St-Michel" in chapter 9.
- **Touring Burgundy during the Grape Gathering:** Medieval lore and legend permeate the harvests in Burgundy, where thousands of workers (armed with vintner's shears and baskets) head over the rolling hills to gather the grapes that have made the region's wines so famous. You can sample the local wines in the area restaurants, which always stock impressive collections. See chapter 13.
- **Schussing down the Alps:** France offers world-class skiing and luxurious resorts. Our favorites are Chamonix, Courchevel, and Megève. Here you'll find cliffs only experts should brave, as well as runs for intermediates and beginners. The après-ski scene roars into the wee hours. See chapter 15.
- **Marveling at the Riviera's Modern-Art Museums:** Since the 1890s, when Signac, Bonnard, and Matisse discovered St-Tropez, artists and their patrons have been drawn to the French Riviera. Experience an unforgettable drive across southern Provence, interspersing museum visits with wonderful meals, sunbathing, and stops at the area's architectural and artistic marvels. Highlights are Aix-en-Provence (Cézanne's studio), Biot (the Léger Museum), Cagnes-sur-Mer (the Museum of Modern Mediterranean Art), Cap d'Antibes (the Grimaldi Château's Picasso Museum), La Napoule (the Henry Clews Museum), and Menton (the Cocteau Museum). In addition, Nice, St-Paul-de-Vence, and St-Tropez all have impressive modern-art collections. See chapters 16 and 17.

2 The Best Romantic Escapes

- **Deauville** (Normandy): Using the resort of Deauville to propel herself to stardom, Coco Chanel added greatly to its sense of glamour and romance. Try your hand at the casinos, ride horses, stroll along the elegant boardwalk, or simply revel in the resort's sense of style and nostalgia. See "Deauville" in chapter 9.
- **La Baule** (Brittany): Consider an escape with your significant other to La Baule, a coastal resort in southern Brittany. The salt air; the moody, windswept Atlantic; and the Belle Epoque architecture help justify the name of its 8km (5-mile) beach, La Côte d'Amour. See "La Baule" in chapter 10.
- **Talloires** (The French Alps): The bracing climate, the history that goes back to the Middle Ages, and the Gallic flair of the innkeepers make for a memorable stay. The accommodations include a converted medieval

monastery, and the village's cuisine is superb. See "Talloires" in chapter 15.

- **Les Baux** (Provence): During the Middle Ages, troubadours sang ballads to audiences at the fortress of Les Baux. The romantic tradition continues today, with escapists from all over congregating in the rocky, arid landscape. The town has an abundance of romantic hideaways. See "Les Baux" in chapter 16.
- **St-Tropez** (Côte d'Azur): Any blonde feels like Brigitte Bardot in sunny St-Tropez, and the number of scantily clad satyrs and nymphs in town during summer could perk up the most sluggish libido. The real miracle here is that the charm of the place manages to survive its hype and the hordes of visitors. See "St-Tropez" in chapter 17.

3 The Best Driving Tours

- **La Route des Crêtes** (Alsace-Lorraine): The Vosges, one of the oldest mountain ranges in France, once formed a boundary with Germany. Richly forested with hardwood trees and firs, they skirt the western edge of the Rhine and resemble the Black Forest. La Route des Crêtes (the Crest Road), originally chiseled out of the mountains as a supply line, begins west of Colmar, at the Col du Bonhomme. High points are Münster (home of the cheese), Col de la Schlucht (a resort with panoramas as far as the Jura and the Black Forest), and Markstein. At many points along the way, you can stop and strike out on a well-marked hiking trail. See "La Route des Crêtes" in chapter 12.
- **La Côte d'Or** (Burgundy): Stretching only 60km (37 miles) from Santenay to Dijon, this route is for wine lovers. Rows of terraced vines rise in tiers above the D122/N74/D1138 highways (La Route des Grands Crus), passing through the towns of Puligny-Montrachet, Volnay, Beaune, Nuits-St-Georges, Vosne-Romanée, Gevrey-Chambertin, and Marsannay-la-Côte. Travel at your leisure, stopping to sample the noble vintages (look for the signs sprouting from the sides of the highway). See chapter 13.
- **The Gorges of the Ardèche** (The Rhône Valley): The river that carved these canyons (the Ardèche, a tributary of the Rhône) is the most temperamental French waterway: Its ebbs and flows have created the Grand Canyon of France. Riddled with alluvial deposits, grottoes, caves, and canyons more than 285m (935 ft.) deep, the valley is one of France's most unusual geological spectacles. A panoramic road (D290) runs along one rim of the canyons, providing views over a striking, arid landscape. Plan to park and walk a little on some of the well-marked paths. The drive, which you can do in a day even if you make frequent stops, stretches between Vallon-Pont-d'Arc and Pont St-Esprit. See "The Ardèche" in chapter 14.
- **La Route des Grandes Alpes** (The French Alps): One of the most panoramic drives in western Europe stretches south from the lakefront town of Evian to coastal Nice. You'll see Alpine uplands, larch forests, glaciers, and the foothills of Mont Blanc. Plan on driving 2 to 6 days, stopping in such towns as Morzine, Avoriaz, Chamonix, and Megève. The route covers 740km (460 miles) and crosses many of France's dramatic mountain passes. Some sections are passable only in midsummer. See chapter 15.

4 The Best Châteaux & Palaces

- **Château de Chantilly/Musée Condé** (Ile de France): Anne de Montmorency, a constable of France who advised six monarchs, began this palace in 1560. To save costs, he ordered the new building placed atop the foundations of a derelict castle. His descendants enlarged and embellished the premises, added the massive stables, and hired Le Nôtre to design gardens that later inspired Louis XVI to create similar, larger ones at Versailles. See p. 220.
- **Château de Versailles** (Ile de France): Versailles is the most spectacular palace in the world. Its construction was fraught with ironies and tragedies, and its costs were a factor in the bloodbath of the French Revolution. Ringed with world-class gardens and a network of canals whose excavation required an army of laborers, the site also contains the Grand and Petit Trianons as well as miles of ornate corridors lined with the spoils of a vanished era. See p. 195.
- **Palais de Fontainebleau** (Ile de France): Since the days of the earliest Frankish kings, the forest has served as a royal hunting ground. Various dwellings had been erected for medieval kings, but in 1528, François I commissioned the core of the building that subsequent monarchs would enlarge and embellish. Napoleon declared it his favorite château, delivering an emotional farewell to his troops from its exterior staircase after his 1814 abdication. See p. 207.
- **Château d'Azay-le-Rideau** (Loire Valley): Visitors are enthralled by this château's beauty. Poised above the waters of the Indre River, it boasts decorative remnants of medieval fortifications and an atmosphere that prefigures the Renaissance embellishments of later Loire Valley châteaux. See p. 258.
- **Château de Chambord** (Loire Valley): Despite the incorporation (probably by Michelangelo) of feudal trappings in its layout, this château was built for pleasure—a manifestation of the successes of the 21-year-old François I. Begun in 1519 as the Loire Valley's most opulent status symbol, Chambord heralded the end of the feudal age and the dawn of the Renaissance. After military defeats in Italy, a chastened François rarely visited, opting to live in châteaux closer to Paris. See p. 235.
- **Château de Chenonceau** (Loire Valley): Its builders daringly placed this palace, built between 1513 and 1521, on arched stone vaults above the rushing Cher River. Two of France's most influential women, each of whom imposed her will on Renaissance politics and the château's design, fought over Chenonceau. Henri II gave the palace to his mistress, Diane de Poitiers. After the king's death, his widow, Catherine de Médicis, humiliated Diane by forcing her to move to a less prestigious château in nearby Chaumont. See p. 246.

5 The Best Museums

- **Centre Pompidou** (Paris): "The most avant-garde building in the world" is a citadel of 20th-century art, with exhibitions drawn from more than 40,000 works. Everything is here, from Calder's 1928 *Josephine Baker* (one of his earliest versions of the mobile) to a re-creation of Brancusi's Jazz Age studio. See p. 146.

- **Musée d'Orsay** (Paris): The spidery glass-and-iron canopies of an abandoned railway station frame one of Europe's most thrilling museums. Devoted to 19th-century art, it contains paintings by most of the French Impressionists, and sculptures and decorative objects whose design forever changed the way Europe interpreted line, movement, and color. See p. 150.
- **Musée du Louvre** (Paris): The Louvre's exterior is a triumph of grand French architecture, while its interior contains an embarrassment of artistic riches, with more paintings (around 300,000) than can be displayed at one time. The collection retains its dignity despite the thousands who traipse through the corridors every day, looking for the *Mona Lisa* and the *Venus de Milo.* I. M. Pei's controversial Great Pyramid neatly offsets the grandeur of its Cour Carrée. See p. 151.
- **Musée de la Tapisserie de Bayeux** (Bayeux, Normandy): This museum's star is a 900-year-old tapestry named in honor of medieval Queen Mathilda. Housed in a glass case, the Bayeux tapestry is a long band of linen embroidered with depictions of the war machine that sailed from Normandy to conquer England in 1066. See p. 296.
- **Musée Historique Lorrain** (Nancy, Alsace-Lorraine): Few other French museums reflect a province as well as this one. Its collections include 16th-century engravings, 17th-century masterpieces by local painters, exhibits on Jewish history in eastern France, antique furniture, wrought iron, and domestic accessories. See p. 380.
- **Foundation Maeght** (St-Paul-de-Vence, Côte d'Azur): Established as a showcase for modern art by collectors Aimé and Marguerite Maeght, this avant-garde museum features works by Giacometti, Chagall, Braque, Miró, Matisse, and Barbara Hepworth. The multilevel design by the architect José Luís Sert boasts glass walls with views of the Provence landscape. See p. 556.
- **Musée Fabre** (Montpellier, Languedoc): This museum occupies a villa where Molière once presented some of his plays. Today it boasts one of the worthiest collections of French, Italian, and Spanish paintings in the south of France. See p. 612.
- **Musée Toulouse-Lautrec** (Albi, Languedoc): Henri Toulouse-Lautrec was born in Albi in 1864. Much to his family's horror, he moved to a scandalous area in Paris, where he created depictions of the Belle Epoque scene that are treasures today. Also on view are works by Degas, Bonnard, and Matisse. See p. 631.
- **Musée Ingres** (Montauban, the Dordogne): This museum, in a 17th-century bishops' palace, was created in 1867 when Jean-Auguste-Dominique Ingres (one of the most admired classicists since the Revolution) bequeathed to the city more than 4,000 drawings and paintings. See p. 707.

6 The Best Cathedrals

- **Notre-Dame** (Paris): This structure's stone walls symbolize the power of Paris in the Middle Ages. Begun in 1163, Notre-Dame is the cathedral of the nation and a triumph of medieval architecture. It's dazzling in the morning and at sunset, when its image reflects in the Seine. See p. 153.
- **Cathédrale Notre-Dame de Chartres** (Chartres, Ile de France): No less an

artist than Rodin declared this cathedral a French Acropolis. Its site reputedly was holy for the Druids and the ancient Romans. Chartres is one of the world's largest cathedrals, one of the first High Gothic cathedrals, and the first to use flying buttresses. It also has possibly the finest stained-glass windows, more than 2,500 sq. m (27,000 sq. ft.) of glass whose vivid hues and patterns of light are truly mystical. See p. 200.

- **Cathédrale Notre-Dame de Rouen** (Rouen, Normandy): Consecrated in 1063 and rebuilt after a fire in 1200, parts of it are masterpieces of the Flamboyant Gothic style; others are plainer, though equally dignified. This cathedral was immortalized in the 19th century, when Monet painted a series of impressions of the facade. See p. 274.
- **Cathédrale Notre-Dame d'Amiens** (Amiens, the Ardennes): A lavishly decorated example of High Gothic architecture, this cathedral boasts a soaring nave whose roof is supported by 126 breathtakingly slender pillars. It was begun in 1220 to house the head of St. John the Baptist, brought back from the Crusades; at 141m (463 ft.) long, it is the largest church in France. It escaped destruction during the world wars, despite fierce fighting nearby. See p. 349.
- **Cathédrale Notre-Dame de Reims** (Reims, Champagne): One of France's first Christian bishops, St. Rémi baptized Clovis, king of the Franks, on this site in 496. The church memorializing the event was conceived as a religious sanctuary where the French kings would be anointed; it was large, spectacular, and (in our eyes) rather cold. The coronation of every king between 815 and 1825 was celebrated here. Damaged by World War I bombings, the cathedral was restored by American donations during the 1920s and 1930s. See p. 338.

7 The Best Vineyards & Wineries

- If your primary interest is the wines of Bordeaux, contact the **Maison du Vin,** 1 cours du 30-Juillet, 33075 Bordeaux (✆ **05-56-00-22-88;** www.vins-bordeaux.fr), which offers 3-day courses that cost 305€ to 490€ ($397–$637) per person. The price includes lunch each day and an impressive selection of wines, most from the region around Bordeaux.
- **Couly-Dutheil** (12 rue Diderot, Chinon; ✆ **02-47-97-20-20;** www.coulydutheil-chinon.com): Many of its medieval cellars are carved into the rock undulating through the area's forests. Most production here involves Chinon wines (mostly reds), though its Bourgueil and St-Nicolas de Bourgueil wines are growing in popularity in North America. See "Chinon" in chapter 8.
- **Taittinger** (9 place St-Nicaise, Reims; ✆ **03-26-85-84-35;** www.taittinger.com): Taittinger is a grand *marque* of French champagne, one of the few still controlled by members of the family that founded it, in 1930. It's one of the most visitor-friendly houses. See p. 341.
- **Domaines Schlumberger** (100 rue Théodore-Deck, Guebwiller, near Colmar; ✆ **03-89-74-27-00;** www.domaines-schlumberger.com): Established in 1810, these cellars blend early-19th-century brickwork and modern stainless steel; a visit will enhance your understanding of the subtle differences among wines produced by the seven varieties of grape cultivated in Alsace. See "Colmar" in chapter 12.

- **Domaine Maurice Protheau** (Château d'Etroyes, Mercurey; ✆ **03-85-45-10-84;** www.domaine-protheau-mercurey.fr): The 50 hectares (124 acres) of grapevines straddle at least two *appellations contrôlées* (a regulation system that ensures a wine has been produced where the bottles says), so you'll have a chance to contrast reds (both pinot noirs and burgundies), whites, and rosés produced under the auspices of both Rully and Mercurey. Headquarters is in a château built in the late 1700s and early 1800s. See "Autun" in chapter 13.
- **The Winegrowing Region around Bordeaux:** This area is among the most glamorous in France, with a strong English influence, thanks to centuries of trade with London- and Bristol-based dealers. One prestigious grower, **Société Duboscq,** Château Haut-Marbuzet, St-Estephe (✆ **05-56-59-30-54**), welcomes visitors who phone in advance of their arrival Monday to Saturday. Free visits to the cellars are followed by a complimentary *dégustation des vins* of whichever of the company's products a visitor requests. See p. 689.

8 The Best Luxury Hotels

- **Hôtel Ritz** (Paris; ✆ **800/223-6800** in the U.S. and Canada, or 01-43-16-30-30; www.ritzparis.com): This hotel occupies a palace overlooking the octagonal borders of one of the most perfect plazas in France: place Vendôme. The decor is pure opulence. Marcel Proust wrote parts of *Remembrance of Things Past* here, and Georges-Auguste Escoffier perfected many of his recipes in its kitchens. See p. 102.
- **Hôtel Meurice** (Paris; ✆ **01-44-58-10-10;** www.meuricehotel.com) faces the Jardin des Tuileries close to the Place de la Concorde. Over the course of its career, it has catered to everybody from royalty to Salvador Dalí. Massively restored and still celebrated for its glass roofed Winter Garden, it's a pocket of posh. See p. 102.
- **Château d'Artigny** (Montbazon, Loire Valley; ✆ **02-47-34-30-30;** www.artigny.com): The perfume king François Coty once lived and entertained lavishly at this mansion outside Tours—and you can do the same today in one of the poshest hotels in the Loire Valley. Experience the grandeur once enjoyed by Elizabeth Taylor and other celebs, taking in the weekend soirées and musical evenings. See p. 253.
- **Oustau de Baumanière** (Les Baux, Provence; ✆ **04-90-54-33-07;** www.oustaudebaumaniere.com): This Relais & Châteaux property is in the valley at the foot of Les Baux de Provence. Both the cuisine and the accommodations, some of which are in buildings dating from the 16th and 17th centuries, are superb. See p. 490.
- **Grand Hôtel du Cap-Ferrat** (St-Jean-Cap-Ferrat, Côte d'Azur; ✆ **04-93-76-50-52;** www.grand-hotel-cap-ferrat.com): The Grand Hôtel occupies 5.6 prime hectares (14 acres) on one of the world's most exclusive peninsulas. In a Belle Epoque palace, it has hosted royals, aristocrats, and wealthy wannabes since the turn of the 20th century. See p. 579.
- **Hôtel du Cap–Eden Roc** (Cap d'Antibes, Côte d'Azur; ✆ **04-93-61-39-01;** www.edenroc-hotel.fr): Built during the grand Second Empire and set on 8.9 hectares (22 acres) of splendidly landscaped gardens, this hotel is legendary, evoking the F. Scott Fitzgerald classic *Tender Is the Night.* Swimmers revel in a pool

blasted from the dark rock of the glamorous coastline. See p. 550.

- **Hôtel Negresco** (Nice, Côte d'Azur; ✆ **04-93-16-64-00;** www.hotel-negresco-nice.com): Built in 1913 as a layered wedding cake in the château style, the Negresco was a lavish escape for the Edwardian era's most respected and most notorious figures, including Lillie Langtry, the longtime mistress of Britain's Edward VII. After her fall from grace, she sat in the lobby, swathed in veils, refusing to utter a word. Following renovations, the hotel is better now than during its Jazz Age heyday. See p. 569.
- **Hôtel du Palais** (Biarritz, Basque Country; ✆ **800/223-6800** in the U.S. and Canada, or 05-59-41-64-00; www.hotel-du-palais.com): Delectably beautiful, this place was built in 1845 as a pink-walled summer palace for Napoleon III and his empress, Eugénie. The Belle Epoque fantasy has entertained such guests as Edward VII of England, Alfonso XIII of Spain, and the duke of Windsor. See p. 659.

9 The Best Affordable Hotels

- **Hôtel de Lutèce** (Paris; ✆ **01-43-26-23-52;** www.paris-hotel-lutece.com): It slumbers on Paris's "other island," the Ile St-Louis, which usually escapes the crush of visitors on the more popular Ile de la Cité, just across the bridge. You're still in the city, but here you can imagine yourself in a country inn. See p. 105.
- **Les Maisons de Léa** (Honfleur, Normandy; ✆ **02-31-14-49-49;** www.lesmaisonsdelea.com): It overlooks a Norman 18th-century port favored by the French novelist Flaubert. The amenities aren't grand, but the charming setting includes an appealing restaurant, and—more surprising—the price tag is reasonable. See p. 284.
- **Hôtel d'Avaugour** (Dinan, Brittany; ✆ **02-96-39-07-49;** www.avaugourhotel.com): Its exterior looks as antique as the fortifications ringing the medieval harbor, but a major restoration transformed the interior into a cozy getaway on the Norman coast. Add aesthetic appeal, old-time flavor of Dinan's winding alleys, and views of the Channel, and you've got the ingredients for an affordable escape. See p. 316.
- **Ostellerie du Vieux-Pérouges** (Pérouges, Rhône Valley; ✆ **04-74-61-00-88;** www.ostellerie.com): This hotel, described as a museum of the 13th century, is one of the most significant in central France. Composed of a group of 13th-century buildings with low ceilings and thick walls, it evokes the France of another day and doesn't overcharge. See p. 423.
- **Hôtel Clair Logis** (St-Jean-Cap-Ferrat, Côte d'Azur; ✆ **04-93-76-51-81;** www.hotel-clair-logis.fr): The real estate surrounding this converted 19th-century villa is among the most expensive in Europe, but this hotel manages to keep its prices beneath levels that really hurt. When you check into your room (named after a flower in the garden surrounding the place), you'll be in good company: Even General de Gaulle, who knew the value of a centime, stayed here. See p. 580.
- **La Réserve** (Albi, Languedoc; ✆ **05-63-60-80-80;** www.relaischateaux.fr/reservealbi): Scrublands, vineyards, groves of olives, and cypresses surround this dignified farmhouse. It's less expensive than many luxurious hideaways along the nearby Côte d'Azur, and its location is just outside the center of one of our favorite fortified sites in Europe, the town of Albi. See p. 632.

10 The Best Historic Places to Stay

- **Trianon Palace & Spa** (Versailles, Ile de France; ✆ **800/228-3000** in the U.S. and Canada, or 01-30-84-50-00; www.westin.com): Louis XIV nearly bankrupted France during the construction of his nearby palace, but this hotel overlooking its gardens might have been even more influential. In 1919, the Versailles Peace Treaty was ratified by delegates who stayed in the same rooms that house guests today. You'll be pampered at this plush, elegant hotel, which boasts its own spa. See p. 198.
- **Château de Locguénolé** (Hennebont, Brittany; ✆ **02-97-76-76-76;** www.chateau-de-locguenole.com): No professional decorator could accumulate the array of furnishings and artifacts that grace this Breton manor house, which has been occupied by the same family for 500 years. Some visitors think it's the most charming hotel in southern Brittany; you may agree. See p. 321.
- **Manoir du Stang** (La Forêt-Fouesnant, Brittany; ✆ **02-98-56-97-37;** www.manoirdustang.com): Even the ivy that twines across the facade of this 16th-century Breton manor house looks as though it was planted by someone very important, very long ago. Formal gardens segue into forested parkland; modern amenities are juxtaposed with enviable antiques—the place is a gem that happens to be a glamorous hotel. See p. 319.
- **Château de Rochegude** (Rochegude, Provence; ✆ **04-75-97-21-10;** www.chateauderochegude.com): During the thousand years of this château's existence, its owners have included popes, dauphins, and less prominent aristocrats who showered it with taste and money. Today each room is outfitted in a style inspired by a specific emperor or king. The setting is 10 hectares (25 acres) of parkland adjacent to the Rhône, outside Orange. See p. 468.
- **Château de Roussan** (St-Rémy-de-Provence, Provence; ✆ **04-90-92-11-63;** www.chateau-de-roussan.com): One of this château's outbuildings was the home of the psychic Nostradamus, and its main building, sheltered by a stone neoclassical facade erected in 1701, is among the most beautiful in Provence. The château evokes another time, with none of the artificiality of the nearby Côte d'Azur. See p. 478.
- **Château des Alpilles** (St-Rémy-de-Provence, Provence; ✆ **04-90-92-03-33;** www.chateaualpilles.com): The Pichot family built this château in 1827, and it has housed many famous personages, including Chateaubriand. The luxurious hotel, modestly referred to as "a house for paying friends," is a showcase of luxury, refinement, and taste. See p. 479.
- **Château de la Vallée Bleue** (La Châtre, Massif Central; ✆ **02-54-31-01-91;** www.chateauvalleebleue.com): If your room is named for Liszt, Chopin, Flaubert, or Delacroix, it's probably because they slept in the same spot. The château was built by a doctor committed to the well-being of his nearby patient George Sand, the author and feminist trendsetter whose masquerades as a man still provoke curiosity in this part of France. See p. 714.

11 The Best Upscale Restaurants

- **Restaurant Plaza Athénée (Alain Ducasse;** Paris; ✆ **01-53-67-65-00**): A coveted three-star rating from Michelin hardly seemed to challenge this brash chef. Ducasse is the darling of foodies and the spiritual heir of the legendary Escoffier. No one can outdo his pasta bathed in cream, sweetbreads, truffles, and (get this) the combs and kidneys of a proud, strutting cock. See p. 127.
- **Le Grand Véfour** (Paris; ✆ **01-42-96-56-27**): Amid the arcades of the Palais Royal, this has been a dining spot since the reign of Louis XV, attracting such notables as Colette, Victor Hugo, and the forever-loyal Jean Cocteau. Jean Taittinger, of the champagne family, runs it today, and his kitchen brings originality to French classics—everything from pigeon in the style of Rainier of Monaco to French-roasted sole and sea scallops in velvety pumpkin sauce. See p. 119.
- **Taillevent** (Paris; ✆ **01-44-95-15-01**): Dining here is the social and gastronomic high point of a Paris visit. Its premises (an antique house near the Arc de Triomphe) are suitably grand, and its cuisine as appropriately stylish as the Jackie Onassis look-alikes who dine here. See p. 128.
- **Les Crayères** (Reims, Champagne; ✆ **03-26-82-80-80;** www.lescrayeres.com): This restaurant's setting is a lavish but dignified château with soaring ceilings and French Empire decor. Built in 1904 as the home of the Pommery family (of champagne fortune) and surrounded by a 5.6-hectare (14-acre) park, it's maintained by a staff that appreciates the nuances of service rituals. You can retire directly to your room after consuming a bottle or two of the region's bubbly. See p. 342.
- **A la Côte St-Jacques** (Joigny, Burgundy; ✆ **03-86-62-09-70;** www.cotesaintjacques.com): On the edge of Burgundy, beside the river Yonne, this is the quintessential *restaurant avec chambres.* Indulge your taste for well-prepared food and wine, and then totter off to one of the carefully furnished guest rooms in the historic compound. One of our favorite dishes is cassolette of morels and frogs' legs, sublime when accompanied by a half bottle of red burgundy. See p. 388.
- **L'Espérance** (Vézelay, Burgundy; ✆ **03-86-33-39-10;** www.marc-meneau-esperance.com): In a farmhouse at the base of a hill (La Colline de Vézelay) that has been a holy site for thousands of years, L'Espérance is run by one of Europe's most famous chefs, Marc Meneau, and his wife, Françoise. The place combines country comforts with great sophistication. See p. 391.
- **Paul Bocuse** (Collonges-au-Mont-d'Or, near Lyon, Rhône Valley; ✆ **04-72-42-90-90**): Bocuse was the *enfant terrible* of French gastronomy through most of his youth. Today he's the world's most famous chef, catering to Europe's hardest-to-please customers. The cuisine is ostensibly Lyonnais, but Bocuse has never been limited by provincialism, and his mind wanders the world for inspiration. His signature dishes range from pigeon in puff pastry with foie gras to his notable black truffle soup. See p. 416.
- **Hôtel-Restaurant Troisgros** (Roanne, Rhône Valley; ✆ **04-77-71-66-97;** www.troisgros.com): The setting is the dining room of a once-nondescript hotel near a train station. The cuisine is a celebration of the agrarian bounty of France. Mingling regional specialties, the menu attracts diners from as far away as Paris. See p. 422.

- **Auberge du Père-Bise** (Talloires, French Alps; ✆ **04-50-60-72-01;** www.perebise.com): A mysterious alchemy transformed a simple lakeside chalet into an illustrious restaurant. Beside Lac d'Annecy in eastern France, it's outfitted like a provincial home of local gentry, yet it serves elegant food favored by generations of patrons, including the Rothschilds. See p. 440.
- **Le Moulin de Mougins** (Mougins, Côte d'Azur; ✆ **04-93-75-78-24;** www.moulin-mougins.com): Occupying a 16th-century olive mill in a Provence forest, this long-celebrated destination is a showcase for the cuisine of Alain Llorca, one of the most talented and written-about chefs on the French Riviera. He concocts what he calls the "cuisine of the sun." See p. 539.

12 The Best Affordable Restaurants

- **Crémerie-Restaurant Polidor** (Paris; ✆ **01-43-26-95-34**): For many Parisians, the cuisine here evokes dinners their grandmothers might have cooked in the days after World War II. The unpretentious setting, with lace curtains filtering the sunlight, drew even such iconoclasts as André Gide. See p. 139.
- **Les Vapeurs** (Trouville, Normandy; ✆ **02-31-88-15-24**): An anomaly among the Norman coast's high-priced brasseries, this restaurant overlooking the port is no-frills, from its Art Deco decor to its fresh, well-priced seafood. Patrons enjoy the festive ambience. See p. 291.
- **L'Auberge de Pelican** (Dinan, Brittany; ✆ **02-96-39-47-05**): Many visitors drive up from Paris for the day, followed by a dinner here in this old-fashioned Breton establishment, where even the bread is homemade. Dishes with an emphasis on fresh fish are based on time-honored recipes. See p. 316.
- **Brasserie de l'Ancienne Douane** (Strasbourg, Alsace-Lorraine; ✆ **03-88-15-78-78;** www.anciennedouane.fr): In a city known for its Alsatian cuisine, this restaurant is a front-runner in the moderate category. In a medieval building, you can feast on the sauerkraut and foie gras of the region, as well as on a succulent specialty, chicken in Riesling wine. See p. 363.
- **Au Chalet de Brou** (Bourg-en-Bresse, Rhône Valley; ✆ **04-74-22-26-28**): In a town famous for its poultry, this restaurant sits across from the village church. It offers the local birds at amazingly low prices, and food critics travel here from all over France for the hearty roast chicken. See p. 425.
- **Le Bistro Latin** (Aix-en-Provence, Provence; ✆ **04-42-38-22-88**): In Paul Cézanne's hometown, seek out its best and most affordable little bistro, serving classic Provençal cuisine in each of its two intimate dining rooms. Its fixed-price menus are the best deal in town. See p. 496.
- **Chez Servais** (Libourne, Bordeaux wine district; ✆ **05-57-51-83-97**): As you're touring the wine district outside Bordeaux, one of your finest and best-value meals is likely to be in this little market town at the junction of the Dordogne and Isle rivers. The cuisine is a savory blend of classical and modern. See p. 688.

2

A Traveler's Guide to France's Art & Architecture

France's art treasures range from medieval stained glass and Ingres portraits to Monet's Impressionist *Water Lilies;* its architecture encompasses Roman ruins and Gothic cathedrals as well as Renaissance châteaux and postmodern buildings like the Centre Pompidou. This brief overview will help you make sense of it all.

1 Art 101

PREHISTORIC, CELTIC & CLASSICAL (20,000 B.C.–A.D. 500)

After England's Stonehenge, Europe's most famous prehistoric remains are France's **Paleolithic cave paintings.** Created 15,000 to 20,000 years ago, they depict mostly hunting scenes and abstract shapes. Whether the paintings served in religious rites or were simply decorative is anybody's guess.

Important examples of ancient art include:

- **Cave art.** The **caves at Lascaux,** the Sistine Chapel of prehistoric art, have been closed since 1963, but experts have created a replica, Lascaux II. To see the real stuff, visit **Les Eyzies-de-Tayac,** which boasts four caves (Font de Gaume is the best). In the neighboring Lot Valley, outside Cahors, is the **Grotte du Pech-Merle,** with France's oldest cave art (about 20,000 years old).
- **Celtic and classical art.** Little remains of the art of **Celtic** (ca. 1,000 B.C.–A.D. 125) and **Roman** (A.D. 125–500) Gaul. Surviving items—small votive bronzes, statues, jewelry, and engraved weapons and tools—are spread across France's **archaeology museums.** Burgundy preserves the most of Celtic Gaul, including sites at **Dijon, Châtillon-sur-Seine, Alise-Ste-Reine,** and **Auxerre.** To see artifacts of Roman Gaul, visit the southern towns of **Nîmes, Arles, Orange, St-Rémy-de-Provence,** and **Vienne.** You'll also find some sculptures in Paris's **Musée de Cluny.**

ROMANESQUE (900–1100)

Artistic expression in early medieval France was largely church-related. Because Mass was in Latin, images were used to communicate the Bible's lessons to the mostly illiterate people. **Bas-reliefs** (sculptures that project slightly from a flat surface) were used to illustrate key tales that inspired faith in God and fear of sin (the *Last Judgment* was a favorite). These reliefs were wrapped around column capitals and fitted into the **tympanums,** or arched spaces above doorways (the complete door, tympanum, arch, and supporting pillars assemblage is the **portal**).

Worshipers were also interested in specialized saints associated with everyday matters, such as crops, marriage, animals, and health. Chapels were built to house silver and gold **reliquaries** displaying bits of saints to which worshipers could pray. Saintly

statues also began appearing on facades, though this became more of a Gothic convention.

The best examples of Romanesque art include:

- **Sculptures and statues.** The best surviving examples are a *Last Judgment* tympanum by Gislebertus at **St-Lazare** in Autun; 76 Romanesque cloister capitals and one of France's best-carved 11th-century portals at **St-Pierre Abbey** in Moissac near Montauban; the tympanum over the inner main portal of huge **Ste-Madeleine** in Vézelay; reliefs of *Christ and the Evangelists* by Bernard Guildin in the crypt of **St-Semin** in Toulouse; and the wonderfully detailed facade frieze and statues of **St-Pierre** in Angoulême.
- **Wall paintings and frescoes.** You'll find examples at **Notre-Dame** in Le Puy (ca. 1000), **St-Savin** near Poitiers (1100), and **Berzé-la-Ville** (1100) near Cluny.
- **Bayeux Tapestry (1066–1077).** The most notable example of Romanesque artistry is the Bayeux Tapestry, 69m (230 ft.) of embroidered linen telling the story of William the Conqueror's defeat of the English.

GOTHIC (1100–1400)

Late medieval French art remained largely ecclesiastical. Church facades and choir screens were festooned with **statues and carvings,** and the French became masters of **stained glass.** Many painterly conventions began on windowpanes or as elaborate designs in **illuminated manuscript** margins, which developed into altarpieces of the colorful, expressive **International Gothic** style of posed scenes and stylized figures.

In Gothic painting and sculpture, figures tended to be more natural than in the Romanesque, but they were also highly stylized, flowing, and rhythmic. The features and gestures were usually exaggerated for symbolic or emotional emphasis.

The best examples of Gothic art include:

- **Sculpture and statues.** The best-preserved examples are at the cathedrals of **Chartres, Amiens,** and **Reims** (see "Architecture 101," below), and at **Strasbourg,** which boasts one of the most elaborate Gothic portals and rose windows in France.
- **Stained glass.** All of the above churches (especially **Chartres**) contain some of the most stunning stained glass in Europe—though first prize goes to Paris's **Ste-Chapelle.**
- **Painting.** Burgundy was the first French area to embrace the High Gothic painting style of its Flemish neighbors. The great **van der Weyden** left works in **Dijon** and **Beaune** as well as at the **Louvre.** The Dutch **Limbourg Brothers'** *Les Très Riches Heures* (1413–16, finished after their deaths), now in **Château de Chantilly,** is considered a touchstone of the International Gothic style. **Enguerrand Quarton** was the most important French painter of the period. His only documented paintings are *Virgin of Mercy* (1452) at **Chantilly** and a work at the **Musée de l'Hospice** in Villeneuve-lez-Avignon, but most scholars also attribute to him the **Louvre's** *Villeneuve Pietà* (1460).
- **Unicorn Tapestries (1499–1514).** Now in Paris's **Musée de Cluny,** these tapestries shine brightly as a statement of medieval sensibilities while borrowing some burgeoning Renaissance conventions.

THE RENAISSANCE & BAROQUE (1450–1800)

Renaissance means "rebirth"—in this case, that of classical ideals. Humanist thinkers rediscovered the wisdom of ancient Greece and Rome, while artists strove for naturalism, using newly developed techniques like linear perspective. The French had little to do with this movement, which started in Italy and was picked up only in Germany and the Low Countries. However, many Renaissance treasures are in French museums, thanks to collectors such as **François I.**

Not until the 17th-century **baroque** did a few French masters emerge. This period is hard to pin down. In some ways a result of the Catholic Counter-Reformation, it reaffirmed spirituality in a simplified, monumental, and religious version of Renaissance ideals. In other ways, it delved even deeper into classical modes and a kind of superrealism based on using peasants as models and the *chiaroscuro* (contrast of light and dark) of the Italian painter Caravaggio.

Some view those two baroque movements as extensions of Renaissance experiments and find the true baroque in later, complex compositions—explosions of dynamic fury, movement, color, and figures—that are well balanced but in such cluttered abundance as to appear untamed. **Rococo** is this later baroque art gone awry: frothy and chaotic.

Paris's **Louvre** abounds with Renaissance works by Italian, Flemish, and German masters, including **Michelangelo** (1475–1564) and **Leonardo da Vinci** (1452–1519). Leonardo's ***Mona Lisa*** (1503–05), perhaps the world's most famous painting, hangs there. Great baroque and rococo artists include:

- **Nicolas Poussin (1594–1665).** While his mythological scenes presaged the Romantic movement, on a deeper level his balance and predilection to paint from nature had closer connection to (and greater influence on) Impressionists like Cézanne. Find his works in the **Louvre** and in **Nancy.**
- **Antoine Watteau (1684–1721).** A rococo painter of colorful, theatrical works now in the **Louvre,** Watteau began the short-lived *fête galante* style of china-doll figures against stylized landscapes of woodlands or ballrooms.
- **François Boucher (1703–70).** Louis XV's rococo court painter, Boucher studied Watteau and produced decorative landscapes and genre works, now at the **Louvre.**
- **Jean-Honoré Fragonard (1732–1806).** Boucher's student and master of rococo pastel scenes, Fragonard painted pink-cheeked, wispy, genteel lovers frolicking among billowing trees. His famous *The Bathers* hangs in the **Louvre.** More work is in Amiens's **Musée de Picardie.**

NEOCLASSICAL & ROMANTIC (1770–1890)

As the baroque got excessive and the rococo got cute, and as the somber Counter-Reformation got serious about imposing limits on religious art, several artists, like Jacques-Louis David, looked to the ancients. Viewing new excavations of Greek and Roman sites (Pompeii, Paestum) and statuary became integral parts of the Grand Tour through Italy, while the Enlightenment (and growing revolutionary) interest in Greek democracy beat an intellectual path to the distant past. This gave rise to a **neoclassical** style that emphasized symmetry, austerity, clean lines, and classical themes, such as depictions of historical or mythological scenes.

The **Romantics,** on the other hand, felt that both the ancients and the Renaissance had gotten it wrong and that the Middle Ages were the place to be. They idealized tales of chivalry and held a deep respect for nature, human rights, and the nobility of peasantry, as well as a suspicion of progress. Their paintings were heroic, historic, and (melo)dramatic.

The greatest artists and movements of the era include:

- **Jacques-Louis David (1744–1825).** David dropped the baroque after study in Rome exposed him to neoclassicism, which he brought back to Paris and displayed in such paintings as *The Oath of the Horatii* (1784) and *Coronation of Napoléon and Joséphine* (1805–08), both in the **Louvre.**
- **Jean-Auguste-Dominique Ingres (1780–1867).** Ingres trained with David, from whom he broke to adapt a more Greek style. He became a defender of the neoclassicists and the Royal French Academy, and opposed the Romantics. His *Grand Odalisque* (1814) hangs in the **Louvre.**
- **Théodore Géricault (1791–1824).** One of the early Romantics, Géricault painted *The Raft of the Medusa* (1819), which served as a model for the movement. This large, dramatic history painting hangs in the **Louvre.**
- **Eugène Delacroix (1798–1863).** Painted in the Romantic style, his *Liberty Leading the People* (1830), in the **Louvre,** reveals experimentation in color and brush stroke.
- The **Barbizon School.** This group of landscape painters, founded in the 1830s by **Théodore Rousseau** (1812–67), painted from nature at Barbizon, where the **Musée Ganne** is devoted to Rousseau's works. The paintings of **Jean-François Millet** (1814–75), who depicted classical scenes and peasants, hang in his studio nearby and in Paris's **Musée d'Orsay.** You'll find works by **Jean-Baptiste-Camille Corot** (1796–1875), a sort of idealistic proto-Impressionist, in the **Louvre.**

IMPRESSIONISM (1870–1920)

Formal, rigid neoclassicism and idealized Romanticism rankled some late-19th-century artists interested in painting directly from nature. Seeking to capture the fleeting *impression* of light reflecting off objects, they adopted a free, open style characterized by deceptively loose compositions; swift, visible brushwork; and often, light colors. For subjects, they turned away from the historical depictions of previous styles to landscapes and scenes of daily life. Unless specified below, you'll find some of their best works in Paris's **Musée d'Orsay.**

Impressionist greats include:

- **Edouard Manet (1832–83).** His groundbreaking *Picnic on the Grass* (1863) and *Olympia* (1863) weren't Impressionism proper, but they helped inspire the movement with their realism, visible brush strokes, and thick outlines.
- **Claude Monet (1840–1926).** The Impressionist movement began with an 1874 exhibition in which Monet showed his loose, Turner-inspired *Impression, Sunrise* (1874), now in the **Musée Marmottan.** One critic focused on it to lambaste the whole exhibition, deriding it all as "Impressionist." Far from being insulted, the show's artists adopted the word for their movement. Monet's *Water Lilies* hangs in the basement of Paris's **Musée de l'Orangerie.** You can visit his studio and gardens at **Giverny,** north of Paris.
- **Pierre-Auguste Renoir (1841–1919).** Originally Renoir was a porcelain painter, which helps explain his figures' ivory skin and chubby pink cheeks.
- **Edgar Degas (1834–1917).** Degas was an accomplished painter, sculptor, and draftsman—his pastels of dancers and bathers are memorable.
- **Auguste Rodin (1840–1917).** The greatest sculptor of the Impressionist era, Rodin crafted remarkably expressive bronzes, refusing to idealize the human figure as had his neoclassical predecessors. The **Musée Rodin,** his former Paris studio,

contains, among other works, his *Burghers of Calais* (1886), *The Kiss* (1886–98), and *The Thinker* (1880).

POST-IMPRESSIONISM (1880–1930)

Few experimental French artists of the late 19th century were considered Impressionists, though many were friends with those in the movement. The smaller movements or styles are usually lumped together as *post-Impressionist.*

Again, you'll find the best examples of their works at Paris's **Musée d'Orsay,** although the pieces mentioned below by Matisse, Chagall, and the Cubists are in the **Centre Pompidou.**

Important post-Impressionists include:

- **Paul Cézanne (1839–1906).** Cézanne adopted the short brush strokes, landscapes, and light color palette of his Impressionist friends, but his style was more formal and deliberate. He sought to give his art monumentality and permanence, even if the subjects were still lifes (*Nature Morte: Pommes et Oranges,* 1895–1900), portraits (*La Femme a la Cafetière,* 1890–95), and landscapes (*La Maison du Pendu Auvers-sur-Oise,* 1873).
- **Paul Gauguin (1848–1903).** Gauguin could never settle himself or his work, trying Brittany, where he developed **synthetism** (black outlines around solid colors), and hopping around the South Pacific, where he was inspired by local styles and colors, as in *Femmes de Tahiti sur la Plage* (1891).
- **Georges Seurat (1859–91), Paul Signac (1863–1935),** and **Camille Pissarro (1830–1903).** These artists developed **divisionism** and its more formal cousin, **pointillism.** Rather than mixing yellow and blue together to make green, they applied tiny dots of yellow and blue right next to one another so that the viewer's *eye* mixed them together to make green. Seurat's best work in the Orsay is *Le Cirque* (1891), though the lines are softer and subjects more compelling in the nude studies called *Les Poseuses* (1886–87).
- **Henri de Toulouse-Lautrec (1864–1901).** He's most famous for his work with thinned-down oils, which he used to create paintings and posters of wispy, fluid lines anticipating Art Nouveau. He often depicted the bohemian life of Paris (dance halls, cafes, and top-hatted patrons at fancy parties), as in the barely sketched *La Danse Mauresque* (1895); the pastel *Le Lit* (1892) shows his quieter, more intimate side.
- **Vincent van Gogh (1853–1890).** A Dutchman, van Gogh spent most of his career in France. He combined divisionism, synthetism, and a touch of Japanese influence and painted with thick, short strokes. Never particularly accepted by any artistic circle, he is the most popular painter in the world today, even though he sold only one painting in his life. The Orsay contains such works as *Le Chambre de Van Gogh à Arles* (1889), a self-portrait (1887), a portrait of his psychiatrist *Docteur Paul Gachet* (1890), and *La Méridienne* (1889–90).
- **Henri Matisse (1869–1954).** Matisse took a hint from synthetism and added wild colors and strong patterns to create **Fauvism** (a critic described those who used the style as *fauves,* meaning "wild beasts"), such as *Interior, Goldfish Bowl* (1914). He continued exploring these themes even when most artists were turning to cubism. When his health failed, he assembled brightly colored collages of paper cutouts (such as the Pompidou's *Sorrow of the King,* 1952). You'll find several of his works in the **Musée Matisse** in Nice. His masterpiece, the **Chapelle du Rosaire** (1949–51), a chapel he designed and decorated, is near Vence.

- **Georges Braque (1882–1963)** and **Pablo Picasso (1881–1973).** French-born Braque and Spanish-born Picasso painted objects from all points of view at once, rather than using tricks like perspective to fool viewers into seeing three dimensions (in the Pompidou, Braque's *Man with Guitar,* 1914, and Picasso's 1907 study for *Les Demoiselles d'Avignon*). The result was called **cubism** and was expanded upon by the likes of **Fernand Léger** (1881–1955; *Wedding,* 1911) and the Spaniard **Juan Gris** (1887–1927; *Le Petit Déjeuner,* 1915). Braque developed the style using collage (he added bits of paper and cardboard to his images), while Picasso moved on to other styles. You can see work from all of Picasso's periods at museums dedicated to him in **Paris, Antibes,** and **Vallauris,** where Picasso revived the ceramics industry.
- **Marc Chagall (1889–1985).** This Hasidic Jewish artist is hard to pin down. He traveled widely in Europe, the United States, Mexico, and Israel; his painting started from cubism and picked up inspiration everywhere to fuel a brightly colored, allegorical, often whimsical style. You'll find a museum devoted to him in **Nice,** several of his stained-glass windows in the **Cathédrale Notre-Dame d'Amiens,** his painted ceiling in Paris's **Opéra Garnier,** and *To Russia, the Asses and the Others* (1911) in the Pompidou.

2 Architecture 101

While each architectural era has its distinctive features, some elements, floor plans, and terms are common to many of the eras.

From the Romanesque period on, most **churches** consist of either a single wide **aisle** or a central **nave** flanked by two narrow aisles. The aisles are separated from the nave by a row of **columns,** or more accurately by square stacks of masonry called **piers,** connected by **arches.** Sometimes in structures from the Romanesque and Gothic eras, you'll see a second level, the **clerestory,** above these arches (and hence above the low roof over the aisles) punctuated by windows.

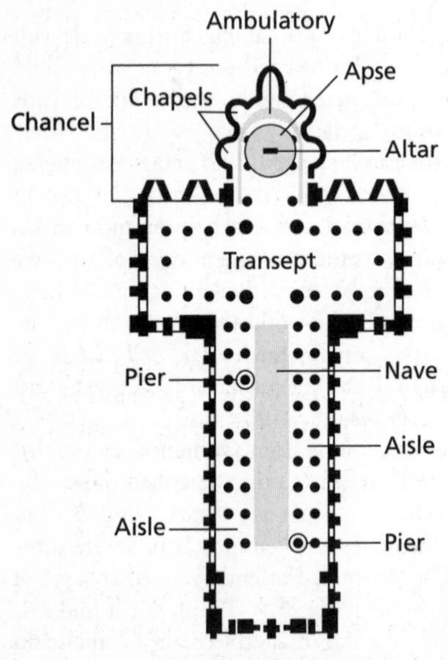

Church Floor Plan

This main nave and aisle assemblage is usually crossed by a perpendicular corridor called a **transept,** placed near the far, east end of the church so that the floor plan looks like a **Latin Cross** (shaped like a crucifix). The shorter, east arm of the nave is called the **chancel;** it often houses the stalls of the **choir** and the **altar.** If the far end of the chancel is rounded off, it is termed an **apse.** An **ambulatory** is a curving corridor outside the altar and the choir area, separating them from the ring of smaller chapels radiating off the chancel and apse.

Some churches, especially those built after the Renaissance, when mathematical proportion became important, have a **Greek Cross** plan, with each axis the same length—like a giant plus sign (+).

Very few buildings (especially churches) were built in one particular style. Massive, expensive structures often took centuries to complete, during which time tastes would change and plans would be altered.

ANCIENT ROMAN (125 B.C.–A.D. 450)

Provence was Rome's first transalpine conquest, and the legions of Julius Caesar quickly subdued the Celtic tribes across France, converting it into Roman Gaul.

Roman architectural innovations include:

- **The load-bearing arch**
- **The use of concrete, brick, and stone**

Nîmes preserves from the 1st century B.C. a 20,000-seat **amphitheater,** a **Corinthian temple** called the "Square House," a fine **archaeology museum,** and the astounding **pont du Gard,** a 47m-long (158-ft.), three-story aqueduct made of cut stones fitted together without mortar.

Pont du Gard, Nîmes

From the Augustan era of the 1st century A.D., **Arles** preserves a 25,000-seat **amphitheater,** a rebuilt **theater,** and a decent **museum.** The nearby **Glanum** excavations outside St-Rémy-de-Provence (which houses its **archaeology museum**) offer a complete, albeit highly ruined, glimpse of an entire Roman provincial town, from a few pre-Roman Gallic remnants and a 20 B.C. arch to the last structures sacked by invading Goths in A.D. 480.

ROMANESQUE (800–1100)

Romanesque churches were large, with a wide nave and aisles to accommodate the faithful who came to hear Mass and worship at the altars of various saints. To support the weight of all that masonry, the walls had to be thick and solid (meaning they could be pierced by only a few small windows) and had to rest on huge piers, giving Norman churches a dark, somber feeling.

Some of the features of this style include:

- **Rounded arches.** These load-bearing architectural devices allowed architects to open up wide naves and spaces, channeling the weight of the stone walls and ceiling across the curve of the arch and into the ground through the columns or pilasters.
- **Thick walls**
- **Infrequent and small windows**
- **Huge piers**

The **Cathédrale St-Bénigne** in Dijon was the first French Romanesque church, but of that era only the crypt remains. The **Cathédrale St-Pierre** in Angoulême has a single large nave, a rounded apse with small radiating chapels, and a pair of transept mini-apses.

GOTHIC (1100–1500)

By the 12th century, engineering developments freed architecture from the heavy, thick walls of the Romanesque and allowed ceilings to soar, walls to thin, and windows to proliferate. The Gothic was France's greatest homegrown architectural style, copied throughout Europe.

Instead of dark, relatively unadorned Romanesque interiors that forced the eyes of the faithful toward the altar, the Gothic interior enticed the churchgoers' gaze upward to high ceilings filled with light. The priests still conducted Mass in Latin, but now peasants could "read" the stories told in stained-glass windows.

The squat, brooding exteriors of the Romanesque fortresses of God were replaced by graceful buttresses and soaring spires, which rose from town centers like beacons of religion.

Some identifiable Gothic features include:

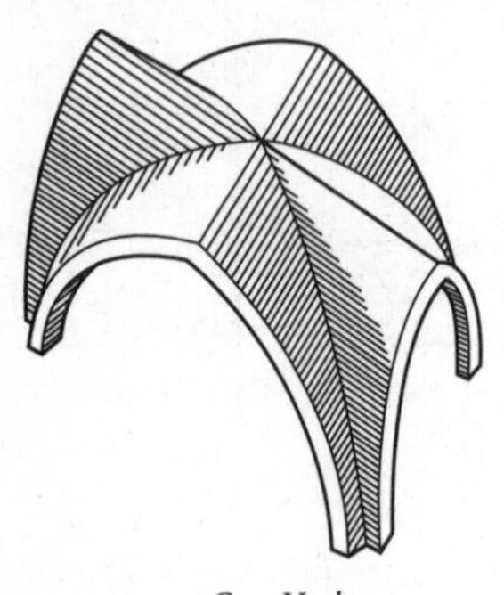

Cross Vault

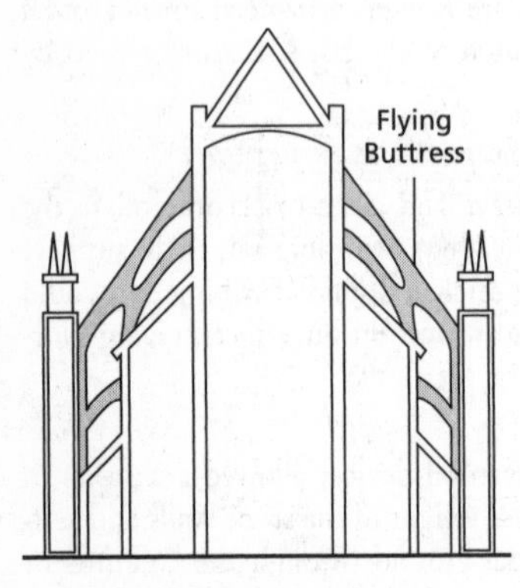

Cross Section of Gothic Church

- **Pointed arches.** The most significant development of the Gothic era was the discovery that pointed arches could carry far more weight than rounded ones.
- **Cross vaults.** Instead of being flat, the square patch of ceiling between four columns arches up to a point in the center, creating four sail shapes, sort of like the underside of a pyramid. The X separating these four sails is often reinforced with ridges called **ribbing.**
- **Flying buttresses.** These free-standing exterior pillars connected by graceful, thin arms of stone help channel the weight of the building and its roof out and down into the ground. Not every Gothic church has evident buttresses.
- **Stained glass.** The multitude and size of Gothic windows allowed them to be filled with Bible stories and symbolism portrayed in colorful patterns of stained glass. The use of stained glass was more common in the later Gothic periods.
- **Rose windows.** These huge circular windows, often the centerpieces of facades, are filled with elegant tracery and "petals" of stained glass.
- **Tracery.** Lacy spider webs of carved stone curlicues grace the pointed ends of windows and sometimes the spans of ceiling vaults.
- **Spires.** These pinnacles of masonry seem to defy gravity and reach toward heaven.
- **Gargoyles.** These are drain spouts disguised as wide-mouthed creatures or human heads.
- **Choir screen.** Serving as the inner wall of the ambulatory and the outer wall of the choir section, the choir screen is often decorated with carvings.

Cathédrale Notre-Dame de Chartres

The **Basilique St-Denis** (1140–44), today in a Paris suburb, was the world's first Gothic cathedral. The statuary, spire, and some 150 glorious stained-glass windows of the **Cathédrale Notre-Dame de Chartres** (1194–1220) make it a must-see, while the **Cathédrale Notre-Dame de Reims** (1225–90) sports more than 2,300 exterior statues and stained glass from 13th-century rose window originals to 20th-century windows by Marc Chagall. The **Cathédrale Notre-Dame d'Amiens** (1220–36) is pure Gothic, its festival of statues and reliefs built with remarkable speed.

Paris's Notre-Dame cathedral (1163–1250) has good buttresses, along with a trio of France's best rose windows, portal carvings, a choir screen of carved reliefs, and spiffy gargoyles (many of which are actually 19th-century neo-Gothic). The *sine qua non* of stained glass is Paris's **Ste-Chapelle** (1240–50).

RENAISSANCE (1500–1630)

In architecture as in painting, the Renaissance came from Italy and was only slowly Frenchified. And as in painting, its rules stressed proportion, order, classical inspiration, and precision to create unified, balanced structures.

Some identifiable Renaissance features include:

- **A sense of proportion**
- **A reliance on symmetry**
- **The use of classical orders.** This specifies three types of column capitals: Doric, Ionic, and Corinthian.

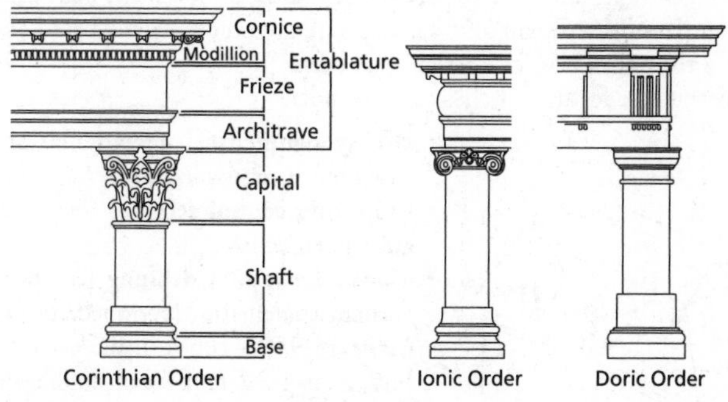

Classical Orders

- **Steeply pitched roofs.** They often feature **dormer windows** (upright windows projecting from a sloping roof).

The Loire Valley and Burgundy are home to many Renaissance **châteaux.** Foremost is the Loire's **Château de Chambord,** started in 1519, probably according to plans by

Leonardo da Vinci (who may have designed its double helix staircase). In contrast, the **Château de Chenonceau,** home to many a French king's wife or mistress, is a fanciful fairy tale built in the middle of a river. The best example in Burgundy is the **Château de Tanlay,** east of Chablis.

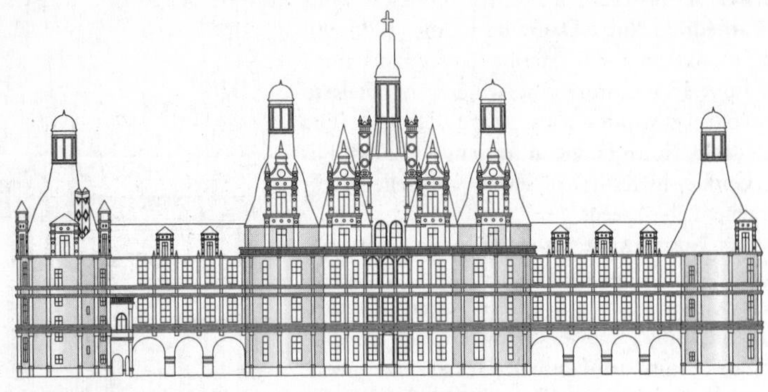

Château de Chambord

CLASSICISM & ROCOCO (1630–1800)

While Italy and Germany embraced the opulent baroque, France took the fundamentals of Renaissance **classicism** even further, becoming more imitative of ancient models. This represents a change from the Renaissance preference of finding inspiration in the classic era.

During the reign of Louis XIV, art and architecture were subservient to political ends. Buildings were grandiose and severely ordered on the Versailles model. Opulence was saved for interior decoration, which increasingly (especially from 1715–50, after the death of Louis XIV) became a detailed and self-indulgent **rococo** (*rocaille* in French). Externally, rococo is noticeable only in a greater elegance and delicacy.

Rococo tastes didn't last long, and soon a **neoclassical** movement was raising structures, such as Paris's **Pantheon** (1758), that were even more strictly based on ancient models than the earlier classicist designs had been.

Some identifiable features of classicism include:

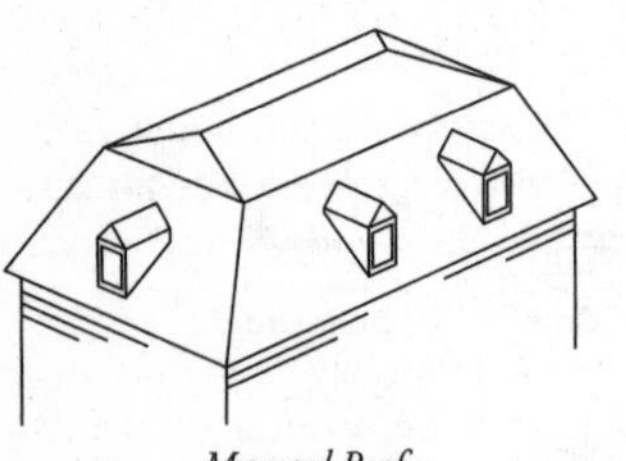

Mansard Roof

- **Highly symmetrical, rectangular structures** based on the classical orders
- **Projecting central sections** topped by triangular pediments
- **Mansard roofs.** A defining feature and true French trademark developed by **François Mansart** (1598–1666) in the early 15th century; a mansard roof has a double slope, the lower longer and steeper than the upper.
- **Dormer windows**
- ***Oeil-de-bouef*** **("ox-eyes").** These small, round windows poke out of the roof's slope.

Mansart built town houses, châteaux, and churches (**Val-de-Grâce** in Paris; the **Palais du Tau** in Reims) and laid out Dijon's **place de la Libération.** But the Parisian architect is chiefly remembered for his steeply sloping namesake, **"mansard" roofs.**

Louis Le Vau (1612–70) was the chief architect of the Louvre from 1650 to 1670 and of the **Château de Vaux-le-Vicomte** (1656–61) outside Paris, a gig that put him and his collaborators—including Mansart, interior decorator **Charles Le Brun** (1619–90), and the unparalleled landscape gardener **André Le Nôtre** (1613–1700)—on Louis XIV's radar and landed them the commission to rebuild **Versailles** (1669–85). Versailles is France's—indeed, Europe's—grandest palace.

Château de Versailles

Rococo architecture is tough to find. In Paris, seek out Delamair's Marais town house, the **Hôtel de Soubise** (1706–12), and the prime minister's residence, the **Hôtel Matignon** (1721), by Courtonne. For rococo decor, check out the **Clock Room** in Versailles.

THE 19TH CENTURY

Architectural styles in 19th-century France began in a severe classical mode. Then they dabbled with medieval revival, delved into modern urban restructuring, and ended with an identity crisis torn between industrial-age advancements and Art Nouveau organic.

The 19th century saw several distinct styles, including:

- **First Empire.** Elegant neoclassical furnishings—distinguished by strong lines often accented with a simple curve—during Napoléon's reign.
- **Second Empire.** Napoléon III's reign saw the eclectic Second Empire reinterpret classicism in a dramatic mode. **Baron Haussmann** (1809–91), who cut broad boulevards through the city's medieval neighborhoods, restructured Paris.
- **Third Republic/early industrial.** Expositions in Paris in 1878, 1889, and 1900 were the catalysts for constructing huge glass-and-steel structures that showed off modern techniques and the engineering prowess of the Industrial Revolution. This produced such Parisian monuments as the **Eiffel Tower (Tour Eiffel)** and **Basilique du Sacré-Coeur.**
- **Art Nouveau.** Architects and decorators rebelled against the Third Republic era of mass production by stressing the uniqueness of craft. They created asymmetrical, curvaceous designs based on organic inspiration (plants and flowers) in such mediums as wrought iron, stained glass, tile, and wallpaper.

Napoléon spent his imperial decade (1804–14) refurbishing the **Palais de Fontainebleau** in First Empire style. The ultimate paean to the classical was the **Arc de Triomphe** (1836), Napoléon's imitation of a Roman triumphal arch.

In the Second Empire, Napoléon III commissioned **Baron Haussmann** in 1852 to remap Paris according to modern urban-planning theories—clearing out the tangles of medieval streets to lay out **wide boulevards** radiating off **grand squares** (the **Etoile** anchored by the Arc de Triomphe is his classic).

In 1889, the French wanted to show how far they had come since the Revolution. They hired **Gustave Eiffel** (1832–1923) to build the world's tallest structure, a temporary 315m-high (1,051-ft.) tower made of riveted steel girders. Everyone agreed it was tall; most thought it was ugly. Its usefulness as a radio transmitter saved Eiffel's tower from being torn down.

Art Nouveau was less an architectural mode than a decorative movement, though you can still find some of the original Art Nouveau Métro entrances designed by **Hector Guimard** (1867–1942) in Paris. (A recently renovated entrance is at the Porte Dauphine station on the no. 2 line.)

THE 20TH CENTURY

France commissioned some ambitious architectural projects in the last century, most of them the ***grand projets*** of the late François Mitterrand. Most were considered controversial, outrageous, or even offensive. Other than a concerted effort to break convention and look stunningly modern, nothing unifies the look of this architecture—except that foreigners designed much of it.

Tour Eiffel, Paris

Britain's **Richard Rogers** (b. 1933) and Italy's **Renzo Piano** (b. 1937) turned architecture inside out—literally—to craft the eye-popping **Centre Pompidou** (1977), Paris's modern art museum. Exposed pipes, steel supports, and plastic-tube escalators wrap around the exterior.

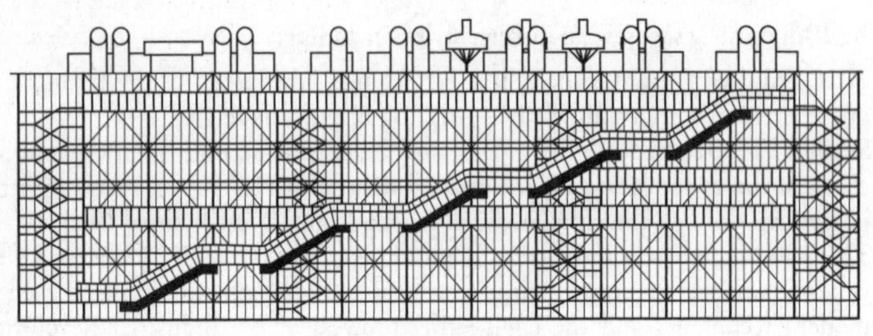

Centre Pompidou, Paris

Chinese-American maestro **I. M. Pei** (b. 1917) was called in to cap the Louvre's new underground Métro entrance with **glass pyramids** (1989), placed smack in the center of the Palais du Louvre's 17th-century courtyard.

In 1989, Paris's opera company moved into the curvaceous, dark glass mound of space of the **Opéra Bastille** (1989), designed by Canadian **Carlos Ott.** (Unfortunately, the acoustics have been lambasted.)

3

Planning Your Trip to France

In the pages that follow, we've compiled everything you need to know to handle the practical details of planning your trip: what documents you'll need, how to calculate the euro, how to find the best airfare, when to go, and more.

1 The Regions in Brief

Though France's 547,030 sq. km (211,209 sq. miles) make it slightly smaller than Texas, no other country has such a diversity of sights and scenery in such a compact area. A visitor can travel through the north's flat, fertile lands; the Loire Valley's green hills; the east's Alpine ranges; the Pyrénées; the Massif Central's plateaus and rock outcroppings; and the southeast's Mediterranean coast. Even more noteworthy are the cultural and historical differences that define each region.

Destinations in France are within easy reach from Paris and each other. **French National Railroads (SNCF)** offers fast service to and from Paris—though trains tend to crawl on routes that do not serve the capital. The train trip from Paris is 4 hours to Alsace, 5 to the Alps, 7 to the Pyrénées, and 8 to the Côte d'Azur—the newer TGVs (high-speed trains) cut that travel time dramatically.

You'll find nearly 71,000km (about 44,100 miles) of roads, mostly in good condition. Try not to travel the Route Nationale network all the time. Nearly all of France's scenic splendors are along secondary roads.

A "grand tour" of France is nearly impossible for the visitor who doesn't have a lifetime to explore. If you want to get to know a province, try to devote at least a week to a specific region; you may have a more rewarding trip if you concentrate on getting to know two or three areas at a leisurely pace rather than racing around trying to see everything. To help you decide where to spend your time, we've summarized the highlights of each region for you.

ILE DE FRANCE (INCLUDING PARIS) The Ile de France is an island only in the sense that rivers—with odd-sounding names such as Essonne, Epte, Aisne, Eure, and Ourcq—and a handful of canals delineate its boundaries (about an 81km/50-mile radius from the center of Paris). France was born in this temperate basin, where the attractions include **Paris, Versailles, Fontainebleau, Notre-Dame de Chartres,** and **Giverny.** Despite industrialization (and Disneyland Paris), pockets of charm remain, including the forests of Rambouillet and Fontainebleau, and the artists' hamlet of Barbizon. For more information, see chapters 5, 6, and 7.

THE LOIRE VALLEY This area includes two ancient provinces, Touraine (centered on Tours) and Anjou (centered on Angers). It was beloved by royalty and nobility until Henry IV moved his court to Paris. Head here to see the most magnificent castles in France. Irrigated by the Loire River and its many tributaries, the valley produces many superb wines. For more information, see chapter 8.

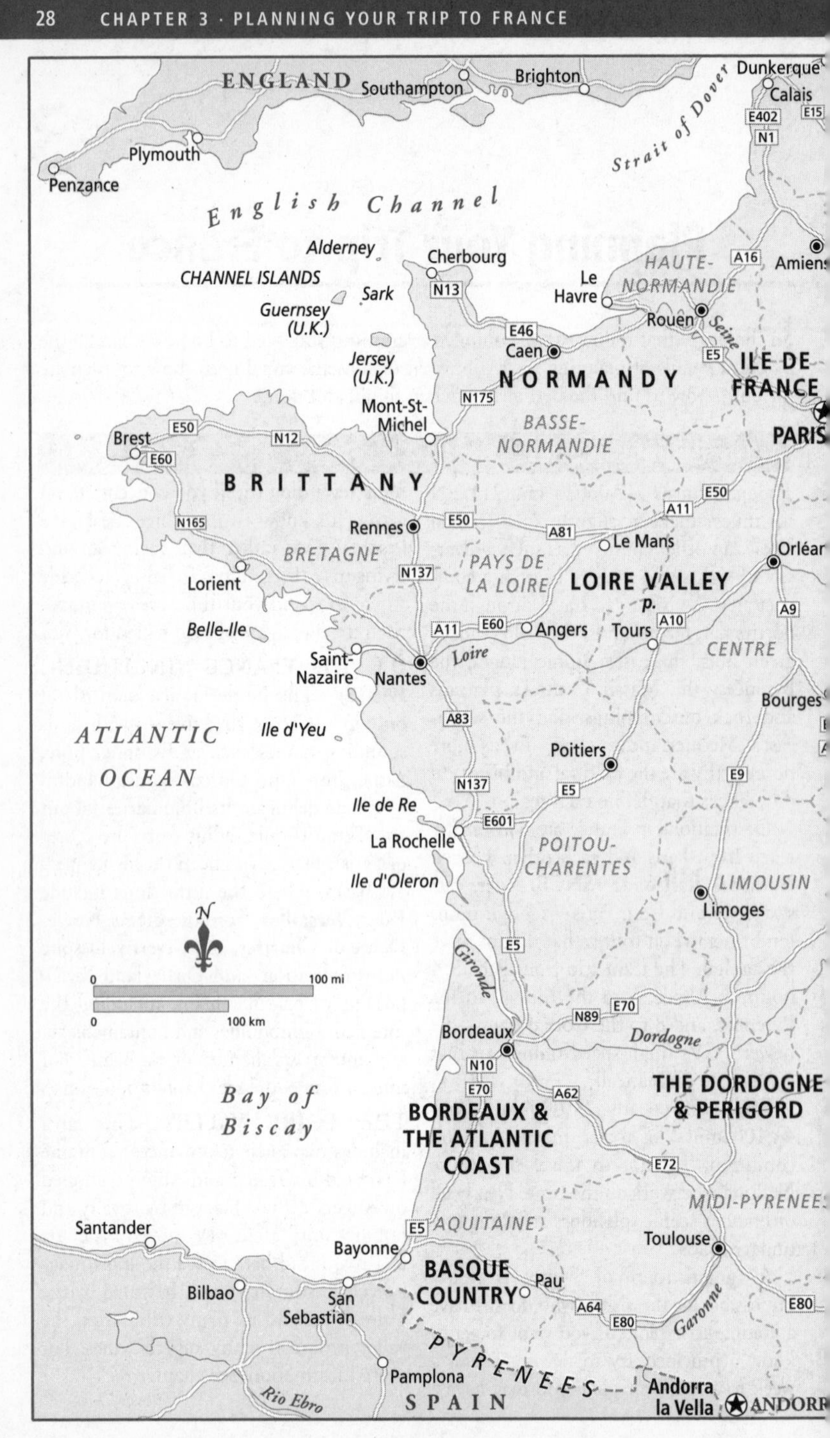

ENGLAND
Southampton
Brighton
Dunkerque
Calais
Strait of Dover
Plymouth
Penzance
English Channel
Alderney
Cherbourg
CHANNEL ISLANDS
Sark
Guernsey (U.K.)
Jersey (U.K.)
Le Havre
HAUTE-NORMANDIE
Amiens
Rouen
Seine
Caen
NORMANDY
ILE DE FRANCE
PARIS
Mont-St-Michel
BASSE-NORMANDIE
Brest
BRITTANY
Rennes
BRETAGNE
Le Mans
Orléan
PAYS DE LA LOIRE
LOIRE VALLEY
Lorient
Belle-Ile
Angers
Tours
CENTRE
Saint-Nazaire
Nantes
Loire
Bourges
ATLANTIC OCEAN
Ile d'Yeu
Poitiers
Ile de Re
La Rochelle
POITOU-CHARENTES
Ile d'Oleron
LIMOUSIN
Limoges
N
0
100 mi
100 km
Gironde
Bordeaux
Dordogne
Bay of Biscay
BORDEAUX & THE ATLANTIC COAST
THE DORDOGNE & PERIGORD
MIDI-PYRENEES
AQUITAINE
Santander
Toulouse
Bayonne
BASQUE COUNTRY
Pau
Bilbao
San Sebastian
Garonne
PYRENEES
Pamplona
Andorra la Vella
ANDORR
Rio Ebro
SPAIN
E402
E15
N1
A16
N13
E46
E5
N175
E50
N12
E60
A11
A81
N165
N137
A10
A9
E60
A83
E9
E601
N89
E70
N10
A62
E72
E80
A64

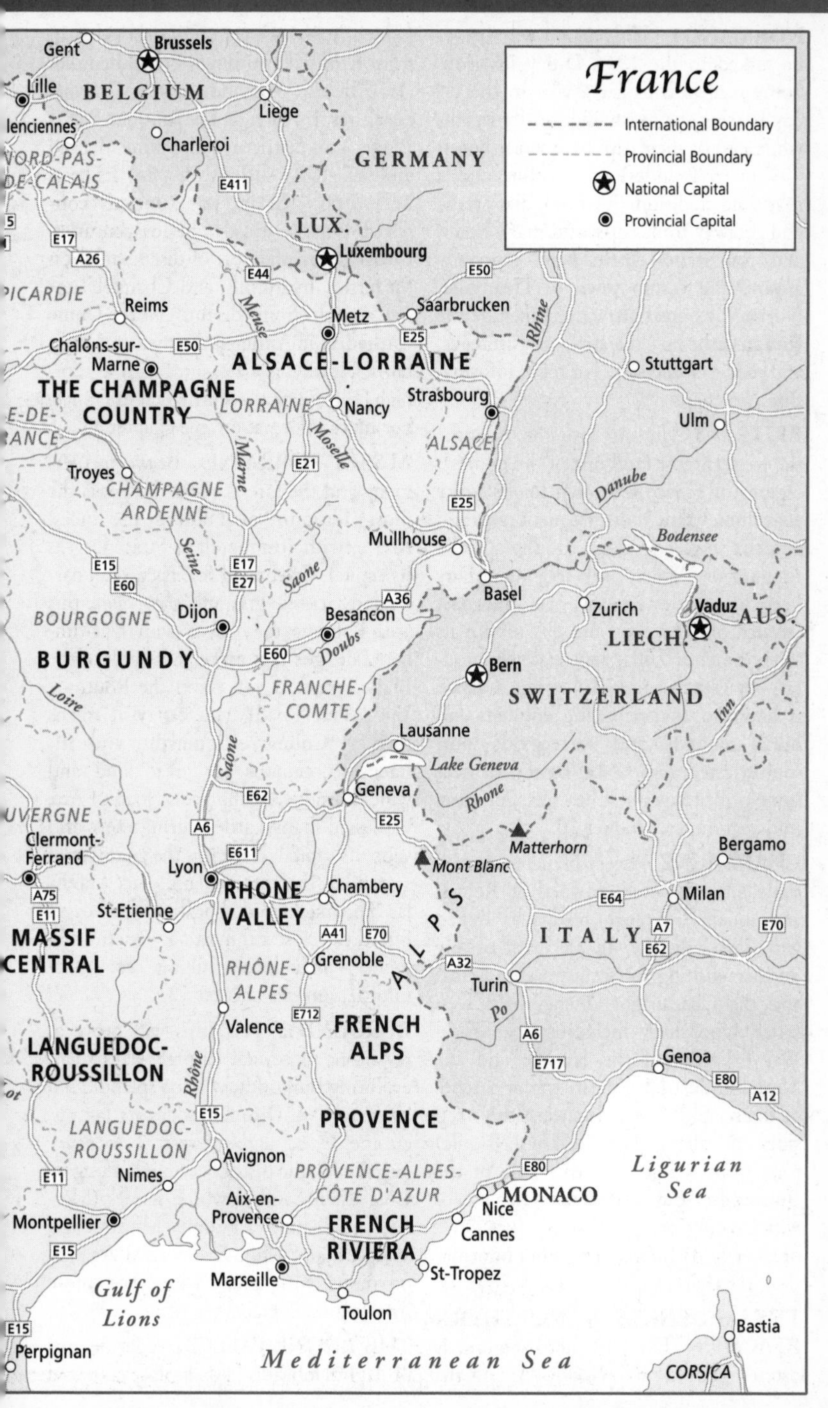
France
International Boundary
Provincial Boundary
National Capital
Provincial Capital
Gent
Brussels
Lille
BELGIUM
Liege
Charleroi
GERMANY
NORD-PAS-DE-CALAIS
LUX.
Luxembourg
PICARDIE
Reims
Metz
Saarbrucken
Chalons-sur-Marne
ALSACE-LORRAINE
THE CHAMPAGNE COUNTRY
LORRAINE
Nancy
Strasbourg
Stuttgart
Ulm
ALSACE
Troyes
CHAMPAGNE ARDENNE
Danube
Bodensee
Mullhouse
Basel
Zurich
Vaduz
AUS.
LIECH.
BOURGOGNE
Dijon
Besancon
BURGUNDY
Bern
FRANCHE-COMTE
SWITZERLAND
Lausanne
Lake Geneva
Geneva
Rhone
Matterhorn
Mont Blanc
AUVERGNE
Clermont-Ferrand
Lyon
RHONE VALLEY
Chambery
Bergamo
Milan
St-Etienne
MASSIF CENTRAL
ITALY
Grenoble
RHÔNE-ALPES
ALPS
Turin
Valence
FRENCH ALPS
Po
LANGUEDOC-ROUSSILLON
Genoa
PROVENCE
Avignon
Nimes
PROVENCE-ALPES-CÔTE D'AZUR
MONACO
Nice
Cannes
Ligurian Sea
Aix-en-Provence
Montpellier
FRENCH RIVIERA
Marseille
St-Tropez
Gulf of Lions
Toulon
Bastia
Perpignan
Mediterranean Sea
CORSICA
Meuse
Rhine
Moselle
Marne
Seine
Saone
Doubs
Loire
Inn
Rhône
E411
E17
A26
E44
E50
E25
E21
E15
E60
E27
A36
E62
A6
E611
A75
E11
A41
E70
A32
E712
E64
A7
E717
E80
A12

NORMANDY This region will forever be linked to the 1944 D-day invasion. Some readers consider a visit to the D-day beaches the most emotionally worthwhile part of their trip. Normandy boasts 599km (372 miles) of coastline and a maritime tradition. It's a popular weekend getaway from Paris, and many hotels and restaurants thrive here, especially around the casino town of **Deauville.** Normandy's great attractions include the **Rouen** cathedral, the abbey of **Jumièges,** and medieval **Bayeux.** For more information, see chapter 9.

BRITTANY Jutting into the Atlantic, the westernmost (and one of the poorest) regions of France is known for its rocky coastlines, Celtic roots, frequent rain, and ancient dialect, akin to the Gaelic tongues of Wales and Ireland. Many French vacationers love the seacoast (rivaled only by the Côte d'Azur) for its sandy beaches, cliffs, and relatively modest—by French standards—prices. **Carnac** is home to ancient Celtic dolmens and burial mounds, and the region's most sophisticated resort, **La Baule,** is near some of Brittany's best beaches. For more information, see chapter 10.

CHAMPAGNE Every French monarch since A.D. 496 was crowned at **Reims,** and much of French history is linked with this holy site. In the path of any invader wishing to occupy Paris, Reims and the Champagne district have seen much bloodshed, including the World War I battles of the Somme and the Marne. Industrial sites sit among patches of forest, and vineyards sheath the steep sides of valleys. The 126km (78-mile) road from Reims to Vertus, one of the **Routes du Champagne,** takes in a trio of winegrowing regions that produce 80% of the world's bubbly. For more information, see chapter 11.

THE ARDENNES & NORTHERN BEACHES This northern region is often ignored by North Americans (which is why we feature it as a side trip from Reims). In summer, French families arrive by the thousands to visit Channel beach resorts such as **Le Touquet-Paris-Plage.** This district is quite industrialized and has always suffered in wars. Its best-known port, Calais, was a bitterly contested English stronghold for centuries. Calais is now the port of disembarkation for ferries, hydrofoils, and Channel Tunnel arrivals from Britain. **Notre-Dame Cathedral** in **Amiens,** the medieval capital of Picardy, is a treasure, with a 42m-high (138-ft.) nave—the highest in France. For more information, see chapter 11.

ALSACE-LORRAINE Between Germany and the forests of the Vosges is the most Teutonic of France's provinces: Alsace, with cosmopolitan Strasbourg as its capital. Celebrated for its cuisine, particularly its foie gras and *choucroute,* this area is home to villages with half-timbered designs that make you think of the Black Forest. If you travel the Route de Vin (Wine Road), you can visit towns such as **Colmar, Riquewihr,** and **Illhaeusern,** famous for great food and wine. Lorraine, birthplace of Joan of Arc, witnessed many battles during the world wars. Its capital, **Nancy,** is the guardian of a grand 18th-century plaza, place Stanislas. The much-eroded peaks of the Vosges forest, the closest thing to a wilderness in France, offer lovely hiking. For more information, see chapter 12.

BURGUNDY Few trips will prove as rewarding as several leisurely days spent exploring Burgundy, with its splendid old cities such as **Dijon.** Besides its famous cuisine (*boeuf* and *escargots à la bourguignonne*), the district contains, along its Côte d'Or, hamlets whose names (Mercurey, Beaune, Puligny-Montrachet, Vougeot, and Nuits-St-Georges) are synonymous with great wine. For more information, see chapter 13.

THE RHONE VALLEY A fertile area of Alpine foothills and sloping valleys in eastern and southeastern France, the upper Rhône Valley ranges from the French suburbs of the Swiss city of Geneva to the northern borders of Provence. The district is thoroughly French, unflinchingly bourgeois, and dedicated to preserving the gastronomic and cultural traditions that have produced some of the most celebrated chefs in French history.

Only 2 hours by train from Paris, the region's cultural centerpiece, **Lyon,** is France's "second city." North of here, you can travel the Beaujolais trail or head for Bresse's ancient capital, **Bourg-en-Bresse,** which produces the world's finest poultry. You can explore the Rhône Valley en route to Provence. Try to visit the medieval villages of **Pérouges** and **Vienne,** 27km (17 miles) south of Lyon; the latter is known for its Roman ruins. For more information, see chapter 14.

THE FRENCH ALPS This area's resorts rival those of neighboring Switzerland and contain incredible scenery: snowcapped peaks, glaciers, and Alpine lakes. **Chamonix** is a famous ski resort facing **Mont Blanc,** western Europe's highest mountain. **Courchevel** and **Megève** are more chic. During the summer, you can enjoy such spa resorts as **Evian** and the restful 19th-century resorts ringing **Lake Geneva.** For more information, see chapter 15.

PROVENCE One of France's most fabled regions flanks the Alps and the Italian border along its eastern end, and incorporates a host of sites that have long been frequented by the rich and famous. Premier destinations are **Aix-en-Provence,** associated with Cézanne; **Arles,** "the soul of Provence," captured by van Gogh; **Avignon,** the 14th-century capital of Christendom during the papal schism; and **Marseille,** a port city established by the Phoenicians (in some ways more North African than French). Provence's gems are the small villages, such as **St-Rémy-de-Provence** (Nostradamus's birthplace) and **Les Baux.** The strip of glittering beach towns along Provence's southern edge is known as the **Côte d'Azur,** or the French Riviera (see the following section). For more information, turn to chapter 16.

THE FRENCH RIVIERA (COTE D'AZUR) The fabled Côte d'Azur (Azure Coast, or Blue Coast) has become quite overbuilt and spoiled by tourism. Even so, the names of its resorts still evoke glamour: **Cannes, St-Tropez, Cap d'Antibes,** and **St-Jean-Cap-Ferrat.** July and August are the most crowded, but spring and fall can be a delight. **Nice** is the biggest city, and most convenient for exploring the area. The principality of **Monaco** occupies only about 2 sq. km (¾ sq. mile). Along the coast are some sandy beaches, but many are rocky or pebbly. Topless bathing is common, especially in St-Tropez, and some of the restaurants are citadels of conspicuous consumption. Dozens of artists and their patrons have littered the landscape with world-class galleries and art museums. For more information, see chapter 17.

LANGUEDOC-ROUSSILLON Languedoc may not be as chic as Provence, but it's less frenetic and more affordable. **Roussillon** is the rock-strewn French answer to Catalonia, just across the Spanish border. The **Camargue** is the marshy delta formed by two arms of the Rhône River. Rich in bird life, it's famous for its grassy flats and such fortified medieval sites as **Aigues-Mortes.** Also appealing are **Auch,** the capital of Gascony; **Toulouse,** the bustling pink capital of Languedoc; and the "red city" of **Albi,** birthplace of Toulouse-Lautrec. **Carcassonne,** a marvelous walled city with fortifications begun around A.D. 500, is the region's highlight. For more information, see chapter 18.

THE BASQUE COUNTRY Since prehistoric times, the rugged Pyrénées have formed a natural boundary between France and Spain. The Basques, one of Europe's most unusual cultures, flourished in the valleys here. In the 19th century, resorts such as **Biarritz** and **St-Jean-de-Luz** attracted the French aristocracy—the empress Eugénie's palace at Biarritz is now a hotel. Four million Catholics make annual pilgrimages to the city of Lourdes. In the villages and towns of the Pyrénées, the old folkloric traditions, permeated with Spanish influences, continue to thrive. For more information, see chapter 19.

THE ATLANTIC COAST Flat, fertile, and frequently ignored by North Americans, this region includes towns pivotal in French history (**Saintes, Poitiers, Angoulême,** and **La Rochelle**), as well as wine- and liquor-producing villages (**Cognac, Margaux, St-Emilion,** and **Sauternes**) whose names are celebrated around the world. **Bordeaux,** the district's largest city, has an economy based on wine merchandising and boasts grand 18th-century architecture. For more information, see chapter 20.

THE DORDOGNE & PERIGORD The land of foie gras and truffles is the site of some of Europe's oldest settlements. For biking or indulging in gourmet meals, the region is among the top vacation spots in France. In the Périgord, the cave paintings at **Les Eyzies** reveal traces of Cro-Magnon settlements. The Dordogne is the second-largest *département* (the French equivalent of an American state). Highlights are the ancient towns of **Périgueux, Les Eyzies-de-Tayac, Sarlat-le-Canéda,** and **Beynac-et-Cazenac.** For more information, see chapter 21.

THE MASSIF CENTRAL The rugged heartland of south-central France, this underpopulated district contains ancient cities, unspoiled scenery, and an abundance of black lava, from which many buildings were created. The largest cities are **Clermont-Ferrand** and **Limoges**—the medieval capitals of the provinces of the Auvergne and the Limousin. **Bourges,** a gateway to the region and once capital of Aquitaine, has a beautiful Gothic cathedral. For more information, see chapter 22.

2 Visitor Information & Maps

Before you go, your best source of information is the **French Government Tourist Office** (www.franceguide.com), which can be reached at the following addresses:

- **United States:** 825 Third Ave., 29th floor, New York, NY 10022 (© **514/288-1904;** fax 212/838-7855); 205 N. Michigan Ave., Chicago, IL 60601 (© **514/288-1904**); or 9454 Wilshire Blvd., Suite 715, Beverly Hills, CA 90212 (© **514/288-1904**).
- **Canada:** 1800 av. McGill College, Suite 490, Montreal, QC H3A 2W9 (© **514/288-2026;** fax 514/845-4868).
- **United Kingdom:** 178 Piccadilly, London W1J 9AL (© **09068/244-123** [60p per min.]; fax 020/7493-6594).
- **Australia:** 25 Blight St., Sydney, NSW 2000 (© **02/9231-5244;** fax 02/9221-8682).

Although AAA has road maps of France, the best are **cartes routiéres** (road maps) published by Michelin. Both map books and fold-outs are available at almost any large bookstore in Paris and other French cities, and are sometimes available at news kiosks. The Michelin maps offer alternative **routes de degagement,** which you can travel to skirt big cities and avoid traffic-clogged highways. We recommend the *France Tourist and Motoring Atlas* (No 20197).

Tips Border Crossings to Monaco

Tiny Monaco (2 sq. km/¾ sq. mile) is an independent nation, but document requirements for travel to Monaco are the same as those for France, and there are virtually no border patrols or passport formalities. For information, contact the **Monaco Government Tourist Office,** 565 Fifth Ave., 23rd floor, New York, NY 10017 (© **800/753-9696** or 212/286-3330; fax 212/286-9890; www.visitmonaco.com); or at The Chambers, Chelsea Harbour, London SW10 OXF (© **020/7352-9962;** fax 020/7352-2103).

USEFUL WEBSITES

- **www.franceguide.com**: The official website of the French Government Tourist Office, with helpful trip-planning information.
- **www.franceway.com**: A helpful site for dining, hotels, and transportation, with detailed Paris listings.
- **www.parisinfo.com**: The website of the Paris Convention and Visitors Bureau provides information on hotels, restaurants, attractions, entertainment, and events. (For more Paris-specific sites, see *Frommer's Paris 2008*.)
- **www.parisfranceguide.com**: This site has plenty of useful information about Paris, with current nightlife, restaurant, music, theater, and events listings.
- **www.chateauversailles.fr**: The best site for the major attractions visited outside Paris.
- **www.normandy-tourism.org**: This site takes you to Normandy, land of Calvados and the D-day beaches, with info including the most visited gardens in the region.
- **www.brittany-bretagne.com**: This site tries to lure you away from Normandy to sample the offerings of its neighbor to the west, with information on places of interest, hotels, transportation, and a calendar of events.
- **www.nice-coteazur.org**: It could be more helpful, but this site provides hotel data and a calendar of events.
- **www.cannes-on-line.com**: This site offers hotel data, a map of Cannes, and a calendar of events.
- **www.sncf.fr**: The official website of the SNCF (French National Railroads) provides timetables and fares, and sells seats online.
- **www.mappy.fr**: This useful site for motorists gives precise directions and toll prices, and estimates the amount of time required to drive to towns and cities in France.

3 Entry Requirements

PASSPORTS

For information on how to get a passport, go to "Passports" in the "Fast Facts: France" section later in this chapter—the websites listed provide downloadable passport applications as well as the current fees for processing passport applications. For an up-to-date, country-by-country listing of passport requirements around the world, go to the "Foreign Entry Requirement" Web page of the U.S. State Department at **http://travel.state.gov**.

It's always wise to have plenty of documentation when traveling with children. For changing details on entry requirements for children traveling abroad, keep up-to-date by going to the U.S. State Department website: http://travel.state.gov/foreignentryreqs.html.

Children of all ages (from birth up) require a passport. Visit **http://travel.state.gov/passport/get/minors/minors_834.html** for a downloadable application; children ages 14 to 17 follow the same rules for a first-time passport applicant (see **http://travel.state.gov/passport/get/first/first_830.html**).

To prevent international child abduction, E.U. governments have initiated procedures at entry and exit points. These often (but not always) include requiring documentary evidence of relationship and permission for the child's travel from the parent or legal guardian not present. Having such documentation on hand, even if not required, facilitates entries and exits. All children must have their own passport. To obtain a passport, the child *must* be present at the center issuing the passport. Both parents must be present as well. If not, then a notarized statement from the parents is required.

Any questions parents or guardians might have can be answered by calling the **National Passport Information Center** at ✆ **877/487-6868** Monday to Friday 8am to 8pm Eastern Standard Time.

MEDICAL REQUIREMENTS

For information on medical requirements and recommendations, see "Health," p. 48.

CUSTOMS

For information on what you can bring into and take out of France, go to **"Customs"** in the **"Fast Facts: France"** section, later in this chapter.

4 When to Go

The best time to visit Paris is in the spring (Apr–June) or fall (Sept–Nov), when things are easier to come by—from Métro seats to good-tempered waiters. The weather is temperate year-round. July and August are the worst for crowds. Parisians desert their city, leaving it to the tourists.

Hotels used to charge off-season rates during the cold, rainy period from November through February; now, they're often packed with business travelers, trade fairs, and winter tour groups, and hoteliers have less incentive to offer discounts. Airfares are still cheaper during these months, and more promotions are available. They rise in the spring and fall, peaking in the summer, when tickets cost the most.

In even-numbered years, don't come to Paris during the first 2 weeks of October without a confirmed hotel room. The weather's fine, but the city is jammed for the auto show.

WEATHER

France's weather varies from region to region and even from town to town. Despite its latitude, Paris never gets very cold—snow is rare. The hands-down winner for wetness is Brittany. Brest (known for the mold—probably caused by the constant damp—that adds flavor to its bleu cheeses) receives a staggering amount of rain between October and December. Rain usually falls in a steady, foggy drizzle and rarely lasts more than a day. May is the driest month.

The Mediterranean coast in the south has the driest climate. When it does rain, it's heaviest in spring and autumn. (Cannes sometimes receives more rainfall than Paris.) Summers are comfortably dry—beneficial to humans but deadly to vegetation, which (unless it's irrigated) often dries and burns up in the parched months.

Provence dreads *le mistral* (an unrelenting, hot wind), which most often blows in the winter for a few days but can last for up to 2 weeks.

Paris's Average Daytime Temperature & Rainfall

	Jan	Feb	Mar	Apr	May	June	July	Aug	Sept	Oct	Nov	Dec
Temp. °F	38	39	46	51	58	64	66	66	61	53	45	40
Temp. °C	3	4	8	11	14	18	19	19	16	12	7	4
Rainfall (in.)	3.2	2.9	2.4	2.7	3.2	3.5	3.3	3.7	3.3	3.0	3.5	3.1

HOLIDAYS

In France, holidays are *jours fériés.* Shops and many businesses (banks and some museums and restaurants) close on holidays, but hotels and emergency services remain open.

The main holidays include New Year's Day (Jan 1), Easter Sunday and Monday, Labor Day (May 1), V-E Day (May 8), Whitmonday (May 19), Ascension Thursday (40 days after Easter), Bastille Day (July 14), Assumption of the Blessed Virgin (Aug 15), All Saints' Day (Nov 1), Armistice Day (Nov 11), and Christmas (Dec 25).

FRANCE CALENDAR OF EVENTS

January

Monte Carlo Motor Rally (Le Rallye de Monte Carlo). The world's most venerable car race. For information, call the Monaco Tourist Office (© **377-92-16-61-16** or 377-93-15-26-00; www.acm.mc). Usually mid-January.

February

Carnival of Nice. Parades, boat races, music, balls, and fireworks are all part of this celebration. The climax is the 114-year tradition of burning King Carnival in effigy, after *Les Batailles des Fleurs* (Battles of the Flowers), when teams pelt each other with blooms. For details, contact the Nice Convention and Visitors Bureau (© **08-92-70-74-07;** fax 04-89-06-48-03; www.nicecarnaval.com). Late February to early March.

March

Foire du Trône, on the Reuilly Lawn of the Bois de Vincennes, 12e, Paris. This mammoth amusement park operates daily from 2pm to midnight. Call © **01-46-27-52-29,** or visit www.foiredutrone.com. End of March to end of May.

International Ready-to-Wear Fashion Shows (Le Salon International de Prêt-à-Porter), Parc des Expositions, Porte de Versailles, 15e, Paris. See what you'll be wearing next season. Call © **01-44-94-70-00,** or visit www.pretparis.com. Early March.

April

International Marathon of Paris. Runners from around the world compete. Call © **01-41-33-14-00,** or visit www.parismarathon.com. Early April.

Les 24 Heures du Mans Moto. This motorcycle race is on a grueling 4km (2½-mile) circuit 4.5km (2¾ miles) south of Le Mans. For information, call l'Automobile Club de l'Ouest (© **02-43-40-24-24**) or the Le Mans Ticket Office (© **04-73-91-85-75;** www.lemans.org). Mid-April.

May

Antiques Show. The annual *Cinq Jours de l'Objet Extraordinaire* show features more than 100 galleries and antiques stores displaying their collections in seven streets on the Left Bank, Carré Rive Gauche. For information, call © **01-42-60-70-10,** or visit www.carrerivegauche.com. Mid-May to early June.

Cannes Film Festival (Festival International du Film). Movie madness transforms this city into a media circus. Admission to the films in competition is by invitation only. Other films play 24 hours a day. Contact the Festival International du Film, 3 rue Amélie, 75007 Paris (✆ **01-53-59-61-00;** www.festival-cannes.org). Two weeks before the festival, its administration moves to the Palais des Festivals, esplanade Georges-Pompidou, 06400 Cannes. Mid-May.

Monaco Grand Prix de Formule. Hundreds of cars race through the narrow streets and winding roads in a blend of high-tech machinery and medieval architecture. Call ✆ **377-93-15-26-00** or 377-92-16-61-16, or visit www.acm.mc. Mid-May.

French Open Tennis Championship, Stade Roland-Garros, 16e, Paris (Métro: Porte d'Auteuil). The Open features 10 days of men's, women's, and doubles tennis on the hot, red, dusty courts. For information, call ✆ **01-47-43-48-00,** or visit www.fft.fr. Late May to early June.

June

Prix du Jockey Club and **Prix Diane-Hermès,** Hippodrome de Chantilly. Thoroughbreds from as far away as Kentucky and Brunei compete in this race. On race days, dozens of trains depart from Paris's Gare du Nord for Chantilly, where racegoers take free shuttle buses to the track. Call ✆ **08-21-21-32-13,** or visit www.france-galop.com for information on these and other Chantilly events. Early June.

Cinéscénie de Puy du Fou, *son-et-lumière,* Château du Puy du Fou, Les Epesses (La Vendée), Brittany. A cast of 2,500 actors, dozens of horses, and laser shows celebrate the achievements of the Middle Ages. Call ✆ **02-51-64-11-11,** or visit www.puydufou.com. Early June to early September.

Festival de St-Denis. A surge of music in the burial place of the French kings, a grim early Gothic monument in Paris's northern suburb of St-Denis. Call ✆ **01-48-13-12-10,** or visit www.festival-saint-denis.fr. Early June to July.

Paris Air Show. France's military-industrial complex shows off its high-tech hardware. Fans, competitors, and industrial spies mob Le Bourget Airport. Call ✆ **01-41-69-20-21,** or visit www.paris-air-show.com. Mid-June in alternate years; next is mid-June 2009.

Les 24 Heures du Mans Voitures, for stock cars, is in the same circuit as the April motorcycle rally, but on a 13km (8-mile) radius. For information, call l'Automobile Club de l'Ouest (✆ **02-43-40-24-24**), or contact the Le Mans Ticket Office (✆ **04-73-91-85-75;** www.lemans.org). Mid-June.

Gay Pride Parade, place de la République to place de la Bastille, Paris. A week of expositions and parties climaxes in a parade patterned after those in New York and San Francisco, followed by a dance at the Palais de Bercy. For more information about gay pride and any other aspect of gay, lesbian, and transgendered life in and around Paris, contact Lesbian and Gay Pride Ile de France, 3 rue Perrée, Box 8, Paris 75003 (✆/fax **01-72-70-39-22;** www.inter-lgbt.org). Late June.

July

Colmar International Festival, Colmar. Classical concerts are held in public buildings of one of the most folkloric towns in Alsace. Call ✆ **03-89-20-68-97,** or visit www.festival-colmar.com. First 2 weeks of July.

Les Chorégies d'Orange, Orange. One of southern France's most important lyric festivals presents oratorios, operas, and choral works in France's best-preserved Roman amphitheater. Call ✆ **04-90-34-24-24,** or visit www.choregies.asso.fr. Early July to early August.

Tips Getting Tickets

Global Tickets can order tickets to many of the musical and theatrical events at the Avignon festival as well as other cultural happenings throughout France. You'll pay a hefty fee (as much as 20%) for the convenience. Contact Global at 234 W. 44th St., Suite 1000, New York, NY 10036 (✆ **800/669-8687;** www.keith prowse.com).

Fête Chopin, Paris. Everything you've ever wanted to hear by the Polish exile, who lived most of his life in Paris. Piano recitals take place in the Orangerie du Parc de Bagatelle, 16e. Call ✆ **01-45-00-22-19,** or visit www. frederic-chopin.com. Early July.

Les Nocturnes du Mont-St-Michel. This is a sound-and-light tour through the stairways and corridors of one of Europe's most impressive medieval monuments. Call ✆ **01-44-61-21-96,** or check out www.monum.fr for more information. Performances are Monday through Saturday evenings from early July to late August.

Tour de France. Europe's most hotly contested bicycle race sends crews of wind tunnel-tested athletes along an itinerary that detours deep into the Massif Central and ranges across the Alps. The finish line is on the Champs-Elysées. Call ✆ **01-41-33-15-00,** or visit www.letour.fr. First 3 weeks of July.

Festival d'Avignon. This world-class festival has a reputation for exposing new talent to critical scrutiny and acclaim. The focus is usually on avant-garde works in theater, dance, and music. Many of the dance and theater performances take place in either the 14th-century courtyard of the Palais des Pâpes or the medieval Cloître (cloister) des Carmes. For information, call ✆ **04-90-27-66-50,** or visit www. festival-avignon.com. Last 3 weeks of July.

Bastille Day. Celebrating the birth of modern-day France, the nation's festivities reach their peak in Paris with street fairs, pageants, fireworks, and feasts. In Paris, the day begins with a parade down the Champs-Elysées and ends with fireworks at Montmartre. July 14.

Paris Quartier d'Eté. For 4 weeks, music rules the Arènes de Lutèce and the Cour d'Honneur at the Sorbonne, both in the Quartier Latin. The dozen or so concerts are grander than the outdoorsy setting; they include performances by the Orchestre de Paris, the Orchestre National de France, and the Baroque Orchestra of the European Union. Call ✆ **01-44-94-98-00,** or visit www.quartierdete.com. Mid-July to mid-August.

Nice Jazz Festival. The most prestigious jazz festival in Europe. Concerts begin in the afternoon and go on until late at night (sometimes all night) on the Arènes de Cimiez, a hill above the city. Contact the Nice Tourist Office (✆ **08-92-70-74-07;** www.nicejazz fest.com). Mid-July.

Festival d'Aix-en-Provence. A musical event par excellence, with everything from Gregorian chant to melodies composed on synthesizers. Recitals are in the medieval cloister of the Cathédrale St-Sauveur. Expect heat, crowds, and traffic. Contact the Festival International d'Art Lyrique et Académie Européenne de Musique (✆ **04-42-17-34-34;** www. festival-aix.com). Month of July.

St-Guilhem Music Season, St-Guilhem le Désert, near Montpellier, Languedoc. A monastery plays host to this festival of baroque organ and choral music. Call ✆ **04-67-57-44-33,** or visit www.saint-guilhem-le-desert.com. Month of July.

August

Festival Interceltique de Lorient, Brittany. Celtic verse and lore are celebrated in the Celtic heart of France. The 150 concerts include classical and folkloric musicians, dancers, singers, and painters. Traditional Breton *pardons* (religious processions) take place in the once-independent maritime duchy. Call ✆ **02-97-21-24-29,** or check www.festival-interceltique.com. Early August.

September

La Villette Jazz Festival. Some 50 concerts are held in churches, auditoriums, and concert halls in the Paris suburb of La Villette. Past festivals have included Herbie Hancock, Shirley Horn, and other international artists. Call ✆ **01-40-03-75-75,** or visit www.jazzlavillette.com. Early to mid-September.

Festival d'Automne, Paris. One of France's most famous festivals is one of its most eclectic, focusing mainly on modern music, ballet, theater, and art. Contact the Festival d'Automne (✆ **01-53-45-17-00;** www.festival-automne.com). Mid-September to late December.

October

Paris Auto Show, Parc des Expositions, Porte de Versailles, 15e, Paris. This is the showcase for European car design, complete with glistening metal, glitzy attendees, lots of hype, and the latest models. Check *Pariscope* for details, or contact the French Government Tourist Office (see "Visitor Information & Maps," earlier in this chapter). You can also get information by calling ✆ **01-56-88-22-40** or visiting www.mondial-automobile.com. Two weeks in October (dates vary).

Perpignan Jazz Festival. Musicians from everywhere jam in what many consider Languedoc's most appealing season. Call ✆ **04-68-35-37-46,** or visit www.jazzebre.com. Month of October.

Prix de l'Arc de Triomphe, Hippodrome de Longchamp, 16e, Paris. France's answer to England's Ascot is the country's most prestigious horse race, culminating the equine season in Europe. Call ✆ **01-44-30-75-00,** or visit www.france-galop.com. Early October.

November

Armistice Day, nationwide. In Paris, the signing of the document that ended World War I is celebrated with a military parade from the Arc de Triomphe to the Hôtel des Invalides. November 11.

Les Trois Glorieuses, Clos-de-Vougeot, Beaune, and Meursault. Three Burgundian towns stage the country's most important wine festival. Though you may not gain access to many of the gatherings, tastings and other amusements will keep you occupied. Reserve early, or visit as day trips from nearby villages. Contact the Office de Tourisme de Beaune (✆ **03-80-26-21-30;** www.ot-beaune.fr). Third week in November.

December

Christmas Fairs, Alsace (especially Strasbourg). More than 60 villages celebrate a traditional Christmas. The events in Strasbourg have continued for some 430 years. Other towns with celebrations are Munster, Sélestat, Riquewihr, Kaysersberg, Wissembourg, and Thann. Call ✆ **03-89-24-73-50,** or visit www.tourism-alsace.com. Late November to December 24.

The Boat Fair (Le Salon Nautique de Paris). Europe's major exposition of what's afloat, at Parc des Expositions, Porte de Versailles, 15e, Paris (✆ **01-41-90-47-22;** www.salonnautiqueparis.com; Métro: Porte de Versailles). Ten days in early December.

Fête des Lumières, Lyon. In honor of the Virgin Mary, lights are placed in windows through the city. Call ✆ **04-72-10-30-30,** or visit www.lumieres.lyon.fr. Early December through early January.

Marché de Noël, Mougins. About 40 merchants, selling all kinds of Christmas ornaments and gifts, descend on this small village in Provence. Call ✆ **04-93-75-87-67,** or visit www.mougins-coteazur.org. Early December.

Fête de St-Sylvestre (New Year's Eve), nationwide. In Paris, this holiday is most boisterously celebrated in the Quartier Latin. At midnight, the city explodes. Strangers kiss and boulevard St-Michel and the Champs-Elysées become virtual pedestrian malls. December 31.

5 Getting There

BY PLANE

The two Paris airports—Orly (airport code: ORY) and Charles de Gaulle (airport code: CDG)—are about even in terms of convenience to the city's center, though taxi rides from Orly may take less time than those from de Gaulle. Orly, the older of the two, is 13km (8 miles) south of the center; Charles de Gaulle is 22km (14 miles) northeast. Air France serves Charles de Gaulle (Terminal 2C) from North America. U.S. carriers land at both airports.

Most airlines charge their lowest fares between November 1 and March 13. Shoulder season (Oct and mid-Mar to mid-June) is a bit more expensive, though we think it's the ideal time to visit France.

THE MAJOR AIRLINES

American Airlines (✆ **800/433-7300;** www.aa.com) has daily flights to Paris from Dallas/Fort Worth, Chicago, Miami, Boston, and New York.

British Airways (✆ **800/247-9297;** www.britishairways.com) offers flights from 18 U.S. cities to Heathrow and Gatwick airports in England. From there, you can book a British Airways flight to Paris.

Continental Airlines (✆ **800/231-0856;** www.continental.com) provides nonstop flights to Paris from Newark and Houston. Flights from Newark depart daily; flights from Houston depart four to seven times a week, depending on the season.

Delta Air Lines (✆ **800/221-1212;** www.delta.com) flies nonstop from Atlanta to Paris every evening and operates daily nonstop flights from Cincinnati and New York. Delta is the only airline offering nonstop service from New York to Nice.

US Airways (✆ **800/428-4322;** www.usairways.com) offers daily nonstop service from Philadelphia to Paris.

The French national carrier, **Air France** (✆ **800/237-2747;** www.airfrance.com), offers daily flights between Paris and such North American cities as Atlanta, Boston, Chicago, Cincinnati, Houston, Los Angeles, Mexico City, Miami, Montreal, New York, Newark, San Francisco, Toronto, and Washington, D.C.

In 2004, Air France acquired control of KLM Royal Dutch Airlines, which is leading to the creation of **Air France-KLM,** the world's biggest airline in terms of revenue. KLM and Air France have coordinated their schedules and fares and are acting as a unit. The merger has led to better connections between flights.

FLIGHTS FROM AUSTRALIA & NEW ZEALAND Getting to Paris

Tips Getting through the Airport

- Arrive at the airport at least 1 hour before a domestic flight and 2 hours before an international flight. You can check the average wait times at your airport by going to the TSA **Security Checkpoint Wait Times** site (waittime/tsa.dhs.gov).
- Know what you can carry on and what you can't. For the latest updates on items you are prohibited to bring in carry-on luggage, go to **www.tsa.gov/travelers/airtravel**.
- Beat the ticket-counter lines by using the self-service electronic ticket kiosks at the airport or even printing out your boarding pass at home from the airline website. Using curbside check-in is also a smart way to avoid lines.
- Help speed up security before you're screened. Remove jackets, shoes, belt buckles, heavy jewelry, and watches and place them either in your carry-on luggage or the security bins provided. Place keys, coins, cellphones, and pagers in a security bin. If you have metallic body parts, carry a note from your doctor. When possible, keep packing liquids in checked baggage.
- Use a TSA-approved lock for your checked luggage. Look for Travel Sentry certified locks at luggage or travel shops and Brookstone stores (or online at www.brookstone.com).

from Australia is difficult, because **Air France** (✆ **02-92-44-21-00;** www.airfrance.fr) has discontinued direct flights. Qantas flies from Sydney to Singapore and other locations with service to Paris. Consequently, on virtually any route, you have to change planes at least once and sometimes twice. **British Airways** (✆ **1300-767-177;** www.britishairways.com) flies daily from Sydney and Melbourne to London, where you can catch one of several connecting flights to Paris. **Qantas** (✆ **612/13-13-13;** www.qantas.com.au) can route passengers from Australia into London, where you make connections for the hop across the Channel. Qantas also flies from Auckland to Sydney and on to London.

FLYING FOR LESS: TIPS FOR GETTING THE BEST AIRFARE

- Passengers who can book their ticket either **long in advance or at the last minute,** or who **fly midweek** or **at less-trafficked hours** may pay a fraction of the full fare. If your schedule is flexible, say so, and ask if you can secure a cheaper fare by changing your flight plans.
- Search **the Internet** for cheap fares. The most popular online travel agencies are **Travelocity.com** (www.travelocity.co.uk); **Expedia.com** (www.expedia.co.uk and www.expedia.ca); and **Orbitz.com**. In the U.K., go to **Travelsupermarket** (✆ **0845/345-5708;** www.travelsupermarket.com), a flight search engine that offers flight comparisons for the budget airlines whose seats often end up in bucket-shop sales. Other websites for booking airline tickets online include **Cheapflights.com, SmarterTravel.com, Priceline.com,** and **Opodo** (www.opodo.co.uk). Meta search sites (which find and then direct you

to airline and hotel websites for booking) include **Sidestep.com** and **Kayak.com**—the latter includes fares for budget carriers like Jet Blue and Spirit as well as the major airlines. **Site59.com** is a great source for last-minute flights and getaways. In addition, most **airlines** offer online-only fares that even their phone agents know nothing about. British travelers should check **Flights International** (✆ **0800/0187050;** www.flights-international.com) for deals on flights all over the world.

- Keep an eye on local newspapers for **promotional specials** or **fare wars,** when airlines lower prices on their most popular routes. You rarely see fare wars offered for peak travel times, but if you can travel in the off months, you may snag a bargain.
- **Consolidators,** also known as bucket shops, are great sources for international tickets, although they usually can't beat Internet fares within North America. Start by looking in Sunday newspaper travel sections; U.S. travelers should focus on the *New York Times, Los Angeles Times,* and *Miami Herald.* U.K. travelers should search in the *Independent, The Guardian,* or *The Observer.* For less-developed destinations, small travel agents who cater to immigrant communities in large cities often have the best deals. ***Beware:*** Bucket shop tickets are usually nonrefundable or rigged with stiff cancellation penalties, often as high as 50% to 75% of the ticket price, and some put you on charter airlines, which may leave at inconvenient times and experience delays. The best specialist consolidator arranging trips to France is **Nouvelles Frontieres,** 5 av. de l'Opera, 1er (✆ **08-25-00-07-47;** www.nouvelles-frontieres.fr), in Paris. We've found the staff here most helpful, and its members will seek out the lowest fares for you. Several reliable consolidators are worldwide and available online. **STA Travel** has been the world's lead consolidator for students since purchasing Council Travel, but their fares are competitive for travelers of all ages. **ELTExpress** (**Flights.com;** ✆ **201/541-3826;** www.eltexpress.com) has excellent fares worldwide, particularly to Europe. They also have "local" websites in 12 countries. **Air Tickets Direct** (✆ **888/858-8884;** www.airticketsdirect.com) is based in Montreal and leverages the currently weak Canadian dollar for low fares; they also book trips to places that U.S. travel agents won't touch, such as Cuba.
- Join **frequent-flier clubs.** Frequent-flier membership doesn't cost a cent, but it does entitle you to better seats, faster response to phone inquiries, and prompter service if your luggage is stolen or your flight is canceled or delayed, or if you want to change your seat. And you don't have to fly to earn points; **frequent-flier credit cards** can earn you thousands of miles for doing your everyday shopping. With more than 70 mileage awards programs on the market, consumers have never had more options. Investigate the program details of your favorite airlines before you sink points into any one. Consider which airlines have hubs in the airport nearest you, and, of those carriers, which have the most advantageous alliances, given your most common routes. To play the frequent-flier game to your best advantage, consult Randy Petersen's **Inside Flyer** (www.insideflyer.com). Petersen and friends review all the programs in detail and post regular updates on changes in policies and trends.

Tips **Don't Stow It—Ship It**

Though pricey, it's sometimes worthwhile to travel luggage-free. Specialists in door-to-door luggage delivery include **Virtual Bellhop** (www.virtualbellhop.com), **SkyCap International** (www.skycapinternational.com), **Luggage Express** (www.usxp.com), and **Sports Express** (www.sportsexpress.com).

LONG-HAUL FLIGHTS: HOW TO STAY COMFORTABLE

- Your choice of airline and airplane will definitely affect your leg room. Find more details about U.S. airlines at **www.seatguru.com**. For international airlines, the research firm Skytrax has posted a list of average seat pitches at **www.airlinequality.com**.
- Emergency exit seats and bulkhead seats typically have the most legroom. Emergency exit seats are usually left unassigned until the day of a flight (to ensure that someone able-bodied fills the seats); it's worth getting to the ticket counter early to snag one of these spots for a long flight. Many passengers find that bulkhead seating (the row facing the wall at the front of the cabin) offers more legroom, but keep in mind that bulkheads are where airlines often put baby bassinets, so you may be sitting next to an infant.
- To have two seats for yourself in a three-seat row, try for an aisle seat in a center section toward the back of coach. If you're traveling with a companion, book an aisle and a window seat. Middle seats are usually booked last, so chances are good you'll end up with three seats to yourselves.
- Ask about entertainment options. Many airlines offer seatback video systems where you get to choose your movies or play video games—but only on some of their planes. (Boeing 777s are your best bet.)
- To sleep, avoid the last row of any section or the row in front of an emergency exit, as these seats are the least likely to recline. Avoid seats near highly trafficked toilet areas. Avoid seats in the back of many jets—these can be narrower than those in the rest of coach. You also may want to reserve a window seat so you can rest your head and avoid being bumped in the aisle.
- Get up, walk around, and stretch every 60 to 90 minutes to keep your blood flowing. See the box "Avoiding 'Economy-Class Syndrome,'" under "Health," p. 48.
- Drink water before, during, and after your flight to combat the lack of humidity in airplane cabins. Avoid alcohol, which will dehydrate you.
- If you're flying with kids, don't forget to carry on toys, books, pacifiers, and chewing gum to help them relieve ear pressure buildup during ascent and descent.

GETTING THERE FROM ELSEWHERE IN EUROPE

BY PLANE

From London, **Air France** (**✆ 0870/142-4343;** www.airfrance.com) and **British Airways** (**✆ 0870/850-9859** in the U.K.; www.britishairways.com) fly frequently to Paris; the trip takes 1 hour. These airlines operate up to 17 flights daily from Heathrow. Many travelers also fly out of the London City Airport in the Docklands.

Direct flights to Paris operate from other U.K. cities such as Manchester and Edinburgh. Contact Air France, British Airways, or **British Midland** (**✆ 0870/**

607-0555; www.flybmi.com). Daily papers often carry ads for cheap flights. Highly recommended **Trailfinders** (© **0845/058-5858;** www.trailfinders.com) sells discount fares.

You can reach Paris from any major European capital. Your best bet is to fly on the national carrier, Air France, which has more connections into Paris from European capitals than any other airline. From Dublin, try **Aer Lingus** (© **800-IRISH-AIR;** www.aerlingus.com), which schedules the most flights to Paris from Ireland. From Amsterdam, try **NWA/KLM** (© **800/225-2525;** www.nwa.com).

BY TRAIN

Paris is one of Europe's busiest rail junctions, with trains arriving at and departing from its many stations every few minutes. If you're in Europe, you may want to go to Paris by train. The cost is relatively low—especially compared to renting a car.

Rail passes as well as individual rail tickets are available at most travel agencies or at any office of **Rail Europe** (© **888/382-7245** in the U.S.; www.raileurope.com) or **Eurostar** (© **800/EUROSTAR** in the U.S.; www.eurostar.com).

BY BUS

Bus travel to Paris is available from London as well as many cities on the Continent. In the early 1990s, the French government established incentives for long-haul buses not to drive into the center of Paris. The arrival and departure point for Europe's largest operator, **Eurolines France,** 28 av. du Général-de-Gaulle, 93541 Bagnolet (© **08-92-89-90-91;** www.eurolines.fr), is a 35-minute Métro ride from central Paris, at the terminus of line no. 3 (Métro: Gallieni), in the eastern suburb of Bagnolet. Despite this inconvenience, many people prefer bus travel.

Long-haul buses are equipped with toilets, and they stop at mealtimes for rest and refreshment.

Because Eurolines does not have a U.S. sales agent, most people buy their ticket in Europe. Any European travel agent can arrange the sale. If you're traveling to Paris from London, contact **Eurolines (U.K.) Ltd.,** 52 Grosvenor Gardens, Victoria, London SW1 0AU (© **0870/580-8080;** www.nationalexpress.com for information or credit card sales).

BY CAR

The major highways into Paris are A1 from the north (Great Britain and Benelux); A13 from Rouen, Normandy, and northwest France; A10 from Bordeaux, the Pyrénées, the southwest, and Spain; A6 from Lyon, the French Alps, the Riviera, and Italy; and A4 from Metz, Nancy, and Strasbourg in the east.

BY FERRY FROM ENGLAND

Ferries and hydrofoils operate day and night, with the exception of last-minute cancellations during storms. Many crossings are timed to coincide with the arrival and departure of trains (especially those between London and Paris). Trains let you off a short walk from the piers. Most ferries carry cars, trucks, and freight, but some hydrofoils take passengers only. The major routes include at least 12 trips a day between Dover or Folkestone and Calais or Boulogne.

Hovercraft and hydrofoils make the trip from Dover to Calais, the shortest distance across the Channel, in just 40 minutes during good weather. The ferries may take several hours, depending on the weather and tides. If you're bringing a car, it's important to make reservations—space below decks is usually crowded. Timetables can vary depending on weather conditions and many other factors.

The leading operator of ferries across the channel is **P&O Ferries** (© **0870/**

Fun Fact Under the Channel

Queen Elizabeth II and the late French president François Mitterrand opened the $15-billion Channel Tunnel in 1994. The tunnel is one of the great engineering feats of our time and is the first link between Britain and the Continent since the Ice Age. The 50km (31-mile) journey takes 35 minutes, with actual time spent in the Chunnel 19 minutes.

The ***Eurostar Express*** has daily passenger service from London to Paris and Brussels. Eurostar tickets are available through **Rail Europe** (✆ **888/382-7245;** www.raileurope.com). In London, make reservations for Eurostar (or any other train in Europe) at ✆ **0870/518-6186.** In Paris, call ✆ **01-70-70-60-88,** and in the United States, call ✆ **800/EUROSTAR,** or visit www.eurostar.com. Chunnel train traffic is competitive with air travel, if you calculate door-to-door travel time. Trains leave from London's Waterloo Station and arrive in Paris at Gare du Nord. The one-way passenger fare between London and Paris averages 71€ to 156€ ($94–$205) second class, 169€ to 211€ ($222–$277) first class.

Fares are complicated and depend on a number of factors. The cheapest one-way fare is Leisure RT, requiring a purchase at least 14 business days before the date of travel and a minimum 2-night stay. A return ticket must be booked to receive this discounted fare.

The Chunnel accommodates not only trains but also cars, buses, taxis, and motorcycles. Prices start at 225€ ($293) round-trip for a small car. **Eurotunnel,** a train carrying vehicles under the Channel (✆ **0870/535-3535** in the U.K.; www.eurotunnel.com), connects Calais, France, with Folkestone, England. It operates 24 hours a day, 365 days a year, running every 15 minutes during peak travel times and at least once an hour at night.

Before boarding Eurotunnel, you stop at a toll booth to pay and then pass through Immigration for both countries at one time. During the ride, you travel in air-conditioned carriages, remaining in your car or stepping outside to stretch your legs. An hour later, you simply drive off.

598-0333 in the U.K.; www.poferries.com). It operates car and passenger ferries between Portsmouth, England, and Cherbourg, France (three departures a day; 4 hr., 15 min. each way during daylight hours, 7 hr. each way at night); and between Portsmouth and Le Havre, France (three a day; 5½ hr. each way). Most popular is the route between Dover, England, and Calais, France (25 sailings a day; 75 min. each way).

6 General Travel Resources

MONEY & COSTS

It's always advisable to bring money in a variety of forms on a vacation: a mix of cash, credit cards, and traveler's checks. You should also exchange enough petty cash to cover airport incidentals, tipping, and transportation to your hotel before you leave home, or withdraw money upon arrival at an airport ATM.

In many international destinations, ATMs offer the best exchange rates. Avoid exchanging money at commercial exchange bureaus and hotels, which often have the highest transaction fees.

France is a very expensive destination. To compensate, you can often find top-value food and lodging. Part of the cost is the value-added tax (VAT in English, TVA in French), which adds between 6% and 33% to everything.

Rental cars (and fuel) are expensive, and flying within France costs more than within the U.S. Train travel is relatively inexpensive, especially with a rail pass. Prices in Paris and on the Riviera are higher than in the provinces. Three of the most visited areas—Brittany, Normandy, and the Loire Valley—have reasonably priced hotels and restaurants offering superb food at moderate prices.

CURRENCY

France's old currency, the franc, disappeared on March 1, 2002, and was replaced by the **euro,** whose official abbreviation is "EUR." Exchange rates of participating countries are locked into a common currency fluctuating against the dollar.

For up-to-the-minute conversion rates, visit **www.xe.com/ucc**. For more about the euro, check out **www.europa.eu.int**.

ATMs

The easiest and best way to get cash away from home is from an ATM (automated teller machine), sometimes referred to as a "cash machine" or a "cashpoint." The **Cirrus** (✆ **800/424-7787;** www.mastercard.com) and **PLUS** (✆ **800/843-7587;** www.visa.com) networks span the globe. Go to your bank card's website to find ATM locations at your destination. Be sure you know your daily withdrawal limit before you depart. ***Note:*** Many banks impose a fee every time you use a card at another bank's ATM, and that fee can be higher for international transactions (up to $5 or more) than for domestic ones (where they're rarely more than $2). In addition, the bank from which you withdraw cash may charge its own fee. For international withdrawal fees, ask your bank. Banks that are members of the **Global ATM Alliance** charge no transaction fees for cash withdrawals at other Alliance member ATMs; these include Bank of America, Scotiabank (Canada, Caribbean, and Mexico), Barclays (U.K. and parts of Africa), and Deutsche Bank (Germany, Poland, Spain, and Italy), and BNP Paribas (France).

Note: If your current PIN is more than four digits, change it to a four-digit (ideally numeric) code. Many European machines do not accept codes that are longer than four digits, and some may not have alphabetic equivalents noted on the keypad.

CREDIT CARDS

Credit cards are another safe way to carry money. They also provide a convenient record of all your expenses, and they generally offer relatively good exchange rates. American Express, Discover, MasterCard, and Visa are all accepted in France. You can withdraw cash advances from your credit cards at banks or ATMs, but high fees make credit card cash advances a pricey way to get cash. Keep in mind that you'll pay interest from the moment of your withdrawal, even if you pay your monthly bills on time. Also, note that many banks now assess a 1% to 3% "transaction fee" on **all** charges you incur abroad (whether you're using the local currency or your native currency).

TRAVELER'S CHECKS

These days, traveler's checks seem less necessary in France because all French cities and towns have ATMs. You can buy traveler's checks at most banks. They are offered in denominations of $20, $50,

The Euro

The **euro** became the official currency of France and 11 other participating countries on January 1, 1999. For details on the euro, check out **www.europa.eu.int/euro.**

The US Dollar and the Euro: One U.S. Dollar was worth approximately .76€ at the time of this writing. Inversely stated, that means that 1 € was worth approximately $1.30.

The British pound, the U.S. Dollar, and the Euro: At press time, 1£ equaled approximately $1.90 and approximately 1.50€

The Canadian dollar, the U.S. Dollar, and the Euro: At press time, one Canadian dollar equaled approximately 86¢, or approximately 66 Eurocents.

Euro	U.S.$	U.K.£	CD$	Euro	U.S.$	U.K.£	CD$
1	1.30	0.67	1.50	75.00	97.50	50.25	112.5
2	2.60	1.34	3.00	100.00	130.00	67.00	150.00
3	3.90	2.01	4.50	125.00	162.50	83.75	187.50
4	5.20	2.68	6.00	150.00	195.00	100.50	225.00
5	6.50	3.35	7.50	175.00	227.50	117.25	262.50
6	7.80	4.02	9.00	200.00	260.00	134.00	300.00
7	9.10	4.69	10.50	225.00	292.50	150.75	337.50
8	10.40	5.36	12.00	250.00	325.00	167.50	375.00
9	11.70	6.03	13.50	275.00	357.50	184.25	412.50
10	13.00	6.70	15.00	300.00	390.00	201.00	450.00
15	19.50	10.05	22.50	350.00	455.00	234.50	525.00
20	26.00	13.40	30.00	400.00	520.00	268.00	600.00
25	32.50	16.75	37.50	500.00	650.00	335.00	750.00
50	65.00	33.50	75.00	1000.00	1300.00	670.00	1500.00

Conversion ratios between the U.S. dollar and other currencies fluctuate, and their differences could affect the relative costs of your trip. Check for updated rates with Universal Currency Converter (**www.xe.com/ucc**).

It's best to exchange currency or traveler's checks at a bank, not a *bureau de change,* hotel, or shop. Traveler's checks (for which you'll receive a better rate than cash) can be changed at all airports and some travel agencies, such as American Express and Thomas Cook. Note the rates, ask about commission fees, and shop around.

$100, $500, and sometimes $1,000. Generally, you'll pay a service charge ranging from 1% to 4%.

The most popular traveler's checks are offered by **American Express** (© **800/807-6233,** or 800/221-7282 for card holders—this number accepts collect calls, offers service in several foreign languages, and exempts Amex gold and platinum cardholders from the 1% fee); **Visa** (© **800/732-1322**)—AAA members can obtain Visa checks for a $9.95 fee (for checks up to $1,500) at most AAA offices or by calling ✆ **866/339-3378;** and **MasterCard** (✆ **800/223-9920**).

Be sure to keep a record of the traveler's checks serial numbers separate from your checks in the event that they are stolen or lost. You'll get a refund faster if you know the numbers.

American Express, Thomas Cook, Visa, and **MasterCard** offer **foreign currency traveler's checks,** useful if you're traveling to one country or to the euro zone; they're accepted at locations where dollar checks may not be.

Another option is the new prepaid traveler's check cards, reloadable cards that work much like debit cards but aren't linked to your checking account. The **American Express Travelers Cheque Card,** for example, requires a minimum deposit, sets a maximum balance, and has a one-time issuance fee of $14.95. You can withdraw money from an ATM (for a fee of $2.50 per transaction, not including bank fees), and the funds can be purchased in dollars, euros, or pounds. If you lose the card, your available funds will be refunded within 24 hours.

TRAVELER INSURANCE

Because France is far from home for most of us, and a number of things can go wrong—lost luggage, trip cancellation, medical emergency—consider various types of insurance.

Check your existing insurance policies and credit card coverage before you buy travel insurance. You may already be covered for lost luggage, canceled tickets, or medical expenses.

The cost of travel insurance varies widely, depending on the cost and length of your trip, your age and health, and the type of trip you're taking, but expect to pay between 5% and 8% of the vacation itself. You can get estimates from various providers through **InsureMyTrip.com**. Enter your trip cost and dates, your age, and other information for prices from more than a dozen companies.

TRIP-CANCELLATION INSURANCE

Trip-cancellation insurance will help retrieve your money if you have to back out of a trip or depart early, or if your travel supplier goes bankrupt. Permissible reasons for trip cancellation can range from sickness to natural disasters to the State Department declaring a destination unsafe for travel.

For more information, contact one of the following recommended insurers: **Access America** (✆ 866/729-6021; www.accessamerica.com); **Travel Guard International** (✆ 800/826-4919; www.travelguard.com); **Travel Insured International** (✆ 800/243-3174; www.travelinsured.com); and **Travelex Insurance Services** (✆ 800/228-9792; www.travelex-insurance.com).

Travel in the Age of Bankruptcy

Airlines go bankrupt, so protect yourself by **buying your tickets with a credit card.** The Fair Credit Billing Act guarantees that you can get your money back from the credit card company if a travel supplier goes under (and if you request the refund within 60 days of the bankruptcy). **Travel insurance** can also help, but make sure it covers against "carrier default" for your specific travel provider. And be aware that if a U.S. airline goes bust midtrip, a 2001 federal law requires other carriers to take you to your destination (albeit on a space-available basis) for a fee of no more than $25, provided you rebook within 60 days of the cancellation.

MEDICAL INSURANCE

For travel overseas, most U.S. health plans (including Medicare and Medicaid) do not provide coverage, and the ones that do often require you to pay for services upfront and reimburse you only after you return home.

As a safety net, you may want to buy travel medical insurance, particularly if you're traveling to a remote or high-risk area where emergency evacuation might be necessary. If you require additional medical insurance, try **MEDEX Assistance** (✆ **410/453-6300;** www.medexassist.com) or **Travel Assistance International** (✆ **800/821-2828;** www.travelassistance.com; for general information on services, call the company's **Worldwide Assistance Services, Inc.**, at ✆ **800/777-8710**).

Canadians should check with their provincial health plan offices or call **Health Canada** (✆ **866/225-0709;** www.hc-sc.gc.ca) to find out the extent of their coverage and what documentation and receipts they must take home in case they are treated overseas.

LOST-LUGGAGE INSURANCE

On international flights (including U.S. portions of international trips), baggage coverage is limited to approximately $9.07 per pound, up to approximately $635 per checked bag. If you plan to check items more valuable than what's covered by the standard liability, see if your homeowner's policy covers your valuables, get baggage insurance as part of your comprehensive travel-insurance package, or buy Travel Guard's "BagTrak" product.

If your luggage is lost, immediately file a lost-luggage claim at the airport, detailing the luggage contents. Most airlines require that you report delayed, damaged, or lost baggage within 4 hours of arrival. The airlines are required to deliver luggage, once found, directly to your house or destination free of charge.

HEALTH

STAYING HEALTHY

General Availability of Healthcare

In general, France is a safe destination. You don't need shots, most food is safe, and the water is potable. If you're concerned, order bottled water. It is easy to get a prescription filled, and nearly all destinations have English-speaking doctors at hospitals with well-trained staffs.

Contact the **International Association for Medical Assistance to Travelers** (**IAMAT;** ✆ **716/754-4883** or, in Canada, 416/652-0137; www.iamat.org) for tips on travel and health concerns in the countries you're visiting, and for lists

---

Avoiding "Economy-Class Syndrome"

Deep vein thrombosis, or as it's known in the world of flying, "economy-class syndrome," is a blood clot that develops in a deep vein. It's a potentially deadly condition that can be caused by sitting in cramped conditions—such as an airplane cabin—for too long. During a flight (especially a long-haul flight), get up, walk around, and stretch your legs every 60 to 90 minutes to keep your blood flowing. Other preventative measures include frequent flexing of the legs while sitting, drinking lots of water, and avoiding alcohol and sleeping pills. If you have a history of deep vein thrombosis, heart disease, or another condition that puts you at high risk, some experts recommend wearing compression stockings or taking anticoagulants when you fly; always ask your physician about the best course for you. Symptoms of deep vein thrombosis include leg pain or swelling, or even shortness of breath.

Healthy Travels to You

The following government websites offer up-to-date health-related travel advice.

- **Australia:** www.dfat.gov.au/travel
- **Canada:** www.hc-sc.gc.ca/index_e.html
- **U.K.:** www.dh.gov.uk/PolicyAndGuidance/HealthAdviceForTravellers/fs/en
- **U.S.:** www.cdc.gov/travel

of local, English-speaking doctors. The United States **Centers for Disease Control and Prevention** (© **800/311-3435;** www.cdc.gov) provides up-to-date information on health hazards by region or country and offers tips on food safety. **Travel Health Online** (www.tripprep.com), sponsored by a consortium of travel medicine practitioners, may also offer helpful advice on traveling abroad. You can find listings of reliable medical clinics overseas at the **International Society of Travel Medicine** (www.istm.org).

WHAT TO DO IF YOU GET SICK AWAY FROM HOME

For travel abroad, you may have to pay all medical costs upfront and be reimbursed later. Medicare and Medicaid do not provide coverage for medical costs outside the U.S. Before leaving home, find out what medical services your health insurance covers. To protect yourself, consider buying medical travel insurance (see "Medical Insurance," under "General Travel Resources," above).

Very few health insurance plans pay for medical evacuation back to the U.S. (which can cost $10,000 and up). A number of companies offer medical evacuation services anywhere in the world. If you're ever hospitalized more than 150 miles from home, **MedjetAssist** (© **800/527-7478;** www.medjetassistance.com) will pick you up and fly you to the hospital of your choice virtually anywhere in the world in a medically equipped and staffed aircraft 24 hours day, 7 days a week. Annual memberships are $225 individual, $350 family; you can also purchase short-term memberships.

U.K. nationals will need a **European Health Insurance Card (EHIC)** to receive free or reduced-costs health benefits during a visit to a European Economic Area (EEA) country (European Union countries plus Iceland, Liechtenstein and Norway) or Switzerland. The European Health Insurance Card replaces the E111 form, which is no longer valid. For advice, ask at your local post office or see www.dh.gov.uk/travellers.

We list **hospitals** and **emergency numbers** under "Fast Facts: France," p. 68.

If you suffer from a chronic illness, consult your doctor before your departure. Pack **prescription medications** in your carry-on luggage and carry them in their original containers, with pharmacy labels—otherwise they won't make it through airport security. Carry the generic name of prescription medicines, in case a local pharmacist is unfamiliar with the brand name.

STAYING SAFE

The most common menace, especially in large cities—particularly Paris—is the plague of pickpockets and gangs of Gypsy children who surround you, distract you, and steal your purse or wallet. Never leave valuables in a car and never travel with your car unlocked. A U.S. State Department travel advisory warns that every car (parked, stopped at a light, or even moving) can be a potential target. It is always prudent to check the U.S. State Department's advisories at http://travel.state.gov.

7 Specialized Travel Resources

TRAVELERS WITH DISABILITIES

Most disabilities shouldn't stop anyone from traveling. There are more options and resources out there than ever before.

Facilities for travelers in France, and nearly all modern hotels, provide accessible rooms. Older hotels (unless they've been renovated) may not provide elevators, special toilet facilities, or wheelchair ramps.

The new TGVs (high-speed trains) are wheelchair accessible; older trains have compartments for wheelchair boarding. On the Paris Métro, passengers with disabilities are able to sit in wider seats. Guide dogs ride free. However, some stations don't have escalators or elevators.

Knowing which hotels, restaurants, and attractions are accessible can save you a lot of frustration. **Association des Paralysés de France,** 17 bd. Auguste-Blanqui, Paris 75013 (✆ **01-40-78-69-66;** www.apf.asso.fr), provides documentation, moral support, and travel ideas for individuals who use wheelchairs. In addition to the Paris office, it maintains an office in each of the 90 *départements* ("mini-states" into which France is divided) and can help find hotels, transportation, sightseeing, house rentals, and (in some cases) companionship for paralyzed or partially paralyzed travelers. It's not, however, a travel agency.

Organizations that offer a vast range of resources and assistance to travelers with disabilities include **MossRehab** (✆ **800/CALL-MOSS;** www.mossresourcenet.org); the **American Foundation for the Blind (AFB;** ✆ **800/232-5463;** www.afb.org); and **SATH (Society for Accessible Travel & Hospitality;** ✆ **212/447-7284;** www.sath.org). **AirAmbulanceCard.com** is now partnered with SATH and allows you to preselect top-notch hospitals in case of an emergency.

Access-Able Travel Source (✆ **303/232-2979;** www.access-able.com) offers a comprehensive database on travel agents from around the world with experience in accessible travel; destination-specific access information; and links to such resources as service animals, equipment rentals, and access guides.

Many travel agencies offer customized tours and itineraries for travelers with disabilities. Among them are **Flying Wheels Travel** (✆ **507/451-5005;** www.flyingwheelstravel.com); and **Accessible Journeys** (✆ **800/846-4537** or 610/521-0339; www.disabilitytravel.com).

Flying with Disability (www.flying-with-disability.org) is a comprehensive information source on airplane travel. **Avis Rent a Car** (✆ **888/879-4273**) has an "Avis Access" program that offers services for customers with special travel needs. These include specially outfitted vehicles with swivel seats, spinner knobs, and hand controls; mobility scooter rentals; and accessible bus service. Be sure to reserve well in advance.

Also check out the quarterly magazine ***Emerging Horizons*** (www.emerginghorizons.com), available by subscription ($16.95 year U.S.; $21.95 outside U.S).

The "Accessible Travel" link at **Mobility-Advisor.com** (www.mobility-advisor.com) offers a variety of travel resources to persons with disabilities.

British travelers should contact **Holiday Care** (✆ **0845-124-9971** in U.K. only; www.holidaycare.org.uk) to access a wide range of travel information and resources for elderly people and those with disabilities.

GAY & LESBIAN TRAVELERS

France is one of the world's most tolerant countries toward gays and lesbians. "Gay Paree" boasts a large gay population, with many clubs, restaurants, organizations, and services.

A helpful source is **La Maison des Femmes,** 163 rue de Charenton, 12e,

Paris (✆ **01-43-43-41-13;** http://maisondesfemmes.free.fr; Métro: Charonne). It offers information about Paris for lesbians and bisexual women, and sometimes sponsors informal get-togethers. Call for a recorded announcement that gives the hours when someone will be available that particular week.

Lesbian or bisexual women can also pick up a copy of ***Lesbia.*** This publication and others are available at Paris's largest, best-stocked gay bookstore, **Les Mots à la Bouche,** 6 rue Ste-Croix-de-la-Bretonnerie, 4e (✆ **01-42-78-88-30;** www.motsbouche.com; Métro: Hôtel-de-Ville; Mon–Sat 11am–11pm, Sun 2–8pm), which carries publications in both French and English.

The International Gay and Lesbian Travel Association (IGLTA; ✆ 800/448-8550 or 954/776-2626; www.iglta.org) is the trade association for the gay and lesbian travel industry, and offers an online directory of gay- and lesbian-friendly travel businesses and tour operators.

Many agencies offer tours and travel itineraries specifically for gay and lesbian travelers. **Above and Beyond Tours** (✆ **800/397-2681;** www.abovebeyondtours.com) are gay Australia tour specialists. San Francisco–based **Now, Voyager** (✆ **800/255-6951;** www.nowvoyager.com) offers worldwide trips and cruises, and **Olivia** (✆ **800/631-6277;** www.olivia.com) offers lesbian cruises and resort vacations.

Gay.com Travel (✆ **800/929-2268** or 415/644-8044; www.gay.com/travel or www.outandabout.com), is an excellent online successor to the popular ***Out & About*** print magazine. It provides regularly updated information about gay-owned, gay-oriented, and gay-friendly lodging, dining, sightseeing, nightlife, and shopping establishments in every important destination worldwide. British travelers should click on the "Travel" link at **www.uk.gay.com** for advice and gay-friendly trip ideas.

The Canadian website **GayTraveler** (**gaytraveler.ca**) offers ideas and advice for gay travel all over the world.

The following travel guides are available at many bookstores, or you can order them from any online bookseller: ***Spartacus International Gay Guide, 35th Edition*** (Bruno Gmünder Verlag; www.spartacusworld.com/gayguide); ***Odysseus: The International Gay Travel Planner, 17th Edition*** (www.odyusa.com); and the ***Damron*** guides (www.damron.com), with separate, annual books for gay men and lesbians.

SENIOR TRAVEL

Many discounts are available to seniors—men and women of the "third age," as the French say; contact the French Government Tourist Office (see "Visitor Information & Maps," earlier in this chapter) for information.

Seniors (60 and over with proof of age) can get **A La Carte Senior,** available at any rail station or online at www.senior-sncf.com. The pass costs 53€ ($69) and is good for a 50% discount on unlimited rail travel throughout the year. The *carte* also offers reduced prices on some regional bus lines and half-price admission at government-owned museums. There are some restrictions—for example, you can't use it between 3pm Sunday and noon Monday, or from noon Friday to noon Saturday. There's no discount on the Paris network of commuter trains.

Air France offers seniors a 10% reduction on its regular non-excursion fares within France. Some restrictions apply. Discounts of around 10% are offered to passengers ages 62 and older on select Air France international flights. Be sure to ask for the discount when booking.

Members of **AARP,** 601 E St. NW, Washington, DC 20049 (✆ **888/687-2277;** www.aarp.org), get discounts on hotels, airfares, and car rentals. AARP offers members a wide range of benefits, including *AARP: The Magazine* and a monthly newsletter. Anyone over 50 can join.

Many reliable agencies and organizations target the 50-plus market. **Elderhostel** (✆ **800/454-5768;** www.elderhostel.org) arranges worldwide study programs for those aged 55 and over. **ElderTreks** (✆ **800/741-7956** or 416/558-5000 outside North America; www.eldertreks.com) offers small-group tours to off-the-beaten-path or adventure-travel locations, restricted to travelers 50 and older.

Recommended publications offering travel resources and discounts for seniors include: the quarterly magazine ***Travel 50 & Beyond*** (www.travel50andbeyond.com) and the bestselling paperback ***Unbelievably Good Deals and Great Adventures That You Absolutely Can't Get Unless You're Over 50 2005–2006, 16th Edition*** (McGraw-Hill), by Joann Rattner Heilman.

FAMILY TRAVEL

To locate accommodations, restaurants, and attractions that are particularly kid-friendly, refer to the "Kids" icon throughout this guide.

Recommended family travel websites include **Family Travel Forum** (www.familytravelforum.com), a comprehensive site that offers customized trip planning; **Family Travel Network** (www.familytravelnetwork.com), an online magazine providing travel tips; **TravelWithYourKids.com** (www.travelwithyourkids.com), a comprehensive site written by parents for parents offering sound advice for long-distance and international travel with children. A fun read, for recommendations in France and elsewhere, is ***Frommer's 500 Places to Take Your Kids Before They Grow Up*** (Wiley Publishing, Inc.).

WOMEN TRAVELERS

Check out the award-winning website **Journeywoman** (www.journeywoman.com), a "real life" women's travel-information network where you can sign up for a free e-mail newsletter and get advice on everything from etiquette and dress to safety. The travel guide ***Safety and Security for Women Who Travel*** by Sheila Swan and Peter Laufer (Travelers' Tales Guides), offering common-sense tips on safe travel, was updated in 2004.

MULTICULTURAL TRAVELERS

Since the days of the celebrated chanteuse Josephine Baker and, later, the author James Baldwin, France has welcomed African-American travelers. That welcome continues today. A good book on the subject is Tyler Stovall's *Paris Noir.* Another worthwhile resource is the website www.cafedelasoul.com.

Regrettably, anti-Semitism has been on the rise in Europe, especially in France, which has registered a significant increase in incidents against Jews. French Jews (not visitors from abroad) have suffered assaults and attacks against synagogues, cemeteries, schools, and other Jewish property. Officials say they believe that attacks in France are linked to the worsening of the Israeli-Palestinian conflict. Some sources—none official—recommend that travelers conceal Star of David jewelry and other such items to ensure personal safety while traveling in France.

Officially, the government of France welcomes Jewish visitors and promises a vigorous defense of their safety and concerns. The French Government Tourist Office website (www.franceguide.com) has a "Jewish Traveler Guide" section with more information.

8 Sustainable Tourism/Ecotourism

Each time you take a flight or drive a car, CO_2 is released into the atmosphere. You can help neutralize this danger to our planet through "carbon offsetting"—paying someone to reduce your CO_2 emissions by the same amount you've added. Carbon offsets can be purchased in the U.S. from companies such as **Carbonfund.org** (www.carbonfund.org) and **TerraPass** (www.terrapass.org), and from **Climate Care** (www.climatecare.org) in the U.K.

Although one could argue that any vacation that includes an airplane flight can't be truly "green," you can go on holiday and still contribute positively to the environment. You can offset carbon emissions from your flight in other ways. Choose forward-looking companies that embrace responsible development practices, helping preserve destinations for the future by working alongside local people. An increasing number of sustainable tourism initiatives can help you plan a family trip and leave as small a "footprint" as possible on the places you visit.

Responsible Travel (www.responsibletravel.com) contains a great source of sustainable travel ideas run by a spokesperson for responsible tourism in the travel industry. **Sustainable Travel International** (www.sustainabletravelinternational.org) promotes responsible tourism practices and issues an annual Green Gear & Gift Guide.

You can find eco-friendly travel tips, statistics, and touring companies and associations—listed by destination under "Travel Choice"—at the TIES website, www.ecotourism.org. Also check out **Conservation International** (www.conservation.org)—which, with *National Geographic Traveler,* annually presents **World Legacy Awards** (www.wlaward.org) to those travel tour operators, businesses, organizations, and places that have made a significant contribution to sustainable tourism. **Ecotravel.com** is

Frommers.com: The Complete Travel Resource

It should go without saying, but we highly recommend **Frommers.com,** voted Best Travel Site by *PC Magazine.* We think you'll find our expert advice and tips; independent reviews of hotels, restaurants, attractions, and preferred shopping and nightlife venues; vacation giveaways; and an online booking tool indispensable before, during, and after your travels. We publish the complete contents of over 128 travel guides in our **Destinations** section covering more than 3,600 places worldwide to help you plan your trip. Each weekday, we publish original articles reporting on **Deals and News** via our free **Frommers.com Newsletter** to help you save time and money and travel smarter. We're betting you'll find our new **Events** listings (http://events.frommers.com) an invaluable resource; it's an up-to-the-minute roster of what's happening in cities everywhere—including concerts, festivals, lectures and more. We've also added weekly **Podcasts, interactive maps,** and hundreds of new images across the site. Check out our **Travel Talk** area featuring **Message Boards** where you can join in conversations with thousands of fellow Frommer's travelers and post your trip report once you return.

part online magazine and part ecodirectory that lets you search for touring companies in several categories (water-based, land-based, spiritually oriented, and so on).

In the U.K., **Tourism Concern** (www.tourismconcern.org.uk) works to reduce social and environmental problems connected to tourism and find ways of improving tourism so that local benefits are increased.

The **Association of British Travel Agents** (**ABTA;** www.abtamembers.org/responsibletourism) acts as a focal point for the U.K. travel industry and is one of the leading groups spearheading responsible tourism.

The **Association of Independent Tour Operators** (**AITO;** www.aito.co.uk) is a group of interesting specialist operators leading the field in making holidays sustainable.

9 Staying Connected

TELEPHONES

To call France:

1. Dial the international access code: 011 from the U.S.; 00 from the U.K., Ireland, or New Zealand; or 0011 from Australia.
2. Dial the country code 33.
3. Dial the city code, which is always two digits, beginning with a zero, but drop that first zero, and then the eight-digit number.

To make international calls: First dial 00 and then the country code (U.S. or Canada 1, U.K. 44, Ireland 353, Australia 61, New Zealand 64). Next, dial the area code and number. For example, if you wanted to call the British Embassy in Washington, D.C., you would dial ✆ 00-1-202-588-7800.

For directory assistance: Dial ✆ 12 for assistance in French; in English, dial ✆ 0-800/364-775. For international inquiries, dial ✆ 08-36-59-32-12. This will link you with a bilingual (French and English) phone operator. You are allowed to request only two numbers for which you pay a service charge of 3€ ($3.90).

For operator assistance: If you wish to use an operator to call your home country, you dial the toll-free number of ✆ **08-00-99-00** plus the digits of your country code (example: ✆ 08-00-99-00-11 for the U.S. and Canada).

Toll-free numbers: Numbers beginning with 08 and followed by 00 are toll-free. But be careful. Numbers that begin with 08 followed by 36 carry a .35€ (45¢) surcharge per minute.

CELLPHONES

The three letters that define much of the world's wireless capabilities are **GSM** (Global System for Mobile Communications), a big, seamless network that makes for easy cross-border cellphone use throughout Europe and dozens of other countries worldwide. In the U.S., T-Mobile, AT&T Wireless, and Cingular use this quasi-universal system; in Canada, Microcell and some Rogers customers are GSM, and all Europeans and most Australians use GSM. GSM phones function with a removable plastic SIM card, encoded with your phone number and account information. If your cellphone is on a GSM system, and you have a world-capable multiband phone such as many Sony Ericsson, Motorola, or Samsung models, you can make and receive calls across civilized areas around much of the globe. Just call your wireless operator and ask for "international roaming" to be activated on your account. Unfortunately, per-minute charges can be high—usually $1 to $1.50 in western Europe and up to $5 in places such as Russia and Indonesia.

Online Traveler's Toolbox

Veteran travelers usually carry some essential items to make their trips easier. Following is a selection of handy online tools to bookmark and use.

- **Airplane Food** (www.airlinemeals.net)
- **Airplane Seating** (www.seatguru.com and www.airlinequality.com)
- **Foreign Languages for Travelers** (www.travlang.com)
- **Maps** (www.mapquest.com)
- **Subway Navigator** (www.subwaynavigator.com)
- **Time and Date** (www.timeanddate.com)
- **Travel Warnings** (http://travel.state.gov, www.fco.gov.uk/travel, www.voyage.gc.ca, or www.dfat.gov.au/consular/advice)
- **Universal Currency Converter** (www.xe.com/ucc)
- **Visa ATM Locator** (www.visa.com), **MasterCard ATM Locator** (www.mastercard.com)
- **Weather** (www.intellicast.com and www.weather.com)

For many, **renting** a phone is a good idea. While you can rent a phone from any number of overseas sites, including kiosks at airports and at car-rental agencies, we suggest renting the phone before you leave home. North Americans can rent one before leaving home from **InTouch USA** (**© 800/872-7626;** www.intouchglobal.com) or **RoadPost** (**© 888/290-1606** or 905/272-5665; www.roadpost.com). InTouch will also, for free, advise you on whether your existing phone will work overseas; simply call **© 703/222-7161** between 9am and 4pm EST, or go to **http://intouchglobal.com/travel.htm**.

Buying a phone can be economically attractive, as many nations have cheap prepaid phone systems. Once you arrive at your destination, stop by a local cellphone shop and get the cheapest package; you'll probably pay less than $100 for a phone and a starter calling card. Local calls may be as low as 10¢ per minute, and in many countries incoming calls are free.

INTERNET/E-MAIL

WITHOUT YOUR OWN COMPUTER

To find cybercafes in your destination, check **www.cybercaptive.com** and **www.cybercafe.com**.

Most major airports have **Internet kiosks** that provide basic Web access for a per-minute fee that's usually higher than cybercafe prices. Check out copy shops such as **Kinko's** (FedEx Kinko's), which offers computer stations with fully loaded software (as well as Wi-Fi).

WITH YOUR OWN COMPUTER

More and more hotels, resorts, airports, cafes, and retailers are going **Wi-Fi** (wireless fidelity), becoming "hotspots" that offer free high-speed Wi-Fi access or charge a small fee for usage. Most laptops sold today have built-in wireless capability. To find public Wi-Fi hotspots at your destination, go to **www.jiwire.com**; its Hotspot Finder holds the world's largest directory of public wireless hotspots.

For dial-up access, most business-class hotels throughout the world offer dataports for laptop modems, and a few thousand hotels in Europe now offer free high-speed Internet access.

Wherever you go, bring a **connection kit** of the right power and phone adapters, a spare phone cord, and a spare Ethernet network cable—or find out whether your hotel supplies them to guests.

For information about electricity and currents, see "Electricity," in the "Fast Facts: France" section, later in this chapter.

10 Packages for the Independent Traveler

Package tours are simply a way to buy the airfare, accommodations, and other elements of your trip (such as car rentals, airport transfers, and sometimes even activities) at the same time and often at discounted prices.

One good source of package deals is the airlines themselves. Most major airlines offer air/land packages, including **American Airlines Vacations** (© 800/321-2121; www.aavacations.com), **Delta Vacations** (© 800/654-6559; www.deltavacations.com), **Continental Airlines Vacations** (© 800/301-3800; www.covacations.com), and **United Vacations** (© 888/854-3899; www.unitedvacations.com). Several big **online travel agencies**—Expedia, Travelocity, Orbitz, Site59, and Lastminute.com—also do a brisk business in packages.

Franceway (www.franceway.com) puts together French packages, including airfares as well as government-rated three-star hotels from Paris to the Riviera. **Travel in France** (www.travel-in-france.com) is not a travel agency but helps you organize your own French package trip, featuring the best airfares on Air France. It also provides information on hotels in a range of prices. **FirstforFrance.com** can also help you put together a package vacation in France. The site maintains a Travel Centre in Paris where you can make bookings at hotels in a wide range of prices. All your arrangements can be made on the Web.

Travel packages are also listed in the travel section of your local Sunday newspaper. Or check ads in national travel magazines such as *Arthur Frommer's Budget Travel Magazine, Travel + Leisure, National Geographic Traveler,* and *Condé Nast Traveler.*

Tips Ask Before You Go

Before you invest in a package deal or an escorted tour:

- Always ask about the **cancellation policy.** Can you get your money back? Is there a deposit required?
- Ask about the **accommodations choices and prices** for each. Then look up the hotels' reviews in a Frommer's guide and check their rates online for your specific dates of travel. Also find out what types of rooms are offered.
- Request a complete **schedule.** (Escorted tours only)
- Ask about the **size** and demographics of the group. (Escorted tours only)
- Discuss what is included in the **price** (transportation, meals, tips, airport transfers, and so on; escorted tours only)
- Finally, look for **hidden expenses.** Ask whether airport departure fees and taxes, for example, are included in the total cost—they rarely are.

11 Escorted General-Interest Tours

Escorted tours are structured group tours, with a group leader. The price usually includes everything from airfare to hotels, meals, tours, admission costs, and local transportation.

The two largest operators conducting escorted tours of France and Europe are **Globus + Cosmos Tours** (✆ **866/755-8581**; www.globusandcosmos.com) and **Trafalgar** (✆ **800/854-0103**; www.trafalgartours.com). Both have first-class tours that run about $300 a day and budget tours for about $100 a day. The differences are mainly in hotel location and the number of activities. There's little difference in the companies' services, so choose your tour based on the itinerary and date of departure. Brochures are available at travel agencies, and all tours must be booked through travel agents.

Tauck World Discovery, 10 Norden Pl., Norwalk, CT 06855 (✆ **800/788-7885**; www.tauck.com), provides first-class, escorted coach grand tours of France as well as 1-week general tours of regions in France. Its 13-day tour covering the Normandy landing beaches, the Bayeux tapestry, and Mont-St-Michel costs $4,990 per person, double occupancy (land only); an 8-day trip beginning in Nice and ending in Paris is $3,350 per person.

Despite the fact that escorted tours require big deposits and predetermine hotels, restaurants, and itineraries, many people derive security and peace of mind from the structure they offer. Escorted tours—whether they're navigated by bus, motorcoach, train, or boat—let travelers sit back and enjoy the trip without having to drive or worry about details. They take you to the maximum number of sights in the minimum amount of time with the least amount of hassle. They're particularly convenient for people with limited mobility and they can be a great way to make new friends.

On the downside, you'll have little opportunity for serendipitous interactions with locals. The tours can be jam-packed with activities, leaving little room for individual sightseeing, whim, or adventure—plus they often focus on the heavily touristed sites, so you miss out on many a lesser-known gem.

12 Special-Interest Trips

In a country as diverse and popular as France, there are numerous options.

BALLOONING The world's largest hot-air-balloon operator is **Buddy Bombard's Private Europe,** 333 Pershing Way, West Palm Beach, FL 33401 (✆ **800/862-8537** or 561/837-6610; fax 561/837-6623; www.buddybombard.com). It maintains about three dozen hot-air balloons, some in the Loire Valley and Burgundy. The 5-day tours, costing $7,844 per person (double occupancy), incorporate food and wine tasting and all meals, lodging in Relais & Châteaux hotels, sightseeing, rail transfers to and from Paris, and a daily balloon ride over vineyards and fields.

Bonaventura Balloon Co., 133 Wall Rd., Napa Valley, CA 94573 (✆ **800/FLY-NAPA** or 707/944-2822; fax 707/944-2220; www.bonaventuraballoons.com), meets you in Paris and takes you on the high-speed train to Burgundy, where your balloon tour begins. It carries you over the scenic parts of the region. Guests stay in a 14th-century mill, now an inn owned by a three-star chef. A 7- to 9-day trip is $2,695 per person, including sightseeing in Paris, two balloon trips, lodging, cooking classes, wine tasting, and at least one meal per day.

BARGE CRUISES Before the advent of the railways, many crops, building supplies, raw materials, and finished products were barged through France on a series of rivers, canals, and estuaries. Many of these waterways retain their old-fashioned locks and pumps, allowing shallow-draft barges easy access through the idyllic countryside.

French Country Waterways, Ltd., P.O. Box 2195, Duxbury, MA 02331 (© **800/222-1236** or 781/934-2454; www.fcwl.com), leads 1-week tours through Burgundy and Champagne. For double occupancy, the price ranges from $4,095 to $5,995.

Le Boat, 980 Awald Rd., Annapolis, MD 21403 (© **800/992-0291** or 410/972-3008; fax 410/280-2406; www.leboat.com), focuses on regions of France not covered by many other operators. The company's luxury crafts fit through the narrow canals and locks of Camargue, Languedoc, and Provence. Each 6-night tour has 10 passengers in five cabins outfitted with mahogany and brass, plus meals prepared by a *cordon bleu* chef. Prices vary widely; for example, 6 nights in the Upper Loire begin at $3,700 per person, rising to $6,000 in summer.

Go Barging (© **800/394-8630;** www.gobarging.com) operates Great Island Voyages, featuring river cruise ships. Fares start at $2,690 per person (double occupancy) for a 6-night cruise, including room, breakfast, and dinner. Bicycles are carried onboard for sightseeing trips. This company also offers cruises in the Loire Valley and the south of France.

BICYCLING TOURS Some of the best cycling tours of France are offered by **VBT (Deluxe Bicycle Vacations),** 614 Monkton Rd., Bristol, VT 05443 (© **800/245-3868;** www.vbt.com), which offers trips in five of the most scenic parts of France. These range from Burgundy (which combines a barge tour) to the Loire Valley, even Provence and the Normandy Coast. Packages are priced from $2,495 to $3,445 per person.

Classic Adventures, P.O. Box 143, Hamlin, NY 14464 (© **800/777-8090;** fax 585/964-7297; www.classicadventures.com), sponsors 6- to 10-day spring and fall tours of the Loire Valley and the Dordogne. Accommodations are upscale, and tours are van-supported and escorted. The 6-day tour, including room, breakfast, and dinner, is $2,489 per person, and for the Loire Valley, a 10-day tour of the Dordogne costs $3,129.

Euro-Bike & Walking Tours, P.O. Box 990, DeKalb, IL 60115 (© **800/321-6060** or 815/758-8851; www.eurobike.com), offers 10-day tours in the Dordogne ($2,300–$3,830 per person), 11-day tours in Provence ($3,250–$4,340 per person), 6-day tours of Burgundy ($1,580–$2,630 per person), and 8-day tours of the Loire ($2,050–$3,420 per person). All are escorted and include room, breakfast, and dinner.

Go-today.com (a division of Europe Express), 19021 120th Ave. NE, Suite 102, Bothell, WA 98011 (© **800/227-3235;** www.go-today.com), has biking and walking tours of Bordeaux, Burgundy, the Dordogne, the Loire Valley, and Provence. An 8-day self-guided bike tour is $1,599 per person, double occupancy. All tours include overnight accommodations and most meals. Guided tours include van support and a guide; on nonguided tours, you'll always have the name of an English-speaking local contact.

COOKING SCHOOLS The famous/infamous Georges-Auguste Escoffier (1846–1935) taught the Edwardians how to eat. Today the Hôtel Ritz maintains the **Ritz-Escoffier Ecole de Gastronomie Française,** 38 rue Cambon, 75001 Paris (© **01-43-16-30-50;** www.ritzparis.com), which offers demonstration classes of the master's techniques on Saturdays. These cost 125€ ($163) each. Courses, taught in French and English, start at 980€ ($1,274) for 1 week, up to 5,550€ ($7,215) for 6 weeks.

Le Cordon Bleu, 8 rue Léon-Delhomme, 75015 Paris (✆ **800/457-2433** in the U.S., or 01-53-68-22-50; www.cordonbleu.edu), was established in 1895 and is the most famous French cooking school—where Julia Child learned to perfect her *pâté brisée* and *mousse au chocolat.* The best-known courses last 10 weeks, after which you are awarded a certificate. Many enthusiasts prefer a less intense immersion and opt for a 4-day workshop or a 3-hour demonstration class. Enrollment in either is first-come, first-served; costs start at 30€ ($39) for a demonstration and start at 889€ ($1,156) for the 4-day workshop. Classes are in English.

LANGUAGE SCHOOLS The **Alliance Française,** 101 bd. Raspail, Paris 75270 (✆ **01-42-84-90-00;** fax 01-42-84-91-00; www.alliancefr.org), a nonprofit organization with a network of 1,100 establishments in 138 countries, offers French-language courses to some 350,000 students. The school in Paris is open all year; month-long courses range from 350€ to 660€ ($455–$858), depending on the number of hours per day. Request information and an application at least 1 month before your departure. In North America, the largest branch is the **Alliance Française,** 1 N. LaSalle St., Suite 1350, Chicago, IL 60602 (✆ **800/6-FRANCE;** fax 800/491-6980; www.afusa.org).

A clearinghouse for information on French-language schools is **Lingua Service Worldwide,** 42 Artillery Dr., Woodbury, CT 06798 (✆ **800/394-LEARN** or 203/263-6294; www.linguaserviceworldwide.com). Its programs are available in many cities throughout France. They cost $920 to $2,250 for 2 weeks, depending on the city, the school, and the accommodations.

MUSIC TOURS One outfit that coordinates hotel stays in Paris with major musical events, usually in at least one (and often both) of the city's opera houses, is **Dailey-Thorp Travel,** P.O. Box 670, Big Horn, Wyoming 82833 (✆ **800/998-4677** or 307/673-1555; fax 307/674-7474; www.daileythorp.com). Sojourns tend to last 3 to 7 days and, in many cases, tie in with performances in other cities (usually London, Berlin, or Milan). Expect accommodations in deluxe hotels such as the Hôtel du Louvre or the Hôtel Scribe, and a staff that has made arrangements for all the nuts and bolts of your arrival in, and artistic exposure to, Paris.

TENNIS TOURS Die-hard fans around the world set their calendars by the French Open, held at Paris's Roland-Garros stadium. You can book your hotel and tickets to the event on your own, but if you're unsure about scheduling, consider a California-based company, **Advantage Tennis Tours,** 33 White Sail Dr., Suite 100, Laguna Niguel, CA 92677 (✆ **800/341-8687** or 949/661-7331; fax 949/489-2837; www.advantagetennistours.com). They typically book packages including 5 or 6 nights of hotel accommodations in Paris, 2 or 3 days on Center Court, and the skills of a bilingual hostess; rates per person, without airfare, begin at $2,995, double occupancy, depending on your choice of hotel and the duration of your visit.

13 Getting Around France

BY TRAIN

The world's fastest trains link some 50 French cities, allowing you to get from Paris to just about anywhere else in the country in hours. With 39,000km (24,200 miles) of track and about 3,000 stations, SNCF (French National Railroads) is fabled for its on-time performance. You can travel in first or second class by day and in couchette by night. Many trains have dining facilities.

INFORMATION If you plan to travel a lot on European railroads, get the latest copy of the *Thomas Cook Timetable of European Passenger Railroads.* This 500-plus-page book documents all of Europe's main passenger rail services with detail and accuracy. It's available online at www.thomascookpublishing.com.

In the United States: For more information and to purchase rail passes before you leave, contact **Rail Europe** (© **877/272-RAIL;** www.raileurope.com).

In Canada: Call Rail Europe at © **800/361-RAIL.**

In London: SNCF has offices at Rail Europe, 179 Piccadilly, London W1V 0BA (© **0870/584-8848**).

In Paris: For information or reservations, go online (www.sncf.fr). You can also go to any local travel agency. A simpler way to buy tickets is to use the *billetterie* (ticket machine) in every train station. If you know your PIN, you can use a credit card to buy your ticket.

FRANCE RAIL PASSES Working cooperatively with SNCF, Air Inter Europe, and Avis, Rail Europe offers three flexible rail passes to North Americans that can reduce travel costs considerably.

The **France Railpass** provides unlimited rail transport in France for any 3 days within 1 month, at 198€ ($261) in first class and 169€ ($222) in second. You can purchase up to 6 more days for an extra 29€ ($38) per person per day. Children 4 to 11 travel for half-price.

The **France Rail 'n' Drive Pass,** available only in North America, combines good value on both rail travel and Avis car rentals. It is best used by arriving at a major rail depot and then striking out to explore the countryside by car. It includes the France Railpass (see above) and use of a rental car. A 2-day rail pass (first class) and 2 days' use of the cheapest rental car (with unlimited mileage) is $356 per person. The best deal if you're traveling in France with a friend—or even 3 or 4 friends—is the **France Saverpass,** granting 3 days of unlimited travel in a 1-month period. The cost is $223 per person first class or $191 second class. There's also a **France Youthpass** for travelers 25 or under, granting 4 days of unlimited train travel within a month. The cost is $194 in first class or $164 in second class. For those over 60, the **France Senior Pass** offers all the same features as the France Railpass, but with a savings. You get 3 days of unlimited train travel in 1 month for $238, with additional rail days costing only $34. Travel days may be used consecutively or nonconsecutively.

A **France Rail Day Pass** allows you to take day trips from Paris to such cities as Lyon, Reims, Dijon, or Nantes. The cost is $129 in first class or $90 in second class. The pass grants you 1 day of unlimited travel in a 1-month period on the national rail network.

EURAILPASS The Eurailpass permits unlimited first-class rail travel in any country in western Europe except the British Isles (good in Ireland). Passes are available for purchase online (www.eurail.com) and at various offices/agents around the world. Travel agents and railway agents in such cities as New York, Montreal, and Los Angeles sell Eurailpasses. You can purchase them at the North American offices of CIT Travel Service, the French National Railroads, the German Federal Railroads, and the Swiss Federal Railways. It is strongly recommended that you purchase passes before you leave home as not all passes are available in Europe; also, passes purchased in Europe will cost about 20% more. Numerous options are available for travel in France.

The **Eurail Global Pass** allows you unlimited travel in 18 Eurail-affiliated

Tips Have a Seat

Remember that a train ticket does not guarantee you a seat; it merely gets you from one place to another. On crowded trains and during busy times, you'll have to make a **seat reservation** (and pay for the privilege) if you want to be sure of sitting somewhere other than on top of your luggage. Seat reservations cost 10€ ($13) per person.

countries. You can travel on any of the days within the validity period which is available for 15 days, 21 days, 1 month, 2 months, 3 months, and some other possibilities as well. Prices for first-class adult travel are $635 for 15 days, $829 for 21 days, $1,025 for 1 month, $1,449 for 2 months, and $1,789 for 3 months. Children 4 to 11 pay half fare; those 3 and under travel for free.

A **Eurail Global Pass Saver,** also valid for first-class travel in 18 countries, offers a special deal for two or more people traveling together. This pass costs $539 for 5 days, $699 for 21 days, $869 for 1 month, $1,229 for 2 months, and $1,519 for 3 months.

A **Eurail Global Youth Pass** for those 12 to 25 allows second-class travel in 18 countries. This pass costs $415 for 15 days, $539 for 21 days, $669 for 1 month, $945 for 2 months, and $1,165 for 3 months.

Eurail Selectpass: The pass offers unlimited travel on the national rail networks of any three, four, or five bordering countries out of the 22 Eurail nations linked by train or ship. Two or more passengers can travel together for big discounts, getting 5, 6, 8, 10, or 15 days of rail travel within any 2-month period on the national rail networks of any three, four, or five adjoining Eurail countries linked by train or ship. A sample fare: for 5 days in 2 months you pay $405 for three countries.

BY CAR

The most charming châteaux and country hotels always seem to lie away from the main cities and train stations. Renting a car is often the best way to travel around France, especially if you plan to explore it in-depth.

But Europe's rail networks are so well developed and inexpensive that we recommend you rent a car only for exploring areas little serviced by rail, such as Brittany, rural Burgundy, and the Dordogne. Or take trains between cities and rent a car on the days when you want to explore independently.

Driving time in Europe is largely a matter of conjecture, urgency, and how much sightseeing you do along the way. Driving time from Paris to Geneva is 5½ hours minimum. It's 2½ hours from Paris to Rouen, 3½ hours to Nantes, and 4 hours to Lyon. The driving time from Marseille to Paris (771km/479 miles) is a matter of national pride, and tall tales abound about how rapidly the French can do it. Flooring it, you may conceivably get there in 7 hours, but we always make a 2-day journey of it.

RENTALS To rent a car, you'll need to present a passport, a driver's license, and a credit card. You also have to meet the company's minimum-age requirement. (For the least expensive cars, this is 21 at Hertz, 23 at Avis, and 25 at Budget. More expensive cars may require that you be at least 25.) It usually isn't obligatory within France, but certain companies have asked for the presentation of an International Driver's License, even though this is becoming increasingly superfluous in western Europe.

Note: The best deal is usually a weekly rental with unlimited mileage. All car-rental bills in France are subject to a 19.6% government tax. Though the rental company won't usually mind if you drive your car into, say, Germany, Switzerland, Italy, or Spain, it's often forbidden to transport your car by ferry, including across the Channel to England.

In France, **collision damage waiver (CDW)** is usually factored into the overall rate quoted, but you should always verify this, of course, before taking a car on the road. At most companies, the CDW provision won't protect you against theft, so if this is the case, ask about purchasing extra theft protection.

Automatic transmission is a luxury in Europe, so if you want it, you'll pay dearly.

Budget (© **800/472-3325** in the U.S., 800/268-8900 in Canada; www.budget.com) has about 30 locations in Paris and at Orly (© **01-49-75-56-05**) and Charles de Gaulle (© **01-48-62-70-22**). For rentals of more than 7 days, you can usually pick up a car in one French city and drop it off in another, but there are extra charges. Drop-offs in cities within an easy drive of the French border (including Geneva and Frankfurt) incur no extra charge; you can arrange drop-offs in other non-French cities for a reasonable surcharge.

Hertz (© **800/654-3001** in the U.S. and Canada; www.hertz.com) maintains about 15 locations in Paris, including offices at the city's airports. The main office is at 27 place St-Ferdinand, 17e (© **01-39-38-38-38;** Métro: Argentine). Be sure to ask about promotional discounts.

Avis (© **800/331-1084** in the U.S. and Canada; www.avis.com) has offices at both Paris airports and an inner-city headquarters at 5 rue Bixio, 7e (© **01-44-18-10-50;** Métro: Ecole Militaire), near the Eiffel Tower.

National (© **800/CAR-RENT** in the U.S. and Canada; www.nationalcar.com) is represented in Paris by Europcar, one office is at 48 rue de Berri, 8e (© **01-53-93-73-40;** Métro: St. Philippe du Roule). It has offices at both Paris airports and at about a dozen other locations. For the lowest rates, reserve in advance from North America.

Two U.S.-based agencies that don't have Paris offices but act as booking agents for Paris-based agencies are **Kemwel Drive Europe** (© **877/820-0668;** www.kemwel.com) and **Auto Europe** (© **800/223-5555;** www.autoeurope.com). They can make bookings in the United States only, so call before your trip.

GASOLINE Known in France as *essence,* gas is expensive for those accustomed to North American prices. All but the least expensive cars usually require an octane rating that the French classify as *essence super,* the most expensive variety. Depending on your car, you'll need either leaded *(avec plomb)* or unleaded *(sans plomb).*

Beware the mixture of gasoline and oil, called *mélange* or *gasoil,* sold in some rural communities; this mixture is for very old two-cycle engines.

Note: Sometimes you can drive for miles in rural France without encountering a gas station; don't let your tank get dangerously low.

DRIVING RULES Everyone in the car, in both the front and the back seats, must wear seat belts. Children under 12 must ride in the back seat. Drivers are supposed to yield to the car on their right, except where signs indicate otherwise, as at traffic circles.

If you violate the speed limit, expect a big fine. Limits are about 130kmph (81 mph) on expressways, about 100kmph (62 mph) on major national highways, and 90kmph (56 mph) on country roads. In towns, don't exceed 60kmph (37 mph).

Note: It's illegal to use a cellphone while you're driving in France; you will be ticketed if you're stopped.

MAPS For France as a whole, most motorists opt for **Michelin map 989.** For regions, Michelin publishes a series of **yellow maps** that are quite good. Big travel-book stores in North America carry these maps, and they're commonly available in France (at lower prices). In this age of congested traffic, one useful feature of the Michelin map is its designations of alternative *routes de dégagement,* which let you skirt big cities and avoid traffic-clogged highways.

Another recommended option is *Frommer's Road Atlas Europe.*

BREAKDOWNS/ASSISTANCE A breakdown is called *une panne* in France. Call the police at ✆ **17** anywhere in France to be put in touch with the nearest garage. Most local garages offer towing. If the breakdown occurs on an expressway, find the nearest roadside emergency phone box, pick up the phone, and put a call through. You'll be connected to the nearest breakdown service facility.

BY PLANE

France has few domestic competitors. **Air France** (✆ **800/237-2747;** www.airfrance.com) is the 800-pound gorilla, serving about eight cities in France and eight others in Europe. Air travel time from Paris to almost anywhere in France is about an hour.

14 Tips on Accommodations

The French government rates hotels on a one- to four-star system. One-star hotels are budget accommodations; two-star lodgings are quality tourist hotels; three stars go to first-class hotels; and four stars are reserved for deluxe accommodations. In some of the lower categories, the rooms may not have private bathrooms; instead, many have what the French call a *cabinet de toilette* (hot and cold running water and maybe a bidet). In such hotels, bathrooms are down the hall. Nearly all hotels in France have central heating, but in some cases, you might wish the owners would turn it up a little on a cold night.

For apartment, farmhouse, or cottage stays of 2 weeks or more, **Idyll Untours (888-868-6871;** www.untours.com) provides exceptional vacation rentals for a reasonable price—which includes air/ground transportation, cooking facilities, and on-call support from a local resident. Best of all: Untours—named the "Most Generous Company in America" by Newman's Own—donates most profits to provide low-interest loans to underprivileged entrepreneurs around the world (see website for details). At press time, Untour's French offerings included lodging in Alsace, Provence, and Paris. Also check out www.venere.com for more information on accommodations.

RELAIS & CHATEAUX Now known worldwide, this organization of deluxe and first-class hostelries began in France for visitors seeking the ultimate in hotel living and dining in a traditional atmosphere. Relais & Châteaux establishments (there are about 150 in France) are former castles, abbeys, manor houses, and town houses converted into hostelries or inns and elegant hotels. All have a limited number of rooms, so reservations are imperative. Sometimes these owner-run establishments have pools and tennis courts. The Relais part of the organization refers to inns called *relais,* meaning "post house." These tend to be less luxurious than the châteaux, but are often charming. Top-quality restaurants are *relais gourmands.* Throughout this guide, we list our favorite Relais & Châteaux members, but there are many more.

For a catalog of member establishments, send $12 to **Relais & Châteaux** (✆ **800/735-2478;** www.relaischateaux.com).

BED & BREAKFASTS Called *gîtes-chambres d'hôte* in France, these may be one or several bedrooms on a farm or in a village home. Many offer one main meal a day (lunch or dinner).

La Maison des Gîtes de France et du Tourisme Vert, 59 rue St-Lazare, Paris 75439 (✆ **01-49-70-75-75;** www.gites-de-france.fr), lists at least 6,000 *gîtes-chambres d'hôte.* Sometimes these B&Bs aren't as simple as you may think: Instead of a bare-bones farm, you may be in a mansion in the countryside.

CONDOS, VILLAS, HOUSES & APARTMENTS If you can stay for at least a week and don't mind doing your own cooking and cleaning, you may want to rent long-term accommodations. The local French Tourist Board might help you obtain a list of agencies that offer this type of rental (which is popular at ski resorts). In France, one of the best groups of agents is the **Fédération Nationale des Agents Immobiliers,** 106 rue de l'Université, Paris 75007 (✆ **01-47-05-44-36;** www.fnpc.fr).

In the United States, **At Home Abroad, Inc.,** 163 Third Ave., Box 319, New York, NY 10003 (✆ **212/421-9165;** fax 212/533-0095; www.athomeabroadinc.com), specializes in villas on the French Riviera and in the Dordogne as well as places in the Provençal hill towns. Rentals are usually for 2 weeks. You'll receive photographs of the properties and a newsletter.

New York Habitat (✆ **212/255-8018;** fax 212/627-1416; www.nyhabitat.com) rents furnished apartments and vacation accommodations in Paris and the south of France. Bookings should be done at least 3 months in advance (even farther out for the south of France) and can be arranged online or over the phone. Prices in Paris range from 300€ to 8,000€ ($390–$10,444); in the south of France 55€ to 10,000€ ($72–$13,000).

CyberRentals is a worldwide vacation rental website (✆ **512/684-1098;** www.cyberrentals.com) that lists vacation homes, condos, luxury villas, cabins, chalets, and other real estate available for rent by owner. For example, you can find properties such as one typical—and lovely—villa in Gordes in the Provence region that sleeps six and rents for between $1,500 and $3,000 per week, depending on season.

If you want to rent an apartment in Paris, the **Barclay International Group,** 6800 Jericho Turnpike, Syosset, NY 11791 (✆ **800/845-6636** or 516/364-0064; fax 516/364-4468; www.barclayweb.com), can give you access to about 3,000 apartments and villas throughout Paris (and 39 other cities in France), ranging from modest modern units to the most stylish lodgings. Units rent for 1 night to 6 months; all have TVs and kitchenettes, and many have concierge staffs and lobby-level security. The least expensive cost around $95 per night, double occupancy. Discounts are given for a stay of 1 week or longer. Rentals must be prepaid in U.S. dollars or with a U.S. credit or charge card.

Hometours International, Inc., 1108 Scottie Lane, Knoxville, TN 37919 (✆ **865/690-8484;** hometours@aol.com), offers more than 400 moderately priced apartments, apartment hotels, and villas in Paris. On the Riviera, you can rent villas, with pools, at reasonable rates.

HOTEL CHAINS One good moderately priced choice is the **Mercure** chain, an organization of simple, modern hotels throughout France. Even at the peak of the tourist season, a room at a Mercure in Paris rents for as little as 85€ ($111) per night (admittedly, a rarity). For more information on Mercure hotels and its 100-page directory, call (✆ **800/221-4542** in the U.S.; www.mercure.com).

Formule 1 hotels are basic but safe, offering rooms for up to three people for around 29€ ($35) per night. Built from prefabricated units, these air-conditioned, soundproof hotels are shipped to a site and assembled, often on the outskirts of cities such as Paris (27 in the suburbs). There are 150 of these throughout the rest of France.

Mercure and Formule 1 are both owned by the French hotel giant Accor, parent of Motel 6, which Formule 1 resembles. Formule 1's low cost makes it unprofitable for the chain to allow customers to reserve rooms from the United States, so you'll have to reserve upon arrival. For a directory, write to Formule 1/ETAP Hotels, c/o Sishe Hotel, 6–8 rue du Bois-Briard, Evry Cedex 91021 (✆ **08-92-68-56-85;** www.hotelformule1.com).

Other worthwhile economy bets, sometimes with a bit more charm, are the hotels and restaurants of the **Fédération Nationale des Logis de France,** 83 av. d'Italie, Paris 75013 (✆ **01-45-84-83-84;** www.logis-de-france.fr). This is an association of 3,000 hotels, usually country inns convenient for motorists, most rated one or two stars. The association publishes an annual directory.

SURFING FOR HOTELS

In addition to the online travel booking sites **Travelocity, Expedia, Orbitz, Priceline,** and **Hotwire,** you can book hotels through **Hotels.com; Quikbook** (www.quikbook.com); and **Travelaxe** (www.travelaxe.net).

HotelChatter.com is a daily webzine offering smart coverage and critiques of hotels worldwide. Go to **TripAdvisor.com** or **HotelShark.com** for helpful independent consumer reviews of hotels and resort properties.

It's a good idea to **get a confirmation number** and **make a printout** of any online booking transaction.

Throughout France, as in many tourist centers worldwide, hotels routinely overbook, so booking by credit card doesn't automatically hold your room if you arrive later than expected or after 6pm. The hotel clerk always asks when you expect to arrive, and the hotel usually holds the room until that time. Always pad your expected arrival by a few hours to be safe. However, all bets are off after 7pm., and the hotel is likely to give your room away unless you call and specifically ask them to hold it. If you've made a reservation very far in advance, confirm within 24 hours of your expected arrival. If you're experiencing a major delay, alert the hotel as soon as you can.

Beware of billing. Readers report that sometimes in France they booked a room online (say, $100 a night), but were charged $125 when they checked out. Keep your online confirmation in case of a dispute.

SAVING ON YOUR HOTEL ROOM

The **rack rate** is the maximum rate that a hotel charges for a room. Hardly anybody pays this price, however, except in high season or on holidays. To lower the cost of your room:

- **Ask about special rates or other discounts.** You may qualify for corporate, student, military, senior, frequent flier, trade union, or other discounts.
- **Dial direct.** When booking a room in a chain hotel, you'll often get a better deal by calling the individual hotel's reservation desk rather than the chain's main number.
- **Book online.** Many hotels offer Internet-only discounts, or supply rooms to Priceline, Hotwire, or Expedia at rates

House-Swapping

House-swapping is becoming a more popular and viable means of travel; you stay in their place, they stay in yours, and you both get a more authentic and personal view of a destination, the opposite of the escapist retreat many hotels offer. Try **HomeLink International** (Homelink.org), the largest and oldest home-swapping organization, founded in 1952, with more than 11,000 listings worldwide ($75 yearly membership). **HomeExchange.org** ($50 for 6,000 listings) and **InterVac.com** ($69 for more than 10,000 listings) are also reliable.

much lower than the ones you can get through the hotel itself.

- **Remember the law of supply and demand.** You can save big on hotel rooms by traveling in a destination's off-season or shoulder seasons, when rates typically drop, even at luxury properties.
- **Look into group or long-stay discounts.** If you come as part of a large group, you should be able to negotiate a bargain rate. Likewise, if you're planning a long stay (at least 5 days), you might qualify for a discount. As a general rule, expect 1 night free after a 7-night stay.
- **Sidestep excess surcharges and hidden costs.** Many hotels have adopted the unpleasant practice of nickel-and-diming its guests with opaque surcharges. When you book a room, ask what is included in the room rate, and what is extra. Avoid dialing direct from hotel phones, which can have exorbitant rates. And don't be tempted by the room's minibar offerings: Most hotels charge through the nose for water, soda, and snacks. Finally, ask about local taxes and service charges, which can increase the cost of a room by 15% or more.
- Carefully consider your hotel's meal plan. If you enjoy eating out and sampling the local cuisine, it makes sense to choose a **Continental Plan (CP),** which includes breakfast only, or a **European Plan (EP),** which doesn't include any meals and allows you maximum flexibility. If you're more interested in saving money, opt for a **Modified American Plan (MAP),** which includes breakfast and one meal, or the **American Plan (AP),** which includes three meals. If you must choose a MAP, see if you can get a free lunch at your hotel if you decide to do dinner out.
- **Book an efficiency.** A room with a kitchenette allows you to shop for groceries and cook your own meals. This is a big money saver, especially for families on long stays.
- **Consider enrolling in hotel chains' "frequent-stay" programs,** which are upping the ante lately to win the loyalty of repeat customers. Frequent guests can now accumulate points or credits to earn free hotel nights, airline miles, in-room amenities, merchandise, tickets to concerts and events, discounts on sporting facilities—and even credit toward stock in the participating hotel, in the case of the Jameson Inn hotel group. Perks are awarded not only by many chain hotels and motels (Hilton HHonors, Marriott Rewards, Wyndham ByRequest, to name a few), but individual inns and B&Bs. Many chain hotels partner with other hotel chains, car-rental firms, airlines, and credit-card companies to give consumers additional incentive to do repeat business.

LANDING THE BEST ROOM

Somebody has to get the best room in the house. It might as well be you. You can start by joining the hotel's frequent-guest program, which may make you eligible for upgrades. A hotel-branded credit card usually gives its owner "silver" or "gold" status in frequent-guest programs for free. Always ask about a corner room. They're often larger and quieter, with more windows and light, and they often cost the same as standard rooms. When you make your reservation, ask if the hotel is renovating; if it is, request a room away from the construction. Ask about nonsmoking rooms and rooms with views. Be sure to request your choice of twin, queen- or king-size beds. If you're a light sleeper, ask for a quiet room away from vending or ice machines, elevators, restaurants, bars, and discos. Ask for a room that has been recently renovated or refurbished.

If you aren't happy with your room when you arrive, ask for another one. Most lodgings will be willing to accommodate you.

In resort areas, such as the south of France, ask the following questions before you book a room:

- What's the view like? Cost-conscious travelers may be willing to pay less for a back room facing the parking lot, especially if they don't plan to spend much time in their room.
- Does the room have air-conditioning or ceiling fans? Do the windows open? If they do, and the nighttime entertainment takes place alfresco, you may want to find out when showtime is over.
- What's included in the price? Your room may be moderately priced, but if you're charged for beach chairs, towels, sports equipment, and other amenities, you could end up spending more than you bargained for.
- How far is the room from the beach and other amenities? If it's far, is there transportation to and from the beach, and is it free?

15 Tips on Dining

- Most restaurants serve lunch between noon and 2:30pm and dinner from 7 to 10pm. In a cafe, you can get reduced prices on drinks, coffee, and sandwiches if you eat at the stand-up bar rather than a table.
- French cookery reaches perfection when accompanied by wine. The general label on bottles of national wine is known as *Appellation d'Origine Contrôllée* (abbreviated AOC). Wine labels are narrowed down to a particular vine-growing region. Of course, labels are only part of the story: It's the vintage that counts. Some of the most satisfying wines come from unlabeled house bottles or carafes, called *vin de la maison.* They're also the cheapest wines served. Some restaurants include a beverage in their fixed-price menu *(boisson compris).* French beers are cheaper than imported beers. One of the best French beers is Kronenbourg, bottled in Alsace.
- Three-star dining remains quite expensive, with appetizers sometimes priced at 58€ ($75) and dinners easily costing 185€ to 250€ ($241–$325) per person in the top dining rooms. But you can get around that high price tag in many places by **dining at lunch** (when prices are always cheaper) or ordering a prix-fixe meal.
- In France, **lunch** (as well as dinner) tends to be a full-course meal with meat, vegetables, salad, bread, cheese, dessert, wine, and coffee. It may be

difficult to find a restaurant that serves the type of light lunch North Americans usually eat. Cafes, however, offer sandwiches, soup, and salads in a relaxed setting.

- **Coffee** in France is served after the meal and carries an extra charge. The French consider it barbaric to drink coffee during the meal and, unless you order it with milk *(au lait),* it'll be served black. In more conscientious places, it's prepared as the traditional *café filtre,* a slow but rewarding java draw.
- Today's dining **dress code** is more relaxed than in the past, except in first-class and *luxe* establishments. Relaxed doesn't mean sloppy jeans and jogging attire, however. Parisians still value style, even when dressing informally.
- Sometimes service is added to your tab—usually 12% to 15%. If not, look for the words *service non compris* on your bill. That means that the cost of service was not added, and you'll be expected to leave a **tip.**

FAST FACTS: France

American Express The Paris office is at 11 rue Scribe (© **01-47-77-79-28**). It operates as a travel agency, a tour operator, and a mail pickup service every Monday to Friday from 9:30am to 6:30pm, Saturday 9am to 5:30pm. Its banking section, for issues involving American Express credit cards, transfers of funds, and credit-related issues, is open Monday to Saturday from 9am to 6:30pm. In Marseille there's an office at 39 bd. de la Canebiére (© **04-91-13-71-26**); it's open Monday to Friday 9am to 6pm and Saturday 9am to noon and 2 to 5:30pm.

Area Code All French telephone numbers consist of 10 digits, the first two of which are like an area code. If you're calling anywhere in France from within France, just dial all 10 digits—no additional codes are needed. If you're calling from the United States, drop the initial 0 (zero).

ATM Networks See "Money & Costs," p. 44.

Business Hours Business hours are erratic, as befits a nation of individualists. Most banks are open Monday through Friday from 9:30am to 4:30pm. Many, particularly in small towns, take a lunch break. Hours are usually posted on the door. Most museums close 1 day a week (often Tues), and they're generally closed on national holidays. Usual hours are from 9:30am to 5pm. Refer to the individual listings. See "When to Go," earlier in this chapter, for a list of recognized holidays.

Generally, offices are open Monday through Friday from 9am to 5pm, but always call first. In Paris or other big French cities, stores are open from 9, 9:30, or (often) 10am to 6 or 7pm without a break for lunch. Some shops, delis, cafes, and newsstands open at 8am and close at 8 or 9pm. In some small stores, the lunch break can last 3 hours, beginning at 1pm. This is more common in the south than in the north.

Car Rentals See "Getting Around France," p. 59.

Currency See "Money & Costs," p. 44.

Customs **What You Can Bring Into France:** Customs restrictions for visitors entering France differ for citizens of European Union (E.U.) and non-E.U. countries. Non-E.U. nationals can bring in duty-free either 200 cigarettes, 100 cigarillos, 50 cigars, or 250 grams of smoking tobacco. This amount is doubled if you live outside Europe. You can also bring in 2 liters of wine and 1 liter of alcohol over 22%, and 2 liters of wine 22% or under. In addition, you can bring in 60cc of perfume, a quarter liter of eau de toilette. Visitors ages 15 and over can bring in other goods totaling 175€ ($228); for those under 15, the limit is 90€ ($117). Customs officials tend to be lenient about general merchandise as the limits are very low. Citizens of E.U. countries can bring in any amount of goods as long as the goods are intended for their personal use and not for resale.

What You Can Take Home from France:

U.S. Citizens Returning U.S. citizens who have been away for 48 hours or more are allowed to bring back, once every 30 days, $800 worth of merchandise duty-free. You're charged a flat rate of duty on the next $1,000 worth of purchases, and any dollar amount beyond that is subject to duty at whatever rates apply. On mailed gifts, the duty-free limit is $200. Have your receipts or purchases handy to expedite the declaration process. ***Note:*** If you owe duty, you are required to pay on your arrival in the United States, using cash, personal check, government or traveler's check, or money order; some locations also accept Visa or MasterCard.

To avoid having to pay duty on foreign-made personal items you owned before your trip, bring along a bill of sale, insurance policy, jeweler's appraisal, or receipt of purchase. Or you can register items that can be readily identified by a permanently affixed serial number or marking—think laptop computers, cameras, and CD players—with Customs before you leave. Take the items to the nearest Customs office, or register them with Customs at the airport from which you're departing. You'll receive, at no cost, a Certificate of Registration, which allows duty-free entry for the life of the item.

You cannot bring fresh foodstuffs into the U.S.; canned foods are allowed. For specifics on what you can bring back and the corresponding fees, download the invaluable free pamphlet *Know Before You Go* online at **www.cbp.gov**. (Click on "Travel," and then click on "Know Before You Go.") Or, contact the **U.S. Customs & Border Protection (CBP),** 1300 Pennsylvania Ave., NW, Washington, DC 20229 (✆ **877/287-8667**), and request the pamphlet.

Canadian Citizens Canada allows its citizens a C$750 exemption, and you're allowed to bring back duty-free 1 carton of cigarettes, 1 can of tobacco, 40 imperial ounces of liquor, and 50 cigars. In addition, you're allowed to mail gifts to Canada from abroad valued at less than C$60 a day, provided they're unsolicited and don't contain alcohol or tobacco (write on the package UNSOLICITED GIFT, UNDER C$60 VALUE). All valuables, including serial numbers of valuables you already own, such as expensive foreign cameras, should be declared on the Y-38 form before departure from Canada. ***Note:*** The C$750 exemption can be used only once a year and only after an absence of 7 days.

For a clear summary of Canadian rules, write for the booklet *I Declare,* issued by the **Canada Border Services Agency** (✆ **800/461-9999** in Canada, or 204/983-3500; www.cbsa-asfc.gc.ca).

U.K. Citizens Citizens of the U.K. returning from an E.U. country such as France go through a Customs exit (called the "Blue Exit") especially for E.U. travelers. In essence, there is no limit on what you can bring back from an E.U. country, as long as the items are for personal use (this includes gifts) and you have already paid the duty and tax. However, Customs law sets out guidance levels. If you bring in more than these levels, you may be asked to prove that the goods are for your own use. Guidance levels on goods bought in the E.U. for your own use are 3,200 cigarettes, 200 cigars, 400 cigarillos, 3 kilograms of smoking tobacco, 10 liters of spirits, 90 liters of wine, 20 liters of fortified wine (such as port or sherry), and 110 liters of beer.

For information, contact **HM revenue Customs** at ✆ **0845/010-9000** (from outside the U.K., 02920/501-261), or consult their website at www.hmrc.gov.uk.

Australian Citizens The duty-free allowance in Australia is A$900 or, for those under 18, A$450. Citizens can bring in 250 cigarettes or 250 grams of loose tobacco, and 2.25 liters of alcohol. If you're returning with valuables you already own, such as foreign-made cameras, you should file form B263.
A helpful brochure available from Australian consulates or Customs offices is *Know Before You Go.* For more information, call the **Australian Customs Service** at ✆ **1300/363-263,** or log on to www.customs.gov.au.

New Zealand Citizens The duty-free allowance for **New Zealand** is $700. Citizens over 17 can bring in 200 cigarettes, 50 cigars, or 250 grams of tobacco (or a mixture of all three if their combined weight doesn't exceed 250g), plus 4.5 liters of wine and beer, or 1.125 liters of liquor. New Zealand currency does not carry import or export restrictions. Fill out a certificate of export, listing the valuables you are taking out of the country; that way, you can bring them back without paying duty.

Most questions are answered in a free pamphlet available at New Zealand consulates and Customs offices: *New Zealand Customs Guide for Travellers, Notice no. 4.* For more information, contact **New Zealand Customs Service,** The Customhouse, 17–21 Whitmore St., Box 2218, Wellington (✆ **04/473-6099** or 0800/428-786; www.customs.govt.nz).

Driving Rules See "Getting Around France," p. 59.

Drugstores If you need a *pharmacie* during off-hours, have the front-desk staff at your hotel get in touch with the nearest Commissariat de Police. An agent there will have the address of a nearby pharmacy open 24 hours a day. French law requires that the pharmacies in any given neighborhood display the name and location of the one that remains open all night. In Paris, one of the most central all-nighters is **Pharmacy Les Champs "Derhy,"** 84 av. des Champs-Elysées, 8e (✆ **01-45-62-02-41;** Métro: George V).

Electricity Electricity in France runs on 220-volt, 50-cycle AC current. U.S. electricity is 110-volt, 60-cycle current. If you are bringing anything electric, you will need a voltage transformer and a plug adapter. Some appliances have dual voltage, which means that you will only need a plug adapter to run your hair dryer or razor, for example. A switch on the appliance will allow you to change voltages. Adapters and converters are for sale at Radio Shack and luggage and travel stores.

Embassies & Consulates If you have a passport, immigration, legal, or other problem, contact your consulate. Call before you go—they often keep odd hours and observe both French and home-country holidays. The Embassy of the **United States,** 2 av. Gabriel, 8e (✆ **01-43-12-22-22;** Métro: Concorde), is open Monday to Friday 9am to 6pm. The Embassy of **Canada** is at 35 av. Montaigne, 8e (✆ **01-44-43-29-00;** Métro: F-D-Roosevelt or Alma-Marceau), open Monday to Friday 9am to noon and 2 to 5pm. The Embassy of the **United Kingdom** is at 35 rue du Faubourg St-Honoré, 8e (✆ **01-44-51-31-00;** Métro: Concorde or Madeleine), open Monday to Friday 9:30am to 1pm and 2:30 to 5pm. The Embassy of **Ireland** is at 4 rue Rude, Paris 75116 (✆ **01-44-17-67-00;** Métro: Etoile), open Monday to Friday 9:30am to 1pm and 2:30 to 5:30pm. The Embassy of **Australia** is at 4 rue Jean-Rey, 15e (✆ **01-40-59-33-00;** Métro: Bir Hakeim), open Monday to Friday 9:15am to noon and 2:30 to 4:30pm. The embassy of **New Zealand** is at 7 ter rue Léonard-de-Vinci, Paris 75116 (✆ **01-45-01-43-43;** Métro: Victor Hugo), open Monday to Friday 9am to 1pm and 2:30 to 6pm. The embassy of **South Africa,** 59 quai d'Orsay, 7e (✆ **01-53-59-23-89;** Métro: Invalides), is open Monday to Friday 9am to noon.

Emergencies In an emergency while at a hotel, contact the front desk. Most staffs are trained in dealing with a crisis and will do whatever is necessary. If the emergency involves something like a stolen wallet, go to the police station in person. Otherwise, you can get help anywhere by calling ✆ **17** for the police, ✆ **18** for the fire department *(pompiers),* or ✆ **15** for medical emergencies.

Etiquette & Customs **Gestures:** If invited to someone's home, bring flowers, but never in the number of 13, which is said to bring bad luck. Don't bring any white flowers (for weddings), red carnations (bad will), or white lilies or chrysanthemums (for funerals). You can also bring wine, but make sure it's an expensive bottle; anything else is considered insulting.

Avoiding offense: Always try to arrive exactly on time if invited to a French house for dinner. Also, dress well.

Eating & drinking: Don't begin eating until the host or hostess has said *bon appétit.*

Business etiquette: Say *bonjour* or *bonsoir* (good morning or good evening), with either a Monsieur or Madame, when meeting someone, even a shopkeeper. Upon leaving, say *au revoir* (goodbye), even if leaving a shop where you didn't buy anything. Business cards are exchanged after the initial intro.

Holidays See "France Calendar of Events," earlier in this chapter.

Hospitals Dial ✆ **15** for medical emergencies. In Paris, the **American Hospital,** 63 bd. Victor-Hugo, in the suburb of Neuilly-sur-Seine (✆ **01-46-41-25-25;** Métro: Pont-de-Levallois or Pont-de-Neuilly; bus no. 82), operates a 24-hour emergency service. The bilingual staff accepts Blue Cross and other American insurance plans. Hospitals in other major cities include **Hôpital Rouen,** 1 rue de Germont (✆ 02-32-88-89-90), in Rouen; **Hôpital Bretonneau,** 2 bd. Tonnellé (✆ 02-47-47-47), in Tours; **Hôpital Civil de Strasbourg,** 1 place de l'Hôpital (✆ 03-88-11-67-68), in Strasbourg; **Hôpital Edouard Herriot,** 5 place Arsonval (✆ 08-20-08-20-69), in Lyon; **Hôpital de Avignon,** 305 rue Raoul Follereau (✆ 04-32-75-33-33), in Avignon; **Hôpital St- Roch,** 5 rue Pierre Dévoluy (✆ 04-92-03-33-75), in Nice; and **CHU de Rangueil,** av. du Prof. Jean-Poulhes (✆ 05-61-32-25-33), in Toulouse.

Internet Access There are hundreds of cybercafes all over France. For a list of Internet cafes, go to www.cybercaptive.com or www.cybercafe.com. The most popular in Paris seems to be **Luxembourg Micro,** 81 bd. Saint-Michel, 5e (✆ **01-46-33-27-98;** www.luxembourg-micro.com). Open daily 9am to 11pm. Métro: Luxembourg. See "Internet/E-mail" under "Staying Connected," earlier in this chapter.

Language English is increasingly understood in France, especially among young people who have studied it in school. People are more likely to understand English in such centers as Paris and the Riviera than in the more remote provinces. Service personnel in hotels tend to speak English, at least at the front desk. A staff member at most restaurants will speak a bit of English. However, many people you encounter in France do not speak English, and you may want to carry a Berlitz handbook. For some basic vocabulary, refer to the appendix of this guide.

Legal Aid If you get into any legal troubles, contact your consulate. See "Embassies & Consulates," above, for contact information.

Liquor Laws Supermarkets, grocery stores, and cafes all sell alcoholic beverages. The legal drinking age is 16. Persons under 16 can be served an alcoholic drink if accompanied by a parent or legal guardian. Wine and liquor are sold every day of the year. ***Be warned:*** France is very strict about drunk-driving laws. If convicted, you face a stiff fine and a possible prison term of up to 2 years.

Lost & Found To speed the process of replacing your personal documents if they're lost or stolen, make a photocopy of the first few pages of your passport and write down your credit card numbers (and the serial numbers of your traveler's checks, if you're using them). Leave this information with someone at home—to be faxed to you in an emergency—and swap it with your traveling companion. Be sure to tell all of your credit card companies the minute you discover your wallet has been lost or stolen, and file a report at the nearest police precinct. Your credit card company or insurer may require a police report number or record of the loss.

Use the following numbers in France to report your lost or stolen credit card: **American Express** (call collect ✆ **336/393-1111**); **MasterCard** (✆ **08-00-90-13-87;** www.mastercard.com); **Visa** ✆ **08-00-90-11-79;** www.visaeurope.com). Your credit card company may be able to wire you a cash advance immediately or deliver an emergency card in a day or two.

If you need emergency cash over the weekend when all banks and American Express offices are closed, you can have money wired to you via **Western Union** (✆ **800/325-6000;** www.westernunion.com). **Travelers Express/MoneyGram** is the largest company in the U.S. for money orders. You can transfer funds either on line or by phone in about 10 minutes (✆ **800/MONEYGRAM;** www.moneygram.com).

Identity theft and fraud are potential complications of losing your wallet, especially if you lose your driver's license with your cash and credit cards. Notify the major credit-reporting bureaus immediately; placing a fraud alert on your records may protect you against liability for criminal activity. The three major U.S. credit-reporting agencies are **Equifax** (✆ **800/766-0008;** www.equifax.com), **Experian** (✆ **888/397-3742;** www.experian.com), and **TransUnion** (✆ **800/680-7289;** www.transunion.com).

If you've lost all forms of photo ID, call your airline and explain the situation; your carrier may let you board the plane if you have a copy of your passport or birth certificate and a copy of the police report you've filed.

Mail Most post offices in Paris are open Monday through Friday from 8am to 7pm and Saturday from 8am to noon. Allow 5 to 8 days to send or receive mail from your home. Airmail letters within Europe cost .54€ (70¢); to the United States and Canada, .90€ ($1.15). Airmail letters to Australia and New Zealand cost .90€ ($1.15).

You can exchange money at post offices. Many hotels sell stamps, as do local post offices and cafes displaying a red TABAC sign outside.

Newspapers & Magazines Copies of the international edition of ***The Herald Tribune*** are distributed all over France and are sold at newspaper kiosks and at newsstands in the lobbies of first-class or deluxe hotels. Copies of ***Time*** and ***Newsweek*** are also widely sold. A far larger selection of U.K. magazines and newspapers is available. London newspapers arrive in Paris an hour or so after publication.

Passports Allow plenty of time before your trip to apply for a passport; processing normally takes 3 weeks but can take longer during busy periods (especially spring). And keep in mind that if you need a passport in a hurry, you'll pay a higher processing fee.

For Residents of the United States: Whether you're applying in person or by mail, you can download passport applications from the U.S. State Department website at http://travel.state.gov. To find your regional passport office, either check the U.S. State Department website or call the toll-free number of the **National Passport Information Center** (✆ **877/487-2778**) for automated information.

For Residents of Canada: Passport applications are available at travel agencies throughout Canada or from the central **Passport Office,** Department of Foreign Affairs and International Trade, Ottawa, ON K1A 0G3 (✆ **800/567-6868;** www.ppt.gc.ca).

For Residents of Ireland: You can apply for a 10-year passport at the **Passport Office,** Setanta Centre, Molesworth Street, Dublin 2 (✆ **01/671-1633;** www.irlgov.ie/iveagh). Those under age 18 and over 65 must apply for a €12 3-year passport. You can also apply at 1A South Mall, Cork (✆ **021/494-4700**) or at most main post offices.

For Residents of Australia: You can pick up an application from your local post office or any branch of Passports Australia, but you must schedule an interview at the passport office to present your application materials. Call the **Australian Passport Information Service** at ✆ **131-232,** or visit the government website at **www.smarttraveler.gov.au.**

For Residents of New Zealand: You can pick up a passport application at any New Zealand Passports Office or download it from their website. Contact the

Passports Office at ✆ **0800/225-050** in New Zealand or 04/474-8100, or log on to **www.passports.govt.nz**.

Police Call ✆ **17** anywhere in France.

Restrooms If you're in dire need, duck into a cafe or brasserie to use the lavatory. It's customary to make a small purchase if you do so. Paris Métro stations and underground garages usually contain public restrooms, but the degree of cleanliness varies. France still has some "hole-in-the-ground" toilets, so be warned. For reviews and recommendations of the tidiest toilets in France and other places, visit **www.thebathroomdiaries.com**.

Safety Much of the country, particularly central France, the northeast, Normandy, and Brittany, remains relatively safe, though no place in the world is crime-free. Those intending to visit the south of France, especially the Riviera, should exercise caution—robberies and muggings are commonplace. It's best to check your baggage into a hotel and then go sightseeing instead of leaving it unguarded in the trunk of a car, which can easily be broken into. Marseille is among the most dangerous French cities. Also see "Staying Safe" under "Health," earlier in this chapter.

Smoking Although restaurants are required to provide nonsmoking sections, you may find yourself next to the kitchen or the restrooms. The best strategy for avoiding smoke is to sit outside.

Taxes As a member of the European Union, France routinely imposes a value-added tax (VAT in English; TVA in French) on many goods and services. The standard VAT is 19.6% on merchandise, including clothing, appliances, liquor, leather goods, shoes, furs, jewelry, perfumes, cameras, and even caviar. Refunds are made for the tax on certain goods and merchandise, but not on services. The minimum purchase is 184€ ($239) at one time for nationals or residents of countries outside the E.U.

Telephones The French use a ***télécarte,*** or phone debit card, which you can purchase at rail stations, post offices, and other places. Sold in two versions, it allows you to use either 50 or 120 charge units (depending on the card) by inserting the card into the slot of most public phones. Depending on the type of card you buy, the cost starts at 10€ ($13) and goes up from there. You must use this card when making calls within France; coins are no longer accepted. You can use a major credit card in much the same way as a télécarte, but there's a catch: To do so involves a minimum charge of 20€ ($26). The phone system gives you 30 days to use up this 20-euro credit. If possible, avoid making calls from your hotel; some establishments will double or triple the charges.

Time Zone The French equivalent of daylight saving time lasts from April to September, which puts it 1 hour ahead of French winter time. France is usually 6 hours ahead of U.S. Eastern Time, except in October, when U.S. clocks are still on daylight time; then France is only 5 hours ahead. The rest of the year, when it's 9am in New York, it's 3pm in France.

Tipping The law requires all bills to say *service compris,* which means the total includes the tip. But French diners often leave some small change as an additional tip, especially if service has been exceptional.

Some general guidelines: For hotel staff, tip 1.05€ to 1.50€ ($1.35–$1.95) for every item of baggage the porter carries on arrival and departure, and 1.50€ ($1.95) per day for the maid. In cafes, service is usually included. Tip taxi drivers 10% to 15% of the amount on the meter. In theaters and restaurants, give cloakroom attendants at least .75€ to 1.20€ ($1–$1.55) per item. Give restroom attendants in nightclubs and other establishments about .50€ (65¢). Give cinema and theater ushers about .50€ (65¢). For guides for group visits to museums and monuments, 1.50€ ($1.95) is a reasonable tip.

Useful Phone Numbers U.S. Dept. of State Travel Advisory (✆ **202/647-5225,** staffed 24 hr.); U.S. Passport Agency (✆ **202/647-0518**); U.S. Centers for Disease Control International Traveler's Hotline (✆ **404/332-4559**).

Water Drinking water is generally safe, though it's occasionally been known to cause diarrhea. If you ask for water in a restaurant, it'll be served bottled (for which you'll pay) unless you specifically request *l'eau du robinet* (tap water). Your waiter may ask if you'd like your water *avec gas* (carbonated) or *sans gas* (without bubbles).

4 Suggested Itineraries in France

When we first launched this guidebook, founding father Arthur Frommer gave us a warning: "You can get lost in France." And we did—and still do on occasion.

If you have unlimited time, one of the world's great pleasures is getting "lost" in France, wandering about at random, making new discoveries every day off the beaten path. But few of us have this luxury, and so below we present both 1- and 2-week itineraries to help you make the most of your time.

France is so vast and so treasure-filled that you can't even skim the surface in 1 or 2 weeks, so relax and don't even try. Instead, we recommend you enjoy the nuggets—Paris, Versailles, and Mont-St-Michel—among other allures, saving the rest for another day. You may also review chapter 1, "The Best of France," to find out what experiences or sights have special appeal to us and then adjust the itineraries to suit your particular travel plans.

France ranks with Germany in offering Europe's fastest and best-maintained superhighways, and it also has one of the fastest and most efficient public transportation systems in the world, especially in its national train system. For example, the highlights of Normandy and the Loire Valley (the château country) are just 1 or 2 hours away from Paris by train. You can travel from Paris to Nice on the Riviera in 6½ hours—or fly much more quickly, of course.

The itineraries that follow take you to some major attractions and some charming towns. The pace may be a bit breathless for some visitors, so skip a town or sight occasionally to have some chill-out time—after all, you're on vacation. Of course, you can use any of these itineraries as a jumping-off point to develop your own custom-made trip.

1 France in 1 Week

The title of this tour is a misnomer. There is no way you can see France in 1 week. But, you can have a memorable vacation in Paris and see other highlights of France in a week if you budget your time carefully. One week provides enough time—barely—to visit the major attractions of Paris such as the **Musée du Louvre** (world's greatest art gallery), the **Eiffel Tower,** and **Notre-Dame.** After 2 days in Paris, head for the former royal stamping grounds of **Versailles,** followed by Normandy (an easy commute from Paris), visiting such highlights as **D-day beaches,** the cathedral city of **Rouen** (where Joan of Arc was burned alive), the tapestry of **Bayeux,** and the incredible monastery of **Mont-St-Michel.**

France in 1 Week

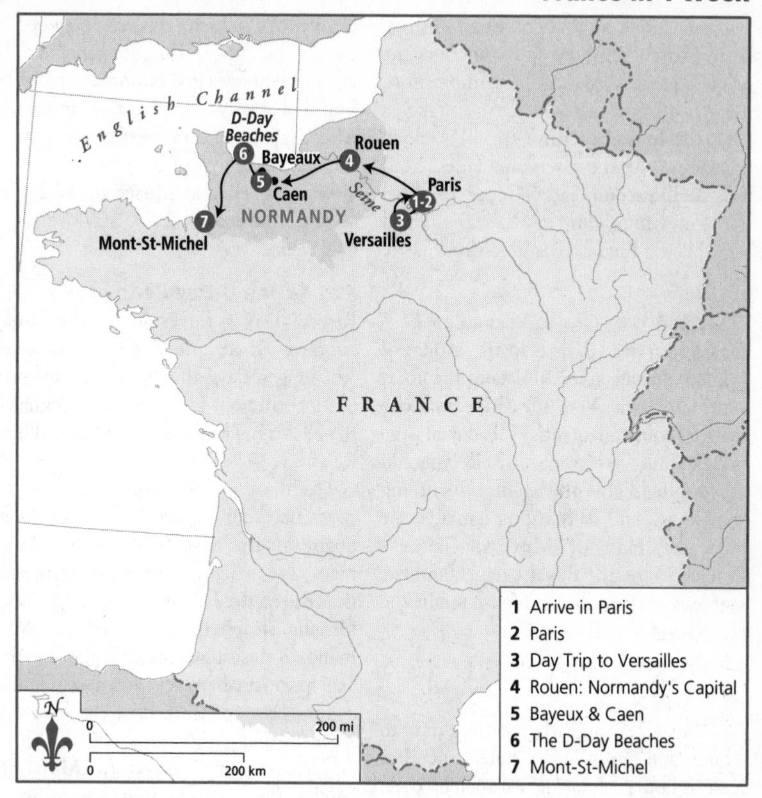

Days 1 & 2: Arrive in Paris ★★★

Take a flight that arrives in Paris as early as possible on **Day 1.** Check into your hotel and hit the nearest cafe for a pick-me-up café au lait and a croissant before sightseeing. Take the Métro to the Palais Royal–Musée du Louvre for a visit to the **Musée du Louvre** (p. 151). Spend at least 2 hours here viewing world-class masterpieces such as Leonardo da Vinci's *Mona Lisa.* After leaving the Louvre, walk south toward the **Quays of the Seine,** spending an hour taking in the tree-shaded banks and panoramic vistas of Paris. Head for that island in the Seine, **Ile de la Cité,** for a lunch in a bistro before exploring its attractions of **Ste-Chapelle** (p. 155) and the monumental **Notre-Dame** (p. 153) and its gargoyles. As the evening fades, head for the **Eiffel Tower** for the greatest cityscape view in Europe.

On **Day 2,** arrive at the **place de la Concorde** (p. 161) and its Egyptian obelisk, and take a stroll up the 1.8km (1-mile) avenue of French grandeur, the **Champs-Elysées,** until you reach the **Arc de Triomphe** (p. 146), which you can scale for another panoramic view of Paris. After, head for the **Ile St-Louis** (p. 92), which, after Cité, is the second island in the Seine. Lacking monumental attractions, this little isle is a sight in itself, with quays to stroll and small side streets where you can discover hidden wonders such as antiques shops and little bistros.

After lunch in one of those bistros, visit **Musée d'Orsay** (p. 150) and the world's greatest collection of Impressionist paintings. After d'Orsay, take a **Bateaux-Mouche** cruise (p. 145) along the Seine. As the afternoon fades, head for **Basilique du Sacré-Coeur** (p. 146) for a crowning view of Paris as the sun sets. Have a final dinner in a Montmartre cafe.

Day ❸: A Day Trip to Versailles ★

Having survived 2 days in the capital of France, bid an adieu and take the RER Line C to the **Versailles/Rive Gauche station.** You can spend a full day at Versailles—and then some—or else you can see the highlights in 3 hours, including the Grands and Petits Appartements, the glittering Hall of Mirrors, Gabriel's Opera House, the Royal Chapel, and the Gardens of Versailles, which contain the Grand and Petit Trianons.

Day ❹: Normandy's Capital of Rouen ★★★

On **Day 4,** take an early-morning train to Rouen and check into a hotel. Spend at least 2 hours exploring its ancient core, especially its **Cathédrale Notre-Dame** (p. 274), immortalized in paintings by Monet. Stand at the **place du Vieux-Marché** (p. 277), where Joan of Arc was executed for heresy in 1431, and then visit the **Eglise St-Maclou** (p. 274), a 1432 church in the Flamboyant Gothic style. After lunch, take a taxi to **Giverny** (p. 217)—it's only 5km (3 miles) southeast of Rouen. At Giverny, visit the **Claude Monet Foundation** (p. 218) and the **Musée d'Art Americain Giverny** (p. 218), returning to your hotel in Rouen for the night.

Day ❺: Bayeux ★★ & Caen ★★★

To expedite the rest of your trip, we recommend renting a car in Rouen. Strike out toward Bayeux, stopping en route to visit **Abbaye de Jumièges** (p. 276), one of the most evocative ruins in France. Even with a stopover, you can easily be in the city of Caen in time for lunch before visiting **Abbaye aux Hommes** (p. 292), founded by William the Conqueror. After Caen, continue west to the city of **Bayeux,** where you can arrive in time to view the celebrated **Musée de la Tapisserie de Bayeux** (p. 296). Stay overnight in Bayeux.

Day ❻: The D-Day Beaches ★★

Reserve **Day 6** for exploring the D-day beaches, where Allied forces launched "the longest day," the mammoth invasion of Normandy in June 1944, that signaled the beginning of the end of Hitler's Third Reich.

From Bayeux, head east to explore the coastline. Your voyage of discovery can begin at the seaside resort of Arromanches-les-Bains, where you can visit the **Musée du Débarquement** (p. 299), **Omaha Beach** (p. 300), and the Normandy American Cemetery (p. 300). You can have lunch in the town of Grandcamp-Maisy (p. 300), later checking out **Utah Beach.**

That evening, drive to **Mont-St-Michel** (less than 2 hr. away) and overnight in the pedestrian village on "The Rock," giving you plenty of time for an early-morning visit to this popular attraction. If it's summer, you can also take an illuminated night tour.

Day ❼: Mont-St-Michel ★★★

You can explore one of the great attractions of Europe, **Mont-St-Michel** (p. 302), in a minimum of 3 hours. This great Benedictine monastery, founded in 966, is best enjoyed by taking an English-language tour that covers the highlights. After viewing the abbey, drop in at **La Mère Poulard** (p. 303) for a legendary omelet. After lunch, return your car to Rouen, where you'll find frequent train service back to Paris and your flight home the following day.

2 France in 2 Weeks

With 2 weeks to explore France, you'll have time to visit several regions—not only Paris, but also the best of the Loire Valley châteaux, the most history-rich town of Provence (Avignon), and several resorts on the Riviera, taking in the beaches, modern-art galleries, and even the principality of Monaco.

For **Days 1 through 7,** follow the "France in 1 Week" itinerary, above.

Day 8: Orléans—Gateway to the Loire Valley ★

On **Day 8,** leave Paris on an early train to **Orléans** (trip time: 1 hr., 15 min.). Heavily bombed in World War II, Orléans is a fairly dull town. Rent a car here and drive west to the **Château de Chambord** (p. 235), the largest château in the Loire Valley, representing the apogee of the French Renaissance architectural style. Allow 2 hours for a visit. Back on the road again, continue southwest to the **Château de Blois** (p. 236), called "the Versailles of the Renaissance" and a virtual illustrated storybook of French architecture. Stay overnight in Blois.

Day 9: Amboise ★★ and Chenonceau ★★★

On the morning of **Day 9,** continue southeast from Blois to **Amboise,** where you can check into a hotel for the night. Visit the 15th-century **Château d'Amboise** (p. 243), in the Italian Renaissance style, and also **Clos-Lucé** (p. 243), last residence of Leonardo da Vinci. In the afternoon, drive southeast to the **Château de Chenonceau** (p. 246), famous for the French dames who have occupied its precincts, including Diane de Poitiers (mistress of the king) and Catherine de Médicis. You can spend 2 hours at the château before driving back to Amboise for the night.

Day 10: Avignon—Gateway to Provence ★★★

From Amboise, get an early start on **Day 10** and drive east to Orléans to return your rental car. You now face a choice: You can take a morning train from Orléans to Paris's Gare d'Austerlitz and then catch the Métro or a taxi to the Gare de Lyon, where you can hop aboard a TGV (fast train) that will put you in Avignon in about 2½ hours. Or, you can take a train from Orléans to Lyon and change trains for Avignon.

Check into a hotel in **Avignon,** capital of Provence. Before the day fades, you should have time to wander through the old city to get your bearings, buy some colorful Provençal fabrics and see one of the smaller sights such as the **Pont St-Bénézet** (also known as the Bridge of Avignon). See p. 469.

Day 11: Avignon to St-Tropez ★★

In the morning, spend 2 hours touring the **Palais des Papes** (p. 471), which was the capital of Christendom during the 14th century when the popes lived here during the so-called "Babylonian Captivity." After lunch in one of Europe's most beautiful medieval cities, rent a car and drive to **St-Tropez** (p. 513). If it's summer, get in some beach time and spend a good part of the early evening in one of the cafes along the harbor, indulging in that favorite French pastime of people-watching.

Day 12: Cannes—Capital of the Riviera Chic ★★★

Before leaving St-Tropez in the morning, check out the Impressionist paintings at **Musée de l'Annonciade** (p. 518). Drive 50km (31 miles) east along the coast until you reach Cannes.

Assuming it's summer, get in some time at the beach, notably at **Plage de la Croisette** (p. 525), and feel free to wear

France in 2 Weeks

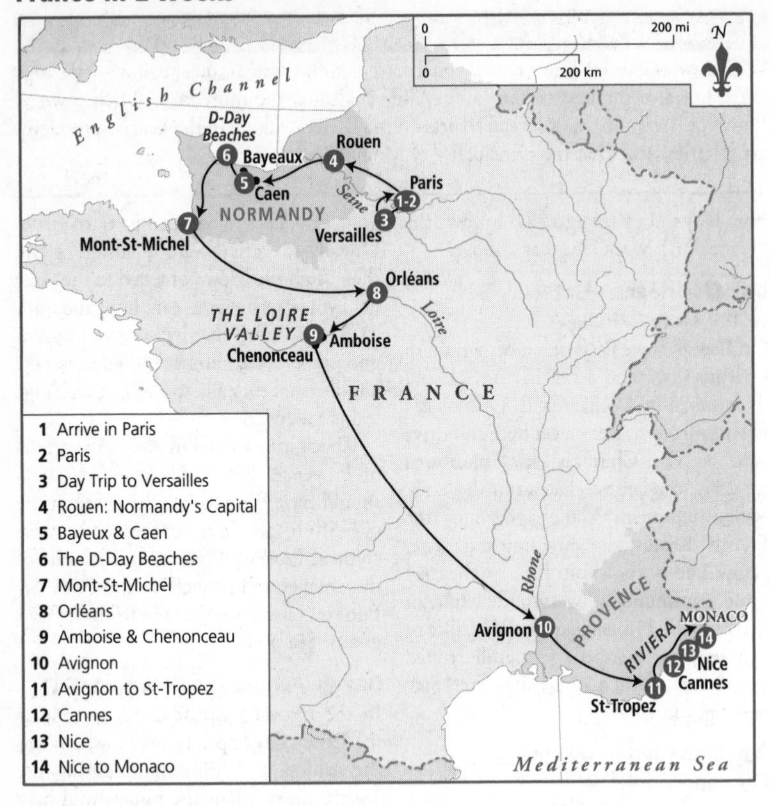

your most revealing swimwear. In the afternoon, take the ferry to **Ile Ste-Marguerite** (p. 513), where the "Man in the Iron Mask" was imprisoned. You can visit his cell. That evening, you may want to flirt with Lady Luck at one of the plush **casinos** (p. 536).

Day ⑬: Nice: Capital of the Riviera ★★★

It's only a 32km (20-mile) drive east from Cannes to **Nice,** the Riviera's largest city. After checking into a hotel (the most affordable along the Riviera), stroll through **Vieille Ville** (p. 565), the Old Town beginning at the foot of "the Rock." Enjoy a snack of *socca,* a round crepe made with chickpea flour that's sold steaming hot by the street vendors. Then head for the **promenade des Anglais** (p. 565), the wide boulevard along the waterfront. Stop in at one of the grand cafes along the water for a light lunch. In the afternoon, head for the best of the hill towns above Nice, notably **St-Paul-de-Vence,** only 31km (19 miles) to the north. Here you can wander its ramparts in about 30 minutes before descending on the greatest modern-art museum in the Riviera, the **Foundation Maeght** (p. 556).

Continue over to Vence (p. 558) for a visit to **Chapelle du Rosaire** (p. 559), where the great Henri Matisse created his artistic masterpiece for some Dominican nuns. From there, it's just 24km (15 miles) southeast to Nice.

Have dinner at a typical bistro, serving a traditional Niçoise cuisine with the inevitable Italian influences.

Day 14: Nice to Monaco ★★★

While still overnighting in Nice, head east for the most hair-raising but thrilling drive in all of France, a trip along the **Grande Corniche** highway that stretches 31km (19 miles) east from Nice to the little resort of **Menton** near the Italian border. Allow 3 hours for this trip. Highlights along this road include **Roquebrune-Cap Martin** and **La Turbie.** The greatest view along the Riviera is at the **Eze Belvedere** at 1,200m (3,937 ft.).

3 France for Families

France offers many attractions for kids. Perhaps your main concern with having children along is pacing yourself with museum time. Our suggestion is to limit **Paris** to 2 days and then spend a day wandering the spectacular grounds and glittering interiors of **Versailles,** 2 days in **Disneyland Paris,** and 2 days on the **Riviera.**

Days 1 & 2: Paris ★★★

Take the kids for a morning visit to **Notre-Dame** (p. 153). The highlight is climbing the 387 narrow and winding steps to the top of one of the towers for a fabulously Quasimodo view of the gargoyles and Paris. After a visit, head for the **Eiffel Tower** (p. 147). In addition to scaling this fantastic monument, you can also order lunch—allow at least 2 hours for your visit, one just to access the elevators on levels one and two. Food is available at the Altitude 95 restaurant on the first floor, but it's a bit pricey for most families. A first-floor snack bar and a second-floor cafeteria offer the best values for the family on a budget.

After touring the tower, take the kids for a donkey ride in the nearby **Champ de Mars,** which also stages the best puppet shows.

In the afternoon, take the children for a stroll through the **Jardin des Tuileries** (p. 156), where there are more donkey rides, ice-cream stands, and a marionette show. At the circular pond, you can rent a toy boat.

Climax your day with a ride along the Seine on the famous **Bateaux-Mouche** (p. 145). Boats have open sun decks.

On **Day 2,** visit the **Musée du Louvre** (p. 151). Even if your kid is not a museum buff and bores easily, your child will surely be intrigued by the many displays. Over the years, we've observed that, even more than the paintings, kids are fascinated by the Egyptian art and antiquities displayed in the Sully and Denon wings, a total of 7,000 items, the largest exhibition of such artifacts outside of Cairo.

After the Louvre, take the Métro to Porte de la Villette, where you can spend 2 or 3 hours at **Cité des Sciences et de l'Industrie** (p. 163). The mammoth structure is home to a planetarium, a 3-D cinema, video workshops, and interactive exhibits.

Space is too tight in this book to document all activities in Paris of interest to children, but you'll want to spend a good 2 hours in the **Jardin d'Acclimatation** in the northern part of the Bois de Boulogne. The visit starts with a ride on a narrow-gauge train through a stretch of wooded park, and attractions include a zoo, a house of mirrors, a puppet theater, a playground, and kiosks selling waffles.

As the afternoon fades, head for **Butte Montmartre** with its fiesta atmosphere. Take the Métro to Anvers and walk to the *funiculaire,* the cable car that carries you to the **Basilique du Sacré-Coeur** (p. 146). Once you arrive at "the top of Paris," follow the crowds to the **place du Tertre,**

France for Families

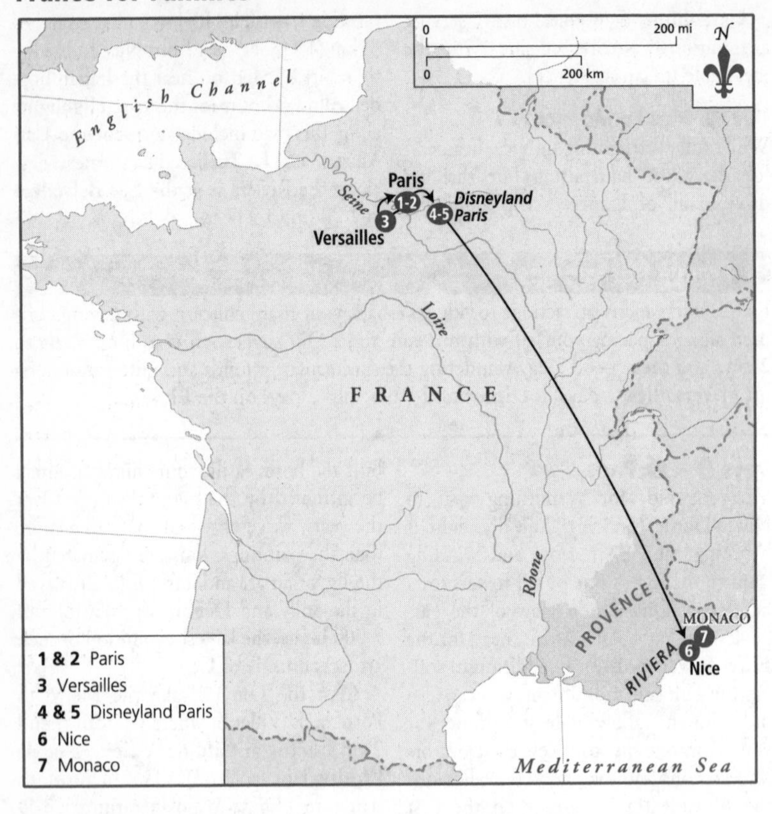

where a Sergeant Pepper–style band often blasts off-key, and you can have a local artist create a sketch of your kids. Finally, reward your brood with ice cream sold on the square.

Day ❸: Versailles ★

Tear yourself away from the glories of Paris for a day spent at the **Château de Versailles** (p. 195). Take the RER line C to the Versailles/Rive Gauche station. Kids delight in the Hall of Mirrors and in the grand apartments. Take the children for a walk through the garden, where they can visit the hamlet where the ill-fated Marie Antoinette strolled with her lambs. You can buy the makings of a picnic lunch in Paris and enjoy it on the grounds, or else you can purchase fast food at one of the stalls placed in discreet corners of the garden.

Return to Paris in time to visit **Parc Zoologique de Paris,** in the Bois de Vincennes on the southeastern outskirts of Paris. Quickly reachable by Métro, this is one of France's greatest zoos, complete with playful animals in natural habitats as well as lions roaming a veldt. There's even a cement mountain similar to Disneyland's Matterhorn.

Days ❹ & ❺: Disneyland Paris ★★★

Disneyland Paris is the top family-vacation destination in France. Allow a full day to see the highlights of the park, plus another day to absorb its secondary adventures. Our recommendation is to visit **Main Street, U.S.A., Frontierland,**

and **Adventureland** on the first day, saving **Fantasyland, Discoveryland,** the entertainment center at **Village Disney,** and **Sleeping Beauty Castle** for the second day. You can stay in the Disney hotels on-site, coming in various price ranges from very expensive to budget. The RER commuter express train A takes you from Etoile in Paris to Marne-la-Vallée/Chessy in 45 minutes.

Day 6: Nice ★★★

Return to Paris and fly to Nice, capital of the French Riviera. If you flew Air France transatlantic, Nice can often be attached as a low-cost extension of your round-trip fare.

In Nice you can check into your hotel for 2 nights, as the city has the most affordable hotels on the Riviera. Set out to explore this old city. The people-watching on the Riviera alone is likely to leave your kids wide-eyed. Beware that they'll see plenty of skin, as topless bathing is rampant. There's always a lot of free entertainment in summer along the boardwalk in Nice, called the **promenade des Anglais** (p. 565).

In the afternoon, journey to the hill town of **St-Paul-de-Vence** (p. 555). This is the most evocative of the hill towns of Nice, and kids delight in touring the ramparts and strolling along the pedestrian-only rue-Grande. You can have a late lunch in the cafeteria of the **Foundation Maeght** (p. 556), the Riviera's greatest modern art museum.

Return to Nice for the evening and take your kids for a stroll through the Old Town, dining in a typical Niçoise bistro.

Day 7: Monaco ★★★

While still based in Nice, head for the tiny principality of Monaco, which lies only 18km (11 miles) east of Nice.

Kids will enjoy the changing-of-the-guard ceremony at **Les Grands Appartements du Palais** (p. 591), where Prince Rainier took his young bride, film star Grace Kelly, years ago. But the best part of Monaco for kids is the **Musée Océanographique de Monaco** (p. 591), one of Europe's biggest aquariums with sharks and other exotic sea creatures. Monaco also has the **Collection des Voitures Anciennes de S.A.S. le Prince de Monaco** (p. 591) and the **Musée National de Monaco** (p. 591), with a mammoth antique doll collection.

Return to Nice that night and prepare for your flight home in the morning.

4 A Wine Lover's Tour of Burgundy

For the aficionado or even the lover of French landscapes, a tour of Burgundy, one of the world's greatest wine-producing regions, is one of the highlights of France. Burgundian vintages have been called *le vin des rois, le roi des vins* (the wine of kings, the king of wines). You can tour the winemaking towns and sample the finest of chardonnays and pinot noirs along the way. The best centers are **Dijon** (capital of Burgundy), **Beaune, Auxerre,** and **Autun.**

Day 1: Chablis to Auxerre ★★

Begin at **Chablis** in Burgundy's northwestern edge. Vineyards surround Chablis, the capital of Basse Bourgogne (Lower Burgundy). The town is now more famous for its wine than for its monuments, but it has two historic churches: the Eglise St-Martin and the Eglise St-Pierre. Chablis is not worth an overnight stop, though 15km (9⅓ miles) to the west along D965, in the hamlet of **Tonnerre,** is **Saint-Père,** one of the best restaurants in the province. After a meal, backtrack about 24km (15 miles) west on D965 (passing through Chablis) to **Auxerre** (p. 386).

Scene of many pivotal moments in French history, Auxerre is the site of one of France's most impressive churches, the Gothic **Cathédrale St-Etienne.** Stay overnight in Auxerre.

Day ❷: Vézelay ★★

Drive south from Auxerre along N151 and then east on D951 to the hamlet of **Vézelay** (p. 389). If there's one must-see Romanesque church in France, it's here. Park at the bottom of the village and climb the cobblestone main street. At the base of the hill is **L'Espérance** ★★★ (p. 391), one of the best restaurants in the world. It's closed Tuesday and at lunch Wednesday, so plan your itinerary accordingly.

You can spend the night in Vézelay; drive 9.5km (6 miles) east on D957 to **Avallon,** or continue south for 56km (35 miles) on well-signposted country roads to **Château-Chinon.** Wherever you spend the night, plan an early departure the following day.

Day ❸: Autun ★★

From Château-Chinon, drive east 32km (20 miles) on D978 to visit one of the oldest towns in France, **Autun** (p. 392).

En route, you may wish to take this detour: Heading east on D978 toward Autun, turn right (south) at Arleuf, going right onto D500. At a fork, turn right toward Glux and follow arrows to Mont Beuvray on D18. Take D274 to reach the summit. After 3km (1¾ miles) of climbing, you'll be at **Oppidum of Bibracte,** home of Eduens, a Gallic tribe. Here Vercingetorix organized the Gauls to fight Caesar's legions in A.D. 52. At this altitude (840m/2,756 ft.), you'll have a splendid view of the wine country of Autun and Mont St-Vincent. Leave Mont Beuvray on D274 and continue northeast to Autun.

At Autun, you'll find a historic town with ruins left by the ancient Romans, as well as a cathedral built in 1120 to hold the remains of St. Lazarus. Spend the night here.

Day ❹: En Route to Beaune ★★

Start early in Autun and be prepared for tours of châteaux, fortresses, vineyards, and other historic sites. Your route will be loaded with appealing detours, so be as flexible as possible as you negotiate a labyrinth of country roads toward Beaune.

Leave Autun on D973 east. After 9.5km (6 miles), turn left onto D326 toward Sully. Here you'll find the **Château de Sully,** once known as the Fontainebleau of Burgundy; it's closed to the public, but a view from the outside may satisfy you. The gardens are open Easter to September daily 8am to 6pm. Leave Sully, following signs to the village of **Nolay.** About 4km (2½ miles) past Nolay, you'll reach the **Château de La Rochepot** (✆ **03-80-21-71-37;** www.larochepot.com), a medieval-style fortress built during the Renaissance (open July–Aug daily 10am–noon and 2–6pm; Apr 2–June and Sept daily 10–11:30am and 2–5:30pm; Oct daily 10–11:30am and 2–4:30pm; closed Nov–Mar). Admission is 6€ ($7.80) for adults and 3.50€ ($4.20) for children ages 6 to 14.

Now head toward **Beaune** on D973, passing some well-known vineyards: Chassagne-Montrachet, Puligny-Montrachet, Meursault, Auxey Durresses, Volnay, and Pommard. En route, you can detour to a restaurant whose setting is as intriguing as its food. **Chagny,** 43km (27 miles) east of Autun and 18km (11 miles) southwest of Beaune, rarely attracts sightseers, and serious foodies from all over stop at **Lameloise,** 36 place d'Arnes (✆ **03-85-87-65-65**), for lamb filet in a rice crepe, Bresse pigeon, lemon soufflé, and one of the broadest selections of burgundies in France. Reservations are required. It's closed Wednesday all day and at lunch on Tuesday and Thursday.

A Wine Lover's Tour of Burgundy

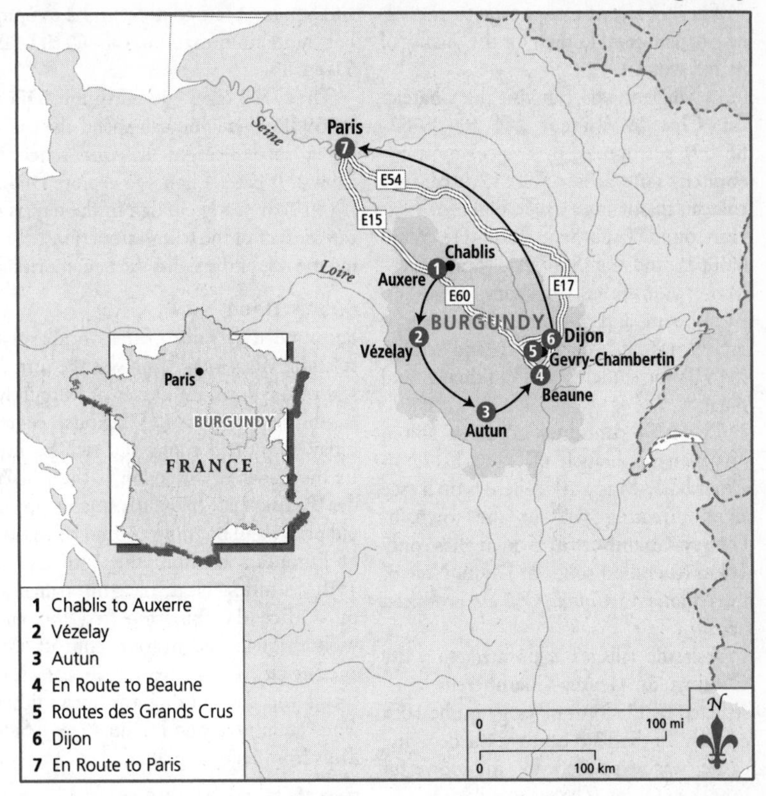

Continue north to Beaune on D973, which changes to N741. You can overnight in Beaune (p. 394). If you arrive early enough in the day, you can explore Beaune's historic attractions in 2½ hours, including **Musée des Beaux-Arts et Musée Marey** (p. 396).

Even more intriguing for the wine connoisseur is a visit to one of the cellars for a tour and a tasting. Our favorite is **Marché aux Vins** (p. 395), housed in a former church. Its cellars are in ancient tombs under the 14th-century church.

Day 5: Route des Grands Crus ★★★

The road visited on this trip is called the *Route des Grands Crus,* or road of the great wines.

Route N74 continues north 44km (27 miles) to Dijon, but you can make a full day of it because of the stopovers along the way.

This route takes you along the most celebrated vineyards of the **Côte d'Or,** which actually stretch from Dijon in the north to Santenay southwest of Beaune, a distance of 60km (37 miles). This is a region of France's greatest wines, and each village has some claim to fame.

As you head north from Beaune, the first village is **Aloxe-Corton,** where Charlemagne once owned vineyards. The emperor is still honored with "a white wine of great character," Corton-Charlemagne, which is still produced here.

The N74 continues north to the village of **Vougeot,** known for the quality of its red wines.

In Vougeot, you can visit the **Château du Clos-de-Vougeot** (✆ **03-80-62-86-09**), surrounded by France's most celebrated vineyards. The 12th-century château maintains a cellar, open for visits year-round (Apr–Sept Mon–Fri 9am–6:30pm and Sat–Sun 9am–5pm; Oct–Mar Mon–Fri 9am–5pm, Sat–Sun 9–11:30am and 2–5pm). Admission is 3.50€ ($6.30) for adults and 2.60€ ($4.70) for students and children 8 and older.

The N74 continues north to Dijon, but you can branch off onto D122 to Chambolle-Musigny, where you'll see signs directing you to the town of **Gevrey-Chambertin,** which lies only 10km (6¼ miles) south of Dijon. Nine of the region's 33 *Grands Crus* are produced here.

Visit the village's main attraction, **Le Château de Gevrey-Chambertin,** constructed by the lords of Vergy in the 10th century. In the 13th century, the decaying castle was expanded by the powerful monks of Cluny. The great hall is impressive, with exposed ceiling beams. Look for the guards' room in the watchtower and the collection of vintage wines in the vaulted cellars. English-language tours, ending with a tasting of the prize vintages, cost 14€ ($18). The château is open Monday and Thursday to Friday 10am to noon and 2 to 5pm, Saturday and Sunday 11am to noon and 2 to 6pm. For more information, call ✆ **03-80-51-84-85.**

The D122 takes you north into **Dijon** (p. 398), where you can spend the night (or a second night if your schedule allows). It takes 4 hours to explore Dijon. If you arrive early enough in the day, you can see half of the town's attractions, visiting the rest of the sights the next morning.

Day 6: Dijon ★★★

Surrounded by some of the world's most splendid vineyards, Dijon was the former seat of the powerful Dukes of Burgundy. A university town and regional center today, it has had a long and rich history. Its monumental attraction is the **Musée des Beaux-Arts** (p. 400), housed in an old palace and boasting a grand collection of European art from the 14th to the 19th centuries. Next, pick up a map at the **Office de Tourisme** (p. 399) and walk through the historic core of this ancient city. Or, better yet, in our view, spend the day touring the magnificent wine country around Dijon (see "Side Trips from Dijon," p. 402).

Day 7: En Route to Paris

Dijon is one of the major transportation hubs in this part of France, and you can easily return to Paris from here. If you're driving, the distance is 312km (194 miles), which you can do in a morning, reaching Paris to the northwest in time for lunch.

5

Settling into Paris

The City of Light always lives up to its reputation as one of the world's most romantic cities. Ernest Hemingway referred to the splendors of Paris as a "moveable feast" and wrote, "There is never any ending to Paris, and the memory of each person who has lived in it differs from that of any other."

Here you can stroll along the Seine and the broad tree-lined boulevards; browse the chic shops and relax over coffee or wine at a cafe; visit the museums, monuments, and cathedrals; or sample the cuisine.

1 Orientation

ARRIVING

BY PLANE Paris has two international airports: **Aéroport d'Orly,** 14km (8⅔ miles) south of the city, and **Aéroport Roissy–Charles de Gaulle,** 23km (14 miles) northeast. A shuttle (16€/$21) makes the 50- to 75-minute journey between the two airports about every 30 minutes.

Charles de Gaulle Airport (Roissy) At Charles de Gaulle (✆ **01-48-62-12-12**), foreign carriers use Aérogare 1, while Air France uses Aérogare 2. From Aérogare 1, you take a moving walkway to the passport checkpoint and the Customs area. A *navette* (shuttle bus) links the two terminals.

The free shuttle buses also transports you to the **Roissy rail station,** from which fast RER (Réseau Express Régional) trains leave every 10 minutes between 5:30am and 11:30pm for Métro stations including Gare du Nord, Châtelet, Luxembourg, Port-Royal, and Denfert-Rochereau. A typical fare from Roissy to any point in central Paris is 8.80€ ($11) per person. Travel time from the airport to central Paris is around 35 to 40 minutes.

You can also take an **Air France shuttle bus** (✆ **08-92-35-08-20** or 01-48-64-14-24) to central Paris for 13€ ($17) one-way, 20€ ($26) round-trip. It stops at the Palais des Congrès (Port Maillot) and continues to place Charles-de-Gaulle–Etoile, where subway lines can carry you to any point in Paris. That ride, depending on traffic, takes 45 to 55 minutes. The shuttle departs about every 20 minutes between 5:40am and 11pm.

The **Roissybus** (✆ **01-58-76-16-16**), operated by the RATP, departs from the airport daily from 8:30am to 5:30pm and costs 8.50€ ($11) for the 45- to 50-minute ride. Departures are about every 15 minutes, and the bus leaves you near the corner of rue Scribe and place de l'Opéra in the heart of Paris.

A **taxi** from Roissy into the city will cost about 50€ to 60€ ($65–$78); from 8pm to 7am the fare is 40% higher. Long orderly lines for taxis form outside each of the airport's terminals.

Paris Arrondissements

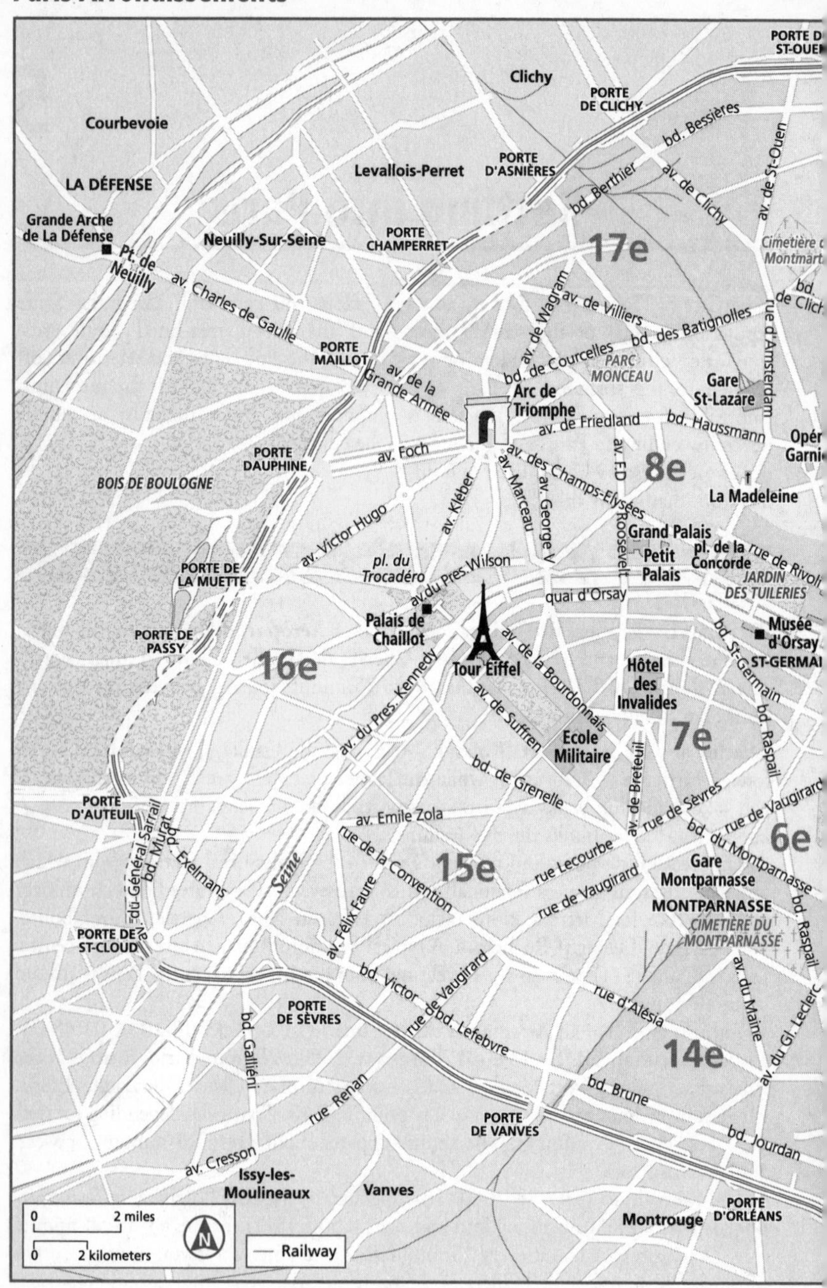

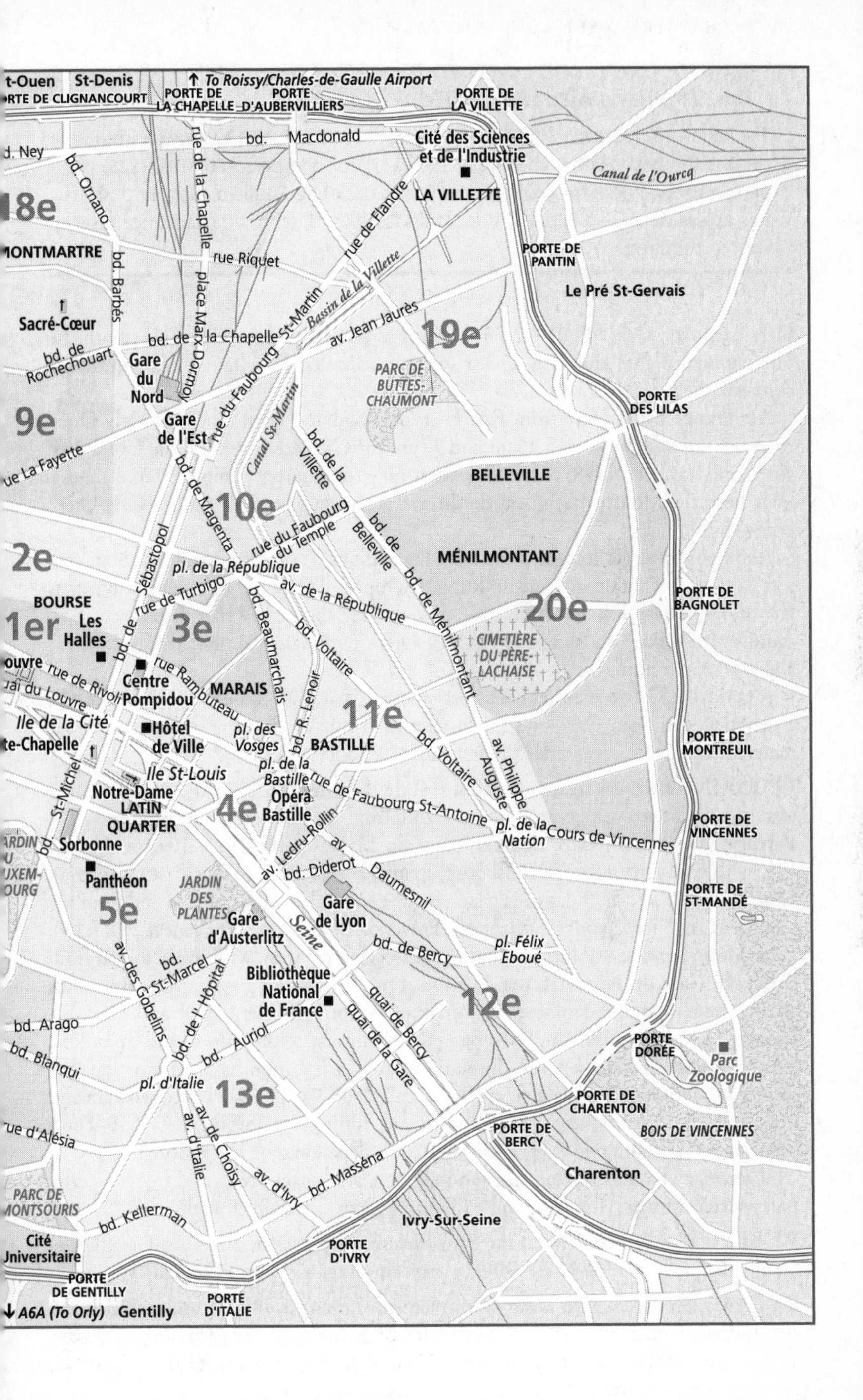

St-Denis
To Roissy/Charles-de-Gaulle Airport
PORTE DE LA CHAPELLE
PORTE D'AUBERVILLIERS
PORTE DE LA VILLETTE
bd. Macdonald
Cité des Sciences et de l'Industrie
Canal de l'Ourcq
LA VILLETTE
18e
bd. Ornano
rue de la Chapelle
rue de Flandre
rue Riquet
bd. Barbès
place Marx Dormoy
PORTE DE PANTIN
Le Pré St-Gervais
Sacré-Cœur
Bassin de la Villette
bd. de la Chapelle
rue du Faubourg St-Martin
av. Jean Jaurès
19e
bd. de Rochechouart
Gare du Nord
PARC DE BUTTES-CHAUMONT
PORTE DES LILAS
9e
Gare de l'Est
Canal St-Martin
bd. de la Villette
BELLEVILLE
bd. de Magenta
10e
rue du Faubourg du Temple
bd. de Belleville
2e
Sébastopol
pl. de la République
MÉNILMONTANT
bd. de Ménilmontant
BOURSE
rue de Turbigo
av. de la République
20e
PORTE DE BAGNOLET
1er
Les Halles
3e
bd. Beaumarchais
bd. Voltaire
CIMETIÈRE DU PÈRE-LACHAISE
rue de Rivoli
Centre Pompidou
rue Rambuteau
MARAIS
Ile de la Cité
Hôtel de Ville
pl. des Vosges
bd. R. Lenoir
11e
BASTILLE
PORTE DE MONTREUIL
Ile St-Louis
pl. de la Bastille
av. Philippe Auguste
Notre-Dame
LATIN QUARTER
4e
Opéra Bastille
rue de Faubourg St-Antoine
pl. de la Nation
Cours de Vincennes
PORTE DE VINCENNES
bd. St-Michel
Sorbonne
av. Ledru-Rollin
bd. Diderot
av. Daumesnil
Panthéon
JARDIN DES PLANTES
Gare de Lyon
PORTE DE ST-MANDÉ
5e
Gare d'Austerlitz
Seine
bd. de Bercy
pl. Félix Eboué
av. des Gobelins
bd. St-Marcel
Bibliothèque National de France
quai de Bercy
12e
bd. Arago
bd. de l'Hôpital
bd. Auriol
quai de la Gare
PORTE DORÉE
Parc Zoologique
bd. Blanqui
pl. d'Italie
13e
PORTE DE CHARENTON
av. de Choisy
av. d'Italie
PORTE DE BERCY
BOIS DE VINCENNES
rue d'Alésia
av. d'Ivry
bd. Masséna
Charenton
bd. Kellerman
Ivry-Sur-Seine
Cité Universitaire
PORTE D'IVRY
PORTE DE GENTILLY
A6A (To Orly)
Gentilly
PORTE D'ITALIE

Tips The Paris Airport Shuttle

The **Paris Airport Shuttle** (✆ **01-53-39-18-18;** fax 01-53-39-13-13; www.parishuttle.com) is the best option. It charges 25€ ($33) for one person or 19€ ($25) per person for two or more going to and from Charles de Gaulle or Orly. Both shuttles accept American Express, Visa, and MasterCard, with 1-day advance reservations required.

Orly Airport Orly (✆ **01-49-75-52-52**) has two terminals—Orly Sud (south) for international flights and Orly Ouest (west) for domestic flights. A free shuttle bus connects them in 3 minutes.

Air France buses leave from Exit E of Orly Sud and from Exit F of Orly Ouest every 12 minutes between 5:45am and 11pm for Gare des Invalides; the fare is 10€ ($13) one-way, 14€ ($18) round-trip. Returning to the airport (about 30 min.), buses leave both the Montparnasse and the Invalides terminal for Orly Sud or Orly Ouest every 15 minutes.

Another way to get to central Paris is to take the RER from points throughout central Paris to the station at Pont-de-Rungis/Aéroport d'Orly for a per-person one-way fare of 3.45€ ($4.50), and from here, take the free shuttle bus that departs every 15 minutes from Pont-de-Rungis to both of Orly's terminals. Combined travel time is about 45 to 55 minutes.

A **taxi** from Orly to central Paris costs about 45€ ($59), more at night. Don't take a meterless taxi from Orly—it's much safer (and usually cheaper) to hire one of the metered cabs, which are under the scrutiny of a police officer.

BY TRAIN Paris has six major stations: **Gare d'Austerlitz,** 55 quai d'Austerlitz, 13e (serving the southwest, with trains to and from the Loire Valley, Bordeaux, the Pyrénées, and Spain); **Gare de l'Est,** place du 11-Novembre-1918, 10e (serving the east, with trains to and from Strasbourg, Reims, and beyond, to Zurich and Austria); **Gare de Lyon,** 20 bd. Diderot, 12e (serving the southeast, with trains to and from the Côte d'Azur [Nice, Cannes, St-Tropez], Provence, and beyond, to Geneva and Italy); **Gare Montparnasse,** 17 bd. Vaugirard, 15e (serving the west, with trains to and from Brittany); **Gare du Nord,** 18 rue de Dunkerque, 15e (serving the north, with trains to and from London, Holland, Denmark, and northern Germany); and **Gare St-Lazare,** 13 rue d'Amsterdam, 8e (serving the northwest, with trains to and from Normandy). Buses operate between the stations, and each station has a Métro stop. For train information and to make reservations, call ✆ **08-92-35-35-35** between 7am and 8pm daily. From Paris, one-way rail passage to Tours costs 38€ to 51€ ($49–$66); one-way to Strasbourg 44€ or 51€ ($57–$66), depending on the routing.

Warning: The stations and surrounding areas are usually seedy and frequented by pickpockets, hustlers, hookers, and addicts. Be alert, especially at night.

BY BUS Most buses arrive at the **Eurolines France** station, 28 av. du Général-de-Gaulle, Bagnolet (✆ **08-92-89-90-91;** www.eurolines.fr; Métro: Gallieni).

BY CAR Driving in Paris is *not* recommended. Parking is difficult and traffic dense. If you drive, remember that Paris is encircled by a ring road, the *périphérique.* Always obtain detailed directions to your destination, including the name of the exit on the *périphérique* (exits aren't numbered). Avoid rush hours.

The major highways into Paris are A1 from the north; A13 from Rouen, Normandy, and other points northwest; A10 from Spain and the southwest; A6 and A7 from the French Alps, the Riviera, and Italy; and A4 from eastern France.

VISITOR INFORMATION

The **Paris Convention and Visitors Bureau** (© **08-92-68-30-00;** .35€/45¢ per minute; www.paris-info.com) has offices throughout the city, with the main headquarters at 25–27 rue des Pyramides, 1er (Métro: Pyramides). It's open Monday to Saturday 10am to 7pm, Sunday and holidays from 11am to 7pm. Less comprehensive branch offices include **Opéra-Grands Magasins,** 11 rue Scribe, 9e (Métro: Opera), open Monday to Saturday 9am to 6:30pm; **Espace Tourisme Ile-de-France,** in the Carrousel du Louvre, 99 rue de Rivoli, 1er (Métro: Palais-Royal–Louvre), open daily 10am to 5pm; in the **Gare de Lyon,** 20 bd. Diderot, Paris 12e (Métro: Gare de Lyon), open Monday to Saturday 8am to 6pm; in the **Gare du Nord,** 18 rue de Dunkerque, 10e (Métro: Gare du Nord), open daily 8am to 6pm; and in **Montmartre,** 21 place du Tertre, 18e (Métro: Abbesses or Lamarck–Caulaincourt), open daily 10am to 7pm. You can walk in at any branch to make a hotel reservation; the service charge is free. The offices are extremely busy year-round, especially in midsummer, so be prepared to wait in line.

CITY LAYOUT

Paris is surprisingly compact. Occupying 2,723 sq. km (1,051 sq. miles), its urban area is home to more than 11 million people. The river Seine divides Paris into the **Rive Droite (Right Bank)** to the north and the **Rive Gauche (Left Bank)** to the south. These designations make sense when you stand on a bridge and face downstream (west)—to your right is the north bank, to your left the south. A total of 32 bridges link the Right Bank and the Left Bank. Some provide access to the two islands at the heart of the city—**Ile de la Cité,** the city's birthplace and site of Notre-Dame; and **Ile St-Louis,** a moat-guarded oasis of 17th-century mansions.

The "main street" on the Right Bank is **avenue des Champs-Elysées,** beginning at the Arc de Triomphe and running to place de la Concorde. Avenue des Champs-Elysées and 11 other avenues radiate like the arms of an asterisk from the Arc de Triomphe, giving it its original name, place de l'Etoile (*étoile* means "star"). It was renamed place Charles-de-Gaulle following the general's death; today, it's often referred to as place Charles-de-Gaulle–Etoile.

FINDING AN ADDRESS Paris is divided into 20 municipal wards called ***arrondissements,*** each with its own city hall, police station, and post office; some have remnants of market squares. Arrondissements spiral out clockwise from the 1st, in the geographical center of the city. The 2nd through the 8th form a ring around the 1st, and the 9th through the 17th form an outer ring around the inner ring. The 18th, 19th, and 20th are at the far northern and eastern reaches of the Right Bank. Arrondissements 5, 6, 7, 13, 14, and 15 are on the Left Bank.

Most city maps are divided by arrondissement, and addresses include the arrondissement number (in Roman or Arabic numerals and followed by "er" or "e"). Paris also has its own version of a zip code. The mailing address for a hotel is written as, for example, "Paris 75014." The last two digits, 14, indicate that the address is in the 14th arrondissement—in this case, Montparnasse.

Numbers on buildings running parallel to the Seine usually follow the course of the river—east to west. On perpendicular streets, building numbers begin low closer to the river.

MAPS If you're staying more than 2 or 3 days, purchase an inexpensive pocket-size book called *Paris par arrondissement,* available at newsstands and bookshops; prices start at 6.50€ ($8.45). This guide provides you with a Métro map, a foldout map of the city, and maps of each arrondissement, with all streets listed and keyed.

THE ARRONDISSEMENTS IN BRIEF

Each of Paris's 20 arrondissements possesses a unique style and flavor. Do note, however, that in this guide we cover hotels in central Paris only; for a wider selection of accommodations in the outer arrondissements, see *Frommer's Paris 2008*.

1er (Musée du Louvre/Les Halles) The **Louvre** lures hordes to the 1st arrondissement, on the Right Bank. This area is home to rue de Rivoli and the **Jeu de Paume** and **Orangerie** museums. Walk through the **Jardin des Tuileries,** laid out by Louis XIV's gardener. Pause to take in the beauty of **place Vendôme.** Zola's "belly of Paris" (Les Halles) is no longer the food-and-meat market; it's now the **Forum des Halles,** a shopping center.

2e (La Bourse) Home to the **Bourse (stock exchange),** this Right Bank district lies between the *grands boulevards* and rue Etienne-Marcel. On weekdays, the shouts of brokers echo across place de la Bourse. Much of the east end of the 2nd is devoted to the **garment district (Le Sentier).** You'll find gems amid the commercialism, and none finer than the **Musée Cognacq-Jay,** 25 bd. des Capucines, featuring work by every artist from Watteau to Fragonard.

3e (Le Marais) This district embraces much of **Le Marais (the Swamp),** one of the best loved of the old Right Bank neighborhoods. Kings have called Le Marais home, and its salons have echoed with the remarks of Racine, Voltaire, Molière, and Mme de Sévigné. It enjoyed a renewal in the 1990s, with galleries and boutiques. One of its chief draws is **Musée Picasso,** a repository of 20th-century art. Le Marais is also the center of Paris's gay and lesbian scene. Rue des Rosiers, with its Jewish restaurants, preserves the memory of the hundreds of Jewish residents who used to reside in Le Marais.

4e (Ile de la Cité/Ile St-Louis & Beaubourg) The 4th has it all: not only the Ile de la Cité, with **Notre-Dame,** the **Sainte-Chapelle,** and the **Conciergerie,** but also the Ile St-Louis, with town houses, courtyards, and antiques shops. Ile St-Louis, a former cow pasture and dueling ground, is home to 6,000 Louisiens, its permanent residents. The area is touristy and crowded.

As the heart of medieval Paris, the 4th evokes memories of Danton, of Robespierre, even of Charlotte Corday stabbing Marat in his bathroom. Here are France's finest **bird and flower markets,** plus the **Centre Pompidou.** After all this, you can retreat to **place des Vosges,** a square of perfect harmony where Victor Hugo penned many masterpieces from 1832 to 1848.

5e (Latin Quarter) The Quartier Latin is Paris's intellectual soul, featuring bookstores, schools, churches, jazz clubs, student dives, Roman ruins, and boutiques. The area got its name because students and professors at the **Sorbonne** (founded in 1253) spoke Latin. As the center of "bohemian Paris," it was the setting for Henry

Murger's novel *La Vie Bohème* (later the Puccini opera *La Bohème*).

Changing times have brought immigrants offering everything from couscous to spring rolls. The 5th borders the Seine, so you'll want to stroll along **quai de Montebello,** where vendors sell everything from antique Daumier prints to copies of Balzac's *Père Goriot.* The 5th also stretches to the **Panthéon,** the resting place of Rousseau, Zola, Hugo, Voltaire, and Jean Moulin, the Resistance leader tortured to death by the Gestapo. Marie Curie is buried here as well.

6e (St-Germain/Luxembourg) For some, this is the most colorful Left Bank quarter. You can see young artists emerging from the **Ecole des Beaux-Arts.** Strolling the boulevards of the 6th, including **St-Germain,** has its own rewards, but the secret of the district lies in its narrow streets, hidden squares, and the **Jardin du Luxembourg,** near Marie de Médicis' **Palais du Luxembourg.** To be authentic, stroll these streets with a loaf of bread from the ovens of **Poilâne,** 8 rue du Cherche-Midi. You'll encounter historical and literary associations, as on **rue Jacob,** where Racine, Ingres, and Hemingway lived. Today's big name could be Spike Lee checking into **La Villa Hôtel** at 29 rue Jacob.

7e (Eiffel Tower/Musée d'Orsay) The **Eiffel Tower** dominates the 7th on the Left Bank. The tower is one of the most recognizable landmarks in the world, but many hated it when it opened in 1889. The 7th is also home to the **Hôtel des Invalides,** which contains Napoleon's Tomb and the Musée de l'Armée. Even visitors with no time to explore should visit the **Musée d'Orsay,** the world's premier showcase of 19th-century French art and culture.

8e (Champs-Elysées/Madeleine) The 8th is the heart of the Right Bank, and its showcase is **avenue des Champs-Elysées,** linking the **Arc de Triomphe** with the obelisk on **place de la Concorde.** Here you'll find fashion houses, hotels, restaurants, and shops. The area is known for having France's (perhaps the world's) superlatives: the best restaurant **(Taillevent),** the sexiest strip joint **(Crazy Horse Saloon),** the most splendid square **(place de la Concorde),** the best rooftop cafe (at **La Samaritaine**), the grandest hotel **(Crillon),** the most impressive arch **(Arc de Triomphe),** the oldest Métro station **(Franklin-D-Roosevelt),** and the most ancient monument (**Obelisk of Luxor,** 3,300 years old). Also here is **La Madeleine** church, which looks like a Greek temple.

9e (Opéra Garnier/Pigalle) Everything from the Quartier de l'Opéra to the strip joints of Pigalle (the infamous "Pig Alley" for World War II GIs) is in the 9th, on the Right Bank. Baron Haussmann's 19th-century redevelopment radically altered it, and the *grands boulevards* are among the most obvious of his works. Another attraction is the **Folies-Bergère,** where cancan dancers have been kicking since 1868 and such entertainers as Mistinguett, Edith Piaf, and Josephine Baker appeared. The **Opéra** (now the Opéra Garnier or Palais Garnier), once the haunt of the Phantom, made the 9th the last hurrah of Second Empire opulence.

10e (Gare du Nord/Gare de l'Est) The two stations, along with cinemas, porno houses, and commercial zones, make the 10th one of the least desirable tourist districts. We avoid it, except for **Brasserie Flo,** for *la formidable choucroute*—sauerkraut with everything.

11e (Opéra Bastille) The **Opéra Bastille,** opened in 1989, is the center of this district. The "people's opera house" stands on the **place de la Bastille,** where on July 14, 1789, Parisians stormed the fortress and released the prisoners.

This area between the Marais, Ménilmontant, and République is "blue-collar chic," and *artistes* walk the sidewalks of rue Oberkampf. Hip Parisians live and work among decaying 19th-century apartments and 1960s public housing with graffiti-spattered walls.

12e (Bois de Vincennes/Gare de Lyon) The 12th is experiencing a renaissance, with new housing, shops, and restaurants. Few out-of-towners came here until the opening of famed restaurant **Au Trou Gascon.** The major attraction is the **Bois de Vincennes,** a sprawling park on the eastern periphery of Paris. It is a favorite of families, who enjoy its zoos and museums, its château and lakes, and the Parc Floral de Paris, with springtime rhododendrons and autumn dahlias. The **Gare de Lyon** is in the 12th, but going here is worthwhile even if you don't have to take a train, as the building is a great architectural monument of Belle Epoque France. The ceiling frescoes and Art Nouveau decor of the station's restaurant, **Le Train Bleu,** are national treasures—and the food's good, too.

13e (Gare d'Austerlitz) Centering on the Gare d'Austerlitz, the 13th may have its fans, though we've yet to meet one. But worth seeing is the **Manufacture des Gobelins,** 42 av. des Gobelins, which makes the famous Gobelins tapestries.

14e (Montparnasse) The northern end of this district on the Left Bank is **Montparnasse,** home of the Lost Generation. One of its monuments is the Rodin statue of Balzac at boulevard Montparnasse and boulevard Raspail. At this corner are **literary cafes** such as La Rotonde, Le Sélect, La Dôme, and La Coupole. Perhaps Gertrude Stein didn't frequent them (she loathed cafes), but other American expats such as Hemingway and Fitzgerald came for a drink or four. At 27 rue de Fleurus, Stein and Alice B. Toklas collected paintings and entertained T. S. Eliot and Matisse.

15e (Gare Montparnasse/Institut Pasteur) A mostly residential district beginning at Gare Montparnasse, the 15th, on the Left Bank, stretches west to the Seine. It's the largest arrondissement but has few attractions, except for the **Parc des Expositions** and the **Institut Pasteur.** Institut Pasteur, 25 rue du Dr. Roux (© **01-45-68-82-82;** Métro: Pasteur), founded by Louis Pasteur in 1887, is a biochemical research center. Parc des Expositions is a fairground that stages special exhibitions.

16e (Trocadéro/Bois de Boulogne) Highlights of the 16th, on the Right Bank, are the **Bois de Boulogne, Jardins du Trocadéro, Musée de Balzac, Musée Guimet** (famous for its Asian collections), and **Cimetière de Passy,** resting place of Manet, Giraudoux, and Debussy. This large arrondissement is known for its well-heeled bourgeoisie, high rents, and posh boulevards. Prosperous, conservative addresses include **avenue d'Iéna** and **avenue Victor-Hugo.** The 16th also includes the best place in Paris to view the Eiffel Tower: **place du Trocadéro.**

17e (Parc Monceau/Place Clichy) One of the most spread-out arrondissements, the 17th, on the Right Bank, flanks the northern periphery of Paris. It incorporates the northern edge of place Charles-de-Gaulle–Etoile in the west, the place Wagram at its center, and the tawdry place Clichy in the east. Highlights are **Parc Monceau,** the **Palais des Congrès** (of interest only if you're attending a convention), and the **Porte Maillot Air Terminal.** The 17th does contain two great restaurants: **Guy Savoy** and **Michel Rostang.**

18e (Montmartre) The 18th, at the far end of the Right Bank, is associated with such names as the **Marché aux Puces de Clignancourt** flea market, **Moulin Rouge, Sacré-Coeur,** and **place du Tertre** (a tourist trap if ever there was one). Utrillo was its native son, Renoir lived here, and Toulouse-Lautrec adopted the area as his own. Today, place Blanche is known for its prostitutes, and Montmartre is filled with honky-tonks, souvenir shops, and bad restaurants.

19e (La Villette) Visitors come to what was once the village of La Villette to see the **Cité des Sciences et de l'Industrie,** a science museum and park. Mostly residential, this district is one of the most ethnic in Paris, home to workers from all parts of the former Empire. A highlight is **Les Buttes Chaumont,** where kids can enjoy puppet shows and donkey rides.

20e (Père-Lachaise Cemetery) This district's greatest landmark is the **Père-Lachaise Cemetery,** resting place of Piaf, Proust, Wilde, Duncan, Stein and Toklas, Bernhardt, Colette, Jim Morrison, and many others. The district is home to Muslims and members of Paris's Sephardic Jewish community, many of whom fled Algeria or Tunisia. With turbaned men selling dates and grains on the street, this arrondissement seems more North African than French.

2 Getting Around

BY METRO (SUBWAY) The Métro (✆ **08-92-68-77-14;** www.ratp.fr) is the most efficient and fastest way to get around Paris. All lines are numbered, and the final destination of each line is clearly marked on subway maps, in the system's underground passageways, and on the train cars. The Métro runs daily from 5:30am to 1:15am. It's reasonably safe at any hour, but beware of pickpockets.

To familiarize yourself with the Métro, check out the color map on the inside back cover of this book. Most stations display a map of the Métro at the entrance. To locate your correct train on a map, find your destination, follow the line to the end of its route, and note the name of the final stop, which is that line's direction. In the station, follow the signs for your direction in the passageways until you see the label on a train. Many larger stations have maps with push-button indicators that light up your route when you press the button for your destination.

Transfer stations are *correspondances*—some require long walks; Châtelet is the most difficult—but most trips require only one transfer. When transferring, follow the orange CORRESPONDANCE signs to the proper platform. Don't follow a SORTIE (exit) sign, or you'll have to pay again to get back on the train.

On the urban lines, one ticket for 1.40€ ($1.80) lets you travel to any point. On the Sceaux, Boissy-St-Léger, and St-Germain-en-Laye lines to the suburbs, fares are based on distance. A *carnet* is the best buy—10 tickets for about 11€ ($14).

At the turnstile entrances to the station, insert your ticket and pass through. At some exits, tickets are also checked, so hold onto yours. There are occasional ticket checks on trains and platforms and in passageways, too.

Value Discount Transit Passes

The **Paris-Visite** (© **08-92-68-77-14**) is valid for 1, 2, 3, or 5 days on public transport, including the Métro, buses, the funicular ride to Montmartre, and RER trains. For access to zones 1 to 3, which includes central Paris and its nearby suburbs, its cost ranges from 8.50€ ($11) for 1 day to 27€ ($35) for 5 days. Get it at RATP (Régie Autonome des Transports Parisiens) offices, the tourist office, and Métro stations.

Another discount pass is **Carte Mobilis,** which allows unlimited travel on bus, subway, and RER lines during a 1-day period for 5.50€ to 19€ ($7.15–$24), depending on the zone. Ask for it at any Métro station.

Most economical, for anyone who arrives in Paris early in the week, is a **Carte Orange.** Sold at large Métro stations, it allows 1 week of unlimited Métro or bus transit within central Paris and its immediate outskirts for 16€ to 44€ ($21–$57). The pass is valid from any Monday to the following Sunday, and it's sold only on Monday, Tuesday, and Wednesday. You'll have to submit a passport-size photo.

RER TRAINS A suburban train system, RER (Réseau Express Regional), passes through the heart of Paris, traveling faster than the Métro and running daily from 5:30am to 12:30am. This system works like the Métro and requires the same tickets. The major stops within central Paris, linking the RER to the Métro, are Nation, Gare de Lyon, Charles de Gaulle–Etoile, Gare-Etoile, and Gare du Nord as well as Châtelet-Les-Halles. All of these stops are on the Right Bank. On the Left Bank, RER stops include Denfert-Rochereau and St-Michel. The five RER lines are marked A through E. Different branches are labeled by a number, the C5 Line serving Versailles-Rive Gauche, for example. Electric signboards next to each track outline all the possible stops along the way. Make sure that the little square next to your intended stop is lit.

BY BUS Buses are much slower than the Métro. The majority run from 6:30am to 9:30pm (a few operate until 12:30am, and 10 operate during early morning hours). Service is limited on Sundays and holidays. Bus and Métro fares are the same; you can use the same tickets on both. Most bus rides require one ticket, but some destinations require two (never more than two within the city limits).

At certain stops, signs list destinations and bus numbers serving that point. Destinations are usually listed north to south and east to west. Most stops are also posted on the sides of the buses. During rush hours, you may have to take a ticket from a dispensing machine, indicating your position in the line at the stop.

If you intend to use the buses a lot, pick up an RATP bus map at the office on place de la Madeleine, 8e, or at the tourist offices at RATP headquarters, 54 Quai de La Rapée, 12e. For detailed recorded information (in English) on bus and Métro routes, call © **01-58-76-16-16,** open Monday to Friday 7am to 9pm.

The RATP also operates the **Balabus,** big-windowed orange-and-white motorcoaches that run only during limited hours: Sunday and national holidays from noon to 8:30pm, from April 15 to the end of September. Itineraries run in both directions between Gare de Lyon and the Grande Arche de La Défense, encompassing some of the city's most beautiful vistas. It's a great deal—three Métro tickets, for 1.40€ ($1.80) each, will carry you the entire route. You'll recognize the bus and the route it follows by the Bb symbol emblazoned on each bus's side and on signs posted beside the route it follows.

BY TAXI It's virtually impossible to get a taxi at rush hour, so don't even try. Taxi drivers are organized into a lobby that limits their number to 15,000.

Watch out for common rip-offs: Always check the meter to make sure you're not paying the previous passenger's fare; beware of cabs without meters, which often wait outside nightclubs for tipsy patrons; and settle the tab in advance.

You can hail regular cabs on the street when their signs read LIBRE. Taxis are easier to find at the many stands near Métro stations. The flag drops at 5.50€ ($7.15), and from 10am to 5pm, you pay .80€ ($1) per kilometer. From 5pm to 10am, you pay 1.10€ ($1.40) per kilometer. On airport trips, you're not required to pay for the driver's empty return ride.

You're allowed several pieces of luggage free if they're transported inside and are less than 5 kilograms (11 lb.). Heavier suitcases carried in the trunk cost 1€ to 1.50€ ($1.30–$1.95) apiece. Tip 12% to 15%—the latter usually elicits a *merci.* For radio cabs, call **Les Taxis Bleus** (© **08-25-16-10-10**) or **Taxi G7** (© **01-47-39-47-39**)—but note that you'll be charged from the point where the taxi begins the drive to pick you up.

BY BOAT The **Batobus** (© **08-25-05-01-01;** www.batobus.com) is a 150-passenger ferry with big windows. Every day between April and December, the boats operate along the Seine, stopping at such points of interest as the **Eiffel Tower, Musée d'Orsay,** the **Louvre, Notre-Dame,** and the **Hôtel de Ville.** Unlike the Bateaux-Mouche (see chapter 6), the Batobus does not provide recorded commentary. The only fare option available is a day pass valid for either 1, 2, or 5 days, each allowing as many entrances and exits as you want. A 1-day pass costs 11€ ($14) for adults, 5€ ($6.50) for students and children under 16; a 2-day pass costs 13€ ($17) for adults, 6€ ($7.80) for students and children under 16; a 5-day pass costs 16€ ($21) for adults, 7€ ($9.10) for students and children under 16. Boats operate daily (closed most of Jan) every 25 to 30 minutes, starting between 10 and 10:30am and ending between 4:30 and 10:30pm, depending on the season of the year.

FAST FACTS: Paris

For additional practical information, see "Fast Facts: France," in chapter 3.

American Express The office at 11 rue Scribe (© **01-47-77-79-28**) is open as a travel agency, a tour operator, and a mail pickup service every Monday to Friday from 9:30am to 6:30pm and Saturday 9am to 5:30pm. Its banking section, for issues involving American Express credit cards, transfers of funds, and credit-related issues, is open Monday to Saturday from 9am to 6:30pm.

Area Code All French telephone numbers consist of 10 digits, the first two of which are like an area code. If you're calling anywhere in France from within France, just dial all 10 digits—no additional codes are needed. If you're calling from the United States, drop the initial 0 (zero).

Currency Exchange American Express can fill most banking needs. Most banks in Paris are open Monday to Friday from 9am to 4:30pm, and a few are open

Saturday; ask at your hotel for the location of the one nearest you. For the best exchange rate, cash your traveler's checks at banks or foreign-exchange offices, not at shops and hotels. Most post offices will change traveler's checks or convert currency. Currency exchanges are also at Paris airports and train stations and along most of the major boulevards. They charge a small commission.

Some exchange places charge favorable rates to lure you into their stores. For example, **Paris Vision,** 214 rue de Rivoli, 1er (© **01-42-60-31-25;** Métro: Tuileries), maintains a minibank in the back of a travel agency, open daily 7am to 9pm. Its rates are a fraction less favorable than those offered for large blocks of money as listed by the Paris stock exchange.

Dentists For emergency dental service, call **S.O.S. Dentaire,** 87 bd. du Port-Royal, 13e (© **01-43-37-51-00;** Métro: Gobelins), Monday to Friday from 6 to 11:30pm and Saturday and Sunday from 9am to midnight. Staff members will arrange an appointment with a qualified dentist either on the day of your call or for early in the morning of the following day. You can also call or visit the **American Hospital** (see "Doctors," below).

Doctors Some large hotels have a doctor on staff. You can also try the **American Hospital,** 63 bd. Victor-Hugo, in the suburb of Neuilly-sur-Seine (© **01-46-41-25-25;** Métro: Pont-de-Levallois or Pont-de-Neuilly; bus no. 82), which operates a 24-hour emergency service. The bilingual staff accepts Blue Cross and other American insurance plans.

Drugstores After hours, have your concierge contact the Commissariat de Police for the nearest 24-hour pharmacy. French law requires one pharmacy in any given neighborhood to stay open 24 hours. You'll find the address posted on the doors or windows of all other drugstores. One of the most central all-nighters is **Pharmacy Les Champs "Derhy,"** 84 av. des Champs-Elysées, 8e (© **01-45-62-02-41;** Métro: George V).

Emergencies For the police, call © **17;** to report a fire, call © **18.** For an ambulance, call © **15** or 01-45-67-50-50.

Police In an emergency, call © **17.** For nonemergency situations, the principal préfecture is at 9 bd. du Palais, 4e (© **01-53-73-53-73;** Métro: Cité).

Post Offices Most post offices in Paris are open Monday to Friday from 8am to 7pm and every Saturday from 8am to noon. One of the biggest and most central is the main post office for the 1st arrondissement, at 52 rue du Louvre (© **01-40-28-76-00;** Métro: Musée du Louvre). It maintains the hours noted above for services that include sale of postal money orders, mail collection and distribution, and expedition of faxes. For buying stamps and accepting packages, it's open on a limited basis 24 hours a day. If you find it inconvenient to go to the post office just to buy stamps, they're sold at the reception desks of many hotels and at cafes designated with red TABAC signs.

Safety Beware of child pickpockets, who prey on visitors around sites such as the Louvre, Eiffel Tower, Notre-Dame, and Montmartre, and who like to pick pockets in the Métro, often blocking the entrances and exits to the escalator. Women should hang onto their purses.

3 Where to Stay

Although Paris hotels are quite expensive, there is some good news. Scores of lackluster lodgings, where the wallpaper dated from the Napoleonic era, have been renovated and offer much better value in the moderate-to-inexpensive price range. The most outstanding examples are in the **7th arrondissement,** where several good-value hotels have blossomed from dives.

By now, the "season" has almost ceased to exist. Most visitors, at least those from North America, visit in July and August. Because many French are on vacation, and trade fairs and conventions come to a halt, there are usually plenty of rooms, even though these months have traditionally been the peak season for European travel. In most hotels, February is just as busy as April or September because of the volume of business travelers and the increasing number of tourists who've learned to take advantage of off-season discount airfares.

Hot weather doesn't last long in Paris, so most hotels, except the deluxe ones, don't provide air-conditioning. To avoid the noise problem when you have to open windows, request a room in the back when making a reservation.

Some hotels offer a continental breakfast of coffee, tea, or hot chocolate; a freshly baked croissant and roll; and butter and jam or jelly. Though nowhere near as filling as a traditional English or American breakfast, it is quick to prepare—it'll be at your door moments after you request it—and can be served at almost any hour. The word "breakfast" in these entries refers to this version.

Rates quoted include service and value-added tax unless otherwise specified. Unless otherwise noted, all hotel rooms have private bathrooms.

RIGHT BANK: 1ST ARRONDISSEMENT (MUSEE DU LOUVRE/LES HALLES)

VERY EXPENSIVE

Hôtel de Vendôme ★★ This jewel box was the embassy of Texas when that state was a nation; the hotel opened in 1998. Though the guest rooms are moderate in size, they're opulent and designed in classic Second Empire style, with luxurious beds; well-upholstered, hand-carved furnishings; and first-rate marble bathrooms with tub/shower combinations. Suites have generous space and such extras as blackout draperies and quadruple-glazed windows. The security is fantastic, with TV intercoms. This hotel's facade and roof are classified as historic monuments by the French government.

1 place Vendôme, Paris 75001. ✆ **01-55-04-55-00.** Fax 01-49-27-97-89. www.hoteldevendome.com. 29 units. High season 604€–674€ ($785–$876) double, 914€ ($1,188) junior suite, from 1,154€ ($1,500) suite; winter 514€–720€ ($668–$936) double, 794€ ($1,032) junior suite, from 974€ ($1,266) suite. AE, DC, MC, V. Parking 25€ ($33). Métro: Concorde or Opéra. **Amenities:** Restaurant; piano bar; room service; massage; babysitting; laundry service; dry cleaning; limited-mobility rooms. *In room:* A/C, TV, minibar, hair dryer, safe.

Hôtel du Louvre ★ *Kids* When Napoleon III inaugurated the hotel in 1855, it was described as "a palace of the people, rising adjacent to the palace of kings." In 1897, Camille Pissarro moved into a room with a view that inspired many of his landscapes. Its decor features marble, bronze, and gilt. Guest rooms feature souvenirs of the Belle Epoque, elegant fabrics, double-glazed windows, comfortable beds, and wood furniture. Suites provide greater dimensions and better exposures, and such upgrades as antiques, trouser presses, and robes. All rooms have well-maintained bathrooms with a choice of tub or shower.

Where to Stay on the Right Bank

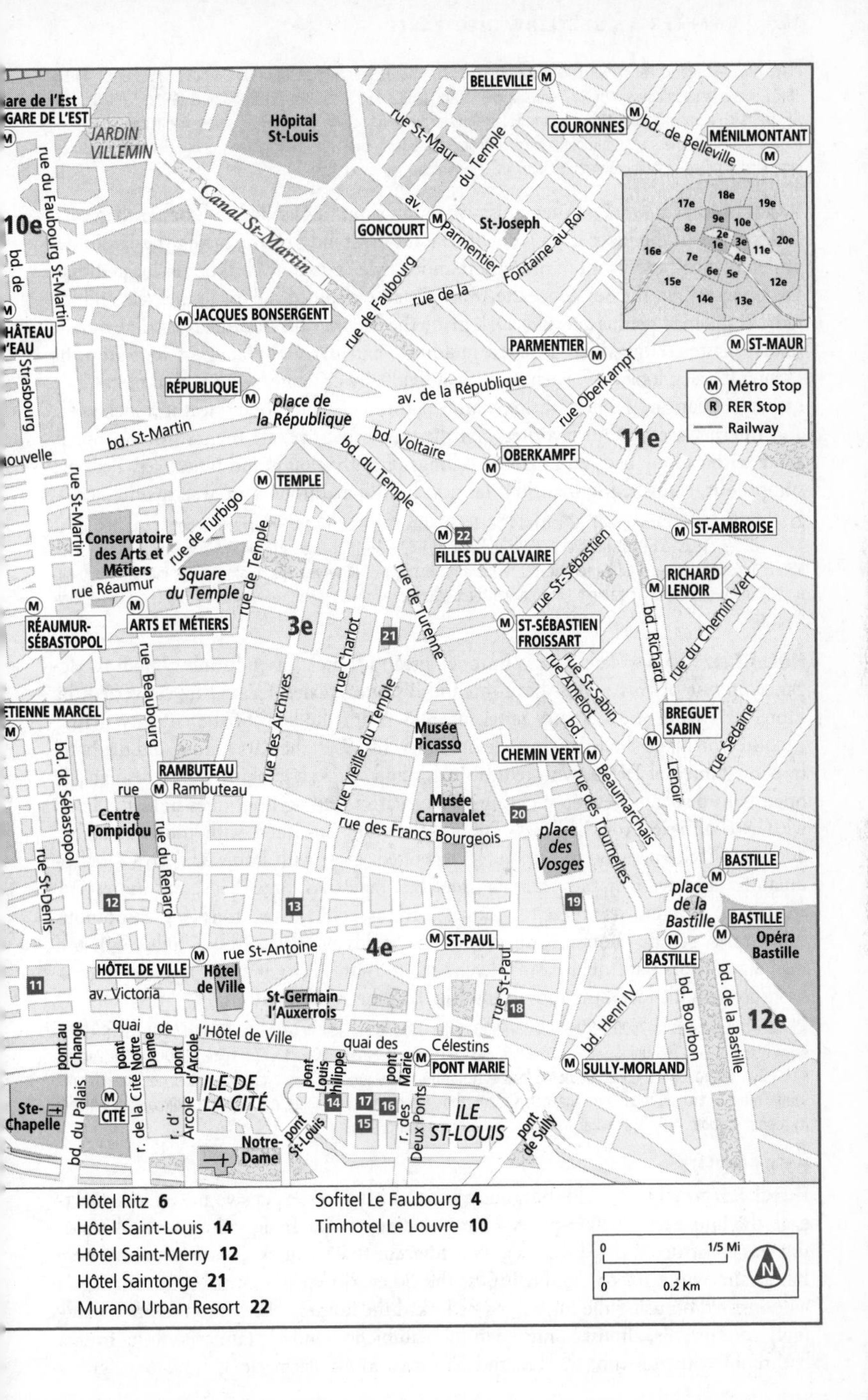
BELLEVILLE
Gare de l'Est
GARE DE L'EST
JARDIN VILLEMIN
Hôpital St-Louis
rue St-Maur
rue du Temple
COURONNES
bd. de Belleville
MÉNILMONTANT
rue du Faubourg St-Martin
Canal St-Martin
10e
bd. de Strasbourg
av. Parmentier
GONCOURT
St-Joseph
rue de la Fontaine au Roi
rue de Faubourg du Temple
17e
18e
19e
9e
10e
8e
2e
3e
11e
20e
16e
1e
7e
4e
6e
5e
12e
15e
14e
13e
JACQUES BONSERGENT
CHÂTEAU D'EAU
PARMENTIER
ST-MAUR
RÉPUBLIQUE
place de la République
av. de la République
rue Oberkampf
Métro Stop
RER Stop
Railway
bd. St-Martin
bd. Voltaire
bd. du Temple
11e
OBERKAMPF
TEMPLE
rue St-Martin
rue de Turbigo
Conservatoire des Arts et Métiers
22
FILLES DU CALVAIRE
ST-AMBROISE
rue St-Sébastien
rue Réaumur
Square du Temple
rue de Temple
rue de Turenne
RICHARD LENOIR
RÉAUMUR-SÉBASTOPOL
ARTS ET MÉTIERS
3e
21
ST-SÉBASTIEN FROISSART
rue du Chemin Vert
rue Beaubourg
rue Charlot
rue St-Sabin
rue Amelot
bd. Richard Lenoir
rue des Archives
ETIENNE MARCEL
rue Vieille du Temple
Musée Picasso
BREGUET SABIN
bd. de Sébastopol
RAMBUTEAU
rue Rambuteau
CHEMIN VERT
bd. Beaumarchais
rue Sedaine
Centre Pompidou
rue du Renard
Musée Carnavalet
20
rue des Francs Bourgeois
place des Vosges
rue des Tournelles
rue St-Denis
BASTILLE
12
13
19
place de la Bastille
BASTILLE
Opéra Bastille
4e
ST-PAUL
rue St-Antoine
HÔTEL DE VILLE
Hôtel de Ville
BASTILLE
11
av. Victoria
St-Germain l'Auxerrois
rue St-Paul
18
bd. Henri IV
bd. Bourbon
bd. de la Bastille
12e
quai de l'Hôtel de Ville
quai des Célestins
pont au Change
pont Notre Dame
pont d'Arcole
pont Louis Philippe
pont Marie
PONT MARIE
SULLY-MORLAND
Ste-Chapelle
bd. du Palais
CITÉ
r. de la Cité
r. d'Arcole
ILE DE LA CITÉ
14
17
16
15
r. des Deux Ponts
ILE ST-LOUIS
pont St-Louis
pont de Sully
Notre-Dame
Hôtel Ritz 6
Hôtel Saint-Louis 14
Hôtel Saint-Merry 12
Hôtel Saintonge 21
Murano Urban Resort 22
Sofitel Le Faubourg 4
Timhotel Le Louvre 10
0
1/5 Mi
0
0.2 Km
N

Place André-Malraux, Paris 75001. ✆ **800/888-4747** in the U.S. and Canada, or 01-44-58-38-38. Fax 01-44-58-38-01. www.hoteldulouvre.com. 177 units. 255€–500€ ($332–$650) double; 700€–1,800€ ($910–$2,340) suite. AE, DC, MC, V. Parking 24€ ($31). Métro: Palais-Royal–Louvre or Louvre–Rivoli. **Amenities:** Restaurant; bar; pool; fitness center; business center; room service; in-room massage; babysitting; laundry service; dry cleaning; nonsmoking rooms; limited-mobility rooms. *In room:* A/C, TV, minibar, hair dryer, safe.

Hôtel Meurice ★★★ After a massive renovation, this landmark is better than ever. It lies between the place de la Concorde and the Grand Louvre, facing the Jardin des Tuileries. The hotel is more media hip, more style conscious, and better located than the George V (in the 8e). Since the 1800s, it has welcomed the royal, the rich, and the radical: the mad genius Salvador Dalí made the Meurice his headquarters. The mosaic floors, plaster ceilings, hand-carved moldings, and Art Nouveau glass roof atop the Winter Garden look new. Each room is individually decorated with period pieces, fine carpets, Italian and French fabrics, marble bathrooms, and modern features such as fax and Internet access. Our favorites, and the least expensive, are the sixth-floor rooms, some with canopy beds and painted ceilings of puffy clouds and blue skies. Beds are sumptuous, furnished in luxurious fabrics, and the bathrooms are well maintained.

228 rue de Rivoli, Paris 75001. ✆ **01-44-58-10-10.** Fax 01-44-58-10-15. www.meuricehotel.com. 160 units. 720€–800€ ($936–$1,040) double; 1,250€–6,300€ ($1,625–$8,190) suite. AE, DC, MC, V. Parking 24€ ($31). Métro: Tuileries or Concorde. **Amenities:** 2 restaurants; bar; gym; full-service spa; room service; massage; babysitting; laundry service; dry cleaning; nonsmoking rooms; limited-mobility rooms. *In room:* A/C, TV, fax, minibar, hair dryer, safe.

Hôtel Ritz ★★★ The Ritz is Europe's greatest hotel, an enduring symbol of elegance on one of Paris's most beautiful and historic squares. César Ritz converted the Hôtel de Lazun into a luxury hotel in 1898. With the help of the culinary master Escoffier, he made the Ritz a miracle of luxury. In 1979, the Ritz family sold the hotel to Mohammed al Fayed, who refurbished it and added a cooking school. An arcade lined with display cases representing 125 of Paris's leading boutiques links the hotel with two annexed town houses. Public salons are furnished with museum-caliber antiques. Each guest room is uniquely decorated, most with Louis XIV or XV reproductions; all have fine rugs, marble fireplaces, tapestries, brass beds, and more. The spacious bathrooms are the city's most luxurious, with deluxe toiletries, sumptuous tubs, scales, private phones, cords to summon maids and valets, robes, full-length and makeup mirrors, and dual basins. Ever since Edward VII got stuck in a too-narrow bathtub with his lover, the tubs at the Ritz have been deep and big.

15 place Vendôme, Paris 75001. ✆ **800/223-6800** in the U.S. and Canada, or 01-43-16-30-30. Fax 01-43-16-45-38. www.ritzparis.com. 168 units. 680€–770€ ($884–$1,001) double; from 900€ ($1,170) suite. AE, DC, MC, V. Parking 44€ ($57). Métro: Opéra, Concorde, or Madeleine. **Amenities:** Restaurant; 4 bars; nightclub; indoor pool; health club; sauna; room service; in-room massage; babysitting; laundry service; dry cleaning; nonsmoking rooms; limited-mobility rooms. *In room:* A/C, TV, minibar, hair dryer, iron/ironing board, safe.

EXPENSIVE

Hôtel Burgundy ★ The Burgundy is one of the less expensive hotels in a mortgage-the-house sea of super-priced accommodations. The frequently renovated building was constructed in the 1830s as two adjacent town houses—one a pension where Baudelaire wrote poetry in the 1860s, the other a bordello. British-born managers who insisted on using the English name linked the houses. The bedrooms are exceedingly comfortable, almost homelike in their ambience, and contain everything from a bathroom with full tub, shower, and bathrobe to an alarm clock. This once-grand

Parisian residence lies in the heart of Paris between Madeleine and the Opera; the Louvre and major department stores are only a short walk away.

8 rue Duphot, Paris 75001. ✆ **01-42-60-34-12.** Fax 01-47-03-95-20. www.burgundyhotel.com. 89 units. 173€–238€ ($225–$309) double, 318€–353€ ($413–$459) suite. AE, DC, MC, V. Métro: Madeleine or Concorde. **Amenities:** Restaurant; bar; room service; babysitting; laundry service; dry cleaning. *In room:* TV, minibar, hair dryer.

MODERATE

Hôtel Britannique *Value* Conservatively modern and plush, this is a much-renovated 19th-century hotel near Les Halles and Notre-Dame. The place is not only British in name, but seems to cultivate English graciousness. The guest rooms are small but immaculate and soundproof, with comfortable beds and well-maintained bathrooms. A satellite receiver gets U.S. and U.K. television shows. The reading room is a cozy retreat.

20 av. Victoria, Paris 75001. ✆ **01-42-33-74-59.** Fax 01-42-33-82-65. www.hotel-britannique.fr. 39 units. 168€–193€ ($218–$251) double; 247€–288€ ($321–$374) suite. AE, DC, MC, V. Métro: Châtelet. **Amenities:** Bar; room service; laundry service; dry cleaning. *In room:* A/C, TV, minibar, hair dryer, safe.

INEXPENSIVE

Timhotel Le Louvre This hotel and its sibling in the 2e, the Timhotel Palais-Royal, 3 rue de la Banque (✆ **01-42-61-53-90;** fax 01-42-60-05-39; Métro: Bourse), are part of a breed of government-rated two-star family-friendly hotels cropping up in France. These Timhotels share the same manager and temperament. Though the rooms at the Palais-Royal branch are a bit larger than the ones here, this branch is so close to the Louvre that it's almost irresistible. The ambience is modern, with monochromatic rooms and wall-to-wall carpeting. Each unit's bathroom comes with a tub and shower.

4 rue Croix des Petits-Champs, Paris 75001. ✆ **01-42-60-34-86.** Fax 01-42-60-10-39. www.timhotel.fr. 56 units. 99€–150€ ($129–$195) double. AE, DC, MC, V. Métro: Palais-Royal. **Amenities:** Restaurant (breakfast only); nonsmoking rooms; limited-mobility rooms. *In room:* A/C, TV.

RIGHT BANK: 3RD ARRONDISSEMENT (LE MARAIS)

EXPENSIVE

Murano Urban Resort ★ *Finds* This hotel oddity, not everyone's cup of tea but charming for some, opened in late 2004. Composed of two abandoned buildings—one a run-down five-story apartment house, the other a three-story parking garage—that were interconnected and upgraded into a new and coherent whole, the result is a trendsetting, aggressively minimalist hotel whose angular sense of design may impress you with its purity. The decorative theme, as conceived by Lyon-based designer Raymond Morel, revolves around the transparency of Murano glass. A Murano glass chandelier is in the green-toned lobby, another is on the ground floor, and very large glass-framed mirrors are in some of the upper hallways. The mirrors and chandeliers are metaphors for how guests can play with light in their respective, and otherwise sparsely furnished, units: Up to three sets of curtains in any room filter sunlight in patterns that range from gauzy and bright to complete blackouts. Additionally, individual settings switch on and off a spectrum of lights in up to six colors. Collectively, they create the semblance of noonday sun; individually and separately, they create moods that range from cheerful to pensive, depending (in theory) on an occupant's mood. Two suites have small swimming pools on their private outdoor terraces.

13 bd. du Temple, Paris 75003. ✆ **01-42-71-20-00.** Fax 01-42-71-21-01. www.muranoresort.com. 52 units. 400€–650€ ($520–$845) double; from 750€ ($975) suite. AE, DC, MC, V. Métro: Filles du Calvaire. **Amenities:** Restaurant; bar; fitness center; spa; Jacuzzi; car-rental facilities; room service; nonsmoking rooms; photo service; limited-mobility rooms. *In room:* A/C, TV, hair dryer, safe.

INEXPENSIVE

Hôtel des Chevaliers Half a block from the place des Vosges, this hotel occupies a corner building whose 17th-century vestiges have been elevated into high art. These include the remnants of a well in the cellar, a stone barrel vault covering the breakfast area, and Louis XIII accessories that'll remind you of the hotel's origins. Each guest room is comfortable and well maintained, and all bathrooms come with both tub and shower. Units on the top floor have exposed ceiling beams. Some are larger than others, with an extra bed making them suitable for those traveling with a child or for three people on the road together.

30 rue de Turenne, Paris 75003. ✆ **01-42-72-73-47.** Fax 01-42-72-54-10. www.chevaliers-paris-hotel.com. 24 units. 150€ ($195) double; 165€ ($215) triple. AE, MC, V. Métro: Chemin Vert or St-Paul. **Amenities:** Bar; laundry service; dry cleaning. *In room:* A/C, TV, minibar, hair dryer, safe.

Hôtel Saintonge ★ *Finds* Its rooms are small, but this hotel has a coziness that you may appreciate, especially if you're attracted to beamed ceilings, patches of exposed masonry, and charmingly claustrophobic hallways. It rises seven stories above a quiet neighborhood in the Marais, one of many 17th-century private houses that are now hotels or apartments. Breakfast is served beneath the vaulted ceiling of what used to be a cellar-level storage area; the lobby boasts hand-hewn beams and a tile floor. Most guest rooms have tall windows; units on the uppermost floor have angled ceilings that evoke an artist's studio in a garret. Most of the tiled bathrooms hold only a shower, no bathtub.

16 rue Saintonge, Paris 75003. ✆ **01-42-77-91-13.** Fax 01-48-87-76-41. 23 units. 115€ ($150) double; 170€ ($221) suite. AE, DC, MC, V. Métro: Filles du Calvaire or République. **Amenities:** Room service; babysitting; laundry service; dry cleaning; nonsmoking rooms; limited-mobility rooms. *In room:* TV, minibar, hair dryer, safe.

RIGHT BANK: 9TH ARRONDISSEMENT (OPERA GARNIER/PIGALLE)

EXPENSIVE

Hotel Amour The dramatic transformation of what had previously been a somewhat nondescript hotel brought it into sync with the increasingly hip neighborhood, just off the rue des Martyrs, which contains it. It's the kind of hotel that services the needs of suburbanites looking for lodgings in the town center on a weekend, or young business travelers looking for a buzz in the lobby even before replicating a buzz in their bedroom upstairs. And in this case, there's a lot to be entertained and amused by within a venue that the "nouveau chic" has deemed worth hanging out in. Bedrooms are each outfitted with a very comfortable mattress—they come from the same company that supplies the (much more expensive) Hôtel Ritz—and no TV and no telephone. Each of the decors varies widely, including some with a minimalist white-on-white decor with touches of *faux* baroque; others with works by graffiti artists applied directly to the walls. Overall, the place has an oddball charm that's generating a lot of press in Paris these days.

8 rue Navarin, Paris 75009. ✆ **01-48-78-31-80.** www.hotelamour.com. 20 units. 90€–190€ ($117–$247) double. AE, MC, V. Metro: St-Georges. **Amenities:** Restaurant; bar; room service. *In room:* A/C, minibar, Wi-Fi, no phone.

RIGHT BANK: 4TH ARRONDISSEMENT (ILE DE LA CITE/ ILE ST-LOUIS & BEAUBOURG)

EXPENSIVE

Hôtel Bourg Tibourg ★ *Finds* Don't come here expecting large rooms with lots of elbowroom: What you get is a sophisticated and supercharged color palette, a sense of high-profile design, and a deliberately cluttered venue that looks like an Edwardian town house as decorated by an obsessive-compulsive on psychedelic hallucinogens. It is set behind an uncomplicated, cream-colored facade in the Marais and marked only with a discreet brass plaque and a pair of carriage lamps. Its rooms were radically overhauled by superstar decorator Jacques Garcia. Bedrooms are genuinely tiny but rich with neo-romantic, neo-Gothic, and, in some cases, neo-Venetian swirls and curlicues. Each is quirky, idiosyncratic, richly upholstered, and supercharged with tassels, faux leopard skin, and lavish window treatments.

19 rue du Bourg-Tibourg, Paris 75004. ✆ **01-42-78-47-39.** Fax 01-40-29-07-00. www.hotelbourgtibourg.com. 30 units. 220€–250€ ($286–$325) double; 350€ ($455) suite. Parking 26€ ($34). AE, DC, MC, V. Métro: Hôtel de Ville. **Amenities:** Room service; laundry service. *In room:* A/C, TV, minibar, hair dryer, safe.

Hôtel du Jeu de Paume ★ This small-scale hotel encompasses a pair of 17th-century town houses accessible through a timbered passageway from the street outside. The rooms are a bit larger than those of some nearby competitors. Originally, the hotel was a clubhouse used by members of the court of Louis XIII, who amused themselves with *les jeux de paume* (an early form of tennis) nearby. Public areas are outfitted in a simple version of Art Deco. Guest rooms are freshly decorated in sleek contemporary style, with elegant materials such as oaken floors, and fine craftsmanship. Some have wood-beamed ceilings. All contain well-maintained bathrooms with tub/shower combinations. The most luxurious units are the five duplexes and two junior suites, each individually decorated and opening onto an indoor courtyard.

54 rue St-Louis en l'Ile, Paris 75004. ✆ **01-43-26-14-18.** Fax 01-40-46-02-76. www.jeudepaumehotel.com. 30 units. 230€–335€ ($299–$436) double; 395€–545€ ($514–$709) suite. AE, DC, MC, V. Métro: Pont Marie. **Amenities:** Bar; gym; sauna; room service; babysitting; laundry service; dry cleaning. *In room:* TV, minibar, hair dryer, safe.

Hôtel Saint-Louis ★ *Value* Proprietors Guy and Andrée Record maintain a charming family atmosphere at this antiques-filled hotel in a 17th-century town house. The hotel represents an incredible value considering its prime location on Ile St-Louis. Expect cozy, slightly cramped rooms, each with a small bathroom containing a tub/shower combination. With mansard roofs and old-fashioned moldings, the top-floor units sport tiny balconies that afford sweeping views. The breakfast room is in the cellar, which has 17th-century stone vaulting.

75 rue St-Louis-en-l'Ile, Paris 75004. ✆ **01-46-34-04-80.** Fax 01-46-34-02-13. 19 units. 140€–220€ ($182–$286) double. MC, V. Métro: Pont Marie or St-Michel-Notre-Dame. **Amenities:** Babysitting. *In room:* TV, hair dryer, safe.

MODERATE

Hôtel de Lutèce This hotel feels like a country house in Brittany. The lounge, with its old fireplace, is furnished with contemporary paintings and antiques, which also fill each guest room. Each unit comes with either tub or shower. The suites, though larger than the doubles, are often like doubles with extended sitting areas. Each is tastefully furnished, with an antique or two. The hotel is comparable in style and amenities to the Deux-Iles (see below), which is under the same ownership.

65 rue St-Louis-en-l'Ile, Paris 75004. ✆ **01-43-26-23-52.** Fax 01-43-29-60-25. www.paris-hotel-lutece.com. 23 units. 185€ ($241) double; 205€ ($267) triple. AE, MC, V. Métro: Pont Marie or Cité. **Amenities:** Laundry service; dry cleaning. *In room:* A/C, TV, hair dryer, safe.

Hôtel des Deux-Iles ★ This is an unpretentious but charming choice in a great location. In a restored 18th-century town house, the hotel has elaborate decor, with bamboo and reed furniture and French Provincial touches. The guest rooms are on the small side, but the beds are very comfortable and the bathrooms well maintained, with tubs or shower units. A garden off the lobby leads to a basement breakfast room, which has a fireplace.

59 rue St-Louis-en-l'Ile, Paris 75004. ✆ **01-43-26-13-35.** Fax 01-43-29-60-25. www.deuxiles-paris-hotel.com. 17 units. 170€ ($221) double. AE, MC, V. Métro: Pont Marie. **Amenities:** Room service; laundry service; dry cleaning; nonsmoking rooms. *In room:* A/C, TV, hair dryer, safe.

Hôtel Saint-Merry ★ *Finds* The rebirth of this once-notorious brothel as a charming, upscale hotel is an example of the area's gentrification. It contains only a dozen rooms, each relatively small, but accented with neo-Gothic detail, exposed stone, 18th-century ceiling beams, and lots of quirky architecture. Suites, much larger than doubles, have upgraded furnishings. All units contain tiled bathrooms with showers or tubs; some have a TV and a minibar. According to the staff, the clientele here is about 50% gay males; the other half is straight and involved in the arts scene in the surrounding neighborhood. Before it became a bordello, it was conceived as the presbytery of the nearby Church of Saint-Merry.

78 rue de la Verrerie, Paris 75004. ✆ **01-42-78-14-15.** Fax 01-40-29-06-82. 12 units. 160€–230€ ($208–$299) double; 335€–400€ ($436–$520) suite. AE, MC, V. Métro: Hôtel de Ville or Châtelet. **Amenities:** Room service; babysitting; laundry service; dry cleaning. *In room:* TV (in some), minibar (in some), hair dryer, safe.

INEXPENSIVE

Hôtel de la Place des Vosges ★ *Value* Built about 350 years ago, during the same era as the majestic square it's named for (a 2-min. walk away), this is a well-managed, small-scale property with reasonable prices and lots of charm. The structure was once used as a stable for the mules of Henri IV. Many of the small guest rooms have beamed ceilings, tiled bathrooms (with tub or shower), small TVs hanging from the ceiling, and a sense of cozy, well-ordered efficiency. The most desirable and expensive of the accommodations is the top-floor room no. 60, overlooking the rooftops of Paris, with a luxurious private bathroom.

12 rue de Birague, Paris 75004. ✆ **01-42-72-60-46.** Fax 01-42-72-02-64. 16 units. 120€–140€ ($156–$182) double. AE, DC, MC, V. Métro: Bastille. **Amenities:** Room service; nonsmoking rooms. *In room:* TV, hair dryer, safe.

Hôtel du 7e Art The hotel occupies one of many 17th-century buildings in this neighborhood classified as historic monuments. Don't expect grand luxury: Rooms are cramped and outfitted with the simplest furniture, relieved by 1950s-era movie posters. Each has white walls, and some—including those under the sloping mansard-style roof—have exposed ceiling beams. All have small bathrooms with either a tub or shower. The five-story building has a lobby bar and a breakfast room, but no elevator. The "7th Art" is a reference to filmmaking.

20 rue St-Paul, Paris 75004. ✆ **01-44-54-85-00.** Fax 01-42-77-69-10. 23 units. 85€–145€ ($111–$189) double. AE, DC, MC, V. Métro: St-Paul. **Amenities:** Bar; coin-operated laundry. *In room:* A/C, TV, hair dryer, safe.

RIGHT BANK: 8TH ARRONDISSEMENT (CHAMPS-ELYSEES/MADELEINE)

VERY EXPENSIVE

Four Seasons Hotel George V ★★★ The George V's history is as gilt-edged as they come. It opened in 1928 in honor of George V of England. During the liberation of Paris, it housed Dwight D. Eisenhower. In its latest incarnation, with all its glitz and glamour, the hotel is one of the best in the world. After its acquisition by Saudi Prince Al Waleed and a 2-year renovation, it reopened under the banner of Toronto-based Four Seasons. The guest rooms are about as close as you'll come to residency in a well-upholstered private home on which teams of decorators have lavished vast amounts of attention and money. The beds rival those at the Ritz and Meurice in comfort. The 245 units come in three sizes. The largest are magnificent; the smallest are, in the words of a spokesperson, *"très agreeable."* Each unit has a large bathroom with a shower and tub. Security is tight—a fact appreciated by sometimes-notorious guests.

31 av. George V, Paris 75008. ✆ **800/332-3442** in the U.S. and Canada, or 01-49-52-70-00. Fax 01-49-52-70-10. www.fourseasons.com. 245 units. 710€–910€ ($923–$1,183) double; 1,350€ ($1,755) suite. Parking 40€ ($52). AE, DC, MC, V. Métro: George V. **Amenities:** 2 restaurants; 2 lounges; indoor pool; fitness center; spa; sauna; room service; massage; babysitting; laundry service; dry cleaning; nonsmoking rooms; limited-mobility rooms. *In room:* A/C, TV, minibar, hair dryer, safe.

EXPENSIVE

Hôtel de la Trémoille ★ In the heart of Paris and a 2-minute walk from the Champs-Elysées, this Right Bank address is preferred by fashionistas as it lies in the heart of the haute couture district. Built in the 19th century, the hotel opened again in 2002 following a $23-million renovation that returned the swank address to much of its original elegance and charm. It blends modern and traditional styles. Originally a private residence, the hotel is outfitted in a Louis XV style, all in woodwork and tapestries. In the old days, you might have encountered General de Gaulle or Orson Welles. Today Johnny Depp is a regular visitor. Rooms are cozy and comfortable, each decorated in harmonies of tawny, ocher, gray, and white, with much use of silks, synthetic furs, and mohair. Bathrooms, done in elegant gray-and-black marble, contain tubs and showers.

14 rue de la Trémoille, Paris 75008. ✆ **01-56-52-14-00.** Fax 01-40-70-01-08. www.hotel-tremoille.com. 93 units. 420€–575€ ($546–$748) double; from 625€ ($813) suite. AE, DC, MC, V. Métro: Alma-Marceau. **Amenities:** Restaurant; bar; fitness center; sauna; room service; laundry service; dry cleaning. *In room:* A/C, TV, minibar, hair dryer, safe.

Hôtel Pershing Hall ★★★ On a hyperstylish street that parallels the avenue Montaigne, this hotel was created when one of France's most celebrated modern designers, Andrée Putnam, radically altered a late-19th-century town house. She had fascinating raw materials: The five-story town house was built in 1890 by the *comte* de Paris, the heir apparent to the French monarchy, as a home for his mistress. During World War I, it was the Paris headquarters of U.S. Gen. John Pershing. The warm, artfully spartan interior reflects the rectilinear style favored by the woman who designed the original decor of Air France's Concorde. Putnam employed quarried stone, tile, mosaics, and hardwoods; a subtle color scheme of warm beiges and grays; bead curtains; bathtubs with claw-and-ball feet; and comfortable, subtly contemporary furniture. Accommodations at the nearby George V are slightly larger, but rooms here have a serene simplicity that contrasts with those competitors' grand style.

49 rue Pierre Charron, Paris 75008. ✆ **01-58-36-58-00.** Fax 01-58-36-58-01. www.pershing-hall.com. 26 units. 420€–500€ ($546–$650) double; 720€–1,000€ ($936–$1,300) suite. AE, DC, MC, V. Métro: George V. **Amenities:** Restaurant; bar; gym; spa; sauna; babysitting; laundry service; dry cleaning; nonsmoking rooms; limited-mobility rooms. *In room:* A/C, TV, minibar, hair dryer, safe.

Sofitel Le Faubourg Cozy, well-upholstered, and businesslike, this hotel in the heart of Paris was created by linking two buildings dating from the 18th and 19th centuries. Celebrity guests such as David Bowie seem to appreciate its low-key but high-quality accommodations and the personalized service. It's decorated throughout with a mixture of modern and traditional French styles, with feng shui touches. Rooms come in various sizes but are comfortable, quiet, and of a decent size, even the short-stay one-person rooms, which, though small, are not claustrophobic. If you want a specific feature—a balcony, a view, high ceilings—inquire about it when booking.

15 rue Boissy d'Anglais, Paris 75008. ✆ **800/SOFITEL** or 01-44-94-14-14. Fax 01-44-94-14-28. www.sofitel.com. 174 units. 465€–558€ ($605–$725) double; from 995€ ($1,294) suite. AE, DC, MC, V. Parking 29€ ($38). Métro: Concorde. **Amenities:** Restaurant; bar; fitness center; *hammam* (steam bath); business center; room service; laundry service; dry cleaning; nonsmoking rooms; limited-mobility rooms. *In room:* A/C, TV, minibar, hair dryer, safe.

MODERATE

Hôtel du Ministère ★ The Ministère is a winning choice near the Champs-Elysées, though it's far from Paris's cheapest budget hotel. The guest rooms are on the small side, but they are comfortable and well maintained; many have oak beams and fine furnishings. Try to avoid rooms on the top floor, which are too cramped. Each unit's bathroom holds a tub/shower combo. Junior suites are only slightly larger than regular doubles, but the extra space may be worth it.

31 rue de Surène, Paris 75008. ✆ **01-42-66-21-43.** Fax 01-42-66-96-04. www.ministerehotel.com. 28 units. 179€–209€ ($233–$272) double. AE, MC, V. Métro: Madeleine. **Amenities:** Bar; room service; laundry service; dry cleaning; nonsmoking rooms. *In room:* A/C, TV, minibar, hair dryer, safe.

Hôtel Galileo ★ *Finds* This is one of the 8th's most charming hotels. Proprietors Roland and Elisabeth Buffat have won friends from all over with their Hôtel des Deux-Iles and Hôtel de Lutèce on St-Louis-en-l'Ile (see above). A short walk from the Champs-Elysées, the town house is the epitome of French elegance and charm. The medium-size rooms are a study in understated taste. Beautifully kept bathrooms hold a tub or shower. The most spacious rooms are nos. 103, 203, 303, 403, and 503, with a glass-covered veranda you can use even in winter. For this neighborhood, the prices are moderate.

54 rue Galilée, Paris 75008. ✆ **01-47-20-66-06.** Fax 01-47-20-67-17. www.galileo-paris-hotel.com. 27 units. 174€ ($226) double. AE, DC, MC, V. Parking 23€ ($30). Métro: Charles-de-Gaulle–Etoile or George V. **Amenities:** Laundry service; dry cleaning; limited-mobility room. *In room:* A/C, TV, minibar, hair dryer, safe.

Hôtel Queen Mary ★ Meticulously renovated inside and out, this early-1900s hotel has an iron-and-glass canopy, wrought iron, and the kind of detailing normally reserved for more expensive hotels. The public rooms have touches of greenery and reproductions of antiques; guest rooms contain upholstered headboards, comfortable beds, and mahogany furnishings, plus a carafe of sherry. All units are renovated, and most come with a tub/shower combination (six have showers only). Suites and triples are slightly more spacious than regular doubles and are beautifully furnished.

9 rue Greffulhe, Paris 75008. ✆ **01-42-66-40-50.** Fax 01-42-66-94-92. www.hotelqueenmary.com. 36 units. 189€–219€ ($246–$285) double; 299€ ($389) triple. AE, DC, MC, V. Métro: Madeleine or Havre-Caumartin. **Amenities:** Bar; room service; limited-mobility rooms. *In room:* A/C, TV, minibar, hair dryer, safe.

Résidence Lord Byron *Kids* Off the Champs-Elysées on a curving street of handsome buildings, the Lord Byron may not be as grand as other hotels in the neighborhood, but it's more affordable. Unassuming and a bit staid, it offers exactly what repeat guests want: a sense of luxury, solitude, and understatement. Beds are old-fashioned, and bathrooms are well kept; most have shower units. It's a fine choice for families, who often book suites for the larger living space. You can eat breakfast in the dining room or in the shaded inner garden.

5 rue Chateaubriand, Paris 75008. ✆ **01-43-59-89-98.** Fax 01-42-89-46-04. www.escapade-paris.com. 31 units. 175€–195€ ($228–$254) double; 265€ ($345) suite. AE, DC, MC, V. Parking 20€ ($26). Métro: George V. RER: Etoile. **Amenities:** Room service; babysitting; laundry service; dry cleaning. *In room:* A/C, TV, minibar, hair dryer, safe.

RIGHT BANK: 16TH ARRONDISSEMENT (TROCADERO/BOIS DE BOULOGNE)

EXPENSIVE

Sofitel Trocadéro Dokhan's ★★ If not for the porters walking through its public areas carrying luggage, you might suspect that this well-accessorized hotel was a private home. It's in a stately 19th-century Haussmann-style building vaguely inspired by Palladio and contains accessories such as antique paneling, Regency-era armchairs, and chandeliers. Each guest room has a different decorative style, with antiques or good reproductions, lots of personalized touches, triple-glazed windows, and beautifully maintained bathrooms with tubs. Beds are often antique reproductions with maximum comfort. Suites have larger living space and spacious bathrooms with such extras as makeup mirrors and luxe toiletries.

117 rue Lauriston, Paris 75116. ✆ **01-53-65-66-99.** Fax 01-53-65-66-88. www.sofitel.com. 45 units. 220€–450€ ($286–$585) double; from 850€ ($1,105) suite. AE, DC, MC, V. Parking 30€ ($39). Métro: Trocadéro. **Amenities:** Champagne bar; room service; massage; babysitting; laundry service; dry cleaning; nonsmoking rooms. *In room:* A/C, TV, fax, minibar, hair dryer, safe.

INEXPENSIVE

Au Palais de Chaillot Hôtel When Thierry and Cyrille Pien, brothers trained in the States, opened this hotel, budget travelers flocked here. Located between the Champs-Elysées and Trocadéro, the town house was restored from top to bottom, and the result is a contemporary yet informal variation on Parisian chic. The guest rooms come in various shapes and sizes and are furnished with a light touch, with bright colors and wicker. Room nos. 61, 62, and 63 afford partial views of the Eiffel Tower. Each room comes with a neatly tiled, shower-only bathroom (tubs in junior suites).

35 av. Raymond-Poincaré, Paris 75016. ✆ **01-53-70-09-09.** Fax 01-53-70-09-08. www.chaillotel.com. 28 units. 125€–145€ ($163–$189) double; 170€ ($221) junior suite; 20€ ($26) extra bed. AE, DC, MC, V. Métro: Victor Hugo or Trocadéro. **Amenities:** Room service; laundry service. *In room:* A/C, TV, hair dryer, safe.

RIGHT BANK: 18TH ARRONDISSEMENT (MONTMARTRE)

EXPENSIVE

Kube Rooms & Bars ★ *Finds* It's relatively new, it's comfortable, it's being talked about within trendy circles of Paris, and it manages to combine its lodgings with a youth-obsessed dance club sensibility. Design-savvy clients usually appreciate the way the architect (in-the-news Raymond Morel) made repeated use of the cube, a form that the owners refer to as "the most modern of shapes." The hotel occupies the six-story premises of what was built in the late 1800s as the administrative headquarters of a now-defunct brewery *(Les bières de la Meuse).* There's a restaurant and a dance lounge on the street level, where a DJ spins tunes most evenings from a mezzanine that looks down on the dance floor of hard-partying 20-somethings.

Bedrooms (and everything else about the place) seem to revel in the concept of the cube as a newly re-conceived decorative device. Rectangular beds are lit from below and appear to float. Expect shag-covered sofas, fuzzy faux-fur slippers in tones of high-voltage yellow, and a sense of compact efficiency that, despite the minimalist angularity and self-conscious sense of "design," is hard to ignore. Instead of room keys, guests are electronically fingerprinted. On the premises is the Ice Kube Bar, a conversational oddity whose bartop is fashioned from—you guessed it—ice. For a per-person price of 38€ ($49), clients pre-reserve a 30-minute block of time within the deep freeze, receive a lecture on the odder natures of the place from a bundled-up staff, are assigned thermally insulated parkas, and are offered as much vodka, served within goblets fashioned from ice, as they can drink within the pre-assigned 30-minute block.

3–5 Passage Ruelle, Paris 75018. ✆ **01-42-05-20-00.** Fax 01-42-05-21-01. www.kubehotel.com. 41 units. 300€–350€ ($390–$455) double; 400€–750€ ($520–$975) suite. AE, DC, MC, V. Parking 30€ ($39). Metro: La Chapelle. **Amenities:** Restaurant; bar/lounge with a DJ several nights a week; fitness center; laundry service/dry cleaning. *In room:* A/C, TV, safe, hair dryer, Wi-Fi.

LEFT BANK: 5TH ARRONDISSEMENT (LATIN QUARTER)

MODERATE

Grand Hôtel Saint-Michel Built in the 19th century, this hotel is larger and more businesslike than many town house–style inns nearby. It basks in the reflected glow of Brazilian dissident Georges Amado, whose memoirs recorded his 2-year sojourn in one of the rooms. The hotel completed a renovation and moved from government-rated two- to three-star status, and continues to renovate on a regular basis. The public areas are tasteful, with portraits and rich upholsteries. All but four rooms have tub/shower combinations. The improvements enlarged some rooms, lowering their ceilings and adding amenities, but retained old-fashioned touches such as wrought-iron balconies (on the fifth floor). Triple rooms have an extra bed and are suitable for families. Others have only shower, toilet, and sink. Sixth-floor rooms offer views over the rooftops.

19 rue Cujas, Paris 75005. ✆ **01-46-33-33-02.** Fax 01-40-46-96-33. 45 units. 170€ ($221) double; 220€ ($286) triple. AE, DC, MC, V. Métro: Cluny–La Sorbonne. RER: Luxembourg or St-Michel. **Amenities:** Bar; room service; babysitting; laundry service; dry cleaning; limited-mobility rooms. *In room:* A/C, TV, minibar, hair dryer, safe.

Hôtel Abbatial Saint-Germain The origins of this hotel run deep: Interior renovations have revealed such 17th-century touches as dovecotes and oak beams. A restoration made the public areas appealing and brought the small guest rooms, furnished in faux Louis XVI, up to modern standards. Rooms were again restored in 2005. All the beds are fitted with immaculate linens. All windows are double-glazed, and the fifth- and sixth-floor units enjoy views over Notre-Dame. The neatly kept bathrooms are equipped with showers.

46 bd. St-Germain, Paris 75005. ✆ **01-46-34-02-12.** Fax 01-43-25-47-73. www.abbatial.com. 43 units. 145€–189€ ($189–$246) double. AE, MC, V. Parking 19€ ($25). Métro: Cluny–La Sorbonne. **Amenities:** Room service; babysitting; nonsmoking rooms. *In room:* A/C, TV, minibar, hair dryer, safe.

INEXPENSIVE

Familia-Hôtel This hotel has been family-run for decades. Many personal touches make the place unique. Finely executed sepia-colored frescoes of Parisian scenes grace the walls of 14 rooms. Eight units have restored stone walls, and seven boast balconies with delightful views over the Quartier Latin. Half of the bathrooms come with tubs as well as showers. The dynamic owners renovate the rooms as often as needed to maintain a high level of comfort.

11 rue des Ecoles, 5 Paris 7500. ✆ **01-43-54-55-27.** Fax 01-43-29-61-77. www.hotel-paris-familia.com. 30 units. 97€–127€ ($126–$165) double; 154€ ($200) triple; 176€ ($229) quadruple. Parking 20€ ($26). AE, DC, MC, V. Métro: Jussieu or Maubert-Mutualité. **Amenities:** Car rental; nonsmoking rooms. *In room:* TV, minibar, hair dryer.

Hôtel le Home Latin *Value* This mansard-roofed hotel, one of Paris's most famous budget hotels, has been known since the 1970s for its simple lodgings. The functional rooms are renovated; some have small balconies overlooking the street. Those facing the courtyard are quieter than those on the street. The elevator only goes to the fifth floor, but to make up for the stair climb, the sixth floor's *chambres mansardées* offer a romantic location under the eaves and panoramic views.

15–17 rue du Sommerard, Paris 75005. ✆ **01-43-26-25-21.** Fax 01-43-29-87-04. www.homelatinhotel.com. 54 units. 106€ ($138) double; 127€ ($165) triple. AE, DC, MC, V. Métro: St-Michel or Maubert-Mutualité. *In room:* TV, hair dryer.

Hôtel Moderne Saint-Germain ★ In the heart of the Quartier Latin, between the Pantheon and St-Michel, the Hôtel Moderne is better than ever since it ended the 20th century with a complete overhaul. Though the rooms are small, this is one of the neighborhood's better government-rated three-star hotels. Its charming owner, Mme Gibon, maintains spotless accommodations. In the units fronting rue des Ecoles, double-glazed windows hush the traffic. About half of the bathrooms have a tub as well as a shower. Guests can use the sauna and Jacuzzi at the Hôtel Sully next door.

33 rue des Ecoles, Paris 75005. ✆ **01-43-54-37-78.** Fax 01-43-29-91-31. www.hotel-paris-stgermain.com. 45 units. 150€ ($195) double; 180€ ($234) triple. AE, DC, MC, V. Parking 26€ ($34). Métro: Maubert-Mutualité. **Amenities:** Fitness center; room service; laundry service; dry cleaning; nonsmoking rooms. *In room:* A/C, TV, hair dryer.

Hôtel Saint-Christophe This hotel, in one of the Quartier Latin's undiscovered areas, offers a gracious English-speaking staff. It was created in 1987 when an older hotel was connected to a butcher shop. All the small- to medium-size rooms are renovated, with Louis XV–style furniture and carpeting.

17 rue Lacépède, Paris 75005. ✆ **01-43-31-81-54.** Fax 01-43-31-12-54. www.charm-hotel-paris.com. 31 units. 110€–150€ ($143–$195) double. AE, DC, MC, V. Métro: Place Monge. **Amenities:** Nonsmoking rooms. *In room:* TV, minibar, hair dryer.

LEFT BANK: 6TH ARRONDISSEMENT (ST-GERMAIN/LUXEMBOURG)

VERY EXPENSIVE

L'Hôtel ★ Ranking just a notch below the Relais Christine (see below), this is one of the Left Bank's most charming boutique hotels. Once a 19th-century fleabag, its previous distinction was that Oscar Wilde died in one of its bedrooms. In 2006, superstar aesthete Jacques Garcia redecorated the hotel, retaining its Victorian-baroque sense. Guest rooms vary in size, style, and price; all have nonworking fireplaces and fabric-covered walls. All the sumptuous beds have tasteful fabrics and crisp linens. About half the bathrooms are small, tubless nooks. Room themes reflect China, Russia, Japan, India, or high-camp Victorian. The Cardinal room is all scarlet, the Viollet-le-Duc room is neo-Gothic, and the room where Wilde died is Victorian. The cellar holds a small swimming pool and *hammam* (steam bath).

13 rue des Beaux-Arts, Paris 75006. ✆ **01-44-41-99-00.** Fax 01-43-25-64-81. www.l-hotel.com. 20 units. 255€–740€ ($332–$962) double; 640€–740€ ($832–$962) suite. AE, DC, MC, V. Métro: St-Germain-des-Prés. **Amenities:** Restaurant; bar; indoor pool; steam room; room service; babysitting; laundry service; dry cleaning. *In room:* A/C, TV, minibar, hair dryer, safe.

Relais Christine ★★ This hotel is in a former 16th-century Augustinian cloister. From a cobblestone street, you enter a symmetrical courtyard and find an elegant reception area with sculpture and Renaissance antiques. Each room is uniquely decorated with wood beams and Louis XIII-style furnishings; the rooms come in a range of styles and shapes. Some are among the Left Bank's largest, with extras such as mirrored closets, plush carpets, thermostats, and some balconies facing the courtyard. The least attractive rooms are in the interior. Bed configurations vary, but all mattresses are on the soft

Where to Stay on the Left Bank

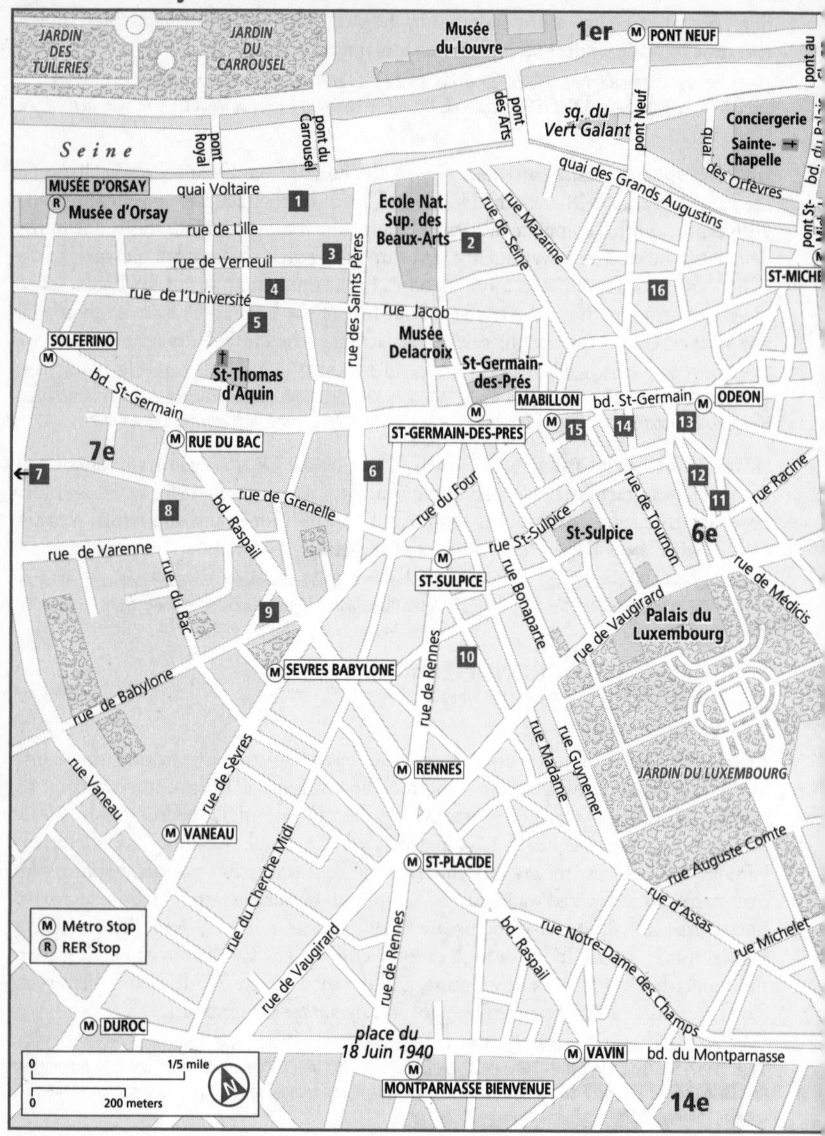

side, offering comfort with quality linens. Each unit comes with a tub and shower. Since 2003, at least four, and usually five, of the rooms have been renovated each year.

3 rue Christine, Paris 75006. ✆ **01-40-51-60-80.** Fax 01-40-51-60-81. www.relais-christine.com. 51 units. 335€–450€ ($436–$585) double; 530€–750€ ($689–$975) duplex or suite. AE, DC, MC, V. Free parking. Métro: Odéon or St-Michel. **Amenities:** Bar; gym; room service; massage; babysitting; laundry service; dry cleaning; nonsmoking rooms. *In room:* A/C, TV, minibar, hair dryer, safe.

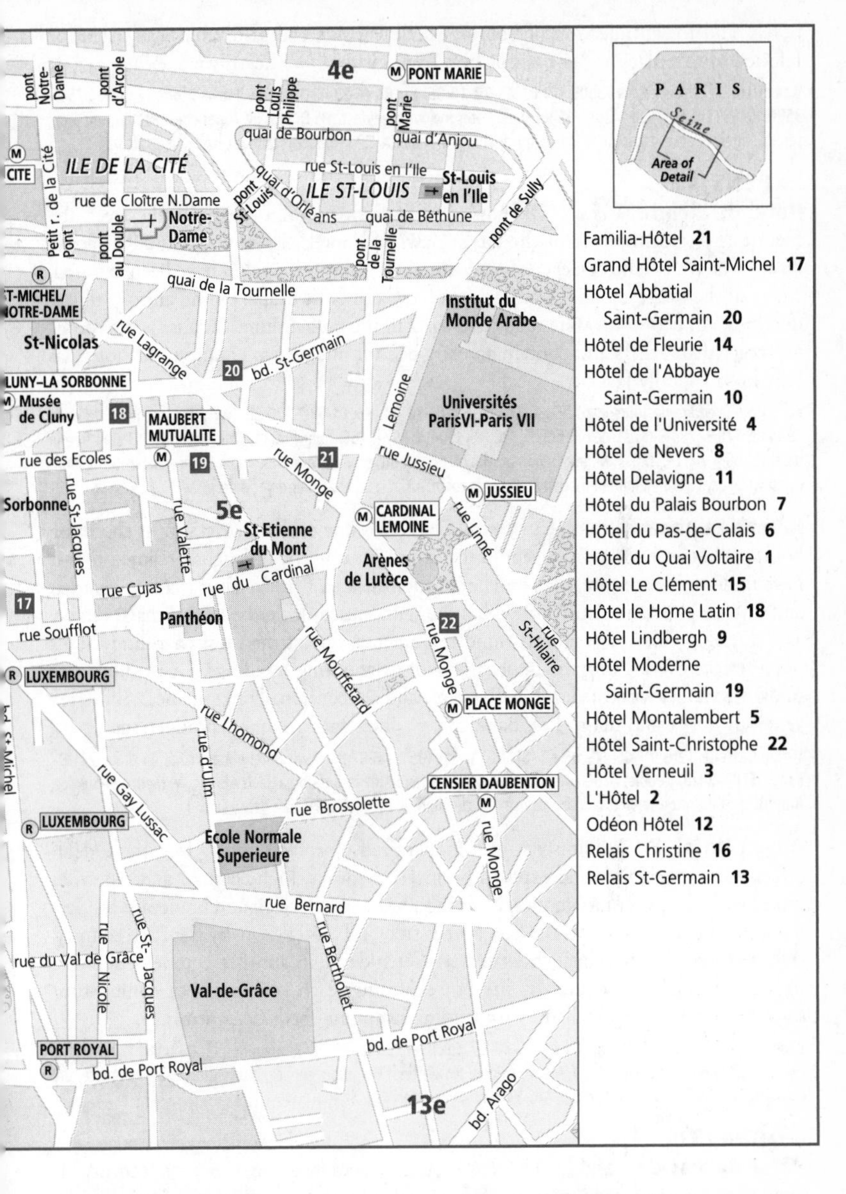

Relais St-Germain ★★ It's difficult to exaggerate the charm of this deeply personalized and intimate hotel created from side-by-side 17th-century town houses. You'll navigate your way through a labyrinth of narrow and winding hallways to soundproof bedrooms that are spacious and artfully and individually decorated in a style that evokes late-19th-century Paris at its most sensual. Two of the rooms have outdoor terraces. Come here for a discreet escape from the anonymity of larger, less personalized hotels, and for an injection of boutique-style Parisian charm. Even *Vogue* magazine referred to this place as "an oasis of Left-Bank charm." We heartily agree.

9 carrefour de l'Odéon, Paris 75006. ✆ **01-43-29-12-05.** Fax 01-46-33-45-30. www.hotelrsg.com. 22 units. 275€–360€ ($358–$468) double; 420€ ($546) suite. Rates include breakfast. AE, DC, MC, V. **Amenities:** Restaurant; room service; Internet access; laundry service; dry cleaning. *In room:* A/C, TV, dataport minibar, hair dryer, safe.

EXPENSIVE

Hôtel de Fleurie ★ *Kids* Off boulevard St-Germain on a colorful little street, the Fleurie is one of the best of the city's "new" old hotels; its statuary-studded facade recaptures 17th-century elegance, and the stone walls in the salon have been exposed. Many of the well-maintained guest rooms have elaborate draperies and antique reproductions. All bedrooms were renovated early in the millennium. Because some rooms are larger than others and contain an extra bed for one or two children, the hotel has long been a family favorite.

32–34 rue Grégoire-de-Tours, Paris 75006. ✆ **01-53-73-70-00.** Fax 01-53-73-70-20. www.fleurie-hotel-paris.com. 29 units. 170€–280€ ($221–$364) double; 305€–350€ ($397–$455) family room. Children under 13 stay free in parent's room. AE, DC, MC, V. Métro: Odéon or Mabillon. **Amenities:** Bar; car rental; room service; babysitting; laundry service; dry cleaning; limited-mobility rooms. *In room:* A/C, TV, minibar, hair dryer, safe.

Hôtel de l'Abbaye Saint-Germain ★ This is one of the district's most charming boutique hotels, built as a convent in the early 18th century. Its brightly colored rooms have traditional furniture, plus touches of sophisticated flair. In front is a small garden and in back a verdant courtyard with a fountain, raised flower beds, and masses of ivy and climbing vines. If you don't mind the expense, one of the most charming rooms has a terrace overlooking the upper floors of neighboring buildings. Guest rooms are midsize to large, with tiled, full bathrooms, and are continually maintained. Suites are generous in size and full of Left Bank charm, often with antique reproductions.

10 rue Cassette, Paris 75006. ✆ **01-45-44-38-11.** Fax 01-45-48-07-86. www.hotel-abbaye.com. 44 units. 221€–330€ ($287–$429) double; 410€–462€ ($533–$601) suite. Rates include breakfast. AE, MC, V. Métro: St-Sulpice. **Amenities:** Bar; room service; laundry service; dry cleaning. *In room:* A/C, TV, hair dryer, safe.

Odéon Hôtel ★ Reminiscent of a modernized Norman country inn, the Odéon offers rustic touches such as exposed beams, stone walls, high ceilings, and tapestries mixed with contemporary fabrics. Near the Théâtre de l'Odéon and boulevard St-Germain, the Odéon stands on the first paved street in Paris (1779). By the 20th century, this area began attracting such writers as Gertrude Stein and her coterie. The guest rooms are small to medium in size but charming; each comes with a combo tub/shower. The beds are excellent, with reading lamps and bedside controls.

3 rue de l'Odéon, Paris 75006. ✆ **01-43-25-90-67.** Fax 01-43-25-55-98. www.odeonhotel.fr. 33 units. 170€–270€ ($221–$351) double. AE, DC, MC, V. Métro: Odéon. **Amenities:** Bar; room service; babysitting; laundry service; dry cleaning; nonsmoking rooms. *In room:* A/C, TV, hair dryer, safe.

MODERATE

Hôtel du Pas-de-Calais The Pas-de-Calais goes back to the 17th century. It retains its elegant facade, with wooden doors leading to a "plant wall" gracing the lobby. Novelist Chateaubriand lived here in the early 1800s, but its most famous guest was Jean-Paul Sartre, who struggled with the play *Les Mains Sales* (Dirty Hands) in room no. 41. The hotel is a bit weak on style. Rooms are small; inner units surround a courtyard with two garden tables and several trellises. Each bathroom has a tub and shower.

59 rue des Sts-Pères, Paris 75006. ✆ **01-45-48-78-74.** Fax 01-45-44-94-57. www.hotelpasdecalais.com. 38 units. 160€–230€ ($208–$299) double; 300€ ($390) suite. AE, DC, MC, V. Parking 25€ ($33). Métro: St-Germain-des-Prés or Sèvres-Babylone. **Amenities:** Bar; room service; babysitting; laundry service; dry cleaning; nonsmoking rooms; limited-mobility rooms. *In room:* A/C, TV, hair dryer, safe.

INEXPENSIVE

Hôtel Delavigne Despite modernization, you still get a sense of the 18th-century origins of this building next to the Luxembourg Gardens. The public areas feature a rustic use of chiseled stone, some of it original. The high-ceilinged guest rooms are tasteful, often with upholstered headboards, sometimes with wood furniture, and sometimes with Spanish-style wrought iron.

1 rue Casimir-Delavigne, Paris 75006. ✆ **01-43-29-31-50.** Fax 01-43-29-78-56. www.hoteldelavigne.com. 34 units. 140€–155€ ($182–$202) double; 170€ ($221) triple. AE (accepted for Internet reservations only), MC, V. Métro: Odéon. **Amenities:** Room service; massage; babysitting; laundry service; dry cleaning. *In room:* TV, hair dryer, safe.

Hôtel Le Clément This hotel sits on a narrow street within sight of the towers of St-Sulpice church. The building dates to the 1700s and was renovated several years ago. Guest rooms are comfortably furnished but often small, although in 2000 some walls were knocked down, creating larger units.

6 rue Clément, Paris 75006. ✆ **01-43-26-53-60.** Fax 01-44-07-06-83. www.hotel-clement.com. 28 units. 117€–150€ ($152–$195) double; 145€–150€ ($189–$195) suite. AE, DC, MC, V. Métro: Mabillon. **Amenities:** Bar; room service. *In room:* A/C, TV, hair dryer, safe.

LEFT BANK: 7TH ARRONDISSEMENT (EIFFEL TOWER/MUSEE D'ORSAY)

VERY EXPENSIVE

Hôtel Montalembert ★★ Unusually elegant for the Left Bank, the Beaux Arts Montalembert dates from 1926. Its decor borrows elements of Bauhaus and postmodern design. Renovated in 2003, the guest rooms are spacious, except for some standard doubles that are small unless you're a very thin model. Frette linens decorate roomy beds topped with cabana-stripe duvets crowning deluxe French mattresses. The bathrooms are luxurious, with deep tubs, Cascais marble, and tall pivoting mirrors.

3 rue de Montalembert, Paris 75007. ✆ **800/786-6397** in the U.S. and Canada, or 01-45-49-68-68. Fax 01-45-49-69-49. www.montalembert.com. 56 units. 350€–450€ ($455–$585) double; 580€–800€ ($754–$1,040) suite. AE, DC, MC, V. Parking 39€ ($51). Métro: Rue du Bac. **Amenities:** Restaurant; bar; access to nearby health club; room service; laundry service; dry cleaning. *In room:* A/C, TV, minibar, hair dryer, safe.

MODERATE

Hôtel de l'Université ★ Long favored by well-heeled parents of North American students studying in Paris, this 300-year-old, antiques-filled and much-renovated town house sits in a discreetly upscale neighborhood. You'll sleep well here on comfortable beds. Each bathroom holds a tub/shower combination. Room no. 54 is a favorite, containing a rattan bed, period pieces, and a terrace. Another charmer is room no. 35, which has a nonworking fireplace and opens onto a courtyard with a fountain. In 2004, many of the bathrooms were renovated.

22 rue de l'Université, Paris 75007. ✆ **01-42-61-09-39.** Fax 01-42-60-40-84. www.hoteluniversite.com. 27 units. 165€–180€ ($215–$234) double. AE, DC, MC, V. Métro: St-Germain-des-Prés. **Amenities:** Room service. *In room:* A/C, TV, minibar, hair dryer, safe.

Hôtel Le Tourville ★ This well-managed, personalized hotel is in a 1930s town house between the Eiffel Tower and Les Invalides. Guest rooms hold original art, antique furnishings or reproductions, and wooden furniture with modern, sometimes bold, upholstery. Four rooms, including the suite, have private terraces. Beds are queen-size or twins. About half of the well-maintained bathrooms have tub/shower combinations, and most were renovated in 2004. The staff is well trained, with personalities that make you want to linger at the reception desk. Breakfast is the only meal served.

16 av. de Tourville, Paris 75007. ✆ **01-47-05-62-62.** Fax 01-47-05-43-90. www.hoteltourville.com. 30 units. 170€–250€ ($221–$325) double; 330€ ($429) suite. AE, MC, V. Métro: Ecole Militaire. **Amenities:** Bar; room service; laundry service; dry cleaning; nonsmoking rooms; limited-mobility rooms. *In room:* A/C, TV, hair dryer.

Hôtel Verneuil ★ *Finds* Small-scale and personal, this hotel, in the words of a critic, "combines modernist sympathies with nostalgia for *la vieille France.*" In a 17th-century town house, it offers a creative, intimate jumble of charm and coziness, with a mixture of antique and contemporary furniture. Guest rooms feature *trompe l'oeil* ceilings, antique beams, quilts, and fabric-covered walls.

8 rue de Verneuil, Paris 75007. ✆ **01-42-60-82-14.** Fax 01-42-61-40-38. www.hotelverneuil.com. 26 units. 155€–210€ ($202–$273) double. AE, DC, MC, V. Métro: St-Germain-des-Prés. **Amenities:** Bar; room service; babysitting; laundry service; dry cleaning. *In room:* A/C (in some), TV, minibar, hair dryer, safe.

INEXPENSIVE

Grand Hôtel L'Evêque Built in the 1930s, this hotel draws many English-speaking guests who appreciate its proximity to the Eiffel Tower. The pastel-colored guest rooms retain an Art Deco feel. They have just enough space to be comfortable, and their double-insulated windows overlook a courtyard in back or the street in front. Suites are only slightly larger double rooms and are no better than the standard. The small bathrooms contain shower units.

29 rue Cler, Paris 75007. ✆ **01-47-05-49-15.** Fax 01-45-50-49-36. www.hotel-leveque.com. 50 units. 90€–115€ ($117–$150) double; 130€ ($169) triple. AE, MC, V. Métro: Ecole Militaire. **Amenities:** Breakfast room. *In room:* A/C, TV, hair dryer, safe.

Hôtel de Londres Eiffel Small and charming, this independently run hotel is just a 2-minute walk from the Eiffel Tower. Completely renovated, it is "dressed" in colors of yellow and raspberry, which are far more harmonious and elegant than the combination sounds. In a residential district (one of the best in Paris), the bedrooms are midsize and tastefully decorated, each with an individual decoration. The top floors open onto views of the Eiffel Tower, which is illuminated at night. Bathrooms are small but well equipped, with either a tub or shower.

1 rue Augereau, Paris 75007. ✆ **01-45-51-63-02.** Fax 01-47-05-28-96. www.londres-eiffel.com. 30 units. 150€–165€ ($195–$215) double. AE, DC, MC. Metro: Ecole Militaire. Parking 34€ ($44). **Amenities:** Rooms for those w/limited mobility. *In room:* A/C, TV, minibar, hair dryer.

Hôtel de Nevers This is one of the neighborhood's historic choices—it was a convent from 1627 to 1790. The building is *classé,* meaning any restoration must respect the original architecture. That precludes an elevator, so you'll have to use the beautiful wrought-iron staircase. The cozy, pleasant guest rooms contain a mix of antique and reproduction furniture. Room nos. 10 and 11 are especially sought after for their terraces overlooking a corner of rue du Bac or a rear courtyard. About half of the units have tub/shower combinations in the bathrooms.

83 rue du Bac, Paris 75007. ✆ **01-45-44-61-30.** Fax 01-42-22-29-47. 11 units. 89€–99€ ($116–$129) double. MC, V. Métro: Rue du Bac. **Amenities:** Room service. *In room:* TV, minibar, hair dryer.

Hôtel du Palais Bourbon The stone walls of this 18th-century building aren't nearly as grand as those of the embassies and private homes nearby. But don't be put off by the tight entrance hall and dark hallways. Though the guest rooms on the upper floors are larger, all rooms are pleasantly decorated, with carefully crafted built-in furniture. Each bathroom has both a tub and a shower.

49 rue de Bourgogne, Paris 75007. ✆ **01-44-11-30-70.** Fax 01-45-55-20-21. www.hotel-palais-bourbon.com. 32 units. 110€–125€ ($143–$163) double; 145€ ($189) triple; 162€ ($211) quad. Rates include breakfast. MC, V. Métro: Varenne. **Amenities:** Room service (breakfast only); laundry service; dry cleaning; nonsmoking rooms. *In room:* A/C, TV, minibar, hair dryer, safe.

Hôtel du Quai Voltaire Built in the 1600s as an abbey and transformed into a hotel in 1856, the Quai Voltaire is best known for its illustrious guests. Wilde, Wagner, and Baudelaire occupied room nos. 47, 55, and 56, respectively. Pissarro painted Le Pont Royal from the window of his fourth-floor room. Many guest rooms in this modest inn have been renovated; most overlook the bookstalls and boats of the Seine. Most units have a tub and shower.

19 quai Voltaire, Paris 75007. ✆ **01-42-61-50-91.** Fax 01-42-61-62-26. www.quaivoltaire.fr. 33 units. 124€–132€ ($161–$172) double; 159€ ($207) triple. AE, DC, MC, V. Parking 24€ ($31). Métro: Musée d'Orsay or Rue du Bac. **Amenities:** Bar; room service; laundry service. *In room:* Hair dryer.

Hôtel Lindbergh A 5-minute walk from St-Germain-des-Prés, this hotel offers streamlined, simple guest rooms. About two-thirds of the bathrooms contain tubs as well as showers and were recently renovated. Breakfast is the only meal served, and the staff will point out good restaurants nearby—an inexpensive bistro, Le Cigale, is quite close.

5 rue Chomel, Paris 75007. ✆ **01-45-48-35-53.** Fax 01-45-49-31-48. www.hotellindbergh.com. 26 units. 116€–160€ ($151–$208) double; 156€–180€ ($203–$234) triple; 166€–190€ ($216–$247) quad. AE, DC, MC, V. Parking 27€ ($35). Métro: Sèvres-Babylone or St-Sulpice. **Amenities:** Room service; laundry service; dry cleaning; limited-mobility room. *In room:* TV, hair dryer.

Hôtel Saint-Dominique Part of this place's charm derives from its division into three buildings connected through an open-air courtyard. The most visible used to be an 18th-century convent—you can still see ceiling beams and structural timbers in the reception area. The guest rooms aren't large, but each is warm and simply decorated.

62 rue St-Dominique, Paris 75007. ✆ **01-47-05-51-44.** Fax 01-47-05-81-28. www.hotelstdominique.com. 34 units. 93€–121€ ($121–$157) double. AE, MC, V. Métro: Latour-Maubourg or Invalides. **Amenities:** Room service. *In room:* TV, minibar, hair dryer, safe.

NEAR THE AIRPORTS

ORLY

Hilton Paris Orly Airport ★ Boxy and bland, the Hilton at Orly is a well-maintained, especially convenient business hotel. Incoming planes can't penetrate the guest rooms' sound barriers, giving you a decent shot at a night's sleep. (Unlike the 24-hr. Charles de Gaulle Airport, Orly is closed to arriving flights from midnight to 6am.) The rooms are standard for a chain hotel; each was renovated in the late 1990s, with a tub/shower combination.

Aéroport Orly, 267 Orly Sud, Orly Aérogare Cedex 94544. ✆ **800/445-8667** in the U.S. and Canada, or 01-45-12-45-12. Fax 01-45-12-45-00. www.hilton.com. 351 units. 130€–210€ ($169–$273) double; 205€–285€ ($267–$371) suite. AE, DC, MC, V. Parking 14€ ($18). Free shuttle bus between hotel and both Orly terminals. **Amenities:** Restaurant; bar; fitness center; sauna; room service; babysitting; laundry service; dry cleaning; nonsmoking rooms; limited-mobility rooms. *In room:* A/C, TV, hair dryer.

ROISSY/CHARLES DE GAULLE

Hôtel Campanile de Roissy This hotel is less expensive than most other lodgings near the airport. A thin overlay of cheerful-looking, rustic artifacts barely masks its cement-and-glass design. Generally, this is an efficiently decorated and not particularly stylish place to stay, with a well-meaning but overworked staff. Each unit comes with a small, shower-only bathroom.

Parc de Roissy, Val-d'Oise 95700. ✆ **01-34-29-80-40.** Fax 01-34-29-80-39. www.campanile.fr. 260 units. 65€–135€ ($85–$176) double. AE, DC, MC, V. Free shuttle to and from Roissy. **Amenities:** Restaurant; bar; laundry service; dry cleaning; nonsmoking rooms; limited-mobility rooms. *In room:* TV, hair dryer.

Hôtel Sofitel Paris Aéroport CDG ★ Many travelers pass happily through this bustling, somewhat anonymous member of the French chain. It employs a multilingual staff accustomed to accommodating international business travelers. The conservatively furnished guest rooms are soundproof havens against the all-night roar of jets. Suites are larger and have more comfort, although they are not especially elegant and are consistent with the chain format. Each unit comes with a tiled bathroom with tub and shower.

Aéroport Charles de Gaulle, Zone Central, B.P. 20248, Roissy 95713. ✆ **800/221-4542** in the U.S. and Canada, or 01-49-19-29-29. Fax 01-49-19-29-00. www.sofitel.com. 350 units. 275€–465€ ($358–$605) double; from 950€ ($1,235) suite. AE, DC, MC, V. Parking 12€ ($16). Free shuttle to and from airport. **Amenities:** Restaurant; bar; fitness center; indoor pool; business center; room service; laundry service; dry cleaning; nonsmoking rooms; limited-mobility rooms. *In room:* A/C, TV, minibar, hair dryer, safe.

4 Where to Dine

Our best piece of advice—even if your budget is lean—is to splurge on one grand French meal (and to make reservations well in advance). A meal at a place such as **Taillevent, Alain Ducasse,** or **Carré des Feuillants** is something you'll always remember.

Three-star dining remains quite expensive. The 100€ ($130) main course (*entree* means "appetizer" in French; don't confuse entrees with main courses) is no longer a novelty, and first courses can exceed 50€ ($65); in the top dining rooms, the total bill easily surpasses 175€ to 200€ ($228–$260) per person. You can get around that high price tag in many places by ordering a fixed-price menu, perhaps for a "mere" 90€ ($117), or by heading for one of the not-so-celebrated but equally stellar dining rooms—**Pierre Gagnaire,** for example, instead of the legendary Alain Ducasse.

One question we're often asked is whether you can dine badly in Paris. The answer is an emphatic yes. We get complaints from readers who cite haughty service and mediocre food at outrageous prices. Often, complaints are about places catering mostly to tourists. We'll help you avoid them by sharing our favorite discoveries. While others are fighting it out for a table at one of the less-than-wonderful places, you can enjoy finer fare off the beaten track.

In the past, suits and ties were a given, and women always wore smart dresses or suits. Well, you can kiss your suits *au revoir.* Except in first-class and deluxe places, attire is more relaxed, but that doesn't mean sloppy jeans and workout clothes. Parisians still value style, even when dressing informally.

Restaurants are required by law to post their menus outside, so peruse them carefully. The fixed-price menu remains a solid choice if you want to have some idea of what your bill will be when it's presented by the waiter (whom you call *monsieur,* not *garçon*).

Part of the fun of a trip to Paris is enjoying the experience of an old-fashioned, family-run bistro. Just when bistros seemed to be dying, new-wave chefs started moving in, reviving them with excellent food at affordable prices.

RIGHT BANK: 1ST ARRONDISSEMENT (MUSEE DU LOUVRE/LES HALLES)

VERY EXPENSIVE

Carré des Feuillants ★★★ MODERN FRENCH This is a bastion of perfection, an enclave of haute gastronomy. When chef Alain Dutournier turned this 17th-century convent between the place Vendôme and the Tuileries into a restaurant, it was an overnight success. The interior is artfully simple, with a vaguely Asian feel shared by a series of small, monochromatic dining rooms that overlook a flowering courtyard and a glassed-enclosed kitchen. You'll find a sophisticated reinterpretation of cuisine from France's southwest, using seasonal ingredients and lots of know-how. Examples include a cappuccino of chestnuts with white truffles; a "cake" of Jerusalem artichokes studded with foie gras and black truffles; and grilled monkfish with crispy potatoes and French caviar (yes, they're producing caviar now in the Gironde region of France), served with a cabbage lasagna and horseradish sauce.

14 rue de Castiglione (near place Vendôme and the Tuileries), 1er. ✆ **01-42-86-82-82.** Fax 01-42-86-07-71. Reservations required far in advance. Main courses 55€–70€ ($72–$91); fixed-price lunch 65€–165€ ($85–$215); fixed-price dinner 165€ ($215). AE, DC, MC, V. Mon–Fri noon–2:30pm and 7:30–10pm. Closed Aug. Métro: Tuileries, Concorde, Opéra, or Madeleine.

Le Grand Véfour ★★★ TRADITIONAL FRENCH This is the all-time winner: a great chef, the most beautiful restaurant decor in Paris, and a history-infused citadel of classic French cuisine. This restaurant has been around since Louis XV. Napoleon, Danton, Hugo, Colette, and Cocteau dined here—as the brass plaques on the tables testify—and it's still a gastronomic experience. Guy Martin, chef for the past decade, bases many items on recipes from the French Alps. He prepares such heavenly dishes as filet of lamb cooked with sweet Muscat wine, carved into rib sections, and served with the smoked essence of its own juice. The desserts are often grand, such as *gourmandises au chocolat* (medley of chocolate) served with chocolate sorbet.

17 rue de Beaujolais, 1er. ✆ **01-42-96-56-27.** Fax 01-42-86-80-71. Reservations required (recommended at least 10 days in advance). Main courses 75€–100€ ($98–$130); fixed-price menu 78€ ($101) lunch, 265€ ($345) dinner. AE, DC, MC, V. Mon–Fri 12:30–1:45pm; Mon–Thurs 8–9:30pm. Closed Aug. Métro: Louvre–Palais-Royal or Pyramides.

EXPENSIVE

Chez Vong ★ CANTONESE This is the kind of Les Halles restaurant you head for when you've had your fill of grand cuisine and pretensions. The decor is a soothing mix of greens and browns, steeped in a Chinese-colonial ambience that evokes early 1900s Shanghai. Menu items feature shrimp and scallops served as spicy as you like, including a super-hot version with garlic and red peppers; "joyous beef" with pepper sauce; chicken in puff pastry with ginger; and an array of fish dishes. The whims of fashion have deemed this one of the restaurants of the moment, so it's full of folks from the worlds of entertainment and the arts.

10 rue de la Grande-Truanderie, 1er. ✆ **01-40-26-09-36.** Reservations recommended. Main courses 25€–30€ ($33–$39); fixed-price lunch Mon–Fri 23€ ($30). AE, DC, MC, V. Mon–Sat noon–2:30pm and 7pm–midnight. Métro: Etienne-Marcel or Les Halles.

Where to Dine on the Right Bank

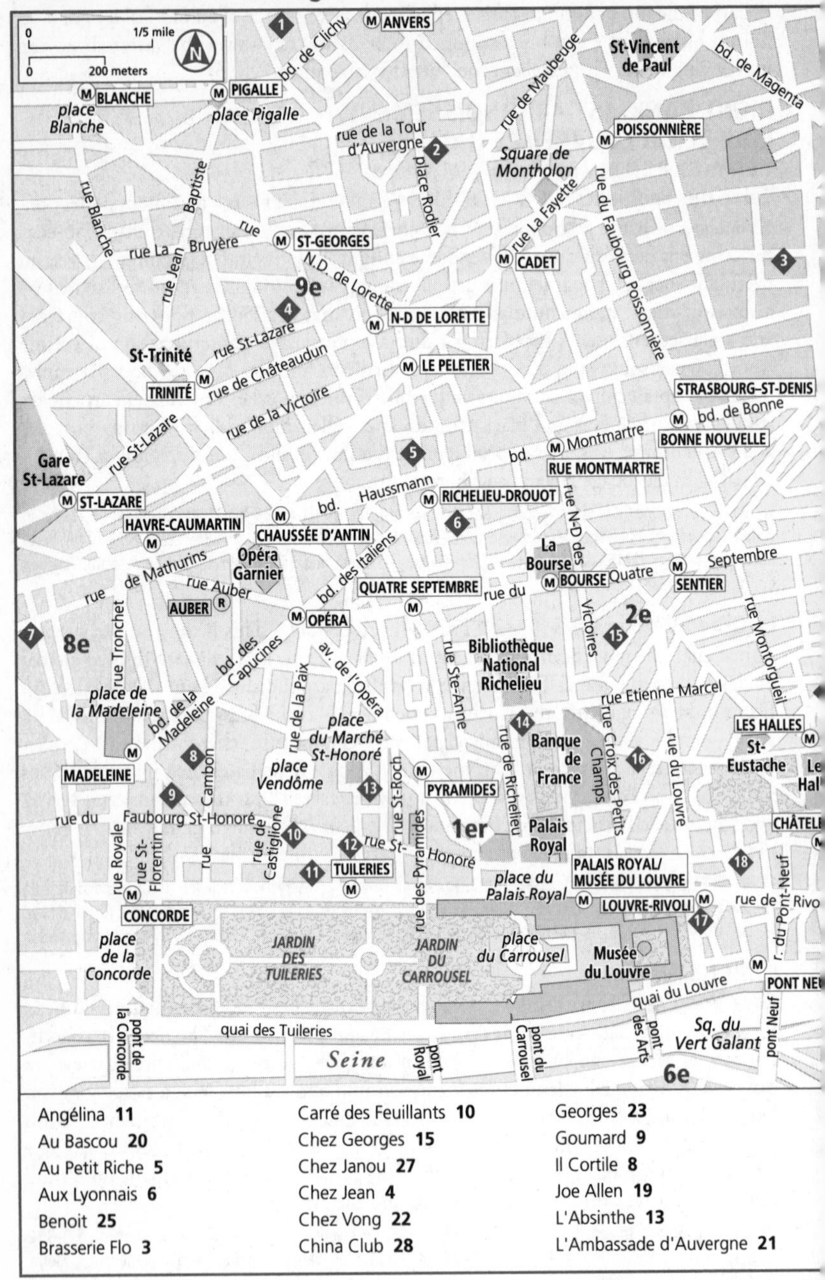

- Angélina **11**
- Au Bascou **20**
- Au Petit Riche **5**
- Aux Lyonnais **6**
- Benoit **25**
- Brasserie Flo **3**
- Carré des Feuillants **10**
- Chez Georges **15**
- Chez Janou **27**
- Chez Jean **4**
- Chez Vong **22**
- China Club **28**
- Georges **23**
- Goumard **9**
- Il Cortile **8**
- Joe Allen **19**
- L'Absinthe **13**
- L'Ambassade d'Auvergne **21**

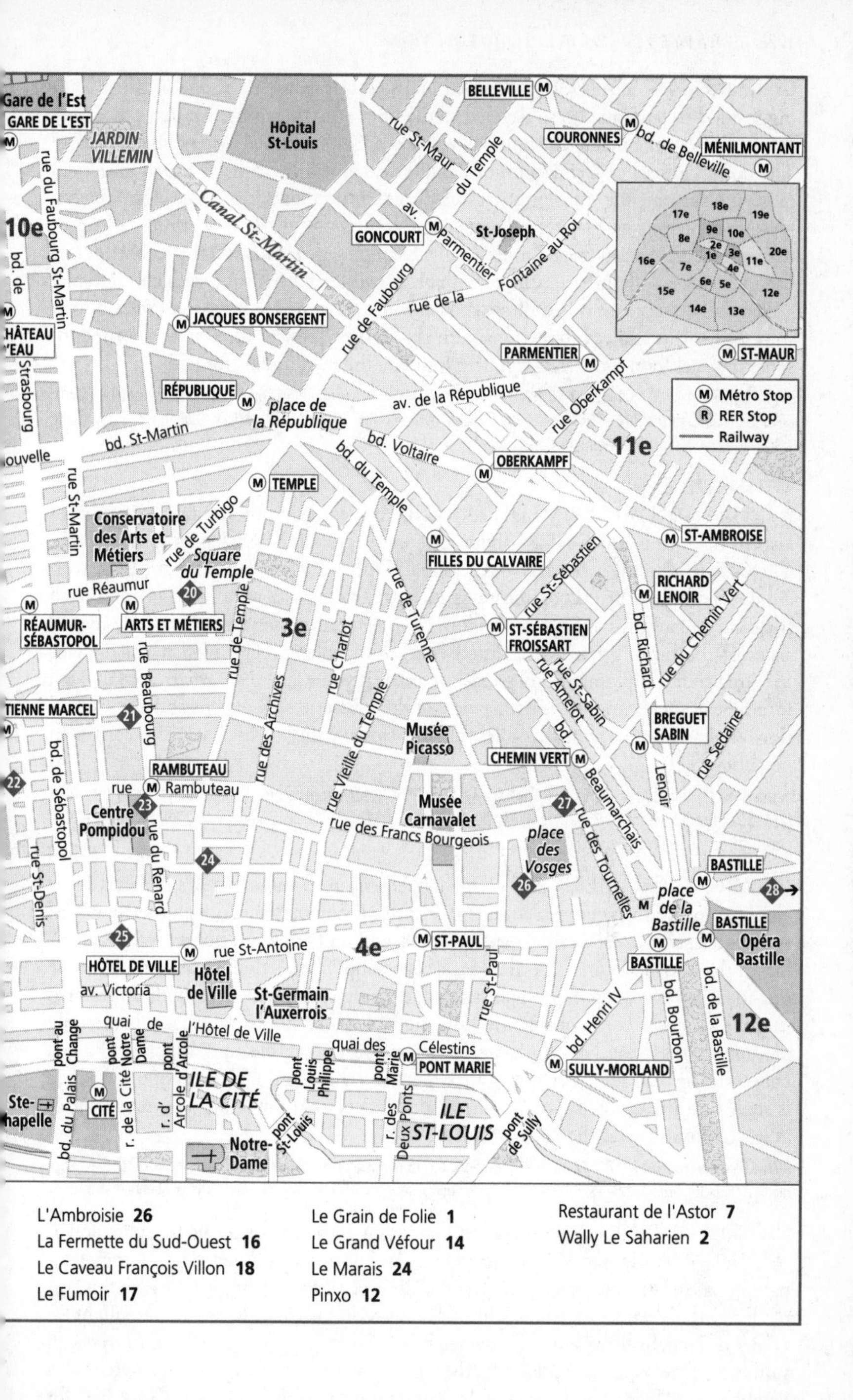

L'Ambroisie **26**
La Fermette du Sud-Ouest **16**
Le Caveau François Villon **18**
Le Fumoir **17**
Le Grain de Folie **1**
Le Grand Véfour **14**
Le Marais **24**
Pinxo **12**
Restaurant de l'Astor **7**
Wally Le Saharien **2**

Goumard ★★★ SEAFOOD Opened in 1872, this landmark is one of Paris's leading seafood restaurants. It's so devoted to the fine art of preparing fish that other food is banned from the menu (the staff will verbally present a limited roster of meat dishes). The decor consists of a collection of Lalique crystal fish in artificial aquariums. Even more unusual are the restrooms, classified as historic monuments; the Art Nouveau master cabinetmaker Majorelle designed the commodes in the early 1900s. Much of the seafood is flown in from Brittany daily. Examples are *craquant* (crisp-cooked) crayfish in herb salad, flash-fried scallops with black truffles, lobster soup with coconut, and grilled turbot salad on a bed of artichokes with tarragon. Nothing (no excess butter, spices, or salt) is allowed to interfere with the natural flavor of the sea. Be prepared for some unusual food—the staff will help translate the menu items for you.

9 rue Duphot, 1er. ✆ **01-42-60-36-07.** Fax 01-42-60-04-54. www.goumard.com. Reservations required far in advance. Main courses 39€–75€ ($51–$98); fixed-price menu 46€ ($60). AE, DC, MC, V. Daily noon–2:30pm and 7:30–10:30pm. Métro: Madeleine or Concorde.

MODERATE

Il Cortile ★★ ITALIAN/MEDITERRANEAN Flanking the verdant courtyard of a small hotel, this much-talked-about restaurant serves the best Italian food in Paris. The cuisine is fresh, inventive, and seasonal. Dishes are from throughout Italy, with emphasis on the north. Look for items such as farfalle pasta with squid ink and fresh shellfish, and award-winning guinea fowl (spit-roasted and served with artfully shaped slices of the bird's gizzard, heart, and liver) with polenta. The French and Italian-speaking staff is diplomatic and good-humored. If you want to see what's cooking, ask for a seat in the dining room with a view of the rotisserie, where hens and guinea fowl slowly spin. In warm weather, tables fill an enclosed patio—a luxury in this congested neighborhood.

In the Hôtel Castille, 37 rue Cambon, 1er. ✆ **01-44-58-45-67.** Reservations recommended. Main courses 20€–40€ ($26–$52); fixed-price menu 95€ ($124). AE, DC, DISC, MC, V. Mon–Fri 12:30–2:30pm and 7:30–10:30pm. Métro: Concorde or Madeleine.

Joe Allen ★ Kids AMERICAN The first American restaurant in Les Halles is aging well. Joe Allen long ago invaded the place with his hamburger. Though the New York restaurateur admits "it's a silly idea," it works, and it's Paris's best burger. While listening to the jukebox, you can order black-bean soup, chili, sirloin steak, ribs, or apple pie. Joe Allen is getting more sophisticated, catering to modern tastes with dishes such as grilled salmon with coconut rice and sun-dried tomatoes. His saloon is the only place in Paris serving New York cheesecake and real pecan pie, and, thanks to French chocolate, he believes his brownies are better than those in the U.S. A popular brunch is served on weekends. If you haven't made a reservation for dinner, expect a wait of at least 30 minutes at the New York Bar.

30 rue Pierre-Lescot, 1er. ✆ **01-42-36-70-13.** Reservations recommended for dinner. Main courses 16€ ($21); fixed-price menu 23€ ($30); brunch 22€ ($29). AE, MC, V. Daily noon–1am; Sat–Sun brunch noon–4pm. Métro: Etienne-Marcel.

L'Absinthe FRENCH This airy and charming location has a pair (upstairs/downstairs) of gracefully paneled dining rooms. An enormous antique clock dominates a panorama over the animated dining room. Best of all for foodies who follow this sort of thing, there's an association within this upscale bistro with one of the mightiest names of French gastronomy: It's owned by Caroline, daughter of Michel Rostang. In summer, tables spill outside onto the all-pedestrian, see-and-be-seen stretch of a neighborhood loaded with some of the world's most upscale boutiques. Come here for well-prepared though not particularly innovative bistro-style food. The best examples include crayfish ravioli, scallops sautéed with bacon and sherry, poached codfish with a garlicky aioli sauce, and a served-pink version of standing rack of veal. Service is quirky, a wee bit judgmental, and, at its worst, a bit cranky.

24 place du Marché St-Honoré, 1er. ✆ **01-49-26-90-04.** Reservations recommended. Fixed-price menu 29€–36€ ($38–$47). AE, DC, MC, V. Mon–Fri noon–2pm; Mon–Sat 7:15–10:30pm. Métro: Tuileries.

Le Fumoir ★ INTERNATIONAL This upscale brasserie is in an antique building a few steps from the Louvre. It's one of the most fashionable places in Paris for a bite or drink. You can order salads, pastries, and drinks at off-hours, and platters of more substantial food—such as codfish with onions and herbs, calves' liver with onions, and herring in mustard-flavored cream sauce—at mealtimes.

6 rue de l'Amiral-Coligny, 1er. ✆ **01-42-92-00-24.** Reservations recommended. Main courses 18€–28€ ($23–$37). AE, MC, V. Salads, pastries, and snacks daily 11am–2pm; full menu Mon–Fri 7:30–11:30pm and Sat–Sun 7:30pm–midnight. Métro: Louvre-Rivoli.

Pinxo ★ *Finds* SOUTHWESTERN FRENCH This is the cost-conscious brasserie that's associated with mega-chef Alain Dutournier's terribly stylish, and much more expensive, Carré des Feuillants, which is about a 5-minute walk on a parallel nearby street. At Pinxo, a good-looking waitstaff clad in black karate uniforms (or pajamas, perhaps) encourages clients to share starters and platters with their tablemates. Sharing is relatively easy, since whatever appears on a plate is replicated, sometimes with variations, three times. The setting manages to elevate kitchen drudgery to a high, and high-tech, art form, with a wooden floor, white walls, and views directly into an all-black open kitchen-cum-theater. Most foods here are grilled or at least prepared with heart-healthy cooking oils. Examples include a mixture of Aquitaine beef on the same plate as a steak, a tartare, and a blood sausage, all accompanied with foie gras. Filet of goose comes with watercress, cannelloni, sliced star fruit, and mushrooms; and platters are piled high with, among others, tuna seviche, herring, and crabmeat spring rolls.

In the Plaza-Paris-Vendôme Hôtel, 9 rue d'Alger, 1er. ✆ **01-40-20-72-00.** Reservations recommended. Main courses 16€–26€ ($21–$34). AE, MC, V. Daily 12:15–2:30pm and 7:15–11:30pm. Métro: Tuileries.

INEXPENSIVE

Angélina TEA/TRADITIONAL FRENCH In the high-rent area near the Inter-Continental, this *salon de thé* (tea salon) combines fashion-industry glitter and bourgeois respectability. The carpets are plush, the ceilings are high, and the accessories have the right amount of patina. The waitresses bear silver trays with pastries, drinks, and tea or coffee to marble-topped tables. Lunch usually offers a salad and a *plat du jour* such as *salade gourmande* with foie gras and smoked breast of duck on a bed of fresh salad greens. Despite the powerful appeal of tea and coffee as a midday pick-me-up, an enduring favorite here is hot chocolate, priced at 6.50€ ($8.45) for a pot suitable for one person. The specialty accompaniment, designed to go well with tea, is the Mont Blanc, a combination of chestnut cream and meringue.

226 rue de Rivoli, 1er. ✆ **01-42-60-82-00.** Reservations not accepted for tea. Pot of tea for 1 6€ ($7.80); sandwiches and salads 6€–14€ ($7.80–$18); main courses 14€–18€ ($18–$23). AE, MC, V. Mon–Sat 8am–6:45pm; Sun 9am–6:45pm. Métro: Tuileries or Concorde.

La Fermette du Sud-Ouest ★ SOUTHWESTERN FRENCH This restaurant, which occupies the site of a 1500s convent, is in the heart of one of Paris's oldest neighborhoods. After the Revolution, the convent was converted into a coaching inn, preserving the original stonework and massive beams. La Fermette prepares rich, savory stews and confits celebrating agrarian France, and serves them on the ground floor and on a mezzanine resembling a choir loft. Menu items include ever-popular magret of duckling with flap mushrooms, *andouillettes* (chitterling sausages), and a sometimes startling array of *cochonailles* (pork products and byproducts) you probably need to be French to appreciate. Cassoulet and *pot-au-feu* are enduring specialties.

31 rue Coquillière, 1er. ✆ **01-42-36-73-55.** Reservations recommended. Main courses 12€–21€ ($16–$27); fixed-price lunch 15€ ($20); fixed-price dinner 23€ ($30). MC, V. Mon–Sat noon–2pm and 7:30–10pm. Métro: Les Halles.

Le Caveau François Villon FRENCH The food here is competently prepared but not particularly noteworthy, and the tables in the cellar-level dining room are claustrophobically close. But there's something fun and spontaneous about the place, so much so that readers have shared how much fun they've had and what they've garnered from French humor and conviviality. The masonry in the basement dates from the late 1400s, around the time when François Villon, the restaurant's namesake, was composing his French-language poetry. Try to get a table in the cellar, where a guitarist entertains every working night from 8:30pm until closing. Menu items change with the seasons, but are likely to include the house version of foie gras, a spinach salad with caramelized bacon, an assortment of terrines and pâtés made from chicken or pork, salmon cooked in orange-flavored butter sauce, and a grilled confit of duckling with a galette of potatoes. The entertainment is convivial and, at times, a bit bawdy.

64 rue de l'Arbre Sec, 1er. ✆ **01-42-36-10-92.** Reservations recommended. Fixed-price lunches 20€–26€ ($26–$34); fixed-price dinners 26€ ($34). AE, DC, MC, V. Tues–Fri noon–2:15pm; Mon–Sat 7pm–midnight. Métro: Louvre.

RIGHT BANK: 2ND ARRONDISSEMENT (LA BOURSE)

MODERATE

Chez Georges TRADITIONAL FRENCH Three generations of the same family run this bistro, which opened in 1964. At lunch it's packed with stock exchange members. It serves *la cuisine bourgeoise* (comfort food). Waiters bring around bowls of appetizers, such as celery rémoulade, to get you started. You can follow with sweetbreads with morels, duck breast with cèpe mushrooms, cassoulet, or *pot-au-feu.* A delight is sole filet with a sauce made from Pouilly wine and crème fraîche.

1 rue du Mail, 2e. ✆ **01-42-60-07-11.** Reservations required. Main courses 25€–33€ ($33–$43). AE, MC, V. Mon–Fri noon–2pm and 7–10pm. Closed Aug. Métro: Bourse.

INEXPENSIVE

Aux Lyonnais ★ LYONNAIS/FRENCH After a meal here, you'll know why Lyon is called the gastronomic capital of France. There is no better Lyonnais bistro in Paris than this time-mellowed place vaguely associated with Alain Ducasse. The day's menu is based on the freshest produce available that morning. It's offered against an 1890s bistro backdrop of potted palms, etched glass, and globe lamps. Inventiveness and solid technique characterize such dishes as parsleyed calves' liver, pike dumplings (the best in Paris), skate meunière, and peppery coq au vin with crème fraîche macaroni. Foie gras is a starter, or you can opt for a charcuterie platter. The best for last: a heaven-sent Cointreau soufflé.

32 rue St-Marc, 2e. ✆ **01-42-96-65-04.** Reservations required. Main courses 22€–25€ ($29–$33); 3-course fixed-price menu 28€–32€ ($36–$42). AE, DC, MC, V. Tues–Fri noon–1:30pm; Tues–Sat 7:30–10pm. Métro: Grands-Boulevards.

RIGHT BANK: 3RD ARRONDISSEMENT (LE MARAIS)

INEXPENSIVE

Au Bascou ★ *Finds* BASQUE The succulent cuisine of France's "deep southwest" is the specialty here, where art objects, oil paintings, and tones of ocher celebrate the beauty of the region, and hanging clusters of pimentos add spice to the air. For a ray of sunshine, try *pipérade basquaise,* a spicy omelet loaded with peppers and onions; pimentos stuffed with purée of codfish; *axoa* of veal (shoulder of calf served with pimento-and-pepper-based green sauce); or thick-sliced filet of cod served with essence of tomatoes.

38 rue Réaumur, 3e. ✆ **01-42-72-69-25.** Reservations recommended. Main courses 16€ ($21); fixed-price menu 16€–18€ ($21–$23). AE, DC, MC, V. Mon–Fri noon–2pm and 8–10:30pm. Closed Aug and week of Christmas. Métro: Arts-et-Métiers.

Chez Janou PROVENÇAL On one of the 17th-century streets behind place des Vosges, a pair of cramped but cozy dining rooms filled with memorabilia from Provence make up this loud and somewhat raucous bistro. The service is brusque and sometimes hectic. Dishes include shrimp with pastis sauce, *brouillade des pleurotes* (baked eggs with oyster mushrooms), spinach salad with goat cheese, fondue of ratatouille, gratin of mussels, and simple but savory magret of duck with rosemary. You can enjoy these specialties on a covered terrace.

2 rue Roger-Verlomme, 3e. ✆ **01-42-72-28-41.** Reservations recommended. Main courses 13€–18€ ($17–$23); fixed-price lunch 14€ ($18). AE, MC, V. Daily noon–3pm and 7:30pm–midnight. Métro: Chemin Vert.

L'Ambassade d'Auvergne ★ AUVERGNAT/FRENCH You enter this rustic tavern through a bar with heavy oak beams, hanging hams, and ceramic plates. It showcases the culinary bounty of France's most isolated region, the Auvergne, whose pork products are widely celebrated. Try chicory salad with apples and pieces of country ham; pork braised with cabbage, turnips, and white beans; or grilled tripe sausages with mashed potatoes and cantal cheese with garlic. Nonpork specialties are pan-fried duck liver with gingerbread, perch steamed in verbena tea, and roasted rack of lamb with wild mushrooms. Dessert may be a poached pear with crispy almonds and caramel sauce.

22 rue de Grenier St-Lazare, 3e. ✆ **01-42-72-31-22.** Reservations recommended. Main courses 14€–22€ ($18–$29); fixed-price menu 28€ ($36). AE, MC, V. Daily noon–2pm and 7:30–10:30pm. Métro: Rambuteau.

RIGHT BANK: 4TH ARRONDISSEMENT (ILE DE LA CITE/ ILE ST-LOUIS & BEAUBOURG)

VERY EXPENSIVE

L'Ambroisie ★★★ FRENCH One of Paris's most talented chefs, Bernard Pacaud draws attention with his vivid flavors and gastronomic skill. Expect culinary perfection but a cool reception at this 17th-century town house. Pacaud's tables are nearly always filled with repeat diners wondering where his imagination will take him next. The dishes change seasonally and may include fricassee of Breton lobster with chestnuts, served with purée of pumpkin; turbot braised with endive, served with julienne of black truffles; or one of our favorites, *poulard de Bresse demi-deuil homage à la Mère Brazier* (chicken roasted with black truffles and truffled vegetables). An award-winning dessert is *tarte fine sablée* (a delicate small biscuit) served with bitter chocolate and vanilla ice cream.

9 place des Vosges, 4e. ✆ **01-42-78-51-45.** Reservations required far in advance. Main courses 80€–140€ ($104–$182). AE, MC, V. Tues–Sat noon–1:30pm and 8–9:30pm. Métro: St-Paul or Chemin Vert.

MODERATE

Benoit ★ TRADITIONAL FRENCH Every mayor of Paris has dined here since the restaurant was founded in 1912 by the grandfather of the present owner, who still occasionally purchases Beaujolais in casks and bottles it in his own cellars. The setting is theatrical, and the service can be attentive or arrogant, depending on a delicate chemistry that longtime fans of this place understand. Prices are higher than you'd expect for bistro fare, but diners keep coming back. The satisfying cuisine is full of flavor, based on time-tested classics. Traditional crowd pleasers include salmon that's both marinated and smoked; snails served in their shells with garlic butter; slow-cooked pot roast with carrots; and cassoulet, a white-bean and pork dish that's fabulous on a cold day.

20 rue St-Martin, 4e. ✆ **01-42-72-25-76.** Reservations required. Main courses 25€–40€ ($33–$52); fixed-price lunch 38€ ($50). AE. Daily noon–2pm and 7:30–10pm. Métro: Hôtel de Ville.

Georges ★ INTERNATIONAL The Centre Pompidou is again in the spotlight; all of artsy Paris is talking about this place. Georges is in a large space on the top floor of Paris's most comprehensive arts complex, with bay-window views over most of the city. The decor is minimalist and postmodern, with lots of brushed aluminum and stainless steel. Tables are made from sandblasted glass, lit from below, and accessorized with hypermodern cutlery. Menu items are mostly Continental, with hints of Asia. Some combinations surprise—macaroni with lobster, for example. Others seem exotic, including roasted ostrich steak. Aside from these dishes, some of the best items on the menu are roasted scallops with lemon butter, and tuna steak spiced with coriander. There's also a luscious version of sole meunière. To get here, head for the exterior elevator to the left of the Pompidou's main entrance. Tell the guard you have a reservation; otherwise, you may not be allowed up.

Centre Pompidou, 6th Floor, 19 rue Beaubourg, 4e. ✆ **01-44-78-47-99.** Reservations required for dinner, recommended for lunch. Main courses 15€–43€ ($20–$56). AE, DC, MC, V. Wed–Mon 11am–midnight. Métro: Rambuteau.

INEXPENSIVE

Le Marais FRENCH/FISH Housed in a 17th-century building whose stonework forms part of the earth-toned decor, this is a convenient stopover during the day while you're exploring the Marais. Flavorful, healthful meals come in generous portions. Choose from a variety of soups and freshly made salads. You can also select from burgers and grilled meats. Service is fast and efficient, and you don't have to linger all day over lunch if you have a busy agenda for the afternoon.

54 rue Ste-Croix-de-la-Bretonnerie, 4e. ✆ **01-48-87-48-71.** Main courses 8.50€–14€ ($11–$18); fixed-price menu 19€ ($25). MC, V. Mon–Sat noon–midnight. Métro: Hôtel de Ville. RER: Châtelet–Les Halles.

RIGHT BANK: 8TH ARRONDISSEMENT (CHAMPS-ELYSEES/MADELEINE)

VERY EXPENSIVE

Le Cinq ★★★ FRENCH Since it was established in 1928 in honor of the king of England, a world-class dining venue has always been associated with the Hôtel George V. The majestic, high-ceilinged dining room evokes the Grand Trianon at Versailles. Within a gray and very pale pink dining room that shimmers with gold inlays, your dining needs are supervised by a sophisticated staff that intuitively understands the needs and priorities of the hotel's widely divergent international clientele. Within 3 years of this restaurant's birth, it had been awarded three coveted stars by the Michelin Guide. The menu changes frequently, but enduring favorites include a tarte of artichokes and black Périgord truffles;

a fricassee of Breton crayfish with coriander and lime sauce; and a classic that has been on the menu since the days of Mistinguett and Piaf, Bresse chicken stuffed with crayfish and herbs.

In the Four Seasons Hotel George V, 31 av. George V, 8e. ✆ **01-49-52-71-54.** Fax 01-49-52-71-81. Reservations recommended 4 weeks in advance for dinner, 1 week in advance for lunch. Main courses 53€–120€ ($69–$156); fixed-price lunches 75€–120€ ($98–$156); fixed-price dinners 120€–210€ ($156–$273). AE, DC, MC, V. Daily noon–2:30pm and 6:30–10:30pm. Métro: George V.

Les Elysées du Vernet ★★★ PROVENÇAL This restaurant is a gastronomic wonder. It has a panoramic glass ceiling, a gray-and-green translucent dome designed by Gustav Eiffel, the architect who conceived the famous tower. Chef Eric Brifford keeps the crowds lined up with menu items that focus on Provençal models and change every 2 months, based on whatever is fresh. Begin your meal with a truffle-studded tart or perhaps a salad of scallops served with caviar and a mango-flavor vinaigrette. Move on to a casserole of wild boar *(cochon noir)* from the Pyrénées with wild mushrooms; or perhaps a whole red snapper, simply grilled and succulent, and served with butter or hollandaise sauce, according to your wishes. Dessert may be a soft lemon-flavor pastry, prepared like a soufflé and served with mascarpone sauce.

In the Hôtel Vernet, 25 rue Vernet, 8e. ✆ **01-44-31-98-98.** Reservations required. Main courses 45€–88€ ($59–$114); *menu gastronomique* 130€ ($169). AE, DC, MC, V. Tues–Fri 12:30–2pm; Mon–Fri 7:30–10pm. Métro: George V.

Pierre Gagnaire ★★★ MODERN FRENCH If you're able to get a reservation, it's worth the effort. The menus are seasonal to take advantage of France's rich bounty; owner Pierre Gagnaire demands perfection, and the chef has a dazzling way with flavors and textures. Stellar examples are crayfish cooked tempura-style with thin-sliced flash-seared vegetables and sweet-and-sour sauce; and turbot cooked in a bag and served with fennel and Provençal lemons. Chicken with truffles comes in two stages—first the breast in wine-based aspic, then the thighs chopped into roughly textured pieces. For dessert, try chocolate soufflé served with a frozen parfait and pistachios.

6 rue Balzac, 8e. ✆ **01-58-36-12-50.** Fax 01-58-36-12-51. Reservations required. Main courses 65€–120€ ($85–$156); fixed-price menu 90€ ($117) lunch, 260€ ($338) dinner. AE, DC, MC, V. Mon–Fri noon–1:30pm; Sun–Fri 7:30–10pm. Métro: George V.

Restaurant Plaza Athénée (Alain Ducasse) ★★★ MODERN & TRADITIONAL FRENCH Few other chefs have catapulted to international fame as quickly as Alain Ducasse. Marketing and glitter are also involved, but what you'll find in this world-renowned hotel is a lobby-level hideaway that top-notch decorator Patrick Jouin originally created around the turn of the millennium, and then artfully redecorated, much to the fascination of haute Paris, in late 2004. The six-star chef, Alain Ducasse, who supervises the kitchens here, divides his time between Paris, Monaco, New York, and Tokyo. In this, his Parisian stronghold, he emphasizes "rare and precious ingredients," whipping up flavorful and very expensive combinations of caviar, lobster, crayfish, truffles (both black and white), and shellfish. Cuisine is vaguely Mediterranean and decidedly contemporary, yet based on traditional models. Examples include chilled crayfish served with Osetra caviar; succulent versions of Bresse chicken with truffles; and thick, oozing slabs of pork crisp-grilled to perfection, making ample use of lard. The wine list is superb, with some selections deriving from the best vintages of France, Germany, Switzerland, Spain, California, and Italy.

In the Hôtel Plaza Athénée, 25 av. Montaigne, 8e. ✆ **01-53-67-65-00.** Fax 01-53-67-65-12. Reservations required 4–6 weeks in advance. Main courses 80€–150€ ($104–$195); fixed-price menus 220€–320€ ($286–$416). AE, DC, MC, V. Thurs–Fri 12:45–2:15pm; Mon–Fri 7:45–10:15pm. Closed mid-July to Aug 22 and 10 days in late Dec. Métro: Alma-Marceau.

Taillevent ★★★ MODERN & TRADITIONAL FRENCH Taillevent opened in 1946 and has climbed steadily in excellence; today it ranks as Paris's outstanding all-around restaurant, challenged only by Lucas-Carton and Pierre Gagnaire. The grand 19th-century town house off the Champs-Elysées has paneled rooms and crystal chandeliers. The place is small, which results in personal attention to every facet of the operation and in a discreet atmosphere. You may begin with *boudin* (sausage) of Breton lobster à la Nage, cream of watercress soup with Sevruga caviar, or duck liver with spice bread and ginger. Main courses include red snapper with black olives, Scottish salmon cooked in sea salt with a sauce of olive oil and lemons, and cassoulet of crayfish. The wine list is among the best in Paris.

15 rue Lamennais, 8e. ✆ **01-44-95-15-01.** Fax 01-42-25-95-18. Reservations required 4–6 weeks in advance. Main courses 34€–90€ ($44–$117); *dégustation* 140€–190€ ($182–$247). AE, DC, MC, V. Mon–Fri noon–2:30pm and 7–10pm. Closed Aug. Métro: George-V.

EXPENSIVE

Ladurée ★ TRADITIONAL FRENCH Ladurée, acclaimed since 1862 as one of Paris's grand cafes, adds a touch of class to the neighborhood. This offshoot of the original near La Madeleine caters to an international set wearing everything from Givenchy to Gap. The stylish, somewhat chaotic venue changes from tearoom to full-fledged restaurant at least twice each day. The Belle Epoque setting is ideal for sampling Ladurée's macaroons—not the coconut version familiar to Americans but two almond meringue cookies, flavored with vanilla, coffee, strawberry, pistachio, or another flavor, held together with butter cream. The talented chefs constantly adjust to take advantage of the freshest ingredients. The menu may include crisp, tender pork filet with potato-and-parsley purée; sea bass with leeks; and marinated red mullet on a salad of cold ratatouille. For an accompaniment to your tea, consider a *plaisir sucre,* a chocolate confection decorated with spun sugar. The only downside: Service isn't always efficient.

75 av. des Champs-Elysées, 8e. ✆ **01-40-75-08-75.** Reservations required for restaurant. Main courses 29€–44€ ($38–$57); fixed-price lunch 27€–32€ ($35–$42); fixed-price dinner 32€ ($42); fixed-price breakfast 16€–24€ ($21–$31); pastries from 6€ ($7.80). AE, DC, MC, V. Daily 7:30am–1am. Métro: George V.

La Maison Blanche ★★ FRENCH/PROVENÇAL Twin brothers Jacques and Lauren Pourcel were celebrated famous chefs in the southerly province of Languedoc before heading north to Paris. The setting is the envy of any restaurant in the world: Positioned on the uppermost (seventh) floor of the Art Deco–style Theatre des Champs-Elysées, it has a contemporary, all-white and purple decor, sweeping views across the Seine, and two dining rooms. Clientele tends to be rich, non-French, and a bit pretentious, but in light of the brilliant food and the sublime setting, who cares? The menu changes with the seasons and the inspiration of the chefs, but stellar examples include filet of grilled sole with citrus sauce; rack of roasted lamb with sesame seeds; and filet of partridge cooked on the bone with caramelized turnips and Szechuan-style spicy peppers, dressed with a syrup of licorice-flavored blackberries.

15 av. Montaigne, 8e. ✆ **47-23-55-99.** Reservations required. Main courses 38€–73€ ($49–$95); fixed-price lunch with wine 65€ ($85). AE, DC, MC, V. Mon–Fri noon–1:45pm; daily 8–10:45pm. Métro: Alma-Marceau.

L'Angle du Faubourg ★★ FRENCH Throughout the 1980s and early 1990s, a reservation at the ultra-upscale Taillevent was sought after by diplomats, billionaires, and demimondaines from around Europe. In 2001, the Taillevent's owner, M. Vrinat, opened a cost-conscious bistro that capitalized on Taillevent's reputation, but at much lower prices. Lunches here tend to be efficient, relatively quick, and businesslike; diners are more leisurely, even romantic. The restaurant has an ultramodern dining room, additional seating in the cellar, and a menu that simplifies Taillevent's lofty culinary ideas. The best examples include cream of endive soup with mustard grains; marinated salmon; risotto with ingredients that change weekly (during our visit, it was studded with braised radicchio); and a grilled, low-fat version of *daurade* (bream), served with artichokes and a reduction of mushrooms, appreciated by diet-conscious *photo-modèles* who stop in between bouts of shopping. Dessert may be old-fashioned rice pudding.

195 rue du Faubourg St-Honoré, 8e. ✆ **01-40-74-20-20.** Reservations required. Main courses 19€–35€ ($25–$46); fixed-price menu 35€–70€ ($46–$91). AE, DC, MC, V. Mon–Fri noon–2:30pm and 7–10:30pm. Métro: Terme or Etoile.

Restaurant de l'Astor ★ FRENCH The vaguely Art Deco decor by superstar Frederick Mechiche includes tones of black and champagne. The view incorporates sightings of some of France's leading politicians, many of whom walk the short distance from the dining room to the Elysée Palace and government ministries nearby. And the cuisine, as conceived and concocted by Laurent Delarbre (voted *meilleur ouvrier de France* in 2004), is utterly sublime. Menu items change with the seasons, but may include, among other items, cream of coconut soup with a tartare of pig's foot and fried slices of foie gras; roasted scallops with a comfit of fennel and licorice; game tart; and rosettes of lamb basted with champagne and served with bacon-studded lard. Everything here is artfully presented, often with a kind of reverential hush.

In the Hôtel Saint-Honoré, 11 rue d'Astorg, 8e. ✆ **01-53-05-05-05.** Reservations recommended. Main courses 31€–34€ ($40–$44); set-price lunches 47€ ($61); set-price dinners 50€–70€ ($65–$91). AE, DC, MC, V. Mon–Fri noon–2pm and 7:30–10pm. Metro: Madeleine.

Spoon, Food & Wine ★ INTERNATIONAL This hypermodern venture by star chef Alain Ducasse is both hailed as a "restaurant for the millennium" and condemned as surreal and a bit absurd. Despite that, there can be a 2-week wait for a dinner reservation. This upscale but affordable restaurant may be the least pretentious and most hip of Ducasse's ventures. The somewhat claustrophobic dining room blends Parisian and Californian references, and the menu (which changes every 2 months) roams the world. Examples include deliberately undercooked grilled squid (part of it evokes sushi) with curry sauce; grilled Waguy beef (an Australia-derived version of Kobe beef); and spareribs with a devil's marmalade. Vegetarians appreciate stir-fried dishes in which you can mix and match up to 15 ingredients. Desserts feature Parisian versions of such U.S.-inspired dishes as cheesecake and doughnuts drenched with bitter chocolate.

In the Hôtel Marignan-Elysée, 14 rue Marignan, 8e. ✆ **01-40-76-34-44.** Reservations recommended 1–2 weeks in advance. Main courses 10€–40€ ($13–$52). AE, DC, MC, V. Mon–Fri noon–2pm and 7–10:30pm. Métro: Franklin-D-Roosevelt.

MODERATE

Citrus Etoile ★ FRENCH This is a good example of a hip, well-connected, and stylish restaurant-of-the-minute, where part of the fun involves seeing and being seen by the politically connected and trend-conscious crowd. The decor is minimalist, black, white, and orange, a bemused blend of the best of California (former home of the owners and inspiration for some of the cuisine) and France. If you opt for a meal here, you'll be in good hands: Chef Gilles Epié used to be a caterer and private chef in Hollywood before returning to Paris with his fashion-model wife Elizabeth (an American, who supervises the dining room) to open this in-vogue dining venue near the Arc de Triomphe. Menu items are health-conscious, artfully simple, "uncluttered," and flavorful. Begin with asparagus with salmon caviar, lime juice, and crumbled egg yolks; braised scallops with Parmesan cheese and olive oil; or perhaps some slices of foie gras with truffles and port-wine sauce. Delightful main courses include John Dory, served with its skin on a bed of laurel leaves with grated Parmesan cheese; breast of pigeon with foie gras and green cabbage; and lobster cooked in a bouillon of green asparagus and tarragon.

6 rue Arsène Houssaye, 8e. ✆ **01-42-89-15-51.** Reservations recommended. Main courses 16€–31€ ($21–$40); set menus 29€–38€ ($38–$49). AE, MC, V. Mon–Fri 12:30–2:30pm and 7:30–10:30pm. Metro: Etoile.

INEXPENSIVE

Bar des Théâtres FRENCH Its local patrons in the 8th arrondissement have long called this bar/restaurant "The Temple of the God Steak Tartare." For those daring souls who still eat this blood-rare red-meat specialty, this long-established restaurant, which opened at the end of World War II, is said to make the best. Even though it's situated in the most lethally priced district of Paris, it has over the years kept its prices within reason. Across the street is the Théâtre des Champs-Elysées, and many of its performers, especially actors and musicians, make the bar their "local" while appearing here. The chef also specializes in a delectable *magret de canard* (duckling), and you can even order caviar and foie gras, but those items would put this into a very expensive category.

6 av. Montaigne, 8e. ✆ **01-47-23-34-63.** Reservations recommended. Main courses 15€–25€ ($20–$33). AE, DC, MC, V. Daily 6am–2am. Metro: Alma Marceau.

RIGHT BANK: 9TH ARRONDISSEMENT (OPERA GARNIER/PIGALLE)

EXPENSIVE

Au Petit Riche ★ FRENCH/LOIRE VALLEY (ANJOU) When this restaurant opened in 1865, it was to complement the very large and then-solvent Café Riche, which at the time stood next door. After the Café burned down, the restaurant continued to attract lawyers, set designers, and machinists from the nearby Opera Garnier, eventually becoming a well-known restaurant in its own right. Today the decor of old Paris is still here, with the original gas lamps and time-mellowed paneling. Expect an impressive roster of Loire Valley wines, and food that combines Loire Valley classics with traditional French fare. Examples include traditional roasted rack of veal; a long-standing house special of tartare of beef; roasted whitefish in meat drippings; a traditional and succulent version of roasted rack of lamb; and seasonal game dishes such as civet of rabbit.

25 rue Le Peletier, 9e. ✆ **01-47-70-68-68.** Reservations recommended. Main courses 15€–30€ ($20–$39); fixed-price lunch 27€ ($34); fixed-price dinner 30€ ($38). AE, DC, MC, V. Mon–Sat noon–2:15pm and 7pm–midnight. Métro: Le Peletier or Richelieu-Drouot.

Chez Jean ★ FRENCH The crowd is young, the food is sophisticated, and the vintage 1950s aura makes you think that American expatriate novelist James Baldwin will arrive any minute. A brasserie has occupied this site since around 1900. Surrounded by well-oiled pine panels and polished copper, you can choose from some of grandmother's favorites as well as more modern dishes. Owner Jean-Frederic Guidoni worked for more than 20 years at one of the world's most expensive restaurants, Taillevent, but within his own milieu, he demonstrates his own innovative touch at prices that are much more reasonable. For starters, consider a succulent version of Brazilian-style shrimp resting on toast that's been smeared with pulverized olives, capers, and pork sausage; or a savory version of a cheesy Alpine staple, *raclette,* made with mustard sauce and *Curé Nantais* cheese; scallops sautéed with Chinese noodles and chanterelles and served with slices of pink grapefruit; and slow-braised pork cooked for 7 hours, and served on a bed of carrots, apricots, and comfit of lemon. Our most recent dessert was an inspired brownie with a clementine-flavored sorbet and "perfumed juices."

8 rue St-Lazare, 9e. ✆ **01-48-78-62-73.** Reservations recommended far in advance. Main courses 25€–34€ ($33–$44); fixed-price menu 34€ ($44). AE, DC, MC, V. Mon–Fri noon–2:30pm and 7:30–10:30pm. Métro: Notre-Dame de Lorette, Opéra, or Cadet.

Wally Le Saharien ALGERIAN Head to this dining room—lined with desert photos and tribal artifacts crafted from ceramics, wood, and weavings—for an insight into the spicy, slow-cooked cuisine that fueled the colonial expansion of France into North Africa. The fixed-price dinner menu begins with a trio of starters: spicy soup, stuffed and grilled sardines, and a savory *pastilla* (puff pastry) of pigeon. Next comes any of several kinds of couscous or a *méchouia* (slow-cooked tart) of lamb dusted with an optional coating of sugar. *Merguez,* the cumin-laden spicy sausage of the North African world, factors importantly into any meal, as do homemade (usually honey-infused) pastries. End your meal with traditional mint-flavor tea.

36 rue Rodier, 9e. ✆ **01-42-85-51-90.** Reservations recommended. A la carte main courses (lunch only) 19€–23€ ($25–$30); fixed-price dinner 44€ ($57). MC, V. Tues–Sat noon–2pm and 7–10pm. Métro: Anvers.

RIGHT BANK: 10TH ARRONDISSEMENT (GARE DU NORD/GARE DE L'EST)

MODERATE

Brasserie Flo ★ ALSATIAN This remote restaurant is hard to find, but once you arrive (after walking through passageway after passageway), you'll see that *fin de siècle* Paris lives on. The restaurant opened in 1860 and has changed its decor very little. The specialty is *la formidable choucroute* (a mound of sauerkraut with boiled ham, bacon, and sausage) for two. Onion soup and sole meunière are always good, as are warm foie gras and guinea hen with lentils. Look for the plats du jour, ranging from roast pigeon to veal fricassee with sorrel, and filet of beef with foie gras.

7 cour des Petites-Ecuries, 10e. ✆ **01-47-70-13-59.** Reservations recommended. Main courses 15€–30€ ($20–$39); fixed-price menus 21€–31€ ($27–$40). AE, DC, MC, V. Daily noon–3pm and 7pm–1am. Métro: Château d'Eau or Strasbourg-St-Denis.

RIGHT BANK: 11TH ARRONDISSEMENT (OPERA BASTILLE)

MODERATE

Bistrot Paul Bert ★ TRADITIONAL FRENCH Some critics define this as the best moderately priced restaurant in this area. Expect a crowded, noisy, usually convivial ambience where necks strain to read the blackboard specials, and where overworked, independent-minded waiters don't suffer fools of any nationality lightly. Menu items evoke the classic traditions that have flourished here at least since the 1950s. Classics include chicken braised in yellow wine from the Jura; veal kidneys in mustard sauce; monkfish served with an herb-flavored cream sauce; and braised filet of sea bass with risotto whose ingredients change virtually every day.

18 rue Paul-Bert, 11e. ✆ **01-43-72-24-01.** Reservations recommended. Main courses 10€–20€ ($13–$26); fixed-price lunch 16€–32€ ($21–$42); fixed-price dinner 32€ ($42). MC, V. Tues–Sat noon–2:30pm and 7:30–11pm. Closed Aug. Métro: Faidherbe-Chaligny.

RIGHT BANK: 12TH ARRONDISSEMENT (BOIS DE VINCENNES/GARE DE LYON)

MODERATE

China Club ★ CHINESE/CANTONESE Evoking 1930s Hong Kong, this favorite is still going strong, laughing at upstart new Asian restaurants and serving some of the best Asian cuisine in Paris. The food is mainly Cantonese, prepared with flair. The menu is vast, with plenty of choices. Nearly everything is good, especially sautéed shrimp and calamari, Shanghai chicken, and red rice sautéed with vegetables. Before dinner, you might want to enjoy a drink in the upstairs smoking lounge. Downstairs, the Sing Song club has live music, including something called Sino-French jazz on Thursday, Friday, and Saturday.

50 rue de Charenton, 12e. ✆ **01-43-43-82-02.** Main courses 13€–29€ ($17–$38); fixed-price dinner 28€ ($36). AE, DC, MC, V. Sun–Thurs 7pm–2am; Fri–Sat 7pm–3am. Closed July 20–Aug 20. Métro: Bastille.

INEXPENSIVE

Swann & Vincent ITALIAN This is the kind of Italian trattoria (albeit with a French accent) that readers write to us about, praising both the quality of the food and the sense of cheerful amiability that brightens up evenings in a neighborhood not often frequented by foreign visitors. The setting evokes an old-time Parisian brasserie from the turn of the 20th century, thanks to paneled walls, bordeaux-colored banquettes, big mirrors, and a prominent bartop crafted from ocher-colored marble. You can begin your meal with a fried combination of calamari and shrimp; or perhaps a visit to the antipasti buffet, for a medley of mostly fish and vegetarian starters. After that, you'll be tempted with a wide array of pastas. Tagliatelle with Gorgonzola or with shellfish is popular, as is ravioli with several choices of stuffing. Main courses include roasted racks of lamb or pork, and veal cutlets prepared *alla milanese* (fried in butter with bread crumbs), *alla parmigiana* (with a layer of cheese), or simply braised and served with lemon-butter or mushroom sauce.

7 rue St-Nicolas, 12e. ✆ **01-43-43-49-40.** Reservations recommended. Fixed-price lunch (Mon–Fri only) 15€ ($20); main courses 12€–16€ ($16–$21). MC, V. Daily noon–2:45pm and 7:30–11:45pm. Métro: Ledru-Rolin.

RIGHT BANK: 16TH ARRONDISSEMENT (TROCADERO/BOIS DE BOULOGNE)

VERY EXPENSIVE

Hiramatsu ★ *Finds* FRENCH Other than the fact that chef Hiroyuki Hiramatsu and most of his staff are Japanese, the only Asian touch at this restaurant is a hot, wet towel that arrives before the meal, in the Japanese style. Everything else is unabashedly French: the contemporary-looking dining room, seating just 40, that's outfitted in mostly monochromatic tones of black and white; rows of windows, each set with shimmering panes of red and blue cut glass; a minisalon where smokers can run in for a quick toke and/or a pre- or postdinner drink (the dining room is nonsmoking); and a polite staff wearing gray-and-white uniforms. Menu items change frequently, but they're always artfully presented. Examples include lightly smoked and marinated salmon served with *fines herbes,* deliberately undercooked crayfish served with a mousseline of mushrooms and a watercress-and-truffle salad, fried scallops served with a "brick" of rhubarb and a splash of champagne sauce, and saddle of roasted venison in puff pastry with vanilla and walnut gnocchi and a purée of celeriac and green apples.

52 rue de Longchamps, 16e. ✆ **01-56-81-08-80.** Reservations required. Main courses 38€–60€ ($50–$78); fixed-price lunch 48€ ($62); fixed-price dinner 95€–130€ ($124–$169). AE, DC, MC, V. Mon–Fri 12:30–2pm and 7:30–9:30pm. Métro: Trocadéro.

MODERATE

La Butte Chaillot ★ *Value* TRADITIONAL FRENCH This baby bistro showcases culinary high priest Guy Savoy and draws a crowd from the affluent neighborhood's corporate offices. Diners congregate in posh but congested areas. Menu items change weekly (sometimes daily) and betray a strange sense of mass production not unlike that found in a luxury cruise liner's dining room. Examples are a sophisticated medley of terrines; a "low-fat" version of chunky mushroom soup; a salad of snails and herbed potatoes; succulent rack of lamb; and roasted rabbit with sage and a compote of onions, bacon, and mushrooms. A starkly contemporary stainless-steel staircase leads to extra seating in the cellar.

110 bis av. Kléber, 16e. ✆ **01-47-27-88-88.** Reservations recommended. Main courses 16€–27€ ($21–$35); fixed-price menus 33€ ($43). AE, DC, MC, V. Sun–Fri noon–2:30pm; daily 7–11pm. Métro: Trocadéro.

RIGHT BANK: 17TH ARRONDISSEMENT (PARC MONCEAU/PLACE CLICHY)

VERY EXPENSIVE

Guy Savoy ★★★ TRADITIONAL FRENCH One of the hottest chefs in Europe, Guy Savoy serves the kind of food he likes to eat, prepared with consummate skill. We think he has a slight edge over his rival Michel Rostang (see below), though Ducasse, at least in media coverage, surpasses them both. The decor is sober, monochromatic, and deliberately understated for the superb and fussed-over food. Although the superb meals comprise as many as nine courses, the portions are small; you won't necessarily be satiated at the end. The menu changes with the seasons and may include cream soup of lentils and crayfish; cream of artichoke soup with Parmesan and black truffles; roasted rack of veal served with truffle-studded mashed potatoes; or sea bass grilled in a salt shell and served with a sauce of sweet herbs. If you come in the right season, you may have a chance to order game such as mallard and venison. Savoy is fascinated with mushrooms and has been known to serve a dozen types, especially in autumn. An example includes a delectable pan-fried combination of mussels and wild mushrooms.

18 rue Troyon, 17e. ✆ **01-43-80-40-61.** Fax 01-46-22-43-09. Reservations for dinner required 1 month in advance; 2–3 days in advance for lunch. Main courses 72€–160€ ($94–$208); *menu dégustation* 230€–285€ ($299–$371). AE, DC, MC, V. Tues–Fri noon–2pm; Tues–Sat 7–10:30pm. Métro: Charles-de-Gaulle–Etoile or Ternes.

Michel Rostang ★★★ FRENCH Michel Rostang is one of Paris's most creative chefs, the fifth generation of a distinguished French "cooking family." His restaurant has four dining rooms paneled in mahogany, cherrywood, or pearwood; some have frosted Lalique crystal panels. Changing every 2 months, the menu offers modern improvements on *cuisine bourgeoise.* Truffles are the dish of choice in midwinter, and you'll find racks of suckling lamb from the salt marshes of France's western seacoasts in spring; in game season, look for pheasant and venison. Year-round staples are quail eggs with sea urchins; fricassee of sole; quenelles of whitefish with a lobster sauce; and Bresse chicken with mushroom purée and a salad composed of the chicken's thighs.

20 rue Rennequin, 17e. ✆ **01-47-63-40-77.** Fax 01-47-63-82-75. Reservations required 1 week in advance. Main courses 60€–98€ ($78–$127); fixed-price menu 70€–230€ ($91–$299) lunch, 175€–230€ ($228–$299) dinner. AE, DC, MC, V. Tues–Fri 12:30–2:30pm; Mon–Sat 7:30–10:30pm. Closed 3 weeks in Aug. Métro: Ternes.

MODERATE

Restaurante Caïus ★ *Value* TRADITIONAL FRENCH This chic place is popular for business lunches and dinners, also drawing residents and shoppers from the neighborhood. It's ringed with wood paneling and banquettes. The owner, Jean-Marc Notelet, has brought renewed vigor to the kitchen. The dining room is a showcase for the chef's enticing cuisine, which is based on flavor-filled local foodstuffs, spices, and judicious use of pepper. We were intrigued by shrimp roasted with paprika and *chermoula* seasonings (typically including cumin, coriander, and saffron); a confit of beef flavored with chocolate and Fava beans, known for their intense flavor, and served with braised and puréed celeriac; just-caught red tuna with fennel and Asian soya; and roasted cod with French *haricots verts* (green beans) and a comfit of fresh citrus sauce.

6 rue d'Armaillé, 17e. ✆ **01-42-27-19-20.** Reservations recommended. Main courses 19€–21€ ($25–$27); fixed-price lunch 23€ ($30); fixed-price dinner 38€ ($50). AE, DC, MC, V. Mon–Fri noon–2:30pm; Mon–Sat 7:30–10pm. Métro: Charles-de-Gaulle–Etoile.

RIGHT BANK: 18TH ARRONDISSEMENT (MONTMARTRE)

INEXPENSIVE

Le Grain de Folie ORGANIC/VEGETARIAN This place may be a bit difficult to find, but it's worth the search. Simple and wholesome, the cuisine is inspired by France, Greece, California, Turkey, and India. The menu includes an array of theme salads, cereals, tarts, terrines, and casseroles. Dessert selections might include an old-fashioned tart or a fruit salad. You can choose one of an array of wines or a frothy glass of vegetable juice to accompany your meal. The decor includes potted plants and exposed stone. Marie-Cécite is the charming owner.

24 rue de Lavieuville, 18e. ✆ **01-42-58-15-57.** Reservations recommended. Main courses 10€–12€ ($13–$16); fixed-price menus 12€–16€ ($16–$21). No credit cards. Tues–Sat 12:30–2:30pm and 7:30–11pm; Sun 11:30am–10pm. Métro: Abbesses.

LEFT BANK: 5TH ARRONDISSEMENT (LATIN QUARTER)

MODERATE

Brasserie Balzar ★ TRADITIONAL FRENCH Opened in 1898, Brasserie Balzar is battered but cheerful, with some of Paris's most colorful waiters. The menu makes almost no concessions to modern cuisine; it includes onion soup, pepper steak, sole meunière, sauerkraut with ham and sausage, pigs' feet, and fried calves' liver served without garnish. Be warned that if you want just coffee or a drink, you probably won't get a table at mealtimes. But the staff, accustomed to many patrons' odd hours, will be happy to serve you dinner in the midafternoon.

49 rue des Ecoles, 5e. ✆ **01-43-54-13-67.** Reservations strongly recommended. Main courses 18€–31€ ($23–$40). AE, DC, MC, V. Daily noon–11:45pm. Métro: Odéon or Cluny–La Sorbonne.

Marty ★ *Finds* MODERN FRENCH Charming, with a stone-trimmed decor that's authentic to the era (1913) when it was established, this restaurant has been "discovered" by new generations of restaurant-goers. Named after its founders, Etienne and Marthe Marty, its fame now extends beyond the 5th arrondissement. Service is attentive, and there are lots of Jazz Age murals on the walls. Food is savory, satisfying, and unfussy. Views from the hideaway tables on the mezzanine sweep over the entire human comedy, which is loud, large, and animated, unfolding above and below you. Begin your meal with tartare of sea bream flavored with anise and lime, lobster ravioli with sherry vinegar, or fresh oysters. Continue with suprême of guinea fowl with vegetable moussaka, a platter that combines grilled squid with grilled strips of red mullet, fried scallops with garlic butter sauce, or perhaps tuna with raspberries and pepper sauce. Dessert might include a soup of red fruits with orange-flavored liqueur.

20 av. des Gobelins, 5e. ✆ **01-43-31-39-51.** Main courses 19€–27€ ($25–$35); fixed-price menu 33€ ($43). AE, DC, MC, V. Daily noon–3pm and 7–11pm. Métro: Gobelins.

INEXPENSIVE

Breakfast in America AMERICAN DINER Connecticut-born Hollywood screenwriter Craig Carlson opened this replica of a down-home U.S.-based diner in 2003, building it with funds from members of the California film community who donated memorabilia from some of their films. Its self-proclaimed mission involves dispensing proper, rib-sticking breakfasts and diner food to a generation of Parisians who assume, prior to their visits here, that coffee comes only as espresso, and that meal quantities are rigidly limited. To their delight, coffee cups here are "bottomless," and food items, especially breakfast items, evoke the good old days of America's bountiful agrarian past. The venue replicates a 1950s-era railway car, replete with scarlet-and-black Naugahyde banquettes, faux windows with mirrored insets, and an unabashedly Americanized staff. Breakfast (heaping portions of the egg-and-waffle-and-bacon combinations, as well as omelets) is served all day. Also available are a half-dozen variations of burgers, as well as tacos, club sandwiches and BLTs, veggie wraps, spinach tortillas, and blue-plate specials such as steak with shrimp. A full-service bar is on-site.

17 rue des Ecoles, 5e. ✆ **01-43-54-50-28.** Reservations not accepted. Breakfast platters 5.95€–9.50€ ($7.75–$12); fixed-price Sunday brunch 15€ ($20); lunch and dinner platters and "blue-plate specials" 6.50€–10€ ($8.45–$13). MC, V. Daily 8:30am–10:30pm. Métro: Cardinal Lemoine or Jussieu.

Coco de Mer ★ *Finds* SEYCHELLE ISLANDS The theme of this restaurant tugs at the emotions of Parisians who have spent their holidays on the beaches of the Seychelles in the Indian Ocean. It contains several dining rooms, one of which is outfitted like a beach, with a sand-covered floor, replicas of palm trees, and a scattering of conch shells. Menu items feature such exotic dishes as tartare of tuna flavored with ginger, olive oil, salt, and pepper; and smoked swordfish, served as carpaccio or in thin slices with mango mousse and spicy sauce. Main courses focus on fish, including *boirzoes* (a species of red snapper) imported from the Seychelles. Dessert might be a *crème de banana gratinée.*

34 bd. St-Marcel, 5e. ✆ **01-47-07-06-64.** Reservations recommended. Main courses 14€–20€ ($18–$26); fixed-price menus 30€–40€ ($39–$52). AE, DC, MC, V. Tues–Sat noon–3pm; Mon–Sat 7:30pm–midnight. Métro: Les Gobelins or St-Marcel.

Perraudin TRADITIONAL FRENCH Everything about this place—decor, cuisine, prices, and service—attempts to duplicate an early-1900s bistro. This one was built in 1870 as an outlet for coal and wine. It evolved into the wood-paneled bistro you see today, where little has changed since Zola was buried in the Panthéon nearby. The walls look marinated in tea; the marble-topped tables, mirrors, and vaudeville posters have been here forever. Reservations aren't made in advance: Diners usually drink a glass of kir at the zinc-topped bar as they wait. (Tables turn over quickly.) Onion tart, pumpkin soup, and terrine are all good appetizers. The menu includes roast leg of lamb with *dauphinois* potatoes, *boeuf bourguignon,* and grilled salmon with sage sauce. The charming, lovely owner and chef, Mme Rameau, has fed many of the grandest scholars and professors in Europe. She accepts reservations only for early-bird

Where to Dine on the Left Bank

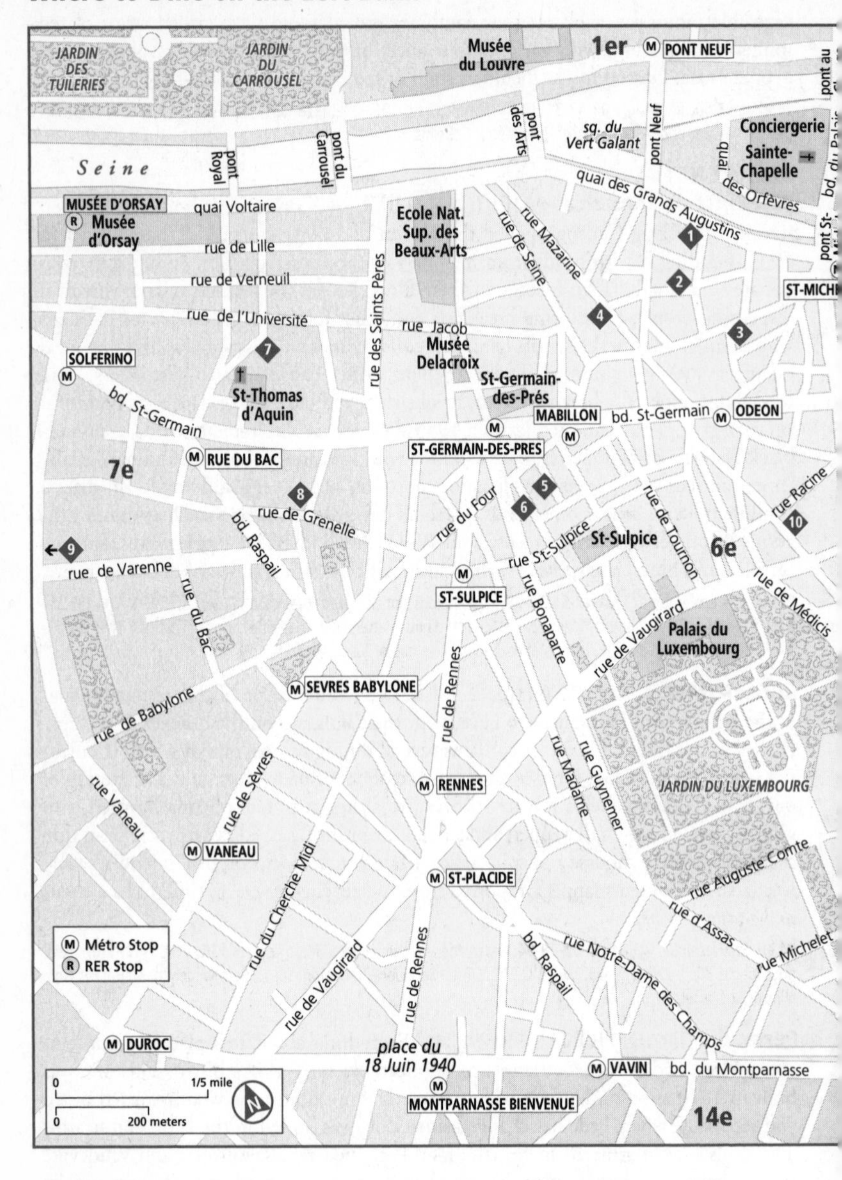

diners between 7 and 8pm. Diners arriving after that must wait at the zinc bar for a table to become available.

157 rue St-Jacques, 5e. ✆ **01-46-33-15-75.** Main courses 16€–29€ ($21–$38); fixed-price menu 18€ ($23) lunch, 28€ ($36) dinner. MC, V. Mon–Sat noon–2:15pm and 7–10pm. Closed 3 weeks in Aug. Métro: Cluny–La Sorbonne. RER: Luxembourg.

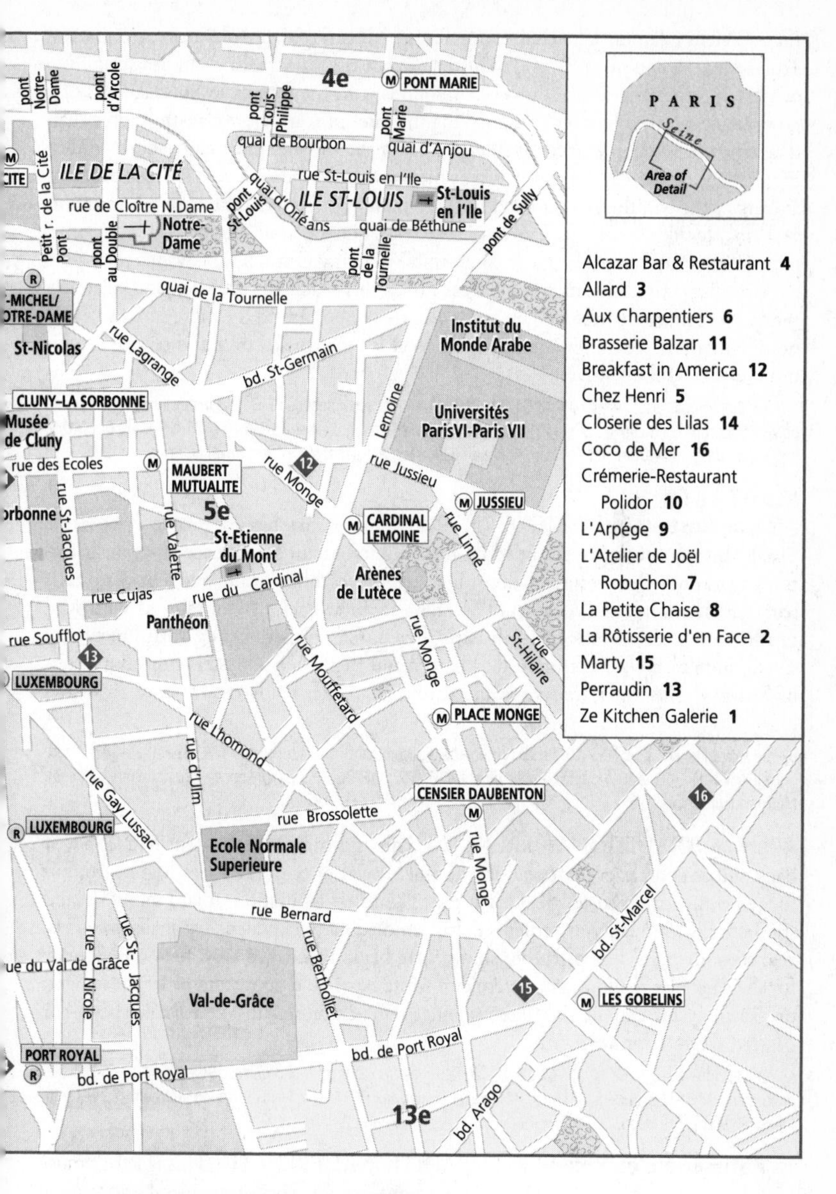

LEFT BANK: 6TH ARRONDISSEMENT (ST-GERMAIN/LUXEMBOURG)

EXPENSIVE

Closerie des Lilas ★ TRADITIONAL FRENCH Opened in 1847, the Closerie was a social and culinary magnet for the avant-garde. The famous people who have sat in the "Pleasure Garden of the Lilacs" include Gertrude Stein and Alice B. Toklas,

Ingres, Henry James, Chateaubriand, Picasso, Hemingway, Apollinaire, Lenin and Trotsky (at the chess board), and Whistler. Today, the crowd may include a sprinkling of stars and the star-struck. The place resounds with the sometimes-loud sounds of a jazz pianist every night after 7pm, making the interior seem more claustrophobic than it is. If you're asked to wait for a table, you can make the wait more enjoyable by ordering the world's best champagne julep at the bar. It's also possible to have just coffee or a drink at the bar, though the food is better than ever. Try veal kidneys with mustard, veal ribs in cider sauce, steak tartare, pikeperch quenelles, or filet of beef with green peppercorn sauce. You'll be more comfortable here if you realize in advance that there are two distinctly different seating areas inside this place: the crowded and relatively inexpensive brasserie (also known as *le bateau*—the boat); and the more expensive and nominally more sedate restaurant, where food is more fussed over and service is a bit more formal and attentive.

171 bd. du Montparnasse, 6e. ✆ **01-40-51-34-50.** Reservations recommended 2–3 days in advance (for restaurant only). Restaurant main courses 35€–45€ ($46–$59); brasserie main courses 19€–24€ ($25–$31). AE, DC, MC, V. Restaurant daily noon–2pm and 7–11pm. Brasserie daily 11:30am–1am. Métro: Port Royal or Vavin.

MODERATE

Alcazar Restaurant ★ MODERN FRENCH Paris's highest-profile *brasserie de luxe* is this high-tech place funded by British restaurateur Sir Terence Conran. It features a red-and-white futuristic decor in a street-level dining room and a busy upstairs bar (La Mezzanine de l'Alcazar). The menu includes rack of veal sautéed with wild mushrooms, roasted rack of lamb with thyme, Charolais duckling with honey and spices, monkfish with saffron in puff pastry, and shellfish and oysters from the waters of Brittany. The wines are stylish and diverse, and the trendy crowd tends to wear a lot of black.

62 rue Mazarine, 6e. ✆ **01-53-10-19-99.** Reservations recommended. Main courses 18€–32€ ($23–$42); fixed-price lunch 20€–30€ ($26–$39); fixed-price dinner 40€ ($52). AE, DC, MC, V. Daily noon–3pm and 7pm–midnight. Métro: Odéon.

Allard ★ TRADITIONAL FRENCH This old-time bistro, opened in 1931, is back and as good as ever after a long decline. It was once the city's leading bistro, but today's competition is too great for it to reclaim that reputation. Allard serves the old specialties, with quality ingredients deftly handled by the kitchen. Try snails, foie gras, veal stew, or frogs' legs or turbot in a beurre blanc sauce. We head here on Monday for the cassoulet Toulousian (casserole of white beans and goose and other meats) and on Saturday for coq au vin. The cassoulet remains one of the Left Bank's best. For dessert, we vote for *tarte* Tatin.

41 rue St-André-des-Arts, 6e. ✆ **01-43-26-48-23.** Reservations required. Main courses 19€–39€ ($25–$51); fixed-price menu 24€–32€ ($31–$42) lunch, 32€ ($42) dinner. AE, DC, MC, V. Mon–Sat noon–3pm and 7:30–11pm. Métro: St-Michel or Odéon.

La Rôtisserie d'en Face ★ *Value* TRADITIONAL FRENCH This is Paris's most popular baby bistro, operated by Jacques Cagna, whose expensive namesake restaurant is across the street. The informal postmodern decor features high-tech lighting, yellow walls, and red banquettes. The simply prepared food is very good and employs high-quality ingredients. It includes several types of ravioli, pâté of duckling *en croûte* (in a pastry) with foie gras, fish, scallops, *friture d'éperlans* (tiny fried freshwater fish), and smoked Scottish salmon with spinach. Cagna's Barbary duckling in red-wine sauce is incomparable.

2 rue Christine, 6e. ✆ **01-43-26-40-98.** Reservations recommended. Main courses 22€ ($29); fixed-price menu 25€–29€ ($33–$38). AE, DC, MC, V. Mon–Fri noon–2:30pm; Mon–Sat 7–11pm. Métro: Odéon or St-Michel.

Ze Kitchen Galerie ★ *Finds* FRENCH/INTERNATIONAL The owner and head chef of this restaurant trained in haute Parisian gastronomy under culinary czar Guy Savoy. Since William Ledeuil established this place in 2001, he's attracted the likes of First Lady Laura Bush, who dined here in 2002. The setting is a colorful loft space in an antique building, with an open kitchen. Most of the paintings on display are for sale (the place doubles as an art gallery). Menu items, like the paintings, change about every 5 weeks. Appetizers are subdivided into pastas, soups, and fish, and main courses are divided into meats and fish that are usually grilled *à la plancha* (with a cooking implement—*la plancha*—that resembles a griddle). The best examples include platters of oysters, mussels, and sea urchins served with herb sauce and *crostini* (literally, little toasts); and grilled shoulder of wild boar with tamarind sauce.

4 rue des Grands-Augustins, 6e. ✆ **01-44-32-00-32.** Reservations recommended. Main courses 22€–30€ ($29–$39); fixed-price lunch with wine 23€–34€ ($30–$44). AE, DC, MC, V. Mon–Fri noon–2:30pm; Mon–Sat 7–11pm. Métro: St-Michel.

INEXPENSIVE

Aux Charpentiers TRADITIONAL FRENCH This old bistro, which opened more than 130 years ago, attracts those seeking the Left Bank of yesteryear. It was once the rendezvous spot of the master carpenters, whose guild was next door. Nowadays, it's where young men take dates. Though the food isn't imaginative, it's well prepared in the best tradition of *cuisine bourgeoise*—hearty but not effete. Appetizers include pâté of duck and rabbit terrine, and we recommend roast duck with olives for the main course. The plats du jour recall French home cooking: salt pork with lentils, *pot-au-feu,* and stuffed cabbage. The wine list has a selection of bordeaux, including Château Gaussens.

10 rue Mabillon, 6e. ✆ **01-43-26-30-05.** Reservations required. Main courses 19€–25€ ($25–$33); fixed-price lunch 20€ ($25); fixed-price dinner 26€ ($34). AE, DC, MC, V. Daily noon–3pm and 7–11:30pm. Métro: St-Germain-des-Prés or Mabillon.

Chez Henri LYONNAIS This is that cozy bistro, all wood and velvet, that you hope to find in Paris. Chez Henri also specializes in the dishes of the Lyon region, still hailed as the gastronomic center of France. The elegantly decorated place is warm and welcoming, and they will feed you well, all at a reasonable price. Slow-cooked lamb with prunes and potatoes gratin is worth crossing town to devour, as is the *magret de canard* (duckling) with honey and delicate fish dishes such as red mullet in a cream sauce are always excellent. We like to finish off with crème brûlée, based on a coveted and carefully guarded family recipe.

16 rue Princesse, 6e. ✆ **01-43-33-51-12.** Reservations recommended. Main courses 12€–18€ ($16–$23). MC, V. Daily noon–2:30pm and 7–11:30pm. Metro: Mabillon.

Crémerie-Restaurant Polidor ★ *Kids* TRADITIONAL FRENCH Crémerie Polidor is the most traditional bistro in the Odéon area, serving *cuisine familiale.* Its name dates from the early 1900s, when it specialized in frosted cream desserts, but the restaurant can trace its history to 1845. The Crémerie was André Gide's favorite, and Joyce, Hemingway, Valéry, Artaud, and Kerouac also dined here. The place still attracts students and artists, who head for the rear. Peer beyond the lace curtains and brass hat racks to see drawers where, in olden days, regular customers used to lock up their cloth napkins. Overworked but smiling waitresses serve the 19th-century cuisine. Try pumpkin soup followed by *boeuf bourguignon, confit de canard,* or *blanquette de veau* (veal stew). For dessert, order a chocolate, raspberry, or lemon tart—the best in all Paris.

41 rue Monsieur-le-Prince, 6e. ✆ **01-43-26-95-34.** Main courses 11€–16€ ($14–$21); fixed-price menu (Mon–Fri) 12€–30€ ($16–$39) lunch, 20€–30€ ($26–$39) dinner. No credit cards. Daily noon–2:30pm; Mon–Sat 7pm–12:30am; Sun 7–11pm. Métro: Odéon.

LEFT BANK: 7TH ARRONDISSEMENT (EIFFEL TOWER/MUSEE D'ORSAY)

VERY EXPENSIVE

L'Arpège ★★★ MODERN FRENCH L'Arpège is best known for Alain Passard's specialties—no restaurant here serves better food. Surrounded by etched glass, burnished steel, monochromatic oil paintings, and pearwood paneling, you can enjoy specialties such as couscous of vegetables and shellfish; lobster braised in the yellow wine of the Jura; braised monkfish in a mustard sauce; pigeon roasted with almonds and honey-flavored mead; and carpaccio of crayfish with caviar-flavored cream sauce. While Passard is loath to include red meat on his menus, it does appear from time to time, in Kobe beef and (during late autumn and early winter) venison. But he focuses on fish, shellfish, poultry, and—his current passion—vegetables. These he elevates to levels unequalled by any other chef in Paris. The signature dessert is a candied tomato stuffed with 12 kinds of dried and fresh fruit, served with anise-flavored ice cream.

84 rue de Varenne, 7e. ✆ **01-47-05-09-06.** Fax 01-44-18-98-39. Reservations required 2 weeks in advance. Main courses 48€–180€ ($62–$234). AE, DC, MC, V. Mon–Fri 12:30–2:30pm and 8–10:30pm. Métro: Varenne.

EXPENSIVE

L'Atelier de Joël Robuchon ★★ FRENCH Upon his retirement in the mid-1990s, Joël Robuchon was hailed around the world as the greatest chef in France. Well, he's back, but in a style and format that's either swank and stylish or a bit unnerving, depending on your point of view. All of the restaurant's 41 seats are pulled up to a bar-style countertop that completely surrounds an open kitchen. The only reservations accepted are for the earliest seating (6:30pm). You may start with pumpkin and cauliflower soup with smoky bacon, or divine chicken-liver terrine. Among the sublime main courses are caramelized quail glazed with shallot-perfumed sauce; buttery, tender langoustines in pastry; ravioli of crayfish with foie gras sauce; and a succulent version of sole meunière. Duckling comes roasted, braised, and flavored with spices such as ginger, nutmeg, and cinnamon. The fish and shellfish are shipped fresh from Brittany.

5–7 rue de Montalembert, 7e. ✆ **01-42-22-56-56.** Reservations required. Main courses 30€–70€ ($39–$91); fixed-price menu 110€ ($143). MC, V. Daily 11:30am–3:30pm and 6:30pm–midnight. Métro: Rue du Bac.

Le Chamarré ★★★ *Finds* FRENCH/MAURITIAN Come here for food that appeals to your brain as much as your palate. Opened in 2002, Le Chamarré immediately shot into the Parisian consciousness, thanks to the inspired cuisine of a pair of French and Mauritian chefs. The restaurant's name translates as "nuances of color," and its French cuisine is subtly influenced by the heat, aromas, and flavors of Mauritius, an island in the Indian Ocean. The decorative interest comes from high-tech lighting whose colors and filters (oranges, blues, reds, and yellows) evoke the luminary spectrum of the skies over the island. Try chicken with curry, Indian rice and herbs;

line-caught sea bass served with an emulsion of limes and comfit of leeks with banana leaves; grilled octopus with garlic; Breton lobster braised in bouillabaisse; and French-derived grilled slices of suckling veal with fried mushroom and walnut oil. Desserts are unusual, with ingredients you may not associate with sweets, such as sliced and fried eggplant with vanilla sauce and laurel-flavored ice cream, and a rum-soaked *savarin* (spongecake) served with ice cream that's flavored with an infusion of Basmati rice.

13 bd. de la Tour-Maubourg, 7e. ✆ **01-47-05-50-18.** Reservations required. Main courses 25€–35€ ($33–$46); fixed-price lunch 40€ ($52); fixed-price dinner 65€–130€ ($85–$169). AE, DC, MC, V. Mon–Fri noon–2:30pm and 7:30–10:30pm; Sat 7:30–10:30pm. Closed Aug. Métro: Invalides.

Le Violon d'Ingres ★★★ FRENCH This restaurant is Paris's *pièce de résistance.* Chef-owner Christian Constant is "the new Robuchon." Those fortunate enough to dine in Violon's warm atmosphere rave about the artistic dishes. They range from pan-fried foie gras with gingerbread and spinach salad to more elegant main courses such as lobster ravioli with crushed vine-ripened tomatoes; roasted veal in light, creamy milk sauce served with tender spring vegetables; and even a selection from the rotisserie, including spit-roasted leg of lamb rubbed with fresh garlic and thyme. The service is charming and discreet; the wine selection, well chosen. The Constant family has virtually tied up the dining rituals along rue St-Dominique, with less expensive and less formal restaurants flanking Le Violon d'Ingres on either side, including Café Constant (see below).

135 rue St-Dominique, 7e. ✆ **01-45-55-15-05.** Fax 01-45-55-48-42. Reservations required at least 2 days in advance. Main courses 40€–46€ ($52–$60); *menu dégustation* 110€ ($143); fixed-price lunch 50€–110€ ($65–$143); fixed-price dinner 80€–110€ ($104–$143). AE, DC, MC, V. Tues–Sat noon–2:30pm and 7–10:30pm. Métro: Invalides or Ecole-Militaire.

MODERATE

La Petite Chaise FRENCH This is Paris's oldest restaurant, opened as an inn in 1680 by the baron de la Chaise at the edge of a hunting preserve. (According to lore, the baron used the upstairs bedrooms for afternoon dalliances, between fox and pheasant hunts.) Very Parisian, the "Little Chair" offers a world of cramped but attractive tables, old wood paneling, and ornate wall sconces. A vigorous chef has brought renewed taste and flavor to this longtime favorite, and the four-course set menu offers a large choice of dishes in each category. Examples are magret of duck with sweet-and-sour sauce; *pot-au-feu,* whose ingredients change with the seasons; and grilled sea bass on a bed of fennel with a light butter sauce.

36 rue de Grenelle, 7e. ✆ **01-42-22-13-35.** Reservations recommended. Main courses all 19€ ($25). Fixed-price menu 19€–31€ ($25–$40). MC, V. Daily noon–2pm and 7–11pm. Métro: Sèvres-Babylone or Rue du Bac.

INEXPENSIVE

Café Constant ★ *Value* FRENCH This is the least expensive of the trio of nearly adjacent restaurants established along the rue St-Dominique by mega-chef Christian Constant, whose mainstream, ultraluxe restaurant (Le Violin d'Ingres) is also recommended. It prides itself on fast service, fast turnover, and well-prepared but not particularly complicated cuisine, which is a good value within this posh and expensive neighborhood. Within two separate dining rooms, one on the ground floor and a smaller one upstairs, you can order main courses such as a *terrine de kako,* made with pork and foie gras and served with lentils and vinaigrette sauce; a tartare of oysters and salmon, flavored with ginger; and veal scallops *"cordon bleu"* that are layered with ham and cheese, breaded, and fried. Desserts are simple, including a chocolate tart and rice pudding. Reservations aren't accepted except for large groups, so most diners are asked to wait at the wood-topped bar for a table to become available. Waits are usually not very long.

139 rue St-Dominique, 7e. ✆ **01-47-53-73-34.** Reservations accepted only for groups of 5 or more. Main courses 12€ ($16). MC, V. Tues–Sat noon–2:30pm and 7–10:30pm. Métro: Invalides.

LEFT BANK: 14TH ARRONDISSEMENT (GARE MONTPARNASSE)

MODERATE

La Cagouille ★ *Finds* FRENCH/SEAFOOD Don't expect to find meat at this temple of seafood—owner Gérard Allamandou refuses to feature it. Everything about La Cagouille is a testimonial to a modern version of the culinary arts of La Charente, the flat sandy district on the Atlantic south of Bordeaux. In a trio of oak-sheathed dining rooms, you'll sample seafood prepared as naturally as possible, with no fancy sauces or elaborate techniques. Allamandou's preferred fish is red mullet, which may appear sautéed in oil or baked in rock salt. The name derives from the regional symbol of La Charente, the sea snail, whose preparation its namesake elevates to a fine culinary art. Look for a vast assemblage of French, mostly white, wines and at least 150 cognacs.

10–12 place Constantin-Brancusi, 14e. ✆ **01-43-22-09-01.** Reservations recommended. Main courses 20€–35€ ($26–$46); fixed-price menu 26€–42€ ($34–$55). MC, V. Daily noon–2:30pm and 7:30–10:30pm. Métro: Gaité.

L'Assiette SOUTHWESTERN FRENCH Everything here appeals to a nostalgic crowd seeking down-to-earth prices and flavorful food. Every meal is a set lunch or dinner. The place was a charcuterie in the 1930s and maintains some of its old accessories. Mitterrand used to drop in for oysters, crayfish, sea urchins, and clams. The food is inspired by Paris's long tradition of bistro cuisine, with a few twists. Examples are chanterelle mushroom salad; *rillettes* (roughly textured pâté) of mackerel; very fresh fish; and homemade desserts, including a crumbly version of apple cake with fresh North African figs. Particularly delicious is *petit salé* (stew with vegetables) of duckling with wine from the Poitou region of west-central France.

181 rue du Château, 14e. ✆ **01-43-22-64-86.** Reservations recommended. Fixed-price menus 50€ ($65). AE, MC, V. Sat–Sun noon–2:30pm; Tues–Sun 8–10:30pm. Closed Aug. Métro: Gaité.

5 The Top Cafes

Whatever your pleasure—reading, meeting a lover, writing your memoirs, nibbling a hard-boiled egg, or drinking yourself into oblivion—you can do it at a French cafe. (For the top wine bars, see "Paris After Dark," in chapter 6.)

Brasserie Lipp, 151 bd. St-Germain, 6e (✆ **01-45-48-53-91;** Métro: St-Germain-des-Prés), has an upstairs dining room, but it's more fashionable to sit in the back room. For breakfast, order traditional black coffee and croissants. At lunch or dinner, the specialty is pork and *choucroute*—the best in Paris. The food is only so-so. Open daily 9:30am to 2am. Restaurant service is available only from 12:45 to 11:45pm, and it's fashionable to arrive late.

Across from the Centre Pompidou, avant-garde **Café Beaubourg,** 100 rue St-Martin, 4e (✆ **01-48-87-63-96;** Métro: Rambuteau or Hôtel-de-Ville), boasts soaring concrete columns and minimalist decor by the architect Christian de Portzamparc. The food is passable, but it's the location that keeps this cafe humming. In summer, tables spill onto the sprawling terrace, providing a panoramic view of the neighborhood's goings-on. Open Sunday to Wednesday 8am to 1am, Thursday to Saturday 8am to 2am.

Jean-Paul Sartre came to **Café de Flore,** 172 bd. St-Germain, 6e (✆ **01-45-48-55-26;** Métro: St-Germain-des-Prés), where it's said he wrote his trilogy *Les Chemins de la Liberté* (The Roads to Freedom). The cafe is still going strong, though celebrities have moved on. Open daily from 7:30am to 1:30am.

Next door, the legendary **Deux Magots,** 6 place St-Germain-des-Prés, 6e (✆ **01-45-48-55-25;** Métro: St-Germain-des-Prés), is still the hangout for sophisticated residents and a tourist favorite in summer. Inside are two Asian statues that give the cafe its name. It's open daily from 7:30am to 1:30am.

Fouquet's, 99 av. des Champs-Elysées, 8e (✆ **01-47-23-50-00;** Métro: George V), is the premier cafe on the Champs-Elysées. Outside, a barricade of potted flowers separates cafe tables from the sidewalk. Inside are a grill room, private rooms, and a restaurant. The cafe and grill room are open daily from 8am to 2am; the restaurant and the slightly less formal grill are open daily from noon to 3pm and 7pm to midnight.

At **La Coupole,** 102 bd. Montparnasse, 14e (✆ **01-43-20-14-20;** Métro: Vavin), the crowd ranges from artists' models to young men dressed like Rasputin. People come here to see and be seen. Perhaps order a coffee or cognac VSOP at a sidewalk table, repeating a ritual that has continued since the place was established in 1927. The dining room serves food that is sometimes good, sometimes indifferent. It serves a buffet breakfast Monday through Friday from 8:30 to 10:30am. Open daily from 8:30am to 1am.

Café de la Musique, in the Cité de la Musique, place Fontaine Aux Lions, 213 av. Jean-Jaurès, 19e (✆ **01-48-03-15-91;** Métro: Porte de Pantin), attracts a crowd devoted to music. The recorded sounds in the background are likely to be more diverse and eclectic than in any other cafe in Paris. The red-and-green-velour setting may remind you of a modern opera house. On the menu you'll find pasta with shellfish, pork in cider sauce, and stingray in black butter sauce. Open daily 8am to 2am.

In the Marais, **La Belle Hortense,** 31 rue Vieille du Temple, 4e (✆ **01-48-04-71-60;** Métro: Hôtel de Ville or St-Paul), is the most literary cafe in a legendary literary neighborhood. It offers an erudite and accessible staff; an inventory of French literary classics as well as modern tomes about art, psychoanalysis, history, and culture; and two high-ceilinged, 19th-century rooms little changed since the days of Baudelaire and Balzac. The zinc-covered bar serves wine for 3€ to 8€ ($3.90–$10) a glass. It's open daily as a cafe and bookstore from 5pm to 2am.

6

Exploring Paris

Paris is one of those cities where the street life—shopping, strolling, and hanging out—should claim as much time as sightseeing. A gourmet picnic in the Bois de Boulogne, a sunrise pilgrimage to the Seine, an afternoon at a flea market—Paris bewitches you with these experiences. For all the Louvre's beauty, you'll probably remember the Latin Quarter's crooked alleyways better than the 370th oil painting of your visit.

The best way to discover Paris is on foot. Walk along the avenue des Champs-Elysées, tour the quays of the Seine, wander the Ile de la Cité and Ile St-Louis, browse the shops and stalls, and stroll the squares and parks. A walk at dawn can be enthralling as you see the city come to life: Merchants wash shop fronts, cafes begin serving coffee and croissants, and vegetable and fruit vendors start setting up their stalls and arranging their produce.

Paris is also a shopper's city—with everything from tony boutiques to colorful street markets. We've covered the best of the best in this chapter.

For sheer variety, there's nothing like Paris nightlife. Nowhere else will you find such bars, clubs, cabarets, jazz dives, music halls, and honky-tonks. (For information about the cafe scene, see chapter 5.)

ORGANIZED TOURS

Before plunging into sightseeing on your own, you may want to take the most popular get-acquainted tour in Paris: **Cityrama,** 149 rue St-Honoré, 1er (✆ **01-44-55-61-00;** Métro: Palais-Royal–Musée du Louvre). On a double-decker bus with enough windows for Versailles, you take a 2-hour ride through the city. While you don't go inside any attractions, you get a look at the outside of Notre-Dame and the Eiffel Tower, among other sites, and a good feel for the city. Earphones provide commentary in eight languages. Tours depart daily at 10am, 11am, 2pm, and 3pm. A 1½-hour orientation tour is 17€ ($22) adults and 8.50€ ($11) children. A morning tour with interior visits to the Louvre costs 39€ ($51). Half-day tours to Versailles (59€/$77) and Chartres (55€/$72) are a good value and relieve some of the hassle associated with visiting those monuments. A joint ticket that includes Versailles and Chartres costs 95€ ($124). A tour of the nighttime illuminations leaves daily at 10pm in summer, 7pm in winter, and costs 22€ ($29); it tends to be tame and touristy.

The **RATP** (✆ **08-92-68-77-14;** www.ratp.fr), which runs regular public transportation, also operates the **Balabus,** a fleet of orange-and-white big-windowed motorcoaches. The only drawback is their limited operating times: Sunday and national holidays from 12:30 to 8:30pm, from April to the end of September. Itineraries run in both directions between Gare de Lyon and the Grand Arche de La Défense. Three Métro tickets will carry you along the entire route. You'll recognize the bus, and the route it follows, by the *Bb* symbol on its side and on signs posted along its route.

Value The Museum Discount Card

If you're a culture buff, consider buying a **Paris Museum Pass,** which admits you to some 70 museums in Paris and its environs. You do the math—if you plan to visit three or four museums, the card is usually worth the investment. A pass good for 2 days costs 30€ ($39); for 4 consecutive days, 45€ ($59); and for 6 consecutive days, 60€ ($78). Cards are available at all major museums and Métro stations. For more information, contact **Association InterMusees,** 4 rue Brantôme, 3e (✆ **01-44-61-96-60;** www.parismuseumpass.fr; Métro: Rambuteau).

A boat tour on the Seine provides vistas of the riverbanks and some of the best views of Notre-Dame. Many boats have sun decks, bars, and restaurants. **Bateaux-Mouche** (✆ **01-40-76-99-99;** www.bateaux-mouches.fr; Métro: Alma-Marceau) cruises depart from the Right Bank of the Seine, adjacent to pont de l'Alma, and last about 75 minutes. Tours leave daily at 20- to 30-minute intervals from 10am to 11pm between April and September. Between October and March, there are at least five departures daily between 11am and 9pm, with a schedule that changes according to demand and the weather. Fares are 8€ ($10) for adults and 4€ ($5.20) for children 4 to 13. Dinner cruises depart daily at 8:30pm, last 2 hours, and cost 95€ to 125€ ($124–$163). On dinner cruises, jackets and ties are required for men.

The amusingly named **Fat Tire Bike Tours–Paris,** 24 rue Edgar Faure, 15e (✆ **01-56-58-10-54;** www.fattirebiketoursparis.com), is a Texas-based company that offers guided English-speaking bike tours of the City of Light. This is a great way to get oriented to Paris, as you cycle by such monuments as the Eiffel Tower or Napoleon's impressive tomb. Night tours are also available. Day tours start daily at 11am from mid-February to mid-December; a second tour starts daily at 3pm April to October. Night tours run daily at 7pm mid-March to October; during March and the first 2 weeks of November, night tours run Tuesday, Thursday, Saturday, and Sunday at 7pm. Day tours cost 24€ ($31) per person, and night tours are 28€ ($36) each.

The first audio-guided tours of Paris have been launched by **Audio Visit,** which takes you through such famous neighborhoods as the Champs-Elysées district, Louvre/Opéra, and Montmartre. English commentaries are available, costing 8€ ($10) per half-day or 15€ ($20) for both audio guide and bike during the same time frame. Rentals of the audio guide are available at the Syndicat d'Initiative de Montmartre, 21 place du Tertre, 18e; Paris Story, 11 bis, rue Scribe, 9e; and Maison Roue Libre, Forum de Halles, 1 Passage Montdétour, 1er. For more information, call **04-78-29-60-72,** or visit www.audiovisit.com.

Context:Paris (✆ **888/467-1986** in the U.S., or 06-13-09-67-11; www.contextparis.com) is an organization of graduate students and art-history professors who lead thematic walking tours of the city. Tours range from 1-hour orientation "chats" to 4-hour in-depth visits of the Louvre. Being academics, the guides try to create a college seminar feeling without being too obtuse and scholarly. Context:Paris also rents cellphones, arranges transportation, and organizes culinary excursions. Prices vary widely depending on what itinerary you select, but many tours cost 50€ to 60€ ($65–$78) per person.

1 The Top Attractions

Arc de Triomphe ★★★ At the western end of the Champs-Elysées, the Arc de Triomphe is the largest triumphal arch in the world, about 49m (161 ft.) high and 44m (144 ft.) wide. Don't cross the square to reach it! With a dozen streets radiating from the "Star," the traffic circle is vehicular roulette. It's the busiest traffic hub in Paris. Instead, take the underground passage.

The arch has witnessed some of France's proudest moments—and some of its more humiliating defeats, as in 1871 (when Paris capitulated in the Franco-Prussian War) and 1940, when news cameras captured the memory of German troops marching under the arch.

Commissioned by Napoleon in 1806 to commemorate his Grande Armée's victories, the arch wasn't completed until 1836, under Louis-Philippe. Four years later, Napoleon's remains—brought from his grave on St. Helena—passed under the arch en route to his tomb at the Hôtel des Invalides. Since then it has become the focal point for state funerals. It's also the site of the Tomb of the Unknown Soldier, where an eternal flame burns.

Of the sculptures decorating the monument, the best known is Rude's *Marseillaise,* also called *The Departure of the Volunteers.* J. P. Cortot's *Triumph of Napoleon in 1810,* along with the *Resistance of 1814* and *Peace of 1815,* both by Etex, also adorn the facade. The arch is engraved with the names of hundreds of generals who commanded troops in Napoleonic victories.

You can take an elevator or climb the stairway to the top, where there's an exhibition hall with lithographs and photos depicting the arch throughout its history. From the observation deck, you have a panoramic view of the Champs-Elysées as well as such landmarks as the Louvre, Eiffel Tower, and Sacré-Coeur.

Place Charles-de-Gaulle–Etoile, 8e. ✆ **01-55-37-73-77.** www.monum.fr. Admission 10€ ($13) adults, 8€ ($10) under 25, free for children 18 and under. Apr–Sept daily 10am–11pm; Oct–Mar daily 10am–10:30pm. Métro: Charles-de-Gaulle–Etoile. Bus: 22, 30, 31, 52, 73, or 92.

Basilique du Sacré-Coeur ★★★ Montmartre's crowning achievement is Sacré-Coeur, with its gleaming white domes and *campanile* (bell tower), though its view of Paris takes precedence over the basilica itself. Like other Parisian landmarks, it has been the subject of much controversy. It was attacked for its ornate architecture, which was denounced in the Parisian press as more of a wedding cake than a church.

After France's defeat by the Prussians in 1870, the basilica was planned as an offering to cure the country's misfortunes; rich and poor alike contributed. Construction began in 1873, but the church wasn't consecrated until 1919. The interior is decorated with mosaics, the most striking of which are the ceiling depiction of Christ and the mural of the Passion at the back of the altar. The crypt contains what some believe is a piece of the sacred heart of Christ—hence the church's name.

On a clear day, the vista from the dome can extend for 56km (35 miles). You can also walk around the inner dome of the church, peering down like a pigeon (a few of which will likely be there to keep you company).

Place St-Pierre, 18e. ✆ **01-53-41-89-09.** www.sacre-coeur-montmartre.com. Free admission to basilica; joint ticket to dome and crypt 5€ ($6.50) adults. Basilica daily 6am–11pm; dome and crypt daily 9am–6pm. Métro: Abbesses; take elevator to surface and follow signs to funicular.

Centre Pompidou ★★★ The dream of former president Georges Pompidou, this center for 20th-century art, designed by Richard Rogers and Renzo Piano, opened in

1977 in the old Beaubourg neighborhood and became the focus of controversy. Its bold exoskeletal architecture and the brightly painted pipes and ducts crisscrossing its transparent facade (green for water, red for heat, blue for air, and yellow for electricity) were jarring. Perhaps the detractors were right all along—within 20 years, the building began to deteriorate so badly that a major restoration was called for. The center was relaunched in 2000.

The Centre Pompidou encompasses four separate attractions. The **Musée National d'Art Moderne (National Museum of Modern Art)** offers a large collection of 20th-century art. With some 40,000 works, this is the big draw, although it can display only about 850 works at one time. If you want to view some real charmers, see Alexander Calder's 1926 *Josephine Baker,* one of his earlier versions of the mobile, an art form he invented. Marcel Duchamp's *Valise* is a collection of miniature reproductions of his fabled dada sculptures and drawings; they're displayed in a carrying case. Every time we visit we have to see Salvador Dalí's *Portrait of Lenin Dancing on Piano Keys.*

In the **Public Information Library,** the public has free access to a million French and foreign books, periodicals, films, records, slides, and microfilms in nearly every area of knowledge. The **Center for Industrial Design** emphasizes contributions in the fields of architecture, visual communications, publishing, and community planning; and the **Institute for Research and Coordination of Acoustics/Music** brings together musicians and composers interested in furthering the cause of music, both contemporary and traditional.

Finally, you can visit a re-creation of the Jazz Age studio of Romanian sculptor **Brancusi (l'Atelier Brancusi),** which is configured as a mini-museum that's slightly separate from the rest of the action.

Place Georges-Pompidou, 4e. ✆ **01-44-78-12-33.** www.centrepompidou.fr. Admission 10€ ($13) adults, 8€ ($10) students, free for children under 18. Wed–Mon 11am–9pm. Métro: Rambuteau, Hôtel de Ville, or Châtelet–Les Halles.

Eiffel Tower ★★★ This may be the single most recognizable structure in the world—it's the symbol of Paris. Weighing 7,000 tons but exerting about the same pressure on the ground as a person sitting in a chair, the tower was not meant to be permanent. Gustave-Alexandre Eiffel, the engineer whose fame rested mainly on his iron bridges, built it for the Universal Exhibition of 1889. (He also designed the framework for the Statue of Liberty.)

The tower, including its 17m (56-ft.) TV antenna, is 317m (1,040 ft.) tall. (The advent of wireless communication in the early 1890s preserved the tower from destruction, because it was the best place in the city for antennas.) On a clear day you can see it from 64km (40 miles) away. Its open-framework construction ushered in the almost-unlimited possibilities of steel construction, paving the way for skyscrapers. Skeptics said it couldn't be built, and Eiffel wanted to make it soar higher. For years it remained the tallest man-made structure on earth.

You can visit the tower in three stages: Taking the elevator to the first landing, you'll have a view over the rooftops of Paris. A cinema, museum, restaurants, and bar are open year-round. The second landing provides a panoramic look at the city (on this level is Le Jules Verne restaurant, a great place for lunch or dinner). The third landing offers the best view, allowing you to identify monuments and buildings. On the ground level, in the eastern and western pillars, you can visit the 1899 elevator machinery when the tower is open.

To get to **Le Jules Verne** (✆ **01-45-55-61-44**), take the private south foundation elevator. You can enjoy an aperitif in the piano bar and then take a seat at one of the

Top Paris Attractions

MONTMARTRE
19
bd. de Clichy
place Pigalle
bd. de Rochechuart
av. Trudaine
rue Condorcet
rue Pigalle
rue N.D. de Lorette
rue Blanche
Casino de Paris
Ste-Trinité
Gare du Nord
rue de Dunkerque
bd. de Magenta
rue La Fayette
St-Vincent de Paul
rue de Chabrol
Gare de l'Est
rue de Paradis
St-Laurent
Notre-Dame de Lorette
Lazare
Folies Bergère
rue La Fayette
rue du Faubourg Poissonnière
rue du Faubourg St-Denis
bd. de Strasbourg
rue du Faubourg St-Martin
rue du Faubourg St-Martin
av. Jean Jaurès
rue Armand Carrel
avenue Secrétan
St-Joseph
St-Georges
place du Colonel Fabien
PARC DES BUTTES-CHAUMONT
bd. de la Villette
rue de le Grange
rue St-Maur
quai de Jemmapes
quai de Valmi
bd. Haussmann
Opéra Garnier
bd. des Italiens
bd. Montmartre
bd. des Capucines
place de l'Opéra
bd. de Bonne Nouvelle
rue du 4 Septembre
rue St-Augustin
rue de Richelieu
Bourse des Valeurs
rue de Cléry
rue d'Abukir
rue du Mail
bd. St-Martin
place de la République
rue du Faubourg du Temple
St-Joseph
place Vendôme
rue des Petits Champs
rue Réaumur
Conservatoire des Arts et Métiers
avenue de la République
St-Roch
Palais Royal
place A. Malraux
rue de Valois
rue du Louvre
rue Turbigo
rue de Sébastopol
rue St-Martin
rue Beaubourg
rue du Temple
bd. du Temple
bd. Voltaire
TUILERIES
Bourse du Commerce
Forum des Halles
13
14
rue des Archives
Archives Nationales
rue de Turenne
LE MARAIS
St-Ambroise
place du Carrousel
Musée du Louvre
12
rue de Rivoli
pont Royal
quai des Tuileries
quai Voltaire
pont du Carr.
quai Malaquais
pont des Arts
Théâtre du Châtelet
rue St-Martin
St-Merri
18
St-Denis
bd. Beaumarchais
rue du Chemin Vert
Ecole Nationale des Beaux-Arts
quai de Conti
pont Neuf
Seine
pont au Change
pont N. Dame
Hôtel de Ville
rue St-Antoine
16
place des Vosges
bd. Richard Lenoir
rue de la Roquette
Théâtre de la Bastille
ST-GERMAIN-DES-PRÉS
7
11
15
quai des Grands Augustins
ILE DE LA CITÉ
quai de l'Hôtel de Ville
St-Gervais
St-Paul
bd. St-Germain
Cloître N.Dame
10
pont St-Louis
quai St-Michel
Notre-Dame
ILE ST-LOUIS
place de la Bastille
17
rue du Faubourg St-Antoine
rue du Four
St-Sulpice
quai de la Tournelle
pont de la Tornelle
St-Louis
bd. Henry IV
Opéra Bastille
8
Sorbonne
rue Saint Jacques
rue des Ecoles
bd. St-Germain
pont de Sully
quai Henry IV
bd. Bourdon
bd. de la Bastille
rue de Lyon
rue de Charenton
avenue Daumesnil
rue de Vaugirard
Palais du Luxembourg
JARDIN DU LUXEMBOURG
QUARTIER LATIN
Institut du Monde Arabe
quai Saint Bernard
Université Paris VII
Panthéon
9
av. L. Rollin
bd. Diderot
rue de Bercy
Gare de Lyon
rue d'Assas
bd. Raspail
bd. St-Michel
rue Gay Lussac
JARDIN DES PLANTES
pont d'Austerlitz
Université Paris V
rue d'Ulm
Gare d'Austerlitz
quai d'Austerlitz
Seine
quai de la Rapée
bd. du Montparnasse
rue Claude Bernard
rue Buffon
St-Médard
rue Censier
Université Paris III
DU MONTPARNASSE
bd. de Port Royal
bd. Saint Marcel
bd. de l'Hôpital
pont de Bercy
quai de Bercy
bd. Raspail
Observatoire de Paris
bd. Arago
rue Jeanne d'Arc
0
1/2 mi
0
0.5 km
N

dining room's tables, all of which provide an inspiring view. The menu changes seasonally, offering fish and meat dishes that range from filet of turbot with seaweed and buttered sea urchins to veal chops with truffled vegetables. Reservations are recommended.

You can ice-skate inside the Eiffel Tower, doing figure eights while taking in views of the rooftops of Paris. Skating takes place on an observation deck 57m (187 ft.) aboveground. The rectangular rink is a bit larger than an average tennis court, holding 80 skaters at once—half the capacity of New York City's Rockefeller Center rink. Admission to the rink and skate rentals is free once you pay the initial entry fee below. The rink is open for 6 weeks during December and January.

Insider tip: The least expensive way to visit the tower is to walk up the first two floors for 3.80€ ($4.95) adults or 3€ ($3.90) ages 25 and under. With this route, you also bypass the long lines for the elevator.

Champ de Mars, 7e. ✆ **01-44-11-23-23.** www.tour-eiffel.fr. Admission to 1st landing 4.20€ ($5.45), 2nd landing 7.70€ ($10), 3rd landing 11€ ($14). Stairs to 2nd floor 3.80€ ($4.95). Sept–May daily 9:30am–11:45pm; June–Aug daily 9am–12:45am. Fall and winter, stairs open only to 6pm. Métro: Trocadéro, Ecole Militaire, or Bir Hakeim. RER: Champ de Mars–Tour Eiffel.

Hôtel des Invalides (Napoleon's Tomb) ★★★ The glory of the French military lives on in the Musée de l'Armée. The Sun King decided to build the "hotel" to house soldiers with disabilities. It wasn't entirely a benevolent gesture, because the veterans had been injured, crippled, or blinded while fighting Louis's battles. This massive building program was launched in 1670. Eventually a Jules Hardouin-Mansart gilded dome crowned the structure.

The best way to approach the Invalides is from the Right Bank across the pont Alexandre-III. Included in the collections (begun in 1794) are Viking swords, Burgundian basinets, 14th-century blunderbusses, Balkan khandjars, American Browning machine guns, war pitchforks, salamander-engraved Renaissance serpentines, musketoons, and grenadiers. You can even see General Daumesnil's wooden leg. There are suits of armor worn by kings and dignitaries, including the famous "armor suit of the lion" that was made for François I. The displays of swords are among the world's finest.

Crossing the Cour d'Honneur (Court of Honor), you'll come to **Eglise du Dôme,** designed by Hardouin-Mansart for Louis XIV. He began work on the church in 1677, though he died before its completion. In the Napoleon Chapel is the hearse used at the emperor's funeral on May 9, 1821.

To accommodate the Tomb of Napoleon—made of red porphyry, with a green granite base—architect Visconti had to redesign the high altar. First buried at St. Helena, Napoleon's remains were returned to Paris in 1840 and then locked inside six coffins. Surrounding the tomb are a dozen Amazon-like figures representing his victories. Almost lampooning the smallness of the man, everything is awesome: You'd think a real giant was buried here, not a symbolic one. The statue of Napoleon in his coronation robes stands 2.5m (8¼ ft.) tall.

Place des Invalides, 7e. ✆ **01-44-42-37-72.** www.invalides.org. Admission to Musée de l'Armée, Napoleon's Tomb, and Musée des Plans-Reliefs 7.50€ ($9.75) adults, 5.50€ ($7.15) students, free for children under 18. Oct–Mar daily 10am–5pm; Apr–Sept daily 10am–6pm; June–Aug daily 10am–7pm. Closed Jan 1, May 1, Nov 1, and Dec 25. Métro: Latour-Maubourg, Varenne, Invalides, or St-Francois-Xavier.

Musée d'Orsay ★★★ The neoclassical Gare d'Orsay train station has been transformed into one of the world's great museums. It contains an important collection devoted to the pivotal years from 1848 to 1914. Across the Seine from the Louvre and the Tuileries, it is a repository of works by the Impressionists as well as the Symbolists, Pointillists, Realists, and late Romantics. Artists represented include van Gogh, Manet, Monet, Degas, and Renoir. It houses thousands of sculptures and paintings across 80 galleries, plus Belle Epoque furniture, photographs, objets d'art, architectural models, and a cinema.

One of Renoir's most joyous paintings is here: *Moulin de la Galette* (1876). Another celebrated work is by the American James McNeill Whistler—*Arrangement in Gray and Black: Portrait of the Painter's Mother.* The most famous piece in the museum is Manet's 1863 *Déjeuner sur l'herbe* (Picnic on the Grass), which created a scandal when it was first exhibited; it depicts a nude woman picnicking with two fully clothed men in a forest. Two years later, his *Olympia,* lounging on her bed wearing nothing but a flower in her hair and high-heeled shoes, met with the same response.

1 rue de Bellechasse or 62 rue de Lille, 7e. ✆ **01-40-49-48-14.** www.musee-orsay.fr. Admission 9€ ($12) adults, 7€ ($9.10) ages 18–24, free ages 17 and under. Tues–Wed and Fri–Sun 9:30am–6pm; Thurs 9:30am–9:45pm. Closed Dec 25, Jan 1, and May 1. Métro: Solférino. RER: Musée d'Orsay.

Musée du Louvre ★★★ The Louvre is one of the world's largest and greatest museums—and now more beautiful than ever since the facade has been thoroughly cleaned. The $1.2-billion Grand Louvre Project, a 15-year undertaking, is officially complete, but refurbishment of individual galleries and paintings continues. For up-to-the-minute data on what is open and about to open, check out the museum's website (www.louvre.fr).

The collection is staggering. You'll have to resign yourself to missing some masterpieces; you simply can't see everything. People on one of those Paris-in-a-day tours race to glimpse the *Mona Lisa* (in her own special room) and the *Venus de Milo.* Those with an extra 5 minutes go in pursuit of *Winged Victory,* the headless statue discovered at Samothrace that dates from about 200 B.C.

To enter the Louvre, you pass through the 21m (69-ft.) **I. M. Pei glass pyramid** in the courtyard. Commissioned by Mitterrand and completed in 1989, it received mixed reviews. The pyramid allows sunlight to shine on an underground reception area and shelters shops and restaurants beneath the Jardin du Carrousel.

Pressed for time? Take a **guided tour** (in English), which lasts about 90 minutes. The short tour, which is your only option if you visit on Monday, covers the "highlights of the highlights." Tours start under the pyramid at the station marked ACCUEIL DES GROUPES.

The collections are divided into eight departments: Asian antiquities; Egyptian antiquities; Greek, Etruscan, and Roman antiquities; Islamic art; sculpture; paintings; prints and drawings; and objets d'art. In 1997, President Jacques Chirac inaugurated nearly 10,000 sq. m (about 107,000 sq. ft.) of gallery space, most of it in the Sully wing, including a new presentation of Egyptian antiquities. It gave 60% more space to the world of the pharaohs, a culture that has fascinated the French since Napoleon's occupation of Egypt in 1798.

Other areas include freshly restored rooms of Greek, Etruscan, and Roman antiquities. **The Grand Galerie,** a 180m (591-ft.) hall opening onto the Seine, is dedicated to mostly Italian paintings from the 1400s to the 1700s, including works by Raphael and Leonardo da Vinci.

The **Richelieu Wing** houses the collection of northern European and French paintings, decorative arts, French sculpture, Oriental antiquities (a rich collection of Islamic art), and the grand salons of Napoleon III. Originally constructed from 1852 to 1857,

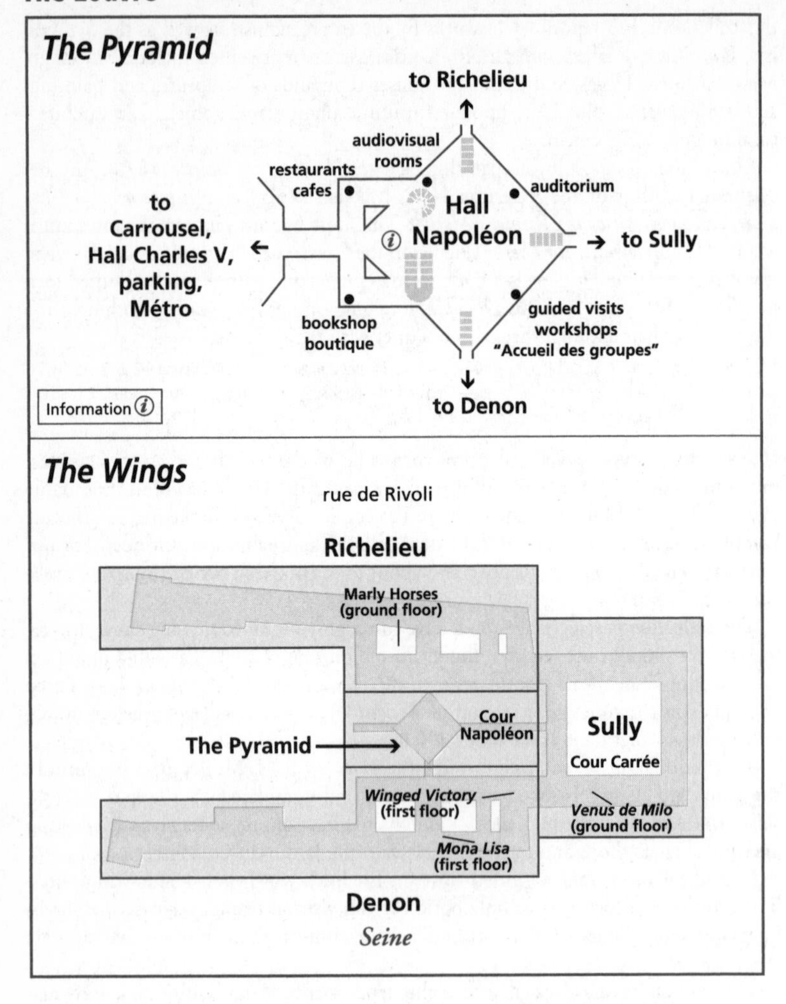

this wing has been virtually rebuilt. In its 165 rooms, plus three covered courtyards, some 12,000 works of art are displayed. Of the Greek and Roman antiquities, the most notable (aside from *Venus* and *Winged Victory*) are fragments of the Parthenon's frieze.

We love Mona and Venus, but our eternal passion burns for Jacques-Louis David's *Portrait of Madame Récamier,* depicting Napoleon's opponent at age 23; on her comfortable sofa, she reclines in the style of classical antiquity. Other favorites of ours are *Ship of Fools,* by Hieronymus Bosch, in the Flemish galleries; *Four Seasons,* by Nicolas Poussin, the canonical work of French classicism; Eugène Delacroix's *Liberty Leading the People,* perhaps the ultimate endorsement of revolution (Louis-Philippe purchased the painting and hid it during his reign); and Paolo Veronese's gigantic *Wedding Feast at Cana,* showing (if nothing else) how stunning color can be when applied by a master.

Tips Leaping over the Louvre Line

If you don't want to wait in line at the entrance to the Louvre pyramid, or use the automatic ticket machines, you can order tickets over the phone (✆ **08-92-68-46-94**) with a credit card. You can also order advance tickets and take a virtual tour at www.louvre.fr. Tickets can be mailed to you in the U.S., or you can pick them up at any Paris branch of the FNAC electronics chain.

When you tire of strolling the galleries, you may like a pick-me-up at the Richelieu Wing's **Café Richelieu** (✆ **01-49-27-99-01**) or at **Café Marly,** 93 rue de Rivoli, 1er (✆ **01-49-26-06-60**), where we suggest a cafe crème, a club sandwich, a pastry, or something from the bistro menu.

34–36 quai du Louvre, 1er. Main entrance in the glass pyramid, Cour Napoléon. ✆ **01-40-20-53-17,** 01-40-20-50-50 for operator, or 08-92-68-46-94 for advance credit card sales. www.louvre.fr. Admission 8.50€ ($11), free for children under 18; free to all 1st Sun of every month. Sat–Mon and Thurs 9am–5:30pm; Wed and Fri 9am–9:30pm. 1½-hr. English-language tours (Mon and Wed–Sun) 6€ ($8), free for children under 13 with museum ticket. Métro: Palais-Royal–Musée du Louvre.

Musée Picasso ★★★ When it opened in the restored Hôtel Salé in Le Marais, the press hailed it as a "museum for Picasso's Picassos," meaning those he chose not to sell. Superior to a similar museum in Barcelona, it offers an unparalleled view of the artist's career, including his fabled gaunt blue figures and harlequins. This museum is one of Paris's most popular attractions. The world's greatest Picasso collection, acquired by the state in lieu of $50 million in inheritance taxes, consists of 203 paintings, 158 sculptures, 16 collages, 19 bas-reliefs, 88 ceramics, and more than 1,500 sketches and 1,600 engravings, plus 30 notebooks. These works span some 75 years of Picasso's life and changing styles.

The range of paintings includes a 1901 self-portrait and embraces such masterpieces as *Le Baiser* (The Kiss). Another masterpiece is *Reclining Nude and the Man with a Guitar.* It's easy to stroll through seeking your favorite work—ours is the delightfully wicked *Jeune garçon à la langouste* (Young Man with a Lobster). The museum also owns several studies for *Les Demoiselles d'Avignon,* the painting that launched cubism in 1907.

In the Hôtel Salé, 5 rue de Thorigny, 3e. ✆ **01-42-71-25-21.** www.musee-picasso.fr. Admission 9.50€ ($12) adults, 7.50€ ($9.75) seniors and ages 18–25, free for children under 18. Apr–Sept Wed–Mon 9:30am–6pm; Oct–Mar Wed–Mon 9:30am–5:30pm. Closed Dec 25 and Jan 1. Métro: St-Paul, Filles du Calvaire, or Chemin Vert.

Notre-Dame ★★★ For 6 centuries, it has stood as a Gothic masterpiece of the Middle Ages. We actually feel that Notre-Dame is more interesting outside than in. You'll have to walk around the entire structure to appreciate this "vast symphony of stone" with its classic flying buttresses. Better yet, cross the bridge to the Left Bank and view it from the quay.

From the square parvis (the courtyard in front), you can view the trio of 13th-century sculpted portals. On the left, the Portal of the Virgin depicts the signs of the zodiac and the Virgin's coronation. The central Portal of the Last Judgment is in three levels: The first shows Vices and Virtues; the second, Christ and his Apostles; and the third, Christ in triumph after the Resurrection. On the right is the Portal of Ste-Anne, depicting such scenes as the Virgin enthroned with Child. Over the central portal is a

Notre-Dame de Paris

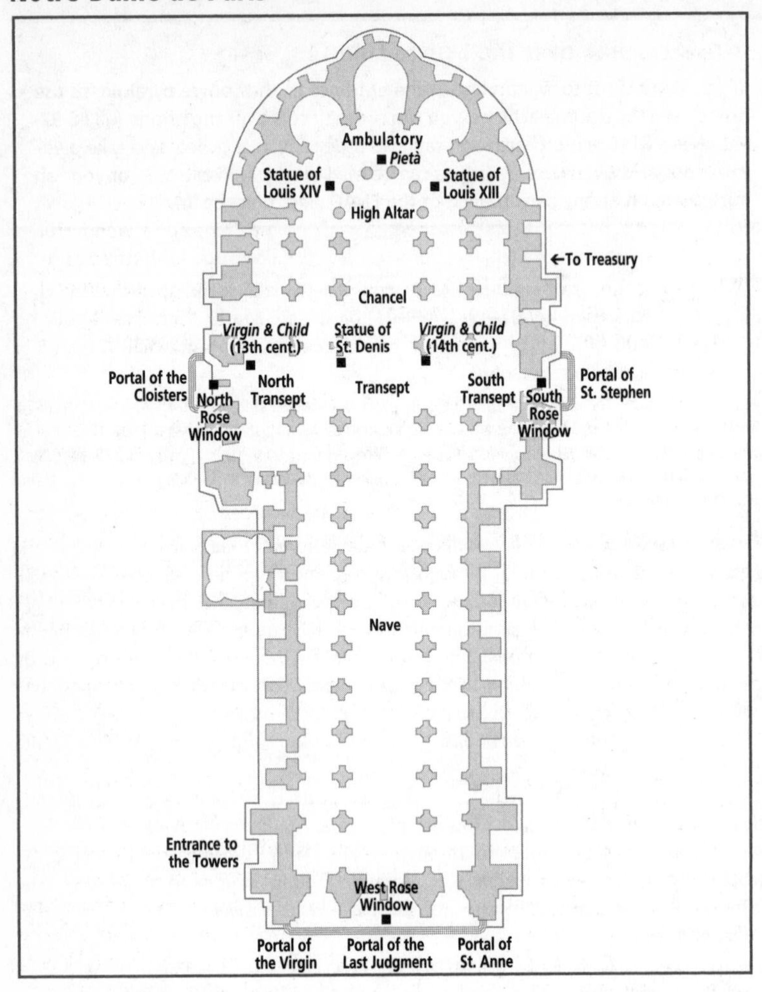

remarkable rose window, 9m (30 ft.) in diameter, forming a showcase for a statue of the Virgin and Child. Equally interesting is the Cloister Portal (around on the left), with its 13th-century Virgin, a unique survivor of many that originally adorned the facade. (Unfortunately, the Child she's holding is decapitated.)

If possible, view the interior at sunset. Of the three giant medallions that warm the austere cathedral, the north rose window in the transept, from the mid–13th century, is best. The interior is typical Gothic, with slender, graceful columns. The carved-stone choir screen from the early 14th century depicts biblical scenes. Near the altar stands the 14th-century Virgin and Child. Behind glass in the treasury is a display of vestments and gold objects, including crowns. Notre-Dame is especially proud of its relic of the True Cross and the Crown of Thorns.

Moments **A Nighttime Walk & an "Abomination"**

When Viollet-le-Duc designed the flying buttresses of the cathedral of Notre-Dame, they were denounced as "horrendous," "a blight of Paris," and an "abomination." Now they are one of the structure's most interesting architectural features. On the Ile de la Cité, wander through the garden in the rear of the cathedral. Near the square Jean XXIII, cross the pont de l'Archevêche and follow quai de Montebello along the Left Bank of the Seine for a wonderful perspective, especially when the *bateaux-mouches* light up the buttresses as they pass along. You'll end up at the place St-Michel, where you can order a nightcap in a cafe.

To visit the gargoyles immortalized by Victor Hugo (where Quasimodo lurked), you have to scale steps leading to the twin square towers, rising to a height of 68m (223 ft.). Once here, you can inspect those devils (some sticking out their tongues), hobgoblins, and birds of prey.

Approached through a garden behind Notre-Dame is the **Memorial des Martyrs Français de la Déportation** (✆ **01-46-33-87-56**), jutting out on the tip of the Ile de la Cité. This memorial honors the French martyrs of World War II, who were deported to camps such as Auschwitz and Buchenwald. In blood red are the words (in French): FORGIVE, BUT DON'T FORGET. It's open June to September daily 10am to noon and 2 to 7pm, and off season daily 10am to noon and 2 to 5pm; admission is free.

6 place du parvis Notre-Dame, 4e. ✆ **01-42-34-56-10.** www.monum.fr. Free admission to the cathedral. Towers 5.50€ ($7.15) adults, 4.50€ ($5.85) seniors and ages 18–25, free for children under 18. Treasury 5.50€ ($7.15) adults, 4.50€ ($5.85) seniors and ages 5–25, free for children under 5. Cathedral year-round daily 8am–6:45pm. Towers and crypt Apr–Sept daily 9:30am–6:30pm (until 11pm Sat–Sun June–Aug); Oct–Mar daily 10am–5:30pm. Museum Wed and Sat–Sun 2–5pm. Treasury Mon–Sat 2:30–6:30pm; Sun 1:30–5:30pm. Métro: Cité or St-Michel. RER: St-Michel.

Ste-Chapelle ★★★ Come here to see one of the world's greatest examples of Flamboyant Gothic architecture—"the pearl among them all," as Proust called it—and brilliant stained-glass windows with a lacelike delicacy. The reds are so red that Parisians have been known to use the phrase "wine the color of Ste-Chapelle's windows." Ste-Chapelle is Paris's second-most important monument from the Middle Ages (after Notre-Dame); it was erected to enshrine relics from the First Crusade, including the Crown of Thorns, two pieces from the True Cross, and the Roman lance that pierced the side of Christ. St. Louis (Louis IX) acquired the relics from the emperor of Constantinople and is said to have paid heavily for them, raising money through unscrupulous means.

Viewed on a bright day, the 15 stained-glass windows depicting Bible scenes seem to glow ruby red and Chartres blue. The walls consist almost entirely of the glass. Built in only 5 years, beginning in 1246, the chapel has two levels. You enter through the lower chapel, supported by flying buttresses and ornamented with fleurs-de-lis. The servants of the palace used the lower chapel, and the upper chamber was for the king and his courtiers; the latter is reached by ascending a narrow spiral staircase.

Ste-Chapelle stages **concerts** in March to November; tickets cost 19€ to 25€ ($25–$33). Call ✆ **01-44-07-12-38** from 11am to 6pm daily for details.

Palais de Justice, 4 bd. du Palais, 4e. ✆ **01-53-40-60-80.** www.monum.fr. 6.50€ ($8.45) adults, 4.50€ ($5.85) ages 18–25, free 17 and under. Daily 9am–5pm. Métro: Cité, St-Michel, or Châtelet–Les Halles. RER: St-Michel.

2 Musée de Louvre/Les Halles: The 1st Arrondissement (Right Bank)

The 1st arrondissement is first for a reason: Several of the city's top attractions are here, including the **Louvre** and the Tuileries. It's also home to **Les Halles,** the major fruit, meat, and vegetable market of Paris for 8 centuries. But the smock-clad vendors, carcasses of beef, and baskets of vegetables all belong to the past. Today, the action has moved to a modern steel-and-glass structure at Rungis, a suburb near Orly. Here is **Les Forum des Halles** (Métro: Les Halles; RER: Châtelet–Les Halles), which opened in 1979. This large complex, much of it underground, houses dozens of shops, restaurants, and movie theaters.

For many visitors, a night on the town still ends in the wee hours with the traditional bowl of onion soup at Les Halles, usually at **Au Pied de Cochon (Pig's Foot)** or **Au Chien Qui Fume (Smoking Dog).**

There's much to see in Les Halles, beginning with the **Eglise St-Eustache,** 2 rue du Jour, 1er (✆ **01-42-36-31-05;** www.saint-eustache.org; Métro: Les Halles), with another entrance on rue Rambuteau. In the old days, cabbage vendors came here to pray for their produce. The Gothic-Renaissance church dates from the mid–16th century yet wasn't completed until 1637. It has been known for its organ recitals since Liszt played here in 1866. Inside is the black marble tomb of Jean-Baptiste Colbert, minister of state under Louis XIV. A statue of the statesman rests on top of his tomb, flanked by Coysevox's *Abundance* (a horn of flowers) and J. B. Tuby's *Fidelity.* The church is open daily 9:30am to 7pm. There's an organ concert Sunday at 5:30pm.

Jardin des Tuileries ★★ These spectacular, statue-studded gardens are as much a part of Paris as the Seine. Le Nôtre, Louis XIV's gardener and planner of the Versailles grounds, designed them. Some of the gardens' most distinctive statues are the 18 enormous bronzes by Maillol in the Jardin du Carrousel, a subdivision of the Jardins des Tuileries placed there in 1964 and 1965, under the direction of then–Culture Minister André Malraux. About 100 years before that, Catherine de Médicis ordered a palace built here, connected to the Louvre; other occupants have included Louis XVI and Napoleon. Twice attacked by Parisians, it was burned to the ground in 1871 and never rebuilt. The trees are arranged according to designs, and the paths are arrow-straight. Breaking the sense of order and formality are bubbling fountains.

Seemingly half of Paris wanders the Tuileries on a warm spring day, admiring the daffodils and tulips. As you walk toward the Louvre, you'll enter the **Jardin du Carrousel,** dominated by the **Arc de Triomphe du Carrousel.** Pierced with three walkways and supported by marble columns, the monument honors Napoleon's Grande Armée, celebrating its victory at Austerlitz on December 5, 1805. The arch is surmounted by statuary, a chariot, and four bronze horses.

Bordering place de la Concorde, 1er. ✆ **01-40-20-90-43** or 01-42-96-19-30. Métro: Tuileries.

Jeu de Paume After knowing many roles, this museum has become a center for photography and video, exploring "the world of images, their uses, and the issues they raise." Its exhibitions not only display photography but mechanical or electronic images. It is now of the finest museums of its type in the world and presents ever-changing exhibitions, many of them daringly avant-garde.

For years the national gallery in the Jeu de Paume, in the northeast corner of the Tuileries gardens, was one of the treasures of Paris, displaying some of the finest works of the Impressionists. In 1986 that collection was hauled off to the Musee d'Orsay to the regret of many. Following a $12.6-million face-lift, this Second Empire building has been transformed into a series of state-of-the-art galleries.

Originally, in this part of the gardens, Napoleon III built a ball court on which *jeu de paume,* an antecedent of tennis, was played—hence the museum's name. The most infamous period in the national gallery's history came during the Nazi occupation, when it served as an "evaluation center" for works of modern art. Paintings from all over France were shipped to the Jeu de Paume; art condemned by the Nazis as "degenerate" was burned.

1 Place de la Concorde, 8e. ✆ **01-47-03-12-50.** Admission 6€ ($7.80) adults, 3€ ($3.90) students and children. Tues noon–9pm; Wed–Fri noon–7pm; Sat–Sun 10am–7pm. Metro: Concorde.

Musée de l'Orangerie ★ In the Tuileries stands this gem among galleries. It has an outstanding collection of art and one celebrated painting on display: Claude Monet's exquisite *Nymphéas* (1915–27), in which water lilies float amorphously on the canvas. The water lilies are displayed as the artist intended them to be—lit by sunlight in large oval galleries that evoke the shape of the garden ponds at his former Giverny estate.

Creating his effects with hundreds and hundreds of minute strokes of his brush (one irate 19th-c. critic called them "tongue lickings"), Monet achieved unity and harmony, as he did in his Rouen Cathedral series and his haystacks. Monet continued to paint his water landscapes right up until his death in 1926, although he was greatly hampered by failing eyesight.

The renovated building also houses the art collections of two men, John Walter and Paul Guillaume, who are not connected to each other, except that they were both married at different times to the same woman. Their collection includes more than 24 Renoirs, including *Young Girl at a Piano.* Cézanne is represented by 14 works, notably *The Red Rock,* and Matisse by 11 paintings. The highlight of Rousseau's nine works displayed here is *The Wedding,* and the dozen paintings by Picasso reach the pinnacle of their brilliance in *The Female Bathers.* Other outstanding paintings are by Utrillo (10 works in all), Soutine (22), and Derain (28).

Jardin des Tuileries, 1er. ✆ **01-44-77-80-07.** Admission 6.50€ ($8.45) adults, 4.50€ ($5.85) students under 26. Free first Sun of every month. Wed–Mon 12:30–7pm (until 9pm Fri). Metro: Concorde.

Musée des Arts Décoratifs In the northwest wing of the Louvre's Pavillon de Marsan, this museum holds a treasury of furnishings, fabrics, wallpaper, objets d'art, and items displaying living styles from the Middle Ages to the present. Notable are the 1920s Art Deco boudoir, bathroom, and bedroom done for couturier Jeanne Lanvin by the designer Rateau, plus a collection of the works donated by Jean Dubuffet. Decorative art from the Middle Ages to the Renaissance is on the second floor; collections from the 17th, 18th, and 19th centuries occupy the third and fourth floors. The fifth floor has specialized centers, such as wallpaper and drawings, and exhibits detailing fashion, textiles, toys, crafts, and glass trends.

Palais du Louvre, 107 rue de Rivoli, 1er. ✆ **01-44-55-57-50.** www.legartsdecoratifs.fr. Admission 8€ ($10) adults, 6.50€ ($8.45) ages 18–25, free for children under 18. Tues–Fri 11am–6pm; Sat–Sun 10am–6pm. Métro: Palais-Royal or Tuileries.

Palais Royal At the demolished Café Foy in the Palais Royal, the outraged Camille Desmoulins jumped on a table and shouted for the mob "to fight to the death." The date was July 13, 1789. The renown of the Palais Royal goes back even farther. The gardens were planted in 1634 for Cardinal Richelieu. It later became the residence of the ducs d'Orléans. Philippe-Egalité, a cousin of Louis XVI, built his apartments on the grounds and later rented them to prostitutes. By the 20th century, such artists as Cocteau and Colette rented the apartments. (A plaque at 9 rue Beaujolais marks the entrance to Colette's apartment.) Today, the Palais Royal contains apartments, shops, and a few restaurants such as **Le Grand Véfour** (p. 119). Note sculptor Daniel Buren's prison-striped columns, added in 1986, and Pol Bury's steel-ball sculptures decorating the fountains.

Rue St-Honoré, on place du Palais-Royal, 1er. No Phone. Free admission. Métro: Palais-Royal–Musée du Louvre.

3 Le Marais: The 3rd Arrondissement (Right Bank)

When Paris began to overflow the confines of the Ile de la Cité in the 13th century, the citizenry settled in Le Marais, a marsh flooded regularly by the Seine. By the 17th century, the Marais had reached the pinnacle of fashion, becoming the center of aristocratic Paris. At that time, most of its great *hôtels particuliers* (mansions)—many now restored or being spruced up—were built by the finest craftspeople in France.

In the 18th and 19th centuries, the fashionable deserted the Marais in favor of Faubourg St-Germain and Faubourg St-Honoré. Industry took over the quarter, and the once-elegant hôtels became tenements. There was talk of demolishing this sector, but in 1962, the Comité de Sauvegarde du Marais saved the district. The Centre Pompidou sparked the neighborhood's regeneration.

No longer "the Swamp" (its English name), the Marais, in the 3rd arrondissement and part of the 4th, is trendy once again, filled with tiny twisting streets, gay and straight bars, and cutting-edge designer shops.

In **place de la Bastille** on July 14, 1789, a mob attacked the Bastille and sparked the French Revolution. Nothing remains of the Bastille, built in 1369. Many prisoners—some sentenced by Louis XIV for "witchcraft"—were kept within; the best known was the "Man in the Iron Mask." When the fortress was stormed, only seven prisoners were discovered (the marquis de Sade had been transferred to an asylum 10 days earlier). Authorities had discussed razing it anyway, so the attack was more symbolic than anything else. What it started will never be forgotten. Bastille Day is celebrated every July 14. In the center of the square is the **Colonne de Juillet (July Column),** honoring the victims of the 1830 July Revolution, which put Louis-Philippe on the throne. The God of Liberty, a winged nude with a star emerging from his head, crowns the tower.

Not far away, **place des Vosges** ★★★, 4e (Métro: St-Paul or Chemin Vert), is Paris's oldest square and once its most fashionable. It was called the Palais Royal in the days of Henri IV, who planned to live here—but his assassin, Ravaillac, had other ideas. Henri II was killed while jousting on the square in 1559, in the shadow of the Hôtel des Tournelles. His widow, Catherine de Médicis, had the place torn down. Place des Vosges, once a dueling ground, was one of Europe's first planned squares. Its *grand siècle* red-brick houses are ornamented with white stone, and its covered arcades allowed people to shop even in the rain—an innovation at the time. In the 18th century, chestnut trees were added, sparking a controversy that continues to this day: Critics say that the addition spoils the perspective.

As you stroll the Marais, you might want to seek out the **Hôtel de Rohan,** 87 rue Vieille-du-Temple (✆ **01-40-27-60-09** or 01-40-27-62-56), once occupied by the fourth Cardinal Rohan, who was involved in the scandal that framed Marie Antoinette for buying a priceless diamond necklace. The main attraction is the 18th-century

Salon des Singes (Monkey Room). In the courtyard is a stunning bas-relief of a nude Apollo and four horses against exploding sunbursts. The hotel (mansion), which is administered by France's National Archives, can be visited only during special exhibitions announced in Paris newspapers.

At 47 rue Vieille-du-Temple is the **Hôtel des Ambassadeurs de Hollande,** where Beaumarchais wrote *The Marriage of Figaro.* Never occupied by the Dutch embassy, it is one of the most splendid mansions in the area and is closed to the public.

Although the facade of the 17th-century **Hôtel de Beauvais,** 68 rue François-Miron, was damaged during the Revolution, it remains one of the most charming in Paris. A plaque commemorates the fact that Mozart inhabited the mansion in 1763. To visit inside, speak to the Association du Paris Historique, on the ground floor of the building, any afternoon.

Hôtel de Sens, 1 rue de Figuier (✆ **01-42-78-14-60**), was built from the 1470s to 1519 for the archbishops of Sens. Along with the Hôtel de Cluny, it's the only domestic architecture remaining from the 15th century. Long after the archbishops had departed in 1605, the scandalous Queen Margot, wife of Henri IV, occupied it. Her "younger and more virile" new lover slew the discarded one as she looked on. Today, the mansion houses the Bibliothèque Forney. The gate is open Tuesday to Saturday 1:30 to 7pm.

Work began on the **Hôtel de Bethune-Sully,** 62 rue St-Antoine (✆ **01-44-61-21-50**), in 1625. In 1634, the duc de Sully, who had been Henri IV's minister of finance, acquired it. After a strait-laced early life, Sully broke loose, adorning himself with diamonds and garish rings—and a bride who had a preference for younger men. The mansion was acquired by the government after World War II and holds the National Office of Historical Monuments and Sites. Recently restored, the relief-studded facade is appealing. There's daily admittance from 9am to 7pm to the courtyard and the garden that opens onto place des Vosges.

The **rue des Rosiers (Street of the Rosebushes)** is one of the most colorful of the streets remaining from the old Jewish quarter. The Star of David shines here, Hebrew letters flash (in neon), shops run by Moroccan or Algerian Jews sell couscous, bearded men sit in doorways, restaurants serve kosher meals, and signs appeal for Jewish liberation.

Shoppers will delight in such places as **Passage de Retz,** 9 rue Charlot (✆ **01-48-04-37-99;** www.passagederetz.com), an avant-garde gallery that was established in 1994 and has the most amusing exhibitions in the Marais. At **Hier, Aujourd'hui, et Demain,** 14 rue de Bretagne (✆ **01-42-77-69-02**), you'll fall in love with 1930s Art Deco.

The 3rd arrondissement is also home to the **Musée Picasso** (see "The Top Attractions," earlier in this chapter).

Musée Carnavalet–Histoire de Paris ★★ The history of Paris comes alive here in intimate terms—down to the chessmen Louis XVI used to distract himself in the days before he went to the guillotine. A renowned Renaissance palace, the mansion was built in 1544 by Pierre Lescot and Jean Goujon and acquired by Mme de Carnavalet. The great François Mansart transformed it between 1655 and 1661. It's best known because one of history's most famous letter writers, Mme de Sévigné, moved here in 1677. Fanatically devoted to her daughter (until she had to live with her), she poured out nearly every detail of her life in letters, virtually ignoring her son. A native of the Marais, she died at her daughter's château in 1696. In 1866 the city turned the building into a museum.

23 rue de Sévigné, 3e. ✆ **01-44-59-58-58.** www.carnavalet.pans.fr. Free admission. Special exhibits 4.50€ ($5.85) adults, 3.80€ ($4.95) students. Tues–Sun 10am–6pm. Métro: St-Paul or Chemin Vert.

4 Where Paris Was Born: Ile de la Cité & the 4th Arrondissement

Medieval Paris, that architectural blending of grotesquerie and Gothic beauty, began on this island in the Seine. Explore as much of it as you can, but at least visit **Notre-Dame** (see "The Top Attractions," earlier in this chapter), the Ste-Chapelle, and the Conciergerie. The 4th arrondissement is on the Right Bank, opposite the island.

Conciergerie ★★ This is the most sinister building in France. Though it had a long, regal history before the Revolution, it's visited today chiefly by those wishing to bask in the Reign of Terror's horrors. The Conciergerie conjures images of the days when tumbrels hauled victims to the guillotine. You approach the Conciergerie through its twin towers, the Tour d'Argent and Tour de César, though the 14th-century vaulted Guard Room is the actual entrance. Also from the 14th century is the vast, dark, foreboding Salle des Gens d'Armes (People at Arms), transformed from the days when the king used it as a banquet hall.

Few of the prisoners in the Conciergerie's history endured tortures as severe as those inflicted on Ravaillac, who assassinated Henri IV in 1610. He got the full treatment—pincers in the flesh, hot lead and boiling oil poured on him. This was also where Marie Antoinette awaited her trial and eventual beheading.

1 quai de l'Horloge, 4e. ✆ **01-53-40-60-93**. www.monum.fr. Admission 6.50€ ($8.45) adults, 4.50€ ($5.85) ages 18–25, free for children under 18. Daily 9:30am–6pm. Métro: Cité, Châtelet, or St-Michel. RER: St-Michel.

5 The Champs-Elysées, Paris's Grand Promenade: The 8th Arrondissement (Right Bank)

In late 1995, after 2 hard, dusty, and costly years of construction, great improvements in Paris's most prominent triumphal promenade were unveiled. The *contre-allées* (side lanes that had always been clogged with parked cars) were removed (new underground garages alleviate the parking problem), lighting was added, pedestrian sidewalks were widened, and new trees were planted. Now the Grand Promenade truly is grand again—with the exception of all of those fast-food joints.

Musée Jacquemart-André ★★ *Finds* This is the best decorative-arts museum in Paris, though it's no place to take the kids (unless they're aspiring decorators). Plan at least 2 hours. The museum is the legacy of the André family, prominent Protestants in the 19th century. The family's last scion, Edouard André, spent most of his adult life stationed abroad in the French army, returning to marry Nélie Jacquemart, a well-known portraitist. They compiled a collection of French 18th-century decorative art and European paintings in an 1850s town house, which they continually redecorated according to the fashions of their time.

In 1912, Mme André willed the house and its collections to the Institut de France, which paid for extensive renovations and enlargements completed in 1996. The collection's highlights are works by Bellini, Carpaccio, and Uccelo; Houdon busts; Gobelin tapestries; Savonnerie carpets; della Robbia terra cottas; awesome antiques; and works by Rembrandt *(The Pilgrim of Emmaus),* Van Dyck, Rubens, Watteau, Fragonard, and Boucher. After a major restoration, one of the most outstanding exhibits is a group of three mid-18th-century frescoes by Giambattista Tiepolo; this is the only museum in France with frescoes by the Venetian master. The works depict spectators on balconies viewing Henri III's arrival in Venice in 1574. Take a break from the Gilded Age opulence with a cup of tea or a tart in Mme André's dining room, hung with 18th-century tapestries.

Where Royal Heads Rolled

The eastern end of the Champs-Elysées is one of the world's grand squares, **place de la Concorde,** an octagonal traffic hub built in 1757 to honor Louis XV. The statue of the king was torn down in 1792 and the name changed to place de la Révolution. It's dominated by an **Egyptian obelisk** from Luxor, the oldest man-made object in Paris; it was carved around 1200 B.C. and given to France in 1829 by the viceroy of Egypt.

During the Reign of Terror, Dr. Guillotin's invention was erected on this spot, where it claimed thousands of lives—from Louis XVI, who died bravely, to Mme du Barry, who went kicking and screaming. Before the leering crowds, Marie Antoinette, Robespierre, Danton, Mlle Roland, and Charlotte Corday lost their heads. (You can still lose your life on place de la Concorde if you chance the frantic traffic and try to cross over.)

For a spectacular sight, look down the Champs-Elysées—the view is framed by Coustou's Marly horses, which once graced the gardens at Louis XIV's Château de Marly. (These are copies; the originals are in the Louvre.) On the opposite side, Coysevox's winged horses flank the gateway to the Tuileries. On each side of the obelisk are fountains with bronze-tailed mermaids and bare-breasted sea nymphs. Gray-beige statues ring the square, honoring the cities of France. To symbolize Strasbourg's fall to Germany in 1871, that city's statue was covered with a black drape that wasn't lifted until the end of World War I. Two of the palaces on place de la Concorde are today the Ministry of the Marine and the deluxe Hôtel de Crillon. Jacques-Ange Gabriel designed them in the 1760s.

158 bd. Haussmann, 8e. ✆ **01-45-62-11-59.** www.musee-jacquemart-andre.com. Admission 9.50€ ($12) adults, 7€ ($9.10) children 7–17, free for children under 7. Daily 10am–6pm. Métro: Miromesnil or St-Philippe-du-Roule.

Place Vendôme ★★ Always aristocratic and often royal, place Vendôme enjoyed its golden age during the Second Empire. Fashion designers such as Worth introduced the crinoline here. Louis Napoleon lived here, wooing his empress, Eugénie de Montijo, at the Hôtel du Rhin. In its halcyon days, Strauss waltzes echoed across the plaza. In time they were replaced by cannon fire. A column crowned by Napoleon dominates the square. There was a statue of the Sun King until the Revolution, when it was replaced by *Liberty.*

Then came Napoleon, who ordered that a sort of Trajan's Column be erected in honor of his victory at Austerlitz. It was made of bronze from captured Russian and Austrian cannons. After Napoleon's downfall, the statue was replaced by one of Henri IV, everybody's favorite king and every woman's favorite man. Later Napoleon mounted it again, in uniform and without the pose of a Caesar.

The Communards of 1871, who detested royalty, pulled down the statue. Courbet is said to have led the raid, for which he was jailed and fined the cost of restoring the statue. He couldn't pay it and was forced into exile in Switzerland. Eventually, the statue of Napoleon, wrapped in a Roman toga, won out.

Place Vendôme, 8e. Métro: Opéra.

6 Montmartre: The 18th Arrondissement (Right Bank)

From the 1880s to just before World War I, Montmartre enjoyed its golden age as the world's best-known art colony, where *la vie de bohème* reigned supreme. Following World War I, pseudoartists flocked here, with tourists hot on their heels. The real artists had long gone to such places as Montparnasse.

Before its discovery, Montmartre was a sleepy farming community, with windmills dotting the landscape. Those who find the trek up to Paris's highest elevations too much of a climb may prefer to ride **Le Petit Train de Montmartre,** which passes all the major landmarks; it seats 55 passengers and offers English commentary. Board at place Blanche (near the Moulin Rouge); the fare is 5.50€ ($7.15) adults, 3.50€ ($4.55) children under 13. Trains run daily 10am to 6pm; until midnight in July and August. For information, contact **Promotrain,** 131 rue de Clignancourt, 18e (© **01-42-62-24-00**).

The simplest way to reach Montmartre is to take the Métro to Anvers and then walk up rue du Steinkerque to the **funicular,** which runs to the precincts of Sacré-Coeur every day from 6am to 12:30am. The fare is one Métro ticket. Except for Sacré-Coeur (see "The Top Attractions," earlier in this chapter), Montmartre has only minor attractions; it's the historic architecture and the atmosphere that are compelling.

Specific attractions to look for include the **Bateau-Lavoir (Boat Warehouse),** on place Emile-Goudeau. Gutted by fire in 1970, it has been reconstructed. Picasso once lived here and, in the winter of 1905 and 1906, painted one of the world's most famous portraits, *The Third Rose* (Gertrude Stein).

L'Espace Montmartre Salvador-Dalí, 11 rue Poulbot, 18e (© **01-42-64-40-10**), presents Dalí's phantasmagorical world with 330 original works, including his 1956 *Don Quixote* lithograph. It's open daily from 10am to 6pm (July–Aug until 9:30pm); admission is 10€ ($13) for adults, 7€ ($9.10) seniors and students, 6€ ($7.80) for ages 8 to 18, and free for children under 8.

One of the most famous churches here is the **Eglise St-Pierre** on rue du Mont-Cenis. The church was consecrated in 1147; two columns in the choir stall are the remains of a Roman temple. Among the sculptured works, note the nun with the head of a pig, a symbol of sensual vice. At the entrance are three bronze doors sculpted by Gismondi in 1980: The middle door depicts the life of St. Peter; the left is dedicated to St. Denis; and the right honors the Holy Virgin.

Musée de Vieux Montmartre, 12 rue Cortot, 18e (© **01-49-25-89-39**), exhibits a wide collection of mementos. Dufy, van Gogh, Renoir, and Suzanne Valadon and her son, Utrillo, once occupied this 17th-century house. It's open Tuesday to Sunday 10am to 6pm; admission is 7€ ($9.10) for adults, 5.50€ ($7.15) for students, 3.50€ ($4.55) ages 10 to 18. Free for children 9 and under.

Cimetière de Montmartre ★ Novelist Alexandre Dumas and Russian dancer Vaslav Nijinsky are just a few of the famous composers, writers, and artists interred here. The remains of the great Stendhal are here, as are Hector Berlioz, Heinrich Heine, Edgar Degas, Jacques Offenbach, and even François Truffaut. We like to pay our respects at the tomb of Alphonsine Plessis, the courtesan on whom Dumas based his Marguerite Gautier in *La Dame aux Camélias.* Emile Zola was interred here, but his corpse was taken to the Panthéon in 1908. In 1871, the cemetery became the site of the mass burials of victims of the Siege and the Commune.

20 av. Rachel (west of the Butte Montmartre and north of bd. de Clichy), 18e. © **01-53-42-36-30.** Sun–Fri 8am–6pm; Sat 8:30am–6pm (until 5:30pm in winter). Métro: La Fourche.

7 La Villette: The 19th Arrondissement (Right Bank)

Cité des Sciences et de l'Industrie ★★ *Kids* Opened in 1986, this science complex, designed to "modernize mentalities" as part of the process of modernizing society, is so vast that a single visit gives only a glimpse of its scope. Some exhibits have an overlay of Gallic humor, including seismographic activity presented as the comic-strip adventures of a jungle explorer. The silver-skinned Géode (a geodesic dome) is a 34m (112-ft.) sphere with a 370-seat theater. Explora, a permanent exhibit, spreads over the three upper levels; its displays revolve around four themes: the universe, life, matter, and communication. The Cité has a multimedia library, a planetarium, and an "inventorium" for children.

At Cinaxe, sophisticated audio systems and oversize screens combine to enhance the sensations of film scenes. The experience includes episodes representing what you'd see, for example, in an airplane flying over mountains or if you were on the nose cone of a rocket.

The *Argonaute* is a submarine built in 1905 as part of a scientific experiment and a forerunner of the giant nuclear subs whose construction was partially based on ideas developed here. It was disarmed in 1982 and would have been demolished but for its purchase by the Musée de la Villette. Today, it's a source of pride, although it's firmly mounted on concrete and is never submerged.

La Cité des Enfants consists of three sections, one each for ages 3 to 5 and ages 6 to 12, plus a special section about electricity. This is an adventure playground, with watersports, a butterfly greenhouse, robots, an ant farm, interactive TVs, and even a Techno Cité that explains the workings of computers and other machines.

The Cité is in **Parc de La Villette,** Paris's largest park, with 54 hectares (133 acres) of greenery. You'll find a belvedere, a video workshop for children, and information about exhibitions, along with a cafe and restaurant.

In the Parc de La Villette, 30 av. Corentine-Cariou, La Villette, 19e. ✆ **01-40-05-70-00.** www.cite-sciences.fr. Cité Pass (entrance to all exhibits) 7.50€ ($9.75) adults, 5.50€ ($7.15) ages 7–24, free 6 and under. Tues–Sat 10am–6pm; Sun 10am–7pm. Métro: Porte de La Villette.

Musée de la Musique Housed in the stone-and-glass Cité de la Musique, this museum is a tribute to the rich musical traditions of many ages and cultures. You can view 4,500 instruments, as well as paintings, engravings, and sculptures that relate to musical history. One appealing section of mandolins, lutes, and zithers evokes music from the 17th century. It's all here: cornets disguised as snakes, antique music boxes, even an electric guitar. As part of the permanent collection, models of the world's great concert halls and interactive display areas give you a chance to hear and better understand the art and technology of musical heritage.

In the Cité de la Musique, 221 av. Jean-Jaurès, 19e. ✆ **01-44-84-44-84.** www.cite-musique.fr. Admission 7€ ($9.10) adults, 5.60€ ($7.30) students 19–25, 3.50€ ($4.55) children under 19. Tues–Sat noon–6pm; Sun 10am–6pm. Métro: Porte de Pantin.

8 The Latin Quarter: The 5th Arrondissement (Left Bank)

This is the precinct of the **University of Paris** (the **Sorbonne**), where students meet and fall in love over coffee and croissants. Rabelais called it the *Quartier* Latin because the students and professors spoke Latin in the classrooms and on the streets. The sector teems with belly dancers, restaurants from Vietnamese to Balkan, cafes, bookstalls, and *caveaux.*

A good starting point is **place St-Michel** (Métro: St-Michel), where Balzac used to get water from the fountain when he was a youth. This center was the scene of much Resistance fighting in the summer of 1944. The quarter centers on **boulevard St-Michel** (known as "Boul' Mich"), to the south.

La Sorbonne The University of Paris—everybody calls it the Sorbonne—was founded in the 13th century, and by the 14th century it had become the most prestigious university in the West, drawing such professors as Thomas Aquinas. Reorganized by Napoleon in 1806, the Sorbonne today is the premier university of France. At first glance it may seem architecturally undistinguished; it was rather indiscriminately reconstructed at the turn of the 20th century. Not so the **Eglise de la Sorbonne,** built in 1635 by Le Mercier at the center of the Sorbonne. It contains the marble tomb of Cardinal Richelieu, a work by Girardon based on a Le Brun design. At his feet is the remarkable statue *Science in Tears.*

Bd. St-Michel. Métro: St-Michel.

Musée National du Moyen Age (Thermes de Cluny) ★★ This museum has two draws: the world's finest collection of art from the Middle Ages, including jewelry and tapestries; and the well-preserved manor house, built atop Roman baths, that holds the collection. In the cobblestone **Cour d'Honneur,** you can admire the Flamboyant Gothic building, with its clinging vines, turreted walls, gargoyles, and dormers with seashell motifs. Along with the Hôtel de Sens in the Marais, this is all that remains in Paris of domestic medieval architecture.

The Cluny was the mansion of a 15th-century abbot. By 1515, it was the home of Mary Tudor, the widow of Louis XII and daughter of Henry VII of England and Elizabeth of York. Seized during the Revolution, it was rented in 1833 to Alexandre du Sommerard, who adorned it with medieval works of art. After his death in 1842, the government bought the building and the collection.

Most people come to see the **Unicorn Tapestries** ★★★, the world's most outstanding tapestries. They were discovered a century ago in the Château de Boussac in the Auvergne. Five of the six tapestries seem to deal with the senses (one depicts a unicorn looking into a mirror held by a maiden). The sixth shows a woman under an elaborate tent, her pet dog resting on an embroidered cushion beside her. The lovable unicorn and its friendly companion, a lion, hold back the flaps. The red-and-green background forms a rich carpet of spring flowers, fruit-laden trees, birds, rabbits, donkeys, dogs, goats, lambs, and monkeys.

Downstairs are the ruins of the Roman baths, dating from around A.D. 200. You can wander through a display of Gallic and Roman sculptures and an interesting marble bathtub engraved with lions.

Insider tip: The garden represents a return to the Middle Ages. It was inspired by the luxuriant detail of the museum's most fabled treasure, the 15th-century tapestry of *The Lady of the Unicorn.* It's small but richly planted.

In the Hôtel de Cluny, 6 place Paul-Painlevé, 5e. ✆ **01-53-73-78-00** or 01-53-73-78-16. www.musee-moyenage.fr. Admission 7.70€ ($10) adults, 5.70€ ($7.40) ages 18–25, free for children under 18. Wed–Mon 9:15am–5:45pm. Métro: Cluny–La Sorbonne, Saint-Michel, or Odéon.

Panthéon ★★ Some of the most famous men in the history of France (Victor Hugo, for one) are buried in austere grandeur here, on the crest of the mount of Ste-Geneviève. In 1744, Louis XV vowed that if he recovered from a mysterious illness, he would build a church to replace the Abbaye de Ste-Geneviève. He recovered—and

Mme de Pompadour's brother hired Soufflot for the job. He designed the church in the form of a Greek cross, with a dome reminiscent of St. Paul's in London. When Soufflot died, his pupil Rondelet carried out the work, completing the structure 9 years after his master's death.

After the Revolution, the church was converted into a "Temple of Fame," a pantheon for great men. Mirabeau was buried here, though his remains were later removed. Marat was another temporary tenant. Voltaire's body was exhumed and placed here—and allowed to remain. In the 19th century, the building changed roles many times—it was a church, then a pantheon, and again a church. After Hugo was buried here, it became a pantheon once more. Other men entombed include Jean-Jacques Rousseau, Emile Zola, and Louis Braille.

In 1995, the ashes of scientist Marie Curie were entombed, "the first lady so honored in our history for her own merits," in the words of François Mitterrand. Another woman, Sophie Bertholet, was buried here first, alongside her chemist husband, Marcellin, but not as a personal honor to her.

The finest frescoes, by Puvis de Chavannes, are at the end of the left wall before you enter the crypt. One illustrates Ste-Geneviève bringing supplies to relieve the victims of the famine. The best depicts her white-draped head looking out over moonlit medieval Paris, the city whose patroness she became.

Place du Panthéon, 5e. ✆ **01-44-32-18-00.** www.monum.fr. Admission 7.50€ ($9.75) adults, 4.80€ ($6.25) ages 18–25, free for children under 18. Apr–Sept daily 10am–6:30pm; Oct–Mar daily 10am–6pm (last entrance 45 min. before closing). Métro: Cardinal Lemoine or Maubert-Mutualité.

9 St-Germain-des-Prés: The 6th Arrondissement (Left Bank)

This area was the postwar home of existentialism, associated with Jean-Paul Sartre, Simone de Beauvoir, Albert Camus, and the intellectual, bohemian crowd that gathered at the Café de Flore, the Brasserie Lipp, and Les Deux-Magots. The black-clad poet Juliette Greco was known as *la muse de St-Germain-des-Prés,* and to Sartre she was the woman with "millions of poems in her throat." Her long hair and uniform of black slacks, black turtleneck sweater, and sandals launched a fashion trend adopted by young women from Paris to California.

In the 1950s, new names appeared—Françoise Sagan, Gore Vidal, and James Baldwin—but by the 1960s, tourists had become entrenched at the cafes. Today, St-Germain-des-Prés retains a bohemian street life, full of bookshops, art galleries, *caveaux* nightclubs, bistros, and coffeehouses.

Eglise St-Germain-des-Prés ★★ Outside, it's a handsome early 17th-century town house; inside, it's one of Paris's oldest churches, dating from the 6th century when a Benedictine abbey was founded on the site. The columns in the triforium are all that remain from that period. Restoration of the Chapelle St-Symphorien—the site of a pantheon for Merovingian kings—began in 1981. During that work, unknown Romanesque paintings were discovered on the chapel's triumphal arch. The Romanesque tower, topped by a 19th-century spire, is the most enduring landmark in St-Germain-des-Prés. Patrons of Les Deux-Magots, across the way, hardly notice the church bells.

The Normans nearly destroyed the abbey at least four times. The present building has a Romanesque nave and a Gothic choir with fine capitals. Among the people interred at the church are Descartes (well, his heart at least) and Jean-Casimir, the king of Poland who abdicated his throne.

Moments Gregorians Unplugged

Eglise St-Germain-des-Prés stages concerts on the Left Bank. Boasting fantastic acoustics and a medieval atmosphere, the unamplified sound will thrill you. Call © **01-42-64-83-16.** Arrive about 45 minutes before a performance for a good seat. Tickets range from 15€ to 50€ ($20–$65).

When you leave the church, turn right onto rue de l'Abbaye and have a look at the 17th-century (and very pink) Palais Abbatial.

3 place St-Germain-des-Prés, 6e. © **01-55-42-81-33.** www.eglise-sgp.org. Free admission. Mon–Sat 8am–7:45pm; Sun 9am–8pm. Métro: St-Germain-des-Prés.

Eglise St-Sulpice ★★ Pause first on the rue St-Sulpice. The 1844 fountain by Visconti displays the likenesses of four bishops of the Louis XIV era: Fenelon, Massillon, Bossuet, and Flechier. Work on the church itself, once Paris's largest, began in 1646 as part of the Catholic revival in France. Although the body of the church was completed in 1745, work on the bell towers continued until 1780, when one was finished and the other left incomplete. One of its most notable treasures is Servandoni's rococo Chapelle de la Vierge (Chapel of the Madonna), which contains a Pigalle statue of the Virgin. The church houses one of the world's largest organs; it has 6,700 pipes and has been played by such musicians as Charles-Marie Widor and Marcel Dupré.

The main draw is the Delacroix frescoes in the Chapel of the Angels (on your right as you enter). Seek out his Jacob wrestling (or is he dancing?) with an angel. On the ceiling, St. Michael has his own troubles with the devil, and another mural depicts Heliodorus being driven from the temple. Painted in the final years of his life, the frescoes were a high point in the baffling career of Delacroix.

Rue St-Sulpice, 6e. © **01-46-33-21-78.** Free admission. Daily 7:30am–7:30pm. Métro: St-Sulpice.

10 The Eiffel Tower/Musée d'Orsay: The 7th Arrondissement (Left Bank)

From place du Trocadéro, you can stand between the two curved wings of the Palais de Chaillot and gaze out on a panoramic view. At your feet are the Jardins du Trocadéro, centered by fountains. Directly in front, pont d'Iéna spans the Seine, leading to the **Eiffel Tower.** Beyond, stretching as far as your eye can see, is the **Champ-de-Mars,** once a military parade ground and now a garden with arches, grottoes, and cascades. Also in this area are the **Musée d'Orsay** (see "The Top Attractions," earlier in this chapter) and the **Musée Rodin.**

Le Musée du quai Branly ★★★ The architect, Jean Nouvel, said he wanted to create something "unique, poetic, and disturbing." And so he did with the opening of this $265-million museum, which took a decade to launch. There was even scandal: The terra-cotta figures from Nigeria turned out to be smuggled. At long last under one roof nearly 300,000 tribal artifacts from Africa, Asia, Oceania, and the Americas have been assembled. Galleries stand on sculpted pillars that evoke totem poles. Set in a lush, rambling garden on the left Bank in the shadow of the Eiffel Tower, this is the greatest monument to popular culture to open in Paris since Pompidou.

Housed in four spectacular buildings with a garden walled off from the quai Branly are the art, sculpture, and cultural materials of a vast range of non-Western civilizations,

Finds **Looking for a Quick Escape?**

The little alley behind the Musée Rodin winds down to a pond with fountains, flower beds, and even sandpits for children. It's one of the most idyllic hidden spots in Paris.

separating into different sections that represent the traditional cultures of Africa, East and Southeast Asia, Oceania, Australia, the Americas, and New Zealand. The pieces here come from the now-defunct Musée des Arts Africains et Oceaniens, the Louvre, and the Musée de l'Homme. Temporary exhibits are shown off in boxes all along the 600-foot exhibition hall. Incredible masterpieces are on display made by some very advanced traditional civilizations; some of the most impressive exhibits present lifelike tribal masks of different cultures, whose emotional expressions are described in English. Allow 2 hours for a full visit; also take a stroll in their carefully manicured garden, or have a coffee in their small cafeteria across from the main building. There are numerous entrances to the museum grounds from the area near the Eiffel Tower; the main entrance is on quai Branly.

27–37 quai Branly and 206–208 rue de Université, 7e. ✆ **01-56-61-70-00.** Admission 8.50€ ($11) adults, 6€ ($7.80) students 18–26 and seniors, free for children 17 and under. Tues–Sun 10am–6:30pm (until 9:30pm Thurs). Métro: Alma-Marceau. RER: Pont d'Alma.

Musée National Auguste Rodin ★★ This beautiful house and its gardens are a repository of the work of Auguste Rodin (1840–1917). Though his works were first thought obscene, he is considered the master of French 19th-century sculpture. After his death, the government purchased Rodin's 18th-century mansion, where he had his studio from 1910 to 1917. The rose gardens were restored to their original splendor, making a perfect setting for Rodin's most memorable works.

In the courtyard are three world-famous creations: *The Gates of Hell, The Thinker,* and *The Burghers of Calais.* Rodin's first major public commission, *The Burghers* commemorated the heroism of six burghers who in 1347 offered themselves as hostages to Edward III in return for his ending the siege of their port. *The Thinker,* in Rodin's own words, "thinks with every muscle of his arms, back, and legs, with his clenched fist and gripping toes." Inside the mansion, the sculptures, plaster casts, reproductions, originals, and sketches reveal the freshness and vitality of this remarkable man. Upstairs are two versions of the celebrated and condemned nude of Balzac, his bulky torso rising from a tree trunk. Also here are many versions of Rodin's last major work, his *Monument to Balzac* (a large one stands in the garden). Generally overlooked is a room devoted to Camille Claudel, Rodin's mistress and a towering artist in her own right. His pupil, model, and lover, she created such works as *Maturity, Clotho, The Waltz,* and the *Gossips.*

In the Hôtel Biron, 77 rue de Varenne, 7e. ✆ **01-44-18-61-10.** www.musee-rodin.fr. Admission 6€ ($7.80) adults, 4€ ($5.20) ages 18–25, free for children under 18. Apr–Sept Tues–Sun 9:30am–5:45pm; Oct–Mar Tues–Sun 9:30am–4:45pm. Métro: Varenne, Invalides, or Saint-Francois-Xavier.

11 Montparnasse: The 14th Arrondissement (Left Bank)

For the Lost Generation, life centered on the Left Bank cafes. Hangouts such as the Dôme, Coupole, Rotonde, and Sélect became legendary. Artists, especially American expatriates, turned their backs on touristy Montmartre. Picasso, Modigliani, Hemingway,

Tips A Museum in the 15th (Left Bank)

Musée Bourdelle ★, 16 rue Antoine-Bourdelle, 15e (✆ **01-49-54-73-74;** Métro: Montparnasse-Bienvenüe), is devoted to the work of Emile-Antoine Bourdelle (1861–1929), a student of Rodin. The museum displays his drawings, paintings, and sculptures, and you can wander through his studio, garden, and house. The most notable exhibits are the 21 studies he did of Beethoven. The original plaster casts of some of his greatest works are also on display. Though some exhibits are badly captioned, you'll still feel the impact of Bourdelle's genius. Admission to the permanent collection is 4.50€ ($5.85) adults, 3€ ($3.90) seniors and students, 2.20€ ($2.85) ages 14 to 25, and free for kids 13 and under. It's open Tuesday to Sunday, 10am to 6pm.

and Man Ray came this way. Fitzgerald was here when he was poor (when he was in the chips, he hung out at Le Ritz). Faulkner, Isadora Duncan, Miró, Joyce, Ford Madox Ford, and even Trotsky came here.

The life of Montparnasse still centers on its cafes and nightclubs, many only a shadow of what they used to be. Its heart is at the crossroads of boulevards Raspail and de Montparnasse, one of the settings of Hemingway's *The Sun Also Rises.* Rodin's controversial statue of Balzac swathed in a large cape stands guard over the prostitutes who cluster around the pedestal. Balzac seems to be the only one in Montparnasse who doesn't feel the impact of time and change.

Cimetière de Montparnasse ★ In the shadow of the Tour Montparnasse lies this burial ground of yesterday's celebrities, debris-littered and badly maintained. A map (to the left of the main gateway) directs you to the most famous occupants: Simone de Beauvoir and Jean-Paul Sartre, who share a gravesite. Others buried here include Samuel Beckett, Guy de Maupassant, Alfred Dreyfus, auto tycoon André Citroën, Camille Saint-Saëns, and Man Ray.

3 bd. Edgar-Quinet, 14e. ✆ **01-44-10-86-50.** Mon–Fri 8am–6pm; Sat 8:30am–6pm; Sun 9am–6pm (until 5:30pm Nov–Mar). Métro: Edgar-Quinet.

Tour Montparnasse ★★ Towering over the entire arrondissement is the Tour Montparnasse, rising 206m (76 ft.)—like the Eiffel Tower, a landmark on the Paris skyline. Completed in 1973, it was denounced by some critics as "bringing Manhattan to Paris." The city passed an ordinance outlawing any more structures of this size in the heart of Paris. Today, the tower houses a mammoth underground shopping mall and a train station. You can ride an elevator to the 56th floor and then climb three flights to the rooftop terrace. At viewing tables, you can pick out all the landmarks, from Sacré-Coeur to the Défense area in the distance. A bar and restaurant are also on this floor.

33 av. du Maine, 14e. ✆ **01-45-38-52-56.** www.tourmontparnasse56.com/uk. Admission 9€ ($12) adults, 6.50€ ($8.45) students, 4€ ($5.20) children 7–15 (2nd child is 4.60€/$6), 3rd child is 2.80€/$3.65), free for children 6 and under. Apr–Sept daily 9:30am–11:30pm; Oct–Mar daily 9:30am–10:30pm. Métro: Montparnasse-Bienvenüe.

12 Parks, Gardens & Cemeteries

See p. 156 for details on the **Tuileries. Cimetière de Montmartre** can be found on p. 162; and the **Cimetière de Montparnasse** on p. 168.

Bois de Boulogne ★★ Kids This is one of the most spectacular parks in Europe. If you had a week, you could spend it all in the Bois de Boulogne and still not see everything. Spend your time strolling along the many hidden pathways or traversing the park in a horse-drawn carriage.

Porte-Dauphine is the main entrance, but you can take the Métro to Porte-Maillot as well. West of Paris, the park was once a forest for royal hunts. In the 19th century, carriages bearing elegant damsels with their escorts rumbled along avenue Foch. Nowadays, it's more likely to attract middle-class picnickers.

When Napoleon III gave the grounds to the city in 1852, Baron Haussmann developed them. Separating Lac Inférieur from Lac Supérieur is the Carrefour des Cascades (you can stroll under its waterfall). The Lower Lake contains two islands connected by a footbridge. From the east bank, you can take a boat there, perhaps stopping at the cafe-restaurant on one of them. Restaurants in the Bois are numerous, elegant, and expensive. The Pré-Catelan contains a deluxe restaurant of the same name and a Shakespearean theater in a garden said to have been planted with trees mentioned in the bard's plays.

The **Jardin d'Acclimatation** (✆ **01-40-67-90-82;** www.jardindacclimatation.fr), at the northern edge of the park, is for children, with a small zoo, an amusement park, and a narrow-gauge railway. Two racetracks, **Longchamp** and **Auteuil,** are in the park. The annual Grand Prix is run in June at Longchamp (site of a medieval abbey). Fashionable Parisians turn out, the women attired in their finest haute couture and hats. North of Longchamp is the Grand Cascade, the artificial waterfall of the Bois de Boulogne.

In the 24-hectare (59-acre) **Bagatelle Park** (✆ **01-43-28-47-63**), which charges a 2€ ($2.60) admission for adults and .50€ (65¢) for students, the *comte* d'Artois (later Charles X) made a wager with Marie Antoinette that he could erect a small palace in less than 3 months. He hired nearly 1,000 craftsmen and irritated the local populace by requisitioning all shipments of stone and plaster arriving through the west gates of Paris. He hired *ébenistes* (cabinetmakers), painters, and the Scottish landscape architect Thomas Blaikie—and won his bet. If you're in Paris in late April, go to the Bagatelle to look at the tulips. In late May, one of the finest rose collections in Europe is in full bloom. If you can, visit in September, when the light is less harsh than in summer, or even in February, when, stripped of much of its greenery, the park assumes its true shape. ***Note:*** Beware of muggers and knife-carrying prostitutes at night.

Porte-Dauphine, 16e. ✆ **01-40-67-90-82.** Métro: Les-Sablons, Porte-Maillot, or Porte-Dauphine.

Cimetière du Père-Lachaise ★★ This cemetery has been called the "grandest address in Paris." Everybody from Sarah Bernhardt to Oscar Wilde (his tomb is by Epstein) was buried here. So were Balzac, Delacroix, and Bizet, as well as Chopin and Molière. Rock star Jim Morrison's tombstone reportedly draws the most visitors—and causes the most disruption. If you search hard enough, you can find the tombs of Abélard and Héloïse, the ill-fated lovers of the 12th century.

Spreading over more than 44 hectares (109 acres), Père-Lachaise was acquired by the city in 1804. Nineteenth-century French sculpture abounds, recalling a time when families tried to outdo others in ornamentation and cherubic ostentation. Some French socialists still pay tribute at the Mur des Fédérés, the anonymous gravesite of the Communards who were executed on May 28, 1871. Several monuments honor the French who died in the Resistance or in Nazi concentration camps.

Royal Remains at St-Denis

In the 12th century, Abbot Suger placed an inscription on the bronze doors of Basilique St-Denis: MARVEL NOT AT THE GOLD AND EXPENSE, BUT AT THE CRAFTSMANSHIP OF THE WORK. The first Gothic building in France that can be dated precisely, St-Denis was the "spiritual defender of the State" during the reign of Louis VI ("the Fat"). The facade, with its crenellated parapet similar to the fortifications of a castle, has a rose window. The windows, in stunning colors—mauve, purple, blue, and rose—were restored in the 19th century.

St-Denis, the first bishop of Paris, was patron saint of the French monarchy. Royal burials began here in the 6th century and continued until the Revolution. The sculptures around the four tombs—some two stories high—span the country's artistic development from the Middle Ages to the Renaissance. The guided tour (in French only) takes you through the crypt. François I was entombed at St-Denis. His funeral statue is nude, although he demurely covers himself with his hand.

Other kings and queens here include Louis XII and Anne of Brittany, Henri II, and Catherine de Médicis. Revolutionaries stormed through, smashing many statues and dumping royal remains in a ditch in the garden. They were reburied under the main altar during the 19th century. In a bizarre twist, following a Mass in 2004, the heart of the 10-year-old heir to the French throne, Louis XVII, was laid to rest at St-Denis, near the graves of his parents, Marie Antoinette and Louis XVI. Ceremonies recognizing the royal heart put to rest decades of rumor and legend surrounding the child's death. Genetic testing has persuaded even the most cynical historians that the person who might have been the future King Louis XVII never escaped prison. The boy died of tuberculosis in 1795, his body ravaged by tumors. The child's corpse was dumped into a common grave, but not before a doctor secretly carved out his heart and smuggled it out of prison in a handkerchief. The heart was compared to DNA from hair trimmed from Marie-Antoinette during her childhood in Austria. It was a perfect match.

The Basilique St-Denis is in a northern suburb of Paris at place de l'Hôtel-de-Ville, 2 rue de Strasbourg (© **01-48-09-83-54;** Métro: Basilique St-Denis). Admission is 6.50€ ($8.45) for adults, 4.50€ ($5.85) for seniors and students 18 to 25, and free for children under 18. It's open April to September Monday to Saturday 10am to 6:15pm, Sunday from noon to 6:15pm; October to March Monday to Saturday 10am to 5:15pm, Sunday noon to 5:15pm. Free organ concerts are presented on Sundays at 10am. It's closed January 1, November 1 and 11, and December 25.

Note: A free map is available at the newsstand across from the main entrance; it will help you find the well-known gravesites.

16 rue de Repos, 20e. © **01-55-25-82-10.** www.pere-lachaise.com. Mon–Fri 8am–6pm; Sat 8:30am–6pm; Sun 9am–6pm (until 5:30pm Nov to early Mar). Métro: Père-Lachaise or Philippe Auguste.

Jardin du Luxembourg ★★ Kids Hemingway told a friend that the Jardin du Luxembourg "kept us from starvation." In his poverty-stricken days in Paris, he wheeled a baby carriage through the gardens because it was known "for the classiness of its pigeons." When the gendarme left to get a glass of wine, the writer would eye his victim, lure it with corn, and snatch it. "We got a little tired of pigeon that year," he confessed, "but they filled many a void."

Before it became a feeding ground for struggling artists, the Luxembourg Gardens knew greater days. They are the finest formal gardens on the Left Bank (some say in all of Paris). Marie de Médicis, the much-neglected wife and later widow of the roving Henri IV, ordered the **Palais du Luxembourg** built on this site in 1612. She planned to live here with her "witch" friend, Leonora Galigäi.

The queen didn't get to enjoy the Luxembourg Palace for very long. Her son, Louis XIII, forced her into exile after he discovered that she was plotting to overthrow him. She died in Cologne in poverty. (The 21 paintings she commissioned from Rubens for her palace are now in the Louvre.) For 10€ ($13), you can visit the palace Monday, Friday, and Saturday at 10:30am to 2:30pm, but you must call ✆ **01-44-54-19-49** to make a reservation.

The gardens are the main draw. They're mostly in the classic French style: well groomed and laid out, the trees planted in designs. Urns and statuary encircle the central water basin. One statue honors Ste-Geneviève, the patroness of Paris, depicted with pigtails reaching to her thighs. Bring the kids and soak in the atmosphere. You can sail a toy boat, ride a pony, attend a Grand Guignol puppet show, or even play boules with a group of elderly men who aren't afraid of looking like a cliché from 1928, complete with black berets and Gauloises.

6e. ✆ **01-44-54-19-49.** Métro: Odéon. RER: Luxembourg.

Parc Monceau Eighteenth- and 19th-century mansions, some evoking Proust's *Remembrance of Things Past,* ring much of the park. It was built in 1778 by the duc d'Orléans, or Philippe-Egalité, as he became known, and opened to the public during Napoleon III's Second Empire. Today you'll find mothers and nurses wheeling baby carriages around the park.

Parc Monceau originally held an Egyptian-style obelisk, a medieval dungeon, an Alpine farmhouse, a Chinese pagoda, a Roman temple, an enchanted grotto, various chinoiseries, and a waterfall. The fairy-tale touches have largely disappeared, except for a pyramid and an oval *naumachie* (a place for a mock sea battle) fringed by a colonnade. Solid statuary and monuments, one honoring Chopin, have replaced many of the fantasies. In spring, the tulips and magnolias alone are worth the airfare to Paris.

8e. ✆ **01-42-27-39-56.** Free admission. Métro: Monceau or Villiers.

13 Paris Underground

Les Catacombs ★ Every year an estimated 50,000 tourists explore some 1,000 yards (914m) of underground tunnel to look at six million ghoulishly arranged skeletons. First opened to the public in 1810, this "empire of the dead" is now illuminated by overhead electric lights.

In the Middle Ages, the Catacombs were quarries; in 1785, city officials decided to use them as a burial ground. The bones of several million persons were moved here from their previous resting places, because the overcrowded cemeteries were considered

Moments Memorial to a Princess

Place de l'Alma (Métro: Alma-Marceau) has been turned into a tribute to the late Diana, princess of Wales, who was killed in an auto accident August 31, 1997, in a nearby underpass. The bronze flame in the center is a replica of the one in the Statue of Liberty and was a gift from the *International Herald Tribune* to honor Franco-American friendship. Many bouquets and messages (and even graffiti) still surround the flame.

Paris has also opened the **Center for Nature Discovery, Garden in Memory of Diana, Princess of Wales,** 21 rue des Blancs-Manteaux, 7e. The small park, which you can visit daily during daylight hours, is devoted to teaching children about nature and gardening, and contains flowers, vegetables, and decorative plants. Admission is free.

health menaces. In 1830, the prefect of Paris closed the Catacombs to the viewing public, considering them obscene and indecent. In World War II, the Catacombs were the headquarters of the French Resistance.

1 place Denfert-Rochereau, 14e. ✆ **01-43-22-47-63.** Admission 5€ ($6.50) adults, 3.10€ ($4.05) seniors, 2.50€ ($3.25) ages 14–25, free for children under 14. Tues 11am–4pm; Wed–Sun 9am–4pm. Métro: Denfert-Rochereau.

The Sewers of Paris (Les Egouts) ★ Some sociologists assert that the sophistication of a society can be judged by the way it disposes of waste. If that's true, Paris receives good marks for its network of sewers. Victor Hugo is credited with making them famous in *Les Misérables.* "All dripping with slime, his soul filled with a strange light," Jean Valjean makes his flight through the sewers of Paris. Hugo also wrote, "Paris has beneath it another Paris, a Paris of sewers, which has its own streets, squares, lanes, arteries, and circulation."

In the early Middle Ages, drinking water was taken directly from the Seine, while wastewater was poured onto fields or thrown onto the unpaved streets, transforming the urban landscape into a sea of smelly mud.

Around 1200, the streets of Paris were paved with cobblestones, with open sewers down the center. These helped spread the Black Death, which devastated the city. In 1370, a vaulted sewer was built in the rue Montmartre, draining effluents into a tributary of the Seine. During the reign of Louis XIV, improvements were made, but waste disposal in Paris remained deplorable.

During the early 1800s, 30km (19 miles) of sewer were added beneath the Parisian landscape. By 1850, the Industrial Revolution made the manufacturing of iron pipe and digging equipment more practical. Baron Haussmann developed a system that used separate underground channels for drinking water and sewage. By 1878, it was 580km (360 miles) long. Beginning in 1894, under the guidance of Belgrand, the network was enlarged, and new laws required that discharge of all waste and storm-water runoff be funneled into the sewers. Between 1914 and 1977, 966km (600 miles) of sewers were added beneath the pavements of Paris.

Today, the network of sewers is 2,093km (1,300 miles) long. Within its cavities, it contains freshwater mains, compressed-air pipes, telephone cables, and pneumatic tubes. Every day, a plant in the suburb of Achères processes 1.3 million cubic yards of wastewater.

The *égouts* (sewers), as well as telephone and telegraph pneumatic tubes, are built around four principal tunnels, one 5.5m (18 ft.) wide and 4.5m (15 ft.) high. It's like an underground city, with the street names clearly labeled. Each branch pipe bears the number of the building to which it is connected.

Tours of the sewers begin at Pont de l'Alma on the Left Bank, where a stairway leads into the bowels of the city. However, you often have to wait in line as long 30 minutes. Visiting times may change in bad weather, when a storm can make the sewers dangerous. The tour consists of a movie on sewer history, a visit to a small museum, and a short trip through the maze.

Pont de l'Alma, 7e. © **01-53-68-27-82.** Admission 4€ ($5.20) adults; 3.20€ ($4.15) seniors, students, and children 5–12; free for children under 5. May–Sept Sat–Wed 11am–5pm; Oct–Apr Sat–Wed 11am–4pm. Métro: Alma-Marceau. RER: Pont de l'Alma.

14 Shopping

Shopping is the local pastime. The City of Light is one of the rare places in the world where shopping surrounds you on almost every street. The windows, stores, and people (and even their dogs) brim with energy, creativity, and a sense of expression. You don't have to buy anything, just peer in the *vitrines* (display windows), absorb cutting-edge ideas, witness new trends, and take home an education in style.

BUSINESS HOURS

Shops are usually open Monday through Saturday from 10am to 7pm, but hours vary, and Paris doesn't run at full throttle on Monday morning. Small shops sometimes take a 2-hour lunch break and may not open until after lunch on Monday. While most stores open at 10am, some open at 9:30am or even 11am. Thursday is the best day for late-night shopping, with stores open until 9 or 10pm.

Sunday shopping is currently limited to tourist areas and flea markets, though there's growing demand for full-scale Sunday hours, a la the United States and the United Kingdom. The big department stores are now open for the five Sundays before Christmas; otherwise, they're dead on *dimanche.*

The **Carrousel du Louvre** (© **01-42-86-88-52**), an underground mall adjacent to the Louvre, is open daily 11am to 7:30pm. The tourist shops that line rue de Rivoli across from the Louvre are open Sunday, as are antiques villages, flea markets, and several food markets. The Virgin Megastore on the Champs-Elysées pays a fine in order to stay open on Sunday. It's *the* teen hangout.

GREAT SHOPPING AREAS

1er & 8e These two quartiers adjoin each other and form the heart of Paris's best Right Bank shopping neighborhood. This area includes the famed **rue du Faubourg St-Honoré,** with the big designer houses, and **avenue des Champs-Elysées,** where the mass-market and teen scenes are hot. At one end of the 1er is the **Palais Royal**—one of the city's best-kept shopping secrets, where an arcade of boutiques flanks the garden of the former palace.

On the other side of town, at the end of the 8e, is **avenue Montaigne,** 2 blocks of the fanciest shops in the world, where you float from one big name to another.

2e Behind the Palais Royal lies the **Garment District** (Sentier) and a few upscale shopping secrets such as **place des Victoires.** This area also holds a few *passages,* alleys filled with tiny stores such as **Galerie Vivienne** on rue Vivienne.

3e & 4e The difference between these two arrondissements gets fuzzy, especially around **place des Vosges,** center stage of the Marais. Even so, they offer several dramatically different shopping experiences.

On the surface, the shopping includes the real-people stretch of **rue de Rivoli** (which becomes **rue St-Antoine**). **BHV** (Bazar de l'Hôtel de Ville), which opened in 1856, is the major department store in this area; it has seven floors and lies adjacent to Paris's City Hall at 52–64 rue de Rivoli (© **01-42-74-90-00**). Many shoppers will also be looking for **La Samaritaine,** 19 rue de la Monnaie, once the most famous department store in France. It occupied four noteworthy buildings erected between 1870 and 1927. These buildings have been sold and are undergoing renovation to be completed in 2012. The new owner has not made his intentions clear about the future of this Parisian landmark.

Hidden in the **Marais** is a medieval warren of tiny, twisting streets chockablock with cutting-edge designers and up-to-the-minute fashions and trends. Start by walking around place des Vosges to see galleries, designer shops, and fabulous finds, and then dive in and get lost in the area leading to the Musée Picasso.

Finally, the 4e is also home of **place de la Bastille,** an up-and-coming area for artists and galleries where you'll find the newest entry on the retail scene, the **Viaduc des Arts** (which stretches into the 12e).

6e & 7e Whereas the 6e is one of the most famous shopping districts in Paris—it's the soul of the Left Bank—much of the good stuff is hidden in the zone that becomes the wealthy residential 7e. **Rue du Bac,** stretching from the 6e to the 7e in a few blocks, stands for all that wealth and glamour can buy. The street is jammed with art galleries, home-decor stores, and gourmet food shops.

9e To add to the fun of shopping the Right Bank, the 9e sneaks in behind the 1er, so if you choose not to walk toward the Champs-Elysées and the 8e, you can head to the big department stores in a row along **boulevard Haussmann** in the 9e. Here you'll find the two big French icons, **Au Printemps** and **Galeries Lafayette,** and a large branch of Britain's **Marks & Spencer.**

SHOPPING A TO Z

ANTIQUES Directly across from the Louvre, **Le Louvre des Antiquaires,** 2 place du Palais-Royal, 1er (© **01-42-97-27-27;** Métro: Palais-Royal), is the largest repository of antiques in central Paris. More than 200 dealers display their wares on three floors, specializing in objets d'art and small-scale furniture of the type that Mme de Pompadour might have favored. You may find 30 matching Baccarat crystal champagne flutes from the 1930s, a Sèvres tea service dated 1773, or a small Jean Fouquet pin of gold and diamonds. Too stuffy? No problem. There's always the 1940 Rolex with the aubergine crocodile strap.

Village St-Paul, 23–27 rue St-Paul, 4e (no phone; Métro: St-Paul), isn't an antiques center but a cluster of dealers in a hole-in-the-wall hide-out; the rest of the street, stretching from the river to the Marais, is lined with dealers, most of whom close on Sunday. The Village St-Paul *is* open on Sunday, and hopping. Inside the courtyards and alleys are every dreamer's visions of hidden Paris: dealers selling furniture and other decorative items in French Provincial and, to a much lesser extent, formal styles.

ART **Galerie Adrien Maeght,** 42 rue du Bac, 7e (© **01-45-48-45-15;** www.maeght.com; Métro: Rue-du-Bac), is among the most famous names, selling contemporary art on a Left Bank street. In addition to major works, it sells posters beginning

Finds An Open-Air Canvas Gallery

The **Paris Art Market,** at the foot of Montparnasse Tower, 14e (✆ **01-53-57-42-60**), is like an open-air gallery and has done much to restore the reputation of Montparnasse as a *quartier* for artists. Some 100 artists participate, including painters, sculptors, photographers, and even jewelers and hat makers. Head for the mall along the boulevard Edgar Quinet for the best work. Open Sunday from 10am to 7:30pm (Métro: Montparnasse).

at 8€ ($10), signed and numbered lithographs from 80€ to 500€ ($104–$650), and books on art and artists.

The **Viaduc des Arts,** 119 av. Daumesnil (between rue de Lyon and av. Diderot), 12e (✆ **01-44-75-80-66;** www.viaduc-des-arts.com; Métro: Bastille, Ledru-Rollin, Reuilly-Diderot, or Gare-de-Lyon), occupies the vaulted spaces beneath one of the 19th-century railway access routes into the Gare de Lyon. Around 1990, crafts artists, including furniture makers, potters, glass blowers, and weavers, began occupying the niches beneath the viaduct, selling their wares to homeowners and representatives of Paris's decorating trades. Trendsetting home-furnishing outfits have since rented additional space. Stretching for more than 2 blocks between the Opéra Bastille and the Gare de Lyon, it offers the possibility of seeing what Parisians consider chic in home decorating.

BOOKS The most famous bookstore on the Left Bank was **Shakespeare and Company,** home to the legendary Sylvia Beach, "mother confessor to the Lost Generation." Hemingway, Fitzgerald, and Gertrude Stein were all patrons. Anaïs Nin often stopped in. At one point Beach helped Henry Miller publish *Tropic of Cancer,* a book so notorious in its day that returning Americans trying to slip a copy through Customs often had it confiscated as pornography. Long ago, the shop moved from rue de l'Odéon to 37 rue de la Bücherie, 5e (✆ **01-43-25-40-93;** www.shakespeareco.org; Métro: St-Michel), where expatriates swap books and literary gossip.

Scattered over two floors of tightly packed inventory, the **Village Voice Bookshop,** 6 rue Princesse, 6e (✆ **01-46-33-36-47;** www.villagevoicebookshop.com; Métro: Mabillon), specializes in new English-language books, so it's a favorite among expatriate Yankees and Brits. It's near some of the Left Bank gathering places described in Gertrude Stein's *The Autobiography of Alice B. Toklas.*

Taschen, 2 rue de Buci, 6e (✆ **01-40-51-79-22;** Métro: Odeon), is a Germany-based publishing house that's known for coffee-table books. Erudite, high-profile, and glossy, most of them focus on architecture, art, photography, or eroticism. If you're in the market for a sweeping overview of the organization's past projects, this is the store for you. It is one of only two retail outlets in the world solely devoted to Taschen products (the other is in Cologne). Prices range from 7€ ($8.40) for a simple but provocative paperback to 5,000€ ($6,500) for a blockbuster collection of fashion photographs focusing on the best works of Helmut Newton.

W. H. Smith France, 248 rue de Rivoli, 1er (✆ **01-44-77-88-99;** www.whsmith.fr; Métro: Concorde), is France's largest store devoted to English and American books, magazines, and periodicals. You can get the *Times* of London and the Sunday *New York Times,* available Monday afternoon. There's a fine selection of maps and travel guides.

CHILDREN'S CLOTHES, SHOES & TOYS **Au Nain Bleu,** 408 rue St-Honoré, 8e (© **02-42-65-20-00;** www.aunainblue.com; Métro: Concorde or Madeleine), is the world's fanciest toy store. But don't panic; in addition to the expensive stuff, there are rows of penny candy–style cheaper toys in jars.

Bonpoint, 15 rue Royale, 8e (© **01-47-42-52-63;** Métro: Concorde), is part of a chain that helps parents transform their darlings into models of well-tailored conspicuous consumption. Though you'll find some garments for real life, the primary allure of the place lies in its tailored, traditional—and expensive—garments by the "Coco Chanel of the children's garment industry," Marie-France Cohen. The shop sells clothes for boys and girls from newborn to age 16.

Prices are a whole lot lower at **Orchestra Kazibao,** 18 rue Vignon, 9e (© **01-42-66-24-74** or 01-42-66-24-72; Métro: Madeleine), which carries selections for toddlers to 14-year-olds. Kids will love the fashions, which are wearable, washable, and affordable. It's only a short walk from place de la Madeleine.

CHINA & CRYSTAL Purveyor to kings and presidents of France since 1764, **Baccarat,** 11 place des Etats-Unis, 16e (© **01-40-22-11-22;** Métro: Boissière or Iéna), and 11 place de la Madeleine, 8e (© **01-42-65-36-26;** Métro: Madeleine), produces world-renowned full-lead crystal dinnerware, jewelry, chandeliers, and statuary. The Madeleine branch is more glamorous but not as well stocked. It carries porcelain and crystal from other manufacturers, such as Christofle.

Lalique, 11 rue Royale, 8e (© **01-53-05-12-12;** www.cristallalique.fr; Métro: Concorde), famous for its clear- and frosted-glass sculpture, Art Deco crystal, and perfume bottles, has recently branched out into other merchandise—for example, silk scarves meant to compete with Hermès and leather belts with Lalique buckles.

And then there's **Limoges-Unic & Madronet,** 34 rue de Paradis, 10e (© **01-47-70-34-59;** www.limoges-unic-madronet.com; Métro: Gare-de-l'Est). In two shops a 3-minute walk from each other, you'll find Limoges china and anything else you might need for the table—glass, crystal, and silver. It pays to drop into both stores, whose inventories vary according to the season and the whims of the buyers.

CHOCOLATE Some of Paris's most delicious chocolates can be found at **Christian Constant,** 37 rue d'Assas, 6e (© **01-53-63-15-15;** Métro: St-Placide). Particularly appealing are combinations of chocolate meringue, chocolate mousse, and bitter chocolate *feuilles d'automne* (autumn leaves).

Racks and racks of chocolates are priced individually or by the kilo at **La Maison du Chocolat,** 225 rue du Faubourg St-Honoré, 8e (© **01-42-27-39-44;** www.lamaisonduchocolat.com; Métro: Ternes), though it'll cost you about 100€ ($130) for a kilo. Note the similarity to Hermès when it comes to the wrapping and ribbon (and prices). The chocolate pastries are affordable; the store even has its own chocolate milk. There are five other branches around Paris.

CRAFTS One of the few regional handicrafts stores in Paris worth going out of your way to find, **La Tuile à Loup,** 35 rue Daubenton, 5e (© **01-47-07-28-90;** www.latuilealoup.com; Métro: Censier-Daubenton), carries beautiful pottery and faïence from many regions of France. Look for figures of Breton folk on the faïence of Quimper, as well as garlands of fruits and flowers from the *terre vernissée* (varnished earth, a charming way to define stoneware) from Normandy, Savoy, Alsace, and Provence. Prices begin at 4.50€ ($5.85) for a sachet of Provençal lavender and climb to 1,500€ ($1,950) for a bulky but undeniably beautiful wall plaque.

DEPARTMENT & DIME STORES After you've admired the architecture of one of Europe's most famous department stores, step inside **Au Printemps,** 64 bd. Haussmann, 9e (✆ **01-42-82-50-00;** www.printemps.com; Métro: Havre-Caumartin; RER: Auber). Inside the main building is **Printemps de la Mode,** which occupies the bulk of the structure, and a housewares shop, **Printemps de la Maison.** Upstairs are wares of every sort, especially clothing. An affiliated store across the street is **Le Printemps de l'Homme,** the menswear division. Behind the main store is a branch of **Monoprix,** Printemps's workaday but serviceable dime store, which contains a grocery. Check out the magnificent stained-glass dome, built in 1923, through which kaleidoscopic light cascades into the sixth-floor cafe. English-speaking interpreters are stationed throughout the store and at the Welcome Desk in the basement of the main building. ***Note:*** Foreign visitors who show their passport receive a flat 10% discount.

A two-part department store, **Au Bon Marché,** 24 rue de Sèvres, 7e (✆ **01-44-39-80-00;** www.lebonmarche.fr; Métro: Sèvres-Babylone), is on the Left Bank in the midst of all the chic boutiques. No. 38 houses a gourmet grocery store; no. 22 is a source for your general shopping needs.

Colette, 213 rue St-Honoré, 1er (✆ **01-55-35-33-90;** www.colette.fr; Métro: Pyramides), is Paris's new store of the moment, a swank citadel for a la mode fashion that has made the elegant but staid rue St-Honoré less stuffy. For cutting-edge design, this is the place to go; you'll see fashions by young talents such as Marni and Lucien Pellat-Finet, furnishings by such designers as Tom Dixon, and even zany Japanese accessories. Here's a tip: Even if you don't buy anything, head for the tea salon downstairs for fresh quiches, salads, and cakes.

At **Galeries Lafayette,** 40 bd. Haussmann, 9e (✆ **01-42-82-34-56;** Métro: Chaussée-d'Antin; RER: Auber), stand under "the Dome"—a stained-glass cupola that towers above the arcaded store. Built in 1912, Galeries Lafayette consists of several stores: **Lafayette Hommes** men's store, **Lafayette Sports, Galeries Lafayette Mariage** (for wedding accessories), and two other general-merchandise stores, both known simply as **"GL."** One floor above street level is one of the fanciest grocery stores in town, **Gourmet Lafayette,** with prices that are slightly less than those at Fauchon.

FASHION: CUTTING-EDGE CHIC **Azzedine Alaïa,** 7 rue de Moussy, 4e (✆ **01-42-72-19-19;** Métro: Hôtel-de-Ville), showcases the collection of the darling of 1970s French fashion. Alaïa revived body consciousness and put the ooh-la-la in Paris chic; he specializes in evening dresses. If you can't afford the current collection, try the stock shop around the corner at 18 rue de Verrerie, which sells last year's leftovers at serious discounts.

Dolce & Gabbana, 22 av. Montaigne, 8e (✆ **01-42-25-68-78;** Métro: Alma-Marceau), occupies most of the ground floor of a soaring skyscraper that houses the executive offices of the LVMH (Louis Vuitton/Moet-Hennessy) group. It showcases the entire line of sexy, sporty, haute men's and women's clothing.

Supporters of the high-camp, high-fashion mogul **Jean-Paul Gaultier** describe him as an avant-garde classicist without allegiance to the aesthetic restrictions of the French bourgeoisie. Detractors call him a glorified punk rocker with a gimmicky allegiance to futurist models as interpreted by *Star Trek.* Whatever your opinion, it's always refreshing and insightful for a fashion buff to check out what France's most iconoclastic designer is doing. There's a branch of his store at 6 rue Vivienne, 2e (✆ **01-42-86-05-05;** Métro: Bourse), but the main branch, and biggest inventory, is at 44 av. George V, 8e (✆ **01-44-43-00-44;** Métro: George V).

FASHION: DISCOUNT & RESALE **Anna Lowe,** 104 rue du Faubourg St-Honoré, 8e (✆ **01-42-66-11-32** or 01-40-06-02-42; www.annalowe.com; Métro: Miromesnil), is one of the top boutiques for women who wish to purchase Chanel or Versace at a discount. Many clothes are runway samples; some have been gently worn.

The inventory at **Réciproque,** 88–123 rue de la Pompe (between av. Victor-Hugo and av. Georges-Mandel), 16e (✆ **01-47-04-30-28,** 01-47-27-93-52, or 01-47-04-82-24; Métro: Pompe), is scattered over five buildings. Everything is secondhand, in sections devoted to Chanel, Versace, Lacroix, Hermès, and Mugler. Women will find gowns, suits, sportswear, and shoes. Men should go to no. 101. Everything has been worn, but in some cases that means only on runways or during photo shoots.

French film stars often shop at **Défilé des Marques,** 171 rue de Grenelles, 7e (✆ **01-45-55-63-47;** Métro: Latour-Maubourg), but anyone can pick up Laurent, Dior, Lacroix, Prada, Chanel, Versace, Hermès, and others at a fraction of the original price. Hermès scarves are sold here as well. Low prices derive from the owners' skill at picking up used clothing in good condition from last year's collections, from collections of many years ago, or from estate sales.

FASHION: FLAGSHIPS The **Chanel** boutique, 29 rue Cambon, 1er (✆ **01-42-86-28-00;** Métro: Concorde or Tuileries), carries classic Chanel as well as pieces with Karl Lagerfeld's interesting twist.

During the decade (1947–57) that he directed his empire, **Christian Dior,** 30 av. Montaigne, 8e (✆ **01-40-73-73-73;** Métro: Franklin-D-Roosevelt), was the only couturier whose name was known throughout the Western Hemisphere. The house has continued to thrive since its reorganization into a small-scale version of a department store, with sections devoted to men's, women's, and children's clothing; gift items; makeup and perfume; and so on. Unlike some of the other big-name fashion houses, Dior is very approachable.

One of the most recognizable accessories in France is an opulent silk scarf or tie from **Hermès,** 24 rue du Faubourg St-Honoré, 8e (✆ **01-40-17-46-00** or 01-40-17-47-17; Métro: Concorde). You'll find them in abundance, along with everything else (bags, purses, and so forth) endorsed by the legendary saddle maker, at the flagship branch.

Louis Vuitton, 6 place St-Germain-des-Prés, 6e (✆ **01-45-49-62-32;** Métro: St-Germain-des-Prés), is the most interestingly decorated branch of Vuitton in Paris. Antiques and fine hardwoods evoke the grand age of travel, when steamships and railway cars hauled the affluent to exotic places. It stocks a wide inventory of purses, suitcases, and trunks with the traditional monogram, plus new lines of Vuitton leather goods crafted from beige cowhide. The store also sells writing instruments as well as a *Carnet du Voyage,* a do-it-yourself scrapbook with watercolors and space to preserve your memories.

FASHION: VINTAGE COUTURE At **Didier Ludot,** 24 Galerie de Montpensier, in the arcades surrounding the courtyard of the Palais Royal, 1er (✆ **01-42-96-06-56;** Métro: Palais-Royal), fashion historians salivate at the inventory of the haute couture of yesteryear. In this stylish shop, at prices that rival what you'd expect to pay for a serious antique, you'll find a selection of gowns and dresses created between 1900 and 1980 for women who looked fabulous at Maxim's, at cocktail parties on the avenue Foch, in Deauville, or wherever.

FOOD At place de la Madeleine stands one of the most popular sights in the city—not La Madeleine church but **Fauchon,** 26 place de la Madeleine, 8e (✆ **01-70-39-38-00;**

Métro: Madeleine). It offers a wider choice of upscale gourmet products than anyplace else in the world. Areas are devoted to candy, pastries, and bread; fresh fruits and veggies; dry and canned goods; fresh fish and meats; awe-inspiring takeaway food; and wine.

Fauchon's main competitor, **Hédiard,** 21 place de la Madeleine, 8e (© **01-43-12-88-88;** www.hediard.fr; Métro: Madeleine), opened in 1854. It's a series of salons filled with almost Disneyesque displays meant to give the store the look of an old-fashioned spice emporium. Hédiard is also rich in coffees, teas, and jams. Upstairs is a superb restaurant, **La Table d'Hédiard** (© **01-43-12-88-99**), open Monday to Friday 8:30am to 10pm, Saturday noon to 10:30pm.

Le Maison du Miel (the House of Honey), 24 rue Vignon, 9e (© **01-47-42-26-70;** www.lamaisondumiel.com; Métro: Madeleine, Havre-Caumartin, or Opéra), has been a family tradition since before World War I. The entire store is devoted to products made from honey: vinegar, mustard, soap, regional varieties of nougat, and various edible honeys. It's around the corner from Fauchon and worth the walk.

JEWELRY Well-dressed women around the world wear fabulous gemstones from **Van Cleef & Arpels,** 22 place Vendôme, 1er (© **01-53-45-35-50;** Métro: Opéra or Tuileries). One of the firm's specialties is yellow diamonds, whose color resembles amber but whose fire is unmistakably brilliant. Floral motifs, in platinum or gold with vibrant hues, are also a trademark.

LEATHER One of the most glamorous leather purveyors, established by an Italian entrepreneur on place Vendôme in 1905, is **Morabito,** 55 rue François, 1er (© **01-53-23-90-40;** Métro: George V). Today it sells chicer-than-thou handbags at prices that begin at 480€ ($624), as well as suitcases—some of the best in Paris—for men and women.

LINGERIE Undergarments manufactured and sold by **Cadolle,** 4 rue Cambon, 1er (© **01-42-60-94-22;** www.cadolle.fr; Métro: Concorde), are among the world's most comfortable and opulent. Herminie Cadolle invented the brassiere in 1889, and in 1911, she moved to this location near the former headquarters of Coco Chanel, whose "emaciated" styles she disliked. Today, her great-granddaughters manage the store. What's new here? The magic word is corsets, preferably in black, worn with long skirts or slacks. Fashioned out of everything from velvet to satin, they're almost guaranteed to turn heads day or night.

MALLS **Carrousel du Louvre,** 99 rue de Rivoli, 1er (© **01-43-16-47-10;** Métro: Palais-Royal–Musée du Louvre), combines a convenient location, a food court, handy boutiques, and plenty of museum gift shops with a touch of culture. Always mobbed, this is one of the few shopping venues allowed to open on Sunday. The easiest way to get here is to enter from rue de Rivoli. It has a Virgin Megastore, the Body Shop, and several big-name boutiques, such as Courrèges and Lalique. Check out Diane Claire for the fanciest souvenirs you've ever seen. A branch of the Paris Convention and Visitors Bureau is next door to Virgin.

Forget about the street address of **Forum des Halles,** 1–7 rue Pierre-Lescot, 1er (no phone; Métro: Etienne-Marcel or Châtelet–Les Halles). This mall fills an entire block where the old produce market, Les Halles, once stood. Now it's a crater of modern metal with layers of boutiques around a courtyard. There's one of everything here—but the feel is sterile, without a hint of *joie de vivre.*

MARKETS Artists love to paint the **Marché aux Fleurs,** place Louis-Lépine, Ile de la Cité, 4e (Métro: Cité); photographers love to click away. The stalls are ablaze with color, each a showcase of flowers (most of which escaped the fate of being hauled to the perfume factories of Grasse in the French Riviera). The Flower Market is along the Seine, behind the Tribunal de Commerce. On Sunday, this is a bird market.

Paris's famous flea market, **Marché aux Puces de Clignancourt,** avenue de la Porte de Clignancourt (no phone; www.marchesauxpuces.fr; Métro: Porte-de-Clignancourt; then turn left, cross bd. Ney, and walk north on av. de la Porte de Clignancourt), is a complex of almost 3,000 stalls and shops in St-Ouen, a suburb north of the 18th arrondissement. It sells everything from antiques to junk, new to vintage clothing. Beware of pickpockets and troublemakers while shopping the market.

The first clues that you're here are the stalls of cheap clothing along avenue de la Porte de Clignancourt. Hold off spending until you get to rue des Rosiers, and then turn left. Vendors start bringing out their offerings around 9am Saturday to Monday and take them in around 6pm. Hours are a tad flexible, depending on weather and crowds. Monday is traditionally the best day for bargain seekers—attendance is smaller and merchants demonstrate a greater desire to sell.

First-timers at the flea market always ask two things: "Will I get any real bargains here?" and "Will I get fleeced?" It's all relative. Obviously dealers have already skimmed the best. And it's true that the same merchandise displayed here will sell for less out in the provinces. But for the visitor who has only a few days to spend in Paris—and only half a day for shopping—the flea market is worth the experience. Vintage French postcards, old buttons, and bistroware are quite affordable; each market has its own personality and an aura of Parisian glamour that can't be found elsewhere. Most of the markets have toilets; some have a central office to arrange shipping. Cafes, pizza joints, and even a few restaurants are scattered throughout. Almost without exception, they are bad. The exception is **Le Soleil,** 109 av. Michelet, St. Ouen (© **01-40-10-08-08**); it was converted from a cafe into a family-run restaurant by Louis-Jacques Vannucci. Catering to flea-market shoppers, the restaurant looks flea-market decorated as well. The food is excellent, especially the sautéed chicken in light cream sauce, green bean salad with tomato cubes, and fresh Norman cod and the tiny mussels cooked in a rich broth. Charging 25€ ($33) for a main course, it is open daily for lunch noon to 3pm and Friday to Saturday for dinner 8 to 11pm.

Then there's the **Marché aux Puces de la Porte de Vanves,** avenue Georges-Lafenestre, 14e (Métro: Porte-de-Vanves). Like a giant yard sale, this bazaar sprawls along two streets. It's Paris's best flea market—dealers swear by it. There's little in terms of formal antiques, and few large pieces of furniture. You'll do better if you collect old linens, secondhand Hermès scarves, toys, costume jewelry, or perfume bottles. Asking prices tend to be high, because dealers prefer to sell to nontourists. On Sundays, there's a food market one street over. Closed on Monday.

Marché Buci, rue de Buci, 6e (Métro: St-Germain-des-Prés), is a traditional French food market held at the intersection of two streets. It's only 1 block long, but what a block it is. Seasonal fruits and vegetables dance across tabletops while chickens spin on the rotisserie. One stall is devoted to big bunches of fresh flowers. Avoid Monday morning, when very little is open.

MUSIC The chain called **FNAC,** with a branch at 136 rue de Rennes, 6e (© **01-49-54-30-00;** Métro: St-Placide), is for anyone looking for CDs, records and tapes, computers, photo equipment, TVs, and stereos. It's known for its wide selection and competitive prices. The ticket service sells tickets for most of the venues and concerts in the city. There are eight other locations in Paris.

Virgin Megastore, 52–60 av. des Champs-Elysées, 8e (✆ **01-49-53-50-00;** Métro: Franklin-D-Roosevelt), is one of the anchors that helped rejuvenate the Champs-Elysées. The landmark building houses the city's largest music store as well as a bookstore and cafe. The ticket service can make reservations for plays, concerts, and sporting events. Other branches are in the Carrousel du Louvre (see "Malls," above), at both airports, and in Gare Montparnasse.

PERFUME, COSMETICS & TOILETRIES Almost every working woman around place de la Madeleine shops at **Catherine,** 7 rue Castiglione, 1er (✆ **01-42-61-02-89;** Métro: Concorde). They appreciate its discounts and lack of pretension. It resembles a high-volume pharmacy more than a boutique; *flacons* of perfume move in and out fast. You get a 30% discount on most makeup and perfume and a 20% discount on brands such as Chanel and Dior.

You'll find some of the best deals in cosmetics at **maki,** 9 rue Mansart, 9e (✆ **01-42-81-33-76;** Métro: Blanche). In the middle of a theater area, it's where actors and models come for quality products at discounted prices. The staff will often give advice on makeup.

Though you can buy its scents in any discount parfumerie, we recommend visiting the source of some of the world's most famous perfumes: **Parfums Caron,** 34 av. Montaigne, 8e (✆ **01-47-23-40-82;** www.parfumscaron.com; Métro: Franklin-D-Roosevelt). Established in 1904, it quickly gained a reputation as the choice of temptresses.

SHOES Called a "merging of James Bond with Helmut Newton," **Rodolphe Menudier,** 14 rue de Castiglione, 1er (✆ **01-42-60-86-27;** Métro: Concorde or Tuileries), is the most written-about and envied new shoe designer in haute Paris. Menudier's men's and women's footwear would make any foot fetishist salivate. Formerly a shoe designer for Balenciaga and Chanel, he launched his own line from a boutique near place Vendôme. Whether you want the look of a vamp (red patent-leather stiletto heels with asymmetrical laces) or something grande dame-ish, if you don't mind paying upwards of 300€ ($390) a pair, this is the store for you.

WINES **Les Caves Taillevent,** 199 rue du Faubourg St-Honoré, 8e (✆ **01-45-61-14-09;** Métro: Charles de Gaulle–Etoile), is a temple to the art of making fine French wine. Associated with one of Paris's grandest restaurants, Taillevent, it occupies the street level and cellar of an antique building in a neighborhood awash with memories of the French empire. Stored here are more than 25,000 bottles of wine—some at around 5.50€ ($7.15).

15 Paris After Dark

THE PERFORMING ARTS

Announcements of shows, concerts, and operas are on kiosks all over town. You can find listings in *Pariscope,* a weekly entertainment guide, and in the English-language *Boulevard,* a bimonthly magazine. Performances start later in Paris than in London or New York—anywhere from 8 to 9pm—and Parisians tend to dine after the theater. (But you may not want to follow suit, because many of the less expensive restaurants close as early as 9pm.)

There are many ticket agencies in Paris, mostly near the Right Bank hotels. *Avoid them if possible.* You can buy the cheapest tickets at the theater box office. Tip the usher who shows you to your seat in a theater or movie house.

For information and tickets to just about any show in Paris (also Dijon, Lyon, and Nice), **Keith Prowse** has a New York office if you'd like to make arrangements before you go. It's at 234 W. 44th St., Suite 1000, New York, NY 10036 (✆ **800/669-8687;** www.keithprowse.com). The Paris office is at 7 rue de Clichy, 9e (✆ **01-42-81-88-98;** Métro: Place de Clichy). They will mail tickets to your home, fax confirmation, or leave tickets at the box office in Paris. There's a markup of 20% (excluding opera and ballet) over box-office price, plus a U.S. handling charge of $8. Hotel and theater packages are also available.

Several agencies sell tickets for cultural events and plays at discounts of up to 50%. One is the **Kiosque Théâtre,** 15 place de la Madeleine, 8e (no phone; www.kiosquetheatre.com; Métro: Madeleine), offering day-of-performance tickets for about half-price. Tickets for evening performances are sold Tuesday to Saturday 12:30 to 8pm. For matinees, tickets are sold Saturday 12:30 to 2pm and Sunday 12:30 to 4pm.

For easy access to tickets for festivals, concerts, and the theater, try one of two locations of the **FNAC** electronics-store chain: 136 rue de Rennes, 6e (✆ **01-49-54-30-00;** Métro: St. Placide); or 1–7 rue Pierre-Lescot, in the Forum des Halles, 1er (✆ **01-40-41-40-00;** Métro: Châtelet–Les Halles).

THE TOP VENUES

Opéra Garnier ★★★, place de l'Opéra, 9e (✆ **08-92-89-90-90** or 01-40-01-18-50; www.operadeparis.fr; Métro: Opéra), is the premier stage for dance and opera. Because of competition from the Opéra Bastille, the original opera has made great efforts to present more up-to-date works, including choreography by Jerome Robbins, Twyla Tharp, and George Balanchine. The architect Charles Garnier designed this rococo wonder in the heyday of the empire. The facade is adorned with marble and sculpture, including *The Dance* by Carpeaux. Restoration has returned the Garnier to its former glory: Its boxes and walls are lined with flowing red and blue damask, the ceiling (painted by Marc Chagall) has been cleaned, and air-conditioning has been added. The box office is open Monday to Saturday 10:30am to 6:30pm.

The controversial building known as the **Opéra Bastille** ★★★, place de la Bastille, 120 rue de Lyon (✆ **08-92-89-90-90** or 01-40-01-17-89; www.operadeparis.fr; Métro: Bastille), was designed by the Canadian architect Carlos Ott, with curtains created by fashion designer Issey Miyake. The showplace was inaugurated in July 1989 (for the Revolution's bicentennial), and on March 17, 1990, the curtain rose on Hector Berlioz's *Les Troyens.* Since its much-publicized opening, the opera house has presented works such as Mozart's *Marriage of Figaro* and Tchaikovsky's *Queen of Spades.* The main hall is the largest French opera house, with 2,700 seats, but music critics have lambasted the acoustics. The building contains two additional concert halls, including an intimate room seating 250, usually used for chamber music. Both traditional opera performances and symphony concerts are presented here. Call to find out about occasional free concerts on French holidays.

New York has its Carnegie Hall, but for years Paris lacked a permanent home for its orchestra. That is, until 2006 when the restored **Salle Pleyel** ★★★, 252 rue du Faubourg-St-Honoré, 8e (✆ **01-42-52-13-13;** Métro: Miromesnil), opened once again. Built in 1927 by the piano-making firm of the same name, Pleyel was the world's first concert hall designed exclusively for a symphony orchestra. Ravel, Debussy, and Stravinsky performed their masterpieces here, only to see the hall devastated by fire less than 9 months after its opening. The original sound quality was never recovered because of an economic downturn. In 1998, real estate developer

Hubert Martigny purchased the concert hall and pumped $38 million into it, restoring the Art Deco spirit of the original and also refining the acoustics it once knew. Nearly 500 seats were removed to make those that remained more comfortable. The Orchestre Philarmonique de Radio France and the Orchestre de Paris now have a home worthy of their reputations, and the London Symphony Orchestra makes Pleyel its venue in Paris. Tickets range from 10€ to 130€ ($13–$169), and seniors and young people under 27 can arrive an hour before a concert and fill any available seat for just 10€ ($13). Reservations are made by phone Monday to Friday 10am to 6pm.

The Art Deco **Théâtre des Champs-Elysées,** 15 av. Montaigne, 8e (✆ **01-49-52-50-50;** www.theatrechampselysees.fr; Métro: Alma-Marceau), which attracts the haute couture crowd, books both national and international orchestras as well as operas and ballets. Events are held year-round, except in August. The box office is open Monday to Saturday 1 to 7pm.

Conceived by the Mitterrand administration, **Cité de la Musique** ★★★, 221 av. Jean-Jaurès, 19e (✆ **01-44-84-45-00,** or 01-44-84-44-84 for tickets and information; www.cite-musique.fr; Métro: Porte-de-Pantin), has been widely applauded. At the city's northeastern edge in what used to be a run-down neighborhood, the $120-million stone-and-glass structure, designed by Christian de Portzamparc, incorporates a network of concert halls, a library and research center, and a museum. The complex stages a variety of concerts, ranging from Renaissance to 20th-century programs.

Even those with only a modest understanding of French can delight in a sparkling production of Molière at the **Comédie-Française,** 2 rue de Richelieu, 1er (✆ **08-25-10-16-80;** www.comedie-francaise.fr; Métro: Palais-Royal–Musée du Louvre), established to keep the classics alive and to promote important contemporary authors. The box office is open daily from 11am to 6:30pm; the hall is dark from July 21 to September 5. The Left Bank annex is the **Comédie-Française-Théâtre du Vieux-Colombier,** 21 rue du Vieux-Colombier, 4e (✆ **01-44-39-87-00;** Métro: Sèvres-Babylone or Saint-Sulpice). Although its repertoire can vary, it's known for presenting some of the most serious French dramas in town.

International stars appear in the cavernous **Olympia,** 28 bd. des Capucines, 9e (✆ **01-55-27-10-00** or 08-92-68-33-68; www.olympiahall.com; Métro: Opéra or Madeleine). Yves Montand appeared once—the performance sold out 4 months in advance—but today you're more likely to catch Gloria Estefan. A typical lineup may include an English rock group, Italian acrobats, a well-known French singer, a dance troupe, an American juggler or comedy team (doing much of their work in English), plus the featured star. A witty emcee and an onstage band provide smooth transitions between acts.

FOLK MUSIC

Au Lapin Agile ★ Picasso and Utrillo once patronized this cottage near the top of Montmartre, formerly known as the Café des Assassins. It has been painted by numerous artists, including Utrillo, and Steve Martin used it as a setting for a play. For decades, it has been the heart of French folk music. You'll sit at wooden tables in a dimly lit room with walls covered by bohemian memorabilia, listening to French folk tunes, love ballads, army songs, sea chanteys, and music-hall ditties. You're encouraged to sing along, even if it's only the "oui, oui, oui—non, non, non" refrain of "Les Chevaliers de la Table Ronde." The best singalongs are on weeknights after tourist season ends. Open Tuesday through Sunday from 9pm to 2am. 22 rue des Saules, 18e. ✆ **01-46-06-85-87.** www.au-lapin-agile.com. Cover (includes 1 drink) 24€ ($31), 17€ ($22) students. Métro: Lamarck Caulaincourt.

NIGHTCLUBS & CABARETS

These places are all outrageously expensive, but they provide some of the most lavish, spectacular floor shows anywhere.

Crazy Horse Saloon ★★ This sophisticated strip joint has thrived for decades thanks to good choreography and a sly, flirty theme that celebrates and exalts the female form. Each number features gorgeous girls outfitted in outrageous costumes. If you opt for dinner, it will be a tasteful, well-prepared event served with flair at Chez Francis, a restaurant under separate management a few steps from the cabaret. Shows, which last 1 hour and 45 minutes, are attended by men and some women. 12 av. George V, 8e. ✆ **01-47-23-32-32.** www.lecrazyhorseparis.com. Cover (includes 2 drinks) 90€ ($117); dinner spectacle 135€–170€ ($176–$221). Métro: Alma-Marceau.

Folies-Bergère Folies-Bergère is a Paris institution; foreigners have flocked here since 1886. Josephine Baker, the African-American singer who used to throw bananas into the audience, became "the toast of Paris" here. According to legend, the first GI to reach Paris in 1944 asked for directions to the club.

Since the naughty Belle Epoque days when the cancan was likely to be performed by women who didn't necessarily wear underpants, Folies-Bergère has witnessed many changes, many modernizations, and an attempt in the mid-1990s to become a "legitimate" dramatic theater. (It didn't work particularly well—audiences preferred the cabaret that had made the place famous.)

In 2002, Folies-Bergère reverted to its original role, mounting 2-hour revues in a state-of-the-art 1,600-seat theater that showcases an appreciation for the (partially clothed) elegance and allure of *la femme.* Be prepared for G-strings and brassieres that management refers to as *léger, léger* (very light), lots of feathers and sequins, and all the ooh-la-la razzmatazz you'd expect. Each show includes two female singers performing in a mixture of French and English, a juggler, and lots of mostly female flesh. The acts are charming, but if you're looking for artful nudity presented with unabashed Parisian permissiveness, head for the Crazy Horse. The restaurant serves dinner, but most spectators opt to skip the meal and focus on the show, which usually starts at 9pm, Tuesday through Sunday. 32 rue Richer, 9e. ✆ **01-44-79-98-60** or 08-92-68-16-50. www.foliesbergere.com. Tickets 25€–84€ ($33–$109). Métro: Grands Boulevards or Cadet.

Lido de Paris The Lido competes with the best Las Vegas has to offer. Its $15-million production, *C'est Magique,* reflects a dramatic reworking of the classic Parisian cabaret show, with eye-popping special effects, water technology using more than 60,000 gallons per minute, and even aerial and aquatic ballet. The show, the most expensive ever produced in Europe, uses 70 performers, $4 million in costumes, and a $2-million lighting design with lasers. There's even an ice rink and swimming pool that appears and disappears. The 45 topless Bluebell Girls, those legendary showgirls, are still here. Chef Paul Bocuse is the consultant for the culinary offerings. 116 bis av. des Champs-Elysées, 8e. ✆ **800/227-4884** in the U.S., or 01-40-76-56-10. www.lido.fr. Dinner dance (7:30pm) and show (11:30pm) 140€–210€ ($182–$273); show only (9:30 and 11:30pm) 100€ ($130). Price includes half-bottle of champagne per person. Métro: George V.

Moulin Rouge The establishment that Toulouse-Lautrec immortalized is still here, but the artist would probably have a hard time recognizing it. Colette created a scandal here by offering an on-stage kiss to Mme de Morny, but shows today have a harder time shocking audiences. Try to get a table—the view is much better on the main floor than from the bar. Expect a combination of strip routines, the saucy sexiness of *la Belle Epoque,* and the permissiveness of Paris between the wars. Handsome men and girls, virtually all topless, keep the place going. Dance finales usually include two dozen of the belles doing a topless cancan. Revues begin nightly at 9 and 11pm. 82 bd. Clichy, place Blanche, 18e. ✆ **01-53-09-82-82.** www.moulinrouge.fr. Cover including champagne 87€–97€ ($113–$126); 7pm dinner and show 140€–170€ ($182–$221). Métro: Blanche.

Nouveau Casino Some Paris-watchers consider this the epitome of the hyper-hip countercultural scene that blossoms along the rue Oberkampf every night. In a former movie theater adjacent to the Café Charbon, it's a large, drafty space centered on a dance floor and an enormous bar crafted to resemble an iceberg. Live concerts take place nightly between 8pm and 1am; on Friday and Saturday, the party continues from 1am until dawn with a DJ who spins some of the most avant-garde dance music in Paris. Celebrity spotters have picked out Prince Albert of Monaco and such French-language film stars as Vincent Cassel and Mathieu Kassovitz. 109 rue Oberkampf, 9e. ✆ **01-43-57-57-40.** www.nouveaucasino.net. Admission to concerts 12€–13€ ($16–$17); to disco 5€–20€ ($6.50–$26). Métro: St-Maur, Parmentier, or Ménilmontant.

LE COOL JAZZ

The great jazz revival that long ago swept America is still going strong here, with Dixieland or Chicago rhythms pounding out in dozens of jazz cellars, mostly called *caveaux.* Most clubs are on the Left Bank near the Seine, between rue Bonaparte and rue St-Jacques. For the latest details, look for publications such as *Jazz Hot, Jazz Magazine,* or *Pariscope.*

Baiser Salé This appealing club is housed in a cellar lined with jazz-related paintings, a large bar, and videos that show jazz greats of the past (Charlie Parker, Miles Davis) Everything is mellow and laid-back, with an emphasis on the music. Genres include Afro-Caribbean, Afro-Latino, salsa, merengue, rhythm and blues, and sometimes fusion. 58 rue des Lombards, 1er. ✆ **01-42-33-37-71.** www.lebaisersale.com. Cover Tues–Sun 8€ ($10) or 16€ ($21) after 10pm. Free Mon. Métro: Châtelet.

Caveau des Oubliettes ★ It's hard to say which is more intriguing—the entertainment and drinking or the setting. An *oubliette* is a dungeon with a trap door at the top as its only opening, and they couldn't have given this place a more suitable name. Located in the Latin Quarter, just across the river from Notre-Dame, this nightspot is housed in a genuine 12th-century prison, complete with dungeons, spine-tingling passages, and scattered skulls, where prisoners were tortured and sometimes pushed through portholes to drown in the Seine. The *caveau* is beneath the subterranean vaults that many centuries ago linked it with the fortress prison of Petit Châtelet. Today, patrons laugh, drink, talk, and flirt in the narrow *caveau* or else retreat to the smoke-filled jazz lounge. There's a free jam session every night, perhaps Latin jazz or rock. At some point on Friday and Saturday nights concerts are staged (a cover is assessed at this time). Open daily 5pm to 2am. 52 rue Galande, 5e. ✆ **01-46-34-23-09.** Cover 10€ ($13) Fri–Sat. Métro: St-Michel.

Le Bilboquet This restaurant/jazz club/piano bar, where the film *Paris Blues* was shot, offers some of the best music in the city. Jazz is featured daily, 9:30pm to 1:30am, in a wood-paneled room with a copper ceiling, brass-trimmed bar, and Victorian candelabra on the upper level in the restaurant. The menu is limited but classic French;

dinner will run you 55€ ($66) and is served Monday to Saturday 8pm to 2am. 13 rue St-Benoît, 6e. ✆ **01-45-48-81-84.** Cover 18€ ($23). Métro: St-Germain-des-Prés.

New Morning Jazz maniacs come to drink, talk, and dance at this enduring club. It's sometimes a scene, attracting such guests as Spike Lee and Prince. The place is especially popular with jazz groups from central and southern Africa. It opens nightly at 8pm, with concerts beginning at 9pm. 7 rue des Petites-Ecuries, 10e. ✆ **01-45-23-51-41.** www.newmorning.com. Cover 17€–21€ ($22–$27). Métro: Château-d'Eau.

Slow Club ★★ One of the most famous jazz cellars in Europe, with medieval ceiling vaults that make the music reverberate in an evocative way, this venue hosts a revolving set of artists who tend to focus on New Orleans–style jazz. The hip folks who flock here are mostly in their 30s and early 40s. The club schedules live music Thursday through Saturday; on Wednesday it features recorded music, everything from swing to rock 'n' roll. Open 10pm to 3:30am. 130 rue de Rivoli, 1er. ✆ **01-42-33-84-30.** Cover 13€ ($17). Métro: Châtelet, Louvres-Rivoli.

DANCE CLUBS

The area around the Eglise St-Germain-des-Prés is full of dance clubs. They come and go so quickly that last year's disco inferno could be a hardware store by now—but new ones will spring up to take the place of the old. For the most up-to-date information, look for publications such as *Time Out, Pariscope,* or *L'Officiel des Spectacles.*

Batofar ★ Self-consciously proud of its status as a club that virtually everybody views as hip, Batofar sits on a converted barge that floats on the Seine, sometimes attracting hundreds of gyrating dancers, most of whom are in their 20s and 30s. House, garage, techno, and live jazz by groups that hail from (among other places) Morocco, Senegal, and Germany sometimes add to the mix. Come here for an insight into late-night Paris at its most raffish and countercultural, and don't even try to categorize the patrons. Beer will cost around 8.50€ ($11) a bottle. Open Tuesday to Saturday from 6pm to 3 or 4am, depending on business. Closed November to March. Facing 11 quai François Mauriac, 13e. ✆ **01-53-60-17-30.** Cover 12€–16€ ($14–$19). Métro: Quai de la Gare.

Cab ★★ If you've ever wanted to dance in a basement under the Louvre, it doesn't get much classier than this joint patronized by French models, Arab businessmen, women with a past, and children of the rich. Dim lighting illuminates black leather furniture, and there are two bars with shiny black or glass surfaces. There is also a trio of seating areas. Music is house and electro, with various hip-hop songs and other American hits mixed in. Open Wednesday and Friday to Sunday 11:30pm to 4:30am. Place du Palais royal, 1er. ✆ **01-58-62-56-25.** Cover 20€ ($26), including 1 drink. Métro: Palais Royal-Musée du Louvre.

La Java This bal-musette dance hall was once one of the most important in Paris; Piaf and Maurice Chevalier made their names here. Today, you can still waltz on what one critic called "retro fetish night," or even tango on Sunday afternoon. Brazilian and Latin themes predominate on some nights. Overall, it's one of the best places in Paris for the old-fashioned pleasure of arm-in-arm dancing. 105 rue du Faubourg du Temple, 11e. ✆ **01-42-02-20-52.** www.batofar.org. Cover 5€–22€ ($6.50–$29). Métro: Belleville, Goncourt.

La Loco Next to the Moulin Rouge, this club is popular with American students and is especially busy on Sunday. People dance to rock and techno, though occasionally metal concerts are staged. La Loco is one of the largest clubs in Paris. In the *sous-sol* (the basement, the coolest of the three levels), you can even see the remnants of an old railway line (hence the name). The Bar Americain looks more Roman with fake statuary and columns crowned by lions. Daily 11pm to 5am. 90 bd. De Clichy, 18e. ✆ **01-53-41-88-88.** Cover 5€–20€ ($6.50–$26). Métro: Blanche.

Le New Riverside This Left Bank cellar from the 18th century attracts droves of jaded clubgoers who appreciate the indestructible premises and classic rock from the 1970s. Expect patrons ages 20 to 40; women, especially when unaccompanied, are almost always admitted free. Open daily 11am to dawn. 7 rue Grégoire-de-Tours, 6e. ✆ **01-43-54-46-33.** Cover (includes 1 drink) 12€–15€ ($16–$20) for men and after midnight Fri–Sat for women. Métro: Odéon or Mabillon.

Les Bains Douches The name, "The Baths," comes from this hot spot's former function as a Turkish bath that attracted gay clients, none more notable than Marcel Proust. It may be hard to get in if the doorman doesn't think you're trendy and *très chic.* Yes, that was Jennifer Lopez we saw whirling around the floor. Dancing begins at midnight, and a supper club–like restaurant is upstairs. Meals cost 40€ to 50€ ($52–$65). On certain nights this is the hottest party atmosphere in Paris, and Mondays are increasingly gay, although sexual preference is hardly an issue at this club. Open Monday to Saturday 11pm to 6am. 7 rue du Bourg-l'Abbé, 3e. ✆ **01-48-87-01-80.** www.lesbainsdouches.net. Cover 10€–20€ ($13–$26). Métro: Etienne Marcel.

ROCK

Bus Palladium A single room with a very long bar, this rock-'n'-roll temple has varnished hardwoods and fabric-covered walls that barely absorb the reverberations of nonstop recorded music. You won't find techno, punk, jazz, blues, or soul here. It appeals to hard-core, mostly heterosexual, rock wannabes ages 25 to 35. Alcoholic drinks cost 5€ to 15€ ($6.50–$20); on Tuesdays, women drink free. It's open Tuesday to Saturday 11pm to 5am. 6 rue Fontaine, 9e. ✆ **01-53-21-07-33.** Cover 12€–20€ ($16–$26) for men and Fri–Sat for women. Métro: Blanche or Pigalle.

SALSA

Les Etoiles Since 1856, this old-fashioned music hall has shaken with the sound of performers at work and patrons at play. Its newest incarnation is as a restaurant discothèque where the music is exclusively salsa and the food Cuban. Expect simple but hearty portions of fried fish, shredded pork or beef, rice, beans, and flan, as bands from Venezuela play to a crowd that already knows or quickly learns how to dance to Latin American rhythms. 61 rue du Château d'Eau, 10e. ✆ **01-47-70-60-56.** Cover (includes meal) 20€–30€ ($26–$39); for nondiners (includes drink) 10€ ($13). Métro: Château d'Eau.

WINE BARS

Many Parisians prefer the wine bar to the traditional cafe or bistro—the food is often better and the ambience more inviting.

Au Sauvignon This tiny spot has tables overflowing onto a covered terrace and a decor that features old ceramic tiles and frescoes done by Left Bank artists. Wines range from the cheapest Beaujolais to the most expensive Puligny-Montrachet. A glass of wine costs 4.50€ to 6€ ($5.85–$7.80). To go with your wine, choose an Auvergne specialty, such as goat cheese or a terrine. Fresh Poilâne bread is ideal with ham, pâté, or goat cheese. Open daily 8am to 10pm. Closed in August. 80 rue des Sts-Pères, 7e. ✆ **01-45-48-49-02.** Métro: Sèvres-Babylone or Saint Sulpice.

After-Dark Diversions: Dives, Drag, & More

On a Paris night, the cheapest entertainment, especially if you're young, is "the show" at the tip of Ile de la Cité, behind Notre-Dame. A sort of Gallic version of the Sundowner Festival in Key West, Florida, it attracts just about everyone who ever wanted to try his or her hand at performance. The spontaneous entertainment usually includes magicians, fire-eaters, jugglers, mimes, and music makers from all over, performing against the backdrop of the illuminated cathedral. This is one of the greatest places in Paris to meet young people in a sometimes-euphoric setting.

Also popular is a stroll along the Seine after 10pm. Take a graveled pathway down to the river from the Left Bank side of pont de Sully, close to the Institut du Monde Arabe, and walk to the right, away from Notre-Dame. This walk, which ends near place Valhubert, is the best place to see spontaneous Paris in action at night. Joggers and saxophone players come here, and many Parisians arrive for impromptu dance parties.

To quench your thirst, wander onto Ile St-Louis and head for the **Café-Brasserie St-Regis,** 6 rue Jean-du-Bellay, 4e, across from pont St-Louis (© **01-43-54-59-41;** Métro: Pont Marie). If you want to linger, you can order a *plat du jour* or a coffee at the bar. But try doing as the Parisians do: Get a 3€ ($3.90) beer to go *(une bière à emporter)* and take it with you on a stroll around the island. The cafe is open daily until midnight.

Les Bacchantes This place prides itself on offering more wines by the glass—at least 90—than any other wine bar in Paris; prices range from 2€ to 6€ ($2.60–$7.80). It also does a hefty restaurant trade in well-prepared *cuisine bourgeoise.* Its cozy, rustic setting—with paneling and chalkboards announcing vintages and platters—attracts theatergoers before and after performances at the Théâtre Olympia, as well as anyone interested in carefully chosen vintages from esoteric or small-scale winemakers. Wines are mainly from France, but you'll also find examples from neighboring countries. 21 rue Caumartin, 9e. © **01-42-65-25-35.** Métro: Havre-Caumartin.

Willi's Wine Bar ★★ Journalists and stockbrokers head for this popular wine bar in the financial district. It offers about 300 kinds of wine, including a dozen specials you can taste by the glass for 3€ to 18€ ($3.90–$23). Lunch is the busiest time; on quiet evenings, you can better enjoy the warm ambience. Daily specials are likely to include lamb brochette with cumin or Lyonnais sausage in truffled vinaigrette, plus a spectacular dessert such as chocolate terrine. A fixed-price menu costs 19€ to 25€ ($25–$33) at lunch, 34€ ($44) at dinner. The restaurant is open Monday to Saturday noon to 2:30pm and 7 to 11pm; the bar, Monday to Saturday noon to midnight. 13 rue des Petits-Champs, 1er. © **01-42-61-05-09.** www.williswinebar.com. Métro: Bourse, Pyramides, or Palais-Royal.

BARS & PUBS

Bar du Crillon ★★ Though some visitors consider the Bar du Crillon too self-consciously elegant, its social and literary history is remarkable. Hemingway set a climactic

If you're caught waiting for the Métro to start running again at 5am, try the **Sous-Bock Tavern,** 49 rue St-Honoré, 1er (✆ **01-40-26-46-61;** Métro: Les Halles or Louvres-Rivoli), open daily from 11am to 5am. Young drinkers gather here to sample from 250 varieties of beer or 20 varieties of whiskey. The dish to order is a platter of mussels—curried, with white wine, or with cream sauce; they go well with the brasserie-style fries.

If drag shows aren't your cup of tea, how about *Last Tango in Paris*? At **Le Tango,** 11 rue au Maire, 3e (✆ **01-42-72-17-78;** Métro: Arts et Métiers), memories of Evita and Argentina live on. On-site is a ballroom called *La Boîte à Frissons.* The evening starts at 10:30pm, with couples dancing until 12:30am, featuring the waltz, the tango, *pasadoble,* the polka, rock 'n' roll, and cha-cha. After that, the dance floor turns into a disco. The cover is 7€ ($9.10). It's open Friday and Saturday from midnight to 5am.

If you're looking for a sophisticated, laid-back venue, consider the **Sanz-Sans,** 49 rue du Faubourg St-Antoine, 4e (✆ **01-44-75-78-78;** Métro: Bastille or Ledru Rollin), a multi-ethnic playground where the children of prominent Parisians mingle, testifying to the unifying power of jazz. In this red-velvet duplex, the most important conversations seem to occur over margaritas on the stairway or the back-room couches. The later it gets, the sexier the scene becomes.

scene of *The Sun Also Rises* here, and over the years it has attracted diplomats from the U.S. Embassy as well as visiting heiresses, stars, starlets, and wannabes. Sonia Rykiel decorated the bar. Another option down the hall is the Edwardian-style **Jardin d'Hiver,** where you can order tea, cocktails, or coffee. In the Hôtel de Crillon, 10 place de la Concorde, 8e. ✆ **01-44-71-15-39.** Métro: Concorde.

Bar Hemingway/Bar Vendôme In 1944, during the liberation of Paris, Ernest Hemingway made history by ordering a drink at the Ritz Bar while gunfire from retreating Nazi soldiers was still audible in the streets. Today the Ritz commemorates the event with bookish memorabilia, rows of newspapers, and stiff drinks. Look for the bar's entrance, and homages to other writers such as Proust, near the hotel's rue Cambon entrance. If you develop a thirst in the daytime, when the Bar Hemingway isn't open, head for the Bar Vendôme, near the hotel's place Vendôme entrance. The setting is just as cozy and woodsy, albeit a bit more grand. In the Hôtel Ritz, 15 place Vendôme, 1er. ✆ **01-43-16-33-65.** Métro: Opéra or Concorde.

Barrio Latino This multilevel emporium of good times, Gallic flair, and Latin charm occupies a space designed by Gustav Eiffel in the 19th century. Tapas bars and dance floors are on the street level *(rez-de-chaussée)* and third floor *(3eme étage);* a Latin restaurant is on the second floor *(2eme étage).* Staff members roll carts loaded with tapas around the floors, selling them like hot dogs at an American baseball game. The restaurant specializes in food that French palates find refreshing: Argentine steaks, Brazilian *feijoada* (a bean-based dish that's similar to cassoulet), and Mexican chili, all of which taste wonderful with beer, caipirinhas, *Cuba libres* (rum and coke), or rum punches. The clientele is mixed, mostly straight, partly gay. 46 rue du Faubourg St-Antoine, 12e. ✆ **01-55-78-84-75.** Cover 20€ ($26) for nondiners Thurs–Sat after 9pm. Métro: Bastille.

Buddha Bar The food is mediocre, but that doesn't seem to matter to the *fashionistas* who frequent this place. A giant Buddha presides over the vast dining room, where a combination of Japanese sashimi, Vietnamese spring rolls, Chinese lacquered duck, and various Asian fusion dishes are served. Many patrons come here to drink at the lacquered bar, found upstairs from the street-level dining room. From the upper perch you can observe the action of the swanky international patrons below. The music is spacey, the atmosphere electric, and some of the prettiest women and handsomest hunks in Paris are in attendance nightly. The location is near the Champs Elysées and place de la Concorde. 8 rue Boissy d'Anglais, 8e. ✆ **01-53-05-90-00.** Daily 4pm–2am. Métro: Concorde.

Harry's New York Bar ★ At *sank roo doe noo,* as the ads tell you to instruct your cabdriver, is the most famous bar in Europe—possibly in the world. Opened on Thanksgiving Day 1911 by an expatriate named MacElhone, it's where members of the World War I ambulance corps drank themselves silly. In addition to being Hemingway's favorite, Harry's is where the white lady and sidecar cocktails were invented; it's also the reputed birthplace of the bloody mary and the headquarters of a loosely organized fraternity of drinkers known as the International Bar Flies.

The historic core is the street-level bar, where CEOs and office workers loosen their ties on more or less equal footing. Daytime crowds are from the neighborhood's insurance, banking, and travel industries; evening crowds include pre- and post-theater groupies and night owls who aren't bothered by the gritty setting and unflattering lighting. A softer, somewhat less macho ambience reigns in the cellar, where a pianist provides music Tuesday to Saturday from 10pm to 2am. 5 rue Daunou, 2e. ✆ **01-42-61-71-14.** Métro: Opéra.

Le Bar de L'Hôtel A Left Bank hotel is home to the city's most romantic bar. Oscar Wilde checked out long ago, but the odd celebrity still shows up: We were once 15 minutes into a conversation before realizing we were speaking to Jeanne Moreau. Drinks are expertly mixed, the place sleek and chic, and conversations are held at a discreet murmur. It would be hard to find a better place for a romantic rendezvous. In L'Hôtel, 13 rue des Beaux-Arts, 6e. ✆ **01-44-41-99-00.** Métro: St-Germain-des-Prés.

Man Ray This chic rendezvous off the Champs-Elysées is dedicated to the photographer and American dadaist Man Ray, who felt more comfortable roaming Montparnasse than the 8th. Many of his photos decorate the club. This spot is a media favorite, because its owners include Johnny Depp, Sean Penn, and John Malkovich. The discreet entry is through wrought-iron doors with virtually no sign. In the basement is a restaurant presided over by two winged Indonesian goddesses. The bar upstairs is big and bustling, and the club often schedules jazz. 32 rue Marbeuf, 8e. ✆ **01-56-88-36-36.** www.manray.fr. Métro: Franklin-D-Roosevelt.

Mojito Habana Amid a decor that evokes colonial Havana under Batista, with lots of green upholsteries, wood panels, and deep sofas, you'll find a three-tiered place with a restaurant (it charges around 50€/$65 for a full meal); a piano bar (music begins at 11pm every night the place is open, and at 10pm on Tues); and a cigar lounge. Jazz concerts are featured Tuesday night. Cocktails, including *Cuba libres,* cost 13€ ($17) each. Entrance is always free. And the music that's in the background is international rock and pop, not solely salsa and merengue. It's open Monday to Saturday from noon to 5am, and it attracts a lot of nattily dressed business travelers. 19 rue de Presbourg, 16e. ✆ **01-45-00-84-84.** Métro: Etoile.

Rosebud The popularity of this place known for a bemused and indulgent attitude toward anyone looking for a drink and some talk hasn't diminished since the 1950s. The name refers to the beloved sled of Orson Welles's *Citizen Kane.* Around the corner from Montparnasse's famous cafes and thick in associations with Sartre and de Beauvoir, Ionesco, and Duras, Rosebud draws a crowd ages 35 to 65, though the staff has recently noticed the appearance of students. Drop in at night for a glass of wine, a shot of whiskey, or a hamburger or chili con carne. 11 bis rue Delambre, 14e. ✆ **01-43-35-38-54** or 01-43-20-44-13. Métro: Vavin.

GAY & LESBIAN CLUBS

Gay life centers on Les Halles and Le Marais, with the greatest concentration of gay and lesbian clubs, restaurants, bars, and shops between the Hôtel-de-Ville and Rambuteau Métro stops. Gay dance clubs come and go so fast that even the magazines devoted somewhat to their pursuit—***3 Keller*** and ***Exit,*** distributed free in gay bars and bookstores—have a hard time keeping up. ***Lesbia*** is a monthly national lesbian magazine.

Amnesia Café The Amnesia's function and crowd may change during the day, but you'll always find a cadre of local gays. This cafe/tearoom/bistro/bar includes two bar areas, a mezzanine, and a cellar bar, Amni-Club, open in the evening. The drinks of choice are beer, cocktails, and *café amnesia,* a specialty coffee with whiskey and Chantilly cream. Deep armchairs, soft pillows, and 1930s accents create an ambience conducive to conversation. Open daily 11am to 2am, Friday and Saturday until 3am. 42 rue Vieille-du-Temple, 4e. ✆ **01-42-72-16-94.** Métro: Hôtel de Ville or St. Paul.

La Champmeslé With dim lighting, background music, and comfortable banquettes, La Champmeslé offers a cozy meeting place for women and a few (about 5%) "well-behaved" men. Paris's leading women's bar is in a 300-year-old building with exposed stone, ceiling beams, and 1950s-style furnishings. Thursday night, one of the premier lesbian events in Paris, a cabaret, begins at 10pm. 4 rue Chabanais, 2e. ✆ **01-42-96-85-20.** Métro: Pyramides or Bourse.

7

Side Trips from Paris: Versailles, Chartres & the Best of the Ile de France

Château de Versailles, the Cathédrale Notre-Dame de Chartres, and the Palais de Fontainebleau draw countless tour buses to this region. They're the stars of the Ile de France. Some lesser-known but equally stunning spots also await you. You can find everything from Romanesque ruins, Gothic cathedrals, and feudal castles to 18th-century châteaux, forests such as Fontainebleau and Chantilly, sleepy villages, and an African game reserve. For kids of all ages, there's Disneyland Paris. Finally, this region is a haven for artists, so you can visit the painted worlds of Corot, Renoir, Degas, Monet, and Cézanne.

You can experience everything we describe here on a day trip or an overnight from Paris. For even more day trips, check out *Frommer's Paris 2008.*

1 Versailles ★

21km (13 miles) SW of Paris, 71km (44 miles) NE of Chartres

Back in the *grand siècle,* all you needed was a sword, a hat, and a bribe for the guard at the gate. Provided you didn't look as if you had smallpox, you'd be admitted to the Château de Versailles, where you could stroll through salon after glittering salon and watch the Sun King, gossiping, dancing, plotting, and flirting. Louis XIV was accorded about as much privacy as an institution.

Today, Versailles would welcome the return of Louis XIV and his fat treasury. You wouldn't believe it to look at the glittering Hall of Mirrors, but Versailles is down-at-the-heels. You get to see only half its treasures; the rest—including the Musée de France, with its 6,000 paintings and 2,000 statues—are closed to the public. Some 3.2 million visitors arrive annually, spending about 2 hours here.

ESSENTIALS

GETTING THERE To get to Versailles, catch the **RER** line C5 to Versailles-Rive Gauche at the Gare d'Austerlitz, St-Michel, Musée d'Orsay, Invalides, Ponte de l'Alma, Champ de Mars, or Javel stop, and take it to the Versailles/Rive Gauche station. The trip takes 35 to 40 minutes. The round-trip fare is 5.50€ ($7.15); Eurailpass holders travel free on the RER but need to show the pass at the ticket kiosk to receive a RER ticket. **SNCF trains** make frequent runs from Gare St-Lazare and Gare Montparnasse in Paris to Versailles. Trains departing from Gare St-Lazare arrive at the Versailles/Rive Droite railway station; trains departing from Gare Montparnasse arrive at Versailles/Chantiers station.

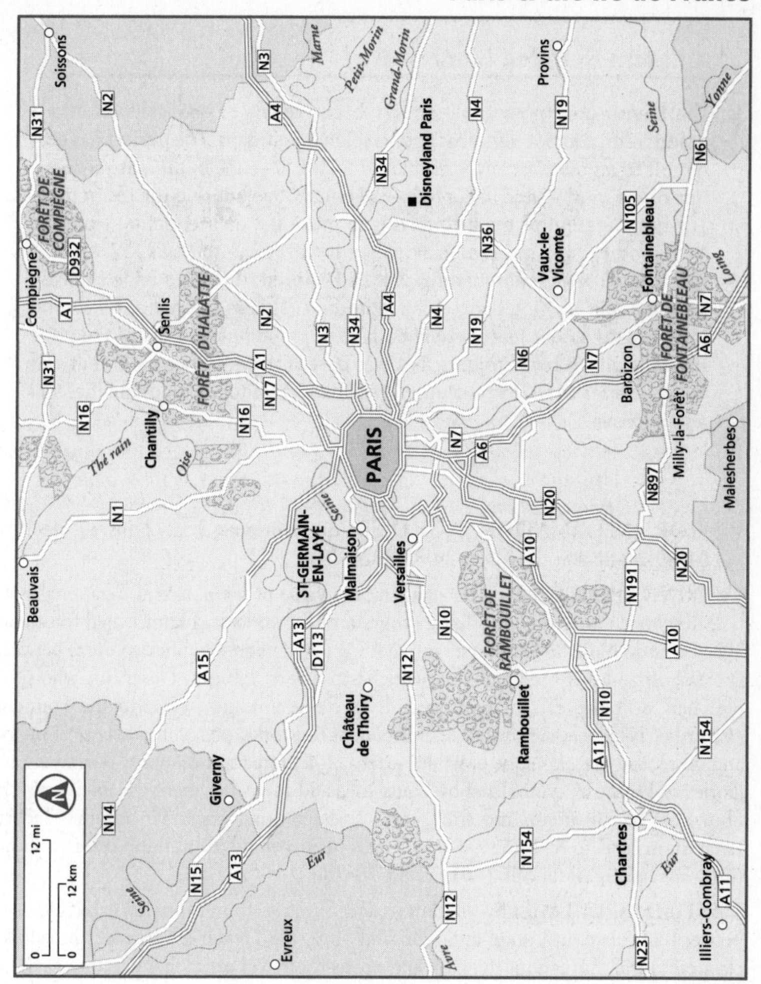

Both Versailles stations are within a 10-minute walk of the château, and we recommend the walk as a means of orienting yourself to the town, its geography, its scale, and its architecture. If you can't or don't want to walk, you can take bus B, or (in midsummer) a shuttle bus marked CHATEAU from either station to the château for either a cash payment of around 2€ ($2.60; drop the coins directly into the coin box near the driver) or the insertion of a valid ticket for the Paris Métro. Because of the vagaries of the bus schedules, we highly recommend the walk. Directions to the château are clearly signposted from each railway station.

If you're **driving,** exit the *périphérique* (the ring road around Paris) on N10 (av. du Général-Leclerc), which will take you to Versailles; park on place d'Armes in front of the château.

A Return to Faded Glory

The French government will pour the equivalent of $455 million into a grand restoration of Versailles and its splendid gardens. The project has gotten off to a slow start and is estimated to last 17 years, but the attraction—one of the most visited in Europe—will remain open during the restoration. The grand design of the architects is to make the palace, dating from the 17th century, look much as it did when it was home to Louis XIV, XV, and the ill-fated XVI. Some features will be removed, such as a wide staircase ordered built by King Louis-Philippe in the château's last major rebuilding in the 1830s. Other features will be added, including a replica of the *grille royale* (a gilded royal insignia that was part of the entrance gate) that was torn out after the 1789 revolution. Facilities for visitors with disabilities will also improve.

VISITOR INFORMATION The **Office de Tourisme** is at 2 bis av. de Paris (✆ **01-39-24-88-88;** fax 01-39-24-88-89).

EVENING SPECTACLES Recognizing the value of the palace as a national symbol, the French government offers a program of fireworks and illuminated fountains, "Les Fêtes de Nuit de Versailles," on about 7 to 10 widely publicized dates between late August and early September, usually beginning at 9:30pm. Observers, who sit in bleachers near the palace's boulevard de la Reine entrance, close to the Fountain *(Bassin)* of Neptune, are treated to a display of fireworks, prerecorded classical music, and up to 200 players (none of whom utters a line) in period costume, portraying the glories of France as symbolized by Louis XIV and the courtiers of the *ancien régime.* Shows are big on pomp and strong on visuals, and last about 90 minutes. Tickets range from 30€ to 85€ ($39–$111). Gates open around 90 minutes prior to showtime. For information, call ✆ **01-30-83-78-98.**

DAYTIME SPECTACLES Saturdays and Sundays from April to early October, between 11:30am and noon and 3:30 and 5pm, the French government broadcasts classical music throughout the park and opens the valves on as many fountains as are currently in operation as part of a program known as *Les Grands Eaux Musicals de Versailles.* The spectacles showcase the landscaping vision of the palace's designers and encourage participants to walk, promenade, or meander the vast park, enjoying the juxtaposition of supremely grand architecture with lavish waterworks. Afternoon events include water coming out of more jets than during the somewhat less lavish morning events. Admission to any part of the park during these spectacles costs 7€ ($9.10) adults or 5.50€ ($7.15) ages 10 to 18, free for children under 10. For information, call ✆ **01-30-83-78-88.**

You can purchase tickets to all spectacles at Versailles up until about a half-hour prior to the day or night of any performance from the ticket office in the *Accueil-Billeterie* on Place d'Armes, immediately across from the main facade of the palace, or from any French branch of the FNAC department store (FNAC's central phone number is ✆ **01-55-21-57-93**).

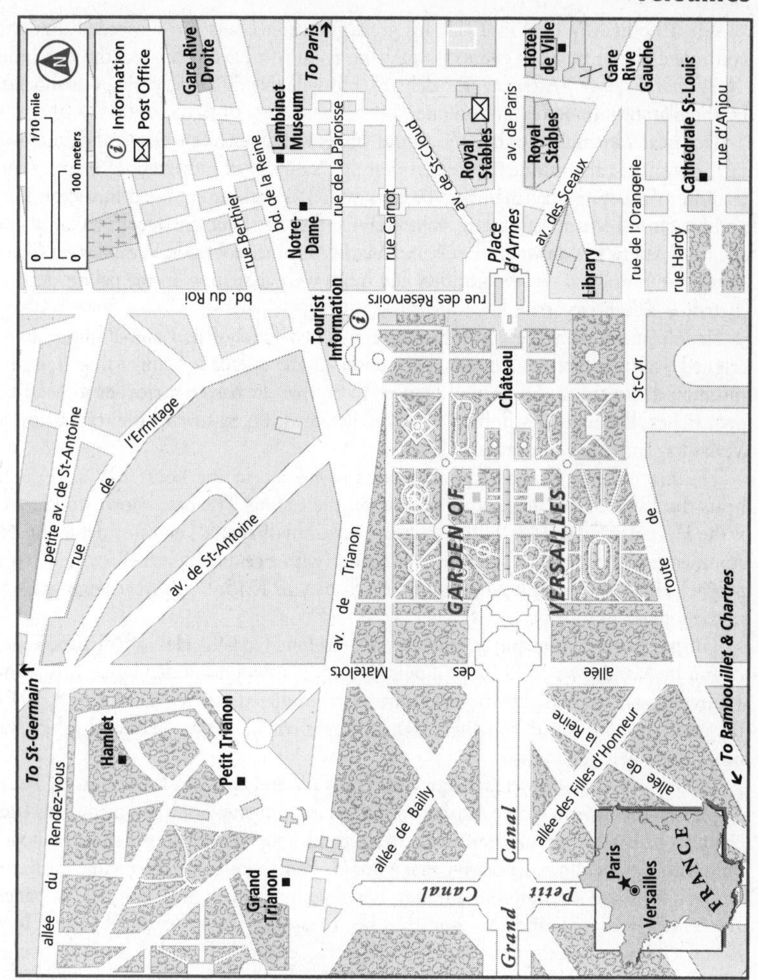

EXPLORING THE CHATEAU & GARDENS

Château de Versailles ★★★ Within 50 years, the Château de Versailles was transformed from Louis XIII's hunting lodge into an extravagant palace. Begun in 1661, its construction involved 32,000 to 45,000 workmen, some of whom had to drain marshes and move forests. Louis XIV set out to build a palace that would be the envy of Europe and created a symbol of opulence copied, yet never duplicated, the world over.

Wishing (with good reason) to keep an eye on the nobles of France, Louis XIV summoned them to live at his court. Here he amused them with constant entertainment and lavish banquets. To some he awarded such tasks as holding the hem of his robe. While the aristocrats played at often-silly intrigues and games, the peasants on the estates sowed the seeds of the Revolution.

When Louis XIV died in 1715, his great-grandson Louis XV succeeded him and continued the outrageous pomp, though he is said to have predicted the outcome: *"Après moi le déluge"* (After me, the deluge). His wife, Marie Leszczynska, was shocked by the blatant immorality at Versailles.

The next monarch, Louis XVI, found his grandfather's behavior scandalous—in fact, on gaining the throne he ordered that the "stairway of indiscretion" (secret stairs leading to the king's bedchamber) be removed. The well-intentioned but weak king and his queen, Marie Antoinette, were well liked at first, but the queen's frivolity and spending led to her downfall. Louis and Marie Antoinette were at Versailles on October 6, 1789, when they were notified that mobs were marching on the palace. As predicted, *le déluge* had arrived.

Napoleon stayed at Versailles but never seemed fond of it. Louis-Philippe (who reigned 1830–48) prevented the destruction of the palace by converting it into a museum dedicated to the glory of France. To do that, he had to surrender some of his own riches. Decades later, John D. Rockefeller contributed toward the restoration of Versailles, and work continues today.

The magnificent **Grands Appartements** ★★★ are in the Louis XIV style; each bears the name of the allegorical painting on the ceiling. The best known and largest is the **Hercules Salon** ★★, with a ceiling painted by François Lemoine, depicting the Apotheosis of Hercules. In the **Mercury Salon** (with a ceiling by Jean-Baptiste Champaigne), the body of Louis XIV was put on display in 1715; his 72-year reign was one of the longest in history.

The most famous room at Versailles is the 71m-long (233-ft.) **Hall of Mirrors** ★★★. Begun by Mansart in 1678 in the Louis XIV style, it was decorated by Le Brun with 17 arched windows faced by beveled mirrors in simulated arcades. On June 28, 1919, the treaty ending World War I was signed in this corridor. The German Empire was proclaimed here in 1871.

The royal apartments were for show, but Louis XV and Louis XVI retired to the **Petits Appartements** ★★ to escape the demands of court etiquette. Louis XV died in his bedchamber in 1774, a victim of smallpox. In a second-floor apartment, which you can visit only with a guide, he stashed away first Mme de Pompadour, and then Mme du Barry.

Louis XVI had a sumptuous **Library,** designed by Jacques-Ange Gabriel. Its panels are delicately carved, and the room has been restored and refurnished. The **Clock Room** contains Passement's astronomical clock, encased in gilded bronze. Twenty years in the making, it was completed in 1753. The clock is supposed to keep time until the year 9999. At age 7, Mozart played for the court in this room.

Gabriel designed the **Opéra** ★★ for Louis XV in 1748, though it wasn't completed until 1770. In its heyday, it took 3,000 candles to light the place. Hardouin-Mansart built the harmoniously gold-and-white **Royal Chapel** in 1699, dying before its completion. Louis XVI married Marie Antoinette here in 1770, while he was the dauphin.

In 2005, a previously off-limits section of the vast palace was opened to the public for the first time by an act of the Parliament. The decision adds some 270,000 sq. ft. of the south wing to public access. Up to now, the area had been reserved for use by Parliament itself. Among the rooms opened up is the mammoth **Battle Gallery,** which at 119m (390 ft.) is the longest hall at Versailles. The gallery displays monumental paintings depicting all of France's great battles ranging from the founding of the monarchy by Clovis, who reigned in the 5th and 6th centuries, through the Napoleonic wars in the early 19th century.

Spread across 100 hectares (247 acres), the **Gardens of Versailles** ★★★ were laid out by landscape artist André Le Nôtre. At the peak of their glory, 1,400 fountains spewed forth. *The Buffet* is an exceptional fountain, designed by Mansart. One fountain depicts Apollo in his chariot pulled by four horses, surrounded by Tritons rising from the water. Le Nôtre created a Garden of Eden using ornamental lakes and canals, geometrically designed flower beds, and avenues bordered with statuary. On the mile-long **Grand Canal,** Louis XV used to take gondola rides with his favorite of the moment.

A walk across the park takes you to the pink-and-white-marble **Grand Trianon** ★★, designed by Hardouin-Mansart for Louis XIV in 1687. Traditionally it has been lodging for VIPs, though de Gaulle wanted to turn it into a weekend retreat. Nixon slept here in the room where Mme de Pompadour died. The original furnishings are gone, replaced today by mostly Empire pieces.

Gabriel, the designer of place de la Concorde in Paris, built the **Petit Trianon** ★★ in 1768 for Louis XV. Louis used it for his trysts with Mme du Barry. In time, Marie Antoinette adopted it as her favorite residence, a place to escape the rigid life at the main palace. Many of the current furnishings, including a few in her rather modest bedchamber, belonged to the ill-fated queen.

Late 2004 witnessed the opening of *Les Grandes Ecuries* (the Stables), immediately opposite the château's main front facade, where horses and carriages of the kings were housed. Visitors can watch a team of up to a dozen students, with their mounts, strut their stuff during hour-long riding demonstrations within the covered 17th-century amphitheater of the historic stables. However, don't go with any expectations that the horsemanship will re-create exclusively 17th- and 18th-century styles. The focus is on showmanship and equestrian razzmatazz rather than exact period replication. Hour-long demonstrations are conducted Thursday to Sunday at 10am and 11am, when entrance costs 8€ ($9.60). An additional presentation every Saturday and Sunday at 2:30pm costs 16€ ($19). Admission to this event provides the only official way a visitor to Versailles can easily gain entrance to the stables.

✆ **01-30-83-78-00.** www.chateauversailles.fr. Palace 14€ ($18) adults; 10€ ($13) adults after 4pm, seniors over 59, and ages 18–25. Both Trianons 16€ ($21) adults; 10€ ($13) adults after 3:30pm, seniors over 59, and ages 18–25. Everything free for children under 18. Palace Apr–Oct Tues–Sun 9am–6:30pm; Nov–Mar Tues–Sun 9am–5:30pm. Trianons Tues–Sun noon–6pm. Grounds daily dawn–dusk.

Musée Lambinet ★ *Finds* Often overlooked by visitors to Versailles, the Musée Lambinet is filled with treasures seized from the French court during the Revolution. Here are all the antiques, the carved wood paneling, even religious art and other objets d'art so beloved by Marie Antoinette and the mistresses of Louis XV. The sumptuous mansion from 1751 is also filled with paintings (no great masterpieces, however), weaponry, and rare porcelain (look for the Du Barry rose). Also on view are rare displays illustrating the lives of Jean-Paul Marat, the radical journalist, and his murderer, Charlotte Corday, as depicted in stage plays and films.

54 bd. De la Reine. ✆ **01-39-50-30-32.** Admission 5.30€ ($6.90). Tues–Sun 2–5:45pm.

SHOPPING

Founded by the Sun King himself, Louis XIV, **Marché Notre-Dame,** place du Marché Notre-Dame (✆ **01-30-97-84-89**), is the major public market in Versailles, housed in a series of red-brick buildings. The present look dates from the 19th century. Indoor shops selling local cheeses and fresh fruits are open daily, but the outdoor stalls in the center of the square flourish only on Tuesday, Friday, and Sunday, from about

7am to 2pm. It's best to go before noon; some of the stalls start shutting down in the early afternoon.

Close to the mammoth market, **Passage de la Geôle** (© **01-30-21-15-13**) is open Friday to Sunday from 10am to 7pm, housing antiques shops selling furniture and objets d'art at "all prices."

WHERE TO STAY

VERY EXPENSIVE

Trianon Palace & Spa ★★★ This luxe hotel is the grandest in the Ile de France. A Westin property, it was built in 1910 on land that had sheltered a Capucine monastery during the *ancien régime.* The setting is lovely—the 2-hectare (5-acre) garden borders the gardens of the Petit Trianon at Versailles. In 1919, it was the headquarters of the peace conference of Woodrow Wilson, Lloyd George, Georges Clemenceau, and other world leaders. Since then, guests have included John D. Rockefeller, Queen Elizabeth II, and Marlene Dietrich, who made headlines by wearing pants in the dining room. The hotel is in a classically designed palace, last restored in the early 1990s and connected to a late-20th-century annex (Le Pavillon) by an underground tunnel. Accommodations in both buildings are decorated in traditional style with reference to château living, using rich fabrics and a mixture of antiques and reproductions. Amenities and electronic accessories are top-of-the-line. Each luxurious bathroom holds a tub/shower combination. The hotel has joined with Phytomer, a top name in French beauty care, to create an outstanding spa.

1 bd. de la Reine, Versailles 78000. © **800/228-3000** in the U.S. and Canada, or 01-30-84-50-00. Fax 01-30-84-50-01. www.westin.com. 192 units. 460€–510€ ($598–$663) double; 650€–1,140€ ($845–$1,482) suite. AE, DC, DISC, MC, V. Free parking. **Amenities:** 2 restaurants; cafe; bar; indoor pool; tennis courts; health club; spa; sauna; business services; room service; babysitting; laundry service; dry cleaning; nonsmoking rooms; limited-mobility rooms. *In room:* A/C, TV, minibar, hair dryer, iron, safe.

MODERATE

Novotel Château de Versailles A 15-minute walk north of one of the side wings of the château, this chain hotel, built in 1988, has a modern facade with columns and large windows. It's not too expensive and is a convenient choice for visitors to Versailles. The renovated bedrooms come in two different styles—the classically French Harmonie or the far more contemporary Novation. Each has a well-kept private bathroom with tub or shower.

4 bd. St-Antoine, Le Chesnay 78150. © **01-39-54-96-96.** Fax 01-39-54-94-40. www.accor-hotels.com. 105 units. 99€ ($129) double; 155€ ($202) suite. Children under 12 stay free in parent's room. AE, DC, MC, V. Parking 10€ ($13). **Amenities:** Restaurant; bar; business services; room service; laundry service; dry cleaning; nonsmoking rooms; limited-mobility rooms. *In room:* A/C, TV, beverage maker, minibar, hair dryer, safe.

WHERE TO DINE

La Flottille (© **01-39-51-41-58**) is the only restaurant inside the park (at the head of the Grand Canal), with a sweeping view over some of Europe's most famous landscaping. Both restaurant and snack-bar service is available. In warm weather, the traditional French cuisine is also served at outside tables. Reservations recommended.

VERY EXPENSIVE

Les Trois Marches ★★★ MODERN FRENCH The food here is of the highest order—and so are the prices. Chef Gérard Vié, known for the inventiveness of his *cuisine bourgeoise,* serves the finest food in Versailles. His greenhouse-inspired dining room is remarkable for its expanses of glass and its intimate size (55 seats). In summer, you can dine under the canopy on the front terrace. Begin with lobster salad flavored with fresh herbs and served with an onion soufflé; foie gras of duckling; galette of potatoes with bacon, chardonnay, and Sevruga caviar; or citrus-flavored scallop bisque. The chef is a great innovator, especially when it comes to main courses: pigeon roasted and flavored with rosé and accompanied by celeriac and truffles; North Atlantic lobster served with carrot juice and creamy lobster bisque; filets of John Dory served with braised eggplant, squid, and squid ink; or filet of sea bass with a "cake" of eggplant. Some patrons find the staff a bit too stiff and patronizing.

In the Hôtel Trianon Palace, 1 bd. de la Reine. ✆ **01-39-50-13-21.** Reservations required. Main courses 75€–100€ ($98–$130); fixed-price lunch 58€ ($75) Tues–Fri only; fixed-price dinner 160€–180€ ($208–$234). AE, DC, MC, V. Tues–Sat 1–2pm and 7:30–9:30pm. Closed Aug.

MODERATE

Le Potager du Roy ★ MODERN FRENCH Philippe Letourneur spent years perfecting a distinctive cuisine that now adds novelty to the dining scene in Versailles. Letourneur rotates his skillfully prepared menu with the seasons. Examples are foie gras with vegetable-flavored vinaigrette, cream of lentil soup with scallops, roasted duck with *navarin* of vegetables, and roasted codfish with roasted peppers in the style of Provence. Looking for something unusual and earthier? Try fondant of pork jowls with comfit of fresh vegetables.

1 rue du Maréchal-Joffre. ✆ **01-39-50-35-34.** Reservations required. Main courses 26€–33€ ($34–$43); fixed-price menu 40€ ($52). AE, MC, V. Tues–Sat noon–1:30pm and 7:30–9:30pm.

INEXPENSIVE

Le Restaurant du Roi ★ Value PROVENÇAL SEAFOOD/FRENCH This informal seafood bistro is in an 18th-century building overlooking the western facade of Versailles. Though the cuisine isn't opulent, it's charming and very French. Specialties include stuffed baby mullet with sweet basil sauce, a gratin of scallops and shrimps in fish broth, filet of sea wolf grilled with caramelized onions, and sautéed scallops with vinegar crafted from aged banyuls dessert wine. Carnivores appreciate the main courses, the best of which is magret of duckling dressed with aged vinegar. Care and imagination go into the cuisine, and the service is professional and polite.

1 av. de St-Cloud. ✆ **01-39-50-42-26.** Reservations required. Main courses 15€–16€ ($20–$21); fixed-price menu 16€–27€ ($21–$35) lunch, 20€–27€ ($26–$35) dinner. AE, MC, V. Tues–Sun noon–2pm; Tues–Sat 7–11pm.

VERSAILLES AFTER DARK

O'Paris Pub, 15 rue Colbert, off place d'Armes (✆ **01-39-50-36-12**), is an Irish pub where you can order the best brews in town. A bit more upmarket, **Bar à Vins-Restaurant Le Ducis,** 13 rue Ducis (✆ **01-39-49-96-51**), offers a mellow atmosphere on a summer evening, with tables spilling onto a side street. A bottle of wine and a good companion should get you through an evening, enhanced perhaps by a plate of food selected from the chalkboard menu.

2 The Glorious Cathedral of Chartres ★★★

98km (61 miles) SW of Paris, 76km (47 miles) NW of Orléans

Many observers feel that medieval architecture reached its pinnacle in the world-renowned cathedral at Chartres. Come to see its architecture, its sculpture, and—most of all—its stained glass, which gave the world a new color, Chartres blue.

The ancient town of Chartres also played a role in World War II. Jean Moulin, a Resistance hero and friend of de Gaulle, refused to sign a document under torture stating that French troops committed atrocities. The Gestapo killed him in 1943 (he's buried in the Panthéon in Paris). To view the town's monument to Moulin, head down rue du Cheval-Blanc from the cathedral until it becomes rue Jean-Moulin (the monument is ahead on your right). Other street names, including boulevard de la Résistance, commemorate the World War II resistance movement. Allow 1 hour for the cathedral, 1½ hours for the town.

ESSENTIALS

GETTING THERE From Paris's Gare Montparnasse, **trains** run directly to Chartres, taking less than an hour. Tickets cost 25€ ($33) round-trip. Call ✆ **08-92-35-35-35.** If **driving,** take A10/A11 southwest from the *périphérique,* and follow signs to Le Mans and Chartres. (The Chartres exit is clearly marked.)

VISITOR INFORMATION The **Office de Tourisme** is on place de la Cathédrale (✆ **02-37-18-26-26;** fax 02-37-21-51-91).

SEEING THE CATHEDRAL

Cathédrale Notre-Dame de Chartres ★★★ Rodin reputedly once sat for hours on the sidewalk, admiring the cathedral's Romanesque sculpture. His opinion: Chartres is the French Acropolis. When it began to rain, a kind soul offered him an umbrella—which he declined, so transfixed was he.

The cathedral's origins are uncertain; some suggest it grew up over a Druid site that later became a Roman temple. As early as the 4th century, a Christian basilica was here. A fire in 1194 destroyed most of what had then become a Romanesque cathedral, sparing the western facade and crypt. The cathedral today dates principally from the 13th century, when it was rebuilt with the efforts of kings, princes, churchmen, and pilgrims from all over Europe. One of the world's greatest High Gothic cathedrals, it was the first to use flying buttresses.

French sculpture in the 12th century broke into full bloom when the **Royal Portal ★★★** was added. The portal is a landmark in Romanesque art. The sculptured bodies are elongated, often formalized beyond reality, in long, flowing robes. But the faces are amazingly (for the time) lifelike, occasionally betraying Mona Lisa smiles. In the central tympanum, Christ is shown at the Second Coming, with his descent depicted on the right, his ascent on the left. Before you enter, admire the Royal Portal and walk around to both the North Portal and the South Portal; both date from the 13th century. They depict such scenes as the expulsion of Adam and Eve from the Garden of Eden.

Inside is a celebrated choir screen (parclose); work on it began in the 16th century and lasted until 1714. The niches, 40 in all, contain statues illustrating scenes from the life of the Madonna and Christ—everything from the Massacre of the Innocents to the Coronation of the Virgin.

But few rushed visitors ever notice the screen; they're too transfixed by the light from the **stained glass ★★★**. Covering an expanse of more than 2,500 sq. m (27,000 sq. ft.), the peerless glass is truly mystical. It was spared in both world wars because of a decision to remove it piece by piece. Most of it dates from the 12th and 13th centuries. It's difficult to single out one panel or window—depending on the position of the sun, the images change constantly; however, an exceptional one is the 12th-century *Vierge de la Belle Verrière* (Virgin of the Beautiful Window) on the south side. Of

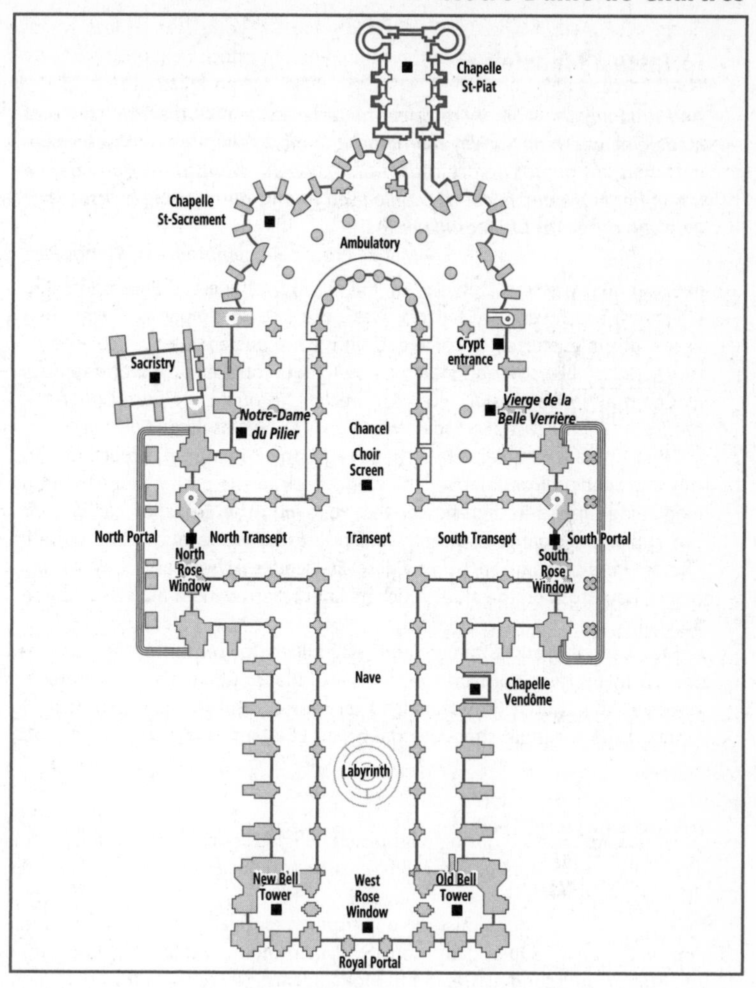

course, there are three fiery rose windows, but you couldn't miss those even if you tried.

The nave—the widest in France—still contains its ancient labyrinth. The wooden *Notre-Dame du Pilier* (Our Lady of the Pillar), to the left of the choir, dates from the 14th century. The crypt was built over 2 centuries, beginning in the 9th. Enshrined within is *Notre-Dame de Sous Terre* (Our Lady of the Crypt), a 1976 Madonna that replaced one destroyed during the Revolution.

Try to take a tour conducted by Malcolm Miller (© **02-37-28-15-58;** fax 02-37-28-33-03; millercharters@aol.com), an Englishman who has spent 3 decades studying the cathedral and giving tours in English. His rare blend of scholarship, enthusiasm, and humor will help you understand and appreciate the cathedral. He usually conducts 75-minute tours at noon and 2:45pm Monday to Saturday for 10€ ($13) per

To Taste a Madeleine

And suddenly the memory returns. The taste was that of the little crumb of madeleine which on Sunday mornings at Combray (because on those mornings I did not go out before church-time), when I went to say good day to her in her bedroom, my aunt Léonie used to give me, dipping it first in her own cup of real or of lime-flower tea.

—Marcel Proust, *Remembrance of Things Past*

Illiers-Combray, a small town 87km (54 miles) southwest of Paris and 24km (15 miles) southwest of Chartres, was once known simply as Illiers. Then Proust groupies started to come and signs were posted: ILLIERS, LE COMBRAY DE MARCEL PROUST. Illiers was and is a real town, but Proust made it world famous as Combray in his masterpiece, *A la recherche du temps perdu (Remembrance of Things Past).* So today the town is known as Illiers-Combray.

The taste of a madeleine launched Proust on his immortal recollection. To this day, readers from all over the world flock to the pastry shops to eat a madeleine dipped in lime-flower tea. Following the Proustian canon, you can explore the gardens, streets, and houses he wrote about and visited. The town is epitomized by its Eglise St-Jacques, where as a boy, Proust placed hawthorn on the altar, which he later referred in his novels as l'Eglise St-Hilaire.

Members of Proust's family had lived in Illiers for centuries. His grandfather, François, was born on rue du Cheval-Blanc. At 11 place du Marché, opposite the church (now headquarters for a local insurance company), François ran a candle shop. His daughter, Elisabeth, married Jules Amiot,

person. Tours are canceled during pilgrimages, religious celebrations, and large funerals. French-language tours (6.20€/$8.05) start at 10:30am and 3pm from Easter to October and at 2:30pm the rest of the year.

If you're fit enough, don't miss the opportunity, especially in summer, to climb to the top of the tower. Open daily from 8:30am to noon and 2 to 7:30pm, it costs 4.60€ ($6) for adults and 3.10€ ($4.05) for students. You can visit the crypt, gloomy and somber but rich with medieval history, only as part of a French-language tour. The cost is 3.10€ ($4.05) per person.

16 Cloître Notre-Dame. ✆ **02-37-21-75-02.** www.monum.fr. Free admission to cathedral. Daily 8:30am–7:30pm.

EXPLORING THE TOWN

Next to the cathedral is the **Musée des Beaux-Arts de Chartres** ★, 29 Cloître Notre-Dame (✆ **02-37-36-41-39**), open May 3 to October 30 Wednesday to Monday from 10am to noon and 2 to 6pm (closed Sun morning); the rest of the year, it's open only until 5pm. Admission is 3€ ($3.90) for adults, free for children 18 an under. In a former Episcopal palace, the building at times competes with its exhibitions. The collection covers mainly the 16th to the 20th centuries and includes works by old masters such as Zurbarán, Watteau, and Brosamer. Of particular interest is David Ténier's *Le Concert.*

who ran a shop a few doors away. Down from Paris, young Marcel would visit his aunt at 4 rue du St-Esprit, which has been renamed rue du Docteur-Proust, honoring Marcel's grandfather.

Musée Marcel Proust/Maison de Tante Léonie, 4 rue du Docteur-Proust (✆ **02-37-24-30-97**), contains the world's most concentrated dose of Proust memorabilia and the objects and memories that helped spark his creative vision. In his novels, this was Aunt Léonie's home, filled with antimacassars and antiques, and typical of the bourgeois comforts of its day. Upstairs are the bedrooms where the young Marcel and his Aunt Léonie slept. Today they contain souvenirs of key episodes in his novels. Also important is a re-creation of the Salon Rouge, which Proust maintained at 102 bd. Haussmann, Paris, 8e, filled with furniture owned by his parents and grandparents. Especially significant are the documents and objects, some of them particularly emotive and evocative, left to the museum by Celeste Albaret, wife of Proust's chauffeur, and his protector, guardian, and "handler" the last 9 years of his life. The museum is open for French-language guided tours Tuesday through Sunday only, at 2:30 and 4pm. During July and August, there's an additional tour Tuesday to Sunday at 11am. Tours are 5€ ($6.50) for adults, 3€ ($3.90) for students, free for children under 12. Closed from mid-December to mid-January.

In the center of town, a sign guides you to other Proustian sights, all open 24 hours a day without charge.

At the foot of the cathedral, the lanes contain gabled houses. Humped bridges span the Eure River. From the Bouju Bridge, you can see the lofty spires in the background. Our favorite stroll is along **rue du Pont-St-Hilaire** ★, which offers the best vista of the old rooftops that lie beneath the towering cathedral. The street of St-Hilaire is east of the Gothic **church of St-Pierre,** on rue St-Pierre, a 10-minute stroll south of the cathedral. Two evocative streets of old Chartres, each a 3-minute walk south of the cathedral, are **rue du Cygne** and **rue des Ecuyers.** To the east, the most charming old quartier is **St. André,** once home to cobblers and tanners. Most of the buildings are restored but date from the 1700s and are known for their embossed doorways crowned by bull's-eye glass.

SHOPPING Your best shopping bet in Chartres is place des Epars. This pedestrian area is home to most of the apparel shops and even some haute couture boutiques. Along rue Noël-Balay is a small mall with about 15 shops you may find interesting, especially if it's raining. Many shops selling regional items line the narrow streets that fan southeast from the cathedral.

At **Galerie du Vitrail,** 17 Cloître Notre-Dame (✆ **02-37-36-10-03**), you'll find a huge selection of stained glass. **Lassaussois Antiquités,** 17 rue des Changes (✆ **02-37-21-37-74**), specializes in antique objets d'art and contemporary furnishings. If antique lace is your passion, stop by **Ariane,** 39 rue des Changes (✆ **02-37-21-20-68**),

Moments A Free Concert

If you visit Chartres on a Sunday afternoon in July or August, the church features free organ concerts at 4:45pm, when the filtered light brings the cathedral's western windows to life.

which also sells handmade sweaters, elegant linens, costume jewelry, and children's clothing.

WHERE TO STAY

Grand Monarque Best Western The most appealing and desirable hotel in Chartres occupies an imposing civic monument whose 600-year-old foundations and infrastructures were "gentrified" sometime in the 19th century with white stucco, neoclassical detailing, and touches of the baroque. Functioning as an inn since its original construction in the 15th century, and expanded and improved many times since then, the hotel remains under the direction of a local family. It attracts guests who enjoy its old-world charm—such as Art Nouveau stained glass and Louis XV chairs in the dining room. The guest rooms are decorated with reproductions of antiques; most have sitting areas. Suites have air-conditioning. Bathrooms are motel standard with a tub/shower combination. The hotel has an old-fashioned, unremarkable restaurant.

22 place des Epars, Chartres 28005. ✆ **800/528-1234** in the U.S., or 02-37-18-15-15. Fax 02-37-36-34-18. www.bw-grand-monarque.com. 55 units. 118€–170€ ($153–$221) double; 200€ ($260) suite. AE, DC, MC, V. Parking 8€ ($10). **Amenities:** 2 restaurants; brasserie; bar; room service; laundry service; dry cleaning; nonsmoking rooms. *In room:* TV, minibar, hair dryer.

Hôtel Châtelet This modern hotel has many traditional touches. The rustic guest rooms are inviting, with reproductions of Louis XV and Louis XVI furniture. The larger, more expensive units face a garden and avoid street noise. But many windows along the front (street) side of the hotel open onto a view of the cathedral. Each room comes with a tidy, tiled bathroom with shower and tub. In chilly weather, there's a log-burning fire in one of the salons. Breakfast is the only meal served, but numerous restaurants are close by.

6–8 av. Jehan-de-Beauce, Chartres 28000. ✆ **02-37-21-78-00.** Fax 02-37-36-23-01. www.hotelchatelet.com. 48 units. 65€–81€ ($85–$105) double. Extra person 9.15€ ($12). AE, DC, MC, V. Parking 6€ ($7.80). **Amenities:** Bar; room service; limited-mobility rooms. *In room:* TV, minibar, hair dryer.

WHERE TO DINE

La Vieille Maison ★★ MODERN FRENCH Even if the food here wasn't superb, the 14th-century building could be visited for its historical value. The dining room, outfitted in the Louis XIII style, is centered on a narrow ceiling vault, less than 2m (6 ft.) across, crafted of chiseled white stone blocks during the 800s. Bruno Letartre, the only *maître cuisinier de France* in Chartres, supervises the cuisine. The menu changes four or five times a year, reflecting the seasonality of the Ile de France and its produce. Recent examples have included foie gras of duckling, roasted crayfish with Indian spices, foie gras served on sliced rye bread, brochettes of lobster and scallops with spaghetti, and noisettes of venison fried with Jamaican and Szechuan pepper and wild mushrooms. Dessert raves go to a thin apple-and-fig tart served with walnut-flavored ice cream.

5 rue au Lait. ✆ **02-37-34-10-67**. www.lavieillemaison.fr. Reservations recommended. Main courses 22€–28€ ($29–$36); fixed-price menu 33€–49€ ($43–$64). MC, V. Wed–Sun noon–2:15pm; Tues–Sat 7–10pm. Closed 1 week in Aug.

Le Geôrges ★★ FRENCH The best food, and the most upscale dining ambience, in Chartres is now featured by the town's best hotel, an also-recommended establishment with roots that go back to the 15th century, when the site served food and drink (not as elegant as what you'll find today) to weary travelers and postal workers. Set on the hotel's street level, within a formal, high-ceilinged dining room outfitted in soft reds and grays, it contains an unusual collection of cast-iron/board models, each about as big as a laptop computer, of antique ovens, bigger versions of which might have fed the masons who labored on the nearby cathedral. Menu items change with the seasons, but usually include savory portions of *pâté de Chartres,* made with a combination of minced meats (including wild duck) baked in a giant puff pastry; a steamed combination of crayfish with scallops in wine sauce; and a superb version of roasted veal "Grand Monarque," served with a casserole of mushrooms and cheese. Also interesting is lobster "prepared in the style of perch," with a reduction of apple-flavored Calvados and Newberg (that is, lobster) sauce. Desserts are sumptuous and the cheese trolley will warm the heart of any Francophile.

In the Grand Monarque Best Western, 22 place des Epars. ✆ **02-37-18-15-15**. Reservations recommended. Fixed-price menus 39€–55€ ($51–$72). AE, DC, MC, V. Tues–Sun noon–2:45pm; Tues–Sat 7:30–10pm.

CHARTRES AFTER DARK

For an evening of theater or modern dance from September to June, try the **Théâtre Municipal,** boulevard Chasles (✆ **02-37-23-42-79**). From time to time, you can catch a jazz or rock concert as well. **Forum de la Madeleine,** avenue Joseph Pichard (✆ **02-37-88-45-00**), presents light fare and usually has a busier performance season. For dancing, go to **Le Privilège,** 1 place St-Pierre (✆ **02-37-35-52-02**), where you'll find a range of dance music from zouk to disco.

3 Barbizon: The School of Rousseau ★★

56km (35 miles) SE of Paris, 9.5km (6 miles) NW of Fontainebleau

In the 19th century, this village on the edge of the forest of Fontainebleau was a refuge for artists such as Rousseau, Millet, and Corot, many of whom couldn't find acceptance in conservative Paris salons. In Barbizon, they turned to nature, and painted realistic pastoral scenes. These artists attracted a school of lesser painters, including Daubigny, Diaz, Charles Jacques, Decamps, Paul Huet, Troyon, and others. Today, Barbizon attracts fashionable Parisians for *le weekend.* Some complain about its prices, but others just enjoy the sunshine and clean air. Even with hordes of galleries and souvenir shops, the town retains much of its traditional atmosphere.

ESSENTIALS

GETTING THERE Barbizon doesn't have a railway station, so the most direct **train** route is from Paris to Fontainebleau (see below), doubling back to Barbizon on one of two buses a day. The round-trip fare to Fontainebleau is 15€ ($20). Bus fare to Barbizon costs 1.40€ ($1.80). For information and schedules, call ✆ **01-64-10-29-20.**

VISITOR INFORMATION The **Office de Tourisme** is at 41 Grande-Rue (✆ **01-60-66-41-87**).

MUSEUMS

Maison et Atelier de Jean-François Millet This museum is devoted to the best-known Barbizon painter, who settled here in 1849. Millet painted religious, classical, and especially peasant subjects. Here you'll see his etching of *The Man with the Hoe,* as well as some original furnishings.

27 Grande-Rue. ✆ **01-60-66-21-55.** www.barbizon-france.com. Admission 3€ ($3.90). Mon and Wed–Sat 9:30am–12:30pm and 2–5:30pm.

Musée Auberge Ganne The inn that housed most of the Barbizon artists during their late-19th-century sojourns here was L'Auberge du Père-Gannes. In the mid-1990s, through collaboration with Paris's Musée d'Orsay, it became the Musée Ganne, a showcase for Rousseau, who began painting landscapes directly from nature (novel at the time) and settled in Barbizon in the 1840s.

92 Grande-Rue. ✆ **01-60-66-22-27.** www.barbizon-france.com. Admission 3€ ($3.90) adults, 2.50€ ($3.25) students, free for children under 16. Mon and Wed–Sun 10am–12:30pm and 2–5:30pm.

WHERE TO STAY

Hostellerie du Bas-Bréau ★★★ This member of Relais & Châteaux is one of France's great old inns (it opened in the 1840s), set amid shady trees and courtyards. Many artists and writers stayed here, notably Robert Louis Stevenson, who scattered anecdotes of the inn throughout his novels. Napoleon III and his empress, Eugénie, came in 1868 to purchase some paintings. Since then, the hotel has maintained its role as a glamorous competitor in the district through several enlargements and refurbishments. It's furnished with antiques and reproductions. In the colder months, guests gather around the fireplace in the living room. Guest rooms contain antiques and comfortable beds; units in the rear open directly onto semiprivate terraces. The luxurious bathrooms have tub/shower combos.

22 Grande-Rue, Barbizon 77630. ✆ **01-60-66-40-05.** Fax 01-60-69-22-89. www.bas-breau.com. 21 units. 250€–280€ ($325–$364) double; 420€–480€ ($546–$624) suite. AE, DC, MC, V. **Amenities:** Restaurant; bar; outdoor pool; room service; babysitting; laundry service; dry cleaning; limited-mobility rooms. *In room:* A/C, TV, minibar, hair dryer, safe.

Hostellerie La Clé d'Or ★ *Finds* Encircled by a stone wall, the grounds of this century-old hotel include a garden and a stone terrace full of plants that flower in a wash of pinks and yellows in spring and summer. The terrace leads to many of the guest rooms, which are cozy, a bit small, and outfitted in an unglitzy, country-comfortable style that incorporates traditional furniture and subtly patterned upholstery. Other units provide a bit more architectural flair under A-frame ceilings with exposed heavy wooden beams. Note that in some units, a curtain of sorts replaces the bathroom door.

73 Grande-Rue, Barbizon 77360. ✆ **01-60-66-40-96.** Fax 01-60-66-42-71. 16 units. 70€–93€ ($91–$121) double; 133€ ($173) suite. AE, DC, MC, V. **Amenities:** Restaurant; English-style bar; business services; limited room service. *In room:* TV, minibar, hair dryer.

WHERE TO DINE

We also recommend the restaurant at the **Hostellerie du Bas-Bréau** (see "Where to Stay," above).

Le Relais de Barbizon *Value* TRADITIONAL FRENCH Many prefer dining at this down-to-earth restaurant to meals at pricier inns. Offering excellent value, Le Relais is a tavern in a building boasting 300-year-old walls, with a provincial dining room centering on a fireplace. In sunny weather, tables are set in the rear yard, with a trellis, an arbor, and trees. Typical choices are quenelle (a kind of dumpling) of pike, coq au vin, breast of duckling with cherries or seasonal fruit, grilled beef, and, in autumn, venison, rabbit, and pheasant.

2 av. Charles-de-Gaulle. © **01-60-66-40-28.** Reservations recommended on weekends. Main courses 13€–20€ ($17–$26); fixed-price menu 22€–40€ ($29–$52). MC, V. Thurs–Tues noon–2pm; Thurs–Mon 7–9:30pm. Closed last 2 weeks of Aug and 2 weeks at Christmas.

4 Fontainebleau: Refuge of Kings ★★★

60km (37 miles) S of Paris, 74km (46 miles) NE of Orléans

Napoleon called the Palais de Fontainebleau the house of the centuries. Napoleon stood on its horseshoe-shaped exterior staircase and bade farewell to his army before his departure to exile on Elba. That scene has been the subject of countless paintings, including Vernet's *Les Adieux*.

After Versailles, a visit to Fontainebleau can be a bit of a letdown. French kings originally came to Fontainebleau because of its proximity to great hunting. François I converted it from a hunting lodge into a palace fit for a king. Versailles, on the other hand, is the creation of the French monarchy at its pinnacle of splendor, prestige, and power.

Set in 20,000 hectares (50,000 acres) of verdant forest, Fontainebleau remains a country retreat for Parisians who come for horseback riding, picnicking, and hiking. It's not as crowded with tourists, so it's more peaceful than Versailles. Allow 2½ hours to see everything in Fontainebleau.

ESSENTIALS

GETTING THERE **Trains** to Fontainebleau depart from the Gare de Lyon in Paris. The trip takes 45 minutes each way and costs 7.50€ ($9.75) one-way. Fontainebleau's railway station lies 3km (1¾ miles) north of the château, in the suburb of Avon. A local bus (marked simply CHATEAU and part of line A) makes the trip to the château at 15-minute intervals Monday through Saturday and at 30-minute intervals on Sunday; the fare is 1.40€ ($1.80) each way. If you're **driving,** take A6 south from Paris, exit onto N191, and follow signs.

VISITOR INFORMATION The **Office de Tourisme** is at 4 rue Royale, Fontainebleau (© **01-60-74-99-99**), opposite the main entrance to the château.

SEEING THE CHATEAU & GARDENS

Musée National du Château de Fontainebleau ★★★ Napoleon joined the parade of French rulers who used the Palais de Fontainebleau as a resort, hunting in its magnificent forest. Under François I (who reigned 1515–47), the hunting lodge was enlarged into a royal palace in the Italian Renaissance style. The style got botched, but many artists, including Cellini, came from Italy to work for the French monarch.

Under François I's patronage, the School of Fontainebleau (led by the painters Rosso, Fiorentino, and Primaticcio) increased in prestige. These artists adorned one of the most outstanding rooms at Fontainebleau: the 63m-long (207-ft.) **Gallery of François I** ★★★. (Restorers under Louis-Philippe didn't completely succeed in ruining it.) Surrounded by pomp, François I walked the length of his gallery while artisans tempted him with their wares, job seekers asked favors, and courtesans attempted to lure him from the duchesse d'Etampes. The stucco-framed panels depict such scenes as Jupiter carrying off Europa, the Nymph of Fontainebleau (with a lecherous dog peering through the reeds), and the king holding a pomegranate, a symbol of unity.

Moments Hiking along Trails Left by French Kings

The Forest of Fontainebleau is riddled with *sentiers* (hiking trails) made by French kings and their entourages who went hunting in the forest. A *Guide des Sentiers* is available at the tourist information center (see above). Bike paths also cut through the forest. You can rent bikes at the Fontainebleau-Avon rail depot. At the station, go to the kiosk, **A La Petite Reine (© 01-60-74-57-57).** The cost of a regular bike is 13€ ($17) per half-day, 20€ ($26) for a full day. The kiosk is open Monday to Friday from 9:30am to 6pm, Saturday and Sunday from 10am to 7pm.

However, the frames compete with the pictures. Everywhere is the salamander, symbol of the Chevalier King.

If it's true that François I built Fontainebleau for his mistress, then Henri II, his successor, left a memorial to the woman he loved, Diane de Poitiers. Sometimes called the Gallery of Henri II, the **Ballroom (La Salle de Bal)** ★★★ is the château's second splendid interior. The monograms H & D are interlaced in the decoration. At one end of the room is a monumental fireplace supported by two bronze satyrs, reproduced in 1966 (the originals were melted down during the Revolution). A series of 16th-century frescoes depict mythological subjects.

An architectural curiosity is the **Louis XV Staircase** ★★. Primaticcio originally decorated the ceiling for the bedroom of the duchesse d'Etampes. When an architect added the stairway, he simply ripped out her bedroom floor and used the ceiling to cover the stairway. Of the preserved Italian frescoes, one depicts the Queen of the Amazons climbing into Alexander the Great's bed.

Fontainebleau found renewed glory under Napoleon. You can wander much of the palace on your own, visiting sites that evoke his 19th-century heyday. They include the throne room, the room where he abdicated (the abdication document displayed is a copy), his offices, his bedroom (look for his symbol, a bee), and his bathroom. Some of the smaller rooms, especially those containing his personal mementos and artifacts, are accessible by guided tour only. The furnishings in the grand apartments of Napoleon and Joséphine are marvelous.

The **Musée Chinois (Chinese Museum),** which is open only erratically, usually, but not always, on weekends (a function of staff shortages), holds the Empress Eugénie's collection of Chinese treasures, including Far Eastern porcelain, jade, and crystal.

After your trek through the palace, visit the **gardens** and especially the carp pond; the gardens, however, are only a prelude to the forest of Fontainebleau and not nearly as spectacular as those surrounding Versailles.

Place du Général-de-Gaulle. © **01-60-71-50-70.** www.musee-chateau-fontainebleau.fr. Combination ticket including private *appartements* 6.50€ ($8.45) adults, 4.50€ ($5.85) students 18–25; ticket to *petits appartements* and Napoleonic rooms 3€ ($3.90) adults, 2.30€ ($3) students 18–25, free for children under 14. June–Sept Wed–Mon 9:30am–6pm; Oct–May Wed–Mon 9:30am–5pm.

WHERE TO STAY

Grand Hôtel de l'Aigle-Noir (The Black Eagle) ★ This mansion, once the home of Cardinal de Retz, sits opposite the château. The formal courtyard entrance has a high iron/board grille and pillars crowned by black eagles. It became a hotel in

1720 and is the finest lodging in Fontainebleau, far superior in amenities and style to the Hôtel Napoléon (see below). The rooms are decorated with Louis XVI, Empire, or Régence-era antiques or reproductions, with plush beds and elegant bathroom amenities. All but four units have a tub/shower combination. Enjoy a drink in the Napoleon III–style piano bar before dinner.

27 place Napoléon-Bonaparte, Fontainebleau 77300. ✆ **01-60-74-60-00.** Fax 01-60-74-60-01. www.hotelaiglenoir.fr. 18 units. 160€–170€ ($208–$221) double; 260€–380€ ($338–$494) suite. AE, DC, MC, V. Parking 9€ ($12). **Amenities:** Restaurant; bar; indoor pool; sauna; room service; fitness center; laundry service; dry cleaning; nonsmoking rooms; 2 limited-mobility rooms. *In room:* A/C, minibar, hair dryer.

Hôtel de Londres With a historic 1850s-era facade, and owned and managed since 1932 by generations of the same family, this hotel enjoys one of the best locations in town for anyone who's fascinated by the architecture of the château of Fontainebleau. It's directly in front of the cour des Adieux, site of Napoleon's farewell to his troops before his exile to Elba. The hotel occupies two of the building's three floors. The well-maintained rooms are tastefully and cozily outfitted, mostly with Louis XVI furniture, and have extra-long beds and tiled bathrooms. Other than breakfast, no meals are served.

1 place du Général-de-Gaulle, Fontainebleau 77300. ✆ **01-64-22-20-21.** Fax 01-60-72-39-16. www.hoteldelondres.com. 12 units. 110€–160€ ($143–$208) double. AE, MC, V. Closed 1 week in Aug and Dec 18–Jan 7. **Amenities:** Bar; laundry service; dry cleaning; nonsmoking rooms. *In room:* TV, hair dryer.

Hôtel Napoléon This classically designed hotel—the number-two choice in Fontainebleau, and renovated in 2004—is a short walk from the château. The lobby has Oriental rugs, arched windows, and a garden tearoom. An inviting bar features an ornate oval ceiling, Louis-Philippe chairs, and a neoclassical fireplace. The renovated guest rooms are filled with reproductions of antiques and flowered headboards. All are comfortable, but those facing the courtyard are larger and more tranquil. All units have full bathrooms.

9 rue Grande, Fontainebleau 77300. ✆ **01-60-39-50-50.** Fax 01-64-22-20-87. www.hotelnapoleon-fontainebleau.com. 57 units. 130€–150€ ($169–$195) double; 210€ ($273) suite. AE, DC, MC, V. Parking 9€ ($12). **Amenities:** Restaurant; bar; room service; laundry service; dry cleaning; limited-mobility rooms. *In room:* TV, minibar, hair dryer.

WHERE TO DINE

In addition to the options below, **La Table des Maréchaux,** in the Hôtel Napoléon (see above), is a superb choice.

Le Caveau des Ducs TRADITIONAL FRENCH This reasonably priced restaurant occupies a former storage cellar. It sits underground, beneath a series of 17th-century stone vaults built by the same masons who laid the cobblestones of rue de Ferrare. Although the food is simple, the setting—with lots of wood and flickering candles—is dramatic. Menu items include staples such as snails in garlic butter, roast leg of lamb with garlic-and-rosemary sauce, and virtually everything that can be concocted from the body of a duck (terrines, magret, and confits). Filet of rump steak with brie sauce is tasty, as are platters of sole, crayfish tails, and salmon on a bed of pasta. Especially flavorful are strips of veal in morel-studded cream sauce on a bed of pasta.

24 rue de Ferrare. ✆ **01-64-22-05-05.** Reservations recommended. Main courses 16€–25€ ($21–$33); fixed-price menu 24€–39€ ($31–$51). AE, MC, V. Daily noon–2pm and 7–10pm.

Le François-1er (Chez Bernard) ★ TRADITIONAL FRENCH The premier dining choice in Fontainebleau has Louis XIII decor, winemaking memorabilia, and walls that the owners think are about 200 years old. If weather permits, sit on the terrace overlooking the château and the cour des Adieux. In game season, the menu features hare, duck liver, and partridge. Other choices include a cassoulet of snails with flap mushrooms and garlic-flavored cream sauce, magret of duckling with cassis sauce, *rognon de veau* (veal kidneys) with mustard sauce, and a salad of baby scallops with crayfish. Chef Bernard Crogiez's cuisine is meticulous, with an undeniable flair.

3 rue Royale. ✆ **01-64-22-24-68.** Reservations required. Main courses 17€–28€ ($22–$36); fixed-price lunch Mon–Fri only 15€ ($20); fixed-price dinner 29€ ($38). AE, MC, V. Tues–Sat noon–2:30pm; Mon–Sat 7:30–9:45pm.

5 Vaux-le-Vicomte: Life before Versailles

47km (29 miles) SE of Paris, 19km (12 miles) NE of Fontainebleau

Though it's close to Paris, Vaux-le-Vicomte is hard to reach by mass transit. By **car,** take N6 southeast from Paris to Melun, which is 6km (3¾ miles) west of the château. By **train,** take the 45-minute ride from Gare de Lyon to Melun (14€/$18 round-trip), and then a taxi from the station 6.5km (4 miles) to Vaux-le-Vicomte (14€/$18 each way). Once there, allow 2 hours to see the château.

The nearest **tourist office** is in the Hotel de Ville, 18 rue Paul Doumer, Melun (✆ **01-64-52-64-52**); it's open Tuesday through Saturday 9:15am to 12:15pm and 1 to 5pm.

SEEING THE CHATEAU

Château de Vaux-le-Vicomte ★★★ The château was built in 1656 for Nicolas Fouquet, Louis XIV's finance minister. The king wasn't pleased that Fouquet was able to live so extravagantly, and then he discovered that the minister had embezzled funds from the treasury. Fouquet was arrested, and Louis hired the same artists and architects who had built Vaux-le-Vicomte to begin creating Versailles. If you visit both, you'll see the striking similarities.

One of the stateliest French châteaux that's still privately owned, Vaux-le-Vicomte belongs to Patrice, *comte* de Vogüé, whose ownership dates back many generations. He lives in one of the outbuildings, not in the main building, which is open for tours.

The view of the château from the main gate reveals the splendor of 17th-century France. On the south side, a majestic staircase sweeps toward the gardens, designed by Le Nôtre. The Grand Canal, flanked by waterfalls, divides the greenery. The château is furnished with 17th-century pieces. The entrance hall leads to 12 staterooms, including the oval rotunda. Many rooms are hung with Gobelin tapestries and decorated with painted ceiling and wall panels by Le Brun, with sculpture by Girardon. A self-guided tour of the interior includes Fouquet's personal suite, the huge basement and wine cellar, the servants' dining room, and the copper-filled kitchen.

Included in the admission fee is entrance to the château's carriage museum **(Musée des Equipages)** in the stables. Some 25 restored 18th- and 19th-century carriages are on display, each accessorized with mannequin horses and people.

Candlelight evenings **(Des Soirées à Chandelles)** take place every Saturday from May to mid-October between 8pm and midnight, and every Friday in July and August from 8pm to midnight. During the events, all electricity to the château is cut off, and thousands of candles illuminate both the château and its gardens. The effect has been called mystical—a memorable re-creation of the way of life that prevailed during the building's heyday. Admission during candlelight evenings is 16€ ($21) for adults, 13€ ($17) for students and children 6 to 15, free for children under 6.

77950 Maincy. ✆ **01-64-14-41-90.** www.vaux-le-vicomte.com. Admission 13€ ($16) adults, 10€ ($13) students and children 6–16, free for children under 6. Audio guide rental 1.50€ ($1.95). Mid-Mar to mid-Nov daily 10am–6pm. Closed mid-Nov to mid-Mar.

WHERE TO DINE

Auberge de Crisenoy MODERN FRENCH You are more likely to find locals from Melun than fellow visitors at this auberge, and that's part of its charm. Behind the solid stone walls of a former private home, the two dining rooms (on separate floors), plus an additional 10 tables on a mezzanine, overlook a garden. The menu items are based on modern interpretations of French classics and change every 3 months. The best examples include foie gras with white grapes, toast, and compote of apples; filet l'agneau with red wine, pears, and new onions; and well-seasoned cassoulet of crayfish with spinach and mussels, served in a copper pot placed directly on the table.

Grande Rue, Crisenoy. From Vaux-le-Vicomte, follow N36 toward Meaux for 2.5km (1½ miles). ✆ **01-64-38-83-06.** Reservations recommended. Fixed-price lunch Tues–Fri only 23€ ($30); fixed-price dinner 30€ ($39) and 47€ ($61). MC, V. Tues–Sun noon–1:45pm; Tues and Thurs–Sat 7:30–9pm. Closed 1 week at Christmas, 1 week in Mar, and 3 weeks in Aug.

La Table de Saint Just TRADITIONAL FRENCH Dine here, and you're bound to be charmed. The original masonry from the 17th-century farmhouse, including artfully crafted oak beams, is intact. It occupies one of the farmhouses once associated with the **Château de Vaux-le-Pénil,** a Renaissance castle that today is privately occupied, widely known in the region, but closed to casual visitors, and only a few steps away. Menu items change with the seasons, but may include foie gras in a shell of caramelized apples, served with comfit of celery and acidified apples; lobster salad with orange sauce; scallops roasted with truffles; and roasted rack of lamb with moussaka of fresh vegetables.

Ferme Saint Just, Vaux-le-Pénil. From Vaux-le-Vicomte, drive 5.5km (3½ miles) west, following signs to Melun, then to Maincy, and then to Vaux-le-Pénil. ✆ **01-64-52-09-09.** Reservations recommended. Main courses 22€–33€ ($29–$43); fixed-price menu 39€–63€ ($51–$82). AE, MC, V. Tues–Sat noon–1:30pm and 7:30–9:30pm. Closed 3 weeks in Aug, 1 week at Christmas, and 1 week in May.

6 Disneyland Paris ★★★

32km (20 miles) E of Paris

After provoking some of the most enthusiastic and controversial reactions in recent French history, the multimillion-dollar Disneyland Paris opened in 1992. It's one of the world's most lavish theme parks, conceived on a scale rivaling that of Versailles. European journalists initially accused it of everything from cultural imperialism to the death knell of French culture.

But after godly amounts of public relations and financial juggling, Disneyland Paris has become France's number-one tourist attraction, with 50 million visitors annually. It accounts for 4% of the French tourism industry's foreign-currency sales. About 40% of the visitors are French, half from Paris. Disneyland Paris looks, tastes, and feels like the ones in California and Florida—except for the $10 cheeseburgers *"avec pommes frites."*

Situated on a 2,000-hectare (5,000-acre) site (about one-fifth the size of Paris) in the suburb of Marne-la-Vallée, the park incorporates the most successful elements of its Disney predecessors and European flair. The park in Florida is larger than the Paris property, with a greater number of attractions and rides, but Disneyland Paris does a decent job of re-creating the Magic Kingdom. In 2002, the Paris park added **Walt Disney Studios,** focusing on the role of movies in popular culture. Take 1 day for the highlights, 2 days for more depth.

ESSENTIALS

GETTING THERE The RER commuter express **rail** network (Line A) stops within walking distance of the park. Board the RER in Paris at Charles-de-Gaulle–Etoile, Châtelet–Les Halles, or Nation. Get off at Line A's last stop, Marne-la-Vallée/Chessy, 45 minutes from central Paris. The round-trip fare is 12€ ($16). Trains run daily, every 10 to 20 minutes from 5:30am to midnight.

Shuttle buses connect Orly and Charles de Gaulle airports with each hotel in the resort. Buses depart the airports every 30 to 45 minutes. One-way transport to the park from either airport is 14€ ($18) for adults, 12€ ($16) for children 3 to 11.

If you're **driving,** take A4 east from Paris and get off at Exit 14, DISNEYLAND PARIS. Parking begins at 8€ ($10) per day, but is free if you stay at one of the park hotels. A series of moving sidewalks speeds up pedestrian transit from parking areas to the park entrance.

VISITOR INFORMATION All the hotels we recommend offer general information on the theme park. For details and reservations at any of its hotels, contact the **Disneyland Paris Guest Relations Office,** located in City Hall on Main Street, U.S.A. (✆ **01-60-30-60-53** in English, or 08-25-30-60-30 in French; www.disneyland paris.com). For information on Disneyland Paris and specific details on the many other attractions and monuments in the Ile de France and the rest of the country, contact the **Maison du Tourisme,** Disney Village (B.P. 77705), Marne-la-Vallée (✆ **01-60-43-33-33**).

ADMISSION Admission varies depending on the season. In peak season, a 1-day park ticket costs 44€ ($57) for adults, 36€ ($47) for children 3 to 12, free for children under 3; a 2-day park-hopper ticket is 95€ ($124) for adults, 78€ ($101) for kids; and a 3-day park-hopper ticket is 119€ ($155) for adults, 98€ ($127) for kids. Peak season is from mid-June to mid-September as well as Christmas and Easter weeks. Entrance to Disney Village is free, though there's usually a cover charge at the dance clubs.

HOURS Hours vary throughout the year, but most frequently are 10am to 8pm. Be warned that autumn and winter hours vary the most; it depends on the weather. It's good to phone ahead if you're contemplating a visit at this time.

SEEING DISNEYLAND

Disneyland Paris is a total vacation destination. In one enormous unit, the park includes five "lands" of entertainment; a dozen hotels; a campground; an entertainment center (**Disney Village,** with six restaurants of its own); a 27-hole golf course; and dozens of restaurants, shows, and shops. The Disney Village entertainment center

---

Tips FASTPASS Those Long Lines

Disneyland Paris has instituted a program that's done well at the other parks. With the **FASTPASS** system, visitors to the various rides reserve a 1-hour time block. Within that block, the waiting is usually no more than 8 minutes.

For Those with Another Day: Walt Disney Studios

Next to Disneyland Paris, **Walt Disney Studios** (✆ **01-60-30-60-30**) takes guests on a behind-the-scenes interactive discovery of film, animation, and television.

The main entrance to the studios, called the **Front Lot,** consists of "Sunset Boulevard," an elaborate sound stage complete with hundreds of film props. The **Animation Courtyard** allows visitors to learn the trade secrets of Disney animators, and the **Production Courtyard** lets guests take a look behind the scenes of film and TV production. At **Catastrophe Canyon,** guests are plunged into the heart of a film shoot. Finally, the **Back Lot** is home to special effects and stunt workshops. A live stunt show features cars, motorbikes, and jet skis.

This ode to Hollywood and the films it produced since the end of its "golden age" has a roller coaster, the Rock 'n' Roller Coaster, featuring the music of Aerosmith, which combines rock memorabilia with high-speed scary twists and turns (completely in the dark); and a reconstruction of one of the explosion scenes in the Hollywood action film *Armageddon.*

Admission is 42€ ($55) for adults, 34€ ($44) for children. Hours are daily from 9am to 6pm (opens at 10am during certain seasons of the year).

is illuminated inside by a spectacular gridwork of lights suspended 18m (59 ft.) above the ground. The complex contains dance clubs, shops, restaurants (one of which offers a dinner spectacle based on the original *Buffalo Bill's Wild West Show*), bars for adults trying to escape their children, a French Government Tourist Office, a post office, and a marina.

Visitors stroll amid flower beds, trees, reflecting ponds, fountains, and a large artificial lake flanked with hotels. An army of smiling employees and Disney characters—many of whom are multilingual, including Buffalo Bill, Mickey and Minnie Mouse, and, of course, the French-born Caribbean pirate Jean Laffite—are on hand to greet the thousands of *enfants.* You'll see characters from *Aladdin, The Lion King, Pocahontas,* and *Toy Story.* As Disney continues to churn out animated blockbusters, look for the newest stars to appear in the theme park.

Main Street, U.S.A. abounds with horse-drawn carriages and barbershop quartets. Steam-powered railway cars embark from the Main Street Station for a trip through a Grand Canyon diorama to **Frontierland,** with its paddle-wheel steamers reminiscent of Mark Twain's Mississippi River. Other attractions are the Critter Corral petting zoo and the Lucky Nugget Saloon, which is inspired by the gold rush era, with the steps and costumes of the cancan show originated in the cabarets of turn-of-the-20th-century Paris.

The park's steam trains chug past **Adventureland**—with its swashbuckling pirates, Swiss Family Robinson treehouse, and reenacted *Arabian Nights* legends—to **Fantasyland.** Here you'll find the **Sleeping Beauty's Castle (Le Château de la Belle au Bois Dormant),** whose pinnacles and turrets are an idealized (and spectacular) interpretation of French châteaux. In its shadow are Europeanized versions of *Blanche*

Neige et les Sept Nains (Snow White and the Seven Dwarfs), Peter Pan, Dumbo, Alice (from Wonderland), the Mad Hatter's Teacups, and Sir Lancelot's Magic Carousel.

Visions of the future are in **Discoveryland,** where tributes to invention and imagination draw from the works of Leonardo da Vinci, Jules Verne, H. G. Wells, the modern masters of science fiction, and the *Star Wars* series.

WHERE TO STAY

You can easily make Disney a day trip from Paris—the transportation links are excellent—or you can spend the night.

The resort's six theme hotels share a reservation service. In North America, call ✆ **407/W-DISNEY.** In France, contact the **Central Reservations Office,** Euro Disney Resort, S.C.A., B.P. 105, F-77777 Marne-la-Vallée Cedex 4 (✆ **01-60-30-60-30;** www.disneylandparis.com).

VERY EXPENSIVE

Disneyland Hotel ★★ Mouseketeers who have rich daddies and mommies frequent Disney's poshest resort. At the park entrance, this flagship four-story hotel is Victorian, with red-tile turrets and jutting balconies. The spacious guest rooms are plushly furnished but evoke the image of Disney, with cartoon depictions and candy-stripe decor. The beds are king-size, double, or twin; in some rooms armchairs convert to beds. Accommodations in the rear overlook Sleeping Beauty's Castle and Big Thunder Mountain. Some less desirable units open onto a parking lot. The luxurious bathrooms have marble vanities, showers and tubs, and twin basins. On the Castle Club floor, you get free newspapers, all-day beverages, and access to a well-equipped private lounge.

Disneyland Paris, B.P. 111, F-77777 Marne-la-Vallée Cedex 4. ✆ **01-60-45-65-89.** Fax 01-60-45-65-33. www.disneylandparis.com. 496 units. 323€–501€ ($420–$651) double; from 850€ ($1,105) suite. Rates include breakfast. AE, DC, MC, V. **Amenities:** 2 restaurants; bar; health club w/indoor pool; Jacuzzi; sauna; room service; babysitting; laundry service; dry cleaning; nonsmoking rooms; limited-mobility rooms. *In room:* A/C, TV, minibar, hair dryer, safe.

EXPENSIVE

Hotel New York ★ Inspired by the Big Apple, this hotel centers on a nine-story "skyscraper" flanked by the Gramercy Park Wing and the Brownstones Wing. (Their exteriors resemble row houses.) This convention hotel is less family-friendly than others at the resort. Guest rooms are comfortable, with Art Deco accessories, New York–inspired memorabilia, and roomy combination bathrooms with twin basins and tub/shower combos. Try for one of the units fronting Lake Buena Vista.

Disneyland Paris, B.P. 100, F-77777 Marne-la-Vallée Cedex 4. ✆ **01-60-45-75-92.** Fax 01-60-45-73-33. www.disneylandparis.com. 565 units. 214€–333€ ($278–$433) double; from 565€ ($735) suite. Rates include breakfast. AE, DC, MC, V. **Amenities:** 2 restaurants; bar; indoor and outdoor pools; exercise room; sauna; room service; babysitting; nonsmoking rooms; limited-mobility rooms. *In room:* A/C, TV, minibar, hair dryer, safe.

Newport Bay Club ★★ You expect to see the reincarnation of Joe Kennedy walking along the veranda with its slated roofs, awnings, and pergolas. It's very Hyannisport here. It's also the biggest hotel in France. With a central cupola, balconies, and a blue-and-cream color scheme, it recalls a harborfront New England hotel (ca. 1900). The layout features nautically decorated rooms in various shapes and sizes. The most spacious are the corner units. The combination bathrooms are roomy, with deluxe toiletries and tub and shower.

Disneyland Paris, B.P. 105, F-77777 Marne-la-Vallée Cedex 4. ✆ **01-60-45-56-55.** Fax 01-60-45-55-33. www.disneylandparis.com. 1,093 units. 172€–272€ ($224–$356) double; from 395€ ($514) suite. Rates include breakfast. AE, DC,

MC, V. **Amenities:** 2 restaurants; bar; indoor and outdoor pools; health club; sauna; room service; nonsmoking rooms; limited-mobility rooms. *In room:* A/C, TV, minibar, safe.

MODERATE

Hotel Cheyenne/Hotel Santa Fe *Kids* Next door to each other near a re-creation of Texas's Rio Grande, these Old West–style lodgings are the resort's least expensive hotels. The Cheyenne consists of 14 two-story buildings along Desperado Street; the desert-themed Santa Fe encompasses four "nature trails" winding among 42 adobe-style pueblos. The Cheyenne is a favorite among families, offering a double bed and bunk beds. Children have an array of activities, including a play area in a log cabin with a lookout tower and a section where you can explore the "ruins" of an ancient Anasazi village. The only disadvantage, according to some parents, is the absence of a pool.

More recently constructed, but charging the same prices, is the nearby **Kyriad Hotel,** a government-rated two-star hotel designed for families that evokes the aesthetics and layout of a French country inn. Whenever the Cheyenne and the Santa Fe are full, Disney usually directs the overflow to the Kyriad.

Disneyland Paris, B.P. 115, F-77777 Marne-la-Vallée Cedex 4. ✆ **01-60-45-63-12** (Cheyenne) or 01-60-45-79-22 (Santa Fe). Fax 01-60-45-62-33 (Cheyenne) or 01-60-45-78-33 (Santa Fe). www.disneylandparis.com. 2,000 units. Hotel Cheyenne 82€–177€ ($107–$230) double; Hotel Santa Fe 67€–150€ ($87–$195) double. Rates include breakfast. AE, DC, MC, V. **Amenities:** Restaurant; bar; babysitting; nonsmoking rooms; limited-mobility rooms. *In room:* A/C, TV.

WHERE TO DINE

Disneyland Paris offers a gamut of cuisine in more than 45 restaurants and snack bars. You can live on burgers and fries, or you can experiment at the following upscale restaurants.

Auberge de Cendrillon TRADITIONAL FRENCH This is a fairy-tale version of Cinderella's country inn, with a glass couch in the center. A master of ceremonies wearing a plumed tricorn hat, embroidered tunic, and lace ruffles welcomes you. There are corny elements, but the chefs go out of their way to make a big deal of French cuisine. For the most part, they succeed admirably. The appetizers set the tone. Our favorites are warm goat-cheese salad with lardons and the smoked salmon platter. Either will put you in the mood for a French classic such as loin of lamb roasted under a zesty mustard coating or flavorful sautéed veal medallions. Because the restaurant follows the park's seasonal schedule, lunch is usually easier to arrange than dinner. There's a lunchtime buffet, served only between 11:30am and around 2:20pm, every day at a price of 22€ ($29) for adults and 10€ ($13) for children ages 3 to 11.

Fantasyland. ✆ **01-64-74-24-02.** Reservations recommended. Main courses 20€–27€ ($26–$35); fixed-price menu 29€ ($38) adults, 10€ ($13) children. AE, DC, MC, V. Mid-July to Aug daily 11:30am–9:30am; rest of the year daily 11:30am–4pm.

California Grill ★★ *Kids* CALIFORNIAN/FRENCH The resort's showcase restaurant serves cuisine that's the equivalent of the fare at a one-Michelin-star restaurant. Focusing on the lighter specialties for which the Golden State is famous, with many concessions to French palates, the elegant restaurant accommodates both adults and children gracefully. Even French food critics are impressed with oysters prepared with leeks and salmon. We also embrace the appetizer of foie gras with roasted red peppers and the roasted pigeon with braised Chinese cabbage and black-rice vinegar. Another winning selection is fresh salmon roasted over beechwood and served with a sprinkling of walnut oil, sage sauce, asparagus, and fricassee of forest mushrooms.

Many items are specifically for children. If you want a quiet, mostly adult venue, go here as late as your hunger pangs will allow.

In the Disneyland Hotel. ✆ **01-60-45-65-76.** Reservations required. Fixed-price menu 44€–71€ ($57–$92); children's menu 15€ ($20). AE, DC, MC, V. Daily 6:30–10:30pm.

Inventions *Value* INTERNATIONAL This may be the only buffet restaurant in Europe where animated characters from the Disney films (including Mickey and Minnie) go table-hopping. With views over a park, the restaurant contains four enormous buffet tables devoted to starters, shellfish, main courses, and desserts. Selections are wide, portions can be copious, and no one leaves hungry. Don't expect *grande cuisine*—that's the domain of the more upscale California Grill (see the previous listing), in the same hotel. What you'll get is a sense of American bounty and culinary generosity, with ample doses of cartoon fantasy.

In the Disneyland Hotel. ✆ **01-60-45-65-83.** Lunch buffet 35€ ($46) adults, 18€ ($23) children 7–11, 16€ ($21) children 3–6; dinner buffet 46€ ($60) adults, 24€ ($31) children 7–11, 18€ ($23) children under 7. AE, DC, MC, V. Daily 12:30–3pm and 6–10:30pm.

DISNEYLAND AFTER DARK

The premier theatrical venue is **Le Legende de Buffalo Bill** in Disney Village (✆ **01-60-45-71-00**). The twice-per-night stampede of entertainment recalls the show that once traveled the West with Buffalo Bill and Annie Oakley. You'll dine at tables arranged amphitheater-style around a rink where sharpshooters, runaway stagecoaches, and dozens of horses and Indians ride fast and perform alarmingly realistic acrobatics. A Texas-style barbecue, served in an assembly line by waiters in 10-gallon hats, is part of the experience. Despite its corny elements, it's not without its charm. Wild Bill is dignified and the Indians are suitably brave. Shows start at 6:30 and 9:30pm; the cost (dinner included) is 59€ ($77) for adults and 39€ ($51) for children 3 to 11.

7 The Remarkable Zoo of Château de Thoiry

40km (25 miles) W of Paris

Château et Parc Zoologique de Thoiry ★★ Known throughout Europe for its synthesis of the French Renaissance and modern pop culture, this attraction draws more visitors in a year than the Louvre or Versailles. The centerpiece of the estate is a 16th-century château, owned for generations by the family of the *vicomte* de la Panouse. Its architect, Philibert de L'Orme, conceived it as a transparent bridge of light, with the sun rising or setting in the center of its central archway during the summer and winter solstices. The creative and hardworking caretakers are Paul de la Panouse and his Minnesota-born wife, Annabelle. Displays include two original manuscripts of unpublished waltzes by Chopin; antique paintings and furniture; at least 600 letters exchanged during the *ancien régime* between the monarchs of France and Spain; letters to French aristocrats from Benjamin Franklin; and the financial records of France from 1745 to 1750. But despite its status as a treasure-trove of culture and documentation, the château is not as popular as the 485 hectares (1,200 acres) of land around it, 121 hectares (300 acres) of which have been transformed into a safari-inspired nature preserve.

Many of the more than 1,000 animals in the park—including elephants, giraffes, zebras, monkeys, rhinoceroses, alligators, lions, tigers, kangaroos, bears, and wolves—roam wild over fenced-off fields. Others, including many birds, are more ornamental, strutting peacefully in or near beautiful formal gardens. For part of your exploration, you'll drive, slowly, in your own (nonconvertible) car over a network of roads. Other subdivisions, including a lion park, require strolling through a Plexiglas tunnel, parts of which are aboveground, parts of which are buried to allow migrations of wildlife from one part of the park to another.

Thoiry-en-Yvelines 78770. Take Autoroute de l'Ouest (A13) toward Dreux. Exit at Bois-d'Arcy onto the N12 and follow signs on N12 and D11 to Thoiry. ✆ **01-34-87-52-25.** www.thoiry.tm.fr. Admission to château 6€ ($7.80) adults, 5€ ($6.50) students and children 3–12. Admission to nature reserve and park 26€ ($34) adults, 19€ ($24) students and children 3–12. May–Aug daily 10am–6pm; Feb–Apr and Sept–Oct daily 10am–5pm; Nov–Jan daily 11am–5pm.

WHERE TO STAY & DINE

Auberge de Thoiry ★ *Kids* In the heart of the village of Thoiry, some 183m (600 ft.) from the entrance to the safari park, this establishment dates from about 1890, when it was a postal relay station. It was later renovated into a charming hotel. Owner Jean-Paul le Moal decorated each guest room to evoke an animal (dog, tortoise, hippopotamus, and so forth). The hotel's low-key charm, its appeal to adults and children, its reasonable rates, and its restaurant—the best in town—make it quite enjoyable. Many of the original structure's stone walls and ceiling beams were preserved during renovations in the late 1990s, and painting techniques make the walls look much older than they really are. The restaurant's fixed-price menus cost 20€ to 25€ ($26–$33) Monday to Friday dinner, 13€ ($16) lunch; 25€ ($33) lunch and dinner on weekends.

38 rue de la porte St-Martin, Thoiry 78770. ✆ **01-34-87-40-21.** Fax 01-34-87-49-57. 12 units. 59€–81€ ($77–$105) double; 128€ ($166) family suite. DC, MC, V. Free parking. **Amenities:** Restaurant; bar; limited room service. *In room:* TV.

8 Giverny: In the Footsteps of Monet

81km (50 miles) NW of Paris

On the border between Normandy and the Ile de France, the Claude Monet Foundation preserves the estate where the great painter lived for 43 years. The restored house and its gardens are open to the public. Budget 2 hours to explore the museum and gardens at Giverny.

ESSENTIALS

GETTING THERE It takes a morning to get to Giverny and to see its sights. Take the Paris-Rouen **train** from Paris's Gare St-Lazare to the Vernon station, where a taxi can take you the 5km (3 miles) to Giverny. Vernon itself lies 40km (25 miles) southeast of Rouen. Perhaps the easiest way to get there is on a full-day **bus tour,** for 65€ ($85) per person, which focuses on Monet's house and garden. Tours depart at 1:45pm Tuesday to Saturday between April and October. You can arrange tours in the summer through **Cityrama,** 149 rue St-Honoré, 1er (✆ **01-44-55-61-00;** Métro: Palais-Royal–Musée du Louvre), or year-round through **American Express,** 11 rue Scribe, 9e (✆ **01-47-14-50-00;** Métro: Opéra).

If you're **driving,** take the Autoroute de l'Ouest (Port de St-Cloud) toward Rouen. Leave the autoroute at Bonnières, and then cross the Seine on the Bonnières Bridge. From here, a direct road with signs leads to Giverny. Expect it to take about an hour; try to avoid weekends. Another approach is to leave the highway at the Bonnières exit and go toward Vernon. Once there, cross the bridge over the Seine and follow signs to Giverny or Gasny (Giverny is before Gasny). This is easier than going through Bonnières, where there aren't many signs.

SHOW ME THE MONET

Claude Monet Foundation ★★★ Born in 1840, the French Impressionist was a brilliant innovator, excelling in presenting the effects of light at different times of day. Some critics claim that he "invented light." His paintings of the Rouen cathedral and of water lilies, which one critic called "vertical interpretations of horizontal lines," are just a few of his masterpieces.

Monet came to Giverny in 1883. Many of his friends visited him at this house (known as Le Pressoir), including Clemenceau, Cézanne, Rodin, Renoir, Degas, and Sisley. When Monet died in 1926, his son, Michel, inherited the house but left it abandoned. The gardens became almost a jungle, inhabited by river rats. In 1966, Michel died and left house and gardens to the Académie des Beaux-Arts. It wasn't until 1977 that Gerald van der Kemp, who restored Versailles, decided to work on Giverny. A large part of it was restored with gifts from U.S. benefactors, notably the late Lila Acheson Wallace, former head of *Reader's Digest.*

The house is open to the public. It contains Monet's collection of 18th- and 19th-century Japanese prints as well as antique (though not original) furnishings. From the painter's bedroom window, you'll have a stunning view of the gardens. You can stroll the garden and view the thousands of flowers, including the *nymphéas.* The Japanese bridge, hung with wisteria, leads to a setting of weeping willows and rhododendrons. Monet's studio barge was installed on the pond.

84 Rue Claude-Monet Parc Gasny. ✆ **02-32-51-28-21.** www.fondation-monet.com. Admission 5.50€ ($7.15) adults, 4€ ($5.20) students, 3€ ($3.90) children 7–18, free for children under 7. Apr–Oct Tues–Sun 9:30am–6pm. Closed Nov–Mar.

Musée d'Art Americain Giverny ★ *Finds* About 100 yards (92m) from Monet's former house and gardens, this museum showcases the U.S.-born artists, mainly Impressionists, who were influenced by Monet and lived at Giverny. Among the more famous painters were John Singer Sargent and William Metcalf, who often summered at Giverny, writing about "its glories" to other artists. The American painters came from 1887 onward, drawn more by the charm of the village than by the presence of Monet. An estimated 100 artists came to live in Giverny, although they did not have much contact, if any, with Monet. He considered these American painters "a nuisance."

An endowment by Daniel and Judith Terra of Chicago supports the museum. Daniel was an avid collector of Impressionist art until his death in 1996.

99 rue Claude-Monet. ✆ **02-32-51-94-65.** www.maag.org. Admission 5.50€ ($7.15) adults, 4€ ($5.20) seniors and students, 3€ ($3.90) children 12–18, free for children under 12. Free to all 1st Sun of each month. Apr–Oct Tues–Sun 10am–6pm. Closed Nov–Mar.

WHERE TO STAY

La Musardiere Giverny is becoming so popular with visitors that many local homes are opening as B&Bs. We find this small inn to be the best of the lot. A short walk from Monet's museum and gardens, it is a former manor house. An attraction in summer is the terraced and arbored garden.

A scenic park filled with ancient trees surrounds the hotel and restaurant. The mansard-roofed building dates from 1880 and was around in Monet's time. Many of the antique features and architectural adornments are still in place. *Musardiere* is French for a place for "idling or dawdling along," and that is just what you do here. Each medium-size guest room, attractively and comfortably furnished, has a small bathroom with tub or shower. The hotel also operates its own restaurant and creperie where fixed-price menus cost 26€ to 36€ ($34–$47).

123 Rue Claude-Monet, Giverny 27620. ✆ **02-32-21-03-18.** Fax 02-32-21-60-00. 11 units. 59€–77€ ($77–$100) double; 92€–106€ ($120–$138) suite. AE, DC, MC, V. Free parking. **Amenities:** Restaurant; bar. *In room:* TV, hair dryer.

WHERE TO DINE

Auberge du Vieux Moulin TRADITIONAL FRENCH This is a convenient lunch stop near the Monet house. The restaurant is in a stone building with a pair of flowering terraces. The Boudeau family maintains a series of dining rooms filled with original Impressionist paintings. Specialties range from escalope of salmon with sorrel sauce to aiguillettes of duckling with peaches. The kitchen doesn't pretend that the food is anything more than good country fare with a dash of panache. The charm of the staff helps a lot, too. You can walk here from the museum in about 5 minutes; leave your car in the museum lot.

21 rue de la Falaise. ✆ **02-32-51-46-15.** Reservations recommended. Main courses 16€–19€ ($21–$25); fixed-price menu 15€–35€ ($20–$46). AE, MC, V. Dec–Oct daily noon–3pm and 7–10pm.

Baudy FRENCH We hesitate to recommend this place because of the never-ending buses arriving from Paris, but it's a local legend and deserves a look. During the town's 19th-century heyday, the American painters used the pink villa as their lodging. In Monet's time, this place was an *epicerie-buvette* (casual hangout) run by the painter's friends, Angelina and Gaston Baudy. Metcalf was the first artist to arrive on Mme Baudy's doorstep, and in time a string of other painters followed. Artists such as Cézanne could be found wandering around the rose garden here. The place no longer has its "legendary two tables," at which Mme Baudy fed the artists, but it plays host to virtually all visitors to Giverny, feeding them simply prepared, traditional French cuisine, including big, freshly made salads and a changing array of hot food.

81 rue Claude-Monet. ✆ **02-32-21-10-03.** Reservations recommended. Main courses 11€–16€ ($14–$21); fixed-price menu 19€ ($24). MC, V. Tues–Sat 10am–7pm; Sun 10am–3pm. Closed Nov–Mar.

Restaurant Les Fleurs ★ FRENCH Capably managed by Michel and Annie Graux, this pleasant, popular restaurant does a large percentage of its business with art lovers. The Claude Monet Foundation is just across the river in Giverny. On the main street of Vernon, 4.8km (3 miles) southwest of the museum, the restaurant focuses on flavorful, familiar *cuisine bourgeoise* that many diners remember fondly from their childhoods. Chef Michel served an apprenticeship with culinary mega-star Alain Ducasse. Menu items include fresh fish, such as sea bass served with saffron sauce; a flavorful risotto of the day; and sweetbreads braised with Parmesan. Other dishes include fresh scallops with lobster-flavored cream sauce; a platter devoted to different preparations of duckling; and a variety of meats grilled, simply and flavorfully, *à la plancha.*

71 rue Sadi-Carnot, Vernon. From the Claude Monet Foundation in Giverny, drive 5km (3 miles) southwest, crossing the Seine, and follow signs to Vernon. ✆ **02-32-51-16-80.** Reservations recommended. Main courses 14€–20€ ($18–$26); fixed-price menu 24€–47€ ($31–$61). AE, MC, V. Tues–Sun noon–2:30pm; Tues–Sat 7:30–10pm. Closed May 1 and Aug 31.

9 Chantilly: A Day at the Races ★★★

42km (26 miles) N of Paris, 50km (31 miles) SE of Beauvais

This is a resort town for Parisians who want a quick weekend getaway. Known for its frothy whipped cream and its black lace, it also draws visitors to its racetrack and château.

Two of the great French horse races, **Le Prix du Jockey Club** and the **Prix Diane-Hermès,** take place at the Hippodrome on the first and second Sundays of June, respectively. Thoroughbreds from as far away as Kentucky and Brunei, as well as entrants sponsored by old and new European money, compete in a very civil format that's broadcast throughout France.

ESSENTIALS

GETTING THERE **Trains** depart frequently for Chantilly from Gare du Nord in Paris. The ride takes about 30 minutes; the round-trip cost is 15€ ($20). On race days, free shuttle buses take fans from the Chantilly station to the track. Alternatively, RER line D will get you from Métro stop Châtelet–Les Halles to Chantilly in about 45 minutes.

VISITOR INFORMATION The **Office Tourisme** is at 60 av. du Maréchal-Joffre (✆ **03-44-67-37-37;** www.chantilly-tourisme.com).

SEEING THE CHATEAU & MUSEUMS

Château de Chantilly/Musée Condé ★★★ Once the seat of the grand Condé, head of the Bourbon-Condé dynasty, this château and the museum within it are on an artificial lake. Approach on the same forested drive that Louis XIV rode for a banquet prepared by his chef, Vatel. (One day when the fish didn't arrive on time, Vatel committed suicide.) The château is French Renaissance, with gables and towers, but part was rebuilt in the 19th century. A forest once filled with stag and boar skirts it.

In 1886, the château's owner, the duc d'Aumale, bequeathed the park and palace to the Institut de France, along with his art collection and library. The château houses sumptuous furnishings as well as works by artists such as Memling, Van Dyck, Botticelli, Poussin, Watteau, Ingres, Delacroix, Corot, Rubens, and Vernet. See Raphael's *Madonna of Lorette, Virgin of the House d'Orléans,* and *Three Graces* (sometimes called the *Three Ages of Woman*). A series of about 40 miniatures represents the foremost French painter of the 15th century, Jean Fouquet. A copy of the rose diamond that received worldwide attention when it was stolen in 1926 is occasionally on display in the jewel collection. One of the most celebrated Condé acquisitions is the Limbourg brothers' *Les Très Riches Heures du Duc de Berry,* a 15th-century illuminated manuscript illustrating the months of the year, which is not always on view.

The château was built about 1560 by Jean Bullant for a member of the Montmorency family. The stables (see below), a hallmark of French 18th-century architecture, were constructed to house 240 horses, with adjacent kennels for 500 hounds. If you have time, take a walk in the garden laid out by Le Nôtre. A hamlet of rustic cottages and the Maison de Sylvie, a graceful building constructed in 1604 and rebuilt by Maria-Felice Orsini, are in the park.

If you don't want to see the château and its museum, you can visit the gardens (4€/$5.20 adults, 3.50€/$4.55 children 13–17, 2.50€/$3.25 children 4–12). Once you're in the garden, you can ride a narrow-gauge electric railway (touristy and loaded with children) through the park, or take a boat ride with lots of other passengers on the château's ornamental lake. Either of these requires a supplement of 7.50€ to 9€ ($9.75–$12) per person, depending on the duration of your ride and the age of the passenger.

Chantilly. ✆ **03-44-62-62-62.** www.chateaudechantilly.com. Admission to the château, museum, and gardens 8€ ($10) adults, 7€ ($9.10) children 13–17, 3.50€ ($4.55) children 4–12. Audio guides 2€ ($2.60). Nov to mid-Mar Mon and Wed–Fri 10:30am–12:45pm and 2–5pm, Sat–Sun 10:30am–5pm; mid-Mar to Apr and Sept–Oct Mon and Wed–Fri 10:30am–12:45pm and 2–6pm, Sat–Sun 10am–6pm; May–Aug Wed–Mon 10am–6pm.

Les Grandes Ecuries/Musée Vivant du Cheval ★★ This museum occupies the restored Grandes Ecuries, the stables built between 1719 and 1735 for Louis-Henri, prince de Bourbon and prince de Condé, who occupied the château. Besides being fond of horses, he believed in reincarnation and expected to come back as a horse in his next life, so he built stables fit for a king.

The stables and an adjoining kennel fell into ruin, but they've been restored as a museum of the living horse, with thoroughbreds housed alongside old breeds of draft horses, Arabs and Hispano-Arabs, and farm horses. Exhibits trace the horse's association with humans and include a blacksmith shop and displays of saddles, equipment for the care of horses, and horse-race memorabilia.

Daily equestrian displays (Apr–Oct) last about 30 minutes and explain how the horse is ridden and trained (11:30am, 3:30pm, and occasionally 5:15pm).

Chantilly. ✆ **03-44-57-40-40.** www.museevivantducheval.fr. Admission 8.50€ ($11) adults, 7.80€ ($10) children 13–17, 6.50€ ($8.45) children 4–12, free for children under 4. Apr–Oct Mon and Wed–Fri 10:30am–5:30pm, Sat–Sun and holidays 10:30am–6pm; Nov–Mar Mon and Wed–Fri 2–5pm, Sat–Sun 10:30am–5:30pm.

WHERE TO STAY

Best Western Hôtel du Parc This 1987 hotel is in the center of town, close to a host of restaurants and sights. There are grander châteaux in Chantilly, but if you want a midtown location, this is your finest choice. The contemporary lobby, dominated by mirrors and chrome, gives way to an inviting English-style bar, with plenty of dark wood and leather. The medium-size guest rooms have built-in furnishings and glass doors that open onto private balconies. About half of the small bathrooms have both tub and shower. Overall, expect a no-frills experience that's pleasant but nothing special.

36 av. du Maréchal-Joffre, Chantilly 60500. ✆ **800/528-1234** in the U.S. and Canada, or 03-44-58-20-00. Fax 03-44-57-31-10. www.bestwestern.fr. 57 units. 100€–150€ ($130–$195) double; 130€–180€ ($169–$234) suite. AE, DC, MC, V. Parking 8€ ($10). **Amenities:** Bar; room service; laundry service; dry cleaning; nonsmoking rooms. *In room:* TV, coffeemaker, hair dryer.

Château de Chaumontel ★ This hotel-restaurant from the late 16th century lies 8km (5 miles) south of Chantilly. Accented with conical towers and slate roofs, it was once the hunting lodge of the prince de Condé. In 1956, it became a hotel. Rooms range from units with high, sloping ceilings and antique beams to elegant replicas of a chamber you'd find in a manor house. Most bathrooms have tubs and showers. Surrounded by a moat and a landscape dotted with wildflowers, the château is as evocative a site as any in this region. The rustic dining room serves excellent meals.

21 rue André-Vassord, Chaumontel 95270. Take N16 south for 6.5km (4 miles). ✆ **01-34-71-00-30.** Fax 01-34-71-26-97. www.chateau-chaumontel.fr. 18 units. 79€–142€ ($103–$185) double; 157€ ($204) suite. Extra bed 12€ ($16). AE, DC, MC, V. **Amenities:** Restaurant; bar; bike rentals; room service; laundry service; dry cleaning. *In room:* TV, hair dryer.

Château de la Tour ★★ A wealthy Parisian banking family built this elegant turn-of-the-20th-century château with a 4.8-hectare (12-acre) park as a weekend getaway. During World War II, it was the home of the German l'Etat Major, and in 1946, it became a luxury hotel. The likes of Edith Piaf, Tino Rossi, and Jean Gabin met and mingled in the restaurant. Today, celebrities and sports personalities still frequent the château. In 1990, it gained a new wing; guests can choose rooms with a modern flavor or a more traditional ambience. All units are large and feature hardwood floors, high ceilings, and first-class furnishings, and half of the units are air-conditioned.

Most of the well-maintained bathrooms have a tub/shower combination. Public areas feature two wood-burning fireplaces.

Chemin de la Chaussée, Chantilly-Gouvieux 60270. ✆ **03-44-62-38-38.** Fax 03-44-57-31-97. www.lechateaudelatour.fr. 41 units. 140€–215€ ($182–$280) double. AE, DC, MC, V. Free parking. **Amenities:** Restaurant; bar; outdoor pool; tennis court; bike rentals; room service; babysitting; laundry service. *In room:* A/C, TV, minibar, hair dryer.

WHERE TO DINE

The restaurant at the **Château de la Tour** (see above) is open to the public for lunch and dinner.

La Ferme de Condé TRADITIONAL FRENCH The most appealing restaurant in Chantilly is in a 100-year-old stone-sided former Anglican church. It's on the periphery of town, about a mile north of the château. Antique farm implements, racks of wine bottles, and barrels give the space a cozy feel. The cuisine is old-fashioned, with variations based on seasonal ingredients and the chef's inspiration. Examples include a terrine *de basse cour,* combining poultry, rabbit, and duck; sweetbread with morels; and a succulent version of suckling pig roasted on a spit and served with fresh thyme and veal kidneys in mustard-flavored cream sauce. Also look for fricassee of scallops with white wine and herbs, and salmon *verdurette,* served with cream sauce and fresh local herbs.

42 av. du Maréchal-Joffre. ✆ **03-44-57-32-31.** Reservations recommended. Main courses 17€–25€ ($22–$33); fixed-price menu 24€–28€ ($31–$36). AE, DC, MC, V. Daily noon–2pm and 7–10pm.

10 Senlis ★★

52km (32 miles) S of Paris, 100km (62 miles) S of Amiens

Sleepy Senlis, which some Parisians treat as a suburb, is a quiet township surrounded by forests. Its memories are many and regal. Barbarians no longer threaten its walls as they did in the 3rd century, and gone are the kings of France, from Clovis to Louis XIV, who passed through or took up temporary residence. You can tie a visit to this town with a trek to Chantilly (see above). Today, the core of Vieux Senlis is an archaeological bonanza that attracts visitors from all over the world. Budget 2 hours to see Senlis.

ESSENTIALS

GETTING THERE Approximately 20 **trains** daily depart from Paris's Gare du Nord for Chantilly (see above). In front of the railway station in Chantilly, **bus** no. 15 (marked SENLIS) has a schedule that coincides with the arrival of trains from Paris. The round-trip bus and train fare is 16€ ($21). Total travel time from downtown Paris to Senlis is 45 to 60 minutes.

VISITOR INFORMATION The **Office de Tourisme** is on place parvis Notre-Dame (✆ **03-44-53-06-40;** www.ville-senlis.fr).

SEEING THE SIGHTS

Medieval streets loaded with antique masonry and evocative doorways run throughout the city. One of the most interesting is the **rue du Chat-Harét;** from its center, it affords a view over the ruined château and the Gallo-Roman foundations. The **rue des Cordeliers** is the site of a (since demolished) medieval convent, and nos. 14 and 10 on that street are particularly beautiful and old, but neither is open to the public.

Cathédrale Notre-Dame de Senlis ★★ This cathedral has a 13th-century spire that rises 77m (253 ft.) and dominates the countryside. The severe western facade contrasts with the Flamboyant Gothic southern portal. A fire swept the structure in 1504, and much rebuilding followed. A 19th-century overlay was applied to the original structure, begun in 1153. Before you enter, walk around to the western porch to see the sculptures. Depicted in stone is a calendar of the seasons, along with scenes showing the ascension of the Virgin. The builders of the main portal imitated the work at Chartres. In the forecourt are memorials to Joan of Arc and Marshal Foch.

3 Place Notre-Dame. ✆ **03-44-53-01-59.** Free admission. Daily 8:30am–7pm.

Château Royal et Parc and Musée de la Vénerie (Hunting Museum) ★ A short walk from the cathedral stands this curious archaeological ruin. Its stones have more royal associations than virtually anywhere else in France. The most impressive aspect remaining today is a massive Gallo-Roman wall, in some places more than 6m (20 ft.) tall. It encircles an area of about 6 hectares (15 acres), some of them occupied by parts of medieval Senlis. Of the wall's 28 original watchtowers, 16 remain. Within the circumference, the best-preserved fortification of its kind in France, are the ruins of a château that was occupied, or at least visited, by virtually every monarch of France from Hughes Capet (in the 10th c.) to Henri IV (late Renaissance). Abandoned by the monarchs around 1600, the château was demolished after the French Revolution. Today, you can wander freely among the ruins, imagining the grandeur of life as it used to be.

The complex's highlight, in the verdant park that surrounds the ruin, is the **Prieuré St-Mauritius,** a monastery that not only honors a saint but also was founded by one, Louis IX. It houses the **Musée de la Vénerie (Hunting Museum),** where you'll see hunting-related works of art from the 15th century to the present. Exhibits include arms, horns, trophies, drawings, engravings, and old hunting suits and costumes, all of which evoke the passion and pageantry that used to surround royal hunting expeditions. You can visit the museum only as part of a 1-hour tour (in French); tours begin every hour on the hour.

Senlis. ✆ **03-44-32-00-81.** Free admission to the park. Admission to the Hunting Museum including guided tour 4.25€ ($5.55) adults, 2€ ($2.60) students and children 12–18, free for children under 12. Mon, Wed, Thurs, Fri 10am–noon and 2–6pm; Sat–Sun 11am–1pm and 2–6pm.

Musée d'Art et d'Archeologie No other site in Senlis depicts the ancient Roman occupation of Gaul in such vivid terms. In the partially Gothic former home of the local bishop, the museum, which opened in 1989, contains most of the archaeological artifacts of the Gallo-Romans in the region. It also includes rare sculptures and church art from the Middle Ages. One floor above street level, you'll find paintings, some by local artists working in an untrained style that art historians refer to as "naive," executed between the 17th and 20th century.

Place Notre-Dame. ✆ **03-44-32-00-83.** Admission 4€ ($5.20) adults, 2€ ($2.60) students and children 16–18, free for children under 16. Mon and Thurs–Fri 10am–noon and 2–6pm; Wed 2–6pm; Sat–Sun and holidays 11am–1pm and 2–6pm.

WHERE TO STAY & DINE

Hostellerie de la Porte Bellon In a town of lackluster inns, this is a good oasis for the night. The stately but relatively inexpensive hotel was built as a convent 300 years ago and later functioned as a coaching inn. A short walk east of Senlis's historic core, it has three floors of big-windowed guest rooms and a facade dotted with old-fashioned shutters and window boxes filled with pansies and geraniums. At the entrance is an unusual 19th-century glass vestibule inspired by an English greenhouse. Accommodations have comfortable beds and cheerful wallpaper, but are a bit spartan. Most have a tub/shower combination.

51 rue Bellon, Senlis 60300. ✆ **03-44-53-03-05.** Fax 03-44-53-29-94. 19 units. 65€–82€ ($85–$107) double; 195€ ($254) 3-bedroom suite. AE, MC, V. Closed Dec 18–Jan 8. **Amenities:** Restaurant; bar. *In room:* TV, dataport.

Vieille Auberge *Value* TRADITIONAL FRENCH This building has held a restaurant since 1558, when it served burned and greasy food to wayfarers and pilgrims headed for the nearby cathedral. Today, considerably cleaned up, it has Louis-Philippe furniture and one large candlelit dining room that consists of three separate spaces. The refined, rustic dining areas have stone walls and heavy tables. During warm months, guests can sit on a small terrace. The staff takes pride in serving classic French dishes, which may include such favorites as monkfish *tournedos* in piquant pepper sauce, filet of beef in country wine sauce accompanied by a vegetable crepe, and duck filet with foie gras and whole-grain mustard sauce. Though the cuisine isn't worth a special drive from Paris, the restaurant is memorable for its atmosphere and perfectly prepared dishes.

8 rue Long Filet. ✆ **03-44-60-95-50.** Reservations recommended Fri–Sat. Main courses 16€–22€ ($21–$29); fixed-price menu 22€–32€ ($29–$42). AE, DC, MC, V. Wed–Mon noon–2pm; Wed–Sat and Mon 7–9:30pm.

11 Compiègne ★★★

81km (50 miles) N of Paris

A visit to this Oise River valley town is usually combined with an excursion to Senlis, a quiet township with medieval streets surrounded by forests, some 32km (20 miles) away. The most famous dance step of all time was photographed in a forest about 6.5km (4 miles) from town: Hitler's "jig of joy" on June 22, 1940, heralded the ultimate humiliation of France and shocked the world.

Like Senlis, this town north of Paris lives for its memories—not all pleasant. Many come to visit the 14,160-hectare (35,000-acre) forest of Compiègne. With its majestic vistas, venerable trees, and ponds, it merits exploration.

ESSENTIALS

GETTING THERE **Trains** run frequently from the Gare du Nord in Paris. The ride takes 50 minutes. The station is across the river from the town center. A round-trip ticket costs 24€ ($31). If you're **driving,** take the Paris-Lille motorway (A1 or the less convenient E15) for 81km (50 miles).

VISITOR INFORMATION The **Office de Tourisme** is located at 28 Hôtel-de-Ville (✆ **03-44-40-01-00**).

SEEING THE SIGHTS

An imposing statue of **Joan of Arc,** who was taken prisoner at Compiègne by the Burgundians on May 23, 1430, stands in the town square.

Musée National du Château de Compiègne ★★★ In its heyday, Compiègne attracted royalty and two Bonaparte emperors. But this wasn't always a place of pageantry. Louis XIV once said: "In Versailles, I live in the style befitting a monarch. In Fontainebleau, more like a prince. At Compiègne, like a peasant." But the Sun

King returned again and again. His successor, Louis XV, started rebuilding the château, based on plans by Gabriel. The king died before work was completed, and Louis XVI and Marie Antoinette expanded it.

Napoleon's second wife, Marie-Louise, arrived at Compiègne to marry him; in a dining room, which you can visit only on the guided tour, she had her first meal with the emperor. Accounts maintain that she was paralyzed with fear of the older man (Napoleon was in his 40s; she was 19). After dinner, he seduced her and is said to have only increased her anxiety.

During the Second Empire, Compiègne reached its pinnacle. Under Napoleon III and Eugénie, the hunting season was the occasion for balls and parties. Women in elegant hoop skirts danced to Strauss waltzes; Offenbach's operas echoed through the chambers and salons; and Eugénie, who fancied herself an actress, performed in the palace theater for her guests.

On the tour, you'll see the gold-and-scarlet Empire Room, where Napoleon spent many a troubled night, and his library, known for its secret door. In the Queen's Chamber, Marie-Louise used the "horn of plenty" bed.

Various wings of the château hold museums. They include the **Musée National de la Voiture (National Automobile Museum),** which exhibits about 150 vehicles, from Ben-Hur chariots to a Citroën "chain-track" vehicle. The château also contains a series of rooms defined as either the **Musée de l'Imperatrice Eugénie,** the Musée du Second Empire, or the Musée Napoléon III, depending on who happens to be talking about it. It's devoted to sculpture, paintings (including some by Carpeaux), and furniture, as well as mementos and documents showcasing life, politics, values, and morals of France's Industrial Revolution and its Gilded Age.

Place du Palais. ✆ **03-44-38-47-02.** www.musee-chateau-compiegne.fr. Admission (including access to museums) 5.50€ ($7.15) adults, 4€ ($5.20) students 18–25, free for children under 18. Wed–Mon 10am–6pm.

Château de Pierrefonds ★★ One of the Compiègne forest's most evocative medieval buildings lies 12km (7½ miles) north of the town. (To reach it from the center, follow signs to Soissons.) Originally built in the 1100s as a château-fortress, it was later bought by Napoleon. Surrounded by a moat, it looks feudal, with rounded towers capped by funnel-shaped pointed roofs. Artifacts from the Middle Ages are displayed inside. Save time for a stroll through the tiny village of Pierrefonds at the base of the château. Here, half-timbered houses recall the château's medieval heyday.

In the Forêt de Compiègne. ✆ **03-44-42-72-72.** http://perso.wanadoo.fr/espace-libre/pierrefonds.html. Admission 6.50€ ($8.45) adults, 4.50€ ($5.85) students 18–25, free for children under 18. May–Aug daily 9:30am–6pm; Sept–Apr daily 10am–1pm and 2–5:30pm.

Musée de la Figurine Historique (Museum of Historical Figurines) ★ Housed in one of Compiègne's finest monuments, the Flamboyant Gothic Hôtel de Ville, built from 1499 to 1503, this museum boasts a collection of about 100,000 tin soldiers, from a Louis XIV trumpeter to a World War II soldier. The Battle of Waterloo, staged in miniature on a landscape with thousands of figurines, is depicted in all its gore.

Place de l'Hôtel-de-Ville. ✆ **03-44-40-72-55.** Admission 2€ ($2.60) adults, 1€ ($1.30) seniors and students, free for children under 18. Tues–Sat 9am–noon; Tues–Sun 2–6pm (until 5pm Nov–Feb).

Wagon de l'Armistice (Wagon du Maréchal-Foch) ★★ In 1940, in one of the most perverse twists of fate in European history, Hitler forced the vanquished French to capitulate in the same rail coach where German officials signed the Armistice on

November 11, 1918. The triumphant Nazis transported the coach to Berlin, and then to Ordüff in the Thuringian Forest, where an Allied bomb destroyed it in April 1945. In Compiègne's suburb of Rethondes, 6.5km (4 miles) to the south, you can visit a replica that recounts the events of 1918 and 1940 in graphic detail, assisted by newspapers, photos, maps, and slide shows.

Rte. de Soissons, Rethondes. ✆ **03-44-85-14-18.** Admission 4€ ($5.20) adults, 2€ ($2.60) children 7–14, free for children under 7. Apr to mid-Oct Wed–Mon 9am–12:30pm and 2–6:30pm; mid-Oct to Mar Wed–Mon 9am–noon and 2–5:30pm.

WHERE TO STAY

The **Rôtisserie du Chat Qui Tourne** (see "Where to Dine," below) also rents rooms.

Hostellerie du Royal-Lieu ★ This half-timbered inn is the best choice for food and lodging close to the town, about 2km (1¼ miles) away. Guest rooms are medium in size, sleekly designed, and the bathrooms are tidily organized. The rooms and the restaurant's terrace overlook a garden. Meals in the elegantly rustic dining room may include four-fish stew with red butter, or brochette of quail with black olives and polenta. Prices range from 23€ to 46€ ($30–$60). Dessert soufflés are available if you order them 30 minutes in advance.

9 rue de Senlis, Compiègne 60200. Follow signs southwest toward Senlis until you reach rue de Senlis, a 5-min. drive east of the town center. ✆ **03-44-20-10-24.** Fax 03-44-86-82-27. www.host-royallieu.com. 20 units. 83€ ($108) double; 105€ ($137) suite. AE, DC, MC, V. **Amenities:** Restaurant; bar; room service. *In room:* TV, hair dryer.

WHERE TO DINE

The restaurant at the **Hostellerie du Royal-Lieu** is also open to the public.

Rôtisserie du Chat Qui Tourne TRADITIONAL FRENCH The name, "Inn of the Cat That Turns the Spit," dates from 1665. The bar and a country inn–style dining room are downstairs. The *menu gastronomique* is likely to include *foie gras de canard* (duck), then *cassolette de Roguens* (veal kidneys), followed by either *poulet rôti à la broche* (chicken roasted on a spit) or *tournedos* of salmon with mushrooms, a cheese, and dessert. Other well-received menu items include a savory version of leek *tarte* and pigeon in puff pastry.

In the Hôtel de France, 17 rue Eugène-Floquet, Compiègne 60200. ✆ **03-44-40-02-74.** Reservations recommended. Main courses 15€–20€ ($20–$26); fixed-price menu 18€–45€ ($23–$59). AE, MC, V. Tues–Sun noon–2pm; Tues–Sat 7–9:30pm.

8

The Loire Valley

Bordered by vineyards, the winding Loire Valley cuts through the land of castles deep in France's heart. Medieval crusaders returning here brought news of the opulence of the East, and soon they began rethinking their surroundings. Later, word came from Italy of an artistic flowering led by Leonardo and Michelangelo. Royalty and nobility built châteaux in this valley during the French Renaissance, and an era of pomp reigned until Henri IV moved his court to Paris, marking the Loire's decline.

The Loire is blessed with attractions, including medieval, Renaissance, and classical châteaux, Romanesque and Gothic churches, and treasures such as the Apocalypse Tapestries. There's even the castle that inspired *Sleeping Beauty.* Trains serve some towns, but the best way to see this region is by car.

1 Orléans ★

119km (74 miles) SW of Paris, 72km (45 miles) SE of Chartres

After suffering damage in World War II, many Orléans neighborhoods were rebuilt in dull styles, so visitors who hope to see how it looked when the Maid of Orléans (Joan of Arc) was here are likely to be disappointed. Today, this city of 200,000 has lost a lot of its importance to Tours, but signs of restoration bring hope for the future.

ESSENTIALS

GETTING THERE Ten **trains** per day arrive from Paris's Gare d'Austerlitz (trip time: 1 hr., 15 min.); there are also a dozen connections from Tours (trip time: 50 min.). The one-way fare from Tours to Orléans is 15€ ($20). Orléans lies on the road between Paris and Tours. If you're **driving** from Paris, take A10 south; from Tours, take A10 north.

VISITOR INFORMATION The **Office de Tourisme** is at 2 place de L'Etape (✆ **02-38-24-05-05;** www.ville-orleans.fr).

EXPLORING THE TOWN

Orléans is the chief town of Loiret, on the Loire, and beneficiary of many associations with the French aristocracy. It gave its name to ducs and duchesses of Orléans. In 1429, **Joan of Arc** relieved the city from attacks by the Burgundians and the English. That deliverance is celebrated every year on May 8, the anniversary of her victory. An equestrian statue of Jeanne d'Arc stands on place du Martroi. From the square, you can drive down rue Royal (rebuilt in 18th-c. style) across pont George-V (erected in 1760). A simple cross marks the site of the Fort des Tourelles, which Joan of Arc and her men captured.

Finds **Biking Your Way through the Loire**

Once you're in Tours, you can rely on public transport to see much of the Loire. You can also rent a bicycle—the region is relatively flat. **Amstercycles,** 5 rue du Rempart, Tours (✆ **02-47-61-22-23**), rents mountain bikes and all-purpose bikes for 13€ to 21€ ($17–$27) per day. A deposit (usually a credit card imprint) is required. The shop is only 46m (150 ft.) from the rail station. A full-day excursion that may interest some experienced mountain bikers involves a 35km (22-mile) jaunt from Tours to Chenonceaux, following a rugged path that for the most part meanders beside the Cher River. Amstercycles provides a map for this itinerary and advice about how best to navigate the bumps. The railway station at Tours doesn't check baggage, so the shop guards bags. The service, available to customers and noncustomers, costs 2€ ($2.60) per day and is available from May to September Monday to Saturday 9am to 12:30pm and 2 to 7pm, Sunday 6 to 7pm only. Off-season hours are erratic.

An excellent itinerary involves riding 17km (11 miles) west of Tours to the Jardins de Villandry. The relatively flat and scenic road takes you along the bank of the Cher River. From here, continue 8km (5 miles) to the Château de Langeais, also a lovely route. If you want to head east from Tours, consider the 24km (15-mile) excursion to Amboise. This route is more densely trafficked and not as bucolic. The tourist office provides maps.

Near rue Royale is **place du Châtelet,** with many boutiques, including a Galeries Lafayette. Look for fashionable clothing, jewelry, books, and leather goods. For antiques, walk along **rue de Bourgogne,** where a host of dealers offer everything from objets d'art to furniture.

Cathédrale Ste-Croix ★ Begun in 1287, after an earlier Romanesque church here collapsed from old age, the cathedral was burned by the Huguenots in 1568. Henri IV laid the first stone of the present building in 1601, and work continued until 1829. The cathedral boasts a 17th-century organ and woodwork from the early 18th century in its chancel, the masterpiece of Jules Hardouin-Mansart and other artists associated with Louis XIV. You'll need to take the guided tour to see the chancel, the crypt, and the treasury, with its Byzantine enamels, gold work from the 15th and 16th centuries, and Limoges enamels.

Place Ste-Croix. ✆ **02-38-77-87-50.** Free admission; tip the guide 1€ ($1.30) if you take a guided tour. June–Aug daily 9:15am–7pm; Sept daily 9:15am–5:45pm; Jan–May and Oct–Dec daily 9:15am–noon and 2:15–5:45pm.

Eglise St-Aignan One of the most frequently altered churches in the Loire Valley, St-Aignan was consecrated in 1509 in the form you see today. It possesses one of France's earliest vaulted hall crypts, complete with polychromed capitals. Scholars of pre-Romanesque art view the place with interest; its 10th- and 11th-century aesthetics are rare. Aboveground, the church's Renaissance-era choir and transept remain, but the Protestants burned the nave during the Wars of Religion. In a wood-carved shrine are the remains of the church's patron saint.

The Loire Valley

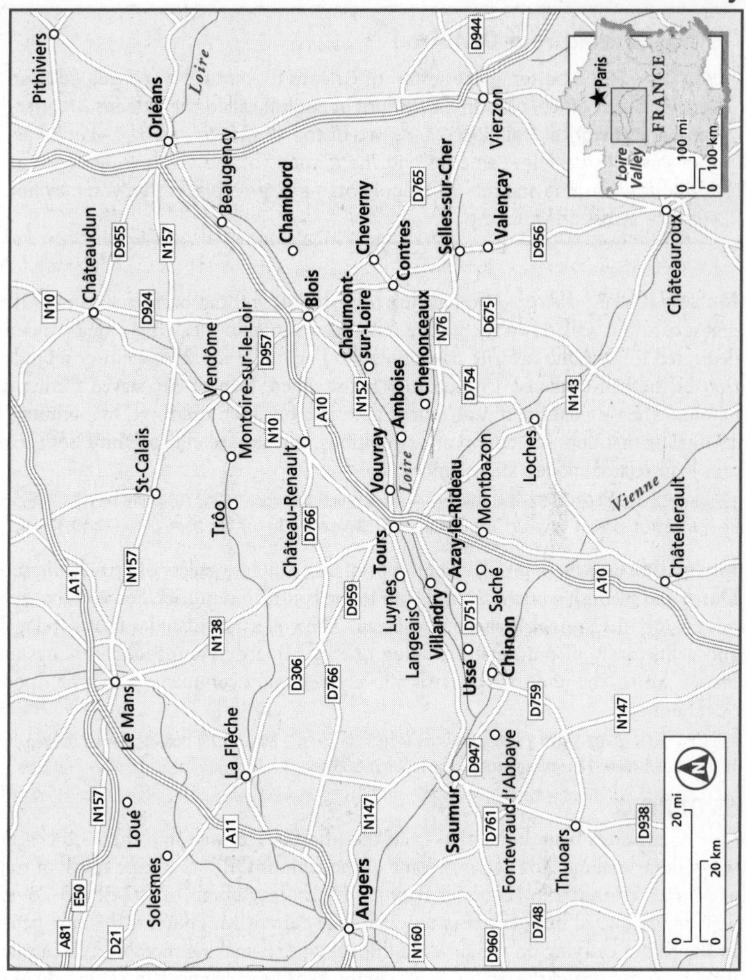

Place St-Aignan. No phone; ask at tourist office. Free admission. Church hours vary; usually open only during Mass. Crypt July–Aug daily 1–6pm.

Hôtel Groslot This Renaissance mansion was begun in 1550 and embellished in the 19th century. François II (first husband of Mary, Queen of Scots) lived here during the fall of 1560 and died on December 5. Between the Revolution and the mid-1970s, it functioned as the town hall. Marriage ceremonies, performed by the town's magistrates, still occur here. It was here that Charles IX met his lovely Marie Touchet. The statue of Joan of Arc praying was the work of Louis Philippe's daughter, Princesse Marie d'Orléans. In the garden you can see the remains of the 15th-century Chapelle St-Jacques.

Place de l'Etape (northwest of the cathedral). ✆ **02-38-79-22-30.** Free admission. July–Sept Mon–Fri 9am–7pm, Sat 5–8pm; Oct–June Mon–Fri and Sun 10am–noon and 2–6pm.

Tips Blazing Your Own Trail

You may gain a better appreciation of Orléans if you take a self-guided tour. At the tourist office, pick up a brochure in English called the **Orléans Architectural and Historical Trail** (2€/$2.60). Two of the 43 sites on the trail—Louis Pasteur Park on rue Jules-Lemaitre and the gardens of the Vieille Intendance at rue Alsace-Lorraine and rue des Huguenots—are great places that you may not stumble across on your own.

Maison Jeanne-d'Arc After visiting the Groslot, you can backtrack to the cathedral square and walk down rue Jeanne-d'Arc, across rue Royale, to see a small museum dedicated to Orléans's favorite mademoiselle. The house is a 20th-century reproduction of the half-timbered 15th-century house where Joan of Arc stayed during her heroics. The original house was much modified, but then destroyed by bombing in 1940. The first floor has temporary exhibitions, and the second and third floors contain Joan-related models and memorabilia.

3 place de Gaulle. ✆ **02-38-52-99-89.** www.jeannedarc.com.fr. Admission 2€ ($2.60) adults, 1€ ($1.30) students, free for children under 16. May–Oct Tues–Sun 10am–12:30pm and 1:30–6:30pm; Nov–Apr Tues–Sun 1:30–6pm.

Musée des Beaux-Arts ★★ This is primarily a picture gallery of French and some Dutch and Flemish works from the 16th to the late 19th centuries. Some of the works once hung in Cardinal Richelieu's château. The collection includes busts by Pigalle and a fine array of portraits, including one of Mme de Pompadour. Among non-French works, the undisputed star is a lovely Velázquez commemorating the Apostle St. Thomas.

Place Ste. Croix. ✆ **02-38-79-21-55.** Admission 4€ ($5.20) adults, 2.50€ ($3.25) students, free for children under 16. Tues–Sat 9:30am–12:15pm and 1:30–5:45pm; Sun 2–6:30pm.

SHOPPING

One of the city's main industries, from the Middle Ages well into the 20th century, was vinegar making. You can buy some of the famous Orléans vinegar north of town at **Martin Pouret,** 236 Faubourg Bannier, Fleury-les-Aubrais (✆ **02-38-88-78-49**). The family-owned business dates to 1797. The current M. Pouret is the only person in the region carrying on the slow, traditional vinegar-making method. You can do a wine tasting at one of the region's most comprehensive wine merchants, **Cave de Marc & Sebastien,** 7 place du Châtelet (✆ **02-38-62-94-11**), in the heart of the commercial center, just north of the Loire and west of rue Royale.

WHERE TO STAY

Hôtel d'Arc This four-story hotel, built in the 1920s, with an Art Deco facade and old-fashioned elevator, sits in the middle of the town and is close to the railway station and the pedestrian-only shopping streets. The guest rooms feature ceiling moldings and paneling. Most are of average size; the largest units have numbers that end in 2. Half of the bathrooms come with a tub and shower. Most rooms are peaceful, but avoid those that face rue de la République, which tend to be noisy. Although the hotel has no restaurant, it serves breakfast in an ornate room with a carved marble fireplace.

37 rue de la République, 45000 Orléans. ✆ **02-38-53-10-94.** Fax 02-38-81-77-47. www.hoteldarc.fr. 36 units. 90€–116€ ($117–$151) double. AE, DC, MC, V. **Amenities:** Laundry service; dry cleaning; nonsmoking rooms. *In room:* TV, minibar, hair dryer.

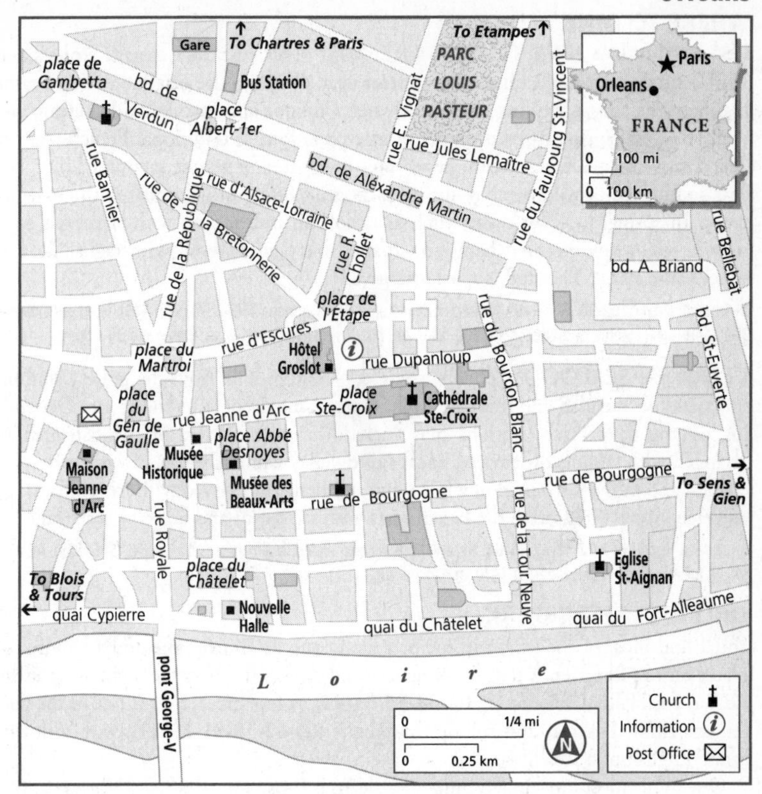

Hôtel Mercure Orléans ★ If you seek modern comfort, this is the town's finest address. Along the river, adjacent to pont Joffre, the eight-story bandbox structure is within walking distance of place du Martroi and its Joan of Arc statue. Though rather impersonal—it's favored by businesspeople—it offers the best rooms in the city. Most units are in chain-hotel style and of medium size. All have tiled bathrooms with tubs and showers. The on-site restaurant serves French and Loire Valley specialties.

44–46 quai Barentin, 45000 Orléans. ✆ **02-38-62-17-39.** Fax 02-38-53-95-34. www.accorhotels.com. 111 units. 114€–145€ ($148–$189) double; 196€ ($255) suite. Parking 5€ ($6.50). AE, DC, MC, V. **Amenities:** Restaurant; bar; outdoor pool; room service; babysitting; laundry service; dry cleaning; nonsmoking rooms; 1 limited-mobility room. *In room:* A/C, TV, minibar, hair dryer.

Hôtel St-Martin *Value* If you prefer simplicity to opulence and think of a hotel room only as a place in which to sleep and shower, then this is the choice for you. The place is well scrubbed, the rooms old-fashioned with a battered charm. The century-old three-story complex consists of two buildings divided by a courtyard. Each offers good-size, sparsely furnished rooms that contain built-in armoires. Only three units have bathrooms with both tub and shower. Some have TVs. Half the rooms overlook the garden behind the hotel, where you can sit and enjoy a nonalcoholic drink.

52 bd. Alexandre-Martin, 45000 Orléans. ✆ **02-38-62-47-47.** Fax 02-38-81-13-28. www.hotel-orleans-st-martin.com. 21 units, 15 with bathroom. 39€ ($51) double without bathroom; 53€ ($69) double with bathroom. MC, V.

WHERE TO DINE

Les Antiquaires ★★★ CLASSIC FRENCH This rustically elegant stone-sided 14th-century mansion is on a narrow street near the river. The original ceiling beams highlight the cozy, appealing interior. Owners Philippe and Pascale Bardau create virtually flawless cuisine based on modern interpretations of traditional French recipes. The creative menu changes with the seasons. In autumn or winter, savor the Loire Valley's abundance of wild game in dishes such as *estouffade* of wild boar with red-wine sauce. In spring, look for dishes such as ravioli of fresh morels with asparagus tips, roasted scallops with cured ham, and roasted baby goat served with tagliatelle and sweet garlic sauce. The staff is most attentive.

2–4 rue au Lin. ✆ **02-38-53-63-48.** Reservations required. Main courses 21€–33€ ($27–$43); fixed-price menus 38€ ($49) Tues–Fri only, and 48€–72€ ($62–$94). AE, MC, V. Tues–Sun noon–2pm; Tues–Sat 7:30–10pm.

L'Etage Kids SEAFOOD This brasserie, a 5-minute walk from the railway station, specializes in shellfish and fresh seafood; its maritime decor suits the menu. Depending on the day's catch, options may include heaping platters of shellfish artfully arranged with strands of seaweed, local Loire Valley whitefish roasted with baby vegetables, and mussels steamed in white wine and herbs and served with french fries. An endlessly popular dessert is the banana tart with ice cream and hot chocolate sauce.

6 rue Jean Hupea. ✆ **02-38-62-45-64.** Reservations recommended. Main courses 12€–18€ ($16–$23). AE, DC, MC, V. Tues–Fri noon–2pm; Tues–Sat 7–10pm. Closed Aug.

ORLEANS AFTER DARK

You'll find most of the action in the bars along **rue de Bourgogne** and a handful of places on **rue Bannier.** A trendy young crowd dances and drinks the night away at the **Le Ka,** Les Halles Châtelet (✆ **02-38-53-81-83**). A few streets over is one of the better jazz clubs, **Paxton,** 264 rue de Bourgogne (✆ **02-38-81-23-29**), with a down-home English pub feel.

One of the most intriguing venues in Orléans is **Cats,** 2 rue des Trois-Maries (✆ **02-38-54-68-68**). Four nights a week (Wed–Sat) at 9pm, it presents what the owners call a *cafe-concert;* you're likely to see (French-language) comedians, songsters, and satirists. Even more unusual is the setting, 10m (33 ft.) underground: Originally constructed in the 12th century as a chapel, it was gradually buried as workmen piled rubble from the construction of the nearby cathedral on top. From 1500, after its deconsecrating, until 1794, it functioned as a cellar for the production and storage of vinegar, and later as the wine cellar of a private home. Cover ranges from 4€ to 15€ ($5.20–$20), depending on the featured artists.

2 Châteaudun

103km (64 miles) SW of Paris, 43km (27 miles) SW of Chartres

Austere and foreboding, **Château de Châteaudun** ★★, place Jean-de-Dunois (✆ **02-37-94-02-90**), rises on a stone table over a tributary of the Loire. Begun in the Middle Ages, the château is a mix of medieval and Renaissance architecture, with towering chimneys and dormers. After a fire in the 18th century, Hardouin, Louis XV's architect, directed the town's reconstruction and turned over the castle to the homeless, who stripped it of its finery. In 1935, the government acquired the fortress and launched a restoration. Even today, it's not richly furnished, but fine tapestries depicting scenes such as the worship of the golden calf now cover its walls. The château's most admirable features are two carved staircases. Inside the Ste-Chapelle, dating from the Middle Ages, are more than a dozen 15th-century robed statues. In 2002, the curators added a permanent exhibit honoring Jean Dunois, a comrade in arms to Joan of Arc.

The château is open daily April through September from 9:30am to 1pm and 2 to 6pm (until 7pm July–Aug), October to March from 10am to 12:30pm and 2 to 5:30pm. Admission is 6.50€ ($8.45) for adults, 4.50€ ($5.85) for ages 18 to 25, and free for children under 18. Allow 1½ hours to see the château.

ESSENTIALS

GETTING THERE Four to 15 **buses** per day arrive from Chartres (trip time: 45 min.), depending on the day of the week and the season. The one-way fare is about 12€ ($16). For schedules, call the station, Gare Routière, Chartres, at © **02-37-18-59-00.** There are about six **trains** per day, departing from Paris's Gare d'Austerlitz, charging around 20€ ($26) each way, and arriving 90 minutes later in Châteaudun. Check with the Office de Tourisme for schedules. If you're **driving** from Paris, head southwest along A10 and exit at Phivars. Then take N10, following signs for Châteaudun.

VISITOR INFORMATION The **Office de Tourisme** is at 1 rue de Luynes (© **02-37-45-22-46;** www.ville-chateaudun.com).

WHERE TO STAY

Hôtel St-Michel This hotel's tradition of housing guests dates to the early 19th century, when it was a coaching inn. Today it is Châteaudun's best inn, although that's not saying a lot. The staff is less than helpful, but the place is decent. Guest rooms are functional in design and simply, though comfortably, furnished. Most have a small, shower-only bathroom. Breakfast is served in the lounge, in your room, or in the greenhouse-style winter garden.

28 place du 18-Octobre and 5 rue Péan, Châteaudun 28200. © **02-37-45-15-70.** Fax 02-37-45-83-39. www.citotel.com/hotels/chateaudun.html. 19 units, 17 with bathroom. 44€ ($57) double without bathroom; 56€ ($73) double with bathroom. AE, DC, MC, V. Parking 7€ ($9.10). **Amenities:** Gym; sauna; room service; nonsmoking rooms. *In room:* TV, minibar.

3 Beaugency ★

150km (93 miles) SW of Paris, 85km (53 miles) NE of Tours

On the right bank of the Loire, the town of Beaugency boasts a 14th-century bridge that's unusual because each of its 26 arches is in a different style. The heart of town is an archaeological garden called the City of the Lords, named after the counts who enjoyed great power in the Middle Ages. A major medieval event took place here: the 1152 annulment of the marriage of Eleanor of Aquitaine and her cousin, Louis VII. This remarkable woman later became queen consort of Henry II of England, bringing southwestern France as her dowry. She was the mother of Richard the Lion-Hearted. (The film *The Lion in Winter* dramatizes these events.) Allow 2 hours to see Beaugency.

The 15th-century **Château Dunois/Le Musée des Arts et Traditions Populaires de l'Orléanais** (Musée Daniel Vannier), 2 place Dunois (© **02-38-44-55-23**), contains a folklore museum of the Orléans district. The collection includes antique toys, hairpieces, furniture, costumes, paintings, and sculpture. The museum is open Wednesday through Monday from 10am to noon and 2 to 5pm (to 6:30pm in summer). Admission is 5.50€ ($7.15) for adults, 2.50€ ($3.25) for children 6 to 17, and free for children under 6. April to September, admission includes a mostly French-language guided tour that runs six times daily during open hours. The château is brooding, foreboding, and impressive, its historical links stretching back to almost-mystical medieval antecedents. It was built on the foundations of an earlier château from about A.D. 1000, known as the Château des Sires de Beaugency (château of the lords of Beaugency), whose feudal power extended throughout the region. Astride the street (la rue du Pont) that leads to one of the château's secondary entrances, the Voûte St-Georges (St. George's Vault) is an arched gateway from the earlier château. ***Note:*** At press time, the château was closed for renovations. Be sure to check its status before heading here.

Eglise Notre-Dame, place Saint-Fermin, would have been a good example of 12th-century Romanesque architecture if Gothic touches hadn't been added. Originally, it was attached to a Benedictine abbey. Nearby, the **Tour St-Fermin,** with a panoramic view of the valley, is all that remains of a church that stood on place Saint-Fermin. A trio of bells is in this tower, whose spire rises 54m (177 ft.). These attractions are open daily from 7am to 7pm; admission is free.

The 10th-century **Eglise St-Etienne,** place du Martroi, is one of the oldest churches in France. Now deconsecrated, it is owned by the municipality and is open only for temporary expositions of painting and sculpture.

ESSENTIALS

GETTING THERE If you're **driving** from Blois to Beaugency, take D951 northeast. About 20 **trains** per day run between Beaugency and either Blois or Orléans; each trip takes 20 minutes, and the one-way fare starts at 5€ ($6.50). For railway information, call ✆ **08-92-35-35-35.** From Orléans, about eight **buses** a day make the trip to Beaugency. For bus schedules and information, call the station in Orléans (✆ **02-38-53-94-75**).

VISITOR INFORMATION The **Office de Tourisme** is at 3 place du Dr.-Hyvernaud (✆ **02-38-44-54-42**).

WHERE TO STAY & DINE

Abbaye de Beaugency ★ This government-rated three-star hotel offers the most historic accommodations in Beaugency. Built in 1640 as a monastery, it retains the stone window and door frames of its original construction, and an elegant brick facade that may remind you of a château. A hotel since 1935, it sits beside the Loire, within view of the town's oldest bridge. Guest rooms are large and bright, and each bathroom has both a tub and shower.

2 quai de l'Abbaye, Beaugency 45190. ✆ **02-38-44-67-35.** Fax 02-38-44-87-92. www.hotel-abbaye-beaugency.com. 17 units. 108€ ($140) double; 106€–124€ ($138–$161) apt. AE, DC, MC, V. **Amenities:** Restaurant; bar; room service; nonsmoking rooms. *In room:* TV.

La Tonnellerie ★ *Finds* About 1.5km (1 mile) south of the center of Beaugency, this well-managed hotel is intimate and charming. It was originally built as a manor house in the 19th century, and it retains its original L-shaped design, walled garden, and sense of the era of Balzac and Flaubert. The Laura Ashley–furnished rooms are comfortable and traditional. Bathrooms are small, all with tubs and shower stalls. The Pouey family can arrange visits to the château, golf, hiking, cycling, or a trip to a winery.

12 rue des Eaux-Bleues, Tavers, Beaugency 45190. ✆ **02-38-44-68-15.** Fax 02-38-44-10-01. www.tonelri.com. 20 units. 84€–201€ ($109–$261) double; 124€–234€ ($161–$304) apt or suite. AE, DC, MC, V. Closed Dec 20–Jan 15. Take A10, exit at Beaugency, and then take N152 to Beaugency/Tavers. **Amenities:** Restaurant; guests-only bar; outdoor pool; babysitting. *In room:* TV, hair dryer, Wi-Fi.

4 Chambord

191km (119 miles) SW of Paris, 18km (11 miles) E of Blois

When François I said, "Come on up to my place," he meant the **Château de Chambord** ★★★, 41250 Bracieux (✆ **02-54-50-40-00;** www.chambord.org). Some 2,000 workers began "the pile" in 1519. What emerged after 20 years was the pinnacle of the French Renaissance, the largest château in the Loire Valley. It was ready for the visit of Charles V of Germany, who was welcomed by nymphets in transparent veils tossing wildflowers in his path. Monarchs such as Henri II and Catherine de Médicis, Louis XIII, and Henri III came and went from Chambord, but none loved it like François I. The state acquired Chambord in 1932.

The château is in a park of more than 5,260 hectares (13,000 acres), enclosed by a wall stretching some 32km (20 miles). Four monumental towers dominate Chambord's facade. The three-story keep has a spectacular terrace from which the ladies of the court used to watch the return of their men from the hunt. The keep also encloses a corkscrew staircase, superimposed upon itself so that one person may descend and a second ascend without ever meeting. The apartments of Louis XIV, including his redecorated bedchamber, are also in the keep.

The château is open daily April to September 9am to 6:15pm, October to March 9am to 5:15pm. Admission is 8.50€ ($11) for adults, 6€ ($7.80) for ages 18 to 25, and free for children under 18. At the tourist office, you can pick up tickets for the summer *son-et-lumière* presentation, *Jours et Siècles* (Days and Centuries). The price is 12€ ($16). Allow 1½ hours to visit the château.

ESSENTIALS

GETTING THERE It's best to **drive** to Chambord. Take D951 northeast from Blois to Ménars, turning onto the rural road to Chambord. You can also rent a **bicycle** in Blois and ride the 18km (11 miles) to Chambord, or take a **tour** to Chambord from Blois in summer. From June 15 to September 15, **Transports du Loir et Cher** (✆ **02-54-58-55-44**) operates bus service to Chambord, leaving Blois at 9am and 1:30pm with return trips at 1 and 6pm.

VISITOR INFORMATION The **Office de Tourisme** on place St-Michel (✆ **02-54-33-39-16**) is open mid-June to October.

WHERE TO STAY & DINE

Hôtel du Grand-St-Michel Across from the château, and originally built as a kennel for the royal hounds, this inn is the only one of any substance in town. Try for a front room overlooking the château, which is dramatically floodlighted at night. Accommodations are plain but comfortable, with provincial decor and shower-only bathrooms. Most visitors arrive for lunch, which in summer is served on a terrace. The marvelous collection of Loire wines is so good that it almost overshadows the regional cooking. High points from the menu include stew of wild boar (in late autumn and winter), breast of duckling in green-peppercorn sauce, and several local pâtés and terrines, including coarsely textured, flavorful *rillettes* of regional pork.

103 place St-Michel, Chambord 41250, near Bracieux. ✆ **02-54-20-31-31.** Fax 02-54-20-36-40. 40 units. 52€–110€ ($68–$143) double. MC, V. Free parking. Closed mid-Nov to mid-Dec. **Amenities:** Restaurant; tennis court. *In room:* TV.

5 Blois

180km (112 miles) SW of Paris, 60km (37 miles) NE of Tours

This town of 55,000 receives half a million visitors yearly, primarily to visit the **Château de Blois** ★★★. If time remains after a visit to the château, you may want to walk around the town. It's a piece of living history, with cobblestone streets and restored white houses with slate roofs and red-brick chimneys. Blois (pronounce it "Blwah") hugs a hillside overlooking the Loire. Some of its "streets" are mere alleyways originally laid out in the Middle Ages, or lanes linked by a series of stairs. Allow 1½ hours to see Blois.

ESSENTIALS

GETTING THERE The Paris-Austerlitz line via Orléans runs six **trains** per day from Paris (trip time: 1 hr. plus transfer waiting time at Orléans), costing 22€ ($29) one-way; from Tours, 8 to 13 trains arrive per day (trip time: 1 hr.) at a cost of 8.50€ ($11) one-way. For information and schedules, call ✆ **08-92-35-35-35.** The train station is at place de la Gare. From June to September, you can take a **bus** (✆ **02-54-78-15-66**) from the Blois train station to tour châteaux in the area, including Chambord, Chaumont, Chenonceau, and Amboise. If you're **driving** from Tours, take RN152 east to Blois. If you'd like to explore the area by **bike,** go to **LeBlond Claude,** 44 levée des Tuileries (✆ **02-54-74-30-13**), where rentals cost 13€ ($17) per day. You have to leave your passport, a credit card, a driver's license, or a deposit of 250€ ($325).

VISITOR INFORMATION The **Office de Tourisme** is at 23 place du Château (✆ **02-54-90-41-41;** www.loiredeschateaux.com).

EXPLORING THE TOWN & THE CHATEAU

If you have time for shopping, head for the area around **rue St-Martin** and **rue du Commerce** for high-end items such as clothing, perfume, shoes, and jewelry. Find a one-of-a-kind piece of jewelry or have something created by the master jeweler **Philippe Denies,** 3 rue St-Martin (✆ **02-54-74-78-24**). If you prefer antique jewelry, stop by **Antebellum,** 12 rue St-Lubin (✆ **02-54-78-38-78**), and browse its selection of precious and semiprecious stones set in gold and silver. For something less serious, stop at **Au Paradis des Enfants,** in a 15th-century house at 2 rue des Trois-Clefs (✆ **02-54-78-09-68**); you'll find toys in every shape and size. If you want to acquire a copy of the tapestries at nearby châteaux, you'll find a wide range at **Tapisserie Langlois,** Voûte du Château (✆ **02-54-78-04-43**). Chocoholics flock to **Jeff de Bruges,** 77 rue du Commerce (✆ **02-54-74-26-44**), and **Max Vauché,** 50 rue du Commerce (✆ **02-54-78-23-55**). On Saturday morning, a **food market** is on rue St-Lubin and place Louis XII, lining several blocks in the center of town at the foot of the château.

Moments **Let the Horse Lead the Way**

You can take a 25-minute **horse-and-buggy ride** through the old town of Blois for 6€ ($7.80) for adults and 5€ ($6.50) for children 2 to 12. The carriage departs from place du Château during May, June, and September on weekends and holidays from 2 to 6pm; in July and August, it leaves daily from 11am to 7pm. For more details, call the tourist office.

Château de Blois ★★★ A wound in battle earned him the name Balafré (Scarface), but he was quite a ladies' man. In fact, on the misty morning of December 23, 1588, the duc de Guise had just left a warm bed and the arms of one of Catherine de Médicis's ladies-in-waiting. His archrival, King Henri III, had summoned him, but when the duke arrived, only the king's minions were about. The guards approached with daggers. Wounded, the duke made for the door, where more guards awaited him. Staggering, he fell to the floor in a pool of his own blood. Only then did Henri emerge from behind the curtains. "Mon Dieu," he reputedly exclaimed, "he's taller dead than alive!" The body couldn't be shown: The duke was too popular. Quartered, it was burned in a fireplace.

The murder of the duc de Guise is only one of the events associated with the Château de Blois, begun in the 13th century by the *comte* de Blois. Blois reached the apex of its power in 1515, when François I moved to the château. For that reason, Blois is often called the "Versailles of the Renaissance," the second capital of France, and the "city of kings." Blois soon became a palace of exile. Louis XIII banished his mother, Marie de Médicis, to the château, but she escaped by sliding into the moat down a mound of dirt left by the builders.

If you stand in the courtyard, you'll find the château is like an illustrated storybook of French architecture. The Hall of the Estates-General is a beautiful 13th-century work; Louis XII built the Charles d'Orléans gallery and the Louis XII wing from 1498 to 1501. Mansart constructed the Gaston d'Orléans wing between 1635 and 1637. Most remarkable is the François I wing, a French Renaissance masterpiece, containing a spiral staircase with ornamented balustrades and the king's symbol, the salamander.

The château presents a *son-et-lumière* show in French from May to September, usually beginning at 10:30pm (but sometimes earlier, depending on the school calendar). As a taped lecture plays, colored lights and readings evoke the age in which the château was built. The show costs 9.50€ ($12) for adults, 4.50€ ($5.85) for children 7 to 15, and is free for children under 7.

41000 Blois. ✆ **02-54-90-33-33.** www.ville-blois.fr. Admission 7€ ($9.10) adults, 5€ ($6.50) students 12–25, 3€ ($3.90) children 6–17, free for children under 6. Daily Apr–Oct daily 9am–6pm; Nov–Mar daily 9am–12:30pm and 2–5:30pm. Closed Dec 25 and Jan 1.

WHERE TO STAY

Some of the best rooms in town are at **Le Médicis** (see "Where to Dine," below).

Holiday Inn Garden Court ★ *Kids* This leading hotel, built in 1996, sits in the heart of town. It offers all the modern amenities and a certain traditional charm. The rooms are furnished with contemporary flair and offer chain-hotel standardized comfort. Each unit has a well-equipped bathroom with tub and shower. In summer, guests flock to a terrace overlooking the hotel garden.

26 av. Maunoury, Blois 41000. ✆ **800/465-4329** in the U.S. and Canada, or 02-54-55-44-88. Fax 02-54-74-57-97. www.holiday-inn.com. 78 units. 75€–96€ ($98–$125) double. Children under 12 stay free in parent's room. AE, DC, MC, V. Free parking. Bus: 1. **Amenities:** 2 restaurants; bar; business services; room service; babysitting; laundry service; dry cleaning; nonsmoking rooms; limited-mobility rooms. *In room:* A/C, TV, minibar, hair dryer.

Hôtel le Savoie This modern 1930s-era hotel is both inviting and livable, from its courteous staff to its guest rooms, which are small but quiet and cozy. Bathrooms are small but have sufficient shelf space; each has a shower. In the morning, a breakfast buffet is set up in the bright dining room.

6–8 rue du Docteur-Ducoux, Blois 41000. ✆ **02-54-74-32-21.** Fax 02-54-74-29-58. www.hotel-blois.com. 24 units. 41€–54€ ($53–$70) double. MC, V. **Amenities:** Bar; room service; babysitting; laundry service; nonsmoking rooms. *In room:* TV, minibar.

Mercure Centre ★ This is one of the best-located hotels in Blois—three stories of reinforced concrete and big windows beside the quays of the Loire, a 5-minute walk from the château. Rooms never rise above the chain format and roadside-motel look, but they are roomy and soundproof. Bathrooms come with tub/shower combinations.

28 quai St-Jean, Blois 41000. ✆ **02-54-56-66-66.** Fax 02-54-56-67-00. www.mercure.com. 96 units. 112€–119€ ($146–$155) double. AE, DC, MC, V. Parking 7€ ($8.40). Bus: Quayside marked PISCINE. **Amenities:** Restaurant; bar; indoor pool; Jacuzzi; sauna; business services; room service; babysitting; laundry service; dry cleaning; nonsmoking rooms; limited-mobility rooms. *In room:* A/C, TV, minibar, hair dryer.

WHERE TO DINE

Au Rendez-vous des Pêcheurs ★★ TOURAINE/SEAFOOD This restaurant occupies a 16th-century house and old grocery a short walk from the château. Chef Christophe Cosme enjoys a reputation for quality, generous portions, and creativity. He prepares two or three meat dishes, including roasted chicken with a medley of potatoes and mushrooms and comfit of garlic, and succulent line-caught whitefish in puff pastry. These appear alongside a longer roster of seafood dishes, such as poached filet of *sandre* (a freshwater fish; "zander" in English) served with fresh oysters, and freshwater eel in puff pastry with figs.

27 rue du Foix. ✆ **02-54-74-67-48.** Reservations required. Main courses 22€–25€ ($29–$33); fixed-price menu 28€–74€ ($36–$96). AE, MC, V. Tues–Sat 12:15–1:30pm; Mon–Sat 7:15–9:30pm. Closed 2 weeks in Jan and 3 weeks in Aug.

Le Médicis ★ TRADITIONAL FRENCH Christian and Annick Garanger maintain one of the most sophisticated inns in Blois, just 1km (⅔ mile) from the château. It's ideal for a gourmet meal or an overnight stop. Fresh fish is the chef's specialty. Typical main courses are asparagus in mousseline sauce, scampi ravioli with saffron sauce, and suprême of perch with morels. Chocolate in many manifestations is the dessert specialty. The Garangers rent 12 elegant rooms with air-conditioning, TV, minibar, and hair dryer. Double rates are 120€ to 150€ ($156–$195).

2 allée François 1er, Blois 41000. ✆ **02-54-43-94-04.** Fax 02-54-42-04-05. www.le-medicis.com. Reservations required. Main courses 14€–31€ ($18–$40); fixed-price menu 22€–68€ ($29–$88). AE, MC, V. Daily noon–2pm and 7–9pm. Closed Jan and Sun night Nov–Mar. Bus: 2.

L'Orangerie du Château ★★★ Kids TOURAINE Next to the château, one of the castle's former outbuildings holds the grandest and best restaurant in the area. Chef Jean-Marc Molveaux presides over a floral-themed dining room. Faithful customers and the most discerning foodies visiting Blois delight in his filet mignon with truffles. You can also sample his lovely medley of shellfish and nuts in cream sauce, or perfectly roasted monkfish flavored with fresh thyme. Everything tastes better with a Sauvignon de Touraine. For dessert, our favorite is melted chocolate and pistachio with crème fraîche.

1 av. Jean-Laigret. ✆ **02-54-78-05-36.** Reservations required. Main courses 22€–34€ ($29–$44); fixed-price menu 31€–65€ ($40–$85); children's menu 15€ ($20). AE, MC, V. Thurs–Tues noon–1:45pm; Thurs–Sat and Mon–Tues 7:15–9:15pm. Closed mid-Feb to mid-Mar.

BLOIS AFTER DARK

There's not much in the way of nightlife in Blois, but you could saunter down to the fun and friendly **L'Hendrix Café,** 1 rue du Puits-Châtel (✆ **02-54-58-82-73**), for a drink. Another possibility is **Le Platinum,** 19 rue des Ponts-Chartrains (✆ **02-54-74-11-54**), a lounge and dance club with mirrored walls. Expect everything from Egyptian belly dancers to drag shows. Mixed drinks cost from 7€ ($9.10), and hours are daily 5pm to 2am.

6 Cheverny

192km (119 miles) SW of Paris, 19km (12 miles) SE of Blois

The upper crust heads to the Sologne area for the hunt as if the 17th century had never ended. However, 21st-century realities—like formidable taxes—can't be entirely avoided, so the **Château de Cheverny** ★★★ (✆ **02-54-79-96-29;** www.chateau-cheverny.fr) must open some of its rooms to visitors.

Unlike most of the Loire châteaux, Cheverny is the residence of the original owner's descendants. The family of the *vicomte* de Sigalas can trace its lineage to Henri Hurault, the son of the chancellor of Henri III and Henri IV, who built the first château in 1634. Upon finding his wife carrying on with a page, he killed the page and offered his spouse a choice: She could swallow poison or have his sword plunged into her heart. She elected the less bloody method. Then he had the castle torn down and the present one built for his second wife. Designed in classic Louis XIII style, it boasts square pavilions flanking the central pile.

You'll be impressed by the antique furnishings, tapestries, and objets d'art. A 17th-century French artist, Jean Mosnier, decorated the fireplace with motifs from the legend of Adonis. The Guards' Room contains a collection of medieval armor; also on display is a Gobelin tapestry depicting the abduction of Helen of Troy. In the king's bedchamber, another Gobelin traces the trials of Ulysses. Most impressive is the stone stairway of carved fruit and flowers.

The château is open daily October to March 9:45am to 5pm; April to June and September 9:15am to 6:15pm; and July and August 9:15am to 6:45pm. Admission is 6.80€ ($8.85) for adults, 5€ ($6.50) for students, 3.40€ ($4.40) for children 7 to 14, and free for children under 7. Allow 2 hours to see Cheverny.

ESSENTIALS

GETTING THERE Cheverny is 19km (12 miles) south of Blois, along D765. It's best reached by **car** or on a **bus tour** from Blois with **Transports du Loir et Cher** (✆ **02-54-58-55-44**). From the railway station at Blois, a bus departs for Cheverny once a day at noon, returning to Blois 4 hours later, according to an oft-changing schedule. Most visitors find it a lot easier to take their own car or a **taxi** from the railway station at Blois.

WHERE TO STAY & DINE

Les Trois Marchands TRADITIONAL FRENCH This coaching inn, more comfortable than St-Hubert (see below), has been handed down for many generations. Jean-Jacques Bricault owns the three-story building, which has awnings, a mansard roof, a glassed-in courtyard, and sidewalk tables under umbrellas. In the tavern-style main dining room, the menu may include foie gras, lobster salad, frogs' legs, fresh asparagus in mousseline sauce, game dishes, or fish cooked in a salt crust. The inn rents 24 well-furnished, comfortable rooms with TVs for 42€ to 55€ ($55–$72) for a double.

60 place de l'Eglise, Cour-Cheverny 41700. ✆ **02-54-79-96-44.** Fax 02-54-79-25-60. www.hoteldes3marchands.com. Dining room main courses 16€–30€ ($19–$36); fixed-price menu 23€–35€ ($30–$46). Le Grill main courses 12€–22€ ($16–$28). AE, DC, MC, V. Tues–Sun noon–2:15pm and 7:30–9:15pm. Closed mid-Feb to mid-Mar.

St-Hubert TRADITIONAL FRENCH About 457m (1,500 ft.) from the château, this inn was built in the 1950s in the provincial style. The least expensive menu may include terrine of quail, pikeperch with beurre blanc, cheeses, and a fruit tart. The most expensive may offer lobster; an aiguillette of duckling prepared with grapes; casserole of seafood with shellfish sauce; and, in season, thigh of roebuck in pepper sauce. The St-Hubert offers 20 conservatively decorated rooms with TVs for 50€ to 72€ ($65–$94) for a double.

122 rte. Nationale, Cour-Cheverny 41700. ✆ **02-54-79-96-60.** Fax 02-54-79-21-17. www.hotel-sthubert.com. Main courses 14€–30€ ($18–$39); fixed-price menu 19€–30€ ($25–$39). AE, MC, V. Daily 12:15–2pm and 7:30–9pm. Closed Sun night off season.

7 Valençay

233km (145 miles) SW of Paris, 56km (35 miles) S of Blois

Château de Valençay ★★ (✆ **02-54-00-15-69**) is one of the Loire's most handsome Renaissance châteaux. Talleyrand acquired it in 1803 on the orders of Napoleon, who wanted his minister of foreign affairs to receive dignitaries in style. The d'Estampes family built Valençay in 1550. The dungeon and west tower are of this period, as is the main body of the building, but other wings were added in the 17th and 18th centuries. The effect is grandiose, with domes and turrets.

The private apartments are open to the public; they're sumptuously furnished, mostly in the Empire style but with Louis XV and Louis XVI trappings as well. A star-footed table in the main drawing room is said to have been the one on which the final agreement of the Congress of Vienna was signed in June 1815 (Talleyrand represented France).

Visits to Valençay are more detailed (and last about 45 min. longer) than those to other châteaux in the valley. The Musée de Talleyrand that used to stand here is closed, but some of the collection is displayed in the new rooms of the castle. After your visit to the château, you can walk through the garden and deer park.

Admission to the castle, car museum, and park is 8.50€ ($11) for adults, 6.50€ ($8.45) for students, 4.50€ ($5.85) for children 7 to 17, and free for children under 7. It's open April to June daily 9:30am to 6pm; July to August daily 9:30am to 7:30pm; September to March by reservation only. Allow 1½ hours to see the castle.

Within 182m (597 ft.) of the château, the **Musée de l'Automobile,** route du Blois, 12 av. de la Résistance (✆ **02-54-00-07-74**), features a collection of more than 60 antique automobiles. Of special interest is a Bédélia (ca. 1914). The tandem-style automobile (the driver rode behind the passenger) with a pulley-operated two-speed gearshift is the rarest in the collection. The Bédélia, like 80% of the cars in the collection, was made in France.

Admission to the car museum only is 5€ ($6.50) for adults, 2.50€ ($3.25) for children 7 to 17, free for children under 7. Hours are July and August daily 10:30am to 12:30pm and 1:30 to 7:30pm; mid-March to June, September, and October daily 10am to 12:30pm and 2 to 6pm. The museum is closed from November to mid-March.

ESSENTIALS

GETTING THERE If you're **driving** from Tours, take N76 east, turning south on D956 to Valençay. From Blois, follow D956 south. SNCF operates **rail** service from Blois. For information, call ✆ **08-92-35-35-35.**

VISITOR INFORMATION The **Office de Tourisme** is at 2 av. de Résistance (✆ **02-54-00-04-42**).

WHERE TO STAY & DINE

Hôtel Le Relais du Moulin The town's best overnight choice is a 5-minute walk from the entrance to the château. It's also immediately adjacent to a stream and the now-disabled water wheel of an 18th-century textile mill that, during the age of Talleyrand and Napoleon, produced fabrics for curtains, clothing, and upholsteries. The hotel has a cream-colored facade, bedrooms outfitted with contemporary-looking furniture and tones of pale yellow and soft red, and views that overlook the château, the river, vineyards, and/or the park surrounding the hotel and the château. Fixed-price menus in the dining room cost from 18€ to 38€ ($23–$49), and focus on traditional and well-prepared French food.

95 rte. Nationale, Valençay 36600. ✆ **02-54-00-38-00.** Fax 02-54-00-38-79. www.hotel-lerelaisdumoulin.com. 54 units. 58€–66€ ($75–$86) double. AE, DC, MC, V. Closed Nov–Mar. **Amenities:** Restaurant; bar; indoor pool; exercise room; sauna; room service; limited-mobility rooms. *In room:* TV, minibar (in some).

8 Chaumont-sur-Loire

200km (124 miles) SW of Paris, 40km (25 miles) E of Tours

On the morning when Diane de Poitiers first crossed the drawbridge, the **Château de Chaumont** ★★ (✆ **02-54-51-26-26**) looked grim. Henri II, her lover, had recently died. The king had given her Chenonceau, but his angry widow, Catherine de Médicis, forced her to trade her favorite château for Chaumont, with its battlements and pepper-pot turrets. Inside, portraits reveal that Diane deserved her reputation as forever beautiful. Another portrait—of Catherine looking like a devout nun—invites unfavorable comparisons.

Charles d'Amboise built Chaumont (Burning Mount) during the reign of Louis XII. Overlooking the Loire, it's approached by a long walk up from the village through a tree-studded park. The castle spans the period between the Middle Ages and the Renaissance, and its prize exhibit is a collection of medallions by the Italian artist Nini. A guest of the château, he made medallion portraits of kings, queens, nobles, and dignitaries—including Benjamin Franklin, who once visited. In the bedroom occupied by Catherine de Médicis, you can see a portrait of the Italian-born queen. The superstitious Catherine housed her astrologer, Cosimo Ruggieri, in one of the tower rooms (a portrait of him remains). He reportedly foretold the disasters awaiting her sons. In Ruggieri's room, a tapestry depicts Medusa with a flying horse escaping from her head.

The château is open daily (except Jan 1, May 1, Nov 1 and 11, and Dec 25) May 8 to September 11 9:30am to 6:30pm, April to May 7 and September 12 to September 30 10:30am to 5:30pm, and October to March 10am to 5pm. Admission is 6.10€ ($7.95) for adults, 4.10€ ($5.35) for students and children under 19. Allow 2 hours to see Chaumont.

ESSENTIALS

GETTING THERE Seventeen **trains** per day travel to Chaumont from Blois (trip time: 15 min.) and Tours (about 45 min.). The one-way fare is 4.50€ ($5.85) from Blois, 8.80€ ($11) from Tours. The railway station serving Chaumont is in Onzain, a nice 1½ miles walk north of the château. For transportation information, call ✆ **08-92-35-35-35.**

VISITOR INFORMATION The **Office de Tourisme** is on rue du Maréchal-Leclerc (✆ **02-54-20-91-73;** www.chaumontsurloire.info).

WHERE TO STAY & DINE

Hostellerie du Château *Value* Most visitors to the château who want to stay close to the castle have to go to hotels nearby. This completely renovated half-timbered inn offers lodgings directly in front of the gateway to the château. Accommodations open onto the riverbank of the Loire; ask for a room with a view. The rooms are modestly yet comfortably furnished, and each has a small bathroom with shower. In the summer you can enjoy regional specialties in the restaurant and swim in the terrace-flanked pool.

2 rue Maréchal de-Lattre-de-Tassigny, Chaumont-sur-Loire 41150. ✆ **02-54-20-98-04.** Fax 02-54-20-97-98. www.hostelleriedu-chateau.com. 15 units. 70€–92€ ($91–$120) double. MC, V. **Amenities:** Restaurant; bar; outdoor pool; room service; babysitting; laundry service. *In room:* TV, hair dryer.

La Domaine des Hauts de Loire ★★ Less than 3km (1¾ miles) from the Château de Chaumont, this Relais & Châteaux property sits on the opposite side of the Loire. The manor house was built by the owner of a Paris-based newspaper in 1840 and called, rather coyly, a "hunting lodge." It's the most appealing stopover in the neighborhood, with rooms decorated in Louis Philippe or Empire style. More than half of the rooms are in the slightly less desirable half-timbered annex that was originally the stables. All have a tub and shower.

The stately dining room is open to nonguests who phone in advance. Its well-prepared food is a local favorite. The menu includes a salad of marinated eel with shallot-flavored vinaigrette, scampi served in celery-based consommé with roasted chestnuts and fried ham, carpaccio of scallops with Iberian ham, roasted pikeperch with parsley sauce and coconut, and pigeon roasted with rutabaga and served with the oil from smoked nuts. Main courses range from 46€ to 66€ ($55–$79), with fixed-price menus offered at 70€, 90€, and 150€ ($84, $108, and $180).

Rte. d'Herbault, Onzain 41150. ✆ **02-54-20-72-57.** Fax 02-54-20-77-32. www.domainehautsloire.com. 36 units. 110€–290€ ($143–$377) double; 320€–450€ ($416–$585) suite. AE, DC, MC, V. Closed Dec–Feb. **Amenities:** Restaurant; bar; outdoor pool; room service; laundry service; dry cleaning; 1 limited-mobility room. *In room:* TV, minibar, hair dryer, safe.

9 Amboise

219km (136 miles) SW of Paris, 35km (22 miles) E of Tours

Amboise is on the banks of the Loire in the center of vineyards known as Touraine-Amboise. The good news: This is a real Renaissance town. The bad news: Because it is so beautiful, tour buses overrun it, especially in summer. Many townspeople still talk about Mick Jagger's purchase of a nearby château. An earlier resident was Leonardo da Vinci, who spent his last years here.

ESSENTIALS

GETTING THERE Amboise is on the Paris-Blois-Tours rail line, with about a dozen **trains** per day from both Tours and Blois. The trip from Tours takes 20 minutes and costs 4.30€ ($5.60) one-way; from Blois, it takes 20 minutes and costs 5.70€ ($7.40) one-way. About five conventional trains a day leave from Paris's Gare d'Austerlitz (trip time: 3 hr.), and several TGVs (trip time: 2 hr., 15 min.) depart from the Gare Montparnasse for St-Pierre-des-Corps, less than a kilometer (½ mile) from Tours. From

St-Pierre-des-Corps, you can transfer to a conventional train to Amboise. Fares from Paris to Amboise start at 25€ ($33). For information, call ✆ **08-92-35-35-35.**

If you prefer to travel by bus, **Fil Vert Buses** (www.touraine-filvert.com), which operates out of the Gare Routière in Tours, just across from the railway station, runs about 8 to 11 **buses** every day between Tours and Amboise. The one-way trip takes about 35 minutes and costs 2.10€ ($2.75).

If you're **driving** from Tours, take N152 east to D32 and then turn south, following signs to Amboise.

VISITOR INFORMATION The **Office de Tourisme** is on quai du Général-de-Gaulle (✆ **02-47-57-09-28**).

EXPLORING THE TOWN

Château d'Amboise ★★ This 15th-century château, which dominates the town, was the first in France to reflect the Italian Renaissance. A combination of Gothic and Renaissance styles, it is associated with Charles VIII, who built it on a rocky spur separating the valleys of the Loire and the Amasse.

You enter on a ramp that opens onto a panoramic terrace fronting the river. At one time, buildings surrounded this terrace, and fetes took place in the enclosed courtyard. The castle fell into decline during the Revolution, and today only about a quarter of the once-sprawling edifice remains. You first come to the Flamboyant Gothic **Chapelle de St-Hubert,** distinguished by its lacelike tracery. Today, tapestries cover the walls of the château's grandly furnished rooms. The **Logis du Roi** (king's apartment) is open to visitors. It was built against the **Tour des Minimes** (also known as the Tour des Cavaliers), which was noteworthy for its ramp up which horsemen could ride. The other notable tower is the Heurtault, which is broader than the Minimes, with thicker walls.

✆ **02-47-57-00-98.** www.chateau-amboise.com. Admission 8.50€ ($11) adults, 7€ ($9.10) students, 5€ ($6.50) ages 8–18, free for children 7 and under. July–Aug daily 9am–7pm; Apr–June daily 9am–6:30pm; Sept–Oct daily 9am–6pm; Nov 1–15 daily 9am–5:30pm; Nov 16–Jan 31 daily 9am–noon and 2–4:45pm; Feb 1–Mar 15 daily 9am–noon and 1:30–5:30pm; Mar 16–31 daily 9am–6pm.

Château du Clos-Lucé ★ Within 3km (1¾ miles) of the base of Amboise's château, this brick-and-stone building was constructed in the 1400s. It later served as a retreat for Anne de Bretagne, who, according to legend, spent a lot of time praying and meditating. Later, François I installed "the great master in all forms of art and science," Leonardo himself. Da Vinci lived here for 3 years, until his death in 1519. (The paintings of Leonardo dying in François's arms are probably symbolic; the king was supposedly out of town at the time.) Today, the site functions as a small museum, offering insights into Leonardo's life and a sense of the decorative arts of the era. The manor contains furniture from his era; examples of his sketches; models for his flying machines, bridges, and cannon; and even a primitive example of a machine gun.

2 rue de Clos-Lucé. ✆ **02-47-57-00-73.** www.vinci-closluce.com. May–Nov admission 12€ ($16) adults, 9.50€ ($12) students and seniors, 7€ ($9.10) children 6–15, 30€ ($39) family ticket (2 adults, 2 children), free for children under 6; Nov–Apr admission 9€ ($12) adults, 7€ ($9.10) students and seniors, 6€ ($7.80) children 6–15, 28€ ($36) family ticket (2 adults, 2 children), free for children under 6. Jan daily 10am–5pm; Feb–Mar and Nov–Dec daily 9am–6pm; Apr–June and Sept–Oct daily 9am–7pm; July–Aug daily 9am–8pm. Closed Jan 1 and Dec 25.

ATTRACTIONS ON THE OUTSKIRTS

The region around Amboise has attractions that resemble a mix of Disney's Magic Kingdom and the court of the Renaissance kings. The most frequently visited attraction, the

Aquarium du Val de Loire, Parc des Mini-Châteaux (✆ **02-47-23-44-57**), lies 9.5km (6 miles) west of Amboise. It has more than 10,000 freshwater and saltwater fish, including about a half-dozen sharks. Admission is 13€ ($17) for adults and 8.50€ ($11) for children 4 to 14. Open daily 10:30am to 6pm.

At the same address (same phone) is the **Parc des Mini-Châteaux,** which holds replicas of France's most famous castles built at 1/25 the size of the originals. Chambord, for example, is less than 3.5m (11 ft.) tall. It's all very patriotic—a sort of learning game that teaches French schoolchildren the glories of their *patrimoine* (heritage) and collects some of the most celebrated architecture in Europe. Admission is 13€ ($17) for adults, 8.50€ ($11) for students and children 4 to 16, and free for children under 4.

The aquarium is open daily year-round; the Parc des Mini-Châteaux is open from April to mid-November, with occasional closures based on the school calendar. Hours vary according to the season—call ahead for information.

To get here from Amboise, follow signs to Tours and take RD751 along the southern bank of the Loire. The aquarium is 1km (2/3 mile) beyond the village of Lussault-sur-Loire (it's clearly marked).

WHERE TO STAY

Belle-Vue Although its rooms aren't particularly plush, this modest, old-fashioned inn gives a sense of the basic conservatism of the Loire Valley of 25 years ago. Built of stone nearly 250 years ago, it sits in the shadow of the château. The clientele is mostly interested in touring the châteaux. Guest rooms are small, nostalgically furnished, and comfortable. Breakfast is the only meal served.

12 quai Charles-Guinot, Amboise 37400. ✆ **02-47-57-02-26.** Fax 02-47-30-51-23. 30 units. 58€–75€ ($75–$98) double. MC, V. Closed Nov 15–Mar 15. **Amenities:** Bar; room service; limited-mobility rooms. *In room:* TV.

Le Château-de-Pray ★ This 1224 château 1.6km (1 mile) west of the town center resembles a tower-flanked castle on the Rhine. You'll find antlers, hunting trophies, and a paneled drawing room with a fireplace and a collection of antique oils. Rooms in the main building were renovated in 1998 and are conservative and comfortable. The more spacious chambers are near the ground floor. Small but well-organized bathrooms contain tubs and showers. Try to avoid the four rooms in the 1990s annex; they're impersonally furnished and lack character. The restaurant, open to nonguests, offers fixed-price menus (30€–55€/$39–$72) of excellent Loire cuisine; reservations are required.

Rte. de Chargé (D751), Amboise 37400. ✆ **02-47-57-23-67.** Fax 02-47-57-32-50. http://praycastel.online.fr. 19 units. 98€–175€ ($127–$228) double; 155€–230€ ($202–$299) suite. AE, DC, MC, V. Free parking. Closed Nov and Jan. **Amenities:** Restaurant; babysitting; laundry service; dry cleaning. *In room:* TV, hair dryer.

Le Choiseul ★★★ This 18th-century hotel, in the valley between a hillside and the Loire, is the best address in Amboise and offers the best cuisine. Guest rooms, 25 of which are air-conditioned, are luxurious; though modernized, they retain their old-world charm. The small bathrooms contain combination tub/showers. The formal dining room has a view of the Loire and welcomes nonguests who phone ahead. The cuisine is better than that in Tours or the surrounding area: deluxe, international, classic French, and regional, utilizing the freshest ingredients (fixed-price menus at 45€–59€/$59–$77). The grounds boast a garden with flowering terraces.

36 quai Charles-Guinot, Amboise 37400. ✆ **02-47-30-45-45.** Fax 02-47-30-46-10. www.le-choiseul.com. 32 units. 125€–270€ ($163–$351) double; 290€–335€ ($377–$436) suite. AE, DC, MC, V. **Amenities:** Restaurant; bar; outdoor pool; bicycles; room service; babysitting; laundry service; dry cleaning. *In room:* A/C, TV, minibar, hair dryer.

Le Fleuray ★ *Finds* One of the most appealing hotels in the region is this well-maintained pink stucco manor house. Managed by English expatriates Peter and Hazel Newington, with their children Jordan and Cassie, it was built in the mid-1800s as the centerpiece of a farm. It's a marvel of country-living grandeur, partly because of the masses of geraniums, marigolds, and flowering vines that adorn the masonry in warm weather. Mick Jagger has discovered the place; he stays here whenever he feels another nervous breakdown coming on. Guest rooms are cozy and homelike, dotted with antique accessories evoking an elegant but not terribly formal English country house, though you shouldn't expect a lot of modern amenities. Bathrooms are compact and well organized with showers.

Don't miss the restaurant; local residents flock here. Items on the fixed-price menus (28€–38€/$36–$49) include dates stuffed with warm Roquefort cheese, pork pâté with onions and chutney, and Creole-style chicken in curry-flavored cream sauce garnished with pineapples.

Rte. Dame Marie, Cangey 37530, near Amboise. ✆ **02-47-56-09-25.** Fax 02-47-56-93-97. www.lefleurayhotel.com. 14 units. 78€–115€ ($101–$150) double. MC, V. Free parking. From Amboise, take N152 northeast of town, following signs to Blois; 12km (7½ miles) from Amboise, turn onto D74, direction Cangey. **Amenities:** Restaurant; bar; outdoor pool; room service; nonsmoking rooms; limited-mobility rooms. *In room:* TV, hair dryer.

Le Manoir Les Minimes ★★ This restored 18th-century mansion is a welcoming, cozy hotel built on the foundation of an ancient convent. On the river's edge, in the shadow of the château, it is surrounded by acres of gardens. Inside, furnishings are elegant in both the public and private rooms, with much use made of antiques. You can dine in the garden if weather permits. The most desirable rooms are in the main building; a comfortable, well-furnished trio of units is in an annex, although these lack character. Our favorite unit is no. 10, a corner suite with panoramic views. Many of the second-floor bedrooms open onto views of the Loire. The best-value rooms are smaller and on the third floor. Each room has its individual decor and comes with an elegant bathroom with tub.

34 quai Charles Guinot, Amboise 37400. ✆ **02-47-30-40-40.** Fax 02-47-30-40-77. www.manoirlesminimes.com. 15 units. 118€–165€ ($153–$215) double; 260€–445€ ($338–$579) suite. V. Closed Nov 14–Mar 10. **Amenities:** Breakfast room; room service; garden. *In room:* A/C, TV, minibar, safe.

Le Manoir Saint Thomas ★ *Finds* Antonella and Bertrand Pautout have installed a government-rated four-star hotel in a manor that dates originally from the 12th century. The living conditions have never been better around here; there's even a heated swimming pool in the garden. Rooms are spacious with luxury bathrooms and are completely modernized, although the antique character has been retained. Parquet floors, period fireplaces, and stained-glass windows evoke the past. The hotel is only a 2-minute walk from the royal château and is close to the former home of Leonardo da Vinci.

1 mail Saint Thomas, Amboise 37400. ✆ **02-47-23-21-82.** Fax 02-47-23-24-96. www.manoir-saint-thomas.com. 10 units. 110€–160€ ($143–$208) double; 160€–270€ ($208–$351) suite. Off-season reductions Nov–Mar. AE, MC, V. **Amenities:** Outdoor pool; room service. *In room:* A/C, TV, minibar, hair dryer.

Le Vieux Manoir ★★ *Finds* Americans Gloria and Bob Belknap fell in love with France and this 18th-century manor, which they restored and turned into an elegant B&B. They accommodate guests in beautifully furnished rooms with country antiques, exposed oak beams, stone walls, and tile floors. Accommodations are named after various legends, from George Sand and Colette to Joséphine and Mme du Barry. A 17th-century structure with old oak beams and exposed stone walls also houses guests; with a fully equipped kitchen, it's ideal for families. A glass conservatory overlooks a manicured garden. Bathrooms, lined with locally made tiles, are the finest in Amboise; they have period mirrors and washstands and heavy German fixtures with tub/shower combinations.

13 rue Rabelais, Amboise 37400. ✆ **02-47-30-41-27.** Fax 02-47-30-41-27. www.le-vieux-manoir.com. 6 units, 2-bedroom cottage. 125€–190€ ($163–$247) double; 195€–280€ ($254–$364) cottage for 4. Rates include breakfast. MC, V. **Amenities:** Nonsmoking rooms. *In room:* TV.

WHERE TO DINE

The finest dining choice is **Le Choiseul** (see above). The restaurant at **Le Fleuray** is also excellent (see "Where to Stay," above).

Brasserie de l'Hôtel de Ville *Kids* FRENCH In the town's historic core, a short walk from the château, this bustling Paris-style brasserie has enjoyed a solid reputation since the early 1990s. It attracts local office workers and art lovers visiting the historic sites during the day, and boisterous groups of friends at night. Expect a noisy environment focused on rows of banquettes, hassled waiters, and steaming platters that emerge relatively quickly from the overworked kitchen. Menu items include a full range of old-fashioned cuisine that many locals remember from their childhoods. Examples include such mainstream staples as sole meunière, grilled beefsteak with french fries, *pot-au-feu,* calves' liver, and dishes from France's Southwest, including a savory version of cassoulet.

3 rue François 1er. ✆ **02-47-57-26-30.** Reservations recommended. Main courses 7.30€–16€ ($9.50–$21) fixed-price menu 11€–15€ ($14–$20); children's menu 7€ ($9.10). AE, DC, MC, V. Daily 10am–3pm and 7–9:30pm.

10 Chenonceaux

224km (139 miles) SW of Paris, 26km (16 miles) E of Tours

A Renaissance masterpiece, the **Château de Chenonceau** ★★★ (✆ **02-47-23-90-07;** www.chenonceau.com) is best known for the *dames de Chenonceau,* who once occupied it. (The village, whose year-round population is less than 300, is spelled with a final "x," but the château isn't.)

In 1547, Henri II gave Chenonceau to his mistress, Diane de Poitiers. For a time this remarkable woman was virtually queen of France, infuriating Henri's dour wife, Catherine de Médicis. Diane's critics accused her of using magic to preserve her celebrated beauty and to keep Henri's attentions from waning. Apparently Henri's love for Diane continued unabated, and she was in her 60s when he died in a jousting tournament in 1559.

When Henri died, Catherine became regent (her eldest son was still a child) and forced Diane to return the jewelry Henri had given her and to abandon her beloved home. Catherine added her own touches, building a two-story gallery across the bridge—obviously inspired by her native Florence.

Chenonceau is one of the most remarkable castles in France because it spans an entire river. The way the waters of the Cher surge and foam beneath its vaulted medieval foundations has been described as mystical. Many visitors consider this their favorite château in all of France.

Gobelin tapestries, including one depicting a woman pouring water over the back of an angry dragon, cover many of the château's walls. The chapel contains a marble *Virgin and Child* by Murillo as well as portraits of Catherine de Médicis in black and white. There's even a portrait of the stern Catherine in the former bedroom of her rival, Diane de Poitiers. In François I's Renaissance bedchamber, the most interesting portrait is that of Diane as the huntress Diana.

The history of Chenonceau is related in 15 tableaux in the **Musée de Cire** (wax museum), located in a Renaissance-era annex a few steps from the château. Open the same hours as the château, it charges admission of 3.50€ ($4.55). Diane de Poitiers, who, among other things, introduced the artichoke to France, is depicted in three tableaux. One portrays Catherine de Médicis tossing out her husband's mistress.

Throughout most of the busy tourist season (mid-Mar to mid-Sept), the château is open daily from 9am to 7pm; September 16 to September 30, it's open daily from 9am to 6:30pm; rest of the year 9am to 5 or 6pm. Admission is 8€ ($10) for adults, and 6.50€ ($8.45) for students and children 7 to 15. A *son-et-lumière* show, *The Era of the Ladies of Chenonceau,* starts at 10:15pm daily in July and August; admission is 6€ ($7.80) and free for children under 7. Allow 2 hours to see this château.

ESSENTIALS

GETTING THERE Four daily **trains** run from Tours to Chenonceaux (trip time: 30 min.), costing 6.25€ ($8.15) one-way. The train deposits you at the base of the château; from there, you can walk or take a taxi. If you're **driving,** from the center of Tours, follow the directions east until you reach the N76, which will take you to the signposted turnoff for Chenonceaux.

VISITOR INFORMATION The **Syndicat d'Initiative** (tourist office), 1 rue du Dr. Bretonneau (✆ **02-47-23-94-45**), is open year-round.

WHERE TO STAY

Auberge du Bon-Laboureur ★★ This inn, within walking distance of the château, is your best bet for a comfortable night's sleep and some of the best cuisine in the Loire Valley. Founded in 1786, the hotel maintains the flavor of that era, thanks to thick walls, solid masonry, and a scattering of antiques. The author Henry James stopped here in 1882, and the inn won his praise. Most guest rooms are small, especially on the upper floors; each comes with a private bathroom with shower or tub. The rear garden has a guesthouse and formally planted roses. The place is noted for its restaurant. In fair weather, tables are set up in the courtyard, amid trees and flowering shrubs.

6 rue du Dr. Bretonneau, Chenonceaux, Bléré 37150. ✆ **02-47-23-90-02.** Fax 02-47-23-82-01. www.amboise.com/laboureur. 24 units. 85€–140€ ($111–$182) double; 145€–185€ ($189–$241) suite. AE, DC, MC, V. Closed mid-Nov to mid-Feb. **Amenities:** Restaurant; bar; outdoor pool; room service; babysitting; laundry service; dry cleaning. *In room:* A/C, TV, hair dryer, safe.

Hostellerie de la Renaudière *Kids* This welcoming family-run hotel is in a converted 18th-century private residence. The convenient location in the middle of town is 8 minutes on foot from the château. The front rooms open onto rail tracks; if you're a light sleeper, request a room in the rear. Each of the intimate, cozily furnished guest rooms has a little bathroom with shower. Kid-friendly innkeepers Isabella and Joel Camus provide toys in the garden. The restaurant serves excellent regional dishes, many based on ancient Loire recipes.

24 rue du Dr. Bretonneau, Chenonceaux, Bléré 37150. ✆ **02-47-23-90-04.** Fax 02-47-23-90-51. www.chenonceau-renaudiere.com. 67€–94€ ($87–$122) double; 90€–120€ ($117–$156) apt. AE, DC, MC, V. Closed mid-Nov to late Feb. **Amenities:** Restaurant; outdoor heated pool; gym; room service; limited-mobility rooms. *In room:* TV, fridge, hair dryer.

La Roseraie ★ *Value* La Roseraie is the most charming hotel in Chenonceaux, with individually decorated rooms and well-kept gardens. Each unit contains a small bathroom with shower. In the 1940s, guests included Winston Churchill, Eleanor Roosevelt, and Harry Truman. During World War II, the innkeeper gained fame with the Allies because of his role in smuggling Churchill's nephew out of Vichy-occupied France.

The English-speaking innkeepers, the exceptionally charming Laurent and Sophie Fiorito, have banned smoking from their excellent dining room. It's open to the public for lunch and dinner. Our favorite dishes include house-style foie gras, magret of duckling with pears and cherries, and an unusual and delicious invention—*emincée* (a dish made with braised meat) of rump steak with wine-marinated pears.

7 rue du Dr. Bretonneau, Chenonceaux, Bléré 37150. ✆ **02-47-23-90-09.** Fax 02-47-23-91-59. www.charmingroseraie.com. 17 units. 52€–95€ ($68–$124) double; 72€–180€ ($94–$234) quad; 180€ ($234) apt. AE, DC, MC, V. Closed mid-Nov to Mar 1. **Amenities:** Restaurant; bar; outdoor pool; laundry service; dry cleaning. *In room:* TV.

WHERE TO DINE

Hostellerie de la Renaudière and **La Roseraie** (see above) boast very good restaurants.

Au Gateau Breton TRADITIONAL FRENCH The sun terrace in back of this 2-century-old Breton-type inn, a short walk from the château, is a refreshing place for dinner or tea. Gravel paths run among beds of pink geraniums and lilacs, and bright umbrellas adorn the red tables. In cool months, meals are served in the rustic dining rooms. Make a meal of the home cooking and cherry liqueur, a specialty of the region. Worthwhile dishes include small chitterling sausages of Tours, *poulet Tourangelle* (fried chicken with a mushroom-flavored cream sauce), chicken with Armagnac sauce, and coq au vin. Medallions of veal with mushroom-cream sauce are excellent. Tasty pastries are sold in the front room.

16 rue du Dr. Bretonneau. ✆ **02-47-23-90-14.** Fax 02-47-23-92-57. Reservations required July–Aug. Main courses 8€–20€ ($10–$26); fixed-price menus 13€–22€ ($16–$29). MC, V. Apr–Sept daily noon–2:30pm, Thurs–Mon 7–10pm; Nov–Mar Thurs–Tues noon–2:30pm.

11 Tours ★

232km (144 miles) SW of Paris, 113km (70 miles) SW of Orléans

Though it doesn't boast a major château, Tours, at the junction of the Loire and Cher rivers, is the traditional center for exploring the valley. Pilgrims en route to Santiago de Compostela in northwest Spain once stopped here to pay homage at the tomb of St-Martin, the Apostle of Gaul, who was bishop of Tours in the 4th century. One of the most significant conflicts in world history, the 732 Battle of Tours, checked the Arab advance into Gaul.

Tours (pop. 138,000) is known for its food and wine. Many of its buildings were bombed in World War II, and 20th-century apartment towers have taken the place of châteaux. However, because Tours is at the doorstep of some of the most magnificent châteaux in France, it makes a good base from which to explore. Most Loire Valley towns are rather sleepy, and Tours is where the action is, with busy streets and cafes. A quarter of the residents are students, who add a vibrant touch to a soulless commercial enclave. Allow a morning or an afternoon to see Tours.

ESSENTIALS

GETTING THERE Most of the trains bound for Tours, including all TGVs (as many as 14 per day), depart from Paris's Gare Montparnasse, although a very limited

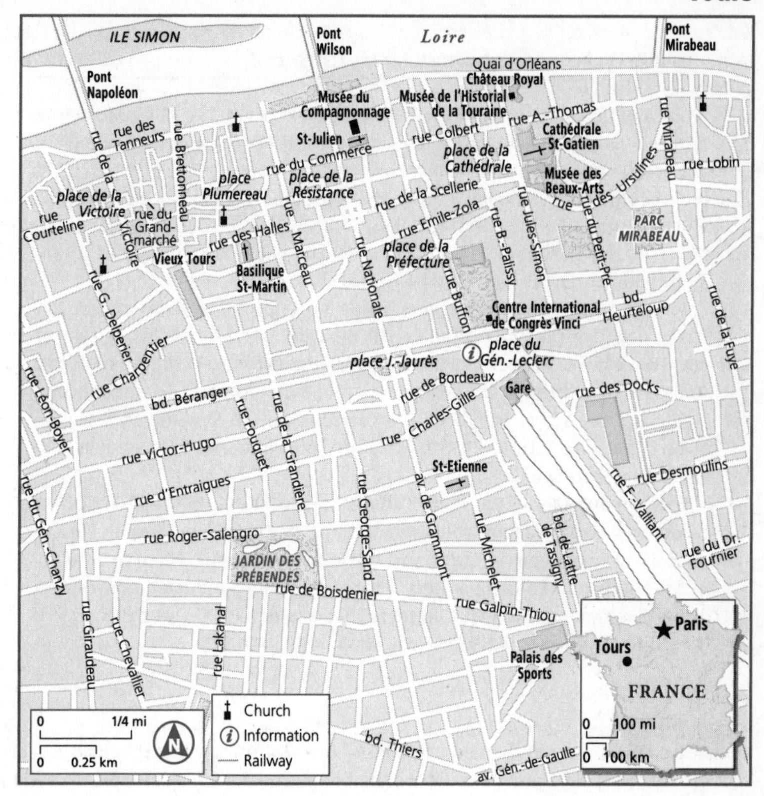

number of trains, including some of the slow and conventional commuter trains, depart from Gare d'Austerlitz. One-way fares range from 27€ to 49€ ($35–$64). Many, but not all, of the conventional (non-TGV) trains pull into the center of Tours, at the **Gare Tours Centre Ville,** place du Maréchal-Leclerc, 3 rue Edouard-Vaillant. Some conventional trains and virtually all the TGV trains, however, arrive at the isolated railway station of **Tours/St-Pierre-des-Corps,** about 6km (3¾ miles) east of the center of Tours. If your train drops you off here, know in advance that at least one (and during peak hours, several) *navettes* (buses) await every TGV train for free ongoing transport to the center of Tours.

If you're **driving,** take highway A10 to Tours.

VISITOR INFORMATION The **Office de Tourisme** is at 78 rue Bernard-Palissy (✆ **02-47-70-37-37;** www.ligeris.com).

GETTING AROUND

It's easy to walk from one end of central Tours to the other, and most of the good hotels are near the train station. For taxi service, call **Taxi Radio** (✆ **02-47-20-30-40**). Car-rental offices in or near the train station include **Avis,** inside the station (✆ **02-47-20-53-27**), open daily 8am to noon and 1:15 to 7pm; and **Europcar,** 7 rue Bernard-Palissy (✆ **02-47-20-30-40**), open daily 8am to noon and 2 to 7pm. You can rent a bike

Moments **Fun-Filled Ways to Get Around**

For a commentary-filled English-language overview of Tours, its monuments, and its layout, ride through the streets of the city aboard a simulated train with rubber wheels. It operates from Easter to mid-October, daily at 10am, 11am, 2pm, 3pm, 4pm, 5pm, and 6pm. Tickets, available at the tourist office or onboard, cost 6€ ($7.80) for adults and 3€ ($3.90) for children under 12. Rides (about 50 min.) begin and end in front of the tourist office, 78–82 rue Bernard-Palissy (✆ **02-47-70-37-37**).

An old-fashioned alternative is a ride on one of the horse-drawn carriages *(Les Calèches)* operated by **Fil Bleu** (✆ **02-47-66-70-70**). A pair of slow-moving workhorses pull the wagon-like conveyances, which hold up to 10 passengers, through the city's medieval neighborhoods. There's no commentary. Tickets cost 2€ ($2.60) per person. May to September, rides are given Tuesday to Saturday at 10am, 11am, 3pm, 4pm, and 5pm; and on Sunday at 3, 4, and 5pm.

Daily in July and August, the tourist office (✆ **02-47-70-37-37**) offers guided old-town walking tours in a mixture of French and English. The 2-hour excursions depart from the tourist office, usually at 10am or 2:30pm. April to June and September and October tours are conducted only on Saturday, Sunday, and holidays. Reservations are required. The cost is 5.50€ ($7.15) for adults and 4.50€ ($5.85) for children 6 to 12.

at **Amstercycles,** 5 rue du Rempart (✆ **02-47-61-22-23;** www.amstercycles.com), at a cost of 14€ ($18) per day. A passport deposit is required. Open May to September Monday to Saturday 9am to 12:30pm and 1 to 7pm, Sunday 9am to 12:30pm and 6 to 7pm.

EXPLORING THE CITY

The heart of town is **place Jean-Jaurès.** The principal street is **rue Nationale,** running north to the Loire River. Head west along rue du Commerce and rue du Grand-Marché to Vieux Tours/Vieille Ville (old town).

Cathédrale St-Gatien This cathedral honors a 3rd-century evangelist and has a Flamboyant Gothic facade flanked by towers with bases from the 12th century. The lanterns date to the Renaissance. The choir is from the 13th century, with new additions built in each century through the 16th. Sheltered inside is the handsome 16th-century tomb of Charles VIII and Anne de Bretagne's two children. Some of the glorious stained-glass windows are from the 13th century.

5 place de la Cathédrale. ✆ **02-47-70-21-00.** Free admission. Daily 8:30am–7pm.

Musée des Beaux-Arts This fine provincial museum in the Palais des Archevêques is worth a visit just to see its lovely rooms and gardens. There are old masters here as well, including works by Degas, Delacroix, Rembrandt, and Boucher. The sculpture collection includes works by Houdon and Bourdelle. You can tour the gardens for free, daily from 7am to 8:30pm.

18 place François-Sicard. ✆ **02-47-05-68-73.** Admission 4.50€ ($5.85) adults, 2.50€ ($3.25) seniors and students, free for children under 13. Wed–Mon 9am–12:45pm and 2–6pm. Bus: 3.

SHOPPING: TO THE MARKET WE GO

In the pedestrian area of rue de Bordeaux, from the magnificent train station to rue Nationale, you'll find dozens of mall-type shops and department stores selling clothes, shoes, jewelry, leather goods, and the like. Up rue Nationale toward the river are more shops and upscale boutiques, and a small mall with chain stores. Rue Nationale continues across the river, but turn left on rue du Commerce toward the old town center. You'll want to explore the streets and courtyards for regional specialties, books, toys, and crafts. A hotbed for antiques is east of rue Nationale (toward the cathedral), along rue de la Scellerie.

Of the more than 30 markets here, the most animated are the **gourmet market (Marché Gourmand),** the first and third Friday of each summer month, 4 to 10pm, place de la Résistance; the **antiques market,** the first and third Friday of the month in the pedestrian zone on rue de Bordeaux, and the fourth Sunday of the month, a larger version of the event with more *brocante* than genuine antiques; the **flower market,** Wednesday and Saturday 8am to 6pm, boulevard Béranger; and the **craft market (Marché Artisanal),** Saturday 9am to 1pm, place des Halles. **Traditional food markets** take place Tuesday to Sunday mornings at various locations; ask at the tourist office. The covered market, **Les Halles et Grand Marché,** with a huge selection of fresh local meat, cheese, and produce, is at place Gaston-Pailhou Monday to Saturday 6am to 7pm and Sunday 6am to 1pm.

WHERE TO STAY

Best Western Le Central Off the main boulevard, this old-fashioned hotel is within walking distance of the river and cathedral, surrounded by gardens, lawns, and trees. Built in 1850, it is a more modest and economical choice than others in town. The Tremouilles family offers comfortable rooms at reasonable rates. Accommodations come in a variety of shapes and sizes; a renovation in 2003 improved them and updated the plumbing in the small bathrooms. Half of the guest rooms have tub/shower combos, the others only showers.

21 rue Berthelot, Tours 37000. ✆ **800/528-1234** in the U.S. and Canada, or 02-47-05-46-44. Fax 02-47-66-10-26. www.bestwestern.com. 37 units. 97€–137€ ($126–$178) double; 173€–230€ ($225–$299) suite. AE, DC, MC, V. Parking 10€ ($13). Bus: 1, 4, or 5. **Amenities:** Bar; room service; babysitting; business center; laundry service; dry cleaning; nonsmoking rooms; limited-mobility rooms. *In room:* A/C, TV, minibar, hair dryer, iron, beverage maker.

Hôtel de l'Univers This hotel was erected in 1853, making it the oldest in town. It has been upgraded to government-rated four-star status, making it the best in the town center. Its midsize rooms, outfitted in a conservative contemporary style, have monochromatic and tasteful soft color schemes. The bathrooms, with shower and tub, have also been renewed. On weekdays, the hotel fills with business travelers; on weekends, it hosts many area brides and grooms.

5 bd. Heurteloup, Tours 37000. ✆ **02-47-05-37-12.** Fax 02-47-61-51-80. www.hotel-univers.fr. 85 units. 197€–270€ ($256–$351) double; 344€–398€ ($447–$517) suite. AE, DC, MC, V. Parking 10€ ($13). Bus: 1, 4, or 5. **Amenities:** Room service; laundry service; dry cleaning; limited-mobility rooms. *In room:* A/C, TV, minibar, hair dryer.

Hôtel du Manoir On a quiet street near the train station, this 19th-century residence is a comfortable place to stay. The cheerful reception area reflects the quality of the rooms. Though small to average in size, all units have windows that let in lots of light and afford views of the neighborhood or the hotel courtyard. Most have simple furnishings. About half the rooms have tub/shower combos; the other half have only showers.

2 rue Traversière, Tours 37000. ✆ **02-47-05-37-37.** Fax 02-47-05-16-00. manoir37@wanadoo.fr. 20 units. 48€–60€ ($62–$78) double. AE, DC, MC, V. Parking 4.50€ ($5.85). Bus: 3 or 70. *In room:* A/C, TV, Wi-Fi.

WHERE TO DINE

Restaurants can be pricey, but you can keep costs low at **La Souris Gourmande,** 100 rue Colbert (✆ **02-47-47-04-80**), where the chef is respected for the diversity of his cheese selection. Try it in half a dozen fondues. You may be asked to join a communal table. Main courses cost 11€ to 15€ ($14–$20). At the raffish but cheerful bistro **Le Lapin qui Fume,** 90 rue Colbert (✆ **02-47-66-95-49**), a fixed-price menu costs 20€ ($26).

EXPENSIVE

La Roche le Roy ★★ MODERN FRENCH One of the hottest chefs in town, Alain Couturier, blends new and old techniques in a gabled 15th-century manor south of the town center. Couturier's repertoire includes scalloped foie gras with lentils, cod with saffron cream sauce, pan-fried scallops with truffle vinaigrette, and *matelote* (stew) of eel with Chinon or Bourgueil wine. His masterpiece is suprême of pigeon with "roughly textured" sauce. For dessert, try a slice of warm orange-flavored chocolate served with coffee-flavored sherbet.

55 rte. St-Avertin. ✆ **02-47-27-22-00.** Reservations recommended. Main courses 24€–32€ ($31–$42); fixed-price lunch 34€ ($44), fixed-price dinner 55€–75€ ($72–$98). AE, MC, V. Tues–Sat noon–1:45pm and 7:30–9:30pm. Closed 1 week in Feb and 3 weeks in Aug. From the center of town, take av. Grammont south (follow signs to St-Avertin–Vierzon). The road crosses a bridge but doesn't change names. The restaurant is beside that road, on the southern periphery of Tours.

MODERATE

La Rôtisserie Tourangelle TRADITIONAL FRENCH This has been a local favorite since shortly after World War II. In the commercial heart of Tours, it has two dining rooms and an outdoor terrace for warm-weather dining. The ever-changing menu may include homemade foie gras and whitefish caught in the Loire and served with beurre blanc. Regional ingredients mix well with the local wines, as exemplified by pikeperch with sabayon; a *beuchelle Tourangelle,* a ragout composed of local red wine from the Loire Valley mixed with veal sweetbreads and kidneys; and *magret de canard* (duckling) served with a "jam" of red Chinon wine. In summer, strawberry parfait with raspberry coulis is a perfect finish.

23 rue du Commerce. ✆ **02-47-05-71-21.** Reservations required. Main courses 15€–17€ ($20–$22); fixed-price menu 16€–41€ ($21–$53). MC, V. Lunch Tues–Fri and Sun 10am–1:30pm; dinner Tues–Sat 6:30–9:30pm. Bus: 1, 4, or 5.

Les Tuffeaux *Value* TRADITIONAL FRENCH Although the cuisine at La Rôtisserie Tourangelle (see above) has a slight edge, this restaurant in an 18th-century house is one of the best in Tours. Menu items change three times a year, depending on the inspiration of chef Gildas Marsollier. He prepares classics but also experiments, with offerings such as noisettes of roasted rabbit with bacon and almonds, crisp grilled crayfish with partridge-stuffed ravioli, and braised turbot with gratinéed *viennoise* of Comté cheese. Roasted filet of pigeon with pink grapefruit is an enduring favorite.

19 rue Lavoisier. ✆ **02-47-47-19-89.** Reservations required. Main courses 15€–24€ ($20–$31); fixed-price menu 25€–36€ ($33–$47). AE, DC, MC, V. Mon–Tues and Thurs–Sat noon–1:30pm; Mon–Sat 7:30–9:30pm. Bus: 1, 4, or 5.

INEXPENSIVE

La Brasserie Buré TRADITIONAL FRENCH A 5-minute walk east of the center of Tours, this somewhat unimaginative brasserie specializes in shellfish and regional recipes. It has a busy bar and a front terrace, with tables inside on the street level and mezzanine. Menu items include six well-flavored versions of sauerkraut; a wide choice of grilled meats, including steak au poivre; foie gras and smoked salmon; and a tempting array of desserts.

1 place de la Résistance. ✆ **02-47-05-67-74.** Main courses 13€–21€ ($17–$27); fixed-price menu (Mon–Fri) 19€ ($25). AE, DC, MC, V. Daily noon–2:30pm and 7pm–midnight. Bus: 1 or 5.

Le Petit Patrimoine TRADITIONAL FRENCH Despite the proliferation of newer, trend-conscious restaurants along rue Colbert, this pocket-size, long-established restaurant exudes a powerful, albeit quirky and idiosyncratic, appeal. Outfitted in a rustic and old-fashioned style that might have been inspired by someone's early-20th-century grandmother, it has ceiling beams, old masonry walls, and a sense of respect for old-fashioned French aesthetics and values. Your hosts, each a distinct personality known by clients as either independent-minded or curmudgeonly, depending on their mood of the moment, will propose dishes that include a savory *matelote* of veal with baby vegetables, a salad of *rillons* (a meat byproduct made from bacon), grilled beefsteaks with goat cheese, and a *torte Tourangelle* composed of pastry casing filled with goat cheese and the above-mentioned *rillons.*

58 rue Colbert. ✆ **02-47-66-05-81.** Reservations recommended. Main courses 8€–14€ ($10–$18); fixed-price menu 15€–31€ ($20–$40). AE, DC, MC, V. Mon–Sat noon–2pm and 7–10pm.

WHERE TO STAY & DINE NEARBY

Château Belmont (Jean Bardet) ★ MODERN FRENCH In three rooms of a 19th-century château, this restaurant is the creation of the Michelin two-star chef Jean Bardet, who considers all meals here "an orchestration of wines, alcohol, food, and cigars." That's not to say that you must partake of all four to have one of the best meals in the region. Specialties include lobster ragout, sliced sea bass with comfit of tomatoes and artichoke hearts, sliced pork with caviar, consommé of crab with squid ink, and scallops with a purée of shallots and truffle cream. The duck giblets and lobster accompanied by a red-wine and orange sauce are reason enough to visit.

The rest of the château, a 21-room luxury hotel, is the domain of Bardet's wife, Sophie. The spacious, air-conditioned rooms are individually decorated; they have high ceilings, fireplaces, TVs, minibars, and antique furnishings. Some have private balconies that open onto the gardens. Bathrooms are luxurious, with tub/shower combinations. A double room costs 145€ to 400€ ($189–$520).

57 rue Groison, Tours 37100. ✆ **02-47-41-41-11.** Fax 02-47-51-68-72. www.jeanbardet.com. Reservations recommended. Main courses 38€–115€ ($49–$150); fixed-price menu 60€–165€ ($78–$215). AE, DC, MC, V. May–Oct Tues–Fri and Sun noon–2pm, daily 7:30–9:30pm; Nov–Apr Tues–Sun noon–2pm, Tues–Sat 7:30–9:30pm.

Château d'Artigny ★★★ This is the grandest address in the Loire Valley. About 1.5km (1 mile) west of the hamlet of Montbazon, the château was built between 1912 and 1920 for perfume and cosmetics king François Coty, who lived and entertained lavishly. Set in a forest, overlooking formal gardens, in an obscure villa near Paris, the Château de Champlatreux, the château combines Jazz Age ostentation and 18th-century French aesthetics. The drawing room and corridors are furnished with fine antiques, Louis XV–style chairs, and bronze statuary. The grounds contain acres of parks and a large garden with a reflecting pool. Guest rooms are outfitted in period style, with many antiques, comfortable mattresses, and all the perks of upscale country living. Only 31 units are in the main building; the others are in four annexes—a former chapel, gatehouse, mill, and staff dormitory.

Rte. d'Azay-le-Rideau (D17), Montbazon 37250. From Tours, take N10 south for 11km (6¾ miles) to Montbazon, and then take D17 1.5km (1 mile) southeast. ✆ **02-47-34-30-30.** Fax 02-47-34-30-39. www.artigny.com. 65 units. 160€–330€ ($208–$429) double; 420€ ($546) junior suite. Half board 78€ ($101) per person. AE, DC, MC, V. **Amenities:** Restaurant; bar; outdoor pool; 2 tennis courts; mini-golf; fitness center; spa; sauna; room service; babysitting; laundry service; dry cleaning. *In room:* TV, minibar, hair dryer, Wi-Fi.

Château de Beaulieu ★★ At this 17th-century estate, you can experience the lifestyle of another era. Beyond the entrance, a double curving stairway leads to the reception hall. Guest rooms have mahogany and chestnut furniture, decorative fireplaces, and good plumbing. Nine are in the château (we recommend these); the others, a bit more sterile, are in a turn-of-the-20th-century pavilion a stone's throw away. All have elegant beds outfitted with comfortable mattresses.

67 rue de Beaulieu, Joué-les-Tours 37300. Take D86 from Tours, and then D207 toward Beaulieu, 7km (4⅓ miles) southwest of Tours. ✆ **02-47-53-20-26.** Fax 02-47-53-84-20. www.chateaudebeaulieu37.com. 19 units. 90€–135€ ($117–$176) double. Half board 170€–215€ ($221–$280) for 2. AE, MC, V. **Amenities:** Restaurant; bar; 3 tennis courts (across road). *In room:* A/C, TV, minibar, hair dryer.

TOURS AFTER DARK

Long a student town, Tours has a lively young population. Even during summer, when most students have left, a youthful crowd rules the hot spots. **Place Plumereau** (often shortened to "place Plume"), a square of medieval buildings, houses a riot of restaurants and bars. In the warmer months, the square explodes with tables, which fill with people who like to people-watch (and be watched themselves). In addition to the bars and clubs around the place Plumereau, an even trendier street, **rue Colbert,** has emerged as a hip and fashionable street. Rue Colbert lies in the heart of Tours, midway between the place Plumereau and the cathedral.

A popular site is **Le Louis XIV,** 37 rue Briçonnet (✆ **02-47-05-77-17**), a stylish bar where meeting new friends and companions is not out of the question. The hottest place in town is **L'Excalibur,** 35 rue Briçonnet (✆ **02-47-64-76-78**), with a disco beat and video system. A clientele of all ages, many from the surrounding countryside, heads to **Le Pyms,** 170 av. de Grammont (✆ **02-47-66-22-22**), an alternative disco open Wednesday to Sunday from 11pm to at least 5am. A bar that tends to be loaded with a selection of the town's students is **Le Club 71,** 71 rue Georges-Courteline (✆ **02-47-37-01-54**).

And if you're gay, relatively energetic, and like to dance, check out the town's most popular gay bar and disco, **Le G.I.,** 13 rue Lavoisier (✆ **02-47-66-29-96**). Positioned on a dark street in a safe but somewhat run-down neighborhood, it attracts a local, mostly male crowd that packs the place on weekends.

Tips Château-hopping Made Easy

Several tour companies in Tours arrange visits to four or five castles per day, departing daily at 9am. Costs range from 40€ to 45€ ($52–$59), depending on the company. The best tours are offered by **Saint-Elol Excursions** (✆ **02-47-37-08-04**) and by **Quart de Tours** (✆ **06-30-65-52-01**). The price does not include admission to the châteaux, but participation in the tour qualifies you for reduced group rates. Some visitors combine two half-day tours into a full day of château hopping. Because trains from Paris take only 55 minutes each way, this makes a worthwhile side trip.

12 Loches ★★

258km (160 miles) SW of Paris, 40km (25 miles) SE of Tours

Forever linked to legendary beauty Agnès Sorel, Loches is the *cité médiévale* of the valley, situated in the hills on the banks of the Indre. Known as the acropolis of the Loire, the château and its satellite buildings form a complex called the **Cité Royale** ★. The House of Anjou, from which the Plantagenets descended, owned the castle from 886 to 1205. The kings of France occupied it from the mid–13th century until Charles IX became king in 1560.

Château de Loches ★★, 5 place Charles-VII (© **02-47-59-01-32**), is remembered for the *belle des belles* (beauty of beauties) Agnès Sorel. Inside is her tomb, where two angels guard her velvet cushion. In 1777, the tomb was opened, but all that remained of the 15th-century beauty were a set of dentures and some locks of hair. Maid of honor to Isabelle de Lorraine, she was singled out by Charles VII to be his mistress and had great influence on the king until her mysterious death. Afterward, Fouquet painted her as a practically topless Virgin Mary, with a disgruntled Charles VII looking on. (The original is in Antwerp; the château has a copy.) The château also contains the oratory of Anne de Bretagne, decorated with ermine tails. One of its outstanding treasures is a triptych of *The Passion* (1485) from the Fouquet school.

You can visit the château without a guide daily. It's open April to September from 9am to 7pm, October to March from 9:30am to 5pm.

The ancient keep, or *donjon,* of the *comtes* d'Anjou (© **02-47-59-07-86**) is open the same hours as the château. The Round Tower of Louis XI contains rooms used for torture; a favorite method involved suspending the victim in an iron cage. In the 15th century, the duke of Milan, Ludovico Sforza, was imprisoned in the Martelet and painted frescoes on the walls to pass the time; he died here in 1508.

Tickets to the château or the dungeon cost 5€ ($6.50) for adults, 3.50€ ($4.55) for students, and 2.50€ ($3.25) for children 7 to 18. A combination ticket to both costs 7€ ($9.10) for adults, 4.50€ ($5.85) for students, and 3.50€ ($4.55) for children ages 7 to 18. Children under 7 enter free.

The château is the site of a *son-et-lumière* show depicting **Merlin the Magician,** "a fairy tale from the age of chivalry." The French-language show runs 15 times during July and August, beginning promptly at 10:30pm in July and 10pm in August. It includes a cast of local residents in medieval costumes, mingling history, lore, and legend into a highly entertaining program. Tickets are 12€ ($16) for adults, 6€ ($7.80) for children 6 to 12, and free for children under 6. Schedules vary and are announced only a few months prior to the event; contact the tourist office in Loches (see below).

Nearby, the Romanesque **Collégiale St-Ours (Collegiate Church of St-Ours),** 1 rue Thomas-Pactius (© **02-47-59-02-36**), spans the 10th to 15th centuries. Sculpted figures, damaged but still attractive, decorate the portal. Stone pyramids *(dubes)* surmount the nave; the carving on the west door is exceptional. The church is open daily from 9am to 7pm, except during class; admission is free.

Finally, you may want to walk the ramparts and enjoy the view of the town, including a 15th-century gate and Renaissance inns.

Allow 3 hours to see Loches.

ESSENTIALS

GETTING THERE Six to 10 **buses** run daily from Tours; the 45-minute trip costs 7.50€ ($9.75) one-way. The one-way **train** fare from Tours is 8.20€ ($11). For bus information, call ✆ **02-47-05-30-49;** for train schedules, call ✆ **08-91-35-35-35.** If you're **driving** from Tours, take N143 southeast to Loches.

VISITOR INFORMATION The **Office de Tourisme** is near the bus station on place de la Marne (✆ **02-47-91-82-82;** www.loches-tourainecotesud.com).

WHERE TO STAY & DINE

Loches is short on inns and good restaurants. If you're here for lunch, we recommend the 18th-century **Hôtel George-Sand,** 39 rue Quintefol (✆ **02-47-59-39-74;** fax 02-47-91-55-75; www.hotelrestaurant-georgesand.com), for its Touraine cuisine, including filet of pikeperch from the Loire. It also rents 20 rooms; doubles go for 42€ to 96€ ($55–$125), suites for 110€ ($143).

Grand Hotel de France ★ This charming hotel was a postal relay station until the mid–19th century. In 1932, it gained three floors and became an inn. Before the turn of the 21st century, management upgraded and redecorated the guest rooms, added new beds, and restored the small bathrooms. The most tranquil rooms overlook the courtyard. You can dine in the wood-paneled dining room or under the parasols in the courtyard.

6 rue Picois, Loches 37600. ✆ **02-47-59-00-32.** Fax 02-47-59-28-66. www.hoteldefrance.com. 17 units. 55€–70€ ($72–$91) double. AE, DC, MC, V. Parking 5€ ($6.50). Closed Jan 5–Feb 13. **Amenities:** Restaurant; bar; room service. *In room:* TV.

13 Villandry

253km (157 miles) SW of Paris, 32km (20 miles) NE of Chinon, 18km (11 miles) W of Tours, 8km (5 miles) E of Azay-le-Rideau

The 16th-century-style gardens of the Renaissance **Château de Villandry** ★★★, 3 rue Principale, 37510 Villandry (✆ **02-47-50-02-09**), are celebrated throughout the Touraine. A trio of superimposed cloisters with a water garden on the highest level, they were restored by the Spanish doctor and scientist Joachim Carvallo, grandfather of the present owner.

The grounds contain 17km (11 miles) of boxwood sculpture, which the gardeners cut to style in only 2 weeks each September. Every square of the gardens is like a geometric mosaic. The borders symbolize the faces of love: tender, tragic (represented by daggers), and crazy (with a labyrinth that doesn't get you anywhere). Pink tulips and dahlias suggest sweet love; red, tragic; and yellow, unfaithful. All colors signify crazy love. The vine arbors, citrus hedges, and walks keep six men busy full-time. One garden contains all the French vegetables except the potato, which wasn't known in France in the 16th century.

A feudal castle once stood at Villandry. In 1536, Jean Lebreton, François I's chancellor, built the present château, whose buildings form a U and are surrounded by a moat. Near the gardens is a terrace from which you can see the small village and its 12th-century church. A tearoom on-site, **La Doulce Terrasse** (✆ **02-47-50-02-10;** www.chateauvillandry.com), serves traditional Loire cooking, including hot dishes, freshly baked bread, homemade ice cream, and cocktails made from fresh fruit.

Admission to the gardens, including a guided tour of the château, costs 8€ ($10) for adults, 5€ ($6.50) for children 8 to 18, and is free for children under 8. Visiting the gardens separately, without a guide, costs 5.50€ ($7.15) for adults and 3.50€ ($4.55) for children 8 to 18. The gardens are open daily from 9am to between 5 and 7:30pm, depending on the hour of sunset; the château is open daily from 9am to between 4:30 and 6:30pm, depending on a complicated seasonal schedule. Tours are conducted in French; leaflets are available in English.

Villandry has no train service. The nearest connection from Tours is at the town of Savonnières. From Savonnières, you can walk along the Loire for 4km (2½ miles) to reach Villandry, rent a **bike** at the station, or take a **taxi.** You can also **drive,** following D7 from Tours. Allow 1½ hours to see Villandry.

WHERE TO STAY & DINE

Le Cheval Rouge MODERN FRENCH The well-known dining stopover near the château extends a congenial welcome. The conservatively decorated dining room lies about 91m (300 ft.) from the banks of the Cher. Specialties include Quiche Tourangel (made with pork byproducts including chitterling sausages), a flavorful version of eel stew, medallions of veal with morels, and turbot with hollandaise sauce. The inn also rents 39 rooms, all with private bathroom and phone. A double is 40€ to 62€ ($52–$81).

37510 Villandry. ✆ **02-47-50-02-07.** Fax 02-47-50-08-77. www.lecheval-rouge.com. Reservations recommended. Main courses 18€–29€ ($23–$38); fixed-price menu 18€–35€ ($23–$46). AE, DC, MC, V. Daily noon–2pm and 7:30–9pm.

14 Langeais

259km (161 miles) SW of Paris, 26km (16 miles) W of Tours

On December 6, 1491, Anne de Bretagne "arrived at Langeais carried in a litter decked with gold cloth, dressed in a gown of black trimmed with sable. Her wedding gown of gold cloth was ornamented with 160 sables." Her marriage to Charles VIII was Langeais's golden hour.

Château de Langeais ★★ This is a medieval fortress, a formidable gray pile that dominates the town. It's one of the few châteaux actually on the Loire. The facade is forbidding, but once you cross the drawbridge, you'll find the apartments so richly decorated that they soften the effect. The castle dates from the 9th century, when the Black Falcon erected the first dungeon in Europe; the ruins survive. The present structure was built in 1465. The interior is well-preserved and furnished thanks to Jacques Siegfried, who not only restored it over 20 years but also bequeathed it to the Institut de France in 1904.

Anne de Bretagne and Charles VIII's symbols—scallops, fleurs-de-lis, and ermine—set the motif for the Guard Room, and seven tapestries known as the Valiant Knights cover the walls of the Wedding Chamber.

In a bedchamber known as The Crucifixion, the 15th-century black-oak four-poster bed is reputed to be one of the earliest known. The room takes its name from a tapestry of the Virgin and St. John on flower-bedecked ground. A rare Flemish tapestry hangs in the Monsieur's Room. The Chapel Hall was built by joining two stories under a ceiling of Gothic arches. In the Luini Room is a large 1522 fresco by that artist, removed from a chapel on Lake Maggiore, Italy. It depicts Saint Francis of Assisi and Saint Elizabeth of Hungary with Mary and Joseph. The Byzantine Virgin in the drawing room is thought to be an early work of Cimabue, the Florentine artist. Finally, the tapestry of the *Thousand Flowers* is a celebration of spring, a joyous riot of growth and symbol of life's renewal. Allow 1½ hours to go through the château.

Langeais 37130. ✆ **02-47-96-72-60.** Admission 8€ ($10) adults, 7€ ($9.10) students and ages 18–25, 5€ ($6.50) for children 10–18. July 14–Aug 20 daily 9:30am–8pm; Apr–July 14 and Aug 21–Oct 15 daily 9am–6:30pm; Oct 16–Mar daily 10am–5:30pm.

ESSENTIALS

GETTING THERE Seven **trains** per day stop here en route from Tours or Saumur. Transit time from Tours is 20 minutes. For schedules and information, call ✆ **08-92-35-35-39.** If you're **driving** from Tours, take N152 southwest to Langeais.

VISITOR INFORMATION The **Office de Tourisme** is at place du 14-Juillet (✆ **02-47-96-58-22**).

WHERE TO STAY & DINE

Hotel Hosten et Restaurant Errard ★ This ivy-draped country inn in the center of town was built in 1853. In 2002, it added a neighboring house, creating a hotel-restaurant complex. The restaurant, which has received many honors, is elegant and formal, the hotel that houses it a bit more relaxed. Guest rooms are rustic and comfortable, and some (particularly the suites in the annex) are surprisingly large. Most of the well-maintained tiled bathrooms have tub/shower combinations. Guests dine indoors or at tables in the open courtyard under umbrellas and flowering trees. The *menu de prestige* includes *matelote* of eel with Bourgueil red wine, and stuffed venison. Dessert may be pear mousse with Jamaican pepper ice cream.

2 rue Gambetta, Langeais 37130. ✆ **02-47-96-82-12.** Fax 02-47-96-56-72. www.errard.com. 10 units. 65€–75€ ($85–$98) double; 92€–109€ ($120–$142) apt. AE, MC, V. Parking 5€ ($6.50). Closed Dec–Jan. **Amenities:** Restaurant; bar. *In room:* TV.

La Duchesse Anne On the eastern outskirts of town, this hotel opened in the 18th century as a coaching inn, providing food and shelter for people and horses. Guest rooms are decorated with flowered wallpaper and filled with comfortable, traditional furniture. Units vary in size and shape, and most of the tiled bathrooms have tubs and showers. Garden tables are set out for dining. The cuisine reflects the traditions of the Loire Valley. It includes flavorful but not experimental dishes such as fresh salmon with beurre blanc, and guinea fowl with Bourgueil wine sauce. From April to October, the restaurant is open for lunch and dinner daily; the rest of the year, it's closed Monday and Friday for lunch.

10 rue de Tours, Langeais 37130. ✆ **02-47-96-82-03.** Fax 02-47-96-68-60. 15 units. 56€ ($73) double. AE, MC, V. **Amenities:** Restaurant; bar; room service. *In room:* TV.

15 Azay-le-Rideau

261km (162 miles) SW of Paris, 21km (13 miles) SW of Tours

Its machicolated towers and blue-slate roof pierced with dormers shimmer in the moat, creating a reflection like a Monet painting. The defensive medieval look is all for show: the Renaissance **Château d'Azay-le-Rideau** ★★, 19 rue Balzac, 37190 Azay-le-Rideau (✆ **02-47-45-42-04;** www.monum.fr), was created as a residence at an idyllic spot on the Indre River. Gilles Berthelot, François I's finance minister, commissioned the castle, and his spendthrift wife, Philippa, supervised its construction. So elegant was the creation that the Chevalier King grew jealous. Berthelot was accused of misappropriation of funds and forced to flee, and the château reverted to the king. He didn't live here, but granted it to "friends of the Crown." It became the property of the state in 1905.

Before you enter, circle the château and note the perfect proportions of the crowning achievement of the Renaissance in the Touraine. Check out its most fancifully ornate feature, the bay enclosing a grand stairway with a straight flight of steps. The Renaissance interior is a virtual museum.

Finds For Literary Fans: An Ode to Balzac

Four kilometers (3 miles) east of Azay-le-Rideau (take D17), you can visit **Saché,** the hometown of Honoré de Balzac. Here he wrote *The Lily of the Valley* and declared that his affection for the Touraine was like "the love of the artist for his art." Of interest to fans is the **Musée Balzac,** in the 19th-century Château de Saché, Saché 37190 (✆ **02-47-26-86-50**). The small château contains the writer's bedrooms, preserved as they were when he lived here. A collection of Balzac's notes, first editions, etchings, letters, and cartoons are on display, as is a copy of Rodin's sculpture of the writer. The castle and museum are open daily April to September from 10am to 6pm, October to March 9:30am to 12:30pm and 2 to 5:30pm. Admission is 4.50€ ($5.85) for adults, 3.50€ ($4.55) for seniors and students, 2€ ($2.60) for children 7 to 18, and free for children under 7.

From the second-floor Royal Chamber, look out at the gardens. This bedroom, also known as the Green Room, is believed to have housed Louis XIII. The adjoining Red Chamber contains a portrait gallery that includes *Lady in Red* and Diane de Poitiers (Henri II's favorite) in her bath.

The château is open daily in July and August 9:30am to 7pm; April to June and September to October 9:30am to 6pm; and November to March 10am to 12:30pm and 2 to 5:30pm. Admission is 7.50€ ($9.75) for adults, 4.80€ ($6.25) for ages 18 to 25, and free for children under 18. Allow 2 hours for a visit.

In warm weather, *son-et-lumière* performances feature recorded music and lights beaming on the exterior of the château. The shows, which last about an hour, begin at 10:30pm from May to July, at 10pm in August, and at 9:30pm in September. Tickets are 12€ ($16) for adults, 7€ ($9.10) for ages 18 to 25, 5€ ($6.50) for ages 12 to 17, and free for children under 12.

ESSENTIALS

GETTING THERE To reach Azay-le-Rideau, take the **train** from Tours or Chinon. From either starting point, the trip time is about 30 minutes and the one-way fare is 4.75€ ($5.70). Both Tours and Chinon have express service to Paris. For SNCF bus and rail schedules to Azay-le-Rideau, call ✆ **08-91-35-35-35.** If you're **driving** from Tours, take D759 southwest to Azay-le-Rideau.

Because trains arrive at Azay-le-Rideau's railway station in relatively small numbers, some visitors prefer to travel to the railway station at nearby Tours, switching to any of the frequent buses between Tours's railway station and Azay. Operated by Ste. TER, a subsidiary of the SNCF, the company charges 4.50€ ($5.85) each way. For more information, call ✆ **08-92-35-35-35.**

VISITOR INFORMATION The **Office de Tourisme** is on place de L'Europe (✆ **02-47-45-44-40;** www.ot-paysazaylerideau.com).

WHERE TO STAY & DINE

L'Aigle d'Or ★ TRADITIONAL FRENCH Owners Jean-Luc and Ghislaine Fèvre work in the kitchens and dining room of this century-old house, which has been the best restaurant in town for nearly 2 decades. The restaurant is in the village center, about .3km (¼ mile) from the château. The service is professional, the welcome charming, and the food the best in Azay. In a dining room accented with ceiling beams, a fireplace, and pastel colors, you'll enjoy dishes including crayfish with foie gras and *blanquette* (stew) of Loire Valley whitefish prepared with one of the region's white wines. Desserts are made fresh daily. In summer, the party expands onto an outdoor terrace.

10 av. Adélaïde-Riché. ✆ **02-47-45-24-58.** Reservations recommended. Main courses 14€–22€ ($18–$29); fixed-price lunch 24€–44€ ($31–$57); children's menu 10€ ($13). V. Thurs–Tues noon–1:30pm; Thurs–Sat and Mon 7:30–9pm.

Le Grand Monarque The ivy that covers the exterior of this hotel—less than 150m (492 ft.) from the château—seems to protect it from the modern world. As you enter the manor house, with its dark ceiling beams, you'll be transported to a different era. The large guest rooms are outfitted with antiques. Units in the annex aren't as well decorated but are more tranquil. Half the well-maintained bathrooms hold tub/shower combinations. You can enjoy a casual evening in the lounge area or in the dining room.

The superb restaurant features such dishes as brochette of crayfish with sesame sauce, suprême of *sandre* in shallot-flavored broth, and galette of pig's foot *en confit.* Look for specialties that include a terrine of stingray with celery, steak of mullet prepared with the local wine of Azay, and a kettle of crayfish with a bouillon of mushrooms. Fixed-price menus range from 28€ to 55€ ($36–$72). During warmer months, you can dine out on the courtyard terrace. In February, March, October, and November, the restaurant closes on Sunday night, all day Monday, and for Tuesday and Friday lunch.

3 place de la République, Azay-le-Rideau 37190. ✆ **02-47-45-40-08.** Fax 02-47-45-46-25. www.legrandmonarque.com. 26 units. 52€–150€ ($68–$195) double; 165€–185€ ($215–$241) suite. AE, MC, V. Parking 15€ ($20). Closed Dec–Jan. **Amenities:** Restaurant; bar; room service; babysitting; laundry service. *In room:* TV, hair dryer, Wi-Fi.

16 Chinon ★★

283km (176 miles) SW of Paris, 48km (30 miles) SW of Tours, 31km (19 miles) SW of Langeais

In the film *Joan of Arc,* Ingrid Bergman sought out the dauphin as he tried to conceal himself among his courtiers. This took place in real life at the Château de Chinon, one of the oldest fortress-châteaux in France. Charles VII centered his government at Chinon from 1429 to 1450. In 1429, with the English besieging Orléans, the Maid of Orléans prevailed upon the dauphin to give her an army. The rest is history. The seat of French power stayed at Chinon until the end of the Hundred Years' War.

Today, Chinon remains a tranquil village known mainly for its delightful red wines. After you visit the attractions, we recommend taking a walk along the Vienne River; definitely stop to taste the wine at one of Chinon's terraced cafes. Allow 3 hours to see Chinon.

ESSENTIALS

GETTING THERE The SNCF runs about 10 **trains** and four **buses** every day to Chinon from Tours (trip time: about 1 hr.). Call ✆ **08-92-35-35-35** for information and schedules. Both buses and trains arrive at the train station, which lies at the edge of the very small town. If you're **driving** from Tours, take D759 southwest through Azay-le-Rideau to Chinon.

VISITOR INFORMATION The **Office de Tourisme** is at place Hofheim (✆ **02-47-93-17-85;** www.chinon.com).

Finds **In Pursuit of the Grape**

Chinon is famous for its wines, which crop up on prestigious lists around the world. Supermarkets and wine shops throughout the region sell them; families that have been in the business longer than anyone can remember maintain the two most interesting stores. At **Caves Plouzeau,** 94 rue Haute-St-Maurice (✆ **02-47-93-16-34;** www.plouzeau.com), the 12th-century cellars were dug to provide building blocks for the foundations of the château. The present management dates from 1929; bottles of red or white wine cost from 8€ to 14€ ($10–$18). You're welcome to climb down to the cellars. They are open for wine sales and visits from April to September, Tuesday to Saturday from 11am to 1pm and 3 to 7pm.

The cellars at **Couly-Dutheil,** 12 rue Diderot (✆ **02-47-97-20-20**), are suitably medieval; many were carved from rock. This company produces largely Chinon wines (mostly reds), and it's proud of the Bourgueil and St-Nicolas de Bourgueil, whose popularity in North America has grown in recent years. Tours of the caves and a *dégustation des vins* (wine tasting) require an advance call and cost 8€ ($10) per person. Visits are conducted April to September Monday to Friday 8am to noon and 2 to 5:45pm.

EXPLORING THE TOWN & CHATEAU

On the banks of the Vienne, the town of Chinon consists of winding streets and turreted houses, many built in the 15th and 16th centuries in the heyday of the court. For the best view, drive across the river and turn right onto quai Danton. From this vantage point, you'll be able to see the castle in relation to the village and the river. The most typical street is rue Voltaire, lined with 15th- and 16th-century town houses. At no. 44, Richard the Lion-Hearted died on April 6, 1199, from a wound suffered during the siege of Chalus in Limousin. The Grand Carroi, in the heart of Chinon, served as the crossroads of the Middle Ages.

Château de Chinon ★★ The château consists of three buildings, two of which have been partially restored (they're still missing roofs). One of the restored buildings, Château du Milieu, dates from the 11th to the 15th centuries and contains the keep and clock tower, which houses a museum of Joan of Arc. A moat separates Château du Milieu from the other, Château du Coudray, which contains the Tour du Coudray, where Joan of Arc once stayed. In the 14th century, the Knights Templar were imprisoned here (they're responsible for the graffiti) before meeting violent deaths. Some of the grim walls from other dilapidated edifices remain, although many buildings—including the Great Hall where Joan of Arc sought out the dauphin—have been torn down.

Between rue St-Maurice and Av. Francois Mitterand. ✆ **02-47-93-13-45.** Admission 6€ ($7.80) adults, 4.50€ ($5.85) students and children 7–18, free for children under 7. Château Apr–Sept daily 9am–7pm; Oct–Mar daily 9:30am–5pm. Closed Jan 1 and Dec 25.

Musée de la Devinière The most famous son of Chinon, François Rabelais, the earthy and often bawdy Renaissance writer, lived on rue de la Lamproie. (A plaque marks the spot where his father practiced law and maintained a home and office.) This site, in the suburb of La Devinière, 5.5km (3½ miles) west of Chinon, was an isolated cottage at the time of his birth. It was maintained, because of local superstition and custom, for the sole purpose of delivering the children of the Rabelais clan into the world.

The museum has three floors of exposition space, each focusing on an aspect of Rabelais, his times, and his role in Chinon. In two neighboring buildings, you'll find exhibits on aspects of life during the Middle Ages, including an unusual display on medicinal plants. Regrettably, the theater presentations that showcased some of Rabelais's literary achievements are no longer presented.

La Devinière, on D117 near N751. ✆ **02-47-95-91-18** for information on theatrical performances. Admission 4.50€ ($5.85) adults, 3€ ($3.90) students, 2.50€ ($3.25) children 7–18, free for children under 7. May–Sept daily 10am–7pm; Mar 14–Apr daily 9:30am–12:30pm and 2–6pm; Oct–Mar 13 daily 9:30am–12:30pm and 2–5pm. From Chinon, follow the road signs pointing to Saumur and the D117.

WHERE TO STAY

Hostellerie Gargantua ★ This 15th-century mansion has a terrace with a château view. The grand building was once a courthouse where the father of François Rabelais worked as a lawyer in the 15th century. Art historians admire the building's early Renaissance staircase and its chiseled-stone details. The traditional guest rooms have been renovated and are comfortably furnished and well kept. Half of the old-fashioned bathrooms contain tubs. Try to stop here for a meal, served in a medieval hall. You can sample Loire *sandre* prepared with Chinon wine or duckling with dried pears and smoked lard, followed by a medley of seasonal red fruits in puff pastry.

73 rue Voltaire, Chinon 37500. ✆ **02-47-93-04-71.** Fax 02-47-93-08-02. www.hostelleriegargantua.com. 7 units. 49€–75€ ($64–$98) double. AE, DC, MC, V. Closed mid-Nov to mid-Dec. **Amenities:** Restaurant; bar; room service; babysitting; laundry service. *In room:* TV, Wi-Fi.

Hôtel Diderot ★ *Finds* Within a 5-minute walk of the town's historic core, this is a comfortable hotel with strands of ivy climbing romantically up its stone front. Although the foundations date from the 14th century, the building was radically altered in the 1700s; today, you'll see remnants of thick wall and ceiling beams throughout the public rooms and in some of the guest rooms. Rooms are midsize to spacious, outfitted in Henry II or Napoleon III style, usually with big windows letting in maximum sunlight. One of the architectural highlights is a magnificent 15th-century fireplace in the breakfast room, where you'll enjoy as many as 52 kinds of jams and jellies as part of your morning ritual. Françoise and Laurent are the congenial hosts. The hotel's name derives not from the philosopher but from the rue Diderot, a few steps away.

4 rue du Buffon, Chinon 37500. ✆ **02-47-93-18-87.** Fax 02-47-93-37-10. www.hoteldiderot.com. 27 units. 52€–73€ ($68–$95) double. AE, DC, MC, V. Parking 6€ ($7.80). **Amenities:** Bar; babysitting; laundry service; dry cleaning; nonsmoking rooms; limited-mobility rooms. *In room:* TV, hair dryer, Wi-Fi.

Hôtel Le Plantagenet This 19th-century mansion in the center of town has been transformed into a well-run hotel. The hotel opens onto views of the river Vienne and lies close to the medieval heart of Chinon. Rooms are midsize and filled with character, each tastefully and comfortably furnished, and each with a private bathroom with tub or shower. The grace note of the hotel is its private garden and terrace, where you can enjoy a drink. Some rooms, just as good as those in the main building, are in an annex manor house, the Maison Bourgeoise.

12 place Jeanne d'Arc, Chinon 37500. ✆ **02-47-93-36-92.** Fax 02-47-98-48-92. www.hotel-plantagenet.com. 32 units. 48€–65€ ($62–$85) double. AE, DC, MC, V. **Amenities:** Bar. *In room:* A/C (in 6 units), TV, hair dryer.

WHERE TO DINE

Au Plaisir Gourmand ★★ TRADITIONAL FRENCH This is the premier restaurant in the area. Owner Jean-Claude Rigollet used to direct the chefs at the fabled Les Templiers in Les Bézards. The 18th-century building contains an intimate dining room. Menu items are likely to include roasted duck with foie gras sauce, oxtail in Chinon red-wine sauce, and sautéed crayfish with a spicy salad. For dessert, try prunes stuffed in puff pastry.

2 rue Parmentier. ✆ **02-47-93-20-48.** Reservations required. Main courses 15€–30€ ($20–$39); tasting menu 28€–39€ ($36–$51). AE, V. Wed–Sun noon–1:30pm; Tues–Sat 7:30–9pm. Closed mid-Feb to mid-Mar.

L'Oceanic SEAFOOD/FRENCH As its name implies, this restaurant specializes in fresh seafood, even though Chinon is inland. Marie-Paule and Patrick Descoubes change the specialties daily based on what's fresh and good at the marketplace. Locals as well as visitors appreciate the value and the reliable cooking techniques. A particularly delicious meal may include cassoulet of lobster and scallops with vanilla-flavored butter, carpaccio of sea scallops with fried leeks and herb-flavored vinaigrette, stingray with Camembert sauce, and roasted filets of codfish with Muenster cheese cream sauce. If you don't like fish, the owners prepare delicious steak.

13 rue Rabelais. ✆ **02-47-93-44-55.** Reservations required. Main courses 10€–40€ ($13–$52); fixed-price menu 24€–34€ ($31–$44). MC, V. Tues–Sun noon–1:30pm; Tues–Sat 7:30–9:30pm.

CHINON AFTER DARK

A charming bar and nighttime hangout is **Le Café Français,** 37 place du Général-de-Gaulle (✆ **02-47-93-32-78**). Behind the Hotel de Ville (town hall), it attracts many good-looking singles. There's a modest admission charge for occasional concerts.

WHERE TO STAY & DINE NEARBY

Château de Marçay ★★★ This Relais & Châteaux property began in the 1100s as a fortress and changed to its present form during the Renaissance. It remained untouched during the region's civil wars. The centerpiece of the wine-producing hamlet of Marçay, it's sumptuously decorated. The main building houses the more opulent lodgings; a handful of less expensive, less dramatic rooms are in an annex a short walk away. About half of the units come with tub and shower; more modern rooms have only a shower. Menu specialties change with the season, and the chef works hard to maintain high standards. The garden terrace and elegantly rustic dining room afford a panoramic view.

Marçay, Chinon 37500. Take D116 for 7km (4⅓ miles) southwest of Chinon. ✆ **02-47-93-03-47.** Fax 02-47-93-45-33. www.chateaudemarcay.com. 34 units. 125€–315€ ($163–$410) double. AE, DC, MC, V. Closed 8 weeks mid-Jan to mid-Mar. **Amenities:** Restaurant; bar; outdoor pool; tennis court; room service; laundry service. *In room:* TV, hair dryer, minibar, safe, Wi-Fi.

Manoir de la Giraudière Built during the mid-1600s, this elegant manor house resembles a small château because of its use of *tuffeau* (the beige stone used in residences of many of the French monarchs). In a 2.4-hectare (6-acre) park surrounded by hundreds of acres of fields and forests, this government-rated two-star establishment offers classic decor and modern comforts. Each good-size room comes with a fine bed and quality linen. About half of the bathrooms contain combination tub/showers; the rest have showers only. Air-conditioning isn't necessary because the thick walls act as natural insulation against heat and cold.

Beaumont-en-Veron, Avoine 37420. Head 5km (3 miles) west of Chinon along D749 toward Bourgueil. ✆ **02-47-58-40-36.** Fax 02-47-58-46-06. www.hotels-france.com/giraudiere. 25 units. 52€–95€ ($68–$124) double; 120€ ($156) suite. AE, DC, MC, V. **Amenities:** Restaurant; bar; babysitting; laundry service. *In room:* TV, hair dryer, Wi-Fi.

17 Ussé

295km (183 miles) SW of Paris, 14km (8⅔ miles) NE of Chinon

At the edge of the dark forest of Chinon in Rigny-Ussé, **Château d'Ussé** ★ (✆ **02-47-95-54-05**) was the inspiration for Perrault's legend of *The Sleeping Beauty (La Belle au bois dormant).* Conceived as a fortress, the complex of steeples, turrets, towers, and dormers was erected at the dawn of the Renaissance on a hill overlooking the Indre River. The terraces, laden with orange trees, were laid out in the 18th century. When the need for a fortified château passed, the north wing was demolished to open up a greater view.

The château was later owned by the duc de Duras and then by Mme de la Rochejacquelin; its present owner, the marquis de Blacas, has opened many rooms to the public. The guided tour begins in the Renaissance chapel, with its sculptured portal and handsome stalls. You then proceed to the royal apartments, furnished with tapestries and antiques. One gallery displays an extensive collection of swords and rifles. A spiral stairway leads to a tower with a panoramic view of the river and a waxwork Sleeping Beauty waiting for her prince to come.

The château is open daily March 20 to September 9:30am to 7pm; October to November 13 and February 20 to March 19 10am to 6pm. Entrance costs 10€ ($13) for adults, 3.50€ ($4.55) for students and children 8 to 16, and is free for children under 8. Allow 1½ hours for the tour. The château is best visited by car or on an organized bus tour from Tours. If you're driving from Tours or Villandry, follow D7 to Ussé.

WHERE TO STAY

Le Clos d'Ussé ★ *Finds* Although most visitors make Ussé a day trip, this little B&B across the street from the castle makes a good overnight stop. The Duchemin family offers well-maintained rooms that are midsize and comfortably furnished; bathrooms have showers. The friendly owners are experts on the lore of the castle.

On D7, Rigny-Ussé 37130. ✆ **02-47-95-55-47.** Fax 02-47-95-55-47. 8 units. 45€–65€ ($59–$85) double. DC, MC. V. Closed Nov–Feb. **Amenities:** Restaurant. *In room:* TV, no phone.

18 Fontevraud-l'Abbaye ★★

304km (189 miles) SW of Paris, 16km (10 miles) SE of Saumur

You'll find the Plantagenet dynasty buried in the **Abbaye Royale de Fontevraud** (✆ **02-41-51-71-41;** www.abbaye-fontevraud.com). The kings, whose male line ended in 1485, were also the *comtes* d'Anjou, and they wanted to be buried in their native soil.

In the 12th-century Romanesque church—with four Byzantine domes—are the remains of two English kings or princes, including Henry II of England, the first Plantagenet king, and his wife, Eleanor of Aquitaine, the most famous woman of the Middle Ages. Her crusading son, Richard the Lion-Hearted, was also entombed here. The Plantagenet line ended with the death of Richard III at the 1485 Battle of Bosworth. The tombs fared badly during the Revolution, when mobs desecrated the sarcophagi and scattered their contents on the floor.

More interesting than the tombs is the octagonal **Tour d'Evraud,** the last remaining Romanesque kitchen in France. Dating from the 12th century, it contains five of its original eight *apsides* (half-rounded indentations originally conceived as chapels), each crowned with a conically roofed turret. A pyramid tops the conglomeration, capped by an open-air lantern tower pierced with lancets.

Robert d'Arbrissel, who spent much of his life as a recluse, founded the abbey in 1099. Aristocratic ladies occupied one part; many, including discarded mistresses of kings, had been banished from court. The four youngest daughters of Louis XV were educated here.

The abbey is open daily June to September 9am to 6pm; April, May, and October from 10am to 5:30pm; and November to March 10am to 5pm. Admission is 6.10€ ($7.95) for adults, 4.10€ ($5.35) for ages 18 to 25, and free for children under 18. Allow 1½ hours for the abbey. Closed January 1, May 1, and November 1 and 11.

ESSENTIALS

GETTING THERE If you're **driving,** take N147 about 4km (2½ miles) from the village of Montsoreau. About five **buses** run daily from Saumur; the one-way fare for the 30-minute trip is 3.80€ ($4.95).

VISITOR INFORMATION The **Office de Tourisme,** allée Ste-Catherine (✆ **02-41-51-79-45**), within the compound of the medieval abbey, is open only from May 15 to September 30.

WHERE TO STAY

Hostellerie du Prieuré St-Lazare ★ *Finds* This is one of the most unusual hotels in Europe, set on 11th-century foundations within the perimeter of the legendary Abbaye Royale in one-time monks' cells. It became a hotel in 1990. The guest rooms are well maintained and monastically simple, with white walls, modern furniture, and exposed sections of cream-colored *tuffeau,* the easy-to-carve rock used to build the abbey during the early Middle Ages. A third of the units come with tub/shower combinations.

Fontevraud-l'Abbaye 49590. ✆ **02-41-51-73-16.** Fax 02-41-51-75-50. www.hotelfp-fontevraud.com. 52 units. 60€–112€ ($78–$146) double; extra bed 15€ ($20). AE, MC, V. Closed Nov 2–Apr. **Amenities:** Restaurant; bar; babysitting. *In room:* TV, minibar.

WHERE TO DINE

The **Hostellerie du Prieuré St-Lazare** (see above) has a good restaurant.

La Licorne ★ MODERN FRENCH For the perfect combination of medieval history and culinary sensuality, visit the abbey and then dine at this 35-seat restaurant on a linden-lined walkway between the abbey and a nearby parish church. Its symmetrical proportions and neoclassical pilasters, built in the 1700s just before what the owners refer to as "La Révolution," evoke the *ancien régime* at its most graceful and opulent. In summer, guests sit in the garden or the elegantly rustic dining room. Chef Jean-Michel Bézille's (aided by Fabrice Bretel) menu almost always includes filet of beef flavored with smoked pork and shallots, roasted *sandre* with Szechuan peppers, crayfish-stuffed ravioli with basil-flavored morel sauce, variations on many of the freshwater fish of the Loire Valley, and luscious desserts such as a warm chocolate tart with pears and lemon-butter sauce.

Allée Ste-Catherine. ✆ **02-41-51-72-49.** Reservations required. Main courses 27€–35€ ($35–$46); fixed-price menu 27€–72€ ($35–$94). AE, DC, MC, V. Tues–Sun noon–2pm; Tues–Sat 7–9pm.

19 Saumur

299km (186 miles) SW of Paris, 53km (33 miles) SE of Angers

Saumur is in a region of vineyards, where the Loire separates to encircle an island; it makes one of the best bases for exploring the western Loire Valley. A small but thriving town, it doesn't entirely live off its past: Saumur produces some 100,000 tons per year of the mushrooms the French adore. Balzac left us this advice: "Taste a mushroom and delight in the essential strangeness of the place." The cool tunnels for the *champignons* also provide the ideal resting place for the celebrated sparkling wines of the region. Enjoy both of these local favorites at a neighborhood cafe.

ESSENTIALS

GETTING THERE **Trains** run frequently between Tours and Nantes, stopping at Saumur. Some 20 trains per day arrive from Tours (trip time: 45 min.); the one-way fare is 9.50€ ($12). Fifteen trains per day pull in from Angers (trip time: 30 min.), costing 6.90€ ($8.95) one-way. The train station is on the north side of town. Most major points of interest, including the château, are on the south bank. From the station, take bus A into town. If you're **driving** from Tours, follow N152 southwest to Saumur.

VISITOR INFORMATION The **Office de Tourisme** is on place de la Bilange (✆ **02-41-40-20-60**), and its hours vary greatly throughout the year.

EXPLORING THE AREA

Of all the Loire cities, Saumur remains the most bourgeois; perhaps that's why Balzac used it for his classic characterization of a smug little town in *Eugénie Grandet.* Saumur is also famous as the birthplace of the *couturière* Coco Chanel.

The men of Saumur are among the best equestrians in the world. Founded in 1768, the city's riding school, **Cadre Noir de Saumur** ★, rue de l'Abbaye (✆ **02-41-53-50-60**), is one of the grandest in Europe, rivaling Vienna's. The stables house some 400 horses. April to September, tours (7€/$9.10) begin at 9:30 to 11am and 2 to 4pm Tuesday to Sunday. Tours depart about every 20 minutes. Morning tours last about 1½ hours and the afternoon tour lasts 1 hour. Some 48km (30 miles) of specialty tracks wind around the town—to see a rider carry out a curvet is a thrill. The performances peak during the **Carrousel de Saumur** ★★ on the last two Saturdays and Sundays in July.

The area surrounding the town has become famous for its delicate sparkling wines. In the center of Saumur, you can wander the many aisles of **La Maison du Vin,** quai Lucien Gauthier (✆ **02-41-38-45-83**), and choose from a large stock direct from the many surrounding vineyards.

An alternative is to travel east of Saumur to the village of St-Hilaire, where you'll find a host of vineyards. One of the better ones is **Veuve Amiot,** 21 rue Jean-Ackerman (✆ **02-41-83-14-14**), where you can tour the wine cellars, taste different vintages, and buy bottles and gift boxes right in the showroom.

Saumur's chief attraction is its château, which takes 1½ hours to tour.

Château de Saumur ★★ In the famous *Les Très Riches Heures du Duc de Berry* at the Château de Chantilly, the 15th-century illuminated manuscript depicts Saumur as a fairy-tale castle of bell turrets and gilded weathercocks. Those adornments are largely gone, however, leaving a stark and foreboding fortress towering on a promontory over the Loire. Under Napoleon, the castle became a prison, then eventually a barracks and munitions depot. The town of Saumur acquired it in 1908 and began preservation efforts that culminated in a complete restoration of the château's western tower and its south wing in 1999.

It now houses an interesting regional museum, **Musée des Arts Décoratifs** ★★, noted for its 16th- to 18th-century ceramics collection. The series of 13th-century enamel crucifixes from Limoges is remarkable. Also here is the **Musée du Cheval** ★, which is devoted to the history of the horse through the ages, complete with stirrups, antique saddles, and spurs.

Saumur 49400. ✆ **02-41-40-24-40.** www.saumur-tourisme.net/chateausaumur_uk.html. Admission 2€ ($2.60) adults, free for children under 11. Oct–Mar daily 10am–1pm and 2–5pm; Apr–Sept daily 10am–1pm and 2–6pm; rest of the year Wed–Mon 10am–1pm and 2–5pm.

WHERE TO STAY

Hotel Adagio Best Western Erected around 1900 and bombed into rubble during World War II, this riverfront hotel was rebuilt in the 1950s using the same honey-colored stone as in its original construction. The large, conservative, comfortably furnished rooms have double-paned windows and high ceilings; some units have air-conditioning. Renovations have destroyed any vestige of old-fashioned France. The staff is hardworking and thoughtful.

94 av. du Général-de-Gaulle, Saumur 49400. ✆ **800/528-1234** in the U.S., or 02-41-67-45-30. Fax 02-41-67-74-59. www.hoteladagio.com. 38 units. 73€–95€ ($95–$124) double; 125€–155€ ($163–$202) suite. AE, DC, MC, V. Parking 7€ ($9.10). **Amenities:** Bar; room service; laundry service; dry cleaning; nonsmoking rooms; limited-mobility rooms. *In room:* A/C, TV, minibar, hair dryer, iron, safe.

Hôtel Anne d'Anjou ★ This 18th-century building was constructed as a family home; its magnificent stairwell below a *trompe l'oeil* ceiling has been designated a historic monument. The rooms in the back overlook the château, and the front faces the Loire. Five units still have their original decor, ranging from Louis XVI to Empire. Accommodations are renovated room by room "as they begin to look a bit tired."

The hotel operates Les Menestrels, one of the most prestigious restaurants in Saumur. Open Monday through Saturday for lunch and dinner, it offers creative fixed-price menus for 35€ to 65€ ($46–$85). The restaurant is in a 16th-century structure with a vaulted cellar, opening onto landscaped gardens.

32–33 quai Mayaud, Saumur 49400. ✆ **02-41-67-30-30.** Fax 02-41-67-51-00. www.hotel-anneanjou.com. 44 units. 95€–185€ ($124–$241) double. AE, DC, MC, V. Parking 10€ ($13). **Amenities:** Restaurant; bar; room service; babysitting; laundry service; nonsmoking rooms; limited-mobility rooms. *In room:* TV, minibar, hair dryer.

Hôtel St-Pierre ★ Nestled among tiny winding roads and built against the Eglise St-Pierre, this hotel overflows with character. It boasts such features as finely upholstered antiques, half-timbered walls, beamed ceilings, stained-glass windows, massive stone fireplaces, and spiral staircases. Guest rooms are individually decorated in the same rich style; even the bathroom walls showcase custom tile designs. Overall, the hotel is an appealing middle-bracket choice in a historic location. The intimate breakfast room opens onto a small garden terrace.

Rue Haute-Saint-Pierre, Saumur 49400. ✆ **02-41-50-33-00.** Fax 02-41-50-38-68. www.saintpierresaumur.com. 14 units. 78€–150€ ($101–$195) double. AE, DC, DISC, MC, V. Free parking. **Amenities:** Bar; room service; babysitting; laundry service; nonsmoking rooms; limited-mobility rooms. *In room:* A/C, TV, minibar, hair dryer, trouser press, Wi-Fi.

Le Prieuré ★★★ This is the grandest address in the region, a bastion of comfort, charm, and grace. The 12th-century priory (now a Relais & Châteaux member), is in a 24-hectare (59-acre) park 8km (5 miles) from town. The hotel has a steep roof, dormer windows, and a large peaked tower. It offers gracious, comfortable rooms; two of the most beautiful are in a 10th-century chapel. The least expensive (and less desirable) rooms are in an outlying pavilion. No matter where, each room comes with fine linen and quality furnishings. The Grand Salon features an ornately carved stone fireplace, crystal chandeliers, oak furniture, and a bar with a fleur-de-lis motif.

The dining room boasts one of the finest views of the Loire, spanning 64km (40 miles)—it's truly beautiful at sunset. The chef wisely recommends filet of beef in wine sauce. Other specialties include grilled filet of Loire salmon and filet of rabbit with goat cheese and fresh herbs. Even if you're not a guest, consider dining here. Main courses cost 22€ to 34€ ($29–$44). The restaurant is open daily from 12:30 to 1:30pm and 7:30 to 9pm.

Chênehutte-les-Tuffeaux 49350. ✆ **02-41-67-90-14.** Fax 02-41-67-92-24. www.prieure.com. 36 units. 167€–280€ ($217–$364) double; 295€–377€ ($384–$490) suite. AE, DC, MC, V. **Amenities:** Restaurant; bar; outdoor pool; minigolf; tennis court; room service; babysitting; laundry service; dry cleaning. *In room:* TV, minibar, hair dryer, Wi-Fi.

Les Terrasses de Saumur Although it was built relatively recently, this hotel has many of the architectural details (a steep slate roof, a U-shaped design ringing a formal courtyard) of a much older building. Rooms are pleasantly furnished, with comfortable beds and modern-looking furniture. There's also a large outdoor swimming pool, rambling green lawns, and plenty of parkland dotted with benches, tables, and chairs. The medium-size guest rooms are standard, with contemporary built-in furniture; the best have private balconies overlooking the Loire Valley. Most units are air-conditioned.

2 rue des Lilas, St-Hilaire-St-Florent, Saumur 49400. ✆ **02-41-67-28-48.** Fax 02-41-67-13-71. www.lesterrassesdesaumur.fr. 23 units. 50€–90€ ($65–$117) double; 90€–150€ ($117–$195) suite. AE, MC, V. **Amenities:** 2 restaurants; bar; 2 outdoor pools; gym; sauna; room service; babysitting; laundry service; dry cleaning; nonsmoking rooms; limited-mobility rooms. *In room:* TV, minibar, hair dryer, safe.

WHERE TO DINE

Le Prieuré and Hôtel Anne d'Anjou's **Les Menestrels** (see above) serve some of the finest cuisine in town.

Les Délices du Château ★★ FRENCH Saumur's finest restaurant is in a restored 12th-century house, a former chapel and soldiers' barracks. On the grounds of the town's massive château, it offers panoramic views of the city and the Loire from its flowery terrace. The impeccably trained staff serves classic cuisine with a personal touch. Superb possibilities include a classic Loire dish: eel stew with pearl onions and white-wine sauce. The menu favors well-balanced flavor combinations exemplified by such dishes as grilled striped bass, sautéed sweetbreads with baby vegetables, filet of beef with foie gras and truffle sauce (surely the most elegant way to serve beef), and utterly delectable baby pigeon with foie gras and wild-mushroom sauce.

Les Feuquières, Saumur 49400, Château de Saumur. ✆ **02-41-67-65-60.** Reservations required. Main courses 18€–22€ ($23–$29); fixed-price menu 45€–73€ ($59–$95). Children's menu 16€ ($21). AE, DC, MC, V. May–Oct daily noon–2:30pm and 7–10pm; Nov–Apr Tues–Sun noon–2:30pm, Wed–Sat 7–10pm.

20 Angers ★★★

288km (179 miles) SW of Paris, 89km (55 miles) E of Nantes

Once the capital of Anjou, Angers straddles the Maine River at the western end of the Loire Valley. Though it suffered extensive damage in World War II, it has been restored, blending provincial charm with a suggestion of sophistication. The bustling regional center is often used as a base for exploring the château district to the west. Young people, including some 30,000 college students, keep this vital city of 260,000 jumping until late at night. Allow 3 hours to see the attractions at Angers.

ESSENTIALS

GETTING THERE Fifteen **trains** per day make the 1- to 2-hour trip from Paris's Gare de Montparnasse; the cost is 43€ to 55€ ($56–$72) one-way. From Tours, 10 trains per day make the 1-hour trip; a one-way ticket is 15€ ($20). The Angers train station, at place de la Gare, is a convenient walk from the château. For train information, call ✆ **08-92-35-35-35.** From Saumur, there are three **bus** connections a day from Monday to Saturday (1½ hr.). Buses arrive at place de la République. Call ✆ **02-41-88-59-25** for schedules. If you're **driving** from Tours, take N152 southwest to Saumur, turning west on D952.

VISITOR INFORMATION The **Office de Tourisme,** 7 place du Président-Kennedy (✆ **02-41-23-50-00;** www.angers-tourisme.com), is opposite the entrance to the château.

EXPLORING THE TOWN

If you have time for shopping, wander to the pedestrian zone in the center of town. Its boutiques and small shops sell everything from clothes and shoes to jewelry and books. For regional specialties, head to **Maison du Vin de l'Anjou,** 5 place du Président-Kennedy (✆ **02-41-88-81-13**), where you can learn about the area's vineyards and buy a bottle or two for gifts or a picnic.

Cathédrale St-Maurice ★★ The cathedral dates mostly from the 12th and 13th centuries; the main tower is from the 16th century. The statues on the portal represent everybody from the Queen of Sheba to David at the harp. The tympanum depicts Christ Enthroned. The stained-glass windows from the 12th through the 16th centuries have made the cathedral famous. The oldest one illustrates the martyrdom of St. Vincent; the most unusual is of St. Christopher with the head of a dog. The Apocalypse Tapestries were once here; now only a few remain, with the majority on display in the nearby château (see below). The 12th-century nave, a landmark in cathedral architecture, is a work of harmonious beauty. If you're interested in a guided tour (offered in English July–Aug), call the church's presbytery at the number below. Tours are conducted erratically, often by an associate of the church, and usually with much charm and humor. The tours are available in French, English, and Italian.

Place Freppel. ✆ **02-41-87-58-45.** Free admission; donations appreciated. Dec–Mar daily 8:30am–5:30pm; Apr–Nov daily 8:30am–7pm.

Château d'Angers ★★★ The moated château, dating from the 9th century, was the home of the *comtes* d'Anjou. The notorious Black Falcon lived here, and in time, the Plantagenets took up residence. From 1230 to 1238, the outer walls and 17 towers were built, creating a fortress. King René favored the château, and during his reign a brilliant court life flourished until he was forced to surrender to Louis XI. Louis XIV turned the château into a prison. In World War II, the Nazis used it as a munitions depot, and the Allies bombed it in 1944.

Visit the castle to see the **Apocalypse Tapestries** ★★★. They weren't always so highly regarded—they once served as a canopy to protect orange trees and were also used to cover the damaged walls of a church. Woven in Paris by Nicolas Bataille from cartoons by Jean de Bruges around 1375 for Louis I of Anjou, they were purchased for a nominal sum in the 19th century. The series of 77 pieces, illustrating the Book of St. John, stretch 100m (328 ft.).

After seeing the tapestries, you can tour the fortress, including the courtyard, prison, ramparts, windmill tower, 15th-century chapel, and royal apartments. Once you've paid the entrance fee, you can take a guided tour focusing on the architecture and history of the château. Throughout most of the year, guided tours depart daily at 10am, 11:30am, 1:15pm, 2:30pm, and 3:30pm, but between September and April, departures are usually (depending on business) at 10:15am and 2:15pm. Each tour lasts 90 minutes, and it can be conducted in four different languages—French, English, German, and Italian.

2 promenade du Bout-du-Monde. ✆ **02-41-86-81-94.** Fax 02-41-87-17-50. www.monum.fr. Admission 7.50€ ($9.75) adults, 4.80€ ($6.25) seniors and students 18–25, free for children under 18. Sept–Apr daily 10am–5:30pm; May–Aug daily 9:30am–6:30pm.

Musée Jean Lurçat ★★ The town's most intriguing museum is in the Ancien Hôpital St-Jean, founded in 1174 to care for the sick. The museum is known for its famous tapestry, *Le Chant du Monde* (The Song of the World), designed by Jean Lurçat and executed in 10 panels between 1957 and 1966. It depicts an abstract conglomeration of beneficent suns, popping champagne bottles, and life cycles of birth and death. You can visit a 17th-century dispensary, with earthenware jars and trivets still on its wooden shelves, and see everything from a Romanesque cloister with a secret garden to a pewter vessel from 1720 that once contained an antidote for snakebites.

4 bd. Arago. ✆ **02-41-24-18-45.** Admission 4€ ($5.20) adults, 3€ ($3.90) students, free for children under 18. June–Sept daily 10am–7pm; Oct–May daily 10am–noon and 2–6pm.

WHERE TO STAY

Hôtel d'Anjou Beside a park, this hotel, built in 1846, is the best choice for overnighting in the area. Although comparable in price to the Quality Hôtel de France, it has more upscale appointments and amenities, along with a better restaurant, Le Salamandre (see "Where to Dine," below). The guest rooms closer to the ground have higher ceilings and are more spacious.

1 bd. Foch, Angers 49100. ✆ **800/528-1234** in the U.S. and Canada, or 02-41-21-12-11. Fax 02-41-87-22-21. www.hoteldanjou.fr. 53 units. 115€–169€ ($150–$220) double; extra bed 30€ ($39). AE, DC, MC, V. Parking 8€ ($10). **Amenities:** Restaurant; bar; laundry service; dry cleaning. *In room:* TV, minibar, safe, Wi-Fi.

L'Hôtel de France This 19th-century hotel, one of the most respected in town, has been run by the Bouyers since 1893. It's the best choice near the railway station. Rooms are soundproof; each is comfortably furnished and well maintained. Bathrooms are very small and hold tubs.

8 place de la Gare, Angers 49100. ✆ **02-41-88-49-42.** Fax 02-41-86-76-70. www.destination-anjou.com/hoteldefrance. 55 units. 94€–133€ ($122–$173) double; 224€ ($291) suite. AE, DC, MC, V. Parking 7€ ($9.10). **Amenities:** 2 restaurants; bar; room service; laundry service; dry cleaning. *In room:* A/C, TV, minibar, hair dryer, safe, Wi-Fi.

WHERE TO DINE

Le Crémet d'Anjou TRADITIONAL FRENCH Located midway between the château and the railway station, this restaurant serves a tried-and-true French menu. Examples include filet of *sandre* cooked in Loire Valley wine; entrecôte of beef marinated in red Bourgueil wine; filet of skate (stingray) with Roquefort sauce; and succulent roasted duckling stuffed with homemade foie gras. The salmon-and-gray-colored dining room is formal, with Louis XVI furniture and glittering chandeliers.

21 rue Delâge. ✆ **02-41-88-38-38.** Reservations recommended. Fixed-price menus 18€–23€ ($23–$30). MC, V. Mon–Fri noon–1:30pm and 7–10pm.

Fun Fact **A Toast with the Home-Brew—Cointreau**

Another libation unique to Angers is Cointreau. **La Distillerie Cointreau,** 2 bd. des Bretonnières (✆ **02-41-31-50-00**), is in the suburb of St-Barthèlemy, a 10-minute drive east of the town center. It has a showroom where you can sample and stock up on the fruity liqueur.

Two brothers in Angers were confectioners who set out to create a drink of "crystal-clear purity." Today, some 13 million bottles of Cointreau are consumed annually. Packaged in a square bottle with rounded corners, Cointreau is made from twice-distilled alcohol from the peels of two types of oranges, bitter and sweet. The factory has turned out the drink since 1849. Cointreau flavors such drinks as the cosmopolitan, the kamikaze, the white lady, and the sidecar.

Le Salamandre ★ CLASSIC FRENCH The salamander was the symbol of Renaissance king François I. In this formal, elegant restaurant, you'll see portraits of and references to that cunning strategist everywhere. Beneath massive sculpted ceiling beams, beside a large wooden fireplace, you'll enjoy the most impeccable service and best food in town. Shining examples include filet of red snapper in lime-flavored cream sauce, crayfish in various presentations, scallops in mushroom cream sauce, roasted turbot with béarnaise sauce, and squid stuffed with crayfish and served with shellfish-flavored cream sauce. The restaurant is in a hotel but not owned by the hostelry.

In the Hotel d'Anjou, 1 bd. Foch. ✆ **02-41-88-99-55.** Reservations recommended. Main courses 20€–27€ ($26–$35); fixed-price menu 26€–46€ ($34–$60) lunch, 36€–46€ ($47–$60) dinner. AE, DC, MC, V. Mon–Sat noon–2pm and 7–9:30pm.

Provence Caffè PROVENÇAL This restaurant celebrates the herbs, spices, and seafood of Provence. The bright decor includes bundles of herbs and souvenirs of the Mediterranean. The chef delights diners with such dishes as risotto served with asparagus and basil or grilled salmon with Provençal herbs.

9 place du Ralliement. ✆ **02-41-87-44-15.** Reservations recommended. Main courses 10€–15€ ($13–$20); fixed-price menu 15€–30€ ($20–$39). MC, V. Tues–Sat noon–2pm and 7–10pm.

ANGERS AFTER DARK

If you head to **place du Ralliement** or **rue St-Laud,** with its many bars and cafes, you'll find yourself in the center of Angers's nightlife. For a great night of beer drinking with friends, go to **Le Kent,** 7 place Ste-Croix (✆ **02-41-87-88-55**). The Irish pub serves some 50 beers and 70 brands of whiskey.

If a night of dancing seems the perfect antidote to a day of château gazing, consider **Disco Le Boléro,** 38 rue St-Laud, adjacent to the place de Ralliement (✆ **02-41-88-61-19**). From June to September, it's open Tuesday to Thursday 11:30pm to 3am, Friday and Saturday 11:30pm to 4am. There's no cover, but beer costs around 8€ ($10). The club attracts a lot of singles, ranging in age from 25 to 45.

At the disco **l'Ecu de Bretagne,** 8 place Vigan (✆ **02-41-48-15-28**), patrons range in age from 20 to 50, and the entrance fee is 10€ ($13).

9 Normandy & Mont-St-Michel

Ten centuries have passed since the Vikings invaded Normandy. The early Scandinavians came to seize the land, but they stayed to cultivate it. The Normans produced great soldiers, none more famous than William the Conqueror, who defeated King Harold at the Battle of Hastings in 1066. The English and the French continued to battle for centuries.

The invasion of June 6, 1944, ravaged much of Normandy. The largest armada ever assembled was responsible for regaining control of Europe from the Nazis. Today, many visitors come to Normandy to see the D-day beachheads.

Some of this province may remind you of a Millet landscape, with cattle grazing in fields and wood-framed houses alongside modern buildings. Not far from the Seine is the hamlet where Monet painted his water lilies. Here and there are stained-glass windows and Gothic architecture that survived the bombardments; however, many great buildings were leveled. Normandy's wide beaches attract families, and in August, the Deauville sands draw the chicest of the chic from Europe and North America. The resort towns of Deauville and Trouville are part of the region known as *La Côte Fleurie* (the Flower Coast), so called because of the profusion of flowers that grow there in the summer.

1 Rouen ★★★

135km (84 miles) NW of Paris, 89km (55 miles) E of Le Havre

The capital of Normandy and the fifth-largest port in France, Rouen is a hub of commerce. It's a bustling, vibrant place, bursting with activity generated by the industries connected to the port and the students at nearby universities and art schools. Former occupants include the writers Pierre Corneille and Gustave Flaubert, Claude Monet (who endlessly painted Rouen's Cathédrale de Notre-Dame), and Joan of Arc ("Oh, Rouen, art thou then my final resting place?"). Today, it's a city of half a million people.

Victor Hugo called Rouen "the city of a hundred spires." Half of it was destroyed during World War II, mostly by Allied bombers, and many Rouennais were killed. During the reconstruction of the old quarters, some of the almost-forgotten crafts of the Middle Ages were revived. The city on the Seine is rich in historical associations: William the Conqueror died here in 1087, and Joan of Arc was burned at the stake on place du Vieux-Marché in 1431.

As in Paris, the Seine splits Rouen into a **Rive Gauche (Left Bank)** and **Rive Droite (Right Bank).** The old city is on the right bank.

ESSENTIALS

GETTING THERE From Paris's Gare St-Lazare, **trains** leave for Rouen about once an hour (trip time: 1½ hr.). The one-way fare is 19€ ($25). The station is at rue Jeanne

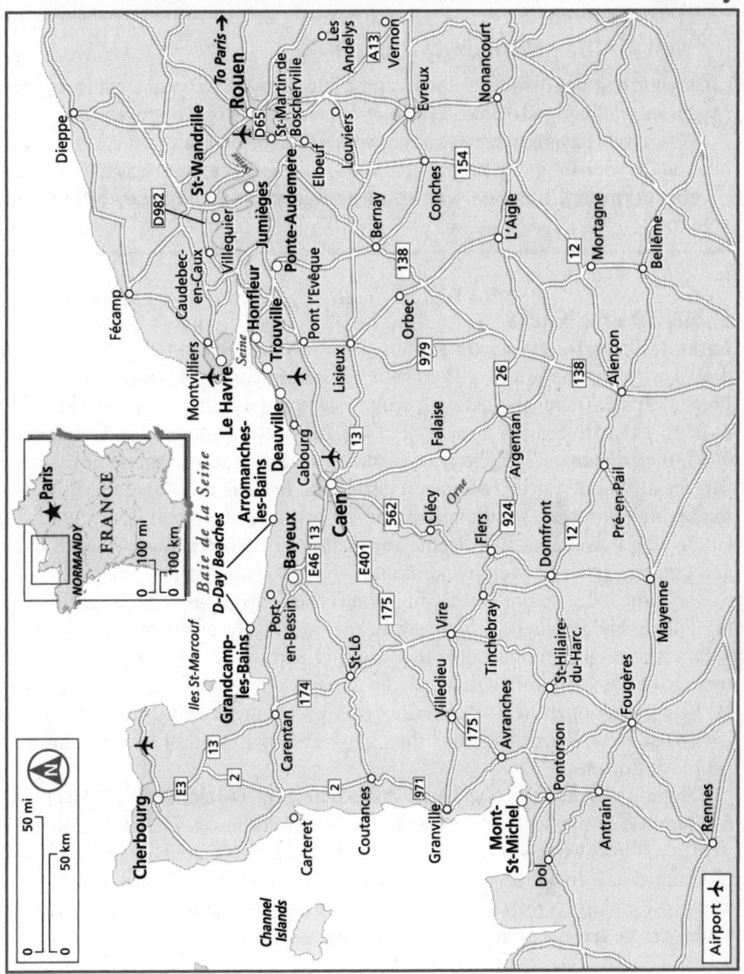

d'Arc. For information, call ✆ **36-35** or **08-92-35-35-35** from outside France, or visit www.voyages-sncf.com. To **drive** from Paris, take A13 northwest to Rouen (trip time: 1½ hr.).

GETTING AROUND The **Métro** is part of the city's MétroBus system (✆ **02-35-52-52-52**). It has one north-to-south line. The most central stations in Old Rouen are Palais de Justice and Gare (Rue Verte). Tickets cost 1.30€ ($1.70) per ride and are good for bus transfers within 1 hour of entering the Métro. Buy tickets from kiosks or automated machines.

VISITOR INFORMATION The **Office de Tourisme** is at 25 place de la Cathédrale (✆ **02-32-08-32-40;** www.rouentourisme.com).

Tips A 4-Day Normandy Itinerary

On your first day, head for Rouen and explore its old town and cathedral. On your second day, go to Caen, William the Conqueror's seat of government. Stay in Caen or in Bayeux, where you can see the local cathedral and the Bayeux tapestry. On your third day (from Caen or Bayeux), explore the D-day beaches. On your fourth day, continue west toward the ancient island-abbey of Mont-St-Michel.

SEEING THE SIGHTS

Cathédrale Notre-Dame de Rouen ★★★ Monet immortalized Rouen's cathedral (particularly the facade, with its galaxy of statues) in his paintings. The main door, **Porte Central,** is embellished with sculptures (some decapitated) depicting the Tree of Jesus. The 12th-century Porte St-Jean and Porte St-Etienne flank it. Consecrated in 1063, the cathedral, a symphony of lacy stonework, was reconstructed after suffering damage in World War II. Two towers distinguish it: **Tour de Beurre** was financed by the faithful who were willing to pay for the privilege of eating butter during Lent. Containing a carillon of 56 bells, the **Tour Lanterne (Lantern Tower)**—built in 1877 and utilizing 740 tons of iron and bronze—rises to almost 150m (492 ft.).

The cathedral's interior is fairly uniform. The choir is a masterpiece, with 14 soaring pillars. The Booksellers' Stairway, in the north wing of the transept, is adorned with a stained-glass rose window that dates, in part, from the 1500s. The 13th-century chancel is beautiful, with simple lines. Especially interesting is the **Chapelle de la Vierge,** adorned with Renaissance tombs of the cardinals d'Amboise. Also entombed is the heart of Richard the Lion-Hearted, a token of his affection for the people of Rouen.

Behind the cathedral is the **Palais de l'Archevêché (Archbishop's Palace),** which was bombed in the war. Now it stands naked against the sky. The broken arches and rosette windows witnessed the trial of Joan of Arc in 1431, and her rehabilitation was proclaimed here in 1456.

Place de la Cathédrale. ✆ **02-35-71-85-65.** www.cathedrale-rouen.net. Free admission. Mon 2–7pm; Tues–Sat 7:45am–7pm; Sun 8am–6pm. Closed during Mass and on bank holidays.

Eglise St-Maclou ★★ St-Maclou was built in the Flamboyant Gothic style, with a step-gabled porch and cloisters, and is known for the 16th-century panels on its doors. Our favorite (to the left) is the *Portail des Fontaines* (Portal of the Fonts). The church was built in 1200, rebuilt in 1432, and consecrated in 1521; its lantern tower is from the 19th century. It sits on a square full of old Norman crooked-timbered buildings. Inside, pictures dating from June 4, 1944, document St-Maclou's destruction and its subsequent restoration.

3 place Barthélémy, behind the cathedral. ✆ **02-35-70-84-90.** Free admission. Mon–Sat 10am–noon and 2–6pm; Sun 3–5:30pm. Closed Jan 1, May 1, July 14, and Nov 11.

Eglise St-Ouen ★★ This church is the outgrowth of a 7th-century Benedictine abbey. Flanked by four turrets, its 115m (377-ft.) octagonal lantern tower is called "the ducal crown of Normandy." The church represents the work of 5 centuries. Its nave is from the 15th century, its choir from the 14th (with 18th-c. railings), and its

stained glass from the 14th to the 16th. On May 23, 1431, Joan of Arc was taken to the cemetery here, and officials sentenced her to be burned at the stake unless she recanted. She signed an abjuration, condemning herself to life imprisonment, but that sentence was later revoked.

Place du Général-de-Gaulle. ✆ **02-32-08-31-01.** Free admission. Mar–Oct Tues–Sat 10am–noon and 2–6pm, Sun 10am–noon and 2–5pm (Nov–Feb closed Thurs–Fri).

Hôtel de Bourgtheroulde This headquarters of a local bank is one of Rouen's showcase Gothic buildings. Built in the 15th century by William the Red and enlarged in the Renaissance, it's noteworthy for its interior courtyard, the only part of the building you can visit regularly. In the courtyard, look back at the octagonal stair tower. The left gallery is entirely Renaissance. The building sometimes opens on weekends for special exhibitions.

15 place de la Pucelle (Square of the Maid). ✆ **02-35-08-64-00.** Free admission. Courtyard Mon–Fri 8am–6pm.

Musée de la Céramique ★★ One of the great treasures here is the collection of 17th- and 18th-century Rouen faïence (opaquely glazed earthenware), which has a distinctive red hue because of the color of the local clay. The exhibits provide a showcase for Masseot Abaquesne, the premier French artist in faïence. An exceptional showcase is devoted to chinoiserie from 1699 to 1745.

A Drive along the Route des Abbayes

Beginning at Rouen, the Seine winds through black forests and lush green countryside along the Route des Abbayes, eventually ending at Le Havre. As you make your way past the ruins of monasteries and châteaux, you'll agree that this is one of the most memorable routes in France.

Ten minutes after leaving Rouen (on D982), you'll arrive at the 11th-century **Abbaye St-George,** in St-Martin de Boscherville. Continue along D982 and then on D65 around the Seine for 19km (12 miles) to Jumièges. One of France's most beautiful ruins, **Abbaye de Jumièges** ★★★ was founded by St. Philbert in the 7th century and rebuilt in the 10th century. The archbishop of Rouen consecrated the abbey church in 1067 in the presence of William the Conqueror. The 30m-high (98-ft.) nave is complete, and two towers 45m (148 ft.) high surround the porch.

Another 16km (10 miles) along the right bank of the Seine is St-Wandrille, 53km (33 miles) northwest of Rouen (take D982 from Jumièges). **Abbaye de St-Wandrille** was founded in 649. Over the centuries, it suffered many attacks (by Vikings, among others). Hardly anything remains of the monastery, save for an 18th-century gate that frames the entrance, and inside cloisters that date from the 14th to the 16th centuries.

From St-Wandrille, continue for 3km (1¾ miles) to **Caudebec-en-Caux** ★, in an amphitheater along the Seine. Nearly destroyed in World War II, it has a Gothic church from the 15th century. Henri IV considered it the handsomest

1 rue Faucon. ✆ **02-35-07-31-74.** Admission 2.30€ ($3) adults, 1.55€ ($2) students, free for children under 18. Wed–Mon 10am–1pm and 2–6pm.

Musée des Beaux-Arts ★★★ This is one of France's most important provincial museums, with more than 65 rooms of art that ranges from medieval primitives to contemporary paintings. You'll find portraits by David and works by Delacroix and Ingres (seek out his *La Belle Zélie*). A Gérard David retable (altarpiece), *La Vierge et les saints* (The Virgin and the Saints), is a masterpiece. One salon is devoted to Géricault, including his portrait of Delacroix. Other works here are by Veronese, Velázquez, Caravaggio, Rubens, Poussin, Fragonard, and Corot, and by Impressionists such as Monet, including several paintings of the Rouen cathedral.

Esplanade de Marcel Duchamp. ✆ **02-35-71-28-40.** Admission 3.80€ ($4.95) adults, 2€ ($2.60) students, free for children under 18. Mon and Wed–Sun 10am–6pm.

Musée Flaubert et d'Histoire de la Médécine Gustave Flaubert, author of *Madame Bovary,* was born in the director's quarters of Rouen's public hospital (his father was the director) in 1821. The room in which he was born is intact. You'll see the glass door that separated the Flauberts from the ward and its patients. Family furniture and medical paraphernalia are also displayed.

51 rue de Lecat. ✆ **02-35-15-59-95.** Admission 3€ ($3.90) adults, 1.50€ ($1.95) for students and ages 18–25, free for children under 18. Tues 10am–6pm; Wed–Sat 10am–noon and 2–6pm. Closed holidays.

chapel in his kingdom. On its west side is a trio of Flamboyant Gothic doorways, crowned by a rose window.

Drive west around the north bank of the Seine to **Villequier** ★, a tranquil village whose late-18th-century manor house functions as a reasonably priced 29-room hotel. It charges 59€ to 72€ ($77–$94) for a double room. For information and reservations, contact the **Château-Hotel de Villequier,** 76490 Villequier (✆ **02-35-95-94-10;** www.chateau-de-villequier.com). Breakfast is the only meal served. In this town, Victor Hugo lost his daughter and her husband, when their boat overturned on the nearby Seine. You can visit the **Musée Victor-Hugo,** quai Victor-Hugo (✆ **02-35-56-78-31**). It has the manuscript of his poem "Contemplations" and excerpts from *The Hunchback of Notre Dame.* The museum is open April to September, Wednesday to Saturday and Monday 10am to 12:30pm and 2 to 6pm, and Sunday 2 to 6pm; October to March, it's open Wednesday to Saturday and Monday 10am to 12:30pm and 2 to 5:30pm, and Sunday 2 to 5:30pm. Adults pay 3€ ($3.90); free for students and children under 18.

Some 53km (33 miles) to the west, along D81 and N182, is **Le Havre** ★★, France's major Atlantic port. The city was repeatedly bombed during World War II, but its recovery has been amazing. From here, you can take boat tours to the lovely resorts of Trouville and Deauville.

Musée Jeanne-d'Arc The life and the martyrdom of Joan of Arc, France's national heroine, are the focus here. In a vaulted cellar, dioramas, waxworks, and commentary in four languages tell the story of her life—from Domrémy, where she was born, to Rouen, where she was burned at the stake. The museum also contains a research library that concentrates on her life and the politics of her era. Visitors can hear, without charge, recorded narration on hand-held devices.

33 place du Vieux-Marché. ✆ **02-35-88-02-70.** www.jeanne-darc.com. Admission 4€ ($5.20) adults, 2.50€ ($3.25) students and children under 18. May–Sept daily 9:30am–7pm; Oct–Apr daily 10am–noon and 2–6:30pm.

Musée Le Secq des Tournelles (Wrought Ironworks Museum) ★ Housed in the 15th-century Eglise St-Laurent, this museum showcases ironwork, a Norman art form. Its collection ranges from what a critic once called "forthright masculine forging to lacy feminine filigree, from Roman keys to the needlepoint balustrade that graced Mme de Pompadour's country mansion." The collection boasts some 14,000 pieces.

2 rue Jacques-Villon. ✆ **02-35-88-42-92.** Admission 2.30€ ($3) adults, 1.55€ ($2) students, free for children under 18. Wed–Mon 10am–1pm and 2–6pm.

Place du Vieux-Marché ★ Joan of Arc was executed for heresy at the Old Marketplace. Tied to a stake, she was burned on May 30, 1431. Her ashes were gathered and tossed into the Seine. A modern church with stained-glass windows from St-Vincent sits in the center of a monumental complex in the square; beside it a bronze cross marks the position of St. Joan's stake.

Finds A Ride on "The Little Train"

The rubber-wheeled **Petit Train** (✆ **02-32-08-32-46**) is the most fun way to see this ancient city. The 40-minute tours leave from the front of the tourist office, 25 place de la Cathédrale (✆ **02-32-08-32-40**). Departures are daily at 10am, 11am, 2pm, 4pm, and 5pm. Tickets cost 6€ ($7.80) for adults and 3€ ($3.90) for children under 13. The train operates from April 1 to October 15, with limited service over the Christmas holidays.

Rue du Gros-Horloge ★★ The "Street of the Great Clock" runs between the cathedral and place du Vieux-Marché. Now a pedestrian mall, it's named for an ornate gilt Renaissance clock mounted on an arch, Rouen's most popular monument. The arch bridges the street and connects to a Louis XV fountain with a bevy of cherubs and a bell tower. At night the bells still toll a curfew.

SHOPPING

Rouen was once one of France's major producers of the fine decorative ceramic ware known as ***faïence de Rouen.*** Examples of both antique and contemporary faïence abound, and it's worth picking up one or two pieces. For contemporary faïence, your best bet is **Faïencerie Carpentier Augy,** 26 rue St-Romain (✆ **02-35-88-77-47**). The well-known studio sells reproductions of historical styles in an array of colors.

Another Rouen specialty is ***les coffret de Rouen.*** The little hand-painted wooden boxes were all the rage during the 18th and 19th centuries. The original versions continue to be popular, but watch out for modern forgeries.

Rouen is also an antiques capital, with more than 80 vendors in the Old Town. The best hunting ground is in Vieux Rouen (the Old Town), along **rue Eau-de-Robec, place Barthélémy, rue Damiette,** and **rue St-Romain.** The city has two **flea markets,** on Saturday and Sunday at place St-Mare, and on Thursday at place des Emmurés. Medium- and large-scale auctions take place year-round at **Les Salles des Ventes,** 25 rue du Général-Giraud (✆ **02-35-71-13-50**) and 20 rue de la Croix-de-Fer (✆ **02-35-71-54-48**).

Other antiques shops worth visiting are **Michel Bertran,** 108 rue Molière (✆ **02-35-98-24-06**), with a good selection of 18th- and 19th-century paintings, especially by School of Rouen Impressionists; **Etienne Bertran,** 110 rue Molière (✆ **02-35-70-79-96**), with its collection of antique books dating to the 1400s; and **Patrick Chasset,** 12 rue de la Croix-de-Fer (✆ **02-35-70-59-97**), for toys and cards from the 1700s and 1800s as well as bottles and glassware. You'll find watercolors by local artists, as well as antique Norman and English engravings, at **Atelier St-Romain,** 28 rue St-Romain (✆ **02-35-88-76-17**).

Lovers of chocolate will discover a veritable paradise at **La Chocolatière,** 18 rue Guillaume-le-Conquérant (✆ **02-35-71-00-79**). The specialty that has attracted local gourmets for as long as anyone can remember is a praline-layered *paillardises,* rich in velvety chocolate that many readers describe as sinful. For millinery, head for **Monique,** 58 rue St-Romain (✆ **02-35-98-07-03**). The mostly original hats run the gamut from funky to refined—and you won't pay Paris prices.

WHERE TO STAY

MODERATE

Hôtel de Dieppe This Best Western property, across from the train station, has been run by the Gueret family since 1880. Although it has been modernized, it's still a traditional French inn. The only problem might be noise, but double-glazed windows help, and the area quiets down after the last train from Paris arrives around 10:30pm. Rooms are compact, with comfortable beds. Half the guest rooms have a full bathroom, the rest just a shower. In **Les Quatre Saisons,** the adjoining rotisserie, you can enjoy dishes such as duckling *à la presse* (pressed duck) and sole poached in red wine.

Place Bernard-Tissot, Rouen 76000. ✆ **800/528-1234** in the U.S. and Canada, or 02-35-71-96-00. Fax 02-35-89-65-21. www.bestwestern.fr. 41 units. 95€–115€ ($124–$150) double. AE, DC, MC, V. Parking 7€ ($9.10). **Amenities:** Restaurant; bar; room service; babysitting; laundry service; dry cleaning; nonsmoking rooms. *In room:* TV, hair dryer, Wi-Fi.

Mercure Centre ★ In a town of lackluster hotels, the Mercure, close to the cathedral, is a fine choice for an overnight stay. The functionally designed rooms, each renovated in late 2004, are almost identical to hundreds of other Mercure accommodations across Europe and are a tad small. Each contains a comfortable bed. Breakfast is the only meal served.

7 rue de la Croix-de-Fer, Rouen 76000. ✆ **02-35-52-69-52.** Fax 02-35-89-41-46. 125 units. 135€–140€ ($176–$182) double; 250€ ($325) suite. AE, DC, MC, V. Parking 10€ ($13). **Amenities:** Bar; room service (drinks only); babysitting; nonsmoking rooms; limited-mobility rooms. *In room:* A/C, TV, minibar, hair dryer, Wi-Fi.

INEXPENSIVE

Hôtel Cardinal *Value* Not only is this hotel ideally located, it's also affordable. It's across from the cathedral (imagine waking up to a view of the majestic structure and the surrounding half-timbered buildings), in the middle of a neighborhood known for antiques, art galleries, and fine dining. With so much to do in the area, you won't mind the hotel's simplicity. Rooms are business-class plain with built-in furnishings and a small bathroom with tub or shower.

1 place de la Cathédrale, Rouen 76000. ✆ **02-35-70-24-42.** Fax 02-35-89-75-14. www.cardinal-hotel.com. 18 units. 58€–76€ ($75–$99) double. MC, V. Parking 5€ ($6.50) nearby. Closed mid-Dec to mid-Jan. **Amenities:** Room service; nonsmoking rooms. *In room:* TV, hair dryer, Wi-Fi.

Hôtel D'Angleterre The traffic noise here can be bad, but the front rooms open onto views of the Seine. Reserve well in advance for July and August, when the hotel is packed. Rooms are small but comfortable and unpretentious. Each comes with a good bed, plus a shower-only bathroom.

21 quai du Havre, Rouen 76000. ✆ **02-35-70-34-95.** Fax 02-35-89-97-12. www.hoteldangleterre.net 37 units. 50€–58€ ($65–$75) double. AE, DC, MC, V. Parking 9€ ($12). **Amenities:** Bar; laundry service; dry cleaning. *In room:* TV, Wi-Fi.

Hôtel de Bordeaux Practically on the banks of the Seine, this hotel offers medium-size and renovated rooms with standard furnishings. They're acceptably comfortable, if a bit sterile-looking. All have views of either the town's medieval rooftops or the cathedral. Rooms on the upper floors afford river views. About half the guest rooms have bathrooms with tubs; the others have showers.

9 place de la République, Rouen 76000. ✆ **02-35-71-93-58.** Fax 02-35-71-92-15. interhotel.rouen@wanadoo.fr. 48 units. 56€–80€ ($73–$104) double. AE, DC, MC, V. Parking 8€ ($10). **Amenities:** Bar; laundry service; dry cleaning; nonsmoking rooms. *In room:* TV, dataport, Wi-Fi.

Hôtel de la Cathédrale Built around a timbered and cobble-covered courtyard, this hotel is on a pedestrian street midway between the cathedral and the Eglise St-Maclou, opposite the Archbishop's Palace where Joan of Arc was tried. The remodeled rooms are well maintained and tastefully furnished, accessible by both stairs and an elevator. All the units contain showers, but only a few come with tubs as well. Breakfast is the only meal served.

12 rue St-Romain, Rouen 76000. ✆ **02-35-71-57-95.** Fax 02-35-70-15-54. www.hotel-de-la-cathedrale.fr. 26 units. 65€–89€ ($85–$116) double. AE, MC, V. Parking 10€ ($13) nearby. **Amenities:** Tea lounge; room service; babysitting; laundry service; nonsmoking rooms. *In room:* TV, hair dryer, Wi-Fi.

Hôtel du Vieux Carré ★ *Finds* In a restored half-timbered 18th-century house, this is one of the most charming and tranquil lodgings in Rouen. After inspecting too many impersonally furnished hotels, we found this one a surprise and a delight. Patrick Beaumont, the enthusiastic and much-traveled owner, has tastefully decorated the midsize guest rooms in comfortable rustic fashion. Unusual for central Rouen, its restaurant opens onto a flower-filled courtyard.

34 rue Ganterie, Rouen 76000. ✆ **02-35-71-67-70.** Fax 02-35-71-19-17. 13 units. 60€ ($78) double. AE, MC, V. **Amenities:** Restaurant (lunch only); tearoom/cafe; laundry service; dry cleaning; limited-mobility rooms. *In room:* TV, Wi-Fi.

WHERE TO DINE

Gill ★★★ MODERN FRENCH The best restaurant in town sits beside the traffic of the Seine's quays. The Art Deco decor, with high-tech lighting and accessories, is an appropriate backdrop for the sophisticated cuisine of Gilles Tournadre. Who can resist ravioli stuffed with foie gras and served in a bouillon sprinkled with fresh truffles? How about terrine of artichoke with fresh truffles or roasted white turbot with fresh asparagus flavored with Parmesan? The best items on the menu are pan-fried foie gras of duckling served with caramelized turnips and a turnip-green salad; a salad of crayfish tails with tomato-and-black-pepper chutney; and the most famous and popular specialty, Rouen-style pigeon with vegetables floating in densely concentrated consommé.

9 quai de la Bourse. ✆ **02-35-71-16-14.** Reservations required far in advance. Main courses 28€–38€ ($36–$49); fixed-price menu 35€–85€ ($46–$111). AE, DC, MC, V. Tues–Sat noon–1:45pm and 7:30–9:30pm. Closed Aug and 2 weeks in Apr.

Les Nymphéas ★★★ MODERN FRENCH One of the most appealing restaurants in Rouen bears the name of a painting by Monet *(Water Lilies).* The setting is a 16th-century half-timbered house that fits gracefully into the centrally located neighborhood (place du Vieux-Marché). The restaurant features sophisticated, savory cuisine. It's celebrated for its warm foie gras with cider sauce; wild duckling Rouennais style, served with wild mushrooms and caramelized onions; and *civet* (stew) of lobster with Sauternes. An award-winning dessert that evokes the Norman countryside is a warm soufflé flavored with apples and Calvados.

7 rue de la Pie. ✆ **02-35-89-26-69.** Reservations required. Main courses 19€–55€ ($25–$72); fixed-price menu 30€–69€ ($38–$90). AE, MC, V. Tues–Sat 12:15–2pm and 7:30–9:45pm. Closed late Aug to mid-Sept.

Maison Dufour ★ NORMAN One of Normandy's best-preserved 15th-century inns has flourished under four generations of the Dufour family since 1906. Dining rooms are decorated with copper pots, woodcarvings, and engravings. The food, reflecting local culinary traditions, is so outstanding that it's hard to single out specialties. The home-smoked salmon, *canard* (duckling) *rouennais,* chopped lamb, John

Dory in cider sauce, and sole Normande are all exemplary. For dessert, try the Calvados-flavored soufflé or a slice of apple tart.

67 bis rue St-Nicolas. © **02-35-71-90-62.** Reservations required. Main courses 15€–28€ ($20–$36); fixed-price lunch 17€–38€ ($22–$49); fixed-price dinner 25€–39€ ($33–$51). AE, MC, V. Tues–Sun noon–1:45pm; Tues–Sat 7–9:30pm.

Pascaline *Value* TRADITIONAL FRENCH This informal bistro is often filled with regulars and has been a favorite since its opening in 1880. The decor hasn't changed much since. The cheapest fixed-price menus are among the best bargains in town. Menu items include seafood dishes such as pavé of monkfish with roughly textured mustard sauce; breast of duck cooked in beer; savory *pot-au-feu maison* (house stew); and, as a *plat du jour,* cassoulet of sausages and lentils. Don't come for refined cuisine—you should expect hearty, time-tested old favorites.

5 rue de la Poterne. © **02-35-89-67-44.** Reservations recommended. Main courses 10€–18€ ($13–$23); fixed-price menu 14€–24€ ($18–$31). AE, MC, V. Daily noon–2pm and 7–11pm.

ROUEN AFTER DARK

Cette Semaine à Rouen, a pamphlet that details the week's entertainment offerings and events, is available free at the tourist office and most hotels.

For highbrow entertainment, **Théâtre des Arts,** 7 rue du Dr.-Rambert (© **02-35-71-41-36**), presents ballet, opera, and classical music. **Théâtre des Deux Rives,** 48 rue Louis-Ricard (© **02-35-89-63-41**), presents plays in French. **Théâtre des Arts/Opéra Léonard de Vinci,** 7 rue du Dr.-Rambert (© **02-35-71-41-36**), has a busy schedule of classical and contemporary opera. A variety of concerts takes place at **Eglise St-Maclou,** 3 rue Dutuit, and **Eglise St-Ouen,** place du Général-de-Gaulle. For information about who's playing, contact the tourist office.

Much of the nightlife, especially pubs, centers on place du Vieux-Marché. The better pubs frequented by 25- to 45-year-olds are the crowded **Café Leffe,** 36 place des Carmes (© **02-35-71-93-30**), and **La Taverne St-Amand,** 11 rue St-Amand (© **02-35-88-51-34**), which has a friendly environment perfect for enjoying a mug of the best Irish, Belgian, or German beer. Across the street, **La Bohème,** 18 rue St-Amand (© **02-35-71-53-99**), is a small discothèque with a cozy, publike ambience. Many students meet at the **Underground Pub,** 26 rue des Champs-Maillets (© **02-35-98-44-84**), which has a street-level bar and an underground bar fitted with wood and British bric-a-brac.

WINE BAR **Le P'tit Zinc,** 20 place du Vieux-Marché (© **02-35-89-39-69**), is a bistro-style wine bar with early-1900s decor and one of the best wine selections in town. Of course, you can order Norman cider as well.

DISCO At **Le Kiosque,** 43 bd. de Verdun (© **02-35-88-54-50**), 20-somethings rule the dance floor. You'll pay a cover of 14€ ($18) to enjoy hard-edged techno music and psychedelic light action. A disco that appeals to a somewhat mature (22–40) crowd is **l'Ibiza,** 29 bd. Des Belges (© **02-35-07-76-20**). Located near place du Vieux-Marché, it has modern decor, a crowded dance floor, occasional karaoke, and a cover charge of 8€ to 12€ ($10–$16), which includes one drink.

GAY & LESBIAN BARS **Le Central,** 138 rue Beauvoisine (© **02-35-07-71-97**), attracts a *très* cool crowd of mostly gay males in their 20s and 30s who prefer the James Dean look. There's a full bar, and the music is house and techno. Pinball machines, video screens, billiards, and darts are other entertainment options. The modern **Le**

Finds Finding Old Normandy in Calvados Country

For a taste of old Normandy, motorists heading from Rouen to Deauville should stop in Pont-Audemer, 50km (31 miles) west of Rouen. On the banks of the River Risle, Pont-Audemer is in the heart of Calvados country. In spite of war damage, Pont-Audemer retains much of its old look, especially if you wander its historic streets, rue de la Licorne (unicorn) and rue de la République. Along rue de la République, look for Eglise St-Ouen, dating from the 11th century.

Chakra, 4 bis bd. Ferdinand-de-Lesseps (© **02-32-10-12-02**), attracts its share of young, well-connected gays and lesbians. It's known for light shows and techno music. A wild crowd parties here until the wee hours, especially on weekends. You'll pay an 8€-to-10€ ($10–$13) cover, which includes one drink.

2 Honfleur ★★

201km (125 miles) NW of Paris, 63km (39 miles) NE of Caen

At the mouth of the Seine opposite Le Havre, Honfleur is one of Normandy's most charming fishing ports. Having escaped major damage in World War II, the working port looks like an antique. Thanks to the pont de Normande, the bridge that links Honfleur to Le Havre, visitors flock here. Honfleur is 500 years older than Le Havre, dating from the 11th century. Artists, including Daubigny, Corot, and Monet, have long favored this township.

ESSENTIALS

GETTING THERE If you're **driving** from Pont l'Evêque or other points south (including Paris), D579 leads to the major boulevard, rue de la République. Follow it to the town center. Driving time from Paris is 2½ hours.

There's no direct **train** service into Honfleur. From Paris, take one of the dozen or so daily trains from Gare St-Lazare to Deauville. From there, bus no. 20 makes the 25-minute ride to Honfleur; the one-way fare is about 3.60€ ($4.70). From Rouen, take the train to Le Havre and transfer to bus no. 50, which costs 6.80€ ($8.85) each way, for the 30-minute ride to Honfleur. Several **buses** run daily between Caen and Honfleur (trip time: 2 hr.); the one-way fare is 11€ ($14). For information, call **Bus Verts** (© **08-10-21-42-14**).

VISITOR INFORMATION The **Office de Tourisme** is on quai Lepaulmier (© **02-31-89-23-30;** www.ot-honfleur.fr).

SEEING THE TOWN

Begin your tour, which should take about an hour, at place de la Porte-de-Rouen. Stroll along the **Vieux Bassin,** the old harbor, taking in the fishing boats and narrow, slate-roofed houses. On the north side of the basin, the former governor's house, **Lieutenance,** dates from the 16th century. Nearby is the **Eglise Ste-Catherine,** place Ste-Catherine (© **02-31-89-11-93**), constructed of timber by 15th-century shipbuilders. The church's wooden belfry is on the other side of the street. The church is open July and August daily from 8am to 8pm; September to June daily 8:30am to noon and 2 to 6pm.

Maisons Satie Opened in 1998, this high-tech museum honors Honfleur's native son Erik Satie in the house where he was born in 1866. Satie was a "complete artist"—he became most famous for his music, but he was also a painter and acted as a muse and inspiration to Picasso, Braque, Cocteau, Debussy, Ravel, and Stravinsky. This is not a traditional museum. The walk-through exhibitions incorporate sound, light, and recordings of Satie's compositions. Visitors wear high-tech helmets that transmit sound, which allows for a degree of play and experimentation in some of the exhibits.

67 bd. Charles V. ✆ **02-31-89-11-11.** Admission 5.10€ ($6.65) adults, 3.60€ ($4.70) ages 10–17, free for children under 10. Apr–Sept Wed–Mon 10am–7pm; Oct–Dec and Feb 16–Mar Wed–Mon 11am–6pm. Closed Jan–Feb 15.

Musée du Vieux Honfleur This place celebrates the unique cultural and aesthetic contributions of Normandy to the rest of Europe. You'll find old furniture, lace head-dresses, embroidery, candle-making equipment, and farm implements, as well as several rooms outfitted with period art and antiques.

Quai St-Etienne. ✆ **02-31-89-14-12.** Admission 3€ ($3.90) adults, 1.80€ ($2.35) students and children 10–18, free for children under 10. July–Aug daily 10am–1pm and 2:30–6:30pm; Apr–June and Sept Tues–Fri 10am–noon and 2–6pm; Oct to mid-Nov and mid-Feb to Mar Tues–Fri 2–5:30pm, Sat–Sun 10am–noon and 2:30–5:30pm. Closed mid-Nov to mid-Feb.

Musée Eugène-Boudin This museum has a good collection of works by the painters who flocked to this port when Impressionism was new. The largest assortment is of the pastels and paintings of Boudin.

Place Erik-Satie. ✆ **02-31-89-54-00.** Admission 5.20€ ($6.75) adults, 3.70€ ($4.80) students and children 10 and over. Mar 15–Sept Wed–Mon 10am–noon and 2–6pm; Oct–Mar 14 Wed–Mon 8:30am–5pm, Sat–Sun 10am–noon and 2:30–5pm. Closed Jan to mid-Feb, July 14, and Dec 25.

NaturoSpace Inaugurated in 1999 on the western outskirts of town, adjacent to the seacoast, Honfleur's modern attraction showcases the flora and butterfly life of some of the most exotic climates on earth. Designed like an enormous greenhouse bursting with tropical plants and butterflies, it contains a labyrinth of walkways that cut through Normandy's approximation of a tropical rainforest. Most visitors spend about an hour in this environment, which is in distinct contrast to the old Norman ethnicity that's otherwise associated with Honfleur.

Bd. Charles V. ✆ **02-31-81-77-00.** Admission 7.40€ ($9.60) adults, 5.80€ ($7.55) students and children under 14. Family package 29€ ($38). Apr–June and Sept daily 10am–1pm and 2–7pm; mid-Jan to Mar and Oct–Nov Wed and Sat–Sun 10am–5:30pm; July–Aug daily 10am–7pm. Closed Dec to mid-Jan.

WHERE TO STAY

Restaurant/Hôtel L'Absinthe (see "Where to Dine," below) also rents rooms.

Castel Albertine ★ *Finds* Management takes great care to maintain the character of this home of Albert Sorel, a 19th-century historian and scholar. The impressive house, of red brick and rose-hued stone, is a 3-minute walk from the port. It is a handsome, welcoming hotel. All of the individually decorated rooms have floor-to-ceiling windows that open onto views of gardens and trees. Each room was renovated in 2002 or 2003, and many have king-size beds. Bathrooms are small but tidily kept, with either a tub or a shower.

19 cours Albert-Manuel, Honfleur 14600. ✆ **02-31-98-85-56.** Fax 02-31-98-83-18. www.honfleurhotels.com. 26 units. 80€–150€ ($104–$195) double. MC, V. Parking 10€ ($13). **Amenities:** Bar; sauna; room service; babysitting; laundry service; dry cleaning; limited-mobility rooms. *In room:* TV, hair dryer.

La Ferme St-Siméon ★★★ An old farmhouse is the focal point of this 17th-century half-timbered slate hotel, one of Normandy's most elegant and prestigious inns. It's in the hills above Honfleur, about 1.5km (1 mile) from the old port. The shimmering water of the English Channel draws artists to the hilltop inn, said to be where Impressionism was born in the 19th century. Much of the hotel has terra-cotta floors, carved wood, and copper and faïence touches. Guest rooms, which are formal and comfortable, have fabric-covered walls. Some rooms contain exposed half-timbering or ceiling beams; others hold canopy-covered beds. Most have antique or heirloom furnishings. Bathrooms are beautifully maintained; about half have tub/shower combinations.

Rte. Adolphe-Marais, Honfleur 14600. ✆ **02-31-81-78-00.** Fax 02-31-89-48-48. www.fermesaintsimeon.fr. 34 units. 220€–450€ ($286–$585) double; 550€–850€ ($715–$1,105) suite. AE, MC, V. **Amenities:** 2 restaurants; bar; indoor pool; spa; sauna; room service; babysitting; laundry service; dry cleaning; nonsmoking rooms; limited-mobility rooms. *In room:* TV, minibar, hair dryer, Wi-Fi.

Les Maisons de Léa ★★ A sense of old-fashioned coziness abounds here. In 1900, the hotel owners enclosed a 16th-century fish market and added plumbing and partitions between what are now comfortable, warmly decorated guest rooms. The renovated rooms have individual color schemes and canopy-covered beds. The accommodations, though modest, are perfect for an overnight stop. All bathrooms contain showers, but only about a third have tubs.

Place Ste-Catherine, Honfleur 14600. ✆ **02-31-14-49-49.** Fax 02-31-89-28-61. www.lesmaisonsdelea.com. 31 units. 102€–160€ ($133–$208) double; 245€–280€ ($319–$364) suite. AE, MC, V. Bus: 20 or 50. **Amenities:** Snack bar; babysitting. *In room:* TV, hair dryer, Wi-Fi.

WHERE TO DINE

La Terrasse et l'Assiette ★★ TRADITIONAL FRENCH Outfitted "in the Norman style" with heavy beams and lots of exposed brick, the gourmet citadel of Honfleur attracts an upscale international clientele. Owner Gérard Bonnefoy churns out dishes that include crayfish with sautéed vermicelli and truffles, an omelet studded with chunks of lobster, unctuous fried foie gras served with lentils, and braised scallops with a purée of Brussels sprouts and smoked-ham sauce. Leave room for *petit gateau moelleux au chocolat* (very moist chocolate-fudge cake). In summer, if the weather is clement, ask for a table on the outdoor terrace, overlooking the historic Eglise Ste-Catherine.

8 place Ste-Catherine. ✆ **02-31-89-31-33.** Reservations recommended. Main courses 28€–35€ ($36–$46); fixed-price menu 28€–49€ ($36–$64). AE, MC, V. Wed–Sun noon–2pm and 7:30–9pm.

Restaurant/Hôtel L'Absinthe ★★ TRADITIONAL FRENCH This tavern, named for the drink preferred by many 19th-century writers, is known for its beautiful decor, extravagant portions, and well-prepared cuisine. Rooms in the 16th-century building have beamed ceilings, parquet floors, and furniture that matches the architectural grandeur. The restaurant consists of two dining rooms (one from the 15th c. with exposed beams and exposed stone, and one from the 17th c. with a stately fireplace). The menu changes frequently. The best menu items include foie gras with caramelized ginger and apples, and sea bass roasted with laurel leaves and red wine.

If you're taken with the place, you can rent a room or the suite. A double runs 105€ to 135€ ($137–$176), and the suite goes for 225€ ($293). Parking costs 11€ ($14).

10 quai de la Quarantaine, Honfleur 14600. ✆ **02-31-89-39-00.** Fax 02-31-89-53-60. www.absinthe.fr. Reservations required. Main courses 30€–42€ ($39–$55); fixed-price menu 33€–65€ ($43–$85). AE, DC, MC, V. Daily 12:15–3pm and 7:15–10pm. Closed Nov 15–Dec 17.

3 Deauville ★★★

206km (128 miles) NW of Paris, 47km (29 miles) NE of Caen

Deauville has been associated with the rich and famous since the duc de Morny, Napoleon III's half-brother, founded it as an upscale resort in 1859. In 1913, it entered sartorial history when Coco Chanel launched her career here, opening a boutique selling tiny hats that challenged the fashion of huge-brimmed hats loaded with flowers and fruit. (Coco's point of view: "How can the mind breathe under those things?")

ESSENTIALS

GETTING THERE There are 6 to 10 daily **rail** connections from Paris's Gare St-Lazare (trip time: 2 hr., 15 min.); prices start at 28€ ($36) one-way. The rail depot lies between Trouville and Deauville, south of town. Take a taxi from the station. **Bus Verts du Calvados** (✆ **08-10-21-42-14**) serves the Normandy coast from Caen to Le Havre. To **drive** from Paris (trip time: 2½ hr.), take A13 west to Pont L'Evêque, and then follow N177 east to Deauville.

VISITOR INFORMATION The **Office de Tourisme** is on place de la Mairie (✆ **02-31-14-40-00;** www.deauville.org).

SPECIAL EVENTS For a week in September, the **Deauville Festival of American Film** (✆ **02-31-14-40-00;** www.festival-deauville.com) honors movies made in the United States. Actors, producers, directors, and writers flock here and briefly eclipse the high rollers at the casinos and the horse-racing and polo crowd.

EXPLORING THE RESORT

Coco Chanel cultivated a tradition of elegance that survives in Deauville and in its smaller and less prestigious neighbor Trouville, on the opposite bank of the Toques (see the next section). Don't expect flash—in its way, restrained and ever-so-polite Deauville is the most British seaside resort in France.

However, in its heart, Deauville is less English than French. It has even been dubbed Paris's 21st *arrondissement.* The crowds here tend to be urban and hip. Deauville is stylish and not (by anyone's definition) inexpensive.

With its golf courses, casinos, deluxe hotels, La Touques and Clairefontaine racetracks, regattas, a yachting harbor, polo grounds, and tennis courts, Deauville is a formidable contender for the business of the upper class. Looking for a charming place to stroll? Head for boutique-lined **rue Eugène-Colas, place Morny** (named for the resort's founder), and **place du Casino.**

BEACHES Expect to spend time on Deauville's boardwalk, **Les Planches,** a promenade running parallel to the beach. Beaux Arts and half-timbered Norman-inspired buildings line its edges. In summer, especially August, parasols dot the beach and oiled bodies cover seemingly every inch of sand. The resort's only beach is **Plage de Deauville,** a strip that's part of La Côte Fleurie.

If you're looking for a gay and nude beach, you'll have to go to **Merville-France-Ville,** 39km (24 miles) from Deauville toward Caen. But considering how permissive most Deauville fans are, many gay travelers feel perfectly comfortable here.

Access to every beach in Normandy is free; in Deauville, you'll pay from 2€ ($2.60) per hour for parking in any of the many public lots beside the sea.

The **Piscine Olympique,** bord de Mer (✆ **02-31-14-02-17**), is a large indoor seawater pool. Depending on the season, bathers pay 4€ to 5€ ($5.20–$6.50) per person. Hours are July and August daily 9:30am to 7:30pm, June and September daily 10am to 7pm, and October through May daily 10:30am to 7pm.

GOLF On Mont Canisy, **Golf Barrière de Deauville** (✆ **02-31-14-24-24**) offers a tranquil country setting tinged by the sea's salty tang. The par-71 18-hole course, one of the largest in Europe, rolls through 5,951m (19,519 ft.) of rapid greens and difficult roughs, with sweeping views of the Auge valley and the sea. In addition to the compound's conventional 18-hole course, a 9-hole course is immediately adjacent, set within a woodland setting, with a par of 36 and greens fees half the rates noted below. The course also has an indoor driving range, a putting green, a practice bunker, private instruction, and a clubhouse with a bar, a restaurant, and an exclusive line of gear. A franchise of the Lucien Barrière chain of resorts, hotels, and casinos, the club includes a palatial half-timbered hotel (see below). According to the season, greens fees for hotel guests are 32€ ($42) Saturday and Sunday and 24€ ($31) Monday to Friday. Nonguests pay 40€ ($52) Saturday and Sunday, 30€ ($39) Monday to Friday.

HORSE RACES/POLO You can watch horses every day from late June to early October. There's either a race at 2pm or a polo match at 3pm. The venues are the **Hippodrome de Deauville La Touques,** boulevard Mauger (✆ **02-31-14-20-00**), in the heart of town near the Mairie de Deauville (town hall); and the **Hippodrome de Deauville Clairefontaine,** route de Clairefontaine (✆ **02-31-14-69-00**), within the city limits, 2km (1¼ miles) west of the center.

SHOPPING

This seaside town has a pedestrian shopping area between the polo field and the port; the main drags are **rue Mirabeau, rue Albert-Fracasse,** and the west end of **avenue de la République.** The leading shops, selling some of the world's most elegant merchandise (with prices to match), cluster on **rue Eugène-Colas, place Morny,** and **place du Casino.** At **La Cave de Deauville,** 48 rue Mirabeau (✆ **02-31-87-35-36**), you'll find a wide selection of apple ciders, Calvados, and the apple aperitif known as *pommeau.*

For an overview of the bounty of the fertile Norman soil, head for the **Marché Publique** (open-air market) in the place du Marché, adjacent to place Morny. From July to mid-September, it's open daily 8am to 1pm. The rest of the year, market days are Tuesday, Friday, Saturday, and occasionally Sunday. In addition to fruits, vegetables, poultry, cider, wine, and cheese, you'll find cookware, porcelain tableware, and cutlery.

WHERE TO STAY

EXPENSIVE

Hôtel du Golf Barrière ★★★ *Kids* Golfers gravitate to this half-timbered hotel created by the Lucien Barrière chain in the late 1980s. The location, in the hills above Deauville, about 3km (1¾ miles) from the center of town, creates an aura of country-club tranquillity. Outfitted in English country-house style, it's one of the few hotels in Normandy with its own golf course. If the links aren't your thing, you might consider the Normandy or Royal hotels (reviewed below, and all three Lucien Barrière properties). The children's center and activities program are the best in Deauville. Rooms come in a wide range of sizes; those in back open onto the links, those in front have better views of the Channel. The best rooms, called "prestige luxe," feature antique-style furnishings, French windows, and spacious bathrooms and balconies.

At New-Golf Club, Mont Canisy, St-Arnoult Deauville 14800. ✆ **02-31-14-24-00.** Fax 02-31-14-24-01. www.lucienbarriere.com. 178 units. 216€–312€ ($281–$406) double; 344€–385€ ($447–$501) junior suite. AE, DC, MC, V. Closed Nov 14–Dec 27 and Jan 3 to mid-Feb. From Deauville, take D278 south for 2.5km (1½ miles). **Amenities:** 2 restaurants; bar; heated outdoor pool; 27-hole golf course; 3 tennis courts; fitness center; sauna; children's center; room service; massage; babysitting; laundry service; dry cleaning; nonsmoking rooms; limited-mobility rooms. *In room:* TV, minibar, hair dryer, safe, Wi-Fi.

Normandy Barrière ★★★ *Kids* This is the most famous hotel in Deauville, with a legendary chic that dates back to the Edwardian age. The Anglo-Norman design includes half-timbering, dovecotes, turrets, and gables; the 1912 building resembles a cozy but stately English country house. A renovation in 2002 updated all the rooms, public areas, and security systems. Because of its extensive facilities for children, including a nursery and babysitting (10€–13€/$13–$17 per hour, per child), it attracts upscale families with children—although that doesn't interfere with the hotel's image as a chic nest for Francophone celebrities. During the Deauville Festival of American Film, it attracts French stars, the press, and jury members. Originally built to house well-heeled gamblers from the nearby casino, it continues to draw the gambling crowd today. Bathrooms are sumptuous.

38 rue Jean-Mermoz, Deauville 14800. ✆ **02-31-98-66-22.** Fax 02-31-98-66-23. www.lucienbarriere.com. 291 units. 288€–398€ ($374–$517) double; 495€–1,200€ ($644–$1,560) suite. AE, DC, MC, V. Parking 25€ ($33) in garage. **Amenities:** Restaurant; children's dining room; bar; heated outdoor pool; 2 tennis courts; fitness room; steam room; room service; babysitting; laundry service; dry cleaning; nonsmoking rooms; limited-mobility rooms. *In room:* TV, minibar, hair dryer, safe, Wi-Fi.

Royal-Barrière ★★★ The Royal adjoins the casino and fronts a park near the Channel. It rises like a palace, with columns and exposed timbers. Although it doesn't have the insider cachet of the Normandy Barrière, it is a grander and more opulent hotel. It's a member of Leading Hotels of the World, and its architecture evokes an Edwardian-era grand palace hotel. The hotel was built in 1913 on architectural principles conceived by Gustav Eiffel (an iron skeleton supports walls and ceilings). Post-millennium the hotel concluded a 5-year renovation program that included virtually every aspect of the establishment, including elegant bathrooms with tubs and showers. The decor of the guest rooms, conceived by mega-designer Jacques Garcia, is a reinterpretation of Directoire and Napoleon III styles. During the Deauville Festival of American Film, the U.S. stars stay here.

Bd. Eugène-Cornuché, Deauville 14800. ✆ **02-31-98-66-33.** Fax 02-31-98-66-34. www.lucienbarriere.com. 290 units. 300€–403€ ($390–$524) double; from 470€–915€ ($611–$1,190) suite. AE, DC, MC, V. Closed Jan to mid-Mar. **Amenities:** 2 restaurants; bar; heated outdoor pool; health club; sauna; room service; laundry service; dry cleaning. *In room:* TV, minibar, hair dryer, safe, Wi-Fi.

INEXPENSIVE

Hôtel Ibis *Value* Built in the 1980s as part of the nationwide chain, the Ibis is on the periphery of Deauville about a half-mile from the casino. The modern building, overlooking the harbor, is one of the best bargains in town. Rooms are comfortable and tidy, but decorated in dull chain style. The small tiled bathrooms contain showers. The restaurant offers a traditional French menu.

9–10 quai de la Marine, Deauville 14800. ✆ **02-31-14-50-00.** Fax 02-31-14-50-05. www.hotelibis.com. 95 units. 60€–99€ ($78–$129) double; 99€–169€ ($129–$220) duplex suite for 2–6 people. AE, DC, MC, V. Parking 10€ ($13). **Amenities:** Restaurant; bar; babysitting; nonsmoking rooms; limited-mobility rooms. *In room:* TV, Wi-Fi.

Hôtel Le Trophée This modern replica of a half-timbered medieval building is in the middle of Deauville, 150m (492 ft.) from the beach. The small rooms have contemporary furniture and private balconies overlooking the shopping streets. Bathrooms are also small. A sun terrace on the roof provides a bird's-eye view of the town and a more private tanning area than the beach. If you plan to eat here, enjoy at least one meal under the stars in the patio courtyard garden. Late in 2004, the hotel transformed what was a private house, immediately across the street, into an annex, creating an additional 15 suites.

81 rue du Général-Leclerc, Deauville 14800. ✆ **02-31-88-45-86.** Fax 02-31-88-07-94. www.letrophee.com. 35 units. 69€–144€ ($90–$187) double; 119€–199€ ($155–$259) suite. AE, DC, MC, V. Parking 8€ ($10). **Amenities:** Restaurant; heated outdoor pool; fitness center; sauna; steam bath; room service; babysitting; limited-mobility rooms. *In room:* TV, minibar, hair dryer, Wi-Fi.

L'Augeval ★ Across from the racetrack and just blocks from the beach and casino, this gem mixes city flair and country charm. The former private villa was built in the early 1900s and sits amid well-kept lawns and gardens. The cozy rooms range from medium to spacious, and each has at least one high-quality antique. Some units have Jacuzzis. Each tiled bathroom holds a tub or shower.

15 av. Hocquart-de-Turtot, Deauville 14800. ✆ **02-31-81-13-18.** Fax 02-31-81-00-40. www.augeval.com. 44 units. 108€–140€ ($140–$182) double; 142€–218€ ($185–$283) suite. AE, DC, MC, V. Parking 8€ ($10). **Amenities:** Bar; small heated outdoor pool; fitness room; room service; babysitting; laundry service; nonsmoking rooms; limited-mobility rooms. *In room:* TV, minibar, hair dryer, safe, Wi-Fi.

WHERE TO DINE

Chez Miocque TRADITIONAL FRENCH This hip cafe near the casino and the boutiques does a bustling business at its sidewalk tables. The English-speaking owner, known as Jack, will welcome you to the convivial bar-type setting for lunch, dinner, or a drink. The place serves hearty brasserie-style food, including succulent lamb stew with spring vegetables, filet of skate with cream-based caper sauce, mussels in white-wine sauce, and steaks. Portions are filling, and the atmosphere can be lively. The dish of the day is always from the sea.

81 rue Eugène-Colas. ✆ **02-31-88-09-52.** Reservations recommended. Main courses 20€–40€ ($26–$52). Set menu 30€ ($39). AE, MC, V. July–Sept daily 9am–midnight; mid-Feb to June and Oct–Dec Fri–Mon noon–4pm and 7pm–midnight. Closed Jan to mid-Feb.

Le Ciro's Barrière ★★★ FRENCH/SEAFOOD Hot on the resort's social scene, Le Ciro's serves Deauville's best seafood. It's expensive but worth it. If you want a bit of everything, ask for the *plateau de fruits de mer,* brimming with lobster and shellfish. For an elaborate appetizer, we recommend lobster salad with truffles. Marmite of scallops with sweet sauterne wine and saffron makes a superb main course. The collection of Bordeaux wine is exceptional. The ambience is airy, stylish, and evocative of the Belle Epoque heyday of Deauville.

Casino de Deauville, promenade des Planches. ✆ **02-31-14-31-31.** Fax 02-31-88-32-02. Reservations required. Main courses 16€–72€ ($21–$94); fixed-price menu 40€ ($52). AE, DC, MC, V. Thurs–Mon 12:30–2:30pm and 7:30–9:30pm. Closed Jan 4–27.

Le Spinnaker ★ NORMAN Owner-chef Pascal Angenard's charming yellow-and-blue restaurant features regional cuisine. The satisfying specialties include terrine of foie gras with four spices, roast lobster with cider vinegar and cream-enriched potatoes, slow-cooked veal flank, and hot apple tart. Pascal recommends roast turbot flavored with shallots *en confit.* A fine array of wines can accompany your meal. On some nights a dish here or there might not be sublime, but most are excellent.

52 rue Mirabeau. ✆ **02-31-88-24-40.** Reservations required. Main courses 28€–60€ ($36–$78); fixed-price menu 30€–45€ ($39–$59). AE, DC, MC, V. Wed–Sun 12:30–1:30pm and 7:30–10pm. Closed June 21–28, Nov 15–30, and Jan 2–31.

DEAUVILLE AFTER DARK

Opened in 1912, the **Casino de Deauville,** rue Edmond-Blanc (✆ **02-31-14-31-14;** www.lucienbarriere.com), is one of France's premier casinos. Its original Belle Epoque core has been expanded with a theater, a nightclub, three restaurants, and an extensive collection of slot machines *(machines à sous).* The casino distinguishes areas for slot machines from more formal locales containing such games as roulette, baccarat, blackjack, and poker. The slots are open daily from 11am to 2am (to 3am Fri and 4am Sat) and have no dress code; access to this area is free. The areas containing *les jeux traditionnels* (traditional games) are open daily at 4pm and close between 3 and 4am, depending on business and the day of the week. Entrance is free, and you must present a passport or identity card to gain admission. The most interesting nights are Friday and Saturday, when the cabaret theater and all the restaurants are open. The theater presents glittering, moderately titillating shows at 10:30pm on Friday and Saturday. Admission is 25€ ($33) Friday, rising to 29€ ($38) on Saturday.

If it's a dance club you're looking for, head to the high-energy **Y Club,** 14 bis rue Désiré-le-Hoc (✆ **02-31-88-30-91**). For salsa, merengue, and reggae, visit **Brok Café,** 14 av. du Général-de-Gaulle (✆ **02-31-81-30-81**). If you want to re-create the restrained but decadent ambience of the 1970s, consider **Le Régine's,** inside Deauville's casino, rue Edmond-Blanc (✆ **02-31-14-31-96**).

Dancing Les Planches, Le Bois Lauret, Blonville (✆ **02-31-87-58-09**), 4km (2½ miles) from Deauville, is a club where you'll find up-to-date music, a dance floor, and even an indoor swimming pool near an indoor/outdoor bar.

4 Trouville ★★

206km (128 miles) NW of Paris, 43km (27 miles) NE of Caen

Across the Touques River from the fashionable (and expensive) Deauville, Trouville feels more like a fishing port. The town is like Honfleur, but with fewer boutiques and art galleries. Don't expect the grand atmosphere of Deauville; Trouville is more low-key. It's also less dependent on resort euros; when the bathers leave its splendid sands, Trouville continues to thrive—its resident population of fishermen sees to that.

ESSENTIALS

GETTING THERE There are **rail** connections from Gare St-Lazare in Paris to Trouville (see the "Deauville" section, earlier in this chapter). **Bus Verts du Calvados** links Trouville, Deauville, and the surrounding region with the rest of Normandy. For bus information, call the **Gare Routière** (✆ **08-10-21-42-14**). If you're traveling by **car** from Deauville, drive west along D180.

VISITOR INFORMATION The **Office de Tourisme** is at 32 quai Fernand-Moureaux (✆ **02-31-14-60-70;** www.trouvillesurmer.org).

EXPLORING THE TOWN

In the heyday of Napoleon III, during the 1860s, *boulevardiers* used to bring their wives and families to Trouville and stash their mistresses in Deauville. Deauville was just coming into existence; it's a planned city, with straight avenues and a sense of industrial-age orderliness. By contrast, the narrow, labyrinthine alleyways of Trouville hint at its origins as a medieval fishing port.

Our recommendation? Explore Trouville, enjoying its low-key charm, and when you tire of it, join the caravan of traffic that heads across the river to the bright lights and glamour of Deauville.

Les Planches is a stretch of seafront boardwalk dotted with concessions on one side and overlooking the sea on the other. In midsummer, expect lots of flesh sprawled on the sands in various states of undress. There's only one beach, **Plage de Trouville** (though when you've tired of it, you only have to cross the river to reach the Plage de Deauville). On Trouville's seafront is the **Piscine de Trouville,** promenade des Planches (✆ **02-31-14-48-10**), an indoor freshwater pool that gets very crowded in summer. Depending on the season, bathers pay 4€ to 5€ ($5.20–$6.50) per person. Hours are July and August daily from 9:30am to 7:30pm, June and September daily from 10am to 7pm, and October to May daily from 10:30am to 7pm.

SHOPPING

Trouville's main shopping streets are **quai Fernand-Moureaux** and **rue des Bains** (some sections of which are off-limits to conventional traffic). The **rue du Général-de-Gaulle** has a greater concentration of everyday shops such as food outlets and hardware stores. The rue des Bains has its share of boutiques and clothing stores, but stylish shops are more numerous in neighboring Deauville.

WHERE TO STAY

Hôtel Carmen *Value* This highly recommended Logis de France member, run by the Bude family, consists of two connected late-18th-century villas, one designed by a cousin of Georges Bizet. The management requests that guests take the half-board plan (breakfast and dinner). Rooms come in a variety of sizes; although most are rather small, they have comfortable beds, plus small shower-only bathrooms. Some overlook a flower-filled courtyard.

24 rue Carnot, Trouville 14360. ✆ **02-31-88-35-43.** Fax 02-31-88-08-03. 18 units. 86€–100€ ($112–$130) double; 132€–145€ ($172–$189) with half board. AE, DC, MC, V. **Amenities:** Restaurant; bar; room service; nonsmoking rooms. *In room:* TV, minibar, hair dryer, Wi-Fi.

Le Beach Hotel Although a poor relation to the palaces of Deauville, Le Beach Hotel offers comfort at more affordable prices. The seven-story hotel, constructed in 1984, emerges out of a lackluster lot only 45m (148 ft.) from the beach. Its average-size rooms have modern furniture and comfortable beds, plus views of Trouville harbor; most bathrooms have showers only.

1 quai Albert-1e, Trouville 14360. ✆ **02-31-98-12-00.** Fax 02-31-87-30-29. 110 units. 85€–115€ ($111–$150) double; 165€–210€ ($215–$273) suite. AE, DC, MC, V. Parking 8€ ($10). **Amenities:** Restaurant; bar; indoor pool; room service; babysitting; limited-mobility rooms. *In room:* TV, minibar.

WHERE TO DINE

La Petite Auberge NORMAN For an inexpensive, quality meal, head to this Norman bistro a block from the casino. Try cream of cauliflower soup with scallops or a *pot-au-feu* Dieppoise featuring filet of sole, scallops, monkfish, and salmon beautifully simmered together. You can also order grilled beef and chicken thighs braised in cider. Because the bistro seats only 30, reservations are vital in summer.

7 rue Carnot. ✆ **02-31-88-11-07.** Reservations required. Main courses 15€–25€ ($20–$33); fixed-price menu 27€–47€ ($35–$61). MC, V. July Thurs–Tues noon–2:30pm and 7:15–9:30pm; Aug daily noon–2:30pm and 7:15–9:30pm; Sept–June Thurs–Mon noon–2:30pm and 7–10pm.

Les Vapeurs ★★ FRENCH/SEAFOOD This Art Deco brasserie, one of the most popular on the Norman coast, is frequented by stylish Parisians on *le weekend.* Established in 1926, it has been called the Brasserie Lipp of Normandy. The windows face the port, and in warm weather you can dine at sidewalk tables. Seafood—a wide range of shrimp, mussels laced with cream, crinkle-shelled oysters, and fish—is the specialty. Sauerkraut is also popular.

160 bd. Fernand-Moureaux. ✆ **02-31-88-15-24.** Reservations recommended. Main courses 15€–30€ ($20–$39). AE, MC, V. Daily noon–1am.

TROUVILLE AFTER DARK

If the casino in Deauville is too stuffy for you, you'll feel more comfortable in its smaller, less architecturally distinctive sibling in Trouville, **Casino Barrière de Trouville,** place du Maréchal-Foch (✆ **02-31-87-75-00;** www.lucienbarriere.com). It has more of a New Orleans–style environment, with a blues and jazz bar that schedules live music Friday and Saturday night, and a small-scale replica of Bourbon Street. Entrance to the slot machines is free. Entrance to the more formal area—with roulette, blackjack, and craps—costs 11€ ($14) per person. You must present a passport or identity card to gain admission. The formal area is open Sunday to Thursday 8pm to 2am, Friday 8pm to 3am, and Saturday 8pm to 4am. The rest of the casino is open daily from 10am. Men aren't required to wear jackets and ties, but tennis shoes are not allowed.

5 Caen ★★★

238km (148 miles) NW of Paris, 119km (74 miles) SE of Cherbourg

Situated on the banks of the Orne, the port of Caen suffered great damage in the 1944 invasion of Normandy. Nearly three-quarters of its buildings, 10,000 in all, were destroyed, though the twin abbeys founded by William the Conqueror and his wife, Mathilda, were spared. The city today is essentially modern and has many broad avenues and new apartment buildings. Completely different from Deauville and Trouville, the capital of Lower Normandy is bustling, congested, and commercial; it's a major rail and ferry junction. The student population of 30,000 and the hordes of travelers have made Caen more cosmopolitan than ever.

ESSENTIALS

GETTING THERE From Paris's Gare St-Lazare, 12 **trains** per day arrive in Caen (trip time: 1 hr., 50 min.–2½ hr.). One-way fares start at 27€ ($35). One-way fares from Rouen (trip time: 1 hr., 45 min.) start at 20€ ($26). To **drive** from Paris, travel west along A13 to Caen (driving time: 2½ hr.).

VISITOR INFORMATION The **Office de Tourisme** is on place St-Pierre in the 16th-century Hôtel d'Escoville (✆ **02-31-27-14-14;** www.tourisme.caen.fr).

EXPLORING THE CITY

Abbaye aux Dames Founded by Mathilda, wife of William the Conqueror, this abbey embraces Eglise de la Trinité, which is flanked by Romanesque towers. Its spires

Finds

An Excursion to the Forbes Château

Built by François Mansart between 1626 and 1636, the **Château de Balleroy** ★, between Bayeux and Caen, has been owned by the Forbes family for more than 3 decades. The late Malcolm Forbes was an internationally known balloonist, and his dream of opening the world's first balloon museum has been fulfilled at the château. Today the château is the venue for the biannual international ballooning festival.

The museum, in a converted stable, is filled with artifacts related to the history of ballooning. The château also contains many period rooms that abound with elegant art and antiques. Admission to the museum and castle is 6.85€ ($8.90) for adults or 5.35€ ($6.95) for students and children 7 to 18; free for those under 7; entrance to just the grounds costs 3€ ($3.90) for everyone. The museum and park are open year-round, mid-March to mid-October daily 10am to 6pm. Off-season hours are Monday to Friday 10am to noon and 2 to 5pm. The castle is open only from mid-March to mid-October daily 10am to 6pm.

The museum (✆ **02-31-21-60-61;** www.chateauballeroy.com) lies at F-14490 Balleroy outside the village of Balleroy. To reach it from Caen (40km/25 miles), head west along N13, cutting south at the junction with D572, and follow the road to Balleroy, where the château is signposted.

were destroyed in the Hundred Years' War. The 12th-century choir houses the tomb of Queen Mathilda; note the ribbed vaulting.

Place de la Reine-Mathilde. ✆ **02-31-06-98-98.** Free admission. Daily 9am–6pm. Free guided 1-hr. tour of choir, transept, and crypt (in French) daily 2:30 and 4pm.

Abbaye aux Hommes ★★ Founded by William and Mathilda, this abbey is adjacent to the Eglise St-Etienne, which you enter on place Monseigneur-des-Hameaux. During the height of the Allied invasion, residents of Caen flocked to St-Etienne for protection. Twin Romanesque towers 84m (276 ft.) tall dominate the church; they helped earn Caen the appellation "city of spires." A marble slab inside the high altar marks the site of William's tomb. The Huguenots destroyed the tomb in 1562—only a hipbone was recovered. During the French Revolution, the last of William's dust was scattered to the wind. The hand-carved wooden doors and elaborate wrought-iron staircase are exceptional. From the cloisters you get a good view of the two towers of St-Etienne.

Esplanade Jean-Marie-Louvel. ✆ **02-31-30-42-81.** Obligatory tours (in French, accompanied by broken-English translation) 2.20€ ($2.85) adults, 1.10€ ($1.45) students, free for children under 18; daily 9:30 and 11am, 2:30 and 4pm. Ticket office for tours daily 8am–4pm.

Caen Memorial (Le Mémorial de Caen) The memorial is 10 minutes away from the Pegasus Bridge and 15 minutes from the landing beaches. The museum presents a journey through history from 1918 to the present. It's an ideal place to relax. You can walk through International Park, have a meal or drink at the restaurant, or browse through the boutique. Expect to spend at least 2½ hours at this site—anyone intrigued by 20th-century European history will be fascinated. One wing is dedicated to a depiction of the American and global role after World War II. Its photo documentaries and exhibits illustrate the Cold War, the construction and collapse of the Berlin Wall, and the assault of military weapons (especially nuclear testing) on the environment.

Esplanade Dwight-Eisenhower. © **02-31-06-06-44.** www.memorial-caen.fr. Admission Apr–Sept 17€ ($21) adults, 16€ ($20) students and children 10–18; Oct–Mar 17€ ($21) adults, 15€ ($19) students and children 10–18; free to World War II veterans, those with war disabilities, war widows, and children under 10. Daily 9am–7pm (until 8pm mid-July to mid-Aug). Closed Jan 1–30 and Dec 25.

Le Château de Caen This complex was built on the ruins of a fortress erected by William the Conqueror in 1060. Enter the grounds at esplanade de la Paix. The gardens are ideal for strolling and, from the ramparts, a panoramic view of Caen unfolds. Within the compound are two museums. The **Musée de Normandie** (© **02-31-30-47-50;** www.musee-de-normandie.caen.fr) displays artifacts from Normandy, including archaeological finds, along with a collection of regional sculpture, paintings, and ceramics. Admission is free, and it's open Wednesday to Monday from 9:30am to 12:30pm and 2 to 6pm. Also within the walls is the **Musée des Beaux-Arts** (© **02-31-30-47-70;** www.ville-caen.fr/mba), with a collection of works—though not their finest—by Old Masters including Veronese and Rubens. Admission is free except for temporary exhibits costing 3€ to 5€ ($3.90–$6.50). It's open Wednesday to Monday 9:30am to 6pm.

SHOPPING

Caen has some good boutique-lined shopping streets, including **boulevard du Maréchal-Leclerc, rue St-Pierre,** and **rue de Strasbourg. Antiques** hunters should check out the shops along rue Ecuyère and rue Commerçantes, and the antiques show at the **Parc aux Expositions,** rue Joseph-Philippon (© **02-31-29-99-99**), in early May. The **markets** at place St-Sauveur on Friday morning and place Courtonne on Sunday morning also sell secondhand articles.

For custom-built reproduction antique furniture, visit **La Reine Matilde,** 47 rue St-Jean (© **02-31-85-45-52**); it also sells decorative items, including a selection of bed linens and curtains. **Le Chocolaterie Hotot,** 13 rue St-Pierre (© **02-31-86-31-90**), has a cornucopia of chocolate products as well as local jams and jellies. At **Le Comptoir Normand,** 7 rue de Geôle (© **02-31-86-34-13**), you'll find many regional items, including Calvados and various charcuterie products such as tripe in the style of Caen.

For objets d'art and paintings, check out **L'Atelier,** 33 rue Montoir-Poissonnerie (© **02-31-44-49-38**), which showcases the work of local painter Gérard Boukhezer. To browse through inventories of wine and *eaux-de-vie* from throughout France, head for **Nicolas,** rue Bellivet 10 (© **02-31-85-24-19**).

WHERE TO STAY

Le Manoir d'Hastings (see "A Nearby Dining Choice," below) also rent rooms.

Holiday Inn Caen City Centre ★ This is the best hotel in town, with a flavor that's both French and international. Across from the racecourse, the hotel predates World War II. It was enlarged and modernized in 1991, when it adopted the Holiday Inn logo. Rooms are predictable, comfortable, and well maintained. Some have air-conditioning and coffeemakers, and most have minibars. Americans visiting the D-day beaches favor the cozy bar.

Place du Maréchal-Foch, Caen 14000. © **800/465-4329** in the U.S., or 02-31-27-57-57. Fax 02-31-27-57-58. www.holiday-inn.com. 88 units. 85€–150€ ($111–$195) double. AE, DC, MC, V. **Amenities:** Restaurant; bar; room service; babysitting; dry cleaning; nonsmoking rooms; limited-mobility rooms. *In room:* TV, coffeemaker, minibar, trouser press, hair dryer, Wi-Fi.

Hôtel de France The exterior of this 1950s brick building is plain, but windows that open to flower boxes add a bit of charm. Rooms are functional, with new furnishings added in 2005; each has a small bathroom with shower. The public areas have a provincial charm. This hotel is a favorite with tour groups.

10 rue de la Gare, Caen 14000. ✆ **02-31-52-16-99.** Fax 02-31-83-23-16. 47 units. 62€–81€ ($81–$105) double. AE, MC, V. Free parking. *In room:* A/C, TV, coffeemaker, Wi-Fi.

Hôtel des Quatrans *Value* This agreeable, unpretentious hotel was rebuilt after World War II, and thanks to continual renovations, it's one of Caen's best bargains. Don't expect luxury: The hotel has four floors of old-fashioned rooms that offer basic amenities, including small, shower-only bathrooms. A buffet breakfast, available in the breakfast room or delivered to your room, is the only meal served.

17 rue Gémare, Caen 14300. ✆ **02-31-86-25-57.** Fax 02-31-85-27-80. www.hotel-des-quatrans.com. 47 units. 62€ ($81) double. MC, V. **Amenities:** Restaurant; bar; business center. *In room:* TV, Wi-Fi.

Hôtel Kyriad This hotel is a reliable bargain. The original was destroyed during a World War II bombing raid. Rebuilt several years later, it's surrounded by a commercial area of shops and restaurants as well as more tranquil pedestrian streets. Massively renovated in 2004, after it joined the Kyriad chain, the hotel offers bedrooms in attractive color schemes such as soft yellows and reds. All the guest rooms contain bathrooms with showers, and nearly three-fourths also have tubs. There's no restaurant, but an independent grill-style restaurant across the street offers inexpensive half-board plans for hotel guests.

1 place de la République, Caen 14000. ✆ **02-31-86-55-33.** Fax 02-31-79-89-44. 47 units. 65€–70€ ($85–$91) double. AE, MC, V. Parking 6.20€ ($8.05). **Amenities:** Bar; nonsmoking rooms; limited-mobility rooms. *In room:* A/C, TV, coffeemaker, hair dryer, Wi-Fi.

A NEARBY LODGING CHOICE

Château d'Audrieu ★★ This château in a park offers the most luxurious accommodations near Caen. It was built of local stone *(pierre de Caen)* at the beginning of the 18th century. During the invasion, some of the fiercest fighting took place around it. Notice the gashes in the trees in the park. The château functioned as a private home until 1976, when it became a hotel. Rooms are lovely and well appointed with antiques; some have Jacuzzis. Beds have tasteful linens. Bathrooms are spacious, with tub/shower combinations.

Audrieu 14250. From Caen, take N13 west for 18km (11 miles), and then D158 for 3km (1¾ miles) to Audrieu. ✆ **02-31-80-21-52.** Fax 02-31-80-24-73. www.chateaudaudrieu.com. 29 units. 150€–295€ ($195–$384) double; 455€ ($592) suite. AE, DC, MC, V. Closed Dec 9–Feb 4. **Amenities:** Restaurant; bar; outdoor heated pool; room service; babysitting; laundry service; dry cleaning; nonsmoking rooms; limited-mobility rooms. *In room:* TV, minibar, hair dryer, Wi-Fi.

WHERE TO DINE

Le Carlotta FRENCH/SEAFOOD This is a well-established brasserie, one of the best known in town, with a high-volume turnover and a penchant for seafood. Within a decor inspired by the Art Deco movement of the 1920s, you'll find yourself in a bustling, sometimes animated venue where tried-and-true menu items include platters of shellfish, especially oysters; snails in garlic-flavored butter sauce; filets of cod with stewed hearts of artichokes; strips of duck breast with parsley sauce; braised oxtail with truffles and mashed potatoes; filet of haddock with lemon-flavored butter sauce; and roasted shoulder of lamb *en confit,* served with Middle Eastern spices and mashed potatoes. Desserts usually include a homemade version of tiramisu and a gratin of seasonal berries.

16 quai Vendeuvre. ✆ **02-31-86-68-99.** Reservations recommended. Main courses 18€–25€ ($23–$33); set menus 22€–36€ ($29–$47). AE, MC, V. Mon–Sat noon–3pm and 6–10:30pm.

Le Petit B *Value* FRENCH/NORMAN A growing number of local diners are enthusiastic about this place, which is set in a 17th-century house in the center of town. Its fixed-price menu, with loads of good choices, is a great deal. You might begin with *terrine maison* or a slice of Norman-style Camembert tart, followed by a seafood brochette, and ending with chocolate mousse.

15 rue de Vaugueux. ✆ **02-31-93-50-76.** Reservations recommended for dinner Fri–Sat. Main courses 15€ ($20); fixed-price menu 25€ ($33). AE, DC, MC, V. Daily noon–2:30pm and 7pm–midnight.

A NEARBY DINING CHOICE

Le Manoir d'Hastings ★★ FRENCH/NORMAN This restaurant, 6.5km (4 miles) north of Caen, occupies a 17th-century monastery with an enclosed Norman garden. It's one of Normandy's most famous and charming inns, and a magnet for Parisians seeking a rustically elegant getaway. Many dishes are twists on Norman favorites, such as cider-cooked lobster with Nantua sauce, delicately flavored sea bass, and filet of monkfish poached in port. Beef filets are stuffed with foie gras, scallops are braised in the local apple-based liqueur *pommeau,* and filets of turbot and sea bass are served on the same platter and drenched in champagne sauce. For dessert, try *tarte Normande* flambéed with Calvados.

The manor also offers 15 rooms in a stone-sided annex. Each has a garden view, bathroom with tub, TV, minibar, and phone. A double goes for 80€ to 100€ ($104–$130). Rooms were overhauled and upgraded in the late 1990s, with improvements in the mattresses, furnishings, and fabrics. The hotel lies very close to Pegasus Bridge, one of the first strategic targets liberated by Allied soldiers after the invasion of Normandy in 1944.

Av. Côte-de-Nacre, Bénouville 14970. From Caen, follow signs north for Ouistreham and turn onto RD35. Stay on this road for 10km (6¼ miles), following signs to Bayeux and Bénouville; the manor is next to the village church. ✆ **02-31-44-62-43.** Fax 02-31-44-76-18. Reservations required. Main courses 14€–22€ ($18–$29); fixed-price lunch (Tues–Fri only) 22€ ($29); fixed-price dinner 29€–55€ ($38–$72). AE, DC, MC, V. Tues–Sun noon–2pm; Tues–Sat 7–9:30pm. Closed 2 weeks in Feb and Oct 23–Nov 16.

CAEN AFTER DARK

Take a walk down rue de Bras, rue St-Pierre, and the north end of rue Vaugueux to size up the action. If you want to connect with the hip 18-to-35 crowd, go to **Le Chic,** rue des Prairies St-Gilles (✆ **02-31-94-48-72**), where disco music begins at 10:30pm. **Le Carré,** 32 quai Vendeuvre (✆ **02-31-38-90-90**), is outfitted in tones of bordello red. The disco caters to patrons over 27 with rock 'n' roll, cutting-edge techno, and a goodly assortment of music from the '70s and '80s. Upstairs, there's a hip and often charming "Bar de Nuit."

Pub Concorde, 7 rue Montoir-Poissonnerie (✆ **02-31-93-61-29**), stocks more than 150 beers. Intensely connected to the hip and trendy night-soul of Caen is an Irish-style pub, **O'Donnell's,** 20 quai Vendeuvre (✆ **02-31-85-51-50**). It's the site of televised European soccer matches, live Irish rock-'n'-roll shows, and lots of animated dialogues among locals and regulars. The live music is every Friday night; otherwise,

Finds A Proustian Remembrance of "Balbec"

Torn from the pages of Marcel Proust's *Remembrance of Things Past,* the resort of "Balbec" was really Cabourg, 24km (15 miles) northeast of Caen. Fans still come to this Second Empire resort, much of which looks as it did in the Belle Epoque. Guests can check into the 1907 **Grand Hotel,** promenade Marcel Proust, 14390 Cabourg (✆ **02-31-91-01-79;** fax 02-31-24-03-20; www.grandhotel-cabourg.com), a holdover from the opulent days of the 19th century. One room, "La Chambre Marcel Proust," has been restored from a description in *Remembrance.* A double costs from 150€ to 296€ ($195–$385), with a suite going for 350€ to 610€ ($455–$793).

a DJ rules the night. Open Monday to Wednesday 4:30pm to 2:30am, Thursday to Saturday 4:30pm to 4am, and Sunday 4:30pm to midnight.

6 Bayeux ★★

267km (166 miles) NW of Paris, 25km (16 miles) NW of Caen

The ducs de Normandie sent their sons to this Viking settlement to learn the Norse language. Bayeux has changed a lot since then, but was spared from bombardment in 1944. This was the first French town liberated, and the citizens gave de Gaulle an enthusiastic welcome when he arrived on June 14. The town is filled with timbered houses, stone mansions, and cobblestone streets.

Visitors wanting to explore sites associated with "the Longest Day" flood the town, because many memorials (not to mention the beaches) are only 9.5 to 19km (6–12 miles) away. Shops line the cozy little streets. Many sell World War II memorabilia, and more postcards and T-shirts than you'll ever need.

ESSENTIALS

GETTING THERE Twelve **trains** depart daily from Paris's Gare St-Lazare. The 2½-hour trip to Bayeux costs 31€ ($41). Most trains stop in Caen. Travel time between Caen and Bayeux is about 20 minutes and costs 7.90€ ($10). To **drive** to Bayeux from Paris (trip time: 3 hr.), take A13 to Caen and E46 west to Bayeux.

VISITOR INFORMATION The **Office de Tourisme** is at pont St-Jean (✆ **02-31-51-28-28;** www.bayeux-bessin-tourism.com).

SPECIAL EVENTS The town goes wild on the first weekend in July during **Fêtes Médiévales;** the streets fill with wine and song during 2 days of medieval revelry. For information, call ✆ **02-31-92-03-30.**

SEEING THE SIGHTS

Musée de la Tapisserie de Bayeux ★★★ The most famous tapestry in the world is actually an embroidery on linen, 69m (226 ft.) long and .5m (20 in.) wide, depicting 58 scenes in eight colors. Contrary to legend, it wasn't made by Queen Mathilda, the wife of William the Conqueror, but was probably commissioned in Kent and created by unknown embroiderers between 1066 and 1077. The first mention of the embroidery was in 1476, when it decorated the nave of the Cathédrale Notre-Dame de Bayeux.

Housed in a Plexiglas case, the embroidery tells the story of the conquest of England by William the Conqueror, including such scenes as the coronation of Harold as the Saxon king of England, Harold returning from his journey to Normandy, the surrender of Dinan, Harold being told of the apparition of a comet (a portent of misfortune), William dressed for war, and the death of Harold. The decorative borders include scenes from *Aesop's Fables.*

Admission to the museum includes access to an annex whose collections are not as spectacular. The **Collections Baron Gérard** is housed in **Le Musée de l'Hôtel du Doyen,** 6 rue Lambert le Forestier (✆ **02-31-92-14-21**). Exhibitions feature examples of regional lacework, porcelain, and religious and secular paintings, many of them created within this region.

Centre Guillaume-le-Conquérant, 13 rue de Nesmond. ✆ **02-31-51-25-50.** Admission 7.50€ ($9.75) adults, 3€ ($3.90) students, free for children under 10. May–Aug daily 9am–7pm; mid-Mar to Apr and Sept–Oct daily 9am–6:30pm; Nov to mid-Mar daily 9:30am–12:30pm and 2–6pm.

Musée Memorial de la Bataille de Normandie This museum deals with the military and human history of the Battle of Normandy (June 6–Aug 22, 1944). In a low-slung building designed like a bunker are 132m (433 ft.) of window and film displays, plus a diorama. Wax soldiers in uniform, along with the tanks and guns used to win the battle, are on exhibit. Across from the museum, the **Commonwealth Cemetery** (✆ **03-21-21-77-00**) lies on the northwestern perimeter of Bayeux, containing 4,144 graves of soldiers from throughout the British Commonwealth, all of them killed during the Battle of Normandy.

Bd. Fabian Ware. ✆ **02-31-51-46-90.** Admission 6€ ($7.80) adults, 4€ ($5.20) students and children, free for children under 10. May–Sept 15 daily 9:30am–6:30pm; Sept 16–Apr 10am–12:30pm and 2–6pm.

Notre-Dame de Bayeux ★★ This cathedral was consecrated in 1077 and partially destroyed in 1105. Romanesque towers from the original church rise on the western side. The central tower is from the 15th century. The nave is a fine example of Norman Romanesque style. The 13th-century choir, a perfect example of Norman Gothic style, is rich in sculpture and has Renaissance stalls. The crypt was built in the 11th century and then sealed, its existence unknown until 1412.

Rue du Bienvenu. ✆ **02-31-92-14-21.** Free admission. Daily 8:30am–6pm (to 7pm July–Aug).

WHERE TO STAY

Best Western Grand Hôtel de Luxembourg ★ After Le Lion d'Or (see below), this Best Western is the area's finest hotel. The restored interior has terrazzo floors; the decor combines neoclassical and Art Deco design. Rooms range in size from small to medium and have been overhauled with an eye to modern comfort, including fine bed linens. All units come with small bathrooms with showers, and more than half also have tubs.

25 rue des Bouchers, Bayeux 14400. ✆ **800/528-1234** in the U.S. and Canada, or 02-31-92-00-04. Fax 02-31-92-54-26. www.hotels-bayeux-14.com. 27 units. 90€–140€ ($117–$182) double; 150€–200€ ($195–$260) suite. AE, MC, V. Parking 8€ ($10). **Amenities:** Restaurant; bar; room service; laundry service; nonsmoking rooms; limited-mobility rooms. *In room:* TV, dataport, Wi-Fi.

Hôtel d'Argouges This much-improved hotel underwent major renovations in 2004. Now a government-rated two-star hotel, it's even more comfortable than it was before. It consists of a pair of 18th-century town houses, set across a garden from one another, with exposed beams, thick walls, and sloping ceilings. Rooms are comfortable, intimate, and cozy, with old-fashioned furniture and modern conveniences. All the bathrooms were upgraded with tub/shower combinations. Breakfast is the only meal served, but at least three restaurants are within a 2-minute walk. In good weather, you can wander in the garden.

21 rue St-Patrice, Bayeux 14402. © **02-31-92-88-86.** Fax 02-31-92-69-16. dargouges@aol.com. 28 units. 52€–120€ ($68–$156) double; 130€–240€ ($169–$312) suite. AE, DC, MC, V. Parking 2€ ($2.60). **Amenities:** Room service; babysitting; nonsmoking rooms; limited-mobility rooms. *In room:* TV, hair dryer, Wi-Fi.

Le Lion d'Or ★★★ This old-world hotel, originally built in 1734, is the best in town. It has an open courtyard with lush flower boxes decorating the facade. As befits an old inn, rooms come in various shapes and sizes. The midsize bathrooms are well equipped; each has a shower and more than half have tubs. Guests are required to take at least one meal here, but that shouldn't be a problem—the traditional cuisine is delicious. The restaurant serves lots of reasonably priced wines.

71 rue St-Jean, Bayeux 14400. © **02-31-92-06-90.** Fax 02-31-22-15-64. www.liondor-bayeux.fr. 28 units. 86€–194€ ($112–$252) double. AE, DC, MC, V. Closed Dec 20–Jan 20. Parking 5€ ($6.50). **Amenities:** Restaurant; bar; fitness center; babysitting; laundry service; limited-mobility rooms. *In room:* TV, minibar, safe (in some).

WHERE TO DINE

Le Pommier ★ *Value* NORMAN One of the most appealing restaurants in Bayeux's historic zone occupies an 18th-century building. Ceiling beams, stone ceiling vaults, and exposed masonry enhance the trio of dining rooms. The establishment is devotedly Norman, with cuisine that reflects the region's long tradition of baking with apples (the name translates as "the apple tree") and cream (though its use is limited to make the food a bit healthier). The health-conscious staff is proud that the dishes "aren't drowned in gravies and sauces." Menu items evolve with the seasons. You can usually expect dishes such as foie gras of duckling; rabbit stew braised in cider; and a platter that contains two kinds of fish served with chitterling sausage and a sauce of cream and chitterling drippings.

38 rue des Cuisiniers. © **02-31-21-52-10.** Fax 02-31-21-06-01. Reservations recommended. Main courses 12€–24€ ($16–$31); fixed-price menu 16€–29€ ($21–$37) at lunch or dinner. AE, MC, V. Apr–Sept daily noon–2:30pm and 7–9:30pm; Oct–Mar Thurs–Mon noon–2pm and 7–9:30pm.

Les Amaryllis ★ *Value* NORMAN This venue is outfitted like a Norman garden and the cuisine is top-notch, based on very fresh local ingredients. Highlights include a starter of diced potatoes and apples, studded with pieces of chitterling sausage and bound together with puff pastry. A long-standing specialty of the house is braised stingray served with a comfit of shallots, as well as lamb, in season, from the salt marshes of Normandy.

32 rue St-Patrice. © **02-31-22-47-94.** Reservations recommended. Main courses 13€–25€ ($17–$33); fixed-price menu 17€–30€ ($22–$39). MC, V. June–Aug Tues–Sun noon–2pm and 7–9:30pm; Sept–Dec and Feb–May Tues–Sun noon–2pm, Tues–Sat 8–10pm. Closed Jan.

7 The D-Day Beaches ★★

Arromanches-les-Bains: 272km (169 miles) NW of Paris, 11km (6¾ miles) NW of Bayeux; Grandcamp-Maisy (near Omaha Beach): 299km (186 miles) NW of Paris, 56km (35 miles) NW of Caen

During a rainy week in June 1944, the greatest armada ever—soldiers and sailors, warships, landing craft, tugboats, jeeps—assembled along the southern coast of England. At 9:15pm on June 5, the BBC announced to the French Resistance that the invasion was imminent, signaling the underground to start dynamiting the railways. Before midnight, Allied planes began bombing the Norman coast. By 1:30am on June 6 ("the Longest Day"), members of the 101st Airborne were parachuting to the ground on German-occupied French soil. At 6:30am, the Americans began landing on the beaches, code-named Utah and Omaha. An hour later, British and Canadian forces made beachheads at Juno, Gold, and Sword.

The Nazis had mocked Churchill's promise in 1943 to liberate France "before the fall of the autumn leaves." When the invasion did come, it was swift, sudden, and a surprise to the formidable "Atlantic wall." Today, veterans walk with their children and grandchildren across the beaches where "Czech hedgehogs," "Belgian grills," pillboxes, and "Rommel asparagus" (all military barriers or structures) once stood.

ESSENTIALS

GETTING THERE The best way to get to the D-day beaches is to **drive.** Public transportation is unreliable. The trip takes about 3 hours from Paris. Take A13 west to Caen, and continue west along A13 to Bayeux. From Bayeux, travel north along D6 until you reach the coast at Port-en-Bessin. From here, D514 runs along the coastline; most D-day sites are west of Port-en-Bessin. Parking is not a problem, and most of the designated areas along the roadway are free. It's best to visit on a weekday, because weekends (especially in summer) can be crowded with tourists and sunbathers.

Bus service from Bayeux is uneven and usually involves long delays. **Bus Verts** (**© 08-10-21-42-14**) runs to Port-en-Bessin and points west, and bus no. 75 offers service year-round to Arromanches and other points in the east. Bus no. 70 travels west (June–Sept only) from Bayeux toward Omaha Beach and the American cemetery.

If you don't have a car, the best way to see the D-day beaches is on a **tour. Normandy Tours,** Hotel de la Gare, Bayeux (**© 02-31-92-10-70;** www.normandy-tours-hotel.com), runs a 4- to 5-hour tour (in English) to Arromanches, Omaha Beach, the American Military Cemetery, and Pointe du Hoc for 39€ ($51) adults and 34€ ($44) students and seniors. **D-Day Tours,** 52 rte. de Porte en Bessin, Bayeux (**© 02-31-51-70-52;** www.d-daybeaches.com), offers tours with a bit more pizazz and guides who speak better English. A half-day trip costs 45€ ($59) for adults and 40€ ($52) for students; a full-day trip is 75€ ($98) for adults and 70€ ($91) for students. The company picks you up at your hotel in Bayeux. A final option, **Battlebus** (**© 02-31-22-28-82;** www.battlebus.fr), conducts a full-day tour encompassing all sites and beaches that were pivotal during the D-day landing and Battle of Normandy; cost is 80€ ($104) per person. Most participants have found this latter option the best tour of all—simultaneously riveting, exhausting, and stimulating.

VISITOR INFORMATION The **Office de Tourisme,** 4 rue du Maréchal-Joffre, Arromanches-les-Bains (**© 02-31-21-47-56**), is open year-round.

RELIVING THE LONGEST DAY

Start your exploration at the seaside resort of **Arromanches-les-Bains.** In June 1944, this was a fishing port until the 50th British Division took it. A mammoth prefabricated port known as Winston was towed across the Channel and installed to supply the Allied forces. "Victory could not have been achieved without it," Eisenhower said. The wreckage of that artificial harbor is just off the beach, **Plage du Débarquement.** **Musée du Débarquement,** place du 6-Juin (**© 02-31-22-34-31;** www.normandy 1944.com), in Arromanches, features maps, models, a cinema, photographs, and a diorama of the landing, all with English commentary. Admission is 6.50€ ($8.45) for adults and 4.50€ ($5.85) for students and children. From June to August, hours are daily 9am to 7pm; September Monday to Saturday 9am to 6pm, Sunday 10am to 6pm; April Monday to Saturday 9am to 12:30pm and 1:30 to 6pm, Sunday 10am to 12:30pm and 1:30 to 6pm; May Monday to Saturday 9am to 7pm, Sunday 10am to 7pm; October and March daily 9:30am to 12:30pm and 1:30 to 5:30pm; November to December and February daily 10am to 12:30pm and 1:30 to 5pm. Closed December 24 to December 26 and 31, and January.

Moving along the coast, you'll arrive at **Omaha Beach,** where you can still see the war wreckage. "Hanging on by their toenails," the men of the 1st and 29th American Divisions occupied the beach that June day. The code name Omaha became famous; until then the beaches had been called St-Laurent, Vierville-sur-Mer, and Colleville. A monument commemorates the heroism of the invaders. Covering some 70 hectares (173 acres) at Omaha Beach, the **Normandy American Cemetery** (✆ **02-31-51-62-00;** www.abmc.gov) is filled with crosses and Stars of David in Lasa marble. The remains of 9,386 American military were buried here on territory now owned by the United States, a gift from the French nation. The cemetery opened its new visitor center earlier this year, 63 years after D-day. The $30 million center houses film and photo exhibits, artifacts, and interactive displays. Admission is free. The cemetery is open daily from 9am to 5pm; the visitor center until 6pm (both closed Dec. 25 and Jan. 1).

Farther along the coast you'll see the jagged lime cliffs of the **Pointe du Hoc.** A cross honors a group of American Rangers, led by Lt. Col. James Rudder, who scaled the cliffs using hooks to get at the pillboxes (gun emplacements). The scars of war are more visible here than at any other point along the beach. Farther along the Cotentin Peninsula is **Utah Beach,** where the 4th U.S. Infantry Division landed at 6:30am. The landing force was nearly 3km (1¾ miles) south of its intended destination, but Nazi defenses were weak. By midday the infantry had completely cleared the beach. A U.S. monument commemorates their heroism.

Nearby, you can visit the hamlet of **Ste-Mère-Eglise,** which was virtually unknown outside of France before paratroopers dropped from the sky. In Ste-Mère-Eglise is Kilometer "0" on the Liberty Highway, marking the first of the milestones the American armies reached on their way to Metz and Bastogne.

WHERE TO STAY & DINE AT GRANDCAMP-MAISY

Hôtel Duguesclin TRADITIONAL FRENCH We recommend this Norman inn for lunch or even an overnight stay. The fish soup, grilled scallops, Norman sole (when it's available), and grilled turbot with white butter are excellent. Everything tastes better with the dining room's country bread and Norman butter.

The hotel rents 23 simple, comfortable rooms, all with bathroom, phone, and TV. Accommodations have a shower or tub (sometimes both). A double costs 45€ to 60€ ($59–$78).

4 quai Crampon, Grandcamp-Maisy 14450. ✆ **02-31-22-64-22.** Fax 02-31-22-34-79. Reservations recommended. Main courses 12€–32€ ($16–$42); fixed-price menu 15€–32€ ($20–$42). AE, MC, V. Daily noon–2pm and 7–9pm.

La Marée NORMAN Set beside the port, this small, nautically decorated restaurant serves mostly fish and only fish caught in the English Channel or within a reasonable distance out in the Atlantic, guaranteeing a local culinary experience. During nice weather, the dining room expands onto a terrace.

5 quai Henri Chéron. ✆ **02-31-21-41-00.** Reservations required. Main courses 22€–27€ ($29–$35); fixed-price menu 14€–25€ ($18–$33). AE, MC, V. Daily 12:30–2:30pm and 7–9:30pm. Closed Jan 1–Feb 7.

WHERE TO STAY AT ARROMANCHES

Hôtel d'Angleterre *Value* This traditional hotel is the best place to stay in the area and has stood for 3 centuries as a historic coaching inn. Explorer Henry Russell used it as a base for his mountain explorations from 1864 to 1874. The Auibiban family offers midsize to spacious bedrooms with private bathrooms. In the restaurant, regional products are used in the crafting of traditional recipes.

Route de Luchon, Arreau 65240. ✆ **02-62-98-69-66.** Fax 05-62-98-69-66. www.hotel-angleterre-arreau.com. 9 units. 112€–200€ ($146–$260) double. V. **Amenities:** Restaurant; outdoor pool. *In room:* TV.

Hotel de la Marine There has been a hotel on this spot since 1837, although the one you see today wins over any of its earlier incarnations when it comes to comfort and style. Renovated in 2005, the hotel directly faces the beach that played a keynote role during the U.S. invasion of Normandy and offers many of the charming details of a Norman private country estate. Bedrooms are rustically outfitted with colorful fabrics and solid, traditional furnishings. In midsummer, half board is required. The restaurant appeals even to nonresidents. It's open daily noon to 2pm and 7 to 9:30pm, and serves set-price thoroughly French meals priced at 22€ to 35€ ($29–$46) each.

1 quai du Canada, Arromanches les Bains 14117. ✆ **02-31-22-34-19.** Fax 02-31-22-98-80. www.hotel-de-la-marine.fr. 33 units. Oct–Apr 72€–90€ ($94–$117) double. May–Sept 75€–160€ ($98–$208) per person, double occupancy. Rates include breakfast and dinner. Free parking. AE, MC, V. **Amenities:** Restaurant; bar; laundry service/dry cleaning. *In room:* TV, hair dryer, iron, safe.

8 Mont-St-Michel ★★★

324km (201 miles) W of Paris, 129km (80 miles) SW of Caen, 76km (47 miles) E of Dinan, 48km (30 miles) E of St-Malo

Massive walls measuring more than half a mile in circumference surround one of Europe's great attractions, the island of Mont-St-Michel. Connected to the shore by a causeway, it crowns a rocky islet at the border between Normandy and Brittany. The rock is 78m (256 ft.) high.

ESSENTIALS

GETTING THERE The most efficient way to reach Mont-St-Michel is to **drive.** From Caen, follow A84 southwest to Pontorson, continuing a few more kilometers to Avranches; from there, merge onto D43, following signs to its end at Mont-St-Michel. Total driving time from Paris is about 4½ hours.

There are no direct trains between Paris and Mont-St-Michel. We suggest taking the high-speed **TGV train** from Paris's Gare Montparnasse to Rennes, where you can transfer to the **bus** run by the **SNCF** (✆ **36-35** or **08/92-35-35-35;** www.voyages-sncf.com) for the 75-minute trip to Mont-St-Michel. Depending on the season, two to five buses a day run to Rennes for 4.50€ ($5.85) per person. Another company, **Les Courriers Bretons** (✆ **02-99-19-70-70;** www.lescourriersbretons.fr), also operates buses that make the 75-minute ride to Mont-St-Michel from St-Malo two to five times a day for 9.20€ ($12) per person.

VISITOR INFORMATION The **Office de Tourisme** is in the Corps de Garde des Bourgeois (the Old Guard Room of the Bourgeois), at the left of the town gates (✆ **02-33-60-14-30;** www.ot-montsaintmichel.com). The tourist office is open daily year-round except Christmas and New Year's.

EXPLORING MONT-ST-MICHEL

You'll have a steep climb up Grande Rue, lined with 15th- and 16th-century houses, to reach the **abbey** (© **02-33-89-80-00;** www.monum.fr). Those who make it to the top can begin their exploration of the Marvel of the West. In the 8th century, St. Aubert, the bishop of Avranches, founded an oratory on this spot. A Benedictine monastery, founded in 966 by Richard I, replaced it. That burned in 1203. Philip Augustus financed the building of an abbey in the 13th century.

Ramparts encircle the church and a three-tiered ensemble of 13th-century buildings called **La Merveille** that rise to the pointed spire of the abbey church. This terraced complex is one of Europe's most important Gothic monuments, a citadel in which the concept of an independent France was nurtured during the darkest years of the English occupation of Aquitaine.

On the second terrace of La Merveille is one of Mont-St-Michel's largest and most beautiful rooms, a 13th-century hall known as the **Salle des Chevaliers.**

Crowning the mountain's summit is the **Eglise Abbatiale** (not to be confused with the parish church, Eglise St-Pierre, lower on the mountain). Begun in the 11th century, the abbey church consists of a Romanesque nave and transept, plus a choir in Flamboyant Gothic style. The rectangular refectory dates from 1212, and the cloisters with their columns of pink granite are from 1225.

The abbey is open daily May to September 9am to 6pm, and October to April 9:30am to 5pm. From June to September, it's also open Monday to Saturday 9pm to 1am (last entrance at midnight). Mass begins at 12:15pm Tuesday to Sunday. Entrance during daytime or nighttime tours includes a guided group tour, but you can also wander around on your own. Year-round, day or night visits, with or without the tour, cost 8€ ($10) for adults, 5€ ($6.50) for students and ages 18 to 25, and free for children under 18.

Guided tours in French depart at intervals of 30 to 45 minutes, depending on the season. There are usually two to four English-language tours per day. Everything is closed January 1, May 1, and December 25.

Archeoscope, chemin de la Ronde (© **02-33-89-01-85**), is a small theater that presents *L'Eau et La Lumière* (Water and Light), celebrating the legend and lore of Mont-St-Michel and its role as a preserver of French medieval nationalism. The 30-minute shows begin every 30 to 60 minutes between 9:30am and 5:30pm. An unusual diversion is the adjacent **Musée de la Mer,** Grande Rue (© **02-33-89-02-02**). It showcases marine crafts throughout history; the ecology of the local tidal flats; and illustrations of the French government's ongoing project intended to reactivate the tidal cleansing of the nearby marshes. **Musée Grevin (Musée Historique de Mont-St-Michel),** chemin de la Ronde (© **02-33-89-02-02**), traces the history of the abbey.

A museum that's worth a visit is the **Logis Tiphaine,** Gardé Rue (© **02-33-89-02-02**), a 15th-century home originally under the control of the Duguesclin family, noted defenders of the fortress from English intrigue. In the building, next to the Eglise St-Pierre, you'll find furniture and accessories from that era, and a sense of pride at the fortress's durability as a bastion of all things French.

A combined ticket for all four of these attractions costs 7€ ($9.10) for adults and 3€ ($3.90) for students. Admission is free for children under 16. Other than the Archeoscope, whose hours are noted above, the museums are open daily from 9am to 5pm.

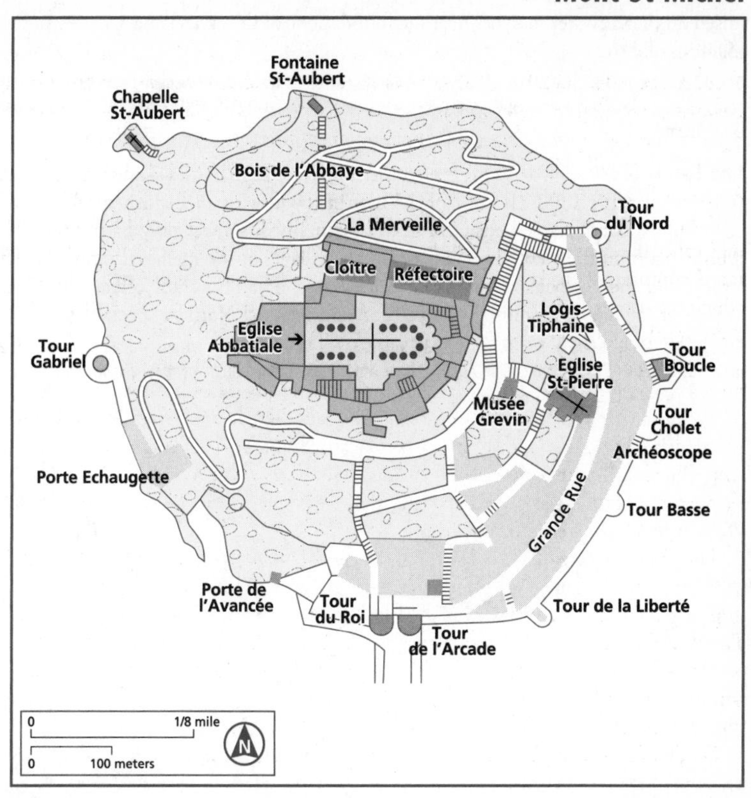

WHERE TO STAY & DINE

Hôtel du Mouton-Blanc Occupying a pair of buildings, parts of which date from the 14th century, this inn stands between the sea and the basilica. Renovated in 2006, the inn has accepted guests since the 1700s. Rooms are small but cozy. Eight are in a comfortable annex, where all units have small bathrooms with showers. The seven better-equipped units in the main building have bathrooms with both tubs and showers. A rustic Norman-style dining room sits on a terrace overlooking the sea. Popular dishes include succulent omelets with seafood, delectable mussels in white wine and garlic, and two marvelous versions of lamb—one roasted in its own juice, the other on a skewer.

Grande Rue, Mont-St-Michel 50116. ✆ **02-33-60-14-08.** Fax 02-33-60-05-62. 15 units. 70€ ($91) double; 102€ ($133) suite. AE, MC, V. **Amenities:** Restaurant; bar. *In room:* TV.

La Mère Poulard NORMAN This country inn is a shrine to those who revere the omelet that Annette Poulard created in 1888, when the hotel was founded. It's under the same ownership as the more rustic Les Terrasses Poulard (see below). Annette Poulard's secret has been passed on to the inn's operators: The beaten eggs are cooked over an oak fire in a long-handled copper skillet. The frothy mixture creates more of an open-fire soufflé than an omelet. Other specialties are *agneau du pré salé* (lamb raised on the saltwater marshes near the foundations of the abbey) and an array of fish, including lobster.

Grande Rue, Mont-St-Michel 50116. ✆ **02-33-89-68-68.** Fax 02-33-89-68-69. www.mere-poulard.com. Reservations recommended. Main courses 30€–38€ ($39–$49); fixed-price menu 45€–65€ ($59–$85). AE, DC, MC, V. Daily noon–10pm.

Les Terrasses Poulard This inn consists of two village houses—one medieval, the other built in the 1800s. It's one of the best in town, with an English-speaking staff, cozy rooms, comfortable beds, and neatly maintained, shower-only bathrooms. The rates depend on the view: the main street, the village, or the medieval ramparts. The largest and most expensive rooms have fireplaces. The restaurant offers a sweeping view over the bay to accompany its seafood and regional Norman specialties.

Grande Rue, Mont-St-Michel 50116. ✆ **02-33-89-02-02.** Fax 02-33-60-37-31. www.terrasses-poulard.com. 29 units. 100€–280€ ($130–$364) double. AE, DC, MC, V. **Amenities:** Restaurant. *In room:* TV, minibar.

Brittany

In this ancient northwestern province, Bretons cling to their traditions. Deep in *l'Argoat* (the interior), many older folks live in stone farmhouses, as their grandparents did, and on special occasions the women wear starched-lace headdresses. The Breton language is spoken, but the Welsh and Cornish understand it better than the French. Sadly, it may die out altogether.

Nearly every village and hamlet has its own *pardon,* a religious festival that can attract thousands of pilgrims in traditional dress. The best known are on May 19 at Treguier (honoring St-Yves); on the second Sunday in July at Locronan (honoring St-Ronan); on July 26 at St-Anne-d'Auray (honoring the "mothers of Bretons"); and on September 8 at Le Folgoet (honoring *ar foll coat*—"idiot of the forest").

Like the prow of a ship, Brittany juts into the sea. Traditionally, the province is divided into Haute-Bretagne and Basse-Bretagne. Promontories, coves, and beaches stud the rocky coastline, some 1,207km (750 miles) long. The interior is a land of hamlets, farmhouses, and moors covered with yellow broom and purple heather. We suggest first-time visitors stick to the coast, where you can see salt-meadow sheep grazing. If you're coming from Mont-St-Michel, you can use St-Malo, Dinan, or Dinard as a base. Visitors from the château country of the Loire can explore the coastline of southern Brittany.

Brittany is a resort region. Many families visit for the beaches. British tourists frequent Dinard, although the water can be choppy and cold, with high waves. La Baule in the south is warmer, with a great beach, restaurants, and the best hotels in the region.

1 St-Malo ★★★

414km (257 miles) W of Paris, 69km (43 miles) N of Rennes, 13km (8 miles) E of Dinard

Built on a granite rock in the Channel, St-Malo is joined to the mainland by a causeway. It's popular with the English, especially Channel Islanders, and its warm brown sands give it a modest claim to being a beach resort. The peninsula curves around a natural harbor that comprises several smaller basins. The walled city radiates outward from the town's château and its spiritual centerpiece, the Cathédrale St-Vincent, both of which lie near the peninsula's tip. The curse of St-Malo is the swarm of tour buses and their passengers engulfing the narrow streets. But there's charm here, though it's "merely the mock," having been virtually rebuilt after damage during World War II. The challenge is to appreciate that charm while contending with so many other travelers on the same pursuit.

ESSENTIALS

GETTING THERE From Paris's Gare Montparnasse, about nine TGV **trains** per day make the journey via Rennes, where you transfer. Trip time is 3 hours; a one-way ticket costs around 43€ ($56). For information, call © **08-92-35-35-35.** If you're **driving** from Paris, take A13 west to Caen and continue southwest along N175 to the town of Miniac Morvan. From there, travel north on N137 directly to St-Malo. Driving time is 5 to 6 hours from Paris.

VISITOR INFORMATION The **Office de Tourisme** is on esplanade St-Vincent (© **08-25-13-52-00;** www.saint-malo-tourisme.com). You must show a passport to take the car-ferry trips and tours to the Channel Islands or *Les Iles Anglo-Normandes.*

SPECIAL EVENTS One of the most important Breton *pardons* is at St-Malo, usually the third weekend in January: the **Pardon of the Newfoundland Fishing Fleet (Pardon de St-Ouen).** The town's **Festival de la Musique Sacrée,** from mid-July to mid-August, offers evening concerts twice a week presented in the cathedral. Call © **02-99-56-05-38** for more information.

EXPLORING THE CITY

Walk along the **ramparts** ★★★ for the best view of the bay and the islets at the mouth of the Rance. These walls were built over several centuries; some date from the 14th century. They were reconstructed in the 17th century and restored in the 19th. You can begin at the 15th-century **Porte St-Vincent.**

At the harbor, you can book tours of the **Channel Islands.** Car ferries leave for the English island of Jersey, from March to October, with **Condor** (© **08-25-13-51-35;** www.condorferries.com), and year-round with **Emeraude Jersey Lines** (© **08-25-13-51-80;** www.emeraudeferries.com). The round-trip fare for a pedestrian without a car from St-Malo is 50€ ($65).

At low tide, a 15-minute stroll leads to the **Ile du Grand-Bé** ★★, the site of the tomb of Chateaubriand, who was born in St-Malo, "deserted by others and completely surrounded by storms." The tomb, marked by a cross, is simple, unlike the man it honors, but the view of the Emerald Coast makes up for it.

The "Bastille of the West," the **Château de St-Malo** ★★, Porte St-Vincent (© **02-99-85-34-33**), and its towers shelter the **Musée de l'Histoire de St-Malo** (© **02-99-40-71-57**). It abounds with insights into the role of St-Malo, as well as souvenirs of the pirates Duguay-Trouin and Surcouf, the most famous of the privateers. Admission costs 5.10€ ($6.65) for adults and 2.55€ ($3.30) for students and children under 18. It's open April to September daily 10am to 12:30pm and 2 to 6pm, October to March Tuesday to Sunday 10am to noon and 2 to 6pm.

After you visit the château, try to carve out some time for wandering through the narrow streets and alleyways of St-Malo's historic core. Memories of the town's origins as a medieval fishing village confront you at nearly every turn.

St-Malo's **Cathédrale St-Vincent,** 12 rue St-Benoît (© **02-99-40-82-31**), is known for its 1,160-nave vault. It's of the Angevin or Plantagenet style, elegantly marking the transition between Romanesque and Gothic. The cathedral also has a Renaissance facade (the west), with additions from the 18th century and a 15th-century tower. The 14th-century choir is surmounted by a triforium with trefoiled arches and flanked by chapels. Admission is free. Open June to August Monday to Saturday 9:45am to 7pm, Sunday 9:30am to 6pm (Sept–May closed noon–2pm).

BEACHES Along the coast, long stretches of sand intersperse with rocky outcroppings that suggest fortresses protecting Brittany from Atlantic storms. You can swim wherever you like, but beware of the very strong undertow. If you're staying in St-Malo, the two best beaches are **Plage de Bon Secours,** near the northern tip of the

Brittany

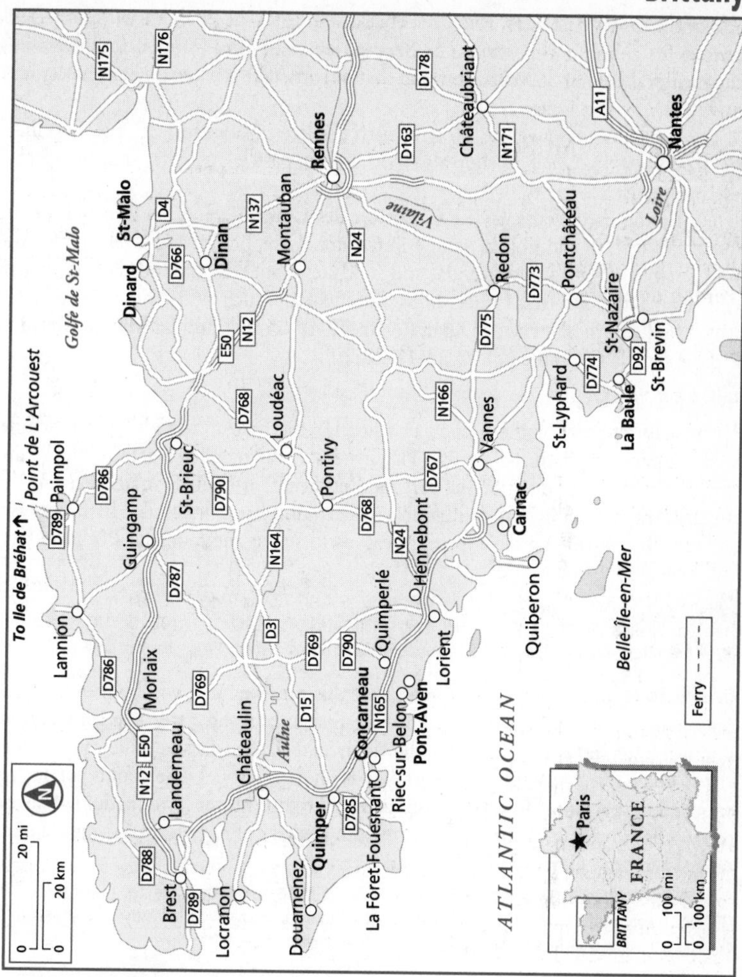

Vieille Ville (old town), and **La Grande Plage du Sillon,** a longer stretch of sand at the eastern perimeter of the Vieille Ville.

SHOPPING If you're in St-Malo on Tuesday or Friday between 8am and 1pm and want to experience a great Breton **market,** head for the place de la Poissonerie and the Halles au Blé, in the heart of the old city. You can't miss the activity, the bustle, and the hawking of country-fresh produce, cheese, fish, and dozens of household items, including dishware, cooking utensils, and handicrafts.

For **boutique shopping,** head to rue St-Vincent, rue Porcon, rue Broussais, rue Georges Clemenceau, rue Ville Pépin, and rue de Dinan. You'll find everything from the trendy to the trashy. Check out **Marin-Marine,** 5 Grand' Rue (✆ **02-99-40-90-32**), for quality men's and women's fashions that include great Breton wool sweaters, one of the town's best buys. Rue Clemenceau and rue Ville Pépin lie within the 19th-century neighborhood known as **St-Servan,** less than 1km (⅔ mile) southwest from the medieval core of St-Malo. To reach that district, take bus no. 2 from the center of St-Malo.

For last-minute souvenirs, stop by **Aux Délices Malouins,** 12 rue St-Vincent (✆ **02-99-40-55-22**). This shop also specializes in pastries, cookies, and chocolates in the regional style.

For Breton handicrafts, try **Le Comptoir des Cotonniers,** 6 rue Broussais (✆ **02-99-40-57-01**). In addition to hand-painted stoneware, books, and Gaelic CDs, you'll find Breton lace, Celtic souvenirs, and food items such as almond-flavored pastries and sugarcoated galettes. Other shops offering crafts such as Breton pottery include **Aux Arts Celtiques,** 4 rue de Dinan (✆ **02-99-40-05-41**), and **La Manne Bretonne,** 2 place Guy la Chambre (✆ **02-23-18-28-20**).

WHERE TO STAY

Hôtel Central Near the harbor, this hotel is the best of a lackluster lot. It offers well-planned, standardized rooms. The structure was rebuilt of granite blocks after World War II, like much of the surrounding neighborhood. Don't expect old-time touches; the furnishings are contemporary. Each unit has a small, tiled bathroom with shower. One of the most compelling reasons to stay is the food: **La Pêcherie** serves well-prepared seafood.

6 Grand' Rue, St-Malo 35400. ✆ **800/528-1234** or 02-99-40-87-70. Fax 02-99-40-47-57. www.hotel-central-st-malo.com. 50 units. 98€–130€ ($127–$169) double; 130€–165€ ($169–$215) suite. AE, DC, MC, V. Parking 15€ ($20). **Amenities:** Restaurant; bar; room service; nonsmoking rooms. *In room:* TV, minibar, hair dryer, Wi-Fi.

Hôtel de la Cité You'd never guess that this inn is new. It was built in 18th-century style following the plan of a building that once stood here. The contemporary interior, however, is no match for the richly embellished facade. Like most modern chain hotels, it offers solid comfort but is short on style. The rooms range from cramped to spacious. Most bathrooms come with tub/shower combinations. Those on the top floor break away from the norm with angled ceilings. As a saving grace, many units open onto views of the oft-turbulent sea.

Place Vauban, St-Malo 35412. ✆ **02-99-40-55-40.** Fax 02-99-40-10-04. www.hotelcite.com. 41 units. 72€–101€ ($94–$131) double. AE, DC, MC, V. Parking 12€ ($16). **Amenities:** Bar; room service; babysitting; laundry service; dry cleaning; limited-mobility rooms. *In room:* A/C, TV, hair dryer, minibar, safe.

Hôtel Elizabeth Adjacent to the medieval ramparts of the old town, this stone-sided hotel was built in the 17th century as a baronial private home. Traditional artifacts and antiques evoke old-time Brittany at its most authentic. The cozy, renovated guest rooms have mellow-grained paneling and comfortable but unpretentious period-reproduction furniture. Bathrooms have touches of marble and tub/shower combinations. Breakfast (the only meal available) is served in a cellar under stout antique ceiling beams.

2 rue des Cordiers, St-Malo 35400. ✆ **02-99-56-24-98.** Fax 02-99-56-39-24. www.st-malo-hotel-elizabeth.com. 10 units. 120€–185€ ($156–$241) double. Rates include breakfast. AE, DC, V. Parking 10€–15€ ($13–$20). **Amenities:** Room service; nonsmoking rooms. *In room:* TV, minibar, hair dryer.

Hôtel France et Chateaubriand This hotel, inside the walls of old St-Malo, is a good example of Napoleon III architecture. Guest rooms range from cozy to spacious and feature such details as cove moldings, plaster ceiling reliefs, and chandeliers. All contain period reproductions, and most have panoramic ocean views. The units all have neatly tiled tub/shower combinations. In the chic bar with gold-trimmed Corinthian columns, you can chat over drinks and listen occasionally to the pianist on the baby grand.

Place Chateaubriand, St-Malo 35412. ✆ **02-99-56-66-52.** Fax 02-99-40-10-04. www.hotel-chateaubriand-st-malo.com. 80 units. 76€–139€ ($99–$181) double. AE, DC, MC, V. Parking 12€ ($16). **Amenities:** Restaurant; cafe; bar; room service; babysitting; laundry service; dry cleaning; nonsmoking rooms; limited-mobility rooms. *In room:* A/C, TV, hair dryer, Wi-Fi.

WHERE TO DINE

Both **Hôtel Central** and **Hôtel France et Chateaubriand** (see "Where to Stay," above) have restaurants.

A la Duchesse Anne ★★★ TRADITIONAL FRENCH Year after year, this restaurant delivers the finest food in town. Built into the ramparts, it offers summer dining under a canopy amid hydrangeas. Main courses include fish soup with chunks of fresh seafood, spiced and cooked in an iron pot; Cancale oysters; grilled turbot with beurre blanc; and a superb version of grilled lobster. The tempting desserts may include *fantaisie du chocolat*—several chocolate-based desserts artfully arranged on a platter.

5 place Guy-La-Chambre. ✆ **02-99-40-85-33.** Reservations required. Main courses 20€–48€ ($26–$62). Fixed-price menu 70€ ($91). MC, V. May–Nov Thurs–Tues 12:15–1:30pm and 7:15–9:30pm. Closed Dec–Jan.

Le Chalut ★★ SEAFOOD/FRENCH This restaurant is *the* place to go for fresh seafood. Chef Jean-Philippe Foucat's flavorful cuisine, based on fresh ingredients, includes a tart with layers of salmon and scallops, sprinkled with lime juice; John Dory with wild mushrooms, essence of lobster, and fresh coriander; and succulent line-caught sea bass with sherry sauce and braised endive. For dessert, try gâteau of bitter chocolate with almond paste or homemade ice cream flavored with malt whiskey.

8 rue de la Corne-de-Cerf. ✆ **02-99-56-71-58.** Reservations required. Main courses 22€–26€ ($29–$34); fixed-price menu 24€–61€ ($31–$79). AE, MC, V. Wed–Sun noon–1:30pm and 7–9:30pm.

ON THE OUTSKIRTS

Le Relais Gourmand O. Roellinger ★★★ BRETON/SEAFOOD After cooking with some of France's grandest chefs, including Guy Savoy and Gérard Vié, Olivier Roellinger struck out on his own. His restaurant in the town of Cancale attracts serious foodies from all over; many Parisians even travel 402km (250 miles) to enjoy the remarkable chef's work. His restaurant lies on the western flank of the Bay of Mont St-Michel (see chapter 9, "Normandy & Mont-St-Michel"), 16km (10 miles) west of St-Malo.

In a former family home, the restaurant lies behind a wall in the upper town. A domed conservatory opens onto a garden with a duck pond. Roellinger accurately calls his cuisine *marine, potagere, et épicée*—of the sea, the kitchen garden, and the spice cabinet. Start, perhaps, with a light cream-of-coconut soup studded with crayfish and garnished with exotic spices; and follow with brochettes of sweetbreads with laurel, grilled over charcoal and drizzled with essence of quince. The restaurant is the centerpiece of a sprawling compound of at least seven historic buildings, some of them dating from the 1760s, and each scattered within the village of Cancale and along its nearby coastline. Collectively known as "Les Maisons de Bricourt," they include two separate hotels (Le Château Richeux and the Hotel les Rimains), which jointly contain 15 comfortable and expensively decorated accommodations. Doubles cost between 165€ and 295€ ($215–$384) each.

1 rue Duguesclin, Cancale. From St-Malo, take av. Pasteur along the seafront and continue west toward D201, following signposts toward Cancale. ✆ **02-99-89-64-76.** www.maisons-de-bricourt.com. Reservations required. Fixed-price menu 100€–170€ ($130–$221). AE, DC, MC, V. Thurs–Mon noon–1:30pm and 7:30–9pm. Closed mid-Dec to mid-Mar.

ST-MALO AFTER DARK

For an evening of gambling, head to the **Casino,** 2 chaussée du Sillon (✆ **02-99-40-64-00**). You can also order dinner, sometimes accompanied by live music. The informally elegant dress code calls for jackets on men.

For dancing, consider **l'Escalier,** La Buzardière (✆ **02-99-81-65-56**), open Thursday to Saturday from midnight to 5am. The cover doesn't exceed 10€ to 13€ ($13–$17). You'll need a car or taxi—the club is in the countryside, 5km (3 miles) east of town. A disco, **Le 109,** 3 rue des Cordiers (✆ **02-99-56-81-09**), is in a vaulted cellar that's at least 300 years old. It isn't as fashionable as L'Escalier, but it's accessible without a car. Open daily 10pm to 3am.

On weekends, and in search of nightlife, many young Bretons head for Rennes, but if you're interested in seeing the town's biggest disco, check out **Number One,** at L'Etanchet, just outside the hamlet of Pleurtuit (✆ **02-99-88-81-17**). Housed in an isolated farmhouse on the outskirts of St-Malo, it contains a bar, a dance floor, and a revolving series of lights that evoke a 1980s disco. It's open Friday and Saturday nights, and on the evening before national holidays. Cover is 10€ ($13) and includes the first drink.

Popular bars include **L'Aviso,** 12 rue du Point du Jour (✆ **02-99-40-99-08**), which specializes in beers from everywhere; and **Cunningham's,** 2 rue des Hauts Sablons (✆ **02-99-81-48-08**), outfitted like the interior of a yacht. If you're on a pub crawl, hunt for **Le O'Flaherty's,** 18 rue des Cordiers (✆ **02-99-56-87-54**), a real Irish pub with a French twist. It serves six different draft beers and more than 20 whiskeys. **Pub Saint Patrick,** 24 rue Sainte-Barbe (✆ **02-99-56-66-90**), offers 50 different Irish whiskeys along with brew from Brittany. It regularly schedules concerts.

Also appealing is **La Caravelle,** 95 bd. De Rochebonne (✆ **02-99-56-39-83**), a piano bar, 2km (1¼ miles) east of St-Malo, with a fine view of the sea.

2 Dinard ★★★

417km (259 miles) W of Paris, 23km (14 miles) N of Dinan

Dinard (not to be confused with its inland neighbor, Dinan) sits on a rocky promontory at the top of the Rance River, opposite St-Malo. Ferries ply the waters between the two resorts. Victorian Gothic villas, many now hotels, overlook the sea, and gardens and parks abound. The old is still best; for a look at what the Edwardians admired, go down the pointe de la Vicomte at the resort's southern tip or stroll along the promenade.

One of France's best-known resorts, Dinard offers well-sheltered bathing and healthful sea air in *La Manche* ("the Sleeve," as the French call the English Channel). During the Victorian era, Dinard, once a fishing port, became popular with the English, who wanted a Continental holiday that was "not too foreign."

ESSENTIALS

GETTING THERE If you're **driving,** take D186 west from St-Malo to Dinard. SNCF **trains** go only as far as St-Malo; from there, take one of the 10 to 14 buses that depart from the St-Malo rail station daily for the 20-minute ride to Dinard. The one-way fare is 3.20€ ($4.15). **Buses** arrive from many large cities in Brittany, including Rennes. For information, call **Compagnie T.I.V.** (© **02-99-82-26-26**). Between April and November, **Compagnie Corsaire,** Gare Maritime de la Bourse, St. Malo (© **02-23-18-15-15**), operates ferryboats from St-Malo to Dinard. The trip takes 10 minutes and costs 3.70€ ($4.80) one-way. During the same months, the company operates a **ferry** from Dinan to Dinard. The trip takes 90 minutes and costs 18€ ($23) one-way. A **taxi** to Dinard from St-Malo is another option; it costs 20€ ($26) during the day and 28€ ($36) after 7pm and on holidays. For information, call © **02-99-46-75-75.**

VISITOR INFORMATION The **Office de Tourisme** is at 2 bd. Féart (© **02-99-46-94-12;** fax 02-99-88-21-07; www.ot-dinard.com).

SPECIAL EVENTS From early June to mid-September, *musique-et-lumière* adds the drama of floodlights and recorded jazz, pop, or classical music to walks along the city's flowered seafront promenade du Clair-de-Lune.

ENJOYING THE RESORT

A 10-minute walk from the town's historic core to the Pointe du Moulinet encircles most of the old town and encompasses views as far away as St-Malo.

BEACHES & SWIMMING Dinard's main beach is **Plage de l'Ecluse** or **La Grande Plage,** the strip of sand between the peninsulas that defines the edges of the old town. Favored by families and vacationers, it's crowded on hot days. Smaller and more isolated is **Plage de St-Enogat** (you pass through the village of St-Enogat on the 20-min. hike east from Dinard). **Plage du Prieuré,** a 10-minute walk from the center, has many trees that shade the sand. Because there's such a difference between high and low tides, the municipality has built swimming pool–style basins along the Plage de L'Ecluse and the Plage du Prieuré beaches to catch seawater during high tide. Most people trek along the salt flats at low tide to bathe in the sea.

Looking for a pool that's covered, heated, filled with seawater, and open year-round? Head for the **Piscine Olympique,** boulevard du Président-Wilson (© **02-99-46-22-77**), next to the casino. Entrance is 4.20€ ($5.45) for adults, 3.30€ ($4.30) for children 5 to 16, and free for children under 5. From July to mid-September, it's open Monday to Saturday 10am to 12:30pm and 3 to 7:30pm, Sunday 10am to 12:30pm and 3 to 6:30pm. The rest of the year, it runs on a varying schedule according to the needs of school groups and swim teams.

GOLF About 8km (5 miles) west of Dinard at St-Briac is one of the finest courses in Brittany, the par-68, 18-hole **Le Dinard Golf** (© **02-99-88-32-07**). It's on sandy terrain studded with tough grasses and durable trees and shrubs. Greens fees are 40€ to 70€ ($52–$91), depending on the season. It rents clubs—though it's wiser to bring your own—as well as carts.

SHOPPING For shops and boutiques, concentrate on rue du Maréchal-Leclerc, rue Levavasseur, and boulevard Féart. The **Line Boutique,** 13 bd. du Président-Wilson (© **02-99-46-11-21**), is an upscale clothing shop only for women. In the 15th-century house containing **Atelier du Prince Noir,** 70 av. George-V (© **02-99-46-29-99**), you'll find paintings and sculptures by some of the most talented artists in France. The gallery is closed from October to April. Another worthwhile destination is **Marinette,** 29 rue Jacques-Cartier (© **02-99-46-82-88**), in a former Protestant church. The high-ceilinged showrooms feature upscale porcelain, stoneware, kitchen utensils, gift items, and fresh flowers.

WHERE TO STAY

Altaïr and **Roche Corneille** (see "Where to Dine," below) also rent rooms.

Grand Hôtel Barrière de Dinard ★★ Dinard's largest hotel, a member of the Lucien Barrière chain, dates from 1859. Its location, a 2-minute walk from the town center, commands an excellent view of the harbor. It rises in two wings, separated by a heated outdoor pool. Most rooms have balconies and are equipped with traditional furnishings and combination tub/showers. The inviting bar is a popular spot before and after dinner.

46 av. George-V, Dinard 35801. ✆ **02-99-88-26-26.** Fax 02-99-88-26-27. www.lucienbarriere.com. 90 units. 143€–283€ ($186–$368) double; 283€–443€ ($368–$576) junior suite. AE, DC, MC, V. Closed mid-Nov to Mar. **Amenities:** Restaurant; bar; 2 pools (1 indoor, 1 outdoor); fitness center; sauna; room service; babysitting; laundry service; nonsmoking rooms; limited-mobility rooms. *In room:* TV, minibar, hair dryer, safe.

Hôtel Printania Originally built in 1920, and a longtime favorite of nostalgia buffs, writers, and artists, the Printania lies a 2-minute walk from the beaches. On August 15, 1944, a bombing raid damaged the hotel. The main villa boasts terraces and a glassed-in veranda with potted palms. The guest rooms contain antiques and Breton decorations. Some have *des lits Bretons* (Brittany-style beds), which surround the occupant with either curtains or paneled doors. Each of the old-fashioned but well-kept bathrooms contains a tub and shower.

5 av. George-V, Dinard 35800. ✆ **02-99-46-13-07.** Fax 02-99-46-26-32. www.printaniahotel.com. 57 units. 55€–90€ ($72–$117) double; half board 52€–70€ ($68–$91) per person. MC, V. Closed mid-Nov to mid-Mar. **Amenities:** Restaurant; bar. *In room:* TV.

Villa Reine-Hortense ★★ Though not as grand as the Grand, this is our second choice in Dinard. The hotel on the beach was built in 1860 as a retreat for one of the Russian-born courtiers of Queen Hortense de Beauharnais, daughter of Joséphine de Beauharnais (who married Napoleon) and mother of Napoleon III. It offers glamorously outfitted public salons and guest rooms decorated in either Louis XV or Napoleon III style. Most units have private balconies; all have tub/shower combinations. One high-ceilinged room (no. 4) has Hortense's silver-plated bathtub, dating from the early 1800s. Breakfast is the only meal served.

19 rue de la Malouine, Dinard 35800. ✆ **02-99-46-54-31.** Fax 02-99-88-15-88. www.villa-reine-hortense.com. 8 units. 150€–235€ ($195–$306) double; 310€–385€ ($403–$501) suite. AE, DC, MC, V. Closed Oct–Mar. **Amenities:** Bar; laundry service. *In room:* TV, hair dryer.

WHERE TO DINE

Another choice is the restaurant at the **Grand Hôtel Barrière de Dinard** (see "Where to Stay," above).

Altaïr ★ *Value* TRADITIONAL FRENCH Patrick Leménager serves excellent cuisine that includes sea scallops in puff pastry with coriander sauce; fresh salmon with herbs; oysters with apple cream, pulverized crayfish, and herbs; and caramelized apple soufflé. The portions are generous, the atmosphere is intimate, and most prices are reasonable. In warm weather, you may dine on the terrace. The Altaïr also rents 22 standard rooms with TVs and shower-only bathrooms. A double with half board is 55€ to 68€ ($72–$88) per person.

Finds An Idyll on an Ile

Ile de Bréhat is home to some 300 hearty folk who live most of the year in isolation—until the summer crowds arrive. The tiny island (actually two islands, Ile Nord and Ile Sud, linked by a bridge, Le Pont Vauban) is in the Golfe de St-Malo, north of Paimpol. A visit to Bréhat is an adventure, even to the French. The only settlement on the islands is Le Bourg, in the south. The only bona fide beach is a strip of sand at Guerzido.

Walking is the primary activity, and it's possible to stroll the footpaths around the island in a day. Cars other than police and fire vehicles aren't allowed. Tractor-driven carts carry visitors on an 8km (5-mile) circuit of Bréhat's two islands, charging 13€ ($17) for the 45-minute jaunt. A number of places rent bikes, but they aren't necessary.

The rich flora here astonishes many visitors, who get off the ferry expecting a windswept island, only to discover a more Mediterranean clime. Flower gardens are in full summer bloom, though both the gardens and houses appear tiny because of the scarcity of land. At the highest point, Chapelle St-Michel, you'll be rewarded with a panoramic view.

The tourist office, place du Bourg, Le Bourg (✆ **02-96-20-04-15**), is open Monday to Saturday from mid-June to mid-September.

To reach Paimpol, **drive** west on D768 from Dinard to Lamballe, then take E50 west to Plérin, and D786 north to Paimpol. To reach the island, take D789 4km (2½ miles) north of Paimpol, where the peninsula ends at the Pointe de l'Arcouest. From Paimpol, 5 to 10 **CAT buses** make the 10-minute run to the point for a one-way fare of 3€ ($3.90). Then catch one of the **ferries** operated by **Les Vedettes de Bréhat** (✆ **02-96-55-79-50;** www.vedettesdebrehat.com). Ferries depart about every 30 minutes in summer, two or three times per day in the off season; the round-trip costs 8€ ($10). Visitors in April, May, June, and September will find the island much less crowded than in July and August. Cars are not allowed on the ferry.

18 bd. Féart, Dinard 35800. ✆ **02-99-46-13-58.** Fax 02-99-88-20-49. Reservations recommended. Main courses 18€–32€ ($23–$42); fixed-price menu 15€–49€ ($20–$64). AE, DC, MC, V. Thurs–Sun noon–2pm; Tues–Sun 7–9:30pm.

Hôtel Roche Corneille ★ FRENCH The dining room of this historic blue-and-white villa (ca. 1870) is known to locals for unpretentious, savory, and very fresh food, expertly prepared by the genteel resident owners, Francois and Elizabeth Garrigue. If you opt for a meal in the sea-fronting dining room, whose decor derives from high ceilings and striped upholstery, you'll be in good company. Long before its transformation into a hotel, and its extensive renovation, it was occupied by extended members of the Romanoff family (the tsars of pre-Revolutionary Russia) and an armada of staff every summer during a 3-week holiday by the sea. Menu items are affordable and inviting. The best examples include house-marinated salmon on a platter of avocados and hearts of artichoke in a truffled vinaigrette; roasted lamb from the salt marshes of nearby Mont-St-Michel; magret of duckling with honey and spices; and heaping platters, artfully draped in seaweed, of very fresh shellfish. A slice of thin tarte Tatin always makes an appealing dessert.

Upstairs, the establishment maintains 28 comfortable midsize bedrooms, each well-maintained, cozy, and with a tiled bathroom, minibar, TV, and phone. Doubles cost from 90€ to 160€ ($117–$208), depending on the season.

4 rue Georges-Clemenceau, Dinard 35800. ✆ **02-99-46-14-47.** Fax 02-99-46-40-80. www.dinard-hotel-roche-corneille.com. Reservations recommended. Main courses 13€–30€ ($17–$39); fixed-price menu 28€ ($36). AE, DC, MC, V. Daily noon–2:30pm and 7–9:30pm. The restaurant (but not the hotel) is closed Dec to mid-Mar.

DINARD AFTER DARK

Like many of Brittany's seaside towns, Dinard has a **Municipal Casino,** 4 bd. du Président-Wilson (✆ **02-99-16-30-30**). It's liveliest from Easter to late October, when all its facilities, including a room for roulette and blackjack, are open. The rest of the year, only the slot machines operate. Hours for the slots are Sunday to Thursday from 10am to 3am, Friday and Saturday from 10am to 4am. Admission to the slot machines is free. Management encourages men to wear ties, especially in the roulette and blackjack areas; the entrance fee for those areas is free. Also on the premises is **La Brasserie,** a bar and bistro that's open year-round. Closed 2 weeks in February and 2 weeks in October. An alternative (not within the casino) is **Le Metro-Dôme,** Le Haut-Chemin (✆ **02-99-46-46-46**), a bar-bistro that has earned the loyalty of many residents thanks to a good selection of wine and an amiable ambience. It lies on the outskirts of town on the road to St-Malo.

In the evenings from June to September, the **promenade du Clair-de-Lune** attracts a huge crowd of strollers for the *musique-et-lumière,* when the buildings and flowers along the promenade are illuminated and musical groups of just about every ilk—from rock to blues to jazz—perform.

3 Dinan ★★

396km (246 miles) W of Paris, 52km (32 miles) NW of Rennes

Once a stronghold of the ducs de Bretagne, Dinan is one of the best-preserved towns in Brittany. It's noted for houses built on stilts over the sidewalks. The 18th-century granite dwellings provide a sharp contrast to the medieval timbered houses in this walled town with a once-fortified château. Dinan (pop. 14,000) is one of Brittany's prettiest towns—it's not overrun like St-Malo.

ESSENTIALS

GETTING THERE Dinan has a railway station, but few SNCF **trains** stop here. Railway passengers usually travel to Rennes, Dinard, or St-Malo, and then transfer to one of the SNCF **buses** (about five a day from each) that line up in front of the railway stations. The one-way bus fare from Rennes is 8.80€ ($11), from St-Malo 6.60€ ($8.60), and from Dinard 4.70€ ($6.10). For information about bus service to Dinan, call the town's Gare Routière, adjacent to the railway station, about 1km (⅔ mile) west of the center (✆ **02-96-39-21-05**). If you're **driving** from Dinard, take highway D166 south to Dinan.

VISITOR INFORMATION The **Office de Tourisme** is at 9 rue du Château (✆ **02-96-87-69-76;** fax 02-96-87-69-77; www.dinan-tourisme.com).

SPECIAL EVENTS The most activity occurs on the third weekend of July, during the **Fêtes des Remparts,** held in even-numbered years (2008 is the next one). Duels from the age of chivalry are staged, and locals don medieval apparel for carousing in the streets of the city's historic core.

EXPLORING THE TOWN

For a panoramic view of the valley, head for the **Jardin Anglais (English Garden),** a terraced garden that huddles up to the ramparts. A Gothic-style bridge spans the Rance River; damaged in World War II, it has since been restored. Dinan's most typical and one of its most appealing streets is the sloping **rue du Jerzual,** flanked with some buildings dating from the 15th century. The street ends at **Porte du Jerzual,** a 13th- and 14th-century gate. **Rue du Petit-Fort** and place des Merciers contain a number of 15th-century *maisons.*

Dominating the city's ramparts, **Château Musée de Dinan,** rue du Château (✆ **02-96-39-45-20**), contains a 14th-century keep and a 15th-century tower, built to withstand sieges. In the stones, you'll see the space for the portcullis and the drawbridge. Inside, you can view an exhibition on the architecture and art of the city, including sculpture from the 12th to the 15th centuries. Admission is 4.25€ ($5.55) for adults, 1.70€ ($2.20) for children 12 to 18, and free for children under 12. It's open June to September daily 10am to 6:30pm, October to May daily 1:30 to 5:30pm (closed Jan).

Tour de l'Horloge (clock tower), on rue de l'Horloge (✆ **02-96-87-02-26**), boasts a clock made in 1498 and a bell donated by Anne de Bretagne in 1507. You'll have a view of Dinan from the 23m (75-ft.) belfry. Admission is 2.80€ ($3.65) for adults, 1.80€ ($2.35) for children 12 to 18, and free for children under 12. Open daily July to August 10am to 6:30pm and mid-May to June and September daily 10am to 6:30pm.

The heart of Bertrand du Guesclin, who defended the town when the duke of Lancaster threatened it in 1359, is entombed in a place of honor in the **Basilique St-Sauveur,** place St-Sauveur (✆ **02-96-39-06-67**). Note the basilica's Romanesque portals and ornamented chapels. It's open daily from 9am to 6pm.

REGIONAL CRAFTS Dinan has attracted craftspeople and artists for at least 20 years. The densest concentration of studios is along the **rue du Jerzual** and the **rue Apport,** where art objects are crafted from glass, wood, silk, leather, and clay. Our favorite shopping street is Jerzual. Other good streets include **place des Merciers** and **place des Cordeliers.** You may be able to buy an item directly from the artisan, but it's more efficient to visit galleries that sell objects by an assortment of the artisans. Two of the best are **Galerie St-Sauveur,** 12 rue de l'Apport (✆ **02-96-85-26-62**), and **Galerie Phonographe,** 2 rue de l'Apport (✆ **02-96-39-38-38**), where wide cross sections of paintings and crafts help provide perspective on the arts in Dinan. St-Sauveur specializes in avant-garde paintings and sculptures by living artists. Phonographe is more regional in flavor, selling lots of Breton land- and seascapes and watercolors.

WHERE TO STAY

Hôtel Arvor *Value* This is a comfortable, relatively inexpensive hotel in a 14th-century Jacobin convent. During renovation in the 1990s, most of the building's interior was demolished and rebuilt. The result is comfortable, contemporary-looking guest rooms with small, shower-only bathrooms. They retain none of their original medieval characteristics, but provide a cozy haven in one of Dinan's oldest neighborhoods. Breakfast is the only meal served, but many inviting restaurants lie within a short walk.

5 rue Pavie, Dinan 22100. ✆ **02-96-39-21-22.** Fax 02-96-39-83-09. www.hotel-arvor-dinan.com. 24 units. 49€–72€ ($64–$94) double. MC, V. Closed Jan. *In room:* TV, hair dryer, iron, Wi-Fi.

Hôtel d'Avaugour ★★ Set on the town ramparts, this is one of the town's best hotels. It's hard to believe that a pair of gutted stone-fronted buildings has been transformed into an up-to-date hotel. Guest rooms are decorated in a style that reflects the historical charm of the area. The rooms contain fabrics inspired by 18th-century design, furniture reflecting the heritage of Dinan, canopied beds, and midsize bathrooms (most with tubs and showers). Half the units overlook the square; the others face the garden.

1 place du Champs-Clos, Dinan 22100. ✆ **02-96-39-07-49.** Fax 02-96-85-43-04. www.avaugourhotel.com. 24 units. 84€–179€ ($109–$233) double; 150€–300€ ($195–$390) suite. MC, V. Closed Nov 10 to mid-Feb. *In room:* TV, hair dryer.

WHERE TO DINE

L'Auberge de Pelican ★ FRENCH/BRETON This traditional restaurant's decor is contemporary but the food is often based on time-honored recipes, all of which are homemade, even the bread. Our favorite dish is the casserole of fresh fish served daily with beurre blanc or "white butter." Fat, succulent scallops from the bay are also a worthy choice for seafood lovers. But the chef prepares meat and poultry dishes equally well, particularly the magret of canard (duckling) with figs and a tender, well-flavored filet of beef with truffles.

3 rue Haute Voie. ✆ **02-96-39-47-05.** Reservations recommended. Main courses 12€–60€ ($16–$78); fixed-price menus 17€–52€ ($22–$68). AE, MC, V. July–Aug Tues–Fri and Sun noon–2pm, daily 7–10pm; Sept–June Tues–Sun noon–2pm, Tues–Wed and Fri–Sun 7–10pm.

ON THE OUTSKIRTS

Jean-Pierre Crousil ★★ *Finds* BRETON/NORMAN Those who think there's nothing left to discover on the Breton coast can drive to this restaurant tucked away in the hamlet of Plancoët, 28km (17 miles) from St-Malo and 17km (11 miles) from Dinan. A smooth beginning is foie gras en terrine in sauterne wine jelly. The most lavish dish is lobster roasted in Calvados, which imparts a wonderfully rich, aromatic flavor. We are fond of duck served in thick, rosy slices; farmhouse quail; and *pigoneaux de nid au Port* (pigeons in potato baskets with port-wine sauce). The chef also prepares turbot with beurre blanc, and scallops in dishes that change depending on his inspiration for the evening.

20 Les Quais, Plancoët. ✆ **02-96-84-10-24.** Reservations required. Main courses 30€–60€ ($39–$78); fixed-price menus 25€–120€ ($33–$156). Mon–Fri fixed-price lunch 35€ ($46). AE, MC, V. Wed–Sun noon–1:30pm; Wed–Sat 7:30–9:15pm. From Dinan, take rue des Rouairies west, and follow signs to Plancoët.

DINAN AFTER DARK

The densest concentration of cafes and bars in Dinan lines the **rue de la Cordonnerie,** nicknamed *la rue de la soif* ("the street where you go when you're thirsty") by long-ago sailors.

An appealing destination is **Le Bistrot d'en Bas,** 20 rue Haute-Voie (✆ **02-96-85-44-00**). It offers about a dozen reds and whites by the glass and at least 15 kinds of *tartine* (grilled open-faced sandwiches), served with a salad, for 6.50€ ($8.45) each. The town's only disco, open Friday and Saturday nights from midnight to 5am, is **Le Zéphire,** 98 rue de Brest (✆ **02-96-39-12-79**), a fuchsia-colored, dimly lit stone-trimmed room about 4km (2½ miles) north of the town center. Cover is 10€ ($13) and includes one drink. Expect all kinds of music, including disco, techno, new wave, and old-fashioned rock 'n' roll.

4 Quimper ★★

570km (354 miles) W of Paris, 205km (127 miles) NW of Rennes

The town that pottery built, Quimper, at the meeting of the Odet and Steir rivers, is the historic capital of Brittany's most traditional region, La Cornouaille. Today, its faïence decorates tables from Europe to the United States. Skilled artisans have been turning out Quimperware since the 17th century, using bold provincial designs. You can tour one of the ateliers; inquire at the tourist office (see below). Today Quimper is rather smug and bourgeois, home to some 63,000 Quimperois, who walk narrow streets spared from World War II damage.

ESSENTIALS

GETTING THERE Slow **trains** (Les Corails) from Paris's Montparnasse station take 7 hours. Speedy TGVs take only 4½ hours from Paris. By all means, skip the slow train and opt for the TGV; the one-way fare is 75€ ($97). For information, call ✆ **08-92-35-35-35.** If you're **driving,** the best route is from Rennes: Take E50/N12 west to just outside the town of Montauban, continue west along N164 to Châteaulin, and head south along N165 to Quimper.

VISITOR INFORMATION The **Office de Tourisme** is on place de la Résistance (✆ **02-98-53-04-05;** www.quimper-tourisme.com).

SPECIAL EVENTS For 8 days in late July, the **Festival de Cornouaille** adds a traditional flavor to the nightlife scene with Celtic and Breton concerts throughout the city. For information, contact the Office de Tourisme.

EXPLORING THE TOWN

In the summer, the tourist office organizes a 90-minute walking tour of the city *(des circuits de ville).* It costs 5€ ($6.50). Tours in French depart daily at 10:30am from in front of the tourist office; tours in English start at 2pm on Tuesday and Friday only.

In some quarters, Quimper maintains its old-world atmosphere, with footbridges spanning the rivers. At place St-Corentin is the **Cathédrale St-Corentin** ★★ (✆ **02-98-95-06-19**), characterized by two towers that climb 75m (246 ft.). The cathedral was built from the 13th to the 15th century; the spires were added in the 19th. Inside, note the 15th-century stained glass. Open May to October Monday to Saturday 8:30am to noon and 1:30 to 6:30pm, Sunday 8:30am to noon and 2 to 6:30pm; November to April Monday to Saturday 9am to noon and daily 1:30 to 6pm.

Also on the square is the **Musée des Beaux-Arts** ★★, 40 place St-Corentin (✆ **02-98-95-45-20**). The collection includes work by Rubens, Boucher, Fragonard, and Corot, plus an exceptional exhibit from the Pont-Aven school (Bernard, Sérusier, Lacombe, Maufra, Denis). Admission is 4.50€ ($5.85) for adults, 2.50€ ($3.25) for ages 12 to 26, and free for children under 12. The museum is open July and August daily from 10am to 7pm; April through June and September and October, Monday and Wednesday to Sunday 10am to noon and 2 to 6pm; and November to March, Monday and Wednesday to Saturday 10am to noon and 2 to 6pm, Sunday 2 to 6pm.

Musée Departemental Breton, 1–3 rue Roi Gradlon (✆ **02-98-95-21-60**), is in the medieval Palais des Éveques de Cornouailles (Palace of the Bishops of Cornwall), adjacent to the cathedral. The museum showcases the evolution of Breton costumes, with examples of local handicrafts, archaeology, and furniture. It is open June to October daily 9am to 6pm; November to May Tuesday to Saturday 9am to noon and daily

2 to 5pm. Admission is 3.80€ ($4.95) for adults, 2.50€ ($3.25) for ages 18 to 25, and free for children under 18.

Musée de Faïence Jules Verlingue, 14 rue Jean-Baptiste-Bouquet (✆ **02-98-90-12-72**), has a fun collection of the city's signature pottery. The museum is open mid-April to mid-October, Monday to Saturday 10am to 6pm. Admission is 4€ ($5.20) adults and 2.30€ ($3) children 7 to 18.

SHOPPING

When artisans from Rouen settled in Quimper, the city became forever associated with ceramics. It produces the most recognized and the most popular French porcelain. Typical are chunky white pieces painted with blue-and-yellow Breton figures, fruits, and flowers. The most popular feature a male *Breton* or a female *Bretonne,* both in profile and in traditional Breton costume. Today, that 19th-century design is copyrighted and fiercely protected.

The best shopping streets are **rue Kereon** and **rue du Parc,** where you'll find Breton products including pottery, dolls and puppets, clothing made from regional cloth and wool, jewelry, lace, and beautiful Breton costumes.

One of three sites that produce stoneware is open for tours. Monday through Friday from 9am to 4:30pm, five to seven tours a day depart from the visitor information center of **HB-Henriot Faïenceries de Quimper,** rue Haute, Quartier Locmaria (✆ **02-98-90-09-36;** www.hb-henriot.com). Tours, in English or French or both, last 40 to 45 minutes and cost 3.50€ ($4.55) for adults, 2€ ($2.60) for children 8 to 14, and are free for children under 8. On-site, a store sells the most complete inventory of Quimper porcelain in the world. You can invest in first-run (nearly perfect) pieces or slightly discounted "seconds," with nearly imperceptible flaws. Anything you buy can be shipped.

For other Breton pottery and pieces of the faïence once heavily produced in this area, visit **François le Villec,** 4 rue Roi-Gradlon (✆ **02-98-95-31-54**). Here you'll find quality tablecloths, linens, and other household linens.

Another good choice for Breton items is **La Galerie le Cornet à Dés,** 1 rue Ste-Thérèse (✆ **02-98-53-37-51**). It stocks hand-painted porcelain and antique and contemporary paintings, mostly of Quimper landscapes.

WHERE TO STAY

Hôtel Gradlon ★ *Value* The town's most consistently reliable hotel is this 19th-century landmark. The frequently renovated hotel has a simple modern annex a few steps away. The decor is simple, angular, and solid, with framed posters of Breton landscapes and monuments, and lots of varnished-wood trim. Guest rooms are simple and comfortable. The tiled bathrooms have tubs and showers.

30 rue de Brest, Quimper 29000. ✆ **02-98-95-04-39.** Fax 02-98-95-61-25. www.hotel-gradlon.com. 22 units. 95€–110€ ($124–$143) double; 130€–155€ ($169–$202) suite. AE, DC, MC, V. Closed late Dec to mid-Jan. Parking 8.50€ ($11). **Amenities:** Bar; babysitting; laundry service; nonsmoking rooms; limited-mobility rooms. *In room:* TV, minibar, hair dryer, Wi-Fi.

Hôtel Océania *Kids* In a garden 1.5km (1 mile) southwest of the town center, the Océania, despite its blandness, is the best choice for families. Built in the 1980s with comfortable, standardized rooms, its Breton-style slate roof would be the envy of any homeowner. It's ideal for motoring families (the pool is a magnet in summer) and is the best business-oriented hotel in the region. Each unit has lots of space, a writing desk, and a midsize bathroom with tub and shower.

2 rue du Poher, Quimper 29000. From town center, follow signs to rte. Pont-l'Abbé. ✆ **02-98-90-46-26.** Fax 02-98-53-01-96. www.hotel-sofibra.com. 92 units. 105€–130€ ($137–$169) double. 1 or 2 children under 16 stay free in parent's room. AE, DC, MC, V. **Amenities:** Restaurant; bar; heated outdoor pool; room service; babysitting; non-smoking rooms; limited-mobility rooms. *In room:* TV, hair dryer.

WHERE TO DINE

Acacias ★ *Kids* BRETON/SEAFOOD This is Quimper's leading restaurant. In a contemporary-looking dining room, it focuses on seafood and very fresh fish, but offers a scattering of meat dishes. Your meal may include roasted crayfish with sweet spices, delectable smoked John Dory perfumed with algae, fondant of pigs' foot with exotic mushrooms, and roasted pigeon with baby vegetables. Customers rave about the dessert specialty of local strawberries marinated in spiced wine. The wine list features 150 to 200 mostly French vintages.

85 bd. Creac'h Gwen. From Quimper, drive 2km (1¼ miles), following signs to Benodet. ✆ **02-98-52-15-20.** Reservations recommended. Main courses 30€–60€ ($39–$78); fixed-price menu 25€–45€ ($33–$59); children's menu 12€ ($16). MC, V. Sun–Fri 12:30–2:30pm; Mon–Fri 7–9pm. Closed May 1–7.

L'Ambroisie ★ *Kids* BRETON/FRENCH Although it's surpassed by Acacias, this restaurant remains one of the most respected and sought-after in Quimper. A 5-minute walk north of the cathedral, the airy ocher-and-gold dining room has contemporary furniture and large paintings in a style inspired by the English neo-surrealist Francis Bacon. Menu items incorporate Breton traditions, with an occasional contemporary twist. The finest examples include a crusty buckwheat galette stuffed with spiced crabmeat, braised scallops with asparagus and citrus sauce, and filet of John Dory on an artfully contrived bed of vegetable ragout.

49 rue Elie Fréron. ✆ **02-98-95-00-02.** Reservations recommended. Main courses 25€–35€ ($33–$46); fixed-price menu 22€–69€ ($29–$90); children's menu 15€ ($20). MC, V. Tues–Sun noon–1:30pm; Tues–Sat 7:30–9:15pm.

WHERE TO STAY & DINE NEARBY

In an orchard district 13km (8 miles) from Quimper, the sleepy village of **La Forêt-Fouesnant** produces the best cider in the province and is home to one of Brittany's finest manor houses.

Manoir du Stang ★★★ To get to this 16th-century ivy-covered manor, you travel down a tree-lined avenue, through a stone gate, and into a courtyard. On your right is a formal garden; stone terraces lead to 10 hectares (25 acres) of woodland. M. and Mme Hubert provide gracious lodging in period rooms. Guests stay in the main building or in the even older but less-desirable annex, which has a circular stone staircase. Your room is likely to be furnished with silk and fine antiques; each midsize bathroom comes with a combination tub/shower. One luxury is the maid who brings your breakfast on a tray each morning.

La Forêt-Fouesnant 29940. Drive 1.5km (1 mile) north of the village center and follow signs from N783; access is by private road. ✆/fax **02-98-56-97-37.** www.manoirdustang.com. 24 units. 99€–150€ ($129–$195) double. No credit cards. Free parking. Closed Oct–Apr. **Amenities:** Bar. *In room:* Hair dryer.

QUIMPER AFTER DARK

The steadfastly Celtic bar **Céili Pub,** 4 rue Aristide-Briand (✆ **02-98-95-17-61**), has lots of polished wood, regional music, and happy people—join in a game of darts with one of the regulars. **St. Andrew's Pub,** 11 place Styvel (✆ **02-98-53-34-49**), with its wood-and-leather interior, 30 varieties of beer, and 37 whiskeys, attracts many Brits and Americans.

The young and stylish flock to **Les Naïades Discothèque,** boulevard Creac'h Gwen (✆ **02-98-53-32-30**), where you can dance to the latest tunes. It sometimes charges a cover.

5 Concarneau ★★

539km (335 miles) W of Paris, 93km (58 miles) SE of Brest

This port is a favorite of painters, who never tire of capturing the subtleties of the fishing fleet. It's also our favorite of the coast communities—primarily because it doesn't depend on tourists. Its canneries produce most of the tuna in France. Walk along the quays, especially in the evening, and watch the Breton fishers unload their catch; later, join them for a pint of cider in the taverns.

ESSENTIALS

GETTING THERE There's no **rail** service to Concarneau. If you're **driving,** the town is 21km (13 miles) southeast of Quimper along D783. A **bus** (✆ **02-98-56-96-72**) runs from Quimper to Concarneau (trip time: 30 min.); the one-way fare is 2€ ($2.60). The bus from Resporden, site of another SNCF railway station, runs 8 to 10 times per day (trip time: 20 min.) for a fare of 2€ ($2.60).

VISITOR INFORMATION The **Office de Tourisme** is on quai d'Aiguillon (✆ **02-98-97-01-44;** www.tourismeconcarneau.fr).

EXPLORING THE AREA

The town is built on three sides of a natural harbor whose innermost sheltered section is the **Nouveau Port.** In the center of the harbor is the heavily fortified **Ville-Close,** an ancient hamlet surrounded by ramparts, some from the 14th century. From the quay, cross the bridge and descend into the town. Souvenir shops have taken over, but don't let that spoil it for you. You can spend an hour wandering the alleys, gazing up at the towers, peering at the stone houses, and stopping in secluded squares.

For a splendid view of the port, walk the **ramparts.** They're open to pedestrians mid-June to mid-September daily 10am to 9:30pm; mid-April to mid-June daily 10am to 6pm; March to mid-April and mid-September to November daily 10am to noon and 2 to 6pm. Access to the ramparts is closed December to February and whenever icy rain makes them slippery. The cost is .80€ ($1.05) per adult and .40€ (50¢) for children under 13 (free Sept–May).

Also in the old town is a fishing museum, **Musée de la Pêche,** 3 rue Vauban (✆ **02-98-97-10-20**). The 17th-century building has ship models and exhibits tracing the development of the fishing industry; you can also view the ship *Hemerica.* Admission is 6€ ($7.80) for adults and 4€ ($5.20) for students and children under 15. It's open in July and August daily 9:30am to 8pm, September to June daily 10am to noon and 2 to 6pm; closed for 3 weeks in January.

BEACHES Concarneau's largest, most beautiful beach, popular with families, is **Plage des Sables Blancs,** near the historic core. Within a 10-minute walk are **Plage de Cornouaille** and two small beaches, **Plage des Dames** and **Plage de Rodel,** where you'll find fewer families with children. The wide-open **Plage du Cabellou,** 5km (3 miles) west of town, is less crowded than the others.

SEA EXCURSIONS Boat rides are usually fine between June and September, but they're treacherous the rest of the year. During midsummer, you can arrange deep-sea fishing with the captain of the ***Santa Maria*** (✆ **02-98-50-69-01**). For excursions along the coastline of southern Brittany, contact **Vedettes Glenn** (✆ **02-98-97-10-31**) or **Vedettes de l'Odet** (✆ **02-98-57-00-58**).

WHERE TO STAY

Hôtel des Halles *Finds* The tourist board gives only two stars to this cement-sided 1960s-era hotel, which is short on historical charm. Yet it's affordable and warm, with guest rooms that are cozier than you may expect. The frequently upgraded rooms have white ceiling beams and wood paneling, plus small shower-only bathrooms. The location, a short distance from the fortifications encircling the town's historic core, is convenient. The city's covered food market, Les Halles (open daily 8am–1pm), is a short walk away. Breakfast is the only meal served.

Place de l'Hôtel de Ville, Concarneau 29900. ✆ **02-98-97-11-41.** Fax 02-98-50-58-54. www.hoteldeshalles.com. 22 units. 49€–69€ ($64–$90) double. AE, MC, V. **Amenities:** Nonsmoking rooms. *In room:* TV, hair dryer.

WHERE TO DINE

La Coquille ★ TRADITIONAL FRENCH This 4-decade-old restaurant occupies one end of a stone-sided harborfront building; guests dine in a trio of rooms with stone walls, ceiling beams, and century-old oil paintings from the school of Pont-Aven. Seafood is the focus at La Coquille, and much of what is on the menu is offered simply because the fish is so fresh and succulent. A particularly excellent dish is a scallop tart with shellfish and cream sauce. The service is bistro style, with a cheerful, old-fashioned panache enhanced by the harbor view.

1 rue du Moros, at Nouveau Port. ✆ **02-98-97-08-52.** Reservations required Sat–Sun and in summer. Main courses 17€–70€ ($22–$91); fixed-price menu 29€–60€ ($38–$78). AE, DC, MC, V. Tues–Sun noon–1:30pm; Tues–Sat 7:30–9:30pm.

WHERE TO STAY & DINE NEARBY

On the outskirts of the once-fortified town of **Hennebont,** 56km (35 miles) southeast of Concarneau, is the most delightful hotel in all of southern Brittany.

Château de Locguénolé ★★★ This country estate is owned by the same family that ran it some 5 centuries ago. Following a devastating fire, the 15th-century château was rebuilt in its present form in 1805. Now a Relais & Châteaux member, with views over coastline and an inlet, it's filled with antiques, tapestries, and paintings. Guest rooms vary in size and style, but each has a harmonious color scheme and, season permitting, sprays of flowers. The converted maids' rooms are smaller, yet still charming; some units are in a converted 1720 Breton cottage. Bathrooms have tub/shower combinations.

Rte. de Port-Louis en Kervignac, Hennebont 56700. From Hennebont, follow signs to château, 4km (2½ miles) south. ✆ **02-97-76-76-76.** Fax 02-97-76-82-35. www.chateau-de-locguenole.com. 22 units. 112€–295€ ($146–$384) double; 330€–410€ ($429–$533) suite. AE, DC, MC, V. Closed Jan 2–Feb 11. **Amenities:** Restaurant; sauna; room service; outdoor pool; babysitting; laundry service; dry cleaning. *In room:* TV, minibar, hair dryer, safe, Wi-Fi.

6 Pont-Aven ★

522km (324 miles) W of Paris, 32km (20 miles) SE of Quimper, 16km (10 miles) S of Concarneau

Paul Gauguin loved this village, with its white houses along the gently flowing Aven River. In the late 19th century, many painters followed him here, including Maurice Denis, Paul Sérusier, and Emile Bernard. The theories and techniques developed at the time have been known ever since as the School of Pont-Aven.

Moments In the Footsteps of Gauguin

In 1886, Paul Gauguin blazed the trail to the Breton village of Pont-Aven, and in time lesser artists followed. One of Gauguin's most memorable works, *The Yellow Christ,* exemplified the credo of the School of Pont-Aven. Breaking from mainstream Impressionism, Pont-Aven artists emphasized purer colors ("as true as nature itself"). They shunned perspective and simplified human figures.

The tourist office sells a walking-tour guide (.50€/65¢) that directs you on a trail once trod by the artists who drew inspiration from the sea and landscapes of this region.

Musée Municipal de Pont-Aven, place de l'Hôtel de Ville (© **02-98-06-14-43**), provides one of the best overviews of the 19th-century painters. Expect muted greens and blues and lots of Breton patriotism as interpreted through the most famous artistic movement to emerge from Brittany. Admission is 4€ ($5.20) for adults, 2.50€ ($3.25) for people under 25, and free to children under 18. The museum is open in July and August daily 10am to 7pm, September to December and February to June daily 10am to 12:30pm and 2 to 6pm (closed Jan).

In the 16th-century **Chapelle de Trémalo,** lieu-dit Trémalo (© **02-98-06-02-94**), 1.2km (¾ mile) north of the town center, you can admire the crucifix that inspired Gauguin's paintings *The Yellow Christ* and *Self-Portrait with the Yellow Christ* (in the Musée d'Orsay). The owners of the private chapel unlock it every morning at 9am and close it between 7 and 8pm, depending on their whim and the season. The location is signposted, and entrance is free.

ESSENTIALS

GETTING THERE If you're **driving** from Quimper, go southeast on N165 and follow signs into Pont-Aven. From Quimperlé, head west along D783. SNCF **trains** stop at Quimperlé, where you can transfer to between four and six daily **buses** for the 30-minute ride to Pont-Aven. The one-way fare is 2€ ($2.60). For train information, call the Pont-Aven tourist office (see below) or © **08-92-35-35-35,** or visit www.voyages-sncf.com.

VISITOR INFORMATION The **Office de Tourisme** is at 5 place de l'Hôtel-de-Ville (© **02-98-06-04-70;** www.pontaven.com).

WHERE TO STAY & DINE

Le Moulin de Rosmadec ★★★ *Finds* TRADITIONAL FRENCH For a charming setting, nothing in Brittany compares to this 15th-century stone mill. Meals are served in a bi-level dining room with antique furnishings or, in good weather, on a flower-filled "island" terrace. The owners, M. and Mme Sébilleau, serve carefully prepared specialties such as ragout of freshwater crayfish. Among the proficiently prepared dishes are *croustillant de pigeon* (crisply baked pigeon in puff pastry) and grilled lobster. Well worth ordering is stir-fried crayfish in its natural juices or a tart layered with red snapper and a confit of tomatoes. A traditional and tasty favorite is grilled John Dory with fresh artichokes.

The Moulin rents four comfortable double rooms for 85€ to 115€ ($111–$150). Each has a TV and a tidy bathroom with tub and shower. Because of the location at the end of a cul-de-sac, the accommodations are quiet and calm.

Pont-Aven 29123. ✆ **02-98-06-00-22.** Reservations recommended. Main courses 24€–32€ ($31–$42); fixed-price menu 35€–50€ ($46–$65); *menu tradition* (with oysters and lobster) 74€ ($96). MC, V. Thurs–Tues 12:30–2pm and 7:30–9pm. Closed Feb, 2 weeks in Oct, and Sun night Sept–June.

7 Carnac ★

486km (302 miles) W of Paris, 37km (23 miles) SE of Lorient, 100km (62 miles) SE of Quimper

Aside from being a seaside resort, Carnac is home to the hundreds of huge stones in the **Field of Megaliths ("Les Alignements")** that date from Neolithic times. Scholars have debated their purpose for centuries, although most suggest they had astronomical or religious significance to the people of the area. One theory is that some of the stones marked burial sites. In all, the town contains 2,732 menhirs (monumental stones), some of them rising to heights of 20m (66 ft.). They stand in 11 more or less straight lines in at least three separate fields.

Out of fear of vandalism, the local tourist authorities have fenced in the megaliths, and now allow visitors to wander freely among the menhirs *only* between October and March, when the park is open daily from 10am to 5pm, and when the entrance is free. From April to September, the park can be visited only as part of a rigidly controlled 1-hour guided tour, priced at 4€ ($5.20) per person (3€/$3.90 for students or anyone under 25). Tours are usually in French but, depending on the perceived need, may include some additional commentary in English; or, during high season, there may even be an all-English tour offered, but nothing is guaranteed. The only way to be sure involves calling the Parc's Visitor Center *(Maison des Mégalithes)* for a rundown on the tours that will be arranged on the day of your intended visit.

At Carnac Ville, **Musée de Préhistoire,** 10 place de la Chapelle (✆ **02-97-52-22-04**), displays collections from 450,000 B.C. to the 8th century. Admission is 5€ ($6.50) for adults, 2.50€ ($3.25) for children 6 to 18, and free for children under 6. Between June and September, the museum is open daily 10am to 12:30pm and 1:30 to 7pm. The rest of the year, it's open Thursday to Tuesday 10am to 12:40pm and 1:30 to 6pm.

Even if Carnac didn't possess these monuments, its pine-studded sand dunes would be worth the trip. Protected by the Quiberon Peninsula, **Carnac-Plage** is a family resort beside the ocean and along the waterfront boulevard de la Plage. And in May and June, the fields—especially around the megaliths—are resplendent with golden broom.

The center of Carnac is about .8km (½ mile) from the sea. From the main square, rue du Tumulus leads north from the center of town to the **Tumulus St-Michel,** a Celtic burial chamber 1.2km (¾ mile) from the center (it is closed to the public).

ESSENTIALS

GETTING THERE **Driving** is the most convenient way to get to Carnac. From Pont-Aven, travel east along N165, passing through Hennebont. At the intersection with D768, continue south along the signposted road to Carnac. From Lorient, take N165 east to Auray, and turn south on D768 to Carnac.

Links to Carnac by public transport are inconvenient, as there's no SNCF railway station in town. Instead, travelers, depending on the origin of their train and the season, get off the SNCF network at either Quiberon or Auray, two nearby towns, both of which lie on the SNCF lines. An additional option, available only between June and August, involves getting off in the hamlet of Plouharnel. From any of the above-mentioned towns, buses make between two and seven departures per day for the center of

Carnac. One-way transit into Carnac by bus from any of the above-mentioned hamlets ranges from 4€ to 5.50€ ($4.80–$6.60) per person, depending on the point of origin. Know in advance that the SNCF itself will usually advise you, when you buy your ticket to Carnac from other points throughout France, which of the above-mentioned hamlets is the most convenient for your descent.

For information about rail transits throughout the region, call © **08-92-35-35-35.** For more information about bus transit from any of the above-mentioned hamlets into Carnac, call © **02-97-21-28-29.**

VISITOR INFORMATION The **Office de Tourisme,** 74 av. des Druides (© **02-97-52-13-52;** www.carnac.fr), is open year-round.

SHOPPING

Carnac has two shopping areas: one along the beachfront called Carnac-Plage, and the other about 2.5km (1½ miles) inland in Carnac proper. Along the beach you'll find souvenir shops; venture down avenue des Druids and avenue de l'Atlantique for more specialized galleries and antiques stores. Other good areas are rue St-Cornély and place de l'Eglise, with a host of clothing and shoe stores, antiques dealers, and jewelers.

L'Enfant d'Armor, 2 place de l'Eglise (© **02-97-52-06-87**), offers an array of Breton embroidery. It's open from April to September. **Opale,** 10 rue St-Cornély (© **02-97-52-28-31**), sells unique creations of jewelry combining silver and semiprecious and precious stones, as well as mother-of-pearl. Go to **Clémentine,** avenue de l'Atlantique (© **02-97-52-96-34**), if you're in the market for quality household linens, porcelain, Breton fabric, and dishware.

WHERE TO STAY & DINE

Auberge le Ratelier ★ *Finds* BRETON A short walk from the center of Carnac Ville, this vine-covered, time-mellowed inn is one of our favorite dining stops in the area. It highlights local seafood, often using recipes handed down from generation to generation. Other dishes have been modernized—gazpacho with fresh prawns, seasoned with basil from the garden; and sea bream, flavored with lemon grass and served with potatoes. The owners are proud of their dessert specialty, a candied fruit ice cream with strawberries and honey.

The inn offers eight small, simple guest rooms, comfortably furnished and quite affordable. Doubles cost 45€ to 55€ ($59–$72).

4 chemin du Douët. © **02-97-52-05-04.** www.le-ratelier.com. Reservations required. Main courses 14€–32€ ($18–$42); fixed-price menu 18€–43€ ($23–$56). MC, V. Apr–Sept daily noon–2:30pm and 7:30–9:30pm; Oct–Mar Thurs–Mon noon–2:30pm and 7:30–9:30pm.

Hôtel Lann-Roz Within walking distance of the water, this oasis for the budget-minded is surrounded by a garden and lawns. The midsize guest rooms are modest yet comfortably furnished; the small bathrooms have tub/shower combinations. The dining room, which is open to the public, serves generous portions of regional food. Examples include fresh Breton tuna with basil and fresh noodles, a rillette (chunky terrine) of fish with shrimp and beurre blanc, and house-smoked salmon with creamy chive sauce. Dessert may be an apple and caramelized rhubarb tart.

36 av. de la Poste, Carnac 56340. © **02-97-52-10-48.** Fax 02-97-52-24-36. www.lannroz.com. 22 units. 47€–80€ ($61–$104) double. MC, V. Restaurant closed Jan 1–Apr 1. **Amenities:** Restaurant; bar. *In room:* TV.

Hôtel Le Diana ★ Located on the most popular beach, the Diana is the most reliable and best hotel in Carnac. The spacious, contemporary rooms have balconies that

Moments **The Wild, Wild Coast**

If you take D768 south from Carnac and follow it onto the peninsula (formerly an island) connected to the mainland by a narrow strip of alluvial deposits, you'll come to the port of **Quiberon,** with its white-sand beach. You'll probably see the rugged Breton fishers hauling in their sardine catch.

This entire coast—the **Côte Sauvage,** or Wild Coast—is dramatic and rugged; the ocean breaks with fury against the reefs. Winds, especially in winter, lash across the dunes, shaving the short pines that grow here. On the landward side, the beach is calm and relatively protected.

Sixteen kilometers (10 miles) west of Brittany's shoreline is Belle-Ile-en-Mer, an outpost of sand, rock, and vegetation the French love for summer holidays. For information, contact the **Office de Tourisme,** Quai Bonnelle Le Palais (✆ **02-97-31-81-93**). Depending on the season, 4 to 12 ferries depart daily from Port Maria in Quiberon (✆ **08-20-05-60-00**). The trip takes 45 minutes; a round-trip ticket costs 24€ ($31) for adults and 14€ ($18) for children under 25. In summer, you must reserve space for your car, as well as for passengers. The ferry docks at Le Palais, a fortified 16th-century port that is the island's window to the rest of France. Storm-wracked and eerie, the topography consists of rocky cliffs, a reef-fringed west coast, and the Grotte de l'Apothicairerie, a cave (closed to visitors) whose name derives from stalactites shaped like apothecary jars. Despite a scattering of hotels and seasonal restaurants, the island feels isolated. A drive around the periphery is about 56km (35 miles).

You'll find excellent accommodations in **Port de Goulphar,** on the southern shore on an inlet framed by cliffs. The standout is the 39-unit Relais & Châteaux property **Castel Clara,** Port de Goulphar, 56360 Bangor (✆ **02-97-31-84-21;** fax 02-97-31-51-69; www.castel-clara.com). Ideal service and first-class cuisine add to the sense of peace. The rooms are comfortable, with TVs and balconies facing the sea. The hotel also offers a terrace with a solarium around a heated seawater pool. Depending on the season, rates per person (including half board) range from 222€ to 315€ ($289–$410). The hotel is closed from mid-December to mid-February.

face the sea, comfortable beds, summery furniture, and small bathrooms with tub/shower combinations. The seafood restaurant also faces the water. Fixed-price menus cost 25€ ($33) each.

21 bd. de la Plage, Carnac Plage 56340. ✆ **02-97-52-05-38.** Fax 02-97-52-87-91. www.lediana.com. 31 units. 161€–245€ ($209–$319) double; 295€–420€ ($384–$546) suite. AE, DC, MC, V. Closed Nov–Apr. **Amenities:** Restaurant; bar; outdoor pool; exercise room; sauna; room service; babysitting; laundry service; dry cleaning; limited-mobility rooms. *In room:* TV, minibar, hair dryer, safe, Wi-Fi.

CARNAC AFTER DARK

Carnac doesn't stay up very late, but a few places are worth checking out. The **Whiskey Club,** 8 av. des Druides (✆ **02-97-52-10-52**), operates in an old stone house with two floors devoted to entertainment. The first offers an atmosphere conducive to conversation over drinks; the second is home to dancing and music. **Les Chandelles,** avenue de l'Atlantique (✆ **02-97-52-90-98**), pulls in a young, flashy crowd. The club plays mainly disco and charges a 10€ ($13) cover. As at most discos in France, no jeans or sneakers are allowed. The professional crowd gathers at **Petit Bedon,** 106 av. des Druides (✆ **02-97-52-11-62**). With its mixture of African and Mexican decor, this is the place to dance to '60s rock. There's no cover, but a beer will set you back 6.50€ ($8.45).

8 La Baule ★★★

452km (281 miles) W of Paris, 79km (49 miles) NW of Nantes

Founded during the Victorian seaside craze, La Baule remains as inviting as the Gulf Stream that warms the waters of its 8km (5-mile) crescent of white-sand beach. Occupying the Côte d'Amour (Coast of Love), it competes with Biarritz as the Atlantic coast's most fashionable resort. La Baule is essentially French, drawing only a small number of foreigners.

Gambler François André founded the casino and major resort hotels here. Pines grow on the dunes, and villas on the outskirts draw a chic crowd from late June to mid-September; if you arrive at any other time, you may have La Baule all to yourself. While the movie stars and flashy rich go to Deauville or Cannes, La Baule draws a more middle-class crowd, but the more reserved wealthy also come here—as the yachts in the harbor testify.

The town is north of a popular stretch of beachfront. The two main boulevards run parallel through the long, narrow town; the one closer to the ocean changes its name six times—at its most famous point, it's called boulevard de l'Océan.

Other than a rock outcropping much weathered by Atlantic storms, the beaches here are clean and sandy-bottomed, providing safe swimming and lots of options for admiring flesh in all states of fitness.

Avenue du Général-de-Gaulle and **avenue Louis-Lajarrige** have the best shops and boutiques. Next to the casino on esplanade de François-André, you'll find a minimall with 40 or so French chain stores and boutiques.

ESSENTIALS

GETTING THERE If you're **driving** from Nantes, take N165 northwest to Savenay and continue west along D773 to La Baule. The **train** trip from Nantes takes about an hour and costs 12€ ($16) one-way. The town's most convenient railway station is La Baule–Escoublac, in the heart of town. Try to avoid getting off at La Baule–Les Pins, which is 4km (2½ miles) northeast of the commercial center. For train information, call ✆ **08-92-35-35-35.**

VISITOR INFORMATION The **Office de Tourisme** is at 8 place de la Victoire (✆ **02-40-24-34-44;** www.labaule.fr).

WHERE TO STAY

Castel Marie-Louise ★★★ This turn-of-the-20th-century Breton manor offers grand lodgings in an oceanfront park. The public rooms are furnished in French Provincial style, with tapestries of animals. Most upper-floor units come with balconies; two are in a tower, each with a private terrace. Each sumptuous bathroom holds a tub and shower. Furnishings reflect several styles: Louis XV, Directoire, and rustic. The excellent chef is reason enough to stay here, and even if you aren't a guest, you may want to stop in for a meal of regional fare that dares to be different. Specialties are lobster, home-smoked salmon, and half-baked chocolate cake.

1 av. Andrieu, La Baule 44504. ✆ **02-40-11-48-38.** Fax 02-40-11-48-35. www.castel-marie-louise.com. 31 units. 160€–303€ ($208–$394) double; 385€–570€ ($501–$741) suite. Half board 78€ ($101) per person. AE, DC, MC, V. Closed mid-Nov to Dec. Parking 12€ ($16) July–Aug. **Amenities:** Restaurant; bar; nearby golf; room service; babysitting; limited-mobility rooms. *In room:* TV, minibar, hair dryer, safe.

Hôtel Bellevue-Plage This hotel is reliable, if not exciting, with a tranquil position in the center of the shoreline around the bay. Built around 1937, it has lost many of its original Art Deco features to renovation. The current modern, durable decor, often in tones of pale blue, is appropriate for a beach hotel. The comfortable rooms have small bathrooms with tub/shower combinations. Guests gravitate to the rooftop solarium and the ground-floor restaurant, which has a sweeping view. You'll also find a beach, sailboats for rent, and access to spa facilities.

27 bd. de l'Océan, La Baule 44500. ✆ **02-40-60-28-55.** Fax 02-40-60-10-18. www.hotel-bellevue-plage.fr. 35 units. 95€–180€ ($124–$234) double; 115€–185€ ($150–$241) suite. AE, DC, MC, V. Closed Jan. **Amenities:** Restaurant; bar; exercise room; sauna; room service; babysitting; laundry service. *In room:* TV, minibar, Wi-Fi.

Hôtel La Palmeraie ★ *Finds* In high-priced La Baule, this is a reasonably priced charmer. Built in the 1930s and renovated in the 1990s, it's named after eight large palms that thrive in the garden, thanks to the mild climate. Decorated in festive pink and white, La Palmeraie is near a beach and luxuriant with flowers in summer. The rooms are attractively decorated, often with English-style pieces. Each has high ceilings and dignified (sometimes antique) furniture. The only drawback: The soundproof rooms aren't all that soundproof. Half board is obligatory in July and August; the food, however, is hardly in the league of that at the first-class hotels. The management and staff are helpful and even friendly.

7 allée des Cormorans, La Baule 44500. ✆ **02-40-60-24-41.** Fax 02-40-42-73-71. www.hotel-lapalmeraie-labaule.com. 22 units. 56€–95€ ($73–$124) double; 85€–139€ ($111–$181) suite. Half board (required July–Aug) 65€–81€ ($85–$105) per person. AE, DC, MC, V. Closed Oct 1–Apr 1. **Amenities:** Restaurant; bar; babysitting. *In room:* TV, hair dryer.

WHERE TO DINE

Castel Marie-Louise (see "Where to Stay," above) also has a restaurant.

Barbade *Value* CLASSIC FRENCH With its verdant plants and big windows, Barbade looks like an oversize greenhouse. It offers competent, well-flavored cuisine that's fairly priced, particularly compared to many of the more expensive establishments nearby. Menu items include sole meunière, grilled dorado, stuffed oysters, a hefty chunk of baked goat cheese with a crisp outer skin, and the chef's pride, freshwater crayfish in puff pastry.

Bd. René Dubois (at the corner of av. Ramblais). ✆ **02-40-42-01-01.** Reservations recommended. Main courses 22€–35€ ($29–$46); fixed-price menus 15€ ($20) lunch, 32€ ($42) dinner. MC, V. Daily noon–3pm; Mon–Sat 8–11pm. Closed Nov–Feb.

LA BAULE AFTER DARK

The most visible nighttime venue is the **Casino de La Baule,** esplanade de Lucien Barrière (✆ **02-40-11-48-28**). Some areas are stylish, but it can't compete with the glamour of Deauville. Entrance to the slot machine area, open daily from 10am to 4am, is free. This section is open daily 9pm to 4am. The casino has a brasserie that serves lunch and dinner daily, as well as a sometimes-crowded disco, **L'Indiana** (✆ **02-40-11-48-28**), open nightly mid-June to mid-September, and Thursday to

Saturday mid-September to mid-June. Hours are midnight to 6am. The cover is 11€ ($14) and includes a drink.

Le Théâtre, 10 av. Pavie (✆ **02-40-60-41-00**), is the biggest, splashiest disco in town, noteworthy for the phallic-looking pillar rising from the big dance floor. It's close to the casino, in the heart of La Baule's resort neighborhood. From June to September it's open nightly from 11pm to 4am. The rest of the year, it's open only Thursday to Sunday (same hours). The region's only gay disco is **Le Petit Navire,** 5 rue du Général LeClerc (✆ **02-40-42-51-59**), in the resort community of Le Pouliguen, just 3km (1¾ miles) west of La Baule. Most of the crowd here comes just to drink and chat.

A stroll down avenue du Général-de-Gaulle or avenue Maréchale-de-Lattre-de-Tassigny will uncover any number of interesting bars and pubs. Newcomers feel welcome at **Le Bax,** 12 av. de Pavie (✆ **02-40-60-90-00**), a cozy environment that survives despite the seasonal clientele. Other choices include **Klimt Café,** 157 av. du Général-de-Gaulle (✆ **02-40-24-14-46**), and **Le Sailor,** 305 av. Maréchale-de-Lattre-de-Tassigny (✆ **02-40-60-24-49**). **Antidote,** 104 av. du Général-de-Gaulle (✆ **02-40-11-04-03**), is open only June to September.

9 Nantes ★★★

385km (239 miles) W of Paris, 325km (202 miles) N of Bordeaux

Nantes is Brittany's largest town, although in spirit it seems closer to the Loire Valley's château country. The mouth of the Loire is 48km (30 miles) away, and here it divides into several branches. Nantes is a busy port that suffered great damage in World War II. It's best known for the Edict of Nantes, issued by Henri IV in 1598, which guaranteed religious freedom to Protestants (it was later revoked). Many famous people, from Molière to Stendhal, have lived here. But Nantes hardly rests on its illustrious past. Now home to high-tech industries, it has some 30,000 college students and a population of half a million.

Built on the largest of three islands in the Loire, the city expanded in the Middle Ages to the northern edge of the river, where its center lies today. The most prominent building, the **Château des Ducs de Bretagne,** rises high above the wide boulevard quai de la Fosse, and regrettably will be closed for renovations throughout the life of this edition. Only the exterior can be viewed, except during temporary exhibitions. At one end of this boulevard is the train station; at the other are the promenades beside the Loire.

ESSENTIALS

GETTING THERE The **TGV** (fast train) from Paris's Gare Montparnasse takes about 2½ hours to get to Nantes and costs 51€ ($66). Beware of slower trains, which can take up to 5½ hours. For information, call ✆ **08-92-35-35-35.** Nantes's **Gare SNCF,** 27 bd. de Stalingrad, is a 5-minute walk from the town center. If you're **driving,** take A11 for 385km (239 miles) west of Paris. The trip takes about 3 hours. **Aéroport Nantes-Atlantique** (✆ **02-40-84-80-00**) is 12km (7½ miles) southeast of town. **Air France** (✆ **02-51-25-02-78**) offers daily flights from Paris. A shuttle bus between the airport and the Nantes train station takes 25 minutes and costs 6€ ($7.80). A taxi from the airport costs 25€ ($33) and takes about 15 minutes.

VISITOR INFORMATION The **Office de Tourisme** is at 3 cours Olivier de Clisson Commerce (✆ **08-92-46-40-44;** fax 02-40-89-11-99; www.nantes-tourisme.com).

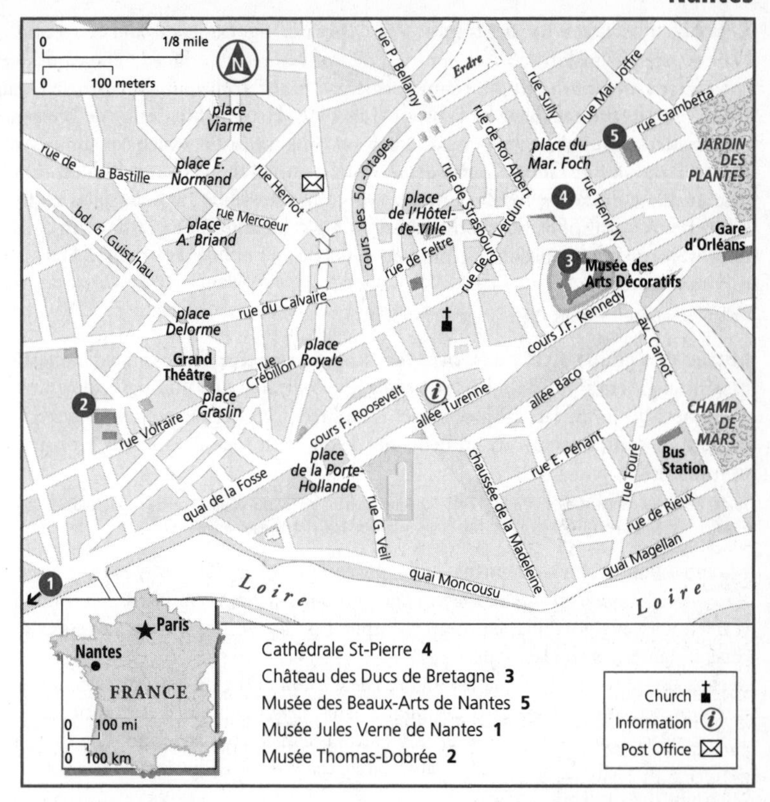

EXPLORING THE CITY

At the tourist office, you can buy a **Carte Nantes Décourvertes,** which allows you to enter museums and ride any of the city's public conveyances, including buses, trains, and some of the boats (summer only) that cruise along the river Erdre through the town. The pass costs 14€ ($18) for 1 day, 24€ ($31) for 2 days, and 30€ ($39) for 3 days.

Cathédrale St-Pierre ★★ Begun in 1434, this cathedral wasn't finished until the end of the 19th century, but it remained architecturally harmonious—a rare feat. Two square towers dominate the facade; more impressive is the 100m-long (328-ft.) interior. Its *pièce de résistance* is Michel Colomb's Renaissance tomb of François II, duc de Bretagne, and his second wife, Marguerite de Foix. Also noteworthy is the tomb of Gen. Juchault de Lamoricière, a Nantes native and a great African campaigner; sculptor Paul Dubois completed the tomb in 1879. After a 1972 fire destroyed the roof, the interior was restored. The white walls and pillars contrast with the rich colors of the stained-glass windows. The crypt, from the 11th century, shelters a museum of religions; at press time it was closed due to terrorist threats.

Place St-Pierre. ✆ **02-40-47-84-64.** Free admission. Summer daily 8:30am–7pm; off season daily 8:30am–6pm.

Château des Ducs de Bretagne ★★ Between the cathedral and the Loire is Nantes's second major sight, where the Edict of Nantes was signed. The castle was constructed in the 9th or 10th century, enlarged in the 13th century, destroyed, and rebuilt into its present shape by François II in 1466. His daughter, Anne de Bretagne, continued the work. Large towers and a bastion flank the castle, which contains a symmetrical section (the Grand Gouvernement) built during the 17th and 18th centuries. The duchesse du Berry, royal courtesan, was imprisoned here, as was Gilles de Retz ("Bluebeard"), one of France's most notorious mass murderers. The castle's rich collections were recently shaped into a museum of the history of Nantes from the 17th century to the present.

4 place Marc-Elder. Call Tourist Office for more information.

Musée des Beaux-Arts de Nantes ★ In one of western France's most interesting provincial galleries, you'll find an unusually fine collection of sculptures and paintings from the 12th to the late 19th centuries. The street level is devoted to mostly French modern or contemporary art created since 1900, with special emphasis on painters from the 1950s and 1960s.

10 rue Georges-Clemenceau. ✆ **02-51-17-45-00.** Admission 3.50€ ($4.55) adults, 1.50€ ($1.95) students 19–26, free for children under 19; free to all 1st Sun of every month. Wed–Mon 10am–6pm.

Musée Jules Verne de Nantes The novelist Jules Verne *(Journey to the Center of the Earth, Around the World in Eighty Days)* was born in Nantes in 1828. This museum is filled with memorabilia and objects inspired by his writings, from ink spots to a "magic" lantern with glass slides.

Fans also seek out Verne's house at 4 rue de Clisson in the Ile-Feydeau, which is privately owned and not open to the public. That neighborhood is a historic, mostly 18th-century area in the heart of the town. It was named after an island (l'Ile Feydeau) that became part of "mainland" Nantes after the river was diverted into a series of canals during the 18th century.

3 rue de l'Hermitage. ✆ **02-40-69-72-52.** Admission 3€ ($3.90) adults, 1€ ($1.30) for students, free for children under 7. Wed–Mon 10am–noon and 2–6pm.

Musée Thomas-Dobrée This 19th-century neo-Romanesque mansion was built by Thomas Dobrée, an important collector and traveler. It stands in the town center, adjacent to the 15th-century manor of Jean V, where the bishops of Nantes occasionally lived. You'll see Dobrée's eclectic collection, gathered during the height of France's Gilded Age, including prehistoric and medieval antiquities, Flemish paintings from the 15th century, ecclesiastical relics, paintings by masters such as Dürer, art objects from India, and the Dobrée family jewels. The collection and building were deeded to the Département de Loire-Atlantique after the death of M. Dobrée in 1894.

18 rue Voltaire. ✆ **02-40-71-03-50.** Admission 3€ ($3.90) adults; 1.50€ ($1.95) seniors, students, and children. Tues–Fri 1:30–5:30pm; Sat–Sun 2:30–5:30pm.

SHOPPING

Nantes overflows with shops and boutiques. The principal shopping streets are rue du Calvaire, rue Crébillon, rue Boileau, rue d'Orléans, rue de la Marne, rue de Verdun, and passage Pommeraye. Most of these encompass the shopping districts around place Graslin, place Royale, the château, and the cathedral. One of the prime areas for antiques is around place Aristide-Briand and rue Mercoeur.

Moments The Secret Garden of Nantes

Two blocks east of the cathedral, you can visit one of France's most beautiful gardens, the **Jardin des Plantes,** boulevard Stalingrad, adjacent to Gare SNCF (✆ **02-40-41-98-67**). The northern entrance is close to the Musée des Beaux-Arts, the southern border across from the train station. Admission is free. It's open daily 8am to 8pm.

Interesting antiques dealers include **Ecritoire Antiquités Poidras,** 12 rue Jean-Jaurès (✆ **02-40-47-78-18**), offering 18th- and 19th-century furniture and decorative pieces such as historic mantels.

For unusual gifts, check out the stores of two master artisans: **Maison Devineau,** 2 place Ste-Croix (✆ **02-40-47-19-59**), which brings the art of waxworking to a new level, "growing" bushels of fruits, flowers, and vegetables from liquid wax; and **Georges Gautier,** 9 rue de la Fosse (✆ **02-40-48-23-19**), a historic boutique established in 1823 with the town's best chocolates.

WHERE TO STAY

Hôtel de France ★ *Finds* Classified by the government as a historic monument, this well-run, beautifully maintained hotel dates from the 1700s. Many of the accommodations are decorated with reproductions of Louis XV– or Louis XVI–style furnishings. The comfortable midsize guest rooms have small bathrooms with a tub and shower. A few of the guest rooms are quite spacious, with high ceilings. The hotel is on a pedestrian-only street flanked with shops.

24 rue Crébillon, Nantes 44000. ✆ **02-40-73-57-91.** Fax 02-40-69-75-75. www.oceaniahotels.com. 74 units. 55€–160€ ($72–$208) double. Free parking. AE, MC, V. **Amenities:** Restaurant; bar; room service; nonsmoking rooms. *In room:* TV, minibar.

Hôtel Graslin *Value* The Graslin is on a steep old street near the harbor, in the center of town. There's a definite lassitude to the place, but the owners and managers, M. and Mme Roche, have given it many homelike touches. It offers more for the money than almost any other hotel in its price category. The comfortable rooms are bland and functional, with small, shower-only bathrooms.

1 rue Piron, Nantes 44000. ✆ **02-40-69-72-91.** Fax 02-40-69-04-44. www.ifrance.com/graslin. 47 units. 60€–87€ ($78–$113) double. AE, DC, MC, V. **Amenities:** Laundry service; dry cleaning; nonsmoking rooms. *In room:* TV, hair dryer, safe.

L'Hôtel Within sight of the château and the cathedral, this hotel is, for the price, a perfect base in Nantes. Built in the 1980s, the place is neat and modern but maintains an inviting atmosphere. The hotel boasts firm beds, rich colors, and contemporary furnishings. Some units have private balconies overlooking the château, while others open onto a garden and terrace. Each neatly tiled bathroom has a tub or shower. You'll find a paneled sitting area with couches and chairs next to the reception desk, as well as a softly lit breakfast room with terrace views.

6 rue Henri-IV, Nantes 44000. ✆ **02-40-29-30-31.** Fax 02-40-29-00-95. www.nanteshotel.com. 31 units. 79€ ($103) double. AE, MC, V. Parking 8€ ($10). **Amenities:** Room service; laundry service; dry cleaning; nonsmoking rooms; limited-mobility rooms. *In room:* A/C, TV, minibar, hair dryer, Wi-Fi.

WHERE TO DINE

La Cigale FRENCH/SEAFOOD This is Nantes's most historic and charming brasserie, decorated in a Belle Epoque style that has changed little since the place opened in 1895 across from the landmark Théâtre Graslin. Menu items may include platters of fresh shellfish, *confit des cuisses de canard* (duckling), and fresh scallops with green peppers and emulsified butter. The sprawling restaurant is usually quite loud, and the staff members tend to be overworked.

4 place Graslin. ✆ **02-51-84-94-94.** Reservations recommended. Main courses 14€–22€ ($18–$28); fixed-price menu 17€–26€ ($21–$34) MC, V. Daily 7:30am–12:30am. Bus: 11 or 34.

L'Atlantide ★★★ MODERN FRENCH On the fourth floor of the complex that houses the city's chamber of commerce, this panoramic restaurant, with views over the semi-industrial landscape, serves the finest cuisine in the area. The world-renowned designer Jean-Pierre Wilmotte created the nautical-looking enclave with lots of mirrors, but Jean-Yves Gueho's innovative cooking is what draws patrons. Menu items, steeped in the traditions of both the Loire Valley and the Breton coast, may include lobster salad with yellow-wine sauce; potato and herb tart capped with foie gras; Breton turbot with Cantonese spices; and braised sweetbreads with Anjou wine. An excellent dessert is bananas braised in local beer. The cellar is known for some of the finest vintages of Loire Valley wine anywhere, with an emphasis on Anjous and muscadets.

Centre des Salorges, 16 quai Ernest-Renaud. ✆ **02-40-73-23-23.** Reservations required. Main courses 28€–70€ ($36–$91); fixed-price dinner 35€–95€ ($46–$124). AE, V. Mon–Fri noon–2:30pm; Mon–Sat 8–9:45pm. Closed 1st 3 weeks of Aug and Dec 23–Jan 3.

Villa Mon Rêve MODERN FRENCH This restaurant, in a stone-sided 19th-century villa built by a prosperous producer of fruits and vegetables, is in a .4-hectare (1-acre) garden awash with roses in summer. Chef Gérard Ryngel's repertoire includes regional specialties and his own creations: wild duck with Bourgueil wine sauce, *sandre* (fish) from the Loire with beurre blanc, frogs' legs sautéed in white wine, and gazpacho studded with chunks of lobster. An unusual dish is roasted duckling with caramelized muscadet wine. The wine list features more than 40 local choices.

Rte. des Bords-de-Loire, Basse-Goulaine. ✆ **02-40-03-55-50.** Reservations recommended. Main courses 18€–32€ ($23–$42); fixed-price menu 22€–44€ ($29–$57). AE, DC, MC, V. Daily noon–1:30pm and 7–9:30pm. Closed 2 weeks in Feb and 2 weeks in early Nov. Take D751 8km (5 miles) south of Nantes.

NANTES AFTER DARK

When the sun goes down, the town turns into one big party. On **place du Bouffay, place du Pilori,** and **rue Kervégan,** you'll find lots of cafes and pubs, many with live music and fun people. A younger crowd rules **rue Scribe.**

The hippest location in Nantes, and the town's leading cultural center, is **Le Lieu Unique,** 2 rue de la Biscuiterie (✆ **02-51-82-15-00**). Converted from a 19th-century biscuit factory, the venue's presentations range from plays (in French) to art exhibitions. Admission is free to the dimly lit, concrete-floored bar at ground level, which is frequented by students and artists. A packed floor of young people dance to the sounds of DJs. Beer is cheap, only 2€ ($2.60) a mug. The bar is open Monday 11am to 8pm; Tuesday to Thursday 11am to 2am; Friday and Saturday 11am to 3am, and Sunday 3 to 8pm.

Catch some live blues, jazz, or rock at **L'Univers Café,** 16 rue Jean-Jacques-Rousseau (✆ **02-40-73-49-55**), or techno and disco at **Quai West,** 3 quai François-Mitterrand (✆ **02-40-47-68-45**), open all night. A great piano bar with a dance floor and occasional jazz concerts is **Le Tie Break,** 1 rue des Petites-Ecuries (© **02-40-47-77-00**).

The pump-it-up dance scene has a huge following of everyone from students to seniors. **Balapapa,** 24 quai François-Mitterrand (© **02-40-48-40-29**), has a real cabaret feel. In two rooms, it plays a mix ranging from big band to funk, and it attracts a crowd just as diverse. The cover is 14€ ($18). The over-30 crowd heads to the vintage 1970s disco **L'Evasion,** 3 rue de l'Emery (© **02-40-47-99-84**). Other popular discos are **Le Duplex,** place Emile-Zola (© **02-40-58-01-04**); **Le Royal Club Privé,** 7 rue des Salorges (© **02-40-69-11-10**); and **Wilton's Club,** 23 rue Rieux (© **02-40-12-01-13**). Don't wear jeans to any of these places, and be prepared to pay 10€ to 15€ ($13–$20) to get in.

The favorite with gays and lesbians is **Le Petit Marais,** 15 rue Kervégan (© **02-40-20-15-25**), where people meet and talk in a friendly atmosphere that welcomes everything from leather to lace. **Le Temps d'Aimer,** 14 rue Alexandre-Fourny (© **02-40-89-48-60**), is mixed and gay-friendly. This disco with its small dance floor attracts a sophisticated crowd. The most you'll pay to get in is 10€ ($13). Newer than either of the above-mentioned bars is a mostly gay pub, **L'Egout et les Couleurs,** 2 rue Kervégan (© **02-40-20-58-58**).

11

The Champagne Country

Taking about 3 days, you can take the Autoroute de l'Est (N3) from Paris and explore a region of cathedrals, historic battlefields, great food, and vineyards, topping your tour with a glass or two of bubbly. On the Routes du Champagne, you can drive to the wine-producing center of Epernay, on to Reims, 145km (90 miles) northeast of Paris. After visiting Reims and its cathedral, you can head toward Verdun, of World War I fame.

1 La Ferté-sous-Jouarre

66km (41 miles) E of Paris, 82km (51 miles) SW of Reims

The little town of La Ferté-sous-Jouarre and the village of Jouarre are twin communities—you can't tell where one ends and the other begins. Although La Ferté-sous-Jouarre, which took its name from a now-gone 10th-century fortress, played a role in French history, it is of little interest today and is worth a visit chiefly for the lodging at Château des Bondons (see below).

In the village of Jouarre, 3km (1¾ miles) south of La Ferté-sous-Jouarre, you can visit a 12th-century Benedictine abbey and explore one of the oldest crypts in France. At the **Tour et Crypt de l'Abbaye de Jouarre,** 6 rue Montmorin (✆ **01-60-22-06-11**), those interested in medieval history will appreciate the documents referring to the Royal Abbey of Jouarre as well as the stones in the Merovingian crypt, which evoke the 7th century. There's also a collection of prehistoric artifacts, remnants of the Roman occupation, and sculptural fragments. Each of these monuments is a medieval treasure. Entrance to the crypt costs 4.50€ ($5.85) for adults and 4€ ($5.20) for students and children under 18. Entrance to the tower is 4.50€ ($5.85) for adults and 4€ ($5.20) for students and children under 18. One floor above the crypt, a small-scale museum, **Musée Briard,** showcases the medieval history of the region of Brie. Entrance to the museum costs 2.50€ ($3.25) for adults and 2€ ($2.60) for children.

The crypt is the star of the three attractions, the tower somewhat less famous and evocative. All three sites are open Wednesday to Monday 10:15am to noon and 2 to 4:15pm.

ESSENTIALS

GETTING THERE If you're **driving,** take N3 along the Marne. About 10 **trains** per day make the 55-minute run from Paris's Gare de l'Est, stopping at La Ferté-sous-Jouarre. From there, take a taxi 3km (1¾ miles) south to Jouarre and its abbey. For train reservations and schedules, call ✆ **08-92-35-35-35,** or visit www.voyages-sncf.com.

VISITOR INFORMATION The **Office de Tourisme** in Jouarre is on rue de la Tour, adjacent to the tower and the abbey (✆ **01-60-22-64-54;** fax 01-60-22-65-15; www.tourisme-jouarre.com).

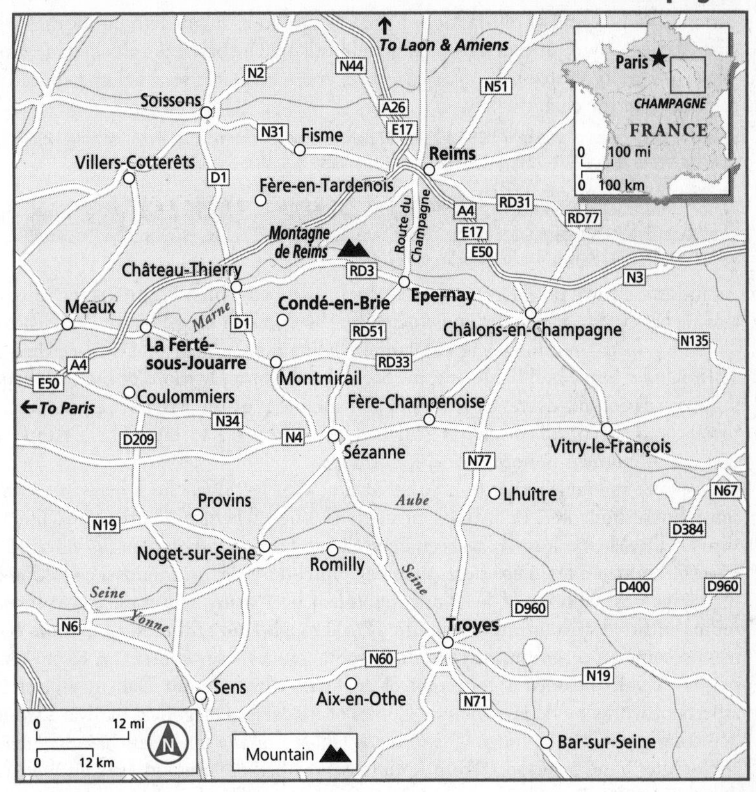

WHERE TO STAY

Château des Bondons ★★ Surrounded by a 24-hectare (59-acre) park and forest, this château dates from the French Revolution. The doomed Louis XVI and Marie-Antoinette were brought here following their arrest at Varennes in June 1791. They were then taken to Paris and executed. Not much of the furniture is original to the building; an English aesthetic, complete with chintz upholstery and British antiques, characterizes the public areas. As befits a château, guest rooms come in a variety of shapes, but they are all comfortable, filled with old and new furnishings, plus tub/shower combinations.

47–49 rue des Bondons, La Ferté-sous-Jouarre 77260. Follow signs to Montménard; take D70 for 2.5km (1½ miles) east of the town center. ✆ **01-60-22-00-98.** Fax 01-60-22-97-01. castel@chateaudesbondons.com. 14 units. 55€–62€ ($72–$81) double. AE, DC, MC, V. **Amenities:** Restaurant; bar; room service; laundry service; dry cleaning. *In room:* TV, minibar, hair dryer, Wi-Fi.

WHERE TO DINE

Château des Bondons (see above) has a restaurant.

Le Plat d'Etain TRADITIONAL FRENCH This homelike, conservative restaurant caters to the gastronomic needs of art-history lovers who make the pilgrimage to see the famous Merovingian crypt, which is nearby. It has exposed ceiling beams, lacy curtains, and tokens of old-fashioned France. The food might remind locals of the style of cuisine once prepared by their grandmothers. The best examples include *blanquette de veau* (veal stew), *boeuf bourguignon,* and whatever is seasonal and appeals to the whims of the chef.

6 place Auguste-Tinchant, Jouarre. ✆ **01-60-22-06-07.** Reservations recommended. Main courses 10€–25€ ($13–$33); fixed-price menus 12€–26€ ($16–$34). MC, V. Daily noon–2pm; Mon–Sat 6:30–9pm.

2 Château-Thierry

90km (56 miles) E of Paris, 9.5km (6 miles) SW of Reims

An industrial town on the Marne's right bank, Château-Thierry contains the ruins of a castle believed to have been constructed for the Frankish king Thierry IV. Château-Thierry gained fame for being the farthest point the German offensive reached in 1918. Under heavy bombardment, the Second and Third Divisions of the U.S. Expeditionary Force aided French troops. The battlefields of the Marne are just west of town; thousands of Allied soldiers who died in World War I are buried here. Atop Hill 204 is a monument honoring American troops.

The poet and fable writer Jean de la Fontaine (1621–95) was born here, in a stone-sided house built in 1452. Today, it contains one of France's most-visited literary shrines, the **Musée Jean-de-la-Fontaine,** 12 rue Jean de la Fontaine (✆ **03-23-69-05-60**). Located a few steps from place de l'Hôtel-de-Ville, it contains a collection of his mementos, editions of his works published over many centuries, and a trio of rooms outfitted with furniture from the 17th through 19th centuries. Each room centers on some aspect of the effect of de la Fontaine on those centuries. A recent temporary exhibit included a collection of engravings by Salvador Dalí that illustrate aspects of works by de la Fontaine. Copies of his fables (allegorical barnyard stories depicting the foibles of humans) and *contes* (short stories a lot racier than the fables) are for sale in the bookshop. From April to September, the museum is open Wednesday to Monday 9am to noon and 2 to 6pm. From October to March, it's open Wednesday to Monday 10am to noon and 2 to 5pm. Admission is 3.40€ ($4.40) for adults, 2.10€ ($2.75) students, and 1.70€ ($2.20) for children under 18; it's free to everyone on Wednesday.

If you're interested in World War I, head 8km (5 miles) northwest of Château-Thierry to the **Bois de Belleau (Belleau Wood).** The Battle of Belleau Wood marked the second clash between American and German troops in World War I and demonstrated the bravery of the U.S. soldiers. After a 2-week struggle, the Second Division of the U.S. Expeditionary Force under Maj. Gen. Omar Bundy took the woods. Though the Germans suffered many losses and some 1,650 prisoners were taken, U.S. casualties were appalling—more than 8,000 American troops were wounded, killed, or missing. In 1923, the battleground was dedicated as a memorial to the men who gave their lives here. The **American cemetery,** also known as Le Cimetière de Belleau (✆ **03-23-70-70-90**), contains 2,288 graves. You'll also see a chapel that was damaged in World War II. Entrance is free; it's open 24 hours daily.

ESSENTIALS

GETTING THERE If you're **driving,** take A4 southwest from Reims or northeast from La Ferté-sous-Jouarre. There are **trains** from Paris's Gare de l'Est (16€/$19 one-way) and Reims (16€/$21 one-way); each trip takes 1 hour. For information, call ✆ **08-92-35-35-35.**

VISITOR INFORMATION The **Office de Tourisme** is at 11 rue Vallée (✆ **03-23-83-10-14;** fax 03-23-83-14-74; www.otsichateau-thierry.com).

WHERE TO STAY

Ile-de-France This modern hotel is the leading choice in an area of not-so-hot options. In 2004 the hotel shrank from 50 units to just 32, making all the accommodations larger and more comfortable. In a park overlooking the Marne Valley, near the ruins of the town's château, the four-story structure boasts balconies and dormers, a view of the town, and well-maintained guest rooms. About half of the bathrooms have tubs as well as showers.

Rte. de Soissons, Château-Thierry 02400. ✆ **03-23-69-10-12.** Fax 03-23-83-49-70. www.hotel-iledefrance.fr. 32 units. 70€–90€ ($91–$117) double; 140€ ($182) suite. AE, DC, MC, V. **Amenities:** Restaurant; bar; fitness center; spa; indoor pool; business center; room service; babysitting; laundry service; nonsmoking rooms; limited-mobility rooms. *In room:* TV, hair dryer.

WHERE TO DINE

Auberge Jean-de-la-Fontaine TRADITIONAL FRENCH The town's best restaurant is filled with paintings on wood panels dedicated to the fables of la Fontaine. The menu changes every 2 to 3 months; it may include dishes such as salmon smoked in-house or an appetizer of duck "in all its states" (breast, smoked thigh with confit of gizzards, and a slice of liver). Main courses range from warm pâté of freshwater *sandre* (fish) with Breton lobster to a regional dish of chitterling sausages garnished with pigs' foot. Dessert may be crème brûlée with bitter almonds.

10 rue des Filoirs. ✆ **03-23-83-63-89.** Reservations required. Fixed-price menu 12€–15€ ($16–$20). MC, V. Sun–Fri 12:30–2pm; Tues–Sat 7:30–9pm. Closed Jan 1–16 and first 3 weeks of Aug.

3 Condé-en-Brie ★

89km (55 miles) E of Paris, 24km (15 miles) W of Epernay

West of Epernay, **Château de Condé** ★, rue du Château, 02330 Condé-en-Brie (✆ **03-23-82-42-25**), was bequeathed to the *comte* de Sade in 1814 and remained in his family until 1983. The name gained notoriety from the works of the marquis, an innovative writer *(Justine, Juliette, The 120 Days of Sodom)* whose sexual practices as described in his works gave us the word *sadism.*

Enguerrand of Coucy built the castle in the late 12th century. A part of the old keep—two big rooms with great chimneys and thick walls—survives. Cardinal de Bourbon, a member of the royal family, reconstructed the castle in the Renaissance style early in the 16th century. His nephew, Louis de Bourbon, called himself the Prince de Condé, most likely because he had many fond childhood memories of the place. After sustaining damage in the 18th century, the château was rebuilt for the marquis de La Faye. The Italian architect Servandoni invited artists Boucher and Watteau to do frescoes and paintings, which you can see today. Servandoni decorated the largest room, making it a theater for music and entertainment. The present castle is exceptional, with its paintings, woodwork, chimneys, and so-called Versailles floor.

In 1994, the new owners, the de Rocheforts, discovered several Watteau frescoes behind mirrors installed during the 18th century. Now, at the push of a button, the mirrors open to reveal the previously hidden treasures.

Admission is 8€ ($10) for adults, 4€ ($5.20) for children 6 to 13, and free for children 5 and under. The castle is open only during the afternoon, and only between mid-April and mid-October, Tuesday to Sunday from 2:30 to 5:30pm. Visits are self-guided, conducted with the help of a free leaflet outlining the history of the building and some of its most important features. It's closed to casual visitors between mid-October and mid-April. Families with children sometimes opt to collectively follow a self-guided treasure hunt, whereby the gift at the end of the hunt is a key that opens a treasure chest loaded with candy and simple toys.

If you're **driving** between Château-Thierry and Epernay on N3, head south at Dormans, and follow the signs to Condé-en-Brie.

4 Reims ★★★

143km (89 miles) E of Paris, 45km (28 miles) NW of Châlons-en-Champagne

Reims (pronounced *Rahns*), an ancient Roman city, was important when Caesar conquered Gaul. French kings came here to be crowned, and it's said that the French nation was born here in A.D. 498. Joan of Arc escorted Charles VII here in 1429, kissing the silly man's feet. But don't let its ancient background mislead you: As you approach Reims, you'll pass through prefabricated suburbs that look like eastern European apartment-house blocks. There are gems in Reims, including the cathedral, but you must seek them out.

Most visitors come to Reims because it's the center of a winegrowing district; its bubbly is present at celebrations all over the world. The city (pop. 191,000) is filled with swank restaurants, ritzy champagne houses, large squares, and long, tree-lined avenues. The champagne bottled here has the lightest and most subtle flavor in the world. Make an effort to linger, and explore the vineyards and wine cellars, the Gothic monuments, and the battlefields.

ESSENTIALS

GETTING THERE If you're **driving** from Paris, take A4 east. **Trains** depart from Paris's Gare de l'Est every 1½ hours (trip time: 1½ hr.); the one-way fare is 22€ ($29). Five trains per day arrive from Strasbourg (trip time: 3 hr.; one-way fare 52€/$67). For information, call ✆ **08-36-35-35-35,** or visit www.voyages-sncf.com.

VISITOR INFORMATION The **Office de Tourisme** is at 2 rue Guillaume-de-Machault (✆ **03-26-77-45-00;** fax 03-26-77-45-19; www.reims-tourisme.com).

EXPLORING THE CITY

Basilique St-Rémi ★★ This church dates from 1007, making it the oldest in Reims. Though an example of classic medieval French masonry, it's often unfavorably compared to the more spectacular cathedral. Within the complex is the former royal abbey of St-Rémi, who as the guardian of the holy ampula used to anoint the kings of France. The abbey now functions as a museum, with an extensive collection covering the history of Reims, regional archaeology, and military history. Architect Louis Duroché designed the majestic ornamental front of the main quadrangle and the Grand Staircase (1778), where you can admire a portrait of the young Louis XV in his coronation robes. The church also contains a Romanesque nave leading to a magnificent choir crowned with pointed arches. The nave, the transepts, one of the towers, and the aisles date from the 11th century; the portal of the south transept is in early-16th-century Flamboyant Gothic style. Some of the stained glass in the apse is from the 13th century. The tomb of St. Rémi is elaborately carved with Renaissance figures and columns.

Reims

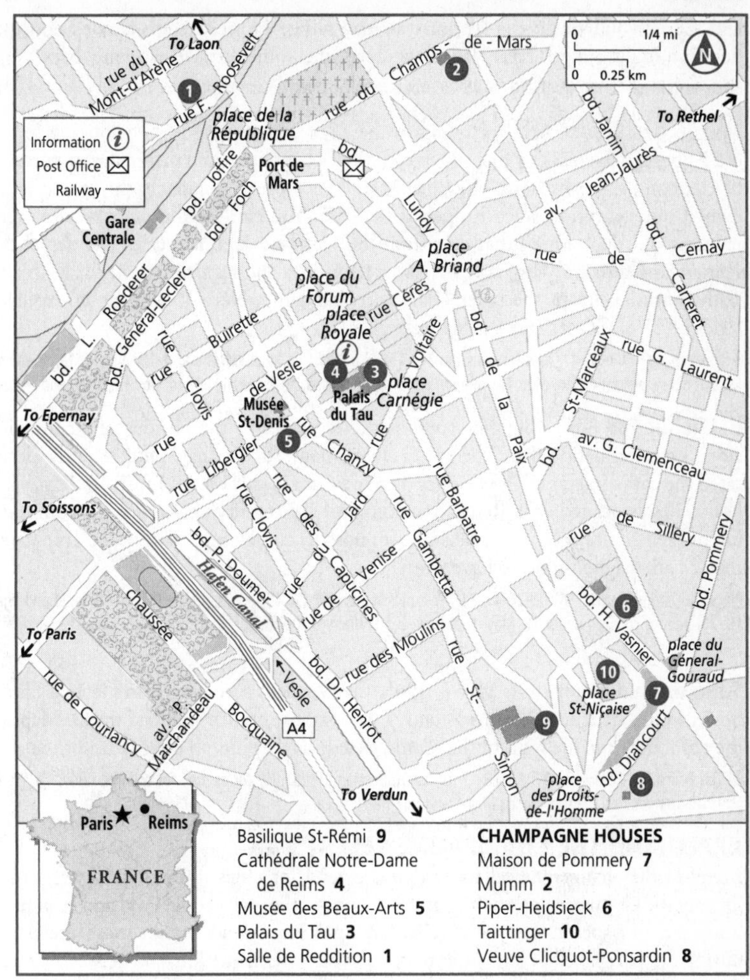

53 rue St-Simon. Basilique: ✆ **03-26-85-31-20.** Free admission. Daily 8am–7pm. Musée: ✆ **03-26-85-23-36.** Admission 3€ ($3.90) adults, free for children under 12. Mon–Fri 2–6:30pm; Sat–Sun 2–7pm.

Cathédrale Notre-Dame de Reims ★★★ One of the world's most famous cathedrals was restored after World War I, funded largely by contributions from John D. Rockefeller; it escaped World War II relatively unharmed. Built on the site of a church that burned in 1211, it was intended as a sanctuary where French kings would be anointed. St-Rémi, the bishop of Reims, baptized Clovis, the king of the Franks, here in A.D. 496. All the kings of France from Louis the Pious in 815 to Charles X in 1825 were crowned here.

Laden with statuettes, its three western facade portals are spectacular. A rose window above the central portal is dedicated to the Virgin. The right portal portrays the Apocalypse and the Last Judgment; the left, martyrs and saints. At the western facade's northern door is a smiling angel. Lit by lancet windows, the immense nave has many bays.

Place du Cardinal-Luçon. ✆ **03-26-77-45-25.** Free admission. Daily 7:30am–7:30pm.

Musée des Beaux-Arts Housed in the 18th-century buildings belonging to the old Abbaye St-Denis, this fine provincial gallery contains more than a dozen portraits of German princes by both "the Elder" and "the Younger" Cranach; the museum has owned this collection since it opened in 1795. You can see the *toiles peintes* (light painting on rough linen) that date from the 15th and 16th centuries and depict the *Passion du Christ* and *Vengeance du Christ.* Paintings and furniture from the 17th and 18th centuries are in the salles Diancourt and Jamot-Neveux. There's an excellent series of 27 of Corot's tree-shaded walks.

8 rue Chanzy. ✆ **03-26-47-28-44.** Admission 3€ ($3.90) adults, free for students and children under 18; free to all 1st Sun of every month. Wed–Mon 10am–noon and 2–6pm. Closed Jan 1, May 1, July 14, Nov 1 and 11, and Dec 25.

Palais du Tau ★★ Built in 1690 as the residence of the bishops of Reims, this stone mansion beside the cathedral contains many statues that, until recently, decorated the cathedral facade. (The ones there now are mostly copies.) Also on display are holy relics associated with Reims, including a 12th-century chalice for the communion of French monarchs and a talisman supposedly containing a relic of the True Cross that Charlemagne is said to have worn.

Place du Cardinal-Luçon. ✆ **03-26-47-81-79.** Admission 6.50€ ($8.45) adults, 4.50€ ($5.85) students and ages 18–25, free for children under 18. May–Sept Tues–Sun 9:30am–6:30pm; Sept–Oct Tues–Sun 9:30am–12:30pm and 2–5:30pm.

Salle de Reddition On May 7, 1945, the Germans surrendered to General Eisenhower in this structure, which was once a schoolhouse near the railroad tracks. Maps of the rail routes line the walls of the rooms, exactly as they did on the day of surrender.

12 rue Franklin-D-Roosevelt. ✆ **03-26-47-84-19.** Admission 3€ ($3.90) adults, free for children under 18. Wed–Mon 10am–noon and 2–6pm. Closed May 1 and July 14.

EXPLORING THE CHAMPAGNE CELLARS ★★

Many of the champagne cellars of Reims extend for miles through chalky deposits. During the German siege of 1914 and throughout the war, people lived and even published a daily paper in them. The cellars are open year-round, but are most interesting during the fall grape harvest. After that, the wine is fermented in vats in the caves and then bottled with a small amount of sugar and natural yeast. The yeast feeds on the sugar and causes a second fermentation that produces those fabulous bubbles. The winegrowers wait until the sparkle has "taken" before they move the bottles to racks or pulpits. For about 3 months, *remueurs* (migrant workers) turn them every day, which brings the impurities (dead yeast cells and other matter) toward the cork. Eventually the sediments are removed and the wine is given its proper dosage (sugar dissolved in wine), depending on the desired sweetness. The process takes 4 or 5 years and takes place in caves that are 30m (98 ft.) deep, where the temperature is a constant 50°F (10°C).

Maison de Pommery Among the most visited cellars are those under the Gothic-style buildings and gardens of the Maison de Pommery. A magnificent 116-step stairway leads to a maze of galleries dug into the chalk; the complex is more than 18km (11 miles) long and about 30m (98 ft.) below ground. Various stages of champagne making are shown, and the end product is for sale in the gift shop.

Place du Général-Gouraud. ✆ **03-26-61-62-55.** www.pommery.com. Admission 10€–15€ ($13–$20); free for children under 12. Reservations required. Daily 9:30am–7pm.

Mumm Founded in 1827, Mumm welcomes visitors with a video that explains how champagne is made. An in-house museum exhibits casks and illustrates the ancient role of the vintner. A guide will lead visitors into a labyrinth of tunnels and storage cellars in the chalky bedrock; they contain a vast inventory—almost 25 million bottles—of slowly fermenting champagne.

34 rue du Champ-de-Mars. ✆ **03-26-49-59-70.** www.mumm.com. Tours (in English) 7.50€ ($9.75) adults, free for children under 16. Reservations required. Mar–Oct daily 9–11am and 2–5pm.

Piper-Heidsieck This firm, one of the oldest champagne houses in the world, was established in 1785. You explore the cellars in an electric-powered car known as *une nacelle* (it holds five passengers) and enjoy a tasting at the end of the tour. The cellars were dug throughout the 19th century directly into the chalky substrata. More than 13 million bottles are in inventory. Champagne is available in the gift shop.

51 bd. Henri-Vasnier. ✆ **03-26-84-43-44.** www.piper-heidsieck.com. Admission 8€ ($10) adults, 4.50€ ($5.85) children 6–18, free for children under 6. Mar–Dec daily 9:30–11:45am and 2–5pm; Jan–Feb Mon–Fri 9:30–11:45am and 2–5pm.

Taittinger Taittinger is a grand *marque* of French champagne, one of the few still controlled by members of the family that founded it (in 1930). It's one of the most visitor-friendly champagne houses. The Romanesque cellars were dug from the site of Gallo-Roman chalk mines in use from the 4th to the 13th century. Tours—including a film, a guided cellar visit, and anecdotes about Reims, the champagne-making process, and Taittinger family lore—last about an hour.

9 place St-Nicaise. ✆ **03-26-85-84-35.** www.taittinger.com. Admission 7€ ($9.10) adults, free for children under 12. Mar–Nov Mon–Fri 9:30am–1pm and 2–5:30pm, Sat–Sun 9–11am and 2–5pm; Dec–Feb Mon–Fri 9:30am–noon and 2–4:30pm.

Veuve Clicquot–Ponsardin One of the most memorable and successful logos in France shows a 19th-century matriarch, Nicole Ponsardin, outfitted in dowdy but expensive finery. She remained firmly in control of the *maison de champagne* that bears her name from 1866 (when her husband died) to 1895. You can visit some of the 26km (16 miles) of underground galleries as part of guided tours that last 75 to 90 minutes.

1 place des Droits-de-l'Homme. ✆ **03-26-89-53-90.** www.veuve-clicquot.com. Admission 8€–11€ ($10–$14). Reservations required. Apr–Sept Mon–Sat 10am–6pm. Closed Sat Oct–Mar.

SHOPPING

The main shopping district is around the cathedral. Nearby streets to browse are the long **rue de Vesle,** the **cours Langlet,** and **place Drouet d'Erlon.**

You'll want to include champagne on your shopping list. Many people opt to visit one of the major houses in town; others drive along the **Routes du Champagne.** This is where you'll find the smaller champagne makers. When you're making the rounds, know that most houses prefer that you take the tour and not just stop in the shop. If you do take the tour, you'll at least get a glass of bubbly at the end. Bottles are priced individually, but you can get discounts if you buy three or six bottles. If you're looking for a good deal, you may want to buy at a store in town, such as **Le Marché aux Vins, Pérardel,** 3 place Léon-Bourgeois (✆ **03-26-40-12-12**). It stocks one of the most comprehensive inventories of champagne in Reims, with 150 types of bubbly from more than 100 companies. They include many superb brands for 12€ to 27€ ($16–$35) per bottle, which are virtually never advertised in North America. Excellent, lesser-known brands include Deutz, Billecart Salmon, Henriot, Guy Charlemagne, and Erick de Sousa. Staff members speak English.

Another specialty is the light, delicious little pink cookie known as *biscuit de Reims.* The best place to find this treat is **La Maison Fossier/Biscuits Fossier,** 25 cours Langlet (✆ **03-26-47-59-84**). For chocolate and candied specialties, try **La Petite Friande,** 15 cours Langlet (✆ **03-26-47-50-44**), where you can purchase liqueur-filled chocolate champagne bubbles and corks.

Parc des Expositions (✆ **03-26-84-69-69**), route de Châlons-en-Champagne (4km/2½ miles east of Reims), plays host to a flea market the first Sunday of every month except July and August. On the first weekend of April, there's a huge "Euro" flea market, with more than 500 vendors, in the same location. The organization responsible for these events is **Artcom/Puces de Reims,** 82 rue Jacquart (✆ **03-26-02-04-06**).

WHERE TO STAY

EXPENSIVE

Grand Hotel des Templiers ★★ This chic hotel a short walk from the cathedral is small, but it's your best inner-city bet. In a restored 1800s mock-Gothic house, antiques, ornate ceilings, and hand-carved woodwork create an inviting ambience. The guest rooms maintain the 19th-century atmosphere, with color-coordinated fabrics and bold-print wall coverings. Each comes with a quality bed and well-maintained bathroom, most often with both tub and shower.

22 rue des Templiers, Reims 51100. ✆ **03-26-88-55-08.** Fax 03-26-47-80-60. 18 units. 190€–280€ ($247–$364) double; 350€ ($455) suite. AE, DC, MC, V. Bus: G or H. **Amenities:** Bar; indoor heated pool; sauna; laundry service; nonsmoking rooms; limited-mobility rooms. *In room:* A/C, TV, minibar, hair dryer, safe.

Les Crayères ★★★ In Reims, there's no better place to stay or dine than here, one of the finest châteaux in eastern France. Located in a 5.6-hectare (14-acre) park, it has 5.5m (18-ft.) ceilings, paneling, and luxurious furnishings. The guest rooms, with terraces and all the amenities, are individually decorated in a country-manor style and usually available when a champagne mogul isn't in residence. The bathrooms hold deluxe toiletries and tub/shower combinations. The restaurant is the greatest in the region (see "Where to Dine," below).

64 bd. Henri-Vasnier, Reims 51100. ✆ **03-26-82-80-80.** Fax 03-26-82-65-52. www.lescrayeres.com. 20 units. 290€–490€ ($377–$637) double; 500€–530€ ($650–$689) suite. AE, DC, MC, V. Closed Dec 20–Jan 11. **Amenities:** Restaurant; bar; tennis court; room service; babysitting; laundry service; dry cleaning; nonsmoking rooms; limited-mobility rooms. *In room:* A/C, minibar, hair dryer, safe, Wi-Fi.

MODERATE

L'Assiette Champenoise ★★ *Finds* About 3km (1¾ miles) southwest from Reims in the suburb of Tinqueux, this is the second-best hotel and restaurant in the area. Built in the 1970s among century-old trees, it occupies part of a former Norman estate, standing in a 1.6-hectare (4-acre) park. The well-maintained rooms are attractively furnished in a mix of French traditional and modern style; bathrooms have tub/shower combinations. Many visitors come here just for the rustic dining room. Chef Arnaud Lallement's cuisine covers a medley of classics, some with an innovative twist. Try John Dory with ragout of vegetables, suckling veal with seven vegetables, or grilled duck liver with fondue of tomatoes. Homemade foie gras is always a reliable starter.

40 av. Paul-Vaillant-Couturier, Tinqueux 51430. From Reims, take A4 west toward Paris and exit at SORTIE 22–TINQUEUX; av. Paul-Vaillant-Couturier will lead you directly to Tinqueux. ✆ **03-26-84-64-64.** Fax 03-26-04-15-69. www.assiette champenoise.com. 55 units. 142€–282€ ($185–$367) double; 250€ ($325) suite. AE, DC, MC, V. Free parking. **Amenities:** Restaurant; bar; indoor pool; sauna; laundry service; limited-mobility rooms. *In room:* TV, minibar, hair dryer, safe.

INEXPENSIVE

Best Western Hôtel de la Paix Located between the train station and the cathedral, this is the only modern hotel in France with a medieval chapel (built for Benedictine nuns in the 1200s) overlooking its garden and pool. Constructed in 1946, it has been enlarged since then. The rooms in this pleasant chain hotel are contemporary and well maintained, and many are air-conditioned. Furnishings are a bit sterile, but the beds are comfortable and most bathrooms have tub/shower combinations. The hotel's **Taverne de Maître Kanter** (✆ **03-26-47-00-45**) serves excellent meals daily at lunch and dinner. The cuisine may include sauerkrauts, fish, grills, oysters, and casseroles.

9 rue Buirette, Reims 51100. ✆ **800/528-1234** in the U.S. and Canada, or 03-26-40-04-08. Fax 03-26-47-75-04. www.bestwestern-lapaix-reims.com. 175 units. 115€–150€ ($150–$195) double. AE, DC, MC, V. Parking 10€ ($13). Bus: G or H. **Amenities:** Restaurant; bar; indoor pool; fitness center; sauna; room service; nonsmoking rooms. *In room:* A/C, TV, minibar, hair dryer, beverage maker.

Grand Hôtel de l'Univers In the heart of Reims, across from the train station, this five-story hotel offers small- to average-size guest rooms outfitted in a basic manner. All but three bathrooms have tub/shower combinations. This area can get noisy, but rooms have double-paned windows. You can have breakfast in the American-style piano bar, where an automated piano plays melodies whenever you press a button, or dinner in the small but well-managed restaurant, which specializes in traditional French cuisine and offers fixed-price menus.

41 bd. Foch, Reims 51100. ✆ **03-26-88-68-08.** Fax 03-26-40-95-61. www.hotel-univers-reims.com. 42 units. 64€–90€ ($83–$117) double. AE, DC, MC, V. **Amenities:** Restaurant; bar; room service; laundry service; limited-mobility rooms. *In room:* TV, minibar, hair dryer, safe.

Grand Hôtel du Nord This late-19th-century hotel is a former relay station for the postal service. The high-ceilinged guest rooms are renovated and decorated in comfortable contemporary style. The hotel lies in a pedestrian-only zone in Reims's historic core, a 10-minute walk from the cathedral and just steps from the rail station. All but five rooms have showers; the rest have tub/shower combos. Two steps from the entrance, lively place Drouet-d'Erlon has many boutiques, cafes, and cinemas. The hotel is also near the cathedral, the basilica, and various museums.

75 place Drouet-d'Erlon, Reims 51100. ✆ **03-26-47-39-03.** Fax 03-26-40-92-26. www.hotelreims.com. 50 units. 60€–70€ ($78–$91) double. AE, DC, MC, V. Parking 6€ ($7.80). Take A4 (A26) to Reims-Centre. Bus: G or H. **Amenities:** Nonsmoking rooms. *In room:* TV, hair dryer.

Mercure Reims Cathédrale ★ *Value* This chain hotel from the 1970s sits on the banks of the Marne Canal, a 5-minute walk from the town center and the cathedral. It's near the entrance to the highway, so it's easy to find. The good-size rooms, each renovated in 2001, have all the modern conveniences, including bathrooms with tubs and showers; some boast views of a waterway. Furnishings are standard motel style.

31 bd. Paul-Doumer, Reims 51100. ✆ **03-26-84-49-49.** Fax 03-26-84-49-84. www.mercure.com. 126 units. 123€ ($160) double; 168€ ($218) suite. AE, DC, MC, V. Parking 10€ ($13). **Amenities:** Restaurant; bar; room service; babysitting; laundry service; nonsmoking rooms. *In room:* A/C, TV, minibar, hair dryer, beverage maker.

WHERE TO DINE

L'Assiette Champenoise (see "Where to Stay," above) has an excellent restaurant.

Le Chardonnay ★★ TRADITIONAL FRENCH This cozy establishment serves superb cuisine in a restored building managed by members of the Lange family. You're likely to be greeted by Chantal and her daughters, the team that oversees the dining room, which overlooks a flowering courtyard. The cuisine is remarkably consistent, with sauces often based on a generous use of local wines. Examples include *suprême de volailles de brest aux crustacés* (chicken breast with shellfish), fricassee of lobster with tarragon vinegar, and nuggets of venison in a red wine-mushroom sauce.

184 av. d'Epernay. Drive 1.5km (1 mile) south of Reims's center, following signs to Epernay. ✆ **03-26-06-08-60.** Reservations recommended. Main courses 20€–32€ ($26–$42); fixed-price menu 28€–66€ ($36–$86); *menu champagne* for 2 (includes bottle of a *champagne de marque*) 140€ ($182). AE, DC, MC, V. Tues–Fri noon–2:30pm; Tues–Sat 7:30–10pm.

Les Crayères ★★★ MODERN FRENCH There is no restaurant to equal this one in the entire champagne country—and the setting is elegant too (see hotel recommendation above). The restaurant installed in the château originated as a hyper-upscale *maison bourgeoise* (actually a mini-château) back in 1903. The cuisine here has always been a magnet for the champagne barons of the area, and the restaurant is the number-one choice for wine buyers from around the world. Under the superb direction of the talented culinary artist, Didier Elena, the cuisine is as sublime as ever. Launch your meal with ravioli stuffed with escargots or sample another appetizer that is celestial in its taste—three different preparations of foie gras, including one presented au naturel. The wild turbot and the grilled lobster are ineffably delicate, and the roast duck with honey vinegar sauce is earthy, regional, and a delight.

64 bd. Henri-Vasnier. ✆ **03-26-82-80-80.** Fax 03-26-82-65-52. Reservations required a few days in advance for weekday dinners, at least a month in advance for weekend dinners. Main courses 50€–75€ ($65–$98); fixed-price menus (including red bordeaux and champagne) 220€–250€ ($286–$325). AE, DC, MC, V. Daily noon–2pm and 7–9:30pm.

WHERE TO STAY & DINE NEARBY

Château de Fère ★★ MODERN FRENCH This fabulous restaurant occupies a turreted 16th-century château in a park. The only restaurant in Champagne with superior cuisine is Les Crayères (see above). Begin in the garden, sipping an aperitif or a glass of champagne with juice from freshly crushed raspberries. Your meal may consist of specialties such as foie gras of duckling with confit of ginger and a sauce made from the dessert wine Muscats de Venise, nuggets of suckling lamb cooked in a truffle-and-parsley-flavored crust, and deliberately undercooked Scottish salmon in lemon-flavored sweet-and-sour sauce. The desserts are mouthwatering, but we prefer the *boulette d'Avesnes,* a cone of cheese flecked with herbs and crushed peppercorns, coated with paprika.

Also available are 25 guest rooms with minibars, TVs, and dataports. Doubles are 150€ to 350€ ($195–$455); suites, 230€ to 400€ ($299–$520).

Rte. de Fismes (D967), Fère-en-Tardenois 02130. From Reims (35 min.), take E46 northwest toward Soissons. At Fismes, take D367 toward Fère-en-Tardenois and follow signs to Château de Fère. About 2.5km (1½ miles) north of the restaurant, you'll see the ruins of a 12th-century castle, also called the Château de Fère. ✆ **03-23-82-21-13.** Fax 03-23-82-37-81. www.chateaudefere.com. Reservations required. Main courses 25€–70€ ($33–$91); fixed-price menu 49€–88€ ($64–$114). AE, DC, MC, V. Daily 12:30–2pm and 7:30–9:30pm. Closed mid-Jan to Feb 15.

Moments The Route de Champagne

Whether for hiking or biking, the Montagne de Reims or *Route de Champagne* is the best place to experience the beauty of this vineyard-studded region. Montagne de Reims is a forested plateau south of Reims, where the slopes produce the grapes used to make bubbly.

Armed with a map from the tourist office in Reims or Epernay, you can explore this area along trails called *sentiers de Grandes Randonnées,* along the top of the northern plateau of Montagne de Reims.

These trails are called GRs. Because you're not likely to have time to visit all of them, we recommend routes GR14 and GR141. They form a loop of some 50km (31 miles) around the plateau's eastern section, taking in such towns as Verzy. Several train stations along the way, including a convenient one at Verzy, offer opportunities to take you back to Reims or Epernay should you tire before finishing the full loop.

REIMS AFTER DARK

Reims has the most vibrant nightlife in the region. The best place to start is **place Drouet-d'Erlon,** home to the city's premier clubs. This is a university town—for the most part, students rule the night. Just follow them to the best venues.

For a beer and a heavy dose of noise and rowdy students, head to the **Glue Pot,** 49 place Drouet-d'Erlon (© **03-26-47-36-46**). At **Au Bureau,** 80 place Drouet-d'Erlon (© **03-26-40-33-06**), a mixed-age crowd congregates in an Irish-style pub that has more than 120 types of beer. In the exotic **Au Lion de Belfort,** 37 place Drouet-d'Erlon (© **03-26-47-48-17**), stuffed heads of hippos, elephants, and the like keep watch. For a more sedate experience, try **L'Escalier,** 7 rue de Chativesle (© **03-26-84-95-14**), where the atmosphere is more conducive to conversation with locals and other tourists.

The best dance floors in town are at **Aquarium,** 93 bd. Général-Leclerc (© **03-26-47-34-29**), which attracts a mixed-age crowd (25–40); and **Le Tigre,** 2 bis av. Georges-Clemenceau (© **03-26-82-64-00**), with its decor of old French cars placed like artwork against the brick walls and mirrors. Young gays and lesbians go to **Bar Lilas,** 75 rue des Courcelles (© **03-26-47-02-81**). Everybody wears jeans; the cover at any of these clubs is 9€ to 10€ ($12–$13). For casino action, head to **Le Multicolore,** 17 rue Lesage (© **03-26-47-45-82**). It offers such games as poker, blackjack, and roulette daily from 10pm to 3am (until 6am Fri–Sat).

Comédie de Reims, chaussée Bocquaine (© **03-26-48-49-10**), has a varied schedule; tickets cost 12€ to 19€ ($16–$25) for adults and 5€ to 8€ ($6.50–$10) for children.

5 Side Trips from Reims: Laon ★★ & Amiens ★★★

Laon: 45km (28 miles) NW of Reims, 119km (74 miles) SE of Amiens, 138km (86 miles) NE of Paris; Amiens: 109km (68 miles) NW of Reims, 121km (75 miles) N of Paris, 114km (71 miles) SW of Lille

Savvy travelers know that this pristine area offers restful alternatives to the tourist meccas of Paris and the Riviera. The landscape of the low-lying region adjacent to Belgium's border will be familiar to admirers of Matisse, who found much inspiration here. Laon and Amiens are the area's major draws.

From Reims, **Laon** is a logical first stop, particularly for those traveling by rail, who must transfer en route to Amiens. This site is the north's most intriguing for its history and setting on a ridge above the plain and the Ardon River. Over the years, it has witnessed much turbulence.

Amiens, on the Somme River, has been a textile center since medieval days. Its old town is a warren of jumbled streets and canals. Amiens is renowned for its Gothic cathedral, one of the finest in France.

Beyond Amiens and Laon, the heavily forested **Ardennes** attracts lovers of nature and French poetry alike. Rimbaud lived and wrote here; writers such as Victor Hugo, George Sand, and Alexandre Dumas expounded upon its beauty in their writings. The sandy beaches of **Le Touquet-Paris-Plage** are the most fashionable and best equipped of the many resorts along the Channel. A mini–Monte Carlo, it was dubbed the "playground of kings" in the days before World War II. Many other stops merit a look if you have the time.

LAON

Arguably the most intriguing town in the north of France, Laon perches on a ridge that rises 98m (322 ft.) above the plain and the Ardon River. The capital of the *département* (mini-state) of Aisne, Laon has a long, turbulent history, attributable in large part to its remarkable location.

ESSENTIALS

GETTING THERE If you're **driving** from Reims, go 45km (28 miles) north on A26. **Trains** arrive from Paris's Gare du Nord at least 15 times a day (trip time: 1½–2 hr.). Others arrive from Reims seven times a day (trip time: 45 min.). For information and schedules, call ✆ **08-92-35-35-85.**

VISITOR INFORMATION The **Office de Tourisme** is on place Gautier de Montagne (✆ **03-23-20-28-62;** fax 03-23-20-68-11; www.tourisme-paysdelaon.com).

EXPLORING THE TOWN

The Romans, recognizing Laon's strategic value, had it fortified. Vandals, Burgundians, Franks, and many others later besieged it. German troops entered in 1870 and in the summer of 1914, holding it until the end of World War I. Medieval ramparts still surround the town. They appear to have survived intact from the Middle Ages and provide a ready-made itinerary for touring Laon. They aren't sound enough to be climbed on and must be admired from below.

You don't have to huff and puff as you head from Laon's **Basse Ville** to its **Haute Ville,** thanks to a cable-operated tram, **Poma** (✆ **03-23-79-07-59**), that shuttles passengers up and down the hill at 2½-minute intervals. It departs from the rail station on place de la Gare and ascends to the Hôtel-de-Ville on place du Général-Leclerc. It operates Monday to Saturday 7am to 8pm. The cost is 1€ ($1.30) one-way, 1.50€ ($1.95) round-trip. After visiting the cathedral, stroll down pedestrian-only **rue Châtelaine,** Laon's major shopping street.

Cathédrale Notre-Dame de Laon ★★ Most visitors head to this cathedral with the carved oxen on its facade. Having escaped World War I unharmed, it inhabits the spot where an ancient basilica stood until it burned in 1111. The structure has six towers, four of which are complete. Inside are stained-glass panels dating from the 13th century, and an 18th-century choir grille. Tours (available in French only) are conducted from Easter to October on Saturday and Sunday at 3pm (arrange through the tourist office). Prerecorded 2-hour audiotape tours are 3€ ($3.90).

8 rue du Cloître, off place Aubry. ✆ **03-23-20-26-54.** Free admission to cathedral; tours 6€ ($7.80). Daily 8:30am–6:30pm.

Musée Archéologique Municipal ★ This museum was founded in 1861 and remained rather sleepy until 1937, when it gained a collection of 1,700 artifacts (mainly from Greece, Rome, Egypt, Cyprus, and Asia Minor) as well as a collection of French painting and sculpture. The latest attraction is an annex in the courtyard of the museum, where you can visit the restored Chapelle Romaine des Templiers (Chapel of the Templars), originally associated with the Crusades of the Knights Templar. The chapel is noteworthy for its medieval stonework.

32 rue Georges-Ermant. ✆ **03-23-20-19-87.** Admission 3.50€ ($4.55) adults, free for children under 18. June–Sept Tues–Sun 11am–6pm; Oct–May Tues–Sun 2–6pm.

WHERE TO STAY

Hostellerie St-Vincent At the edge of the city, near the point where the road from Reims (A26) enters the Basse Ville, this simple government-rated two-star hotel is the most modern and best in town. It offers basic but comfortable guest rooms and has a good restaurant on premises.

111 av. Charles-de-Gaulle, Laon 02000. ✆ **03-23-23-42-43.** Fax 03-23-79-22-55. www.stvincent-laon.com. 47 units. 57€ ($74) double. AE, MC, V. **Amenities:** Restaurant; bar; room service; limited-mobility rooms. *In room:* TV, dataport.

Hôtel de la Bannière de France This revered hotel, built in 1685, is in the most historic part of Laon, Haute Ville. Behind its antique-looking facade, it has a modernized interior and the ambience of a traditional French hotel. The rooms are small but cozy and comfortably furnished, with shower-only bathrooms. The personality of the owner, Mme Lefevre, is obvious in the traditional restaurant.

11 rue Franklin-D-Roosevelt, Laon 02000. ✆ **03-23-23-21-44.** Fax 03-23-23-31-56. www.hoteldelabannieredefrance.com. 18 units. 59€–70€ ($77–$91) double. AE, DC, MC, V. Parking 6.50€ ($8.45). Closed May 1 and Dec 20–Jan 20. **Amenities:** Restaurant; bar; nonsmoking rooms. *In room:* TV, hair dryer, dataport.

WHERE TO DINE

Hostellerie St-Vincent and **Hôtel de la Bannière de France** (see "Where to Stay," above) contain good restaurants.

Brasserie du Parvis PICARD/FRENCH The allure here is the location opposite the main facade of the cathedral. In warm weather, the outdoor tables facing the church are hard to snag. Inside, the owners redecorate frequently, focusing on whatever festival or event happens to be on the minds of local residents—eclipses of the sun or moon, medieval festivals, and the like. Menu items include *ficelle Picard,* a kind of crepe made with ham and mushrooms; a pungent tart of local maroilles cheese; and a very ethnic version of chitterling sausages, *les andouillettes de Troyes,* with mustard sauce. More appetizing, at least to North American palates, is chicken cutlet with mushroom cream sauce.

Place du Parvis Laon. ✆ **03-23-20-27-27.** Reservations recommended. Main courses 6€–18€ ($7.80–$23); fixed-price menu 12€–30€ ($16–$39). MC, V. Daily 11:30am–10pm (until 11pm July–Aug). Closed Wed and Sun nights Nov 15–Mar 15.

AMIENS

A textile center since medieval times, Amiens was the ancient capital of Picardy. It sits on the south bank of the Somme, where it is divided into a series of canals and irrigation networks. The old town, a jumble of narrow streets crisscrossed by canals, is rundown and seedy but still worth exploring. The city's focal point is its world-famous Gothic cathedral, one of France's finest.

ESSENTIALS

GETTING THERE If you're **driving** from Reims, take A26 north 45km (28 miles) to Laon, and then head west on N44 to N32, which becomes D934 to Amiens. The distance is 109km (68 miles); however, the trek may take you more than 1½ hours because of the country roads you'll be on after you exit A26. Amiens is adjacent to the main autoroute (A1) connecting Paris with Lille. Driving time from Paris is about 90 minutes. Those coming from the northern suburbs of Paris prefer A16, which passes near Amiens on its way to Calais.

Reaching Amiens by **train** from Reims requires a transfer in Laon or Tergnier. There are only three trains a day, which take 80 minutes to 3 hours, depending on the schedule.

Many visitors arrive straight from Paris—Amiens is on the main line connecting Paris's Gare du Nord with Lille. Depending on the season, four or five trains a day make the 65-minute trip (each way); the fare is 18€ ($23) one-way. The rail station in Amiens is at place Alphonse-Fiquet, a 10-minute walk from the old town. For information and schedules, call ✆ **08-92-35-35-35.**

VISITOR INFORMATION The **Office de Tourisme** is at 6 bis rue Dusevel (✆ **03-22-71-60-50;** fax 03-22-71-60-51; www.amiens.com/tourisme).

EXPLORING THE TOWN

Julius Caesar praised the fertility of the fields around Amiens. During the Middle Ages, **Les Hortillonnages** ★, an expanse of almost 242 hectares (598 acres) at the eastern edge of the core, was set aside for the cultivation of all kinds of herbs, fruits, and vegetables. Irrigated by a web of canals fed by the Somme, the district is still producing foodstuffs. Not long ago, the harvest was floated on barges and in shallow-bottomed boats to be sold on the Quai Bélu, near the cathedral. Although today the produce comes from the fields into the town center by truck, the ritual retains its medieval name, the **Marché sur l'Eau** (though locals increasingly refer to it as **Marché St-Leu**). The tradition continues every Saturday from 8:30am to 1pm, when the river's quays are transformed into a huge outdoor vegetable market.

A few paces north of the cathedral, straddling both banks of the Somme, is a cluster of carefully restored 13th- and 14th-century houses in a labyrinth of narrow cobblestone streets. Known as the **Quartier St-Leu,** this is a neighborhood of gift shops, antiques shops, art galleries, boutiques, and cafes.

Jules Verne, author of *20,000 Leagues Under the Sea* and *Journey to the Center of the Earth,* is buried in Amiens at the **Cimetière de la Madeleine,** rue St-Maurice, northwest of the town center. The representation of Verne on the Beaux Arts tomb appears to be physically rising from the dead. The cemetery is open daily from 9am to 7pm. Verne's home is at 2 rue Charles-Dubois (✆ **03-22-45-37-84;** www.jules-verne.net). It's now a research center documenting his life and literary achievements, but the management discourages visitors.

More amenable to the idea of receiving visitors is the town's newest museum, **L'Imaginaire Jules-Verne,** 36 rue de Noyon (✆ **03-22-45-45-75;** www.jules-verne.net). A 2-minute walk from the railway station, the museum is dedicated to perpetuating insights into the writer's quirky but profound imagination. Admission is 3€ ($3.90) for adults, 1.50€ ($1.95) for students and children 8 to 18, and free for anyone under 8. It's open Tuesday to Sunday, afternoons only, from 3 to 7pm. Be warned that this museum's exhibitions are in French only, and that exhibitions focus on his (sometimes relatively obscure) novels.

Cathédrale Notre-Dame d'Amiens ★★★ At 141m (463 ft.) long, this cathedral is the largest church in France. It was begun in 1220 by Robert de Luzarches and completed around 1270. Its original purpose was to house the head of St. John the Baptist, brought back from the Crusades in 1206. Two unequal towers were added later—the south one in 1366, the north one in 1402. The renowned architect Viollet-le-Duc restored the cathedral in the 1850s.

The cathedral is the crowning example of French Gothic architecture. In John Ruskin's *Bible of Amiens* (1884), which Proust translated into French, he extolled the door arches. The portals of the west front are lavishly decorated, important examples of Gothic cathedral sculpture. Two galleries surmount the portals; the upper has 22 statues of kings. The large rose window is from the 16th century.

Inside are carved stalls and a Flamboyant Gothic choir screen. Local artisans made these stalls, with some 3,500 figures, in the early 16th century. Slender pillars—126 of them—hold up the interior of the church, the zenith of the High Gothic in the north of France. The cathedral escaped destruction in World War II. In 1996, the *Portail de la Mère-Dieu* (Portal of the Mother of God), to the right of the cathedral's main entrance as you look over the facade, was restored at enormous expense.

Place Notre-Dame. ✆ **03-22-71-60-56.** Free admission. Guided tours 5.50€ ($7.15), free for children under 19 at 10:45am and 4:30pm. Apr–Sept Mon and Wed–Sun 7:30am–noon and 2–7pm; Oct–Mar daily 7:30am–noon and 2–5pm. Audio-guided tours are available in English for 4€ ($5.20).

Musée de Picardie ★★ This museum occupies a building constructed from 1855 to 1867. The palace of the Napoleonic dynasty, inaugurated by Napoleon III, consists of three sections, including one devoted to archaeology. Other sections include exhibits on the Roman occupation of Gaul, the Merovingian era, ancient Greece, and Egypt. One collection documents the Middle Ages with ivories, enamels, objets d'art, and sculpture. The sculpture and painting collection traces the European schools from the 16th to the 20th centuries, with works by El Greco, Maurice Quentin de La Tour, Guardi, and Tiepolo. Fragonard's *Les Lavandières* is his most beautiful work here.

48 rue de la République. ✆ **03-22-97-14-00.** Admission 4€ ($5.20) adults, 2.50€ ($3.25) students, free for children under 16; 4€–6€ ($5.20–$7.80) surcharge may apply for temporary exhibitions. Tues–Sun 10am–12:30pm and 2–6pm.

WHERE TO STAY

Le Carlton ★ From a glance at this hotel's Napoleon III architecture, you'll see that it's the stellar choice in Amiens. Though geared toward business travelers, its guest rooms are luxurious, with rich furniture and hand-painted frescoes depicting nostalgic scenes within Amiens's antique medieval St-Leu district. Appointments include fine linens and bathrooms with tub/shower combinations. The public areas, all featuring polished dark wood, range from an English bar to a brasserie-style restaurant.

42 rue de Noyon, Amiens 80000. ✆ **03-22-97-72-22.** Fax 03-22-97-72-00. www.lecarlton.fr. 24 units. 75€–105€ ($98–$137) double; 135€ ($176) suite. AE, DC, MC, V. **Amenities:** Restaurant; bar; room service; nonsmoking rooms; limited-mobility rooms. *In room:* TV, hair dryer, Wi-Fi.

Mercure Amiens *Value* Overall, this hotel provides good value, unbeatable location, and the cost-consciousness of the Accor group. It sits opposite the main facade of the cathedral. The building has a stately facade and some antique beams in the guest rooms, and the interior has a clean, modern look. The pricier rooms contain cramped but cozy sitting areas; the less expensive units are smaller and more functional. Some have windows overlooking the cathedral. Rooms rarely rise above standard motel level, but they come with comfortable beds and bathrooms with tub/shower combinations.

17–19 place au Feurre, Amiens 80000. ✆ **03-22-22-00-20.** Fax 03-22-91-86-57. www.mercure.com. 47 units. 96€–106€ ($125–$138) double. AE, DC, MC, V. Free parking overnight, 1€ ($1.30) during the day. **Amenities:** Bar; nonsmoking rooms; limited-mobility rooms. *In room:* A/C, TV.

WHERE TO DINE

Les Marissons ★ PICARD/FRENCH Two or three places around town match the quality of the food here, but none offers such a charming setting. The restaurant sits in a 15th-century building adjacent to one of the city's oldest bridges, pont de la Dodane. The cuisine is elegantly presented. Chef Antoine Benoit's specialties include a unique terrine *(pâté d'estran)* made from chunks of locally raised lamb mixed with sheep's cheese and wrapped in puff pastry, sea bass with apricots, roast lamb *pré salé* (salt from the marshes), scallops baked in their shells, and veal kidneys with rosemary sauce. In summer, you can dine in the garden.

Pont de la Dodane, Quartier St-Leu. ✆ **03-22-92-96-66.** www.le-marissons.fr. Reservations recommended. Main courses 21€–32€ ($27–$42); fixed-price menu 19€–53€ ($25–$69). AE, DC, MC, V. Mon–Fri noon–1:45pm; Mon–Sat 7:30–9:30pm.

AMIENS AFTER DARK

You'll find the largest number of nightspots around quai Bélu in the St-Leu district. Try **Bar le Must,** 48 rue du Don (✆ **03-22-92-37-78**), where you can absorb the fusion of live piano music and alcohol.

If you're big on musical events, head for the 1950 Picard-style house next to the train station, **Le Grand Wazoo,** 5 rue Vulfran-Warmé (✆ **03-22-91-64-91**). Named in honor of a Frank Zappa album, this club draws a mixed crowd intent on listening to local musicians as well as more famous groups. It's open Monday through Saturday 6pm until 1am. Concerts (usually heavy metal, acid rock, and techno) take place about three times a week, usually on Friday and Saturday. When there's live music, cover ranges from 2€ to 5€ ($2.60–$6.50); otherwise, admission is free.

While you're checking out the scene along the canal area, stop in the old medieval house that's home to the restaurant/wine bar **La Queue de Vache (The Cow's Tail),** 51 quai Bélu (✆ **03-22-91-38-91**). Containing no more than 30 seats on two different levels, the restaurant and wine bar offers snacks and full-fledged meals, with main courses priced at 10€ to 20€ ($13–$26). It pours about 30 wines, many sold by the glass. Platters of sausage, terrines, and cheeses go well with the wine, but if you want a full platter, consider a hearty portion of roasted *magret de canard* (duck). Every first Tuesday of the month, there's live New Orleans–style jazz.

For dancing, your best bet is **Le Lipstick,** 9 rue des Francs-Muriers (✆ **03-22-97-96-71**). It attracts a youth-conscious, high-energy crowd that likes punk rock and dancing. Entrance may be free on slow nights, or may cost around 10€ to 12€ ($13–$16) when a live band plays. A theme bar, **Le Texas Café,** 13 rue des Francs-Muriers (© **03-22-72-19-79**), offers a roster of stiff drinks and a karaoke machine.

Nelson's Pub, 5 quai Bélu (© **03-22-91-56-00**), and its next-door neighbor, **Le Newport,** 3 quai Bélu (no phone), play recorded rock 'n' roll in environments favored by thirsty conversationalists. A short walk away is **Le Squale,** 18 rue de Dodane (© **03-22-72-20-46**), a pub with pinewood planks and a decor that reminds some Francophiles of the interior of a wine barrel.

If you're gay and on the loose in Amiens, **Red and White,** rue de la Dodane, in the Quartier St-Leu (no phone), offers the chance to meet and talk with like-minded folks who might have dropped in for an after-dinner drink or to hear some music. Its opening and closing times tend to be erratic.

6 Epernay

140km (87 miles) E of Paris, 26km (16 miles) S of Reims

On the left bank of the Marne, Epernay rivals Reims as a center for champagne. Although it only has one-sixth Reims's population, Epernay produces nearly as much champagne. It boasts an estimated 322km (200 miles) or more of cellars and tunnels. These caves are vast vaults cut into the chalk rock on which the town is built. Represented in Epernay are such champagne companies as Moët et Chandon (the largest), Pol Roger, Mercier, and de Castellane.

Epernay's main boulevards are the elegant residential avenue de Champagne, rue Mercier, and rue de Reims, all radiating from place de la République. Two important squares in the narrow streets of the commercial district are place Hughes-Plomb and place des Arcades.

Epernay has been destroyed or burned by invading armies nearly two dozen times. Few of its buildings have survived. However, check out the neoclassical villas and Victorian town houses on avenue de Champagne.

ESSENTIALS

GETTING THERE If you're **driving** to Epernay from Reims, head south on E51. Eighteen **trains** per day arrive from Paris's Gare de l'Est (trip time: 1 hr., 15 min.); the one-way fare is 19€ ($25). From Reims, there are 16 trains per day (trip time: 25 min.; 5.60€/$7.30 one-way). For information, call © **08-92-35-35-35,** or visit www.voyages-sncf.com. The major **bus** link is STDM Trans-Champagne (© **03-26-65-17-07** in Epernay), operating four buses per day Monday to Saturday between Châlons-en-Champagne and Epernay (trip time: 45 min.).

VISITOR INFORMATION The **Office de Tourisme** is at 7 av. de Champagne (© **03-26-53-33-00;** fax 03-26-51-95-22; www.ot-epernay.fr).

EXPLORING THE TOWN

Boutiques and shops abound in the pedestrian district of **place des Arcades, rue du Général-Leclerc, rue St-Thibault, rue St-Martin,** and **rue Porte Lucas.** You'll find stores selling gifts, clothes, antiques, books, and regional food items.

For champagne, you can go to the individual houses along avenue de Champagne (see below) or try one of the stores that represent a variety of houses. Two of the best are **La Cave Salvatori,** 11 rue Flodoard (© **03-26-55-32-32**), and **Le Domaine des**

Crus, 2 rue Henri Dunant (✆ **03-26-54-18-60**), known for a staggering array of champagnes.

For regional antiques from the 18th and 19th centuries, try **Antiquités Jocelyne Huzette,** 35 rue Blandin (✆ **03-26-54-58-52**).

For champagne gift items such as flutes and corks, as well as table decorations and linens, visit **De-ci-de-ca,** 34 rue du Général-Leclerc (✆ **03-26-55-67-68**). **Fromm Jacques,** 33 rue St-Thibault (✆ **03-26-55-25-64**), and **Camaieu,** 12 rue de Professeur Langevin (✆ **03-26-51-83-83**), sell garden ornaments, souvenirs, and art objects commemorating the historic medievalism of Amiens. Camaieu is not to be confused with another well-recommended store with the same name, **Camaieu,** which specializes in women's clothing, at 14 rue St-Thibault (✆ **03-26-52-72-18**).

Champagne de Castellane Across from Mercier (see below), this champagne house, unlike the two recommended below, gives you a closer view of how champagne is actually produced. You see workers doing it all—corking, labeling, even removing sediment. The museum on-site may be a bit dull, but the climb to the tower (237 steps) for a panoramic view of the area is not. The tower is from 1904 and has become the symbol of Epernay. A tasting of the house Brut Croix Rouge is included after the tours, some of which are conducted in English (depending on demand).

63 av. de Champagne. ✆ **03-26-51-19-19.** Admission 1€ ($1.30), free for ages 16 and under. Apr–Dec daily 10am–noon and 2–6pm. Closed Jan–Mar.

Mercier Mercier is near Moët et Chandon, and you can visit them both on the same day. Mercier conducts tours in English of its 18km (11 miles) of tunnels from laser-guided trains. The caves contain one of the world's largest wooden barrels, with a capacity of more than 200,000 bottles. No reservation is necessary if there are fewer than 10 in your group.

70 av. de Champagne. ✆ **03-26-51-22-22.** www.champagne-mercier.fr. Admission 6.50€ ($8.45). Late Mar to mid–Nov daily 9:30–11:30am and 2–4:30pm. Closed rest of year.

Moët et Chandon Champagne Cellars A staff member gives guided tours in English, describing the champagne-making process and filling you in on champagne lore: Napoleon, a friend of Jean-Rémy Moët, used to stop by for thousands of bottles on his way to battle. The only time he didn't take a supply was at Waterloo—and look what happened there. At the end of the tour, you're given a glass of bubbly. No reservations are necessary, except for large groups.

20 av. de Champagne. ✆ **03-26-51-20-20.** www.moet.com. Admission 11€–23€ ($14–$30). Early May to early Nov daily 9:30–11:30am and 2–4:30pm; early Nov to Apr Mon–Fri 9:30–11:30am and 2–4:30pm.

WHERE TO STAY

Les Berceaux (see "Where to Dine," below) also rents rooms.

Best Western Hôtel de Champagne This simple 1970s inn lies about 180m (591 ft.) from the Moët et Chandon showroom, near place de la République. Some rooms are outfitted in modern style; others look vaguely inspired by Louis XV. Each room has a small bathroom with shower. A buffet breakfast is served every morning.

30 rue Eugène-Mercier, Epernay 51200. ✆ **800/528-1234** in the U.S. and Canada, or 03-26-53-10-60. Fax 03-26-51-94-63. www.bw-hotel-champagne.com. 30 units. 90€–115€ ($117–$150) double. AE, DC, MC, V. Free parking. **Amenities:** Bar; fitness center; sauna; laundry service; nonsmoking rooms. *In room:* A/C, TV, minibar, hair dryer, safe, Wi-Fi.

Royal Champagne ★★★ Constructed around an 18th-century relay station for the postal system, this hotel is a member of the Relais & Châteaux group. The establishment's historic core contains the reception area, bar, and dining facilities; guest rooms are in town house–style accommodations overlooking the nearby vineyards. The units are rustic and very comfortable, exemplifying the coziness of wine-country living. Each comes with a sumptuous bed with fine linen, plus a combination tub/shower.

The chef is known for classic dishes with an innovative twist. The food is exceptional, with specialties such as lobster ragout, John Dory with a purée of celery and truffle-flavored cream sauce, and roast lamb with garlic.

Champillon Bellevue 51160. ✆ **03-26-52-87-11.** Fax 03-26-52-89-69. Drive 8km (5 miles) north from Epernay toward Reims on the rte. du Vignoble (N2051) to Champillon. www.royalchampagne.com. 25 units. 205€–355€ ($267–$462) double; 335€–380€ ($436–$494) suite. AE, DC, MC, V. **Amenities:** Restaurant; bar; room service; babysitting; laundry service; dry cleaning. *In room:* A/C, TV, minibar, hair dryer, safe.

WHERE TO DINE

The food at **Royal Champagne** (see "Where to Stay," above) is excellent.

Les Berceaux ★★★ CHAMPENOISE Chef-owner Patrick Michelon serves generous portions of flavorful, conservative regional cuisine. The menu changes seasonally and always features fresh produce and superior cuts of fish, meat, and game. Particularly scrumptious are such dishes as Pyrénéan suckling lamb roasted on a spit; snails in champagne sauce; roast filet of John Dory; and galette of roasted and minced pigs' feet in puff pastry, served with potatoes. At an on-site wine bar, Bistrot le 7, you can sample an assortment of vintages by the glass. It showcases local wines, especially champagne. If Les Berceaux errs at all, it tends to be a bit pretentious, a flaw that you may be able to overcome with a touch of humor.

Available upstairs are 28 comfortable guest rooms, each with TV. A double with a tub/shower combination rents for 95€ ($124).

13 rue des Berceaux, Epernay 51200. ✆ **03-26-55-28-84.** Fax 03-26-55-10-36. www.lesberceaux.com. Reservations recommended. Main courses 27€–38€ ($35–$49); fixed-price menu 30€–64€ ($39–$83). AE, DC, MC, V. Wed–Sun noon–2pm and 7–9pm.

EPERNAY AFTER DARK

Start out at the chic cafe and bar **Le Progrès,** 5 place de la République (✆ **03-26-55-22-72**). For a glass of wine or even Scotch (something you don't see enough of in this wine-crazed region), consider a visit to **Le Chriss Bar,** 40 rue de Sézanne (✆ **03-26-57-87-18**). A place that rocks and rolls a bit later into the night, sometimes with live music, is **Le Garden Club,** 5 av. Foch (✆ **03-26-54-20-30**), which has an atmosphere more in tune with Paris than with Epernay.

12

Alsace-Lorraine

The provinces of Alsace and Lorraine, with ancient capitals at Strasbourg and Nancy, have been the object of many disputes between Germany and France. Alsace has been called "the least French of French provinces," more reminiscent of the Black Forest across the Rhine. In fact, it became German from 1870 until after World War I and was ruled by Hitler from 1940 to 1944. These days, both provinces are back under French control, though they remain somewhat independent.

In the Vosges Mountains you can follow **La Route des Crêtes (Crest Road)** or skirt the foothills, visiting the wine towns of Alsace. In its cities and cathedrals, the castle-dotted landscape evokes a past filled with military glory or defeat. Lorraine is Joan of Arc country, and many of its towns still suggest their medieval heritage.

No clear-cut line delineates Alsace from Lorraine. Alsace is more German. Lorraine, with its rolling landscape, appears more French in character.

1 Strasbourg ★★★

488km (303 miles) SE of Paris, 217km (135 miles) SW of Frankfurt

The capital of Alsace, Strasbourg is one of France's greatest cities and the birthplace of *pâté de foie gras.* Here Rouget de Lisle first sang "La Marseillaise," the French national anthem.

Strasbourg is one of France's major ports, only 3km (1¾ miles) west of the Rhine. In addition to being the site of the Council of Europe, Strasbourg is home to the European Parliament, which convenes at the Palais de l'Europe.

In 1871, Strasbourg was absorbed by Germany and made the capital of the territory of Alsace-Lorraine. It reverted to France in 1918. One street is a perfect illustration of the city's identity crisis: More than a century ago it was avenue Napoléon. In 1871, it became Kaiser-Wilhelmstrasse, and then boulevard de la République in 1918. In 1940, it became Adolf-Hitler-Strasse, and it ended up as avenue du Général-de-Gaulle in 1945.

One of the most happening cities in France, Strasbourg is home to the University of Strasbourg, once attended by the likes of Goethe, Napoleon, and Pasteur. Today, some 40,000 students follow in their footsteps.

ESSENTIALS

GETTING THERE The **Strasbourg-Entzheim Airport** (Aéroport International Strasbourg; ✆ **03-88-64-67-67;** www.strasbourg.aeroport.fr), 15km (9⅓ miles) southwest of the city center, receives daily flights from many European cities, including Paris, London, Rome, Vienna, and Moscow. You can get from the airport to the town center by using **shuttle buses** and **city trams.** They run at 40-minute intervals all day long. The one-way cost is 5.10€ ($6.65). Take a shuttle bus to the south side of Strasbourg, to a

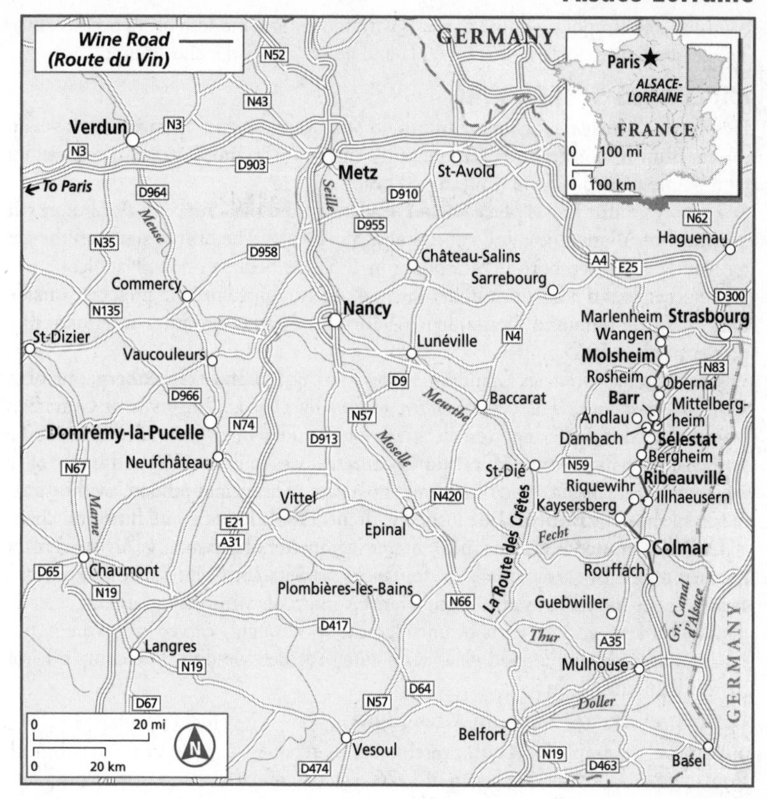

junction point known as Baggersee. From there, you'll continue to the town center on tram line A. Combined travel time is between 35 and 40 minutes each way. For information, call © **03-88-77-70-70.**

At least 16 **trains** a day arrive from Paris's Gare de l'Est (trip time: 4 hr.); the one-way fare is 50€ ($65). For information and schedules, call © **36-35** or © **08-92-35-35-35** from outside France.

By **car,** the giant A35 crosses the plain of Alsace, with occasional references to its original name, the N83. It links Strasbourg with Colmar and Mulhouse.

VISITOR INFORMATION The **Office de Tourisme** is on place de la Cathédrale (© **03-88-52-28-28;** fax 03-88-52-28-29; www.ot-strasbourg.fr).

SPECIAL EVENTS **Wolf Music,** 24 rue de la Mésange (© **03-88-32-43-10**), arranges ticket sales for two festivals: the **Festival of Classical Music** (© **03-88-15-29-29**), for 2 weeks in June, and the **Festival de Jazz** (© **03-88-15-29-29**), July 1 to July 3. Both feature international artists and draw large crowds. Ticket prices begin at 19€ ($25) and go on sale in mid-April. The Association Musica (© **03-88-23-47-23;** www.festival-musica.org) organizes the **Festival International des Musiques d'Aujourd'hui.** It takes place from the end of September to the first week of October and combines contemporary music concerts with movies and modern opera performances. Tickets are 5.50€ to 16€ ($7.15–$21) and go on sale at the end of June.

EXPLORING STRASBOURG

Despite war damage, much remains of Old Strasbourg, including covered bridges and towers from its former fortifications, plus many 15th- and 17th-century dwellings with painted wooden fronts and carved beams.

The city's traffic hub is **place Kléber** ★, dating from the 15th century. Sit here with a tankard of Alsatian beer and get to know Strasbourg. The bronze statue in the center is of J. B. Kléber, born in Strasbourg in 1753; he became one of Napoleon's most noted generals and was buried under the monument. Apparently his presence offended the Nazis, who removed the statue in 1940. This Alsatian bronze was restored to its proper place in 1945.

From here, take rue des Grandes-Arcades southeast to **place Gutenberg,** one of the city's oldest squares. The central statue (1840) by David d'Angers is of Gutenberg, who perfected his printing press in Strasbourg in the winter of 1436 and 1437. The former town hall, now the **Hôtel du Commerce,** was built in 1582 and is one of the most significant Renaissance buildings in Alsace. The neighborhoods within a few blocks of the city's **cathedral** are loaded with medieval references and historical charm.

La Petite France ★★ is the most interesting quarter of Strasbourg. A virtual island, it's surrounded by scenic canals on four sides, and its 16th-century houses reflect in the waters of the Ill River. In "Little France," old roofs with gray tiles have sheltered families for ages, and the cross-beamed facades with roughly carved rafters are in typical Alsatian style. For a good view, walk along rue des Moulins, branching off from rue du Bain-aux-Plantes.

Cathédrale Notre-Dame de Strasbourg ★★★ The city's crowning glory is an outstanding example of Gothic architecture, representing a transition from the Romanesque. Construction began in 1176. The pyramidal tower in rose-colored stone was completed in 1439; at 141m (463 ft.), it's the tallest one from medieval times. This cathedral is still in use. Religious ceremonies, particularly on feast days, meld perfectly with the architectural majesty. Individual tourists can visit the tower only in the summer (you may have to wait to climb it). The Office de Tourisme (see above) organizes tours for groups; call for the schedule.

Four large counterforts divide the **main facade** ★★★ into three vertical parts and two horizontal galleries. Note the **rose window,** which looks like stone lace. The facade is rich in decoration: On the portal of the south transept, the *Coronation and Death of the Virgin* in one of the two tympanums is the finest such medieval work. In

---

Finds Exploring Strasbourg by Boat

One of the most romantic ways to spend time in Strasbourg is to take an excursion on the **Ill River** from the Palais de Rohan. The 75-minute cruises cost 7.40€ ($9.60) for adults and 3.70€ ($4.80) for children. They include recorded commentary in six languages. From April to October, rides depart at 30-minute intervals daily between 9:30am and 9pm, May to September 9:30am to 10pm. Between December and March, departures are at 10:30am, 1pm, 2:30pm, and 4pm. For information, call Batorama, 15 rue de Nantes (✆ **03-88-84-13-13**).

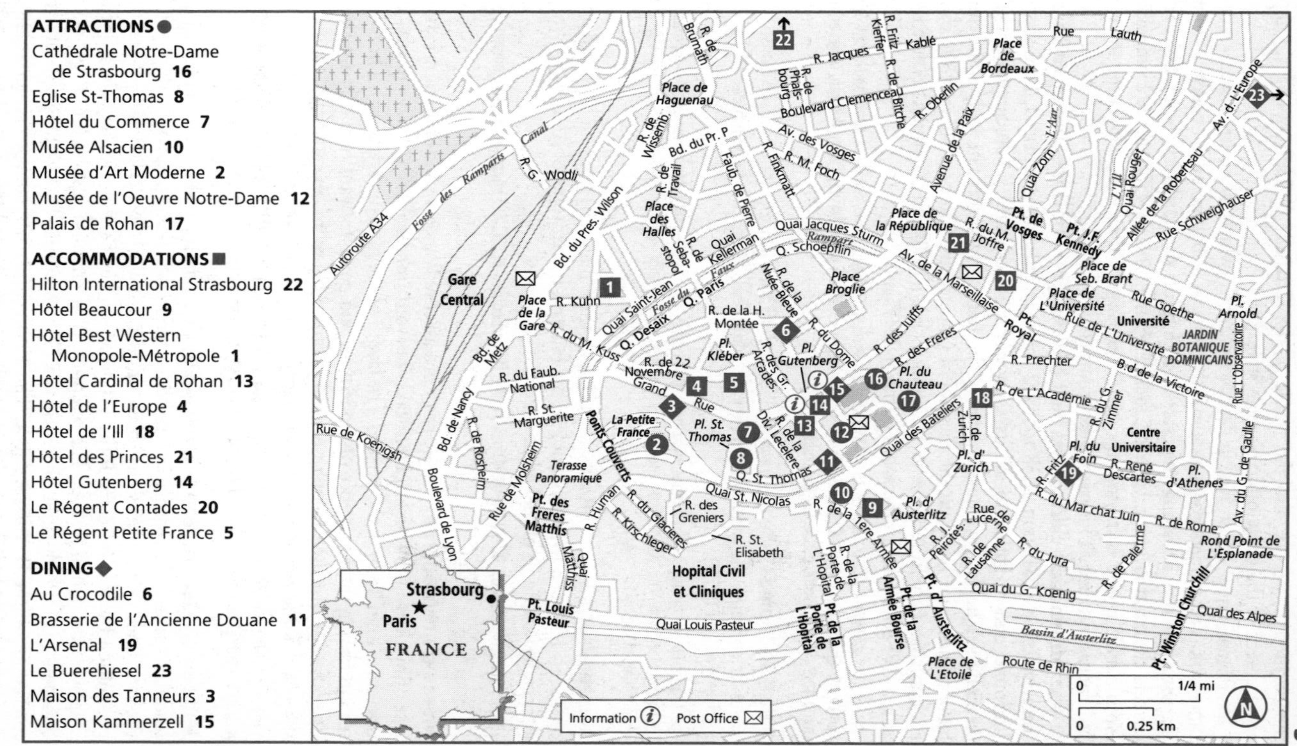
ATTRACTIONS
Cathédrale Notre-Dame de Strasbourg 16
Eglise St-Thomas 8
Hôtel du Commerce 7
Musée Alsacien 10
Musée d'Art Moderne 2
Musée de l'Oeuvre Notre-Dame 12
Palais de Rohan 17
ACCOMMODATIONS
Hilton International Strasbourg 22
Hôtel Beaucour 9
Hôtel Best Western Monopole-Métropole 1
Hôtel Cardinal de Rohan 13
Hôtel de l'Europe 4
Hôtel de l'Ill 18
Hôtel des Princes 21
Hôtel Gutenberg 14
Le Régent Contades 20
Le Régent Petite France 5
DINING
Au Crocodile 6
Brasserie de l'Ancienne Douane 11
L'Arsenal 19
Le Buerehiesel 23
Maison des Tanneurs 3
Maison Kammerzell 15
Information
Post Office
0
1/4 mi
0.25 km
N
Strasbourg
Paris
FRANCE
Gare Central
Place de la Gare
Place de Haguenau
Place des Halles
Place de la République
Place Broglie
Pl. Kléber
Pl. Gutenberg
Pl. du Chauteau
Pl. St. Thomas
La Petite France
Ponts Couverts
Terasse Panoramique
Pt. des Freres Matthis
Pt. Louis Pasteur
Hopital Civil et Cliniques
Pt. de la Porte de L'Hopital
Pt. de la Armée Bourse
Pt. d' Austerlitz
Place de L'Etoile
Pl. d' Austerlitz
Pl. d' Zurich
Pl. du Foin
Centre Universitaire
Pl. d'Athenes
Rond Point de L'Esplanade
Pt. Winston Churchill
Place de L'Université
Université
JARDIN BOTANIQUE DOMINICAINS
Pl. Arnold
Place de Seb. Brant
Pt. J.F. Kennedy
Pt. de Vosges
Pt. Royal
Place de Bordeaux
Autoroute A34
Boulevard de Lyon
Bd. de Nancy
Bd. du Pres. Wilson
Boulevard Clemenceau
Av. des Vosges
Avenue de la Paix
Av. de la Marseillaise
Quai Jacques Sturm
Quai des Bateliers
Quai St. Nicolas
Quai Louis Pasteur
Quai du G. Koenig
Quai des Alpes
Route de Rhin
Bassin d'Austerlitz
Rue de Koenigsh
Av. d. L'Europe
Allée de la Robertsau
Rue Schweighauser
B.d de la Victoire
Av. du G. de Gaulle
Canal
Fosse des Remparts

the north transept, see also the facade of the **Chapelle St-Laurence,** a stunning achievement of the late Gothic German style.

A Romanesque **crypt** lies under the chancel, which is covered with square stonework. The stained-glass window is the work of Max Ingrand. The **nave** is majestic, with windows depicting emperors and kings on the north Strasbourg aisle. Five chapels cluster around the transept, including one built in 1500 in the Flamboyant Gothic style. In the south transept stands the **Angel Pillar** ★★, illustrating the Last Judgment, with angels lowering their trumpets.

The **astronomical clock** ★ was built between 1547 and 1574. It stopped during the Revolution, and from 1838 to 1842 the mechanism was replaced. Each day at 12:30pm, crowds gather to see its show of allegorical figures. On Sunday, Apollo drives his sun horses; on Thursday, you see Jupiter and his eagle. The body of the clock has a planetarium based on the theories of Copernicus. Close-up views of the clock are available daily from noon to 12:30pm; tickets (1.50€/$1.95 adults, .80€/$1.05 ages 5–18) go on sale in the south portal at 11:45am.

Place de la Cathédrale. ✆ **03-88-32-75-78** for times of services. Cathedral Mon–Sat 7–11:40am and 12:40–7pm; Sun 12:45–6pm. Tower (✆ 03-88-43-60-40) Apr–Oct daily 9am–5:30pm; Nov–Mar daily 9am–4:30pm. Tower admission 4.40€ ($5.70) adults, 2.20€ ($2.85) children under 18.

Eglise St-Thomas Built between 1230 and 1330, this Protestant church boasts five naves. It contains the **mausoleum** ★★ of Maréchal de Saxe, a masterpiece of French art by Pigalle (1777).

Rue Martin-Luther (along rue St-Thomas, near pont St-Thomas). ✆ **03-88-32-14-46.** www.eglise-st-thomas.org. Free admission. May–Oct daily 10am–noon and 2–6pm; Nov–Dec daily 10am–noon and 2–5pm; Feb–Apr daily 2–5pm. Closed Jan.

Musée Alsacien ★ This museum occupies three mansions from the 16th and 17th centuries. It's like a living textbook of the folklore and customs of Alsace, containing arts, crafts, and tools of the old province.

23 quai St-Nicolas. ✆ **03-88-52-50-01.** Admission 4€ ($5.20) adults, 2€ ($2.60) students, free for children under 18. Wed–Mon noon–6pm.

Musée d'Art Moderne In the heart of La Petite France, this is Strasbourg's showcase of modern European art. Don't take the word "modern" too literally—the collection dates from 1870 to the present. The layout of the museum starts with a historical section tracing the emergence of modern art and going forward to the 21st century. Other facilities include a graphic art and photography room, an art library, a museum shop, and a cafe-restaurant on the terrace.

1 place Jean-Hans Arp. ✆ **03-88-23-31-31.** Admission 5€ ($6.50) adults, 2.50€ ($3.25) students under 25 and seniors, free for children under 18. Tues–Wed and Fri 11am–7pm; Thurs noon–10pm; Sun 10am–6pm.

Musée de l'Oeuvre Notre-Dame ★★★ This museum illustrates the art of the Middle Ages and Renaissance in Strasbourg and Alsace. Some pieces were displayed in the cathedral, where copies have been substituted. The most celebrated is a stained-glass head of Christ from about the 11th century. There's also a window depicting an emperor from around 1200. The sculpture is of great interest, as are the works of Strasbourg goldsmiths from the 16th and 17th centuries. The winding staircase and interior are in the Renaissance style. The 13th-century hall contains sculptures from the cathedral, including the wise and foolish virgins from 1280.

3 place du Château. ✆ **03-88-52-50-00.** Admission 4€ ($5.20) adults, 2€ ($2.60) students, free for children under 18. Tues–Sun 10am–6pm.

Palais de Rohan ★★ This palace south of the cathedral was built from 1732 to 1742. It's an example of supreme elegance and proportion. Noted for its facades and rococo interior, it's one of the crowning design achievements in eastern France. On the first floor is a fine-arts museum (Musée des Beaux-Arts) with works by Rubens, Rembrandt, Van Dyck, El Greco, Goya, Watteau, Renoir, and Monet. On the street level is a decorative-arts museum that exhibits ceramics and the original machinery of the cathedral's first astronomical clock. Also on the premises are collections of artifacts excavated from nearby digs, focusing especially on art and utilitarian objects from the Roman and early medieval (Merovingian) eras.

2 place du Château. ✆ **03-88-52-50-00.** Admission for 1 museum 4€ ($5.20) adults, 2€ ($2.60) students, free for children under 18; combo ticket 6€ ($7.80) adults, 3€ ($3.90) students, free for children under 18. Wed–Mon 10am–6pm.

SHOPPING

Strasbourg overflows with antiques shops, artisans, craftspeople, and beer makers. Every well-accessorized home in Alsace owns some of the napkins, aprons, tablecloths, and tea and bath towels of the Beauvillé textile mills. **Nappes d'Alsace,** 6 rue Mercière, near the cathedral (✆ **03-88-22-69-29**), has one of the widest selections of textiles in town.

Bastian, 22–24 place de la Cathédrale (✆ **03-88-32-45-93**), specializes in the charming 18th- and 19th-century ceramic tureens that Alsace produced in abundance. Look for ragout pots in the forms of a cabbage, a trout, a boar's head, or a turkey, painted in bright colors. There's also a selection of Louis XV and Louis XVI furniture, crafted in the region during the 18th and 19th centuries following Parisian models from the same era.

Bastian's main competitor is **Ville et Campagne,** 23 quai des Bateliers (✆ **03-88-36-96-84**), in a Renaissance-style 17th-century building across from the Palais de Rohan. Standout items are polychromed Alsatian antiques (especially 18th- and 19th-c. armoires and chests), Louis- and Directoire-style furnishings, statues, and antique paintings.

One of the most appealing shops in Strasbourg is **Arts et Collections d'Alsace,** 4 place du Marché aux Poissons (✆ **03-88-14-03-77**), which offers copies of art objects and utilitarian ware from museums and private collections through Alsace. You'll see upscale gift items for the home and kitchen, made from pottery, stone, wrought iron, glass, copper, and carved wood. The shop also sells fabric by the meter or yard.

A name in pottery that you're likely to encounter is **Soufflenheim,** a provincial rococo pattern—usually in blues and reds—named after the Alsatian village north of Strasbourg where the style originated. To get there, take N63 north of the center of Strasbourg for 24km (15 miles). In the village, ceramics and pottery have been made since the Bronze Age. Soufflenheim is home to at least a dozen outlets selling cake molds, tureens, saucers and cups, dinnerware, and more, usually in rustic patterns. One of the most prominent retailers is **Gérard Wehrling,** 64 rue de Haguenau (✆ **03-88-86-65-25**), known for pottery that can withstand the rigors of modern ovens, microwaves, and refrigerators. Expect to pay 51€ to 100€ ($66–$130) for a large casserole (which is not recommended for freezers).

If you're driving, you may want to check out the villages of Obernai, Illhaeusern, Ribeauvillé, and Schiltigheim. The last is beer-drinking territory; the others offer country wares and antiques.

WHERE TO STAY

EXPENSIVE

Hilton International Strasbourg ★★★ The luxurious, seven-story steel-and-glass Hilton—the best hotel in the city—stands over a university complex opposite the Palais de la Musique et des Congrès. The decor incorporates five kinds of Iberian marble, much of it chosen to resemble the ruddy sandstone of the famous cathedral, which is visible from the hotel. The midsize guest rooms are decorated in standard international chain style—comfortable but not outstanding. They contain tasteful artwork and have spacious marble-trimmed bathrooms with tub/shower combinations.

Av. Herrenschmidt, Strasbourg 67000. Take the Strasbourg-Centre exit from the autoroute and follow signs to the Wacken, Palais des Congrès, and Palais de l'Europe. ✆ **800/445-8667** in the U.S. and Canada, or 03-88-37-10-10. Fax 03-88-36-83-27. www.hilton-strasbourg.com. 243 units. 115€–325€ ($150–$423) double; from 465€ ($605) suite. AE, DC, MC, V. Parking 19€ ($25). **Amenities:** 2 restaurants; 2 bars; room service; babysitting; laundry service; nonsmoking rooms; limited-mobility rooms. *In room:* A/C, TV, minibar, hair dryer, safe (in some), Wi-Fi.

Le Régent Petite France ★★ This well-run hotel offers serious competition to the Hilton. Many guests choose it for its more comfortable rooms and atmosphere. This site was once an ice factory, and many of the old steam machines remain. The marble lobby sets the tone, with ice-cream colors and potted palms. Guest rooms come in various sizes, the best of which are quite spacious and open onto river views. The luxurious beds are among the city's finest, and the bathrooms are state-of-the-art, with tub/shower combinations. The staff is one of the most professional in Strasbourg.

5 rue des Moulins, Strasbourg 67000. ✆ **800/223-5652** in the U.S. and Canada, or 03-88-76-43-43. Fax 03-88-76-43-76. www.regent-petit-france.com. 72 units. 169€–315€ ($220–$410) double; 229€–485€ ($298–$631) suite. AE, DC, MC, V. **Amenities:** Restaurant; bar; fitness club; Jacuzzi; sauna; room service; babysitting; laundry service; dry cleaning; nonsmoking rooms; limited-mobility rooms. *In room:* A/C, TV, minibar, hair dryer, safe, Wi-Fi.

MODERATE

Hôtel Beaucour ★★ This hotel is geared toward business travelers, but anyone will find it ideal—it's the city's most tranquil lodging. At the end of a private street a few blocks east of the cathedral, within what used to be an umbrella factory, it occupies a 17th-century building with timbered ceilings. Every guest room contains a whirlpool tub and a fax hookup, plus a bathroom with tub and shower. Furnishings are of standard international style, but comfortable. The hotel maintains an affiliation with at least two restaurants a short walk away. The concierge, who seems to know all the city's secrets, will make reservations for you.

5 rue des Bouchers, Strasbourg 67000. ✆ **03-88-76-72-00.** Fax 03-88-76-72-60. www.hotel-beaucour.com. 49 units. 139€ ($181) double; 167€–186€ ($217–$242) suite. AE, DC, MC, V. Parking 7€ ($9.10). **Amenities:** Babysitting; laundry service; dry cleaning; limited-mobility rooms. *In room:* TV, minibar, hair dryer, iron, Wi-Fi.

Hôtel Best Western Monopole–Métropole This hotel is on a quiet street near the train station. Its lobby features a scattering of antiques, among them a 17th-century armoire and a statue of a night watchman. An extension of the salon displays oil portraits of 18th-century Alsatian personalities and glass cases with pewter tankards and candlesticks. Breakfast (the only meal available) is served in the high-ceilinged Alsatian-style dining room. The guest rooms are comfortable, with crisp white linens and (in most) air-conditioning. Each unit is unique; some have Alsatian-style antiques. Some bathrooms have tubs; the rest have showers.

16 rue Kuhn, Strasbourg 67000 ✆ **800/528-1234** in the U.S. and Canada, or 03-88-14-39-14. Fax 03-88-32-82-55. www.bw-monopole.com. 90 units. 100€–134€ ($130–$174) double; 150€ ($195) suite. AE, DC, MC, V. Parking 12€

($16). **Amenities:** Bar; babysitting; laundry service; dry cleaning; nonsmoking rooms; limited-mobility rooms. *In room:* TV, minibar, hair dryer, iron, safe, Wi-Fi.

Hôtel Cardinal de Rohan ★ *Value* In the pedestrian zone steps from the cathedral, this five-story hotel is one of the city's best values and within walking distance of the Palais de Rohan. The 17th-century building was rebuilt shortly after World War II. It offers a choice of elegantly furnished rooms, the cheapest of which are small and have a French bed called a *matrimonial* (a standard double bed). Guest-room decor ranges from Louis XV to a regional Alsatian look with lots of wood paneling. All units come with shower-only bathrooms.

17–19 rue du Maroquin, Strasbourg 67060. ✆ **03-88-32-85-11.** Fax 03-88-75-65-37. www.hotel-rohan.com. 36 units. 72€–135€ ($94–$176) double. AE, DC, MC, V. **Amenities:** Babysitting; laundry service; dry cleaning; nonsmoking rooms. *In room:* TV, minibar, hair dryer, safe, Wi-Fi.

Hôtel de l'Europe Behind a half-timbered facade a 3-minute walk west of the cathedral, this is one of the best-located government-rated three-star hotels in town. Its roots go back to the 15th century, when it functioned as a coaching inn; it was enlarged with the annexation of an 18th-century house next door. Frequently renovated, it's comfortable and unpretentious, with all the electronic gadgets you may want. Units run the gamut from modern to a half-timbered fantasy directly under the roof (room no. 404), where angled beams evoke the original construction. Each of the accommodations has a tiled and tidily maintained bathroom, most with tub and shower, the rest with shower only.

38–40 rue du Fossé-des-Tanneurs, Strasbourg 67000. ✆ **03-88-32-17-88.** Fax 03-88-75-65-45. www.hotel-europe.com. 60 units. 61€–184€ ($79–$239) double. AE, DC, MC, V. Parking 13€ ($17). **Amenities:** Room service; babysitting; nonsmoking rooms. *In room:* A/C, TV, minibar (in some), hair dryer, safe, Wi-Fi.

Hôtel des Princes *Value* A 15-minute walk from the center of town, the Hôtel des Princes enjoys a three-star government rating and is one of the best bargains in the city. The management is helpful; the renovated rooms are furnished comfortably but simply. About half have tub/shower combos, the other half just showers. Continental breakfast is the only meal served.

33 rue Geiler, Quartier du Conseil de l'Europe, Strasbourg 67000. ✆ **03-88-61-55-19.** Fax 03-88-41-10-92. www.hotel-princes.com. 43 units. 110€–125€ ($143–$163) double. AE, MC, V. **Amenities:** Babysitting; laundry service; dry cleaning; nonsmoking rooms. *In room:* TV, minibar.

Le Régent Contades ★★ *Finds* Our favorite moderately priced choice is this glorified B&B, in a five-story structure with dormers, close to the cathedral. Diplomats may consider it a secret, but word is out. The stylish hostelry has an intelligent, helpful staff. The guest rooms are furnished in a romantic style with a variety of monochromatic colors that include pink, blue, or soft browns or reds. The most spacious units are in a new wing. Most bathrooms hold tub/shower combos (the rest have showers). Breakfast is the only meal served.

8 av. de la Liberté, Strasbourg 67000. ✆ **03-88-15-05-05.** Fax 03-88-15-05-15. www.regent-contades.com. 47 units. 109€–255€ ($142–$332) double; 169€–420€ ($220–$546) suite. Parking 18€ ($23). AE, DC, MC, V. **Amenities:** Bar; fitness center; sauna; room service; laundry service; nonsmoking rooms; limited-mobility rooms. *In room:* A/C, TV, minibar, hair dryer, safe, Wi-Fi.

INEXPENSIVE

Hôtel de l'Ill *Value* A 5-minute walk from the cathedral, this government-rated two-star hotel is a good deal. The former restaurant added rooms in the 1920s. In the

1990s, the property became a hotel and gained a modern wing. An inviting, unpretentious place, it offers quiet, comfortably furnished rooms decorated in either modern or Alsatian traditional style. Two rooms at the rear have a private terrace or balcony opening onto a view of neighboring gardens. Each room comes with a tidily kept, shower-only bathroom, but no amenities other than a phone (some have a TV). The breakfast room is decorated Laura Ashley–style—well, except for the cuckoo clock.

8 rue des Bateliers, Strasbourg 67000. ✆ **03-88-36-20-01.** Fax 03-88-35-30-03. 27 units. 57€–67€ ($74–$87) double. MC, V. Parking 7€ ($9.10). **Amenities:** Nonsmoking rooms; limited-mobility rooms. *In room:* TV, Wi-Fi.

Hotel Gutenberg ★ *Finds* Just off place Gutenberg, this many-windowed hotel is both a bargain and a discovery. The renovated mansion exudes old-fashioned charm—the sculptured walls date to 1745—yet is completely modern (with soundproofing). M. Hyboux, the owner, welcomes guests to "the capital of Europe." Many of the guest rooms, with flowery draperies and upholstered furniture, have wooden beams. Each comes with a tiled bathroom with shower. The most romantic accommodations, evoking old France, are on the fifth floor under timbers.

31 rue des Serruriers, Strasbourg 67000. ✆ **03-88-32-17-15.** Fax 03-88-75-76-67. www.hotel-gutenberg.com. 42 units. 65€–98€ ($85–$127) double. MC, V. *In room:* A/C (in some), TV, Wi-Fi.

WHERE TO DINE

VERY EXPENSIVE

Au Crocodile ★★★ ALSATIAN A beautiful sky-lit restaurant, Au Crocodile serves the most inventive food in Strasbourg. Only two restaurants in this region equal it: Le Buerehiesel (see below) and the Auberge de l'Ill (see "Colmar," later in this chapter). An especially appealing feature is the fixed-price menus that revolve around creative themes, which have included Egypt and Victor Hugo. Chef Emile Jung offers a wide array of inventive dishes. Some of the best include strips of duckling cooked in a sauce of red wine and a reduction of the bird's blood; sautéed scallops with purée of celery and Indian-style (Marsala-style) spiced butter sauce; delicate local freshwater whitefish *(sandre)* served in sauerkraut; and duck liver cooked in a salt crust. Our major problem comes only when the bill (*la note,* as the French say) arrives—especially when we indulge in the high-priced wines.

10 rue de l'Outre. ✆ **03-88-32-13-02.** www.au-crocodile.com. Reservations required. Main courses 40€–80€ ($52–$104); fixed-price lunch 57€–112€ ($74–$146); fixed-price dinner 86€–145€ ($112–$189). AE, DC, MC, V. Tues–Sat noon–2pm and 7:30–9:30pm. Closed last 3 weeks of July and Dec 24–Jan 8.

Le Buerehiesel ★★★ MODERN FRENCH Also known as Le Restaurant Westermann, Buerehiesel is famous for Antoine Westermann's *cuisine moderne* and for its prime location in l'Orangerie, a park at the end of the allée de la Robertsau planned by the landscape artist Le Nôtre, who gave the park to Joséphine during her marriage to Napoleon. The decor, slightly modernized in recent years, includes richly grained wooden ceilings and a conservatively modern design. The kitchen recycles heirloom recipes in innovative and exciting ways. Of special merit are foie gras of goose with truffles; frogs' legs fried with local herbs; ravioli stuffed with confit of onions; and steamed sea bass with a marinade of crisp, al dente vegetables and aromatic herbs. Appealingly old-fashioned, and prepared for only two diners at a time, is one of the Alsace's most classic recipes, *poularde baeckoffe:* Consisting of a top-quality Bresse hen that's slow-cooked in a covered ceramic dish, it comes in versions appropriate to both summer (with potatoes, artichoke hearts, and a confit of lemons) and winter (with leeks, potatoes, and truffles). Don't miss a spectacular dessert, bitter chocolate in puff pastry, served with essence of bitter oranges preserved in their own juices and Grand Marnier.

4 parc de l'Orangerie. ✆ **03-88-45-56-65.** www.buerehiesel.com. Reservations required. Main courses 61€–130€ ($79–$169); fixed-price 5-course menu 136€ ($177), 7-course menu 180€ ($234). AE, DC, MC, V. Tues–Sat noon–2pm and 7–9:45pm. Closed 1st 3 weeks of Jan and 1st 3 weeks of Aug.

MODERATE

L'Arsenal ALSATIAN This restaurant in a late-19th-century building that was originally a private house often counts European Parliament members among its patrons. The inventive regional menu changes often but may feature young rabbit and gooseliver in jelly, veal escalope and calves' feet in red-wine sauce, duck roasted with pears and local wine, or salmon on a bed of sauerkraut. A specialty is *kugelhof* (pastry shell), which is normally a sweet dish—the chef here fills it with escargots and mushrooms. The pig's foot stuffed with foie gras is the best rendering of this dish in town.

11 rue de l'Abreuvoir. ✆ **03-88-35-03-69.** Reservations required. Main courses 16€–23€ ($21–$30); fixed-price lunch 23€–30€ ($30–$39); fixed-price dinner 30€ ($39). AE, MC, V. Mon–Fri noon–1:30pm and 7–9pm. Closed Aug.

Maison des Tanneurs ★ ALSATIAN In La Petite France, this restaurant abounds with flowers and antiques that create a warm atmosphere, and has a terrace that opens onto the canal. The restaurant has been called "La Maison de la Choucroute," because its sauerkraut-and-pork platter is the finest in the area. But the chef prepares many other tasty dishes, including snails cooked Alsatian style with local white wine, a traditional version of Strasbourg foie gras, and guinea fowl stuffed with green peppers. We recommend crayfish tails in court bouillon and *coq au Riesling* (chicken cooked in white wine, with noodles).

42 rue du Bain-aux-Plantes. ✆ **03-88-32-79-70.** www.maison-des-tanneurs.com. Reservations required. Main courses 16€–25€ ($21–$33). AE, DC, MC, V. Tues–Sat noon–1:45pm and 7–10pm (also Sun noon–2pm in Dec). Closed 3 weeks in Jan.

Maison Kammerzell ★ *Kids* ALSATIAN The gingerbread Maison Kammerzell is an attraction as well as a fantastic restaurant. The carved-wood framework was constructed during the Renaissance, the overhanging stories in 1589. We suggest *la choucroute formidable,* the Alsatian specialty prepared with goose fat, Riesling wine, and Strasbourg sausages. The owner, Guy-Pierre Baumann, also offers homemade foie gras, guinea hen with mushrooms, medallion of young wild boar, and other regional dishes. A concession to modern cuisine is the chef's version of sauerkraut with fish. Families will want to take advantage of the free meals for children under 10 at lunch, which makes the place popular with big broods. If you'd rather eat your sauerkraut in relative peace, come for dinner.

16 place de la Cathédrale. ✆ **03-88-32-42-14.** www.maison-kammerzell.com. Reservations required. Main courses 15€–24€ ($20–$31); fixed-price menu 29€–45€ ($38–$59). AE, DC, MC, V. Daily noon–2:30pm and 7–11pm.

INEXPENSIVE

Brasserie de l'Ancienne Douane ★★ *Value* ALSATIAN This is the largest and most colorful dining spot in Strasbourg. Established in the oldest part of town as part of a historical renovation, it offers 600 seats indoors and 200 seats on a terrace. The high-ceilinged rooms are somewhat formal, with Teutonic chairs and heavily timbered ceilings. Among the Alsatian specialties are the well-known "sauerkraut of the Customs officers" and the foie gras of Strasbourg. Onion pie and ham knuckle with potato salad and horseradish are also popular.

6 rue de la Douane. ✆ **03-88-15-78-78.** www.anciennedouane.fr. Reservations recommended. Main courses 14€–25€ ($18–$33); fixed-price menu 18€–50€ ($23–$65). AE, DC, MC, V. Daily 11:30am–2:30pm and 6:30–11pm.

WHERE TO STAY & DINE NEARBY

Many visitors head north 12km (7½ miles) to La Wantzenau, which has very good restaurants. From Strasbourg, take D468 along the west bank of the Rhine.

Relais de la Poste ★★★ FRENCH/ALSATIAN The leading restaurant in this citadel of fine dining is a cozy half-timbered 18th-century house in the heart of the little Alsatian village. The chefs depend on the changing seasons for their inspiration. They prepare traditional dishes with a modern twist, lighter versions of old favorites. Their succulent concoctions include boned and stuffed quail with a sauce of morels, and fried turbot *"osso buco"* with Szechuan peppercorn sauce. Two superb appetizers are fresh gooseliver and game terrine. Other memorable dishes include pikeperch in lobster sauce with basil noodles, and salmon tournedos with white beans.

The inn also rents 18 comfortably furnished guest rooms, each in a rustic style, for a double rate of 77€ to 122€ ($100–$159).

21 rue du Général-de-Gaulle, La Wantzenau 67610. ✆ **03-88-59-24-80.** Fax 03-88-59-24-89. www.relais-poste.com. Main courses 23€–45€ ($30–$59); fixed-price menu 45€–130€ ($59–$169). AE, DC, MC, V. Tues–Fri and Sun noon–2pm; Tues–Sat 7–10pm. Closed first 2 weeks of Jan.

STRASBOURG AFTER DARK

A bastion of outdoor entertainment is **place de la Cathédrale,** where you can find an assortment of performers and artists. Dancers perform spontaneously against the illumination of the cathedral. From mid-July to early August, additional folk dances take place in La Petite France on Monday night in the places des Tripiers, Tuesday in the place Benjamin Zix, and Wednesday in the place du Marché aux Cochons de Lait. Performance dates vary; check with the Office de Tourisme (✆ **03-88-52-28-28;** www.ot-strasbourg.fr) for a schedule.

THE PERFORMING ARTS For opera and ballet, seek out the **Opéra du Rhin,** 19 place Broglie (✆ **03-88-75-48-23;** www.operanationaldurhin.fr); tickets cost 11€ to 75€ ($14–$98). The **Orchestre Philharmonique de Strasbourg** performs at the Palais de la Musique et des Congrès, place de Bordeaux (✆ **03-88-15-09-00;** www.philharmonique-strasbourg.com). Tickets cost 6€ to 50€ ($7.80–$65). The **Théâtre National de Strasbourg** plays a busy schedule at 1 av. de la Marseillaise (✆ **03-88-24-88-00;** www.tns.fr). Tickets cost 16€ to 33€ ($21–$43).

CLUBS Head to the streets surrounding place de la Cathédrale: rue des Frères, rue des Soeurs, and rue de la Croix. One of your best bets is **Le Gayot,** 18 rue des Frères (✆ **03-88-36-31-88**), with occasional guest performers. **Jeannette et les Cycleux,** 3 rue des Tonneliers (✆ **03-88-23-02-71**), is a wine bar with a juke box playing rock 'n' roll and other hits from America in the 1950s. Entrance is free.

Le Seven, 25 rue des Tonneliers (✆ **03-88-32-77-77**), has a below-street-level dance floor that features all types of music except disco. The place packs in a stylish crowd ages 20 to 35. Cover ranges from 10€ to 15€ ($13–$20).

One of the biggest and most visible discos in the region, **Le Chalet,** 376 rte. de Wantzenau (✆ **03-88-31-18-31**), lies 8km (5 miles) north of Strasbourg. The 8€-to-18€ ($10–$23) cover buys the first drink and access to two huge and distinctly different sections. One is designed for techno fans, another for less harsh dance music, with a good mix of disco classics. Open 10pm to 4am Thursday to Saturday. To get there, follow signs to Wantzenau.

2 La Route du Vin (Wine Road) ★★★

The fastest route between Strasbourg and Colmar, 68km (42 miles) south, is N83. But if you have time, the famous Route du Vin makes a rewarding experience. It rolls through 60 charming villages. Along the way are inns where you can sample wine, take a leisurely meal, or spend the night.

The Wine Road runs along the Vosges foothills, with medieval towers and feudal ruins evoking faded pageantry. The vine-covered slopes sometimes reach a height of 435m (1,427 ft.), and an estimated 20,000 hectares (50,000 acres) of vineyards line the road. Some 30,000 families earn their living tending the grapes. The best time to go is for the harvest in September and October. The well-marked route starts at Marlenheim.

MARLENHEIM

This agreeable town, noted for its Vorlauf red wine, is 21km (13 miles) west of Strasbourg on N4. Even if you can't drive the full length of the Wine Road, you may want to visit for the excellent inn.

WHERE TO STAY & DINE

Le Cerf ★★★ In the heart of this medieval village, occupying a half-timbered building at least 300 years old, this hotel offers pleasantly furnished rooms adjoining an excellent restaurant. Michel Husser and his wife, Cathy, will feed you elegant, esoteric, and upscale menu items that include, depending on the mood of the chef, such dishes as a fricassee of crayfish and wild mushrooms, a gratin of mushrooms with Riesling, an exotic version of sauerkraut that supplements the normal roster of pork and sausage with smoked foie gras, and a roulade of lobster with spinach and a broth that's brewed from the lobster shells. The restaurant, but not the hotel, is closed on Tuesday and Wednesday year-round.

30 rue du Général-de-Gaulle, Marlenheim 67520. ✆ **03-88-87-73-73.** Fax 03-88-87-68-08. www.lecerf.com. 14 units. 90€–140€ ($117–$182) double; 200€ ($260) suite. AE, DC, MC, V. Free parking. **Amenities:** Restaurant. *In room:* A/C, TV, hair dryer.

Finds **Biking the Wine Road**

To rent bikes, visit **Association Velo Emploi,** 10 rue des Bouchers (✆ **03-88-24-05-61**). Subsidized by the city of Strasbourg, this place offers among the cheapest rentals anywhere. Half-day rentals cost 5€ ($6.50), full-day rentals 8€ ($10). Open April to September daily 9:30am to 12:30pm and 1:30 to 7pm; October to March Monday to Friday 10am to 5pm. A security deposit of 100€ ($130) is required.

The Strasbourg tourist office provides maps showing bike routes that fan out from the city into the countryside, with emphasis on cycle lanes (*les pistes cyclables* in French) that prohibit cars. One of these is a 27km (17-mile) stretch that runs southwest from Strasbourg to the wine hamlet of Molsheim. It has a forest on one side, the banks of the Brûche River (a tributary of the Rhine) on the other, and little car traffic.

WANGEN

One of the jewels of the route, Wangen (30km/19 miles from Strasbourg) has a city gate crowned by a tower and twisting, narrow streets. It's one of the most typical of the wine towns. The road from Wangen winds down to Molsheim.

MOLSHEIM ★

Molsheim (32km/20 miles from Strasbourg) retains its ramparts and a Gothic-Renaissance church built from 1614 to 1619. The Guild of Butchers erected its *Alte Metzig* (town hall), which has a turret, gargoyles, and a loggia. The belfry houses a clock with allegorical figures striking the hour. The local **Office de Tourisme** is at 19 place de l'Hôtel de Ville (✆ **03-88-38-11-61**).

ROSHEIM ★

Nestled behind medieval fortifications, this town (31km/19 miles from Strasbourg) has a 12th-century Romanesque house and the Eglise St-Pierre et St-Paul, also Romanesque, from 2 centuries later; it's dominated by an octagonal tower. Medieval walls and gate towers evoke Rosheim's past. The **Office de Tourisme** is at place de la République (✆ **03-88-38-11-61**).

OBERNAI ★★

The patron saint of Alsace, Obernai, was born here, 32km (20 miles) from Strasbourg. With its timbered houses and colorful marketplace, **place du Marché,** this town is one of the most interesting stops on the Wine Road. There's a **market** on Thursday from 8am to noon; go early. **Place de l'Etoile** abounds with flowers, and the **Hôtel de Ville** has a delightful loggia. An old watchtower, the **Tour de la Chapelle,** is from the 13th and 16th centuries. The town's six-pail **fountain** is one of the most spectacular in Alsace. The **Office de Tourisme** is at place du Beffroi (✆ **03-88-95-64-13**).

WHERE TO STAY & DINE

Le Parc ★★ This contemporary hotel offers fine dining and many facilities you'd find in a spa, with a traditional Alsatian motif and architectural style. City dwellers seeking R&R appreciate the well-furnished, spacious guest rooms, each with a combination tub/shower bathroom. The well-managed restaurant serves dishes that vary depending on what's in the local markets. That may include monkfish with mushrooms, duckling with apples and cèpes (flap mushrooms), crayfish salad, salmon in red-wine sauce, and rich fruit desserts.

169 rte. d'Ottrott, Obernai 67210. ✆ **03-88-95-50-08.** Fax 03-88-95-37-29. www.hotel-du-parc.com. 62 units. 115€–225€ ($150–$293) double; 260€–325€ ($338–$423) suite. AE, MC, V. Closed 2 weeks in late June to mid-July and mid-Dec to mid-Jan. **Amenities:** Restaurant; bar; cigar bar; indoor and outdoor pools; Jacuzzi; sauna; steam room; spa; business center; room service; laundry service; dry cleaning; limited-mobility rooms. *In room:* A/C, TV, hair dryer, safe, Wi-Fi.

BARR

The grapes for some of the finest Alsatian wines, sylvaner and Gewürztraminer, are harvested here. The castles of Landsberg and Andlau stand high above the town. Barr (37km/23 miles from Strasbourg) has many pleasant old-timbered houses. The charming **place de l'Hôtel-de-Ville** has a town hall from 1640. Call ✆ **03-88-08-66-65** for tourist information at 1 Rue des Bouchers.

MITTELBERGHEIM

Mittelbergheim, 43km (27 miles) from Strasbourg, is a special village. Houses in the Renaissance style border its **place de l'Hôtel-de-Ville.**

WHERE TO STAY & DINE

Winstub Gilg ★ This is an excellent inn. Though parts of the building date from 1614, its showpiece is a two-story stone staircase, classified as a historic monument. Medieval stonemasons who worked on the cathedral at Strasbourg carved it. Each attractively furnished guest room has a combination tub/shower. Chef Vincent Reuschlé attracts a loyal following with regional specialties such as onion tart, sauerkraut, and foie gras in brioche. Main courses include stewed kidneys and sweetbreads, rack of lamb cooked pink, duck with oranges, and, in season, roast pheasant with grapes. The hotel and restaurant close in January and from June 21 to July 8. The rest of the year, the restaurant closes on Tuesday and Wednesday.

1 rte. du Vin, Mittelbergheim, Barr 67140. ✆ **03-88-08-91-37.** Fax 03-88-08-45-17. www.hotel-gilg.com. 15 units. 52€–85€ ($68–$111) double. AE, DC, MC, V. **Amenities:** Restaurant. *In room:* TV.

ANDLAU

This gardenlike resort, 42km (26 miles) from Strasbourg, was the site of an abbey founded in 887 by the disgraced wife of Emperor Charles the Fat. It has now faded into history, but a church remains that dates from the 12th century. In the tympanum are noteworthy Romanesque carvings. The **Office de Tourisme,** 5 rue du Général-de-Gaulle (✆ **03-88-08-22-57;** www.pays-de-barr.com), is open Monday to Friday 9am to noon.

WHERE TO DINE

Au Boeuf Rouge TRADITIONAL FRENCH This bustling, unpretentious bistro has a busy bar and a comfortably battered dining room. Its menu of time-tested specialties includes homemade terrines, gamecock, fresh fish, and a tempting dessert cart. Noted chef Pierre Kieffer prepares a fabulous quenelle of brochet, a local whitefish, according to his grandmother's recipe. While the fare is reliable and consistent, it isn't the most innovative cookery on the wine trail, excepting his seasonal version of wild boar with cassis sauce and spaetzle. For dessert, have a slice of Baettelman, an Alsatian cake baked with apples and cherries. There's also a wine *stube* (tavern) on-site to the right as you enter. From March to October, you can sit on the terrace in front.

6 rue du Dr.-Stoltz, Andlau. ✆ **03-88-08-96-26.** Reservations recommended. Main courses 15€–25€ ($20–$33); fixed-price menu 15€–28€ ($20–$36). AE, DC, MC, V. Oct–July 12 Fri–Wed 11:30am–2:30pm, Fri–Tues 6–9:30pm; July 13–Sept 30 daily 11:30am–2:30pm and 6–9:30pm. Closed 10 days in Feb and 3 weeks June–July.

DAMBACH

In the midst of its vineyards, Dambach (48km/30 miles from Strasbourg) is one of the delights of the Wine Road. The town, formally Dambach-la-Ville, has ramparts and three fortified gates. Its timbered houses are gabled with galleries, and many contain oriels. Wrought-iron signs still tell you if a place is a bakery or a butcher shop. A short drive from the town is the **Chapelle St-Sebastian,** with a 15th-century ossuary. **The Office de Tourisme** (✆ **03-88-92-61-00**) is in La Mairie (town hall), place du Marché.

SELESTAT ★

Sélestat lies 52km (32 miles) from Strasbourg. It was once a free city, a center of the Renaissance, and the seat of a great school. Towered battlements enclose the town. The **Bibliothèque Humaniste,** 1 rue de la Bibliothèque (✆ **03-88-58-07-20**), houses a collection of manuscripts, including Sainte-Foy's *Book of Miracles.* It's open Monday and Wednesday to Friday from 9am to noon and 2 to 6pm, Saturday from

9am to noon. (In July and Aug, it's also open Sat–Sun 2–5pm.) Admission is 3.70€ ($4.80) for adults, 2.20€ ($2.85) for students, and free for children under 12.

The Gothic **Eglise St-George** has some fine stained glass and a gilded and painted stone pulpit. Also try to visit the 12th-century **Eglise Ste-Foy,** built of red sandstone in the Romanesque style. One of the town's most noteworthy Renaissance buildings is the **Maison de Stephan Ziegler** in the Rue de Verdun.

The **Office de Tourisme** is in La Commanderie St-Jean, boulevard du Général-Leclerc (✆ **03-88-58-87-20**).

From Sélestat, you can detour about 750m (2,460 ft.) up an isolated peak to **Château Haut-Koenigsbourg** (✆ **03-88-82-50-60**), a 15th-century castle. It's the largest in Alsace and affords an eagle's-nest view. It once belonged to the Hohenstaufens. During the Thirty Years' War, the Swedes dismantled it. In 1901, the then-ruined pile was offered as a gift by the city of Sélestat to the German Kaiser, Wilhelm II, who rebuilt it at massive personal expense. At the end of World War I, it was ceded back to the French nation as part of the Treaty of Versailles. Admission is 7.50€ ($9.75) for adults, 4.80€ ($6.25) for students 18 to 25, and free for children under 18. During April, May, and September, it's open daily 9:30am to 5:30pm; during June, July, and August, it's open daily 9:30am to 6:30pm. During October and March, it's open daily 9:45am to 5pm. And from November to February, it's open daily 9:45am to noon and 1 to 5pm.

WHERE TO DINE NEARBY

La Couronne ★★★ ALSATIAN This charming family-run place serves deftly prepared dishes reflecting the bounty of Alsace. A flower-filled vestibule leads to a trio of dining rooms. The chefs know the classics but give a personal twist to most dishes, using market-fresh ingredients in skillful concoctions that look as delectable as they taste. They prepare light, modern interpretations of Alsatian dishes without heavy sauces and fats. The restaurant has a fine cellar of Alsatian wines. Menu choices may include noisettes of roebuck (from midsummer to Christmas), ragout of fish, foie gras, *omble chevalier* (whitefish from Lake Geneva) with sauerkraut and cumin-laced potatoes, and frogs' legs served with freshwater-shrimp flan.

45 rue de Sélestat-Baldenheim. From Sélestat, go 9km (5⅗ miles) east on D21; when the road forks, bear right and take D209 to the village of Baldenheim. ✆ **03-88-85-32-22.** Reservations required. Main courses 15€–30€ ($20–$39); fixed-price menu 32€–68€ ($42–$88). MC, V. Tues–Wed and Fri–Sun noon–2:30pm; Tues–Wed and Fri–Sat 7–9:30pm. Closed 1st week of Jan and mid-July to Aug.

BERGHEIM

Renowned for its wines, this town (85km/53 miles from Strasbourg) has kept part of its 15th-century fortifications. You can see timbered Alsatian houses and a Gothic church.

RIBEAUVILLE ★

At the foot of vine-clad hills, Ribeauvillé (87km/54 miles from Strasbourg) is picturesque, with old shop signs, pierced balconies, turrets, and flower-decorated houses. The town is noted for its Riesling and Gewürztraminer wines. See its Renaissance fountain and **Hôtel de Ville,** place de la Mairie, which has a collection of silver-gilt medieval and Renaissance tankards known as *hanaps.*

Guided tours showcase the *hanaps,* the building's architecture, and the history of the town. The free 90-minute tours run from May to September, on Sunday and Tuesday through Friday at 10am, 11am, and 2pm. On tour days at 3pm, the same guide leads a 90-minute walking tour of the town. Tours are in French, German, or halting English.

Also of interest in Ribeauvillé is the **Tour des Bouchers** ("butcher's tower"), built in stages from the 13th to the 16th century.

Every year on the first Sunday in September, visitors fill the town for its **Jour des Menetriers (Day of the Minstrels).** Beginning at 3pm and lasting almost 2½ hours, it features a parade of flute players from Alsace, the rest of France, Switzerland, and Germany, and as many as 600 parade participants. You can stand anywhere to watch the spectacle, but seats on the medieval stone benches line either side of the parade route.

WHERE TO STAY & DINE

Clos St-Vincent ★★★ This is one of the most elegant choices along Route du Vin. Most of the individually decorated guest rooms have a balcony or terrace, but you get much more than a view of the Haut-Rhin vineyards and summer roses. The rooms, ranging from medium to large, are furnished with grand comfort; each has a bed covered in fine linen and a bathroom with state-of-the-art plumbing and combination tub/shower. Some have air-conditioning. The Chapotin family's cuisine is exceptional: hot duck liver with nuts, turbot with sorrel, roebuck (in season) in hot sauce, and veal kidneys in pinot noir. The wines are smooth, especially the popular Riesling and Gewürztraminer.

Rte. de Bergheim, Ribeauvillé 68150. ✆ **03-89-73-67-65.** Fax 03-89-73-32-20. www.leclossaintvincent.com. 24 units. 105€–200€ ($137–$260) double; 185€–270€ ($241–$351) suite. AE, MC, V. Closed Nov 15–Mar 15. **Amenities:** Restaurant; bar; indoor pool; room service; babysitting, limited-mobility rooms. *In room:* TV, minibar, hair dryer, safe, Wi-Fi.

RIQUEWIHR ★★★

Surrounded by some of the finest vineyards in Alsace, this town (89km/55 miles from Strasbourg) appears much as it did in the 16th century. With well-preserved walls and towers and wine presses, it's one of the most rewarding destinations along the route.

You can see Gothic and Renaissance houses, with balconies, gables, and carved doors and windows. The most interesting are **Maison Liebrich** (1535), **Maison Preiss-Zimmer** (1686), and **Maison Kiener** (1574). Try to peer into some of the courtyards, where time seems frozen. **Tour de Dolder (Dolder Belfry Tower)** is from 1291. Riquewihr contains at least four minor museums, plus a handful of other quasi-museums that the average short-term visitor may, without missing a lot, opt to skip. Two of the most important, however, and even these are worth only a very brief visit, include the pentagonal **Musée de la Tour des Voleurs,** in the rue des Juifs, which is the site of a medieval torture chamber, and the **Musée Dolder,** which showcases a handful of civic exhibits from the earliest days of the city's medieval history. A combined ticket to both museums costs 3€ ($3.90) for adults and 2€ ($2.60) for students and persons under 18. Both monuments are open April to October only, Wednesday to Monday 10am to noon and 2 to 5:30pm and for 2 weeks in December. For more information about either of these very minor museums, contact the local **Office de Tourisme,** 1 Grand'Rue in nearby Ribeauvillé (✆ **08-20-36-09-22**). Another minor museum within Riquewihr is the **Musée de la Communication,** a site also known as the **Alsace Postal History Museum** (✆ **03-89-47-93-80**). Set within the thick stone walls of the Château de Riquewihr, which was originally built in 1539 by the Duke of Wurttemberg, it costs 4€ ($5.20) for adults, 3.50€ ($4.55) for students, and

2.50€ ($3.25) for children under 18. Hours are the same, with the same annual closing, as the two other museums noted immediately above.

WHERE TO STAY & DINE

Auberge du Schoenenbourg ★★★ FRENCH We highly recommend the food here. You'll dine in a garden surrounded by vineyards at the edge of the village. Chef François Kiener, assisted by Christophe Schriber, offers a delectable array of tantalizing fare. *Foie gras maison* is de rigueur, but salmon soufflé with sabayon truffles is an elegant surprise. Try panache of fish with sorrel, ravioli of snails with poppy seeds, or tournedos in puff pastry with mushrooms and foie gras. Especially flavorful is a platter of both smoked and fresh salmon, served with creamy horseradish sauce and herb-flavored sauerkraut.

Although the restaurant does not rent rooms, the 58-room **Hôtel Le Schoenenbourg** is next door on rue du Schoenenbourg (✆ **03-89-49-01-11;** fax 03-89-47-95-88; www.hotel-schoenenbourg.fr). It offers comfortably furnished guest rooms for 80€ to 117€ ($104–$152) in a double, 210€ ($273) in a suite.

2 rue de la Piscine. ✆ **03-89-47-92-28.** Reservations required. Main courses 25€–33€ ($33–$43); fixed-price menu 32€ ($42) Mon–Fri only, and 44€–78€ ($57–$101). AE, MC, V. Year-round Sun noon–2pm; Mar–Oct daily 7–10pm; Nov–Apr Thurs–Tues 7–10pm. Closed Jan.

KIENTZHEIM

Kientzheim (90km/56 miles from Strasbourg) is known for its wine, two castles, timber-framed houses, and walls from the Middle Ages. From here, it's just a short drive to Kaysersberg, also known for its vineyards. Tourist info can be found in Kaysersberg.

KAYSERSBERG ★★

Once a free city of the empire, Kaysersberg (93km/58 miles from Strasbourg) lies at the mouth of the Weiss Valley, between two vine-covered slopes; it's crowned by a castle ruined in the Thirty Years' War. From one of the many ornately carved bridges, you can see the city's medieval fortifications along the top of one of the nearby hills. Many of the houses are Gothic and Renaissance, and most have half-timbering, wrought-iron accents, leaded windows, and multiple designs carved into reddish sandstone.

In the cafes, you'll hear a combination of French and Alsatian. The age of the speaker usually determines the language—the older ones remain faithful to the dialect of their grandparents.

Dr. Albert Schweitzer was born here in 1875; his house is near the bridge over the Weiss. You can visit the **Musée du Docteur Schweitzer,** 126 rue du Général de Gaulle (✆ **03-89-47-36-55**), from April to November, daily from 9am to noon and 2 to 6pm (closed Dec–Mar). Admission is 2€ ($2.60) adults and 1€ ($1.30) for students and children under 12.

The **Office de Tourisme** is at 39 rue du Général-de-Gaulle (✆ **03-89-78-22-78;** www.kaysersberg.com).

WHERE TO STAY & DINE

Au Lion d'Or FRENCH/ALSATIAN This 1521 building boasts an exceptionally beautiful decor. A carved lion's head adorns the oak door leading into the restaurant, which has a beamed ceiling, stone detailing, brass chandeliers, and a massive fireplace. If you eat at an outdoor table, you'll have a view of one of Alsace's prettiest streets. The classic Alsatian dishes include wild game, foie gras (which Alsatians claim to have invented), and yummy pork dishes, often with hams and sausage. Sauerkraut, served in its traditional meat-and-potato form or with fish, is an enduring specialty and a favorite with the loyal clientele.

66 rue du Général-de-Gaulle. ✆ **03-89-47-11-16.** www.auliondor.fr. Reservations required. Main courses 13€–20€ ($17–$26); fixed-price menu 18€–36€ ($23–$47). AE, MC, V. May–Oct Thurs–Tues noon–2:30pm, Thurs–Mon 6:30–9:30pm; Feb–Apr and Nov–Dec Thurs–Mon noon–2:30pm and 6:30–9:30pm. Closed Feb.

Le Chambard ★★★ FRENCH/ALSATIAN The regional cuisine here is so good, it's worth planning a stop. You'll recognize the restaurant by the gilded wrought-iron sign above the cobblestones. Exposed stone and polished wood accent the rustic interior. Regional specialties with Mediterranean influences attest to the mastery of the kitchen. The imaginative chef, Olivier Nasti, presents impeccably flavored and sophisticated cuisine. The restaurant is known for sauerkraut served with a host of (mostly smoked) pork specialties, as well as foie gras and pungent Münster cheese. Other choices include a "cake" of eggplant with goose foie gras, an upscale version of traditional Alsatian stew made with foie gras, and traditional Alsatian cake *(kugelhof)* with cinnamon-flavored ice cream. The cellar stocks the best local vintages.

A 20-room hotel annex, built in 1981 to match the other structures on the street, has a massive Renaissance fireplace that was transported from another building. A double goes for 117€ to 151€ ($152–$196).

9–13 rue du Général-de-Gaulle, Kaysersberg 68240. ✆ **03-89-47-10-17.** Fax 03-89-47-35-03. www.lechambard.com. Reservations required. Main courses 31€–68€ ($40–$88); fixed-price menu 22€–75€ ($29–$98). AE, MC, V. Thurs–Sun noon–2pm; Tues–Sun 7–9pm.

AMMERSCHWIHR

Ammerschwihr, 9km (5⅗ miles) north of Colmar (79km/49 miles from Strasbourg), is a good stop to cap off your Wine Road tour. Once a free city of the empire, the town was almost destroyed in 1944 and has been reconstructed in the traditional style. More and more travelers visit to sample the wine, especially Käferkopf. Check out the town's gate towers, 16th-century parish church, and remains of early fortifications.

WHERE TO STAY & DINE

A l'Arbre Vert ★ *Value* At least part of this hotel's charm derives from the close supervision of Joël and Evelyne Tournier, chef and *maître d'hôtel,* respectively, who represent at least three generations of attentive, family-managed service. Public rooms are delightful, loaded with regional artifacts and coziness. Guest rooms were renovated in 2003, and each is clean, well maintained, and comfortable, with a shower-only bathroom. The restaurant, which is closed every Tuesday, is open to nonresidents and serves very good Alsatian specialties, including savory scallop of gooseliver with pinot noir, cassoulet of snails with mushrooms, and crisp-baked salmon with leeks. Some of the best warm dessert soufflés in the region emerge, steaming, from the kitchens, many laden with whatever fresh fruit happens to be in season at the time. (In midwinter, look for a superb version with oranges, clementines, or lemons.)

7 rue des Cigognes, Ammerschwihr 68770. ✆ **03-89-47-12-23.** Fax 03-89-78-27-21. www.arbre-vert.net. 19 units. 51€–72€ ($66–$94) double. Half board 57€–69€ ($74–$90) per person double occupancy. AE, DC, MC, V. Closed mid-Feb to mid-Mar. **Amenities:** Restaurant; bar. *In room:* TV.

Aux Armes de France ★★★ FRENCH/ALSATIAN This is the best restaurant along the Wine Road. Although you can rent one of 10 rooms here (doubles go for 67€–82€/$87–$107), the real reason to come is the cuisine. In a flower-filled setting, Philippe Gaertner and his staff attract many French and German gourmets. A specialty is fresh foie gras served in its own golden aspic. Main courses include classics with imaginative variations, such as roebuck (in season) in hot sauce, and lobster fricassee with cream and truffles. Spicy duckling is savory, as is filet of sole with fresh noodles. Terrine of lobster and calf's head in aspic *(presskopf)*, which we've never seen in any other restaurant in France, is a particular enticement for adventurous gastronomes.

1 Grand'Rue, Ammerschwihr 68770. © **03-89-47-10-12.** Fax 03-89-47-38-12. www.aux-armes-de-france.com. Reservations required. Main courses 20€–30€ ($26–$39); fixed-price menu 25€–44€ ($33–$57). AE, DC, MC, V. Fri–Tues noon–2pm and 7:30–9pm.

ROUFFACH

Rouffach is south of Colmar. One of the highest of the Vosges Mountains, Grand-Ballon shelters the town from the winds that bring rain, which makes for a dry climate and a special grape. We include it here because of the excellent vineyard **Clos St-Landelin** (© **03-89-78-58-00;** www.mure.com), on the Route du Vin, at the intersection of RN83 and route de Soultzmatt. A clerical estate from the 6th century until the Revolution, it has been celebrated over the centuries for the quality of its wine. Clos St-Landelin covers 21 hectares (52 acres) at the southern end of the Vorbourg Grand Cru area. Its steep slopes call for terrace cultivation.

The soil that produces these wines is anything but fertile. Loaded with pebbles, sand, and limestone, the high-alkaline earth produces low-yield, scraggly vines whose fruit goes into superb Rieslings, Gewürztraminers, and pinot noirs. Members of the Muré family have owned these vineyards since 1648. In their cellar is a 13th-century wine press, the oldest in Alsace, and one of only three like it in France. (The other two are in Burgundy.) The family welcomes visitors who want to tour the cellars and ask about the wine, which is for sale. It's open Monday to Thursday 8am to 6:30pm, Friday 8am to 7pm, and Saturday 10am to 1pm and 2 to 6pm.

3 Colmar ★★★

440km (273 miles) SE of Paris, 140km (87 miles) SE of Nancy, 71km (44 miles) SW of Strasbourg

One of the most attractive towns in Alsace, Colmar abounds with medieval and early Renaissance buildings, half-timbered structures, gables, and gracious loggias. Tiny gardens and wash houses surround many of the homes. Its old quarter looks more German than French, filled with streets of unexpected twists and turns. As a gateway to the Rhine country, Colmar is a major destination for travelers heading south from Strasbourg. Near the vine-covered slopes of the southern Vosges, it's the third-largest town in Alsace.

Colmar has been so well restored that it's Alsace's most beautiful city, far more pleasing than Strasbourg. It's hard to tell that Colmar was hard hit in two world wars.

ESSENTIALS

GETTING THERE If you're **driving,** take N83 from Strasbourg; trip time is 1 hour. Because of the narrow streets, we suggest that you park and walk. Leave the car in the Champ-de-Mars, or in the underground Place Rapp for a fee of around 1.10€ ($1.45) per hour, northeast of the railway station, and then walk a few blocks east to the old city; or park in the lot designated PARKING VIEILLE VILLE, accessible from rue de l'Est at the edge of the Petite Venise neighborhood, and walk a few blocks southeast to reach the old city. **Trains** link Colmar to Nancy, Strasbourg, and Mulhouse, as well as to Germany via Strasbourg, across the Rhine. Twenty-one trains per day arrive from Paris's Gare de l'Est (trip time: 4–6 hr.); the one-way fare is 55€ ($72). For information, call © **36-35** or **08-92-35-35-35** from outside France.

VISITOR INFORMATION The **Office de Tourisme** is at 4 rue Unterlinden (© **03-89-20-68-92;** www.ot-colmar.fr).

For information on wines, vintages, and winery visits, contact the **CIVA** (Alsace Wine Committee), Maison du Vin d'Alsace, 12 av. de la Foire-aux-Vins (© **03-89-20-16-20**). It's usually open Monday to Friday 9am to noon and 2 to 5pm. Make arrangements far in advance.

SPECIAL EVENTS Alsatian **folk dances** on place de l'Ancienne-Douane begin at 8:30pm on Tuesday from mid-May to mid-September. If you want to listen to classical music, visit during the first 2 weeks in July for the **Festival International de Musique de Colmar** (© **03-89-20-68-97;** www.festival-colmar.com), which schedules 24 concerts in venues around the city, such as churches and public monuments. **Les Mardis de la Collégiale,** at place de la Cathédrale (© **06-71-06-50-18**), offers concerts every Tuesday at 8:45pm from the end of July to mid-September. Tickets for these events cost 10€ to 15€ ($13–$20). You can get complete information on any of the events in town at the Office de Tourisme.

EXPLORING COLMAR

Colmar boasts lots of historic houses, many half-timbered and, in summer, accented with geranium-draped window boxes. One of the most beautiful is the **Maison Pfister,** 11 rue des Marchands, at the corner of rue Mercière, a building with wooden balconies (1537). On the ground floor is a wine boutique owned by a major Alsace winegrower, **Muré,** proprietor of the vineyard Clos St-Landelin (© **03-89-41-33-61**).

If you take pont St-Pierre over the Lauch River, you'll have an excellent view of Old Colmar and can explore **Petite Venise,** which is filled with canals.

SHOPPING Head for the old town of Colmar, particularly rue de Clefs, Grand' Rue, rue des Têtes, and rue des Marchands.

Antiques abound, and you'll find a large grouping of stores in the old town, especially along rue des Marchands. Shops that deserve particular attention include **Geismar Dany,** 32 rue des Marchands (© **03-89-23-30-41**), specializing in antique painted furniture, and **Antiquités Guy Caffard,** 56 rue des Marchands (© **03-89-41-31-78;** www.caffard-antiquities.com), with its mishmash of furniture, postcards, books, toys, bibelots, and the like. Also worth noting are **Lire & Chiner,** 36 rue des Marchands (© **03-89-24-16-78;** www.lire-et-chiner.fr), and **Antiquité Arcana,** 13 place l'Ancienne Douane (© **03-89-41-59-81**).

One of the most appealing stores is **Arts et Collections d'Alsace,** 1 rue des Tanneurs (© **03-89-24-09-78**), which offers copies of art objects and utilitarian wares of yesteryear. There are items for the home and kitchen, made from wrought iron, pottery, glass, copper, carved wood, and fabric.

WINERIES Because Colmar is one of the gateways to the wine-producing Rhine country, local wine is one of the best purchases you can make. If you don't have time to visit the vineyards along the Wine Road, stop in at **Cave du Musée,** 11 rue Kléber (© **03-89-23-85-29**), for one of the largest selections of wines and liqueurs from the region and the rest of France.

You can drive to one of the most historic vineyards in Alsace-Lorraine. **Domaines Schlumberger** (© **03-89-74-27-00;** www.domaines-schlumberger.com) lies 26km

(16 miles) southwest of Colmar in Guebwiller. The cellars, established by the Schlumberger family in 1810, are an unusual combination of early-19th-century brickwork and modern stainless steel. These grapes become such famous wines as Rieslings, Gewürztraminers, muscats, sylvaners, and pinots (blanc, gris, and noir). Views of the vineyards and tasting rooms are available without an appointment, but group tours of the cellars are conducted only when a staff member is available. Call before you go to find out when that might be. Closed 2 weeks in August and December 22 to January 2.

Eglise des Dominicains This church contains one of Colmar's most famous treasures: Martin Schongauer's painting *Virgin of the Rosebush,* or *Vierge au buisson de rose* (1473), all gold, red, and white, with fluttering birds. Look for it in the choir.

Place des Dominicains. ✆ **03-89-24-46-57.** Admission 1.30€ ($1.70) adults, 1€ ($1.30) students, free for children under 13. Apr–Dec daily 10am–1pm and 3–6pm. Closed Jan–Mar.

Eglise St-Martin ★ In the heart of Old Colmar is a collegiate church begun in 1230 on the site of a Romanesque church. It has a choir erected by William of Marburg in 1350 and a steeple that rises to 70m (230 ft.).

Place de la Cathédrale. ✆ **03-89-41-27-20.** Free admission. Daily 8:30am–6:30pm. Closed to casual visitors during Mass.

Musée Bartholdi Statue of Liberty sculptor Frédéric-Auguste Bartholdi was born in Colmar in 1834. This small, memento-filled museum is in the house where he was born. It has Statue of Liberty rooms containing plans and scale models, and documents related to its construction and other works regarding U.S. history. Bartholdi's Paris apartment, with furniture and memorabilia, has been reconstructed here. The museum supplements its exhibits with paintings of Egyptian scenes that Bartholdi collected during his travels in 1856.

30 rue des Marchands. ✆ **03-89-41-90-60.** www.musee-bartholdi.com. Admission 4.30€ ($5.60) adults, 2.70€ ($3.50) students and children 12–18, free for children under 12. Wed–Mon 10am–noon and 2–6pm. Closed Jan–Feb, May 1, Nov 1, and Dec 25.

Musée d'Unterlinden (Under the Linden Trees) ★★ This former Dominican convent (1232), the chief seat of Rhenish mysticism in the 14th and 15th centuries, became a museum around 1850, and it's been a treasure house of the art and history of Alsace ever since.

The jewel of its collection is the **Issenheim Altarpiece (Le Retable d'Issenheim)** ★★★, created by Würzburg-born Matthias Grünewald, "the most furious of realists," around 1515. His colors glow, and his fantasy will overwhelm you. One of the most exciting works in German art, it's an immense altar screen with two-sided folding wing pieces—designed to show the Crucifixion, then the Incarnation, framed by the Annunciation and the Resurrection. The carved altar screen depicts St. Anthony visiting the hermit St. Paul; it also shows the Temptation of St. Anthony, the most beguiling part of a work that contains some ghastly birds, weird monsters, and loathsome animals. The demon of the plague is depicted with a swollen belly and purple skin, his body blotched with boils; a diabolical grin appears on his horrible face.

Other attractions include the magnificent altarpiece (dating back to 1470) of Jean d'Orlier by Martin Schongauer, a large collection of religious woodcarvings and stained glass from the 14th to the 18th centuries, and Gallo-Roman lapidary collections, including funeral slabs. The armory collection contains ancient arms from the Romanesque to the Renaissance, featuring halberds and crossbows.

1 rue d'Unterlinden. ✆ **03-89-20-15-58.** www.musee-unterlinden.com. Admission 7€ ($9.10) adults, 5€ ($6.50) students and children 12–17, free for children under 12. May–Oct daily 9am–6pm; Nov–Apr Wed–Mon 9am–noon and 2–5pm. Closed national holidays.

WHERE TO STAY

Rooms are also available in **La Maison des Têtes** (see "Where to Dine," below).

Grand Hôtel Bristol This 1926 red sandstone "grand hotel" has been totally renovated. Right at the train station, it provides well-maintained rooms with both modern and provincial decor. Accommodations are rather standardized and not quite as grand as the name of the hotel suggests. Most of the tidy, midsize bathrooms have tub/shower combinations.

7 place de la Gare, Colmar 68000. ✆ **03-89-23-59-59.** Fax 03-89-23-92-26. www.grand-hotel-bristol.com. 70 units. 100€–146€ ($130–$190) double. AE, DC, MC, V. **Amenities:** 2 restaurants; bar; room service; babysitting; laundry service; dry cleaning; nonsmoking rooms; 1 limited-mobility room. *In room:* TV, minibar, hair dryer, Wi-Fi.

Hostellerie Le Maréchal ★★ Three 16th-century houses make up this hotel, the most tranquil in town. You climb a wide staircase to reach the guest rooms, most of which are air-conditioned. In the east wing is a small, partially timbered room with a sloping ceiling. Accommodations are small but neatly organized, each with a tiled bathroom, most with tub/shower combinations. The restaurant has a fireplace in winter; in summer, seating moves to the terrace, where you can enjoy a water view. Feast on stuffed quail, good beef and veal dishes, and lamb Provençal, all accompanied by Tokay and Alsatian wines.

4–6 place des Six-Montagnes-Noires, Colmar 68000. ✆ **03-89-41-60-32.** Fax 03-89-24-59-40. www.hotel-le-marechal.com. 30 units. 105€–225€ ($137–$293) double; 255€ ($332) suite. AE, MC, V. **Amenities:** Restaurant; room service; laundry service; dry cleaning; nonsmoking rooms. *In room:* TV, minibar, hair dryer, safe, Wi-Fi.

Le Colombier ★ Originally built as a half-timbered house in the 14th century, this building is among the town's finest hotels. Very old beams and masonry contrast pleasantly with contemporary lighting and furniture. The staff is engaging and helpful. If the government-rated three-star hotel had a restaurant (breakfast is the only meal served), it would surely earn four-star status. With the exception of the cozy unit beneath the steeply pitched pinnacle of the roof, all of the guest rooms have high ceilings; they vary in size and shape. Each contains comfortable appointments and fine linen, plus a small but tidy shower-only bathroom. Some rooms overlook the canals of Petite Venise; others open onto a half-timbered courtyard.

7 rue Turenne, Colmar 68000. ✆ **03-89-23-96-00.** Fax 03-89-23-97-27. www.hotel-le-colombier.fr. 27 units. 79€–150€ ($103–$195) double; 150€–230€ ($195–$299) suite. AE, DC, MC, V. **Amenities:** Bar; limited-mobility rooms. *In room:* A/C, TV, minibar, hair dryer, safe, Wi-Fi.

WHERE TO DINE

Chez Hansi *Value* ALSATIAN Set within two rooms of a half-timbered house dating from 1532, this is the most historic and most folklorically charming restaurant in a town that's loaded with worthy competitors. Even its name is a reference to the pen name (Hansi) of Jean-Jacques Waltz, a 19th-century illustrator, who in his artwork elevated Alsatian kitsch to an art form rivaled in America by Norman Rockwell. You'll find this hypertraditional place in the Vieille Ville, beneath massively beamed ceilings and a staff whose females are clad in dirndls. Come here for steaming and heaping platters of *choucroute* (sauerkraut garnished with pork products), foie gras, onion tarte, *pot-au-feu* that's redolent with gravy and chunks of beef, and, for the ultra-adventurous, calf-head *(tete de veau)* garnished with an apple in its mouth.

23 rue des Marchands. ✆ **03-89-41-37-84.** Reservations recommended. Main courses 16€–25€ ($21–$33); set-price menus 18€–44€ ($23–$57). MC, V. Fri–Tues 11:45am–1:45pm and 6:45–9:30pm. Closed Jan.

La Maison des Têtes ★★★ TRADITIONAL FRENCH This Colmar monument, named for the sculptured heads on its stone facade, is the town's leading hotel and one of its top restaurants. It opens off a covered cobblestone drive and courtyard. The 17th-century house lies in the center of town, near the Unterlinden Museum. The dining rooms are decorated with aged-wood beams and paneling, Art Nouveau lighting fixtures, and stained glass and leaded windows. The excellent food includes foie gras with truffles, *choucroute,* seasonal roebuck with morels and dried fruits, roasted duck with two spices, and fresh trout or Rhine salmon braised in Riesling. The Alsatian wines are sublime. There are also 21 nicely furnished rooms with minibars and TVs; some have Jacuzzis. Rates are 91€ to 230€ ($118–$299) for a double, 207€ to 269€ ($269–$350) for a suite.

In the Hôtel des Têtes, 19 rue des Têtes, Colmar 68000. ✆ **03-89-24-43-43.** Fax 03-89-24-58-34. www.la-maison-des-tetes.com. Reservations required. Main courses 16€–28€ ($21–$36); fixed-price menu 30€–36€ ($39–$47); *menu dégustation* 58€ ($75). AE, DC, MC, V. Wed–Sun noon–2pm; Tues–Sat 7–9:30pm. Closed Feb.

WHERE TO STAY & DINE NEARBY

Gourmets flock to Illhaeusern, 18km (11 miles) from Colmar, east of the N83 highway, to dine at the Auberge de l'Ill, one of France's great restaurants. The signs for the restaurant, beside the main highway, are difficult to miss.

Auberge de l'Ill ★★★ MODERN FRENCH This is the greatest restaurant in eastern France. Run by the Haeberlin family in their 19th-century farmhouse, Auberge de l'Ill combines the finest Alsatian specialties with *cuisine moderne* and classic offerings. You can enjoy your aperitif or coffee under the weeping willows in a beautiful garden with a river view. Chef Marc Haeberlin takes dishes of Alsatian origin and makes them into *grande cuisine*—freshwater eel stewed in Riesling, *matelotes* (small glazed onions) in Riesling, and an inventive foie gras. His partridge, pheasant, and duckling are among the best in Europe. Two unsurpassed choices are braised slices of pheasant and partridge served with winey game sauce, chestnuts, wild mushrooms, and Breton cornmeal; and salmon soufflé. A divine starter is mousseline of frogs' legs with white-wine and chive sauce; you may follow that with mallard duckling lacquered with spices and served with a confit of red cabbage and figs. Some dishes require 24 hours' notice, so inquire when you make reservations.

You can spend the night in one of 13 rooms at the **Hôtel des Berges,** in a delightfully furnished, air-conditioned room overlooking the Ill River. The rates are 262€ to 300€ ($341–$390) for a double, 350€ to 520€ ($455–$676) for a suite, and 465€ ($605) for a decade-old cottage on the grounds.

Rue de Collonges, Illhaeusern 68970. ✆ **03-89-71-89-00.** Fax 03-89-71-82-83. www.auberge-de-l-ill.com. Reservations required (1 week in advance for summer weekends). Main courses 35€–135€ ($46–$176); fixed-price menu 110€–142€ ($143–$185). AE, DC, MC, V. Wed–Sun noon–2pm and 7–9pm. Closed early Feb to mid-Mar.

COLMAR AFTER DARK

Head for the seductive **La Fiesta/Le Cotton Club,** place de la Gare (✆ **03-89-23-43-04**). Popular and busy, this nightclub consists of two strikingly different venues: On street level, La Fiesta is a bar with lots of suds, margaritas, and a busy after-work scene. Upstairs, there's a cocktail lounge with a dance floor and a calmer, more urban (think Paris or Berlin) ambience. For a mellow atmosphere, try the piano bar **Louisiana Club,** 3A rue Berthe-Molly (© **03-89-24-94-18**), where you can groove to authentic blues and jazz.

4 La Route des Crêtes ★★★

From Basel, Switzerland, to Mainz, Germany, a distance of some 242km (150 miles), the Vosges Mountains stretch along the west side of the Rhine Valley, bearing a similarity to the Black Forest of Germany. Many German and French families spend their summer vacation exploring the Vosges. Travelers with less time may want to settle for a quick look at the ancient mountains that once formed the boundary between France and Germany. They are filled with tall hardwood and fir trees, and a network of twisting roads with hairpin curves traverses them. The depths of the mountain forests are the closest France comes to wilderness.

EXPLORING THE AREA

You can explore the mountains by heading west from Strasbourg, but there's a more interesting route from Colmar. La Route des Crêtes (Crest Road) begins at **Col du Bonhomme,** west of Colmar. The French High Command created it during World War I to carry supplies over the mountains. From Col du Bonhomme, you can strike out on this magnificent road, once the object of bitter fighting but today a series of panoramic vistas, including one of the Black Forest.

By **Col de la Schlucht,** 62km (39 miles) west of Colmar, you'll have climbed 1,472m (4,829 ft.). Schlucht is a summer and winter resort, one of the most beautiful spots in the Vosges, with a panoramic view of the Valley of Münster and the slopes of Hohneck. As you skirt the edge of this glacier-carved valley, you'll be in the midst of a land of pine groves with a necklace of lakes. You may want to turn off the main road and go exploring in several directions; the scenery is that tempting. But if you're still on the Crest Road, you can circle **Hohneck,** one of the highest peaks at 1,590m (5,217 ft.), dominating the Wildenstein Dam of the Bresse winter-sports station.

At **Markstein,** you'll come to another resort. From here, take N430 and then D10 to **Münster,** where the savory cheese is made. You'll go via the Petit-Ballon, a landscape of forest and mountain meadows with grazing cows. Finally, **Grand-Ballon,** at 1,400m (4,593 ft.), is the highest point you can reach by car in the Vosges. Get out of your car and go for a walk—if it's a clear day, you'll be able to see the Jura, with the French Alps beyond.

WHERE TO STAY & DINE IN MUNSTER

Au Chêne Voltaire This chalet-style inn, built in 1939 and renovated many times, lies in an isolated section of the forest. Most of the modern, no-frills rooms are in a building separate from the rustic core that contains the popular restaurant, which is open to the public (closed Wed–Thurs). The hotel isn't a destination; it's just good to keep in mind if you need to rest for the night before pressing on in the morning. Each unit comes with a small, shower-only bathroom, a balcony, and clean, comfortable, no-nonsense furniture. Set-price menus in the dining room go for 18€ ($23).

Rte. du Chêne-Voltaire, Luttenbach, Münster 68140. Take D10 less than 2.5km (1½ miles) southwest from the center of Münster. © **03-89-77-31-74.** Fax 03-89-77-45-71. 20 units. 46€–77€ ($60–$100) double. MC, V. **Amenities:** Outdoor swimming pool; sauna. *In room:* TV, balcony.

5 Nancy ★★★

370km (230 miles) E of Paris, 148km (92 miles) W of Strasbourg

Nancy, in France's northeast corner, was the capital of old Lorraine. The city was built around a fortified castle on a rock in the swampland near the Meurthe River. A canal a few blocks east of the historic center connects the Marne to the Rhine.

The city is serenely beautiful, with a history, cuisine, and architecture all its own. It once rivaled Paris as the center for the design and production of Art Nouveau. Nancy has three faces: the medieval alleys and towers around the old Palais Ducal where Charles II received Joan of Arc, the rococo golden gates and fountains, and the dull modern sections.

With a population of 100,000, Nancy remains the hub of commerce and politics in Lorraine. Home to a large university, it's a center of mining, engineering, metallurgy, and finance. Its 30,000 students, who have a passion for *le cool jazz,* keep Nancy jumping at night.

ESSENTIALS

GETTING THERE **Trains** from Strasbourg arrive every hour (trip time: 1 hr.); the one-way fare is 22€ to 30€ ($29–$39). Trains from Paris's Gare de l'Est pull in about every 2 hours (trip time: 3 hr.); the one-way fare is 45€ ($59). Because of new high-speed train service, travel time from Paris to Nancy (plus nine other cities in Lorraine) can be cut in half. For information and schedules, call ✆ **36-35** or **08-92-35-35-35** from outside France. If you're **driving** to Nancy from Paris, follow N4 east (trip time: 4 hr.).

VISITOR INFORMATION The **Office de Tourisme** is at place Stanislas (✆ **03-83-35-22-41;** fax 03-83-35-90-10; www.ot-nancy.fr).

SPECIAL EVENTS Serious jazz lovers come to town for 2 weeks in October to attend **Jazz Pulsations** (✆ **03-83-35-40-86;** www.nancyjazzpulsations.com). Some kind of performance takes place every night around sundown in a tent in the Parc de la Pépinière, a very short walk from the place Stanislas. Tickets cost 10€ to 25€ ($13–$33).

EXPLORING NANCY

A **Passe-Musée** is a combination ticket that allows entrance to three of the town's most visited attractions, all for a net price of 8€ ($10) per person, with no discounts for students or children. Included in the pass is access to the Musée de l'Ecole de Nancy, the Musée des Beaux-Arts, and the Musée Historique Lorraine (which is also known as the Musée des Arts et Traditions Populaires). Ask about the ticket at the tourist office.

The most monumental square in eastern France, and the heart of Nancy, is **place Stanislas** ★★★, named for Stanislas Leszczynski, the last of the ducs de Lorraine, ex-king of Poland, and father-in-law of Louis XV. His 18th-century building programs transformed Nancy into one of Europe's most palatial cities. The square stands between Nancy's two most notable neighborhoods: the **Ville Vieille** (old town), in the medieval core in the northwest, centered on the cathedral, Grande-Rue, and the labyrinth of narrow, meandering streets that funnel into it; and the **Ville Neuve,** in the southwest. Built in the 16th and 17th centuries, when streets were laid out in straight lines, Ville Neuve centers on rue St-Jean.

Place Stanislas was laid out from 1752 to 1760 according to the designs of Emmanuel Héré. Its ironwork gates are magnificent. The square is fabled for the brilliant and fanciful railings, the work of Jean Lamour. His gilded railings with flowery

Nancy

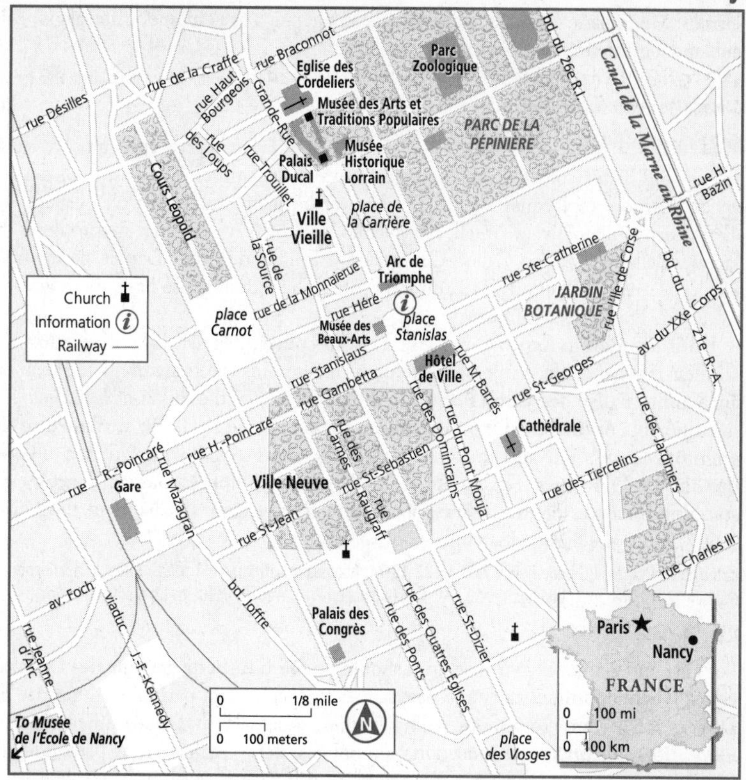

decorations and crests evoke Versailles. In 2005 cars were banished from the plaza, making it an all-pedestrian zone.

The **Arc de Triomphe,** constructed by Stanislas from 1754 to 1756 to honor Louis XV, adjoins the place de la Carrière, a tree-lined promenade leading to the 1760 **Palais du Gouvernement.** This governmental palace adjoins the **Palais Ducal,** built in 1502 in the Gothic style with Flamboyant Gothic balconies.

Musée de l'Ecole de Nancy ★ In a turn-of-the-20th-century building is a museum displaying the works of Emile Gallé, the greatest artist of the Nancy style. See Gallé's celebrated "Dawn and Dusk" bed and our favorite, the "mushroom lamp." Works by Eugène Vallin, another outstanding artist, are also on display.

36–38 rue Sergent-Blandan. ✆ **03-83-40-14-86.** www.ecole-de-nancy.com. Admission 6€ ($7.80) adults, 4€ ($5.20) students, free for children under 18. Free for students on Wed. Wed–Sun 10:30am–6pm. Guided tours in French available Fri–Sun.

Musée des Beaux-Arts ★★ Built in the 1700s, this is an outstanding regional museum, encompassing the Collection Galilée, works displayed in Paris between 1919 and 1930. It boasts a rare Manet portrait of the wife of Napoleon III's dentist—remarkable because of its brilliance and intensity. There are also works by Delacroix,

Utrillo, Modigliani, Boucher, and Rubens. Italians such as Perugino, Caravaggio, Ribera, and Tintoretto are represented as well.

3 place Stanislas. ✆ **03-83-85-30-72.** Admission 6€ ($7.80) adults, 4€ ($5.20) students and children. Free for students on Wed. Wed–Mon 10am–6pm.

Musée Historique Lorrain ★★★ This is one of France's great museums, covering the art and history of the Lorraine region from ancient times. The first floor devotes an entire room to Jacques Callot, an engraver born in Nancy in 1592. Galerie des Cerfs displays tapestries. You'll see a collection of 17th-century masterpieces by Jacques Bellange, Jacques Callot, Georges de la Tour, and Claude Deruet, dating from when the duchy was known as a cultural center. The museum also has a room devoted to eastern France's Jewish history.

Until the Revolution this was a Franciscan convent. Franciscans were known as Cordeliers—hence the name of the church that adjoins the museum. The Flamboyant Gothic **Eglise des Cordeliers** ★ is the burial site of the dukes of Lorraine. The most notable of the burial monuments are those of René II (1509; attributed to the sculptor Mansuy Gauvain) and a reclining statue of his second wife, Philippa of Gueldres, by Ligier Richier. The limestone rendering of Philippa is one of Nancy's most stunning examples of Renaissance portraiture. The octagonal Chapel of the Dukes (1607) holds the baroque sarcophagi.

In the Palais Ducal, 64 Grande-Rue. ✆ **03-83-32-18-74.** Admission 3.10€ ($4.05) adults, 2.30€ ($3) students and children 12–18, free for children under 12. Free for students on Wed. Wed–Mon 10am–12:30pm and 2–6pm.

SHOPPING

For glitz and glamour, your first stops should be **rue Gambetta** and **rue des Dominicains,** where boutiques carry the best names in fashion and perfume. Along **rue St-Dizier,** you'll run across shops selling clothes, shoes, jewelry, and leather goods at more affordable prices. Two additional shopping streets—each running perpendicular to those noted above, and each with what's usually viewed as cheaper and less glamorous merchandise—are the **rue St-Jean** and **rue St-Geroges.** The Old Town is home to boutiques that carry antiques, arts and crafts, and bric-a-brac, as well as clothing and jewelry.

For chic women's clothing, accessories, and shoes, try **Vanessa,** 14 rue Gambetta (✆ **03-83-32-85-88**). From the sophisticated to the trendy, men seek out **Alto Stratus,** 34 rue des Dominicains (✆ **03-83-30-17-33**), and **Tolub,** 9 rue Gambetta (✆ **03-83-32-98-14**).

Many of Nancy's antiques shops specialize in Art Nouveau. Visit **Denis Rugat,** 13 rue Stanislas (✆ **03-83-35-20-79**), for the best pieces. Another good outlet is **Galerie d'Art International,** 17 rue Amerval (✆ **03-83-35-06-83**). Both stock inventories of Lalique crystal, brightly colored vases, and enameled boxes made with a technique known locally as *les émaux de Longwy,* plus an assortment of glass-shaded lamps. And if you're a longtime fan of the glassmaking techniques of the late 19th century, you'll find more glass and crystal by Daum, at more reasonable prices, than virtually anywhere else in France. The company's premier outlet is **Boutique Daum,** 14 Place Stanislas (✆ **03-83-32-21-65**), where the most perfect specimens from the Daum factory are sold at prices that are usually about 30% less than what you'd pay in other glass galleries in France. Each piece, a work of art in its own right, is signed "Daum." In contrast, and for prices that are about 30% to 40% less than what's sold in the above-mentioned boutique, you can head to Daum's factory outlet, **Magasin d'Usine**

Daum, 17 rue Cristallerie (✆ **03-83-30-80-24**), a 5-minute walk from the Place Stanislas. Their "slightly flawed" factory seconds are gift-wrapped and sold, each signed with the more enigmatic (and less prestigious) NANCY.

WHERE TO STAY

Albert-1er-Astoria Near the back of the railway station, this hotel was built after World War II and has an annex just around the corner. Guests select this efficiently operated, government-rated two-star hotel for its reasonable prices and central location. It offers comfortable but not particularly plush guest rooms, outfitted in contemporary style with a monochromatic color scheme. Each has a shower-only bathroom. The hotel has a pleasant garden. Breakfast is the only meal served.

3 rue de l'Armée-Patton, Nancy 54000. ✆ **03-83-40-31-24.** Fax 03-83-28-47-78. www.albert1-astoria.com. 83 units. 50€–75€ ($65–$98) double. AE, DC, MC, V. Parking 6.50€ ($8.45). **Amenities:** Nonsmoking rooms. *In room:* TV, hair dryer, safe, Wi-Fi.

Grand Hôtel de la Reine ★★★ This is the grandest hotel in Nancy. The 18th-century mansion was built simultaneously with the monumental square that contains it. The hotel is one of the showplaces of the Concorde chain, which operates such bastions of luxury as Paris's Hôtel de Crillon. The Louis XV–style guest rooms boast draped testers over comfortable beds, Venetian-style chandeliers, and gilt-framed mirrors. All accommodations contain roomy bathrooms with tub/shower combos. Units overlooking place Stanislas are expensive. If you can live without a view, some suites (those overlooking the hotel's back and sides) are cheaper than the most expensive double. The elegant and very grand Stanislas restaurant serves classic and modern dishes.

2 place Stanislas, Nancy 54000. ✆ **800/777-4182** in the U.S. and Canada, or 03-83-35-03-01. Fax 03-83-32-86-04. www.hoteldelareine.com. 42 units. 145€–295€ ($189–$384) double; 360€ ($468) suite. AE, DC, MC, V. Parking 16€ ($21). **Amenities:** Restaurant; bar; room service; babysitting; laundry service; dry cleaning; nonsmoking rooms; limited-mobility rooms. *In room:* A/C, TV, minibar, beverage maker, hair dryer, Wi-Fi.

Hôtel de Guise ★ *Finds* The interior of this 17th- and 18th-century stone-fronted town house was ripped apart and renovated with great care to retain the stone floors and monumental staircase that Nancy's nobility used for grand entrances and exits during the *ancien régime.* Local antiques (at least in the public areas) enhance the architecture. Guest rooms vary in style—Art Deco, Louis XV, Napoléon 1er, or French Empire. Each has a bathroom sheathed in (usually) white tiles and a shower, and about half have tub/shower combinations. Thanks to the building's U-shaped floor plan, many rooms overlook either the street or a pleasant front courtyard. The hotel itself has very few amenities, but its location in the heart of Nancy's historic core ensures a wide selection of restaurants, attractions, and bars within a short walk.

18 rue de Guise, Ville Vieille, Nancy 54000. ✆ **03-83-32-24-68.** Fax 03-83-35-75-63. www.hoteldeguise.com. 48 units. 60€–77€ ($78–$100) double; 85€–99€ ($111–$129) suite. AE, MC, V. **Amenities:** Nonsmoking rooms; limited-mobility rooms. *In room:* TV, Wi-Fi.

Park Inn ★★ Rising above every other building in Nancy, this 1970s seven-story hotel opposite the train station caters to business and leisure travelers. Functional and efficient, with a hardworking staff, it's a top choice for Nancy but lacks the style of the Grand Hôtel de la Reine. The chain style of the guest rooms offers comfort, predictability, and warmth, with firm beds and serviceable bathrooms that hold tub/shower combinations.

11 rue Raymond-Poincaré, Nancy 54000. ✆ **03-83-39-75-75.** Fax 03-83-32-78-17. www.parkinn.com. 192 units. 89€–119€ ($116–$155) double; 144€ ($187) suite. AE, DC, MC, V. Parking 9€ ($12). **Amenities:** Restaurant; bar;

room service; laundry service; dry cleaning; nonsmoking rooms; limited-mobility rooms. *In room:* A/C, TV, minibar, hair dryer, Wi-Fi.

WHERE TO DINE

The **Park Inn** hotel and **Grand Hôtel de la Reine** (see "Where to Stay," above) have decent restaurants.

Le Capucin Gourmand ★★ TRADITIONAL FRENCH This is the leading grand restaurant of Nancy, a 5-minute walk of place Stanislaus, and offers diners a warm, cozy decor with tones of gray and wood paneling. Former president Jacques Chirac raves about the cuisine served here. On our last visit we savored such creations as minced scallops and truffles pressed into patties and served with a walnut-oil vinaigrette; a "marble" of foie gras with exotic mushrooms; and a turbot steak that was "clothed" in baby vegetables. A signature dish is a civet of rabbit *à la royale*—in a sauce of its own blood mixed with red wine and just a hint of bitter chocolate. Another equally commendable dish is a noisette of venison Grand Veneur. For dessert, a "passion of chocolate" came with baked fresh figs marinated in honey and served with a yogurt-flavored ice cream.

31 rue Gambetta. ✆ **03-83-35-26-98.** www.lecapu.com. Reservations required. Main courses 24€–40€ ($31–$52); fixed-price menu 28€–58€ ($36–$75). AE, MC, V. Tues–Fri and Sun noon–2pm; Tues–Sat 7:30–10pm.

Le Grand Café Foy TRADITIONAL FRENCH This restaurant occupies the second floor of a building that borders place Stanislas. Outfitted with exposed timbers and Louis XIII furnishings, it is independent of a simple street-level brasserie (Café Foy) that serves less appealing food. The menu is a stylish roster of dishes such as roasted rabbit with violet-flavored mustard sauce, foie gras (a specialty of the house), braised lobster with a compote of fennel and veal juices, and local freshwater fish baked in a potato crust. Try a dessert that's unusual and heavenly: honey mousse cake prepared with brandy.

1 place Stanislas. ✆ **03-83-32-15-97.** www.grandcafefoy.fr. Reservations recommended. Main courses 12€–25€ ($16–$33); fixed-price menu 20€–32€ ($26–$42). MC, V. Daily noon–2pm and 7–11pm. Closed 2 weeks in Feb.

Les Pissenlits (The Dandelions) *Value* TRADITIONAL FRENCH At this cost-conscious brasserie, the food is simple but flavorful and artfully prepared. Chef Jean-Luc Mengin's specialties are likely to include *matelote* of freshwater zander with shallots, dandelion salad with bacon and creamy vinaigrette, and aiguillettes of duckling with spice-flavored honey sauce. The chef's wife, Danièle, is one of the few accredited female wine stewards in France. Art Nouveau antiques, many of them crafted in Nancy, fill the dining room.

27 rue des Ponts. ✆ **03-83-37-43-97.** www.les-pissenlits.com. Reservations recommended. Main courses 12€–16€ ($16–$21); fixed-price menu 19€–36€ ($25–$47). MC, V. Tues–Sat 11:45am–2:30pm and 7:15–10:30pm.

NANCY AFTER DARK

As night approaches, most of the student population heads to the Old Town. **Le Blue Note III,** 3 rue des Michottes (✆ **03-83-30-31-18**), has a room for rock performances, a piano bar, a lounge with a fireplace and comfy armchairs, and a rowdy beer hall. It's open Wednesday through Sunday. Entrance is free except on Friday and Saturday night, when there's a 10€ ($13) cover. Women enter free on those nights before 12:30am.

Nancy's most popular dance club is **Les Caves du Roy,** 9 place Stanislas (✆ **03-83-35-24-14**), where a techno crowd flails around in a chrome-and-metallic space.

The hottest nightclub in the region is a converted warehouse in the suburb of Vandoeuvre, 4km (2½ miles) south of the center of town. **Le Circus,** 42 rue Jean-Mermoz (✆ **03-83-57-53-85;** www.circusmedia.fr), sits near the town's wholesale food market (le Marché en Gros). It features fire-eaters, jugglers, and techno music. Expect up to 2,000 revelers on a Friday or Saturday night, when the cover is 11€ ($14) and includes the first drink. It's open Friday to Saturday from 11pm to 5am.

6 Domrémy-la-Pucelle

443km (275 miles) SE of Paris, 10km (6¼ miles) NW of Neufchâteau

Most often visited on a day trip, Domrémy is a plain village that would have slumbered in obscurity but for the fact that Joan of Arc was born here in 1412. Today, it's a pilgrimage center attracting tourists from all over the world.

A residence traditionally considered her family's house is known as **Maison Natale de Jeanne d'Arc,** 2 rue de la Basilique (✆ **03-29-06-95-86**). Here you can see the chamber where she was born. A museum beside the house shows a film depicting St. Joan's life. The house is open April to September daily 9am to noon and 1:30 to 6:30pm; October to March Wednesday to Monday 10am to noon and 2 to 5pm. Admission is 3€ ($3.90) for adults, free for children under 10. Closed in January.

Adjacent to the museum, on rue Principale, is **Eglise St-Rémi;** recent repairs have masked its 12th-century origins. All that remains from the age of Joan of Arc are a baptismal font and some stonework. On a slope of the Bois-Chenu 1.5km (1 mile) uphill from the village is a monument steeped in French nationalism, the **Basilique du Bois-Chenu.** It was begun in 1881 and consecrated in 1926. To reach it, follow signs from the center and along rue de la Basilique.

ESSENTIALS

GETTING THERE If you're **driving,** take N4 southeast of Paris to Toul, and then A31 south toward Neufchâteau/Charmes. Then take N74 southwest (signposted in the direction of Neufchâteau). At Neufchâteau, follow D164 northwest to Coussey. From there, take D53 into Domrémy.

There is no railway station in Domrémy—you must take one of four **trains** daily going to either Nancy or Toul, where you can make bus and rail connections to Neufchâteau, 9.5km (6 miles) away. You can also take a **taxi,** MBM Assistance 88 (✆ **03-29-06-12-13**), for about 20€ ($26) each way.

7 Verdun ★★

261km (162 miles) E of Paris, 66km (41 miles) W of Metz

Built on both banks of the Meuse and intersected by a series of canals, Verdun has an old section, the Ville Haute, on the east bank, which includes the cathedral and Episcopal palace. Today, stone houses on narrow cobblestone streets give Verdun a medieval appearance. However, most visitors come to see the famous World War I battlefields, 3km (1¾ miles) east of the town, off N3 toward Metz.

ESSENTIALS

GETTING THERE Two **trains** arrive daily from Paris's Gare de l'Est; you'll have to change at Châlons-en-Champagne. Several daily trains also arrive from Metz, after a change at Conflans. The one-way fare from Paris is 35€ ($46); from Metz, it's 12€ ($16). For train information and schedules, call ✆ **36-35** or **08-92-35-35-35** from outside France. **Driving** is easy; Verdun is several miles north of the Paris-Strasbourg autoroute (A4).

VISITOR INFORMATION The **Office de Tourisme** is on place de la Nation (✆ **03-29-84-18-85;** fax 03-29-83-99-93; www.verdun-tourisme.com). It's closed on bank holidays.

TOURING THE BATTLEFIELDS

At this garrison town in eastern France, Maréchal Pétain said, "They shall not pass!" And they didn't. Verdun is where the Allies held out against a massive assault by the German army in World War I. Near the end of the war, 600,000 to 800,000 French and German soldiers died battling over a few miles along the muddy Meuse between Paris and the Rhine. Two monuments commemorate these tragic events: Rodin's *Defense* and Boucher's *To Victory and the Dead.*

The local tourist office offers maps and advice on two carefully delineated, and separate, tours of the brutal and bloody battlefields that helped define World War I. They include the *Circuit Champs de Bataille Rive Droite,* which encompasses the better-known battlegrounds on the River Meuse's right bank. They'll provide a map for self-guided tours, whose estimated length is about 4 hours, that will include, on the Meuse's right bank, a 32km (20-mile) run, taking in **Fort Vaux,** where Raynal staged a heroic defense after sending his last message by carrier pigeon. After passing a **French cemetery** of 16,000 graves—an endless field of crosses—you arrive at the **Ossuaire de Douaumont,** where the bones of those blown to bits were embedded. Nearby, at the **Fort de Douaumont,** the "hell of Verdun" was unleashed. From the roof you can look out at a vast field of corroded tops of "pillboxes." Then you proceed to the **Tranchée des Baïonettes (Trench of Bayonets).** Bayonets of French soldiers entombed by a shell burst form this unique memorial.

Within a few paces of the Tranchée des Baïonettes, you'll see the premises of the **Mémorial de Verdun** (built around 1967), Fleury Devant Douaumont (✆ **03-29-84-35-34;** www.memorial-14-18.com), a museum that commemorates the weapons, uniforms, photographs, and geography of one of the bloodiest battles of World War I. From February to mid-December, it's open daily from 9am to noon and 2 to 6pm (closed mid-Dec to Jan). Entrance is 7€ ($9.10) for adults and students, 3.50€ ($4.55) for children 11 to 16, free for children under 11.

The second self-guided tour, known as ***Circuit Champs de Bataille Rive Gauche*** (or *Circuit de l'Argonne*), also requires about 4 hours, and during its 97km (60 miles), it focuses on mostly outdoor sites, as opposed to the monuments and museums that are included in the tour's first 2 hours. It takes in the **Butte de Montfaucon,** a hill on which Americans erected a memorial tower, and the **Cimetière Américain at Romagne,** with some 15,000 graves.

Because public transportation is inadequate, only visitors with cars should attempt to make these circuits.

WHERE TO STAY & DINE

Château des Monthairons ★★ This hotel, operated by the Thouvenin family, occupies an 1857 château crafted of blocks of pale stone. Guest rooms vary in shape and size, most with locally made furniture. All have luxury beds and quality linens. Bathrooms boast generous shelf space and tub/shower combinations. On the property are a pair of 15th-century chapels, a nesting ground for herons, and opportunities for canoeing and fishing.

Rte. D34, Dieue-sur-Meuse 55320. ✆ **03-29-87-78-55.** Fax 03-29-87-73-49. www.chateaudesmonthairons.fr. 25 units. 90€–225€ ($117–$293) double; 280€ ($364) suite. AE, DC, MC, V. Drive 12km (7½ miles) south of Verdun on D334. Closed Jan–Feb 8. **Amenities:** Restaurant; bar; limited-mobility rooms, children's play area. *In room:* TV, minibar, hair dryer, Wi-Fi.

Hostellerie du Coq Hardi ★★ This is our favorite hotel in town, composed of four connected 18th-century houses near the Meuse. It contains church pews, antiques, and a Renaissance fireplace. Most of the well-maintained guest rooms have been decorated in regional style. Each has a comfortable bed and an efficient but small bathroom, mainly with tub and shower. The dining room serves the best food in town. It has a painted ceiling, Louis XIII chairs, and two deactivated World War I bombshells at its entrance. Specialties are *salade Coq Hardi* (with green mustard and pine nuts), Challons duck, cassoulet of snails in champagne, and preparations of foie gras.

8 av. de la Victoire, Verdun 55100. ✆ **03-29-86-36-36.** Fax 03-29-86-09-21. www.coq-hardi.com. 35 units. 95€–135€ ($124–$176) double; 215€–230€ ($280–$299) suite. AE, MC, V. Free parking. **Amenities:** 2 restaurants; bar; room service; nonsmoking rooms; limited-mobility rooms. *In room:* TV, minibar, hair dryer, Wi-Fi.

13

Burgundy

Castles rising from vineyards and medieval churches mark the landscape of Burgundy, the land of the good life for those who savor fine cuisine and wine in historic settings. Burgundy was once an independent province; its Valois dukes spread their might across Europe from 1363 to 1477. In preserving its independence, Burgundy weathered many struggles, notably under Charles the Bold, always in conflict with Louis XI. When Charles died in 1477, Louis annexed the duchy. Burgundy later suffered more upheaval, including much damage to its cities during the Franco-Spanish wars that began in 1636. Peace finally held in 1678.

At the time of the Revolution, Burgundy had disappeared as a political entity and was divided into the *départements* (mini-states) of Yonne, Saône-et-Loire, and Côte-d'Or. The ducs de Bourgogne are but a memory, but they left a legacy of vintage red and white wines to please and excite the palate. The major winegrowing regions of Burgundy are Chablis, Côte de Nuits, Côte de Beaune, Côte de Chalon, Mâconnais, and Nivernais.

1 Auxerre ★★

154km (96 miles) SE of Paris, 148km (92 miles) NW of Dijon

Auxerre was founded by the Gauls and enlarged by the Romans. On a hill overlooking the Yonne River, it's the capital of Lower Burgundy and home to many vineyards, some of which produce Chablis. Joan of Arc spent several days here in 1429. Napoleon met Maréchal Ney here in 1815, on the former emperor's return from Elba. Louis XVIII had sent Ney to stop Napoleon, but Ney embraced him and turned his army against the king. For that, Ney was later shot.

This city is a sleepy place. Its 42,000 residents will admit that not a lot happens around here—and that's how they like it.

ESSENTIALS

GETTING THERE Visitors often **drive** here because Auxerre is near A6/E1 (Autoroute du Soleil). Many **trains** between Paris (Gare de Lyon) and Lyon stop at Auxerre. There are 12 trains per day from Paris (the fare is 22€/$29 one-way) and 19 from Lyon (40€/$52 one-way); trip time from either city is 3 to 5 hours. For train information, call ✆ **08-92-35-35-35.**

VISITOR INFORMATION The **Office de Tourisme** is at 1–2 quai de la République (✆ **03-86-52-06-19;** fax 03-86-51-23-27; www.ot-auxerre.fr).

EXPLORING AUXERRE

The railway station is at the eastern edge of town, about 1.5km (1 mile) from the historic center. Most of Auxerre is on the western bank of the Yonne. Its heart is between

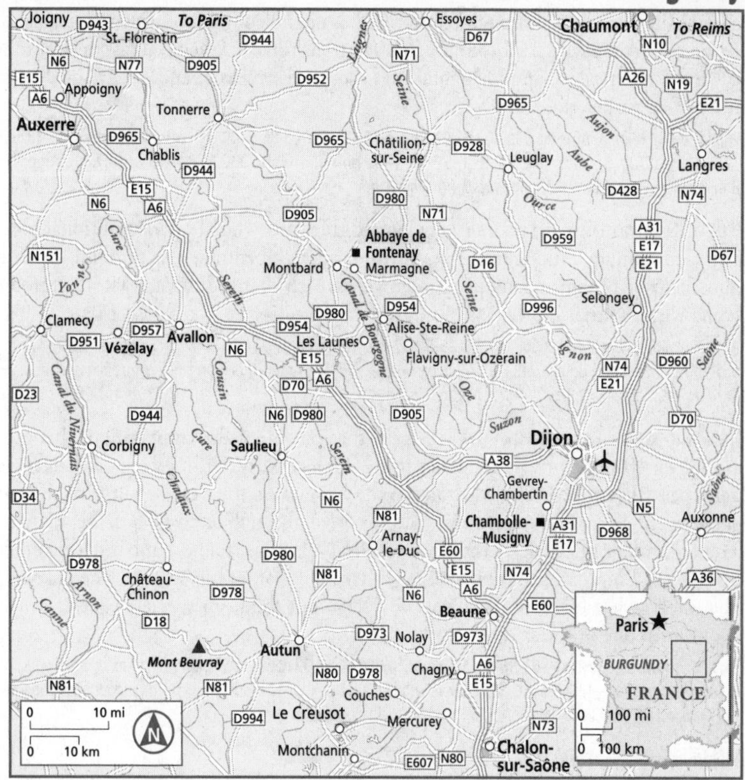

place du Maréchal-Leclerc (where you'll find the Hôtel de Ville [city hall]) and the Cathédrale St-Etienne.

Cathédrale St-Etienne ★★ Pay a visit to the Flamboyant Gothic Cathédrale St-Etienne, begun in the 13th century but not completed until the 16th. The front facade is remarkable, with sculptured portals. The stained glass, some of it original, is famous. In the crypt, which is all that remains of the Romanesque church that stood on this site, you can see 11th-century frescoes.

Every Sunday in July and August, organ concerts run from 5 to 6pm; admission is free. Daily from June to August at 10pm and in September at 9:30pm, a 70-minute sound-and-light show relates the history of the church. It's presented in English, French, and German and costs 5€ ($6.50) for adults and is free for children under 14.

Place St-Etienne, Toulousse 31000. ✆ **03-86-52-23-29.** Free admission to church. Combined admission to crypt and treasury 4€ ($5.20), free for children under 14. June–Aug Mon–Sat 9am–6pm, Sun 2–5pm; Sept–May Mon–Sat 10am–noon and 2–6pm.

WHERE TO STAY

Hôtel Le Maxime This family-run hotel boasts attractive, high-ceilinged rooms, many with views of the river or the old city. Most units retain their original wall and ceiling beams. Built as a private villa in 1855, the gracious, old-fashioned inn has been a hotel since 1900. A thorough renovation has upgraded the accommodations. All the bathrooms come with a tub/shower combination. You can take breakfast in your room or in the quiet salon, amid Oriental rugs, polished paneling, and a sense of the gentility of an earlier era.

2 quai de la Marine, Auxerre 89000. ✆ **03-86-52-14-19.** Fax 03-86-52-21-70. www.lemaxime.com. 25 units. 77€–108€ ($100–$140) double; 130€–165€ ($169–$215) suite. AE, DC, MC, V. Parking 6€ ($7.80). **Amenities:** Bar; laundry service; dry cleaning. *In room:* TV, minibar, hair dryer.

Hôtel Normandie This centrally located three-story hotel offers traditional hospitality, combining antique furnishings with modern amenities. The tranquil, comfortably furnished rooms open onto garden views; each unit is different. Most bathrooms come with multijet showers only, but some have tubs.

41 bd. Vauban, Auxerre 89000. ✆ **03-86-52-57-80.** Fax 03-86-51-54-33. www.hotelnormandie.fr. 47 units. 65€–90€ ($85–$117) double. AE, DC, MC, V. Parking 6€ ($7.80). **Amenities:** Bar; small gym; sauna; room service. *In room:* A/C, TV, minibar, hair dryer.

Le Parc des Maréchaux ★★ A gem that outshines the competition, this was a Napoleon III–style private residence in the 19th century, set in its own .4-hectare (1-acre) park. The most secluded choice in the area, it's on the western outskirts of town, surrounded by century-old trees. The decor in the public areas and the lounge is French Empire; the style of the guest rooms is less consistent—a mixture of contemporary and Empire. Each room comes with a combination tub/shower. The only available meal is breakfast, but the staff will serve hot food, on special request, in your room or in one of the salons.

6 av. Foch, Auxerre 89000. ✆ **03-86-51-43-77.** Fax 03-86-51-31-72. www.hotel-parcmarechaux.com. 25 units. 84€ ($109) double; 120€–136€ ($156–$177) triple or quad. AE, DC, MC, V. **Amenities:** Heated outdoor pool; room service. *In room:* TV, minibar.

WHERE TO DINE

Le Jardin Gourmand ★★ FRENCH The most sophisticated restaurant in town specializes in *cuisine moderne du marché* (modern market cuisine), employing the freshest ingredients to create artfully presented menus that change, often radically, eight times a year. The setting is an 1870 house a 10-minute walk from the cathedral. In summer, an awning shades an outdoor terrace. Pierre Boussereau and Olivier Laplaine are devoted to cultivating fresh salad greens and herbs in their garden, and use them to garnish such platters as carpaccio of duck liver. Other dishes may include leg of pheasant stuffed with poultry livers and served with braised cabbage and hazelnut oil; scallops with a mousse of green beans; smoked lamb served *à la plancha* with pepperoni-studded salsa and saffron-fried potatoes; calves' liver served with thickened veal stock and fresh cardamom; and red mullet with a sauce of thickened fish stock and star anise.

56 bd. Vauban. ✆ **03-86-51-53-52.** www.lejardingourmand.com. Reservations required. Main courses 35€–45€ ($46–$59); fixed-price menus 40€ ($52), 50€ ($65), 60€ ($78), and 85€ ($111). AE, MC, V. Thurs–Mon noon–1:45pm and 7:30–9:15pm. Closed Nov 7–29.

WHERE TO STAY & DINE NEARBY

A la Côte St-Jacques ★★★ FRENCH/BURGUNDIAN This is one of the top Relais & Châteaux members in France, with a 300-year-old foundation, a clientele that has included Catherine Deneuve and several French presidents, and a well-engrained sense of comfort and culinary style. Specialties include sea scallops roasted with caramelized spices, braised endive, and zabaglione; roast duckling with a lasagna of chestnuts, exotic mushrooms, foie gras, and mousseline of beets; terrine of Brittany oysters; and smoked sea bass served with Sevruga caviar.

The restaurant and 22 opulent rooms—air-conditioned, contemporary, very comfortable, and decorated with individual color schemes and parquet floors—lie in modern quarters adjacent to the Yonne River. Ten less expensive, non-air-conditioned rooms lie on an older site. An underground tunnel, fashioned from rocks salvaged from old buildings, connects the two sections. Rates run 150€ to 375€ ($195–$488) for a double and 440€ to 560€ ($572–$728) for a suite. Each has a TV, minibar, hair dryer, and safe; there's also an indoor pool and sauna.

14 Faubourg de Paris (N6), Joigny 89300. From Auxerre, head north on N6 (toward Sens) for 27km (17 miles). ✆ **03-86-62-09-70.** Fax 03-86-91-49-70. www.cotesaintjacques.com. Reservations required. Main courses 48€–90€ ($62–$117); fixed-price lunch 83€–160€ ($108–$208); fixed-price dinner 160€–195€ ($208–$254). AE, DC, MC, V. Daily 12:15–2:45pm and 7:15–9:45pm. Hotel and restaurant closed Jan 5–22.

2 Vézelay ★★

217km (135 miles) SE of Paris, 52km (32 miles) S of Auxerre

Vézelay, a living museum of French antiquity, stands frozen in time. For many, the town is the high point of a trip through Burgundy. Because it contained what was believed to be the tomb of St. Mary Magdalene, that "beloved and pardoned sinner," it was one of the great pilgrimage sites of the Christian world.

Today, the medieval charm of Vézelay is widely known throughout France, and visitors virtually overrun the town in summer. The hordes are especially thick on July 22, the official day of homage to La Madeleine.

ESSENTIALS

GETTING THERE If you're **driving** from Paris, take A6 south to Auxerre, then continue south along N151 to Clamecy and turn east on D951 to Vézelay. Five **trains** a day travel from Paris Gare de Lyon via Auxerre to Sermizelles, taking 2½ hours and costing 15€ ($20) one-way. From Sermizelles, a bus makes the run to Vézelay only on Saturday at noon. The rest of the week, take a taxi from Sermizelles, 15 minutes away. For train information and schedules, call ✆ **08-92-35-35-35.**

VISITOR INFORMATION The **Office de Tourisme,** rue St-Etienne (✆ **03-86-33-23-69;** fax 03-86-33-34-00; www.vezelaytourisme.com), is open daily from April to September, and Friday to Wednesday from October to May.

EXPLORING THE TOWN

On a hill 108m (354 ft.) above the countryside, Vézelay is known for its ramparts and houses with sculptured doorways, corbeled staircases, and mullioned windows. The site of the town was an abbey founded by Girart de Roussillon, *comte* de Bourgogne. Pope John VIII consecrated the abbey in 878.

On March 31, 1146, St. Bernard preached the Second Crusade here; in 1190, the town was the rendezvous point for the Third Crusade, drawing such personages as Richard the Lion-Hearted and King Philippe-Auguste of France. Later, St. Louis of France came here several times on pilgrimages.

Park outside the town hall and walk through the medieval streets lined with 15th-, 16th-, and 18th-century houses and flower-filled gardens.

If you're in the mood to shop, head for rue St-Etienne and rue St-Pierre. You'll find an assortment of stores selling religious books and statuary, including **Jerusalem,** 78 rue St-Pierre (✆ **03-86-33-37-43**), and **Le Magasin du Pélerin,** place de la Basilique

(✆ **03-86-33-29-14**). **Galerie Lieber,** 14 rue St-Etienne (✆ **03-86-33-33-90**), specializes in handmade jewelry, using semiprecious and precious stones in both heavy and delicate settings of silver and gold. You may also want to pick up a bottle or two of Vézelay wine at **La Cave Henry de Vézelay,** route de Nanchèvres, St-Père-sous-Vézelay (✆ **03-86-33-29-62**).

Basilique Ste-Madeleine ★★ Built in the 12th century, France's largest and most famous Romanesque church is only 9m (30 ft.) shorter than Notre-Dame de Paris. When you enter the narthex, a vestibule of about 370 sq. m (4,000 sq. ft.), raise your eyes to the doorway depicting Christ giving the apostles the Holy Spirit. From the Romanesque nave, with its traverse arches in white-and-gray stone, you'll see the light Gothic chancel. You can visit the Carolingian crypt, where the tomb of Mary Magdalene formerly rested (today the crypt contains some of her relics). There's a panoramic view from the back terrace.

Place de la Basilique, Vézelay 89450. ✆ **03-86-33-39-50.** Free admission. Daily 7am–8pm.

WHERE TO STAY

L'Espérance (see "Where to Dine," below) also rents luxurious rooms.

Le Compostelle This pleasant hotel is the best of Vézelay's more affordable inns. It's in the center of town, up the hill leading to the basilica, in a late-19th-century building that was transformed into this hotel in 1991. It's reminiscent of an English country house. Guest rooms are midsize and comfortably furnished, with small, shower-only bathrooms. Breakfast is the only meal served.

Place du Champ-de-Foire, Vézelay 89450. ✆ **03-86-33-28-63.** Fax 03-86-33-34-34. le.compostelle@wanadoo.fr. 18 units. 49€–60€ ($64–$78) double. AE, MC, V. Closed Jan 9 to mid-Feb. *In room:* TV.

Poste et Lion d'Or ★ *Value* This local favorite is filled with character and tradition. On the main square, at the bottom of the hill that rises to the basilica, this hotel was built in the 17th century as a postal station. With a terrace and small garden, the Poste et Lion d'Or is a first-class lodging with surprisingly reasonable rates. The functional guest rooms are conservatively outfitted in some cases in a vaguely Louis XVI style. Other than L'Espérance, it's the finest address in town, though only slightly better than Le Pontot (see below).

Place du Champ-de-Foire, Vézelay 89450. ✆ **03-86-33-21-23.** Fax 03-86-32-30-92. www.laposte-liondor.com. 38 units. 68€–89€ ($88–$116) double; 128€–162€ ($166–$211) suite. AE, DC, MC, V. Parking 6€ ($7.80). Closed Jan–Feb. **Amenities:** Bar; laundry service; nonsmoking rooms. *In room:* A/C, TV.

Résidence-Hôtel Le Pontot ★ Near the basilica is this tastefully renovated medieval structure. The guest rooms are decorated in a romantic French style—not to everyone's taste, but a lovely attempt at creating a homelike environment. Rooms range from small to spacious, each outfitted differently from its neighbor, with small, shower-only bathrooms. The hotel has bar service and a charming walled garden where you can eat breakfast (or relax throughout the day), but no restaurant.

Place du Pontot, Vézelay 89450. ✆ **03-86-33-24-40.** Fax 03-86-33-30-05. www.lepontot.com. 11 units. 105€–165€ ($137–$215) double. MC, V. Parking 10€ ($13). Closed Nov–Easter. **Amenities:** Bar. *In room:* TV.

WHERE TO DINE

La Bougainville ★ BURGUNDIAN Not all of us can afford to dine at L'Espérance (see below), so La Bougainville is a more affordable alternative. This elegantly decorated antique house, complete with fireplace, serves as a backdrop for such regional specialties as *oeufs en meurette* (eggs poached in red wine and served with red-wine sauce) or a platter of oysters. After that, you can plunge into *filet de boeuf à la bourguignon* (beef cooked in burgundy with crème fraîche and escargots). The restaurant is also adept at concocting game dishes, such as venison with chestnuts or a delightful hare stew. For dessert, the specialty is *success aux noisettes avec nectarines rôti pralinée* (hazelnut cakes with roasted nectarines and praline ice cream).

26 rue St-Etienne. ✆ **03-86-33-27-57.** Reservations required. Main courses 10€–30€ ($13–$39). MC, V. Thurs–Mon noon–2pm and 7–9pm. Closed Nov–Feb 1.

L'Espérance ★★★ MODERN FRENCH No other restaurant in Burgundy is as frequently assessed and gossiped about as this one, directed by Marc and Françoise Meneau. The restaurant has the feel of an old-fashioned farm and bakery, with Napoleon III decor. Located in a fertile valley, it emanates Burgundian wholesomeness as well as Parisian chic. Flagstone floors and big windows overlooking a garden complement the superb cuisine. Menu items change frequently but are likely to include *cromesquis de foie gras* (in the form of a cube that melts in your mouth), potato galette with caviar, turbot en croûte, and roasted and caramelized filet of veal. The slightly overworked staff struggles valiantly with the traffic generated by the place's fame.

On the premises are 34 well-maintained and comfortable guest rooms in three historic buildings. The accommodations epitomize French country living at its best. Doubles cost 200€ to 300€ ($260–$390), suites 400€ to 470€ ($520–$611).

St-Père-sous-Vézelay, Vézelay 89450. ✆ **03-86-33-39-10.** Fax 03-86-33-26-15. www.marc-meneau-esperance.com. Reservations recommended. Main courses 55€–95€ ($72–$124); fixed-price lunch 100€–250€ ($130–$325); fixed-price dinner 170€–250€ ($221–$325). AE, DC, MC, V. Thurs–Sun noon–2pm; Wed–Mon 7:30–9:30pm. Closed mid-Jan to Mar.

3 Avallon ★

214km (133 miles) SE of Paris, 52km (32 miles) SE of Auxerre, 96km (60 miles) NW of Dijon

This fortified town sits behind ancient ramparts, upon which you can stroll. A medieval atmosphere permeates Avallon, where you'll find many 15th- and 16th-century houses. At the town gate on Grande Rue Aristide-Briand is a clock tower from 1460. The Romanesque **Eglise St-Lazare** dates from the 12th century and has two interesting doorways. The church, open daily from 8am to 7pm, is said to have received the head of St. Lazarus in 1000, thus turning Avallon into a pilgrimage site. Today, Avallon is a destination mainly for its fabulous food.

ESSENTIALS

GETTING THERE If you're **driving,** travel south from Paris along A6 to Auxerre; from Auxerre, take N6 south to Avallon. Seven **trains** arrive daily from Paris Gare de Lyon (trip time: 2½ hr.; one-way fare 30€–50€/$39–$65). For train information, call ✆ **08-92-35-35-35.** Bus service from Dijon takes 2 hours and costs 17€ ($22) one-way; purchase tickets on the bus. For bus information, contact the railway station in Avallon (✆ **03-86-34-01-01**).

VISITOR INFORMATION The **Office de Tourisme** is at 6 rue Bocquillot (✆ **03-86-34-14-19;** www.avallonnais-tourisme.com).

WHERE TO STAY

Château de Vault-de-Lugny ★★★ Between Avallon and Vézelay is this 16th-century moat-encircled château, with a fortress tower and peacocks on the grounds. It emphasizes service, with two staff members to every guest. The accommodations are sumptuous, with canopy beds, antique furnishings, and fireplaces. Luxurious bathrooms hold tub/shower combinations. You can order cocktails in the salon, and then eat dinner by candlelight. Fresh ingredients are the hallmark of the cuisine here. A special *bourguignon* meal of typical regional dishes is offered nightly.

A Vault-de-Lugny, Avallon 89200. Take D957 from Avallon, turn right in Pontaubert (after the church) and follow signs; Vault-de-Lugny is about 3km (1¾ miles) away. ✆ **03-86-34-07-86.** Fax 03-86-34-16-36. www.lugny.fr. 15 units. 160€–510€ ($208–$663) double; 360€–550€ ($468–$715) suite. AE, DC, MC, V. Closed mid-Nov to Apr 6. **Amenities:** Restaurant; bar; indoor pool; room service; babysitting; laundry service. *In room:* TV, minibar, hair dryer, safe.

Moulin des Ruats ★ *Finds* This enchanting country inn sits on the banks of the Cousin. Constructed as a flour mill in the 17th century, it has been a family hotel since 1924. Some guest rooms have exposed beams and intimate alcoves. Each contains a small bathroom with a shower, and some have tubs as well. Try for a room with a balcony overlooking the river. The elegant dining room serves a menu of freshwater fish and boasts a fine wine list and a terrace. The restaurant and the accommodations are equally atmospheric and impressive.

Vallée du Cousin, Avallon 89200. Take D427 3km (1¾ miles) outside town. ✆ **03-86-34-97-00.** Fax 03-86-31-65-47. www.moulin-des-ruats.com. 25 units. 80€–130€ ($104–$169) double; 155€ ($202) apt. AE, DC, MC, V. Closed mid-Nov to mid-Feb. **Amenities:** Restaurant; bar; room service; babysitting. *In room:* TV.

WHERE TO DINE

Les Capucins ★★ BURGUNDIAN Chef-owner Guy Cucurull is king of the cooks in this town long known for its discerning palates. Warm colors and fresh flowers brighten the rustic decor and country furnishings. The restaurant is on a sleepy square just a 12-minute stroll from the heart of town. It's on the ground floor of a little hotel that rents 16 guest rooms for 40€ to 69€ ($52–$90) double, eight containing air-conditioning.

The chef fashions such dishes as red mullet in a purée of apples and potatoes, and tender veal shanks with macaroni gratin. Two typical Burgundian dishes are fat escargots in garlic butter and classic *oeufs en meurette.* For dessert, lemon- and anise-flavored madeleines are served with ice cream.

6 av. Paul-Doumer, Avallon 89200. ✆ **03-86-34-06-52.** Fax 03-86-34-58-47. Main courses 10€–25€ ($13–$33); fixed-price menu 17€–44€ ($22–$57). AE, MC, V. Daily noon–2pm and 7–9:30pm.

4 Autun ★★

293km (182 miles) SE of Paris, 85km (53 miles) SW of Dijon, 48km (30 miles) W of Beaune, 60km (37 miles) SE of Auxerre

Deep in Burgundy, Autun is one of the oldest towns in France. In the days of the Roman Empire, it was called "the other Rome." Some relics still stand, including the remains of the largest theater in Gaul, the Théâtre Romain. It was nearly 150m (492 ft.) in diameter and could hold some 15,000 people. Outside the town, you can see the tower of the 24m-high (79-ft.) Temple de Janus.

Autun is a thriving provincial town of 20,000. Because it's off the beaten track, the hordes go elsewhere. Still, it has its historical associations—Napoleon studied here in 1779 at the military academy (today the Lycée Bonaparte).

ESSENTIALS

GETTING THERE If you're **driving,** take D944 south from Avallon to Château-Chinon. Follow D978 east into Autun. From Lyon, you can take a train (trip time: 45 min.) from the center to the transportation hub at Gare le Creusot; the fare is 26€

($34). From there, three **TGVs** a day make the 50-minute trip to Autun; the fare is 6.50€ ($8.45) one-way. Ten trains a day from Paris's Gare de Lyon (one-way fare: 50€–65€/$65–$85) run to Montchanin–Le Creusot, 40km (25 miles) south of Autun. From there, take a 45-minute bus connection to Autun. In Autun, **buses** arrive at a parking lot by the railway station on avenue de la République. For bus information, call © **03-85-86-92-55.** For railway information, call the station in Autun (© **03-85-52-73-65**) or SNCF (© **03-80-42-11-00**).

VISITOR INFORMATION The **Office de Tourisme** is at 2 av. Charles-de-Gaulle (© **03-85-86-80-38;** fax 03-85-86-80-49; www.autun-tourisme.com).

SEEING THE SIGHTS

Autun was once an important link on the road from Lyon to Boulogne. A legacy of that period is the 17m-high (56-ft.) **Porte d'Arroux,** once the city gate, which has two archways now used for cars and smaller ones used for pedestrians. Also exceptional is the **Porte St-André (St. Andrew's Gate),** northwest of the Roman theater. Rising 20m (66 ft.), it has four doorways and is surmounted by a gallery of 10 arcades.

Cathédrale St-Lazare ★★ On the highest point in Autun, the cathedral was built in 1120 to house the relics of St. Lazarus. On the facade, the tympanum in the central portal depicts the Last Judgment—a triumph of Romanesque sculpture. Inside, a painting by Ingres depicts the martyrdom of St. Symphorien, who was killed in Autun. In the 1860s, Viollet-le-Duc, the architect who restored many monuments of France, had to double the size of some of the columns supporting the roof to avoid a collapse. New capitals matching the Romanesque style of the originals were crafted to top the new columns. The original capitals are on display, more or less at eye level, in the Salle Capitulaire, one flight above street level; especially noteworthy are *La Reveil des Mages* (The Awakening of the Magi) and *La Fuite en Egypte* (The Flight into Egypt).

Place St-Louis. © **03-85-52-12-37.** Free admission. July–Aug daily 8am–7pm; Sept–June daily 8am–6pm.

Musée Rolin ★ This 15th-century mansion was built for a famous lawyer, Nicolas Rolin (b. 1380). An easy walk from the cathedral, the museum displays a collection of Burgundian Romanesque sculpture, as well as paintings and archaeological mementos. From the original Rolin collection are *Nativity* by the Maître de Moulins, and a statue that's a 15th-century masterpiece, *Our Lady of Autun* (*La Vierge d'Autun,* also known as *La Vierge Bulliot* after the benefactor who returned the original statue to the cathedral in 1948).

3 rue des Bancs. © **03-85-52-09-76.** Admission 3.25€ ($4.25) adults, 1.65€ ($2.15) students and children. Apr–Sept Wed–Mon 9:30am–noon and 1:30–6pm; Oct–Mar Wed–Mon 10am–noon and 2–5pm. Closed holidays.

NEARBY ATTRACTIONS

After visiting Autun (if you have a car), you can tour one of Burgundy's finest wineries: **Domaine Maurice Protheau,** Château d'Etroyes, in Mercurey, 40km (25 miles) southeast along D978 (© **03-85-45-10-84**). Among the selections are at least two *appellations contrôlées* (a regulation system that ensures a wine has been produced where the bottles says), so you'll have a chance to immerse yourself in the subtle differences between reds (both pinot noirs and burgundies), whites, and rosés produced under the auspices of Rully and Mercurey. The headquarters of the winery, founded in the 1740s, is a château built in the 1700s and early 1800s. Free tours of the cellars are offered, in French and halting English, daily from 10am to noon and 2 to 7pm (call ahead to confirm). A *dégustation des vins* (wine tasting) and the opportunity to haul a bottle or two away costs 3.50€ ($4.55).

Three kilometers (1¾ miles) away, you can visit the **Château de Rully,** site of the **Domaine de la Bressande** (✆ **03-85-87-20-89**), a well-respected producer of white and some red burgundies. Originally built in the 12th century as a stronghold for the *comte* de Ternay, it offers tours to the public. The owner prefers that you visit the château as part of a group. Individuals can visit in July and August Tuesday to Sunday at 2, 4, and 5pm, but this offering is more limited than the group tour. Either option costs 6€ ($7.80).

WHERE TO STAY & DINE

Hostellerie du Vieux Moulin ★★ This fine hotel, a 10-minute walk north of the town center, also contains Autun's best restaurant. It's at the edge of the Arroux River, in a stone-walled former grain mill built in the 1870s. The hotel boasts a scattering of 19th-century regional antiques and simple but comfortable guest rooms. The small bathrooms have showers and tubs. Reminders of the winemaking trade accent the rooms. Some units have TVs and air-conditioning.

In summer, you can dine at a table overlooking the garden and a stream. Menu items include filet of local *sandre* (whitefish) with basil-flavored cream sauce; Charolais beef simmered in red wine; and tournedos Talleyrand, flavored with shallots and red wine (the dish is named for a local bishop, not the politician). Any of dozens of red burgundies can accompany your meal.

Porte d'Arroux, Autun 71403. ✆ **03-85-52-10-90.** Fax 03-85-86-32-15. 16 units. 63€–85€ ($82–$111) double. MC, V. Closed Dec–Feb. **Amenities:** Restaurant; bar.

Hôtel les Ursulines ★ The best hotel in Autun, the Ursulines offers attractive rooms with views of the countryside and the Morvan mountains. Built in the 1600s as a convent, it gained a comfortable annex in 2000 that holds about half the rooms. Accommodations vary in shape and size, but each comes with a fine bed, quality linens, antique furniture, and a bathroom with a combination tub/shower. Units under the mansard eaves of the old building are the cheapest, smallest, and coziest. The hotel is known for its cuisine.

14 rue Rivault, Autun 71400. ✆ **03-85-86-58-58.** Fax 03-85-86-23-07. www.hotelursulines.fr. 43 units. 69€–130€ ($90–$169) double; 134€–160€ ($174–$208) suite. AE, DC, MC, V. Parking 7€ ($9.10). **Amenities:** Restaurant; bar; babysitting; laundry service. *In room:* A/C (in some), TV, minibar, hair dryer, Wi-Fi.

5 Beaune ★★

316km (196 miles) SE of Paris, 39km (24 miles) SW of Dijon

This is the capital of the Burgundy wine country and one of the best-preserved medieval cities in the district, with a girdle of ramparts. Its history goes back over 2,000 years. Beaune was a Gallic sanctuary, then a Roman town. Until the 14th century, it was the residence of the ducs de Bourgogne. When the last duke, Charles the Bold, died in 1477, Louis XI annexed Beaune.

ESSENTIALS

GETTING THERE If you're **driving,** note that Beaune is a few miles from the junction of four highways—A6, A31, A36, and N6. Beaune has good railway connections with Dijon, Lyon, and Paris. From Paris's Gare de Lyon, there are 11 TGV **trains** per day (trip time: 2 hr.; one-way fare 45€–55€/$59–$72); from Lyon, 11 trains per

Tips Burgundy by Bike

The best way to see this golden land is by bike. Near the Beaune Rail Station, **Bourgogne Randonnées (✆ 03-80-22-06-03;** www.bourgogne-randonnees.com) rents bikes for 15€ ($20) per day.

day (trip time: 1½ hr.; 21€/$25 one-way); and from Dijon, 33 trains per day (trip time: 25 min.; 6.50€/$8.45). For train information and schedules, call ✆ **08-92-35-35-35.**

VISITOR INFORMATION The **Office de Tourisme** is at 6 bd. Perpreuil (✆ **03-80-26-21-30;** fax 03-80-26-21-39; www.ot-beaune.fr).

SPECIAL EVENTS The town comes to life during the third weekend in November, when wine buyers and oenophiles from the world over descend on the old town for a 3-day festival and wine auction called **Les Trois Glorieuses.** The town is packed with wineries offering *dégustations* priced from 20€ to 35€ ($26–$46) for "several" glasses each of a different wine vintage—and with tourists visiting the labyrinth of caves and wine cellars. With all the free spirits (both kinds), visitors crowding the streets can be more than a bit tipsy.

EXPLORING THE TOWN

North of the Hôtel-Dieu, the **Collégiale Notre-Dame,** place du Général Leclerc (✆ **03-80-26-22-70**), is an 1120 Burgundian Romanesque church. Some remarkable tapestries illustrating scenes from the life of the Virgin Mary are on display in the sanctuary. You can view them from Easter to mid-November.

The best shopping streets are rue de Lorraine, rue d'Alsace, rue Maufoux, and place de la Madeleine. For smaller boutiques, stroll down the pedestrian rue Carnot and rue Monge. For antiques, concentrate your efforts around **Quartier du Camp Americain,** 3km (1¾ miles) northeast of the center of Beaune.

Beaune is one of the best towns in the region for sampling and buying Burgundy wines. You can tour, taste, and buy at **Marché aux Vins,** rue Nicolas-Rolin (✆ **03-80-25-08-20**), housed in a 14th-century church. Entrance is 10€ ($13). Its cellars are in and among the ancient tombs, under the floor of the church. A well-stocked competitor, stocking most of the vintages of Burgundy, is **Cordelier,** 6 rue de l'Hôtel-Dieu (✆ **03-80-25-08-85**). Another cellar, **Caves Patriarche Père et Fils,** 7 rue du Collège (✆ **03-80-24-53-78**), is under the former Convent of the Visitandines, with cellars from the 13th, 16th, and 17th centuries.

Musée de l'Hôtel-Dieu ★★ One of the town's most visible antique buildings is the Hôtel-Dieu. It thrived during the Middle Ages under an order of nuns associated with the famous vineyards of Aloxe-Corton and Meursault. It functioned as a hospital until 1970, and some sections still hold a retirement home. The Musée de l'Hôtel-Dieu displays Flemish-Burgundian art such as Rogier van der Weyden's 1443 polyptych ***The Last Judgment*** ★★★. In the Salle des Pauvres (Room of the Poor), you'll find painted, broken-barrel, timbered vaulting and mostly authentic furnishings.

Rue de l'Hôtel-Dieu. ✆ **03-80-24-45-00.** Admission 6€ ($7.80) adults, 3€ ($3.90) ages 10–18, free for children under 10. Apr–Nov 19 daily 9am–6:30pm; Nov 20–Mar daily 9–11:30am and 2–5:30pm.

Musée des Beaux-Arts et Musée Marey Along with a rich Gallo-Roman archaeological section, this museum has paintings from the 16th to the 19th centuries, including Flemish primitives, and pieces by Felix Ziem, a precursor of the Impressionists. Sculptures from the Middle Ages and the Renaissance are also on display. The museum also honors Beaune physiologist Etienne Jules Marey, who discovered the principles of the cinema long before 1895.

6 bd. Perpreuil (Porte Marie de Bourgogne). ✆ **03-80-24-56-78.** Admission (includes Musée du Vin de Bourgogne) 5.40€ ($7) adults, 3.50€ ($4.55) students and children, free for children under 12. Apr–Oct daily 9:30am–6pm. Closed Nov–Mar (except 3rd weekend in Nov).

Musée du Vin de Bourgogne ★ Housed in the former mansion of the ducs de Bourgogne, the Musée du Vin de Bourgogne traces the evolution of the region's winemaking. The collection of tools, objets d'art, and documents is contained in 15th- and 16th-century rooms. On display in the 14th-century press house is a collection of wine presses.

Rue d'Enfer. ✆ **03-80-22-08-19.** Admission 5.40€ ($7) adults, 3.50€ ($4.55) students and children, free for children under 12. Apr–Nov daily 9:30am–5pm; Dec–Mar Wed–Mon 9:30am–6pm.

WHERE TO STAY

Hôtel de la Poste ★ Outside the town fortifications, this traditional hotel rivals but does not surpass the more elegant Hôtel Le Cep (see below). Its origins as an inn go back to 1660; it was radically restored in 1991 and upgraded every year since. The rooms overlook the ramparts or the vineyards, and some have brass beds. The midsize bathrooms have tub/shower combinations. Specialties at the restaurant range from chicken fricassee with tarragon to sole in court bouillon with white butter.

5 bd. Georges-Clemenceau, Beaune 21200. ✆ **03-80-22-08-11.** Fax 03-80-24-19-71. www.hoteldelapostebeaune.com. 36 units. 160€–210€ ($208–$273) double; 290€–450€ ($377–$585) suite. AE, DC, MC, V. Parking 10€ ($13). **Amenities:** 2 restaurants; bar; room service; laundry service; limited-mobility rooms. *In room:* A/C, TV, minibar, hair dryer, safe.

Hôtel Le Cep ★★★ The chic spot for oenophiles is this former residential mansion in the town center, fit for the ducs de Bourgogne. Each antiques-filled guest room is individually decorated and named after a Grand Cru wine of the Côte-d'Or vineyards; our favorites are the Chambre Montrachet and the Chambre Meloisey. On the grounds are two of the loveliest arcaded courtyards in Beaune, one from the 16th century, another from the 14th century. A tower housing one of the city's most beautiful stone staircases rises from here. A former wine cellar is the breakfast room. One of Beaune's finest restaurants is inside the hotel.

27 rue Maufoux, Beaune 21200. ✆ **03-80-22-35-48.** Fax 03-80-22-76-80. www.hotel-cep-beaune.com. 62 units. 160€–200€ ($208–$260) double; from 240€ ($312) suite. AE, DC, MC, V. Parking 13€ ($17). **Amenities:** Restaurant; business center; room service; laundry service; nonsmoking rooms; limited-mobility rooms. *In room:* A/C, TV, minibar, hair dryer, safe.

L'Hostellerie de Bretonnière *Value* This is the best bargain in town. It's well run, with quiet rooms, and 5 minutes on foot from the center of town. The inn was built as a postal relay station around 1900 and became a hotel in 1950. In 2004, management enlarged the hotel with the addition of a seven-unit annex in the garden, containing only duplex suites, each rustically outfitted in a style that evokes the traditions of rural Burgundy. The accommodations in the rear are the most tranquil, though most visitors prefer those overlooking the garden. Rooms are small, but adequate for an overnight; each has a shower-only bathroom. Continental breakfast is available.

43 rue de Faubourg Bretonnière, Beaune 21200. ✆ **03-80-22-15-77.** Fax 03-80-22-72-54. www.hotelbretonniere.com. 32 units. 55€–79€ ($72–$103) double; 95€–110€ ($124–$143) duplex suites. AE, DC, MC, V. Free parking. **Amenities:** Bar. *In room:* TV, hair dryer, Wi-Fi.

L'Hôtel de Beaune ★★ Although Le Cep is more tranquil and luxurious, L'Hôtel (which opened in 2002) is the second-most desirable hotel in town. Marble, mahogany, teak, and Italian stucco abound. Behind the 19th-century exterior, its guest rooms are tastefully furnished and comfortable, though lacking some of Le Cep's glamour. Each of the accommodations here is individually decorated, with lustrous yellow-and-orange quilts on mahogany beds of royal size. Bathrooms are exotically deluxe, with chrome basins set in teak, toilets screened behind smoked-glass doors, showers the size of studies, black Italian marble floors, king-size beds, and mirrored walls. Although the hotel has no restaurant on-site, it maintains an extraordinarily comprehensive wine cellar that, on advance notice, visitors can examine. Wines inside are for sale, either for consumption within the hotel's bar or for take-away.

5 rue Samuel Legay, Beaune 21200. ✆ **03-80-25-94-14.** Fax 03-80-25-94-13. www.lhoteldebeaune.com. 7 units. 180€–335€ ($234–$436) double. AE, DC, MC, V. **Amenities:** Bar; room service; babysitting; laundry service. *In room:* TV, hair dryer, safe, Wi-Fi.

WHERE TO DINE

Hôtel de la Poste (see "Where to Stay," above) has a good restaurant.

Bernard Morillon ★★ TRADITIONAL FRENCH This respected dining room is in a 16th-century house beneath original ceiling beams. Bernard Morillon is the owner-chef, and his wife, Martine, supervises the Directoire–Louis XV dining room. A signature dish is an intricate version of pigeon deboned and reconstructed on a platter, served with gravy enriched with foie gras. There's also superb Bresse chicken with Gevry-Chambertin wine, and ragout of freshwater crayfish. Consider beginning with crusty Burgundy snails served with garlic-and-parsley-flavored cream sauce.

31 rue Maufoux. ✆ **03-80-24-12-06.** Reservations recommended. Main courses 35€–76€ ($46–$99); fixed-price menu 53€–77€ ($69–$100). AE, DC, DISC, MC, V. Wed–Fri and Sun noon–2pm; Tues–Sun 7:30–10pm. Closed Feb.

Jardin des Remparts ★★★ MODERN FRENCH This is the finest restaurant in Beaune, topping even Bernard Morillon. Just outside the city's medieval wall, it's in a 1930s-era Art Deco *maison bourgeoise.* Two pale-yellow-and-green dining rooms open onto a terrace overlooking the garden. Happily, prices for the well-regarded cuisine are a bit lower than you may expect. Menu items are adventurous and creative, and include tartare of beef and minced oysters, whitefish baked in a mushroom crust, and pigeon roasted with licorice and softened caramel.

10 rue de l'Hôtel-Dieu ✆ **03-80-24-79-41.** Reservations recommended. Main courses 25€–48€ ($33–$62); fixed-price lunch 30€ ($39); fixed-price dinner Tues–Thurs 55€–85€ ($72–$111). MC, V. Tues–Sat noon–1:30pm and 7–9pm. Closed Dec 1–Jan 15.

Ma Cuisine ★ *Finds* FRENCH/BURGUNDIAN Open only 4 days a week, Ma Cuisine enjoys a reputation for well-prepared regional food and an impressively varied wine cellar. Fabienne Escoffier presides over the kitchen, and her husband, Pierre, maintains the dining room. The restaurant attracts local residents, many of them wine producers. Your old-fashioned meal may begin with a platter of thin-sliced cured ham with parsley, or compote of rabbit with fresh tarragon. Main courses include spit-roasted and deboned pigeon and beef bourguignon with garlic. Desserts are 19th-century French brasserie favorites: thin-sliced apple or pear tart, crème brûlée, almond cake. The setting, a much-renovated 15th-century stable, is appropriately historic.

Passage Ste-Hélène. ✆ **03-80-22-30-22.** Reservations recommended. Main courses 14€–28€ ($18–$36); fixed-price menu 20€ ($26). MC, V. Mon–Tues and Thurs–Fri noon–1:30pm and 7:30–9pm.

Relais de Saulx ★ FRENCH In a 200-year-old stone-trimmed building named after one of the region's ancient and noble families, Relais de Saulx is decorated with heavy timbers, oil paintings, and all the accouterments you'd expect from one of the region's most respected restaurants. The kitchen prepares traditional Bourguignon cuisine and up-to-date adaptations. Staples are Bresse chicken with morel sauce, scallops with truffle sauce, sea bass with fresh morel, and roast pigeon with sauces and garnishes that vary according to the season.

6 rue Louis-Very. ✆ **03-80-22-01-35.** Reservations required for large groups. Main courses 12€–20€ ($16–$26); fixed-price menu 17€–39€ ($22–$51). AE, DC, MC, V. Tues and Thurs–Sat noon–2pm; Mon–Sat 7–10pm. Closed 1 week in Feb and 2 weeks in Aug.

WHERE TO STAY & DINE NEARBY

Hostellerie de Levernois ★ FRENCH Under Jean Croet and his sons, this became one of the most celebrated restaurants of regional France. New owners are now in charge, and the restaurant is still trying to find its way. It offers grand cuisine in a stone-sided 17th-century *maison bourgeoise* in a 3.2 hectare (8-acre) park. The kitchen doesn't emphasize virtuoso techniques, but it knows what to do with first-class ingredients. On a recent visit, the snails in puff pastry were a pure delight, as was a brochette of crayfish tails with spicy sauce. Chickens for roasting come from Bresse and are acclaimed as the best in France.

The inn rents 18 carefully decorated rooms in a well-designed modern annex. They have TV, air-conditioning, and (in most) tub/shower combos. Doubles cost 180€ to 305€ ($234–$397); the suites go for 245€ to 400€ ($319–$520).

Rte. de Verdun-sur-le-Doubs, Levernois 21200. Take D970 south of Beaune for 3km (1¾ miles), following signs for LONS LE SAUNIER. ✆ **03-80-24-73-58.** Fax 03-80-22-78-00. www.levernois.com. Reservations required. Main courses 41€–49€ ($53–$64); fixed-price lunch 38€ ($49); fixed-price dinner 65€–98€ ($85–$128). AE, DC, MC, V. Apr–Oct Mon–Sat noon–1:30pm and 7–9:30pm; off season Mon and Wed–Sun noon–1:30pm and 7–9:30pm. Closed Feb–Mar.

BEAUNE AFTER DARK

To hear jazz and rock music and flirt with the locals, head to **Le Raisin de Bourgogne,** 164 rte. de Dijon (✆ **03-80-24-69-48**), which fills up early with a 30-plus crowd. If you're in the mood for an ale or two, try the English-style **Pickwick's Pub,** 2 rue Notre-Dame (✆ **03-80-22-55-92**). For a piano bar and karaoke, go to **Why Not,** 74 rue de Faubourg-Madeleine (✆ **03-80-22-64-74**). **Opéra-Night,** rue du Beaumarché (✆ **03-80-24-10-11**), plays booming house music and has an huge dance floor, strobe lights, and mirrors revealing every angle imaginable. A competitor is **Disco Jazz Band,** 11 rte. de Seurre (✆ **03-80-24-73-49**); both dance clubs charge a cover of up to 12€ ($16).

6 Dijon ★★★

312km (194 miles) SE of Paris, 320km (199 miles) NE of Lyon

Dijon is known overseas mainly for its mustard. Located in the center of the Côte d'Or, it's the ancient capital of Burgundy. Here, great wine accompanies good food. Between meals, you can enjoy the art and architecture.

Your first impression, especially if you arrive at the rail station, can be misleading. You may think Dijon is a dreary modern city, but press on to its medieval core and discover old streets and buildings that have been restored. The mayor, François Rebsamen, was elected on a platform that mixed aspects of socialist, communist, and Greenpeace rhetoric. He is committed to the verdancy of Dijon.

ESSENTIALS

GETTING THERE The best way to reach Dijon is by **driving.** From Paris, follow A6 southeast to Pouilly-en-Auxois, and then go east along A38 into Dijon. Dijon also has excellent rail and bus connections to the rest of Europe. A total of 13 TGV **trains** arrive from Paris's Gare de Lyon each day (trip time: 1 hr., 45 min.); the one-way fare is 35€ to 50€ ($46–$65). Trains arrive from Lyon every hour (trip time: 2 hr.; 25€/$33 one-way). For information, call ✆ **08-92-35-35-35.**

VISITOR INFORMATION The **Office de Tourisme** is at 34 rue des Forges (✆ **03-80-44-11-44;** fax 03-80-30-90-02; www.dijon-tourism.com).

SPECIAL EVENTS Between the end of June and the beginning of August, the streets of Dijon experience a lively renaissance when **Estivade** (✆ **03-80-74-51-95**) comes to town. The festival uses the city's streets as a stage for folk dances, music, and theater. It's always a big hit. You can get a schedule of events from the city tourist office (see above) or La Mairie (the town hall; ✆ **03-80-30-51-51**).

SEEING THE SIGHTS

One of the most historic buildings in this ancient province is the **Palais des Ducs et des Etats de Bourgogne,** which symbolizes the independent (or semi-independent, depending on the era) status of this fertile region. Capped with an elaborate tile roof, the complex is arranged around a trio of courtyards. The oldest section, only part of which you can visit, is the **Ancien Palais des Ducs de Bourgogne,** erected in the 12th century and rebuilt in the 14th. The newer section is the **Palais des Etats de Bourgogne,** constructed in the 17th and 18th centuries for the Burgundian parliament. Today, the palace is La Mairie (town hall); all of its newer section and much of its older section are reserved for the municipal government and not open to the public. However, there's a fine museum, the **Musée des Beaux-Arts** (see below).

On N5, 1.5km (1 mile) west from the center of town, stands the **Chartreuse de Champmol,** the Carthusian monastery built by Philip the Bold as a burial place; it's now a psychiatric hospital. Much of it was destroyed during the Revolution. You may not be permitted to enter the building, but you can see the Moses Fountain in the gardens designed by Sluter at the end of the 14th century. The Gothic entrance is superb.

The **Musée Archéologique,** 5 rue du Dr-Maret (✆ **03-80-30-88-54;** www.musees-bourgogne.org), contains findings unearthed from Dijon's archaeological digs. A medieval nunnery, **L'Ancien Couvent des Bernardines,** 17 rue Ste-Anne (✆ **03-80-44-12-69**), is home to two museums. The chapel holds the Musée d'Arts Sacrés, devoted to art from regional churches, and the cloister contains the **Musée de la Vie Bourguignonne** (also known as the Musée Perrin de Puycousin), which exhibits folkloric costumes, farm implements, and some 19th- and early-20th-century storefronts from Dijon's center. Admission is free to all three of these museums. All are open Wednesday to Monday 9am to noon and 2 to 6pm.

Musée des Beaux-Arts ★★ The part of the old palace that you can visit contains one of France's oldest and richest museums. It boasts exceptional sculpture, ducal kitchens from the mid-1400s (with great chimney pieces), a collection of European paintings from the 14th to the 19th centuries, and modern French paintings and sculptures. Take special note of the Salle des Gardes, the banquet hall of the old palace built by Philip the Good (Philippe le Hardi). The tomb of Philip the Bold was created between 1385 and 1411 and is one of the best in France: A reclining figure rests on a slab of black marble, surrounded by 41 mourners.

In the Palais des Ducs et des Etats de Bourgogne, cour de Bar. ✆ **03-80-74-52-09.** Free admission. Temporary expositions cost 3.40€ ($4.40) each. Free to all Sun. May–Oct Wed–Mon 9:30am–6pm; Nov–Apr Wed–Mon 10am–5pm.

Musée Magnin This museum was built in the 19th century as the home of an arts-conscious member of the *grande bourgeoisie.* The city of Dijon inherited the building and its contents following the death of the family's last descendant. It contains an eclectic display of 19th-century antiques and art objects, as well as a collection of paintings accumulated or painted by the former owners.

4 rue des Bons-Enfants. ✆ **03-80-67-11-10.** Admission 3.50€ ($4.55) adults, 2.50€ ($3.25) students and ages 18–25, free for children under 18. Tues–Sun 10am–noon and 2–6pm.

SHOPPING

Your shopping list may include robust regional wines, Dijon mustard, antiques, and the black-currant cordial cassis (try a splash in champagne to make a kir royale). The best shopping streets are rue de la Liberté, rue du Bourg, rue Bossuet, and (for antiques) rue Verrerie.

The market at **Les Halles Centrales,** rue Odebert, sells fruits, vegetables, and foodstuffs on Tuesday, Thursday, and Friday from 8am to noon, and Saturday from 8am to around 5pm. A separate endeavor that specializes in used clothing, kitchen utensils, housewares, and flea-market castoffs, **Les Marchés autour des Halles** operates along the market's periphery Tuesday and Friday from 8am to noon, and Saturday from 8am to around 5pm.

For the ideal picnic lunch, begin at **La Boutique Maille,** 32 rue de la Liberté (**© 03-80-30-41-02**), where you can purchase many varieties of the world-famous mustard. Follow with a visit to the **Crémerie Porcheret,** 18 rue Bannelier (**© 03-80-30-21-05**), to pick up several varieties of regional cheese, including *citeaux,* made by the brothers at a nearby monastery. Finish your journey at one of the three locations of **Mulot et Petitjean,** 1 place Notre-Dame, 16 rue de la Liberté, or 13 place Bossuet (**© 03-80-30-07-10**), where you can pick up a pastry (especially gingerbread) for dessert.

For antiques, try **Monique Buisson,** 21 rue Verrerie (**© 03-80-30-31-19**), which offers a good collection of regional furniture from the 1700s; **Dubard,** 25 bis rue Verrerie (**© 03-80-30-50-81**), for 19th-century garden ornaments and contemporary upholstery fabric. Other choice stops include **Aux Occasions,** 29 rue Auguste-Comte (**© 03-80-73-55-13**), where you can browse through a multitude of mainly English antiques from the 1800s, as well as old and new Oriental rugs. Also appealing is **Antiquaires Golmard,** 3 rue Auguste-Comte (**© 03-80-67-14-15**), which specializes in objects originating on private estates in the region. This store is flexible about trading antiques with individuals and other dealers, making it something of a clearinghouse for unusual antiques from throughout Europe. **Le Consortium,** 16 rue Quentin (**© 03-80-68-45-55**), is one of Dijon's most interesting modern-art galleries.

WHERE TO STAY

Hostellerie du Chapeau-Rouge ★ This Dijon landmark, which has an acclaimed restaurant, is the town's best address. The hotel is filled with 19th-century antiques, and its rooms have modern conveniences and comfortable furnishings. Most of the bathrooms have Jacuzzis. Because no other hotel restaurant in town serves comparable food, you may want to visit here even if you're not a guest. The chef offers Burgundian favorites and more innovative fare. Specialties depend on what's good in any given season.

5 rue Michelet, Dijon 21000. **© 800/528-1234** in the U.S. and Canada, or 03-80-50-88-88. Fax 03-80-50-88-89. www.chapeaurouge.fr. 30 units. 139€–155€ ($181–$202) double; 216€–268€ ($281–$348) suite. AE, DC, MC, V. Parking 10€ ($13). **Amenities:** Restaurant; bar; room service; laundry service; nonsmoking rooms. *In room:* A/C, TV, minibar, coffeemaker, hair dryer, safe.

Hôtel de La Cloche ★ Legends associated with this site go back to the 15th century, but the building evokes a late-19th-century grand hotel, complete with high ceilings and the modernized decor favored by Napoleon III. Located in the center of town, it features pink-and-gray marble floors, Oriental carpets, comfortable and conservative guest rooms with tub/shower combinations, and a lobby bar that's one of the most elegant places of its kind in town, with a view of the garden.

14 place Darcy, Dijon 21000. **© 03-80-30-12-32.** Fax 03-80-30-04-15. www.hotel-lacloche.com. 68 units. 155€–270€ ($202–$351) double; 350€–400€ ($455–$520) suite. AE, DC, MC, V. Free parking. **Amenities:** 2 restaurants; bar; fitness center; sauna; room service; babysitting; laundry service; limited-mobility rooms. *In room:* A/C, TV, minibar, hair dryer, safe.

Moments Side Trips from Dijon

Leave Dijon on A38 heading northwest on a good road in the Vallée de l'Ouche, alongside the Burgundy Canal. At pont de Pany, on the outskirts of Sombernon, exit onto a local highway (D905) and continue northwest. On your left lies the lake of Grosbois. The scenery is typical of agricultural France, with isolated farms, woods, and pastures.

Pass through Vitteaux; just before the next village, Posanges, stands a feudal château. You can't visit it, but it's worth a picture. Continue on D905 until you come to a railroad crossing. On your left is another old castle, now part of a private farm. The next village you reach along D905 is Pouillenay. Follow the signs for a short detour to the hamlet of **Flavigny-sur-Ozerain.** Park your car outside the walls and walk through the old streets.

Leave Flavigny and follow signs for a few miles on country roads to **Alise-Ste-Reine,** the site of what was once Alésia, the camp of the Gallic chieftain Vercingetorix. Alise-Ste-Reine was named after a local Christian who was decapitated for refusing to marry a Roman governor. In the town center stands a statue of Vercingetorix crafted by Millet. You can explore the ruins of a Roman-Gallic town, **Les Fouilles d'Alésia,** and **Le Musée d'Alésia,** which sit side-by-side on the rue de l'Hôpital (✆ **03-80-96-81-03**) at the edge of the village. The museum and ruins are open daily June 30 through August from 9am to 7pm, March 22 to June 29 and September 1 to November 11 from 10am to 6pm (closed Nov 12–Mar 21). A combination ticket costs 6€ ($7.80) for adults, 4.50€ ($5.85) for students and children 6 to 18, and is free for children under 6.

After Alise-Ste-Reine, you can head back to the village of Les Laumes, a railroad center. Before entering the village, make a U-turn to the right and

Hôtel Wilson ★ *Finds* Our favorite nest in Dijon, opening onto a pleasant square, this *ancien relais de poste* (coaching inn) dates from the 17th century and has been tastefully restored. Although it has been modernized and decorated with Burgundian wood furniture, many of the old wood ceiling beams have been exposed, adding authentic charm. All units have small bathrooms, each with a shower and some with tubs.

Place Wilson, Dijon 21000. ✆ **03-80-66-82-50.** Fax 03-80-36-41-54. www.wilson-hotel.com. 27 units. 75€–95€ ($98–$124) double. AE, MC, V. Parking 10€ ($13). **Amenities:** Bar. *In room:* A/C, TV, Wi-Fi.

WHERE TO DINE

Hostellerie du Chapeau-Rouge (see "Where to Stay," above) boasts a marvelous restaurant.

Le Pré aux Clercs ★★★ BURGUNDIAN/FRENCH In an 18th-century house across from the Palais des Ducs, this is one of Burgundy's finest restaurants, with a reputation that dates to 1833. Chef-owner Jean-Pierre Billoux, assisted by his wife, Marie Françoise, prepares meals that have won acclaim. Menu items, served beneath an intricately beamed ceiling, may include such dishes as a terrine of pigeon with a confit of garlic, crayfish prepared with aged sherry vinegar, and roasted duckling with gingerbread stuffing. The array of wines will delight any connoisseur.

take N454 to Baigneux-les-Juifs. After the village of Grésigny, you'll see a farm-fortress surrounded by water on your left.

Go 1.5km (1 mile) farther and turn right toward the **Château de Bussy-Rabutin** (✆ **03-80-96-00-03**). Roger de Rabutin ridiculed Louis XIV's court, for which he spent 6 years in the Bastille. The château, with two towers, has survived mostly intact. The gardens and park are attributed to Le Nôtre. It's open Tuesday to Sunday from 9:15am to noon and 2 to 5pm. Admission is 5.50€ ($7.15) for adults and 15€ ($20) for students and children under 18.

Return to Grésigny, turn right before the farm-fortress, and then go left. Outside the village, turn right toward Menetreux Le Pitois. You're off the main road and into the real countryside. Back on D905, head to **Montbard,** hometown of George-Louis Leclerc, *comte* de Buffon, one of the 18th century's great naturalists and author of *L'Histoire Naturelle,* a 44-volume encyclopedia. The scientist's home is open to visitors, and a mini-museum, **Musée Buffon** (✆ **03-80-92-50-42**), is dedicated to his life and work. It's open only from April to October, Wednesday to Sunday from 10am to noon and 2 to 5pm. The rest of the year, it's closed. The **Hôtel de l'Ecu,** 7 rue Auguste-Carré (✆ **03-80-92-11-66**), serves moderately priced meals in an 18th-century postal relay station; menus cost 18€ to 52€ ($23–$68).

Continue east 9.5km (6 miles) to Marmagne, then turn left on D32 and head toward the **Abbaye de Fontenay** (✆ **03-80-92-18-57**). Isolated in a valley, Fontenay is one of Europe's most unspoiled 12th-century Cistercian abbeys. It is open December to March daily 10am to noon and 2 to 5pm; April to November daily 10am to 5:30pm. Admission is 9€ ($12) for adults, 4.20€ ($5.45) for children and students, and free for children under 7.

13 place de la Libération. ✆ **03-80-38-05-05.** Reservations required. Main courses 25€–45€ ($33–$59); fixed-price lunch 38€ ($49); fixed-price dinner 48€ ($62) and 95€ ($124). AE, DC, MC, V. Tues–Sun noon–1:30pm; Tues–Sat 7:30–9:30pm.

Les Oenophiles ★ TRADITIONAL/MODERN FRENCH You enter this elegant, grand restaurant through an antique courtyard. Stone walls surround a dining room decorated with Oriental carpets and Louis XII chairs. It serves traditional food that's hearty and satisfying, in a style somewhere between old-fashioned and conservatively modern. Specialties include foie gras of duckling in puff pastry, served with compote of figs; marinated scallops and shrimp prepared tempura-style; and scallops and crayfish tails in a medley of spring vegetables and ginger. On the premises is a modern 32-room hotel, Hotel Philippe-le-Bon. Rooms have minibars, air-conditioning, and TVs. Rates for a double are 81€ to 205€ ($105–$267).

18 rue Ste-Anne, Dijon 21000. ✆ **03-80-30-73-52.** Fax 03-80-30-95-51. Reservations required. Main courses 26€–33€ ($34–$43); fixed-price dinner 33€–54€ ($43–$70). AE, MC, V. Mon–Sat noon–1:30pm and 7–9:30pm.

Stéphane Derbord ★★★ FRENCH Given the prices and acclaim of this restaurant, customers have a right to expect perfection—and they get it. Prominently positioned a few steps from the Hôtel Wilson, Stéphane Derbord is the most sought-after restaurant in Dijon. Isabelle Derbord, Stéphane's charming wife, presides over the cozy dining room. Many menu items are accurately called "delectables," including duck liver in a terrine and fresh scallops in pistachio oil. Saône River *sandre* is steamed and served with crayfish and pike dumplings; sea-bass lasagna comes with fennel and lemon-flavored sauce; and chicken is roasted to perfection and served with spicy gravy. And, oh, try that pheasant pie with fresh duck liver.

10 place Wilson. ✆ **03-80-67-74-64.** Reservations required. Main courses 30€–36€ ($39–$47); fixed-price menu 25€–85€ ($33–$111). AE, DC, MC, V. Wed–Sat noon–1:45pm; Mon–Sat 7:30–9:30pm. Closed 1 week in Jan and 2 weeks in Aug.

WHERE TO DINE NEARBY

Joël Perreaut's Restaurant des Gourmets ★★★ FRENCH This restaurant is reason enough to journey outside Dijon to a charming medieval village 6km (3¾ miles) south of Dijon. After Joël and Nicole Perreaut added an annex, modern kitchens, and a dining room, this place became known as one of Burgundy's best restaurants. In a modern room overlooking a garden, you can enjoy a seasonal menu that may include profiteroles of snails with fresh mint sauce, roast duckling with orange sauce and spices, a crosscut section of veal cooked for 7 hours with orange segments and served with Parmesan cheese, and veal sweetbreads with red-wine sauce and purée of mushrooms. The cellar contains more than 600 wines; many are burgundies from lesser-known, small-scale wineries.

8 rue Puits-de-Têt, Marsannay-la-Côte 21160. ✆ **03-80-52-16-32.** Reservations required. Main courses 26€–45€ ($34–$59); fixed-price menu 30€ ($39) and 59€ ($77); *menu surprise* 78€ ($101). AE, DC, MC, V. Wed–Sun noon–2pm; Tues–Sat 7–9:30pm. Closed Jan 17–Feb 9, 1st 2 weeks of Feb, and Aug 1–15. Drive 9.5km (6 miles) south of Dijon on N74, following the signs for Beaune and then Marsannay-la-Côte.

DIJON AFTER DARK

Begin your evening at one of the cafes or brasseries lining place Zola, rue des Godrans, place du Théâtre, or place Darcy, such as the **Concorde,** 2 place Darcy (✆ **03-80-30-69-43**); **Jardin Théâtre,** 1 bis place du Théâtre (✆ **03-80-67-13-59**); or **La Comédie,** 3 place du Théâtre (✆ **03-80-67-11-62**). These spots fill up with young people who start the night with a drink and a look around.

If you prefer a 30s-to-40s crowd that likes to mingle in the low-key atmosphere of a piano bar, try **Hunky Dory,** 5 av. Foch (✆ **03-80-53-17-24**); **Le Messire,** 3 rue Jules-Mercier (✆ **03-80-30-16-40**); or **Le Cintra,** 13 av. Foch (✆ **03-80-53-19-53**), which also has a little disco. For the boisterous (and often sloshed) atmosphere of an Irish pub, head over to **Le Kilkenny,** 1 rue Auguste-Perdrix (✆ **03-80-30-02-48**).

Appealing to a more sedate crowd is **Le Chat Noir,** 20 av. Garibaldi (✆ **03-80-73-39-57**), which emphasizes slower, more romantic music.

The opera season in Dijon stretches from the middle of October to May. The city's premier venue is the **Grand Théâtre de Dijon,** 2 rue Longepierre (✆ **03-80-60-44-44**); call ahead for information on operas, operettas, dance recitals, and concerts. The city's second-most visible cultural venue is the **Théâtre National Dijon-Bourgogne,** rue Danton (✆ **03-80-30-12-12**). Tickets for performances at either theater range from 15€ to 40€ ($20–$52).

7 Saulieu ★

250km (155 miles) SE of Paris, 76km (47 miles) NW of Beaune

Saulieu is interesting, but its food put it on the international map. The town (pop. 3,000) has enjoyed a reputation for cooking since the 17th century. Even Mme de Sévigné praised it in her letters. So did Rabelais.

The main sight is the **Basilique St-Andoche,** place de la Fontaine (✆ **03-80-64-07-03**), which has some interesting decorated capitals. Next door, in the **Musée François-Pompon,** place de la Fontaine, at rue Sallier (✆ **03-80-64-19-51**), you can see works by François Pompon (who died in 1930), the sculptor of animals whose works are featured in Paris's Musée d'Orsay. Pompon's large statue of a bull stands on a plaza off N6 at the entrance to Saulieu. Also in the museum are archaeological remnants from the Gallo-Roman era, sacred medieval art, and old tools illustrating aspects of life in Burgundy several centuries ago. The museum is open from March to December Wednesday through Monday from 10am to 12:30pm and 2 to 6pm, Sunday 10am to 12:30pm and 2:30 to 5pm. Admission is 4€ ($5.20) for adults and 2.50€ ($3.25) for children 12 to 16. It's closed in January and February.

ESSENTIALS

GETTING THERE If you're **driving,** head along N80 from Montbard or N6 from Paris or Lyon. The **train** station is northeast of the town center. For train information and schedules, call ✆ **08-92-35-35-35.** Passengers coming from Paris sometimes opt to take the TGV from the Gare de Lyon, getting off in Montbard, 48km (30 miles) to the north. From Montbard, a series of **buses** carry passengers on to Saulieu about three times a day for a one-way fare of 7.65€ ($9.95). For bus and rail information, call the **Gare SNCF** in Saulieu (✆ **03-80-64-05-32**).

VISITOR INFORMATION The **Office de Tourisme** is at 24 rue d'Argentine (✆ **03-80-64-00-21;** saulieu.tourism@cegetel.net).

WHERE TO STAY & DINE

Le Relais Bernard Loiseau ★★ This former stagecoach stop with one of the best-known restaurants in France is an excellent choice. If you want to stay overnight, you'll find guest rooms with everything from Empire to Louis XV decor. You'll sleep on a comfortable mattress, on a bed that's likely to be 200 years old. All units contain private bathrooms with tubs and showers.

The suicide in 2003 of its famous chef, Bernard Loiseau (rumored to be despondent at the thought of losing a Michelin star), shocked the culinary world and made international headlines. Loiseau's wife, Dominique, and staff are carrying on admirably. The cooking remains in his style: less traditional, leaning away from heavy sauces. The emphasis is on bringing out maximum taste with no excess fat or sugar. All the great burgundies are on the wine list.

Saulieu 21210. ✆ **03-80-90-53-53.** Fax 03-80-64-08-92. www.bernard-loiseau.com. 32 units. 125€–330€ ($163–$429) double; 260€–470€ ($338–$611) suite. AE, MC, V. Closed Jan 10–Feb 10. **Amenities:** Restaurant; bar; indoor and outdoor pools; fitness room; spa; sauna; room service; laundry service; limited-mobility rooms. *In room:* A/C (in some), TV, minibar, hair dryer.

14

The Rhône Valley

The Rhône is as mighty as the Saône is peaceful, and these rivers form a part of the countryside that most travelers experience only briefly as they rush to the Riviera on the Mediterranean Express. This land of mountains and rivers is Beaujolais country, home to Lyon, a fabulous stop for gourmets, and boasts Roman ruins, castles, and the Grand Canyon of France.

The district brims with time-mellowed inns and gourmet restaurants serving cuisine that's among the finest in the world.

1 Lyon ★★★

431km (268 miles) SE of Paris, 311km (193 miles) N of Marseille

At the junction of the turbulent Rhône and the tranquil Saône, Lyon is the third-largest city in France. The city has a population of 400,000, with more than a million more people spread across the large urban area that surrounds it. Lyon is the center of an industrial region—textile manufacturing is especially important. It's a leader in publishing and banking, and it's one of the world's silk capitals. Some of the country's best restaurants, including Paul Bocuse, are in and around Lyon. Such dishes as Lyon sausage, quenelles, and tripe Lyonnais are world famous. The region's succulent Bresse poultry is the best in France.

Lyon has urban sprawl, and some of the most humid summers in France. Still, it's much more relaxed and friendlier than Paris. Parks in full bloom, skyscrapers and sidewalk cafes, a great transport system, and a nightlife fueled by student energy invigorate Lyon, along with talented chefs, both young and old.

Lyon is the best base for exploring the Rhône region. It has the finest food in France and a historic core unequaled in the region.

ESSENTIALS

GETTING THERE If you're arriving from the north by **train,** don't get off at the first station, Gare La Part-Dieu; continue to Gare de Perrache, where you can begin sightseeing. The high-speed TGV takes only 2 hours from Paris; the one-way fare is 50€ to 80€ ($65–$104). Lyon makes a good stopover en route to the Alps or the Riviera. For information, call ✆ **08-92-35-35-35,** or visit www.voyages-sncf.com.

By **plane,** it's a 45-minute flight from Paris to Aéroport Saint-Exupéry (✆ **08-26-80-08-26**), 25km (16 miles) east of the city. **Satobuses** (✆ **04-72-68-72-17**) run from the airport into the center of Lyon every 20 minutes during the day. The 45-minute bus trip costs 8.40€ ($11) each way.

If you're **driving** from Paris, head southeast on A8/E1 into Lyon. From Nice, head west on E1/A7 toward Aix-en-Provence, continuing northwest toward Avignon. Bypass the city and continue north along the same route into Lyon. From Grenoble or the French Alps, head northwest on A48 to A43, which will take you northwest into Lyon.

The Rhône Valley

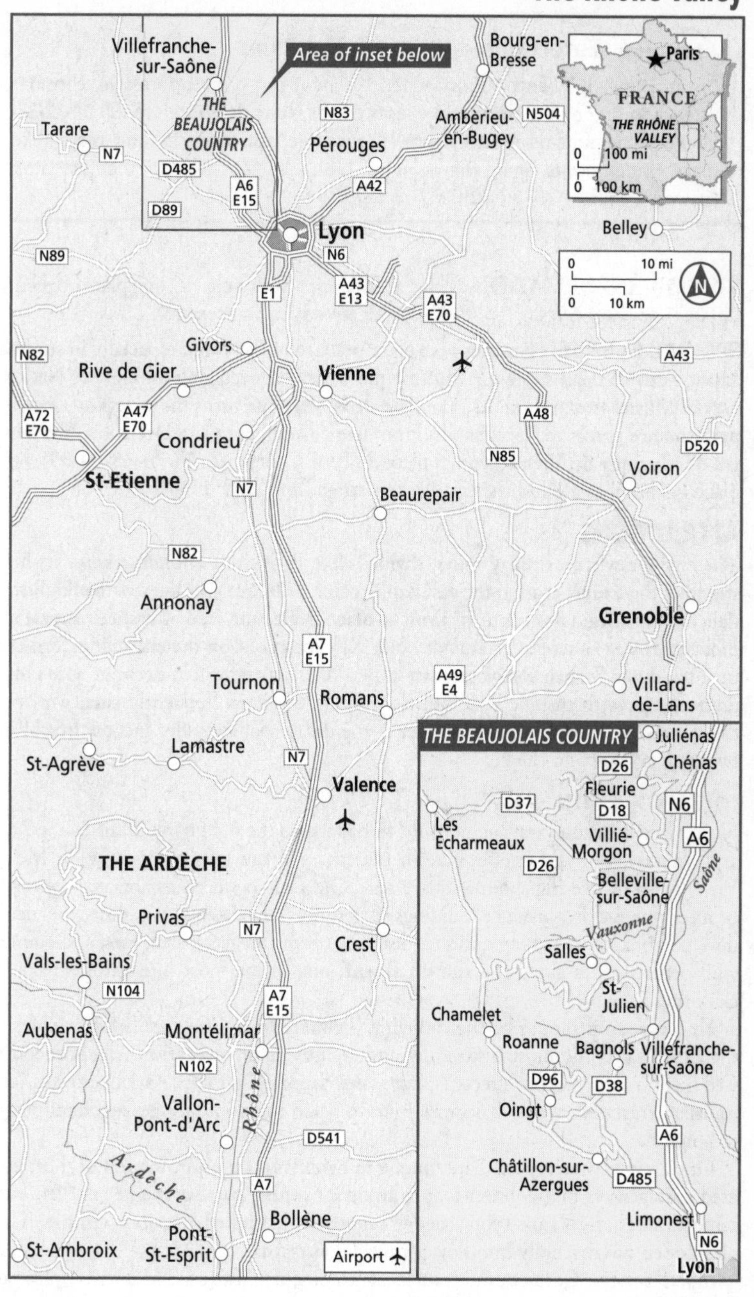

Moments Entertainment among the Ruins

During June, July, and August, when the heat can grow oppressive, consider attending one of the nocturnal events of **Les Nuits de Fourvière** (© **04-72-32-00-00;** www.nuits-de-fourviere.org). Dance recitals, concerts, and plays take place under lights amid the ruins of Lyon's ancient Roman theaters atop Fourvière Hill.

VISITOR INFORMATION The **Office de Tourisme** is on place Bellecour (© **04-72-77-69-69;** fax 04-78-42-04-32; www.lyon-france.com).

SPECIAL EVENTS Festivals take place practically every day, especially in summer. Music festivals reign supreme, with the most popular occurring on France's National Day of Music, around June 21. The **Fête de la Musique** turns the streets of Lyon into performance spaces for local bands. From late November to late December, the **Festival de Musique du Vieux-Lyon,** 5 place du Petit-Collège (© **04-78-38-09-09**), takes place in churches around the city. Tickets range from 18€ to 30€ ($23–$39).

ATTRACTIONS

The city sprawls over many miles, divided, like Paris, into *arrondissements.* Its heart straddles the Saône, around the east bank's place Bellecour and the west bank's Primatiale St-Jean. Begin your tour of Lyon at **place Bellecour,** one of France's largest and most charming squares. A statue of Louis XIV looks out on the encircling 18th-century buildings. Urban sociologists are proud of Lyon's efforts to decorate some of its drab facades with trompe l'oeil murals. Among the most frequently cited works are the facade of the Musée Tony Garnier, 4 rue des Serpollières, 8e, and the fresco "des Lyonnais célèbres" in the 2e.

IN VIEUX LYON ★★★

From place Bellecour, walk across pont Bonaparte to the right bank of the Saône River and **Vieux Lyon.** (From elsewhere in the city, you can take bus no. 28, or Métro: Vieux Lyon.) Covering about a square mile, Old Lyon contains an amazing collection of medieval and Renaissance buildings. After years of existence as a slum, the area is now fashionable, attracting antiques dealers, artisans, weavers, sculptors, and painters who depict scenes along the **rue du Boeuf,** one of the most interesting streets for exploring.

Your first stop should be the cathedral, **Primatiale St-Jean** (see below). North of the cathedral is the most historically and architecturally evocative neighborhood of Old Lyon, with narrow streets, spiral stairs, hanging gardens, soaring towers, and unusual courtyards whose balconies seem to perch precariously atop medieval pilings or columns.

One architectural aspect that's unique to Lyon is its *traboules,* a series of short covered passageways that connect longer avenues running parallel to one another. Scattered throughout Vieux Lyon, they're capped with vaulted masonry ceilings. They often open unexpectedly into flower-ringed courtyards.

Try to see the Gothic arcades of the 16th-century **Maison Thomassin,** place du Change, and the 16th-century **Hôtel du Chamarier,** 37 rue St-Jean, where Mme de Sévigné lived. You can admire these buildings from the outside, but you are not

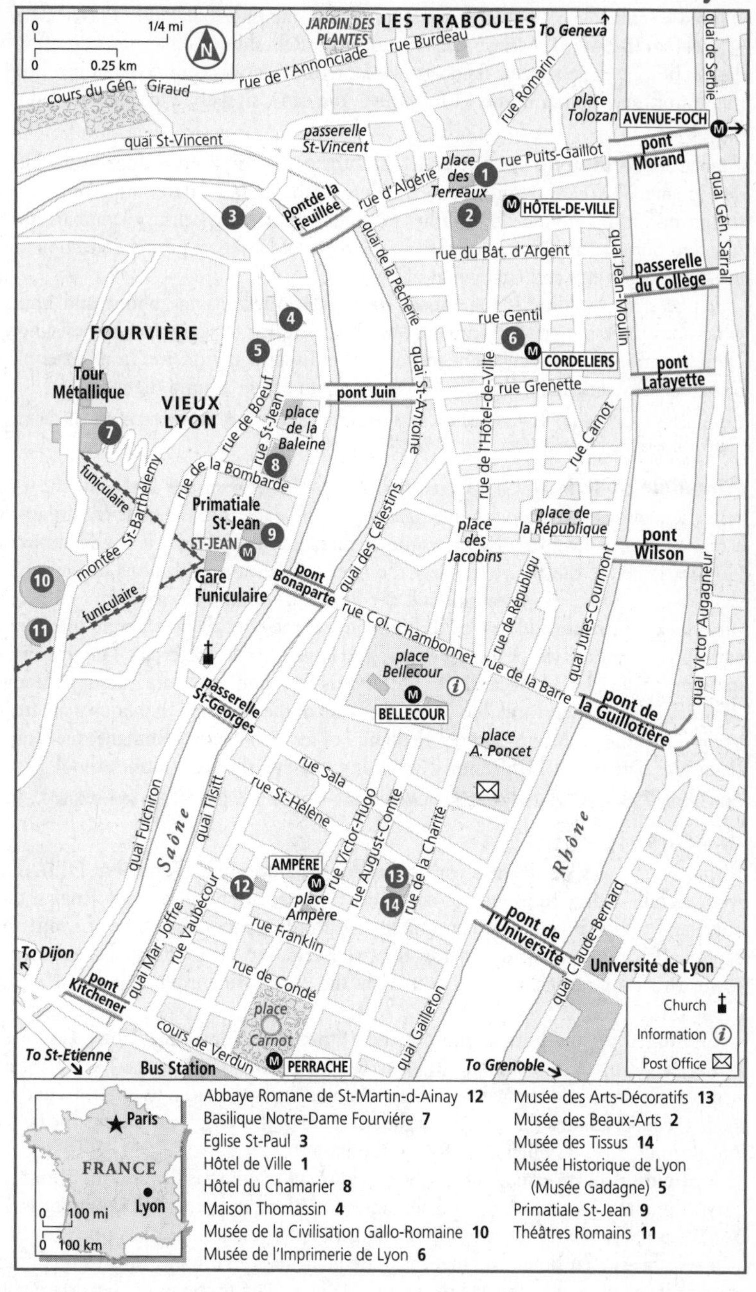
0 1/4 mi
0 0.25 km
N
JARDIN DES PLANTES
LES TRABOULES
To Geneva
rue Burdeau
rue de l'Annonciade
cours du Gén. Giraud
rue Romarin
place Tolozan
AVENUE-FOCH
quai de Serbie
quai St-Vincent
passerelle St-Vincent
pont Morand
rue Puits-Gaillot
place des Terreaux
rue d'Algérie
pontde la Feuillée
HÔTEL-DE-VILLE
quai Gén. Sarrail
quai de la Pêcherie
rue du Bât. d'Argent
quai Jean-Moulin
passerelle du Collège
rue Gentil
FOURVIÈRE
CORDELIERS
Tour Métallique
quai St-Antoine
rue de l'Hôtel-de-Ville
pont Lafayette
VIEUX LYON
pont Juin
rue Grenette
rue de Boeuf
rue St-Jean
place de la Baleine
rue Carnot
funiculaire
rue de la Bombarde
montée St-Barthélemy
Primatiale St-Jean
quai des Célestins
place des Jacobins
place de la République
pont Wilson
ST-JEAN
Gare Funiculaire
pont Bonaparte
rue de République
quai Jules-Courmont
quai Victor Augagneur
rue Col. Chambonnet
place Bellecour
BELLECOUR
rue de la Barre
pont de la Guillotière
passerelle St-Georges
place A. Poncet
rue Sala
rue St-Hélène
quai Fulchiron
Saône
quai Tilsitt
rue Victor-Hugo
rue August-Comte
rue de la Charité
Rhône
AMPÈRE
place Ampère
rue Vaubécour
quai Mar. Joffre
rue Franklin
pont de l'Université
quai Claude-Bernard
Université de Lyon
To Dijon
pont Kitchener
rue de Condé
place Carnot
cours de Verdun
quai Gailleton
To St-Etienne
Bus Station
PERRACHE
To Grenoble
Church
Information
Post Office
Paris
FRANCE
Lyon
0 100 mi
0 100 km
Abbaye Romane de St-Martin-d-Ainay 12
Basilique Notre-Dame Fourviére 7
Eglise St-Paul 3
Hôtel de Ville 1
Hôtel du Chamarier 8
Maison Thomassin 4
Musée de la Civilisation Gallo-Romaine 10
Musée de l'Imprimerie de Lyon 6
Musée des Arts-Décoratifs 13
Musée des Beaux-Arts 2
Musée des Tissus 14
Musée Historique de Lyon (Musée Gadagne) 5
Primatiale St-Jean 9
Théâtres Romains 11

allowed to enter. The neighborhood also contains the **Eglise St-Paul,** 3 place Gerson (© **04-78-28-34-45**), consecrated in A.D. 549. Rebuilding began in 1084 after its destruction by the Saracens. Its octagonal lantern tower was completed in the 1100s, the rest of the premises in the 13th century. You can visit daily 2 to 6pm, and admission is free.

Musée Historique de Lyon (Musée Gadagne) ★ This museum is in the Hôtel de Gadagne, an early-16th-century residence. You'll find interesting Romanesque sculptures on the ground floor. Other exhibits include 18th-century Lyonnais furniture and pottery, antique ceramics from the town of Nevers, a pewter collection, and numerous paintings and engravings of Lyon.

In the same building is the **Musée de la Marionette** (same phone and hours), which has three puppets by Laurent Mourguet, creator of Guignol, the best-known French marionette character. The museum also displays marionettes from other parts of France (Amiens, Lille, and Aix-en-Provence) and from around the world.

1 place du Petit-Collège. © **04-78-42-03-61.** Admission (including Musée de la Marionette) 4€ ($5.20) adults, 2.30€ ($3) students, free for children under 18. Wed–Mon 10:45am–6pm.

Primatiale St-Jean ★ This cathedral was built between the 12th and the 15th centuries, and its exceptional stained-glass windows date from the same era. Its apse is a masterpiece of Lyonnais Romanesque architecture. A highlight is the Flamboyant Gothic chapel of the Bourbons. On the front portals are medallions depicting the signs of the zodiac, the Creation, and the life of St. John. The cathedral's 16th-century clock is intricate and beautiful. It announces the hour daily at noon, 2pm, 3pm, and 4pm in grand style: A rooster crows, and angels herald the event. The treasury is in a wing called **La Manécanterie.** Entrance is free, and hours are Tuesday through Saturday 10am to noon and 2 to 6pm. The wing of the cathedral that houses the treasury is noted for the beauty and severe dignity of its 12th-century Romanesque facade. Its origins date to the 11th century, when it was established as a music school.

Place St-Jean. © **04-78-42-28-25.** Free admission. Mon–Fri 8am–noon and 2–7:30pm; Sat–Sun 8am–noon and 2–5pm.

IN FOURVIERE HILL ★

Rising to the west of Vieux Lyon is **Colline de Fourvière (Fourvière Hill).** The wooded hill—home to numerous convents, colleges, and hospitals; two Roman theaters; and a superb Gallo-Roman museum—affords a panoramic vista of Lyon. You can see the city's many bridges across the two rivers, and the rooftops of the medieval town. In clear weather, you can even view the countryside extending to the snow-capped Alps.

Enthroned on the hill's summit is the 19th-century **Basilique Notre-Dame de Fourvière,** 8 place de Fourvière (© **04-78-25-51-82**), rising fortress-like with four octagonal towers and crenellated walls. Colored mosaics cover its interior, and an ancient chapel adjoins the church. A gilded statue of the Virgin surmounts the belfry. Admission is free; it's open daily 8am to 7pm.

Jardin du Rosaire extends along the hillside between the basilica and the 13th-century Primatiale St-Jean. It's open daily 6am to 9:30pm and promises a pleasant walk. You'll see a vast shelter for up to 200 pilgrims. Additional mobility is provided by a pair of cable-driven funiculars that make frequent (every 10 min.) runs from a point immediately adjacent to the Métro station in Vieux Lyon to the top of Fourvière Hill. Priced at 1.25€ ($1.65) each way, they run daily between 5am and midnight.

The **Théâtres Romains,** 6 rue de l'Antiquaille, Montée de Fourvière, a Roman theater-odeum complex, is in a park south of the basilica. The theater is the most ancient in France, built by order of Augustus from 17 to 15 B.C. and expanded during the reign of Hadrian. The odeum, reserved for musical performances, was once sumptuously decorated; its orchestra floor still contains mosaics of marble and porphyry. The third building was dedicated in A.D. 160 to the goddess Cybele, or Sibella. Only the building's foundations remain. The archaeological site can be visited daily April 15 to September 15 9am to 9pm, off season daily 7am to 7pm. Admission is free.

An altar dedicated to a bull cult and a marble statue of a goddess are on display in the **Musée de la Civilisation Gallo-Romaine,** 17 rue Cléberg (✆ **04-72-38-81-90**), near the archaeological site. The museum's collection of Gallo-Roman artifacts is the finest in France outside Paris. The site is open Tuesday through Sunday 10am to 6pm. Admission is 6€ ($7.80) adults, 4€ ($5.20) students and children 12 to 25, and free for children under 18. Entrance is free on Thursday. Guides are available on Sundays and holidays at 3pm. Performances are given at both theaters in June and July during Les Nuits de Fourvière (see box, p. 408); make reservations at ✆ **04-72-32-00-00.**

ELSEWHERE AROUND THE CITY

In addition to the sites below, you can also visit Lyon's oldest church, the 1107 **Abbaye Romane de St-Martin-d'Ainay,** 11 rue Bourgelat (✆ **04-72-40-02-50**), south of place Bellecour, near place Ampère. Admission is free; hours are daily 8:30 to 11:30am and 3 to 6:30pm. The rue de l'Hôtel-de-Ville extends north from place Bellecour to **place des Terreaux,** dominated by one of the most beautiful of Europe's city halls, the 1746 **Hôtel de Ville.** Its outside is dark and severe; the brilliant interior is closed to the public.

L'Institut & Musée Lumière Film buffs from all over the world come here. The famous Lumière family, including Antoine (1840–1911), Auguste (1862–1954), and Louis (1864–1948), once lived in Lyon. The brothers were chemists, industrialists, and motion-picture pioneers. In Lyon, they founded a factory for producing photographic plates, paper, and chemicals. They invented the Lumière process of color photography and the Cinematographe, an early motion picture camera, in 1895. They produced films, including *La Sortie des Usines Lumière,* released in 1895 and considered the first movie. The complex is dedicated to the memory of the innovators and is a living museum of cinema. Early films are shown, and books, photos, posters, and pre-cinematographic and cinematographic equipment are on display.

25 rue du Premier Film. ✆ **04-78-78-18-95.** www.institut-lumiere.org. Admission 6€ ($7.80) adults, 5€ ($6.50) students and children 7–18, free for children under 7. Tues–Sun 11am–6:30pm. Métro: Montplaisir-Lumière.

Musée de l'Imprimerie de Lyon Occupying a 15th-century mansion, this museum is devoted to Lyon's role in the world of printing. Exhibits include a page from a Gutenberg Bible, 17th- to 20th-century presses, 16th- to 19th-century woodcuts, and engravings. This is one of the most important printing museums in Europe, along with those at Mainz and Antwerp. It has a collection of books from "all epochs," including *incunabula,* books printed before Easter 1500.

13 rue de la Poulaillerie. ✆ **04-78-37-65-98.** Admission 3.80€ ($4.95) adults, 2€ ($2.60) students, free for children under 18. Wed–Sun 9:30am–noon and 2–6pm.

Musée des Arts-Décoratifs ★★ In the 1739 Lacroix-Laval mansion by Soufflot (architect of the Panthéon in Paris), the Musée des Arts-Décoratifs contains furniture and objets d'art from the 17th and 18th centuries. The medieval and Renaissance periods are also represented. Look for a five-octave clavecin by Donzelague, the 18th-century creator of musical instruments.

34 rue de la Charité. ✆ **04-78-38-42-00.** Admission (includes Musée des Tissus; see below) 5€ ($6.50) adults, 3.50€ ($4.55) students, free for children under 18. Tues–Sun 10am–noon and 2–5:30pm. Métro: Ampère.

Musée des Beaux-Arts ★★ On the south side of the place des Terreaux stands the Palais des Arts (also called the Musée de St-Pierre). The former Benedictine abbey was built between 1659 and 1685 in the Italian baroque style. Today, it is home to the Musée des Beaux-Arts, which has an outstanding collection of paintings and sculpture. You enter through a courtyard graced with statuary and shade trees. The ground floor offers a display of 14th-century paintings. The collection also includes Etruscan, Egyptian, Phoenician, Sumerian, and Persian art. Of special note is Perugino's altarpiece. The top floor holds one of France's richest 19th-century collections, with works by artists from Veronese, Tintoretto, and Rubens to Braque, Bonnard, and Picasso. Be sure to see Joseph Chinard's bust of Mme Récamier, the Lyon beauty who charmed Napoleonic Paris by merely reclining, and the Fantin-Latour masterpiece *Reading.*

20 place des Terreaux. ✆ **04-72-10-17-40.** Admission 6€ ($7.80) adults, free for students and children under 18. Tues–Sun 10am–6pm.

Musée des Tissus ★★★ Next door to the Musée des Arts-Décoratifs (see above), in the 1730 Palais de Villeroy, is an even more interesting collection. On view are priceless fabrics from all over the world, spanning 2,000 years. Some of the finest fabrics made in Lyon from the 18th century to the present are displayed. The 15th- and 16th-century textiles embroidered with religious motifs are noteworthy, as are the 17th-century Persian carpets. Look for the partridge-motif brocade from Marie Antoinette's bedchamber at Versailles, as well as a 150-color brocaded satin woven for Queen Victoria, which is decorated with birds of paradise and orchids.

34 rue de la Charité. ✆ **04-78-38-42-00.** Admission (includes Musée des Arts-Décoratifs) 5€ ($6.50) adults, 3.50€ ($4.55) students, free for children under 18. Tues–Sun 10am–5:30pm.

OUTSIDE THE HEART OF THE CITY

One of Lyon's grandest archaeological sites is **Amphithéâtre des Trois-Gauls,** rue du Jardin-des-Plantes, Croix-Rousse (no phone), near the city's northern perimeter. You can view the site only from the outside. At the time of its construction, it was the centerpiece of Condate, a Gallic village that predated the arrival of the Romans by centuries. Various accounts have members of Gallic tribes meeting here in the earliest example of a parliamentary system. Based on that information, France's 2,000th anniversary was celebrated in Lyon in 1989.

On the opposite side of the Rhône, you can explore Lyon's largest public park and garden, the 105-hectare (259-acre) **Parc de la Tête d'Or** (✆ **04-78-89-02-03**). Its largest entrance is on boulevard des Belges. It opened in 1857 and has all the fountains, pedestrian walkways, and statues you'd expect. Surrounded by wealthy neighborhoods, the park has a lake, a zoo, a botanic garden with greenhouses, and a rose garden with some 100,000 plants. It's open daily 7am to 10pm (until 9pm Oct–Apr). Entrance is free.

At Rochetaillée-sur-Saône, 11km (6¾ miles) north of Lyon on D433, the **Musée Français de l'Automobile "Henri Malartre"** is in the Château de Rochetaillée, 645 chemin du Musée (✆ **04-78-22-18-80**). The château was built in 1131 on even older foundations and rebuilt in the 1400s. The curators are proud of the majestic 15th-century staircase, the Romanesque gateway that's part of the original 12th-century design, and a policy that permits photography, smoking, and any motorcycle-fetish garb you care to wear while admiring the collection of vehicles. The collection includes 100 cars dating to 1890, 65 motorcycles from 1903 and after, and 40 bicycles from 1818 and later. Admission to the museum and château is 6€ ($7.80) adults, 3€ ($3.90) students, and free for ages under 18. It is open Tuesday to Sunday 9am to 6pm (until 7pm July–Aug). From Lyon, take bus no. 40, 43, or 70.

SHOPPING

The third-largest city in France offers an array of retail outlets. For boutiques, art galleries, and artists' studios, head to Vieux Lyon and the area around rue de la République, rue Victor Hugo, rue Mercière, and quai St-Antoine. Antiques dealers concentrate around rue Auguste-Comte as it approaches place Bellecour. Also consider venturing to the **Cité des Antiquaires,** 117 bd. Stalingrad (✆ **04-72-69-00-00**), with more than 100 dealers spread over two floors, and merchandise from the 18th century to the 1950s. It's open Thursday, Saturday, and Sunday 10am to 7pm; June and August Sunday hours are 9:30am to 1pm.

Lyon is a bastion of fashion. The densest concentrations of retail shops are along rue Emile Zola, rue de Président-Herriot, and place Kléber. For chic women's couture that rivals anything you'll find in Paris, try **George Rech,** 59 rue du Président-Herriot (✆ **04-78-37-82-90**). More than 300 shops and boutiques fill the largest shopping center in Lyon, the **Centre Commercial de la Part-Dieu,** 17 rue du Dr. Bouchut (✆ **04-72-60-60-60**). Although Lyon is not the major silk center that it used to be, it is home to several silk manufacturers. You'll see a good selection of silk scarves, ties, sashes, and squares at **Hermès,** 96 rue du Président-Herriot (✆ **04-78-42-25-14**).

Bernachon, 42 cours Franklin-Roosevelt (✆ **04-78-24-37-98**), is home to Lyon's best chocolates and pastries. Here you'll find 30 varieties of bite-size pastries known as mini-gâteaux, 30 varieties of petits fours, and even dark, rich chocolates lightly dusted with 24-karat gold. The Bernachon store houses a small restaurant and tearoom, **Bernachon Passion** (✆ **04-78-52-23-65**).

WHERE TO STAY

Alain Chapel (see "Where to Dine," below) rents rooms.

EXPENSIVE

Hôtel la Cour des Loges ★★★ This luxury hotel in Old Lyon occupies four connected houses dating from the 15th and 16th centuries. Among its allures are a rooftop bar and garden, an indoor pool, and a magnificent loggia-ringed courtyard. Most of its beautifully furnished rooms and suites face gardens, the square, or a large, sunny lobby. The size and configuration of the rooms vary, but all are lavishly decorated. Most of the immaculate tiled bathrooms have both tub and shower. The savviest staff in Lyon is courteous and efficient.

2–8 rue du Boeuf, Vieux Lyon 69005. ✆ **04-72-77-44-44.** Fax 04-72-40-93-61. www.courdesloges.com. 62 units. 240€–470€ ($312–$611) double; 510€–600€ ($663–$780) suite. AE, DC, MC, V. Parking 30€ ($39). Métro: St-Jean. **Amenities:** Restaurant; bar; indoor pool; sauna; room service; laundry service; dry cleaning. *In room:* A/C, TV, minibar, hair dryer, Wi-Fi.

Villa Florentine ★★★ Conveniently located in Vieux Lyon, this Relais & Châteaux hotel is an even more stunning choice than Cour des Loges. One of the great city hotels along the Rhône, it is a bastion of taste and luxury. The views from the lounges, terraces, and guest rooms are the most panoramic in town. Converted from a 17th-century convent, the building retains many of its original Italianate architectural details. The accommodations are spacious and comfortable, decorated in a style that blends modern Italian design with Renaissance reproductions. In 2004, the hotel was enlarged with the creation of a nine-unit annex, just across the street, where rooms and suites are a bit larger and more modern than those within the hotel's original core.

25–27 montée Saint-Barthélemy, Lyon 69005. ✆ **04-72-56-56-56.** Fax 04-72-40-90-56. www.villaflorentine.com. 28 units. 195€–390€ ($254–$507) double; from 430€–900€ ($559–$1,170) suite. AE, DC, MC, V. Parking 15€ ($20). **Amenities:** Restaurant; bar; outdoor pool; fitness center; mini-spa; sauna; room service; babysitting; laundry service; dry cleaning; limited-mobility rooms. *In room:* A/C, TV, minibar, hair dryer, safe, Wi-Fi.

MODERATE

Grand Hôtel Mercure Château Perrache ★ This hotel near the Perrache train station offers Lyon's most traditional rooms. The style is polarizing: You will either love or hate this monument to Art Nouveau. Admittedly, the old dame has seen better times. Originally built in 1906 and classified as a national monument, the hotel is one of the genuinely fine examples of Art Nouveau in Lyon. Be aware that some of the bedrooms are more recently renovated than others. Renovated units contain contemporary furnishings, while the older units retain more of their original antique styling. Romantics and nostalgia buffs love the creaky furnishings, the antiques, and the winter garden. Most of the old-fashioned bathrooms have dated bathtubs. The restaurant, Les Belles Saisons, does more than just cater to the tired business traveler; its finely honed Continental and regional dishes are often innovative.

12 cours de Verdun, Lyon 69002. ✆ **800/MERCURE** in the U.S., or 04-72-77-15-00. Fax 04-78-37-06-56. www.mercure.com. 111 units. 112€–199€ ($146–$259) double; 220€–240€ ($286–$312) suite. AE, DC, MC, V. Parking 10€ ($13). Métro: Perrache. **Amenities:** Restaurant; bar; room service; babysitting; laundry service; nonsmoking rooms. *In room:* A/C, TV, minibar, beverage maker, hair dryer, Wi-Fi.

Hôtel Globe et Cécil *Value* Near place Bellecour, this hotel is a good deal because of its location and attentive staff. Built as a private mansion during France's 19th-century Gilded Age, it became a hotel in 1892. Today the six-story property (with elevator) is a government-rated three-star staple. Some of the individually decorated rooms are old-fashioned and charmingly dowdy; others are more modern and efficient. All have tidy shower-only bathrooms. Many restaurants are nearby.

21 rue Gasparin, Lyon 69002. ✆ **04-78-42-58-95.** Fax 04-72-41-99-06. www.globeetcecilhotel.com. 60 units. 145€ ($189) double. Rates include breakfast. AE, DC, MC, V. Parking 3€ ($3.90). Métro: Bellecour. **Amenities:** Laundry service. *In room:* A/C, TV, hair dryer, Wi-Fi.

Mercure Lyon Beaux-Arts In the center of Lyon, this is one of the best moderately priced hotel choices. The lobby evokes the 1930s. The guest rooms, though comfortable, are outfitted in businesslike modern style. Because this is a noisy part of the city, double-glazing on the windows helps shut out traffic sounds; the quieter rooms are in the rear. Each unit comes with a tiled bathroom, and most have a tub. Breakfast is the only meal served, though you may prefer croissants and coffee at one of the cafes on place Bellecour.

75 rue du Président-Herriot, Lyon 69002. ✆ **800/MERCURE** in the U.S., or 04-78-38-09-50. Fax 04-78-42-19-19. www.mercure.com. 75 units. 123€–134€ ($160–$174) double; 157€ ($204) suite. AE, DC, MC, V. Métro: Cordelier. **Amenities:** Bar; room service; babysitting; laundry service; dry cleaning; nonsmoking rooms. *In room:* A/C, TV, minibar, hair dryer, Wi-Fi.

INEXPENSIVE

Collège Hotel *Value* Accommodations in a university dormitory in Lyon are not the spartan affair you might expect; in fact, they are rather comfortable and boast a number of attractive features. Located on the right bank of the Saône within the heart of Vieux Lyon, Collège Hotel offers 39 small but well-furnished bedrooms with immaculate linens and a choice of modern bathrooms (the best ones are the corner units with hand-held showers). Many of the bedrooms open onto private terraces or balconies. Each floor has a 1960s vintage refrigerator from which "boarders" can help themselves to free nonalcoholic drinks. Breakfast is served in the Study Room, with a choice of freshly baked breads and freshly squeezed orange juice. In the evening the teachers' lounge turns into a bar, and the library meeting room contains thousands of books, its blackboard hiding a giant screen. Best of all is a roof garden terrace with its gym. As soon as night falls, the hotel's 130 windows light up as part of a unique light show, enhancing the magnificent 1930s facade.

5 place Saint-Paul, Lyon 69005. ✆ **04-72-10-05-05.** Fax 04-78-27-98-84. www.college-hotel.com. 39 units. 125€ ($163) double; 140€ ($182) triple. AE, MC, V. Parking 12€ ($16). **Amenities:** Roof garden; gym; library. *In room:* A/C, TV.

Hôtel Bayard The foundations of this dignified town house date from the 16th century. The hotel was renovated in 1999, and some guest rooms were decorated in romantic French style, with draped canopies or four-poster beds. Each room is outfitted in a style inspired by a period of French history. Most of the compact private bathrooms have showers and tubs. You enter the hotel through a narrow hallway and climb one flight of stairs to the reception area. Don't be put off by the staff members, who may appear detached.

23 place Bellecour, Lyon 69002. ✆ **04-78-37-39-64.** Fax 04-72-40-95-51. www.hotelbayard.com. 15 units. 79€–109€ ($103–$142) double. Rates include breakfast. AE, DC, MC, V. Parking 10€–12€ ($13–$16). Métro: Bellecour. **Amenities:** Laundry service; nonsmoking rooms. *In room:* TV, Wi-Fi.

Hôtel Bellecordière The small, neatly kept accommodations at this nondescript hotel are no-frills and, at their worst, a bit depressing. Each unit has a compact shower-only bathroom. Breakfast is the only available meal, but many worthwhile restaurants are within a short walk.

18 rue Bellecordière, Lyon 69002. ✆ **04-78-42-27-78.** Fax 04-72-40-92-27. www.hotel-bellecordiere.com. 44 units. 75€ ($98) double. Rates include breakfast. AE, MC, V. Métro: Bellecour. *In room:* TV, hair dryer, Wi-Fi.

La Résidence *Value* Long a favorite with budget travelers, this hotel is in a pedestrian zone in the center of Lyon. Beyond an ornate 19th-century facade, the guest rooms are comfortably though not spectacularly furnished. Half come with tub/shower combinations. For the price, the place offers one of the best bargains in this rather overpriced city. Breakfast is the only meal served, but many restaurants are literally outside the door, as is some of the finest shopping.

18 rue Victor-Hugo, Lyon 69002. ✆ **04-78-42-63-28.** Fax 04-78-42-85-76. www.hotel-la-residence.com. 67 units. 75€–80€ ($98–$104) double; 90€–98€ ($117–$127) suite. AE, DC, MC, V. Métro: Bellecour. **Amenities:** Restaurant; nonsmoking rooms; limited-mobility rooms. *In room:* A/C, TV, minibar, hair dryer, safe.

WHERE TO DINE

The food in Lyon is among the finest in the world—with prices to match. However, we've found that a person of moderate means can often afford the most reasonable fixed-price menu even in the priciest establishments.

VERY EXPENSIVE

Alain Chapel ★★★ MODERN FRENCH This Relais Gourmand property occupies a 19th-century postal station that has evolved into a comfortable, stylish restaurant and lodging. Alain Chapel was one of the world's premier chefs, and after his death, many claimed that the reputation of his restaurant would falter. That hasn't been the case. Chef Philippe Jousse, who trained under Chapel, helps maintain Lyon's status as a gastronomic capital.

Menu items served within a rustically antique-looking setting change with the seasons, but are likely to include lobster salad with pigeon necks and black truffles; Bresse chicken cooked in a pig's bladder, stuffed with foie gras, and drizzled with foie gras sauce; puff pastry with apples and vanilla-flavored bourbon sauce and champagne-flavored sorbet; and a particularly appealing assortment of unusual local cheeses, charmingly presented.

Alain Chapel also has 12 beautiful guest rooms; a double runs 115€ to 135€ ($150–$176).

N83 Mionnay, St-André-de-Corcy 01390. Take N83 20km (12 miles) north of Lyon. ✆ **04-78-91-82-02.** Fax 04-78-91-82-37. www.alainchapel.fr. Reservations required. Main courses 38€–52€ ($49–$68); fixed-price lunch Wed–Thurs and Sat–Sun 60€ ($78); fixed-price dinner 110€–152€ ($143–$198). AE, DC, MC, V. Wed–Thurs and Sat–Sun 12:30–1:30pm; Wed–Sun 7:30–10pm. Closed Jan.

Léon de Lyon ★★★ MODERN FRENCH Located on the street level in a century-old private home, tables fill a series of rooms that have welcomed many a famous guest, from Charles Aznavour to Bill Clinton. The four dining rooms are each outfitted in their own style: one with wood panels, one with stained glass, and each lined with some of the 70 oil paintings in the owner's private collection. The owner, Jean-Paul Lacombe, is a challenger to the top chefs of Lyon, serving regional and modern cuisine with innovative flair. His brilliant use of Lyonnais offal may scare some but will please gastronomes. Offerings may include a terrine that incorporates farm-raised pork with foie gras, quenelles of pikeperch, pheasant soup with foie gras and red beans, or lobster with asparagus. The sorbets made with fresh fruits are a perfect ending.

1 rue Pleney. ✆ **04-72-10-11-12.** Reservations required. Main courses 43€–105€ ($56–$137); fixed-price lunch 59€–120€ ($77–$156); fixed-price dinner 120€–150€ ($156–$195). AE, MC, V. Tues–Sat noon–2pm and 7:30–10pm. Closed Aug 1–21. Métro: Hôtel-de-Ville.

Les Loges FRENCH This hotel restaurant originated with lofty ambitions, a celebrity chef, and a flurry of promotion. In 2003 it dropped the pretense and gradually evolved into a desirable—albeit not particularly cutting-edge—dining room. The flavorful food is beautifully prepared and served in generous portions—well-executed fare that you'd expect from a top-notch steakhouse or hotel dining room. Surrounded by Renaissance-era stone walls, wrought iron, and ornate crystal chandeliers, you may begin with foie gras, marinated salmon, or crabmeat cocktail with guacamole. Continue with grilled lamb, beef, veal, or pork, served with virtually any sauce you specify, or roasted quail in a succulent mixture of herbs and its own juices.

In the Hôtel la Cour des Loges, 6 rue du Boeuf. ✆ **04-72-77-44-44.** Reservations recommended. Main courses 20€–40€ ($26–$52); fixed-price menu 55€–80€ ($72–$104). AE, DC, MC, V. Sun noon–2pm and 7:30–10pm.

Paul Bocuse ★★★ LYONNAIS Paul Bocuse is one of the world's most famous chefs. He specializes in regional cuisine, though long ago he was the leading exponent of nouvelle cuisine (which he later called "a joke"). Because Bocuse, who is now in his 70s, is gone at least part of the time, other chefs carry on with the mass production (for up to 180 diners) of the signature dishes that the master created. There isn't a lot of room for variation. Tired of the conventional facades of most French restaurants, Bocuse commissioned a local artist to paint the history of French cuisine. The tale begins in the 1700s and proceeds through the years to its "defining moment"—a depiction of Bocuse himself.

You can begin your meal with the famous black truffle soup, and then try one of the most enduring dishes in the Bocuse repertoire: Bresse chicken cooked in a pig's bladder. Other options include roast pigeon in puff pastry with baby cabbage leaves and foie gras, and red snapper served in a potato casing. A boutique sells Bocuse's preferred wine, cognac, jams and jellies, coffees and teas, and cookbooks.

40 rue de la Plage, Pont de Collonges, Collonges-au-Mont-d'Or. ✆ **04-72-42-90-90.** Reservations required as far in advance as possible. Main courses 30€–135€ ($39–$176); fixed-price menu 120€–195€ ($156–$254). AE, DC, MC, V. Daily noon–1:30pm and 8–9:30pm. Closed Dec 25 and Jan 1. Take N433 9km (5⅗ miles) north of Lyon.

MODERATE

La Tassée *Value* FRENCH The chef here believes in serving good food at prices most people can afford, rather than dazzling with frills. La Tassée serves huge portions of anything from strips of tripe to game. Favorites include quenelles of *brochet* (pike) with lobster sauce, and sautéed chicken with drizzles of vinegar, served with freshly made pasta. The dining room boasts noteworthy frescoes painted in 1951, when the restaurant opened.

20 rue de la Charité. ✆ **04-72-77-79-00.** www.latassee.fr. Main courses 15€–32€ ($20–$42); fixed-price menu 25€–72€ ($33–$94). AE, MC, V. Sept–June Mon–Sat noon–2pm and 7–10pm; July–Aug Mon–Fri noon–2pm and 7–10pm. Métro: Bellecour.

Le Bistrot de Lyon TRADITIONAL LYONNAIS One of the largest and busiest restaurants in town was established in 1975. It incorporates at least four dining rooms, velvet banquettes, mirrors, and mosaics. The harried staff rushes amiably through the place, hauling giant platters. The kitchen showcases the recipes that made Lyon famous, with "soul food" dishes that include *salade Lyonnais, pot-au-feu,* crispy pigs' trotters, snails in puff pastry, fried steaks with garlic sauce, and a succulent and spicy version of steak tartare.

64 rue Mercière. ✆ **04-78-38-47-47.** Main courses 15€–21€ ($19–$27); fixed-price lunch 17€ ($21); fixed-price dinner 22€–27€ ($29–$34). AE, MC, V. Daily noon–2:30pm and 7pm–1am. Métro: Cordelier.

INEXPENSIVE

Brasserie Georges ★ *Value* FRENCH/LYONNAIS With prices that are reasonable, a historic core that, for a restaurant, is almost unbeatable, and a list of Lyonnais classics that residents travel in from the suburbs for, this is one of the must-visit restaurants of Lyon. It's the oldest in Lyon (founded in 1836), and probably the largest in France (with 450 seats). Turn-of-the-20th-century French poet Lamartine still owes the restaurant 40 francs for a meal he consumed 100 years ago. If you thrill to nest where the proud and mighty have already nested, you can ask specifically for a table that is identified with a plaque as having hosted Ernest Hemingway, the Lumière brothers, Edith Piaf, Rodin, Jean-Paul Sartre, and/or Jules Verne. Other more recent guests have included the Dalai Lama and former president Jacques Chirac. Specialties include standing roast beef, prepared for two diners at a time; snails in garlic butter; heaping platters of smoked salmon; hearty stews whose ingredients (veal, game, fish, shellfish) tend to change with the seasons; and pepper steaks.

Tips Beaucoup Bocuse

A resurgence of interest in chef Paul Bocuse swept across Lyon when Bocuse bought the **Brasserie le Nord** ★, 18 rue Neuve (✆ **04-72-10-69-69**), where he had worked as a teenager. Its prices (22€–30€/$28–$39 per person) signaled that the last of the great chefs had finally decided to go for the mass market. It's one of the most popular places in Lyon for traditional Lyonnais cuisine. A short while later, Bocuse opened a clone of Le Nord, **Brasserie le Sud,** place Antonin Poncet (✆ **04-72-77-80-00**), where the culinary venue celebrates all points south (including Provence and, to a lesser degree, French-speaking North Africa) with a Mediterranean-inspired diet that includes tagines and couscous, and a color scheme of vivid blues and yellows. In 1998, he endorsed the opening of **Brasserie de l'Est,** 14 place Jules-Ferry (✆ **04-37-24-25-26**), a large, bustling place offering Pan-French cuisine and a noisy and animated ambience that evokes the *brasseries de gare* of faraway Paris. And, finally, the Bocuse empire rounded out the four directions of the compass with the establishment of its final bistro, **La Brasserie de l'Ouest,** 1 Quai du Commerce (✆ **04-37-64-64-64**). Actually, its venue is more like the wild, wild American West (that is, California) than you may have expected. There's a hint of Pacific Rim cuisine here, and its layout is described as "American style" with an open kitchen, wide-open vistas, and a bustling kind of theatricality. Each of the four is open for lunch and dinner daily, and prices of main courses at each range from 22€ to 30€ ($28–$39).

30 cours Verdun, Perrache. ✆ **04-72-56-54-54.** Reservations not necessary. Main courses 20€–25€ ($25–$32); fixed-price menus 14€–22€ ($18–$29). AE, DC, MC, V. Daily 11:30am–11:30pm (until 12:30am Fri–Sat). Closed May 1. Métro: Perrache.

Café des Fédérations *Finds* TRADITIONAL FRENCH This is one of the busiest bistros in Lyon, and sometimes the most amusingly raucous. Open only on weekdays and catering to the office-worker crowd, it's operated with panache by a team of hard-working employees who would probably perform beautifully in the trenches of a war zone. The fixed-price menus offer a selection of appetizers, main courses, and desserts. Each evokes old-time Lyonnais cuisine at its least pretentious, with such options as a green salad with bacon and croutons; eggs *en meurette* (poached in red wine); pork chops; *andouillette* (chitterling sausages) served with *gratin dauphinois* (potato croquettes); and several other kinds of sausage, usually with *pommes de terre dauphinoise* (a potato gratin dish with cream and garlic).

8 rue Major-Martin. ✆ **04-78-28-26-00.** Reservations recommended. Fixed-price lunch 18€ ($23); fixed-price dinner 25€ ($32). V. Mon–Fri noon–2pm and 8–10pm. Closed 3 weeks in Aug. Métro: Hôtel-de-Ville.

LYON AFTER DARK

This cosmopolitan hub offers many entertainment and culture options. At any newsstand, pick up a copy of the weekly guide *Lyon-Poche,* which lists happenings and venues around town, from bars to classical concerts.

For the theater or opera buff, Lyon's **Théâtre des Célestins,** place Célestins (✆ **04-72-77-40-00**), is the premier venue for comedy and drama; and the **Opéra,** place de la Comédie (© **08-26-30-53-25**), always has a lively and diverse season. **Halle Tony Garnier,** 20 place Antonin Perrin (© **04-72-76-85-85**), originated as a 19th-century food market. The immense space with excellent acoustics is known for concerts, trade fairs, and temporary art exhibitions.

The best pub in town is the **Smoking Dog,** 16 rue Lainerie (© **04-78-28-38-27**), a happy neighborhood bar with a mixed-age crowd.

Rock 'n' rollers head to the old train station to **Le Boudoir,** 13 place J.-Ferry (© **04-72-74-04-41**), with an up-and-coming yuppie crowd. Another club to check out is **Le Box-Office,** 30 bd. Eugène-Deruelle (© **04-78-95-12-93**), with its brash techno crew. The cover at these clubs ranges from 12€ to 16€ ($16–$21). Jazz enthusiasts gravitate toward a Lyon tradition, **Le Hot Club,** 26 rue Lanterne (© **04-78-39-54-74**).

As you may have expected in a city the size of Lyon, there are a scattering of busy and popular gay bars. Popular spots for men include **La Ruche,** 22 rue Gentil, 2e (© **04-78-37-42-26;** Métro: Cordelier), and **Le Forum,** 15 rue des Quatres Chapeaux, 2e (© **04-78-37-19-74;** Métro: Cordelier), located in the city's historic core. Lesbian women tend to gravitate toward **Bar Le Marais,** 4 rue Thomassin, 2e (© **04-78-92-80-89;** Métro: Cordelier).

2 The Beaujolais Country ★★

The vineyards of Beaujolais start about 40km (25 miles) north of Lyon. This wine-producing region is small—64km (40 miles) long and less than 16km (10 miles) wide—yet it's one of the most famous in France. It's known throughout the world because of the Beaujolais wine craze that began in Paris some 30 years ago. In an average year, this region produces more than 190 million bottles of wine. Some 180 châteaux are scattered throughout this part of France. At many of them, you can sample and buy bottles of Beaujolais.

This region is a colorful and prosperous rural area, with vineyards on hillsides, cottages where the growers live, and historic houses and castles. It has been called the Land of the Golden Stones, but don't expect architectural monuments.

Unlike Alsace, with its Route du Vin, the Beaujolais country doesn't have a defined route. You can branch off in any direction, stopping at whatever point or wine cellar intrigues you. Don't be worried about losing your way after meandering off the A6 superhighway. This is one of the easiest parts of eastern France to negotiate, with clear road signs. If you're in doubt, simply follow the signs to the region's capital and commercial center, Villefranche-sur-Saône.

If you're pressed for time, you can tie the highlights together in a one-way drive, beginning at the region's southern terminus, Villefranche-sur-Saône, known as **Villefranche,** which you can reach from A6 between Mâcon and Lyon. (If you're heading north to south, follow the drive in reverse order, beginning in Juliénas, also off A6.)

Start in Villefranche. After an excursion west on D38 to **Bagnols-en-Beaujolais,** return to Villefranche. From here, take the meandering D504 and D20, which make sharp bends toward the east en route to **St-Julien-sous-Montmelas.** From St-Julien, take D19 to **Salles-en-Beaujolais.** From Salles, take D62 and D19 to **Belleville-sur-Saône.** Then follow D37 and D68 to **Villié-Morgon.** From Villié-Morgon, take D68 and D266 to **Juliénas.**

VILLEFRANCHE-SUR-SAONE—CAPITAL OF BEAUJOLAIS

Go to the **Office du Tourisme,** 96 rue de la Sous-Prefecture, not far from the marketplace (✆ **04-74-07-27-50;** www.beaujolais.com), for a booklet on the Beaujolais country. It includes a map and itineraries and lists the wine-tasting cellars open to the public. It also lists and details some 30 villages.

BAGNOLS-EN-BEAUJOLAIS

To reach Bagnols from Villefranche, head west on D38.

WHERE TO STAY & DINE

Château de Bagnols-en-Beaujolais ★★★ This is lordly living on a grand scale. France's premier château hotel, this one-time Renaissance ruin has been restored by 400 artisans and craftspeople. Antiques, paintings, and art, much from the 17th century, fill the mansion. The individually decorated guest rooms are sumptuous, with antique beds, period velvets, embroidered linen sheets, and down pillows; one unit is named for Mme de Sévigné, who spent a restless night here in 1673. The bathrooms have tiled floors, brass fittings, and luxurious tubs. Although this place does have a pool, it's not for the young and restless—you won't find a gym or tennis courts. La Salle des Gardes serves elegant Continental fare.

Bagnols 69620. ✆ **04-74-71-40-00.** Fax 04-74-71-40-49. www.bagnols.com. 21 units. 370€–450€ ($481–$585) double; from 522€ ($679) suite. AE, DC, MC, V. Closed Jan 2–Mar 25. **Amenities:** Restaurant; lounge; outdoor pool; room service; laundry service; limited-mobility rooms. *In room:* TV, hair dryer, safe, Wi-Fi.

ST-JULIEN-SOUS-MONTMELAS

This charming village is 11km (6¾ miles) northwest of Villefranche (take D504, then D20). Claude Bernard, the father of physiology, was born here in 1813. His small stone house—now the **Musée Claude-Bernard** (✆ **04-74-67-51-44**)—exhibits the scholar's mementos, instruments, and books. From October to February, it's open Wednesday to Sunday 10am to noon and 2 to 5pm; April to September daily 10am to noon and 2 to 6pm; closed March. Admission is 5€ ($6.50) adults, 3€ ($3.90) children 10 to 16, and free for children under 10.

SALLES-EN-BEAUJOLAIS

Eglise de Salles Arbuissonnas ★ (✆ **04-74-67-51-50**) was begun in A.D. 1090 and completed in the 1700s. The religious hideaway is mostly Romanesque, with an occasional Gothic overlay, especially in its doorways. Connoisseurs of Romanesque architecture love the golden ocher color of the limestone. Notice the Salle Capitulaire, where the capitals of columns from throughout the building's history are on display. The church is open May to September daily 9am to 6pm, October to April daily 9am to 5pm. Admission is free. From St-Julien, take D19 a short distance to Salles.

BELLEVILLE-SUR-SAONE

For an excellent dining experience, drive north from Salles on D19 and D62 to Belleville-sur-Saône.

WHERE TO DINE

Le Rhône au Rhin ★ MODERN FRENCH Chef Michel Debize operates this out-of-the-way restaurant (1km/⅔ mile north of the village of Belleville-sur-Saône) in a converted antique house, as a refuge from the more congested regions. As you try the flavorful cuisine, you may surrender to his escapist dream. The decor is contemporary and comfortable, outfitted in warm tones of brown and soft orange. Menu items change with the seasons, but may include terrine of foie gras with apples served in puff pastry, tartare of raw tuna with gazpacho, and a duo of salmon and crayfish in a potato galette.

10 av. du Port. ✆ **04-74-66-16-23.** Reservations required. Main courses 12€–25€ ($16–$33); fixed-price menu 22€–50€ ($29–$65). MC, V. Tues–Sun noon–2pm; Tues and Thurs–Sat 7–9pm.

VILLIE-MORGON

For another dining experience in the Beaujolais country, we suggest driving west from Belleville-sur-Saône on D37, and then north on D18 to Villié-Morgon. The village and the surrounding region contain around 250 wine producers. Their product, at its best, is usually judged among the best Beaujolais wines in France.

In the basement of the **Château de Fontcrenne,** immediately adjacent to the Hôtel de Ville, is the **Caveau de Morgon** (✆ **04-74-04-20-99;** www.morgon.fr). It assembles and "marries" a selection of the Villié-Morgon region's best wines into a well-respected brand name (Caveau de Morgon) whose savvy marketing benefits winegrowers and consumers alike. Whatever you do, don't use the word "blend" to describe this company's product—the word is usually received with something akin to horror. The cellar is open for tours and sales daily 9:30am to noon and 2 to 7pm (closed Jan), and open only Friday to Sunday in February. Admission is free. You'll pay a nominal charge—1€ ($1.30) per glass, 7€ ($9.10) per bottle—for wine you consume.

JULIENAS

Wines are also a reason to travel north on D266 and D68 to Juliénas. This village produces a full-bodied, robust wine. Go to the **Cellier de la Vieille Eglise** (✆ **04-74-04-42-98**), an old church cellar, to sip the wine. A statue of Bacchus with some tipsy, scantily clad girlfriends looks on from what used to be the altar. It's open from Wednesday to Monday from 9:45am to noon and 2:30 to 6:30pm. The local farmers' and winegrowers' cooperative helps support this wine outlet. Admission is free, but expect to pay 6.50€ to 8€ ($8.45–$10) per bottle, depending on the vintage.

3 Roanne

390km (242 miles) SE of Paris, 87km (54 miles) NW of Lyon

This industrial town on the left bank of the Loire is a popular excursion from Lyon and Vichy because it's home to one of France's greatest three-star restaurants, the Hôtel-Restaurant Troisgros (see "Where to Stay & Dine," below).

In a neoclassical mansion built at the end of the 18th century, **Musée Joseph-Déchelette,** 22 rue Anatole-France (✆ **04-77-23-68-77**), offers an exceptional display of Italian and French earthenware from the 16th, 17th, 18th, and 20th centuries, as well as Roanne earthenware. Hours are Wednesday through Monday 10am to noon and 2 to 6pm. On Sunday, the museum is open only in the afternoon, and on Saturday there is no noontime break. Admission is 4€ ($5.20) for adults, 2€ ($2.60) for students, free for ages under 18, and free for everyone on Wednesday afternoon.

ESSENTIALS

GETTING THERE **Trains** and some **buses** serve Roanne from nearby cities, notably Lyon; the train is a lot more convenient. By train, Roanne lies 3 hours from Paris and 1 hour and 10 minutes from Lyon; for information, call ✆ **08-92-35-35-35,** or visit www.voyages-sncf.com. If you're **driving,** follow N7 northwest from Lyon to Roanne. From Paris, follow A6 south to Nemours and continue southwest on N7.

VISITOR INFORMATION The **Office de Tourisme** is at 1 cours de la République (✆ **04-77-71-51-77;** www.leroannais.com).

WHERE TO STAY & DINE

Hôtel-Restaurant Troisgros ★★★ FRENCH/LYONNAIS This Relais & Châteaux is one of the top 10 restaurants in France. It attained that reputation in the 1950s and has since factored into the itineraries of globe-trotting foodies, visiting heads of state, and wealthy people touring the region. Come here with respect for the French *grande bourgeoisie* and the appeal of French culinary finesse. The place is too conservative and devoted to impeccably tailored service for anything radical or provocative.

Decorated in neutral colors and lined with contemporary artwork, the restaurant features superb cuisine at astronomical prices. Pierre (the father) and Michel (the son) Troisgros, the current keepers of the flame, celebrate the bounty of the Lyonnais countryside. Dishes include fried foie gras served with marinated eggplant, salmon with sage sauce, and beef served with Fleurie wine and bone marrow. For dessert, ask to see one of the best assortments of esoteric cheeses in the region, or perhaps enjoy a praline soufflé.

The hotel also rents 16 traditionally furnished rooms; a double costs 175€ to 510€ ($228–$663).

Place Jean Troisgros, Roanne 42300. ✆ **04-77-71-66-97.** Fax 04-77-70-39-77. www.troisgros.com. Reservations required. Main courses 50€–130€ ($65–$169); fixed-price menu 140€–250€ ($182–$325). AE, DC, MC, V. Thurs–Mon noon–1:30pm and 7:30–9:30pm. Closed 2 weeks in Feb and 2 weeks in Aug.

WHERE TO STAY & DINE NEARBY

In the nearby village of **Le Coteau,** you'll find several worthy restaurants. These two are our favorites. To get there, take N7 3km (1¾ miles) south from the center of Roanne.

Auberge Costelloise ★★ FRENCH Chef Christophe Suchon provides what this region needs: an attractive restaurant with fine cuisine and reasonable prices. The restaurant is adjacent to the banks of the headwaters of the Loire, in a dining room ringed with paintings and wood paneling. Choose one of the fixed-price menus, which change weekly. The well-planned menu focuses on fish, including fresh salmon cooked in truffle vinaigrette. *Daurade* (bream) comes in garlic-flavored cream sauce, crayfish is served with saffron-flavored potatoes and a Thai-inspired lemon grass, and red snapper is enhanced by Provençal pistou. You can order fine vintages of Burgundian wines by the pitcher. This is the place to head when you can't afford the dazzling but expensive food at Troisgros.

2 av. de la Libération. ✆ **04-77-68-12-71.** Reservations required. Main courses 25€–29€ ($33–$38); fixed-price menus 35€ ($46) Tues–Fri only, and 40€–66€ ($52–$86). AE, MC, V. Mon–Sat noon–1:30pm and 7:45–9:15pm. Closed Aug 7–Sept 5 and Dec 26–Jan 4.

Hôtel Restaurant Alain Artaud TRADITIONAL FRENCH Popular with locals, who favor it for family celebrations and business meetings, this well-established inn lies in the center of Le Coteau. The turn-of-the-20th-century house was radically renovated in 1999. Specialties include several preparations of Charolais beef. There's also a succulent version of *bourride Marseillaise* (fish stew), and scallops served with beurre blanc and caramelized cabbage.

The 24 guest rooms are contemporary, comfortable, and streamlined. They have air-conditioning, a minibar, satellite TV, and a shower or tub. Doubles cost 65€ to 90€ ($85–$117).

133 av. de la Libération, Le Coteau 42120. ✆ **04-77-68-46-44.** Fax 04-77-72-23-50. www.hotel-artaud.com. Reservations recommended. Main courses 12€–25€ ($16–$33); fixed-price menu 20€–58€ ($26–$75). AE, DC, MC, V. Tues–Sat noon–2pm; Mon–Sat 7:30–9pm. Closed 3 weeks in Aug and Dec 24–Jan 2.

4 Pérouges ★★

464km (288 miles) SE of Paris, 35km (22 miles) NE of Lyon

Saved from demolition by a courageous mayor in 1909 and preserved by the government, this village of craftspeople (pop. 1,119) often attracts movie crews: *The Three Musketeers* (1973) and *Monsieur Vincent* (1948) were filmed here. However, films have not been made here since the 1970s, since French film production moved primarily to Eastern Europe. The town sits on what has been called an "isolated throne," atop a hill northeast of Lyon.

Follow rue du Prince, once the main business street, to place des Tilleuls, at the center of which is the **Arbre de la Liberté (Tree of Liberty),** planted in 1792 to commemorate the Revolution. Nearby, in a 14th-century building, is the **Musée du Vieux-Pérouges,** place de la Halle (✆ **04-74-61-00-88**), displaying such artifacts as hand looms. It's open only from Easter to November 1, daily 10am to noon and 2 to 6pm. Admission is 4€ ($5.20). The price includes access to the museum and, through adjoining doors, to one of the finest houses in the village, the **Maison des Princes de Savoie,** with a watchtower **(La Tour de Guet)** and a replica of a 13th-century garden, the **Jardin de Hortulus.**

Wander through the town, soaking in the atmosphere of a stone village that's remained virtually unchanged.

ESSENTIALS

GETTING THERE It's easiest to **drive** to Pérouges, though the signs for the town, especially at night, are confusing. From Lyon, take route 84 northeast and exit near Meximieux.

VISITOR INFORMATION The **Tourist Office (Syndicat d'Initiative,** Cité de Pérouges; ✆ **04-74-61-01-14;** www.perouges.org) lies adjacent to the entrance of this very small village.

WHERE TO STAY & DINE

Ostellerie du Vieux-Pérouges ★★ *Finds* This is a treasure in a restored group of 13th-century timbered buildings. The Thibaut family runs a museum-caliber inn furnished with cupboards housing pewter plates, iron lanterns hanging from medieval beams, refectory dining tables, and stone fireplaces. The midsize to spacious guest rooms are completely up-to-date, with modern amenities, yet they have an old-fashioned atmosphere and style that recall medieval France.

The restaurant's food is exceptional, especially when accompanied by the local sparkling wine, Montagnieu, which has been compared to Asti Spumante. Specialties include Bresse chicken in morel-studded cream sauce, filet of carp stuffed *à l'ancienne* with pikeperch, and *panache* Pérougien (an omelet stuffed with creamed morels and served with shrimp and crayfish cream sauce). By far the best-selling dessert is a crepe known as a *galette pérougienne à la crème,* from a century-old secret recipe. After dinner, ask for a glass of Ypocras, a unique liqueur made from a recipe dating to the Middle Ages.

Place des Tilleuls, Pérouges 01800. ✆ **04-74-61-00-88.** Fax 04-74-34-77-90. www.ostellerie.com. 28 units. 110€–230€ ($143–$299) double; 260€ ($338) suite. AE, MC, V. **Amenities:** Restaurant; bar; room service; laundry service. *In room:* TV, hair dryer, Wi-Fi.

5 Bourg-en-Bresse

425km (264 miles) SE of Paris, 61km (38 miles) NE of Lyon

The ancient capital of Bresse, this farming and business center on the border between Burgundy and the Jura offers fabulous food.

ESSENTIALS

GETTING THERE Bourg-en-Bresse is accessible by **train** from Paris, Lyon, and Dijon. Fifteen TGV (fast) trains arrive from Paris's Gare de Lyon daily (trip time: 2 hr.). From Lyon (40–80 min.), 10 trains arrive per day. From Dijon (2 hr.), five trains arrive daily. For information, call ✆ **08-92-35-35-35,** or visit www.voyages-sncf.com. If **driving** from Lyon, take A42 or N83 for the 40-minute trip; from Dijon (2 hr.), follow A31 to Mâcon and take A40 to Bourg-en-Bresse.

VISITOR INFORMATION The **Office de Tourisme** is at 6 av. Alsace-Lorraine (✆ **04-74-22-49-40;** www.bourg-en-bresse.org).

SEEING THE SIGHTS

If you have time, visit the **Eglise Notre-Dame,** off place Carriat. Begun in 1505, it contains some finely carved 16th-century stalls. If you'd like to wander around town, check out the 15th-century houses on rue du Palais and rue Gambetta.

Monastère Royal de Brou ★ Art lovers will want to stop at the Eglise de Brou to see its magnificent royal tombs. One of the great artistic treasures of France, this Flamboyant Gothic monastery was built between 1506 and 1532 (the three cloisters between 1506 and 1512, the church between 1513 and 1532) for Margaret of Austria, the ill-fated daughter of Emperor Maximilian. Over the ornate Renaissance doorway, the tympanum depicts Margaret and her "handsome duke," Philibert, who died when he caught a cold on a hunting expedition. The nave and its double aisles are admirable. Look for the ornate rood screen, decorated with basket-handle arching. Ask a guide for a tour of the choir, which is rich in decorative detail; Flemish sculptors and local craftsmen made the 74 choir stalls of oak in just 2 years.

The tombs are the church's treasure. The Carrara marble statues are of Philibert and Margaret. Another tomb is that of Marguerite de Bourbon, mother of Philibert and grandmother of François I, who died in 1483. See also the stained-glass windows inspired by a Dürer engraving and an alabaster retable (altarpiece) depicting *The Seven Joys of the Madonna.* The monastery sometimes mounts expositions of modern art.

63 bd. de Brou. ✆ **04-74-22-83-83.** Admission to church, cloisters, and museum 6.50€ ($8.45) adults, 4.50€ ($5.85) students, free for children under 18. Mid-June to Sept daily 9am–6pm; Apr to mid-June daily 9am–12:30pm and 2–6pm; Oct–Mar daily 9am–noon and 2–5pm. Closed Jan 1, May 1, Nov 1 and 11, and Dec 25.

WHERE TO STAY

Hôtel du Prieuré ★ Erected in 1982, this is the town's most gracious hotel. The angular structure sits on .4 hectare (1 acre) of gardens surrounded by 500-year-old stone walls. This place is especially alluring in spring, when forsythia, lilacs, roses, and Japanese cherries fill the air with their perfume. Most guest rooms are large and tranquil, outfitted in Louis XV, Louis XVI, or French country style. All come with a small bathroom, most with both tub and shower.

49–51 bd. de Brou, Bourg-en-Bresse 01000. ✆ **04-74-22-44-60.** www.hoteldupriere.com. Fax 04-74-22-71-07. 14 units. 78€–90€ ($101–$117) double. AE, MC, V. Free parking. **Amenities:** Room service; nonsmoking rooms. *In room:* TV, hair dryer.

Le Logis de Brou This four-story property has landscaped grounds and is near the road fronting the church. Each comfortable guest room has reproductions of antique furniture, plus a small shower-only bathroom. Jacqueline and Gérard Roger run a fine inn and employ an especially helpful staff.

132 bd. de Brou, Bourg-en-Bresse 01000. ✆ **04-74-22-11-55.** Fax 04-74-22-37-30. www.logisdebrou.com. 30 units. 52€–70€ ($68–$91) double; 129€–153€ ($168–$199) suite. AE, MC, V. Parking 9€ ($12). **Amenities:** Business center; laundry service. *In room:* TV, hair dryer.

WHERE TO DINE

Auberge Bressane ★★ TRADITIONAL FRENCH Bresse poultry is the best in France, and chef Jean-Pierre Vullin specializes in succulent *volaille de Bresse,* served five ways, including a delectable version in cream sauce with morels. You also may enjoy gâteau of chicken liver, fried frogs' legs with garlic and wild mushrooms, quenelles of pikeperch with shrimp, or sea bass with fresh basil, accompanied by regional wines such as Seyssel and Montagnieu.

166 bd. de Brou. ✆ **04-74-22-22-68.** Reservations recommended. Main courses 26€–39€ ($34–$51); fixed-price menus 23€–75€ ($30–$98). AE, DC, MC, V. Wed–Mon noon–1:30pm and 7:15–9:45pm.

Au Chalet de Brou ★★ TRADITIONAL FRENCH You'll find flavorful and relatively inexpensive food at this unpretentious restaurant across from the village's most famous church. Specialties include a "cake" of chicken livers served with essence of tomato; quenelle of pikeperch with lobster sauce; frogs' legs in parsley sauce; and at least a half-dozen kinds of Bresse chicken, served with your choice of morel-flavored cream sauce, raspberry vinegar, or chardonnay sauce. Some purists (including us) opt for it simply grilled in order to appreciate the unadorned flavor of the bird in its own drippings. Dessert may be an apple tart presented, according to your choice, hot or semifrozen.

168 bd. de Brou. ✆ **04-74-22-26-28.** Reservations recommended. Main courses 8€–25€ ($10–$33); fixed-price menu 20€–42€ ($26–$55). AE, MC, V. Sat–Thurs noon–2pm; Tues–Wed and Sun 7–10pm. Closed Dec 20–Jan 20.

6 Vienne ★★

489km (304 miles) SE of Paris, 31km (19 miles) S of Lyon

Gastronomes know Vienne because it boasts one of France's leading restaurants, La Pyramide. Even if you can't afford the haute cuisine, you may want to visit. It's a wine center and the southernmost Burgundian town.

ESSENTIALS

GETTING THERE **Trains** connect Vienne with the rest of France. Some trips require a transfer in Lyon, 20 minutes away. For information, call ✆ **08-92-35-35-35,** or visit www.voyages-sncf.com. **Buses** from Lyon arrive about eight times a day, making many stops and taking about an hour; for information, contact Vienne's Gare Routière (✆ **04-76-00-38-38**), adjacent to the railway station. The one-way bus or train fare from Lyon is 6€ ($7.80). If you're **driving** from Lyon, take N7 (which is more direct) or A7, an expressway that meanders along the banks of the Rhône.

VISITOR INFORMATION The **Office de Tourisme** is at cours Brillier (✆ **04-74-53-80-30;** fax 04-74-53-80-31; www.vienne-tourisme.com).

SPECIAL EVENTS In the first 2 weeks of July, Vienne attracts some of the biggest names in jazz for the annual **Festival du Jazz à Vienne.** Tickets range from 27€ to 30€ ($35–$39). You can get tickets and information from the **Théâtre Antique de Vienne,** 4 rue Chantelouve (✆ **04-74-78-87-87;** www.jazzavienne.com).

SEEING THE SIGHTS

Vienne contains many antique buildings, making it a *ville romaine et médiévale.* Near the center of town on place du Palais is the **Temple d'Auguste et de Livie,** built on the orders of the Roman emperor Claudius and turned into a "temple of reason" during the French Revolution. Another outstanding monument is the **Pyramide du Cirque Romain,** part of the Roman circus. Rising 16m (52 ft.), it rests on a portico with four arches and is sometimes called the tomb of Pilate.

Take rue Clémentine to the **Cathédrale St-Maurice** ★★, place St-Maurice (✆ **04-74-85-60-28**), which dates from the 12th century and wasn't completed until the 15th. It has three aisles but no transepts. Its west front is built in the Flamboyant Gothic style, and inside are many fine Romanesque sculptures.

In the south part of town is the **Eglise St-Pierre** ★, place St-Pierre (✆ **04-74-85-20-35**). A landmark with origins in the 5th century, it's one of the oldest medieval churches in France. Inside, the **Musée Lapidaire** (✆ **04-74-85-20-35**) displays architectural fragments and sculptures from excavations. The museum is open April to October Tuesday to Sunday from 9:30am to 1pm and 2 to 6pm; January to March and November and December Tuesday to Friday from 9:30am to 12:30pm and 2 to 5pm, Saturday and Sunday from 2 to 6pm. Admission is 2.30€ ($3) for adults, 1.70€ ($2.20) for students, and free for children under 18. Closed January 1, May 1, November 1, November 11, and December 25.

A **Roman Theater (Théâtre Romain)** ★, 7 rue du Cirque (✆ **04-74-85-39-23**), has been excavated east of town at the foot of Mont Pipet. Theatrical spectacles were staged here for an audience of thousands. You can visit September and October Tuesday to Sunday 9:30am to 1pm and 2 to 6pm; January to March and November and December Tuesday to Saturday 9:30am to 12:30pm and 2 to 5:30pm, Sunday 1:30 to 5:30pm; April to August daily 9:30am to 1pm and 2 to 6pm. Admission is 6€ ($7.80) for a day pass.

If you have about an hour for a side trip, in Hauterives, south of Vienne, you'll find one of the world's strangest pieces of architecture. The **Palais du Facteur Cheval,** or **Palace of the Mailman Cheval** (✆ **04-75-68-81-19**), the lifelong work of French postman Ferdinand Cheval, is built of stone and concrete and elaborately decorated, often with clamshells. It's an eccentric palace of fantasy and a tribute to the aesthetic value, or mania, of the individual. The work was finished in 1912, when Cheval was 76. Admission is 5.20€ ($6.75) for adults, 4.20€ ($5.45) students, and 3.70€ ($4.80) for children 6 to 16. The palace is open in July and August daily 9:30am to 12:30pm and 1:30 to 7pm; April, May, June, and September daily 9am to 12:30pm and 1:30 to 6:30pm; February, March, October, and November daily 9:30am to 12:30pm and 1:30 to 5:30pm; and December and January 1 to January 14 daily 9:30am to 12:30pm and 1:30 to 4:30pm. It's closed January 15 to January 31.

WHERE TO STAY

La Pyramide Fernand-Point (see "Where to Dine," below) also offers rooms.

Hostellerie Beau-Rivage A Relais du Silence property, this place originated around 1900 as a simple inn that offered food and wine to fishermen who traveled from Lyon to the well-stocked waters of this section of the Rhône. It has evolved into a stylish, nostalgic enclave. The rooms are well furnished; some are larger than you may expect. Most come with a tub/shower combination.

The Rhône passes by the dining terrace. The traditional cuisine is exceptional. Try quenelles of pike; stuffed snails with new potatoes; and delicious suprême of pigeon on a platter with confit of pigeon, roasted foie gras, and turnips. The Côtes du Rhône wines complement the food well.

2 rue du Beau-Rivage, Condrieu 69420. From Vienne, cross the Rhône on N86 and head south 12km (7½ miles); pass through Condrieu and, on the southern outskirts, look for signs on the left. ✆ **04-74-56-82-82.** Fax 04-74-59-59-36. www.hotel-beaurivage.com. 30 units. 110€–145€ ($143–$189) double; 210€–235€ ($273–$306) suite. DC, MC, V. **Amenities:** Restaurant; laundry service. *In room:* A/C, TV, minibar.

WHERE TO DINE

La Pyramide Fernand-Point ★★★ MODERN FRENCH This is the area's premier place to stay or dine, and for many it's the preferred stopover between Paris and the Riviera. The restaurant perpetuates the memory of a superb chef, Fernand Point. Through the continuing efforts of Patrick Henriroux, many of Point's secrets, especially his sauces, have been preserved. Menus change seasonally, but the cuisine is always imaginative. Examples include watercress and zander soup garnished with braised endive; peppered and roasted duckling with red cabbage, wild mushrooms, and liqueur-soaked grapes; and John Dory wrapped in Parma ham, with soya-flavored endive and Tabasco-flavored sabayon. The cheese platter is wonderful, and desserts are as artfully caloric, and as stylish, as anything else in the Rhône Valley.

The hotel offers 25 charming, air-conditioned guest rooms, each with minibar, TV, and dataport. Doubles go for 190€ to 230€ ($247–$299), suites for 250€ to 350€ ($325–$455). Limited-mobility rooms are also available.

14 bd. Fernand-Point, Vienne 38200. ✆ **04-74-53-01-96.** Fax 04-74-85-69-73. www.lapyramide.com. Reservations required. Main courses 48€–80€ ($62–$104); fixed-price menu 98€–195€ ($127–$254). AE, DC, MC, V. Thurs–Mon 12:30–1:30pm and 7:30–9:30pm. Closed Feb and 1 week in mid-Aug.

Les Saveurs du Marché FRENCH This bustling, high-turnover, and slightly rowdy restaurant is known to many of the hardworking laborers of Vienne, who come here for inexpensive lunchtime meals, and for slightly more leisurely and more intricate food at night. Within a 10-minute walk south of the town center, the blue-and-white dining room reflects, so its owners say, the colors of southern France. Along one wall is a massively paneled bar. Menu items change with the seasons and the availability of raw ingredients, but may include a delectable soufflé of pikeperch with fresh mussels, a salad of warm goat cheese, pheasant stew with wild mushrooms, and a savory casserole of spicy scallops and crayfish. Expect good value and a sense of cheerful informality.

34 cours de Verdun. ✆ **04-74-31-65-65.** Reservations recommended. Fixed-price lunch 12€ ($16); fixed-price dinner 19€–39€ ($25–$51). DC, MC, V. Mon–Fri noon–1:45pm and 7:30–9:30pm. Closed Aug.

7 Valence ★

671km (417 miles) SE of Paris, 100km (62 miles) S of Lyon

Valence stands on the left bank of the Rhône between Lyon and Avignon. A former Roman colony, it later became the capital of the Duchy of Valentinois, set up by Louis XII in 1493 for Cesare Borgia.

Today, Valence is a market town and distribution point for Rhône Valley fruit and vegetable producers. It's fitting that François Rabelais, who wrote of gargantuan appetites, spent time here as a student.

Visitors can climb the ruined château atop the white stone **Mont Crussol.** The ruins date from the 12th century. Valence is still the home of the Arsenal, one of France's oldest gunpowder factories.

The most interesting sight is the **Cathédrale St-Apollinaire,** place de Ormeaux (✆ **04-75-43-13-32**), consecrated by Urban II in 1095 and much restored since. Built in the Auvergnat-Romanesque style, the cathedral is on place des Clercs in the center of town. The choir contains the tomb of Pope Pius VI, who died a prisoner here in the 18th century. It's open daily from 8am to 7pm.

Adjoining the cathedral is the **Musée Municipal,** 4 place des Ormeaux (✆ **04-75-79-20-80**), noted for its nearly 100 red-chalk drawings by Hubert Robert done in the 18th century. It's open June to September Tuesday to Saturday 10am to noon and 2 to 6:45pm, and Sunday 2 to 5:45pm; October to May Tuesday to Sunday 2 to 5:30pm. Admission is 5.20€ ($6.75) adults, 2.50€ ($3.25) students, and free for children under 16.

ESSENTIALS

GETTING THERE **Trains** run from Lyon, Grenoble, and Marseille. For information, call ✆ **08-92-35-35-35.** If you're **driving** from Lyon, take A7 south. From Grenoble, follow E711 to outside the town of Voreppe, go southwest along E713, and follow W532 into Valence. From Marseilles, follow A7 north.

VISITOR INFORMATION The **Office de Tourisme** is at parvis de la Gare (✆ **08-92-70-70-99;** fax 04-75-44-90-41; www.tourisme-valence.com).

WHERE TO STAY & DINE

Hôtel-Restaurant Pic ★★★ FRENCH This is the least known of France's great restaurants, although it ranks among the top 10. The cooking and the wine list (featuring regional selections such as Hermitage, St-Péray, and Côtes du Rhône) are exceptional. The villa has a courtyard and a dining room with big tables and ample chairs. Chef Anne-Sophie Pic has been called a fireball in the kitchen, bringing modern (often Asian) touches to classical dishes. Her appetizers, such as chicken skewered on twigs of aromatic rosemary, are a delight. For a main dish you may select frogs' legs cooked with garlic and served with chestnut-stuffed ravioli; *lièvre a la Royale* (hare simmered in a mixture of red wine and its own blood); or guinea fowl stuffed with rosemary, dried tomatoes, black olives, and fennel. Pic pays special attention to fresh vegetables, including fava beans and baby spinach. The desserts are rapturous, from grapefruit sorbet to cold orange soufflé. Menu items change every 3 weeks.

The brasserie, **Restaurant du Cèpe** (✆ **04-75-44-53-86**), serves regional food without a lot of culinary fuss. Full meals, without wine, cost 25€ to 30€ ($33–$39) per person. Pic also rents 15 individually decorated guest rooms. They cost 195€ to 285€ ($254–$371) for a double, 305€ to 395€ ($397–$514) for a suite.

285 av. Victor-Hugo. ✆ **04-75-44-15-32.** Fax 04-75-40-96-03. www.pic-valence.com. Reservations required. Main courses 10€–25€ ($13–$33); fixed-price menu 30€ ($39) lunch Tues–Fri, 115€–155€ ($150–$202) dinner. V. Daily 7:30–2pm.

8 The Ardèche ★★★

The Ardèche occupies the eastern flank of the Massif Central (see chapter 22), a landscape of jagged, much-eroded granite and limestone highlands. Although it defines itself as Le Midi—its southern border lies less than 40km (25 miles) from Avignon and 48km (30 miles) from Nîmes—its culture and landscape are more rooted in the rugged uplands of France's central highlands.

Through its territory flow the streams and rivers that drain the snow and rain of the Massif Central. They include rivers such as the Ligne, Fontolière, Lignon, Tanargue, and, most important, Ardèche. They flow beside, around, and through rocky ravines, feudal ruins, and stone-sided villages perched in high-altitude sites originally chosen for ease of defense in medieval times.

The most famous and visited section of the Ardèche is its southern extremity, with granite-sided ravines 300m (984 ft.) deep, gouged by millions of springtime floodings of the Ardèche River—no wonder it's called the Grand Canyon of France. This area draws thousands of tourists, often with their children, who take driving tours along the highways flanking the ravines.

We recommend that you stop in the southern Ardèche to admire the gorges only briefly. It's better to spend the night in the less touristy northern reaches.

The northern Ardèche, in the 45km (28 miles) of hills and valleys separating the hamlets of Vals-les-Bains and Lamastre, is a soft and civilized wilderness, with landscapes devoted to grape growing, shepherding, and hill trekking.

One writer described **Vallon-Pont-d'Arc,** the gateway to the gorges, as a Gallic version of Gatlinburg, Tennessee. For your overnight stop, we suggest you continue north to the more picturesque towns of Vals-les-Bains or Lamastre.

Fun Fact The Grand Canyon of France

The ebbs and flows of the Ardèche, France's fastest-flowing river, have created the Grand Canyon of France. Littered with alluvial deposits, strewn in ravines whose depth can exceed 285m (935 ft.), the river's final 58km (36 miles), before the waters dump into the Rhône, is one of the country's most unusual geological areas. A **panoramic road (D290)** runs along a rim of these canyons, providing views over an arid landscape of grasses, trees, hardy shrubs, and some of the most distinctive deposits of granite, limestone, and basalt in Europe.

The beautiful driving route, which you can traverse in a few hours even if you stop for sightseeing (follow signs directing you along well-marked footpaths), stretches north to south between the towns of Vallon-Pont-d'Arc and Pont St-Esprit. The meandering corniche roads are a challenge. Look out for other vehicles weaving frighteningly as drivers and passengers admire the scenery and snap photos.

If you want to kayak in the gorges, go between early April and late November, when the waters are green and sluggish and safer than they are during the winter and spring floods. In Vallon-Pont-d'Arc, you'll find at least three dozen rental agencies for everything from plastic kayaks to horses. One of the best, **Aventure Canoës,** place du Marché (B.P. 27), Vallon-Pont-d'Arc 07150 (© **04-75-37-18-14;** www.aventure-canoes.fr), rents canoes and kayaks. A 3-hour *mini-descente* costs around 15€ ($20) per person for use of a canoe or kayak. The ride will take you along a 6.5km (4-mile) route from Vallon-Pont-d'Arc to the downstream hamlet of Chames. A full-day *grande descente* along the 31km (19-mile) downstream route from Vallon-Pont-d'Arc to St-Martin d'Ardèche costs around 24€ ($31) per person. A 2-day trip by canoe or kayak costs 36€ to 47€ ($47–$61) per person, depending on the season and the equipment you choose. Prices include transport by minivan back to Vallon-Pont-d'Arc at the end of the ride. Lunch is not included, so bring your own. Picnic fixings are available at dozens of bakeries and delicatessens near each point of origin.

Despite the appeal of kayaking, most travelers stick with driving along the upper summits of the gorges.

VALS-LES-BAINS

43km (27 miles) W of Montélimar, 138km (86 miles) SW of Lyon

In a depression of the valley of the Volane River, Vals-les-Bains is surrounded by about 150 springs whose existence was discovered around 1600. Scientists have never understood why each spring contains a different percentage of minerals: Most contain bicarbonate of soda, some are almost tasteless, and one—*La Source Dominique*—has such a high percentage of iron and arsenic that it's poisonous. Waters from Dominique are piped away from the town; others are funneled into a Station Thérmale adjacent to the town's casino.

In the park outside the Station Thérmale, a *source intermittante* erupts, Old Faithful style, to a height of around 7.5m (25 ft.) every 6 hours or so. Small crowds gather for eruptions usually at 5:30am, 11:30am, 5:30pm, and 11:30pm.

The Belle Epoque **Casino de Vals-Les-Bains** (© **04-75-88-77-77**), avenue Expilly, is open daily noon to 3am; admission is free. The only casino between Lyon and Aigues-Mortes, it's mobbed on weekends by locals playing roulette or the slot machines, the only options offered. The bistro-style theme restaurant, **Le Venetian,** is open nightly 7pm to midnight and Sunday noon to 3pm.

Other than the scenery, the town's most unusual site is about 23km (14 miles) south, beside the highway to Privas. The 16th-century entrance gate of a ruined feudal château stands here. The views over the confluence of two ravines and the valley are worth the detour.

WHERE TO STAY

Grand Hôtel des Bains This is the largest and best hotel in town. The central wing was built in 1860 in anticipation of a visit from Empress Eugénie. Alas, Eugénie, finding she was comfortable in the nearby resort of Vichy, canceled her visit. The hotel added two additional wings in 1870. It has a cordial staff and well-maintained, conservatively furnished rooms, most with both tub and shower.

3 montée de l'Hôtel-des-Bains, Vals-les-Bains 07600. © **04-75-37-42-13.** Fax 04-75-37-67-02. www.hotel-des-bains.com. 65 units. 69€–97€ ($90–$126) double; 128€–140€ ($166–$182) suite. AE, DC, MC, V. Closed Nov–Mar. **Amenities:** Restaurant; bar; outdoor pool; indoor pool; room service; laundry service; nonsmoking rooms; limited-mobility rooms. *In room:* TV, hair dryer.

WHERE TO DINE

Restaurant Mireille TRADITIONAL FRENCH This tiny (26-seat) restaurant occupies a space below vaulted stone ceilings that for centuries sheltered a herd of goats. Known for its earthy warmth, Mireille serves an ambitious menu of carefully crafted cuisine. Choices range from local mousse of flap mushrooms with scallops to filet of turbot with white butter.

3 rue Jean-Jaurès. © **04-75-37-49-06.** Reservations recommended. Fixed-price menus 13€–25€ ($17–$33). V. Thurs–Tues noon–2pm; Thurs–Mon 7–9pm. Daily in summer (same hours). Closed 2 weeks in Nov.

LAMASTRE

42km (26 miles) N of Vals-les-Bains, 30km (19 miles) W of Valence

Many connoisseurs of Ardèche architecture view Lamastre as the most unaltered and evocative village in the district. Its most important site is its church, in Macheville, the upper part of the village. Built of pink Romanesque stone, it encompasses portions that date from the 12th century, and it's a frequent site of weddings. Most visitors use the town as a base for nature walks and hikes through the surrounding hills and valleys. A series of brown-and-white signs marks each trail.

WHERE TO STAY & DINE

Château d'Urbilhac ★ Its history is rich and illustrious, and if you ask them, the congenial owners (Sylvie and Claude Aillaud) of this massive stone palace will recite dates, names, and conflicts that date back to France's wars of religion during the 16th century. For nearly 30 years, this high-altitude château and its 30 hectares (74 acres) of forest functioned as an upscale hotel with an equally upscale restaurant, but today, things have been scaled back to family-friendly proportions, and meals are available only to residents and their invited guests. One of the high points is the pool, an 80-foot-long watery rectangle that overlooks the valley of the River Doux, far below. Bedrooms are high-ceilinged, rather formal, and furnished with 19th- and early-20th-century antiques. The Aillaud family also rent two houses, one with one bedroom, the other with four, as part of long-term rentals, for families and groups of friends who want to spend a significant block of time within the region.

Lamastre 07270. © **04-75-06-42-11.** Fax 04-75-06-52-75. www.chateaudurbilhac.fr. 11 units. 130€–160€ ($169–$208) double. Rates include breakfast. Dinner 38€ ($49) extra per person. No credit cards. From the center of Lamastre, drive for 2km (1⅓ miles) southeast along Rte. de Vernoux-en-Vivarois. **Amenities:** Restaurant; bar; swimming pool; billiards table; tennis court; bicycle rental. Golf course within 25km (16 miles). *In room:* A/C, TV.

15

The French Alps

No part of France has more dramatic scenery than the Alps; the western ramparts of the mountains and their foothills are truly majestic. From the Mediterranean to the Rhine, they stretch along the southeastern flank of France. The skiing here is the best in Europe. Some resorts are legendary, such as **Chamonix–Mont Blanc,** the capital of Alpine skiing, with its 19km (12-mile) Vallée Blanche run. Mont Blanc, at 4,734m (15,531 ft.), is the highest mountain in western Europe.

Most of this chapter covers the area known as the Savoy (Savoie), taking in the French lake district and the largest Alpine lake, Lac Léman (Lake Geneva).

From January to March, skiers flock to Chamonix–Mont Blanc, Megève, Val d'Isère, and Courchevel 1850; from July to September, spa fans head to Evian-les-Bains and Aix-les-Bains. Grenoble, the capital of the French Alps, is the gateway. Grenoble lies 30 minutes by car from the Grenoble–St-Geoirs airport, 40 minutes from the Lyon-Satolas international airport, and 90 minutes from Geneva's Cointrin airport. The city is connected to the Paris-Lyon-Marseille motorway on the west and to the Chambéry-Geneva motorway on the east.

1 Evian-les-Bains ★★★

576km (358 miles) SW of Paris, 42km (26 miles) NE of Geneva

On the château-dotted southern shore of Lac Léman (Lake Geneva), Evian-les-Bains is one of the leading spa resorts in France. Its lakeside promenade, lined with trees and lawns, has been fashionable since the 19th century. Evian's waters became famous in the 18th century, and the first spa buildings were built in 1839. Bottled Evian is considered useful in everything from baby formula to salt-free diets and is seen as a treatment for gout and arthritis.

In the days when Marcel Proust came to enjoy the Belle Epoque grandeur, Evian was the haunt of the very rich. Proust modeled his "Balbec baths" on Evian's. Today, the spa, with its promenade and elegant casino, attracts a broader range of guests—it's not just for the rich anymore.

In addition to its **spa buildings,** Evian boasts an imposing **Ville des Congrès (Convention Hall)** that has earned the resort the title of "city of conventions." From late April to September, the **Nautical Center** (© **04-50-92-08-40**) on the lake is a popular attraction; it has a 115m (377-ft.) pool with a diving stage, solarium, restaurant, bar, and children's paddling pool.

The major excursion from Evian is a boat trip on Lake Geneva offered by the **Compagnie Générale de Navigation (CGN),** a Swiss outfit whose agent in Evian is the Office du Baigneur, place du Port (© **04-50-75-27-53**). A round-trip ticket from

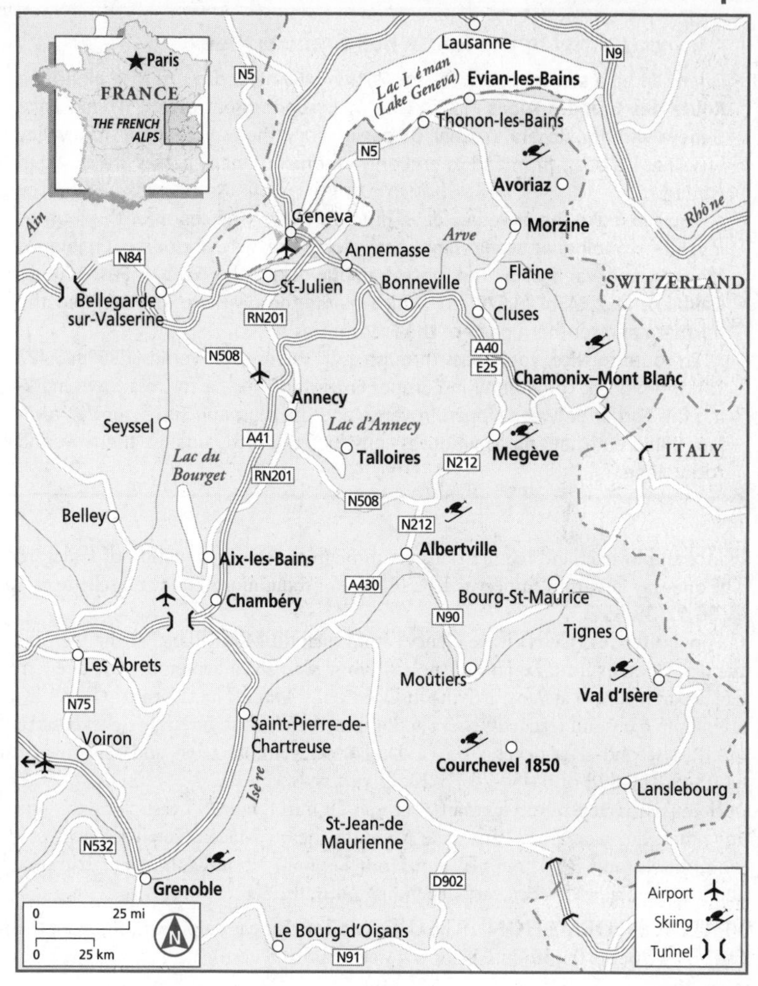

Evian to Lausanne in Switzerland costs 19€ ($25). Contact the company or head for the Office de Tourisme (see below) for other prices and hours. In summer, it also offers night cruises. If you want to see it all, you can tour both the Haut-Lac and the Grand-Lac. The most popular trip is the crossing from Evian to Ouchy-Lausanne, Switzerland (the port for Lausanne), on the north side.

Crescent-shaped **Lake Geneva (Lac Léman)** is the largest lake in central Europe. Covering about 362 sq. km (140 sq. miles), the lake is formed by the Rhône River and is noted for its exceptional blue color.

ESSENTIALS

GETTING THERE The best way to approach Evian-les-Bains by **train** from the French Alps is through the gateway city of Annecy. (Many trains from other parts of

Moments Driving the Route des Grandes Alpes

Evian can be a starting point for the 741km (460-mile) drive to Nice along the **Route des Grandes Alpes** ★★★. One of Europe's great drives, it links Lake Geneva with the Riviera, crossing 35 passes along the way. Leaping from valley to valley, it's open from end to end only in summer (many passes are closed in winter).

You can make the drive in 2 days, but why hurry? The charm of this journey involves stopping at scenic highlights along the way, including Chamonix, Megève, and Val d'Isère. The most dramatic pass is the **Galibier Pass (Col du Galibier)**, at 2,645m (8,678 ft.), which marks the dividing line between the northern and southern parts of the French Alps.

En route to Nice, you'll pass through such towns as St-Veran (1,959m/6,427 ft.), the highest community in Europe; Entrevaux, once a fortress town marking the border between Upper Provence and the Alps; and Touet-sur-Var, a village filled with tall, narrow houses constructed directly against the towering rocky slope.

France and Switzerland require transfers through the railway junction of Bellegarde.) The one-way fare from Annecy is 14€ ($18). For train information and schedules, call ✆ **08-92-35-35-35.**

Popular **ferries (CGN)** leave Geneva from quai du Mont-Blanc, at the foot of the rue des Alpes, or from Le Jardin Anglais. From May 28 to September 21, one ferry a day departs Geneva at 9am, arriving in Evian at 11:45am. The return trip leaves Evian at 5:50pm daily and reaches Geneva at 8:45pm. A first-class, one-way ticket costs 33€ ($43), a second-class ticket 24€ ($31). For ferry information and schedules, call ✆ **0848/811-848** or 04-50-70-73-20, or visit www.cgn.ch.

If you're **driving** from Geneva (trip time: 50 min.), take N5 east along the southern rim of the lake. From Paris, take A6 south. Before Mâcon, you'll see signs pointing to the turnoff for Thonon-Evian. From Thonon, N5 leads to Evian. Trip time is about 5½ hours, which can vary depending on traffic.

VISITOR INFORMATION The **Office de Tourisme** is on place d'Allinges (✆ **04-50-75-04-26;** fax 04-50-75-61-08; www.eviantourism.com).

TAKING THE WATERS AT EVIAN

The clear, cold waters at Evian, legendary for their health and beauty benefits, attract a clientele that possesses both the time and the money to appreciate them.

The most luxurious way to immerse yourself in the resort's hydro-rituals is to check into either of these hotels, both of which maintain private spa facilities open only to well-heeled guests: **Hotel Royal,** boulevard de Royal, or **Hotel Ermitage,** avenue du Léman (contact for both ✆ **04-50-26-85-00;** www.royalparcevian.com). They offer the most expensive packages and are adept at pampering patrons' bodies, souls, and egos.

More reasonably priced are the spa facilities at **Les Thermes de Evian,** place de la Libération (✆ **04-50-75-02-30;** www.lesthermesevian.com). This public spa is adjacent to Débarcadère (the dock), just uphill from the edge of the lake. The hotel spas are more likely to emphasize beauty regimes and stress therapies; the public facility offers a broader range of services, including tanning, massage, and skin and beauty care (but no facilities for overnight guests).

You can indulge yourself with a daylong *thermale,* which provides access to exercise rooms and classes, saunas, steam baths, water from the Evian springs, and two massage sessions. Depending on the program you select, you will spend 45€ to 165€ ($59–$215). You can also spend up to 130€ ($169) extra per day on additional massage, health, and beauty regimes. The spa is open Monday to Saturday usually from 9am to 1:30pm and 2:30 to 6:30pm.

WHERE TO STAY

The **Hôtel-Restaurant Le Bourgogne** (see "Where to Dine," below) also rents rooms.

Hôtel de la Verniaz et ses Chalets ★★★ This glamorous country house, owned by the Verdier family, stands on a hillside with a view of woods, water, and the Alps. The well-furnished rooms are in either the main house or one of the separate chalets; the chalets have their own gardens and more privacy but cost a small fortune. Throughout the hotel, you'll find comfortable, even plush, accommodations. Each unit comes with a luxurious bathroom with combination tub/shower. Main courses in the hotel restaurant run from 19€ to 30€ ($25–$39); fixed-price menus, 38€ to 70€ ($49–$91).

Avenue D'Abondance, à Neuvecelle Eglise, Evian-les-Bains 74500. ✆ **800/735-2478** in the U.S. and Canada, or 04-50-75-04-90. Fax 04-50-70-78-92. www.verniaz.com. 35 units. 102€–275€ ($133–$358) double; 255€–340€ ($332–$442) suite; 280€–590€ ($364–$767) chalet. AE, DC, MC, V. Closed mid-Nov to mid-Feb. **Amenities:** Restaurant; bar; outdoor pool; 2 tennis courts; room service; babysitting; laundry service; dry cleaning; nonsmoking rooms. *In room:* TV, minibar, hair dryer, iron, safe.

WHERE TO DINE

Hôtel-Restaurant Le Bourgogne ★ TRADITIONAL FRENCH Come here for a delectable meal, impeccable service, an attractive setting, and excellent wine. Featured regional wines are Crépy and Rousette. Menu choices in the restaurant are likely to include the house version of foie gras, beef served with morels or a peppercorn sauce, and a poached version of *omble chevalier* (tiny local whitefish) with whiskey sauce. You'll also find robust portions of cassoulet, terrines of oxtail or salmon, magrets of duckling with orange, and steaks.

The inn also offers 30 comfortable rooms with TVs for 71€ to 98€ ($92–$127) double.

Place Charles-Cottet, Evian-les-Bains 74500. ✆ **04-50-75-01-05.** Reservations required. Main courses 19€–25€ ($25–$33); fixed-price menu 12€–46€ ($16–$60). AE, DC, MC, V. Tues–Sun noon–2pm; Tues–Sat 7–10pm. Closed Jan.

EVIAN-LES-BAINS AFTER DARK

In the town center on the south bank of Lake Geneva is the **Casino Royal Evian,** domaine du Royal Club Evian (✆ **04-50-26-87-87**). It's popular with the Swiss from across the lake. It offers blackjack, baccarat, and roulette and has more than 250 slot, roller, and video-poker machines. Jackets for men are preferred. The Jackpot Restaurant and Bar is open until the casino closes.

2 Annecy ★★★

538km (334 miles) SE of Paris, 56km (35 miles) SE of Geneva, 140km (87 miles) E of Lyon

Lac d'Annecy is the jewel of the Savoy Alps. The resort of Annecy, which is the region's capital, makes the best base for touring the Haute-Savoie. Once a Gallo-Roman town, the seat of the *comtes* de Genève, Annecy opens onto one of the best views of lakes and mountains in the French Alps. Since the 1980s, Annecy has become a booming urban center that has managed to preserve its natural setting. In summer, its lakefront promenade is crowded and active.

ESSENTIALS

GETTING THERE If you're **driving,** Annecy is near several highways: From Paris, take A6 southeast to Beaune and connect with A6/N6 south to Mâcon-Nord. Then follow A40 southeast to Seyssel, connecting with N508 going southeast to Annecy. Allow at least 5 hours. From Geneva, follow A40W to St. Julien and take RN201 south toward Annecy. Trip time is 30 minutes.

A car is useful but not essential in the Alps. Annecy has **train** and **bus** service from Geneva, Grenoble, Lyon, and Paris. Nine trains per day arrive from Grenoble (trip time: 2 hr.); the one-way fare is 17€ ($22). About six trains daily arrive from Paris's Gare de Lyon (trip time: 3 hr., 40 min.); the fare is 65€ to 90€ ($85–$117) one-way. For information, call ✆ **08-92-35-35-35.**

There's also a nearby **airport** (✆ **04-50-27-30-06**) in the hamlet of Meythet, with service on Air France from Paris's Orly airport.

VISITOR INFORMATION The **Office de Tourisme** is at 1 rue Jean-Jaurès (✆ **04-50-45-00-33;** fax 04-50-51-87-20; www.lac-annecy.com).

SEEING THE SIGHTS

Built around the river Thiou, Annecy has been called the Venice of the Alps because of the canals that cut through the old part of town, **Vieil Annecy.** You can explore the arcaded streets where Jean-Jacques Rousseau arrived in 1728.

After seeing Annecy, consider a trek to the **Gorges du Fier** ★★ (✆ **04-50-46-23-07;** www.gorgesdufier.com), a dramatic river gorge 9.5km (6 miles) to the west. To reach it, take a train or bus from Annecy's rail station to Poisy. From the station, go about 1.5km (1 mile), following the clearly marked signs. This striking gorge is one of the most interesting sights in the French Alps. A gangway takes you through a gully 3 to 10m (10–33 ft.) wide, cut through the rock by torrents of water; you'll hear the roar of the river at the bottom. Emerging from this labyrinth, you'll be greeted by a huge expanse of boulders. You can visit the gorge from June 15 to September 10, daily 9am to 7pm (last trip at 6:20pm); and from March 15 to June 14 and September 11 to October 15, daily 9am to noon and 2 to 6pm (last trip at 5:20pm). The site is closed to the public October 16 to March 14. A hike through its well-signposted depths takes less than an hour and costs 4.70€ ($6.10) for adults, 2.60€ ($3.40) for children; it's free for kids under 7.

You can also take a cruise on the ice-blue lake for which the town is famous. Tours of **Lac d'Annecy,** offered from Easter to late October, last an hour and cost 11€ ($14). An English-speaking guide points out the sights. Tours depart between one and six times a day, depending on the season. Inquire at the Office de Tourisme (see above), or call the **Compagnie des Bateaux du Lac d'Annecy** (✆ **04-50-51-08-40**).

Château de Montrottier Within walking distance of the gorges, in the hamlet of Montrottier, is the 13th- and 14th-century Château de Montrottier. A one-time feudal citadel partially protected by the rugged geology around it, the château's tower offers a panoramic view of Mont Blanc. A small museum, collected by a local dilettante, showcases pottery, Asian and African costumes, armor, tapestries, and lace antiques, as well as some bronze bas-reliefs from the 16th century.

Kids The Lure of the Hills

The Office de Tourisme (see above) distributes free pamphlets that describe about a dozen easy, family-oriented hiking and biking excursions in the forests around Annecy. More experienced hikers may wish to pick up a free map with a detailed set of challenging walks.

Walks in both categories last 2 to 6 hours. Some begin in the center of Annecy; others require a trip by car or bus from one of several towns in the area—such as Saint-Jorioz or Sevrier, to the west, or Talloires, to the east—to the excursion's origination point. A travel agency in Annecy, **Agence Crolard,** place de la Gare (✆ **04-50-45-08-12**), sells bus tickets to the destinations around Annecy and Lac d'Annecy and Lac Léman. It also arranges excursions by minibus to sites of panoramic interest in July and August.

Lovagny 74330. ✆ **04-50-46-23-02.** www.chateaudemontrottier.com. Admission 7€ ($9.10) adults, 6.20€ ($8.05) students, 4.50€ ($5.85) children 7–15, free for children under 7. Mar 15–May 31 Wed–Mon 2–6pm; June–Aug daily 2–7pm; Sept Wed–Mon 2–6pm; Oct daily 2–6pm. Closed Nov–Mar 14.

Le Palais de l'Ile This is the town's most potent and most frequently photographed visual symbol. Built prior to the 18th century and connected to the "mainland" of Annecy via a bridge, it resembles a miniature château, surrounded by water, despite its long-term use as a prison (and certainly a very cold one) for local malefactors.

3 passage de l'Ile. ✆ **04-50-33-87-30.** Admission 3.30€ ($4.30) adults, 1€ ($1.30) students and persons 12–25, free for children under 12. June–Sept daily 10:30am–6pm; Oct–May Wed–Mon 10am–noon and 2–5pm.

Musée Château d'Annecy This forbidding gray-stone monument, whose 12th-century pinnacle is known as the Queen's Tower, dominates the resort. The château contains a museum of regional artifacts that include alpine furniture, religious art, oil paintings, and modern works. One section is devoted to the geology and marine life of the region's deep, cold lakes.

Place du Château. ✆ **04-50-33-87-30.** Admission 4.80€ ($6.25) adults, 1.80€ ($2.35) ages 12–25, free for children under 12. June–Sept daily 10:30am–6pm; Oct–May Wed–Mon 10am–noon and 2–5pm.

WHERE TO STAY

La Maison de Marc Veyrat (see "Where to Dine," below) also rents rooms.

Au Faisan Doré *Kids* Near the casino at the end of a tree-lined lakefront boulevard, this government-rated three-star hotel is 2 minutes on foot from the lake and Imperial Park. Owned by the Clavel family since 1919, it's a member of the Logis de France chain, which caters to families. The public and private rooms are decorated in the style of the Haute-Savoie region—wooden overhead beams, rustic country furniture, and unpainted wood walls. Each guest room is cozy and comfortable but not extravagant. Half of the units contain combination tub/showers. The chef serves three different fixed-price menus in the adjacent restaurant.

34 av. d'Albigny, Annecy 74000. ✆ **04-50-23-02-46.** Fax 04-50-23-11-10. www.hotel-aufaisandore.com. 40 units. 68€–95€ ($88–$124) double. AE, DC, MC, V. Parking 10€ ($13). Closed Dec 20–Feb 1. **Amenities:** Restaurant; bar. *In room:* TV.

Hôtel du Nord *Value* A government-rated two-star hotel in the center of Annecy, minutes from the train station and Lac d'Annecy, the continually renovated du Nord is one of the town's better bargains. You'll appreciate the modernity of the soundproof rooms; 20 come with showers only, others with tub and shower. The helpful staff speaks English and can direct you to reasonably priced restaurants nearby. Breakfast is the only meal served.

24 rue Sommeiller, Annecy 74000. ✆ **04-50-45-08-78.** Fax 04-50-51-22-04. www.annecy-hotel-du-nord.com. 30 units. 51€–64€ ($66–$83) double. AE, MC, V. *In room:* A/C, TV, dataport.

Hôtel La Demeure de Chavoire ★★ One of the most charming accommodations in the area is at Chavoires, about 3km (1¾ miles) east of Annecy. It's intimate and cozy, decorated with well-chosen Savoy antiques. Large doors lead to the gardens overlooking the lake. The guest rooms have names rather than numbers, and each is uniquely decorated with wood beams. Bathrooms are small but efficient, with shower and tub. Thoughtful service makes this a deserving selection, and it's more tranquil than the hotels in the center of Annecy. The staff will direct you to nearby restaurants.

71 rte. d'Annecy, Veyrier-du-Lac 74290. ✆ **04-50-60-04-38.** Fax 04-50-60-05-36. www.demeuredechavoire.com. 13 units. 145€–195€ ($189–$254) double; 225€–275€ ($293–$358) suite. AE, DC, MC, V. From Annecy, follow signs to Chavoires and Talloires. **Amenities:** Bar; tearoom; spa; room service; babysitting; laundry service; dry cleaning. *In room:* TV, minibar, hair dryer, safe, Wi-Fi.

WHERE TO DINE

La Maison de Marc Veyrat ★★★ MODERN FRENCH Famous throughout France for owner Marc Veyrat-Durebex's excellent and unusual cuisine, this world-class and horrendously priced restaurant occupies a romanticized version of a Savoyard château at the edge of a lake in the village of Veyrier-du-Lac, 1.5km (1 mile) south of Annecy. Guests dine in a posh room with ceiling frescoes.

The chef has been dubbed *l'enfant terrible* of upscale Alpine cuisine. He offers a unique dining experience, marked by an almost ritualistic etiquette. Fortunately, the waitstaff advises you on the order in which the meal and its components are designed to be eaten. For example, a "declination of local cheeses," consisting of three large ravioli, each stuffed with a different cheese—a mild cow cheese, a pungent goat cheese, and a very strong blue—is eaten in ascending order of strength. Other choices include ravioli of vegetables, flavored with rare mountain herbs gathered by M. Veyrat-Durebex and his team; pikeperch sausage; crayfish poached with bitter almonds; and poached sea bass with caviar. Desserts include a miniature chestnut cake served with essence of truffles. The wine list is excellent.

The *auberge* rents 11 expensive and beautifully furnished rooms. Rates are 300€ to 670€ ($390–$871) for a double; a suite costs from 695€ to 880€ ($904–$1,144).

13 vieille rte. des Pensières, Veyrier-du-Lac 74290. From Annecy's lakefront boulevard, follow signs to Veyrier-du-Lac, Chavoires, and Talloires. ✆ **04-50-60-24-00.** Fax 04-50-60-23-63. www.marcveyrat.fr. Reservations required. Main courses 75€–120€ ($98–$156); fixed-price dinner 295€–385€ ($384–$501). AE, DC, MC, V. Sat–Sun noon–1:30pm; Wed–Sun 7:30–9pm. Closed Nov to mid-May.

Le Belvédère FRENCH/SEAFOOD This is one of the most appealing reasonably priced restaurants in town. On a belvedere above Annecy, about 1.5km (1 mile) west of the town center, it provides views that extend up to 8km (5 miles) over mountains and lakes. Menu items include a salad of Breton lobster with freshwater crayfish and strips of foie gras, a platter containing scallops and red mullet with shellfish-flavored butter sauce, and an unusual "duet" of foie gras with a purée of figs and vanilla-flavored bourbon sauce. Dessert may be a "trilogy" of tropical-flavored sorbets.

The 10 simple guest rooms are much less opulent than the restaurant. Rooms go for 75€ to 143€ ($98–$186) double.

7 chemin du Belvédère, Annecy 7400. From downtown Annecy, follow signs leading uphill to Le Semnoz. ✆ **04-50-45-04-90.** www.belvedere-annecy.com. Reservations recommended. Main courses 16€–45€ ($21–$59); fixed-price menu 25€–70€ ($33–$91). AE, MC, V. Thurs–Tues 12:15–1:30pm; Mon and Thurs–Sat 7:30–9:30pm. Closed Jan.

Le Clos des Sens ★★ FRENCH/SAVOYARD The charm of this restaurant derives from its inspired cuisine, based on local ingredients, and its decor, salvaged from several Savoyard chalets. At street level is a contemporary-looking bar; in the upstairs dining room, the food is elaborate, savory, and geared to the cold-weather climate. The best examples include consommé of shrimp studded with chunks of firm crayfish meat; filets of fera (a Lac d'Annecy fish) that are partially smoked, partially marinated; spit-roasted suckling pig served with polenta; and a dessert specialty of caramelized fennel served with tarragon-flavored ice cream. The establishment maintains a quartet of comfortable, cozy bedrooms, each with cable TV, a safe, and minibar (but oddly, no phone), priced from 150€ to 200€ ($195–$260).

13 rue Jean-Mermoz, Annecy-le-Vieux. ✆ **04-50-23-07-90.** www.closdessens.com. Reservations recommended. Main courses 29€–40€ ($38–$52); fixed-price lunch Wed–Fri 29€ ($38); fixed-price dinner 45€–90€ ($59–$117). AE, DC, MC, V. Wed–Sun noon–1:30pm; Tues–Sat 7:30–9:30pm. Closed Jan 1–15, May 1–8, and Sept 1–15.

ANNECY AFTER DARK

In the old town, you'll find bars, cafes, pubs, and (in warmer months) street dances, fairs, and even carnivals. A calmer alternative is an evening of theater or dance at the **Théâtre d'Annecy,** 1 rue Jean-Jaurès (✆ **04-50-33-44-00;** www.bonlieu-annecy.com); tickets cost 15€ to 25€ ($20–$33).

If a long day has left you thirsty, try the traditional Irish pub, **Le Captain Pub,** 11 rue Pont-Morens (✆ **04-50-45-79-80**), with hearty ales on tap. **Le Vieux Necy,** 3 rue Filaterie (✆ **04-50-45-01-57**), attracts a younger, more boisterous crowd.

The best piano bar in town is **Le Duo,** 104 av. de Genève (✆ **04-50-57-01-46**). It's ideal for quiet conversation. Annecy's most visible and popular gay bars are the **Comedy Café and Night Bar,** 13 rue Royale, Galerie des Sorbiers (✆ **04-50-52-82-83**), and the **Happy People Disco,** 48 rue Carnot (✆ **04-50-51-08-66**), where both locals and visitors dance the night away.

For the most elegant evening on the town, head to the **Casino de l'Impérial,** 33 av. d'Albigny (✆ **04-50-09-30-00**), part of the Belle Epoque–style Impérial Palace hotel on a peninsula jutting into Lac d'Annecy. Entrance to the gaming rooms is free; you must present a passport. The casino is open daily noon to 2am (until 4am Sat).

3 Talloires ★★

551km (342 miles) SE of Paris, 32km (20 miles) N of Albertville, 13km (8 miles) S of Annecy

The charming village of Talloires, which dates to 866, is old enough to appear on lists of territories once controlled by Lothar II, great-grandson of Charlemagne. Chalk cliffs surround a bay, and at the lower end a promontory encloses a port. An 18-hole golf course, **Golf Club du Lac d'Annecy** (✆ **04-50-60-12-89;** www.golf-lacannecy.com), and watersports such as boating, swimming, water-skiing, and fishing make this a favorite vacation spot. Talloires also boasts one of France's great restaurants, Auberge du Père-Bise, and a Benedictine abbey founded in the 11th century, now the deluxe Hôtel de l'Abbaye.

ESSENTIALS

GETTING THERE From Annecy, you can reach Talloires by **driving** south along N508 for 13km (8 miles). There are about eight daily **buses** from Annecy to Talloires, which take 35 minutes. In Talloires, buses stop in front of the post office. For bus information, call in Annecy (✆ **04-50-45-73-90**).

VISITOR INFORMATION The **Office de Tourisme** is on rue André-Theuriet (✆ **04-50-60-70-64;** fax 04-50-60-76-59; www.talloires.fr).

WHERE TO STAY

Auberge du Père-Bise and **La Villa des Fleurs** (see "Where to Dine," below) also rent rooms.

Hôtel de l'Abbaye ★★ This 16th-century Benedictine monastery has been a hotel since the French Revolution. It's one of the grand inns of the Alps. With close-up views of the lake, it makes for a memorable stop. It doesn't equal the cuisine or the luxury of the Auberge du Père-Bise (see below), but then again, it's a lot more affordable. The hotel is rich with beamed ceilings, antique portraits, leather chairs, gardens, and carved balustrades. The great corridors lead to converted guest rooms, of which no two are alike. The furnishings include all the Louis periods as well as Directoire and Empire. In 2004, the hotel was thoroughly renovated. All units contain showers, and several have tubs as well. In summer, the restaurant expands onto a shaded lakefront terrace. Overall, this is an extremely pleasant escape from urban life.

Chemin des Moins, Talloires 74290. ✆ **04-50-60-77-33.** Fax 04-50-60-78-81. www.abbaye-talloires.com. 33 units. 110€–300€ ($143–$390) double; 320€–580€ ($416–$754) suite. AE, DC, MC, V. Closed Nov 17 to mid-Feb. **Amenities:** Restaurant; bar; spa; sauna; room service; babysitting; laundry service; dry cleaning. *In room:* TV, minibar, safe.

WHERE TO DINE

Auberge du Père-Bise ★★★ FRENCH Since the 1950s, when it attracted starlets and millionaires (when being a millionaire actually meant something), Auberge du Père-Bise has radiated style and charm. A chalet built in 1901 and renovated many times since, it's one of France's most acclaimed—and expensive—restaurants. In fair weather you can dine under a vine-covered pergola and enjoy the view of mountains and the lake. The kitchen excels at dishes such as mousse of foie gras, layered potatoes with truffles and foie gras, delicate young lamb, and gratin of crayfish tails.

The inn also offers 34 guest rooms with minibars and TV. Rates are 300€ to 400€ ($390–$520) for a double and 580€ ($754) for a suite. Reserve at least 2 months in advance, especially in summer.

Rte. du Port, bord du Lac, Talloires 74290. ✆ **04-50-60-72-01.** Fax 04-50-60-73-05. www.perebise.com. Reservations required. Main courses 30€–95€ ($39–$124); fixed-price menu 80€–170€ ($104–$221). AE, DC, MC, V. Daily noon–2pm and 7–9pm. Closed mid-Nov to mid-Feb.

La Villa des Fleurs *Value* TRADITIONAL FRENCH This *restaurant avec chambres* should be better known, because it's the best place in Talloires for the price. Proprietors Marie-France and Charles Jaegler serve wonderful meals, which often include *salade landaise* with foie gras, and filet of fera (a Lac d'Annecy fish) with sage sauce. The dining room overlooks the water.

Eight simply furnished rooms with minibars and Victorian-era decor are at the top of a winding staircase—there's no elevator. Doubles cost 94€ to 130€ ($122–$169).

Rte. du Port, Talloires 74290. ✆ **04-50-60-71-14.** Fax 04-50-60-74-06. www.hotel-lavilladesfleurs74.com. Reservations required. Main courses 25€–32€ ($33–$42); fixed-price menu 30€–42€ ($39–$55). AE, MC, V. Tues–Sun noon–2pm; Tues–Sat 7–9pm. Closed Nov 29–Feb 6.

4 Aix-les-Bains ★★★

535km (332 miles) SE of Paris, 34km (21 miles) SW of Annecy, 16km (10 miles) N of Chambéry

On the eastern edge of Lac du Bourget, modern Aix-les-Bains is the most fashionable (and largest) spa in eastern France. The hot springs, which offered comfort to the Romans, are said to be useful for treating rheumatism.

ESSENTIALS

GETTING THERE Some 20 **trains** per day arrive from Paris (trip time: 3 hr.); the one-way fare is 69€ to 86€ ($90–$112). Ten daily trains pull in from Annecy (trip time: 30 min.; one-way fare: 6.60€–8.40€/$8.60–$11). For information and schedules, call ✆ **08-92-35-35-35.** For information on **bus** routes in and around the French Alps, including the status of service from Nice to Aix, call the Gare Routière in Chambéry (✆ **04-79-69-11-88**). If you're **driving** to Aix-les-Bains from Annecy, follow RN 201 south.

VISITOR INFORMATION The **Office de Tourisme** is on place Maurice-Mollard (✆ **04-79-88-68-00;** fax 04-79-88-68-01; www.aixlesbains.com).

SEEING THE SIGHTS

Aix is well equipped for visitors, with flower gardens, a casino (the Palais de Savoie), a racecourse, a golf course, and Lac du Bourget, which has a beach. **Thermes d'Aix-les-Bains** (✆ **04-79-35-38-50;** www.thermaix.com) lies in the center of town, near the casino, the Temple of Diana, and the Hôtel de Ville (town hall). Closer to the lake, a string of flower beds and ornamental shrubs border the town's waterside promenades, where you can take a lovely stroll.

Steamboats take visitors on a beautiful 4-hour **boat ride** on Lac du Bourget. The trip travels most of the length of the Canal de Savière (which links the lake with the Rhône) between early February and mid-December, daily or four times a week, depending on the season. Prices for boat rides range from 30€ to 55€ ($39–$72). For departure times, which change almost weekly throughout the season, contact the ferry operator, **Les Bateaux d'Aix** (✆ **04-79-63-45-00**). Boats depart from the piers of Grand Port, 3km (1¾ miles) northwest of the center. You can also take a bus ride from Aix to the town of **Revard,** at 1,524m (5,000 ft.), which affords a panoramic view of Mont Blanc. For information, contact **Trans Savoie** (✆ **04-79-68-32-90**).

Abbaye d'Hautecombe ★★ This is the spiritual centerpiece of the French Alps and the mausoleum of many princes of the House of Savoy. It was built by a succession of monks, beginning in the 1100s, from the Cîteaux, Cistercian, and Benedictine orders. The abbey stands on a promontory over the western edge of Lac du Bourget, almost directly across the water from Aix-les-Bains. Before the 1500s, at least 40 members of the royal family of the Savoy were buried here.

After years of neglect, the church was reconstructed and embellished during the 19th century by Charles-Felix, king of Sardinia, in the Troubadour Gothic style. The fervently religious ecumenical community (Communaute du Chemin Neuf) occupying the abbey organizes seminars, welcomes short- and medium-term devotees, and perpetuates the site's tradition of worship. Pilgrims are welcome to attend daily Mass at noon.

Self-guided half-hour tours with recorded narration, in English and French, depart at 6-minute intervals during open hours. You can drive to the abbey or take a 30-minute boat ride. Four steamers per day leave the landing stage at Aix-les-Bains; the round-trip fare is 12€ ($16) for adults and 8€ ($10) for children under 12.

St-Pierre de Curtille 73310. ✆ **04-79-54-58-80.** Tours cost 3€ ($3.90). Free ages 17 and under. Wed–Mon 10–11:30am and 2–5pm.

Musée Faure This is the town's most interesting museum, with a modern-art collection that includes sculptures by Rodin and works by Degas, Corot, and Cézanne. It's on a hill overlooking the lake and the town.

10 bd. des Côtes. ✆ **04-79-61-06-57.** Admission 4.40€ ($5.70), free for children under 16. Wed–Mon 10am–noon and 1:30–6pm.

WHERE TO STAY

Hostellerie Le Manoir ★ This architecturally interesting site—a 19th-century stable until the present owners transformed it into a hotel—includes paths weaving through turn-of-the-20th-century gardens with outdoor furniture under shade trees. The decor in the midsize-to-spacious guest rooms is old-fashioned—with antique and provincial furniture—yet up-to-date, each different from its neighbors. Bathrooms come with tub/shower combinations. The government rates the Ariana (see below) higher because of its superior facilities, but the Manoir has more French charm and personality. You can order breakfast or dinner on a terrace bordering the garden. Most of the public and guest rooms open onto terraces.

37 rue Georges-1er, Aix-les-Bains 73105. ✆ **04-79-61-44-00.** Fax 04-79-35-67-67. www.hotel-lemanoir.com. 73 units. 94€–164€ ($122–$213) double; 174€ ($226) suite. AE, DC, MC, V. Parking 8.50€ ($11). **Amenities:** Restaurant; bar; indoor pool; fitness center; sauna; limited room service. *In room:* TV, hair dryer, safe, Wi-Fi.

Hôtel Mercure Ariana ★★ The Ariana caters to a spa-oriented crowd that enjoys quiet walks in the surrounding park. The loggia-dotted glass exterior opens into an Art Deco interior highlighted by metal, wood, and fabrics; plenty of white marble; and antique reproductions. Tunnel-like glass walkways connect the hotel's sports facilities to its main core. The guest rooms, renovated during 2004 and 2005, come in a range of sizes and styles, each comfortable and well appointed. Most have good-size bathrooms with tub/shower combination. Café Adelaïde is both a cafe and a restaurant.

111 av. de Marlioz, à Marlioz, Aix-les-Bains 73101. ✆ **04-79-61-79-79.** Fax 04-79-61-79-00. www.mercure.com. 60 units. 98€–142€ ($127–$185) double. AE, DC, MC, V. **Amenities:** Restaurant; bar; indoor pool; 2 nearby tennis courts; health club; sauna; bike rentals; room service; babysitting; laundry service. *In room:* A/C, TV, minibar, hair dryer, Wi-Fi.

WHERE TO DINE

Brasserie de la Poste FRENCH Since the mid-1960s, from a position in the heart of town, immediately across from the railway station and the post office, this cozy brasserie has served bountiful, cost-conscious meals to office workers, day laborers, and commuters. The interior is outfitted in tones of dark bordeaux and dark hardwood paneling, waiters are attentive and hardworking, and food is doled out in generous portions. Long-standing specialties include *choucroute,* slabs of buttery foie gras, cheese-laden *fondues Savoyardes,* frogs' legs in garlic butter, pepper steaks with french fries, and sautéed crayfish.

32 av. Victoria. ✆ **04-79-35-00-65.** Reservations not required. Fixed-price menus 12€–28€ ($16–$36); main courses 8€–20€ ($10–$26). AE, DC, MC, V. Tues–Sun noon–2:30pm; Tues–Sat 7–10pm.

Restaurant du Casino Grand Cercle FRENCH No other setting in Aix-les-Bains provides as rich an environment as this Beaux Arts restaurant in the town casino. For a taste of glamour and glitter in a beautiful place, it's one of the most enjoyable experiences in town. The restaurant occupies a corner of the area reserved for blackjack and roulette, giving diners a close-up view of the gamblers testing their luck. The food is not elaborate; the menu offers conservative but flavorful dishes of veal, beef, and chicken, with a scattering of terrines, soups, and salads. A passport is required for visitors to enter the casino. The slots are open daily 11am to 3am (until 4am Fri–Sat); the gaming rooms are open Tuesday to Thursday 8pm to 3am (until 4am Fri–Sat).

Rue du Casino. ✆ **04-79-35-16-16.** Reservations recommended. Fixed-price menu 28€ ($36). AE, DC, MC, V. Daily 8–11pm.

5 Grenoble ★★★

567km (352 miles) SE of Paris, 55km (34 miles) S of Chambéry, 103km (64 miles) SE of Lyon

The ancient capital of the Dauphine, Grenoble is the commercial, intellectual, and tourist center of the Alps. It's a major stop for travelers, including those driving between the Riviera and Geneva.

A sports capital in winter (and host of the 1968 Winter Olympic Games) and summer, it attracts many foreign students—its university has the largest summer-session program in Europe. Founded in 1339, the University of Grenoble has a student body of some 50,000. The city (pop. 405,000) is also home to four other universities with a large contingent of English and American students, giving the city a cosmopolitan air.

ESSENTIALS

GETTING THERE An important rail and bus junction, Grenoble is easily accessible from Paris and all the cities in this chapter. About 11 **trains** per day arrive from Paris Gare de Lyon (trip time: 3½ hr.); the one-way fare is 68€ to 89€ ($88–$116). Trains arrive almost every hour from Chambéry (trip time: 30 min.; one-way fare is 9.70€/$13). For information, call ✆ **08-92-35-35-35.**

Until 2004, Grenoble's airport accepted Air France flights from Paris and the rest of Europe. But when Air France transferred all of its inbound flights to nearby Lyon, air traffic to the airport in Grenoble virtually dried up. Flights arrive to Grenoble from London and Bristol (England). **EasyJet** and **British Airways** fly only September to April, but **Ryan Air** also flies in summer. For more information contact the center at Grenoble's **Aéroport Grenoble-Isère** (✆ **04-76-65-48-48**), 41km (25 miles) northwest of the city center. A shuttle bus meets every flight and takes passengers to and from Grenoble's center; the cost is 4€ ($5.20) each way. A taxi (✆ **04-76-65-46-18**) to the town center costs 70€ to 100€ ($91–$130).

For information on flying into Lyon, see chapter 14. **Satobus** (✆ **04-72-68-72-17**) meets most flights at the Lyon airport and takes passengers to Grenoble. Travel time is an hour; the fare is 20€ ($26) each way, 15€ ($20) students, and 10€ ($13) ages 4 to 12.

If you're **driving,** take A6 from Paris to Lyon, and then continue on A48 into Grenoble. Depending on conditions, the drive should take 6 to 7 hours.

VISITOR INFORMATION The **Office de Tourisme** is at 14 rue de la République (✆ **04-76-42-41-41;** fax 04-76-00-18-98; www.grenoble-isere-tourisme.com). For information about public transportation in Grenoble, call ✆ **08-20-48-60-00.**

SEEING THE SIGHTS

Grenoble lies near the junction of the Isère and Drac rivers. Most of the city is on the south bank of the Isère, though its most impressive monument, the **Fort de la Bastille,** stands on a rocky hilltop on the north bank. A cable car will carry you from the south bank across the river to the top of the fort. The center of Grenoble's historic section is the **Palais de Justice** and **place St-André.** The more modern part of town is southeast, centered on the contemporary **Hôtel de Ville** (town hall) and the nearby **Tour Perret.**

Begin at **place Grenette,** where you can enjoy a drink or an espresso at a cafe. Don't miss the **place aux Herbes** and the **place St-André,** in the very heart of the *centre ville.* Place St-André, dating from the Middle Ages, is the most evocative square in old Grenoble, with the Palais de Justice on one side and the Eglise St-André on the other. The Palace of Justice was built in many stages. The brick church went up in the 13th century. Two great streets for strolling and browsing are rue de la Poste, in the medieval core, and rue J.-J.-Rousseau, a 5-minute walk southwest of the city.

Enjoy a ride on the **Téléphérique-Grenoble-Bastille** (**© 04-76-44-33-65**), cable cars that take you over the banks of the Isère River and its valley. The cable car operates according to the following schedule: March Monday and Tuesday 11am to 7pm, Wednesday to Friday 9:30am to 7pm, Saturday and Sunday 9:30am to 7:25pm; April, May, and October Monday 11am to 7:25pm, Tuesday 11am to 11:45pm, Wednesday to Saturday 9:30am to 11:45pm, Sunday 9:30am to 7:25pm; June Monday 11am to 11:45pm, Tuesday to Saturday 9:15am to 11:45pm, Sunday 9:15am to 7:25pm; July and August Monday 11am to 12:15pm, Tuesday to Sunday 9:15am to 12:15am; September Monday 11am to 11:45pm, Tuesday to Saturday 9:30am to 11:45pm, Sunday 9:30am to 7:25pm; November to February Monday and Tuesday 11am to 6:30pm, Wednesday to Saturday 10:45am to 6:30pm. A round-trip ticket costs 5.80€ ($7.55) for adults, 4.65€ ($6.05) for students, and 3.75€ ($4.90) for ages 5 to 18. It's closed during the month of January. At the belvedere where you land, you'll have a view of the city, the mountains, and the remains of the Fort de la Bastille. Come for the view, not the fort. You can walk up in an hour or so if you're an Olympic athlete; the beginning of the route is signposted to the west of place St-André. We suggest you take the téléphérique to the top, and then stroll down along the footpath, Montée de Chalmont, that winds through Alpine gardens and past old ruins before reaching a cobblestone walk that leads to the old town.

Musée Dauphinois ★ Housed in the 17th-century convent Ste-Marie-d'en-Haut and enhanced by the convent's cloister, gardens, and baroque chapel, this museum lies across the Isère in the Ste-Marie-d'en-Haut section of town. A collection of ethnographic and historical mementos of the Dauphine region is on exhibit, along with folk arts and crafts. This place is a quick course on life in the Alps—no other museum gives such a detailed view of the people. Furnishings, tools, artifacts, and replicas of Alpine settings are on display. Check out the special exhibition on skiing, tracing the development of the sport from its origins to the 21st century's high-tech innovations.

30 rue Maurice-Gignoux. **© 04-76-85-19-01.** www.musee-dauphinois.fr. Free admission. June–Sept Wed–Mon 10am–7pm; Oct–May Wed–Mon 10am–6pm. Closed Jan 1, May 1, and Dec 25.

Musée de Grenoble ★★★ Founded in 1796, this is one of the country's oldest art museums. It was the first French museum outside of Paris to focus on modern art, a fact appreciated by Picasso, who donated his *Femme Lisant* in 1921. The collection includes Flemish and Italian Renaissance works, but the Impressionist paintings generate the most interest. Note Matisse's *Intérieur aux aubergines* and Léger's *Le Remorqueur.* Ernst, Corot, Klee, Bonnard, Gauguin, Monet—they're all here. On display are a number of older paintings and sculptures, along with artifacts and relics from Greek, Egyptian, and Roman times, including a well-preserved mosaic. The artistic highlight is a sculpted door panel from the 1400s, depicting Jacob and his sons. A collection of 20th-century sculptures occupies the François Mitterrand Esplanade and the Albert Michallon Park surrounding the museum.

5 place de Lavalete. ✆ **04-76-63-44-44.** www.museedegrenoble.fr. Admission 5€ ($6.50) adults, 2€ ($2.60) seniors, students, and children. Wed–Mon 10am–6:30pm.

WHERE TO STAY

Hôtel d'Angleterre Tulip Inn Grenoble In the center of town, this hotel features tall windows and wrought-iron balconies, and opens onto a pleasant square with huge chestnut trees. The stylish salons boast wood-grained walls and ceilings and tropical plants. Some guest rooms look out on the Vercors Massif. Most of the small to midsize units are comfortably furnished and come with shower-only bathrooms; some have Jacuzzi tubs. Breakfast is the only meal served.

5 place Victor-Hugo, Grenoble 38000. ✆ **04-76-87-37-21.** Fax 04-76-50-94-10. www.hotel-angleterre-grenoble.com. 62 units. 100€–170€ ($130–$221) double. AE, DC, MC, V. Free parking. **Amenities:** Restaurant; bar; room service; dry cleaning. *In room:* TV, minibar, coffeemaker, hair dryer, safe, Wi-Fi.

Hôtel Trianon Few other hotels in town have masked a banal 1950s design so effectively. Here, historical decorative styles do the trick. The rooms are cramped but cozy, furnished in just about every Louis style; in a handful, the decor evokes a folkloric grange in the Alps. The midsize bathrooms are equipped with showers, and some have tubs as well. A comfortable, well-managed hotel, Trianon caters to business travelers during the week, so rates drop on weekends. You'll find this hotel a short walk south of the pedestrian-only district in the town center, near a well-known school, the Lycée Champollion.

3 rue Pierre-Arthaud, Grenoble 38000. ✆ **04-76-46-21-62.** Fax 04-76-46-37-56. www.hotel-trianon.com. 38 units. 51€–82€ ($66–$107) double. AE, DC, MC, V. Parking 7€ ($9.10). **Amenities:** Bar; room service. *In room:* TV.

Park Hotel Concorde ★★ This is the most opulent and prestigious hotel in Grenoble, a government-rated four-star legend that welcomes most of the important politicians and entertainment-industry moguls who visit the region. On the lower four floors of a mid-1960s tower mostly devoted to private condominiums, it's a short drive south of Grenoble's commercial center and close to City Hall. Each guest room is decorated differently, with a blend of dignified (sometimes antique) furniture, state-of-the-art lighting, and modern upholstery. All bathrooms have both tub and shower; some also have a Jacuzzi.

10 place Paul-Mistral, Grenoble 38027. ✆ **04-76-85-81-23.** Fax 04-76-46-49-88. www.park-hotel-grenoble.fr. 50 units. 165€–345€ ($215–$449) double; from 690€ ($897) suite. Parking 16€ ($21). AE, DC, MC, V. Tram: A to Chavant. **Amenities:** Restaurant; bar; business center; room service; babysitting; laundry service. *In room:* A/C, TV, minibar, hair dryer, safe, Wi-Fi.

WHERE TO DINE

Auberge Napoléon ★★★ FRENCH No other restaurant in France boasts as intense an association with Napoleon Bonaparte, but that's less important to diners than the fact that the restaurant is the finest in the Grenoble area. In 1815, Napoleon spent the night here at the beginning of a 100-day reign that ended with his defeat by Wellington at the Battle of Waterloo. You'll find enough subtle references to the history of France, from the Revolution to around 1820, to keep a student of French history busy throughout the superb meal. The restaurant seats only 23, in a plush, manicured dining room with upholstered walls and about 20 contemporary floral still lifes by renowned Grenoblois artist Martine Poller. Your host is Avignon-born Frederic Caby, an expert in the history of French cuisine, the exploits of Napoleon, and the nuances of Grenoble. We'd vote the bouillabaisse the best in the Alps. Cuisine is by resident chef Agnès Chotin. Try velvety-smooth crayfish and shrimp cream soup, or duck foie gras terrine. The chef makes a superb filet of beef in game sauce. Filet of pike is served with bacon and accompanied by homemade local pasta from the Savoy—a harmonious combination.

7 rue de Montorge. ✆ **04-76-87-53-64.** www.auberge-napoleon.fr. Reservations recommended. Main courses 26€–39€ ($34–$51); fixed-price menu 47€–97€ ($61–$126). AE, DC, MC, V. Mon–Sat 7:30–10pm. Closed 3 weeks in Aug.

Café de la Table Ronde FRENCH This is the second-oldest cafe in France, after the more famous Procope in Paris. It is still going strong and still serving good, affordable cuisine. Founded in 1739, the cafe has attracted such luminaries as Stendhal and Sarah Bernhardt. It is said to be the spot where Pierre Choderlos de Laclos conceived the plot for his 1784 *Les Liaisons dangereuses.* The menu offers both regional and national cuisine—the ingredients always fresh. We gravitate to the *le poisson du jour* (fresh fish of the day), although the *fondue Savoyarde* with *charcuterie* is a winter delight as is the alpine ham. The cafe conducts concerts and poetry readings.

7 place St-André. ✆ **04-76-44-51-41.** www.cafetableronde.com. Reservations not needed. Main courses 11€–39€ ($14–$51); fixed-price menus 23€–33€ ($30–$43). AE, DC, MC, V. Daily noon–midnight.

Restaurant Pique-Pierre ★ TRADITIONAL FRENCH One of the town's most appealing restaurants, this bastion of culinary finesse, about 1.5km (1 mile) north of the town center, sits in a pleasant garden. Sheathed in burnished paneling, it offers an oft-changing roster of delectable items that include such dishes as crayfish, roasted pigeon in foie gras sauce, scallops au gratin, roasted filet of duckling with red-wine sauce, and seafood salad with salmon and mussels. Of the 10 choices on the dessert list, our favorite is the bittersweet chocolate *tarte.*

Rte. Historique de Stendhal (N75), St-Martin-le-Vinoux. ✆ **04-76-46-12-88.** Fax 04-76-46-43-90. www.pique-pierre.com. Reservations recommended. Main courses 15€–22€ ($20–$29); fixed-price menu 29€–59€ ($38–$77). AE, MC, V. Tues–Sun noon–1:15pm; Tues–Sat 7–9:30pm. Closed last week of July and 1st 3 weeks of Aug. Bus: 3.

ON THE OUTSKIRTS

Restaurant Alain Pic ★★ FRENCH/SAVOYARD The creative statement of a legendary chef, this restaurant occupies a substantial Savoyard house originally built in 1905 in the quiet hamlet of Montbonnot (7km/4⅓ miles north of Grenoble). Three peaks of the Chartreuse mountain group surround the hamlet. In a comfortable dining room outfitted in richly textured Savoyard style, famed chef Alain Pic prepares sublime dishes that include carpaccio of tuna with baby vegetables, fresh foie gras of duckling served with liqueur-marinated grapes, beef layered with foie gras in a sauce of Syrah red wine, sea scallops in champagne sauce, and tuna steaks with sesame seeds and red wine.

876 rue du Général-de-Gaulle (RN90), Lieu-dit Les Mésanges, Montbonnot-Saint-Martin. ✆ **04-76-90-21-57.** Reservations recommended. Main courses 18€–49€ ($23–$64); fixed-price menu 25€ ($33) Tues–Fri only, 40€–52€ ($52–$68) all other times. AE, MC, V. Tues–Fri and Sun noon–2pm; Tues–Sat 7:30–9pm. Closed 2 weeks in late Aug. Bus: 602 from Grenoble.

GRENOBLE AFTER DARK

To get things started, walk to **place St-André, place aux Herbes,** or **place de Gordes.** On a good night, these squares overflow with young people, and the energy level builds in anticipation of an explosion of dancing and partying.

Check out **Le Jazz Club,** 7 rte. de Lyon (✆ **04-76-87-05-67**); if sports bars are more your scene, join wild crowds of students at **Le Couche Tard,** 1 rue Palais (✆ **04-76-44-18-79**), and the **London Pub,** 11 rue Brocherie (✆ **04-76-44-41-90**).

For a great outdoor party, check out **Le Saxo,** 5 place d'Agier (✆ **04-38-37-07-49**). Its patio, with speakers blasting techno and rock into the wee hours, has the feeling of a college party. If you're pumped up and need to cut loose on the dance floor, bop on over to **Coco-Loco-Nae-Vas,** 1 rue Lamartine (✆ **04-76-87-23-48**), where the young rule. The cover of 10€ ($13) is rarely imposed.

Le Styx, 6 place Claveyson (✆ **04-76-44-09-99**), is attuned to cutting-edge music from such centers as London and Los Angeles. Expect a mix of hip-hop, R&B, soul, and techno, but be prepared for anything. The dance floor is too small, but it's popular anyway. Young office workers head here after 5pm to sample one of 70 different cocktails, but beer and pastis are the drinks of choice.

The town's most animated gay disco is **Le Georges V,** 124 cour Berriat (✆ **04-76-84-16-20**), which does most of its business Wednesday to Sunday beginning around 10:30pm.

6 Courchevel 1850 ★★

633km (393 miles) SE of Paris, 52km (32 miles) SE of Albertville, 97km (60 miles) SE of Chambéry

Courchevel has been called a resort of "high taste, high fashion, and high profile," a chic spot where multimillion-dollar chalets sit on pristine pine-covered slopes. Skiers and geographers know it as part of Les Trois Vallées, sometimes called "the skiing supermarket of France." The resort, with 150km (93 miles) of ski runs in Courchevel and 604km (375 miles) of ski runs in the Trois Vallées around it, employs as many workers in winter as in summer, many of whom do nothing more than manicure and maintain the slopes. Courchevel 1850 has excellent resorts and hotels—with price tags to match—so it draws the super-rich. Travelers on average budgets should avoid it and head for more reasonably priced resorts, especially Chamonix (see "Chamonix–Mont Blanc," later in this chapter).

Courchevel consists of four planned ski towns, each designated by its elevation in meters. They are the less fashionable Courchevel 1300 (Le Prez), Courchevel 1550, Courchevel 1650, and, crowning them all, Courchevel 1850. Courchevel maintains three ski schools with a staff of 700 instructors, a labyrinth of chairlifts, and more than 200 ski runs, which are excellent in the intermediate and advanced categories. Also in Les Trois Vallées are the less well-known resorts of **Méribel, Les Menuires, La Tania,** and **Val Thorens,** which you should avoid unless you direly need to save money.

Courchevel 1850 is the most attractive ski mecca in the French Alps. It's also the focal point of a chair-hoist network crisscrossing the Les Trois Vallées region. At the center of one of the largest ski areas in the world, Courchevel sits at the base of a soaring amphitheater whose deep snowfalls last longer than those at most other resorts because it faces north. Expect reliable snow conditions, perfectly groomed runs, vertical cliffs, and enough wide runs to appease the intermediate skier. The glacier skiing draws experts from around the world.

SKI PASSES A 1-day pass (lift ticket) for Courchevel costs 37€ ($47), and a 1-day pass to Les Trois Vallées goes for 43€ ($56). A 3-day pass costs 106€ ($137) for Courchevel, 127€ ($165) for Les Trois Vallées.

Moments Le Snowboarding

Snowboarding (*le snowboarding* in French) is indulged and accepted at even the grandest resorts. For safety reasons, the pistes for snowboards are designated areas segregated from conventional ski runs. In Courchevel, the site is Le Snowpark. Peppered with all the moguls and hillocks a snowboarder would expect, it straddles the side of La Piste des Chenus, running parallel to conventional ski runs and accessible by way of la Telecabine des Chenus. Check with the tourist office for more details.

ESSENTIALS

GETTING THERE If you're **driving** from Paris, take A6 to Lyon, then A42 to Chambéry, and then A430 to Albertville. At Albertville, take N90 to Moutiers, and then follow the narrow roads 915 and 75 into Courchevel. Courchevel 1850 is the last stop on a steep alpine road that dead-ends at the village center. Roads are open year-round, but driving can be treacherous during snowstorms. To go any higher, you'll have to take a cable car from the center of town. Most visitors drive here (you'll need snow tires and chains), but some buses link the city to railway junctions farther down the mountain.

The nearest **train** station is in Moutiers Salins. From Paris's Gare de Lyon, five trains per day leave for Moutiers. The high-speed TGV covers the distance from Paris to Chambéry in about 3 hours. In Chambéry, transfer for Moutiers. From the station in Moutiers, a 1-hour **bus** trip completes the journey to Courchevel. There are five buses per day Monday to Friday and 15 per day on Saturday and Sunday costing between 9.50€ and 12€ ($12–$16).

The nearest international **airport** is at Geneva. From there, you can catch a bus to Courchevel. There are three buses per day Monday through Friday and eight on Saturday and Sunday. The 4-hour ride costs 68€ ($88) one-way. From the airport at Lyon, there are three to five buses a day to Courchevel; the 4-hour trip costs 61€ ($79) one-way.

VISITOR INFORMATION The **Office de Tourisme,** at La Croisette in the heart of town (✆ **04-79-08-00-29;** fax 04-79-08-15-63; www.courchevel.com), provides information on skiing and each of the four Courchevel ski towns.

WHERE TO STAY

VERY EXPENSIVE

Hôtel Bellecôte ★★ This seven-story chalet, with direct access to the slopes, is known for its collection of unusual antiques. Bored with traditional Alpine motifs, the founder scoured the bazaars of Afghanistan and the Himalayas for objects that lend exotic warmth to the wood-sheathed walls and ceilings. Guest rooms are outfitted with lots of varnished paneling, plush accessories, and carved wooden objects from the Far or Middle East. The midsize bathrooms have combination tub/showers. The hotel has its own ski-rental shop.

Full meals in the elegant dining room include cassoulet of sweetbreads with flap mushrooms, frogs' legs Provençal, and chicken with morels. The impressive luncheon buffet has a dazzling array of seafood, such as crayfish and urchins, followed by sauerkraut with pork. The Bellecôte serves the best *fondant au chocolat* in the Alps.

Rue de Bellecôte, Courchevel 1850 73120. ✆ **04-79-08-10-19.** Fax 04-79-08-17-16. www.lebellecote.com. 52 units. 240€–340€ ($312–$442) double; 450€–520€ ($585–$676) suite for 2. Rates include half board. AE, DC, MC, V. Closed mid-Apr to Dec 20. **Amenities:** Restaurant; bar; indoor pool; fitness center; sauna; salon; room service; babysitting; laundry service; dry cleaning. *In room:* TV, minibar, hair dryer, safe, Wi-Fi.

EXPENSIVE

Courcheneige *Kids* This hotel is at the heart of the slopes—you can practically ski from your doorstep. Built like a chalet, with balconies, the hotel has its own ski shop. Guest rooms mostly open onto views of the mountain ranges, including l'Aiguille du Fruit. Most of the midsize bathrooms have tub/shower combinations. Some rooms are large enough for a family of five. Courcheneige is always warm and cozy, especially in the art-filled, elegantly decorated public rooms. The Alpine and international cooking is excellent; meals are sometimes served on the terrace.

Rue Nogentil, Courchevel 1850 73120. ✆ **04-79-08-02-59.** Fax 04-79-08-11-79. www.courcheneige.com. 85 units. 264€–344€ ($343–$447) double; 410€–478€ ($533–$621) suite for 2. Rates include half board. AE, V. Free parking. **Amenities:** Restaurant; bar; fitness center; Jacuzzi; sauna; babysitting; laundry service; dry cleaning; free shuttle bus to ski lifts. *In room:* TV, hair dryer, Wi-Fi.

La Sivolière ★★ The secret of La Sivolière's success is its owner, Madeleine Cattelin, who has a rich knowledge of and appreciation for her native Savoy. The hotel was constructed in the 1970s, with lots of pinewood boards and artfully rustic lichen-covered boulders, and radically upgraded to a four-star hotel in 2004. It's near a small forest in a sunny spot near the ski slopes. Each guest room contains tasteful furnishings. All units come with a shower; some have a tub as well.

Quartier Les Chenus, Courchevel 1850 73120. ✆ **04-79-08-08-33.** Fax 04-79-08-15-73. www.hotel-la-sivoliere.com. 44 units. 300€–730€ ($390–$949) double; 690€ ($897) suite. AE, MC, V. Parking 20€ ($26). Closed late Apr to early Dec. **Amenities:** Restaurant; bar; sauna; indoor pool; room service; babysitting; laundry service; dry cleaning. *In room:* TV.

Le Chabichou ★★ This is one of the town's finest hotels, within easy walking distance of many bars and clubs and boasting a superb restaurant (see "Where to Dine," below). Most of the guest rooms in the gingerbread-trimmed chalet are large and well furnished; their daring modern design may not appeal to everyone, however. Beds offer grand alpine comfort, with quality mattresses and fine linens; the midsize bathrooms are luxurious, with combination tub/showers.

Quartier Les Chenus, Courchevel 1850 73120. ✆ **04-79-08-00-55.** Fax 04-79-08-33-58. www.chabichou-courchevel.com. 42 units. 420€–830€ ($546–$1,079) double; from 640€ ($832) suite for 2. Rates include half board. AE, DC, MC, V. Parking 25€ ($33). Closed May–June and Sept to mid-Nov. **Amenities:** Restaurant; bar; fitness center; sauna; room service; babysitting; laundry service; dry cleaning. *In room:* TV, minibar, hair dryer, safe, Wi-Fi.

Les Ducs de Savoie ★ This hotel, one of the largest in Courchevel, has elaborately scrolled pinewood and rows of picturesque icicles hanging from the protruding eaves. Each spacious, pleasant guest room has a balcony or terrace. Decorated in alpine style, the modern rooms have comfortable beds and combination tub/showers. The property is a few feet from the Téléski (ski lift) of the Jardin Alpin, and you can ski directly to the hotel's vestibule.

Le Jardin Alpin, Courchevel 1850 73120. ✆ **04-79-08-03-00.** Fax 04-79-08-16-30. 73 units. 340€–580€ ($442–$754) double; 325€ ($423) suite for 2. Rates include half board. AE, DC, MC, V. Parking 18€ ($23). Closed Apr 16–Dec 20. **Amenities:** Restaurant; bar; indoor pool; fitness center; business center; Jacuzzi; sauna; massage; babysitting; laundry service; dry cleaning. *In room:* TV, hair dryer, safe, Wi-Fi.

WHERE TO DINE

Chalet des Pierres FRENCH/SAVOYARD This is the best of the lunch restaurants scattered across the slopes. Accented with weathered planking and warmed by open hearths, it sits in the middle of the Des Verdons ski slope, a few paces from the path of whizzing skiers. Lunch can be served on a terrace, but most visitors gravitate to the two-story interior, where blazing fireplaces, hunting trophies, and a hip international crowd contribute to the place's charm. Items include air-dried Alpine meat and sausages, the best *pommes frites* in Courchevel, pepper steak, and *fondue Savoyarde.* Two appealing dishes are the Beaufort cheese tart and a leg of lamb that's suspended, the traditional way, from a string in the chimney and left to slowly cook in the smoke from the smoldering fire.

Au Jardin Alpin. ✆ **04-79-08-18-61.** www.chaletdepierres.com. Reservations required. Main courses 27€–45€ ($35–$59). AE, MC, V. Daily noon–5pm. Closed late Apr to early Dec.

La Bergerie TRADITIONAL FRENCH Its uneven flagstone steps, stacks of firewood, and weathered pine logs and planks testify to La Bergerie's origins as an 1830s shepherd's hut. The ambience is sports-oriented and outdoorsy. Well-prepared menu items include scallops in shallot butter, fondue bourguignonne, raclette made with cheese from small-scale producers in Switzerland, and cheesy Savoyard pasta with ham. An especially refined platter that usually meets with success is pâté of salmon smoked, poached, grilled, and served with lemon-and-caviar crème fraîche.

Rte. de Nogentile. ✆ **04-79-08-24-70.** Reservations required. Main courses 28€–31€ ($36–$40) lunch, 50€–70€ ($65–$91) dinner; fixed-price menu 65€–70€ ($85–$91). AE, MC, V. Restaurant daily noon–3pm; Tues–Sat 8–10pm. Bar and cafe daily 10am–midnight. Closed late Apr to mid-Dec.

Le Bateau Ivre ★★★ MODERN FRENCH This restaurant, one of the greatest in the French Alps, occupies two floors of a hotel in the upper reaches of the resort. The paneled room has parquet floors and big windows that afford a view over the town and its slopes. Enjoyable dishes include *les oeufs cassées* (literally, "broken eggs"), an elegant house specialty accented with roasted crayfish tails and truffles. Also look for frogs' legs in garlic-flavored cream sauce, grilled red snapper with balsamic vinegar and fresh vegetables, polenta with escalopes of foie gras in vinaigrette, and succulent rack of lamb with olives and artichoke hearts. Scallops may be scented with gentian, an Alpine wildflower.

In the Hôtel Pomme-de-Pin, quartier Les Chenus. ✆ **04-79-08-36-88.** Reservations required. Main courses 35€–110€ ($46–$143); fixed-price menu 90€–190€ ($117–$247). AE, DC, MC, V. Sat–Sun 12:30–2:15pm; daily 7:30–10pm. Closed mid-Apr to Dec 20.

Le Chabichou ★★★ MODERN FRENCH This is the second-best restaurant in town (only Le Bateau Ivre is better). Le Chabichou is on the second floor of the hotel of the same name; big windows showcase a view of the slopes. The cuisine includes a number of superlative dishes, such as soup made from "fish from the lake," magret of duckling with honey sauce, divine lobster salad, red mullet with vinaigrette sauce, and velvety risotto with giant prawns.

In Le Chabichou hotel, Quartier Les Chenus. ✆ **04-79-08-00-55.** Reservations required. Main courses 40€–70€ ($52–$91); fixed-price lunch 45€ ($59); fixed-price dinner 90€–180€ ($117–$234). AE, DC, MC, V. Daily 12:30–2pm and 7:30–9:30pm. Closed May–June and Sept–Nov.

COURCHEVEL AFTER DARK

A chic but seasonal resort, Courchevel offers nightlife that roars into the wee hours in midwinter but melts away with the snow. You'll never have to walk far from the center to sample the fun, because the area around **La Croisette** (the departure point for most of the lifts) contains lots of restaurants, bars, and clubs that come and go.

Les Caves de Courchevel, Porte de Courchevel (✆ **04-79-08-12-74**), attracts an upscale crowd. A mock Tyrolean facade of weathered wood hides a club evoking a medieval cloister, with stone arches and columns. From December to April, Les Caves is open nightly for drinks from 11pm to 5am (closed May–Nov). Also appealing is **Piggy's Pub,** rue de la Croisette (✆ **04-79-08-00-71**), where stiff drinks and recorded music contribute to the sensation that you're far, far away from the French Alps. **Rhumerie Le Calico,** Au Forum (✆ **04-79-08-20-28**), is the closest thing in town to a British pub; it's open from December to April only.

7 Megève ★★★

599km (372 miles) SE of Paris, 72km (45 miles) SE of Geneva

Megève is a summer resort set amid forests, foothills, and mountain streams. But it's better known as a cosmopolitan ski resort, with more than 290km (190 miles) of downhill runs plus nearly 81km (50 miles) of cross-country trails.

The village, with its turreted houses around a 17th-century church, suggests that Megève looks much the same as it did at the turn of the 20th century. Hubert de Givenchy claims that the big draw of Megève is its *"parfum d'authenticité,"* from its scent of wood smoke to the sounds of hooves clopping on cobblestones. From 11am to 6am, the center of the old village closes to traffic, except for pedestrians and sledges. You can shop at your leisure, stopping everywhere from the cobbler to the antiques dealer to the many boutiques. The town center contains **place de l'Eglise** and the famous **Hôtel du Mont-Blanc,** south of the main arteries that cut through the valley.

Some of the resort's hotels and one of its most important cable-car depots are in the village of **Mont d'Arbois,** about 1.5km (1 mile) east of the center of Megève, at the end of a steep, narrow, winding road. (In winter, it's unwise to drive up this road without chains and snow tires.)

Tennis, horseback riding, and cable railways add to the attractions, with views of the Mont Blanc area from the top of the chairlifts. Amusement includes a casino, clubs, and shows. Megève has more diversions than most other French winter resorts and is a social center of international status.

ESSENTIALS

GETTING THERE Air France serves Geneva's **Cointrin Airport** (✆ **022/717-82-45**). There's bus service four times a day directly to Megève, 69km (43 miles) southeast of the airport. The 90-minute ride costs 40€ ($52). For information, contact Megève's tourist office (see below) or **Borini & Cie** (✆ **04-50-21-18-24**).

Many visitors come by **train.** Get off at Sallanches, 13km (8 miles) away. From Sallanches, about 8 to 10 buses a day make the trip to Megève at a cost of 6.50€ ($8.45) one-way. For schedules, call ✆ **04-50-21-25-18,** or visit www.sat-montblanc.com. The train journey from Paris (one-way fare: 73€–82€/$95–$107) to Megève is faster on weekends, when the TGV travels directly to Sallanches, taking about 5½ hours. Monday to Friday, the TGV goes only as far as Annecy, after which travelers transfer onto slower trains to Sallanches. Total trip time is around 7½ hours. For train information, contact Megève's tourist office (see below) or the SNCF at ✆ **08-92-35-35-35.**

Buses serve the Autogare SNCF (also known as the Gare Routière de Megève), beside the highway running through the town center.

Moments **Two Megève Highlights**

If you have the stamina, take the 15km (9⅓-mile) footpath called the **Route de la Croix (Way of the Cross)** from the edge of town; it links more than a dozen country chapels. Nothing in Megève is more memorable than the annual **Foire de la Croix,** on the last Sunday of September. It marks the return of the herds from the high alpine pastures. You can taste the farmers' bounty at dozens of stands at the fair, a tradition here since 1282.

If you're **driving** to Megève from Paris, take A6 southeast to Mâcon, connect to A40 east to St-Gervais, and follow N212 south straight into Megève.

Warning: Winter driving conditions can be perilous. Make sure your car has snow tires and chains.

VISITOR INFORMATION The **Office de Tourisme** is at 70 rue Monseigneur-Conseil (✆ **04-50-21-27-28;** fax 04-50-93-03-09; www.megeve.com).

OUTDOOR PURSUITS ON THE SLOPES & BEYOND

You can take a chair hoist to **Mont d'Arbois,** at 1,800m (5,900 ft.), where a panorama unfolds of Mont Blanc as well as the Fis and Aravis massifs. Cable service operates from June 17 to September 5, every half-hour from 9am to 6pm, and costs 10€ ($14) round-trip. To reach the station, take route Edmond-de-Rothschild from the resort's center, past the golf course. Mont d'Arbois is a pocket of greater luxury in an already-posh resort. For information, call ✆ **04-50-21-22-07.**

The **French Ski School,** 176 rue de la Poste (✆ **04-50-21-00-97**), is one of Europe's foremost, with 300 instructors for adults and 32 for children. Classes include the complete French skiing method, modern ski techniques, acrobatic skiing, cross-country skiing, and ski touring. The school is open December 20 to April, daily 9am to 6:30pm.

A similar option is the **Ecole de Ski Internationale,** 273 Rue de la Poste (✆ **04-50-58-78-88**). Facilities include a Chamois gondola, which takes skiers to the mountain from the center of town; the Rocharbois cable car, linking the ski areas of Mont d'Arbois and Rochebrune; and a gondola and chairlift at the Rochebrune Massif. Skiing here appeals to both intermediates and experts. A 1-day ski pass (lift ticket) costs 32€ ($42). Prices for a 3-day pass start at 94€ ($122).

Megève Palais des Sports et des Congrès (Sports Palace and Assembly Hall), route du Jaillet (✆ **04-50-21-15-71**), has two pools, saunas, an outdoor Olympic-size skating rink open year-round, a curling track, a body-building room, a bar, a gymnasium, indoor tennis courts, an auditorium, conference rooms, and a gallery. Hours change with the seasons and event schedule; it's usually open daily 9am to 11pm (closed May–June).

WHERE TO STAY

VERY EXPENSIVE

Chalet du Mont d'Arbois ★★★ Built in 1928 in a design emulating Switzerland's chalets, this is the most opulent and stylish small resort on the mountain. Guest rooms are spacious, sunny, and sumptuous. The good-size bathrooms have tub/shower combinations. The public rooms are the grandest in Megève, with fireplaces, beamed ceilings, and antiques. The restaurant (see "Where to Dine," below) serves modern French cuisine.

447 chemin de la Rocaille, Megève 74120. ✆ **04-50-21-25-03.** Fax 04-50-21-24-79. www.chalet-montarbois.com. 37 units. Winter 455€–969€ ($592–$1,260) double, from 1,100€ ($1,430) suite; off season 319€–807€ ($415–$1,049) double, from 900€ ($1,170) suite. Rates include breakfast. Half board 58€ ($75) per person. AE, DC, MC, V. Closed Apr to mid-June and Oct to mid-Dec. **Amenities:** Restaurant; bar; indoor and outdoor pools; Jacuzzi; sauna; room service; massage; babysitting; laundry service; dry cleaning; limited-mobility rooms. *In room:* TV, minibar, hair dryer, safe.

Les Fermes de Marie ★★★ This unique inn offers the grandest comfort at the resort. It consists of remnants of at least 20 antique barns and crumbling chalets that were assembled and discreetly modernized in a desirable location at the eastern edge of the resort. The result is a compound of appealing, comfortable buildings loaded with atmosphere and eccentricities. The folkloric theme extends to the guest rooms, which look like attractive Alpine cabins and have deluxe beds. Each well-kept bathroom has a combo tub/shower.

Chemin de Riante Colline, Megève 74120. ✆ **04-50-93-03-10.** Fax 04-50-93-09-84. www.fermesdemarie.com. 71 units. Winter 410€–870€ ($533–$1,131) double, from 780€ ($1,014) suite; off season 244€–590€ ($317–$767) double, from 676€ ($879) suite. Rates include half board. AE, DC, MC, V. Closed Apr 22–June 24 and mid-Sept to mid-Dec. **Amenities:** 3 restaurants; bar; indoor pool; health club; Jacuzzi; sauna; room service; babysitting; laundry service; dry cleaning; nonsmoking rooms; limited-mobility rooms. *In room:* TV, minibar, hair dryer, safe.

EXPENSIVE

Au Coin du Feu ★ Modern, spacious, and comfortable, this is one of the best of Megève's middle-bracket (middle for Megève, anyway) hotels. It's under the same management as the more glamorous Les Fermes de Marie (see above). It originated in the mid-1980s, when its owners maneuvered 23 guest rooms into an older chalet. Rooms are cozy and medium-size, with tub/shower combinations. Public areas contain fireplaces (one of them monumental) and lots of exposed stone. You'll find the place within a 10-minute uphill walk of Megève's center, beside the path leading to the Rochebrune cable car.

Rte. du Téléphérique de Rochebrune, Megève 74120. ✆ **04-50-21-04-94.** Fax 04-50-21-20-15. www.coindufeu.com. 23 units. Winter 276€–553€ ($359–$719) double. Rates include half board. AE, DC, MC, V. Closed early Apr to late Dec. **Amenities:** Restaurant; bar w/outdoor terrace; room service; babysitting; laundry service; dry cleaning. *In room:* TV, hair dryer, safe.

MODERATE

Le Fer à Cheval ★★ This is the finest hotel in the center of the village. Its rivals are the pricier Chalet du Mont d'Arbois and Les Fermes de Marie, both outside the town center. This hotel was built in 1960 and has been renovated frequently. Designed like an enlarged chalet, it incorporates many square yards of recycled weathered planking and paneling, all salvaged from antique buildings throughout the region. Genuine Savoyard antiques fill the beautifully maintained guest rooms. The rooms are traditional in style, with quality beds and linens. Most are spacious and sunny, opening onto a view. All units come with midsize bathrooms with combination tub/showers.

36 rte. du Crêt-d'Arbois, Megève 74120. ✆ **04-50-21-30-39.** Fax 04-50-93-07-60. www.feracheval-megeve.com. 56 units. 159€–269€ ($207–$350) double; from 517€ ($672) suite. Rates include half board. AE, MC, V. Closed Apr 8–June 7 and mid-Sept to early Dec. **Amenities:** 2 restaurants; bar; outdoor pool; fitness room; Jacuzzi; sauna; room service; babysitting; laundry service; dry cleaning. *In room:* TV, minibar, hair dryer, safe.

INEXPENSIVE

Hôtel Gai Soleil *Kids* At the base of hills at the southeast edge of town, between Megève's center and the Rochebrune slopes, this hotel was built in 1929 and has been much renovated since. The broad staircase that sweeps down to the front contrasts with the Swiss chalet-inspired design of the rest of the property. Inside, it's warm and colorful, with lots of exposed wood and well-upholstered comfort. Varnished pine highlights the small, cozy rooms; all but six have bathrooms with tub/shower combinations. It also has a heated outdoor pool.

343 rue Crêt-du-Midi, Megève 74120. ✆ **04-50-21-00-70.** Fax 04-50-21-57-63. www.le-gai-soleil.fr. 21 units. 81€–140€ ($105–$182) double. Rates include half board. 20%–50% discount for children. AE, MC, V. Free parking. Closed Sept 14–Dec 14 and Apr 18–June 15. **Amenities:** Restaurant; bar; outdoor pool; exercise room; Jacuzzi; room service. *In room:* TV, minibar, hair dryer.

WHERE TO DINE

Also try the restaurant at **Le Fer à Cheval** (see "Where to Stay," above).

Chalet du Mont d'Arbois ★ MODERN FRENCH Often cited in French fashion magazines as one of the most elegant places in Megève, this restaurant is known for its spit-roasted meats. The flavors and spices of the cuisine suit the bracing climate. Scattered throughout are mementos of the owners, the Rothschilds, and of their association with some of the greatest vineyards in the world. Savory items include foie gras of duckling, *omble chevalier* (local freshwater fish) meunière, spit-roasted turbot served with shellfish-studded risotto, and a dish that never fails to please: spit-roasted Bresse chicken in its own drippings. Part of the menu is devoted to low-fat, low-sodium choices.

In Chalet du Mont d'Arbois resort, 447 chemin de la Rocaille. ✆ **04-50-21-25-03.** Reservations required. Main courses 32€–70€ ($42–$91); fixed-price menu 58€ ($75). AE, MC, V. Daily noon–2pm and 7:30–10pm. Closed Apr to mid-June and Oct to mid-Dec.

L'Alpette SAVOYARD/FRENCH This is the oldest mountain restaurant in the French Alps, opening onto panoramic views of Megève. It's also one of the best choices for Savoyard staples such as alpine ham, steak, and grilled meats (the Savoy lamb is especially delectable). The fine cuisine has a loyal following of both residents and skiers who flock here on a yearly basis. While many patrons prefer to end their meal with one of the regional cheeses, dessert lovers should try a tarte Tatin (thin-crusted apple tart) or a succulent "chocolate pot" made with two kinds of chocolate, orange zest, and Kahlúa.

222 rte. du Téléphérique de Rochebrune. ✆ **04-50-21-03-69.** Reservations recommended. Main courses 19€–32€ ($25–$42). AE, MC, V. Daily 9am–5pm. Closed Apr 30–July 1 and Aug 30 to mid-Dec.

Le Prieuré TRADITIONAL FRENCH The name "priory" dates back as far as A.D. 746, when this place was used as a dining hall for monks. Over the centuries, the building was rebuilt and restored with stones from the local hillside. Today it is one of the best dining choices outside of the hotels. Specialties include *foie gras de canard* and salad made from crab, mussels, and lake fish; and excellent versions of beef stew *(pot-au-feu),* which is simmered for up to 8 hours. An excellent appetizer is melon with locally cured ham, perhaps followed by grilled bass with fennel or magret of duckling flavored with peaches. For dessert, try half-baked chocolate cake.

Place de l'Eglise. ✆ **04-50-21-01-79.** Reservations required. Main courses 20€–30€ ($26–$39); fixed-price menu 24€–38€ ($31–$49). AE, DC, V. Daily noon–2:30pm and 7:30–10pm. Closed June 2–30, Nov 6–Dec 19, and Sun night and all day Mon–Tues in low season.

Les Enfants Terribles TRADITIONAL FRENCH Since the 1950s, this acclaimed restaurant has been a fun and irreverent place to dine. The decor emulates that of an upscale brasserie, thanks to bordeaux-colored banquettes, well-maintained wooden paneling, and a skylight-style ceiling that floods the interior with natural light. On the main square of Megève, the restaurant is warmly outfitted with wood panels and rustic artifacts. The extensive menu encompasses pizzas, pastas, grills, Savoyard raclettes and fondues, veal kidneys, and filets of beef layered with foie gras.

In the Hôtel du Mont-Blanc, place de l'Eglise. ✆ **04-50-58-76-69.** Reservations required. Main courses 18€–31€ ($23–$40); fixed-price lunch 20€–24€ ($26–$31). AE, DC, MC, V. Winter daily noon–midnight; off season Thurs–Mon noon–3pm and 7–11pm. Closed 3 weeks Apr–May and 3 weeks in Oct.

Le Vieux Megève SAVOYARD This cozy chalet, which has functioned since the early '70s as one of the most visible restaurants in the town center, was originally built in 1880 as a farmhouse. Inside, a richly beamed and paneled dining room for up to 80 diners focuses on a massive stone fireplace with lots of alpine accessories and old-fashioned napery in tones of red, and in summer, window boxes seem to blaze with the colors of seasonal flowers. Come here for hearty, rib-sticking cuisine from the high Alps such as a cheese-encrusted version of onion soup, an "alpine salad" of fresh greens, tomatoes, and salted ham, or perhaps a platter of mixed alpine charcuterie, which includes sausages and strips of air-dried beef. Main courses include three different kinds of fondue, old-fashioned raclettes, and a wide assortment of grilled meats, each served with a choice of sauces and french fries. Don't expect haute or particularly innovative cuisine: What you get is alpine charm and tried-and-true regional cuisine that hasn't changed a lot in the past 80 years. Watch for seasonal closings.

58 place de la Résistance. ✆ **04-50-21-15-16-44.** Reservations required. Set-price lunches 23€–25€ ($30–$33); main courses 19€–26€ ($25–$34). MC, V. Daily noon–2pm; dinner seatings at 7, 7:30, and 9:30pm. Closed Sept to mid-Dec and Apr to mid-June.

MEGEVE AFTER DARK

This town is a hotbed of clubs and bars for après-ski fun. The ultimate is **Club de Jazz des 5 Rues,** 19 passage de Cinq Rues (✆ **04-50-91-90-69**), a rendezvous for such jazz notables as Claude Luter and Claude Bolling; it's open only during the peak winter season. **Le Casino,** 115 av. Charles-Feige (✆ **04-50-93-01-83**), is a small, sedate casino—although you can still lose lots of money here. Most vacationers bypass the gaming tables and head for the disco immediately across the street, **Palo Alto** (✆ **04-50-91-82-58**). On the street level, you'll find a restaurant and music that management loosely advises is for persons ages 25 and older; upstairs, the louder and more frenetic scene is recommended for 18- to 25-year-olds. There's no cover charge in either room, but a beer will cost 15€ ($20).

The underground **Les Caves de Megève,** rue Amboise Martin (✆ **04-50-21-30-11**), located at the end of an impossibly narrow staircase, is small and cozy, with a small dance floor. A French celebrity might make a highly theatrical appearance at any minute. No cover, but drinks cost 13€ to 18€ ($17–$23).

8 Chamonix–Mont Blanc ★★★

613km (381 miles) SE of Paris, 82km (51 miles) E of Annecy

At an altitude of 1,027m (3,369 ft.), Chamonix is the historic capital of Alpine skiing. This is the resort to choose if you're not a millionaire. Site of the first Winter Olympic Games, in 1924, Chamonix is in a valley almost at the junction of France, Italy, and Switzerland. Skiers the world over know its 20km (12-mile) **Vallée Blanche run,** one of the most rugged, and the longest, in Europe. With exceptional equipment—gondolas, cable cars, and chairlifts—Chamonix is among Europe's major sports resorts, attracting an international crowd with lots of English and Swedish skiers. Thrill seekers also flock here for mountain climbing and hang gliding. A charming old-fashioned mountain town, Chamonix has a breathtaking backdrop, **Mont Blanc** ★★★, western Europe's highest mountain at 4,734m (15,531 ft.).

The 11km (6¾-mile) **Mont Blanc Tunnel** (✆ **04-50-55-55-00**) has made Chamonix a major stop along one of Europe's busiest highways. The tunnel is the easiest way through the mountains to Italy; motorists stop here even if they aren't interested in skiing or mountain climbing. For vehicles originating in France, the round-trip toll for a car and its passengers is 31€ ($40) one-way; 39€ ($51) round-trip. The return half of the round-trip ticket must be used within 7 days of issue. For information, call ✆ **04-50-55-55-00.**

Chamonix sprawls in a narrow strip along both banks of the Arve River. Its casino, rail and bus stations, and most restaurants and nightlife are in the town center. Cable cars reach into the mountains from the town's edge. Locals refer to Les Praz, Les Bossons, Les Moussoux, Argentière, and Les Pélérins as satellite villages within Greater Chamonix, though technically Chamonix refers to only a section around place de l'Eglise.

ESSENTIALS

GETTING THERE Most (but not all) **trains** coming from other parts of France or Switzerland require a transfer in such nearby villages as St-Gervais (in France) or Martigny (in Switzerland). Passengers change trains in either of these villages before continuing on by train to Chamonix. Passengers from Aix-les-Bains, Annecy, Lyon, Chambéry, Paris, and Geneva pass through those villages. There are six daily connections from Paris (trip time: 7 hr.); the one-way fare is 70€ to 95€ ($91–$124). From Lyon, there are six relatively complicated rail links per day (trip time: 4 hr.). A one-way fare costs 34€ ($41). For more information and schedules for trains throughout France, call ✆ **08-92-35-35-35.**

Year-round, two to six buses a day run from the Geneva airport; the one-way fare is 35€ ($46). Buses arrive and depart from a spot adjacent to the railway station. For information, call **Cie S.A.T.** (✆ **04-50-53-01-15**).

If you're **driving,** you probably won't have to worry about road conditions: Because Chamonix lies on a main road between Italy and the Mont Blanc Tunnel, conditions are excellent year-round. Even after a storm, roads are quickly cleared. From Paris, follow A6 toward Lyon, and then take A40 toward Geneva. Before Geneva, turn south along A40, which runs to Chamonix.

GETTING AROUND Within Chamonix, a local network of small buses (*navettes,* usually painted yellow and blue) make frequent runs from points in town to many of the *téléphériques* (cable cars) and villages up and down the valley. The price of a lift ticket usually includes the fare. Daily ski passes cost 36€ to 47€ ($47–$61), depending on the areas you specify. For information, contact **Chambus** (✆ **04-50-53-05-55;** www.chamonix-bus.com).

VISITOR INFORMATION Chamonix's **Office de Tourisme** is on place du Triangle-de-l'Amitié (✆ **04-50-53-00-24;** fax 04-50-53-58-90; www.chamonix.com).

SPECIAL EVENTS If you're here from mid-July to August, you may want to attend the classical and jazz concerts of the **Semaines Musicales du Mont-Blanc.** Concerts are at the Grand Salle of the Majestic, built during the Belle Epoque as an opulent hotel and later transformed into apartments. Tickets cost 13€ to 20€ ($17–$26) and are available from the Office de Tourisme.

SKIING

With the highest mountain in western Europe, this is an area for the skilled skier. Regrettably, the five main ski areas are not connected by lifts (you must return to the resort and take a different lift to ski a different area), and lines at the most popular areas are the longest in the Alpine world. Weather and snow conditions create crevasses and avalanches that may close sections for days and even threaten parts of the resort.

Skiing is not actually on Mont Blanc, but on the shoulders and slopes across the valley facing the giant. Vertical drops can be spectacular, with lift-serviced hills rising to as high as 3,150m (10,335 ft.). Glacier skiing begins at 3,740m (12,270 ft.). This is not for beginners or timid intermediate skiers, who should head for Les Houches or Le Tour. World-class skiers come here to face the challenges of the high snows of Brévent, La Flégère, and especially Les Grands Montets, a fierce north-facing wall of snow about 3 city blocks wide.

SEEING THE AREA BY CABLE CAR

The belvederes accessible from Chamonix by cable car or mountain railway are famous. For information, contact the **Compagnie du Mont-Blanc,** 35 place de la Mer de Glace (✆ **04-50-53-22-75**).

In town, you can board a cable car for the **Aiguille du Midi** ★★★ and on to Italy—a harrowing full-day journey. The first stage, a 9-minute run to the Plan des Aiguilles at an altitude of 2,263m (7,425 ft.), isn't so alarming. But the second stage, to the Aiguille du Midi station at 3,781m (12,405 ft.), may make your heart leap, especially when the car rises 600m (1,970 ft.) between towers. At the summit, you'll be about 100m (328 ft.) from Mont Blanc's peak. You'll have a commanding view of the aiguilles of Chamonix and Vallée Blanche, the largest glacier in Europe (15km/9⅓ miles long and 6km/3¾ miles wide), and of the Jura and the French, Swiss, and Italian Alps.

You leave the tram station along a chasm-spanning narrow bridge leading to the third cable car and the glacial fields beyond. Or you can end your journey at Aiguille du Midi and return to Chamonix; this excursion takes half a day. Generally, the cable cars operate year-round: in summer, daily 6am to 5pm, leaving at least every 10 minutes; in winter, daily 8:30am to 3:30pm, leaving every 10 minutes. The first stage, to Plan des Aiguilles, costs 12€ ($16) round-trip. The complete round-trip from Chamonix to Aiguille du Midi costs 37€ ($48).

You then cross over high mountains and pass jagged needles of rock and ice bathed in dazzling light. The final trip to **Pointe Helbronner,** Italy—at 3,407m (11,178 ft.)—does not require a passport if you want to leave the station and descend on two more cable cars to the village of Courmayeur. From there, you can go to nearby Entrèves to dine at **La Maison de Filippo** (✆ **01-65-86-97-97;** www.lamaison.com), a "chalet of gluttony." The round-trip from Chamonix to Pointe Helbronner is 54€ ($70); the cable car operates from mid-May to mid-October only.

Another cableway takes you up to **Le Brévent** ★★★, at 2,485m (8,153 ft.). From here, you'll have a first-rate view of Mont Blanc and the Aiguilles de Chamonix. The round-trip excursion takes about 1½ hours. Cable cars operate year-round from 8am to 5pm. Summer departures are at least every 15 minutes. A round-trip costs 20€ ($26).

Another journey takes you to **Le Montenvers** ★★★ (✆ **04-50-53-12-54**), at 1,883m (6,178 ft.). Access is not by cable car but on a **cog railway** known as the ***Train Montenvers–Mer de Glace.*** It departs from the Gare Montenvers–Mer de

Glace, behind Chamonix's Gare SNCF, near the center of town. At the end of the run, you'll have a view of the 6.5km (4-mile) long *mer de glace* ("sea of ice," or glacier). Immediately east of the glacier, Aiguille du Dru is a rock climb notorious for its difficulty. The trip takes 1½ hours, including a return by rail. Departures are 8am to 6pm in summer, until 4:30pm in the off season; service usually operates year-round. The round-trip fare is 20€ ($26).

You can also visit a cave, **La Grotte de Glace,** hollowed out of the *mer de glace;* a cable car connects it with the resort of Montenvers, and the trip takes 3 minutes. The train, cable car, and visit to the cave cost 23€ ($30).

WHERE TO STAY

Chalet Hôtel Le Chantel A 30-minute walk west of the city hall, this white-stucco B&B evokes a Swiss chalet, with dark-stained wood, balconies, and mountain panoramas. It benefits from the care and attention of its owners, who have added touches you'd expect in a private home. The cozy, knotty-pine-paneled rooms are small but homey, without many amenities; each has a comfortable bed and a compact shower-only bathroom.

391 rte. des Pecles, Chamonix 74400. ✆ **04-50-53-06-69.** Fax 04-50-55-52-42. www.skiambiance.co.uk. 8 units. 88€ ($106) double. Rates include breakfast. MC, V. Free parking. **Amenities:** Breakfast lounge. *In room:* No phone.

Hôtel de l'Arve Originally a cafe around the turn of the 20th century, this place is now a comfortable hotel. Most of its stucco facade dates from the 1960s. The interior is simple, with childproof, much-used furniture and accessories. Furnishings in the small to medium guest rooms are functional, and the compact bathrooms contain shower stalls. This is a simple place that offers a friendly welcome, an appreciation for the outdoors, and views of the Arve River from many rooms. The setting is convenient, a 5-minute walk from the town hall.

60 impasse des Anémones, Chamonix 74400. ✆ **04-50-53-02-31.** Fax 04-50-53-56-92. www.hotelarve-chamonix.com. 37 units. 58€–111€ ($75–$144) double. AE, DC, MC, V. Closed mid-Oct to Dec 17. **Amenities:** Restaurant; fitness center; sauna. *In room:* TV.

WHERE TO DINE

Bartavel ITALIAN The place is a sporty, informal pizzeria and brasserie. Service is a bit rough, but that's part of its style. Decorated much like a tavern in Italy, this restaurant offers a range of pastas, salads, soups, and rib-sticking platters designed to go well with cold air and high altitudes. Beer and wine flow liberally. Bartavel attracts many outdoor enthusiasts who appreciate its copious portions and reasonable prices.

26 cours du Bartavel. ✆ **04-50-53-97-19.** Main courses 15€–23€ ($20–$30); pasta and pizzas 7.50€–11€ ($9.75–$14). MC, V. Daily 11:30am–11:45pm. Closed May and Nov.

La Casa Valerio ITALIAN This good-natured restaurant is the domain of longtime Chamonix resident Valerio Comazetto, whose customers have followed him from restaurant to restaurant for 2 decades. You may enjoy a drink at the cozy bar, filled with Chianti bottles and Alpine souvenirs, before proceeding upstairs to the dining room, where red-and-white checked tablecloths set the trattoria mood. You'll find the best pizzas in the region, many redolent of Mediterranean herbs. The restaurant serves up to 25 kinds of fresh-made pasta, including succulent versions with salmon and thin-sliced *jambon de Parme.* More substantial dishes include grilled calamari and mussels in white-wine sauce.

88 rue du Lyret. ✆ **04-50-55-93-40.** Main courses 10€–28€ ($13–$36). AE, DC, MC, V. Daily noon–2am.

Le Chaudron ★ *Value* TRADITIONAL FRENCH You'll find fancier places in town, but for good value, honest cooking, and fine mountain ingredients, Le Chaudron is near the top of our list. Chef Stephan Osterberger cooks in front of you, and you're sure to appreciate his specialties, which include house-style sweetbreads, rabbit stew with juniper berries, several robust beef dishes, and fondues, as well as many salads and desserts. The cellar is filled with well-chosen wines, including Château Mouton-Rothschild and Château Latour.

79 rue des Moulins. ✆ **04-50-53-40-34.** Reservations recommended. Main courses 15€–32€ ($20–$42); fixed-price menu 24€–56€ ($31–$73). MC, V. Daily 7pm–midnight. Closed May–June 15 and Oct–Nov.

Restaurant Albert 1er ★★★ MODERN FRENCH Although the hotel complex that contains this establishment features other, newer eateries, this is the star. You'll dine in one of a trio of cozily decorated dining rooms, with bay windows opening onto views of Mont Blanc and walls accented by rustic artifacts and antique farm implements. Begin with chef Pierre Carrier's broth *(fumet)* of wild mushrooms garnished with ravioli stuffed with foie gras. Main courses include bison steak with green-peppercorn sauce, superb pan-fried scallops with risotto and lobster sauce, locally smoked salmon with caviar-flavored cream sauce, and foie gras of duck with truffled chicken rillettes. Try the honey ice cream with raspberry coulis. In summer, dine alfresco in the garden.

In the Hameau Albert 1er hotel, 119 impasse du Montenvers. ✆ **04-50-53-05-09.** Reservations recommended. Main courses 35€–70€ ($46–$91); fixed-price menus 70€–140€ ($91–$182). AE, DC, MC, V. Fri–Mon 12:30–2pm; Thurs–Tues 7:30–9:30pm. Closed late Oct to early Dec.

Restaurant Matafan ★ FRENCH This stellar restaurant centers on a pentagonal fireplace. Specialties change seasonally but may include *omble chevalier* (lake fish) meunière, medallions of veal in white-truffle sauce, rack of lamb roasted with herbs (for two), and sinful desserts such as a mousse of apples and white chocolate. The excellent cellar contains more than 500 wines, many reasonably priced. In summer, you can lunch next to the pool in the garden. There's music in the adjacent piano bar every night.

In the Hôtel Mont-Blanc, 62 allée du Majéstic. ✆ **04-50-53-05-64.** Reservations required. Main courses 20€–35€ ($26–$46); fixed-price menu 48€–62€ ($62–$81). AE, DC, MC, V. Daily noon–1:30pm and 7–10pm. Closed May and Oct 15–Dec 15.

CHAMONIX AFTER DARK

Nightlife in Chamonix runs the gamut from the classical to riotous. You'll find the most bars and pubs along rue des Moulins and rue Paccard. Chamonix's most popular disco is **Le Garage,** Avenue de l'Aiguille du Midi (✆ **04-50-53-64-49**). Open nightly during the height of winter and summer high seasons, but only Thursday to Sunday during rainy months, it's outfitted with a modern format, very artfully "designed" with lots of chrome, steel, and glass. Clientele here could include just about anyone, reflecting the changing hordes of skiers and mountaineers who swarm through Chamonix at regular intervals. Entrance ranges from 5€ to 10€ ($6.50–$13). The **Casino,** 12 place H.-B.-de-Saussure (✆ **04-50-53-07-65**), has slot machines and roulette and blackjack tables.

9 Val d'Isère ★★

665km (413 miles) SE of Paris, 118km (73 miles) E of Albertville, 130km (81 miles) E of Chambéry

In an open valley, Val d'Isère (1,820m/5,971 ft. above sea level) was originally a hunting station for the ducs de Savoie. It's now a center of some of Europe's most spectacular skiing. Less snobbish than Courchevel and less old-fashioned than Megève, it's a youthful, rather brash resort where virtually everyone comes to enjoy outdoor pursuits. Its fans compare it favorably to Chamonix, which—despite the allure of nearby Mont Blanc and superb skiing—seems to be burdened with longer lift lines and a less accessible layout of ski lifts and slopes.

ESSENTIALS

GETTING THERE & GETTING AROUND **Driving** is the preferred way to get to Val d'Isère. Most motorists come from Albertville, accessible by superhighway from Paris. From Albertville, follow signs to Moutiers, then take RN202 to Bourg-St-Maurice (58km/36 miles) and continue another 31km (19 miles) to Val d'Isère. The meandering RN202 is panoramic and breathtaking—for its views and its lack of guardrails along some sections. During snowfalls, chains on tires are required. When you get to the resort, we strongly advise you park your car and not use it again until you leave. Parking problems are legendary, and without chains, you'll risk getting stuck during snowfalls. You can walk virtually anywhere in town faster than you can drive.

Two dozen red-and-white Train Rouge free **shuttle buses,** each with a capacity of 100 people and their equipment, connect the hamlets at either end of the valley (La Daille and Le Fornet) to the center. The central terminus is the Rond-Point des Pistes. In summer, service is available only in July and August.

Parking lots and garages scattered around the valley are clearly marked. Each charges around 12€ to 14€ ($16–$18) per day, or 50€ to 70€ ($65–$91) per week, depending on the season and the size of your car.

Nearby **airports** include Cointrin, outside Geneva (✆ **04122/798-2000** or 041222/717-8083); Lyon-St-Exupéry (✆ **04-37-25-52-55**); Grenoble (✆ **04-76-65-48-48**); and Chambéry (✆ **04-79-54-49-54**). Bus and limo service are available from these airports; contact Cars Martin (✆ **04-79-06-00-42**).

The nearest **train** station is at Bourg-St-Maurice (✆ **08-92-35-35-35**), an alpine village 31km (19 miles) west of Val d'Isère. For train information, call ✆ **08-92-35-35-35.** From there, Cars Martin (✆ **04-79-06-00-42;** www.altibus.com) **buses** depart 4 to 10 times a day, depending on the season. The one-way fare is 13€ ($17). Or you can take a **taxi** from Bourg-St-Maurice that costs about 75€ ($98) for up to four passengers. Call **Altitude Taxis** (✆ **06-07-41-11-53**), or arrange pickup in advance with your hotel.

VISITOR INFORMATION The resort's **Office de Tourisme,** rue Principale, Val Village (✆ **04-79-06-06-60;** fax 04-79-06-04-56; www.valdisere.com), is a font of information on outdoor activities. The widest spectrum of information on sports is available from the **Club des Sports (Sports Department),** route de la Balme, Quartier Balme B.P. 61, 73152 Val d'Isère (✆ **04-79-06-03-49**).

OUTDOOR PURSUITS ON & OFF THE SLOPES

Don't expect a pristine Alpine village. In Val d'Isère, traffic roars through the town center. Clusters of cheap restaurants, creperies, and more than 125 stores and outlets line the road. Since 1983, some of the worst of the town's architectural sins have been corrected, thanks to tighter building codes and greater emphasis on traditional chalet-style architecture.

Access to Val d'Isère, less than 9.5km (6 miles) from the Italian border, is inconvenient and time-consuming, and parking is a nightmare during busy seasons. But despite the commercialism, the town hums with the sense that its visitors are here to enjoy skiing. And few other European resorts can boast as logical a layout for a far-flung collection of ski slopes.

Val d'Isère is the focal point for a network of satellite resorts scattered around the nearby valleys, including the architecturally uninspired **Tignes** (2,066m/6,778 ft. above sea level), whose layout is divided into four resort-style villages. The most stylish and prosperous of the villages is **Val Claret;** less fortunate and successful are **Tignes le Lac, Tignes les Boisses,** and **Tignes les Brévières.**

Guarding one entrance to Val d'Isère is **La Daille,** a resort of mostly high-rise condominiums and timeshares. At the other end of town is the medieval hamlet of **Le Fornet,** the departure point for gondolas crossing a mountain ridge to the Pissaillas Glacier and another network of ski trails, the Système de Solaise.

All of these satellites lack the cachet and diversity of Val d'Isère's nightlife and dining. Public transport (the Train Rouge; see "Getting There & Getting Around," above) can pick you up and deposit you at the departure point to the terminus of virtually any ski lift or trail in the region.

Val d'Isère is legendary for its "death-defying" chutes and its off-piste walls. These slopes are for experts, but the intermediate skier will also find open snowfields. The best place for intermediates is Tignes, with its wide variety of runs, including the Grande Motte (3,345m/10,974 ft.). Skiers find enough variety here to stay 2 weeks and never revisit the slopes that stretch from the Pissaillas Glacier far above Val d'Isère to Tignes Les Brévières four valleys away.

There are only a few marked expert runs; the more accessible off-piste areas lure experts from all over Europe and the United States. Most of these runs can be reached after short traverses from the Bellevarde, Solaise, and Fornet cable cars in Val d'Isère and the Grande Motte cable car in Val Claret.

In winter, half-day, full-day, and 2-day **ski passes** (lift tickets) sell for 29€ ($38), 40€ ($52), and 72€ ($94), respectively.

At least a dozen **ski schools** flourish in winter. One of the largest and busiest is the **Ecole de Ski Français,** or French National Ski School (✆ **04-79-06-02-34**), with 350 guides and teachers. Somewhat more personal is **Snow Fun** (✆ **04-79-06-16-79**), with 60 guides. Purists usually gravitate to **Top Ski,** galerie des Cimes (✆ **04-79-06-14-80;** www.topskival.com), a small but choice outfit with 24 extremely well-trained guides catering exclusively to Alpine connoisseurs who want to ski off-piste (away from the officially recognized and maintained trails).

Officially, the resort's sports activities slow down or stop altogether between early May and late June, and from early September to mid-November.

WHERE TO STAY

The staff at **Val Hôtel** (✆ **04-79-06-18-90;** fax 04-79-06-11-88), the resort's central reservations network, can book accommodations for you.

Hôtel Altitude This oft-modernized chalet dates to the 1970s, when it was built in Savoyard style. The Altitude is comfortable and cozy, a short walk south of the town center, so you'll be able to escape the crowds. Many guests return each year, occupying elegantly appointed guest rooms with quality beds and fine linens. Each bathroom comes with a combination tub/shower.

Rte. de la Balme, Val d'Isère 73150. ✆ **04-79-06-12-55.** Fax 04-79-41-11-09. www.hotelaltitude.com. 40 units. Winter 92€–155€ ($120–$202) double; off season 68€–102€ ($88–$133) double. Rates include half board. AE, DC, MC, V. Closed May 5–June 30 and Sept 9–Dec 1. **Amenities:** Restaurant; bar; outdoor pool; health club; sauna; room service; babysitting; laundry service; dry cleaning. *In room:* TV, hair dryer.

Hôtel Christiania ★★ This is the best hotel in a town of worthy contenders, and the only government-rated four-star hotel in Val d'Isère. The stylishly designed 1949 lodging was almost completely rebuilt in 1991. However, reminders of its original design appear, most obviously in the *Sputnik*-style furniture in a sunken lobby ringed with exposed stone, varnished pine, and blazing fireplaces. Ski buffs are willing to pay the high prices because of the location, although the hotel doesn't measure up to similarly priced, more atmospheric resorts in Megève and Chamonix. The guest rooms range from midsize to spacious, with pine trim and Alpine touches. Some accommodations contain sleeping lofts or bunk beds. Midsize bathrooms come equipped with tubs and showers. The restaurant offers international and French—especially Savoy—specialties. The refined service is what you'd expect from a hotel of this caliber.

B.P. 48, Val d'Isère 73152. ✆ **04-79-06-08-25.** Fax 04-79-41-11-10. www.hotel-christiania.com. 69 units. 177€–332€ ($230–$432) double; from 252€ ($328) suite. Rates include half board. AE, MC, V. Closed late Apr to Dec 5. **Amenities:** Restaurant; bar; indoor pool; fitness center; sauna; room service; massage; babysitting; laundry service. *In room:* TV, hair dryer.

WHERE TO DINE

La Grande Ourse FRENCH Although it's open for lunch, this restaurant doesn't exhibit its trademark coziness until after dark, when flickering candles and a blazing fireplace generate lots of Savoyard charm. In a small, charming wooden house built in 1937, La Grande Ourse has the resort's most intriguing mural, a depiction of the zodiac on the ceiling of its richly paneled main dining room. Menu items at lunch include grilled meats, pastas, salads, and simple but fortifying dishes of the day. Evening menus offer more sophisticated fare, such as fricassee of guinea fowl with fondant of foie gras, warm foie gras with apples and cider sauce, roast rack of lamb with herbs, large pockets of lobster-stuffed ravioli with lobster sauce, and Savoyard fondue with three cheeses. Dessert may be a *tarte fine* (brandy tart) with apples or a Gallic version of a North American brownie.

B.P. 57, Val d'Isère 73150, Sur le Front de Neige, adjacent to the church. ✆ **04-79-06-00-19.** Reservations recommended at dinner. Main courses 18€–27€ ($23–$35) lunch; 20€–35€ ($26–$46) dinner. AE, DC, MC, V. Daily noon–3pm and Wed–Mon 7:30–9:30pm. Closed mid-May to Nov.

La Vieille Maison ★ *Finds* SAVOYARD Amid relatively new buildings in the hamlet of La Daille, this former farmhouse is one of the valley's oldest chalets. Constructed in 1780, it has lots of exposed stone and old-fashioned style. Menu items are based on Savoyard themes, with hearty cold-weather dishes such as fondues and raclettes, many of which are prepared only for two to four diners. Menu items include *tartiflette,* a succulent dish made from Reblochon cheese, potatoes, onions, butter, and lardons; game dishes, including wild boar steak; such local freshwater fish as *omble chevalier* in white-wine sauce; and raclette garnished with a green salad and a small platter of charcuterie. Hands-on diners sometimes opt for "La Viande à l'Auze"—a superhot slab of rock is placed on your table so that you can sizzle your beef strips yourself.

Vieux Village de la Daille. ✆ **04-79-06-11-76.** Reservations recommended. Main courses 19€–25€ ($25–$33); fixed-price menus 33€–45€ ($43–$59). MC, V. Mon–Sat 7–9:30pm. Closed May–June and Oct–Nov.

VAL D'ISERE AFTER DARK

Most bars are in the town's pedestrian zone or adjacent to rue Principale. **Café Face,** rue Principale (✆ **04-79-06-29-80**), draws an attractive crowd. Its most fun alternative, **Dick's Tea Bar** (✆ **04-79-06-14-87**), just off the rue Principale and opposite the

Hôtel Christiania, is the wildest après-ski joint in the Val d'Isère. Inside you'll find a rustic and cozily appointed timber and stone interior (including an Internet cafe where you can surf things other than the snow) where you can drink as merrily and as uninhibitedly as you want, and—after around 9pm, dance, dance, dance. Although the cover charge of 12€ ($16) is imposed after 1am, the bar is open every day during winter from 3pm to 4am. Hours vary during off season, but even during the slowest period, the place is usually open on Friday and Saturday nights. Smaller and more intimate, without dancing, is a bar that has a neighborhood feel, two pool tables, and lots of English-speaking patrons: **Le Petit Danois,** behind the bus station, off rue Principale (✆ **04-79-06-27-97**).

A SIDE TRIP TO ALBERTVILLE

The rail and highway junction of Albertville lies in **La Vallée de la Tarantaise,** a sinuous valley that climbs 85km (53 miles) along Route 90. Route 90 extends from low-lying Albertville and branches into **La Vallée d'Isère,** whose focal point is the resort of Val d'Isère. Most visitors travel between the two by car, although about five trains a day connect Albertville and Bourg-St-Maurice. From Bourg-St-Maurice, a bus continues for another 30km (19 miles) up to Val d'Isère, leaving at times that coincide with train arrivals. Train passengers should expect a total transit time of 60 to 90 minutes, depending on the day of the week. The one-way fare is around 15€ ($20).

WHERE TO STAY & DINE

Hôtel Million ★★★ TRADITIONAL FRENCH This is the area's finest choice, attracting gastronomes and sports enthusiasts. Set back from the main road, the Hôtel Million was established in 1770 by Jean-Pierre Million (who named it Etoile du Nord). It's a white building with strong horizontal lines and gables on a flagstone-covered square; the anterooms have authentic 19th-century decor, while the dining room has high ceilings and classic furnishings. Some of chef/owner Jose de Anacleto and his wife, Su-Chen's, traditional dishes derive from popular Savoy tastes of the 19th century, in particular frogs' legs, freshwater fish from Lake Annecy, and freshwater crayfish. Other choices include fera (an alpine whitefish) served with wild celery and herb-flavored butter; *foie gras maison;* and filet of John Dory with artichokes and snails.

Twenty-seven spacious, attractive guest rooms are available. Outfitted in rustic alpine style, each contains a TV. Year-round, doubles cost 127€ to 168€ ($165–$218) Sunday to Thursday, 165€ to 195€ ($215–$254) Friday and Saturday.

8 place de la Liberté, Albertville 73200. ✆ **04-79-32-25-15.** Fax 04-79-32-25-36. www.hotelmillion.com. Reservations recommended. Main courses 17€–36€ ($22–$47); fixed-price menu 26€–70€ ($34–$91). AE, DC, MC, V. Tues–Fri and Sun noon–2pm; Tues–Sat 7–10pm.

16

Provence: In the Footsteps of Cézanne & van Gogh

Provence has been called a bridge between the past and the present, which blend in a quiet, often melancholy way. Peter Mayle's *A Year in Provence* and its sequels have played a large role in the popularity of this sunny corner of southern France.

The Greeks and Romans filled the landscape with cities boasting baths, theaters, and arches. Romanesque fortresses and Gothic cathedrals followed. In the 19th century, the light and landscapes attracted painters such as Cézanne and van Gogh.

Provence has its own language and its own customs. The region is bounded on the north by the Dauphine, on the west by the Rhône, on the east by the Alps, and on the south by the Mediterranean. In chapter 17, we focus on the part of Provence known as the Côte d'Azur, or the French Riviera.

For more coverage of the region, see *Frommer's Provence & the Riviera.*

1 Orange ★★

659km (409 miles) S of Paris, 55km (34 miles) NE of Nîmes, 121km (75 miles) NW of Marseille, 26km (16 miles) S of Avignon

Orange gets its name from when it was a dependency of the Dutch House of Orange-Nassau. The last orange grove disappeared 2,000 years ago. The juice that flows in Orange today comes from its vineyards, which turn out a Côtes-du-Rhône vintage. Many wine caves, some of which offer *dégustations* to paying customers, thrive throughout the district. (The tourist office can provide a list.)

Overlooking the Valley of the Rhône, today's Orange (pop. 30,000) boasts Europe's third-largest extant triumphal arch and best-preserved Roman theater. Louis XIV, who toyed with the idea of moving the theater to Versailles, said "It is the finest wall in my kingdom."

ESSENTIALS

GETTING THERE Orange sits on major rail and highway arteries. Some 20 **trains** per day arrive from Avignon (trip time: 20 min.); the one-way fare is around 6€ ($7.80). From Marseille, there are 11 trains per day (trip time: 1 hr., 15 min.), for 20€ ($26) one-way. From Paris, you can catch a TGV train to Orange; the one-way fare is 76€ ($99), and the trip takes 3 hours. For rail information, call ✆ **08-92-35-35-35.** For information on bus routes, contact the **Gare Routière** (✆ **04-90-82-07-35**), place Pourtoules, behind the Théâtre Antique. If you're **driving** from Paris, take A6 south to Lyon, and then A7 to Orange. The 684km (425-mile) drive takes 5½ to 6½ hours.

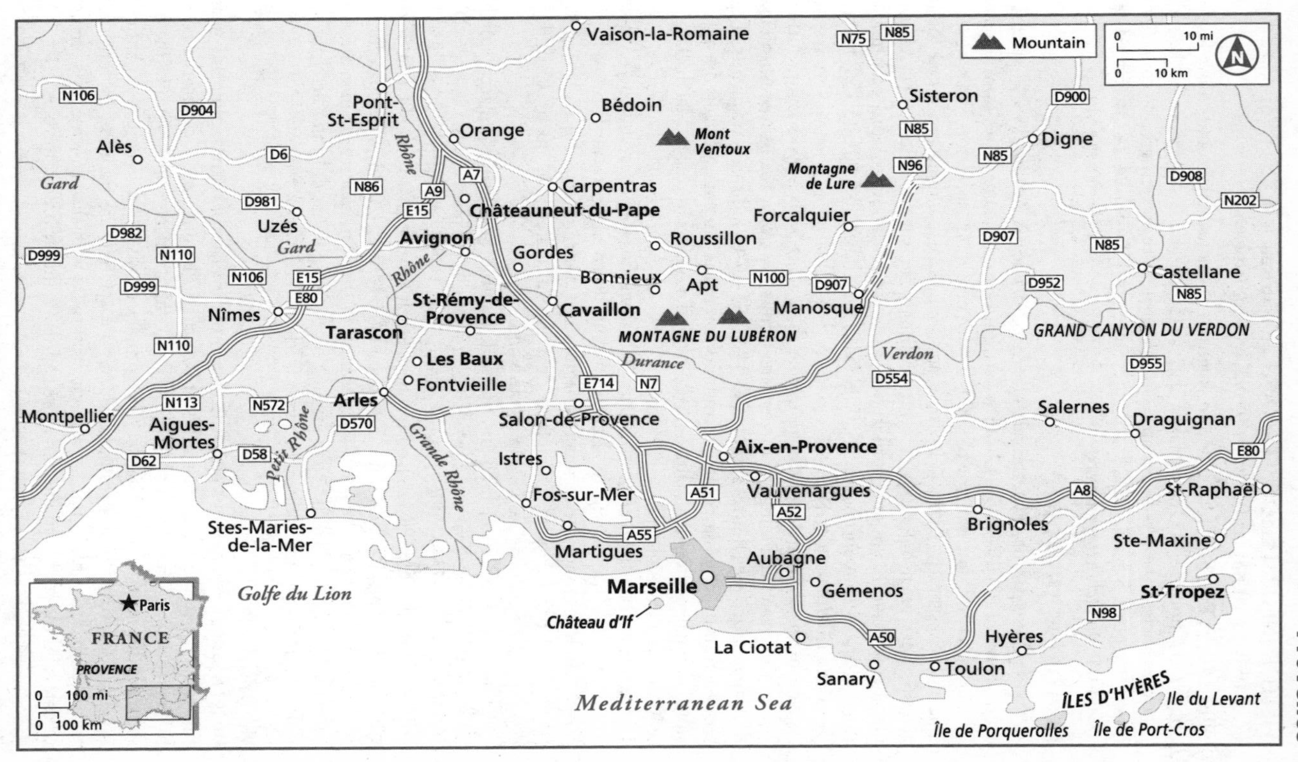
Mountain
0 10 mi
0 10 km
Vaison-la-Romaine
Pont-St-Esprit
Orange
Bédoin
Mont Ventoux
Sisteron
Digne
Montagne de Lure
Alès
Gard
Rhône
Carpentras
Châteauneuf-du-Pape
Forcalquier
Uzés
Avignon
Roussillon
Gordes
Bonnieux
Apt
Castellane
Manosque
Nîmes
St-Rémy-de-Provence
Cavaillon
Tarascon
MONTAGNE DU LUBÉRON
GRAND CANYON DU VERDON
Les Baux
Durance
Verdon
Fontvieille
Arles
Salon-de-Provence
Salernes
Draguignan
Montpellier
Aigues-Mortes
Petit Rhône
Grande Rhône
Aix-en-Provence
Istres
Vauvenargues
Fos-sur-Mer
St-Raphaël
Brignoles
Stes-Maries-de-la-Mer
Martigues
Ste-Maxine
Aubagne
Marseille
Gémenos
St-Tropez
Golfe du Lion
Château d'If
La Ciotat
Hyères
Toulon
Sanary
Mediterranean Sea
ÎLES D'HYÈRES
Île du Levant
Île de Porquerolles
Île de Port-Cros
N75
N85
N106
D904
D900
D6
N96
N85
D908
N86
A7
A9
N202
D981
E15
D982
D907
N110
D999
N106
E15
N100
D907
D952
E80
N110
D955
E714
N7
D554
N113
N572
D570
D62
D58
E80
A51
A8
A52
A55
N98
A50
FRANCE
Paris
PROVENCE
0 100 mi
0 100 km

VISITOR INFORMATION The **Office de Tourisme** is at 5 cours Aristide-Briand (✆ **04-90-34-70-88;** fax 04-90-34-99-62; www.otorange.fr).

SPECIAL EVENTS From July 8 to August 4, a drama, dance, and music festival called **Les Chorégies d'Orange** takes place at the Théâtre Antique, one of the most evocative ancient theaters in Europe. For information or tickets, visit or contact the office, 18 place Sylvain, adjacent to the theater (✆ **04-90-34-24-24;** fax 04-90-11-04-04; www.choregies.asso.fr).

EXPLORING THE TOWN

In the southern part of town, the carefully restored **Théâtre Antique** ★★★, place des Frères-Mounet (✆ **04-90-51-17-60;** www.theatre-antique.com), dates from the days of Augustus. Built into the side of a hill, it once held 8,000 spectators in tiered seats. The theater is nearly 105m (345 ft.) long, 38m (125 ft.) high, and noted for its acoustics. It's open daily: November to February 9:30am to 4:30pm, March and October 9:30am to 5:30pm, April to May and September 9am to 6pm, and June to August 9am to 7pm. Admission is 7.70€ ($10) for adults and 5.80€ ($7.55) for students and children under 18.

West of the theater stood a huge temple that, along with a gymnasium, formed one of the greatest buildings in the empire. Across the street, the **Musée Municipal d'Orange,** place du Théâtre-Antique (✆ **04-90-51-17-60**), displays fragments of the temple. Your ticket to the theater also admits you to the museum, which is open daily April through September 9:30am to 7pm, and October through March 9am to 5:30pm.

Even older than the theater is the **Arc de Triomphe** ★★, on avenue de l'Arc-de-Triomphe. It's decayed, but its decorations and other elements are fairly well preserved. Built to honor the conquering legions of Caesar, it rises 22m (72 ft.) and is nearly 21m (69 ft.) wide. Composed of a trio of arches held up by Corinthian columns, it was used as a dungeon in the Middle Ages.

Before leaving Orange, head for the park **Colline St-Eutrope,** adjacent to the Théâtre Antique, for a view of the valley and its mulberry plantations.

After exploring the town, drive south for 13km (8 miles) along A9 to **Châteauneuf-du-Pape,** where you can have lunch (Tues–Sun) at the **Hostellerie du Château des Fines-Roches,** route d'Avignon (✆ **04-90-83-70-23;** www.chateaufinesroches.com). Although the *hostellerie* was built in the 19th century, its medieval features make it look feudal. If you're pressing on to Avignon, it's only another 13km (8 miles) south along any of three highways (each marked AVIGNON).

WHERE TO STAY

Hôtel Arène ★ *Finds* On a pedestrian street in the shade of century-old plane trees, this hotel sits in the center of the historic district. The bull's-eye location is a compelling reason to stay here. Try to get a room with a balcony opening onto the old square in front; it's more nostalgic. The complex consists of a series of four antique town houses woven into a seamless whole. Guest rooms are traditionally furnished with French decor. Each unit has a private bathroom with shower. Amenities are up-to-date, and the staff is among the more courteous and helpful in town.

Place de Langes, Orange 84100. ✆ **04-90-11-40-40.** Fax 04-90-11-40-45. www.hotel-arene.fr. 35 units. 74€–140€ ($96–$182) double; 122€–160€ ($159–$208) triple. AE, DC, MC, V. Parking 8€ ($10). **Amenities:** Room service; nonsmoking rooms; limited-mobility rooms. *In room:* TV, minibar, hair dryer, safe.

Tips Shopping for *Brocante* in Provence

In France, there's a big difference between antiques and fun old junk. They even have different names. For serious purchases, you may want to stick to well-established antiques stores, found in great abundance all over France.

But if you prefer something more affordable and your idea of fun is a flea market, then what you really want is *brocante.* Your best bet is to head to a town's regular market on a specific day (the markets in Cannes are a good example; see chapter 17).

If you find yourself in Provence on Sunday, head out early (around 9am) for **Isle-sur-la-Sorgue,** a village that specializes in *brocante.* The town is 23km (14 miles) east of Avignon, 11km (6¾ miles) north of Cavaillon, and 42km (26 miles) south of Orange. The *brocante* market, **Foire à la Brocante,** is on Saturday, Sunday, and Monday; Sunday is most fun because there's also a food market. Everything is over by 6pm. If you're driving, try for a parking space in the free outdoor lot, Parking Portalet, adjacent to the fairgrounds. The *brocante* is on the near side of the river, a little farther downstream. Every building on the side of the street facing the river is a warehouse filled with dealers and loot.

Surprisingly for such a small place, Isle-sur-la-Sorgue has a Michelin-starred restaurant: **La Prévôté,** 4 rue J.-J.-Rousseau (✆ **04-90-38-57-29;** www.la-prevote.fr). Technically, this restaurant lies 4km (2½ miles) outside of town, in the hamlet of Lagnes. To get here from Isle-sur-la-Sorgue, follow the signs pointing to Gordes for 4km (2½ miles). It's widely signposted. You should make your lunch reservation before arriving in town. In the rear of a flower-filled courtyard, the chef wows shoppers and locals with sublime cuisine. The *pièce de résistance* is a hot chocolate tart. Fixed-price menus cost 25€ to 65€ ($33–$85) at lunch, 55€ to 65€ ($72–$85) at dinner. Closed 3 weeks in February, Tuesday and Wednesday October to June, and all of November.

Isle-sur-la-Sorgue has an Office de Tourisme at place de la Liberté (✆ **04-90-38-04-78**).

Park Inn This is one of your best bets for general overnight comfort far from the crowds. The well-managed hotel in a 1980s building has wings that curve around a landscaped courtyard. Its well-furnished rooms are arranged around a series of gardens, the largest of which contains a pool. Rooms were renovated in 1999 and have compact modern bathrooms (most with tub/shower combos). The poolside restaurant serves fixed-price menus.

80 rte. de Caderousse, Orange 84100. Drive .8km (½ mile) west of the city center, following directions to Caderousse. ✆ **04-90-34-24-10.** Fax 04-90-34-85-48. www.parkinn.com. 99 units. 85€–130€ ($111–$169) double. AE, DC, MC, V. Free parking. **Amenities:** Restaurant; bar; outdoor pool; room service; laundry service; dry cleaning; nonsmoking rooms; limited-mobility rooms. *In room:* A/C, TV, minibar, hair dryer.

WHERE TO DINE

Le Parvis *Kids* TRADITIONAL FRENCH Jean-Michel Berengier sets the best table in Orange, albeit in a rather austere dining room. He bases his cuisine on prime vegetables and the best ingredients from mountain or sea. Try escalope of braised sea bass with fennel or asparagus, or lamb with garlic cream sauce. A can't-miss dish is foie gras. Fresh and flavorful seafood is prepared in different ways according to the season, and the staff prides itself on its dozens of preparations. The service is efficient and polite, and there's a children's menu.

55 cours Pourtoules. ✆ **04-90-34-82-00.** Reservations required. Main courses 14€–23€ ($18–$30); fixed-price menu 16€–42€ ($21–$55); children's menu 12€ ($16). MC, V. Tues–Sun noon–2:30pm; Tues–Sat 7:30–9:15pm. Closed Nov 7–Dec 3 and Jan 16–Feb 3.

WHERE TO STAY & DINE NEARBY

Château de Rochegude ★★ This Relais & Châteaux member stands on 10 hectares (25 acres) of parkland. The castle is at the edge of a hill, surrounded by vineyards. The 12th-century turreted residence has been renovated by a series of distinguished owners, ranging from a pope to a dauphin. Each room is done in Provençal style, with fabrics and furniture influenced by the region's 18th- and 19th-century traditions. As befits a château, rooms come in many shapes and sizes, and some are quite spacious. All have bathrooms with tub/shower combinations. At the château's restaurant, both the food and the service are exceptional. You can enjoy meals in the stately dining room, barbecue by the pool, and refreshments on sunny terraces. Fixed-price lunches cost 16€ to 31€ ($21–$40), fixed-price dinners 35€ to 85€ ($46–$111).

26790 Rochegude. Take D976 13km (8 miles) north of Orange, following signs toward Gap and Rochegude. ✆ **04-75-97-21-10.** Fax 04-75-04-89-87. www.chateauderochegude.com. 25 units. 170€–355€ ($221–$462) double; 430€–555€ ($559–$722) suite. AE, DC, MC, V. Free parking. Closed Nov. **Amenities:** Restaurant; bar; outdoor pool; tennis court; room service; laundry service; nonsmoking rooms. *In room:* A/C, TV, minibar.

2 Avignon ★★★

684km (425 miles) S of Paris, 81km (50 miles) NW of Aix-en-Provence, 106km (66 miles) NW of Marseille

In the 14th century, Avignon was the capital of Christendom. The pope lived here during what the Romans called the Babylonian Captivity. The legacy left by that court makes Avignon one of the most beautiful of Europe's medieval cities.

Today, this walled city of some 85,000 residents is a major stop on the route from Paris to the Mediterranean. It is increasingly known as a cultural center. Artists and painters have been moving here, especially to rue des Teinturiers. Experimental theaters, galleries, and cinemas have brought diversity to the inner city. The popes are long gone, but life goes on exceedingly well.

ESSENTIALS

GETTING THERE The fastest and easiest way to get here is to **fly** from Paris's Orly Airport to **Aéroport Avignon-Caumont** (✆ **04-90-81-51-51**), 8km (5 miles) southeast of Avignon (trip time: 1 hr.). Taxis from the airport to the center cost 21€ ($27). Call ✆ **04-90-82-20-20.** From Paris, TGV **trains** from Gare de Lyon take 3 hours and 30 minutes. The one-way fare is 94€ ($122). Trains arrive frequently from Marseille (70 min.; 23€/$30); and from Arles (20 min.; 6€/$7.80). For train information, call ✆ **08-92-35-35-35.**

If you're **driving** from Paris, take A6 south to Lyon, and then A7 south to Avignon. If you'd like to explore the area by **bike,** go to **Provence Bike,** 52 bd. St-Roch

Avignon

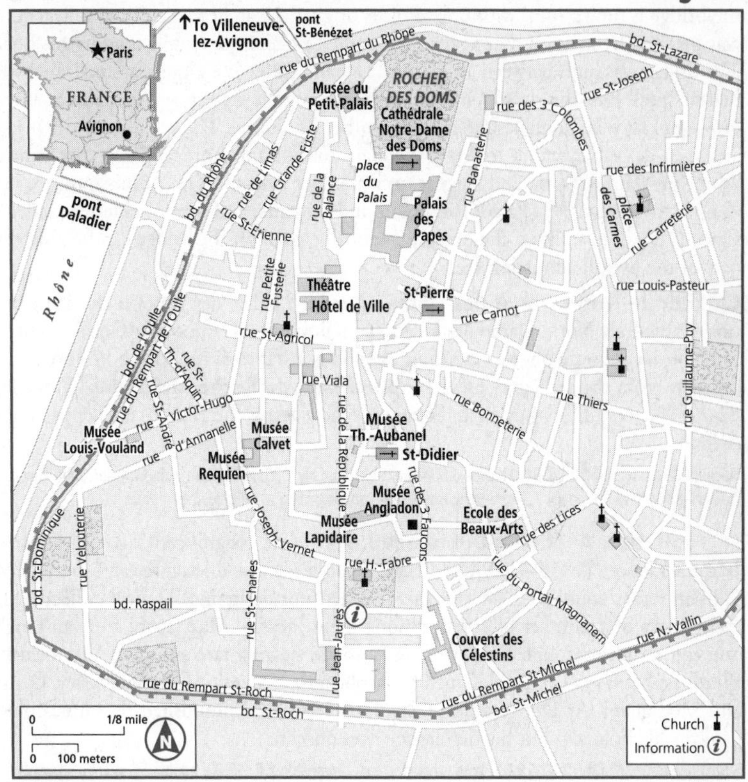

(✆ **04-90-27-92-61;** www.provence-bike.com), which rents all sorts of bikes, including 10-speed road bikes and mountain bikes, for around 9€ to 25€ ($12–$33) per day. A deposit of 150€ to 450€ ($195–$585), in cash or a credit card imprint, is required.

VISITOR INFORMATION The **Office de Tourisme** is at 41 cours Jean-Jaurès (✆ **04-32-74-32-74;** fax 04-90-82-95-03; www.ot-avignon.fr).

SPECIAL EVENTS The biggest celebration is the **Festival d'Avignon,** held July 6 to July 27. The international festival focuses on avant-garde theater, dance, and music. Part of the fun is the bacchanalia nightly in the streets. Tickets cost 10€ to 35€ ($13–$46). Prices for rooms and meals skyrocket, so make reservations far in advance. For information, contact the **Bureaux du Festival,** Espace Saint-Louis, 20 rue du Portail Boquier, Avignon 84000 (✆ **04-90-27-66-50;** www.festival-avignon.com).

SEEING THE SIGHTS IN AVIGNON

Even more famous than the papal residency is the ditty *"Sur le pont d'Avignon, l'on y danse, l'on y danse"* ("On the bridge of Avignon, we dance, we dance"). **Pont St-Bénézet** ★★ (✆ **04-90-85-60-16**) was far too narrow for the *danse* of the rhyme, however. Spanning the Rhône and connecting Avignon with Villeneuve-lèz-Avignon, the bridge is now a ruin, with only 4 of its original 22 arches. According to legend, it was inspired by a vision that a shepherd named Bénézet had while tending his flock. The bridge was built between 1177 and 1185 and suffered various disasters. (In 1669, half of it fell into the river.) On one of the piers is the two-story **Chapelle St-Nicolas**—one story in Romanesque style, the other in Gothic. The remains of the bridge are open daily November to March 9:30am to 5:45pm; April and October 9am to 7pm; July 9am to 9pm; and August to September 9am to 8pm. Admission is 3.50€ ($4.55) for adults, 3€ ($3.90) for seniors and students, and free for children under 8. Once you pay to walk on the bridge, the small chapel on the bridge can be visited as part of the overall admission fee.

Cathédrale Notre-Dame des Doms Near the Palais des Papes is the 12th-century Cathédrale Notre-Dame des Doms, containing the Flamboyant Gothic tomb of some of the apostate popes. Crowning the top is a statue of the Virgin from the 19th century. From the cathedral, enter the **promenade du Rocher-des-Doms** (© **04-90-82-27-96**) to stroll its garden and enjoy the view across the Rhône to Villeneuve-lèz-Avignon.

Place du Palais. © **04-90-86-81-01.** Free admission. Dec–Jan daily 7:30am–5:30pm; Feb–May and Sept–Nov daily 7:30am–6pm; June–Aug daily 7:30am–9pm. Hours may vary according to religious ceremonies.

La Fondation Angladon-Dubrujeaud ★★ The magnificent art collection of Jacques Doucet (1853–1929), the Belle Epoque dandy, dilettante, and designer of Parisian haute couture, is on view here. When not designing, Doucet collected the early works of a number of artists, among them Picasso, Max Jacob, and van Gogh. You can wander through Doucet's former abode viewing rare antiques; 16th-century Buddhas; Louis XVI chairs designed by Jacob; and canvases by Cézanne, Sisley, Degas, and Modigliani. At Doucet's death, his fortune was so diminished that his nephew paid for his funeral—but his rich legacy lives on here.

5 rue Laboureur. © **04-90-82-29-03.** www.angladon.com. Admission 6€ ($7.80) adults, 3€ ($3.90) students and children 14–18, 1.50€ ($1.95) children 7–13. Wed–Sun 1–6pm. Closed Nov.

Musée Calvet ★ In an 18th-century mansion, this museum holds a fine- and decorative-art collection that features the works of Vernet, David, Corot, Manet, and Soutine, plus a collection of ancient silverware. Our favorite oil is Bruegel the Younger's *Le Cortège Nuptial* (The Bridal Procession). Look for a copy of Bosch's *Adoration of the Magi,* plus sculptures by Camille Claudel.

65 rue Joseph-Vernet. © **04-90-86-33-84.** Admission 6€ ($7.80) adults, 3€ ($3.90) students, free for children under 13. Wed–Mon 10am–noon and 2–6pm.

Musée du Petit-Palais The museum contains an important collection of paintings from the Italian schools of the 13th to 16th centuries, with works from Florence, Venice, Siena, and Lombardy. Salons display 15th-century paintings done in Avignon, and several galleries contain Roman and Gothic sculptures.

Place du Palais des Papes. © **04-90-86-44-58.** Admission 6€ ($7.80) adults, 3€ ($3.90) students, free for children under 13. June–Sept Wed–Mon 10am–1pm and 2–6pm; Oct–May Wed–Mon 9:30am–1pm and 2–5:30pm.

Musée Lapidaire A 17th-century Jesuit church houses this collection of Gallo-Roman sculptures. This museum has been called a junkyard of antiquity: Gargoyles, Gallic and Roman statues, and broken pillars confront you at every turn. Most of the pieces have known greater glory and placement (often in temples); use your imagination to conjure up their lost splendor.

27 rue de la République. ✆ **04-90-86-33-84.** Admission 6€ ($7.80) adults, 3€ ($3.90) students 13–18, free for children under 13. Wed–Mon 10am–noon and 2–6pm.

Palais des Papes ★★★ Dominating Avignon from a hilltop is one of the most famous, or notorious, palaces in the Christian world. Headquarters of a schismatic group of cardinals who came close to destroying the authority of the popes in Rome, this fortress-showplace is the monument most frequently associated with Avignon. The guided tour (usually lasting 50 min.) can be monotonous, because most of the rooms have been stripped of their finery. The exception is the **Chapelle St-Jean,** known for its frescoes, which are attributed to the school of Matteo Giovanetti and were painted between 1345 and 1348. These frescoes present scenes from the life of John the Baptist and John the Evangelist. More Giovanetti frescoes are in the Chapelle St-Martial. They depict the miracles of St. Martial, the patron saint of Limousin.

The **Grand Tinel (Banquet Hall)** is about 41m (135 ft.) long and 9m (30 ft.) wide; the pope's table stood on the south side. The **Pope's Bedroom** is on the first floor of the Tour des Anges. Its walls are decorated in tempera foliage on which birds and squirrels perch. Bird cages are painted in the recesses of the windows. In a secular vein, the **Studium (Stag Room)**—the study of Clement VI—was frescoed in 1343 with hunting scenes. Added under the same Clement, who had a taste for grandeur, the **Grande Audience (Great Audience Hall)** contains frescoes of the prophets, also attributed to Giovanetti and painted in 1352. If you have time, consider a visit to the **Musée du Petit-Palais** (see above).

Place du Palais des Papes. ✆ **04-90-27-50-74.** www.palais-des-papes.com. Admission (including tour with guide or recording) 9.50€ ($12) adults, 7.50€ ($9.75) seniors and students, free for children under 8. July daily 9am–8pm; Apr–June and Aug–Oct daily 9am–7pm; Nov–Mar daily 9:30am–5:45pm.

STEPPING BACK IN TIME IN VILLENEUVE-LEZ-AVIGNON ★

The modern world is impinging on Avignon, but across the Rhône, the Middle Ages slumber on. When the popes lived in exile at Avignon, cardinals built palaces *(livrées)* across the river. Many visitors prefer to stay or dine here rather than in Avignon. Villenueve-lez-Avignon lies just across the Rhône from Avignon and is easiest to reach on bus no. 11, which crosses the larger of the two relatively modern bridges, the **pont Daladier.**

For information about the town, contact the **Office de Tourisme,** 1 place Charles David (✆ **04-90-25-61-33;** fax 04-90-25-91-55; www.villeneuvelesavignon.fr/tourisme).

Cardinal Arnaud de Via founded the **Eglise Notre-Dame,** place Meissonier (✆ **04-90-25-46-24**), in 1333. Other than its architecture, the church's most popular attraction is an antique copy (by an unknown sculptor) of Enguerrand Charonton's *Pietà,* the original of which is in the Louvre. The church is open April to September daily 10am to 12:30pm and 2 to 6:30pm; October to March daily 10am to noon and 2 to 5pm. Admission is free.

Chartreuse du Val-de-Bénédiction Inside France's largest Carthusian monastery, built in 1352, you'll find a church, three cloisters, rows of cells that housed the medieval monks, and rooms depicting aspects of their daily lives. Part of the complex is devoted to a workshop (the Centre National d'Ecritures et du Spectacle) for painters and writers, who live in the cells rent-free for up to a year to pursue their craft. Photo and art exhibits take place throughout the year.

Palais des Papes

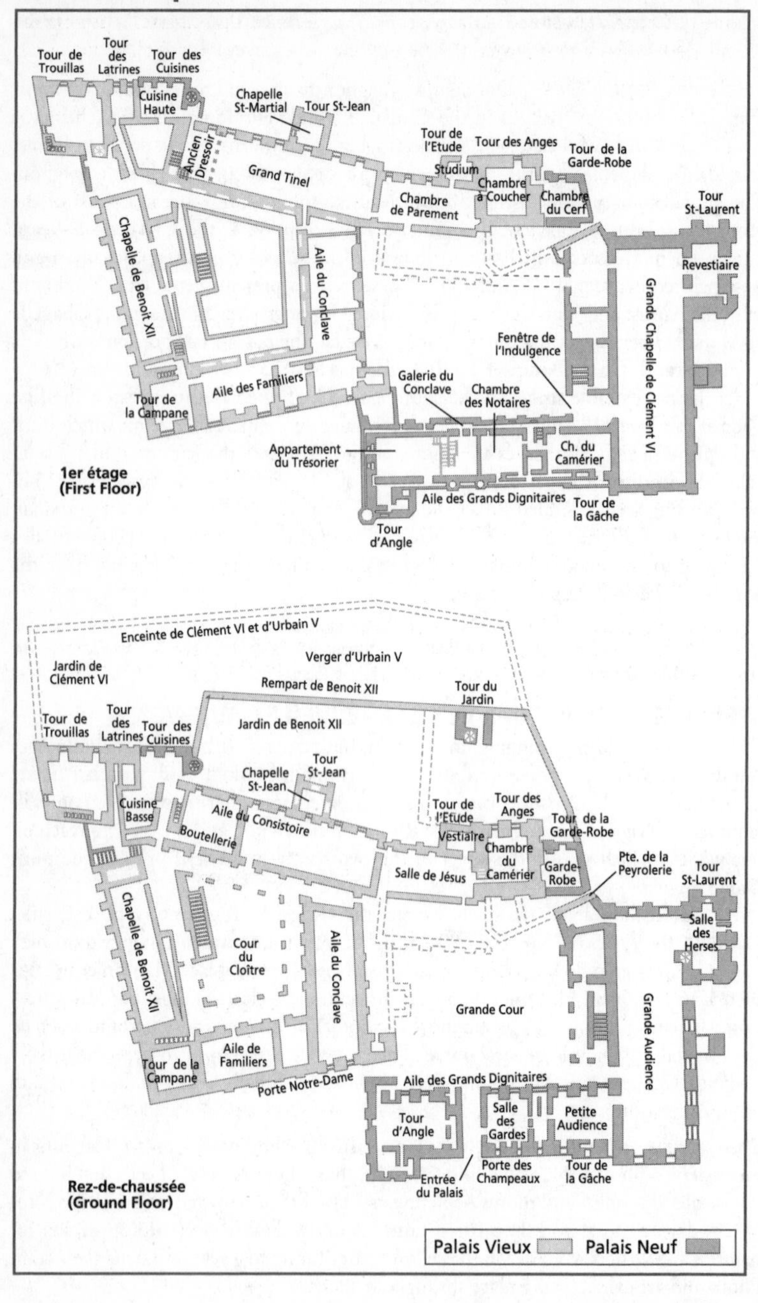

Pope Innocent VI (whose tomb you can view) founded this Charterhouse, which became the country's most powerful. The 12th-century graveyard cloister is lined with cells where the fathers prayed and meditated.

Rue de la République. ✆ **04-90-15-24-24.** Admission 6.50€ ($8.45) adults, 4.50€ ($5.85) students, free for children under 18. Apr–Sept daily 9am–6:30pm; Oct–Mar daily 9:30am–5:30pm.

Fort St-André ★ Crowning the town is Fort St-André, founded in 1360 by Jean-le-Bon to serve as a symbol of might to the pontifical powers across the river. Inside the fort is the Abbaye St-André, opened in the 18th century but now privately owned. Also within the fort you can visit a formal garden, a tranquil setting with a rose-trellis colonnade, fountains, and flowers.

Mont Andaon. ✆ **04-90-25-45-35.** Admission 5€ ($6.50) adults, 3.50€ ($4.55) students and ages 17–25, free for children under 17. Apr–Sept daily 10am–12:30 and 2–6pm; Oct–Mar daily 10am–noon and 2–5pm.

Musée Pierre de Luxembourg (Musée de Villeneuve-lez-Avignon) ★ Villeneuve's most important museum occupies a 14th-century home constructed for a local cardinal. The building was enlarged with a second story in the 1600s. Since its designation as a museum in 1996, it's been the richest repository of medieval painting and sculpture in the region. Its most treasured possessions include a remarkable *Coronation of the Virgin* by Enguerrand Charonton. Painted in 1453, it contains scenes that are Bosch-like in their horror, representing the denizens of hell supplicating the eternally calm mother of Christ. Equally important is a rare 14th-century ivory statue of the Virgin, by an unknown sculptor; it's one of the finest of its type anywhere.

Rue de la République. ✆ **04-90-27-49-67.** Admission 3€ ($3.90) adults, 2€ ($2.60) students and ages 18–25, free for children under 18. Apr–Sept Tues–Sun 10am–12:30pm and 2–6:30pm; Mar and Oct–Jan Tues–Sun 10am–noon and 2–5pm. Closed Feb.

Tour Philippe le Bel Philippe the Fair constructed this tower in the 13th century, when Villeneuve became a French possession; it served as a gateway to the kingdom. If you have the stamina, you can climb to the top for a view of Avignon and the Rhône Valley.

Rue Montée-de-la-Tour. ✆ **04-32-70-08-57.** Admission 1.60€ ($2.10) adults, .90€ ($1.15) students and children 12–17, free for children under 12. Apr–Sept daily 10am–noon and 2–7:30pm; Mar and Oct–Nov Tues–Sun 10am–noon and 2–7pm. Closed Dec–Feb.

SHOPPING

The idea behind **Mistral Les Indiens de Nîmes,** 19 rue Joseph-Vernet (✆ **04-90-86-32-05**), is to duplicate 18th- and 19th-century Provençal fabric patterns. Fabrics are available by the meter and in the form of clothing for men, women, and children. In addition, you can buy kitchenware and furniture inspired by Provence and the steamy wetlands west of Marseille.

The clothing at **Souleiado,** 5 rue Joseph Vernet (✆ **04-90-86-47-67**), derives from traditional Provençal costumes. Most of the clothing is for women. Fabrics are for sale by the meter. The name means "first ray of sunshine after a storm."

Hervé Baume, 19 rue Petite Fusterie (✆ **04-90-86-37-66**), is for those who yearn to set a Provençal table. The place is piled high with a little bit of everything—from Directoire dinner services to handblown crystal hurricane lamps. **Jaffier-Parsi,** 42 rue des Fourbisseurs (✆ **04-90-86-08-85**), is known for its copper saucepans from the Norman town of Villedieu-les-Poêles, which has been making them since the Middle Ages. If you're seeking new perspective on Provençal pottery, go to **Terre è Provence,**

26 rue de la République (✆ **04-90-85-56-45**). You can pick up wonderful kitsch—perhaps terra-cotta plates decorated with three-dimensional cicadas.

Most markets in Avignon are open 6am to 1pm. The biggest covered market with 40 different merchants is **Les Halles,** place Pie, open Tuesday to Sunday. Other smaller **food markets** are on place Parking des Italiens on Sunday, and on place St-Chamand also on Sunday. The **flower market** is on place des Carmes on Saturday, and the **flea market** is in the same place on Sunday.

WHERE TO STAY

EXPENSIVE

Hôtel d'Europe ★★★ This deluxe hostelry, in operation since 1799, is almost the equal of La Mirande (see below), though slightly cheaper. You enter the vine-covered hotel through a courtyard, which holds tables in the warmer months. The grand hall and salons contain antiques, and the good-size guest rooms have handsome decor and period furnishings. Two suites are on the roof, with views of the Palais des Papes. In some twin-bedded rooms, the beds are a bit narrow. Overall, accommodations are comfortable, with touches of Gallic charm. The spacious bathrooms are handsomely equipped, and each has a combination tub/shower. The restaurant, which specializes in traditional French and Provençal cuisine, is one of the best in Avignon.

12 place Crillon, Avignon 84000. ✆ **04-90-14-76-76.** Fax 04-90-14-76-71. www.heurope.com. 44 units. 163€–467€ ($212–$607) double; 792€ ($1,030) suite. AE, DC, MC, V. Parking 15€ ($20). **Amenities:** Restaurant; bar; business services; room service; babysitting; laundry service; dry cleaning; nonsmoking rooms. *In room:* A/C, TV, minibar, hair dryer, safe.

La Mirande ★★★ In the heart of Avignon behind the Palais des Papes, this 700-year-old town house is one of France's grand little luxuries. In 1987, Achim and Hannelore Stein transformed it into a citadel of opulence. The hotel displays 2 centuries of decorative art, from the 1700s Salon Chinois to the Salon Rouge, with striped walls in Rothschild red. Room no. 20 is the most sought-after—its lavish premises open onto the garden. All rooms are stunning, with exquisite decor, hand-printed fabrics on the walls, antiques, bedside controls, and huge bathtubs. The restaurant, among the finest in Avignon, deserves its one Michelin star.

4 place de la Mirande, Avignon 84000. ✆ **04-90-85-93-93.** Fax 04-90-86-26-85. www.la-mirande.fr. 20 units. 295€–520€ ($384–$676) double; 620€–820€ ($806–$1,066) suite. AE, DC, MC, V. Parking 25€ ($33). **Amenities:** Restaurant; bar; room service; babysitting; laundry service; dry cleaning; nonsmoking rooms; limited-mobility rooms. *In room:* A/C, TV, minibar, hair dryer, safe.

MODERATE

Hôtel Clarion Cloître St-Louis ★ This hotel is in a former Jesuit school built in the 1580s. Much of the original premises remain, including the baroque facade, the wraparound arcades, and the soaring ceiling vaults. Guest rooms are more functional; in fact, they're rather dull as a result of renovations. Rooms range from medium-size to spacious, and some have sliding glass doors overlooking the patio. Each unit has modern decor without a lot of extras; all but three have tub/shower combinations.

20 rue du Portail Boquier, Avignon 84000. ✆ **800/CLARION** in the U.S., or 04-90-27-55-55. Fax 04-90-82-24-01. www.cloitre-saint-louis.com. 80 units. 100€–240€ ($130–$312) double; 220€–360€ ($286–$468) suite. AE, DC, MC, V. Parking 10€–15€ ($13–$20). **Amenities:** Restaurant; bar; outdoor pool; room service; nonsmoking rooms; limited-mobility rooms. *In room:* A/C, TV, minibar, hair dryer, safe.

Mercure Pont d'Avignon *Value* This chain hotel is one of the best in Avignon, and it's a good deal for what it offers. It lies within the city walls, at the foot of the Palais des Papes. Rooms are well furnished yet functional; what they lack in style they make up for in comfort. Bathrooms are small, but most contain tub/shower combinations. Breakfast is the only meal served.

Quartier de la Balance, rue Ferruce, Avignon 84000. ✆ **04-90-80-93-93.** Fax 04-90-80-93-94. www.mercure.com. 87 units. 96€–135€ ($125–$176) double. Children under 16 stay free in parent's room. AE, DC, MC, V. Parking 9€ ($12). **Amenities:** Bar; laundry service; dry cleaning; nonsmoking rooms. *In room:* A/C, TV, minibar, hair dryer, safe.

INEXPENSIVE

Hôtel d'Angleterre This three-story Art Deco structure in the heart of Avignon is the city's best budget hotel, with the advantage of being located inside the city ramparts. It was built in 1929 of gray stone, emulating the style that local builders imagined was characteristic of English houses. The rooms are on the small side, but they are comfortably furnished; and most have compact shower-only bathrooms. Breakfast is the only meal served.

29 bd. Raspail, Avignon 84000. ✆ **04-90-86-34-31.** Fax 04-90-86-86-74. www.hoteldangleterre.fr. 39 units. 57€–70€ ($74–$91) double. AE, MC, V. Free parking. Closed Dec 17–Jan 17. **Amenities:** Laundry service; dry cleaning. *In room:* A/C, TV, Wi-Fi.

Hôtel de l'Atelier The name of this 16th-century house (which translates as "the workshop") derives from the weaving machines that produced fabrics here during the 1950s. Since 2003, it has been the domain of Gérard and Annick Burret, who outfit their rooms in as romantic and nostalgic a style as possible. Each of the accommodations, some with high beamed ceilings, comes with a neatly tiled bathroom with shower or bathtub. You'll find the hotel in the heart of Villeneuve-lèz-Avignon, a 2-minute walk from the Pierre de Luxembourg museum. A rear garden with potted orange and fig trees provides fruit for breakfast. A stone fireplace in the duplex lounge blazes on cold winter nights. Continental breakfast is the only meal served.

5 rue de la Foire, Villeneuve-lez-Avignon 30400. ✆ **04-90-25-01-84.** Fax 04-90-25-80-06. www.hoteldelatelier.com. 23 units. 53€–104€ ($69–$135) double. AE, MC, V. Parking 9€ ($12) in nearby garage. **Amenities:** Limited room service. *In room:* TV, hair dryer, safe.

Hôtel le Médiéval About 3 blocks south of the Palais des Papes, this three-story town house from the late 1600s is well maintained and uncomplicated. Under beamed ceilings, the comfortable guest rooms are medium-size to spacious. Most peaceful are the units that overlook the inner courtyard, with its pots of flowers and shrubs. Those that overlook a congested medieval street corner might be noisier, but they have a rough-and-ready charm of their own. Most of the small bathrooms have tub/shower combinations.

15 rue Petite Saunerie, Avignon 84000. ✆ **04-90-86-11-06.** Fax 04-90-82-08-64. www.hotelmedieval.com. 34 units. 55€–70€ ($72–$91) double; extra bed 8€ ($10). MC, V. Closed Dec 22–Feb 3. **Amenities:** Limited room service; nonsmoking rooms. *In room:* TV, hair dryer, Wi-Fi.

WHERE TO DINE

Hôtel d'Europe and **La Mirande** (see "Where to Stay," above) have excellent restaurants.

Brunel PROVENÇAL This flower-filled restaurant is in the heart of Avignon. Managed by the Brunel family, it offers such superb dishes as monkfish with anise-flavored butter; confit of lamb couscous; and tuna steak with coulis of capers and onions. Artichoke hearts accompany grilled John Dory, and even pigs' feet are sublime. The desserts are prepared fresh daily. You can order house wines by the carafe.

46 rue de La Balance. ✆ **04-90-85-24-83.** Reservations required. Main courses 10€–18€ ($13–$23) lunch, 25€–33€ ($33–$43) dinner; fixed-price menu 33€ ($43). AE, MC, V. Tues–Sat noon–2pm and 7:45–10pm. Open Mon–Sat in July. Closed first 2 weeks in Aug and Dec 20–Jan 6.

Christian Etienne ★★★ PROVENÇAL The stone house containing this restaurant was built in 1180, around the same time as the Palais des Papes (next door). Owner Christian Etienne reaches new culinary heights. His dining room contains early-16th-century frescoes honoring the marriage of Anne de Bretagne to the French king in 1491. Several of the fixed-price menus feature themes: Two present seasonal tomatoes, mushrooms, or other vegetables; one offers preparations of lobster; and the priciest relies on the chef's imagination *(menu confiance)* for unique combinations. In summer, look for the vegetable menu entirely based on ripe tomatoes; the main course is a mousse of lamb, eggplants, tomatoes, and herbs. The vegetable menus aren't completely vegetarian; they're flavored with meat, fish, or meat drippings. A la carte specialties include filet of perch with Châteauneuf-du-Pape, rack of lamb with fresh thyme and garlic essence, filet of venison with foie gras, and a dessert of fennel sorbet with saffron-flavored English cream sauce.

10 rue Mons. ✆ **04-90-86-16-50.** www.christian-etienne.fr. Reservations required. Main courses 25€–45€ ($33–$59); fixed-price lunch 35€–115€ ($46–$150); fixed-price dinner 60€–115€ ($78–$150). AE, DC, MC, V. Tues–Sat noon–1:15pm and 7:30-9:15pm. Closed first 2 weeks in Aug and Dec 20–Jan 6.

Hiély-Lucullus ★★ FRENCH Before the arrival of Christian Etienne (see above), this Relais Gourmand property reigned supreme in Avignon. Today it is still formidable competition. The Belle Epoque decor enhances the grand cuisine. Market-fresh products go into innovative dishes such as crayfish-stuffed ravioli flavored with fresh sage and served with pumpkin sauce, filet of female venison with tangy honey sauce, and escalope of sautéed foie gras on toasted rye bread. Lots of fresh fish is imported daily and cooked to perfection. The *pièce de résistance* is *agneau des Alpilles grillé* (grilled Alpine lamb). Dessert may be vanilla-bourbon cream in puff pastry. Carafe wines include Tavel Rosé and Châteauneuf-du-Pape.

5 rue de la République. ✆ **04-90-86-17-07.** Reservations required. Main courses 20€–25€ ($26–$33); fixed-price menu 28€–48€ ($36–$62). AE, MC, V. Daily noon–2pm and 7–10pm.

La Compagnie des Comptoirs ★ MEDITERRANEAN Part of the charm of this place derives from the contrast between its contemporary cuisine and the grandeur of its medieval setting, a 10-minute walk from the Palais des Papes. The menu celebrates France's many colonial influences—spices and techniques from North Africa, Egypt, India, Canada, Louisiana, and parts of Africa. Menu items may include a tart with comfit of onions, thin-sliced smoked swordfish, and orange-flavored vinaigrette; giant prawns slowly cooked with comfit of lemons, coriander, cucumbers, and onions; roasted flank of Provençal bull with anchovy sauce, potato purée, and olive oil; and chicken breasts dredged in pulverized hazelnuts, served with prunes and exotic mushrooms.

The long, narrow, high-ceilinged dining rooms—originally the hallways and courtyards of a 1363 Benedictine convent that was dissolved during the French Revolution—have been meticulously restored. The restaurant is also a nightclub and bar, and the action spills into the gracefully proportioned interior courtyard. Music derives from a changing series of DJs who spin tunes Thursday to Saturday in the bar-lounge from 6pm to 1am.

83 rue Joseph-Vernet. ✆ **04-90-85-99-04.** www.lacompagiedescomptoirs.com. Reservations recommended. Main courses 14€–33€ ($18–$43). AE, DC, MC, V. Tues–Sat noon–2pm and 7:30–11pm.

La Fourchette *Value* FRENCH This bistro offers creative cooking at a moderate price, although it shuts down on the weekends. Its two airy dining rooms have large bay windows that flood the inside with light. You may begin with fresh sardines flavored with citrus, ravioli filled with haddock, or parfait of chicken livers with spinach flan and comfit of onions. For a main course, we recommend monkfish stew with endive, or daube of beef with gratin of macaroni.

7 rue Racine. ✆ **04-90-85-20-93.** Fixed-price lunch 25€–31€ ($33–$40); fixed-price dinner 31€ ($40). MC, V. Mon–Fri 12:15–1:45pm and 7:15–9:45pm. Closed 3 weeks in Aug. Bus: 11.

AVIGNON AFTER DARK

Near the Palais des Papes is **Le Grand Café,** La Manutention (✆ **04-90-86-86-77**), a restaurant-bar-cafe that just may become your favorite watering hole. Behind the Palais des Papes, it's in an entertainment complex in a former military supply warehouse. The dance-club standby is **Les Ambassadeurs,** 27 rue Bancasse (✆ **04-90-86-31-55**); it's more animated than its competitor, **Piano Bar Le Blues,** 25 rue Carnot (✆ **04-90-85-79-71**). Nearby is a restaurant, **Red Zone,** 27 rue Carnot (✆ **04-90-27-02-44;** www.redzonebar.com), that books live performances in the bar area by whatever band happens to be in town. There's also music and dancing at **La Compagnie des Comptoirs** (see "Where to Dine," above).

Winning the award for most unpronounceable name is **Le Woolloomooloo** (it means "black kangaroo" in an Australian Aboriginal dialect), 16 bis rue des Teinturiers (✆ **04-90-85-28-44**). The bar and cafe complement a separate room devoted to the cuisine of France and a changing roster of cuisines from Asia, Africa, and South America. An alternative is **Bokao's Café,** 9 quai St-Lazare (✆ **04-90-82-47-95;** www.bokaos.fr), a restaurant and disco. The most viable option for lesbians and gays is **L'Esclav,** 12 rue de Limas (✆ **04-90-85-14-91**), a bar and disco that are the focal point of the city's gay community.

3 St-Rémy-de-Provence ★

705km (438 miles) S of Paris, 26km (16 miles) NE of Arles, 19km (12 miles) S of Avignon, 13km (8 miles) N of Les Baux

Nostradamus, the physician and astrologer, was born here in 1503. However, St-Rémy is more closely associated with van Gogh. He committed himself to an asylum here in 1889 after cutting off his left ear. Between moods of despair, he painted such works as *Olive Trees* and *Cypresses.*

Come to sleepy St-Rémy not only for its memories and sights but also for a glimpse of small-town Provençal life. It's a market town of considerable charm that draws the occasional visiting celebrity trying to escape the spotlight.

ESSENTIALS

GETTING THERE Local **buses** from Avignon (four to nine per day) take 40 minutes and cost around 5€ ($6.50) one-way. In St-Rémy, buses pull into the place de la République, in the town center. For bus information, call ✆ **04-90-82-07-35.** If you're **driving,** head south from Avignon along D571.

VISITOR INFORMATION The **Office de Tourisme** is on place Jean-Jaurès (✆ **04-90-92-05-22;** fax 04-90-92-38-52; www.saintremy-de-provence.com).

SEEING THE SIGHTS

Monastère St-Paul-de-Mausolée ★★ Visitors can see the 12th-century cloisters of the asylum that van Gogh made famous in his paintings. Now a psychiatric hospital for women, the former monastery is east of D5, a short drive north of Glanum (see below). You can't visit the cell where the artist was confined from 1889 to 1890, but it's worth visiting to explore the Romanesque chapel and cloisters. The circular arches and columns have beautifully carved capitals. On your way to the church, you'll see a bust of van Gogh.

Av. Edgar-le-Roy. ✆ **04-90-92-77-00.** Admission 4€ ($5.20) adults, 3€ ($3.90) students and children 12–16, free for children under 12. Apr–Oct daily 9:30am–6pm; Nov–Mar Tues–Sun 10:30am–5pm.

Ruines de Glanum ★ A Gallo-Roman settlement thrived here during the final days of the Roman Empire. Its monuments include a triumphal arch from the time of Julius Caesar, along with a cenotaph called the Mausolée des Jules. Garlanded with sculptured fruits and flowers, the arch dates from 20 B.C. and is the oldest in Provence. The mausoleum was raised to honor the grandsons of Augustus and is the only extant monument of its type. In the area are entire streets and foundations of private residences from the 1st-century town, plus some remains from a Gallo-Greek town of the 2nd century B.C.

Av. Vincent-van-Gogh. From St-Rémy, take D5 1.5km (1 mile) south, following signs to LES ANTIQUES. ✆ **04-90-92-23-79.** Admission 6.50€ ($8.45) adults, 4.50€ ($5.85) students and ages 18–25, free for children under 18. Apr–Aug daily 10am–6:30pm; Sept–Mar Tues–Sun 10:30am–5pm.

SHOPPING

St-Rémy is a center for home decorating, with many antiques shops and fabric stores on the narrow streets of the old town and the boulevards surrounding it. A couple antiques stores are on the outskirts of town: **Au Broc de St-Ouen,** route d'Avignon (✆ **04-90-92-28-90**), has several dealers; and **Portes Anciennes,** route d'Avignon (✆ **04-90-92-13-13;** www.portesanciennes.com), sells a good selection of antiques and flea-market finds. St-Rémy is known for its great **markets.** On Wednesday morning on the streets of the old town, vendors spread out their wares, including spices, olives, fabrics, and crafts. On Saturday morning, a small vegetable market is held near the Eglise St-Martin on boulevard Marceau.

WHERE TO STAY

Château de Roussan ★★ *Finds* Although other château hotels are more stylish, this one is more evocative of another time. Its most famous resident, the psychic Nostradamus, lived in an outbuilding a few steps from the front door. Today, you'll pass beneath an archway of 300-year-old trees leading to the neoclassical facade, built in 1701. Most rooms are spacious. Expect old-fashioned plumbing with combination tub/showers. The staff can be off-putting, but the sense of mysticism and the historical importance of this place usually compensate for any crabbiness. History will envelop you as you wander the grounds, especially when you come upon the sculptures lining a basin, fed by a stream.

Rte. de Tarascon, St-Rémy-de-Provence 13210. From the center, head in the direction of Tarascon (D99) for 2km (1¼ miles). ✆ **04-90-92-11-63.** Fax 04-90-92-50-59. www.chateau-de-roussan.com. 19 units. 60€–102€ ($78–$133) double. AE, DC, MC, V. **Amenities:** Restaurant; bar; room service; laundry service; computer room; TV room; limited-mobility rooms. *In room:* No phone, but management will provide access to portable phone; hair dryer and iron both available on request.

Château des Alpilles ★★★ For luxury and refinement, this is the only château in the area that can equal Vallon de Valrugues (see below). It sits in the center of a tree-studded park 2km (1¼ miles) from the center of St-Rémy. The Pichot family built it in 1827, and it housed Chateaubriand and other luminaries. When Françoise Bon converted the mansion in 1980, she wanted to create a "house for paying friends." The rooms combine an antique setting with plush upholstery, rich carpeting, and vibrant colors with a garden graced with majestic magnolias. Each guest room boasts whimsical accessories, like a pair of porcelain panthers flanking one of the mantels, and travertine-trimmed bathtubs. Units in the 19th-century annex are as comfortable as those in the main house. The midsize bathrooms have tub/showers.

Ancienne Route du Grès, St-Rémy-de-Provence 13210. ✆ **04-90-92-03-33.** Fax 04-90-92-45-17. www.chateaualpilles.com. 21 units. 170€–250€ ($221–$325) double; 245€–380€ ($319–$494) suite. AE, DC, MC, V. Closed Nov 15–Feb 15. **Amenities:** Restaurant; outdoor pool; 2 tennis courts; sauna; room service; laundry service. *In room:* TV, minibar, hair dryer, safe.

Hostellerie du Vallon de Valrugues ★★★ Surrounded by a park, this hotel has the best accommodations and restaurant in town. Constructed in the 1970s, it resembles a fantasy version of an ancient Roman villa. Owner Jean-Michel Gallon offers beautiful rooms and suites. They have marble bathrooms, all with tub/showers. The property has a putting green, and guests have access to horseback riding. The restaurant's terrace is as appealing as its cuisine, which is winning praise for innovative light dishes, such as John Dory with truffles, and frozen nougat with comfit of fruits. Fixed-price menus are 71€ ($92); a children's menu is 20€ ($26).

Chemin Canto-Cigalo, St-Rémy-de-Provence 13210. ✆ **04-90-92-04-40.** Fax 04-90-92-44-01. www.vallondevalrugues.com. 53 units. 190€–280€ ($247–$364) double; 390€–660€ ($507–$858) suite. AE, MC, V. Closed 3 weeks in Feb. **Amenities:** Restaurant; bar; outdoor pool; 2 tennis courts; gym; sauna; room service; babysitting; laundry service; dry cleaning; nonsmoking rooms; limited-mobility rooms. *In room:* A/C, TV, minibar, hair dryer, safe.

Hôtel du Soleil In 1965, a private home was converted into this amiable, unpretentious hotel, a 4-minute walk south of the town center. The hotel is set in a garden with grand trees and a wrought-iron gazebo. Inside, the assortment of ceiling beams and Provençal accessories evoke the region around you. Guest rooms are simple but convenient, with tasteful furnishings and small, tiled bathrooms (some with both tub and shower). You'll want to spend part of your time beside the pool, ringed by chaise longues.

35 av. Pasteur, 13210 St-Rémy-de-Provence. ✆ **04-90-92-00-63.** Fax 04-90-92-61-07. www.hotelsoleil.com. 24 units. 55€–72€ ($72–$94) double; 75€–90€ ($98–$117) suite. AE, DC, MC, V. Closed Nov to early Mar. **Amenities:** Bar; outdoor pool; limited room service. *In room:* TV, hair dryer, safe.

Hôtel les Ateliers de l'Image Fans refer to this place as "trendy but not posh." It's one of the most unusual hotels in the region, nestled in a 1-hectare (2½-acre) park studded with olive trees and cypresses. The bar and the less expensive guest rooms are in a simple, boxy building that was originally a movie theater. The more luxurious rooms and the restaurant fill the radically restored premises of a 19th-century building that was the town's first bona fide hotel. In both buildings, rooms are comfortable, stylish, and airy, outfitted with minimalist wood and metallic furniture. Many look out on the park and the faraway foothills. Five units are duplex suites, each with a private steam room, and one suite is a "treehouse," supported by the majestic branches of a century-old plane tree and accessible from an upper floor of the main building by a catwalk. Its restaurant, **Chez l'Ami,** fuses French and Asian flavors, and its unique Le Bar (see "St-Rémy after Dark," below) is a nighttime draw.

36 bd. Victor Hugo, St-Rémy-de-Provence 13210. ✆ **04-90-92-51-50.** Fax 04-90-92-43-52. www.hotelphoto.com. 32 units. 165€–380€ ($215–$494) double; 300€–600€ ($390–$780) duplex suite. Rates include breakfast. AE, DC, MC, V. Closed Dec 11–Feb 28. **Amenities:** Restaurant; bar; pool; room service; babysitting; laundry service; nonsmoking rooms; limited-mobility rooms. *In room:* A/C, TV, hair dryer, safe.

La Maison du Village ★★ *Finds* Our favorite nest in this *über* Provençal town is this meticulously restored 18th-century town house in the center of St-Rémy. Warm and welcoming, each unit is a suite with a big sitting area and a luxurious bathroom. They're decorated in soft colors, with tasteful fabrics and wrought-iron beds. The old-fashioned, free-standing bathtubs are large enough for a romantic duo. On request, the innkeepers serve organic meals in the family-style dining room or the little "secret garden" out back. Drinks are served and soft music plays in the communal lounge.

10 rue du Mai 1945, St-Rémy-de-Provence 13210. ✆ **04-32-60-68-20.** Fax 04-32-60-68-21. www.lamaisondu village.com. 5 units. 190€ ($247) double. MC, V. **Amenities:** Lounge; limited room service. *In room:* TV.

WHERE TO DINE

Another great choice is the restaurant at the **Hostellerie du Vallon de Valrugues** (see above).

La Gousse d'Ail PROVENÇAL A small, family-run place, La Gousse d'Ail serves good food at reasonable prices. Specialties include *escargot à la Provençal* (snails with garlic and regional herbs) and vegetarian dishes featuring colorful produce from the market, prepared with light sauces and local herbs. At least 1 day a week the chef prepares the restaurant's famous bouillabaisse. The waitstaff speaks English.

6 bd. Marceau. ✆ **04-90-92-16-87.** www.la-goussedail.com. Reservations recommended. Main courses 15€–20€ ($20–$26); fixed-price lunch 15€ ($20); fixed-price dinner 30€–40€ ($39–$52). AE, MC, V. Fri–Wed noon–2:30pm and 7–10pm. Closed Jan 28–Feb 28.

La Maison Jaune ★★ FRENCH/PROVENÇAL One of the most enduringly popular restaurants in St-Rémy is in the former residence of an 18th-century merchant. Today, in a pair of dining rooms occupying two floors, you'll appreciate cuisine prepared and served with flair by François and Catherine Perraud. In nice weather, additional seats are on a terrace overlooking the Hôtel de Sade. Menu items include pigeon roasted in wine from Les Baux; grilled sardines served with candied lemon and raw fennel; artichoke hearts marinated in white wine and served with tomatoes; and succulent roasted rack of lamb served with tapenade of black olives and anchovies.

15 rue Carnot. ✆ **04-90-92-56-14.** Reservations required. Fixed-price menu 34€–62€ ($44–$81). MC, V. Tues–Sun noon–1:30pm; Tues–Sat 7–9:30pm. Closed Jan–Feb.

ST-REMY AFTER DARK

Le Bar, in the Hôtel les Ateliers de l'Image, 36 bd. Victor Hugo (✆ **04-90-92-51-50**), is an unusual destination in this laid-back town. In a former Art Deco movie theater, it serves party-colored cocktails and occasional bouts of live music from 6pm to midnight.

4 Arles ★★★

725km (450 miles) S of Paris, 35km (22 miles) SW of Avignon, 89km (55 miles) NW of Marseille

Often called the soul of Provence, this town on the Rhône attracts art lovers, archaeologists, and historians. To the delight of visitors, many of the vistas van Gogh painted so luminously remain. The painter left Paris for Arles in 1888, the same year he cut

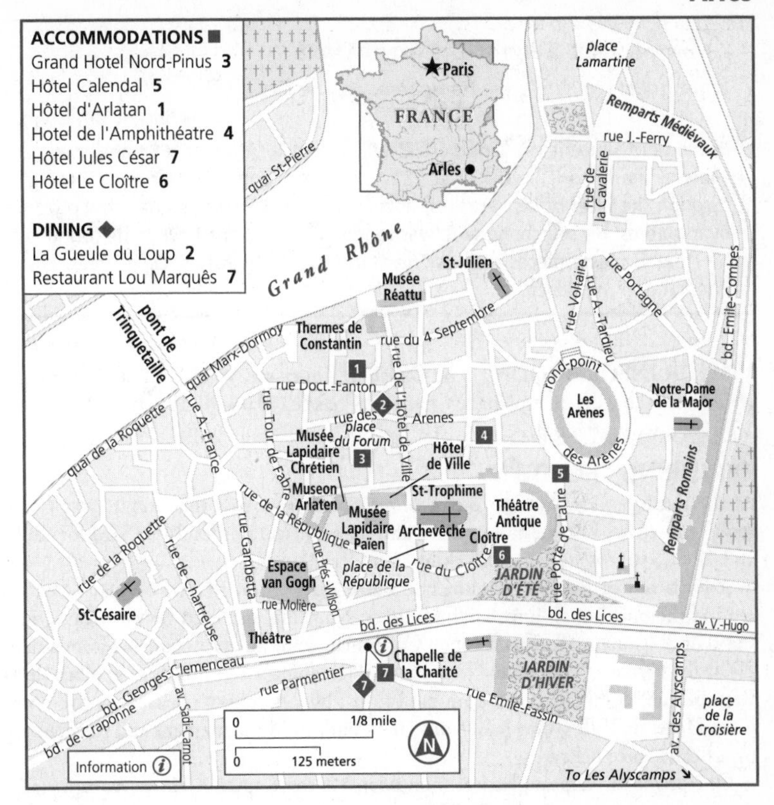

off part of his left ear. He painted some of his most celebrated works here, including *The Starry Night, The Bridge at Arles, Sunflowers,* and *L'Arlésienne.*

The Greeks are said to have founded Arles in the 6th century B.C. Julius Caesar established a Roman colony here. Constantine the Great named it the second capital of his empire in A.D. 306, when it was known as "the little Rome of the Gauls." Arles was incorporated into France in 1481.

Though Arles doesn't possess as much charm as Aix-en-Provence, it's still rewarding to visit, with first-rate museums, excellent restaurants, and summer festivals. The city today, with a population of 55,000, isn't quite as lovely as it was, but it has enough of the antique charm of Provence to keep its appeal alive.

ESSENTIALS

GETTING THERE There are hourly rail connections between Arles and Avignon (20 min.; 6€–10€/$7.80–$13), Marseille (50 min.; 12€/$16), and Nîmes (20 min.; 6.90€/$8.95). For rail schedules and information, call ✆ **08-92-35-35-35.** There are about four **buses** per day from Aix-en-Provence (trip time: 1 hr., 45 min.). For bus information, call ✆ **08-10-00-08-16.** If **driving,** head south along D570 from Avignon.

If you'd like to get around by bicycle, head for **Cycles Peugeot,** 15 rue du Pont (✆ **04-90-96-03-77**), which rents bikes at 30€ ($39) per day.

Moments Van Gogh's "Different Light"

What strikes me here is the transparency of the air.

—Vincent van Gogh

Dutch-born Vincent van Gogh (1853–90) moved to Arles in 1888 and spent 2 years in the historic towns of Les Baux, St-Rémy, and Stes-Maries, recording, through the filter of his neuroses, dozens of Impressionistic scenes now prized by museums. His search, he said, was for "a different light." When he found it, he created masterpieces such as *The Starry Night, Cypresses, Olive Trees,* and *Boats Along the Beach.*

VISITOR INFORMATION The **Office de Tourisme,** where you can buy a *billet global* (see below), is on esplanade Charles-de-Gaulle (✆ **04-90-18-41-20;** fax 04-90-18-41-29; www.arles.org).

EXPLORING THE TOWN

At the tourist office, you can buy a ***billet global*** ★, a pass that admits you to the town's museums, Roman monuments, and major attractions for 14€ ($18) for adults and 12€ ($16) for students and children under 19.

Arles is full of Roman monuments. **Place du Forum,** shaded by plane trees, is around the old Roman forum. The Café de Nuit, immortalized by van Gogh, once stood on this square. You can see two Corinthian columns and fragments from a temple at the corner of the Hôtel Nord-Pinus. Three blocks south of here is **place de la République,** dominated by a 15m-tall (49-ft.) blue porphyry obelisk. On the north is the **Hôtel de Ville** (town hall) from 1673, built to Mansart's plans and surmounted by a Renaissance belfry.

One of the city's great classical monuments is the Roman **Théâtre Antique** ★★, rue du Cloître (✆ **04-90-93-05-23**). Augustus began the theater in the 1st century; only two Corinthian columns remain. The *Venus of Arles* was discovered here in 1651. Take rue de la Calade from city hall. The theater is open May to September daily 9am to 6pm; March, April, and October daily 9 to 11:30am and 2 to 5:30pm; November to February daily 10 to 11:30am and 2 to 4:30pm. Admission is 3€ ($3.90) for adults, 2.20€ ($2.85) for students and children 12 to 18, and free for children under 12. Nearby is the **Amphitheater (Les Arènes)** ★★, rond-pont des Arènes (✆ **04-90-49-36-86**), also built in the 1st century. Sometimes called Le Cirque Romain, it seats almost 25,000 and still hosts bullfights in summer. Visit at your own risk: The stone steps are uneven, and much of the masonry is worn. For a good view, you can climb the three towers that remain from medieval times, when the amphitheater was turned into a fortress. Hours are May to September daily 9am to 7pm; March, April, and October daily 9am to 6pm; November to February daily 10am to 4:30pm. Admission costs 4€ ($5.20) for adults, 3€ ($3.90) for students and children under 19.

Eglise St-Trophime ★ This church is noted for its 12th-century portal, one of the finest achievements of the southern Romanesque style. Frederick Barbarossa was crowned king of Arles here in 1178. In the pediment, Christ is surrounded by the symbols of the Evangelists. The cloister, in Gothic and Romanesque styles, is noted for its medieval carvings.

East side of place de la République. ✆ **04-90-49-38-00.** Free admission to church; cloister 3.50€ ($4.55) adults, 2.60€ ($3.40) students and children 12–18, free for children under 12. Church daily 8:30am–6:30pm. Cloister Nov–Feb daily 10am–4:30pm; Mar–Apr and Oct daily 9am–5:30pm; May–Sept daily 9am–6pm. Closed Jan 1, May 1, Nov 1, and Dec 25.

Les Alyscamps ★ Perhaps the most memorable sight in Arles, this Christian graveyard was once a Roman necropolis. After being converted into a Christian burial ground in the 4th century, it became a setting for legends and was even mentioned in Dante's *Inferno.* Today, it's lined with poplars and studded with ancient sarcophagi. Arlesiens escape here to enjoy a respite from the heat.

Rue Pierre-Renaudel. ✆ **04-90-49-36-87.** Admission 3.50€ ($4.55) adults, 2.60€ ($3.40) children 12–18, free for children under 12. Nov–Feb daily 10–11:30am and 2–4:30pm; Mar–Apr and Oct daily 9–11:30am and 2–5:30pm; May–Sept daily 9am–6pm. Closed Jan 1, May 1, Nov 1, and Dec 25.

Musée de l'Arles et de la Provence Antiques ★★ Half a mile south of the town center within a hypermodern setting built in 1995, you'll find one of the world's most famous collections of Roman Christian sarcophagi, plus a rich ensemble of sculptures, mosaics, and inscriptions from the Augustinian period to the 6th century A.D. Eleven detailed models show ancient monuments of the region as they existed in the past.

Presqu'île du Cirque Romain. ✆ **04-90-18-89-80.** Admission 5.50€ ($7.15) adults, 4€ ($5.20) students and children under 18. Mar–Oct daily 9am–7pm; Nov–Feb daily 10am–5pm. Closed Jan 1, May 1, Nov 1, and Dec 25.

Musée Réattu ★ This collection, which belonged to the local painter Jacques Réattu, has been updated recently with works including etchings and drawings by Picasso. Other pieces are by Alechinsky, Dufy, and Zadkine. Note the Arras tapestries from the 16th century.

10 rue du Grand-Prieuré. ✆ **04-90-49-37-58.** Admission 4€ ($5.20) adults, 3€ ($3.90) students and children 12–18, free for children under 12. May–Sept daily 10am–noon and 2–6:30pm; Mar–Apr and Oct daily 10am–noon and 2–5pm; Nov–Feb daily 1–5:30pm.

Museon Arlaten ★ The poet Frédéric Mistral founded this museum, using the money from his Nobel Prize for literature in 1904. Mistral led a movement to establish modern Provençal as a literary language, and the museum's name is rendered in Provençal style. It's a folklore museum, with regional costumes, furniture, dolls, a music salon, and a room devoted to mementos of Mistral.

29 rue de la République. ✆ **04-90-93-58-11.** Admission 4€ ($5.20) adults, 3€ ($3.90) students and children under 18. June–Aug daily 9:30am–1:30pm and 2–5pm; Sept daily 9:30am–noon; Apr–May Tues–Sun 9:30am–12:30pm and 2–5pm; Oct–Mar Tues–Sun 9:30am–12:30pm and 2–4pm.

Finds ***Le Olé***

Bullfights, or *corridas,* are held about five weekends a year, between Easter and late September. The bull is killed only during the Easter *corridas* (perhaps a reference to the death of Christ?); otherwise, the bull is not killed, making the ritual less bloody than the Spanish version. The Easter event begins at 11am, the others around 5pm. A seat on the stone benches of the Roman amphitheater costs 16€ to 90€ ($21–$117). Tickets are usually available at the amphitheater a few hours beforehand. For advance ticket sales, call ✆ **04-90-96-03-70.**

Finds A Shopping Expedition

In an isolated spot 12km (7½ miles) north of Arles, **Magasin d'Usine Les Olivades,** chemin des Indienneurs, St-Etienne-du-Grès (✆ **04-90-49-18-04**), sits by the road leading to Tarascon. A trek here is worth your while for the wide array of art objects and fabrics inspired by Provence. The inexpensive prices here result from small flaws, most of them not noticeable, in some of the fabric or color runs. Some of the patterns may not be from this season, but from previous outdated seasons, but no one back home will know the difference. Dresses, shirts for men and women, table linens, and fabric are available at Olivades retail outlets throughout Provence, but the selection here is better and cheaper.

WHERE TO STAY

Grand Hôtel Nord-Pinus ★ Few other hotels in town evoke Provence's charm as well as this one, which originated as a bakery at the turn of the 20th century. Occupying a town house on a tree-lined square in the heart of Arles, it has public rooms filled with antiques, an ornate staircase with wrought-iron balustrades, and many of the trappings you'd expect in an upscale private home. Guest rooms are glamorous, even theatrical; they come in a range of shapes, sizes, and decors, and are filled with rich upholsteries and draperies arranged artfully beside oversize French doors. Bathrooms contain combination tub/showers. Many bullfighters and artists have stayed here—their photographs, as well as a collection of safari photos by Peter Beard, decorate the public areas.

14 place du Forum, Arles 13200. ✆ **04-90-93-44-44.** Fax 04-90-93-34-00. www.nord-pinus.com. 27 units. 160€–295€ ($208–$384) double; 450€ ($585) suite. AE, DC, MC, V. Parking 17€ ($22). **Amenities:** Restaurant; bar; room service; laundry service; dry cleaning; nonsmoking rooms. *In room:* TV.

Hôtel Calendal ★ *Value* Because of its reasonable rates, the Calendal is a bargain hunter's favorite. On a quiet square near the arena, it offers high-ceilinged accommodations decorated in bright colors. Most rooms have views of the hotel's garden, filled with palms and palmettos. Each unit comes with a compact shower-only bathroom.

5 rue Porte de Laure, Arles 13200. ✆ **04-90-96-11-89.** Fax 04-90-96-05-84. www.lecalendal.com. 38 units. 89€–119€ ($116–$155) double. Parking 10€ ($13). AE, DC, MC, V. Bus: 4. **Amenities:** Restaurant; bar; room service; laundry service; nonsmoking rooms; limited-mobility rooms. *In room:* A/C, TV, hair dryer.

Hôtel d'Arlatan ★ In the former residence of the *comtes* d'Arlatan de Beaumont, this hotel has been managed by the same family since 1920. It was built in the 15th century on ancient Roman foundations. Rooms are furnished with authentic Provençal antiques and have tapestry-covered walls. Try to get a room overlooking the garden. Those on the ground floor are largest. About two-thirds of the guest rooms have tub/shower combos, and the rest have showers.

26 rue du Sauvage, Arles 13100. ✆ **04-90-93-56-66.** Fax 04-90-49-68-45. www.hotel-arlatan.fr. 48 units. 85€–155€ ($111–$202) double; 175€–245€ ($228–$319) suite. AE, MC, V. Parking 11€–14€ ($14–$18). Closed Jan. **Amenities:** Bar; laundry service; babysitting; limited-mobility rooms. *In room:* A/C, TV, minibar.

Hotel de l'Amphitheatre Originally built in the 1600s, and ideally situated midway between the ancient Roman amphitheater and the Roman theater, this hotel was radically renovated beginning in 2005. Today, it's on the short list of the city's centrally located and particularly charming hotels. The antique atmosphere is filled with hand-hewn wood ceiling beams, bright fabrics, soft lighting, reproductions of Provençal or rococo furniture, and a layout of bedrooms that in some cases feature sweeping views out over the terra-cotta roofs of historic Arles. At press time, some of the cheaper rooms hadn't yet been fully renovated, retaining some of the dowdier fixtures of this building's incarnation as a less glamorous hotel under earlier owners. Our preferred nest here is the Belvedere Suite, whose windows offer 360-degree views over the town. No meals are served other than breakfast, but many dining options lie within a short walk.

5–7 rue Diderot, Arles 13200. ✆ **04-90-96-10-30.** Fax 04-90-93-98-69. www.hotelamphitheatre.fr. 28 units. Oct–Mar 67€–92€ ($87–$120) double; 127€–145€ ($165–$189) suite. Apr–Sept 59€–81€ ($77–$105) double; 101€–117€ ($131–$152) suite. AE, MC, V. **Amenities:** Babysitting; laundry service; dry cleaning. *In room:* A/C, TV, fridge, hair dryer, safe, Wi-Fi.

Hôtel Jules César ★★★ This 17th-century Carmelite convent is now a stately country hotel with one of the best restaurants in town. Although it's in a noisy neighborhood, most rooms face the unspoiled cloister. You'll wake to the scent of roses and the sounds of birds singing. Throughout, you'll find a blend of neoclassical architecture and modern amenities. The decor is luxurious, with antique Provençal furnishings found at auctions in the countryside. The interior rooms are the most tranquil and the darkest, though enlivened by bright fabrics. Most of the downstairs units are spacious; the upstairs rooms are small but have a certain old-world charm. The rooms in the modern extensions are comfortable but lack character. Each bathroom comes with a combination tub/shower.

9 bd. des Lices, Arles Cedex 13631. ✆ **04-90-52-52-52.** Fax 04-90-52-52-53. www.hotel-julescesar.fr. 58 units. 160€–250€ ($208–$325) double; 300€–385€ ($390–$501) suite. AE, DC, MC, V. Parking 13€ ($17). Closed Nov 10–Dec 24. **Amenities:** Restaurant (see "Where to Dine," below); bar; room service; babysitting; laundry service; dry cleaning; nonsmoking rooms; limited-mobility rooms. *In room:* TV, minibar, hair dryer, safe.

Hôtel Le Cloître *Value* This hotel, between the ancient theater and the cloister, offers great value. Originally part of a 12th-century cloister, it still has its original

---

Moments A Homage to Mistral

If you're interested in Frédéric Mistral and how he revitalized the Provençal language, opt for a pilgrimage to the village of Maillane, 15km (9⅓ miles) north of Arles. To get there, follow the signs to Avignon and turn off at the clearly signposted routes to Maillane and the **Musée de Frédéric Mistral,** avenue Lamartine, Maillane (✆ **04-90-95-84-19**). Here, within Mistral's childhood home, you'll find his daily writing implements; evidence of his devotion to his early widowed mother; insights into some of his romantic dalliances with local damsels; a writing desk that had belonged to his close friend, 19th-century novelist and poet Lamartine; and a letter, in French, from then–U.S. president Theodore Roosevelt, bearing the letterhead of the White House in Washington. From October to March, the museum is open Tuesday to Sunday 10 to 11:30am and 2 to 4:30pm; from April to September, Tuesday to Sunday 9:30 to 11:30am and 2:30 to 6:30pm. Entrance is 4€ ($5.20) for adults, 3€ ($3.90) for ages 12 to 18, and free for children under 12.

Romanesque vaultings. Throughout, you'll find a rich Provençal atmosphere, pleasant rooms with high ceilings, and subtle references to the building's antique origins. Guest rooms are lean on amenities except for phones and small, shower-only bathrooms. Some units have TVs available for a supplement of 4.50€ ($5.85) per day; otherwise, there's a TV lounge.

16 rue du Cloître, Arles 13200. www.hotelcloitre.com. ✆ **04-90-96-29-50.** Fax 04-90-96-02-88. 30 units. 47€–78€ ($61–$101) double. AE, MC, V. Parking 5€ ($6.50). Closed Nov 1–Mar 20.

WHERE TO DINE

La Gueule du Loup FRENCH/PROVENÇAL Named for its founder, who, according to local legend, grew to resemble a wolf as he aged, this cozy, well-managed restaurant occupies a stone-fronted antique house in the historic core of Arles, near the ancient Roman arena. Today it's owned by members of the Allard family, who prepare serious gourmet-style French food that's more elaborate than the cuisine at many competitors. The best examples include hearty filet of bull braised in red wine, monkfish in saffron sauce, roasted cod with green and sweet red peppers in saffron sauce, and superb duckling cooked in duck fat and served with flap mushrooms. Reservations are important—the cozy room seats only 30.

39 rue des Arènes. ✆ **04-90-96-96-69.** Reservations recommended. Main courses 8€–22€ ($10–$29); fixed-price dinner 28€ ($36); fixed-price lunch 12€ ($16). MC, V. Easter–Oct Tues–Sat noon–2:30pm, Mon–Sat 7–9:30pm; Nov–Easter Tues–Sat noon–2:30pm and 7–9:30pm. Closed 1 week in Nov and mid-Jan to mid-Feb.

Restaurant Lou Marquès ★★ PROVENÇAL Lou Marquès, at the Hôtel Jules-César, has the best reputation in town. Seating is in the formal dining room or on the terrace. The cuisine features creative twists on Provençal specialties. A first course could be *queues de langoustine en salade vinaigrette d'agrumes et basilic* (crustaceans and salad with citrus-and-basil vinaigrette) or *risotto de homard aux truffes* (lobster risotto with truffles). As a main course, try *pavé de loup en barigoule d'artichaut et à la sauge* (a thick slice of wolf fish with sage-stuffed artichokes) or *filet mignon de veau et ragoût fin de cèpes et salsifis* (veal with a stew of mushrooms and salsify, a long-forgotten oyster-flavored vegetable). For a light dessert, there's *biscuit glacé au miel de lavande* (a small cake glazed with lavender honey).

At the Hôtel Jules César, 9 bd. des Lices. ✆ **04-90-52-52-52.** Reservations recommended. Main courses 30€–90€ ($39–$117); fixed-price lunch 21€–28€ ($27–$36); fixed-price dinner 40€–80€ ($52–$104). AE, DC, MC, V. Daily noon–1:30pm and 7:30–9:30pm. Closed Nov 12–Dec 24.

ARLES AFTER DARK

Because of its relatively small population (around 50,000), Arles doesn't offer as many nightlife options as Aix-en-Provence, Avignon, Nice, or Marseille. The town's most appealing choice is the bar/cafe/music hall **Le Cargo de Nuit,** 7 av. Sadi-Carnot (✆ **04-90-49-55-99**). Open Wednesday to Saturday night, it's a club that later has live music—salsa, jazz, rock 'n' roll—and then disco dancing until 3am. Cover ranges from 8€ to 23€ ($10–$30).

The town's most animated cafe, where most singles go, is **Le Café van Gogh,** 11 place du Forum (✆ **04-90-96-44-56**). Overlooking an attractive plaza, it features live music and an ambience that the almost-young and the restless refer to as *super-chouette,* or "super cool."

5 Les Baux ★★★

715km (444 miles) S of Paris, 19km (12 miles) NE of Arles, 81km (50 miles) N of Marseille

Cardinal Richelieu called Les Baux "a nesting place for eagles." On a wind-swept plateau overlooking the southern Alpilles, Les Baux is a ghost of its former self, though still very dramatic. It was once the citadel of seigneurs who ruled with an iron fist and sent their armies as far as Albania. In medieval times, troubadours from all over the Continent came to this "court of love," where they recited western Europe's earliest-known vernacular poetry. Eventually, Alix of Baux, the "Scourge of Provence," ruled Les Baux, sending his men throughout the land to kidnap people. If no one was willing to pay ransom for one of his victims, the poor wretch was forced to walk a gangplank over the cliff's edge.

Fed up with the rebellions against Louis XIII in 1632, Richelieu commanded his armies to destroy Les Baux. Today, the castle and ramparts are mere shells, though you can see remains of Renaissance mansions. The dry, foreboding countryside around Les Baux, which nestles in a valley surrounded by shadowy rock formations, offers its own fascination. Vertical ravines lie on either side of the town. Vineyards—officially classified as Coteaux d'Aix-en-Provence—surround Les Baux, facing the Alpilles. If you follow the signposted *route des vin,* you can motor through the vineyards in an afternoon, perhaps stopping off at growers' estates.

Now the bad news: Because of the beauty and drama of the area, Les Baux is virtually overrun with visitors; it's not unlike Mont-St-Michel in that respect.

ESSENTIALS

GETTING THERE Les Baux is best reached by car; there is no rail service. From Arles, take the express highway N570 northeast until you reach the turnoff for a secondary road (D17), which will lead you northeast to Fontvieille. From here, just follow the signs east into Les Baux. By **train,** most passengers get off at Arles. Bus service has been discontinued. Taxis in Arles (✆ **06-80-27-60-92**) will take you to Les Baux for around 30€ ($39); be sure to agree upon the fare in advance.

VISITOR INFORMATION The **Office de Tourisme** (✆ **04-90-54-34-39;** fax 04-90-54-51-15; www.lesbauxdeprovence.com) is on Maison du Roy, near the northern entrance to the old city.

EXPLORING THE AREA

Les Baux is one of the most dramatic towns in Provence. You can wander through feudal ruins, called **La Ville Morte (Ghost Village)** ★★★, at the northern end of town. The site of this citadel covers an area at least five times that of Les Baux itself. As you stand at the ruins, you can look out over the Val d'Enfer (Valley of Hell) and even see the Mediterranean in the distance.

You can reach **La Citadelle** ★★, the castle ruins at the bottom of the town, by walking up rue du Château, which leads into the **Château des Baux** (✆ **04-90-54-55-56**). Allow at least an hour to explore. You enter the citadel by going through the **Hôtel de la Tour du Brau,** which houses the Musée du Château. The building was the residence of the powerful Tour de Brau family. The museum has exhibits related to the history of Les Baux, which will help you understand the ruins in the compound. Models of the fortress in medieval times explain how the site has evolved architecturally.

After leaving the Hôtel de la Tour du Brau, you're free to wander through the ruins. You'll take in such sites as the ruined chapel of St-Blaise (now home to a little museum devoted to the olive), replicas of medieval siege engines, grottoes used for storage or lodgings in the Middle Ages, the skeleton of a hospital built in the 16th century, and a cemetery. Finally, the **Tour Sarrazin (Saracen Tower)** offers a view of the village and the citadel compound. Admission to the castle, including the museum and access to the ruins, is 7.50€ ($9.75) for adults, 5€ ($6.50) for students, free for children 17 and under. The site is open in July and August daily 9am to 7:30pm; March to June and in September and October daily 9am to 6:30pm; November to February daily 9:30am to 5pm.

In the village, you can visit the **Yves Brayer Museum,** at the intersection of rue de la Calade and rue de l'Eglise (✆ **04-90-54-36-99;** www.yvesbrayer.com). In a 16th-century house (Hôtel de Porcelet), the museum is devoted to the works of Yves Brayer (1907–90), a figurative painter and a famous native son (he's buried in the village cemetery). His works depict Italy, Morocco, and Spain, along with bullfighting scenes. The museum is open April through September daily 10am to 12:30pm and 2 to 6:30pm; off-season hours are Wednesday to Monday 10am to 12:30pm and 2 to 5:30pm (closed Jan to mid-Feb). Admission is 4€ ($5.20) for adults, 2.50€ ($3.25) for students and children under 13.

Cathédrale d'Images ★ (✆ **04-90-54-38-65**) is one of the most remarkable cathedrals in Provence. It lies in a limestone quarry a quarter-mile north of the village; take route du Val d'Enfer. Outside, you can marvel at the fact that the cathedral is carved out of the stone mountain. It's just as amazing inside, where the limestone surfaces of the large rooms and pillars become three-dimensional screens for a bizarre audiovisual show. Hundreds of projectors splash images from all directions according to themes that change throughout the season. In the past, shows have celebrated the triumphs of the Italian Renaissance, medieval pilgrimages, the works of van Gogh, and Romanesque sculpture and architecture. Photographer Albert Plecy created the site in 1977. It's open daily 10am to 6pm; closed January 2 to February 8. Admission is 7.50€ ($9.75) for adults and 3.50€ ($4.55) for children under 18.

Musée des Santons is in the town's **Ancien Hôtel de Ville,** place Louis Jou (✆ **04-90-54-34-39**). Built in the 16th century as a chapel, La Chapelle des Pénitents Blancs, the museum displays antique and idiosyncratic woodcarvings, each representing a different saint or legend. It's open April to October, daily 9am to 7pm; November to March, daily 9am to 5pm. Admission is free.

Climb to the much-praised **place St-Vincent** for a sweeping view over the Vallon de la Fontaine. This is also the site of the much-respected **Eglise St-Vincent** (no phone), which is open April to October daily 9am to 6:30pm, November to March daily 10am to 5:30pm. Its campanile is called La Lanterne des Morts (Lantern of the Dead). The modern windows were a gift from Rainier of Monaco, when he was the Marquis des Baux during the 1980s. Today, Albert of Monaco fulfills the honorary/ceremonial duties associated with that role. If anything, you're more likely to see Caroline of Monaco, thanks to her residency within a private home in nearby St-Rémy-de-Provence, a few kilometers downhill from here.

The Renaissance-era **Hôtel de Manville,** rue Frédéric Mistral, was built in the 16th century as a private mansion. Today, it is the **Mairie** (town hall) of Les Baux. You can visit its courtyard. It's open the same hours as Musée des Santons (see above). **Fondation Louis Jou** lies in the Renaissance-era **Hôtel Jean-de-Brion,** rue Frédéric Mistral

(✆ **04-90-54-34-17**). It can be visited only by appointment and does not maintain regular hours, even during the times when they're "officially posted" as being open. Those official hours are defined as April to December, every Thursday to Monday, 11am to 1pm and 2 to 6pm. In reality they are less frequent than that, so be sure to call before your arrival. Inside are engravings and serigraphs by the Barcelona-born artist Louis Jou (1882–1968), as well as a few small-scale works by Rembrandt, Dürer, and Goya. Jou frequently visited Paris but considered Les Baux his home from 1917 until his death. He is considered the most important contemporary artist to come out of Les Baux. Admission is 3€ ($3.90) for adults, 1.50€ ($1.95) for children.

WHERE TO STAY

La Riboto de Taven (see "Where to Dine," below) rents rooms.

Auberge de la Benvengudo ★ In a quiet location about 1.5km (1 mile) south of town, this auberge is a 19th-century farmhouse surrounded by sculptured shrubbery, towering trees, and parasol pines. The property has an outdoor pool, a tennis court, and a terrace filled with the scent of lavender and thyme. About half the rooms are in the original building, above the restaurant, and the rest in an attractive stone-sided annex. All are sunny and well maintained. Each has a private terrace or balcony, and some have antique four-poster beds. Five units come with shower only; the others have a combination tub/shower.

Vallon de l'Arcoule, rte. d'Arles, Les Baux 13520. Take RD78 for 1.5km (1 mile) southwest of Les Baux, following signs to Arles. ✆ **04-90-54-32-54.** Fax 04-90-54-42-58. www.benvengudo.com. 25 units. 135€–165€ ($176–$215) double; 190€ ($247) suite. AE, MC, V. Closed Nov 1–Mar 15. **Amenities:** Restaurant; outdoor pool; tennis court; room service; babysitting. *In room:* A/C, TV, hair dryer.

Hostellerie de la Reine-Jeanne *Value* In the heart of the village, this warm, well-scrubbed inn is the best bargain in Les Baux. You enter through a typical provincial French bistro. All the guest rooms are spartan but comfortable, and three have terraces. Bathrooms are cramped and relatively modest, with a shower stall only.

Grand-Rue, Les Baux 13520. ✆ **04-90-54-32-06.** Fax 04-90-54-32-33. www.la-reinejeanne.com. 10 units. 50€–70€ ($65–$91) double. AE, MC, V. Closed Jan 15–31 and Nov 15–30. **Amenities:** Restaurant; bar; limited room service. *In room:* A/C, TV.

La Cabro d'Or ★★★ This is the less famous, less celebrated sibling of the nearby Oustau de Baumanière (see below). You'll find some of the most comfortable accommodations in the region in these five low-slung stone buildings. The original building, a farmhouse, dates from the 18th century. The guest room decor evokes old-time Provence with art and antiques. Some rooms have sweeping views over the countryside, and each comes with a combination tub/shower. The dining room sits in a much-altered agrarian building from the 1800s. The massive ceiling beams are works of art in their own right.

The restaurant is flanked by a vine-covered terrace with views of a pond, a garden, and a rocky and barren landscape that has been compared to the surface of the moon. The cuisine, although not on the level of Oustau de Baumanière's, is sublime—light and flavorful, with a special emphasis on fresh produce. Specialties include a thick roasted slice of foie gras of duckling served with lemon-flavored quince sauce and red port wine, carpaccio of red mullet flavored with olive oil and sea salt, and a lasagna of scallops served with strips of Serrano ham. Main courses range from 39€ to 42€ ($51–$55); the restaurant also features a fixed-price *menu du jour* for 45€ ($59).

Les Baux de Provence 13520. ✆ **04-90-54-33-21.** Fax 04-90-54-45-98. www.lacabrodor.com. 31 units. 150€–260€ ($195–$338) double; 305€–450€ ($397–$585) suite. Off-season discounts (about 25%) available. Half board 80€ ($104) per person. AE, DC, MC, V. Closed mid-Nov to Dec 21. **Amenities:** Restaurant; bar; outdoor pool; 2 tennis courts; babysitting; laundry service; limited-mobility rooms. *In room:* A/C, TV, minibar, hair dryer, iron, safe.

Oustau de Baumanière ★★★ This Relais & Châteaux member is one of southern France's legendary hotels. Raymond Thuilier bought the 14th-century farmhouse in 1945, and by the 1950s, it was a rendezvous for the glitterati. Today, managed by its founder's grandson, it's not as glitzy, but the three stone houses draped in flowering vines are still charming. The plush rooms evoke the 16th and 17th centuries. All units contain large sitting areas, and no two are alike. If there's no vacancy in the main building, the hotel will assign you to one of the annexes. Request Le Manoir, the most appealing. The spacious bathrooms contain tub/shower combinations.

In the stone-vaulted dining room, the chef serves specialties such as ravioli of truffles with leeks, *rossini* (stuffed with foie gras) of veal with fresh truffles, and roast duckling with olives. The award-winning *gigot d'agneau* (lamb) *en croûte* has become this place's trademark. A fixed-price menu costs 175€ ($228).

Les Baux, Maussane-les-Alpilles 13520. ✆ **04-90-54-33-07.** Fax 04-90-54-40-46. www.oustaudebaumaniere.com. 30 units. 250€–300€ ($325–$390) double; 360€–530€ ($468–$689) suite. AE, DC, MC, V. Closed Jan 4–Feb 5. Restaurant closed Wed all day and Thurs at lunch Oct–Mar. **Amenities:** Restaurant; outdoor pool; room service; babysitting; laundry service; limited-mobility rooms. *In room:* A/C, TV, minibar, hair dryer, iron, safe.

WHERE TO DINE

La Cabro d'Or and **Oustau de Baumanière** (see "Where to Stay," above) offer excellent dining.

La Riboto de Taven ★★★ Known for its flawless cuisine and market-fresh ingredients, this is one of the great restaurants of the area, a rival of La Cabro d'Or. The 1835 farmhouse outside the medieval section of town has been owned by two generations of the Novi family. In summer, you can sit outdoors. Brawny flavors and the heady perfumes of Provençal herbs characterize chef Jean-Pierre Novi's cuisine. Menu items may include sea bass in olive oil; fricassee of mussels flavored with basil; lamb *en croûte* with olives; or perhaps, in late autumn and winter, medallions of roebuck served with caramelized root vegetables; plus homemade desserts. The menu changes virtually every day and always features an intelligent and tasteful use of local ingredients and produce.

Accommodations include four rooms within the thick walls of the main *mas* (Provençal farmhouse) costing 160€ to 200€ ($208–$260), and two "cave-dweller junior suites" that have been shoehorned into the grottoes at the far end of the establishment's garden, and which look out across the ravine toward the once-fortified citadel of Les Baux. These go for 250€ ($325). Each of the accommodations is gracefully accessorized with Provençal-style furniture, and each contains a minibar, phone, TV, hair dryer, and bathroom with a tub/shower combo. The property has an swimming pool.

Le Val d'Enfer, Les Baux 13520. ✆ **04-90-54-34-23.** Fax 04-90-54-38-88. www.riboto-de-taven.fr. Reservations required. Fixed-price menu 48€ ($62). AE, MC, V. Thurs–Tues 7:30–9:30pm. Closed Jan–Mar 1.

6 Aix-en-Provence ★★

755km (469 miles) S of Paris, 81km (50 miles) SE of Avignon, 32km (20 miles) N of Marseille, 306km (109 miles) W of Nice

This faded university town is the most charming center in Provence. Founded in 122 B.C. by Roman general Caius Sextius Calvinus, who named the town Aquae Sextiae

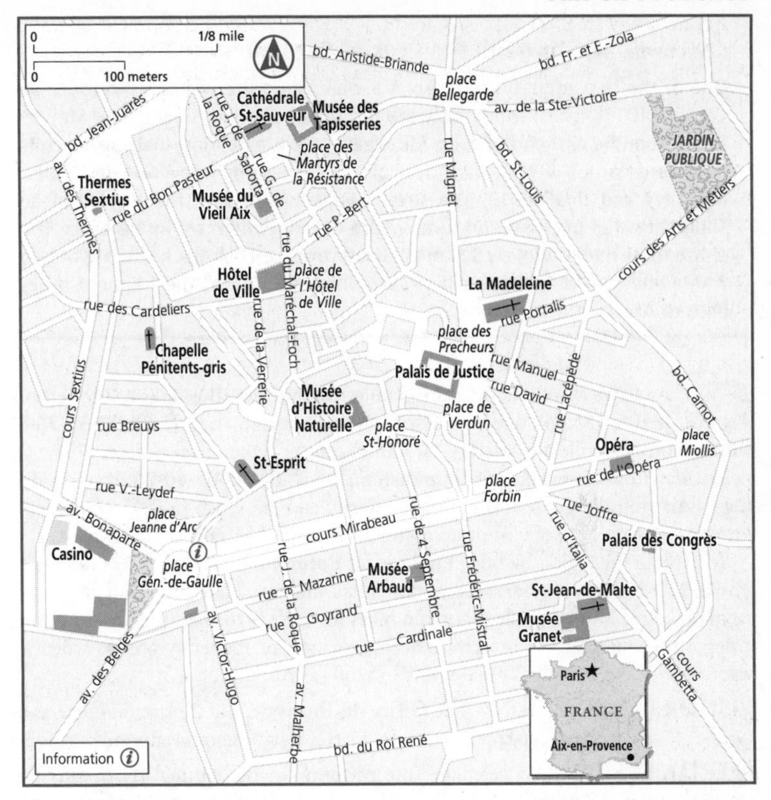

after himself, Aix (pronounced "ex") originated as a military outpost. It became a civilian colony, the administrative capital of a province of the late Roman Empire, the seat of an archbishop, and official residence of the medieval *comtes* de Provence. After the union of Provence with France, Aix remained a judicial and administrative center until the Revolution.

Paul Cézanne, the celebrated son of this old capital of Provence, immortalized the countryside in his paintings. Just as he saw it, Montagne Ste-Victoire looms over the town today, though a string of high-rises now interrupts the landscape.

Today, this city of 150,000 is quiet in winter but active and bustling when the summer hordes pour in. Many local residents are international students. (The Université d'Aix dates from 1413.) Summer is lively, with frequent cultural events, ranging from opera to jazz, from June to August. Aix is an increasingly popular bedroom community for urbanites fleeing Marseille after 5pm.

ESSENTIALS

GETTING THERE The city is easily accessible. Twenty-seven **trains** arrive daily from Marseille; the trip takes 45 minutes and costs 8€ ($10) one-way. Twenty-five trains arrive from Nice; the trip takes 3 to 4 hours and costs 33€ ($43) one-way. There are also 25 trains per day from Cannes (3½ hr.), costing 30€ ($39) one-way. High-speed

Moments Aix through the Eyes of Cézanne

One of the best experiences in Aix is a walk along the well-marked *route de Cézanne* (D17), which winds eastward through the countryside toward Ste-Victoire. From the east end of cours Mirabeau, take rue du Maréchal-Joffre across boulevard Carnot to boulevard des Poilus, which becomes avenue des Ecoles-Militaires and finally D17. The stretch between Aix and the hamlet of Le Tholonet is full of twists and turns where Cézanne often set up his easel. The entire route makes a lovely 5.5km (3⅓-mile) stroll. Le Tholonet has a cafe or two where you can refresh yourself while waiting for one of the frequent buses back to Aix.

TGV trains arrive at Vitroll, 5.5km (3⅓ miles) west of Aix. Bus links to the center of Aix cost 4.10€ ($5.35) one-way. For more information, call ✆ **08-92-35-35-35.** **Buses** from Marseille arrive every 10 minutes; from Avignon, five times a day; and twice a day from Nice. For more information, call ✆ **08-91-02-40-25.** If you're **driving** to Aix from Avignon or other points north, take A7 south to RN7 and follow it into town. From Marseille or other points south, take A51 north into town.

To explore the region by bike, head for **La Rotondo,** 2 av. Des Belges (✆ **04-42-26-78-92**), a short walk northeast of the cours Mirabeau. Here you can rent 10-speed racing bikes or more durable mountain bikes for 20€ ($26) per day. You must leave a deposit—your passport or driver's license, or cash or monetary objects worth the value of the bike, usually 200€ to 300€ ($260–$390).

VISITOR INFORMATION The **Office de Tourisme** is at 2 place du Général-de-Gaulle (✆ **04-42-16-11-61;** fax 04-42-16-11-62; www.aixenprovencetourism.com).

SPECIAL EVENTS Aix celebrates the performing arts, particularly music, more than any other city in the south of France. It offers at least four summer festivals that showcase music, opera, and dance, including the **Aix en Musique** (✆ **04-42-21-69-69;** www.aixenmusique.fr), all summer long, which focuses on symphonic and chamber music, and **Festival International d'Art Lyrique & de Musique** (✆ **04-42-17-34-34;** www.festival-aix.com) in late July, which attracts musicians from all over the world.

EXPLORING THE AREA

Aix's main street, **cours Mirabeau** ★★, is one of Europe's most beautiful. Plane trees stretch across the street like umbrellas, shading it from the hot Provençal sun and filtering the light into shadows that play on the rococo fountains below. Shops and sidewalk cafes line one side of the street; sandstone *hôtels particuliers* (mansions) from the 17th and 18th centuries fill the other. The street begins at the 1860 fountain on place de la Libération, which honors Mirabeau, the revolutionary and statesman. A ring of streets, including boulevard Carnot and cours Sextius, circles the heart of the old quarter (Vieille Ville, or old town). Inside this périphérique is the pedestrian zone.

After touring Aix, you may consider a side trip on D10 15km (9⅓ miles) east to the **Château de Vauvenarges,** the privately owned site of Pablo Picasso's last home. You can't visit the château's interior, but Picasso and one of his wives, Jacqueline Roche, are buried nearby. Stop for a meal at **Au Moulin de Provence,** rue des Maquisards (✆ **04-42-66-02-22**), across the road from the château.

Atelier de Cézanne Cézanne was the major forerunner of cubism. This house, surrounded by a wall and restored by American admirers, is where he worked. Repaired in 1970, it remains much as Cézanne left it in 1906, "his coat hanging on the wall, his easel with an unfinished picture waiting for a touch of the master's brush," as Thomas R. Parker wrote.

9 av. Paul-Cézanne (outside town). ✆ **04-42-21-06-53.** Admission 5.50€ ($7.15) adults, 2€ ($2.60) students and children under 13. Apr–June and Sept daily 10am–noon and 2:30–6pm; July–Aug daily 10am–6pm; Oct–Mar daily 10am–noon and 2–5pm. Closed Jan 1, May 1, and Dec 25.

Cathédrale St-Sauveur ★ The cathedral of Aix is dedicated to Christ under the title St-Sauveur (Holy Savior or Redeemer). Its baptistery dates from the 4th and 5th centuries, and the complex as a whole has seen many additions. It contains a 15th-century Nicolas Froment triptych, *The Burning Bush.* One side depicts the Virgin and Child; the other, Good King René and his second wife, Jeanne de Laval.

Place des Martyrs de la Résistance. ✆ **04-42-23-45-65.** Free admission. Daily 9am–noon and 2–6pm. Mass Sun 10:30am and 7pm.

Chapelle Penitents-gris (Chapelle des Bourras) This 16th-century chapel honoring St. Joseph was built on the ancient Roman Aurelian road linking Rome and Spain. Herbert Maza, founder and former president of the Institute for American Universities, restored the chapel. M. Borricand, rector of a group of local ecclesiastics, arranges visits.

15 rue Lieutaud. ✆ **04-42-26-26-72.** Free admission; donations welcome. Visits by reservation only.

Musée des Tapisseries ★ Three series of tapestries from the 17th and 18th centuries line the gilded walls of this former archbishop's palace. The prelates decorated the palace with *The History of Don Quixote,* by Natoire; *The Russian Games,* by Leprince; and *The Grotesques,* by Monnoyer. The museum also exhibits rare furnishings from the 17th and 18th centuries.

28 place des Martyrs de la Résistance. ✆ **04-42-23-09-91.** Admission 2.50€ ($3.25) adults, free for ages under 25. Wed–Mon 10am–12:30pm and 1:30–5pm. Closed Jan 1, May 1, and Dec 25.

SHOPPING

Opened more than a century ago, **Bechard,** 12 cours Mirabeau (✆ **04-42-26-06-78**), is the most famous bakery in town. It takes its work so seriously that it refers to its underground kitchens as a *laboratoire* (laboratory). Most of the delectable pastries are made fresh every day.

Founded in 1934 on a busy boulevard just east of the center of town, **Santons Fouque,** 65 cours Gambetta, route de Nice (✆ **04-42-26-33-38;** www.santonsfouque.com), stocks the largest assortment of *santons* (wooden figurines of saints) in Aix.

Tips To the Markets We Will Go

Aix offers the best markets in the region. Place Richelme holds a **fruit and vegetable market** every morning. Come here to buy the exquisite products of Provence, such as olives, lavender, local cheeses, and fresh produce. There's a **flower market** Tuesday, Thursday, and Saturday morning on place des Prêcheurs. The **fish market** is daily in the morning on place Richelme.

More than 1,900 figurines are cast in terra cotta, finished by hand, and painted according to 18th-century models. Each of the trades practiced in medieval Provence is represented, including shoemakers, barrel makers, coppersmiths, and ironsmiths, poised to welcome the newborn Jesus. Figurines range in price from 10€ to 950€ ($13–$1,235).

WHERE TO STAY

EXPENSIVE

Hôtel des Augustins ★ Converted from the 12th-century Grands Augustins Convent, this hotel is beautifully restored, with ribbed-vault ceilings, stained glass, stone walls, terra-cotta floors, and an entry hall loaded with Louis XIII furnishings. The reception desk is in a chapel, and paintings and watercolors decorate the public rooms. This place won a spot in history by sheltering an excommunicated Martin Luther on his return from Rome. The rooms are outfitted in a restrained contemporary style, with dark-wood furniture and high ceilings. Each unit comes with a good-size bathroom and combination tub/shower. Breakfast is the only meal served.

3 rue de la Masse, Aix-en-Provence 13100. ✆ **04-42-27-28-59.** Fax 04-42-26-74-87. www.hotel-augustins.com. 97€–240€ ($126–$312) double. AE, MC, V. **Amenities:** Laundry service. *In room:* A/C, TV, minibar.

La Villa Gallici ★★★ This elegant, relentlessly chic inn, which originated in the 18th century as a private home, is the most stylish hotel in town. The rooms, richly infused with the decorative traditions of Aix, are subtle and charming. Some rooms boast a private terrace or garden, and each comes with a combination tub/shower. The villa sits in a large enclosed garden in the heart of Aix, close to one of the best restaurants, Le Clos de la Violette (see "Where to Dine," below). It's a 5-minute walk to the town center.

Av. de la Violette (impasse des Grands Pins), Aix-en-Provence 13100. ✆ **04-42-23-29-23.** Fax 04-42-96-30-45. www.villagallici.com. 22 units. 220€–620€ ($286–$806) double; 420€–780€ ($546–$1,014) suite. AE, DC, MC, V. **Amenities:** Restaurant; bar; outdoor pool; room service; babysitting; laundry service; dry cleaning; limited-mobility rooms. *In room:* A/C, TV, minibar, hair dryer, safe.

MODERATE

Grand Hôtel Nègre Coste This hotel, an 18th-century former town house, is so popular with the musicians who flock to Aix for the summer festivals that it's difficult to get a room at any price. Such popularity is understandable. Flowers cascade from jardinières, and 18th-century carvings surround the windows. Inside, there's a wide staircase, marble portrait busts, and a Provençal armoire. The medium-size soundproof rooms contain interesting antiques. The higher floors overlook cours Mirabeau or the old city. Each unit comes with a compact bathroom with shower; some have tubs as well.

33 cours Mirabeau, Aix-en-Provence 13100. ✆ **04-42-27-74-22.** Fax 04-42-26-80-93. www.hotelnegrecoste.com. 37 units. 75€–145€ ($98–$189) double. AE, DC, MC, V. Parking 10€ ($13). **Amenities:** Room service; laundry service; nonsmoking rooms. *In room:* A/C, TV, minibar, hair dryer, safe.

Novotel Aix Pont de l'Arc *Kids* You'll find this chain hotel at the end of a labyrinthine but well-marked route. The large rooms are designed for European business travelers or families, and each comes with a combination tub/shower. The hotel offers one of the most pleasant dining rooms in the suburbs, **Côté Jardin,** with windows overlooking Rivière Arc de Méyran and a forest.

If this hotel is full, rooms are usually available at the 102-unit **Novotel Aix-Beaumanoir,** rue Marcel Arnaud, périphérique Sud (✆ **04-42-91-15-15;** fax 04-42-91-15-05), a few steps away. Doubles cost 80€ to 108€ ($104–$140); amenities include a restaurant and a pool.

Périphérique Sud, arc de Méyran, Aix-en-Provence 13100. Take the ring road 3km (1¾ miles) south of the town center and exit at Aix-Est 3 Sautets. ✆ **800/221-4542** in the U.S., or 04-42-16-09-09. Fax 04-42-26-00-09. www.accorhotels.com. 80 units. 108€–128€ ($140–$166) double; 145€ ($189) suite. AE, DC, MC, V. **Amenities:** Restaurant; bar; outdoor pool; room service; laundry service; dry cleaning; nonsmoking rooms; limited-mobility rooms. *In room:* A/C, TV, minibar, hair dryer.

INEXPENSIVE

Hôtel Cardinal *Value* Not everything in this hotel is state-of-the-art, but because of the old-fashioned setting (an 18th-c. town house loaded with personalized quirks), a collection of 18th- and 19th-century antiques, and upscale and historically appropriate upholsteries, many clients don't seem to mind. Located in the Mazarin quarter, on the side of the cours Mirabeau that's less frequently visited by foreign visitors, it has touches of nostalgia that many locals associate with old-time Provence. The annex, which lies about 7.5m (25 ft.) away, near an antique church, holds most of the suites, each of which has a simple kitchenette. Bathrooms tend to be small, usually with showers but not bathtubs.

24 rue Cardinale, Aix-en-Provence 13100. ✆ **04-42-38-32-30.** Fax 04-42-26-39-05. 29 units. 69€ ($90) double; 80€–105€ ($104–$137) suite. MC, V. **Amenities:** Room service; nonsmoking rooms. *In room:* TV, hair dryer.

Hôtel des Quatre Dauphins This 18th-century town house is a short walk from place des Quatre Dauphins and the cours Mirabeau. Some original motifs have survived through frequent modernizations. The medium-size guest rooms were refurbished in simplified Provençal style, some with painted ceiling beams and casement windows that overlook the street. Five units come with a compact bathroom with tub/shower, the rest with shower only. You can have breakfast in your room or in a small salon.

54 rue Roux-Alphéran, Aix-en-Provence 13100. ✆ **04-42-38-16-39.** Fax 04-42-38-60-19. 13 units. 68€–85€ ($88–$111) double. AE, MC, V. **Amenities:** Room service. *In room:* A/C, TV, Wi-Fi.

Hôtel La Caravelle *Value* This conservatively furnished hotel, with a bas-relief of a three-masted caravel on its stucco facade, is a 3-minute walk from the center of town. It offers warm hospitality. One nice touch is the breakfast served in the stone-floored lobby. The rooms have double-glazed windows to help muffle the noise. Most bathrooms contain showers only.

29 bd. du Roi-René (at cours Mirabeau), Aix-en-Provence 13100. ✆ **04-42-21-53-05.** Fax 04-42-96-55-46. www.lacaravelle-hotel.com. 31 units. 65€–70€ ($85–$91) double. AE, DC, MC, V. **Amenities:** Room service; laundry service; dry cleaning; nonsmoking rooms. *In room:* A/C, TV, minibar, Wi-Fi.

WHERE TO DINE

VERY EXPENSIVE

Le Clos de la Violette ★★★ MODERN FRENCH This innovative restaurant is a few steps from La Villa Gallici (see "Where to Stay," above) in an elegant neighborhood that most visitors reach by taxi. The Provençal villa has an octagonal reception area and several dining rooms. The stylish, seasonal dishes highlight the flavors of Provence. A stellar example of the innovative cuisine is an appetizer of mousseline of potatoes with sea urchins and fish roe. An elegant dish is braised sea wolf with crisp fried shallots and a "cappuccino" of spicy Spanish sausages. Delightful rack of suckling lamb is stuffed with carrots and chick peas and served under an herb-flavored pastry crust. For dessert, try multilayered sugar cookies with hazelnut and vanilla-flavored cream sauce and thin slices of white chocolate, or a "celebration" of Provençal figs—an artfully arranged platter containing a galette, tart, parfait, and sorbet.

10 av. de la Violette. ✆ **04-42-23-30-71.** www.closdelaviolette.fr. Reservations required. Main courses 43€–48€ ($56–$62); fixed-price lunch 40€ ($52); tasting menu 130€ ($169). AE, MC, V. Tues and Thurs–Sat noon–1:30pm and Mon–Sat 7:30–9:30pm. Closed Aug 1–20.

MODERATE

Antoine Côte Cour PROVENÇAL/ITALIAN This popular trattoria is in an 18th-century town house a few steps from place Rotonde. Regulars include Emanuel Ungaro and many film and fashion types, who mingle with old-time "Aixers." Despite its grandeur, the ambience is unpretentious, even jovial. Crusty bread and small pots of aromatic purées (anchovy and basil) arrive at your table as you sit down. A simple wine, such as Côtes-du-Rhône, goes nicely with the hearty Mediterranean fare. Examples of dishes are memorable pasta Romano flavored with calves' liver, flap mushrooms, and tomato sauce; ravioli with goat cheese; *osso buco;* a selection of *légumes farcies* (such as eggplant and zucchini stuffed with minced meat and herbs); and at least half a dozen kinds of fresh fish.

19 cour Mirabeau. ✆ **04-42-93-12-51.** Reservations recommended. Main courses 15€–30€ ($20–$39). MC, V. Tues–Sat noon–2:30pm; Mon–Sat 7:30pm–midnight.

Chez Maxime GRILLS/PROVENÇAL Set in the heart of Aix's pedestrian shopping zone, this likeable restaurant offers an all-Provençal ambience of bordeaux-colored banquettes, salmon-colored walls, and tables, each shaded by an enormous linden tree, that spill out onto the pavement during clement weather. There's a succulent array of a dozen grills, beefsteaks, and fresh fish, as well as a main course laced with saffron and the flavors of the sea, a *marmite* (stewpot) *de la mer.* Also appealing is house-made foie gras of duckling, a kind of pâté made from beef and Provençal herbs known as *caillette de province,* and such desserts as a *fondant au chocolat.* The wine list features dozens of vintages, many of them esoteric bottles from the region.

12 place Ramus. ✆ **04-42-26-28-51.** Reservations recommended. Main courses 10€–20€ ($13–$26); fixed-price lunch 13€ ($16); fixed-price dinner 18€–34€ ($23–$44). MC, V. Tues–Sat noon–2pm; Mon–Sat 7–10pm. Oct–Mar closed Sun–Mon.

Le Bistro Latin ★★ Value PROVENÇAL This is the best little bistro in Aix-en-Provence for the price. Guests dine in two intimate rooms: a street-level space and a cellar decorated in Greco-Latin style. The staff is young and enthusiastic, taking special pride in their fixed-price menus. Try chartreuse of mussels, a meat dish with spinach-and-saffron cream sauce, scampi risotto, or crepe rack of lamb in an herbed crust.

18 rue de la Couronne. ✆ **04-42-38-22-88.** Reservations recommended. Main courses 14€–18€ ($18–$23); fixed-price lunch 16€ ($21); fixed-price dinner 16€–35€ ($21–$46). MC, V. Tues–Sat noon–2pm; Mon–Sat 7–10:30pm.

AIX AFTER DARK

An easy-to-reach bar that manages to be convenient and hip at the same time lies almost directly across from the city's tourist office. Open daily from 8am until at least 2am, **La Rotonde,** Place Jeanne d'Arc (✆ **04-42-91-61-70**), functions as a bar, a cafe, and a rendezvous point for friends and business associates throughout the day and evening.

People between the ages of 20 and 30 who like animated bar scenes and loud electronic music head for **Le Mistral,** 3 rue Frédéric-Mistral (✆ **04-42-38-16-49**), where techno and house music blares long and loud, all for a cover charge of around 15€ to 18€ ($20–$23)—unless you happen to be gorgeous and female, in which case you'll get in free and, depending on the mood of the staff, you may even receive a free glass or two of champagne.

For jazz that's produced by a changing roster of visiting musicians, head for the **Scat Club,** 11 rue de la Verrerie (✆ **04-42-23-00-23**), a smoky jazz den that's the preferred venue for patrons in their late 30s and 40s. Open Tuesday to Sunday, it maintains notoriously late hours, with live music often not beginning until around midnight. And last but certainly not least is Aix's body-shop bar, **La Joia** (✆ **06-80-35-32-94;** www.joia-club.com), route de l'Enfant, in the hamlet of Les Milles, 8km (5 miles) south of Aix (to get there, follow the signs to Marseille). On-site you'll find a restaurant, several bars, an outdoor swimming pool (the kind where you may opt to jump in topless), a dance floor with both indoor and outdoor sections, and a venue that's more hip than it is chic. Know in advance that long lines await on Fridays and Saturdays. Entrance usually costs 11€ to 16€ ($14–$21), unless you're a star or self-enchanted enough to convince the doorman that you are.

7 Marseille ★★★

771km (479 miles) S of Paris, 187km (116 miles) SW of Nice, 31km (19 miles) S of Aix-en-Provence

Bustling Marseille, with more than a million inhabitants, is the second-largest city in France and the country's premier port. It's been called France's New Orleans and (by Dumas) "the meeting place of the entire world." The city is ancient, founded by Greeks in the 6th century B.C. Marseille is a place of unique sounds, smells, and sights. It has seen wars and destruction, but trade has always been its raison d'être.

Perhaps its most common association is with the national anthem of France, "La Marseillaise." During the Revolution, 500 volunteers marched to Paris, singing this rousing song along the way. The rest is history.

Although Marseille is sprawling, dirty, and slumlike in many respects, it also exhibits much elegance and charm. The **Vieux-Port,** the colorful old harbor, compensates for the dreary industrial dockland nearby. Marseille is also the home of many North and sub-Saharan Africans, creating a lively medley of races and creeds. A quarter of the population is of North African descent.

Marseille is twice the size of Paris, and its age-old problems include a drug industry, smuggling, corruption, the Mafia, and racial tension. Unemployment is on the rise. Nevertheless, it's always fascinating and unlike any other city in France. A city official proclaimed recently: "Marseille is the unbeloved child of France. It's attached to France, but has the collective consciousness of an Italian city-state, like Genoa or Venice." A renaissance of sorts is under way. Tourism has risen, and some cruise ships are again including Marseille as a port of call. Scaffolding and grand construction projects are everywhere—and it's about time.

To the astonishment of much of the country, a poll of French people under 25 years cited Marseille as the number-one French city in which they'd like to live, with Montpellier second. Paris tied for third place with Bordeaux.

ESSENTIALS

GETTING THERE The **airport** (✆ **04-42-14-14-14**), 27km (17 miles) northwest of the city center, receives international flights from all over Europe. From the airport, blue-and-white minivans *(navettes)* make the trip to Marseille's St-Charles rail station, near the Vieux-Port, for 8.50€ ($11). The minivans run daily every 20 minutes from 6am (hourly) or to the arrival of the last flight.

Marseille has **train** connections from all over Europe, with especially good connections to and from Italy. The city is the terminus for the TGV bullet train, which departs daily from Paris's Gare de Lyon (trip time: 3 hr., 15 min.; one-way fare 75€–95€/$98–$124). Some Parisians plan a day trip to the Mediterranean beaches at Marseille, returning to the City of Light for dinner. Local trains leave Paris almost every hour, making a number of stops before reaching Marseille. For information, call © **08-92-35-35-35. Buses** serve the Gare Routière, place Victor Hugo (© **04-91-08-16-40**), adjacent to the St-Charles railway station.

If you're **driving** from Paris, follow A6 south to Lyon, and then continue south along A7 to Marseille. The drive takes about 7 hours. From Provence, take A7 south to Marseille.

GETTING AROUND Parking and car safety are so problematic that your best bet is to park your car in a garage and rely on public transportation.

Métro lines 1 and 2 both stop at the main train station, Gare St-Charles, place Victor Hugo. Individual tickets are for sale at Métro and bus stops for 1.20€ ($1.55) each; they're valid on Métro and bus lines for up to 60 minutes after purchase. If you plan to take public transport several times during your stay, you get a discount if you buy a **Carte Liberté,** valid for either 5 rides for 6€ ($7.80) or 10 rides for 12€ ($16). They're available at any Métro station or **Espace Info** booth. The kiosks provide information about Marseille's public transport system at strategic points throughout the city, usually in or near Métro stations. Information and public-transit maps are available at the main office, **Espace Info,** 6 rue des Fabres (© **04-91-91-92-10**).

The major arteries divide Marseille into 16 *quartiers.* Unlike Paris's *arrondissements,* the designations rarely appear in addresses.

Call © **04-91-02-20-20** for a **taxi.**

VISITOR INFORMATION The **Office de Tourisme** is at 4 la Canebière (© **04-91-13-89-00;** fax 04-91-13-89-20; www.marseille-tourisme.com; Métro: Vieux-Port).

SEEING THE SIGHTS

Many travelers never visit the museums, preferring to absorb the life of the city on its busy streets and at its cafes, particularly those along the main street, **La Canebière.** Known as "can of beer" to World War II GIs, it's the heart and soul of Marseille—and the seediest main street in France. Lined with hotels, shops, and restaurants, it fills with sailors from every nation and people of every nationality, including many Algerians. (Some 100,000 North Africans live in the city and its tenement suburbs, often in communities that resemble *souks.*)

La Canebière winds down to the **Vieux-Port** ★★, dominated by the massive neoclassical forts of St-Jean and St-Nicholas. The port is filled with fishing craft and yachts and ringed with seafood restaurants. For a panoramic view, head to the **Parc du Pharo,** a promontory facing the entrance to the Vieux-Port. From a terrace overlooking the Château du Pharo, built by Napoleon III for his Eugénie, you can clearly see Fort St-Jean and the old and new cathedrals.

One of the most efficient, and easiest, ways to see Marseille's centrally located monuments is aboard the hop-on, hop-off fleet of **Le Grand Tour Buses** (© **04-91-91-05-82;** www.marseillelegrandtour.com). Each bus is painted in highly recognizable shades of white, blue, and yellow, and each sports an open-air deck that you'll either appreciate for its unobstructed view or avoid because of its exposure to the blasting heat of the midsummer sun. The buses run year-round, although more buses run between March and mid-November (about eight per day, usually between 10am and 5pm) than during other times of the year (about four per day, usually every other

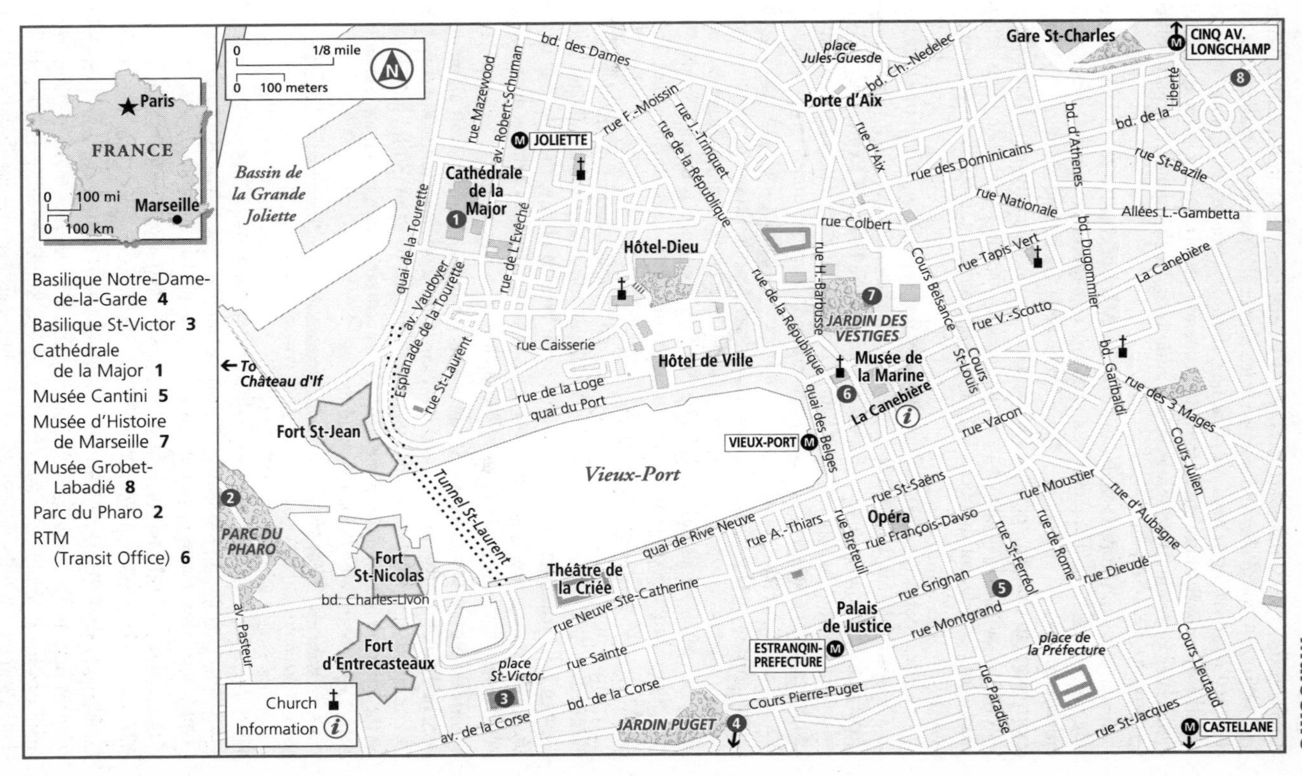

Gare St-Charles
CINQ AV. LONGCHAMP
CASTELLANE
Porte d'Aix
place Jules-Guesde
bd. Ch.-Nedelec
bd. d'Athenes
bd. de la Liberté
rue St-Bazile
Allées L.-Gambetta
La Canebière
rue des 3 Mages
Cours Julien
bd. Dugommier
bd. Garibaldi
rue d'Aubagne
Cours Lieutaud
rue des Dominicains
rue Nationale
rue Tapis Vert
rue V.-Scotto
Cours Belsance
Cours St-Louis
rue Vacon
rue Moustier
rue de Rome
rue Dieudé
rue St-Ferréol
place de la Préfecture
rue St-Jacques
rue Paradise
rue d'Aix
rue Colbert
rue H.-Barbusse
JARDIN DES VESTIGES
Musée de la Marine
La Canebière
rue St-Saëns
rue François-Davso
Opéra
rue Grignan
rue Montgrand
rue Breteuil
Palais de Justice
ESTRANQIN-PREFECTURE
Cours Pierre-Puget
quai des Belges
VIEUX-PORT
rue de la République
rue J.-Trinquet
rue F.-Moissin
Hôtel-Dieu
Hôtel de Ville
rue A.-Thiars
quai de Rive Neuve
Vieux-Port
JARDIN PUGET
bd. des Dames
JOLIETTE
rue Caisserie
rue de la Loge
quai du Port
rue Neuve Ste-Catherine
Théâtre de la Criée
rue Sainte
bd. de la Corse
Cathédrale de la Major
rue de L'Evêché
av. Robert-Schuman
rue Mazewood
Tunnel St-Laurent
place St-Victor
av. de la Corse
rue St-Laurent
Esplanade de la Tourette
av. Vaudoyer
quai de la Tourette
Fort St-Nicolas
bd. Charles-Livon
Fort d'Entrecasteaux
Fort St-Jean
To Château d'If
Bassin de la Grande Joliette
PARC DU PHARO
av. Pasteur
0 1/8 mile
0 100 meters
Church
Information
FRANCE
Paris
Marseille
0 100 mi
0 100 km
Basilique Notre-Dame-de-la-Garde 4
Basilique St-Victor 3
Cathédrale de la Major 1
Musée Cantini 5
Musée d'Histoire de Marseille 7
Musée Grobet-Labadié 8
Parc du Pharo 2
RTM (Transit Office) 6

hour between 10:30am and 4:15pm). There's a one-time fee of 17€ ($22) for adults and 14€ ($18) for seniors and students with proper ID. Ages 4 to 11 and under pay 8€ ($10). Participants can jump off at any of 16 different stops en route, and then climb back onto the next bus in the day's sequence, usually arriving between 1 and 2 hours later, depending on the season. For additional details, contact the tourist office at ✆ **04-91-13-89-00.**

A tourist train, the **Petit Train de la Bonne Mère** (✆ **04-91-25-124-69;** Métro: Vieux-Port), makes two circuits around town. Year-round, train no. 1 makes a 50-minute round-trip to Basilique Notre-Dame-de-la-Garde and Basilique St-Victor. From Easter to October, train no. 2 makes a 40-minute round-trip of old Marseille by way of the cathedral, Vieille Charité, and the Quartier du Panier. The trains depart from quai des Belges at the Vieux-Port. Each trip costs 5€ ($6.50) for adults and 3€ ($3.90) for children.

From quai des Belges at the Vieux-Port, you can take a 25-minute motorboat ride to **Château d'If** for 10€ ($12) round-trip. Boats leave every 60 to 90 minutes, depending on the season. For information, contact the **Frioul If Express** (✆ **04-91-46-54-65;** Métro: Vieux-Port), daily 9am to 6:30pm. On the sparsely vegetated island of Château d'If (✆ **04-91-59-02-30** for information), François I built a fortress to defend Marseille. The site later housed a prison, where carvings by Huguenot prisoners can still be seen. Alexandre Dumas used the château as a setting for the fictional adventures of *The Count of Monte Cristo.* The château's most famous association—with the legendary Man in the Iron Mask—is also apocryphal. The château is open Tuesday through Sunday 9am to 5:30pm (until 6:30pm Apr–Sept). Entrance to the island is 5€ ($6.50) adults, 3.50€ ($4.55) ages 18 to 25, and free for those 17 and under.

If you're driving, continue from the old port to the **corniche Président-J.-F.-Kennedy,** a 4km (2½-mile) promenade. You'll pass villas and gardens and have a good view of the Mediterranean. To the north is the **Port Moderne,** the "gateway to the East." Its construction began in 1844, and a century later the Germans destroyed it. Motorboat trips are conducted along the docks.

Basilique Notre-Dame-de-la-Garde This landmark church crowns a limestone rock overlooking the southern side of the Vieux-Port. It was built in the Romanesque-Byzantine style popular in the 19th century and topped by a 9m (30-ft.) gilded statue of the Virgin. Visitors come for the view—best at sunset—from its terrace. Spread out before you are the city, the islands, and the sea.

Rue Fort-du-Sanctuaire. ✆ **04-91-13-40-80.** www.notredamedelagarde.com. Free admission. Daily 7am–7pm. Métro: Vieux-Port.

Basilique St-Victor ★ This semifortified basilica was built above a crypt from the 5th century, when St. Cassianus founded the church and abbey. You can visit the crypt, which also reflects work done in the 10th and 11th centuries.

Place St-Victor. ✆ **04-96-11-22-60.** Admission to crypt 2€ ($2.60). Church daily 9am–7pm. Crypt daily 9am–7pm. Head west along quai de Rive-Neuve (near the Gare du Vieux-Port). Métro: Vieux-Port.

Cathédrale de la Major This was one of the largest cathedrals (some 135m/443 ft. long) built in Europe in the 19th century. It has mosaic floors and red-and-white marble banners, and the exterior is in a bastardized Romanesque-Byzantine style. The domes and cupolas may remind you of Istanbul. This vast pile has almost swallowed its 12th-century Romanesque predecessor, built on the ruins of a Temple of Diana.

Place de la Major. ✆ **04-91-90-52-87.** Free admission. Hours vary. Métro: Vieux-Port.

Musée Cantini The temporary exhibitions of contemporary art here are often as good as the permanent collection. This museum is devoted to modern art, with masterpieces by Derain, Marquet, Ernst, Masson, Balthus, and others. It also owns a selection of works by important young international artists.

19 rue Grignan. ✆ **04-91-54-77-75.** Admission 3€ ($3.90) adults, 1.50€ ($1.95) students, free for seniors and children under 10. Oct–May Tues–Sun 10am–5pm; June–Sept Tues–Sun 11am–6pm.

Musée d'Histoire de Marseille Visitors may wander through an archaeological garden where excavations are going on, as scholars learn more about the ancient town of Massalia, founded by Greek sailors. To help you more fully realize the era, audiovisual exhibits and a free exhibition room set the scene. A medieval quarter of potters has been discovered and is open to the public. You can also see what's left of a Roman shipwreck excavated from the site.

Centre Bourse, Square Belsunce. ✆ **04-91-90-42-22.** Admission 2€ ($2.60) adults, 1€ ($1.30) students and children 11–18, free for children under 11. Mon–Sat noon–7pm. Métro: Vieux-Port.

Musée Grobet-Labadié ★ This collection, bequeathed to the city in 1919, includes Louis XV and Louis XVI furniture, as well as an outstanding collection of medieval Burgundian and Provençal sculpture. Other exhibits showcase 17th-century Gobelin tapestries; 15th- to 19th-century German, Italian, French, and Flemish paintings; and 16th- and 17th-century Italian and French faïence.

140 bd. Longchamp. ✆ **04-91-62-21-82.** Admission 2€ ($2.60) adults, 1€ ($1.30) students and children 11–18, free for children under 11. June–Sept Tues–Sun 11am–6pm; Oct–May Tues–Sun 10am–5pm. Closed public holidays. Métro: Cinq av. Longchamp.

SHOPPING

Only Paris and Lyon can compete with Marseille for its breadth and diversity of merchandise. Your best bet is a trip to the **Vieux-Port** and the streets surrounding it, where folkloric objects cram the boutiques. Many shops are loaded with souvenirs such as crèche-style *santons.* The best place to buy these is above the Vieux-Port, behind the Théâtre National de la Criée. At **Ateliers Marcel Carbonel,** 47 rue Neuve-Ste-Catherine (✆ **04-91-54-26-58**), more than 600 Nativity-related figures, in half a dozen sizes, sell for 10€ ($13) and up.

Bring a photo to the artists at **Amandine,** 69 bd. Eugène-Pierre (✆ **04-91-47-00-83**), and they'll frost a cake with an amazing likeness. If you don't have a snapshot with you, choose from their images, which include scenes of the Vieux-Port. More traditional pastries and chocolates are at **Puyricard,** 25 rue Francis-Davso (✆ **04-91-54-26-25**), or 30 bd. Georges Clemenceau (✆ **04-91-85-19-87**). The treats include chocolates stuffed with *pâté d'amande* (almond paste) and *confits de fruits* (candied fruit).

Since medieval times, Marseille has thrived on the legend of Les Trois Maries—three saints named Mary, including everyone's favorite ex-sinner, Mary Magdalene. Assisted by awakened-from-the-dead St. Lazarus, they reportedly came ashore near Marseille to Christianize ancient Provence. In commemoration of their voyage, small boat-shaped cookies *(les navettes),* flavored with secret ingredients that include tons of orange zest, orange-flower water, and sugar, are forever associated with Marseille. They're sold throughout the city, most notably at **Le Four des Navettes,** 136 rue Sainte (✆ **04-91-33-32-12;** www.fourdesnavettes.com). Opened in 1791, it sells the cookies for 15€ ($20) per dozen and does very little else besides perpetuate the city's most cherished (and dubious) medieval myth.

Antiques from around Provence are for sale along cours Julien and in La Préfecture neighborhood. One of the best stores is **Antiquités François-Décamp,** 302 rue Paradis (✆ **04-91-81-18-00**). At **Felio,** 4 place Gabriel-Péri (✆ **04-91-90-32-67**), you'll find large-brimmed hats that would have thrilled ladies of the Belle Epoque, as well as berets and other styles of chapeau.

A well-stocked emporium carries virtually every kind of Provençal foodstuff: **Ducs de Gascogne,** 20 cours d'Estienne d'Orves (✆ **04-91-33-87-28;** www.ducsdegascogne.com; Métro: Vieux-Port). Foodstuffs originating in both the southeast and southwest of France are all beautifully packaged, including *calissons* (sugared almond confections), foie gras, jams, honey, olives and olive oil, tapenades, and spices known for centuries throughout the region.

Looking for something that approximates a sun-flooded mall in California, with a Provençal accent? Head for the most talked about real-estate development in the city's recent history, **L'Escale Borély,** avenue Mendès-France. A 25-minute trip south of Marseille (take the Métro to Rond-Point du Prado, and then transfer to bus no. 19; or from the center of Marseille, take bus no. 83, and then walk about a quarter-mile), it incorporates shops, cafes, bars, and restaurants. For more on L'Escale Borély, see "Marseille After Dark," below.

You may not think of Marseille as a place to shop for fashion, but the local industry is booming. Its center is along **cours Julien** and **rue de la Tour,** where you'll find many boutiques and ateliers. Much of the clothing reflects North African influences. Many items are rich, brocaded, and ethnic, cut chic and close to the body.

Here's a sampling of the best markets in Marseille: The **Capucins Market** (daily 8am–7pm), place des Capucins, has fruit, herbs, fish, and food products. **Quai du Port** (daily 8am–1pm) is a fish market on the old port. **Allées de Meilhan,** on La Canebière (Tues and Sat 8am–1pm), sells flowers year-round; from the last Sunday in November through December, vendors sell *santons* here daily 8am to 7pm. On **cours Julien** near Notre-Dame du Mont, you'll find a market with fruits, vegetables, and other foods (Tues, Thurs, Sat 8am–1pm). At the same location, vendors sell stamps (Sun 8am–1pm) and secondhand goods (every other Sun 8am–7pm). Also on cours Julien, there are old-book vendors every other Saturday (8am–3pm), organic products (Fri 8am–1pm), and a flower market (Sat and Wed 8am–1pm).

WHERE TO STAY

VERY EXPENSIVE

Le Petit Nice ★★★ This is the best hotel in Marseille. It opened in 1917, when the Passédat family joined two villas in a secluded area below the street paralleling the beach. The spacious Marina Wing across from the main building offers rooms individually decorated in an antique style, opening onto sea views. The rooms in the main house are more modern and avant-garde. Four units were inspired by the cubist movement, with posh geometric appointments and bright colors. Each unit comes with a luxurious bathroom with tub/shower. The hotel restaurant is beautiful, with a view of the shore and the rocky islands off its coast. In summer, dinner is served in the garden facing the sea.

Corniche Président-J.-F.-Kennedy/Anse-de-Maldormé, Marseille 13007. ✆ **04-91-59-25-92.** Fax 04-91-59-28-08. www.petitnice-passedat.com. 16 units. 190€–550€ ($247–$715) double; 595€–870€ ($774–$1,131) suite. AE, DC, MC, V. Free parking. Métro: Vieux-Port. **Amenities:** Restaurant; bar; outdoor pool; free use of bikes; room service; babysitting; laundry service; dry cleaning; nonsmoking rooms. *In room:* A/C, TV, minibar, hair dryer, safe.

EXPENSIVE

Mercure Beauvau Vieux Port ★★ Although completely restored and up-to-date, this is the oldest hotel in Marseille, having hosted such artsy types as Chopin and George Sand in the 19th century. It is decorated in the various epoch styles of France, including Louis XIII, Napoleon III, and Empire. In the public rooms antique Provençal furnishings are used as accents, whereas the bedrooms, for the most part, have contemporary furnishings that are both tasteful and comfortable. There is no restaurant on-site, but many are available nearby; and the bar, one of the most attractive places in Marseille for a rendezvous, overlooks the port.

4 rue Beauvau, Marseille 13001. ✆ **04-91-54-91-00.** Fax 04-91-54-15-76. www.mercure.com. 72 units. 179€–299€ ($234–$389) double; 409€–449€ ($532–$584) suite. AE, DC, MC, V. Parking 15€ ($20). **Amenities:** Bar; room service; breakfast room; laundry service/dry cleaning. *In room:* A/C, TV, hair dryer, minibar, safe.

Sofitel Marseille Vieux Port ★★★ This government-rated four-star hotel lacks the glamour and style of Le Petit Nice, but it is the highest-rated lodging in the city center. A glistening modern palace, it stands above the embankments of the old port. Some guest rooms have panoramic views of the Vieux-Port; others look out on the boulevard. Rooms are up-to-date, comfortable, and furnished in Provençal style, with a combination tub/shower. All are fairly generous in size. This hotel and its corporate sibling, the Novotel Vieux Port (see below), are in the same building and share a staff and dining facilities.

36 bd. Charles-Livon, Marseille 13007. ✆ **04-91-15-59-00.** Fax 04-91-15-59-50. www.accorhotels.com. 134 units. 235€–315€ ($306–$410) double; 570€–1,000€ ($741–$1,300) suite. AE, DC, MC, V. Parking 15€ ($20). Métro: Vieux-Port. **Amenities:** Restaurant; bar; room service; babysitting; laundry service; dry cleaning; nonsmoking rooms; limited-mobility rooms. *In room:* A/C, TV, minibar, hair dryer, safe.

MODERATE

Hôtel le Corbusier ★ The radical designs of Swiss-born architect Le Corbusier (aka Charles-Edouard Jeanneret, 1887–1965) have long been associated with Marseilles. In 1952, in a location 2km (1¼ miles) south of Marseilles' *Vieux Port,* he designed *l'Unité d'Habitation* (it's also known as *La Cité Radieuse*), a multi-functional, nine-story building that combines shops and apartments for 1,500 residents. Within his original plan, he even included a provision for the inclusion of a hotel, which, beginning in 1959, opened its doors for business to the general public from premises on the building's third and fourth floors. At the time, horrified neighbors referred to the place as *La maison du fada* (House of the Crazy) because it was so ugly. Today, it's viewed as an architectural treasure that vaguely evokes the form of a ship headed out to sea.

Recently, the husband-and-wife team of Alban and Dominique Gérardin spent a ton of money stripping the hotel back to the original combination of expressionism and functionalism for which Le Corbusier is known. They've zealously retained a handful of their studios' original kitchens, each designed by Le Corbusier's now-celebrated collaborator Charlotte Perriand (none of them actually works, but they're highly prized as minimalist statements nonetheless), and outfitted the hotel with the kind of spartan, functional, and often metallic furniture, lighting fixtures, and accessories of which the great designer would have approved. The smallest units are rather cramped, evoking the cabins aboard cruise ships; larger units are more airy and congenial, some with their (non-working) original kitchens. None of the units has a bathroom door, since le Corbusier considered such niceties as frills and "aesthetic diversions." On the premises is a (separately recommended) restaurant, *Le Ventre de l'Architect* (The Architect's Stomach). Guests of the hotel have access to a rooftop jogging track and wading pool, both of them surrounded by the boxy, blocky designs for which Le Corbusier was (and still is) famous. The reception area for this place, clad in blond paneling and floored with slabs of gray and white marble, is on the building's third floor. Take the elevator from the building's lobby to reach it.

On the 3rd and 4th floors of "La Cité Radieuse," 280 bd. Michelet, Marseille 13008. ✆ **04-91-16-78-00.** www.hotellecorbusier.com. 21 units. 59€–105€ ($77–$137) double; 120€ ($156) suite. DC, MC, V. Bus: 21. **Amenities:** Restaurant; bar; jogging track and wading pool; fitness club (all on rooftop); mini-library; laundry service/dry cleaning; baby cribs rentable for 10€ ($13) each. *In room:* A/C, TV, fridge, Wi-Fi.

La Résidence du Vieux Port This old hotel has a touch of raffish charm and an unbeatable location: directly beside the harbor. The guest rooms have loggia-style terraces opening onto the port; the rooms are simple but serviceable, each with a shower unit.

18 quai du Port, Marseille 13001. ✆ **04-91-91-91-22.** Fax 04-91-56-60-88. www.hotelmarseille.com. 50 units. 125€–135€ ($163–$176) double; 165€ ($215) suite. AE, DC, MC, V. Parking 7€ ($9.10). Métro: Vieux-Port. **Amenities:** Cafe; bar; room service; laundry service; dry cleaning; nonsmoking rooms; limited-mobility rooms. *In room:* A/C, TV, minibar, hair dryer, safe.

Novotel Vieux Port *Value* In the same building as the Sofitel (see above), the Novotel broke off from its more upscale affiliate in 1987. Services are less extensive, amenities less plush, and spaces a bit more cramped than at the Sofitel, but because this is one of the most reasonably priced hotels in town, no one seems to mind. The few rooms overlooking the old port tend to fill up first. Each unit is outfitted in chain-hotel style and comes with a small, well-equipped bathroom with tub/shower.

36 bd. Charles-Livon, Marseille 13007. ✆ **04-96-11-42-11.** Fax 04-96-11-42-20. www.accorhotels.com. 110 units. 105€–178€ ($137–$231) double. AE, DC, MC, V. Parking 15€ ($20). Métro: Vieux-Port. **Amenities:** Restaurant; bar; outdoor pool; room service; babysitting; laundry service; dry cleaning; nonsmoking rooms; limited-mobility rooms. *In room:* A/C, TV, minibar, hair dryer.

INEXPENSIVE

Hôtel Mascotte This hotel evokes the grandeur of 19th-century life in Marseille. It's less than 2 blocks from the Vieux-Port, in the heart of town. The sun and mistrals of many seasons have battered the Beaux Arts facade, decorated with ornate corbels and cornices. Renovations have stripped the guest rooms of some of their old-fashioned charm, but have left efficient, soundproof spaces. Each unit has a compact bathroom with a shower and tub. Breakfast is the only meal served, but the neighborhood abounds with dining options.

5 la Canebière, Marseille 13001. ✆ **04-91-90-61-61.** Fax 04-91-90-95-61. www.oceanianhotels.com. 45 units. 88€ ($114) double. AE, DC, MC, V. Parking in nearby public lot 12€ ($14). **Amenities:** Room service; laundry service; dry cleaning; nonsmoking rooms. *In room:* A/C, TV, minibar, hair dryer.

New Hôtel Bompard This tranquil retreat, built after World War II, lies atop a cliff along the corniche, about 3km (1¾ miles) east of the Vieux-Port. Partly because of its garden, it may remind you of a well-appointed private home. A Provençal *mas* (farmhouse) in the garden holds four large rooms that are more luxurious and atmospheric than those in the main building. Some of the beds are baldachin-style (canopied); floors have Provençal tiles; bathrooms are relatively large, with tub/shower combos; and furnishings are romantic. Rooms in the main building are cheap, modern, and streamlined, with tub/shower combos, and not terribly romantic, although about a third were renovated in 2004.

2 rue des Flots Bleus, Marseille 13007. ✆ **04-91-99-22-22.** Fax 04-91-31-02-14. www.new-hotel.com. 49 units. 95€–220€ ($124–$286) standard double; 200€–250€ ($260–$325) Provençal *mas* double. AE, DC, MC, V. Free parking. Bus: 61 or 83. **Amenities:** Restaurant; bar; outdoor pool; room service; laundry service; nonsmoking rooms; limited-mobility rooms. *In room:* A/C, TV, minibar, hair dryer, iron, safe, Wi-Fi.

WHERE TO DINE

EXPENSIVE

Le Petit Nice (see "Where to Stay," above) has a lovely restaurant.

Le Miramar ★★★ SEAFOOD Except for Le Petit Nice (see above), Le Miramar offers the grandest dining in Marseille. Bouillabaisse aficionados flock here to savor a version that will surely be a culinary highlight of your trip. It's hard to imagine that this was once a rough-and-tumble recipe favored by local fishermen, a way of using the least desirable portion of their catch. Actually, it's traditionally two dishes, a saffron-tinted soup followed by the fish poached in the soup. It's eaten with *une rouille,* a sauce of red chiles, garlic, olive oil, egg yolk, and cayenne. The version served here involves lots of labor and just as much costly seafood. The setting is a room with frescoes of underwater life and big windows that open onto the Vieux-Port. It's linked to a terrace that overlooks Marseille's most famous church, Notre-Dame-de-la-Garde.

12 quai du Port. ✆ **04-91-91-10-40.** Reservations recommended. Main courses 31€–48€ ($40–$62); bouillabaisse from 55€ ($72) per person (minimum 2). AE, DC, MC, V. Tues–Sat noon–2:30pm and 7–9:30pm. Métro: Vieux-Port.

Une Table au Sud ★★ MODERN PROVENÇAL One floor above street level, in a modern dining room with views of the Vieux-Port, this restaurant serves some of the most creative cuisine in Marseille. The historically important 19th-century building has sculpted lion heads embellishing its facade. Chef de cuisine Lionel Levy and his wife, Florence, the *maître d'hôtel,* are the creative forces here. Their cuisine changes daily according to the ingredients available at local markets. Menu items include a creamy soup made from chestnuts and sea urchins, and a thick slice of a local saltwater fish known as *denti,* which local gastronomes compare to a *daurade royale* (sea bream) served with flap mushrooms and chicken stock; mullet served with saffron and herb risotto; and roasted squab with Arabica coffee-flavored juices. Depending on the mood of the chef, desserts may include pineapple *dacquoise* (stacked meringue dessert) served with vanilla-flavor whipped cream.

1 quai du Port. ✆ **04-91-90-63-53.** Reservations recommended. Fixed-price lunch 34€ ($41); fixed-price dinner 48€–98€ ($62–$127). AE, MC, V. Tues–Thurs noon–2pm and 7:30–10:30pm; Fri–Sat noon–2pm and 7:30pm–midnight. Closed Aug and Dec 23–27. Métro: Vieux-Port.

MODERATE

Le Comptoir des Favouilles PROVENÇAL/SOUTHWESTERN FRENCH On the opposite side of the building from Les Arcenaulx (see below), this restaurant occupies a former dorm for prisoners who were forced to row the ornamental barges of Louis XIV during his inspections of Marseille's harbor. You'll get a lot for your money—prices are relatively reasonable and ingredients very fresh. Provençal dishes include succulent baked sea wolf prepared as simply as possible—with herbs and olive oil. Particularly noteworthy is bouillabaisse (which, at 45€/$59 per person, is the most expensive main course on the menu) and a delectable combination of saltwater crayfish with foie gras. Desserts usually include roasted figs served with sweet dessert wine.

44 rue Sainte. ✆ **04-96-11-03-11.** Reservations recommended. Main courses 12€–45€ ($16–$59); fixed-price menu 13€ ($17) lunch. AE, DC, MC, V. Mon–Fri noon–2:30pm; Mon–Sat 7:30–10:30pm. Closed mid-July to mid-Aug. Métro: Vieux-Port.

Les Arcenaulx ★ *Finds* PROVENÇAL This is an architectural oddity that serves memorable cuisine. The navies of Louis XIV built these stone warehouses near the Vieux-Port; they now contain this restaurant and two bookstores, run by the charming sisters Simone and Jeanne Laffitte. Look for Provençal cuisine with a Marseillais accent in such dishes as roasted pigeon or duckling with caramelized quince; roasted scallops with hearts of violet artichokes; *daurade* (bream) roasted whole "on its skin"; and filet of beef *rossini,* layered with foie gras. Equally tempting are artichokes *barigoule* (loaded with aromatic spices and olive oil) and a worthy assortment of *petites légumes farcies* (Provençal vegetables stuffed with chopped meat and herbs).

25 cours d'Estienne d'Orves. ✆ **04-91-59-80-30.** Reservations recommended. Main courses 18€–34€ ($23–$44); fixed-price menu 24€–54€ ($31–$70). AE, DC, MC, V. Mon–Sat noon–2pm and 8–11pm. Closed Aug 15–22 and Dec 27–Jan 3. Métro: Vieux-Port.

Le Ventre de l'Architect FRENCH With a westward-facing view of the sea and the setting sun, this is the restaurant that's associated with the hotel that occupies a building that, when designed by Le Corbusier between 1952 and 1954, was considered one of the most revolutionary designs in Europe. You'll benefit from both an architecturally historic setting and menu items that are creative, imaginative, and—if you understand a bit of French—described in ways that would have pleased a 19th-century impressionistic poet. Examples include cream of pumpkin soup; a "pillow" of foie gras "draped" with slices of Serrano ham; a "waltz" of jumbo shrimp with scallops, served with pink risotto; beef medallions "rolled together" with cured ham and served with "herbs from the chef's garden"; and veal chops with braised endives and a purée of violets.

In the Hotel le Corbusier, on the 3rd floor of "La Cité Radieuse," 280 bd. Michelet. ✆ **04-91-16-78-00.** Lunch main courses 18€–25€ ($23–$33); all dinner main courses 28€ ($36); set-price dinner 40€ ($52). Mon–Sat noon–2pm and 8–11pm. DC, MC, V. Bus: 21.

INEXPENSIVE

La Kahena TUNISIAN This is one of the busiest and most-respected Tunisian restaurants in a city that's loaded with worthy competitors. Established in 1976 and set close to the Vieux-Port, it's a two-room enclave of savory North African aromas: minced or grilled lamb, tomatoes, eggplant, herbs, and couscous, so beloved by Tunisian expatriates. The menu lists 10 varieties of couscous, including versions with lamb, chicken, fish, the savory sausages known as *merguez,* and a "complete" version that includes a little bit of each of those ingredients. Also look for *méchouia,* a succulent version of roasted lamb. The restaurant's name, incidentally, derives from a 6th-century-B.C. Tunisian princess who was legendary for uniting all the Berber tribes of North Africa.

2 rue de la République. ✆ **04-91-90-61-93.** Reservations recommended. Main courses 12€–16€ ($16–$21). MC, V. Daily noon–2:30pm and 7:30–11pm. Métro: Vieux-Port.

Toinou SEAFOOD In a massive building that overshadows every other structure nearby, this landmark restaurant serves more shellfish than any other restaurant in Marseille. Inside, a display of more than 40 species of shellfish is laid out for inspection by some of the canniest judges of seafood in France—Toinou's customers. Dining rooms are on three floors, served by a waitstaff who are very entrenched in their *marseillais* accents and demeanors. Don't come here unless you're really fond of shellfish, any species of which can be served raw or cooked. The wine list is extensive, with attractively priced whites from such regions as the Loire Valley.

3 cours St-Louis, 1e. ✆ **04-91-33-14-94.** www.toinou.com. Reservations recommended. Main courses 15€–69€ ($20–$90); fixed-price shellfish platter for two 39€ ($51). DC, MC, V. Daily 11:30am–11:30pm. Métro: Vieux-Port.

MARSEILLE AFTER DARK

For an amusing and relatively harmless exposure to the town's saltiness, walk around the **Vieux-Port,** where cafes and restaurants angle their sightlines for the best view of the harbor.

L'Escale Borély, avenue Mendès-France, is a modern-day equivalent of the Vieux-Port. It's a waterfront development south of the town center, only 20 minutes away (take bus no. 83 or 19). About a dozen cafes, as well as restaurants of every possible ilk, serve many cuisines. They offer views of in-line skaters on the promenade in front and the potential for conversation with friendly strangers, with less likelihood of street crime.

Unless the air-conditioning is powerful, Marseille's dance clubs produce a lot of sweat. Close to Vieux-Port, you can dance and drink at the **Metal Café,** 20 rue Fortia (✆ **04-91-54-03-03**), where 20- to 50-year-olds listen to R&B, house, and techno music recently released in London and Los Angeles. Or try the nearby **Trolley Bus,** 24 quai de Rive-Neuve (✆ **04-91-54-30-45;** www.letrolley.com), best known for its techno, house, hip-hop, jazz, and salsa.

If you miss free-form modern jazz and don't mind taking your chances in the less-than-savory neighborhood adjacent to the city's rail station (La Gare St-Charles—take a taxi there and back), consider dropping into **La Cité de la Musique** (also known as **La Cave à Jazz**), 4 rue Bernard-du-Bois (✆ **04-91-39-28-28**). Other nightlife venues in Marseille evoke Paris, but with lots of extra *méridional* (southern) spice thrown in for extra flavor. Three Marseillais bars that we found particularly intriguing include **Le Pharaon,** Place de l'Opéra (✆ **04-91-54-09-89;** Métro: Vieux-Port), a cozy enclave of deep sofas and armchairs, soft lighting, and—usually—a sense of well-being. Somewhat more bustling and animated is **l'Exit,** 12 quai de Riveneuve (✆ **04-91-54-29-43;** Métro: Vieux-Port), a bar with a terrace that profits from Marseille's sultry nights, and two floors of seething nocturnal energy. And for a bar that prides itself on its wide array of complicated cocktails and tapas, as well as a lot of attractive 30-somethings, consider **l'Interdit,** 9 rue Molière (✆ **06-22-99-51-25;** Métro: Vieux-Port). A place that's loaded with razzmatazz, and appealing for both its dance floor and its cabaret acts, is **Le Circus,** 5 rue du Chantier (✆ **04-91-33-77-22;** Métro: Vieux-Port). A fee of 15€ ($20) gets you entrance into the overall compound, after which you can visit any aspect of the place (cabaret vs. dance floor) that appeals to you at the time.

The gay scene in Marseille isn't as crowded, or as intriguing, as the one in Nice, but its premier gay bar, **The Get Bar-MP Bar,** 10 rue Beauvau (✆ **04-91-33-64-79**), benefits from a long history of being the town's gay bar of record. It's open Tuesday to Sunday 7pm to 3am. An equally valid, and equally gay, option is **The New Can Can,** 3–5 rue Sénac (✆ **04-91-48-59-76;** www.newcancan.com), a broad and sprawling bar-and-disco venue that, at least in Marseille, seems to be everybody's favorite dance-club venue. Technically, the place identifies as a mostly gay venue, but frankly, it gets so many heterosexuals that the gender-specific definitions that dominate many of the town's other nightclubs are—at least here—practically moot. One or another of its subdivisions tends to open nightly at around 8:30pm, and by the weekend, it blossoms into full electronic bloom. It is open Thursday to Sunday 11pm until dawn. There is no cover except on Friday and Saturday nights when 9€ ($12) is levied before midnight, 14€ ($18) after midnight.

8 Toulon

836km (519 miles) S of Paris, 127km (80 miles) SW of Cannes, 68km (42 miles) E of Marseille

This fortress and town is France's principal naval base, the headquarters of the Mediterranean fleet, with hundreds of sailors wandering the streets. It's not as seedy, but also not as intriguing, as Marseille. The beautiful harbor is surrounded by hills and crowned by forts, protected on the east by a breakwater and on the west by the great peninsula of Cap Sicié. The outer roads are known as the Grande Rade and the inner roads as the Petite Rade. A winter resort colony lies on the outskirts. Like Marseille, Toulon has a large Arab population. There's racial tension here, worsened by the closing of the shipyards.

Park your car underground at place de la Liberté, and then walk along boulevard des Strasbourg, turning right onto rue Berthelot. This will take you into the pedestrian-only area in the core of the old city. It's filled with shops, hotels, restaurants, and cobblestone streets—but it can be dangerous at night. The best beach, **Plage du Mourillon,** is 2km (1¼ miles) east of the heart of town.

ESSENTIALS

GETTING THERE & GETTING AROUND **Trains** arrive from Marseille about every 5 to 30 minutes (trip time: 1 hr.); the one-way fare is 10€ ($13). If you're on the Riviera, trains arrive frequently from Nice (trip time: 1 hr., 45 min.) and Cannes (trip time: 80 min.). For information, call ✆ **08-92-35-35-35.**

Three **buses** per day arrive from Aix-en-Provence (trip time: 1 hr., 15 min.); the fare is about 10€ ($13) one-way. For information, call **Sodetrav** (✆ **08-25-00-06-50**). If you're **driving** from Marseille, take A50 east to Toulon. When you arrive, park your car and get around on foot—the Vieille Ville (old town) and most attractions are easy to reach. A municipal **bus** system serves the town as well. A bus map is available at the tourist office. For information, call **Le Réseau Mistral** at ✆ **04-94-03-87-03.**

VISITOR INFORMATION The **Office de Tourisme** is at place Raimu (✆ **04-94-18-53-00;** fax 04-94-24-77-39; www.toulontourisme.com).

EXPLORING THE TOWN

In **Vieux Toulon,** between the harbor and boulevard de Strasbourg (the main axis of town), are many remains of the port's former days. A colorful food market, conducted Tuesday to Sunday from 8am to 1pm, **Le Marché du cours Lafayette,** spills onto the streets around cours Lafayette. Also in old Toulon is the **Cathédrale Ste-Marie-Majeure** (✆ **04-94-92-28-91**), built in the Romanesque style in the 11th and 12th centuries, and expanded in the 17th. Its badly lit nave is Gothic; the belfry and facade are from the 18th century. It's open daily from 7:30am to noon and 2:30 to 7pm.

In contrast to the cathedral, tall modern buildings line quai Stalingrad, opening onto **Vieille d'Arse.** On place Puget, look for the ***atlantes*** **(caryatids),** figures of men used as columns. These interesting figures support a balcony at the **Hôtel de Ville (City Hall)** and are also included in the facade of the naval museum.

Musée de la Marine, place du Ingénieur-Général-Monsenergue (✆ **04-94-02-02-01**), contains figureheads and ship models. Year-round, it's open Wednesday to Monday 10am to 6pm. Admission is 5€ ($6.50) for adults, 3.50€ ($4.55) for students, free for ages under 18.

Musée de Toulon, 113 bd. du Maréchal-Leclerc (© **04-94-36-81-00**), displays works from the 16th century to the present. There's a good collection of Provençal and Italian paintings and religious works. The latest acquisitions include New Realism pieces and minimalist art. It's open Tuesday to Sunday noon to 6pm; admission is free.

After you've covered the top attractions, we suggest taking a drive, an hour or two before sunset, along the **corniche du Mont-Faron.** It's a scenic boulevard along the lower slopes of Mont Faron, providing views of the busy port, the town, the cliffs, and, in the distance, the Mediterranean.

Earlier in the day, consider boarding a **téléphérique,** or funicular (© **04-94-92-68-25**), near the **New Hôtel La Tour Blanche.** It operates Tuesday to Sunday 9:30am to noon and 2 to 6:30pm (closed mid-Nov to Feb 3); the round-trip costs 6.10€ ($7.95) for adults and 4.30€ ($5.60) for children 4 to 10 years old. At the top, enjoy the view and then visit the **Memorial du Débarquement en Provence,** Mont Faron (© **04-94-88-08-09**), which documents the Allied landings in Provence in 1944, among other events. It's open in summer daily 10am to noon and 2 to 4:30pm; from mid-September to June, it's open Tuesday to Sunday 10am to noon and 2 to 4:30pm. Admission is 3.80€ ($4.95) for adults and 1.55€ ($2) for children 8 to 16.

WHERE TO STAY

New Hôtel La Tour Blanche With excellent accommodations, terraced gardens, and a pool, this 1970s hotel is one of the best in Toulon. It lies in the hills about 1.5km (1 mile) north of the center of town, which gives it sweeping views of the port and sea even from the lower floors. Many rooms, especially those overlooking the bay, have balconies. All are comfortably and simply outfitted in international modern style. The compact bathrooms have showers, but only half have tub/shower combinations. Some units have dataports. The restaurant, Les Terrasses, has a panoramic view. Fixed-price menus of traditional Provençal cuisine cost 19€ to 23€ ($25–$30).

Bd. de l'Amiral-Vence, Mont Faron, Toulon 83000. © **04-94-24-41-57.** Fax 04-94-22-42-25. www.new-hotel.com. 75 units. 84€–108€ ($109–$140) double. AE, DC, MC, V. Free parking. Bus: 40. From the town center, follow signs to the Mont Faron téléphérique, and you'll pass the hotel en route. **Amenities:** Restaurant; bar; outdoor pool; room service; babysitting; laundry service; limited-mobility rooms. *In room:* A/C, TV, hair dryer, iron.

WHERE TO DINE

Au Sourd ★ SEAFOOD This restaurant dates back to 1862, and it's still going strong after all these years. The original owner, a former soldier, was nicknamed "Le Sourd," or the deaf one, because his ear had been badly injured during the Crimean War. The interior is the replica of an old Provençal house. There's nothing old about the cuisine: it's among the freshest in the area, especially if you stick to the fish and seafood dishes. The present chefs make the finest bouillabaisse in the area. Equally good is the savory kettle of *bourride,* which is various small fish cooked with onions, tomatoes, and garlic, and flavored with saffron and olive oil. We are also fond of the various fish of the day, which are grilled to perfection. Two other commendable dishes are the sautéed calamari and the fricassee of scallops.

10 rue Molière. © **04-94-92-28-52.** Reservations recommended. Main courses 12€–50€ ($16–$65). Fixed-price menu 28€ ($36). AE, MC, V. Tues–Sat noon–2pm and 7:15–10pm.

Le Jardin du Sommelier ★ FRENCH/PROVENÇAL This is a wine restaurant with some of the finest vintages in the area, but it also turns out a savory cuisine of well-prepared dishes with market-fresh produce. Since 1992, it's been recognized as the leading restaurant of this port city. Much of the chef's repertoire is based on the sea, including a medley of scallops and shrimp au gratin. Meat and poultry dishes are also respected, the best, in our view, being the magret of roast duckling with a Thai preparation. The atmosphere is that of an old Provençal home, and your host is Christian Scalisi, the leading food and wine expert in the area.

20 allées Courbet. ✆ **04-94-62-03-27.** Reservations required. Fixed-price menus 30€–50€ ($39–$65). AE, MC, V. Mon–Fri noon–1:15pm; Mon–Tues and Thurs–Sat 8–9:30pm. Closed Aug.

TOULON AFTER DARK

The temporary home of thousands of sailors is bound to have a nightlife scene that's earthier, and a bit raunchier, than those of equivalent-size towns elsewhere. A rough-and-ready bar that offers stiff drinks, live music, and a complete lack of pretension is **Le Bar 113,** 113 av. de Infanterie de la Marine (✆ **04-94-03-42-41**). At **Bar à Thym,** 32 bd. Cuneo (✆ **04-94-41-90-10**), everybody seems to drink beer, gossip, and listen to live music.

Toulon is also home to one of the region's best-known gay discos, **Boy's Paradise,** 1 bd. Pierre-Toesca (✆ **04-94-09-35-90**), near the train station. Adjacent to the port is the gay **Bar La Lampa,** Port de Toulon (✆ **04-94-03-06-09**), where tapas and live music accompany lots of beer and wine or whiskey.

9 Iles d'Hyères ★

39km (24 miles) SE of Toulon, 119km (74 miles) SW of Cannes

Off the Riviera in the Mediterranean, a little group of islands encloses the southern boundary of the Hyères anchorage. During the Renaissance they were called the Iles d'Or, named for the golden glow the rocks sometimes give off in sunlight. Nothing in the islands today will remind you of the turbulent times when they were attacked by pirates and Turkish galleys, or even of the Allied landings in World War II.

Mass tourism has arrived on these sun-baked islands, with some of the tackiness that accompanies it. Cars are forbidden on all three major islands, and the ferryboats cannot transport them. Expect a Gallic version of Nantucket, with thousands of midsummer day-trippers arriving, often with children, for a day of sun, sand, and people-watching.

Which island is the most appealing? Ile des Porquerolles is the most beautiful. Thinking of heading to Le Levant? You may want to steer clear—only 25% of the island is accessible to visitors. The remainder belongs to the French army and is used frequently for testing missiles.

ESSENTIALS

GETTING TO ILE DE PORQUEROLLES Ferryboats leave from several points along the Côte d'Azur. The most frequent, most convenient, and shortest trip is from the harbor of La Tour Fondue on the peninsula of Giens, a 32km (20-mile) drive east of Toulon. Depending on the season, there are 4 to 20 departures a day. The round-trip fare for the 15-minute crossing is 16€ ($21). For information, call the **Transports Maritimes et Terrestres du Littoral Varois,** La Tour Fondue, 83400 Giens (✆ **04-94-58-21-81**). The next-best option is the ferryboat from Toulon but only between June and September. Other options, each of them available only between June and September, involve taking one of the ferryboats maintained by the **Compagnie Maritime des Vedettes Ile d'Or & Le Corsaire** (✆ **04-94-71-01-02**). Their ferryboats offer crossings from either of *Les Gares Maritimes* in Le Lavandou and Cavalaire.

On any of the venues noted above, round-trip fares to the Ile de Porquerolles cost 30€ ($39) for adults and 23€ ($30) for children 4 to 11.

GETTING TO ILE DE PORT-CROS The most popular ferry route to the island is the 35-minute crossing that departs between four and seven times daily, depending on the season. (From Oct–Mar, there are only three crossings per week.) For information, contact the **Compagnie Maritime des Vedettes** (✆ **04-94-71-01-02**). Round-trip fares cost 27€ ($35) for adults and 21€ ($27) for children 4 to 11. The same company, for approximately the same price, also offers crossings to Port-Cros from Cavalaire, but only between April and September. For no additional fee, vessels will drop passengers at the military installations at Le Levant.

VISITOR INFORMATION Other than temporary, summer-only kiosks without phones that distribute brochures and advice near the ferry docks in Porquerolles and Port-Cros, there are no tourist bureaus on the islands. The offices in Hyères and Toulon try to fill in the gaps. Contact the **Office de Tourisme,** 3 av. Ambroise Thomas, Hyères (✆ **04-94-01-84-50**), or the **Office de Tourisme,** place Raimu, Toulon (✆ **04-94-18-53-00**).

ILE DE PORQUEROLLES ★

This is the largest and westernmost of the Iles d'Hyères. It has a rugged south coast, but the north strand, facing the mainland, has sandy beaches bordered by heather, scented myrtles, and pine trees. The island is about 8km (5 miles) long and 2km (1¼ miles) wide, and is 4.8km (3 miles) from the mainland.

The population is only 400. The island is said to receive 275 days of sunshine annually. It's a land of rocky capes, pine forests twisted by the mistral, sun-drenched vineyards, and pale ocher houses. The "hot spots," if there are any, are the cafes around **place d'Armes,** where everybody gathers.

The island has a violent history of raids, attacks, and occupation by everybody from the Dutch and the English to the Turks and the Spaniards. Ten forts, some in ruins, testify to its fierce past. The most ancient is **Fort Ste-Agathe,** built in 1531 by François I. In time it was a penal colony and a retirement center for soldiers of the colonial wars.

The French government purchased the largest hunk of the island in 1971 and turned it into a national park and botanical garden.

WHERE TO STAY & DINE

Le Relais de la Poste On a small square in the heart of the island's main settlement, this pleasant and unpretentious hotel is the oldest on the island—it opened "sometime in the 19th century" and is managed by the good-natured sixth generation of its founding family. It offers Provençal-style rooms with loggias. Most rooms are small to medium in size, and each comes with fine linen on a twin or double bed. In-room amenities are lean except for a phone. Bathrooms are compact and well organized, with shower stalls. The hotel has a billiard table and a creperie that sells only snack-style dessert crepes and fresh fruit juice.

Place d'Armes, Porquerolles 83540. ✆ **04-98-04-62-62.** Fax 04-94-58-33-57. www.lerelaisdelaposte.com. 30 units. 85€–120€ ($111–$156) double. No credit cards. Closed late Sept to Easter. **Amenities:** Bar; lounge; bike rental.

Mas du Langoustier ★★ In a large park on the island's western tip, this tranquil resort hotel is an old *mas* with a view of a lovely pine-ringed bay. Employees greet guests in a covered wagon by the jetty. Guest rooms, in antique Provençal style, are the most elegantly decorated on the island. Bathrooms are roomy, and most have tub/shower combinations. Should you visit for a meal, the menu is the finest in the Hyère islands, offering mainly seafood in a light nouvelle style. Try *loup* (wolf fish) with Noilly Prat in puff pastry, or tender kid with dried tomatoes roasted in casserole. You can drink and dine on the terraces.

Porquerolles 83400. ✆ **04-94-58-30-09.** Fax 04-94-58-36-02. www.langoustier.com. 50 units. 177€–262€ ($230–$341) double; 267€–312€ ($347–$406) suite. Rates include half board. MC, V. **Amenities:** 2 restaurants; bar; room service; babysitting; laundry service; limited-mobility rooms. *In room:* A/C, TV, minibar, safe. Closed late Sept to late Apr.

ILE DE PORT-CROS ★

Lush subtropical vegetation reminiscent of a Caribbean island makes this a green paradise, 5km (3 miles) long and 2km (1¼ miles) wide. The most mountainous of the archipelago, Port-Cros has been a French national park since 1963. A fire in 1892 devastated the island, which now abounds with pine forests and ilexes. Birders flock here to observe nearly 100 different species. There are many marked trails, mainly for daytrippers. The most popular and scenic is ***sentier botanique;*** the more adventurous and athletic take the 10km (6¼-mile) ***circuit historique*** (you'll need a packed lunch for this one). Divers follow a 274m (899-ft.) trail from Plage de la Palud to the islet of Rascas, where a plastic guide sheet identifies the underwater flora. Thousands of pleasure craft call here annually, which does little to help the island's fragile environment.

WHERE TO STAY & DINE

Le Manoir ★ This is the only bona fide hotel on the island, but despite lack of competition, its owners work hard to make their guests as comfortable as possible. Originally, it functioned as the grandiose home of the family that owned the entire island. Today, the hotel consists of an 18th-century architectural core, plus an annex that contains most of the guest accommodations. Accommodations are simple, and bathrooms come equipped with tub/shower combinations. Some rooms have air-conditioning. The restaurant serves lobster-and-fish terrine, several seasoned meats, and fresh local fish with baby vegetables, as well as regional goat cheese and velvety mousses.

Ile de Port-Cros 83400. ✆ **04-94-05-90-52.** Fax 04-94-05-90-89. lemanoir.portcros@wanadoo.fr. 22 units. 145€–185€ ($189–$241) double; 185€–210€ ($241–$273) suite. MC, V. Closed Oct–Apr. **Amenities:** Restaurant; bar; outdoor pool; room service; laundry service. *In room:* Hair dryer.

17

The French Riviera

Each resort on the Riviera, known as the Côte d'Azur (Azure Coast), offers its own unique flavor and charms. This narrow strip of fabled real estate, less than 201km (125 miles) long and located between the Mediterranean and a trio of mountain ranges, has always attracted the jet set with its clear skies, blue waters, and orange groves.

A trail of modern artists captivated by the light and setting has left a rich heritage: Matisse at Vence, Cocteau at Menton and Villefranche, Picasso at Antibes and seemingly everywhere else, Léger at Biot, Renoir at Cagnes, and Bonnard at Le Cannet. The best collection is at the Foundation Maeght in St-Paul-de-Vence.

The Riviera's high season used to be winter and spring only. In recent years, July and August have become the most crowded, and reservations are imperative. The average summer temperature is 75°F (24°C); in winter it's 49°F (9°C).

The corniches of the Riviera, depicted in countless films, stretch from Nice to Menton. The Alps drop into the Mediterranean here, and roads were carved along the way. The lower road, 32km (20 miles) long, is the Corniche Inférieure. Along this road are the ports of Villefranche, Cap-Ferrat, Beaulieu, and Cap-Martin. The 31km (19-mile) Moyenne Corniche (Middle Road), built between World War I and World War II, runs from Nice to Menton, winding in and out of tunnels and through mountains. The highlight is at Eze. Napoleon built the Grande Corniche—the most panoramic—in 1806. La Turbie and Le Vistaero are the principal towns along the 32km (20-mile) stretch, which reaches more than 480m (1,575 ft.) high at Col d'Eze.

Note: For more extensive coverage of this region, check out *Frommer's Provence & the Riviera.*

1 St-Tropez ★★

874km (543 miles) S of Paris, 76km (47 miles) SW of Cannes

An air of hedonism runs rampant in this sun-kissed town, but the true Tropezian resents the fact that the port has such a bad reputation. "We can be classy too," one native insisted. Creative people along with ordinary folk create a varied atmosphere.

The Brigitte Bardot vehicle, *And God Created Woman,* put St-Tropez on the tourist map, but it has more history. Colette lived here for years, and the diarist Anaïs Nin, confidante of Henry Miller, posed for a little cheesecake on the beach in 1939 in a Dorothy Lamour–style bathing suit.

St-Tropez attracts artists, composers, novelists, and the film colony in the summer. Trailing behind is a flamboyant parade of humanity. Some of the most fashionable yachts, bearing some of the most chic people, anchor here in summer.

In 1995, Bardot pronounced St-Tropez dead, "squatted by a lot of no-goods, drugheads, and villains." But 1997 saw her return, and headlines in France announced that

St-Tropez was "hot once again." (Today she owns two houses in St-Tropez and is occasionally spotted among groups of her friends.) Other celebrities have been showing up, including Oprah, Barbra Streisand, Jack Nicholson, Robert De Niro, and Elton John.

ESSENTIALS

GETTING THERE The nearest rail station is in St-Raphaël, a neighboring resort. At St-Raphaël's Vieux Port, **boats** leave the Gare Maritime de St-Raphaël, rue Pierre-Auble (✆ **04-94-95-17-46**), for St-Tropez (trip time: 50 min.) four or five times a day from April to October. The one-way fare is 11€ ($14). Year-round, 10 to 15 Sodetrav **buses** per day leave from the Gare Routière in St-Raphaël (✆ **04-94-97-88-51**) for St-Tropez. The trip takes 1½ to 2½ hours, depending on the bus and the traffic, which during midsummer is usually horrendous. A one-way ticket costs 9.20€ ($12). Buses run directly to St-Tropez from Toulon and Hyères and from the nearest airport, at Toulon-Hyères, 56km (35 miles) away.

If you **drive,** note that parking in St-Tropez is very difficult, especially in summer. You can park in the **Parking des Lices** (✆ **04-94-97-34-46**), beneath place des Lices; enter on avenue Paul-Roussel. Designed for 300 cars, this lot is free for the first hour, the second hour costs 1€ ($1.30), and the third hour and each hour thereafter costs an additional 1€ ($1.30). A 24-hour sojourn costs 34€ ($44) in summer; in winter there is a slight reduction to 23€ ($30). Many visitors with expensive cars prefer this lot because it's more secure than any other. Charging the same rates, a new garage, **Parking du Nouveau Port,** avenue Charles de Gaulle (✆ **04-94-97-40-31**), stands at the waterfront. Every municipal engineer in St-Tropez has worked hard to funnel incoming traffic toward either of these two underground garages. A car can't enter the resort without seeing prominent signs funneling traffic to either location. To get here from **Cannes,** drive southwest along the coastal highway (RD98), turning east when you see signs pointing to St-Tropez.

VISITOR INFORMATION The **Office de Tourisme** is on quai Jean-Jaurès (✆ **04-94-97-45-21;** fax 04-94-97-82-66; www.ot-saint-tropez.com).

A DAY AT THE BEACH

The hottest Riviera beaches are at St-Tropez. The best for families are closest to the center, including the **Plage de la Bouillabaisse** and **Plage des Graniers.** More daring are the 9.5km (6-mile) crescents at **Plage des Salins** and **Plage de Pampelonne,** some 3km (1¾ miles) from the town center. At Pampelonne there are about 35 businesses on a 4.8km (3-mile) stretch, located about 10km (6¼ miles) from St-Tropez. The concessionaire that's noted as an all-gay venue is the **Aqua Club,** Plage de Pampelonne (✆ **04-94-79-84-35**). You'll need a car, bike, or scooter to get from town to the beach. Parking is 4€ ($5.20) for the day. Famous hedonistic spots along Pampelonne include the cash-only club **La Voile Rouge** (✆ **04-94-79-84-34**), which features bawdy spring break-style entertainment. This is the most outrageous, the sexiest, and the most exhibitionist (not for children) of the beaches of St-Tropez. Also thriving are **Club 55,** 55 bd. Patch, Plage de Pampelonne (✆ **04-94-55-55-55**), and **Nikki Beach,** Plage de Pampelonne (✆ **04-94-79-82-04**). Maintained by an American from Miami, Nikki Beach is wild, frenetic, uninhibited, and about as Floridian a venue as you're likely to find in the south of France. **Plage des Jumeaux** (✆ **04-94-55-21-80**) is another active beach; it draws many families with young kids because it has playground equipment. **Marine Air Sport** (✆ **04-94-97-89-19;** www.marine-air-sport.com) rents

The French Riviera

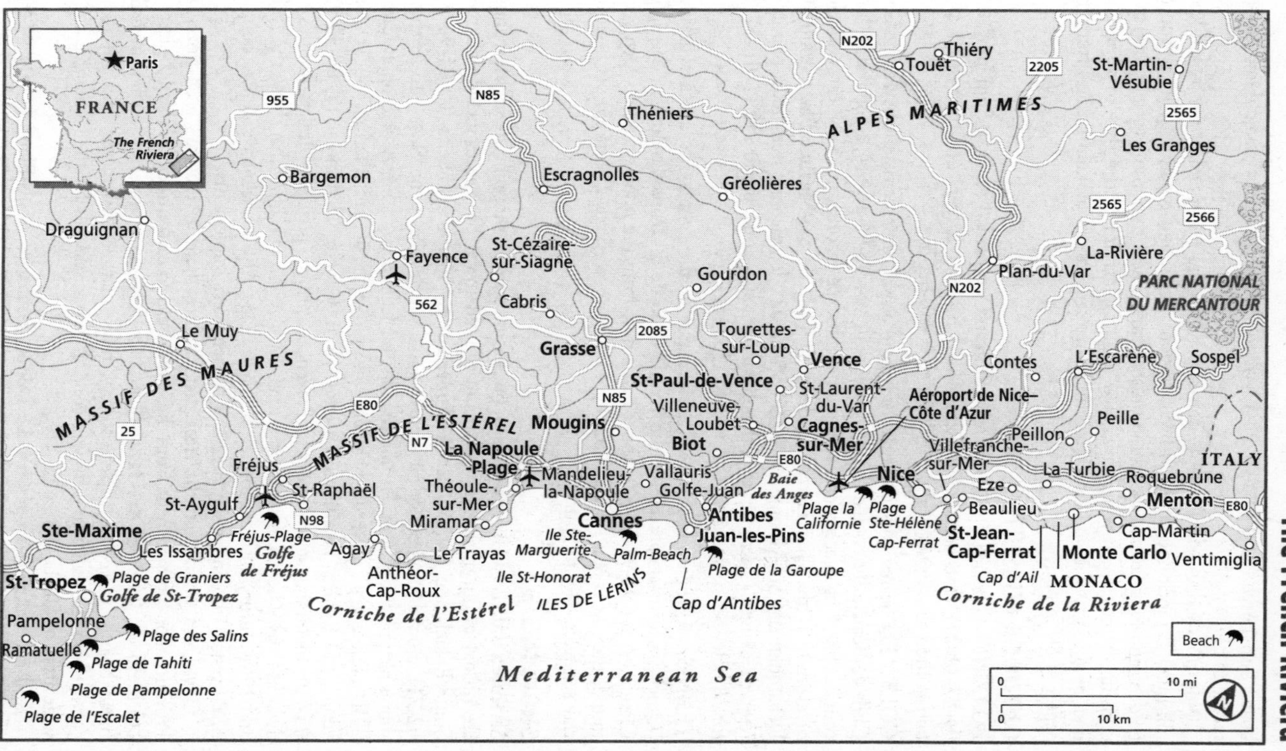

boats; **Sun Force** (© **04-94-79-90-11**) rents jet skis, scooters, water-skiing equipment, and boats.

Notoriously decadent **Plage de Tahiti** occupies the north end of the 5.5km-long (3½-mile) Pampelonne, lined with concessions, cafes, and restaurants. It's a strip of golden sand long favored by exhibitionists wearing next to nothing (or nothing) and cruising shamelessly. If you ever wanted to go topless, this is the place to do it. Gay men tend to gravitate to **Coco Beach** in Ramatuelle, about 6.5km (4 miles) from the center of St-Tropez.

OUTDOOR PURSUITS

BOATING The highly recommended **Suncap Company,** 15 quai de Suffren (© **04-94-97-11-23**), rents boats 5.5 to 12m (18–39 ft.) long. Larger ones come with a captain at the helm. Prices begin at 1,200€ ($1,560) per day.

GOLF The nearest golf course, at the edge of Ste-Maxime, across the bay, is the **Golf Club de Beauvallon,** boulevard des Collines (© **04-94-96-16-98**), a popular 18-hole course. Sprawling over a rocky, vertiginous landscape that requires a golf cart and a lot of exertion is the Don Harradine–designed **Golf de Ste-Maxime-Plaza,** route du Débarquement, Ste-Maxime (© **04-94-55-02-02**). It welcomes nonguests; phone to reserve tee times. Greens fees at both golf courses range from 78€ to 85€ ($101–$111) for 18 holes per person, and 45€ to 90€ ($59–$117) for 9 holes, year-round.

TENNIS Anyone who phones in advance can use the eight courts (artificial grass or "Quick," a form of concrete) at the **Tennis-Club de St-Tropez,** route des Plages, St-Claude (© **04-94-97-15-52**), about half a mile from the resort's center. Open year-round, the courts rent for 20€ ($26) per hour for green set, 25€ ($33) per hour for clay set, from 8am to 9pm.

SHOPPING

St-Tropez is dense with stylish shops, but has no specific shopping street. Most shops are tucked in out-of-the-way corners of the old town. Big names include Hermès, Sonia Rykiel, and Dior. **Galeries Tropéziennes,** 56 rue Gambetta (© **04-94-97-02-21**), crowds hundreds of gift items—some worthwhile, some silly—into its showrooms near place des Lices. The merchandise is Mediterranean, breezy, and sophisticated.

In a resort that's increasingly loaded with purveyors of suntan lotion, touristy souvenirs, and T-shirts, **Jacqueline Thienot,** 10 rue Georges-Clemenceau (© **04-94-97-05-70**), maintains an inventory of Provençal antiques prized by dealers from as far away as Paris. The one-room shop is in an 18th-century building that shows the 18th- and 19th-century antiques to their best advantage. Also for sale are antique examples of Provençal iron and rustic farm and homemaker's implements.

Olives and wood from the trees that produce them have always been prized in Provence. For carvings made from the wood, head to **Autour des Oliviers,** 2 place de l'Ormeau (© **04-94-97-64-31**), which stocks large inventories of kitchen utensils, bread boards, carved crucifixes, pottery, trays, platters, ornaments, and gift items carved from the yellow-and-brown wood. It also stocks salt for the Comargue and a wide array of French olive oils.

And even chic St-Tropez has **Le Dépot,** boulevard Louis-Blanc (© **04-94-97-80-10**), which sells secondhand designer clothes by the likes of Hermès, Moschino, Gaultier, and Chanel. Some of the merchandise even has its original tags.

On Tuesday and Saturday mornings on place des Lices, there's an **outdoor market** with food, clothes, and *brocante.* This is one of the best Provençal markets in the south

St-Tropez

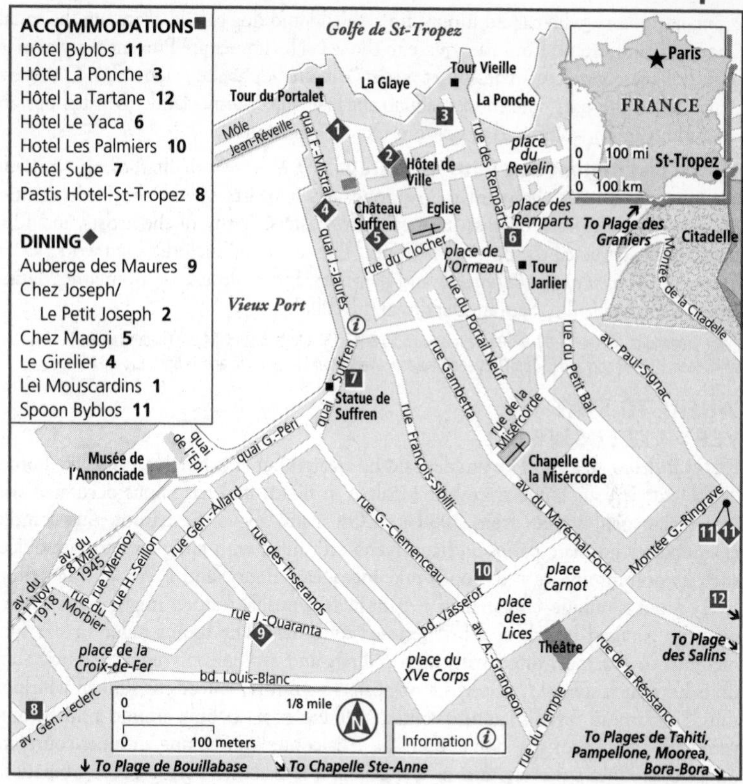

of France, with more than 100 vendors selling everything from tableware to homemade bread. The fish, vegetable, and flower market is down a tiled alley (place aux Herbes) behind the tourist office. It operates daily 8am to noon in summer and Tuesday to Sunday 8am to noon in winter.

EXPLORING THE CITY

Château Suffren is east of the port at the top end of quai Jean-Jaurès. Home to occasional art exhibits, it was built in A.D. 980 by Comte Guillame I of Provence.

Near the junction of quai Suffren and quai Jean-Jaurès stands the bronze **Statue de Suffren,** paying tribute to Vice-Admiral Pierre André de Suffren. Though largely forgotten today, the St-Tropez native was one of the greatest sailors of 18th-century France. In the Vieille Ville (old town), one of the most interesting streets is **rue de la Miséricorde.** It's lined with stone houses that hold boutiques. This street evokes medieval St-Tropez better than any other in town. At the corner of rue Gambetta is the **Chapelle de la Miséricorde,** with a blue, green, and gold tile roof.

Port Grimaud ★ makes an interesting outing. From St-Tropez, drive 4km (2¾ miles) west on A98 to Route 98, and then 1.5km (1 mile) north to the Port Grimaud exit. If you approach the village at dusk, when it's bathed in Riviera pastels, it looks like a 16th-century hamlet. This is a mirage: Port Grimaud is the dream of its promoter,

François Spoerry, who carved it out of marshland and dug canals. Flanking the canals, fingers of land extend from the square to the sea. The homes are Provençal-style, many with Italianate window arches. Boat owners can anchor at their doorsteps. One newspaper called the port "the most magnificent fake since Disneyland." Most shops and restaurants in Port Grimaud close from October to March.

Musée de l'Annonciade (Musée St-Tropez) ★★ Near the harbor, this museum occupies the former chapel of the Annonciade. It boasts one of the Riviera's finest modern-art collections of post-Impressionist masters. Many of the artists, including Paul Signac, depicted the port of St-Tropez. The collection includes such works as Van Dongen's *Women of the Balustrade* and paintings and sculpture by Bonnard, Matisse, Braque, Dufy, Utrillo, Seurat, Derain, and Maillol.

Place Grammont. ✆ **04-94-97-04-01.** Admission 5.50€ ($7.15) adults, 3.50€ ($4.55) children under 12. June–Sept Wed–Mon 10am–noon and 3–7pm; Oct and Dec–May Wed–Mon 10am–noon and 2–6pm. Closed Nov.

WHERE TO STAY

VERY EXPENSIVE

Hôtel Byblos ★★★ The builder said he created "an anti-hotel, a place like home." That's true if your home resembles a palace in Beirut and has salons decorated with Phoenician gold statues from 3000 B.C. On a hill above the harbor, this complex encompasses intimate patios and courtyards. It's filled with antiques and rare objects such as polychrome carved woodwork, marquetry floors, and a Persian-rug ceiling. Every room is unique, and all have elegant beds. Unusual features might include a fireplace on a raised hearth or a bed recessed on a dais. The rooms range in size from medium to spacious, often with high ceilings and antiques or reproductions. Some units have such special features as four-posters with furry spreads or sunken whirlpool tubs. Le Hameau, a stylish annex, contains 10 duplex suites built around a small courtyard with an outdoor spa. Some rooms have balconies overlooking an inner courtyard; others open onto a flowery terrace. Deluxe bathrooms hold tub/shower combinations.

Av. Paul Signac, St-Tropez 83990. ✆ **04-94-56-68-00.** Fax 04-94-56-68-01. www.byblos.com. 97 units, 10 junior suites. 300€–700€ ($390–$910) double; 600€–2,400€ ($780–$3,120) suite. AE, DC, MC, V. Closed mid-Oct to mid-Apr. Parking 30€ ($39). **Amenities:** 2 restaurants; 2 bars; nightclub; outdoor pool; gym; spa; sauna; salon; room service; massage; babysitting; laundry service; dry cleaning; nonsmoking rooms. *In room:* A/C, TV, minibar, hair dryer, safe.

Hôtel La Tartane ★ This small hotel lies between the center of St-Tropez and the Plage des Salins, about a 3-minute drive from each. After a comprehensive upgrade, its government rating jumped from three stars to four, accompanied by a big hike in prices. It has a heated stone-rimmed pool in the garden, attractively furnished public rooms with terra-cotta floors, and attentive, hardworking management. The midsize guest rooms are bungalows surrounding the pool. Each holds a small tiled bathroom with a shower stall or tub/shower combo. Breakfasts are elaborate.

Rte. des Salins, St-Tropez 83990. ✆ **04-94-97-21-23.** Fax 04-94-97-09-16. www.latartane.com. 28 units. 250€–650€ ($325–$845) double; 445€–900€ ($579–$1,170) suite. AE, DC, V. Closed Oct to mid-Apr. **Amenities:** 2 restaurants; bar; outdoor pool; spa; steam bath; salon; massage; laundry service; dry cleaning; free shuttle to beach. *In room:* A/C, TV, minibar, hair dryer, safe.

Hôtel Le Yaca ★ Life here is *la dolce vita.* Built in 1722 off a narrow street in the old part of town, this was the first hotel in St-Tropez. Colette lived for a few weeks here in 1927, and before that it was the temporary address of pre-Impressionists such as Paul Signac. The high-ceilinged reception area overlooks an inner courtyard filled with flowers. Many rooms also have views of this courtyard; all were renovated in the early part of the millennium. Some are on the upper level, with terra-cotta floor tiles and massive ceiling timbers. Each has a comfortable bed, utilitarian furniture, and high ceilings, and most have a roomy bathroom with tub and shower (otherwise only a shower).

1 bd. d'Aumale, St-Tropez 83900. © **04-94-55-81-00.** Fax 04-94-97-58-50. www.hotel-le-yaca.fr. 28 units. 305€–525€ ($397–$683) double; 775€–1,005€ ($1,008–$1,307) suite. AE, DC, MC, V. Closed mid-Oct to mid-Apr. Parking 20€ ($26). **Amenities:** Restaurant; bar; outdoor pool; room service; massage; babysitting; laundry service; dry cleaning; nonsmoking rooms. *In room:* A/C, TV, minibar, hair dryer, safe.

Pastis Hotel-St-Tropez ★★ *Finds* Best-selling author Peter Mayle, whose writings have drawn thousands to visit Provence, occasionally drops by this boutique hotel. Here he is welcomed by two ex-pat Brits, John and Pauline Larkin, who took a portside Provençal house and transformed it into a chic little inn. They have decorated it in a sophisticated eclectic style, even featuring their collection of framed albums including the Sex Pistols and the Rolling Stones. Guests intermingle as they sip an aperitif by the pool in the courtyard. You get the feeling that you're staying in a private home when you lodge here, one discreetly decorated with art. Like the public lounges, the rooms are also furnished in an eclectic mix, and each unit comes with a spacious bathroom as well as a balcony or breakfast terrace. Some accommodations are large enough for extra beds or cots. Indian rugs, Chinese armoires, and beds adorned with Provençal *boutis* spreads enhance the warm, intimate ambience. Although the hotel doesn't have a restaurant, the staff prepares breakfast and light lunches for guests, or even a little supper for those arriving late.

61 av. du Général Leclerc. © **04-98-12-56-60.** Fax 04-94-96-99-82. www.pastis-st-tropez.com. 9 units. 250€–550€ ($325–$715) double. AE, MC, V. Free parking. **Amenities:** Outdoor pool; nonsmoking rooms. *In room:* A/C, TV.

EXPENSIVE

Hôtel La Ponche ★★ The same family has run this hotel overlooking the port for more than half a century. The cozy nest has long been a favorite of ours, as it's the most discreet, most charming, and least celebrity-flashy establishment in town, making Byblos look nouveau riche and a bit strident. It's filled with the original airy paintings of Jacques Cordier, who died in 1978, which add to the atmosphere. The redecorated rooms are well equipped and open onto sea views. Each floor holds two or three rooms. Sun-colored walls with subtle lighting lend a homey feeling. The beds are elegantly appointed with linen and quality mattresses, and the midsize to large bathrooms have tub/shower combinations or a shower only.

Port des Pécheurs, St-Tropez 83990. © **04-94-97-02-53.** Fax 04-94-97-78-61. www.laponche.com. 18 units. 145€–425€ ($189–$553) double; 215€–540€ ($280–$702) suite. AE, MC, V. Parking 21€ ($27). Closed Nov to mid-Feb. **Amenities:** Restaurant; bar; room service; babysitting; laundry service; dry cleaning. *In room:* A/C, TV, minibar, hair dryer, safe.

MODERATE

Hôtel Les Palmiers Accompanied by a verdant garden, this pleasant and practical government-rated three-star hotel was created in 1955 with the union of two once-separate houses, the older of which dates from the late 18th century. One of the best things about it is its location directly astride the heartbeat place des Lices in the center of St-Tropez. Bedrooms are simple and compact, and outfitted in a modernized Provençal theme highlighted with blue, soft orange, and ocher. Christian Guerin is the extroverted owner. There's a bar on the premises, but no restaurant.

24–26 bd. Vasserot (place des Lices), St-Tropez 83991. ✆ **04-94-97-01-61.** Fax 04-94-97-10-02. www.hotel-les-palmiers.com. 25 units. 65€–207€ ($85–$270) double. AE, MC, V. **Amenities:** Room service; laundry service. *In room:* A/C, TV, minibar, hair dryer, safe.

Hôtel Sube If you want to be right on the port, in a location that's perfect for ship- and celebrity-watching, this might be your first choice. It's directly over the Café de Paris bar, in the center of a shopping arcade. The two-story lounge has a beamed ceiling and a glass front, allowing a great view of the harbor. The rooms aren't large but are comfortable and decorated in French Provincial style. The more expensive units have scenic views of the port. Each comes with a private bathroom with a shower and tub.

15 quai Suffren, 83900 St-Tropez. ✆ **04-94-97-30-04.** Fax 04-94-54-89-08. www.hotel-sube.com. 28 units. 90€–250€ ($117–$325) double. AE, MC, V. Parking nearby 30€ ($39). **Amenities:** Cafe; bar. *In room:* A/C, TV.

WHERE TO DINE

EXPENSIVE

Leï Mouscardins ★★★ FRENCH/PROVENÇAL At the end of St-Tropez's harbor, this restaurant has won awards for culinary perfection. The dining room is decorated in formal Provençal style; an adjoining sunroom sits under a canopy. We recommend *moules* (mussels) *marinières* for an appetizer. On the menu are a celebrated Côte d'Azur fish stew, *bourride Provençale,* and an unusual main-course specialty, crushed chestnuts garnished with morels, crayfish, and truffles. The fish dishes are excellent, particularly sauté of monkfish, wild mushrooms, and green beans. Dessert specialties are soufflés made with Grand Marnier or Cointreau.

1 rue Portalet. ✆ **04-94-97-29-00.** Reservations required. Main courses 33€–65€ ($43–$85); fixed-price lunch 58€ ($75); fixed-price dinner 60€–90€ ($78–$117). AE, DC, MC, V. June–Sept daily noon–2pm and 7:30–10pm; Oct–May Wed–Mon noon–2pm and 7:30–9:30pm. Closed Nov 14–Dec 17 and Jan 9–Feb 4.

Spoon Byblos ★★ FRENCH/INTERNATIONAL This is one of the many entrepreneurial statements by Alain Ducasse, considered by some the world's greatest chef—or at least the most acclaimed. Originally launched in Paris, Spoon has traveled everywhere from London to the Riviera. Here it serves the cuisines of many cultures with produce mainly from the Mediterranean. It draws special inspiration from the food of Catalonia, Andalusia, and Morocco, and offers more than 300 wines from around the world. Background music ranges from hip-hop to the hits of the '70s. It's terribly fashionable, although you may grow a bit weary of its self-conscious sense of chic after an hour or two within its ultradesigned premises.

The restaurant opens onto a circular bar made of blue-tinted glass and polished stainless steel. The menu will have you salivating before you even take a bite. Dig into shrimp and squid consommé with a hint of jasmine and orange; spicy king prawns on a skewer; delectable lamb couscous; or spit-roasted John Dory. You may top off a meal with the chef's favorite cheesecake or a slice of Neapolitan with the taste of strawberry, vanilla, and pistachio.

In the Hôtel Byblos, av. Paul-Signac. ✆ **04-94-56-68-20.** Reservations required. Main courses 15€–42€ ($20–$55); fixed-price menu 65€ ($85). AE, DC, MC, V. July–Aug daily 8pm–12:30am; mid-Apr to June and Sept to mid-Oct daily 8–11pm. Closed mid-Oct to mid-Apr.

MODERATE

Auberge des Maures *Value* PROVENÇAL One of our favorite cost-conscious restaurants in an otherwise very expensive town lies close to one end of the all-pedestrian rue Allard. The stone-sided building, highlighted with Provence-specific murals, boasts a rollaway roof and garden seating (both experienced during nice weather). The open kitchen affords views of the staff preparing items such as grilled versions of many kinds of fresh fish and meat; *panache Provençal,* on which are piled deep-fried zucchini blossoms; hearts of artichoke *barigoule;* and a medley of *petits farcis* (stuffed vegetables). The Salinesi family (Evelyn and Phillippe) takes pride in using seasonal, all-fresh ingredients.

4 rue du Docteur Boutin. ✆ **04-94-97-01-50.** www.aubergedesmaures.com. Reservations recommended. Main courses 10€–25€ ($13–$33); fixed-price menu 42€ ($55). AE, DC, MC, V. Daily 7:30pm–1am. Closed Dec–Mar.

Chez Joseph/Le Petit Joseph ★ PROVENÇAL These side-by-side restaurants are serviced by the same kitchen, and the menus are quite similar. Le Petit Joseph is quieter and more romantic, with low-beamed ceilings, an Asian decor, and cozy banquettes. Chez Joseph, where you sit with other patrons at long tables, tends to be completely booked and packed at 10pm. Both restaurants offer outdoor seating, but Le Petit has just a few tables; Chez features a large terrace. The traditional yet creatively presented cuisine emphasizes fish, and the menu changes often. For dessert, the *parfait léger* is a treat—vanilla custard with chocolate powder on a cherry crumble with a scoop of cherry-vanilla ice cream and fresh fruit.

1 place de l'Hôtel-de-Ville. ✆ **04-94-97-01-66.** Reservations recommended at Chez Joseph. Main courses 22€–50€ ($29–$65). AE, MC, V. Daily noon–2pm and 7:30pm–midnight.

Le Girelier PROVENÇAL The Rouets own this portside restaurant, whose blue-and-white color scheme has become a trademark. They serve grilled fish in many versions, as well as bouillabaisse (only for two). Also on the menu are brochette of monkfish, a kettle of spicy mussels, and *pipérade* (a Basque omelet with pimientos, garlic, and tomatoes). Most dishes are moderately priced.

Quai Jean-Jaurès. ✆ **04-94-97-03-87.** Main courses 30€–55€ ($39–$72); fixed-price menu 45€ ($59). AE, DC, MC, V. Daily noon–2pm and 7–11pm. Closed Nov 1–Feb 15.

INEXPENSIVE

Chez Maggi ★★ PROVENÇAL/ITALIAN St. Tropez's most flamboyant gay restaurant and bar also draws straight diners and drinkers. At least half its floor space is devoted to a bar, where patrons range in age from 20 to 60. There are no tables in front. Consequently, cruising at Chez Maggi, in the words of loyal patrons, is *très crazée* and seems to extend for blocks in every direction. Meals are served in an adjoining dining room. Menu items include chicken salad with ginger; goat-cheese salad; *petits farcis provençaux* (vegetables stuffed with minced meat and herbs); brochettes of sea bass with lemon sauce; and chicken curry with coconut milk, capers, and cucumbers.

7 rue Sibille. ✆ **04-94-97-16-12.** Reservations recommended. Main courses 14€–28€ ($18–$36). MC, V. Apr–Sept daily 7pm–3am. Closed Oct to mid-Mar.

ST-TROPEZ AFTER DARK

On the lobby level of the Hôtel Byblos, **Les Caves du Roy,** avenue Paul-Signac (✆ **04-94-97-16-02**), is the most self-consciously chic nightclub in St-Tropez and the most famous in France. Entrance is free, but drink prices begin at a whopping 18€ ($23). It's open nightly from May to late September from 11:30pm until dawn. **Le Papagayo,** in the Résidence du Nouveau-Port, rue Gambetta (✆ **04-94-79-29-50**), is one of the largest nightclubs in town. The decor was inspired by the psychedelic 1960s. Entrance is between 15€ and 18€ ($20–$23), and includes one drink.

Adjacent to Le Papagayo is **Le VIP Room,** in the Résidence du Nouveau-Port (✆ **04-94-97-14-70**), whose upscale male and female patrons may be equally at home in Les Caves du Roy. Cocktails run between 14€ and 15€ ($18–$20). The club is all steel, chrome, mirrors, and glass. Expect an active bar area, dance floor, and the kind of social posturing and preening that can be amusing—or not.

Le Pigeonnier, 13 rue de la Ponche (© **04-94-97-84-26**), rocks, rolls, and welcomes a crowd that's mostly gay or lesbian and between 20 and 50. Most of the socializing revolves around the long, narrow bar, where patrons from all over Europe enjoy chitchat. There's also a dance floor. For another gay hot spot, check out the action at **Chez Maggi** (see "Where to Dine," above).

Below the Hôtel Sube, the **Café de Paris,** sur le Port (© **04-94-97-00-56**), is one of the most popular hangouts. The utilitarian room has early-1900s globe lights, an occasional 19th-century bronze artifact, masses of artificial flowers, and a long zinc bar. The crowd is irreverent and animated. **Café Sénéquier,** sur le Port (© **04-94-97-00-90**), is historic, venerable, snobbish, and, at its worst, off-puttingly stylish.

Le Bar du Port, quai Suffren, adjacent to the Café de Paris (© **04-94-97-00-54**), is breezy, airy, and almost obsessively hip and self-consciously trendy. This cafe-bar attracts a consistently young clientele. Expect lots of table-hopping, stylishly skimpy clothing, recorded music that may make you want to get up and dance, and insights into what's really going on in the minds of French 20-somethings.

If your idea of a night out is sitting in a cafe drinking wine, you can "hang out" at such joints as **Kelly's Irish Pub,** quai F. Mistral, at the bottom end of the Vieux Port (© **04-94-54-89-11**), which draws a mostly foreign crowd. The tavern is casual, not chic. If you're nostalgic for St-Germain-des-Prés, head for the old-fashioned **Le Café,** place des Lices (© **04-94-97-44-69**), with its famous zinc bar. Its glory lies in its location and not because of any innate value as a warm and cozy cafe (it's both a bistro/restaurant and cafe).

2 La Napoule–Plage ★

901km (560 miles) S of Paris, 8km (5 miles) W of Cannes

This secluded resort is on the sandy beaches of the Golfe de la Napoule. In 1919, the fishing village was a paradise for the sculptor Henry Clews and his wife, Marie, an architect. Fleeing America's "charlatans," whom he believed had profited from World War I, the New York banker's son emphasized the fairy-tale qualities of his new home. An inscription over the entrance to his house—now the **Musée Henry-Clews**—reads ONCE UPON A TIME.

The museum is in the **Château de la Napoule** ★, boulevard Henry-Clews (© **04-93-49-95-05;** www.chateau-lanapoule.com), which was rebuilt from the ruins of a medieval château. Clews covered the capitals and lintels with a grotesque menagerie—scorpions, pelicans, gnomes, monkeys, and lizards. Women, feminism, and old age are recurring themes in the sculptor's work, as exemplified by the distorted suffragette depicted in his *Cat Woman.* The artist admired chivalry and dignity as represented by *Don Quixote*—to whom he likened himself. Clews died in Switzerland in 1937, and his body was returned to La Napoule for burial. Marie Clews later opened the château to the public. The château is open February 5 to November 4, daily 10am to 6pm; November 8 to February 6, Saturday and Sunday 10am to 6pm, charging 4€ ($5.20). Tours in French and English are given February 5 to November 5, daily at 11:30am, 2:30pm, 3:30pm, and 4:30pm. There are no tours the rest of the year.

ESSENTIALS

GETTING THERE The waterside community of La Napoule–Plage is part of La Mandelieu–La Napoule, which lies on the **bus** and **train** routes between Cannes and St-Raphaël. The one-way fare, for the bus or train, from Cannes to La Mandelieu–La Napoule is 1.90€ ($2.45). For information and schedules, call ✆ **08-92-35-35-35.** If you're **driving,** take A8 west from Cannes.

VISITOR INFORMATION The **Office de Tourisme** is on avenue Henry-Clews (✆ **04-92-97-99-27;** fax 04-93-93-64-66; www.ot-mandelieu.fr).

WHERE TO STAY

La Calanque The foundations of this government-rated two-star, well-positioned hotel date from the Roman Empire, when it was an aristocrat's villa. The present hotel, run by the same family since 1942, looks like a hacienda, with salmon-colored stucco walls. Guest rooms are small to medium in size, and each has a comfortable bed and bathroom with a tub or shower. The hotel's restaurant spills onto a terrace and offers some of the cheapest fixed-price meals around. Nonguests are welcome.

Av. Henry-Clews, La Napoule 06210. ✆ **04-93-49-95-11.** Fax 04-93-49-67-44. 17 units. 31€–58€ ($40–$75) double. MC, V. Closed mid-Oct to Feb. **Amenities:** Restaurant; bar (guests only). *In room:* A/C (in some), TV.

L'Ermitage du Riou ★★ *Finds* This old Provençal house, the most tranquil choice at the resort, is a seaside government-rated four-star hotel bordering the Riou River and the Cannes-Mandelieu golf club. The rooms are furnished in regional style, with authentic furniture and ancient paintings. The rooms range in size from medium to spacious, and each has an elegant bed and fine linen. The most expensive ones have safes. The good-size bathrooms have tub/shower combinations. Views are of the sea or the golf course.

Av. Henry-Clews, La Napoule 06210. ✆ **04-93-49-95-56.** Fax 04-92-97-69-05. www.ermitage-du-riou.fr. 41 units. 126€–301€ ($164–$391) double; 341€–529€ ($443–$688) suite. AE, DC, MC, V. **Amenities:** Restaurant; bar; outdoor pool; sauna; nonsmoking rooms; limited-mobility rooms. *In room:* A/C, TV, minibar, hair dryer, safe, Wi-Fi.

Sofitel Royal Casino ★★ A member of the Accor group, this Las Vegas–style hotel is on the beach near a man-made harbor, about 8km (5 miles) from Cannes. It was the first French hotel with a casino and the last (before building codes changed) to have a casino directly on the beach. The hotel has one of the most contemporary designs on the Côte d'Azur. Most of the good-size rooms angle toward a sea view; those facing the street are likely to be noisy, despite soundproofing. Each has a well-kept bathroom with a tub/shower combination.

605 av. du Général-de-Gaulle, La Mandelieu–La Napoule 06212. ✆ **800/221-4542** in the U.S. and Canada, or 04-92-97-70-00. Fax 04-93-49-51-50. www.sofitel.com. 213 units. 250€–310€ ($325–$403) double; from 300€–330€ ($390–$429) suite. AE, DC, MC, V. Parking 12€ ($16). **Amenities:** 2 restaurants; 4 bars; nightclub; 2 tennis courts; exercise room; sauna; Turkish bath; room service; babysitting; laundry service; dry cleaning; limited-mobility rooms. *In room:* A/C, TV, minibar, hair dryer.

WHERE TO DINE

La Calanque's restaurant (see "Where to Stay," above) is open to nonguests.

Le Féréol ★ TRADITIONAL/MODERN FRENCH This well-designed restaurant serves most of the culinary needs of the largest hotel (and only casino) in town. Outfitted in nautical style, it offers impressive lunch buffets. At night the room is candlelit and more elegant, and the view through bay windows is soothing. Menu items include Breton artichokes with a "surprise" stuffing that's composed of minced cured ham, cheese, and herbs; a "frivolity" of mushrooms composed of two kinds of exotic mushrooms plus a confit of quail all served atop a warm brioche; filet of John Dory with artichoke hearts, lavender, and scampi; and a succulent version of roasted veal with baby Provençal vegetables and herbs.

In the Sofitel Royal Casino, 605 av. du Général-de-Gaulle. ✆ **04-92-97-70-20.** Reservations recommended. Main courses 20€–78€ ($26–$101); fixed-price lunch 28€ ($37); fixed-price dinner 40€ ($52). AE, DC, MC, V. Sept–June Wed–Sun 12:30–2:30pm and 7–10:30pm. July–Aug daily 12:30–3:30pm and 7–11pm.

L'Oasis ★★★ MODERN FRENCH Here you'll find the most wonderful cuisine on the Western Riviera. At the entrance to the harbor of La Napoule, in a mid-20th-century house with a lovely garden and a re-creation of a medieval cloister, this restaurant became world famous under now-retired Louis Outhier. Today, his protégé, Stéphane Raimbault, prepares sophisticated cuisine. Because Raimbault cooked in Japan for 9 years, many of his dishes are of the "East meets West" variety, with dishes such as crayfish cooked "in the fires of hell" and served with wok-fried baby vegetables; perfectly grilled Mediterranean fish; or a masterful saddle of venison with hazelnuts, pepper sauce, and caramelized pears. The cellar houses one of the finest collections of Provençal wines anywhere. In summer, meals are served under the plane trees in the garden.

Rue Honoré-Carle. ✆ **04-93-49-95-52.** Reservations required. Main courses 35€–55€ ($46–$72); fixed-price lunch 54€–72€ ($70–$94); fixed-price dinner 80€–165€ ($104–$215). AE, DC, MC, V. Daily noon–2pm and 7:30–10pm. Closed Sun dinner and Mon Nov–Mar; closed mid-Dec to mid-Jan.

3 Cannes ★★★

905km (562 miles) S of Paris, 163km (101 miles) E of Marseille, 26km (16 miles) SW of Nice

When Coco Chanel came here and got a suntan, returning to Paris bronzed, she startled the milk-white society ladies, who quickly began copying her. Today the bronzed bodies—clad in nearly nonexistent swimsuits—that line the beaches of this chic resort continue the late fashion designer's example.

ESSENTIALS

GETTING THERE **Trains** from the other Mediterranean resorts, Paris, and the rest of France arrive frequently throughout the day. By train, Cannes is 15 minutes from Antibes and 35 minutes from Nice. The TGV from Paris via Marseille reaches Cannes in about 5½ to 6 breathless hours. The one-way fare from Paris is about 108€ to 110€ ($140–$143). For rail information and schedules, call ✆ **08-92-35-35-35,** or visit www.voyages-sncf.com. **Rapide Côte d'Azur,** place de l'Hôtel de Ville, Cannes (✆ **04-93-39-70-30**), offers bus service to Nice and back every 20 minutes during the day (trip time: 1½ hr.). The one-way fare is 6€ ($7.80).

The Nice **international airport** (✆ **08-20-42-33-33**) is a 30-minute drive northeast. **Buses** pick up passengers at the airport every 40 minutes during the day and drop them at the Gare Routière, place de l'Hôtel de Ville (✆ **04-93-45-20-08**). Bus service from Antibes operates every half-hour.

By **car** from Marseille, take A51 north to Aix-en-Provence, continuing along A8 east to Cannes. From Nice, follow A8 southwest to Cannes.

VISITOR INFORMATION The **Office de Tourisme** is at 1 bd. De La Croisette (✆ **04-93-39-24-53;** fax 04-92-99-84-23; www.cannes.fr).

SPECIAL EVENTS Cannes is at its most frenzied at the end of May, during the **International Film Festival** at the Palais des Festivals on promenade de la Croisette. It attracts not only film stars but also seemingly every photographer in the world. You have a better chance of being named prime minister of France than you do of attending one of the major screenings. (Hotel rooms and tables at restaurants are equally scarce during the festival.) But the people-watching is fabulous. If you find yourself here at the right time, you can join the thousands who line up in front of the Palais des Festivals, where the premieres are held. With paparazzi shouting and gendarmes holding back fans, the guests parade along the red carpet, stopping for a moment to strike a pose. *C'est Cannes!*

You may be able to get tickets for some of the lesser films, which play 24 hours. For information, see "France Calendar of Events," in chapter 3, or visit **www.festival-cannes.org**.

From international regattas and galas to *concours d'élégance* (an extravagant car show) and even a Mimosa Festival (focusing on local handicrafts) in February, something's always happening at Cannes, except in November, which is traditionally a dead month.

A DAY AT THE BEACH

Beach-going in Cannes has more to do with exhibitionism and voyeurism than with actual swimming.

Plage de la Croisette extends between the Vieux Port and the Port Canto. Though the beaches along this billion-dollar stretch of sand aren't in the strictest sense private, they're *payante,* meaning entrance costs 15€ to 22€ ($20–$29). You don't need to be a guest of the Noga Hilton, Martinez, Carlton, or Majestic to use the beaches associated with those hotels, though if you are you'll usually get a 50% discount. A wooden barricade that stops close to the sea separates each beach from its neighbors, making it easy for you to stroll from one to another.

Why should you pay a fee at all? Well, it includes a full day's use of a mattress, a chaise longue (the seafront isn't sandy or even soft, but covered with pebbles and dark-gray shingles), and a parasol, as well as easy access to freshwater showers and kiosks selling beverages. There are also outdoor restaurants where no one minds if you appear in your swimsuit.

For nostalgia's sake, our favorite beach is the one associated with the **Carlton** (see "Where to Stay," below)—it was the first beach we went to, as teenagers, in Cannes. The merits of each of the 20 or so beaches vary daily depending on the crowd, and because every beach allows topless bathing (keep your bottom covered), you're likely to find the same forms of décolletage along the entire strip.

Looking for a free public beach where you'll have to survive without renting chaises or parasols? Head for **Plage du Midi,** sometimes called Midi Plage, just west of the Vieux Port (no phone), or **Plage Gazagnaire,** just east of the Port Canto (no phone). Here you'll find families with children and lots of caravan-type vehicles parked nearby.

OUTDOOR PURSUITS

BICYCLING & MOTOR SCOOTERING Despite the roaring traffic, the flat landscapes between Cannes and satellite resorts such as La Napoule are well suited for riding a bike or motor scooter. At **Cycles Daniel,** 2 rue du Pont Romain (© **04-93-99-90-30**), *vélos tout terrain* (mountain bikes) cost 13€ ($17) a day. Motorized bikes and scooters cost 30€ ($39) per day; renters must be at least 14 years old. For larger

Cannes

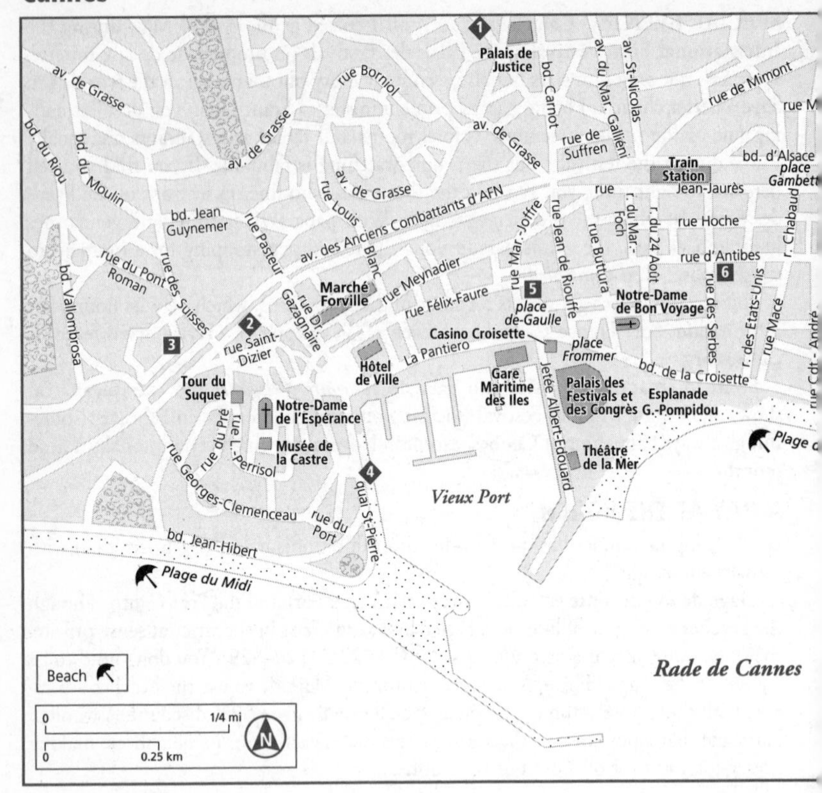

scooters, you must present a valid driver's license. Another purveyor of bikes is **Mistral Location,** 4 rue Georges Clemenceau (✆ **04-93-99-25-25**), which charges 14€ ($18) per day.

BOATING Several companies rent boats of any size, with or without a crew, for a day, a week, or a month. An outfit known for short-term rentals of small craft, including motorboats, sailboats, and canoes, is **Elco Marine,** 110 bd. du Midi (✆ **04-93-47-12-62**). For larger boats, including motor-driven and sailing yachts and craft suitable for deep-sea fishing, try **International Yacht Charter,** 45 La Croisette (✆ **04-92-98-39-93**).

GOLF One of the region's most challenging courses, **Country-Club de Cannes-Mougins,** 175 av. du Golf, route d'Antibes, Mougins (✆ **04-93-75-79-13**), 6.5km (4 miles) north of Cannes, is a 1976 reconfiguration by Dye & Ellis of a 1920s-era course. Noted for the olive trees and cypresses that adorn the flat terrain, it has many water hazards and technical challenges. Since 1981, the par-72 course has played host to the Cannes-Mougins Open, a stop on the PGA European Tour. The course is open to anyone (with proof of handicap) willing to pay greens fees of 100€ ($130) per person. An electric golf cart rents for 45€ ($59), golf clubs for 35€ ($46). Reservations are recommended.

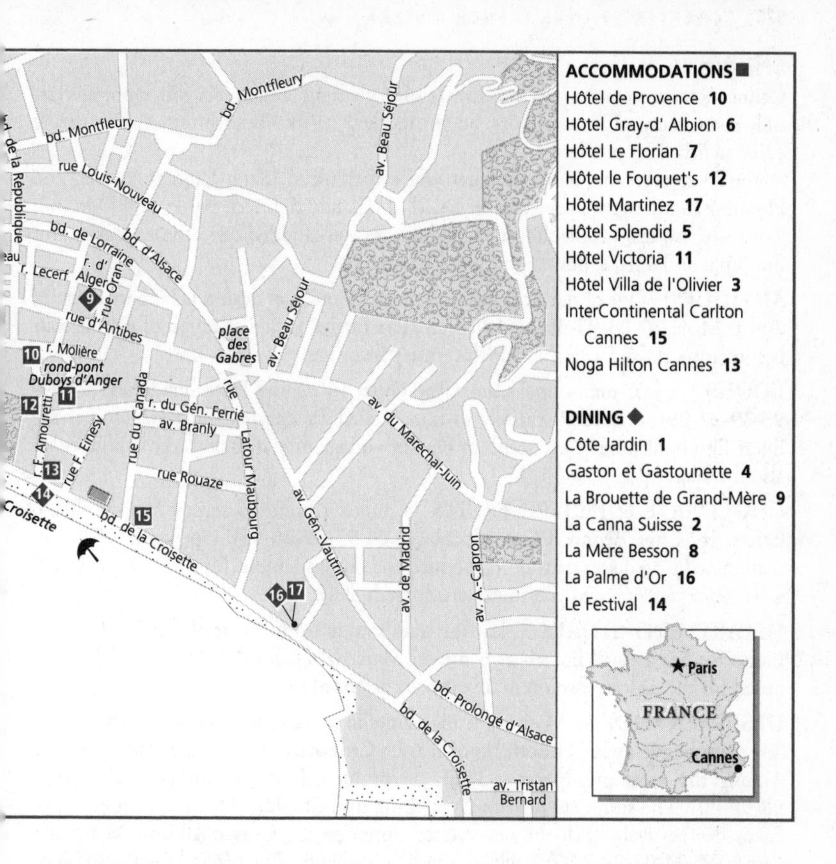

SWIMMING Cannes probably has more privately owned swimming pools, per capita, than anywhere else in France. If your hotel doesn't have one, consider an excursion to the **Piscine Pierre de Coubertin,** avenue P. de Coubertin (✆ **04-93-47-12-94**). Its length of almost 23m (75 ft.) makes this outdoor pool ideal for swimming laps. Because it's used for a variety of civic functions, including practices for local swim teams, hours are limited, so call ahead. Entrance costs 2.15€ ($2.80) for adults, 1.25€ ($1.65) for children 3 to 15.

TENNIS Some resorts have their own courts. The city of Cannes also maintains a half-dozen courts (one made from synthetic resins, five clay-topped); you'll pay 10€ to 15€ ($13–$20) per hour, depending on the court and the time you want to play, plus 3.25€ ($4.25) per hour for lighting. They're at **ASLM Tennis Municipal de la Bastide,** 220 av. Francis Tonner, 06400 Cannes (✆ **04-93-47-29-33**). If those courts are already taken, **ASLM Tennis Municipal Aérodrome,** Aérodrome de Cannes Mandelieu, 06400 Cannes (✆ **04-93-47-29-33**), also maintained by the municipality, charges the same rates for its five clay-topped courts.

SHOPPING

Cannes achieves a blend of resort-style leisure, glamour, and media glitz more successfully than many of its neighbors. So you're likely to find branch outlets of virtually every stylish Paris retailer.

You'll see every big-name designer you can think of (Saint-Laurent, Rykiel, and Hermès) and designers you've never heard of (Claude Bonucci, Basile, and Durrani). There are also real-people shops; resale shops for star-studded castoffs; flea markets for fun junk; and a fruit, flower, and vegetable market.

ANTIQUES One of the city's most noteworthy antiques dealers is **Hubert Herpin,** 20 rue Macé (© **04-93-39-56-18**). This store carries a wide selection of marble statues, marquetry, and 18th- and 19th-century furniture.

BOOKS A year-round bookstore, **Ciné-Folie,** 14 rue des Frères-Pradignac (© **04-93-39-22-99**), is devoted entirely to film. Called *La Boutique du Cinema,* it is the finest film bookstore in the south of France; vintage film stills and movie posters are also for sale.

CHOCOLATE & JELLIED FRUITS Cannes is home to several famous chocolatiers. Try **Chez Bruno,** 13 rue Hoche (© **04-93-39-26-63**). Opened in 1929 and maintained by a descendant of its founder, the shop is famous for *fruits confits* as well as *marrons glacés* (glazed chestnuts), made fresh daily.

DEPARTMENT STORES Near the train station in the heart of Cannes, **Galeries Lafayette** has a small branch at 6 rue du Maréchal-Foch (© **04-97-06-25-00**). It's noted for the upscale fashion in its carefully arranged interiors.

DESIGNER SHOPS Most of the big names in fashion, for both men and women, line **promenade de la Croisette,** known as **La Croisette,** the main drag facing the sea. Among the most prestigious is **Dior,** 38 promenade de la Croisette (© **04-92-98-98-00**). The stores are in a row, stretching from the Hôtel Carlton almost to the Palais des Festivals, with the best names closest to the **Gray-d'Albion,** 38 rue des Ferbes (© **04-92-99-79-79**), which is both a mall and a hotel (how convenient). The stores in the Gray-d'Albion mall include **Hermès.** The two-section mall serves as a cut-through from the primary expensive shopping street, La Croisette, to the less expensive shopping street, **rue d'Antibes.**

FLEA MARKETS Cannes has two regular flea markets. Casual, dusty, and increasingly filled with castaways from estate sales, the **Marché Forville,** conducted in the neighborhood of the same name, near the Palais des Festivals, is a stucco structure with a roof and a few arches but no sides. From Tuesday to Sunday, it's the fruit, vegetable, and flower market that supplies dozens of grand restaurants. Monday is *brocante* day, when the market fills with dealers selling everything from *grandmère*'s dishes to bone-handled carving knives.

On Saturdays, from 8am to 12:30pm, a somewhat disorganized and busy **flea market** takes place outdoors along the edges of the allée de la Liberté, across from the Palais des Festivals. Hours depend on the whims of whatever dealer happens to haul in a cache of merchandise, but it usually begins around 8am and runs out of steam by around 4:30pm. ***Note:*** Vendors at the two flea markets may or may not be the same.

FOOD The street with the greatest density of emporiums selling wine, olives, herbs, cheese, bread, and oils is the appealing **rue Meynadier.**

Tips Seeing Cannes from a *Petit Train*

One of the best ways to get your bearings in Cannes (and to get an idea of the difference between the city's new and old neighborhoods) is to climb aboard a white-sided *Petit Train touristique de Cannes.* The diesel-powered vehicles roll through the streets on rubber tires. They operate every day from 10am to between 7 and 11:30pm, depending on the season (there's no service in Nov). Two itineraries are offered: For views of glittery modern Cannes, board the train at a designated spot in front of either of the town's two casinos for a ride along La Croisette and its side streets. For a ride through the narrow streets of Vieux Cannes (Le Suquet), board the train at a clearly designated site on the seaward side of La Croisette, opposite the Hôtel Majestic. Both tours depart every hour. They last around 45 minutes, depending on traffic, and cost 5€ to 9€ ($6.50–$12) for adults and 2.50€ to 3€ ($3.25–$3.90) for children younger than 10, depending on the tour. (The tour of the old town is the less expensive.) A combination ticket to both tours (good on separate days, if you prefer) costs 8€ ($10) for adults and 5€ ($6.50) for children under 10. For details, call ✆ **04-93-38-39-18.**

A charming old-fashioned shop, **Cannolive,** 16–20 rue Vénizelos (✆ **04-93-39-08-19**), is owned by members of the Raynaud family, which founded the place in 1880. It sells Provençal olives and their byproducts—tapenades that connoisseurs refer to as "Provençal caviar," black "olives de Nice," and green "olives de Provence," as well as three grades of olive oil from regional producers. Oils and food products are at no. 16; gift items (fabrics, porcelain, and Provençal souvenirs) are sold next door.

MARKETS At the edge of the Quartier Suquet, the **Marché Forville** is the town's primary fruit, flower, and vegetable market. On Monday it's a *brocante* market. See "Flea Markets," above.

PERFUME The best and most expensive shop is **Bouteille,** 59 rue d'Antibes (✆ **04-93-39-05-16**). Its prices are higher than its competitors' because it stocks more brands, has a wider selection, and gives away occasional samples. Other shops dot rue d'Antibes. Any may feature your favorite fragrance in a promotional deal. For reasonably priced perfumes, head to the boutiques associated with the Hôtel Gray-d'Albion.

SEEING THE SIGHTS

For many visitors, Cannes might as well consist of only one street, the **promenade de la Croisette**—or just La Croisette—curving along the coast and split by islands of palms and flowers.

A port of call for cruise liners, Cannes is sheltered by hills. Hotels, apartment houses, and boutiques line the seafront. Many of the bigger hotels, some dating from the 19th century, claim part of the beaches for their guests; there are also public areas. Above the harbor, the old town of Cannes sits on Suquet Hill, where you'll see the 14th-century **Tour de Suquet,** which the English dubbed the Lord's Tower.

Nearby is the **Musée de la Castre** ★, in the Château de la Castre, Le Suquet (✆ **04-93-38-55-26**). It contains paintings, sculpture, and works of decorative art.

The ethnography section includes objects from all over, including Peruvian and Maya pottery. There's also a gallery devoted to relics of Mediterranean civilizations, from the Greeks to the Romans, from the Cypriots to the Egyptians. Five rooms hold 19th-century paintings. The museum is open June to August Tuesday to Sunday 10am to 1pm and 3 to 7pm; April, May, and September Tuesday to Sunday 10am to 1pm and 2 to 6pm; and October to March Tuesday to Sunday 10am to 1pm and 2 to 5pm. Admission is 3€ ($3.60), but free the first Sunday of every month.

FERRYING TO THE ILES DE LERINS ★★

Across the bay from Cannes, the Lérins Islands are the major excursion from the port. Ferries depart every half-hour from 7:30am to 30 minutes before sundown. The largest of the ferry companies in Cannes is **Compagnies Estérel-Côte d'Azur,** 1 Port de Cannes (✆ **04-93-39-11-82**). Competitors include **Cie Horizon IV,** CQ (✆ **04-92-98-71-36**); **Société Maritime Cannoise,** Quai St. Pierre (✆ **04-93-38-29-92**); and **Trans-Côte d'Azur,** quai St-Pierre (✆ **04-92-98-71-30**). Departures are from the Gare Maritime des Iles in Cannes. Round-trip fare is 11€ ($14) for adults, 5.50€ ($7.15) for children 5 to 10, and free for children under 5.

ILE STE-MARGUERITE This island was named after St-Honorat's sister, Ste-Marguerite, who lived here with a group of nuns in the 5th century. Today it is a youth center whose members are dedicated to the restoration of the fort—when they aren't sailing and diving. From the dock, you can stroll along the island (signs point the way) to the Fort de l'Ile, built by Spanish troops from 1635 to 1637. Below is the 1st-century-B.C. Roman town where the "Man in the Iron Mask" was imprisoned. You can visit his cell at Ste-Marguerite. As you listen to the sound of the sea, you realize what a forlorn outpost this was.

Musée de la Mer, Fort Royal (✆ **04-93-38-55-26**), traces the history of the island, displaying artifacts of Ligurian, Roman, and Arab civilizations, plus the remains discovered by excavations, including paintings, mosaics, and ceramics. The museum is open April to September Tuesday to Sunday 10:30am to 5:45pm (closing at 4:45pm Oct–Mar). Admission is 3€ ($3.90) for adults, free for students and children under 18.

ILE ST-HONORAT ★★ Only 1.6km (1 mile) long, but richer in history than its sibling islands, the Ile St-Honorat is the site of a monastery whose origins date to the 5th century. The **Abbaye de St-Honorat** ★, Les Iles de Lérins, 06400 Cannes (✆ **04-92-99-54-00**), boasts a combination of medieval ruins and early-20th-century ecclesiastical buildings, and is home to a community of about 30 Cistercian monks. Under controlled circumstances, if space is available, well-intentioned outsiders can visit and spend the night, but only for prayer and meditation. Most visitors opt to wander through the pine forests on the island's western side and sunbathe on its beaches.

WHERE TO STAY

VERY EXPENSIVE

Hôtel Martinez ★★ Although it's a bit less appealing than the Carlton, this is a popular convention hotel and a desirable property for the individual. When the Art Deco hotel was built in the 1930s, it rivaled any other lodging along the coast in sheer size. Over the years, however, it fell into disrepair. But in 1982, the Concorde chain returned the hotel and its restaurants to their former luster, and today it competes with the Noga Hilton. The aim of the decor was a Roaring '20s style, and all units boast full marble bathrooms, wood furnishings, tasteful carpets, quality mattresses,

Fun Fact And It Wasn't Even the Super Bowl

The twin cupolas of the InterContinental Carlton Cannes were modeled on the breasts of the most fabled local courtesan, La Belle Otéro.

and pastel fabrics. Called a hotel within a hotel, the penthouse floor has become the chicest place to stay at the resort, featuring 11 suites, the most sought-after in town following a massive restyling. It has a private beach, one of the finest restaurants in Cannes (La Palme d'Or, reviewed below), and a water-skiing school.

73 bd. de la Croisette, Cannes 06406. ✆ **04-92-98-73-00.** Fax 04-93-39-67-82. www.hotel-martinez.com. 415 units. 270€–950€ ($351–$1,235) double; from 850€ ($1,105) suite. AE, DC, MC, V. Parking 35€ ($46). **Amenities:** 3 summer restaurants; 2 winter restaurants; bar; private beach; outdoor pool; 7 tennis courts nearby; fitness center; spa; sauna; room service; babysitting; laundry service; dry cleaning; nonsmoking rooms; limited-mobility rooms. *In room:* A/C, TV, minibar, hair dryer, safe.

InterContinental Carlton Cannes ★★★ Cynics say that one of the most amusing sights in Cannes is the view from under the grand gate of the Carlton. Here you'll see vehicles of every description dropping off huge amounts of baggage and numbers of fashionable (and sometimes not-so-fashionable) guests. It's the epitome of luxury and has become such a part of the city's heartbeat that to ignore it would be to miss the resort's spirit. The twin gray domes at either end of the facade are often the first things recognized by starlets planning their grand entrances, grand exits, and grand scenes in the hotel's public and private rooms.

Built in 1912, the Carlton once attracted the most prominent members of Europe's *haut monde.* Today the hotel is more democratic, booking lots of conventions and motorcoach tour groups; however, in summer (especially during the film festival) the public rooms still fill with all the voyeuristic and exhibitionistic fervor that seems so much a part of the Riviera. Guest rooms are plush and a bit airier than you may expect. The most spacious rooms are in the west wing, and many upper-floor rooms open onto waterfront balconies. In 2004, the hotel converted what had been a casino into seven of its most luxurious suites. The large bathrooms are in the grand luxe style, with tub/shower combinations.

58 bd. de la Croisette, Cannes 06400. ✆ **04-93-06-40-06.** Fax 04-93-06-40-25. http://cannes.intercontinental.com. 338 units. 260€–950€ ($338–$1,235) double; from 615€ ($800) suite. AE, DC, MC, V. Parking 35€ ($46). **Amenities:** 3 summer restaurants; 1 winter restaurant; 2 bars; health club; sauna; business center; room service; laundry service; dry cleaning; nonsmoking rooms; limited-mobility rooms. *In room:* A/C, TV, minibar, hair dryer, safe.

Noga Hilton Cannes ★ This hotel is far superior to most Hiltons in the U.S. This is one Cannes's most sought-after sites, which the owners acquired after the old Palais des Festivals was demolished. The design of the six-story building, with massive amounts of exposed glass, recalls the best aspects of its older sibling, the Noga Hilton in Geneva. You register in a soaring lobby sheathed with white marble. The soundproof guest rooms are stylish, with balconies, bedside controls, luxury beds, tub/shower combinations, and various electronic accessories; rates vary with the sea view. Many of the appointments evoke the 1930s. Prestige Rooms have large beds and elegant carpeting. Less desirable units are called Cityview and Gardenview rooms.

50 bd. de la Croisette, Cannes 06414. ✆ **800/445-8667** in the U.S. and Canada, or 04-92-99-70-00. Fax 04-92-99-70-11. www.hiltoncannes.com. 234 units. 199€–239€ ($259–$311) double; 389€–429€ ($506–$558) suite. AE, DC,

MC, V. **Amenities:** Restaurant; bar; casino; outdoor pool; shopping arcade; room service; babysitting; laundry service; dry cleaning; nonsmoking rooms; limited-mobility rooms. *In room:* A/C, TV, minibar, coffeemaker, hair dryer, safe.

EXPENSIVE

Hôtel Gray-d'Albion ★★ The smallest of the major hotels isn't on La Croisette. It occupies mostly contemporary, not particularly historic premises and enjoys a four-star rating from the French government. Although it cannot compete on many levels with the larger, better-accessorized palace hotels (such as the Carlton) with which it is often compared, it maintains a conservative, somewhat staid image as solid, dependable, and reliable. Now part of the Lucien Barrière chain, it's uncontroversial, but nonetheless completely respectable. Groups form a large part of its clientele, but it also caters to the individual. The medium-size rooms blend contemporary and traditional furnishings; the generous-size bathrooms have tub/shower combinations. Each unit has a balcony, but the views aren't notable, except from the eighth and ninth floors, which overlook the Mediterranean.

38 rue des Serbes, Cannes 06400. ✆ **04-92-99-79-79.** Fax 04-93-99-26-10. www.lucienbarriere.com. 199 units. 93€–380€ ($121–$494) double; 500€–1,400€ ($650–$1,820) suite. AE, DC, MC, V. **Amenities:** Restaurant; bar; salon; 24-hr. room service in summer (limited in winter); babysitting; laundry service; dry cleaning; nonsmoking rooms; limited-mobility rooms. *In room:* A/C, TV, minibar, hair dryer, safe.

MODERATE

Château de la Tour ★ *Finds* Enveloped by its fine garden, this hotel was created from a former private estate. Lying 252m (825 ft.) from the beaches, the hotel has been elegantly restored and turned into a beautiful gem of accommodations. Guest rooms boast views of the sea and lush gardens below. The small standard rooms are cozy yet comfortable, while superior units get the panoramic views, are more spacious, and are usually accompanied by a balcony or terrace. There is a Provençal elegance and charm found here that's rarely achieved by more modern, impersonal hotels.

10 av. Font de Veyre, Cannes 06150. ✆ **04-93-90-52-52.** Fax 04-93-47-86-61. www.hotel-chateau-tour-cannes.fr. 34 units. Summer 160€–280€ ($208–$364) double; off season 95€–180€ ($124–$234) double. Rates include continental breakfast. AE, MC, V. Free parking. **Amenities:** Restaurant; bar; outdoor pool; Jacuzzi; laundry service; limited-mobility rooms. *In room:* A/C, hair dryer, TV, minibar, safe.

Hôtel Le Fouquet's ★ *Finds* This intimate lodging draws a discreet clientele, often from Paris, who'd never think of patronizing the grand hotels. Riviera French in design and decor, the hotel is several blocks from the beach. Each of the cozy guest rooms, renovated in 2004, is outfitted just a bit differently from its neighbor. They're decorated in bold Provençal colors of ocher and blue, and have contemporary vaguely regional furniture. The owner is often on-site, making the hotel feel like an intimate B&B. Bathrooms, though small, are efficiently organized, with showers and tubs.

2 rond-point Duboys-d'Angers, Cannes 06400. ✆ **04-92-59-25-00.** Fax 04-92-98-03-39. www.le-fouquets.com. 10 units. 110€–280€ ($143–$364) double. AE, DC, MC, V. Parking 12€ ($16). Closed Nov 1–Apr 12. Bus: 1. **Amenities:** Room service; babysitting; laundry service; dry cleaning; nonsmoking rooms. *In room:* A/C, TV, minibar, hair dryer, safe.

Hôtel Splendid ★ *Value* Opened in 1871, and widely renovated in 2004, this is a favorite of scholars, politicians, actors, and musicians. The ornate white building with wrought-iron accents looks out onto the sea, the old port, and a park. The rooms boast antique furniture and paintings; about 15 have kitchenettes. Each comes with a good bed and a small but efficient bathroom with a combination tub/shower. The more expensive rooms have sea views.

4–6 Rue Félix-Faure, Cannes 06400. ✆ **04-97-06-22-22.** Fax 04-93-99-55-02. www.splendid-hotel-cannes.fr. 62 units. 124€–264€ ($161–$343) double. Rates include breakfast. AE, MC, V. Parking 15€ ($20). **Amenities:** Room service; babysitting; nonsmoking rooms; limited-mobility rooms. *In room:* A/C, TV/VCR, hair dryer, safe.

Hôtel Victoria ★ The Victoria, a stylish modern hotel renovated in 2005, offers accommodations with period reproductions and refrigerators. Nearly half the rooms have balconies overlooking a small park and the hotel pool. The accommodations facing the park cost a little more but are worth it. In all units, silk bedspreads, padded headboards, and quality mattresses create a boudoir feel. Each unit has a modern tiled bathroom with a shower or tub/shower combination. After a day on the beach, guests congregate in the paneled bar and sink comfortably into couches and armchairs.

Rond-point Duboys-d'Angers, Cannes 06400. ✆ **04-92-59-40-00.** Fax 04-93-38-03-91. www.hotel-victoria-cannes.com. 25 units. 105€–170€ ($137–$221) double; 235€–420€ ($306–$546) suite. AE, DC, MC, V. Parking 17€ ($22). Closed late Nov to Dec. **Amenities:** Bar; outdoor pool; babysitting; laundry service; dry cleaning; nonsmoking rooms. *In room:* A/C, TV, minibar, hair dryer, safe.

Hôtel Villa de l'Olivier *Finds* Charming and personal, this is a hideaway with a low-key management style. In the 1930s, it was a private villa; in the 1960s it became a hotel, with a wing extending deep into its garden. Today, you'll find buildings with lots of glass overlooking a kidney-shaped pool, and decor combining the French colonial tropics with the romantic late 19th century and Provence. Rooms have upholstered walls, each in a different color and pattern, and lots of Provençal accessories. Bathrooms come in a variety of sizes, each with a combination tub/shower.

5 rue des Tambourinaires, Cannes 06400. ✆ **04-93-39-53-28.** Fax 04-93-39-55-85. www.hotelolivier.com. 24 units. 90€–135€ ($117–$176) double; 260€ ($338) suite. AE, DC, MC, V. Parking 10€ ($13). Closed Nov 22–Dec 27. **Amenities:** Bar; outdoor pool; room service; laundry service; dry cleaning; nonsmoking rooms. *In room:* A/C, TV, hair dryer, Wi-Fi.

INEXPENSIVE

Hôtel de Provence *Value* Built in the 1930s, this hotel is small and unpretentious—a contrast to the intensely stylish, larger hotels with which it competes. Most of the rooms have private balconies, and many overlook the shrubs and palms of the hotel's walled garden. Guest rooms are showing their age but are still comfortable, and for Cannes this is a remarkable bargain. Most of the bathrooms are roomy, and many have tub/shower combinations. In warm weather, breakfast is served under the flowers of an arbor.

9 rue Molière, Cannes 06400. ✆ **04-93-38-44-35.** Fax 04-93-39-63-14. www.hotel-de-provence.com. 30 units. 75€–109€ ($98–$142) double; 115€–139€ ($150–$181) suite. AE, MC, V. Parking 15€ ($20). Closed mid-Nov to mid-Dec. **Amenities:** Bar; room service; laundry service; dry cleaning. *In room:* A/C, TV, minibar, hair dryer, safe.

Hôtel Le Florian This hotel is on a busy but narrow, densely commercial street that leads directly into La Croisette, near the beach. Three generations of the Giordano family have maintained it since the 1950s. The hotel is basic but comfortable, and most rooms are rather small, Provençal in their styling, with decor that dates from 2004. Bathrooms are compact, with showers and renovated plumbing. Breakfast is the only meal available.

8 rue Commandant-André, Cannes 06400. ✆ **04-93-39-24-82.** Fax 04-92-99-18-30. www.hotel-leflorian.com. 32 units. 55€–75€ ($72–$98) double. AE, MC, V. Parking 10€ ($13) nearby. Closed Dec to mid-Jan. Bus: 1. *In room:* A/C, TV, hair dryer.

WHERE TO DINE

VERY EXPENSIVE

La Palme d'Or ★★★ MODERN FRENCH Movie stars on the see-and-be-seen circuit head here during the film festival. It's a sophisticated rendezvous that serves some of the Riviera's finest hotel cuisine. The Taittinger family (of champagne fame) set out to establish a restaurant that could rival the competition—and succeeded. The result is this tawny-colored Art Deco marvel with bay windows, a winter-garden theme, and outdoor and enclosed terraces overlooking the pool, the sea, and La Croisette. Menu items change with the seasons but are likely to include warm foie gras with fondue of rhubarb; filets of fried red mullet with a beignet of potatoes, zucchini, and olive-cream sauce; or crayfish, clams, and squid marinated in peppered citrus sauce. A modernized version of a Niçoise staple includes three parts of a rabbit with rosemary sauce, fresh vegetables, and chickpea rosettes. The most appealing dessert is wild strawberries from Carros with Grand Marnier–flavored *nage* and "cream sauce of frozen milk." The service is worldly without being stiff.

In the Hôtel Martinez, 73 bd. de la Croisette. ✆ **04-92-98-74-14.** Reservations required. Main courses 50€–90€ ($65–$117); fixed-price lunch 60€–145€ ($78–$189); fixed-price dinner 75€–150€ ($98–$195). AE, DC, MC, V. Tues–Sat 12:30–2pm and 8–10pm. Closed Apr 17–May 2 and Nov 5–Dec 5.

EXPENSIVE

Gaston et Gastounette ★ TRADITIONAL FRENCH For views of the marina, this is your best bet. Located in the old port, it has a stucco exterior with oak moldings and big windows, and a sidewalk terrace surrounded by flowers. It serves two different bouillabaisses—a full-blown authentic stewpot prepared only for two diners at a time and a less daunting individualized version designed as an appetizer. Other choices include baby turbot with hollandaise sauce; John Dory filets with wild mushrooms; and an unusual Japanese-style broth flavored with monkfish, saltwater salmon, and chives. Profiteroles with hot chocolate sauce make a memorable dessert.

7 quai St-Pierre. ✆ **04-93-39-47-92.** Reservations required. Main courses 25€–50€ ($33–$65); fixed-price lunch 25€–36€ ($33–$47); fixed-price dinner 38€ ($49). AE, DC, MC, V. Daily noon–2pm and 7–10:30pm. Closed Dec 15–24 and Jan 3–20.

La Mère Besson ★ TRADITIONAL FRENCH The culinary traditions of the late Mère Besson, who opened her restaurant in the 1930s, endure in one of Cannes's favorite places. The specialties are prepared with respect for Provençal traditions. Most delectable is *estouffade Provençal* (beef braised with red wine and rich stock flavored with garlic, onions, herbs, and mushrooms). Every Friday, you can sample a platter with codfish, fresh vegetables, and dollops of the famous garlic mayonnaise (aioli) of Provence. Other specialties are fish soup, *bourride Provençale* (thick fish-and-vegetable stew), and roasted rack of lamb with mint.

13 rue des Frères-Pradignac. ✆ **04-93-39-59-24.** Reservations required. Main courses 19€–30€ ($25–$39); fixed-price dinner 27€–32€ ($35–$42). AE, MC, V. Mon–Sat 7–10:30pm. Bus: 1.

Le Festival ★ TRADITIONAL FRENCH Screen idols and sex symbols flood the front terrace during the film festival. Almost every chair is emblazoned with the names of movie stars (who may or may not have occupied it), and tables are among the most sought-after in town. You can choose from the restaurant or the less formal grill room. Meals in the restaurant may include rack of lamb, *soupe des poissons* (fish soup) with rouille, simply grilled fresh fish (perhaps with aioli), bouillabaisse with lobster, pepper steak, and sea bass flambéed with fennel. Items in the grill are more in the style of an elegant brasserie, served a bit more rapidly and without as much fuss but at more or less the same prices. An appropriate finish in either section may be smooth peach melba.

52 bd. de la Croisette. ✆ **04-93-38-04-81.** Reservations required. Main courses 18€–30€ ($23–$39); fixed-price menu 23€–42€ ($30–$55). AE, DC, MC, V. July–Aug daily 9am–midnight; Sept–June daily 9am–11pm (until midnight during film festival). Closed Nov 18–Dec 28.

MODERATE

La Canna Suisse ★ *Finds* SWISS Two sisters own this small 30-year-old restaurant in Vieux-Cannes. Decked out like a Swiss chalet, it specializes in the cheese-based cuisine of Switzerland's high Alps. Because its cuisine is so suitable to cold-weather dining, the restaurant wisely opts to close during the crush of Cannes' midsummer tourist season. It does great business the rest of the year. The menu features two kinds of fondue—a traditional version concocted from six kinds of cheese and served in a bubbling pot with chunks of bread on skewers, and another that adds mushrooms (morels or cèpes) to the blend. The only other dining options here include raclette and equally savory *tartiflette* (an age-old recipe that combines boiled potatoes with fatback, onions, cream, herbs, and Reblochon cheese). There's a long list of (mostly white) French and Swiss wines, wonderful with these ultratraditional dishes.

23 rue Forville, Le Suquet. ✆ **04-93-99-01-27.** Reservations recommended. Main courses 16€–23€ ($21–$30); fixed-price menu 25€–28€ ($33–$36). AE, MC, V. Mon–Sat 7:30–10:30pm. Closed May 20–Aug.

INEXPENSIVE

Côté Jardin ★ *Value* FRENCH/PROVENÇAL Set near the courthouse (Palais de Justice) in the heart of commercial Cannes, this restaurant attracts loyal locals because of its unpretentious ambience and its reasonably priced and generous portions. You're offered three different choices as seating options: on the street level glassed-in veranda; at a table amid the flowering shrubs of the garden terrace; or upstairs within the cozy Provençal dining room. The best menu items include open-faced ravioli filled with minced beef jowls, filets of red mullet with butter-flavored parsley sauce, a range of grilled and roasted meats and fish, and a dessert of praline and pineapple tart with vanilla-flavored cream sauce.

12 av. St-Louis. ✆ **04-93-38-60-28.** Reservations required, especially in summer. Fixed-price menus 30€–55€ ($39–$72). AE, DC, MC, V. Tues–Sat noon–2pm and 7:30–10pm. Closed 1 week in early Jan.

La Brouette de Grand-Mère *Finds* TRADITIONAL FRENCH Few other restaurants in Cannes work so successfully at establishing a cozy testimonial to the culinary skills of old-fashioned French cooking. Owner Christian Bruno has revitalized the recipes that many of the chic and trendy residents of Cannes remember from their childhoods (or from an idealized version of their childhoods). Memories are evoked, in a way that Proust might have appreciated, through dishes that include a savory meat-and-potato stew known as *pot-au-feu,* roasted quail served with cream sauce, and chicken casserole cooked with beer. Traditional starters may include sausage links, terrines, and baked potatoes stuffed with smoked fish roe and served with a small glass of vodka. Set in the heart of town just behind the Noga Hilton and the InterContinental Carlton, the place offers two dining rooms, each outfitted in Art Deco style in tones of deep red and soft violet and an outdoor terrace.

9 bis rue d'Oran. ✆ **04-93-39-12-10.** Reservations recommended. Fixed-price menu, including aperitif and unlimited wine, 35€ ($46). MC, V. Daily 7:30–11pm. Closed June 11–July 3 and Nov to mid-Dec.

CANNES AFTER DARK

Cannes is invariably associated with permissiveness, filmmakers celebrating filmmaking, and gambling. If gambling is your thing, Cannes has some world-class casinos, each loaded with addicts, voyeurs, and everyone in between. The better established is the **Casino Croisette,** in the Palais des Festivals, 1 jetée Albert-Edouard (✆ **04-92-98-78-00**). Run by the Lucien Barrière group, and a well-respected fixture in town since the 1950s, it's a competitor of the newer **Palm Beach Casino,** place F-D-Roosevelt, Pointe de la Croisette (✆ **04-97-06-36-90**), on the southeast edge of La Croisette. Inaugurated in 1933 and rebuilt in 2002, it features three restaurants and Art Deco decor. It's glossier, newer, and a bit hungrier for new business. Both casinos maintain slot machines that operate daily from 11am to 5am. Suites of rooms devoted to *les grands jeux* (blackjack, roulette, and chemin de fer) open nightly from 8pm to 5am.

Yet a third gambling den, **Casino des Princes,** is more intimate than either of its more flamboyant competitors, occupying the subterranean levels of the Noga Hilton Cannes, 50 bd. de la Croisette (✆ **04-97-06-18-50**). Outfitted in tones of gold and ocher, it is open nightly 8pm to 4am. A government-issued photo ID is necessary, and jackets for men are requested. Adjoining the casino is the hotel's most upscale restaurant, Restaurant/Bar des Princes, open for dinner nightly from 8pm to 2:45am.

The hippest club is **Le Life,** 22 rue Macé (✆ **04-93-99-94-86**), where a multicultural crowd of night owls, mostly younger than 35, come to dance, drink, talk, and flirt. It's open every night 11pm to 4am and charges 16€ ($21) for admission.

The aptly named **Bar des Stars,** in the Restaurant Fouquet's in the Hôtel Majestic Barrière, 14 La Croisette (✆ **04-92-98-77-29**), is where deals go down during the film festival. Directors, producers, stars, press agents, screenwriters, and wannabes crowd in here at festival time. Even when there's no festival, it's a lively place for a drink; its scarlet decor evokes an Art Deco Asian fantasy.

Gays and lesbians will feel comfortable at **Le Vogue,** 20 rue du Suquet (✆ **04-93-39-99-18**), a mixed bar open Tuesday to Sunday from 7:30pm until 2:30am. Another gay option is **Disco Le Sept,** 7 rue Rouguière (✆ **04-93-39-10-36**), where drag shows appear nightly at 1:30am. Entrance is free, except on weekends, when it's 16€ ($21; includes a drink). A lot of straights go here, too.

The most visible gay clientele in Cannes tends to gravitate toward **Le Hype,** 52 bd. Jean-Jaurès (✆ **04-93-39-20-50**), which was re-outfitted late in 2004 in a 1950s-retro venue that includes red vinyl banquettes, white walls, a busy bar, occasional drag shows, and lots of randomly scheduled and somewhat flippant theme parties. Open for drinks and dining daily 6pm to 2:30am, with fixed-price meals priced at 32€ ($42), it's a popular and convivial spot for same-sex socializing. A lot rougher, darker, and more shadowy is the gay male disco, **Le Divan,** 3 rue Rouguière (✆ **04-93-68-73-70**), located within a vaulted cellar that's designed to look a lot older than it really is. This place is not for the timid: If you opt for a visit here, leave your valuables in your hotel safe and remain alert. It's open Tuesday to Sunday 6pm until around 4am, depending on the crowds.

A discreet ambience prevails at **Zanzibar,** 85 rue Félix-Faure (✆ **04-93-39-30-75**). A bartender confided to us, "If a gay man wants to meet a French version of Brad Pitt, especially at festival time, this is the place." The bar is open all night and caters to people of all sexual persuasions. At dawn the doors open, and the last of the drag queens stagger out.

The popular nightclub **Whatnut's Bal-Room,** 7 rue Marceau (✆ **04-93-68-60-58**), in the commercial center of Cannes, got a face-lift. There's a bar area near the entrance and two dance floors that feature radically different music: One is for 1980s-style disco; the other for house, garage, and modern forms of electronic sounds. Patrons are on the young side (18–35), admission is free, and drinks cost 5€ to 10€ ($6.50–$13). Open July to August daily 10:30pm to 5am; September to June Friday to Sunday 10:30pm to 5am.

4 Mougins

903km (561 miles) S of Paris, 11km (6¾ miles) S of Grasse, 8km (5 miles) N of Cannes

This former fortified town on the crest of a hill provides an alternative for those who want to be near the excitement of Cannes but not in the midst of it. Picasso and other artists appreciated the sun-drenched hills covered with gnarled olive trees. The artist arrived in 1936; in time, Jean Cocteau, Paul Eluard, and Man Ray followed. Picasso later decided to move here permanently. He spent the latter part of his life here with his wife Jacqueline. Fernand Léger, René Clair, Isadora Duncan, and even Christian Dior have lived at Mougins.

Mougins is a haven for those who feel that the Riviera is overrun, spoiled, and overbuilt. It preserves the quiet life even though it's a stone's throw from Cannes. Though Mougins looks serene and tranquil, it's actually part of the industrial park of Sophia Antipolis, a center where more than 1,000 companies have offices. Many visitors on a gastronomic tour of the Riviera spend the night here because of the celebrated inn Le Moulin de Mougins (see below).

ESSENTIALS

GETTING THERE The best way to get to Mougins is to **drive.** From Nice, follow E80/A8 west, and then cut north on Route 85 into Mougins. From Cannes, head north of the city along N85. From La Napoule–Plage, head east toward Cannes on N7, and then north at the turnoff to Mougins up in the hills.

In 2005, the French railways, **SNCF,** reactivated an antique rail line stretching between Grasse (the perfume capital) and Cannes, linking the hamlet of Mouans-Sartoux en route. The village of Mouans-Sartoux lies only 457m (1,500 ft.) from the center of Mougins. Rail service costs 2.90€ ($3.75) one-way from either Cannes or Grasse to Mouans-Sartoux. There are several trains per day. Among buses, **Société Tam** (✆ **08-00-06-01-06**) runs buses between Cannes and Grasse. Bus no. 600 stops in Val-de-Mougins, a 10-minute walk from the center of Mougins. One-way fares from either Cannes or Grasse cost 1.55€ ($2). Given the complexities of a bus transfer from Cannes, it's a lot easier just to pay 22€ to 30€ ($29–$39) for a **taxi** to haul you and your possessions northward from Cannes.

VISITOR INFORMATION The **Office de Tourisme** is at 15 av. Jean-Charles-Mallet (✆ **04-93-75-87-67;** fax 04-92-92-04-03; www.mougins-coteazur.org).

SEEING THE SIGHTS

For a look at the history of the area, visit the **Espace Culturel,** place du Commandant-Lamy (✆ **04-92-92-50-42**), in the St. Bernardin Chapel. It was built in 1618 and traces area history from 1553 to the 1950s. It's open December to October, Monday to Friday from 9am to noon and 2 to 5pm, Saturday and Sunday from 11am to 6pm (closed Nov). Admission is free.

You can also visit the **Chapelle Notre-Dame de Vie,** chemin de la Chapelle, 1.5km (1 mile) southeast of Mougins. The chapel, once painted by Churchill, is best known for the priory next door, where Picasso spent his last 12 years. It was built in the 12th century and reconstructed in 1646; it was an old custom to bring stillborn babies to the chapel to have them baptized. The priory is still a private home occupied intermittently by the Picasso heirs. Alas, because of a series of break-ins and ongoing renovations, the chapel is open only during Sunday Mass from 9 to 10am.

Musée de l'Automobiliste ★★ Kids This is one of the top attractions on the Riviera. Founded in 1984 by Adrien Maeght, it's a modern concrete-and-glass structure. It houses exhibitions and one of Europe's most magnificent collections of prestigious automobiles, which includes more than 100 vehicles dating from 1908 to the present. Within two steps of the sea, the museum explores the use of the automobile in both civil and military contexts. Individual cars are on display for historical, aesthetic, technical, or sentimental reasons. Children appreciate the antique toys and antique model cars, and any teenager who has seen pimped-out cars on TV will appreciate the cool quotient of such rare luxury rides as the 1925 Hispano-Suiza H6B and its even more opulent J12 counterpart from 1933.

Aire des Bréguières or 772 Chemin de Font de Currault. ✆ **04-93-69-27-80.** Admission 7€ ($9.10) adults, 5€ ($6.50) children 12–18, free for children 12 and under. Apr–Sept daily 10:30am–7pm; Oct–Mar Tues–Sun 10:30am–6pm.

WHERE TO STAY

Le Moulin de Mougins (see "Where to Dine," below) offers rooms and suites.

Le Manoir de l'Etang ★★ You'll get a strong sense of life in rural Provence within the thick, ivy-covered stone walls of this artfully renovated 19th-century manor house, located within a verdant 4-hectare (10-acre) park a short drive east from the center of Mougins. A mass of nearby olive trees and cypresses seem to showcase a small pond covered with lotuses and waterlilies. New owners massively renovated and upgraded it in 2004, creating a stylish and urban-style renovation, some of it very contemporary-looking, with airy bedrooms that each benefited from some sophisticated decorating. The interior, including the bedrooms, is bright and modern, the perfect place for a hideaway, off-the-record weekend. The in-house restaurant serves artfully conceived food, some platters arranged in ways that qualify them as sculptural statements in their own right. Despite its modernity and its airy and contemporary decorative style, the place still captivates the romance of the old, Romantic Riviera of long ago.

Aux Bois de Font-Merle, 66 allée du Manoir, Mougins 06250. ✆ **04-92-28-36-00.** Fax 04-92-28-36-10. www.manoir-de-letang.com. 21 units. 160€–250€ ($208–$325) double; 325€–360€ ($423–$468) suite; from 360€ ($468) apt for 4. AE, MC, V. Closed late Oct to Apr. **Amenities:** Restaurant; bar; outdoor pool; room service; laundry service; dry cleaning; nonsmoking rooms. *In room:* A/C, TV, minibar.

Le Mas Candille ★★ With a staff that at times might be just a bit too easygoing, this 200-year-old Provençal *mas* (farmhouse) was renovated in 2005 after gaining a well-designed annex in 2001. The public rooms contain many 19th-century furnishings, and some open onto the gardens. Rooms are individually decorated in different styles, including Japanese, medieval, French colonial (Indochina), and Provençal regional. Bathrooms are of good size, with tub/shower combinations. The dining room, with stone detailing and a massive fireplace with a timbered mantel, serves exceptional food. Fresh salads and light meals are available throughout the day. In clement weather, lunch is served on the terrace; dinner is served on the terrace in summer only.

Boulevard Clément Rebuffel, Mougins 06250 ✆ **04-92-28-43-43.** Fax 04-92-28-43-40. www.lemascandille.com. 40 units. 320€–555€ ($416–$722) double; 625€–755€ ($813–$982) suite. AE, DC, MC, V. **Amenities:** 2 restaurants; bar; 2 outdoor pools; gym; spa; room service; laundry service; dry cleaning; nonsmoking rooms; limited-mobility rooms. *In room:* A/C, TV, minibar, hair dryer, safe, Wi-Fi.

WHERE TO DINE

Le Mas Candille is noted for its sublime cuisine; you may want to call to reserve a table. **Le Manoir de l'Etang** also earns praise for its Provençal cuisine. See "Where to Stay," above, for more information about both.

L'Amandier de Mougins Café-Restaurant ★ *Value* NIÇOISE/PROVENÇAL This relatively inexpensive bistro was founded about a decade ago by the world-famous chef Roger Vergé. Today the restaurant carries on admirably under new owners. A mass-market cousin to its exclusive neighbor, this restaurant serves simple platters in an airy stone house. The specialties, based on traditional recipes, may include terrine of Mediterranean hogfish with lemon; tartare of fresh salmon and seviche of tuna with hot spices; or magret of duckling with honey sauce and lemons, served with deliberately undercooked polenta.

Place du Commandant-Lamy. ✆ **04-93-90-00-91.** Reservations recommended. Main courses 28€–45€ ($36–$59); fixed-price lunch 25€ ($33); fixed-price dinner 34€–44€ ($44–$57). AE, DC, MC, V. Daily noon–2pm and 7–9:30pm.

Le Moulin de Mougins ★★★ FRENCH The new chef here has a big toque to fill. In 2004, Alain Llorca took over the celebrated inn, formerly the kingdom of Roger Vergé, a *maître cuisinier de France* and one of the country's top three chefs. After 7 years as chef of the fabled Hôtel Negresco in Nice, Llorca was just the man to succeed Vergé. He employs market-fresh ingredients in his "cuisine of the sun," a reference to Provence's light-drenched countryside.

Cuisine here is earthy but upscale, often with modern twists on old culinary traditions both from Provence and other parts of the French-speaking world. Examples include hearts of artichoke stuffed with marinated seafood; an *accras de morue* (codfish fritters) that one would expect in Martinique; spaghetti with shellfish; roasted Provençal goat with herbs; sweetbreads with mushrooms fried in grease; and a succulent version of magret of duckling with honey sauce, lemons, and polenta.

The inn also rents four suites and three rooms with air-conditioning, minibars, and TVs. Rooms cost 140€ to 190€ ($182–$247) double, suites 300€ to 330€ ($390–$429).

Notre-Dame de Vie, Mougins 06250. ✆ **04-93-75-78-24.** Fax 04-93-90-18-55. www.moulin-mougins.com. Reservations required. Main courses 55€–95€ ($72–$124); fixed-price menu 58€–115€ ($75–$150) lunch, 98€–160€ ($127–$208) dinner. AE, DC, MC, V. Tues–Sun noon–2pm and 7:30–10pm.

5 Grasse ★★

906km (563 miles) S of Paris, 18km (11 miles) N of Cannes, 9.5km (6 miles) N of Mougins, 23km (14 miles) NW of Antibes

Grasse, a 20-minute drive from Cannes, is the most fragrant town on the Riviera. Surrounded by jasmine and roses, it has been the capital of the perfume industry since the Renaissance. It was once a famous resort, attracting such royals as Queen Victoria and Princess Pauline Borghese, Napoleon's lascivious sister.

Today some three-quarters of the world's essences are produced here from foliage that includes violets, daffodils, wild lavender, and jasmine. It takes 10,000 flowers to produce just more than 1 kilogram of jasmine petals. Almost a ton of petals is needed to distill 1 liter of essence. These figures are important to remember when looking at that high price tag on a bottle of perfume.

ESSENTIALS

GETTING THERE **Trains** now run to Grasse from Nice, Cannes, or Antibes. One-way tickets cost 2.10€ ($2.75) from Cannes, 3€ ($3.90) from Antibes, and 7€ ($9.10) from Nice. For train schedules and more information, call ✆ **08-92-35-35-35,** or visit www.voyages-sncf.com. **Buses** pull into town every 30 to 60 minutes daily from Cannes (trip time: 50 min.). The one-way fare is 4€ ($5.20). There are also about 14 buses every day from Nice (1 hr.). The one-way fare is around 6.30€ ($8.20). They arrive at the Gare Routière, place Notre Dame des Fleurs (✆ **04-93-36-08-43**), a 10-minute walk north of the town center. Visitors arriving by **car** take A8, which funnels in traffic from Monaco, Aix-en-Provence, and Marseille.

VISITOR INFORMATION The **Office de Tourisme** is in the Palais des Congrès, 22 cours Honoré Cresp (✆ **04-93-36-66-66;** fax 04-93-36-86-36; www.grasse-riviera.com).

SEEING THE SIGHTS

Musée d'Art et d'Histoire de Provence ★ This museum is in the Hôtel de Clapiers-Cabris, built in 1771 by Louise de Mirabeau, the marquise de Cabris and sister of Mirabeau. Its collections include paintings, four-poster beds, marquetry, ceramics, brasses, kitchenware, pottery, urns, and archaeological finds.

2 rue Mirabeau. ✆ **04-93-36-80-20.** Admission 3€ ($3.90) adults, 1.50€ ($1.95) children 10–16, free for children under 10. June–Sept daily 10am–6:30pm; Oct–May Wed–Mon 10am–12:30pm and 2–5:30pm.

Parfumerie Fragonard ★ One of the best-known perfume factories is named after an 18th-century French painter. This factory has the best villa, the best museum, and the best tour. An English-speaking guide will show you how "the soul of the flower" is extracted. After the tour, you can explore the museum, which displays bottles and vases that trace the industry back to ancient times. If you're shopping for perfume and want to skip the tour, that's okay.

20 bd. Fragonard. ✆ **04-93-36-44-65.** www.fragonard.com. Daily 9am–6pm; Nov–Jan daily 9am–12:30pm and 2–6:30pm.

Parfumerie Molinard This firm is well-known in the United States, where its products are sold at Saks, Neiman Marcus, and Bloomingdale's. In the factory you can witness the extraction of the essence of the flowers. You'll also learn all the details of the process of converting flowers into essential oils. You can admire a collection of antique perfume-bottle labels and see a rare collection of perfume *flacons* by Baccarat and Lalique.

60 bd. Victor-Hugo. ✆ **04-93-36-01-62.** www.molinard.com. Free admission. Apr–Sept daily 9am–6:30pm (until 7pm July–Aug); Oct–Apr Mon–Sat 9am–1pm and 2–6:30pm.

Villa Musée Fragonard The setting is an 18th-century aristocrat's town house with a magnificent garden in back. The collection displayed here includes the paintings of Jean-Honoré Fragonard, who was born in Grasse in 1732; his sister-in-law, Marguerite Gérard; his son, Alexandre; and his grandson, Théophile. Alexandre decorated the grand staircase.

23 bd. Fragonard. ✆ **04-93-36-52-98.** Admission 3€ ($3.90) adults, 1.50€ ($1.95) children 10–16, free for children under 10. June–Sept daily 10am–6:30pm; Oct–May Wed–Mon 10am–12:30pm and 2–5:30pm.

WHERE TO STAY

Hôtel La Bellaudière *Value* Part of the respected Logis de France chain, this unpretentious family-run hotel is 3km (1¾ miles) east of the town center in the hills above Grasse. The stone-sided farmhouse was built in stages beginning 400 years ago, with most of what you see today built in the 1700s. Guest rooms are simple but dignified and outfitted with Provençal motifs, and many boast views of the sea. A garden terrace is lined with flowering shrubs, and guests get a sense of friendly cooperation from the hosts. Fixed-price meals in the dining room cost 20€ to 25€ ($26–$33) each.

78 rte. de Nice, Grasse 06130. © **04-93-36-02-57.** Fax 04-93-36-40-03. 17 units. 54€–68€ ($70–$88) double. AE, DC, MC, V. Free parking. **Amenities:** Restaurant; limited room service. *In room:* TV.

WHERE TO DINE

For inexpensive dining, you can head for **Hôtel La Bellaudière** (see "Where to Stay," above).

La Bastide St-Antoine (Restaurant Chibois) ★★★ FRENCH/PROVENÇAL La Bastide St-Antoine offers one of the grandest culinary experiences along the Riviera. Jacques Chibois and his restaurant have attracted national attention since 1996. In a 200-year-old Provençal farmhouse surrounded by 2.8 hectares (7 acres) of trees and shrubbery, the restaurant serves a sophisticated array of dishes. The best examples are oysters flavored with yucca leaves, a terrine of foie gras with celery, roasted suckling lamb with a fricassee of fresh vegetables and basil, and fresh crayfish with sautéed flap mushrooms. Desserts may include strawberry soup with spice wine or ice cream made with olives and a hint of olive oil. The chef also does wonders with wild duck.

You can stay in one of nine rooms and seven suites, decorated in Provençal style with upscale furnishings and comfortable beds. They have air-conditioning, safes, hair dryers, minibars, and TVs. Doubles cost 200€ to 450€ ($260–$585); suites 530€ to 780€ ($689–$1,014).

48 av. Henri-Dunant. © **04-93-70-94-94.** Fax 04-93-70-94-95. www.jacques-chibois.com. Reservations required. Main courses 32€–60€ ($42–$78); fixed-price lunch Mon–Sat 57€–180€ ($74–$234); fixed-price dinner 140€–180€ ($182–$234). AE, DC, MC, V. Daily noon–2pm and 8–9:30pm.

6 Biot ★

918km (570 miles) S of Paris, 9.5km (6 miles) E of Cagnes-sur-Mer, 6.5km (4 miles) NW of Antibes

Biot has been famous for its pottery since merchants began to ship earthenware jars to Phoenicia and throughout the Mediterranean. Settled by Gallo-Romans, Biot has a long, war-torn history. Somehow the potters persevered at their ancient craft. Biot is also where Fernand Léger painted until the day he died. A magnificent collection of his work is on display at a museum here.

ESSENTIALS

GETTING THERE Biot's **train** station is 3km (1¾ miles) east of the town center. There's frequent service from Nice and Antibes. For rail information and schedules, call © **08-92-35-35-35,** or visit www.voyages-sncf.com. The **bus** from Antibes is even more convenient than the train. For bus information and schedules, call © **04-92-28-58-68** in Antibes. To **drive** to Biot from Nice, take N7 west. From Antibes, follow N7 east.

VISITOR INFORMATION The **Office de Tourisme** is at 46 rue St-Sébastien (© **04-93-65-78-00;** fax 04-93-65-78-04; www.biot.fr).

EXPLORING THE TOWN

If you have time, explore the village. Begin at the **place des Arcades,** where you can see the 16th-century gates and the remains of the town's ramparts. Biot is known for its carnations and roses, which are sold on this lovely square. The **Eglise de Biot,** place des Arcades (✆ **04-93-65-00-85**), dates from the 15th century. It's the work of Italian immigrants who resettled the town after the Black Death. The church is known for two stunning 15th-century retables (altarpieces): the red-and-gold *Retable du Rosaire* by Ludovico Bréa, and the recently restored *Christ aux Plaies* by Canavesio.

Musée d'Histoire Locale et de Céramique Biotoise, 9 rue St-Sebastien (✆ **04-93-65-54-54**), has assembled the best work of local artists, potters, ceramists, painters, and silver- and goldsmiths. It's open Wednesday to Sunday 2 to 6pm; admission is 2.50€ ($3.25) for adults, 1.20€ ($1.55) for children 6 to 16, and free for children under 6.

In the late 1940s, glassmakers created a bubble-flecked glass known as *verre rustique.* It comes in brilliant colors such as cobalt and emerald, and is displayed in many store windows on the main shopping street, **rue St-Sebastien.** The best place to watch the glassblowers and to buy glass, aside from the shops along rue St-Sebastien, is **Verrerie de Biot,** 5 chemin des Combes (✆ **04-93-65-03-00**), at the bottom of town. Tours, costing 6€ ($7.80), are conducted daily from June to August at 11:30am, 4pm, and 5:30pm; September to May daily at 4:30pm. While you're here, you can call at **Galerie International du Verre** (✆ **04-93-65-03-00;** www.verreriebiot.com), where beautifully displayed glassworks are for sale, often at exorbitant prices. Open June to September Monday to Saturday 9:30am to 8pm, Sunday 10am to 1pm and 3 to 7:30pm; October to May Monday to Saturday 9:30am to 6:30pm, Sunday 10am to 1pm and 2:30 to 6:30pm.

The namesake of the **Galerie Jean-Claude Novaro** (also known as Galerie de la Patrimoine), place des Arcades (✆ **04-93-65-60-23**), is known as the Picasso of glass artists. His works are pretty and colorful, though they sometimes lack the diversity and flair of the creations displayed at the Galerie International du Verre. Most of his glass art is for sale. You may also want to shop at **La Poterie Provençale,** 1689 rte. de la Mer (✆ **04-93-65-63-30**), adjacent to the Musée Fernand-Léger, about 3km (1¾ miles) southeast of town. It's one of the last potteries in Provence to specialize in the amphora-like containers known as *jarres.*

Bonzaï Arboretum de la Côte d'Azur Privately owned and maintained by members of the Okonek family, this arboretum and showroom contains the largest collection of bonsai in France. Most of the potted trees sell for between 20€ and 150€ ($26–$195), and most were crafted from artfully tormented-looking versions of local fig, almond, or olive trees. Especially noteworthy are some bonsai versions of rare tropical cypresses and tropical figs, some as tall as 2m (6½ ft.), loaded with aerial root systems and miniaturized trunks and branches that many botanists find fascinating.

299 Chemin de Val de Pôme, Biot 06410. 3km (1¾ miles) south of Biot. ✆ **04-93-65-63-99.** Admission is 4€ ($5.20) for adults or 2€ ($2.60) for students. Wed–Mon 10am–noon and 2–6pm.

Musée National Fernand-Léger ★★ The artist's widow, Nadia Léger, assembled this collection and donated it to the French government after the artist's death in 1955. Léger's mosaic-and-ceramic mural enhances the stone-and-marble facade. On the grounds is a polychrome ceramic sculpture, *Le Jardin d'enfant;* inside are two floors of geometrical forms in pure, flat colors. The collection includes paintings, ceramics, tapestries, and sculptures showing the artist's development from 1905 until his death. His paintings abound with cranes, acrobats, scaffolding, railroad signals, buxom nudes, casings, and crankshafts. The most unusual work depicts a Léger Mona Lisa *(La Giaconde aux Clés)* contemplating a set of keys, a wide-mouthed fish dangling over her head.

Chemin du Val-de-Pôme (on the eastern edge of town, beside the road to the rail station). ✆ **04-92-91-50-30.** www.musee-fernandleger.fr. Admission 4.50€ ($5.85), free for children under 18. July–Sept Wed–Mon 10:30am–6pm; Apr–June Wed–Mon 10am–12:30pm and 2–6pm; Oct–Mar Wed–Mon 10am–12:30pm and 2–5:30pm.

WHERE TO DINE

Le Jarrier ★ PROVENÇAL One of the most enduringly excellent restaurants in Biot was built 300 years ago as a pottery for the *jarres* used to transport and store olive oil and wine. One of its two dining rooms has its walls removed every summer and becomes an open-air terrace with views over the valley. The cuisine is "personalized"—an idiosyncratic and modernized interpretation of Provençal staples. Examples include stuffed zucchini blossoms; several versions of risotto, many of them vegetarian; *daurade* (bream) served with herb-laden vinaigrette; and Challons duckling with lavender-honey sauce and either figs or braised leeks. Even if you don't usually order dessert, consider the comfit of oranges in puff pastry.

30 passage de la Bourgade. ✆ **04-93-65-11-68.** Reservations recommended. Main courses 19€–35€ ($25–$46); fixed-price lunch 23€–47€ ($30–$61); fixed-price dinner 30€–47€ ($39–$61). AE, MC, V. Wed–Sun 12:30–2:30pm and 7:30–11pm.

Les Terraillers ★★★ MEDITERRANEAN This stone-sided restaurant is .8km (about ½ mile) south of Biot, in a 16th-century studio for the production of clay pots and ceramics. The cuisine of chef Claude Jacques, Michael Fulci, and their staff changes with the seasons and is more sophisticated and appetizing than that at many competitors. Examples are a platter containing two preparations of pigeon (thigh and breast cooked in different ways), served with a corn galette and the pigeon's own drippings; "fish of the day" in saffron sauce; roasted scallops with saffron and mussel-flavored cream sauce and leek comfit; a tart with artichoke hearts and tomatoes en comfit with lobster salad; braised John Dory Provençal style, with olive oil and a fricassee of zucchini, artichokes, tomatoes, and olives; and ravioli filled with pan-fried foie gras and served with essence of morels and mushroom duxelles.

11 rte. du Chemin-Neuf. Take rte. du Chemin-Neuf, following signs to Antibes. ✆ **04-93-65-01-59.** Reservations required as far in advance as possible. Main courses 27€–46€ ($35–$60); fixed-price lunch 39€–55€ ($51–$72); fixed-price dinner 59€–75€ ($77–$98). AE, MC, V. June–Sept Fri–Tues noon–2pm and 7–10pm. Closed Oct 25–Dec 2.

7 Golfe-Juan & Vallauris ★

Golfe-Juan: 913km (567 miles) S of Paris, 6.5km (4 miles) E of Cannes. Vallauris: 910km (565 miles) S of Paris, 6.5km (4 miles) E of Cannes

Napoleon and 800 men landed at Golfe-Juan in 1815 to begin his Hundred Days. Protected by hills, this spot beside the coast was also a favored port for the American navy. Today it's a family resort known for its beaches and a noteworthy restaurant (see "Where to Dine," below).

The 2km-long (1¼-mile) RN135 leads inland from Golfe-Juan to Vallauris. Once just a stopover along the Riviera, Vallauris (noted for its pottery) owes its reputation to Picasso. The master "discovered" Vallauris after World War II and occupied a villa known as "The Woman from Wales."

ESSENTIALS

GETTING THERE You can **drive** to Golfe-Juan or Vallauris on any of the Riviera's three east-west highways. Although route numbers are not always indicated, city names are clear once you're on the highway. From Cannes or Antibes, N7 east is the fastest route. From Nice or Biot, take A8/E80 west.

There's a sleepy-looking rail station in Golfe-Juan, on avenue de la Gare. To get here, you'll have to transfer from a **train** in Cannes. The train from Cannes costs 1.80€ ($2.35) each way. For railway information, call © **08-92-35-35-35,** or visit www.voyages-sncf.com. A flotilla of **buses** operated by Envibus (© **04-93-64-18-37**) makes frequent trips from Cannes; the 20-minute trip costs 1€ ($1.30) each way; from Nice, the 90-minute trip costs 1.30€ ($1.70) each way.

VISITOR INFORMATION There's an **Office de Tourisme** (www.vallauris-golfe-juan.fr) on boulevard des Frères-Roustan, Golfe-Juan (© **04-93-63-73-12;** fax 04-93-63-21-07), and another on square du 8-Mai, 1945 Vallauris (© **04-93-63-82-58;** fax 04-93-63-13-66).

A DAY AT THE BEACH

Because of its position beside the sea, Golfe-Juan long ago developed into a warm-weather resort. The town's twin strips of beach are **Plage du Soleil** (east of the Vieux Port and the newer Port Camille-Rayon) and **Plage du Midi** (west of those two). Each stretches 1km (⅔ mile) and charges no entry fee, with the exception of small areas administered by concessions that rent mattresses and chaises and have snack kiosks. Regardless of which concession you select (on Plage du Midi they sport names like Au Vieux Rocher, Palma Beach, and Corail Plage; on Plage du Soleil, Plage Nounou and Plage Tétou), you'll pay 12€ to 38€ ($16–$49) for a day's use of a mattress. Plage Tétou is associated with the upscale Chez Tétou (see "Where to Dine," below). If you don't want to rent a mattress, you can cavort unhindered anywhere along the sands, moving freely from one area to another. Golfe-Juan indulges bathers who remove their bikini tops, but in theory it forbids nude sunbathing.

SEEING THE SIGHTS

Picasso's ***l' Homme au Mouton*** **(Man and Sheep)** is the outdoor statue at place Isnard in front of which Prince Aly Kahn and screen goddess Rita Hayworth were married. The council of Vallauris had intended to enclose this statue in a museum, but Picasso insisted that it remain on the square, "where the children could climb over it and the dogs water it unhindered."

L'Espace Jean Marais If you're a fan of early movies, you'll remember the robust, macho French actor who symbolized for many of us the bonhomie of France's working-class heroes prior to World War II. Jean Marais (1913–98) spent the final 18 years of his life based in Vallauris, painting and sculpting. After his death, the city assembled his paintings and sculptures into this masonry-sided space. Come here for a nostalgic homage to one of France's memorable actors, star of such films as *La Belle et la Bête,* and for an insight into the fact that, indeed, life still continues after an actor's cinematic star has faded.

Av. des Martyrs de la Résistance. © **04-93-63-46-11.** Admission 1.50€ ($1.95). Tues–Sat 9am–12:30pm and 2–5:30pm.

Musée Magnelli, Musée de la Céramique & Musée National Picasso La Guerre et La Paix ★ A chapel of rough stone shaped like a Quonset hut is the focal point of a three-in-one sightseeing highlight. The museum grew from the site of a chapel that Picasso decorated with two paintings: *La Paix* (Peace) and *La Guerre* (War). The paintings offer contrasting images of love and peace on the one hand, and violence and conflict on the other. In 1970, a house painter illegally gained entrance to the museum and substituted one of his designs after whitewashing a portion of the original. When the aging master inspected the damage, he said, "Not bad at all." In 1996, the site added a permanent exposition devoted to the works of the Florentine-born Alberto Magnelli, a pioneer of abstract art. A third section showcases ceramics, both traditional and innovative, from potters throughout the region.

Place de la Libération. ✆ **04-93-64-71-83.** Admission 3€ ($3.90) adults, 1.50€ ($1.95) students, free for children under 16. June–Aug Wed–Mon 10am–6pm; Sept–May Wed–Mon 10am–12:15pm and 2–5pm.

SHOPPING

Galerie Madoura, avenue de Georges et Suzanne Ramié, Vallauris (✆ **04-93-64-66-39**), is the only shop licensed to sell Picasso reproductions. It's open Monday through Friday 10am to 12:30pm and 3 to 6pm. Some of the reproductions are limited to 25 to 500 copies. Another gallery to seek out is the **Galerie Sassi-Milici,** 65 bis av. Georges-Clemenceau (✆ **04-93-64-65-71**), which displays works by contemporary artists.

Market days in Vallauris are Tuesday to Sunday 7am to 12:30pm, at **place de l'Homme au Mouton,** with its flower stalls and local produce. For a souvenir, you may want to visit a farming cooperative, the **Cooperative Nérolium,** 12 av. Georges-Clemenceau (✆ **04-93-64-27-54**). It produces such foods as bitter-orange marmalade and quince jam, olive oils, and scented products such as orange-flower water. Another unusual outlet for local products is the **Parfumerie Bouis,** 50 av. Georges-Clemenceau (✆ **04-93-64-38-27**).

La Boutique de l'Olivier, 46 av. Georges-Clemenceau (✆ **04-93-64-16-63**), specializes in olive-wood objects. They include pepper mills, salad servers, cheese boards, free-form bowls, and bread-slicing boxes. **Terres à Terre,** 58 av. Georges-Clemenceau (✆ **04-93-63-16-80**), is known for its culinary pottery, made of local clay. This is an excellent outlet for terra-cotta pottery. Gratin dishes and casseroles have long been big sellers.

WHERE TO DINE

Chez Tétou ★★★ SEAFOOD In its own amusing way, this is one of the Côte d'Azur's most famous restaurants, capitalizing on the beau monde that came here in the 1950s and 1960s. Retaining its Provençal earthiness despite its high prices, it has thrived in a white-sided beach cottage for more than 65 years. Appetizers are limited to platters of charcuterie or several almost-perfect slices of fresh melon. Most diners order the house specialty, bouillabaisse. Also on the limited menu are grilled sea bass with tomatoes Provençal, sole meunière, and several preparations of lobster—the most famous is grilled and served with lemon-butter sauce, fresh parsley, and basmati rice. Dessert may be a powdered croissant with grandmother's jams (winter) or raspberry-and-strawberry tart (summer).

Av. des Frères-Roustan, sur la Plage, Golfe-Juan. ✆ **04-93-63-71-16.** Reservations required. Main courses 60€–70€ ($78–$91); bouillabaisse 90€ ($117). No credit cards. Thurs–Sun and Tues noon–2:30pm; Thurs–Tues 8–10:30pm. Closed Nov to early Mar.

8 Juan-les-Pins ★★

913km (567 miles) S of Paris, 9.5km (6 miles) S of Cannes

This suburb of Antibes is a resort developed in the 1920s by Frank Jay Gould. People flocked to "John of the Pines" to escape the crassness of Cannes. In the 1930s Juan-les-Pins drew a chic winter crowd. Today it attracts young Europeans from many economic backgrounds in pursuit of sex, sun, and sea, in that order. F. Scott Fitzgerald decried Juan-les-Pins as a "constant carnival." If he could see it now, he'd know he was a prophet.

ESSENTIALS

GETTING THERE Juan-les-Pins is connected by **rail** and bus to most other Mediterranean coastal resorts, especially Nice (trip time: 30 min.; one-way fare: 4€/ $5.20). For rail information and schedules, call ✆ **08-92-35-35-35,** or visit www.voyages-sncf.com. **Buses** arrive from Nice and its airport at 40-minute intervals throughout the day. A bus leaves for Juan-les-Pins from Antibes at place Guynemer (✆ **04-93-34-37-60**) daily every 20 minutes and costs 1.45€ ($1.90) one-way (trip time: 10–15 min.). To **drive** to Juan-les-Pins from Nice, travel along N7 south; from Cannes, follow the signposted roads. Juan-les-Pins is just outside of Cannes.

VISITOR INFORMATION The **Office de Tourisme** is at 51 bd. Charles-Guillaumont (✆ **04-92-90-53-05;** fax 04-93-61-55-13; www.antibesjuanlespins.com).

SPECIAL EVENTS The town offers some of the best nightlife on the Riviera, and the action reaches its height during the annual jazz festival. The 10- to 12-day **Festival International de Jazz,** in mid-July, attracts jazz masters and their fans. Concerts are in a temporary stadium, custom-built for the event in Le Parc de la Pinède. Tickets cost 20€ to 60€ ($26–$78) and can be purchased at the Office de Tourisme in both Antibes and Juan-les-Pins.

A DAY AT THE BEACH

Part of the reason people flock here is that the town's beaches have sand, unlike many of the other resorts along this coast, which have pebbly beaches. **Plage de Juan-les-Pins** is the most central beach. Its subdivisions, all public, include **Plage de la Salis** and **Plage de la Garoupe.** If you don't have a beach chair, go to the concessions operated by each of the major beachfront hotels. Even if you're not a guest, you can rent a chaise and mattress for around 15€ to 18€ ($20–$23). The most chic is the area maintained by the Hôtel des Belles-Rives. Competitors more or less in the same category are La Jetée and La Voile Blanche, both opposite the tourist information office. Topless sunbathing is permitted, but total nudity isn't.

WATERSPORTS

If you're interested in scuba diving, check with your hotel staff, **Easy Dive,** Port Gallice (✆ **04-93-61-26-07**), or **EPAJ,** embarcadère Courbet (✆ **04-93-67-52-59**). A one-tank dive costs 45€ ($54), including all equipment. **Water-skiing** is available at virtually every beach in Juan-les-Pins. Concessionaires include one outfit that's more or less permanently located on the beach of the Hôtel des Belles-Rives. Ask any beach attendant or bartender, and he or she will guide you to the water-skiing representatives who station themselves on the sands. A 10-minute session costs 15€ to 25€ ($20–$33).

WHERE TO STAY

VERY EXPENSIVE

Hôtel des Belles-Rives ★★★ This is one of the Riviera's fabled addresses, on par with the equally famous Juana (see below), though the Juana boasts superior cuisine. It was once a holiday villa occupied by Zelda and F. Scott Fitzgerald, and the scene of many a drunken brawl. It later played host to the illustrious, such as the duke and duchess of Windsor, Josephine Baker, and Edith Piaf. A 1930s aura lingers through recent renovations. Double-glazing and air-conditioning help a lot. As befits a hotel of this age, rooms come in a variety of shapes and sizes, from small to spacious; each has a luxurious bathroom with a combination tub/shower. The lower terraces hold garden dining rooms, a waterside aquatic club with a snack bar and lounge, and a jetty. There are also a private beach and a dock.

33 bd. Edouard Baudoin, Juan-les-Pins 06160. ✆ **04-93-61-02-79.** Fax 04-93-67-43-51. www.bellesrives.com. 44 units. 220€–520€ ($286–$676) double; 345€–730€ ($449–$949) suite. AE, DC, MC, V. Free parking. Closed Jan–Mar 11. **Amenities:** 2 summer restaurants; 1 winter restaurant; 2 bars; courtesy car; room service; babysitting; laundry service; dry cleaning; nonsmoking rooms. *In room:* A/C, TV, minibar, hair dryer, safe.

Hôtel Juana ★★★ This balconied Art Deco hotel, beloved by F. Scott Fitzgerald, is separated from the sea by the park of pines that gave Juan-les-Pins its name. The hotel is constantly being refurbished, as reflected in the attractive rooms with mahogany pieces, well-chosen fabrics, tasteful carpets, and large bathrooms (tub and shower) in marble or tile. The rooms often have such extras as balconies. The hotel has a private swimming club where you can rent a "parasol and pad" on the sandy beach at reduced rates. Nearby is a park with umbrella-shaded tables and palms.

La Pinède, av. Gallice, Juan-les-Pins 06160. ✆ **04-93-61-08-70.** Fax 04-93-61-76-60. www.hotel-juana.com. 40 units. 210€–655€ ($273–$852) double; 248€–1,200€ ($322–$1,560) suite. AE, MC, V. Parking 15€ ($20). Closed Nov 10–Feb 26. **Amenities:** Restaurant; 2 bars; heated outdoor pool; sauna; gym; bike rentals; secretarial services; room service; massage; babysitting; laundry service; dry cleaning; nonsmoking rooms. *In room:* A/C, TV, minibar, hair dryer, iron, safe.

MODERATE

Hôtel des Mimosas This elegant 1870s-style villa sprawls in a tropical garden on a hilltop, a 10-minute walk to a good beach. The decor is a mix of high-tech and Italian-style comfort, with antique and modern furniture. Guest rooms come in a variety of shapes and sizes—some quite small—each with a compact tub/shower bathroom. Try for one of the four rooms with a balcony or the nine rooms with a terrace. A pool sits amid huge palm trees. The hotel is fully booked in summer, so reserve far in advance.

Rue Pauline, Juan-les-Pins 06160. From the town center, drive .4km (¼ mile) west, following N7 toward Cannes. ✆ **04-93-61-04-16.** Fax 04-92-93-06-46. www.hotelmimosas.com. 34 units. 95€–135€ ($124–$176) double. AE, MC, V. Free parking. Closed Oct–May. **Amenities:** Bar; outdoor pool; room service; laundry service; dry cleaning; nonsmoking rooms. *In room:* A/C, TV, minibar, hair dryer, iron, safe.

Hôtel Le Pré Catelan In a residential area near the town park, 200m (656 ft.) from a sandy beach, this year-round Provençal villa (built ca. 1900) features a garden with rock terraces, towering palms, lemon and orange trees, large pots of pink geraniums, and outdoor furniture. The atmosphere is casual, the setting uncomplicated and unstuffy. Furnishings are durable and basic. As is typical of such old villas, guest rooms come in a variety of shapes and sizes. Some have kitchenettes, and more expensive units have terraces. Despite the setting in the heart of town, the garden lends a sense of isolation. Breakfast is the only meal served.

27 av. des Palmiers, Juan-les-Pins 06160. © **04-93-61-05-11.** Fax 04-93-67-83-11. www.precatelan.com. 24 units. 85€–141€ ($111–$183) double; 125€–232€ ($163–$302) suite. AE, MC, V. Parking 7€ ($9.10). **Amenities:** Bar; outdoor pool; babysitting; laundry service; dry cleaning; nonsmoking rooms. *In room:* TV, minibar, hair dryer, safe.

INEXPENSIVE

Hôtel Cecil *Value* A stone's throw from the beach, this well-kept small hotel is one of the best bargains in Juan-les-Pins. It originated in 1929 when a 19th-century villa was radically enlarged with another story and transformed into a hotel. The traditionally furnished rooms are worn yet well kept, ranging from small to midsize, each with a compact tiled bathroom with shower only. The owners provide a courteous welcome and a good meal.

Rue Jonnard, Juan-les-Pins 06160. © **04-93-61-05-12.** Fax 04-93-67-09-14. www.hotelcecilfrance.com. 21 units. Feb–Oct 55€–92€ ($72–$120) double. AE, DC, MC, V. Parking 15€ ($20). Closed Nov 7–Jan 14. **Amenities:** Restaurant; room service; babysitting; nonsmoking rooms. *In room:* A/C, TV, hair dryer.

WHERE TO DINE

Le Bijou Plage *Value* FRENCH/PROVENÇAL This upscale brasserie has flourished beside the seafront promenade since 1923. The marine-style decor includes lots of varnished wood and bouquets of blue and white flowers in a mostly blue-and-white interior. Windows overlook a private beach that's much less crowded than the public beaches nearby. Menu items are sophisticated and less expensive than you'd expect. Examples include excellent bouillabaisse, grilled sardines, risotto with John Dory and truffled butter, steamed mussels with *sauce poulette* (frothy cream sauce with herbs and butter), grilled John Dory with a vinaigrette enriched by a tapenade of olives and fresh basil, and a super-size *plateau des coquillages et fruits de mer* (shellfish and seafood). Don't confuse this informally elegant place with its beachfront terrace, open April 15 to September 15 daily noon to 4pm.

Bd. du Littoral. © **04-93-61-39-07.** Reservations recommended. Main courses 22€–55€ ($29–$72); fixed-price menu 21€–47€ ($27–$61). AE, DC, MC, V. Daily noon–2:30pm and 7:30–10:30pm.

Le Perroquet PROVENÇAL The cuisine is well presented and prepared, and the restaurant's ambience is carefully synchronized to the resort's casual and carnival-like summer aura. It's across from the Parc de la Pinède, and it's decorated with depictions of every imaginable form of parakeet, the restaurant's namesake. Look for savory versions of fish, at its best when grilled simply with olive oil and basil, and served with lemons. A worthwhile appetizer is the *assortiment Provençale,* which includes tapenade of olives, marinated peppers, grilled sardines, and stuffed and grilled vegetables. Steaks may be served with green peppercorns or béarnaise sauce, and desserts include three types of pastries on the same platter.

Av. Georges-Gallice. © **04-93-61-02-20.** Reservations recommended. Main courses 8€–45€ ($10–$59); fixed-price menu 26€–35€ ($34–$46). MC, V. Daily noon–2pm and 7–11pm. Closed Nov–Dec 26.

JUAN-LES-PINS AFTER DARK

For starters, visit the **Eden Casino,** boulevard Baudoin in the heart of Juan-les-Pins (© **04-92-93-71-71**), and try your luck at the roulette wheel or at one of the slot machines. The area containing slot machines is open every day 10am to 5pm. The area containing *les grands jeux* is open daily 8:30pm to 5am. A photo ID is required, preferably in the form of a passport.

For a faux-tropical experience, head to **Le Pam Pam,** route Wilson (✆ **04-93-61-11-05**), where you can sip rum drinks in an atmosphere that celebrates reggae and Brazilian and African music and dance performances.

If you prefer high-energy reveling, check out the town's many discos. **Whisky à Gogo,** boulevard de la Pinède (✆ **04-93-61-26-40**), attracts young trendsetters with its rock beat. In summer it fills up with the young, restless, and horny. Between October and Easter, it's closed. **Le Village,** 1 bd. de la Pinède (✆ **04-92-93-90-00**), boasts an action-packed dance floor and DJs spinning the latest sounds from the international music scene. The cover charge is a stiff 15€ ($20). Free for women before 1am on Friday.

9 Antibes & Cap d'Antibes ★★

913km (567 miles) S of Paris, 21km (13 miles) SW of Nice, 11km (6¾ miles) NE of Cannes

On the other side of the Baie des Anges (Bay of Angels) from Nice is the port of Antibes. The town has a quiet charm unique on the Côte d'Azur. Its harbor is filled with fishing boats and yachts, and in recent years it has emerged as a hot spot. The marketplaces are full of flowers. If you're in Antibes in the evening, you can watch fishers playing the popular Riviera game of boule (similar to boccie).

Spiritually, Antibes is totally divorced from Cap d'Antibes, a peninsula studded with the villas of the super-rich. In *Tender Is the Night,* Fitzgerald described it as a place where "old villas rotted like water lilies among the massed pines."

ESSENTIALS

GETTING THERE **Trains** from Cannes arrive at the rail station, place Pierre-Semard, every 20 minutes (trip time: 15 min.); the one-way fare is 3€ ($3.90). Trains from Nice arrive at the rate of 25 per day (trip time: 18 min.); the one-way fare is around 3.50€ ($4.55). For rail information, call ✆ **08-92-35-35-35,** or visit www.voyages-sncf.com. The **bus** station, La Gare Routière, place Guynemer (✆ **04-93-39-11-39**), receives buses from throughout Provence.

If you're **driving,** follow E1 east from Cannes and take the turnoff to the south for Antibes, which will lead to the historic core of the old city. From Nice, take E1 west until you come to the turnoff for Antibes. From the center of Antibes, follow the coastal road, boulevard Leclerc, south to Cap d'Antibes.

VISITOR INFORMATION The **Office de Tourisme** is at 11 place du Général-de-Gaulle (✆ **04-92-90-53-00;** fax 04-92-90-53-01; www.antibesjuanlespins.com).

SEEING THE SIGHTS

Musée Naval et Napoléonien *Kids* In this stone-sided fort and tower, built in stages in the 17th and 18th centuries, you'll find an interesting collection of Napoleonic memorabilia, naval models, and paintings, many of which were donated by at least two world-class collectors. A toy-soldier collection depicts various uniforms, including one used by Napoleon in the Marengo campaign. A wall painting on wood shows Napoleon's entrance into Grenoble; another shows him disembarking at Golfe-Juan on March 1, 1815. In contrast to Canova's Greek-god image of Napoleon, a miniature pendant by Barrault reveals the general as he really looked, with pudgy cheeks and a receding hairline. In the rear rotunda is one of the many hats worn by the emperor. You can climb to the top of the tower for a view of the coast that's worth the admission price.

Batterie du Grillon, bd. J.-F.-Kennedy. ✆ **04-93-61-45-32.** Admission 3€ ($3.90) adults; 1.50€ ($1.95) seniors, students, and ages 12–25; free for children under 12. Mon–Sat 9:30am–noon; Mon–Fri 2:15–6pm.

Musée Picasso ★★ On the ramparts above the port is the Château Grimaldi, once the home of the princes of Antibes of the Grimaldi family, who ruled the city from 1385 to 1608. Today it houses one of the world's great Picasso collections. Picasso came to town after the war and stayed in a small hotel at Golfe-Juan until the museum director at Antibes invited him to work and live at the museum. Picasso spent 1946 painting here. When he departed, he gave the museum all the work he'd done: 24 paintings, 80 pieces of ceramics, 44 drawings, 32 lithographs, 11 oils on paper, 2 sculptures, and 5 tapestries. In addition, a gallery of contemporary art exhibits Léger, Miró, Ernst, and Calder, among others.

Place du Mariejol. ✆ **04-92-90-54-20.** Admission 6.50€ ($8.45), 4€ ($5.20) children 12–18, free for children under 12. June–Sept Tues–Sun 10am–6pm (until 8pm July–Aug); Oct–May Tues–Sun 10am–noon and 2–5:30pm.

WHERE TO STAY

VERY EXPENSIVE

Hôtel du Cap–Eden Roc ★★★ Legendary for the glamour of its setting and its clientele, this Second Empire hotel, opened in 1870, is surrounded by masses of gardens. It's like a country estate, with spacious public rooms, marble fireplaces, paneling, chandeliers, and upholstered armchairs. The guest rooms are among the most sumptuous on the Riviera, with deluxe beds. Bathrooms are spacious, with brass fittings and tub/shower combinations. Even though the guests snoozing by the pool—blasted out of the cliff-side at enormous expense—appear artfully undraped during the day, evenings are upscale, with lots of emphasis on clothing and style. The world-famous Pavillon Eden Roc, near a rock garden apart from the hotel, has a panoramic sea view. Venetian chandeliers, Louis XV chairs, and elegant draperies add to the drama. Lunch is served on a terrace, under umbrellas and an arbor.

Bd. J.-F.-Kennedy, Cap d'Antibes 06600. ✆ **04-93-61-39-01.** Fax 04-93-67-13-83. www.edenroc-hotel.fr. 130 units. 350€–945€ ($455–$1,229) double; 810€–1,250€ ($1,053–$1,625) suite. No credit cards. Closed mid-Oct to Apr. Bus: A2. **Amenities:** Restaurant; 2 bars; outdoor pool; gym; sauna; secretarial services; room service; massage; babysitting; laundry service; dry cleaning; nonsmoking rooms; limited-mobility rooms. *In room:* A/C, TV (on request), hair dryer, safe.

Hôtel Impérial Garoupe ★★ Within steps of the beach, this hotel is the centerpiece of a small park with rows of pines that block some of the sea views. The heiress to the Moulinex housewares fortune built it in 1993. Gilbert Irondelle, son of the director of Antibes's Grand Hôtel du Cap-Ferrat, has transformed it into a pocket of posh that's less intimidating than his father's more monumental hotel. The luxurious rooms contain contemporary furnishings, luxury beds, and deluxe bathrooms with tub/shower combinations. The in-house restaurant serves French and international cuisine.

60–74 chemin de la Garoupe, Cap d'Antibes 06600. ✆ **800/525-4800** in the U.S., or 04-92-93-31-61. Fax 04-92-93-31-62. www.imperial-garoupe.com. 34 units. 270€–625€ ($351–$813) double; 400€–750€ ($520–$975) suite. AE, DC, MC, V. Bus: A2. **Amenities:** Restaurant; bar; heated outdoor pool; room service; babysitting; laundry service; dry cleaning; nonsmoking rooms; limited-mobility rooms. *In room:* A/C, TV, minibar, hair dryer, Wi-Fi.

MODERATE

Castel Garoupe *Value* We highly recommend this Mediterranean villa, which was built in 1968 on a private lane in the center of the cape. It offers tastefully furnished, spacious rooms with fine beds and compact bathrooms with showers and tubs. Many rooms have private balconies, and each has shuttered windows. Some units have air-conditioning, while others have TVs. There's a tranquil garden on the premises.

959 bd. de la Garoupe, Cap d'Antibes 06160. ✆ **04-93-61-36-51.** Fax 04-93-67-74-88. www.castel-garoupe.com. 28 units. 125€–155€ ($163–$202) double; 155€–276€ ($202–$359) studio apt with kitchenette. AE, MC, V. Closed Nov to mid-Mar. Bus: A2. **Amenities:** 2 bars; outdoor pool; exercise room; room service; babysitting; laundry service; dry cleaning; nonsmoking rooms. *In room:* Dataport, kitchenette, minibar, hair dryer, safe.

Villa Val des Roses ★ *Finds* Two Flemish brothers, Frederik and Filip Vanderhoeven, have created a relaxed place to stay only a minute's walk from the sea with a sandy beach, and just a 10-minute trek from the historic old town. The whitewashed Art Deco villa, a boutique alternative to the larger, grander hotels in the area, is built in the colonial style with such extras as an outdoor pool with a large terrace set against a backdrop of century-old palm trees. There is a light, contemporary feeling to the decor, and each of the accommodations is individually decorated, often in soft, creamy tones; natural wood furnishings are placed throughout. Each accommodation comes with a private terrace or balcony, and there are often marble pillars and views from the modern bathrooms. The hotel opens onto a small alleyway, away from the noise of the boulevards of Antibes. Fish barbecue is served at the hotel's restaurant.

6 chemin des Lauriers, Cap d'Antibes 06160. ✆ **06-85-06-06-29.** Fax 04-92-93-97-24. 7 units. 150€–210€ ($195–$273) double. Rates include continental breakfast. MC, V. Parking 12€ ($16). **Amenities:** Restaurant; outdoor pool; tennis court; nonsmoking rooms; limited-mobility rooms. *In room:* A/C, TV, fridge, safe.

INEXPENSIVE

Hôtel Beau Site This white stucco villa with a tile roof and heavy shutters is surrounded by eucalyptus trees, pines, and palms. Located off the main road, a 7-minute walk from the beach, it has a low wall of flower turns and wrought-iron gates. The interior is like a country inn, with oak beams and antiques. The guest rooms are comfortable and well maintained, and bathrooms are small.

141 bd. J.-F.-Kennedy, Cap d'Antibes 06150. ✆ **04-93-61-53-43.** Fax 04-93-67-78-16. www.hotelbeausite.net. 30 units. 79€–144€ ($103–$187) double. AE, DC, MC, V. Bus: A2. Closed Oct 21–Mar 10. **Amenities:** Bar; pool; room service; babysitting; laundry service; dry cleaning. *In room:* A/C, TV, hair dryer.

WHERE TO DINE

The Zelda and Scott Fitzgerald of today head for the **Eden Roc Restaurant** at the Hôtel du Cap–Eden Roc for grand service and grand cuisine. The dining room at the **Hôtel Impérial Garoupe** (see "Where to Stay," above) is also open to the public.

La Taverne du Saffranier *Value* PROVENÇAL Earthy and irreverent, this brasserie in a century-old building serves a changing roster of savory local specialties. Portions are generous. Examples are a platter of *petits farcis* (stuffed vegetables); a mini-bouillabaisse for single diners; savory fish soup; and an assortment of grilled fish (including sardines) that's served only with a dash of fresh lemon.

Place du Saffranier. ✆ **04-93-34-80-50.** Reservations recommended. Main courses 15€–30€ ($20–$39); fixed-price lunch 14€ ($18). No credit cards. Feb–Mar Tues–Sun noon–2:30pm, Thurs–Sat 7–10:30pm; Apr–May and Oct–Dec Tues–Sun noon–2:30pm, Tues–Sat 7–10:30pm; June–Sept daily noon–2:30pm and 7–10:30pm. Closed Jan.

Le Vieux Murs FRENCH/SEAFOOD This charming Provençal tavern is inside the 17th-century ramparts that used to fortify the old seaport, not far from the Musée Picasso. White paint complements soaring stone vaults, and a glassed-in front terrace overlooks the water. The owner, Philippe Bensimon, and his chef, Thierry Gratarolla, run a warm, welcoming place. They use market-fresh ingredients, especially seafood, which is prepared with flavor and served with style. Daily offerings depend on what's best at the market. Lusty Provençal meat and poultry dishes are menu staples.

Promenade de l'Amiral-de-Grasse. ✆ **04-93-34-06-73.** Reservations recommended. Main courses 20€–35€ ($26–$46); fixed-price menu 42€–70€ ($55–$91). AE, DC, MC, V. Apr–Oct daily noon–2:30pm and 7:30–10:30pm; Nov–Mar Wed–Sun noon–2:30pm, Tues–Sun 7:30–10:30pm.

Restaurant de Bacon ★★★ SEAFOOD The Eden Roc restaurant at the Hôtel du Cap is more elegant, but Bacon serves the best seafood around. Surrounded by ultraexpensive residences, this restaurant on a rocky peninsula offers a panoramic coast view. Bouillabaisse aficionados claim that Bacon offers the best in France. In its deluxe version, saltwater crayfish float atop the savory brew; we prefer the simple version—a waiter adds the finishing touches at your table. If bouillabaisse isn't to your liking, try fish soup with garlic-laden rouille sauce; fish terrine; sea bass; John Dory; or something from a collection of fish unknown in North America, for example, sar, pageot, or denti.

Bd. de Bacon. ✆ **04-93-61-50-02.** Reservations required. Main courses 19€–130€ ($25–$169); fixed-price menu 49€–79€ ($64–$103). AE, DC, MC, V. Wed–Sun noon–2pm; Tues–Sun 8–10pm. Closed Oct to mid-Feb.

10 Cagnes-sur-Mer ★

918km (570 miles) S of Paris, 21km (13 miles) NE of Cannes

Cagnes-sur-Mer, like the Roman god Janus, has two faces. Perched on a hill in the "hinterlands" of Nice, **Haut-de-Cagnes** is one of the most charming spots on the Riviera. At the foot of the hill is an old fishing port and rapidly developing beach resort, **Cros-de-Cagnes,** which lies between Nice and Antibes.

For years Haut-de-Cagnes attracted the French literati, including Simone de Beauvoir, who wrote *Les Mandarins* here. A colony of painters also settled here; Renoir said the village was "the place where I want to paint until the last day of my life." The racecourse is one of the finest in France.

ESSENTIALS

GETTING THERE The **train** depot, Gare SNCF, lies in Cagnes-Ville (the more commercial part of town) at avenue de la Gare. It serves trains that run along the Mediterranean coast, with arrivals every hour from both Nice (trip time: 13 min.; one-way fare 2.50€/$3.25) and Cannes (trip time: 23 min.; 3.85€/$5). For rail information, call ✆ **08-92-35-35-35,** or visit www.voyages-sncf.com. **Buses** from Nice and Cannes stop at Cagnes-Ville and at Béal/Les Collettes, within walking distance of Cros-de-Cagnes. For information, call **The Société de Transports de Cagnes** (✆ **04-93-20-45-05**). The climb from Cagnes-Ville to Haut-de-Cagnes is strenuous; a free minibus runs daily about every 30 minutes year-round from place du Général-de-Gaulle in the center of Cagnes-Ville to Haut-de-Cagnes. By **car** from any of the coastal cities of Provence, follow the A8 coastal highway, exiting at CAGNES-SUR-MER/CROS-DE-CAGNES.

VISITOR INFORMATION The **Office de Tourisme** is at 6 bd. Maréchal-Juin, Cagnes-Ville (✆ **04-93-20-61-64;** fax 04-93-20-52-63; www.cagnes-tourisme.com).

SPECIAL EVENTS Cagnes is the site, for 2 days every August, of a **Medieval Festival *(La Fête Médiévale de Cagnes)*** that dominates the medieval core of Haut-de-Cagnes. Highlights include equestrian tournaments, jousting exhibitions, and knights, knaves, and damsels in medieval costumes. Tickets to the individual festival events sell for between 5.50€ to 14€ ($7.15–$18) each, and, along with festival information, are available at the local tourist office.

EXPLORING THE TOWN

Cros-de-Cagnes, a part of Cagnes-Sur-Mer, is known for its 4km (2½ miles) of seafront, covered with light-gray pebbles smoothed by centuries of wave action. These beaches are **Plages de Cros-de-Cagnes.** As usual, toplessness is accepted but full nudity isn't.

At least five concessions along this expanse rent beach mattresses and chaises for 15€ ($20). The most centrally located are **Tiercé Plage** (**✆ 04-93-20-13-89**), **Le Cigalon** (**✆ 04-93-07-74-82**), **La Gougouline** (**✆ 04-93-31-08-72**), and **Le Neptune** (**✆ 04-93-20-10-59**).

The orange groves and fields of carnations of the upper village provide a beautiful setting for the narrow cobblestone streets and 17th- and 18th-century homes. Drive to the top, where you can enjoy the view from **place du Château** and have lunch or a drink at a sidewalk cafe.

Château-Musée Grimaldi (Musée de l'Olivier & Musée d'Art Moderne Méditerranéen) ★ The Château-Musée was a fortress built in 1301 by Rainier Grimaldi I, a lord of Monaco and a French admiral (his portrait is in the museum). Charts illustrate how the defenses were organized. In the early 17th century, the castle was converted into a gracious Louis XIII château, which now contains two museums. The Museum of the Olive Tree shows the steps involved in cultivating and processing the olive. The Museum of Mediterranean Modern Art displays works by Kisling, Carzou, Dufy, Cocteau, and Seyssaud, among others, and temporary exhibits. In one salon is an interesting trompe l'oeil fresco, *La Chute de Phaeton.* The tower affords a view of the Côte d'Azur.

7 place Grimaldi. **✆ 04-92-02-47-30.** Admission to both museums 3€ ($3.90) adults, 1.50€ ($1.95) students, free for children under 18. May–Sept Wed–Mon 10am–noon and 2–6pm; Oct–Apr Wed–Mon 10am–noon and 2–5pm.

Musée Renoir & Les Collettes ★ Les Collettes has been restored to its appearance when Renoir lived here, from 1908 until his death in 1919. He continued to sculpt here, even though he was crippled by arthritis. He also continued to paint, with a brush tied to his hand and the help of assistants.

The house was built in 1907 in an olive and orange grove. There's a bust of Mme Renoir in the entrance room. You can explore the drawing room and dining room on your own before going up to the artist's bedroom. In his atelier are his wheelchair, easel, and brushes. The terrace of Mme Renoir's bedroom faces a stunning view of Cap d'Antibes and Haut-de-Cagnes. On a wall hangs a photograph of one of Renoir's sons, Pierre, as he appeared in the 1932 film *Madame Bovary.* Although Renoir is best remembered for his paintings, in Cagnes he began experimenting with sculpture. The museum has 20 portrait busts and portrait medallions, most of which depict his wife and children. The curators say they represent the largest collection of Renoir sculpture in the world.

19 chemin des Collettes. **✆ 04-93-20-61-07.** Admission 3€ ($3.90) adults, 1.50€ ($1.95) children 12–18, free for children under 12. May–Sept Wed–Mon 10am–noon and 2–6pm; Oct–Apr Wed–Mon 10am–noon and 2–5pm. Ticket sales end 30 min. before lunch and evening closing hours.

SHOPPING

Terraïo, 12 place du Dr.-Maurel, Haut-de-Cagnes (✆ **04-93-20-86-83**), is a tiny gem. Art critics claim the stoneware in this shop captures the celadon and turquoise tones of the nearby Mediterranean. Artist, owner, and native son Claude Barnoin has spent nearly 25 years perfecting the mixture of copper-based glazes that produce these tones. The ashtrays, dinner services, and showcase pieces produced in the artist's studio (which you cannot visit) are the pride of many French and U.S. collections. Prices run from around 10€ ($13) for a simple ashtray to as much as 550€ ($715) for something spectacular. The shop, which lies just across the square from the Château-Musée Grimaldi, is open daily from 2 to around 6pm, except in midsummer, when it may close for an occasional day.

WHERE TO STAY

IN CAGNES-SUR-MER

Hôtel Le Chantilly *Value* This is the best bargain for those who prefer to stay near the beach. Built in a boxy and angular style in 1960, the hotel's landscaping and homey interior, with Oriental rugs and potted plants, make this place as inviting as possible. Most rooms are small but cozily furnished and well kept, often opening onto balconies; each has a compact tiled bathroom with shower. In fair weather you can enjoy breakfast, the only meal served, on an outdoor terrace.

31 chemin de la Minoterie, Cagnes-sur-Mer 06800. ✆ **04-93-20-25-50.** Fax 04-92-02-82-63. www.ch-demeures.com/chantilly. 20 units. 66€–72€ ($86–$94) double; 75€–107€ ($98–$139) suite. AE, DC, MC, V. Parking 6€ ($7.80). **Amenities:** Room service; babysitting; nonsmoking rooms. *In room:* TV, minibar.

IN HAUT-DE-CAGNES

Le Cagnard ★★★ Several 13th-century houses were joined in the 1960s to form this glamorous Relais & Châteaux property. The dining room is covered with frescoes, and there's a vine-draped terrace. The rooms and salons are furnished with antiques such as provincial chests, armoires, and Louis XV chairs. Each room has its own style: Some are duplexes, others have terraces and views of the countryside. The luxurious bathrooms are spacious, with tub/shower combinations.

The cuisine of chef Jean-Yves Johany has been awarded a Michelin star and is reason enough to make the trip. Fresh ingredients go into delectable dishes. Fixed-price menus cost 48€ to 85€ ($62–$111) at lunch and 70€ to 110€ ($91–$143) at dinner. The hotel is open year-round; the restaurant closes from November to December 15 and on Monday, Tuesday, and Thursday at lunch.

Rue du Pontis-Long, Le Haut-de-Cagnes, Cagnes-sur-Mer 06800. ✆ **04-93-20-73-21.** Fax 04-93-22-06-39. www.le-cagnard.com. 25 units. 150€–270€ ($195–$351) double; 180€–485€ ($234–$631) suite. AE, DC, MC, V. Parking 8€ ($10). **Amenities:** Restaurant; bar; room service; babysitting; laundry service; dry cleaning; nonsmoking rooms. *In room:* A/C, TV, minibar, hair dryer, iron, safe.

WHERE TO DINE

In Haut-de-Cagnes, the hotel **Le Cagnard** (see "Where to Stay," above) has a remarkable restaurant.

IN HAUT-DE-CAGNES

Fleur de Sel FRENCH/PROVENÇAL Energetic owners Philippe and Pascale Loose run this charming restaurant in a 200-year-old stone-sided house in the center of the village. In two ocher-toned dining rooms outfitted with Provençal furniture and oil paintings, you'll enjoy the kind of cuisine that Philippe learned during stints at some of the grandest restaurants of France, including a brief time with Marc Meneau at L'Espérance in Vézelay. Tasty recommendations include foie gras with artichoke hearts in puff pastry; cappuccino of crayfish with paprika and pistachios; scallops braised with spinach; and filet of beef braised in a hearty local red wine, Bellet.

85 Montée de la Bourgade. ✆ **04-93-20-33-33.** Reservations recommended. Main courses 16€–36€ ($21–$47); fixed-price menu 23€–40€ ($30–$52). MC, V. Fri–Tues noon–2pm; Thurs–Tues 7:30–10pm.

Josy-Jo ★★ TRADITIONAL FRENCH Le Cagnard (see "Where to Stay," above) has a more elegant setting, but the food here is comparable. Behind a 200-year-old facade covered with vines and flowers, this Michelin star-rated restaurant was the home and studio of Modigliani and Soutine during their hungriest years. Paintings cover the walls, and the Bandecchi family runs everything smoothly. The menu features grilled meats and a variety of fish. You can enjoy brochette of gigot of lamb with kidneys; calves' liver; homemade terrine of foie gras of duckling; stuffed Provençal vegetables; and an array of salads.

8 place du Planastel. ✆ **04-93-20-68-76.** Reservations required. Main courses 9€–32€ ($12–$42). AE, MC, V. Mon–Fri 12:30–2pm; Mon–Sat 7:30–9:30pm. Closed Nov 19–Dec 22.

IN CROS-DE-CAGNES

Loulou (La Réserve) ★★ FRENCH This restaurant, which like Josy-Jo and Cagnard has a Michelin star, makes the Cagnes area a gourmet enclave. It's across the boulevard from the sea and named for a famous long-departed chef. Brothers Eric and Joseph Campo prepare spectacular versions of fish soup; shrimp steamed and served with fresh ginger and cinnamon; and grilled versions of the catch of the day. These dishes are served as simply as possible, usually with just a drizzling of olive oil and balsamic vinegar. Meat dishes include flavorful veal kidneys with port sauce, and delectable grilled steaks, chops, and cutlets. Dessert may include caramelized-apple tart. The glassed-in veranda in front is a prime people-watching spot.

91 bd. de la Plage. ✆ **04-93-31-00-17.** Reservations recommended. Main courses 23€–84€ ($30–$109); fixed-price menu 39€ ($51). AE, MC, V. Mon–Fri noon–1:30pm and 7:30–9:30pm; Sat 7–9:30pm.

11 St-Paul-de-Vence ★★

926km (575 miles) S of Paris, 23km (14 miles) E of Grasse, 28km (17 miles) E of Cannes, 31km (19 miles) N of Nice

Of all the cliff-side villages of the Riviera, St-Paul-de-Vence is the best known. It gained popularity in the 1920s, when many artists lived here, occupying the 16th-century houses that flank the cobblestone streets. Its ramparts (allow about 30 min. to circle them) overlook flowers and olive and orange trees. They haven't changed much since they were constructed from 1537 to 1547 by order of François I. From the north ramparts you can look out on Baou de St-Jeannet, a sphinx-shaped rock that was painted into the landscape of Poussin's *Polyphème.*

ESSENTIALS

GETTING THERE The nearest **rail** station is in Cagnes-sur-Mer. Some 20 **buses** per day leave from Nice's Gare Routière, dropping passengers off in St-Paul-de-Vence (one-way fare: 4.30€/$5.60), then in Vence. For information, call the **Compagnie SAP** (✆ **04-93-58-37-60**). If you're **driving** from Nice, take the coastal A8 highway east, turn inland at Cagnes-sur-Mer, and follow signs north to St-Paul-de-Vence.

VISITOR INFORMATION The **Office de Tourisme** is at 2 rue Grande (✆ **04-93-32-86-95;** fax 04-93-32-60-27; www.saint-pauldevence.com).

EXPLORING THE TOWN

Note: Driving a car in St-Paul's old town is prohibited, except to drop off luggage at your hotel.

The local tourist office, if you phone at least a day (and sometimes a few hours) in advance, can arrange any of several distinctly themed walking tours of the town's historic core, as well as to some of the town's outskirts. Most tours last for about an hour and are priced at 9€ ($12) each; all of them depart from the tourist office. Depending on your interests, tours may highlight the city's history and architecture, the artists who lived here and the works they created, even the lessons and lore of the French pastime of *pétanques* (also known as *boules*), wherein a practice session with seasoned locals is included as part of the experience. We advise you to approach the experience with an open mind, and to accept substitute tours if the one stressing your particular area of interest is not available during your time in St-Paul. For more information and reservations, contact the local tourist office (see "Visitor Information," above).

The pedestrian-only **rue Grande** is the most evocative street, running the length of St-Paul. Most of the stone houses along it are from the 16th and 17th centuries, and many still bear the coats of arms placed there by the original builders. Today, most of the houses are antiques shops, arts-and-crafts galleries, and souvenir and gift shops; some are still artists' studios.

The village's chief sight is the **Collégiale de la Conversion de St-Paul** ★, constructed in the 12th and 13th centuries and much altered over the years. The Romanesque choir is the oldest part, containing some remarkable stalls carved in walnut in the 17th century. The bell tower was built in 1740. Look to the left as you enter: You'll see the painting *Ste-Cathérine d'Alexandrie,* which has been attributed to Tintoretto. The **Trésor de l'Eglise** is one of the most beautiful in the Alpes-Maritimes, with a spectacular ciborium. Look also for a low relief of the *Martyrdom of St-Clément* on the last altar on the right. In the baptismal chapter is a 15th-century alabaster Madonna. It's open daily 9am to 6pm (to 7pm July–Aug). Admission is free.

Near the church is the **Musée d'Histoire de St-Paul,** place de l'Eglise (**© 04-93-32-41-13**), a museum in a village house that dates to the 1500s. It was restored and refurnished in 16th-century style, with artifacts illustrating the history of the village. It's open daily 10am to 12:30pm and 1:30 to 5:30pm. Admission is 3.40€ ($4.40) adults, 2.10€ ($2.75) students and children 5 to 18, and free for children under 5.

Foundation Maeght ★★★ This avant-garde building houses one of the most modern art museums in Europe. On a hill in pine-studded woods, the Foundation Maeght is like Shangri-La. Nature and the creations of men and women blend harmoniously in this unique achievement of the architect José Luis Sert. Its white concrete arcs give the impression of a giant pagoda.

A stark Calder rises like some futuristic monster on the lawn. In a courtyard, the bronze works of Giacometti, marble statues by Miró, and mosaics by Chagall form a surrealistic garden. Sculpture is displayed inside, but the museum is at its best in a natural setting of terraces and gardens. It's built on several levels, its many glass walls providing an indoor-outdoor vista. The foundation, a gift "to the people" from Aimé and Marguerite Maeght, also provides a showcase for new talent. On the property are a library, a cinema, and a cafeteria. In one showroom you can buy original lithographs by artists such as Chagall and Giacometti, and limited-edition prints.

Outside the town walls. ✆ **04-93-32-81-63.** www.maeght.com. Admission 12€ ($16) adults, 7.50€ ($9.75) students and ages 10–18, free for children under 10. July–Oct daily 10am–7pm; Nov–June daily 10am–12:30pm and 2:30–6pm.

WHERE TO STAY

La Colombe d'Or rents deluxe rooms (see "Where to Dine," below).

VERY EXPENSIVE

Le Mas d'Artigny ★★★ This hotel, one of the Riviera's grandest, evokes a sprawling Provençal homestead set in an acre of pine forests. In the lobby is a constantly changing art exhibit. Each of the comfortably large rooms has its own terrace or balcony, and suites have a private pool with hedges. Bathrooms are deluxe, with tub/shower combinations. The swimming situation is remarkable—guests in the 60 conventional rooms share a large pool, each of the suites has its own 2×6m (6½×20-ft.) pool, and each of the four villas has an even bigger pool. The restaurant has magnificent views of the sea. It employs the flavors of Provence in its French, international, and Provençal specialties, using quality ingredients to shape its harmonious cuisine. The wine cellar deserves a star for its vintage collection, but watch those prices.

Rte. des Salettes, La Colle sur Loup 06480. From the town center, follow signs west about 2km (1¼ miles). ✆ **04-93-32-84-54.** Fax 04-93-32-95-36. www.mas-artigny.com. 85 units. 150€–450€ ($195–$585) double; 670€–1,400€ ($871–$1,820) suite. Off-season discounts (about 30%) available. AE, DC, MC, V. **Amenities:** Restaurant; bar; 27 outdoor pools; tennis court; exercise room; sauna; mountain bikes; room service; babysitting; laundry service; dry cleaning. *In room:* A/C, TV, minibar, hair dryer.

EXPENSIVE

Hôtel Le St-Paul ★★★ Converted from a 16th-century Renaissance residence and retaining many original features, this Relais & Châteaux member is in the heart of the village. The guest rooms, decorated in sophisticated Provençal style, have sumptuous beds and midsize bathrooms with tub/shower combinations. Sitting on the balcony of room no. 30 will help you understood why Renoir, Léger, Matisse, and Picasso were inspired by Provence. Many rooms enjoy a view of the valley with the Mediterranean in the distance. The restaurant has a flower-bedecked terrace sheltered by 16th-century ramparts and a superb dining room with vaulted ceilings.

86 rue Grande, St-Paul-de-Vence 06570. ✆ **04-93-32-65-25.** Fax 04-93-32-52-94. www.lesaintpaul.com. 19 units. 210€–425€ ($273–$553) double; 440€–600€ ($572–$780) suite. AE, DC, MC, V. Closed Dec to mid-Jan. **Amenities:** Restaurant; bar; 3 tennis courts; room service; babysitting; laundry service; limited-mobility rooms. *In room:* A/C, TV, minibar, hair dryer, safe, Wi-Fi.

MODERATE

Auberge Le Hameau ★ *Value* This romantic Mediterranean villa is on a hilltop on the outskirts of St-Paul-de-Vence, on the road to Colle at Hauts-de-St-Paul. Built as a farmhouse in the 1920s and enlarged and transformed into a hotel in 1967, it contains high-ceilinged rooms, each with a compact tub/shower bathroom. You'll have a remarkable view of the surrounding hills and valleys. There are also a vineyard and a sunny terrace with fruit trees, flowers, and a pool.

528 rte. de la Colle (D107), St-Paul-de-Vence 06570. From the town, take D107 about 1km (⅔ mile), following the signs south of town toward Colle. ✆ **04-93-32-80-24.** Fax 04-93-32-55-75. www.le-hameau.com. 17 units. 110€–170€ ($143–$221) double; from 170€ ($221) suite. MC, V. Closed Nov 15–Feb 15. **Amenities:** Bar; outdoor pool; laundry service. *In room:* A/C, TV, hair dryer, safe.

Auberge Les Orangers ★ *Finds* M. Franklin has created a "living oasis" in his villa, which is configured like a highly personalized bed-and-breakfast. The scents of rose, orange, and lemon waft through the air. The main lounge is decorated with original oils and furnished in a provincial style. Expect to be treated like a guest in a private home. The rooms, with antiques and Oriental carpets, have panoramic views; the small bathrooms have tub/shower combinations. Banana trees and climbing geraniums surround the sun terrace.

Quartier les Fumerates, rte. de la Colle (D107), St-Paul-de-Vence 06570. From the town center, follow the signs to Cagnes-sur-Mer for 1km (⅔ mile) south. ✆ **04-93-32-80-95.** Fax 04-93-32-00-32. www.stpaulweb.com/hlo. 10 units. 120€–140€ ($156–$182) double; 160€ ($208) suite. Rates include breakfast. MC, V. Free parking. **Amenities:** Room service; laundry service; babysitting. *In room:* Hair dryer.

Les Bastides St-Paul This hotel is in the hills outside town, 1.5km (1 mile) south of St-Paul and 4km (2½ miles) south of Vence. Spread over two buildings, it offers comfortable carpeted rooms, each accented with regional artifacts and opening onto a terrace and garden. The compact bathrooms hold tub/shower combinations. On the premises is a cloverleaf-shaped pool. Longtime hoteliers Marie José and Maurice Giraudet head the responsive management staff. Breakfast is served anytime you want it.

880 rte. des Blaquières (rte. Cagnes-Vence), St-Paul-de-Vence 06570. From the town center, follow signs toward Cagnes-sur-Mer for 1.5km (1 mile) south. ✆ **04-92-02-08-07.** Fax 04-93-20-50-41. 20 units. 84€–125€ ($109–$163) double. AE, DC, MC, V. **Amenities:** Outdoor pool; room service; babysitting; nonsmoking rooms; limited-mobility rooms. *In room:* A/C, TV, minibar, safe.

WHERE TO DINE

The dining room at the **Hôtel Le St-Paul** features exceptional cuisine based on market-fresh ingredients. For more deluxe dining, consider the restaurant at **Le Mas d'Artigny.** See "Where to Stay," above.

La Colombe d'Or ★ PROVENÇAL For more than a decade, "The Golden Dove" has been St-Paul's most celebrated restaurant—not for cutting-edge cuisine or exotic experiments, but for its remarkable art collection. You can dine amid Mirós, Picassos, Klees, Dufys, Utrillos, and Calders. In fair weather everyone tries for a seat on the terrace. You may begin with smoked salmon or foie gras from Landes if you've recently won at the casino. If not, you can count on a soup made with fresh seasonal vegetables. The best fish dishes are poached sea bass with mousseline sauce, and sea wolf baked with fennel. Tender beef comes with *gratin dauphinois* (potatoes), or you may prefer lamb from Sisteron. A classic finish to any meal is a *soufflé flambé au Grand-Marnier.*

The guest rooms (16 doubles, 10 suites) contain French antiques and Provençal accessories. They're in the original 16th-century stone house and in two wings added in the 1950s, one of which stretches into the garden next to the pool. Some units have exposed stone and ceiling beams; all are comfortable, with air-conditioning, minibars, and TVs. Prices are 220€ to 320€ ($286–$416) for a double, 320€ ($416) for a suite.

1 place du Général-de-Gaulle, St-Paul-de-Vence 06570. ✆ **04-93-32-80-02.** Fax 04-93-32-77-78. www.la-colombe-dor.com. Reservations required. Main courses 14€–42€ ($18–$55). AE, DC, MC, V. Daily noon–2pm and 7:30–10pm. Closed Nov–Dec and Jan 10–20.

12 Vence ★

926km (575 miles) S of Paris, 31km (19 miles) N of Cannes, 24km (15 miles) NW of Nice

Travel into the hills northwest of Nice—across country studded with cypresses, olive trees, and pines, where carnations, roses, oleanders, and other flowers grow in profusion—and Vence comes into view. Outside the town, along boulevard Paul-André, two olive presses carry on their age-old duties. The attraction here is the **Vieille Ville** (old town). Visitors pose for photographs on place du Peyra in front of the **Vieille Fontaine** (old fountain), a feature in several films. The 15th-century square tower is also a curiosity.

If you're wearing sturdy shoes, the narrow, steep streets of the old town are worth exploring. Dating from the 10th century, the cathedral on place Godeau is unremarkable except for some 15th-century Gothic choir stalls. But if it's the right day of the week, most visitors quickly pass through the narrow gates of this once-fortified walled town to see one of Matisse's most remarkable achievements, the Chapelle du Rosaire.

ESSENTIALS

GETTING THERE Frequent **buses** (no. 400 or 94) originating in Nice take 45 minutes to reach Vence; the one-way fare is 1.30€ ($1.70). For information, contact the **Compagnie SAP** (✆ **04-93-80-09-38**). The nearest **rail** station is in Cagnes-sur-Mer, about 10km (6¼ miles) southwest from Vence. From there, about 20 buses per day priced at 1.30€ ($1.70) make the trip to Vence. For train information, call ✆ **08-92-35-35-35,** or visit www.voyages-sncf.com. To **drive** to Vence from Nice, take N7 west to Cagnes-sur-Mer, and then D236 north to Vence.

VISITOR INFORMATION The **Office de Tourisme** is on place Grand-Jardin (✆ **04-93-58-06-38;** fax 04-93-58-91-81; www.ville-vence.fr).

A MATISSE MASTERPIECE

Chapelle du Rosaire ★★ It was a beautiful golden autumn along the Côte d'Azur. The great Henri Matisse was 77, and after a turbulent time he set out to design and decorate his masterpiece—"the culmination of a whole life dedicated to the search for truth," he said. Outside Vence, Matisse created the Chapelle du Rosaire for the Dominican nuns of Monteils. (Sister Jacques-Marie, a member of the order, had nursed him back to health after a serious illness.) From the front you might find it unremarkable and pass it by—until you spot a 12m (39-ft.) crescent-adorned cross rising from a blue-tile roof.

Matisse wrote: "What I have done in the chapel is to create a religious space . . . in an enclosed area of very reduced proportions and to give it, solely by the play of colors and lines, the dimensions of infinity." The light picks up the subtle coloring in the simply rendered leaf forms and abstract patterns: sapphire blue, aquamarine, and lemon yellow. In black-and-white ceramics, St. Dominic is depicted in only a few lines. The most remarkable design is in the black-and-white-tile Stations of the Cross, with Matisse's self-styled "tormented and passionate" figures. The bishop of Nice came to bless the chapel in the late spring of 1951 when the artist's work was completed. Matisse died 3 years later.

The price of admission includes entrance to **L'Espace Matisse,** a gallery devoted to the documentation of the chapel's design and construction from 1949 to 1951. It also contains lithographs and religious artifacts that concerned Matisse.

Av. Henri-Matisse. ✆ **04-93-58-03-26.** Admission 3€ ($3.90) adults, free for children under 12; contributions to maintain the chapel are welcome. Dec 16–Nov 14 Tues and Thurs 10–11:30am; Mon–Thurs and Sat 2–5:30pm. Sun Mass 10am, followed by visit at 10:45am. Closed Nov.

WHERE TO STAY

VERY EXPENSIVE

Le Château du Domaine St-Martin ★★★ If you're heading into the hill towns above Nice and you seek luxury and refinement, this is your address. The château, in

Fun Fact **A Goat of Note**

Le Château du Domaine St-Martin stands on the site of an ancient fortress belonging to the Knights Templars. Local legend has it that this is where the knights buried a store of treasure, including *la chèvre d'or*—a large goat made of solid gold.

a 14-hectare (36-acre) park with terraced gardens, was built in 1936 on the grounds where the "Golden Goat" treasure was reputedly buried. The main building holds the standard units; suites are in the tile-roofed villas. You can walk through the gardens on winding paths lined with tall cypresses, past the chapel ruins and olive trees. The spacious rooms are distinctively decorated, and the large rose-colored bathrooms have tub/shower combinations. The luxurious restaurant has a view of the coast and offers superb French cuisine. In summer, many guests prefer the poolside grill.

Av. des Templiers B.P. 102, Vence 06142. From the town center, follow signs toward Coursegoules and Col-de-Vence for 1.5km (1 mile) north. ✆ **04-93-58-02-02.** Fax 04-93-24-08-91. www.chateau-st-martin.com. 39 units, 6 villas. 350€–825€ ($455–$1,073) double; 735€–1,640€ ($956–$2,132) suite. AE, DC, MC, V. Closed mid-Oct to mid-Mar. **Amenities:** Restaurant; bar; outdoor pool; 2 tennis courts; salon; room service; massage; babysitting; laundry service; dry cleaning; limited-mobility rooms. *In room:* A/C, TV, hair dryer, safe, Wi-Fi.

EXPENSIVE

Hôtel Cantemerle ★ One of the most appealing places in Vence is this artfully designed cluster that resembles an old-fashioned compound of Provençal buildings. Capped with rounded terra-cotta roof tiles, they stand on a lawn dotted with old trees, surrounding a pool. Public areas, stylishly outfitted with Art Deco furniture and accessories, include a paneled bar and a sun-flooded flagstone terrace where meals are served. Rooms aren't overly large but contain unusual reproductions of overscale Art Deco armchairs, louvered wooden closet doors, and balcony-style sleeping lofts with comfortable beds. Most of the good-size bathrooms hold a combination tub/shower. The restaurant serves worthwhile regional and mainstream French cuisine.

258 chemin Cantemerle, Vence 06140. ✆ **04-93-58-08-18.** Fax 04-93-58-32-89. www.relais-cantemerle.com. 28 units. 190€–215€ ($247–$280) double; 50€ ($65) extra bed. Half board 60€ ($78). AE, MC, V. Closed late Oct to mid-Mar. **Amenities:** Restaurant; bar; indoor pool; outdoor pool; gym; sauna; room service; babysitting; laundry service; dry cleaning; 2 limited-mobility rooms. *In room:* A/C, TV, minibar, hair dryer, safe, Wi-Fi.

MODERATE

La Maison du Frêne ★ *Finds* In the heart of Vence, this Provençal guesthouse, now an elegant retreat, was once a private home in the 18th century. Vence has far more lavish and luxurious retreats, but none with this snug, cozy comfort—and at an affordable price. It is an inn collector's gem. Bedrooms are midsize to spacious, and both beautifully and comfortably furnished. An old ash tree planted in front of the house during the reign of François I and the manse itself have been the subject of countless paintings. The original architecture has been preserved, although all the modern comforts have been added. Such men as Matisse, Chagall, Dufy, or Dubuffet have passed by the door or else dropped in. The reception area contains original sculptures and modern paintings, and it's linked to the country kitchen where delicious homemade breakfasts are prepared. Of all the rooms, we prefer the junior suite on the highest level with its sloping ceiling. From the balcony of the bathroom you can look out upon the Matisse Chapel.

1 place du Frêne, Vence 06140. ✆ **06-88-90-49-69.** Fax 04-93-24-37-83. www.lamaisondufrene.com. 4 units. 125€–140€ ($163–$182). No credit cards. Parking 7€ ($9.10). **Amenities:** Nonsmoking rooms. Dinner upon request in winter. *In room:* TV on request, beverage maker, safe.

Le Floréal On the road to Grasse is this pleasant, comfortable hotel with a view of the mountains and a refreshing lack of pretension. Many of the well-furnished rooms look out into the garden, where orange trees and mimosa add fragrance to the breezes. Most accommodations are medium-size, and each is comfortable, with quality mattresses and fine linen. Bathrooms are compact and tiled.

440 av. Rhin-et-Danube, Vence 06140. ✆ **04-93-58-64-40.** Fax 04-93-58-79-69. www.bestwestern.fr. 42 units. 50€–205€ ($65–$267) double. AE, DC, MC, V. Free parking. **Amenities:** Restaurant; bar; pool; sauna; room service; babysitting; laundry service; dry cleaning. *In room:* A/C, TV, hair dryer.

INEXPENSIVE

Auberge des Seigneurs ★ This 400-year-old stone hotel gives you a taste of old Provence. Decorative objects and antiques are everywhere. The guest rooms are well maintained, but the management dedicates its energy to the restaurant. Nevertheless, the Provençal-style rooms are comfortable, with lots of exposed paneling and beams. Two have nonworking fireplaces. The small, tiled bathrooms contain showers. The restaurant is in a stone building that used to be the kitchen of the Château de Villeneuve, where François I spent part of his youth. The specialty is grills prepared on the open spit in view of the dining room, which holds a long wooden table and an open fireplace with a row of hanging copper pots and pans. Fixed-price menus range from 31€ to 35€ ($40–$46).

Place du Frêne, Vence 06140. ✆ **04-93-58-04-24.** Fax 04-93-24-08-01. 6 units. 80€–95€ ($104–$124) double. DC, MC, V. Closed Nov–Mar 15. **Amenities:** Restaurant; bar; room service; nonsmoking rooms. *In room:* Hair dryer, Wi-Fi.

WHERE TO DINE

Auberge des Seigneurs, Hôtel Cantemerle, and **Le Château du Domaine St-Martin** (see "Where to Stay," above) offer excellent dining.

La Farigoule PROVENÇAL In a century-old house that opens onto a rose garden, this restaurant specializes in Provençal cuisine. Menu items are conservative but flavorful: They include *bourride Provençale* (bouillabaisse with a dollop of cream and lots of garlic); shoulder of roasted lamb with a ragout of fresh vegetables, served with fresh thyme; and such fish dishes as dorado with comfit of lemons and fresh, aromatic coriander. In the summer, you can dine in the rose garden.

15 rue Henri-Isnard. ✆ **04-93-58-01-27.** Reservations recommended. Main courses 14€–25€ ($18–$33); fixed-price dinner 22€–40€ ($29–$52). MC, V. Thurs–Mon noon–2pm and 7:30–10pm. Closed Dec 7–Jan 7.

La Table d'Amis Jacques Maximin ★★★ MODERN FRENCH This deluxe dining room is justly hailed as one of the Riviera's grandest restaurants. The setting is an artfully rustic 19th-century manor house that was transformed in the mid-1980s into the private home of culinary superstar Jacques Maximin. Today, it's the target of pilgrimages by foodies and movie stars venturing north from the Cannes Film Festival, including Hugh Grant, Elizabeth Hurley, and Robert De Niro. You can sample a menu devoted to the seasonal produce of the surrounding countryside. Stellar examples are salads made with asparagus and truffles, Canadian lobster, or fresh scallops; line-caught sea wolf Niçoise (with stewed tomatoes and peppers); pigeon breast with cabbage and lentil cream sauce; peppered duck; and some of the best beef dishes in the region. Expect surprises from the capricious chef, whose menu changes virtually every day.

689 chemin de la Gaude. From the historic core of Vence, drive southwest for 4km (2½ miles), following signs to Cagnes-sur-Mer. ✆ **04-93-58-90-75.** Reservations required. Main courses 25€–83€ ($33–$108); fixed-price menu, including wine, 60€ ($78). AE, MC, V. Wed–Sun 12:30–2pm and 7:30–10pm. Closed Nov 12–Dec 12.

13 Nice ★★★

929km (577 miles) S of Paris, 32km (20 miles) NE of Cannes

Nice is the capital of the Riviera, the largest city between Genoa and Marseille. It's also one of the most ancient, founded by the Greeks, who called it Nike (Victory). By the 19th century, the Victorian upper class and tsarist aristocrats were flocking here. But these days it's not as chichi and expensive, especially compared to Cannes. In fact, of all the major French resorts, from Deauville to Biarritz to Cannes, Nice is the most affordable. It's also the best place to base yourself on the Riviera, especially if you're dependent on public transportation. You can go to San Remo, "the queen of the Italian Riviera," and return to Nice by nightfall. From the Nice airport, the second largest in France, you can travel by train or bus along the entire coast to resorts such as Juan-les-Pins and Cannes.

Because of its brilliant sunshine and relaxed living, Nice has long attracted artists and writers, among them Dumas, Nietzsche, Flaubert, Hugo, Sand, and Stendhal. Henri Matisse, who made his home in Nice, said, "Though the light is intense, it's also soft and tender." The city averages 300 days of sunshine a year.

ESSENTIALS

GETTING THERE **Trains** arrive at Gare Nice-Ville, avenue Thiers (✆ **08-92-35-35-35;** www.voyages-sncf.com). From there you can take trains to Cannes, Monaco, and Antibes, with easy connections to anywhere else along the Mediterranean coast. There's a small tourist center at the train station, open Monday through Saturday from 8am to 7pm and Sunday from 9am to 6pm. If you face a long delay, you can eat at the cafeteria and even shower at the station.

Buses to and from Monaco, Cannes, St-Tropez, and other parts of France and Europe serve the main bus station, or **Gare Routière,** 5 bd. Jean-Jaurès (✆ **04-93-85-61-81**).

Transatlantic and intercontinental flights land at **Aéroport Nice–Côte d'Azur** (✆ **08-20-42-33-33**). From there, municipal bus no. 98 departs at 20-minute intervals for the Gare Routière (see above); the one-way fare is 1.50€ ($1.95). Bus nos. 23 and 99 go to Gare SNCF. More luxurious is a yellow-sided shuttle bus *(la navette de l'aéroport)* that charges 4€ ($5.20) for a ride between the airport and the bus station. A **taxi** from the airport into the city center will cost at least 20€ to 30€ ($26–$39) each way. Trip time is about 30 minutes.

Value A Note on Nice Buses

If you plan to use the city's buses, consider buying a 1- or 7-day pass, available from tobacco stands and newspaper kiosks throughout the city. The pass allows unlimited transit on any municipal bus. The price is 4€ ($5.20) for a 1-day pass, 15€ ($20) for 7 days. For additional information, call Société Ligne d'Azur (✆ **08-10-06-10-06**).

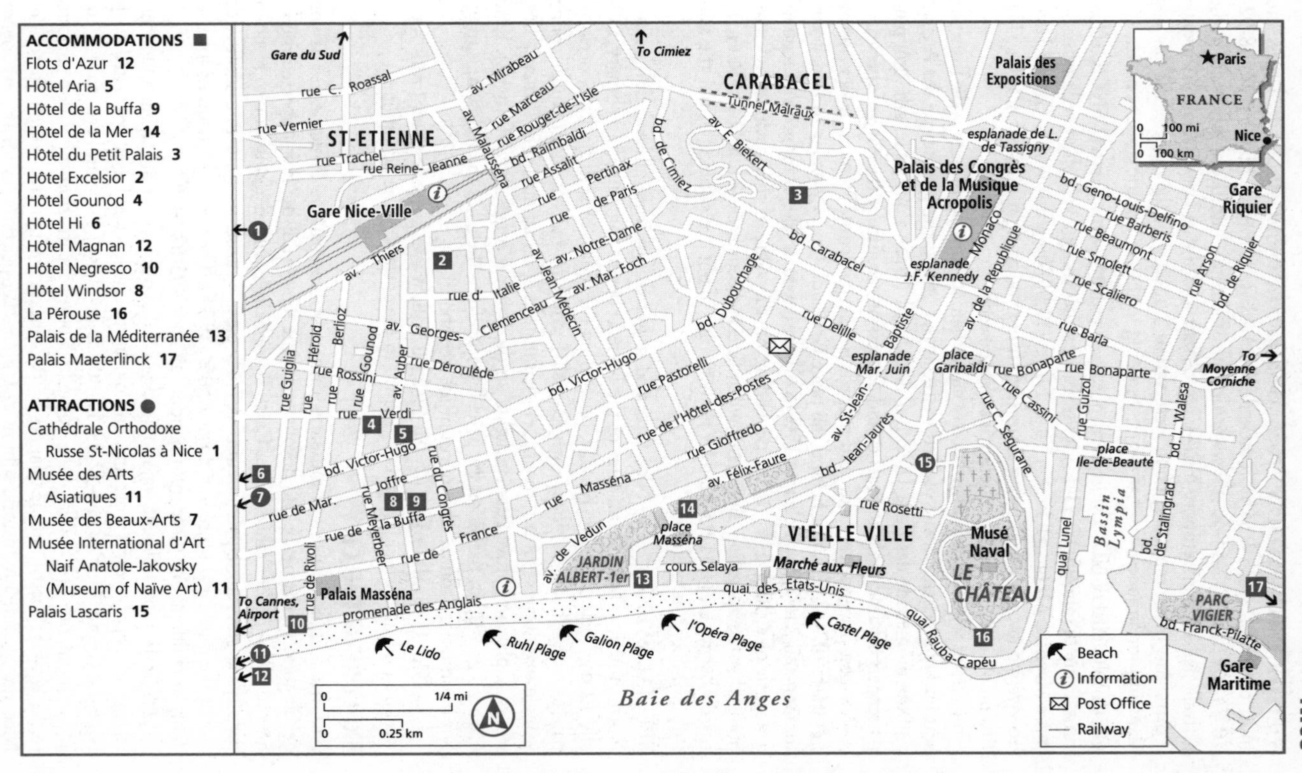
ACCOMMODATIONS
Flots d'Azur 12
Hôtel Aria 5
Hôtel de la Buffa 9
Hôtel de la Mer 14
Hôtel du Petit Palais 3
Hôtel Excelsior 2
Hôtel Gounod 4
Hôtel Hi 6
Hôtel Magnan 12
Hôtel Negresco 10
Hôtel Windsor 8
La Pérouse 16
Palais de la Méditerranée 13
Palais Maeterlinck 17
ATTRACTIONS
Cathédrale Orthodoxe Russe St-Nicolas à Nice 1
Musée des Arts Asiatiques 11
Musée des Beaux-Arts 7
Musée International d'Art Naif Anatole-Jakovsky (Museum of Naïve Art) 11
Palais Lascaris 15
Gare du Sud
To Cimiez
CARABACEL
Palais des Expositions
Paris
FRANCE
Nice
0 100 mi
0 100 km
ST-ETIENNE
Gare Nice-Ville
Tunnel Malraux
esplanade de L. de Tassigny
Palais des Congrès et de la Musique Acropolis
Gare Riquier
esplanade J.F. Kennedy
esplanade Mar. Juin
place Garibaldi
To Moyenne Corniche
place Ile-de-Beauté
Bassin Lympia
VIEILLE VILLE
place Masséna
JARDIN ALBERT-1er
Marché aux Fleurs
Musé Naval
LE CHÂTEAU
PARC VIGIER
Gare Maritime
Palais Masséna
To Cannes, Airport
promenade des Anglais
quai des Etats-Unis
quai Rauba-Capéu
Le Lido
Ruhl Plage
Galion Plage
l'Opéra Plage
Castel Plage
Baie des Anges
0 1/4 mi
0 0.25 km
N
Beach
Information
Post Office
Railway

VISITOR INFORMATION Nice maintains three **tourist offices**, the largest and most central of which is at 5 promenade des Anglais, near place Masséna (© **08-92-70-74-07;** fax 04-92-14-46-49; www.nicetourisme.com). Additional offices are in the arrivals hall of the Aéroport Nice–Côte d'Azur and the railway station on avenue Thiers. Any office can make a hotel reservation (but only for the night of the day you show up) for a modest fee that varies according to the classification of the hotel.

GETTING AROUND Most local buses serve the **Station Central SNCF,** 10 av. Félix-Faure (© **04-93-13-53-13;** www.voyages-sncf.com), a very short walk from the place Masséna. Municipal buses charge 1.45€ ($1.90) for a ride within Greater Nice. To save money, consider buying a *carnet* entitling you to eight rides for 8.30€ ($11). Bus nos. 2 and 12 make frequent trips to the beach.

No point within downtown Nice is more than about a 10-minute walk from the seafronting promenade, site of such well-known quays as the promenade des Anglais and the promenade des Etats-Unis. Bus nos. 2 and 12 run along its length, dropping passengers off at any of the beaches and concessions that front the edge of the sea.

The best place to rent bikes and mopeds is **Energy Scoot,** Promenade des Anglais (© **04-97-07-12-64**), just behind the place Grimaldi. Open Monday to Friday 9am to noon and 2 to 7pm, it charges 15€ ($20) per day for a bike or moped and requires a deposit of at least 54€ ($70), depending on the value of the machine you rent. Somewhat less appealing, but useful when Energy Scoot is closed, is **Nicea Rent,** 12 rue de Belgique (© **04-93-82-42-71**). It charges about the same rates, but the staff isn't always on the premises.

SPECIAL EVENTS The **Nice Carnaval** draws visitors from all over Europe and North America. The "Mardi Gras of the Riviera" begins sometime in February, usually 12 days before Shrove Tuesday, celebrating the return of spring with 3 weeks of parades, *corsi* (floats), *veglioni* (masked balls), confetti, and battles in which young women toss flowers (some throw rotten eggs instead of carnations). The climax, a fireworks display on Shrove Tuesday, lights up the Baie des Anges (Bay of Angels). King Carnival goes up in flames on his pyre, but rises from the ashes the following spring. For information, contact the tourist office (see above).

The **Nice Festival du Jazz** (© **01-47-23-07-58;** www.nicejazzfest.com) runs for a week in mid-July, when jazz artists perform in the ancient Arène de Cimiez.

EXPLORING THE CITY

Nice has a higher density of museums than many comparable French cities. If you decide to forgo the beach and devote your time to some of the best-respected museums in the south of France, buy a **Carte Passe-Musée,** which admits you to seven of the city's largest municipal museums. A 7-day pass, available from the tourist office or any of the municipal museums, costs 7.50€ ($9.75). There are no discounts for students or children. For more information, call © **04-93-62-61-62.**

One of the most efficient ways to quickly gain an overview of the layout and architecture of Nice involves boarding one of the double-decker buses associated with **Nice–Le Grand Tour** (© **04-92-29-17-00**). Every day of the year, between 9:30am and 6:50pm, one of a flotilla of this company's buses departs from a position adjacent to the Jardins Albert I, on the quai des Etats-Unis, for a panoramic 90-minute tour of Nice and its outlying historic suburb of Cimiez. Per-person rates for the experience are 17€ ($22) for adults, 13€ ($17) for students, and 9€ ($12) children 4 to 11. Participants can get off at any of 11 stops en route, opting to reboard any other buses, which follow at 40-minute intervals, after they've explored the neighborhood. Advance reservations aren't necessary.

In 1822, the orange crop at Nice was bad. The workers faced a lean time, so the English residents put them to work building the **promenade des Anglais** ★★, a wide boulevard fronting the bay, split by "islands" of palms and flowers and stretching for about 7km (4⅓ miles). Along the beach are rows of grand cafes, the Musée Masséna, villas, and hotels—some good, others decaying.

Crossing this boulevard in the tiniest bikinis or thongs are some of the world's most attractive bronzed bodies. They're heading for the **beach**—"on the rocks," as it's called here. Tough on tender feet, the beach is made not of sand but of pebbles (and not small ones, either). It's one of the least attractive aspects of the cosmopolitan resort city. Many bathhouses provide mattresses for a fee.

In the east, the promenade becomes **quai des Etats-Unis,** the original boulevard. It's lined with some of the best restaurants in Nice, most offering their own versions of bouillabaisse. Rising sharply on a rock is the site known as **Le Château,** where the ducs de Savoie built their castle, which was torn down in 1706. Even the foundations have disappeared in the wake of Louis XIV's destruction of what was viewed as a bulwark of Provençal resistance to his regime; all that remains are two or three stones. The hill has been turned into a garden of pines and exotic flowers. To reach the site and take in the view, board an elevator; many people take the elevator up, and then walk down. The park is open daily from 8am to dusk.

At the north end of Le Château is the famous old **graveyard** of Nice, known primarily for lavish monuments that form their own enduring art statement. It's the largest one in France. To reach it, you can take a small, canopied **Train Touristique de Nice** (**© 06-16-39-53-51;** fax 04-93-62-85-48), which departs from the Jardin Albert-1er. The 40-minute ride passes many of Nice's most heralded sites, including place Masséna, promenade des Anglais, and quai des Etats-Unis. Departing every 30 to 60 minutes, the train operates daily 10am to 5pm (until 6pm Apr–May and Sept; until 7pm June–Aug). There's no service between mid-November and mid-December and during most of January. The round-trip price is 6€ ($7.80) for adults and 3€ ($3.90) for children under 10.

Continuing east from "the Rock" (the site of Le Château), you reach the **harbor,** where the restaurants are even cheaper and the bouillabaisse is just as good. While lingering over a drink at a sidewalk cafe, you can watch the boats depart for Corsica. The port was excavated between 1750 and 1830. Since then the port has gained an outer harbor, protected by two jetties.

The "authentic" Niçoise live in **Vieille Ville** ★, the old town, beginning at the foot of "the Rock" and stretching to place Masséna. Sheltered by sienna-tiled roofs, many of the Italianate facades suggest 17th-century Genoese palaces. The old town is a maze of narrow streets, teeming with local life and studded with the least expensive restaurants in Nice. Buy an onion pizza *(la pissaladière)* from a vendor. Many of the buildings are painted a faded Roman gold, and their banners are laundry flapping in the sea breezes.

While here, try to visit the **Marché aux Fleurs,** the flower market at cours Saleya. A flamboyant array of carnations, violets, jonquils, roses, and birds of paradise, it operates Tuesday through Sunday 8am to 6pm in summer, and 8am until between 2 and 4pm in winter, depending on the vendors' remaining inventory and energy level.

Nice's commercial centerpiece is **place Masséna,** with pink buildings in the 17th-century Genoese style and fountains with water jets. Stretching from the main square to the promenade is the **Jardin Albert-1er,** with an open-air terrace and a Triton Fountain. With palms and exotic flowers, it's the most relaxing oasis in town.

Cathédrale Orthodoxe Russe St-Nicolas à Nice ★ Ordered and built by none other than Tsar Nicholas II, this is the most beautiful religious edifice of the Orthodoxy outside Russia, and a perfect expression of Russian religious art abroad. It dates from the Belle Epoque, when some of the Romanovs and their entourage turned the Riviera into a stomping ground (everyone from grand dukes to ballerinas walked the promenade). The cathedral is richly ornamented and decorated with icons. You'll spot the building from afar because of its collection of ornate onion-shaped domes. During church services on Sunday morning, the building closes to tourist visits.

Av. Nicolas-II (off bd. du Tzaréwitch). ✆ **04-93-96-88-02.** Admission 3€ ($3.90) adults, 2€ ($2.60) students, free for children under 12. May–Sept daily 9am–noon and 2:30–6pm; Oct–Apr daily 9:30am–noon and 2:30–5pm. From the central rail station, head west along av. Thiers to bd. Gambetta, and then go north to av. Nicolas-II.

Musée des Arts Asiatiques A tribute to the sculpture and paintings of Cambodia, China, India, Tibet, and Japan, this museum opened near the airport in 1998. Inside are some of the best ceramics and devotional carvings ever found; colonials brought many of them back to France during the 19th and early 20th centuries. Of special interest are the accouterments associated with Japan's tea-drinking ceremony and several monumental representations of Buddha.

405 promenade des Anglais. ✆ **04-92-29-37-00.** Admission 4.50€ ($5.85) adults, 2€ ($2.60) ages 18–25, free for children under 15. May to mid-Oct Wed–Mon 10am–6pm; mid-Oct to Apr Wed–Mon 10am–5pm. Bus: 9, 10, or 23.

Musée des Beaux-Arts ★★ The collection is in the former residence of the Ukrainian Princess Kotchubey. It has an important gallery devoted to the masters of the Second Empire and the Belle Epoque, with an extensive collection of 19th-century French experts. The gallery of sculptures includes works by J. B. Carpeaux, Rude, and Rodin. Note the important collection by a dynasty of painters, the Dutch Vanloo family. One of its best-known members, Carle Vanloo, born in Nice in 1705, was Louis XV's premier *peintre.* A fine collection of 19th- and 20th-century art includes works by Ziem, Raffaelli, Boudin, Monet, Guillaumin, and Sisley.

33 av. des Baumettes. ✆ **04-92-15-28-28.** Admission 4€ ($5.20) adults, 2.50€ ($3.25) students, free for children under 18. Tues–Sun 10am–6pm. Bus: 3, 9, 12, 22, 24, 38, 60, or 62.

Musée International d'Art Naïf Anatole-Jakovsky (Museum of Naive Art) ★ This museum is in the beautifully restored Château Ste-Hélène in the Fabron district. The museum's namesake, for years one of the world's leading art critics, once owned the collection. His 600 drawings and canvases were turned over to the institution and opened to the public. Artists from more than two dozen countries are represented by everything from primitive painting to 20th-century works.

Château St-Hélène, av. de Fabron. ✆ **04-93-71-78-33.** Admission 4€ ($5.20) adults, 2.50€ ($3.25) seniors and students, free for children under 19. Wed–Mon 10am–6pm. Bus: 9, 10, 12, or 23; 10-min. walk. Closed Dec 25, Jan 1, and May 1.

Palais Lascaris *Kids* The baroque Palais Lascaris in the city's historic core is associated with the Lascaris-Vintimille family, whose recorded history predates the year 1261. Built in the 17th century, it contains elaborately detailed ornaments. An intensive restoration by the city of Nice in 1946 brought back its original beauty, and the palace is now classified as a historic monument. The most elaborate floor, the *étage noble,* retains many of its 18th-century panels and plaster embellishments. A pharmacy, built around 1738 and complete with many of the original delftware accessories, is on the premises.

15 rue Droite. ✆ **04-93-62-72-40.** Free admission. Wed–Mon 10am–6pm. Bus: 1, 2, 3, 5, 6, 14, 16, or 17.

NEARBY ATTRACTIONS IN CIMIEZ ★★

In the once-aristocratic hilltop quarter of Cimiez, 5km (3 miles) north of Nice, Queen Victoria wintered at the Hôtel Excelsior and brought half the English court with her. Founded by the Romans, who called it Cemenelum, Cimiez was the capital of the Maritime Alps province. Excavations have uncovered the ruins of a Roman town, and you can wander the dig sites. The arena was big enough to hold at least 5,000 spectators, who watched contests between gladiators and wild beasts. To reach this suburb and its attractions, take bus no. 15 or 17 from place Masséna.

Monastère de Cimiez (Cimiez Convent) ★ The convent embraces a church that owns three of the most important works by the locally prominent Bréa brothers, who painted in the late 15th century. See the carved and gilded wooden main altarpiece. In a restored part of the convent where some Franciscan friars still live, the Musée Franciscain is decorated with 17th-century frescoes. Some 350 documents and works of art from the 15th to the 18th centuries are on display, and a monk's cell has been re-created in all its severe simplicity. Also visit the 17th-century chapel. From the magnificent gardens, you'll have a panoramic view of Nice and the Baie des Anges. Matisse and Dufy are buried in the cemetery.

Place du Monastère. ✆ **04-93-81-00-04.** Free admission. Museum Mon–Sat 10am–noon and 3–6pm. Church daily 9am–6pm.

Musée Matisse ★ This museum honors the artist, who died in Nice in 1954. Seeing his nude sketches today, you'll wonder how early critics could have denounced them as "the female animal in all her shame and horror." Most of the pieces in the museum's permanent collection were painted in Nice, and many were donated by Matisse and his heirs. These include *Nude in an Armchair with a Green Plant* (1937), *Nymph in the Forest* (1935–42), and a chronologically arranged series of paintings from 1890 to 1919. The most famous of these is *Portrait of Madame Matisse* (1905), usually displayed near a portrait of the artist's wife by Marquet, painted in 1900. There's also an assemblage of designs he prepared as practice sketches for the Matisse Chapel at Vence. Also here are *The Créole Dancer* (1951), *Blue Nude IV* (1952), and around 50 dance-related sketches he did between 1930 and 1931. The artist's last work, *Flowers and Fruit* (1953), is made of cut-out gouache.

In the Villa des Arènes-de-Cimiez, 164 av. des Arènes-de-Cimiez. ✆ **04-93-53-40-53.** Admission 4€ ($5.20) adults, 2.50€ ($3.25) students, free for children under 18. Wed–Mon 10am–6pm. Closed Jan 1, May 1, and Dec 25.

Musée National Message Biblique Marc Chagall ★★ In the hills of Cimiez, this handsome museum, surrounded by pools and a garden, is devoted to Marc Chagall's treatment of biblical themes. Born in Russia in 1887, Chagall became a French citizen in 1937. The artist and his wife donated the works—the most important Chagall collection ever assembled—to France in 1966 and 1972. On display are 450 of his oils, gouaches, drawings, pastels, lithographs, sculptures, and ceramics; a mosaic; three stained-glass windows; and a tapestry. Chagall decorated a concert room with brilliantly hued stained-glass windows. Temporary exhibits each summer feature great periods and artists of all times.

Av. du Dr.-Ménard. ✆ **04-93-53-87-20.** Admission 5.50€ ($7.15) adults, 4€ ($5.20) students, free for children under 18. July–Sept Wed–Mon 10am–6pm; Oct–June Wed–Mon 10am–5pm.

OUTDOOR PURSUITS

BEACHES Along Nice's seafront, beaches extend uninterrupted for more than 7km (4⅓ miles), going from the edge of Vieux-Port (the old port) to the international airport, with most of the best bathing spots subdivided into public beaches and private concessionaires. None has sand; they're covered with gravel (often the size of golf balls). The rocks are smooth but can be mettlesome to people with poor balance or tender feet. Tucked between the seven public beaches are the private beaches of hotels such as the Beau Rivage. Most of the public beaches consist of two sections: a free area and one where you can rent chaise longues, mattresses, and parasols; use changing rooms; and take freshwater showers. For that, you'll pay 10€ to 12€ ($13–$16) for a half-day, 12€ to 20€ ($16–$26) for a full day. Nude sunbathing is prohibited, but toplessness is common. Take bus no. 9, 10, 12, or 23 to get to the beach.

GOLF The oldest golf course on the Riviera is about 16km (10 miles) from Nice: **Golf Bastide du Roi** (also known as the Golf de Biot), route d'Antibes, Biot (✆ **04-93-65-08-48**). Open daily, this is a flat, not particularly challenging seafront course. (Golfers must cross a highway twice before completing the full 18 holes.) Tee times are 8am to 6pm; you can play until the sun sets. Reservations aren't necessary, though on weekends you should probably expect to wait. Greens fees are 50€ ($65).

SCUBA DIVING The best outfit is the **Centre International de Plongée (CIP) de Nice,** 2 ruelle des Moulins (✆ **06-09-52-55-57** or 04-93-55-59-50), adjacent to the city's old port, between quai des Docks and boulevard Stalingrad. A *baptême* (dive for first-timers) costs 30€ ($39). A one-tank dive for experienced divers, equipment included, is 32€ ($42); appropriate diver's certification is required.

TENNIS The oldest tennis club in Nice is the **Nice Lawn Tennis Club,** Parc Impérial, 5 av. Suzanne-Lenglen (✆ **04-92-15-58-00**). It's open daily 9am to 8pm from mid-October to mid-April (closed winter) and charges 15€ to 25€ ($20–$33) per person for 2 hours of court time. The club has a cooperative staff, a loyal clientele, 13 outdoor clay courts, and 6 outdoor hard-surface courts. There are no indoor courts. Reserve the night before.

SHOPPING

You may want to begin with a stroll through the streets and alleys of Nice's historic core. The densest concentrations of boutiques are along **rue Masséna, place Magenta, avenue Jean-Médecin, rue de Verdun, rue Paradis,** and on the streets around them. A shop of note is **Gigi,** 10 rue de la Liberté (✆ **04-93-87-81-78**), which sells sophisticated clothing for women.

Opened in 1949 by Joseph Fuchs, the grandfather of the present English-speaking owners, the **Confiserie Florian du Vieux-Nice,** 14 quai Papacino (✆ **04-93-55-43-50**), is near the Old Port. The specialty is glazed fruit crystallized in sugar or artfully arranged into chocolates. Look for exotic jams (rose-petal preserves, mandarin marmalade) and the free recipe leaflet, as well as candied violets, verbena leaves, and rosebuds. One of the oldest chocolatiers in Nice, **Confiserie Auer,** 7 rue St-François-de-Paule, near the opera house (✆ **04-93-85-77-98**), was established in 1820. Since then, few of the original decorative accessories have changed. The shop specializes in chocolates, candies, and *fruits confits,* the signature Provençal goodies.

Façonnable, 7–9 rue Paradis (✆ **04-93-87-88-80**), is the original site of a chain with several hundred branches around the world. This is one of the largest, with a wide range of men's suits, raincoats, overcoats, sportswear, and jeans. The look is youthful and conservatively stylish, for relatively slim French bodies. An outlet for women's clothing and sportswear (Façonnable Sport) and the main line of Façonnable women's wear (Façonnable Femmes) lies immediately across the street at 10 rue Paradis (✆ **04-93-88-06-97**).

If you're thinking of indulging in a Provençale *pique-nique,* **Nicola Alziari,** 318 bd. Madeleine (✆ **04-93-44-45-12**), will provide everything from olives, anchovies, and pistous to aiolis and tapenades. It's one of Nice's oldest purveyors of olive oil, with a house brand that comes in two strengths: a light version that aficionados claim is vaguely perfumed with Provence, and a stronger version suited to the earthy flavors and robust ingredients of a Provençal winter. Also for sale are objects crafted from olive wood.

For arts and crafts, head to the **Atelier Contre-Jour,** 3 rue du Pont Vieux (✆ **04-93-80-20-50**). It carries painted-wood handicrafts, including picture frames; painted furniture; and silk lampshades, as well as decorative posters showing the best of their painted work of the past 25 years. **Plat Jérôme,** 34 rue Centrale (✆ **04-93-97-53-54**), stocks varnished pottery. Many artists' studios and galleries are on side streets near the cathedral in the old town.

La Couqueto, 8 rue St-François-de-Paule (✆ **04-93-80-90-30**), sells *santons,* the traditional Provençal figurines. The best selection of Provençal fabrics is at **Le Chandelier,** 7 rue de la Boucherie (✆ **04-93-85-85-19**), where you'll see designs by two of the region's best-known producers of cloth, Les Olivades and Valdrôme.

Nice is also known for its **street markets.** In addition to the flower market, **Marché aux Fleurs** (see "Exploring the City," above), the main flea market, **Marché à la Brocante,** also at cours Saleya, takes place Monday 8am to 5pm. Another flea market on the port, **Les Puces de Nice,** place Robilante, is open Tuesday to Saturday 9am to 6pm.

WHERE TO STAY

VERY EXPENSIVE

Hôtel Negresco ★★★ The Negresco, on the seafront in the heart of Nice, is one of the Riviera's superglamorous hotels. The Victorian wedding-cake hotel is named after its founder, Henry Negresco, a Romanian who died a pauper in Paris in 1920. The country's châteaux inspired both the interior and the exterior, with its mansard roof and domed tower. The hotel's decorators scoured Europe to gather antiques, tapestries, and art. Some of the accommodations, such as the Coco Chanel room, are outfitted in homage to the personalities who stayed here. Others are modeled on literary or musical themes, such as *La Traviata.* In 1998, most of the bathrooms, which all have tubs and showers, were upgraded. Suites and public areas are even grander; they include the Louis XIV salon, reminiscent of the Sun King, and the Napoleon III suite, where swagged walls, a leopard-skin carpet, and a half-crowned pink canopy create a sense of majesty. The most expensive rooms with balconies face the Mediterranean and the private beach. The staff wears 18th-century costumes. The restaurant is one of the Riviera's greatest.

37 promenade des Anglais, Nice Cedex 06007. ✆ **04-93-16-64-00.** Fax 04-93-88-35-68. www.hotel-negresco-nice.com. 145 units. 280€–560€ ($364–$728) double; from 650€–1,800€ ($845–$2,340) suite. AE, DC, MC, V. Free parking.

Amenities: 2 restaurants; bar; fitness center; secretarial services; room service; massage; babysitting; laundry service; dry cleaning; nonsmoking rooms. *In room:* A/C, TV, minibar, hair dryer.

Palais de la Méditerranée ★★★ Long hailed as a Queen of the Nice Riviera, this glittering seaside palace on the promenade des Anglais reigned from 1929 to 1978 and then was shuttered. In its heyday, the hotel's theater stage hosted everyone from Maurice Chevalier to American chanteuse Josephine Baker. Its Art Deco facade was left intact after a restoration, but the interior of this place was gutted and turned into a marble pile with glamorous touches such as plush hallways and such modern amenities as a heated outdoor swimming pool. Monumental chandeliers and stained-glass windows, among other architectural features, were spared in the renovations. Bedrooms, midsize to grandly spacious, are outfitted in a tasteful modern decor, with luxurious bathrooms with tub and shower. Ninety of the bedrooms also open onto sea views. Behind the facade, the hotel's casino has been restored to its Art Deco glamour.

13–15 promenade des Anglais, Nice 06011. ✆ **04-92-14-77-00.** Fax 04-92-14-77-14. www.lepalaisdelamediterranee.com. 188 units. 335€–650€ ($436–$845) double; from 1,590€ ($2,067) suite. AE, DC, MC, V. **Amenities:** Restaurant; bar; casino; 2 pools (indoor and outdoor); fitness center; Turkish bath; solarium; watersports; room service; nonsmoking rooms; limited-mobility rooms. *In room:* A/C, TV, minibar, hair dryer, safe.

Palais Maeterlinck ★★★ On 3.6 hectares (9 acres) of landscape east of Nice, this deluxe hotel occupies a fin de siècle villa inhabited between the world wars by the Belgian writer Maurice Maeterlinck, winner of the Nobel Prize for literature. Although many visitors find the setting sumptuous, the service and experience of the staff pale in comparison to the Negresco's. But on the plus side, it's more tranquil than the hotels in more central locations. It has verdant terraces and a large outdoor pool, set amid banana and olive trees and soaring cypresses. A funicular will carry you down to the rock-strewn beach and marina. Each elegant guest room, decorated in neoclassical Florentine style, is outfitted in a different monochromatic color scheme. All but a few have terraces opening onto views of Cap d'Antibes and Cap-Ferrat, and deluxe bathrooms containing tubs and showers.

30 bd. Maeterlinck, Nice 06300. Drive 6.5km (4 miles) east of Nice along the Basse Corniche. ✆ **04-92-00-72-00.** Fax 04-92-04-18-10. www.palais-maeterlinck.com. 40 units. 245€–360€ ($319–$468) double; from 450€ ($585) suite. AE, DC, MC, V. Free parking. **Amenities:** Restaurant; bar; outdoor pool; fitness center; room service; babysitting; laundry service; dry cleaning; nonsmoking rooms; 1 limited-mobility room. *In room:* A/C, TV, minibar, hair dryer, safe.

EXPENSIVE

Hôtel Hi ★ *Finds* An architectural and decorative "statement," this hotel occupies a former boardinghouse that dates to the 1930s. Spearheaded by Matali Crasset, a onetime colleague of Philippe Starck, a team of architects and engineers created one of the most aggressively avant-garde hotels in the south of France. The angular seven-story hotel opened in 2003. Each of the nine high-tech room "concepts" is different. They range from white-on-white to birch-wood veneer and acid green to cool violet and gray. The unconventional layouts may include a bathtub tucked behind a screen of potted plants or elevated to a position of theatrical prominence. Electronic gizmos include state-of-the-art CD systems. The Japanese word *hi* describes the black mottling on the back of an ornamental carp, which has traditionally been associated with good luck.

3 av. des Fleurs, Nice 06000. ✆ **04-97-07-26-26.** Fax 04-97-07-26-27. www.hi-hotel.net. 38 units. 215€–395€ ($280–$514) double; 680€ ($884) suite. AE, DC, MC, V. Parking 24€ ($31). Bus: 23. **Amenities:** 24-hr. bar and snack bar; rooftop swimming pool; laundry service; nonsmoking rooms; limited-mobility rooms. *In room:* A/C, TV, safe.

La Pérouse ★★ *Finds* Once a prison, La Pérouse has been reconstructed and is now a unique Riviera hotel. Set on a cliff, it's built right in the gardens of an ancient château-fort. No hotel affords a better view over both the old city and the Baie des Anges. In fact, many people stay here just for the view. The hotel resembles an old Provençal home, with low ceilings, white walls, and antique furnishings. The lovely, spacious rooms are beautifully furnished, often with Provençal fabrics. Most have loggias overlooking the bay. The bathrooms are large, clad in Boticino marble, and hold tubs and showers.

11 quai Rauba-Capéu, Nice 06300. ✆ **04-93-62-34-63.** Fax 04-93-62-59-41. www.hotel-la-perouse.com. 62 units. 215€–455€ ($280–$592) double; 660€–905€ ($858–$1,177) suite. AE, DC, MC, V. Parking 24€ ($31). **Amenities:** Restaurant (mid-Apr to mid-Oct); bar; outdoor pool; exercise room; Jacuzzi; sauna; room service; babysitting; laundry service; nonsmoking rooms. *In room:* A/C, TV, minibar, hair dryer, safe.

MODERATE

Hôtel du Petit Palais This whimsical hotel occupies a mansion built around 1890; in the 1970s it was the home of the actor and writer Sacha Guitry (a name that's instantly recognized in millions of French households). It lies about a 10-minute drive from the city center in the Carabacel district near the Musée Chagall. Many of the Art Deco and Italianate furnishings and Florentine moldings and friezes remain intact. The preferred rooms, and the most expensive, have balconies that afford sea views during the day and sunset views at dusk. Bathrooms are small but efficient, and each has a shower and tub. Breakfast is served in a small but pretty salon.

17 av. Emile-Bieckert, Nice 06000. ✆ **04-93-62-19-11.** Fax 04-93-62-53-60. www.guide-gerard.com. 25 units. 85€–170€ ($111–$221) double. AE, DC, MC, V. Parking 10€ ($13). **Amenities:** Bar; room service; babysitting; laundry service; dry cleaning; nonsmoking rooms; limited-mobility rooms. *In room:* A/C, minibar, hair dryer, safe.

Hôtel Gounod ★ A winning choice in the city center, this hotel is a 5-minute walk from the sea. It was built around 1910 in a neighborhood where the street names honor composers. The Gounod boasts ornate balconies, a domed roof, and an elaborate canopy of wrought iron and glass. The attractive lobby and adjoining lounge are festive and stylish, with old prints, copper flowerpots, and antiques. The high-ceilinged guest rooms are quiet; most overlook the gardens of private homes. The tiled bathrooms are small but efficiently organized, mainly with shower units. Suites have safes. Guests have free unlimited use of the pool, cafe-bar, and Jacuzzi at the Hôtel Splendid, next door.

3 rue Gounod, Nice 06000. ✆ **04-93-16-42-00.** Fax 04-93-88-23-84. www.gounod-nice.com. 45 units. 130€–140€ ($169–$182) double; 240€ ($312) suite. AE, DC, MC, V. Parking 14€ ($18). Closed Nov 20–Dec 20. Bus: 8. **Amenities:** Bar; outdoor pool; gym; Jacuzzi; sauna; room service; massage; babysitting; laundry service; dry cleaning; nonsmoking rooms. *In room:* A/C, TV, minibar, hair dryer.

Hôtel Windsor *Value* One of the most arts-conscious hotels in Provence is in a *maison bourgeoise* built by disciples of Gustav Eiffel in 1895. It's near the Negresco and the promenade des Anglais. Each unit is a unique decorative statement by a different artist. The heir and scion of the longtime owners, the Redolfi family, commissioned manifestations of his mystical and mythical visions after years of traveling through Asia, Africa, and South America. In the "Ben" room, for example, a Provençal artist of the same name painted verses of his own poetry, in tones of blue, orange, yellow, and green, on a white background. You can take your chances or select a room based on the photos on the hotel website. Most units have a combination tub/shower. The fifth floor holds the health club, steam room, and sauna. The garden contains scores of tropical and exotic plants and the recorded sounds of birds singing in the jungles of the Amazon.

11 rue Dalpozzo, 06000 Nice. ✆ **04-93-88-59-35.** Fax 04-93-88-94-57. www.hotelwindsornice.com. 54 units. 85€–170€ ($111–$221) double. MC, V. Parking 10€ ($13). Bus: 9, 10, or 22. **Amenities:** Restaurant; bar; outdoor pool; health club; sauna; room service; babysitting; nonsmoking rooms. *In room:* A/C, TV, minibar, hair dryer, safe.

INEXPENSIVE

Flots d'Azur This three-story 19th-century villa is next to the sea and a short walk from the more elaborate and costlier promenade hotels. The rooms vary in size and decor; all have good views and sea breezes. Twelve units have TVs and minibars, and each comes with a tiled bathroom with shower. Double-glazed windows cut down on noise. There's a small sitting room and sun terrace in front, where a continental breakfast is served.

101 promenade des Anglais, Nice 06000. ✆ **04-93-86-51-25.** Fax 04-93-97-22-07. www.flotsdazur.com. 20 units. 67€–107€ ($87–$139) double. MC, V. Free parking. Bus: 23. **Amenities:** Laundry service; dry cleaning; nonsmoking rooms. *In room:* A/C, TV, minibar, hair dryer.

Hôtel Aria The grandiose facade of this stately hotel contrasts distinctly with the simple interior. A 5-minute walk from the railway station, it's unpretentious and charges relatively reasonable rates. Guest rooms are outfitted in cozy Provençal style, with wrought iron and wooden furniture. The five-story building underwent a radical restoration (and earned an upgrade to government-rated three-star status) in 2003. It stands in a small park near the place Mozart, in a neighborhood known as the musicians' quarter (Berlioz, Wagner, Paganini, and Verdi once lived nearby).

15 av. Auber. ✆ **04-93-88-30-69.** Fax 04-93-88-11-35. www.aria-nice.com. 30 units. 89€–119€ ($116–$155) double; 145€–185€ ($189–$241) suite. AE, DC, MC, V. Parking 14€ ($18) in lot across street. Bus: 23. **Amenities:** Laundry; nonsmoking rooms; 1 limited-mobility room. *In room:* A/C, TV, minibar, hair dryer, iron/ironing board.

Hôtel de la Buffa ★ *Value* Lying only a few steps from the promenade des Anglais and the pebbly beaches, this centrally located hotel combines charm with value. Decorated with a certain flair and style, it offers a prevailing family atmosphere. Rooms are tastefully and comfortably furnished, with the larger accommodations suitable for a family of up to four persons. If you wish, a safe and a refrigerator can be installed in your room. All the midsize bathrooms contain showers. Those units facing the streets have double-glazing on their windows. If you wish to partake of discounted meals, an arrangement can be made for you to take half or full board at the adjoining restaurant, which is under different management.

56 rue de la Buffa, Nice 06000. ✆ **04-93-88-77-35.** Fax 04-93-88-83-39. www.hotel-buffa.com. 13 units. 48€–73€ ($62–$95) double; 95€ ($124) quad. AE, DC, V. Bus: 23. *In room:* A/C, TV, fridge in some, hair dryer, safe in some.

Hôtel de la Mer *Value* In the center of Old Nice, this ocher-colored government-rated two-star hotel was built around 1910 and transformed into a hotel in 1947. Ms. Feri Forouzan, the owner, welcomes guests with personal charm. Most rooms are of good size, and all have small bathrooms with showers. Some contain minibars. It's a 2-minute walk to the promenade des Anglais and the seafront. Breakfast is served in one of the public salons or in your room.

4 place Masséna, Nice 06000. ✆ **04-93-92-09-10.** Fax 04-93-85-00-64. hotel-mer@wanadoo.fr. 12 units. 45€–73€ ($59–$95) double. AE, MC, V. Parking 12€ ($16) in nearby lot. Bus: 3, 9, 10, or 12. **Amenities:** Room service; massage. *In room:* A/C, TV.

Hôtel Excelsior The Excelsior's ornate corbels and stone pediments rise grandly a few steps from the railway station. This much-renovated 19th-century hotel has modern decor, most of it from the mid-1990s, and rooms outfitted in tones of Provençal ocher, blue, and brown that have seen a lot of wear but are still comfortable. They have small, shower-only bathrooms. Furnishings, for the most part, are functional and conservative. There's a garden and the beach is a 20-minute walk through the residential and commercial heart of Nice.

19 av. Durante, Nice 06000. ✆ **04-93-88-18-05.** Fax 04-93-88-38-69. www.excelsiornice.com. 42 units. 90€–120€ ($117–$156) double. AE, DC, MC, V. Parking free. Bus: 99. **Amenities:** Nonsmoking rooms. *In room:* A/C, TV, hair dryer.

Hôtel Magnan This well-run modern hotel was built around 1945 and has been renovated frequently. It's a 10-minute bus ride from the heart of town but only a minute or so from the promenade des Anglais and the bay. Many of the simply furnished rooms have balconies facing the sea, and some contain minibars. The look is a bit functional, but for Nice this is a good price, especially considering the comfortable beds. The bathrooms are small, each with a shower stall. Owner Daniel Thérouin occupies the apartment on the top floor, guaranteeing close supervision. Breakfast can be served in your room.

Square du Général-Ferrié, Nice 06200. ✆ **04-93-86-76-00.** Fax 04-93-44-48-31. www.hotelmagnan-nice.com. 25 units. 48€–69€ ($62–$90) double. AE, MC, V. Parking 9.50€ ($12). Bus: 23. **Amenities:** Nonsmoking rooms. *In room:* TV, minibar.

Villa Saint-Exupéry *Value* This former Carmelite monastery has been completely renovated and turned into a first-rate hostel that's the most attractively priced in the area. In winter it's a student residence, but in the busy summer months it turns into a hotel catering to backpackers, seasoned travelers on a budget, artists, musicians, and, of course, students. The restored and comfort-filled villa offers good though very standard hotel rooms (some with kitchenette), as well as some dormitory accommodations at youth hostel-level tariffs. Furnishings are modern and selected more for comfort than style. Echoing its past life, the former chapel preserved its open stage and stained-glass windows. Guests mingle in the public lounge, where there are five computers with free Internet access for guests. Guests are also welcome to use a fully equipped kitchen. Wine, beer, and some other supplies are sold on premise, while a supermarket lies just down the hill.

22 av. Gravier, Nice 06100. ✆ **04-93-84-42-83.** Fax 04-93-52-44-31. www.vsaint.com. 60 units. 32€–55€ ($42–$72) per person in a single or twin-bedded room; 20€–24€ ($26–$31) per person for dormitory bed. MC, V. Rates include continental breakfast. MC, V. Parking 18€–30€ ($23–$39). **Amenities:** Bar; laundry service; cooking facilities; free Internet access in lounge-area computers. *In room:* Kitchenettes (in some).

WHERE TO DINE

VERY EXPENSIVE

Le Chantecler ★★★ TRADITIONAL/MODERN FRENCH This is Nice's most prestigious and best restaurant. In 1989, a redecoration sheathed its walls with panels removed from a château in Pouilly-Fuissé; a Regency-style salon was installed for before- or after-dinner drinks; and a collection of 16th-century paintings, executed on leather backgrounds in the Belgian town of Malines, was imported. A much-respected chef, Bruno Turbot, revised the menu to include the most sophisticated and creative dishes in Nice. They change almost weekly but may include turbot filet served with purée of broad beans, sun-dried tomatoes, and asparagus; roasted suckling lamb served with beignets of fresh vegetables and ricotta-stuffed ravioli; and a melt-in-your-mouth fantasy of marbled hot chocolate drenched in almond-flavored cream sauce.

In the Hôtel Negresco, 37 promenade des Anglais. ✆ **04-93-16-64-00.** Reservations required. Main courses 35€–110€ ($46–$143); fixed-price lunch 45€–80€ ($59–$104); fixed-price dinner 85€–130€ ($111–$169). AE, MC, V. Wed–Sun 12:30–2pm and 8–10pm. Closed Jan to mid-Feb. Bus: 8, 9, 10, or 11.

EXPENSIVE

La Merenda ★★ *Finds* NIÇOISE Because there's no phone, you have to go by this place twice—once to make a reservation and once to dine—but it's worth the effort. Forsaking his chef's crown at Le Chantecler (see above), Dominique Le Stanc opened this tiny bistro serving sublime cuisine. Though he was born in Alsace, his heart and soul belong to the Mediterranean, the land of black truffles, wild morels, sea bass, and asparagus. His food is a lullaby of gastronomic unity, with texture, crunch, richness, and balance. Le Stanc never knows what he's going to serve until he goes to the market. Look for specials on a chalkboard. Perhaps you'll find stuffed cabbage, fried zucchini flowers, or oxtail flavored with fresh oranges. Lamb from the Sisteron is cooked until it practically falls from the bone. Raw artichokes are paired with a salad of mâche. Service is discreet and personable.

4 rue Terrasse. No phone. Reservations required. Main courses 32€–48€ ($42–$62). No credit cards. Mon–Fri seatings at 7:15 and 9:15pm. Closed Feb 5–13 and Aug 1–15. Bus: 8.

MODERATE

Brasserie Flo *Kids* TRADITIONAL FRENCH This is the town's most bustling brasserie. In 1991, the Jean-Paul Bucher group, a French chain noted for its skill at restoring historic brasseries, bought the premises of a faded early-1900s restaurant near place Masséna and injected it with new life. The original frescoes cover the high ceilings. The place (which is affiliated with Brasserie Flo in Paris) is brisk, stylish, reasonably priced, and fun. Menu items include an array of grilled fish, Alsatian-style choucroute, steak with brandied pepper sauce, and fresh oysters and shellfish.

2–4 rue Sacha-Guitry. ✆ **04-93-13-38-38.** Reservations recommended. Main courses 15€–22€ ($20–$29); fixed-price menus 23€–30€ ($30–$39); children's menu 14€ ($18). AE, DC, MC, V. Daily noon–2:30pm and 7pm–midnight. Bus: 1, 2, or 5.

L'Ane Rouge ★★ PROVENÇAL Facing the old port and occupying an antique building whose owners have carefully retained its ceiling beams and stone walls, this is one of the city's best-known seafood restaurants. In the two modern yet cozy dining rooms, you can enjoy traditional specialties such as bouillabaisse, *bourride* (stew), filet of John Dory with roulades of stuffed lettuce leaves, mussels stuffed with bread crumbs and herbs, and salmon in wine sauce with spinach. Service is commendable.

7 quai des Deux-Emmanuels. ✆ **04-93-89-49-63.** Reservations required. Main courses 25€–57€ ($33–$74); fixed-price lunch 33€–70€ ($43–$91); fixed-price dinner 48€–70€ ($62–$91). AE, DC, MC, V. Fri–Tues noon–2pm; Thurs–Tues 7–10:30pm. Closed Feb. Bus: 30.

Le Safari ★ PROVENÇAL/NIÇOISE The decor couldn't be simpler: a black ceiling, white walls, and an old-fashioned terra-cotta floor. The youthful staff is relaxed, sometimes in jeans, and always alert to the latest fashion. Many diners prefer the outdoor terrace overlooking the Marché aux Fleurs, but all appreciate the reasonably priced meals that appear in generous portions. Menu items include a pungent *bagna cauda,* which calls for diners to immerse vegetables in a sizzling brew of hot oil and anchovy paste; grilled peppers bathed in olive oil; *daube* (stew) of beef; fresh pasta with basil; and an omelet with *blettes* (tough but flavorful greens). The unfortunately named *merda de can* (dog poop) is gnocchi stuffed with spinach and is a lot more appetizing than it sounds.

1 cours Saleya. ✆ **04-93-80-18-44.** Reservations recommended. Main courses 14€–30€ ($18–$39); fixed-price menu 28€–35€ ($36–$46). AE, DC, MC, V. Daily noon–11pm. Bus: 1.

INEXPENSIVE

La Petite Maison ★★ *Finds* FRENCH/PROVENÇAL This bustling and noisy tavern in the heart of the old town resides in a 19th-century grocery store. Locals guard the address, hoping it won't be mobbed by tourists. Regulars include Elton John and his longtime companion, who live in a villa a few miles away. It's usually packed with diners wanting to taste the array of Niçoise cuisine, the authenticity of which is virtually unequalled in the city. Try the town's finest zucchini blossom fritters and finish with homemade ice cream flavored with pine nuts and candied orange blossoms. In between, you may enjoy a succulent array of grilled fish, pastas, and steaks, all prepared with the right Mediterranean touches and just enough garlic.

11 rue St.-Francoise de Paule. ✆ **04-93-85-71-53.** Reservations recommended. Main courses 10€–35€ ($13–$46). AE, V. Mon–Sat noon–2:30pm and 7:30pm–midnight.

La Zucca Magica ★ *Finds* VEGETARIAN/ITALIAN The chef at this popular harborside restaurant has been named the best Italian chef in Nice. That this honor should go to a vegetarian restaurant was the most startling part of the news. Chef Marco, who opened his restaurant in 1997 after cooking for many years in Rome, certainly has a fine pedigree—he's a relative of Luciano Pavarotti. He serves refined cuisine at reasonable prices, using recipes from Italy's Piedmont region and updating them with no meat or fish. The red-and-green decor (the colors of Italy) will put you in the mood for the creative cuisine. You'll have to trust Marco, though, because everyone is served the same meal. You can count on savory cuisine using lots of herbs, Italian cheeses, beans, and pasta. Lasagna is a specialty.

4 bis quai Papacino. ✆ **04-93-56-25-27.** Reservations recommended. Fixed-price lunch 22€ ($29); fixed-price dinner 30€ ($39). No credit cards. Tues–Sat 12:30–2pm and 7pm–midnight.

Restaurant L'Estocaficada *Finds* NIÇOISE *Estocaficada* is the Provençal word for stockfish, Europe's ugliest fish. There may be a dried-out, balloon-shaped version on display in the cozy dining room. Brigitte Autier is the owner and chef, and her kitchen is visible from everywhere in the dining room. Descended from a matriarchal line (since 1958) of mother-daughter teams who've managed this place, she's devoted to the preservation of recipes prepared by her Niçoise grandmother. Examples are gnocchi, beignets, several types of *farcies* (tomatoes, peppers, or onions stuffed with herbed fillings), grilled sardines, and bouillabaisse served as a main course or in a mini version. The place also serves pastas, one of which is garnished with three types of cheese.

2 rue de l'Hôtel-de-Ville. ✆ **04-93-80-21-64.** Reservations recommended. Main courses 15€–22€ ($20–$29); fixed-price menu 27€–33€ ($35–$43). AE, MC, V. Tues–Sat noon–2pm and 7:30–10pm. Bus: 1, 2, or 5.

NICE AFTER DARK

Nice has some of the most active nightlife along the Riviera. Evenings usually begin at a cafe. At kiosks around town you can pick up a copy of *La Semaine des Spectacles,* which outlines the week's diversions.

The major cultural center on the Riviera is the **Opéra de Nice,** 4 rue St-François-de-Paule (✆ **04-92-17-40-00**), built in 1885 by Charles Garnier, fabled architect of the Paris Opéra. It presents a full repertoire, with emphasis on serious, often large-scale operas. In one season you might see *Tosca, Les Contes de Hoffmann,* Verdi's *Macbeth,* Beethoven's *Fidelio,* and *Carmen,* as well as a *saison symphonique,* dominated by the Orchestre Philharmonique de Nice. The opera hall is also the major venue for concerts and recitals. Tickets are available (to concerts, recitals, and full-blown operas) a day or two prior to any performance. You can show up at the box office (Mon–Sat 10am–5:30pm, Sun 10am–6pm), or buy tickets in advance with a major credit card by phoning © **04-92-17-40-40.** Tickets run from 9.60€ ($13) for nosebleed (and we mean it) seats to 87€ ($113) for front-and-center seats on opening night.

Near the Hôtel Ambassador, **Le Before,** 18 rue des Congrès (© **04-93-87-85-59**), is an aperitif bar—called *apero-bar*—where a stylish all-ages crowd goes before heading off to more dance-oriented places. The decor is "New York–inspired," with lots of brick similar to what you'd find in a Gotham cellar. Open daily from 6pm to midnight, with cold platters served until 10pm.

Cabaret du Casino Ruhl, in the Casino Ruhl, 1 promenade des Anglais (© **04-97-03-12-22**), is Nice's answer to the more ostentatious glitter of Monte Carlo and Las Vegas. It includes just enough flesh to titillate; lots of spangles, feathers, and sequins; a medley of cross-cultural jokes and nostalgia for the old days of French chanson; and an acrobat or juggler. The 27€ ($35) cover includes one drink; dinner and the show, complete with a bottle of wine per person, costs 60€ ($78). Shows begin Friday and Saturday at 10pm. No jeans or sneakers.

The casino contains an area exclusively for slot machines, open daily from noon to 4am; entrance is free. A more formal gaming room (jacket required, but not a tie) offers blackjack, baccarat, and chemin de fer. Presentation of a government-issued photo ID, preferably a passport, is required. It's open Sunday to Thursday 8pm to 4am, or Friday and Saturday 5pm to 5am.

Le Relais, in the Hôtel Negresco, 37 promenade des Anglais (© **04-93-16-64-00**), is the most beautiful museum-quality bar in Nice, with an oxblood-red ceiling, Oriental carpets, English paneling, Italianate chairs, and tapestries. It was once a haunt of the actress Lillie Langtry. With its piano music and white-jacketed waiters, the bar still attracts a chic crowd.

At many bars in the old town, Americans will feel right at home. They include the **Scarlett O'Hara Irish Pub,** at the corner of rue Rossetti and rue Droite (© **04-93-85-84-66**); **Wayne's,** 15 rue de la Préfecture (© **04-93-13-46-99**); and **William's Pub,** 4 rue Centrale (© **04-93-62-99-63**), which has live music. If you'd rather hang out with French people, try **La Civette,** 29 rue de la Préfecture (© **04-93-62-35-51**), a popular spot for aperitifs. Two nearly adjacent sports bars with roughly equivalent decors, clienteles, and sports priorities are **Chez Wayne,** 15 rue de la Prefecture, off place Rossetti in Vieux Nice (© **04-93-13-46-99**), and **Le Master Home Bar,** 11 rue de la Prefecture (© **04-93-80-33-82**). Both occasionally sponsor live bands, have more widescreens telecasting sporting events than you could possibly take in during one sitting, and offer the option of a rollicking good time. At Chez Wayne, Thursday is karaoke night. When live music is presented at either of these bars, it tends to begin around 9pm. **La Bodeguita,** 14 rue Chavin (© **04-93-92-67-24**), serves tapas, wine by the glass, and lots of beer, and both re-create some of the sun-and-salsa motifs of nightlife at its best in the Caribbean and South America.

GAY NIGHTLIFE

Near the Hôtel Negresco and promenade des Anglais, **Le Blue Boy,** 9 rue Jean-Baptiste Spinetta (✆ **04-93-44-68-24**), is the oldest gay disco on the Riviera. With two bars and two floors, it's a vital stop for passengers aboard the all-gay cruises that call at Nice. The cover is 8€ ($10). Open daily 10:30am to 5pm.

A more trend-conscious gay bar in Nice is **Le Klub,** 6 rue Halevy (✆ **06-60-55-26-61**), near the Casino Ruhl. Entrance costs 9€ ($12) and includes one drink. Expect a hard-dancing, high-energy crowd of mostly gay men, many of them under 35, as well as lots of straight people who come for the nonstop barrage of house music and the focus on dancing.

14 Villefranche-sur-Mer ★

935km (581 miles) S of Paris, 6.5km (4 miles) E of Nice

According to legend, Hercules opened his arms, and Villefranche was born. It sits on a big blue bay that looks like a gigantic bowl, large enough to attract U.S. Sixth Fleet cruisers and destroyers. Quietly slumbering otherwise, Villefranche transforms into an exciting Mediterranean port when the fleet is in. About 7km (4⅓ miles) east of Nice, it's the first town you reach along the Lower Corniche.

ESSENTIALS

GETTING THERE **Trains** arrive from most towns on the Côte d'Azur, especially Nice (every 30 min.), but most visitors **drive** via the Corniche Inférieure (Lower Corniche). For rail information and schedules, call ✆ **08-92-35-35-35,** or visit www.voyages-sncf.com. The Sun Bus company (✆ **04-93-85-61-81**) maintains service at 15-minute intervals aboard line no. 100 from Nice and from Monte Carlo into Villefranche. One-way bus transit from Nice costs 2€ ($2.60); from Monaco the cost is 3€ ($3.90). Buses deposit their passengers in the heart of town, directly opposite the tourist information office.

VISITOR INFORMATION The **Office de Tourisme** is on Jardin François-Binon (✆ **04-93-01-73-68;** fax 04-93-76-63-65; www.villefranche-sur-mer.com).

EXPLORING THE TOWN

The vaulted **rue Obscure** is one of the strangest streets in France. In spirit it belongs more to a North African casbah than to a European port. People live in tiny houses, and occasionally there's an open space, allowing for a courtyard. To get there, take rue de l'Eglise.

Once popular with such writers as Katherine Mansfield and Aldous Huxley, the town is still a haven for artists, many of whom take over the little houses that climb the hillside. More recent arrivals who've bought homes in the area are Tina Turner and U2's Bono.

One artist who came to Villefranche left a memorial: Jean Cocteau, the painter, writer, filmmaker, and well-respected dilettante, spent a year (1956–57) painting frescoes on the 14th-century walls of the Romanesque **Chapelle St-Pierre,** quai de la Douane/rue des Marinières (✆ **04-93-76-90-70**). He presented it to "the fishermen of Villefranche in homage to the Prince of Apostles, the patron of fishermen." One panel pays tribute to the Gypsies of the Stes-Maries-de-la-Mer. In the apse is a depiction of the miracle of St. Peter walking on the water, not knowing that an angel supports him. Villefranche's women, in their regional costumes, are honored on the left side of the narthex. The chapel charges 2€ ($2.60) admission for everyone (adults and children). It is open June to August Tuesday to Sunday 10am to noon and 4 to 8:30pm; September to November 15 Tuesday to Sunday 9:30am to noon and 2 to 6pm; December 16 to May Tuesday to Sunday 9:30am to noon and 2 to 5pm. (It's closed Nov 16–Dec 15.)

WHERE TO STAY

Hôtel Welcome ★ This is as good as it gets in Villefranche. The Welcome was a favorite of author and filmmaker Jean Cocteau. In the six-story villa hotel, with shutters and balconies, everything has been modernized and extensively renovated. Try for a fifth-floor room overlooking the water. All the midsize to spacious rooms are comfortably furnished, each with a small bathroom, and most with a combination tub/shower. The sidewalk cafe is the focal point of town life. The on-site wine bar and the restaurant, St-Pierre, have open fireplaces and fruitwood furniture.

1 quai Amiral-Courbet, Villefranche-sur-Mer 06231. ✆ **04-93-76-27-62.** Fax 04-93-76-27-66. www.welcomehotel.com. 36 units. 93€–205€ ($121–$267) double; 202€–355€ ($263–$462) suite. AE, DC, MC, V. **Amenities:** Bar; room service; babysitting; laundry service. *In room:* A/C, TV, minibar, hair dryer, safe.

WHERE TO DINE

La Mère Germaine FRENCH/SEAFOOD This is the best of the string of restaurants on the port. Plan to relax over lunch while watching fishermen repair their nets. Mère Germaine opened the place in the 1930s, and these days a descendant, Remy Blouin, handles the cuisine, producing bouillabaisse celebrated across the Riviera. We recommend grilled sea bass with fennel, sole Tante Marie (stuffed with mushroom purée), lobster ravioli with shellfish sauce, and beef filet with garlic and seasonal vegetables. Perfectly roasted *carré d'agneau* (lamb) is prepared for two.

Quai Courbet. ✆ **04-93-01-71-39.** Reservations recommended. Main courses 25€–70€ ($33–$91); fixed-price menu 37€ ($48); bouillabaisse 63€ ($82). AE, DC, MC, V. Daily noon–2:30pm and 7–10pm. Closed mid-Nov to Christmas.

15 St-Jean-Cap-Ferrat ★★

939km (583 miles) S of Paris, 9.5km (6 miles) E of Nice

Of all the oases along the Côte d'Azur, no other place has the snob appeal of Cap-Ferrat. It's a 15km (9⅓-mile) promontory sprinkled with luxurious villas and outlined by sheltered bays, beaches, and coves. The vegetation is lush. In the port of St-Jean, the harbor accommodates yachts and fishing boats.

ESSENTIALS

GETTING THERE Most visitors drive or take a **bus** or **taxi** from the rail station at nearby Beaulieu. Buses from the station at Beaulieu depart hourly for Cap-Ferrat; the one-way fare is 1.80€ ($2.35). There's also bus service from Nice. For bus information and schedules, call ✆ **04-93-85-64-44.** By **car** from Nice, take N7 east.

VISITOR INFORMATION The **Office de Tourisme** is on 59 av. Denis-Séméria (✆ **04-93-76-08-90;** fax 04-93-76-16-67; www.ville-saint-jean-cap-ferrat.fr).

SEEING THE SIGHTS

One way to enjoy the scenery here is to wander on some of the public paths. The most scenic goes from **Plage de Paloma** to **Pointe St-Hospice,** where a panoramic view of the Riviera landscape unfolds. You can also wander around the hamlet **St-Jean,** a colorful fishing village with bars, bistros, and inns.

Everyone tries to visit the **Villa Mauresque,** avenue Somerset-Maugham, but it's closed to the public. Near the cape, it's where Maugham spent his final years. When tourists tried to visit him, he proclaimed that he wasn't one of the local sights.

Once the property of King Leopold II of Belgium, the **Villa Les Cèdres** lies west of the port of St-Jean. Although you can't visit the villa, you can go to the nearby **Parc Zoologique,** boulevard du Général-de-Gaulle, northwest of the peninsula (✆ **04-93-76-04-98;** www.zoocapferrat.com). It's open May to September daily 9:30am to 7pm, March, April and October daily 9:30am to 6pm (closed Nov–Feb). Admission is 13€ ($17) for adults and 9€ ($12) for students and children 3 to 10. This private zoo is in the basin of a drained lake. It houses a wide variety of reptiles, birds, and animals in outdoor cages.

Musée Ile-de-France (aka Villa Ephrussi de Rothschild) ★★ Built by Baronne Ephrussi de Rothschild, this is one of the Côte d'Azur's legendary villas. Born a Rothschild, the baronne married a Hungarian banker and friend of her father, about whom even the museum's curator knows little. She died in 1934, leaving the Italianate building and its gardens to the Institut de France on behalf of the Académie des Beaux-Arts. The museum preserves the wealth of her collection: 18th-century furniture; Tiepolo ceilings; Savonnerie carpets; screens and panels from the Far East; tapestries from Gobelin, Aubusson, and Beauvais; Fragonard drawings; canvases by Boucher; Sèvres porcelain; and more. The sprawling gardens contain fragments of statuary from churches, monasteries, and palaces. An entire section is planted with cacti.

Av. Denis-Séméria. ✆ **04-93-01-45-90.** www.villa-ephrussi.com. Admission 9.50€ ($12) adults, 7€ ($9.10) students and children 7–18. Feb–Oct daily 10am–6pm (till 7pm July–Aug); Nov–Jan Mon–Fri 2–6pm, Sat–Sun 10am–6pm.

HITTING THE BEACH

The town's most visible and popular beaches are **Plage Passable,** on the northeastern "neck" of the Cap-Ferrat peninsula, close to where it connects to the French mainland; and **Plage de Paloma,** near the peninsula's southernmost tip, overlooked by the Chapelle St-Hospice. Neither is sandy (the beaches are made of pebbles and gravel), but they do have snack bars, souvenir stands, and restaurants. Most hotel guests opt to remain around their pools, and indeed, many hotels don't have beaches. A noteworthy exception is the Grand Hôtel du Cap-Ferrat (see below), which acquired a rocky beach in the early 1900s.

WHERE TO STAY

EXPENSIVE

Grand Hôtel du Cap-Ferrat ★★★ One of the best features of this early-1900s palace is its location: at the tip of the peninsula in the midst of a 5.6-hectare (14-acre) garden of semitropical trees and manicured lawns. It has been the retreat of the international elite since 1908 and occupies the same celestial status as the Réserve and Métropole in Beaulieu (see the next section, "Beaulieu-sur-Mer"). Its cuisine even equals the Métropole's. Parts of the exterior have open loggias and big arched windows; you can also enjoy the views from the elaborately flowering terrace over the sea. Accommodations look as if the late Princess Grace might settle in comfortably at any minute. They're generally spacious and open to sea views, and most come with a sumptuous bathroom with tub and shower. Rates include admission to the pool, Club Dauphin. The beach is accessible by funicular from the main building. The hotel is open year-round.

71 bd. du Général-de-Gaulle, St-Jean-Cap-Ferrat 06230. ✆ **04-93-76-50-52.** Fax 04-93-76-04-52. www.grand-hotel-cap-ferrat.com. 53 units. 205€–1,325€ ($267–$1,723) double; 845€–2,995€ ($1,099–$3,894) suite. AE, DC, MC, V. Indoor parking 80€ ($96); outdoor parking free. Closed Jan 2–Mar 1. **Amenities:** 2 restaurants; 2 bars; Olympic-size heated outdoor pool; 2 tennis courts; sauna; use of bicycles; room service; babysitting; laundry service; dry cleaning; nonsmoking rooms; limited-mobility rooms. *In room:* A/C, TV, minibar, hair dryer, safe.

La Voile d'Or ★★ Established in 1966, the "Golden Sail" is a tour de force. It offers intimate luxury in a converted 19th-century villa at the edge of the little fishing port and yacht harbor, with a panoramic coast view. It's equal to the Grand Hôtel in every feature except cuisine, which is just a notch lower. The guest rooms, lounges, and restaurant open onto terraces. Accommodations are individually decorated, with hand-painted reproductions, carved gilt headboards, baroque paneled doors, parquet floors, antique clocks, and paintings. The luxurious bathrooms have tub/shower combinations. Guests gather on the canopied outer terrace for lunch, and in a stately room with Spanish armchairs and white wrought-iron chandeliers for dinner.

31 av. Jean-Mermoz, St-Jean-Cap-Ferrat 06230. ✆ **04-93-01-13-13.** Fax 04-93-76-11-17. www.lavoiledor.fr. 45 units. 229€–765€ ($298–$995) double; 449€–847€ ($584–$1,101) suite. Rates include continental breakfast. AE, MC, V. Parking 25€ ($33). Closed Nov 1–Apr 13. **Amenities:** 2 restaurants; bar; 2 saltwater outdoor pools; exercise room; sauna; room service; babysitting; laundry service; dry cleaning. *In room:* A/C, TV, minibar, hair dryer, safe.

MODERATE

Hôtel Brise Marine Built around 1878, this villa with front and rear terraces sits on a hillside. A long rose arbor, beds of subtropical flowers, palms, and pines provide an attractive setting. The atmosphere is casual and informal, and the rooms are comfortably but simply furnished. They have small, tiled bathrooms with shower and tub. You can have breakfast in the beamed lounge or under the rose trellis. The little corner bar serves afternoon drinks.

58 av. Jean-Mermoz, St-Jean-Cap-Ferrat 06230. ✆ **04-93-76-04-36.** Fax 04-93-76-11-49. www.hotel-brisemarine.com. 18 units. 145€–165€ ($189–$215) double. AE, DC, MC, V. Parking 12€ ($16). Closed Nov–Jan. **Amenities:** Bar; room service. *In room:* A/C, TV, minibar, hair dryer, safe.

Hôtel Clair Logis ★ *Value* The grandmother of the present owners created this B&B by adding two outbuildings to the grounds of her early-1900s villa. It's on an otherwise pricey resort strip about a 10-minute walk from the beach. The pleasant rooms, each named after a flower, are scattered over three buildings in the confines of the garden. The most romantic and spacious are in the main building, a comfortably proportioned *maison bourgeoise* built in 1903; the seven rooms in the 1960s annexes are the most modern but have the least character and tend to be smaller and cheaper. The hotel's most famous guest was de Gaulle, who stayed in the Strelitzias (Bird of Paradise) room during many of his retreats from Paris.

12 av. Centrale, St-Jean-Cap-Ferrat 06230. ✆ **04-93-76-51-81.** Fax 04-93-76-51-82. www.hotel-clair-logis.fr. 16 units. 95€–198€ ($124–$257) double. AE, DC, MC, V. Free parking. Closed Jan 10 to early Feb and Nov 1–Dec 15. **Amenities:** Room service; laundry service; nonsmoking rooms; limited-mobility rooms. *In room:* A/C (in some), TV, minibar, hair dryer.

WHERE TO DINE

Capitaine Cook ★ PROVENÇAL/SEAFOOD Next door to the fancy La Voile d'Or hotel (see above), a few blocks uphill from the center of the village, this restaurant specializes in seafood served in hearty portions. You'll have a panoramic view of the coast from the terrace; inside, the decor is maritime and rugged. Oysters, served simply on the half shell or in several creative ways with sauces and herbs, are a specialty.

Roasted catch of the day is the mainstay, but filet mignon is also popular. The staff speaks English.

11 av. Jean-Mermoz. ✆ **04-93-76-02-66**. Main courses 16€–27€ ($21–$35); fixed-price menu 25€–30€ ($33–$39). MC, V. Fri–Tues noon–2pm; Thurs–Tues 7:15–11pm. Closed mid-Nov to Dec.

Le Provençal ★ FRENCH/PROVENÇAL With the possible exception of the Grand Hôtel's dining room, this is the grandest restaurant in town. Near the top of Nice's highest peak, it has the most panoramic view, which can sweep as far as the Italian border. Many of the menu items are credited to the inspiration of "the Provençal" in the kitchens. Selections include marinated artichoke hearts beside half a lobster, *tarte fine* (sweet tart) of potatoes with deliberately undercooked foie gras, rack of lamb with local herbs and tarragon sauce, and crayfish with asparagus and black-olive tapenade. The best way to appreciate the desserts is to order the sampler, *les cinq desserts du Provençal*—five dishes that usually include macaroons with chocolate and crème brûlée.

2 av. Denis-Séméria. ✆ **04-93-76-03-97**. Reservations required. Main courses 25€–67€ ($33–$87); fixed-price menu 70€ ($91). AE, MC, V. Apr–Sept daily noon–2:30pm and 7:30–11pm; Oct–Mar Wed–Sun noon–2:30pm and 7:30–11pm.

Le Sloop FRENCH/PROVENÇAL Le Sloop is the most popular and most reasonably priced bistro in this expensive area. Outfitted in blue and white inside and out, it sits at the edge of the port, overlooking the yachts in the harbor. A meal may begin with a salad of flap mushrooms steeped *en cappuccino* with liquefied foie gras, or perhaps tartare of salmon with aioli and lemon crepes. You may follow with a filet of sea bass served with red-wine sauce, or a mixed fish fry of three kinds of Mediterranean fish, bound together with olive oil and truffles. Dessert may include strawberry soup with sweet white wine and apricot ice cream or any of about seven other choices, each based on "the red fruits of the region." The regional wines are reasonably priced.

Au Nouveau Port. ✆ **04-93-01-48-63**. Reservations recommended. Main courses 24€–44€ ($31–$57); fixed-price menu 30€ ($39). AE, MC, V. July–Aug Thurs–Mon noon–2pm, daily 7–10pm; Sept–June Thurs–Tues noon–2pm and 7–10pm. Closed mid-Nov to mid-Dec.

16 Beaulieu-sur-Mer ★★

939km (583 miles) S of Paris, 9.5km (6 miles) E of Nice, 11km (6¾ miles) W of Monte Carlo

Protected from the north winds blowing down from the Alps, Beaulieu-sur-Mer is often referred to as "La Petite Afrique" (Little Africa). Like Menton, it has the mildest climate along the Côte d'Azur and is popular with the wintering wealthy. English visitors originally staked it out after an English industrialist founded a hotel here between the rock-studded slopes and the sea. Beaulieu is rich with lush vegetation, with palms as well as oranges, lemons, and bananas.

ESSENTIALS

GETTING THERE Most visitors **drive** from Nice on the Moyenne Corniche or the coastal highway. **Trains** connect Beaulieu with Nice, Monaco, and the rest of the Côte d'Azur. For rail information, call ✆ **08-92-35-35-35,** or visit www.voyages-sncf.com.

VISITOR INFORMATION The **Office de Tourisme** is on place Georges-Clemenceau (✆ **04-93-01-02-21;** fax 04-93-01-44-04; www.ot-beaulieu-sur-mer.fr).

FUN ON & OFF THE BEACH

Beaulieu does have a beach scene, but don't expect soft sand. The beaches aren't as rocky as those in Nice or other nearby resorts, but they're still closer to gravel than to sand. The longer of the town's two free public beaches is **Petite Afrique,** adjacent to the yacht basin; the shorter is **Baie des Fourmis,** beneath the casino. **Plage de la Calanque** (© **04-93-01-45-00**) rents mattresses for 8€ ($10) per half-day and sells snacks and drinks.

The town is home to an important church, the late-19th-century **Eglise de Sacré-Coeur,** a quasi-Byzantine, quasi-Gothic mishmash at 13 bd. du Maréchal-Leclerc (© **04-93-01-18-24**). It's open daily 8am to 7pm. At the same address (same phone) is the 12th-century Romanesque chapel of Santa Maria de Olivo, used mostly for temporary exhibits of painting, sculpture, and civic memorabilia. Unlike the Eglise de Sacré-Coeur, the chapel is not an active house of worship and is open only for special exhibitions.

As you walk along the seafront promenade, you can see many stately Belle Epoque villas that evoke the days when Beaulieu was the height of fashion. Although you can't go inside, you'll see signs for **Villa Namouna,** which once belonged to Gordon Bennett, the owner of the *New York Herald,* and **Villa Léonine,** former home of the marquess of Salisbury.

For a memorable 2-hour walk, start north of boulevard Edouard-VII, where a path leads up the Riviera escarpment to **Sentier du Plateau St-Michel.** A belvedere here offers panoramic views from Cap d'Ail to the Estérel. A 1-hour alternative is the stroll along **promenade Maurice-Rouvier.** The promenade runs parallel to the water, stretching from Beaulieu to St-Jean. On one side you'll see the most elegant mansions in well-landscaped gardens; on the other, views of the Riviera landscape and the peninsular point of St-Hospice.

Casino de Beaulieu, avenue Fernand-Dunan (© **04-93-76-48-00**), was built in the Art Nouveau style in 1903. The slot machines are open daily, without charge, 11am to 4am. The *salles des grands jeux* are open Friday and Saturday 11am to 5am, Sunday to Thursday 9pm to 4am. Management strongly recommends that men wear jackets, or at least appropriate clothing. Patrons must present a photo ID.

Also in the casino is a deluxe restaurant, **L'Araucarla** (© **04-93-76-48-05**), which overlooks the Mediterranean. The upscale *brasserie de luxe* serves seasonal gourmet cuisine that may include snails in garlic butter, roast breast of duckling with citrus sauce or figs, and a wide array of grilled fresh fish. It's open Wednesday to Sunday noon to 2pm and Wednesday to Saturday 7pm to midnight.

Villa Kérylos ★★ This is a replica of an ancient Greek residence, painstakingly designed and built by the archaeologist Theodore Reinach. A collection of Greek figurines and ceramics fills the cabinets. Most interesting is the reconstructed Greek furniture, much of which would be fashionable today. One curious mosaic depicts the slaying of the Minotaur and provides its own labyrinth. (If you try to trace the path, expect to stay for weeks.)

Rue Gustave-Eiffel. © **04-93-01-01-44.** www.villa-kerylos.com. Admission 8€ ($10) adults, 6€ ($7.80) seniors and children 7–18, free for children under 7. Feb–Oct daily 10am–6pm (until 7pm July–Aug); Nov–Jan Mon–Fri 2–6pm, Sat–Sun 10am–6pm.

WHERE TO STAY

EXPENSIVE

La Réserve de Beaulieu ★★★ A Relais & Châteaux member, this pink-and-white fin de siècle palace is one of the Riviera's most famous hotels. Here you can sit, have an aperitif, and watch the sunset while a pianist plays Mozart. A number of the lounges open onto a courtyard with bamboo chairs, grass borders, and urns of flowers. The social life revolves around the main drawing room. The individually decorated guest rooms range widely in size and design; most overlook the Mediterranean, and some have a view of the mountains. They come with deluxe beds and luxurious bathrooms with tubs and showers. Some have private balconies. The dining room has a frescoed ceiling, parquet floors, chandeliers, and windows facing the Mediterranean.

5 bd. du Maréchal-Leclerc, Beaulieu-sur-Mer 06310. ✆ **04-93-01-00-01.** Fax 04-93-01-28-99. www.reservebeaulieu.com. 39 units. 170€–590€ ($221–$767) double; 460€–1,020€ ($598–$1,326) suite. AE, DC, MC, V. Parking 33€ ($43). Closed mid-Nov to Dec 20. **Amenities:** Restaurant; bar; outdoor pool; fitness center; gym; salon; room service; massage; babysitting; laundry service; dry cleaning; nonsmoking rooms; billiards. *In room:* A/C, TV, minibar, hair dryer, safe.

Le Métropole ★★ This Italianate villa is second only to La Réserve de Beaulieu (see above). It offers some of the Riviera's most luxurious accommodations. The Relais & Châteaux member sits on .8 hectare (2 acres) of grounds discreetly shut off from the traffic of the resort. Here, you'll enter a world of French elegance, with lots of balconies opening onto sea views, marble accents, Oriental carpets, and a polite staff. The guest rooms are furnished in tasteful fabrics and wallpapers, with deluxe mattresses; the roomy bathrooms have tub/shower combinations. The restaurant has a seaside terrace and bar.

15 bd. du Maréchal-Leclerc, Beaulieu-sur-Mer 06310. ✆ **04-93-01-00-08.** Fax 04-93-01-18-51. www.le-metropole.com. 41 units. 180€–1,125€ ($234–$1,463) double; 620€–1,550€ ($806–$2,015) suite. AE, DC, MC, V. Parking 25€–33€ ($33–$43). Closed Oct 20–Dec 20. **Amenities:** Restaurant; bar; outdoor pool; room service; babysitting; laundry service; dry cleaning; limited-mobility rooms. *In room:* A/C, TV, minibar, hair dryer, safe.

INEXPENSIVE

Hôtel Le Havre Bleu *Value* This is a great bargain if you don't require a lot of services and amenities. Le Havre Bleu has one of the prettiest facades of any inexpensive hotel in town. In a former Victorian villa, the hotel has arched ornate windows and a front garden dotted with flowering urns. The impeccable guest rooms are comfortable and functional. The in-room amenities are few, except for a TV; the compact bathrooms have showers. Breakfast is the only meal served.

29 bd. du Maréchal-Joffre, Beaulieu-sur-Mer 06310. ✆ **04-93-01-01-40.** Fax 04-93-01-29-92. www.lehavreblue.com. 21 units. 60€–77€ ($78–$100) double; 80€–100€ ($104–$130) triple; 94€ ($113) quad. AE, MC, V. Free parking. **Amenities:** Bar; room service; babysitting; laundry service. *In room:* TV.

Hôtel Marcellin The early-20th-century Marcellin is a good budget selection in an otherwise high-priced resort. Built around 1900 for a local family, the sprawling, much-altered villa was divided into two about 25 years ago, and half was converted into this pleasant, cost-conscious hotel (the other half remains a private home). The restored rooms come with homelike amenities and a southern exposure. They're small to midsize, but comfortably furnished. All units have a small tiled bathroom with shower. The location isn't bad, either: in the congested town, near its western periphery, and only a 5-minute walk from the beach. Breakfast is the only meal served, but many restaurants are nearby.

18 av. Albert-1er, Beaulieu-sur-Mer 06310. ✆ **04-93-01-01-69.** Fax 04-93-01-37-43. www.hotel-marcellin.com. 21 units. 60€–99€ ($78–$129) double. MC, V. **Amenities:** Bar; room service; babysitting; limited-mobility rooms. *In room:* A/C, TV, hair dryer.

Inter-Hôtel Frisia Most of the Frisia's rooms, decorated in a modern style, open onto views of the harbor. The waterview units are the most expensive. All rooms have small bathrooms, with a combination tub/shower. Two spacious suites with kitchenettes are in free-standing villas near the hotel's main building. Public areas include a sunny garden and inviting lounges. English is widely spoken here, and the management makes foreign guests feel especially welcome. Breakfast is the only meal served, but many reasonably priced restaurants are nearby.

2 bd. Eugène-Gauthier, Beaulieu-sur-Mer 06310. ✆ **04-93-01-01-04.** Fax 04-93-01-31-92. www.frisia-beaulieu.com. 32 units. 60€–130€ ($78–$169) double; 175€–195€ ($228–$254) suite. AE, MC, V. Closed Nov 13–Dec 17. Parking 9€ ($12). **Amenities:** Bar; room service; babysitting; laundry service; dry cleaning. *In room:* A/C, TV, minibar, hair dryer, safe.

WHERE TO DINE

La Pignatelle *Value* FRENCH/PROVENÇAL Even in this expensive town, you can find an excellent, affordable Provençal bistro. Despite its relatively low prices, La Pignatelle prides itself on the fresh ingredients in its robust cuisine. Specialties include mushroom-stuffed ravioli with truffled cream sauce, succulent *soupe de poissons* from which the kitchen has labored to remove the bones, cassoulet of mussels, monkfish steak garnished with olive oil and herbs, fricassee of sea bass with shrimp, and *petite friture du pays,* which incorporates small fish using old Provençal traditions.

10 rue de Quincenet. ✆ **04-93-01-03-37.** Reservations recommended. Main courses 15€–32€ ($20–$42); fixed-price lunch 13€ ($17); fixed-price dinner 19€–29€ ($25–$38). MC, V. Thurs–Tues noon–2pm and 7–10pm. Closed Nov.

Les Agaves ★★ MODERN FRENCH One of the most stylish restaurants in Beaulieu is in an early-1900s villa across the street from the railway station. U.S.-based publications such as *Bon Appétit* have praised the cuisine. Of note are curry-enhanced scallops with garlic-flavored tomatoes and parsley, terrine of pork with comfit of onions, lobster salad with mango, bouillabaisse, rockfish soup, chopped shrimp with Provençal herbs, and several preparations of foie gras. Filet of sea bass with truffles and champagne sauce is delectable.

4 av. Maréchal Foch. ✆ **04-93-01-13-12.** Reservations recommended. Main courses 20€–35€ ($26–$46); fixed-price menu 36€ ($47). AE, MC, V. Daily 7:30–10pm. Closed Nov 20–30 and Jan 15–22.

BEAULIEU AFTER DARK

The Art Deco–style **Grand Casino de Beaulieu,** 4 av. Fernand-Dunan (✆ **04-93-76-48-00**), encourages jackets for men in its fancier areas, and absolutely forbids tennis shoes. It requires that patrons show a passport. The slot-machine section, where dress is more casual, is free to enter and doesn't require a passport.

17 Eze & La Turbie ★★

942km (585 miles) S of Paris, 11km (6¾ miles) NE of Nice

The hamlets of Eze and La Turbie, though 6.5km (4 miles) apart, are so similar that most tourism officials speak of them as if they're one entity. Both boast fortified feudal cores in the hills overlooking the coast, and both were built during the early Middle Ages to stave off raids from corsairs who wanted to capture harem slaves and laborers. Clinging to the hillsides around these hamlets are upscale villas, many of which have been built since the 1950s by retirees from colder climes. Closely linked, culturally and fiscally, to nearby Monaco, Eze and La Turbie have full-time populations of less than 3,000. The medieval cores of both contain galleries, boutiques, and artisans' shops that have been restored.

Eze is accessible on the Moyenne (Middle) Corniche; La Turbie, by way of the Grande (Upper) Corniche. Signs along the coastal road indicate the direction motorists should take to reach either of the hamlets.

The leading attraction in Eze is the **Jardin d'Eze** ★, boulevard du Jardin-Exotique (✆ **04-93-41-10-30**), a showcase of exotic plants in Eze-Village, at the pinnacle of the town's highest hill. Admission is 5€ ($6.50) for adults, 2.50€ ($3.25) for students and ages 12 to 25, and free for children under 12. In July and August, it's open daily 9am to 8pm; the rest of the year, it opens daily at 9am and closes between 5 and 7:30pm, depending on the time of sunset.

La Turbie boasts a ruined monument erected by Roman emperor Augustus in 6 B.C., the **Trophée des Alps (Trophy of the Alps)** ★. It's near a rock formation known as La Tête de Chien, at the highest point along the Grand Corniche, 450m (1,476 ft.) above sea level. The Roman Senate ordered the creation of the monument, which many locals call La Trophée d'Auguste, to celebrate the subjugation of the people of the French Alps by the Roman armies.

A short distance from the monument is the **Musée du Trophée d'Auguste,** rue Albert-1er, La Turbie (✆ **04-93-41-20-84**), a mini-museum containing finds from digs nearby and information about the monument's restoration. Open May to September daily 9:30am to 1:30pm and 2:30 to 6:30pm, October to April daily 10am to 1:30pm and 2:30 to 5pm. Admission is 5€ ($6.50) for adults, 3.50€ ($4.55) for students and ages 18 to 25, and free for children 17 and under. It's closed January 1, May 1, November, and December 25.

The **Office de Tourisme** is on place du Général-de-Gaulle, Eze-Village (✆ **04-93-41-26-00;** fax 04-93-41-04-80; www.eze-riviera.com).

WHERE TO STAY

Hostellerie du Château de la Chèvre d'Or ★★★ This is one of the grandest resort hotels along the Eastern Riviera. The miniature-village retreat was built in the 1920s in neo-Gothic style. It's a Relais & Châteaux property in a complex of village houses, all with views of the coastline. But unlike most villages in the area, this one doesn't have a beach. The decor of the "Golden Goat" maintains its character while adding modern comfort. The spacious guest rooms are filled with quality furnishings, and the large bathrooms have excellent fixtures, including tub/shower combinations. Even if you don't spend the night, try to visit for a drink in the lounge, which has a panoramic view.

Rue du Barri, Eze-Village 06360. ✆ **04-92-10-66-66.** Fax 04-93-41-06-72. www.chevredor.com. 33 units. 270€–780€ ($351–$1,014) double; from 1,650€ ($2,145) suite. AE, DC, MC, V. Closed mid-Nov to early Mar. **Amenities:** 3 restaurants; bar; outdoor pool; gym; sauna; room service; babysitting; laundry service; dry cleaning. *In room:* A/C, TV, minibar, hair dryer, safe.

WHERE TO DINE

Le Troubadour FRENCH/PROVENÇAL The stone-fronted medieval house that contains this well-known restaurant has, since World War I, housed businesses that have included a bar, a delicatessen, and the local post office. Today, within three dining rooms, each accented with thick ceiling beams, you can order succulent and flavorful dishes that include braised rabbit in aspic, served with warm hearts of artichoke, foie gras, and carrots; a delightful filet of John Dory with stuffed and deep-fried zucchini blossoms; roasted rack of lamb with parsley sauce; and other dishes that each manage to showcase some aspect of the Mediterranean diet. You'll find the place close to the village church, in the upper heights of Eze Village.

4 rue du Brec, Eze Village. ✆ **04-93-41-19-03.** Reservations recommended. Main courses 25€–30€ ($33–$39); fixed-price menus 35€–48€ ($46–$62). MC, V. Tues–Sat 1–2:30pm and 7:30–10pm. Closed late Nov to Christmas, 1 week between late Feb and Mar, and 2 weeks in late June to early July.

18 Monaco ★★★

939km (583 miles) S of Paris, 18km (11 miles) E of Nice

Monaco, according to Somerset Maugham, is defined as "370 sunny acres peopled with shady characters." Katharine Hepburn once called it "a pimple on the chin of the south of France." She wasn't referring to the principality's lack of beauty but rather to the preposterous idea of a little country, a feudal anomaly, taking up some of the choicest Riviera coastline. Monaco became the property of the Grimaldi clan as early as 1297. It has maintained something resembling independence since. In a fit of impatience, the French annexed it in 1793, but the ruling family recovered it in 1814.

Hemmed in by France on three sides and the Mediterranean on the fourth, tiny Monaco maintains its independence. And as almost everybody knows, the Monégasques do not pay taxes. Nearly all their country's revenue comes from tourism and gambling.

Monaco, or more precisely its capital of Monte Carlo, has for a century been a symbol of glamour. The 1956 marriage of Prince Rainier III to American actress Grace Kelly enhanced its status. She had met the prince when she was in Cannes to promote *To Catch a Thief.* Their daughter Caroline was born in 1957; a son, Albert, in 1958; and a second daughter, Stephanie, in 1965. The Monégasques welcomed the birth of Caroline but went wild for Albert, a male heir. According to a 1918 treaty, Monaco would become an autonomous state under French protection should the ruling dynasty become extinct.

Though not always happy in her role, Princess Grace won the respect and admiration of her people. The Monégasques still mourn her death in a 1982 car accident.

In April 2005, Prince Rainier died after suffering ailing health for many years. Upon his father's death, the unmarried Prince Albert became the reigning prince. Unlike his father's storybook marriage to Grace Kelly, Albert remains not only unmarried but also without an heir, even though he's admitted to having a son out of wedlock. However, his illegitimate son cannot ascend to the throne. So concerned was Prince Rainier with this situation that he changed the Monaco constitution in 2002, allowing the crown to pass to one of the princesses or their children if Albert abdicated or died without a child. Currently, Princess Caroline is in line to succeed Albert.

The second-smallest state in Europe (Vatican City is the tiniest), Monaco consists of four parts. The old town, **Monaco-Ville,** on a promontory, "the Rock," 60m (197 ft.) high, is the seat of the royal palace and the government building, as well as the Oceanographic Museum. To the west, **La Condamine,** the home of the Monégasques, is at the foot of the old town, forming its harbor and port sector. Up from the port (Monaco is steep) is **Monte Carlo,** once the playground of royalty and still the center for the wintering wealthy, the setting for the casino and its gardens and the

Tips Reach Out & Touch Someone in Monaco

To call Monaco from within France, dial 00 (the access code for all international long-distance calls from France), followed by the **country code, 377,** and then the eight-digit local phone number. (Don't dial the 33 code; that's the country code for France.)

To call Monaco from North America, dial the international access code, 011, the country code, 377, and then the eight-digit Monaco number.

To call any other country from within Monaco, dial 00 (the international access code), then the applicable country code, and the number. For example, to call Cannes, you would dial 00, 33 (France's country code), 4 (the city code, without the zero), and the eight-digit number.

deluxe hotels. The fourth part, **Fontvieille,** is a neat industrial suburb. **Monte-Carlo Beach,** at the far frontier, is on French soil. It attracts a chic crowd, including movie stars in the skimpiest bikinis and thongs.

Monaco used to be slow in summer, but now July and August tend to be so crowded that it's hard to get a room. The Monégasques court an affluent crowd. But with the decline of royalty, Monaco has had to develop a broader tourism base. You can now stay here moderately, though still not cheaply. As always, you can lose your shirt at the casinos. "Suicide Terrace" at the casino, though not used as frequently as in the old days, is still a real temptation to many.

Even when family fortunes aren't slipping through the fingers of gamblers, the casino has been the subject of legends and the setting for many films. Richard Burton presented Elizabeth Taylor with the huge Kohinoor diamond here. Because Monaco is a tax haven, many celebrities have become residents, including Plácido Domingo, Claudia Schiffer, Boris Becker, and Ringo Starr.

ESSENTIALS

GETTING THERE Monaco has rail, bus, and highway connections from other coastal cities, especially Nice. **Trains** arrive every 30 minutes from Cannes, Nice, Menton, and Antibes. For more rail information, call ✆ **08-92-35-35-35,** or visit www.voyages-sncf.com. Monaco's railway station (Gare SNCF) is on avenue Prince Pierre. It's a long walk uphill from the train station to Monte Carlo. If you'd rather take a **taxi** but can't find one at the station, call ✆ **93-15-01-01.** There are no border formalities when entering Monaco from mainland France. Monaco is a lengthy **drive** from Paris. Take A6 south to Lyon. At Lyon, connect with A7 south to Aix-en-Provence and take A6 south directly to Monaco. If you're already on the Riviera, drive from Nice along N7 northeast. It's only 19km (12 miles), but with traffic, the drive can take 30 minutes.

VISITOR INFORMATION The **Direction du Tourisme et des Congrés** office is at 2A bd. des Moulins (✆ **92-16-61-66;** fax 92-16-61-16; www.monaco-tourisme.com).

SPECIAL EVENTS Two of the most-watched **car-racing events** in Europe are in January (Le Rallye) and May (the Grand Prix). For more information, call ✆ **99-99-30-00.** In June, Monte Carlo is home to a weeklong convention that attracts media moguls from virtually everywhere, **Le Festival International de la Télévision,** Grimaldi Forum, Avenue Princess Grace (✆ **99-99-30-00**). Shows from all over the world are broadcast and judged on their merits.

FUN ON & OFF THE BEACH

BEACHES Just outside the border, on French soil, the **Monte-Carlo Beach Club** adjoins the Monte-Carlo Beach Hotel, 22 av. Princesse-Grace (© **04-93-28-66-66**). The beach club has thrived for years; it's an integral part of Monaco's social life. Princess Grace used to come here in flowery swimsuits, greeting her friends and subjects with humor and style. The sand is replenished at regular intervals. You'll find two large pools (one for children), cabanas, a restaurant, a cafe, and a bar. As the temperature drops in late August, the beach closes for the winter. The admission charge of 45€ to 80€ ($59–$104), depending on the season, grants you access to the changing rooms, toilets, restaurants, and bar, and use of a mattress for sunbathing. A day's use of a cubicle, where you can lock up your street clothes, costs an extra 18€ to 25€ ($23–$33). A fee of 35€ to 90€ ($46–$117) will get you a day's use of a private cabana. Most socializing occurs around the pool's edges. As usual, topless is de rigueur, but bottomless isn't.

Monaco, the quintessential kingdom by the sea, offers swimming and sunbathing at the **Plage de Larvotto,** off avenue Princesse-Grace (© **93-30-63-84**). There's no charge to enter this strip of beach, whose surface is frequently replenished with sand hauled in by barge. Part of it is open, other sections are private.

GOLF The prestigious **Monte Carlo Golf Club,** route N7, La Turbie (© **04-92-41-50-70**), on French soil, is a par-72 course with scenic panoramas. Certain perks (including use of electric carts) are reserved for members. In order to play, nonmembers are asked to show proof of membership in another club and provide evidence of their handicap. Greens fees for 18 holes are 90€ ($117) Monday to Friday, 110€ ($143) Saturday and Sunday. Clubs rent for 20€ ($26). The course is open daily 8am to sunset.

SPA TREATMENTS In 1908, the Société des Bains de Mer launched a seawater (thalassotherapy) spa in Monte Carlo, inaugurated by Prince Albert I. It was bombed during World War II and didn't reopen until 1996. **Les Thermes Marins de Monte-Carlo,** 2 av. de Monte-Carlo (© **92-16-40-40**), is one of the largest spas in Europe. Spread over four floors are a pool, a Turkish *hammam* (steam bath), a healthy restaurant, a juice bar, two tanning booths, a fitness center, a beauty center, and private treatment rooms. A day pass, giving access to the sauna, steam rooms, fitness facilities, and pools, costs 78€ ($101). Massages cost 65€ ($85) for a 30-minute session, 110€ ($143) for a 60-minute session.

SWIMMING Overlooking the yacht-clogged harbor, the **Stade Nautique Rainier-III,** quai Albert-1er, at La Condamine (© **93-30-64-83**), a pool frequented by the Monégasques, was a gift from Prince Rainier to his subjects. It's open May to October daily 9am to 6pm (until midnight July–Aug). Admission for a one-time visit costs 5.40€ ($7) per person; discounts are available if you plan to visit 10 times or more. Between November and April, it's an ice-skating rink. If you want to swim in winter, try the indoor **Piscine du Prince Héréditaire Albert,** in the Stade Louis II, 7 av. de Castellane (© **92-05-42-13**). It's open Monday, Tuesday, Thursday, and Friday 7:30am to 2:30pm; Saturday 1 to 6pm; and Sunday 8am to 1pm. Admission is 3.50€ ($4.55).

TENNIS & SQUASH The **Monte Carlo Country Club,** 155 av. Princesse-Grace, Roquebrune-St-Roman, France (© **04-93-41-30-15**), has 21 clay and 2 concrete tennis courts. The 36€ ($47) fee provides access to a restaurant, health club with Jacuzzi and sauna, putting green, beach, squash courts, and the well-maintained tennis courts.

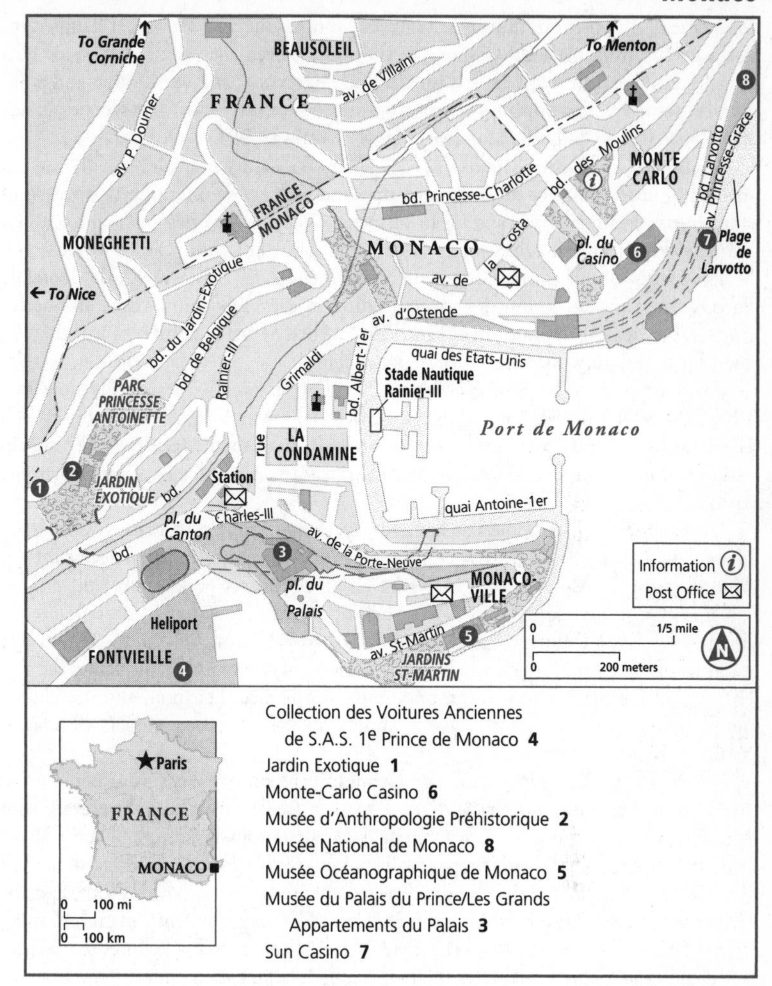

Guests of the hotels administered by the Société des Bains de Mer (Hôtel de Paris, Hermitage, Mirabeau, and Monte Carlo Beach Club) pay half-price. Plan to spend at least half a day, ending a round of tennis with use of any of the other facilities. It's open daily 8am to 8 or 9pm, depending on the season.

SHOPPING

Bijoux Marlene, Les Galeries du Métropole, 207 av. des Spélugues (© **93-50-17-57**), sells only imitation gemstones. They're shamelessly copied from the real McCoys sold by Cartier and Van Cleef & Arpels. Made in Italy of gold-plated silver, the jewelry (the staff refers to it as Les Bijoux Fantaisies) costs 10€ to 1,000€ ($13–$1,300) per piece.

Boutique du Rocher, 1 av. de la Madone (© **93-30-91-17**), is the larger of two boutiques Princess Grace opened in 1966 as the official retail outlets of her charitable foundation. The organization merchandises Monégasque and Provençal handicrafts. A short walk from place du Casino, the shop sells carved frames for pictures or mirrors; housewares; gift items crafted from porcelain, textiles, and wood; toys; and dolls. On the premises are workshops where artisans produce the goods. The second branch is at 25 rue Emile de Loth, Monaco-Ville (✆ **93-30-33-99**).

Argument, 17 bd. des Moulins (✆ **93-50-33-85**), aims at a solid middle-bracket man who simply wants to dress appropriately and look good. You can pick up a swimsuit, shorts, slacks, a blazer, and a pair of socks to replace the ones you ruined on too many walking tours, at prices that won't require that you remortgage your house.

If you insist on ultrafancy stores, you'll find them cheek by jowl with the Hôtel de Paris and the casino, lining the streets leading to the Hôtel Hermitage, and across from the gardens at the mini-mall Park Palace. **Allée Serge-Diaghilev** is just that, an alley, but a very tiny one filled with designer shops.

You don't have to be Princess Caroline to shop in Monaco, especially now that **FNAC** (✆ **93-10-81-81**) has opened in the heart of town. A branch of the big French chain that sells CDs, tapes, and books is at the **Galeries du Métropole,** 17 av. des Spélugues, in the Jardins du Casino, next to the Hôtel Métropole and across from the casino.

The Galeries du Métropole also has a few specialty shops worth visiting. Check out **Geneviève Lethu** (✆ **93-50-09-41**) for colorful and country tabletop accessories or **Manufacture de Monaco** (✆ **93-50-64-63**) for glorious bone china and elegant tabletop items. Two doors away is a branch of the chic but often affordable French linen house **Yves Delorme** (✆ **93-50-08-70**). **Royal Food** (✆ **93-15-05-04**) is a gourmet grocery store, which you'll find down a set of curving stairs hidden in the side entrance of the mall; here you can buy food from France, Lebanon, and the United States, or stock up for *le pique-nique* or for day trips. This market is open Monday to Saturday 10am to 7:30pm.

For real-people shopping, stroll **rue Grimaldi,** the principality's most commercial street, near the fruit, flower, and food market (see below), and **boulevard des Moulins,** closer to the casino, where you'll see glamorous boutiques. There's also a pedestrian thoroughfare with shops less forbiddingly chic than those along boulevard des Moulins: **Rue Princesse-Caroline** is loaded with bakeries, flower shops, and the closest thing you'll find to funkiness in Monaco. Also check out the **Formule 1** shop, 15 rue Grimaldi (✆ **93-15-92-44**), where everything from racing helmets to specialty key chains and T-shirts celebrates the roaring, high-octane racing machines.

No one comes to the Riviera for bargain shopping but, even in chic Monte Carlo, there is **Stock Griffe,** 5 bis av. St-Michel (✆ **93-50-86-06**). It slashes prices on Prada, Pucci, Escada, and the like. A tremendous amount of merchandise is packed into these tiny precincts. The place may be small, but not the discounts, some of which add up to an astonishing 90%. Greater reductions are for older garments that didn't move, but you can also snap up some newer fashions.

MARKETS For a look at the heart and soul of the real Monaco, head to place des Armes for the **fruit, flower, and food market,** which starts daily at 7:30am. The indoor and outdoor market has a fountain, cafes, and hand-painted vegetable tiles beneath your feet. The outdoor market packs up at noon, and some dealers at the indoor market stay open to 2pm. If you prefer bric-a-brac, there's a small but funky (especially for Monaco) flea market, **Les Puces de Fontvieille,** on Saturday 9:30am to 5:30pm on the quai Jean-Charles Rey, immediately adjacent to Port de Fontvieille.

SEEING THE SIGHTS

Collection des Voitures Anciennes de S.A.S. le Prince de Monaco *Kids* Prince Rainier III opened a showcase of his private collection of more than 100 vintage autos, including the 1956 Rolls-Royce Silver Cloud that carried the prince and princess on their wedding day. Monaco shopkeepers gave it to the royal couple as a wedding present. A 1952 Austin Taxi on display was once used as the royal "family car." Other exhibits are a "woodie" (a 1937 Ford station wagon Prince Louis II used on hunting trips); a 1925 Bugatti 35B, winner of the Monaco Grand Prix in 1929; a 1903 De Dion Bouton; and a 1986 Lamborghini Countach.

Les Terrasses de Fontvieille. ✆ **92-05-28-56.** www.palais.mc. Admission 6€ ($7.80) adults, 3€ ($3.90) students and children 8–14, free for children under 8. Daily 10am–6pm. Closed Dec 25.

Jardin Exotique ★★ Built on the side of a rock, the gardens are known for their cactus collection. They were begun by Prince Albert I, who was a naturalist and scientist. He spotted some succulents growing in the palace gardens and created this garden from them. You can also explore the grottoes here, as well as the **Musée d'Anthropologie Préhistorique** (✆ **93-15-29-80**). The view of the principality is splendid.

Bd. du Jardin-Exotique. ✆ **93-15-29-80.** Admission (includes museum) 7€ ($9.10) adults, 3.60€ ($4.70) children 6–18, free for children under 6. Mid-May to mid-Sept daily 9am–7pm; mid-Sept to Nov 14 and Dec 26 to mid-May daily 9am–6pm. Closed Nov 15–Dec 25.

Les Grands Appartements du Palais ★ Most summer day-trippers from Nice want to see the home of Monaco's royal family, the Palais du Prince, which dominates the principality from "the Rock." A tour of the Grands Appartements allows you a glimpse of the Throne Room and some of the art, including works by Bruegel and Holbein, as well as Princess Grace's state portrait. The palace was built in the 13th century, and part dates from the Renaissance. The ideal time to arrive is 11:55am, to watch the 10-minute **Relève de la Garde** (changing of the guard).

In a wing of the palace, the **Musée du Palais du Prince (Souvenirs Napoléoniens et Collection d'Archives)** holds a collection of mementos of Napoleon and Monaco. When the royal residence is closed, this museum is the only part of the palace the public can visit.

Place du Palais. ✆ **93-25-18-31.** www.palais.mc. Combination ticket 6€ ($7.80) adults, 3€ ($3.90) children 8–14, free for children under 8. Palace and museum June–Sept daily 9:30am–6pm; Oct daily 10am–5pm. Museum also open Nov 1–11 daily 10am–5pm; Dec 17–May Tues–Sun 10:30am–noon and 2–4:30pm. Palace closed Nov–May; museum closed Nov 12–Dec 16.

Musée National de Monaco ★ *Kids* In a villa designed in a style similar to that of Charles Garnier (architect of Paris's Opéra Garnier), this museum houses a magnificent collection of antique mechanical toys and dolls. See the 18th-century Neapolitan crib, which contains some 200 figures. This collection, assembled by Mme de Galea, was presented to the principality in 1972; it originated with the 18th- and 19th-century practice of displaying new fashions on doll models.

17 av. Princesse-Grace. ✆ **93-30-91-26.** www.monte-carlo.mc/musee-national. Admission 6€ ($7.80) adults, 3.50€ ($4.55) students and children 6–14, free for children under 6. Easter–Sept daily 10am–6pm; Oct–Easter daily 10am–12:15pm and 2:30–6pm. Closed Jan 1, May 1, Nov 19, Dec 25, and 4 days during Grand Prix.

Musée Océanographique de Monaco ★★ *Kids* Albert I, great-grandfather of the present prince, founded this museum in 1910. In the main rotunda is a statue of Albert in his favorite costume: that of a sea captain. Displayed are specimens he collected during 30 years of expeditions. The aquarium, one of the finest in Europe, contains more than 90 tanks.

The collection is exhibited in the zoology room. Some of the exotic creatures were unknown before he captured them. You'll see models of the ships aboard which he directed his scientific cruises from 1885 to 1914. The most important part of the laboratory has been preserved and re-created as closely as possible. Skeletons of specimens, including a whale that drifted ashore at Pietra Ligure in 1896, are on the main floor. The whale skeleton is remarkable for its healed fractures sustained when a vessel struck the animal as it was drifting on the surface. An exhibition devoted to the discovery of the ocean is in the physical-oceanography room on the first floor. Underwater movies are shown in the lecture room. There is also a shark lagoon.

Av. St-Martin. ✆ **93-15-36-00.** www.oceano.mc. Admission 13€ ($16) adults, 6€ ($7.80) children 6–18, free for children under 6. Apr–Sept daily 9:30am–7pm (until 7:30pm July–Aug); Oct–Mar daily 10am–6pm.

WHERE TO STAY

VERY EXPENSIVE

Hôtel de Paris ★★★ On the resort's main plaza, opposite the casino, this is one of the world's most famous hotels. The ornate facade has marble pillars, and the lounge has an Art Nouveau rose window at the peak of the dome. The decor includes marble pillars, statues, crystal chandeliers, sumptuous carpets, Louis XVI chairs, and a wall-size mural. Elegant fabrics, rich carpeting, classic accessories, and an excellent restaurant make this hotel a favorite of the world's most discerning travelers. The guest rooms come in a variety of styles, with period or contemporary furnishings. Some units are enormous. Bathrooms are large, with marble and elegant brass fittings, plus tub/shower combinations. ***Note:*** The rooms opening onto the sea aren't as spacious as those in the rear.

Place du Casino, Monaco 98007. ✆ **92-16-30-00.** Fax 92-16-26-26. www.montecarloresort.com. 191 units. 400€–940€ ($520–$1,222) double; from 1,995€ ($2,594) suite. AE, DC, MC, V. Valet parking 28€ ($36). **Amenities:** 3 restaurants (see "Where to Dine," below); bar; large indoor pool; fitness center; Thermes Marins spa offering thalassotherapy under medical supervision; 2 saunas; concierge; salon; room service; babysitting; laundry service; dry cleaning; nonsmoking rooms. *In room:* A/C, TV, minibar, hair dryer, safe.

Hôtel Hermitage ★★ Picture yourself sitting in a wicker armchair, enjoying a drink under an ornate stained-glass dome with an encircling wrought-iron balcony. You can do this at the cliff-top Hermitage. The "palace," with its wedding-cake facade, was the creation of Jean Marquet (who also created marquetry). Most rooms have large brass beds and decoratively framed doors that open onto balconies. Even the smallest rooms are medium-size, and the largest one is fit for the biggest movie star with the most trunks. Large mirrors, elegant fabrics and upholstery, deluxe bathrooms with tubs and showers, and sumptuous beds make living here idyllic. In 2003, the hotel added two floors to its century-old main building. Guest rooms are modern and sleek in the styling. High-season rates apply during Christmas, New Year's, Easter, and July and August.

Square Beaumarchais, Monaco Cedex 98005. ✆ **98-06-59-77.** Fax 92-16-38-52. www.montecarloresort.com. 280 units. 320€–528€ ($416–$686) double; 568€–792€ ($738–$1,030) junior suite; from 1,596€ ($2,075) suite. AE, DISC, MC, V. Parking 20€ ($24). **Amenities:** Restaurant; 2 bars; indoor pool; health club; sauna; room service; babysitting; laundry service; dry cleaning; nonsmoking rooms. *In room:* A/C, TV, minibar, hair dryer, safe.

EXPENSIVE

Columbus Monaco Hotel ★★ *Value* In the modern Fontvieille section of Monaco, this stylish, contemporary hotel faces Princess Grace's rose garden and the sea. Guest rooms are done in what owner Ken McCulloch calls "hybrid hip," a style that evokes both Miami and London. Elegant touches include Lartigue photos of the Riviera, high-tech cabinets filled with video games, and chocolate leather furnishings. Guest rooms have deluxe linens and Frette bathrobes. There are some disadvantages: For example, the hotel is in a condo complex whose residents share the pool. However, a boat carries guests to a tranquil sandy beach nearby.

23 av. des Papalins, Monaco 98000. ✆ **92-05-90-00.** Fax 92-05-23-86. www.columbushotels.com. 181 units. 265€–295€ ($345–$384) double; 395€–780€ ($514–$1,014) suite. AE, MC, V. Parking 23€ ($30). **Amenities:** Restaurant (brasserie w/antipasto buffet); bar; outdoor pool; fitness room; business center; salon/barber; room service; babysitting; laundry service; dry cleaning; nonsmoking rooms; limited-mobility rooms. *In room:* A/C, TV, minibar, hair dryer, iron/ironing board, safe.

Fairmont Monte Carlo ★ Although a bit down the scale from the two previous choices, this is also a deluxe palace, built by the Loews Corporation but bought in 1998 by a consortium of local investors and renamed the Monte Carlo Grand Hôtel. Fairmont Hotels & Resorts took over the property in early 2005, renaming it again.

It hugs the coast below the terraces that support the famous casino, on one of the most valuable pieces of real estate along the Côte d'Azur. Architecturally daring when built (some of its foundations were sunk into the seabed, and some of the principality's busiest highways roar beneath it), the resort is viewed as an integral enhancement of Monégasque life. It contains Monaco's highest concentration of restaurants, bars, and nightclubs—think of it as Las Vegas with a Gallic accent. The guest rooms are conservatively furnished. Each has a pastel decor that's flooded with light from big windows and views over the town or the sea. All units contain large bathrooms with tubs and showers.

12 av. des Spélugues, Monaco 98007. ✆ **93-50-65-00.** Fax 93-30-01-57. www.fairmont.com/Montecarlo. 619 units. 199€–389€ ($259–$506) double; from 439€ ($571) suite. AE, DC, MC, V. Parking 29€ ($38). **Amenities:** 4 restaurants; 2 bars; outdoor pool; health club; sauna; room service; babysitting; limited-mobility rooms. *In room:* A/C, TV, minibar, hair dryer, safe.

Hôtel Mirabeau ★★ In the heart of Monte Carlo, next to the casino, the Mirabeau combines modern design with a refined atmosphere. Large mirrors, spacious lighted closets, and sumptuous beds with luxurious mattresses make staying here idyllic; many rooms have terraces with views overlooking the Mediterranean. Although the newest rooms are as fine as those in the main building, many guests prefer older ones for their old-fashioned French decor and street-front exposures. Bathrooms are well appointed, with tub/shower combos.

1 av. Princesse-Grace, Monaco 98000. ✆ **92-16-65-65.** Fax 93-50-84-85. www.montecarloresort.com. 103 units. 320€–528€ ($416–$686) double; 568€–2,124€ ($738–$2,761) suite. AE, DC, MC, V. Parking 24€ ($31). **Amenities:** Restaurant; bar; outdoor pool; gym; sauna; room service; babysitting; laundry service; dry cleaning; nonsmoking rooms. *In room:* A/C, TV, minibar, hair dryer, safe, robes.

Monte-Carlo Beach Hôtel ★ Despite its name, this hotel is in France, not Monaco. The most beautiful of the accommodations is the circular unit above the lobby. Eva Peron stayed here in 1947 during her infamous Rainbow Tour of Europe. Princess Grace came here almost every day in summer to paddle around the pool, a rendezvous for the rich and beautiful. All the spacious rooms are luxurious, right down to the sea views; the beautiful bathrooms have tub/shower combinations. The greatest choice of dining venues is available from June to September, when Le Restaurant serves gourmet meals at lunch and dinner. Le Rivage offers brasserie-style lunches and dinners near the pool. La Potinière features gastronomic lunches. La Vigie, a short walk from the hotel near several piers where yachts can tie up, offers buffets inspired by the cuisine of Provence.

Av. Princesse-Grace, Monte-Carlo Beach, Roquebrune–Cap-Martin 06190. ✆ **98-06-25-25.** Fax 98-06-26-26. www.montecarloresort.com. 47 units. 270€–620€ ($351–$806) double; from 803€ ($1,044) suite. AE, DC, MC, V. Free parking. Closed Nov–Mar. **Amenities:** 3 restaurants; 2 bars; outdoor pool; gym; sauna; room service; babysitting; laundry service; dry cleaning; nonsmoking rooms. *In room:* A/C, TV, minibar, hair dryer, safe.

MODERATE

Hôtel Alexandra This hotel is on a busy, often-noisy street corner in the center of the business district above the Casino Gardens. Its comfortably furnished guest rooms don't generate much excitement, but they're reliable and respectable. The Alexandra knows it can't compete with the giants of Monaco, and doesn't even try, but it attracts those who'd like to visit the principality without spending a fortune.

35 bd. Princesse-Charlotte, Monaco 98000. ✆ **93-50-63-13.** Fax 92-16-06-48. www.monaco-hotel.com/montecarlo/alexandra. 56 units. 135€–170€ ($176–$221) double. AE, DC, MC, V. Parking 7€ ($9.10). **Amenities:** Room service; babysitting. *In room:* A/C, TV, minibar, hair dryer, iron.

INEXPENSIVE

Hôtel de France Not all Monégasques are rich, as a stroll along rue de la Turbie will convince you. Here you'll find some of the cheapest accommodations and eateries in the high-priced principality. This 19th-century hotel, 3 minutes from the rail station, has modest furnishings but is well kept and comfortable. The guest rooms and bathrooms are small, and each unit has a shower.

6 rue de la Turbie, Monaco 98000. ✆ **93-30-24-64.** Fax 92-16-13-34. www.monte-carlo.mc/france. 26 units. 85€–108€ ($111–$140) double. Rates include breakfast. MC, V. Parking 7.50€ ($9.75). **Amenities:** Bar; room service. *In room:* TV, hair dryer.

WHERE TO DINE

VERY EXPENSIVE

Le Louis XV ★★★ FRENCH/ITALIAN In the Hôtel de Paris, the Louis XV offers what one critic called "down-home Riviera cooking within a Fabergé egg." Star chef Alain Ducasse creates refined but not overly adorned cuisine, served by the finest staff in Monaco. Everything is light and attuned to the seasons, with intelligent, modern interpretations of Provençal and northern Italian dishes. You'll find chargrilled breast of baby pigeon with sautéed duck liver, an ongoing specialty known as "Provençal vegetables with crushed truffles," and everything from truffles and caviar to the best stewed salt cod on the coast. Ducasse divides his time between this enclave and his restaurants in Paris and New York. The hotel keeps its collection of rare fine wines in a dungeon chiseled out of the rocks.

In the Hôtel de Paris, place du Casino. ✆ **98-06-88-64.** Reservations recommended. Jacket and tie required for men. Main courses 60€–420€ ($78–$546); fixed-price dinner 110€–210€ ($143–$273). AE, MC, V. Thurs–Mon 12:15–1:45pm and 8–9:45pm; also June–Sept Wed 12:15–1:45pm. Closed Feb 14–Mar 1 and Nov 28–Dec 28.

EXPENSIVE

Baccarat ★ ITALIAN Baccarat is an elegant testimonial to the flavors and presentations of Italy, with an emphasis on Sicily, birthplace of owner-chef Carmelo Gulletta. The avant-garde paintings of Monégasque painter Clérissy line the walls of the vaguely Art Deco space, but the owners say the cuisine is more Italian and less Monégasque than anything else in Monaco. Guletta's French-born, English-speaking wife, Patricia, supervises the dining room. The antipasto selection is the best in the principality, ranging from steamed asparagus with hollandaise to Andalusian gazpacho. The chefs turn out risottos as good as anything in Italy, along with Monaco's most enticing pastas such as savory spaghetti with baby clams. In general, fish dishes such as sole meunière are better than meat and poultry offerings.

4 bd. des Moulins. ✆ **93-50-66-92.** Reservations recommended. Main courses 10€–32€ ($13–$42). AE, MC, V. Daily noon–2:30pm and 7–11pm.

Bar et Boeuf ★★ INTERNATIONAL This restaurant is one of the many jewels in the crown of superchef Alain Ducasse, who is, according to many critics, both a culinary genius and the orchestrator of an upscale international assembly line. Acclaimed restaurant critic Gael Greene has referred to him as "Robo-Chef," and a small number of increasingly vocal critics complain about "franchise sprawl." You can still get a genuinely good meal here, even if none of it is prepared or even supervised by Ducasse. Bar et Boeuf is an upscale Gallic reinvention of a surf-and-turf restaurant. The only fish here is sea bass *(bar),* and the beef is perhaps the most cosseted and fussed-over meat in France. Examples include filets of sea bass with citrus marmalade and an assortment of species of braised celery; filet steak with Sicilian herbs; beef Wellington; and beef with a sauté of *taggiasche* (Italian) olives and wine glaze, served with fried spiny artichokes. The most lavish dish is *tournedos rossini* layered with foie gras and truffles, served with a tartare of truffled foie gras and pan-fried exotic mushrooms.

In the Sporting d'Eté Monte Carlo, av. Princesse-Grace. ✆ **92-16-60-60.** Reservations recommended. Main courses 28€–57€ ($36–$74). AE, DC, MC, V. Late May to late Sept daily 8pm–1am. Closed rest of year.

Le Café de Paris ★ TRADITIONAL FRENCH Its *plats du jour* are well prepared, and its location, the plaza adjacent to the casino and the Hôtel de Paris, allows a front-row view of the comings and goings of the nerve center of Monte Carlo. We find this 1985 re-creation of old-time Monaco a bit too enraptured with the devil-may-care glamour of early-1900s Monte Carlo. Despite that, the Café de Paris continues to draw patrons who appreciate the razzmatazz and all the glass and chrome. Menu items change frequently. Local office workers appreciate the platters, especially at lunchtime, because they can be served and consumed quickly. They range from fresh grilled sea bass to steak tartare with matchstick frites. Adjacent to the restaurant, you'll find (and hear) a jangling collection of slot machines and a predictable cluster of boutiques.

Place du Casino. ✆ **92-16-20-20.** Reservations recommended. Main courses 17€–55€ ($22–$72); fixed-price menu 75€ ($98). AE, DC, MC, V. Daily 8am–3am.

Rampoldi ★ FRENCH/ITALIAN More than any other restaurant in Monte Carlo, Rampoldi is linked to the charming but somewhat dated interpretation of *la dolce vita.* Opened in the 1950s at the edge of the Casino Gardens and staffed with a mix of old and new, it's more Italian than French in spirit. It also serves some of the best cuisine in Monte Carlo. Menu items include an array of pastas, such as tortellini with cream and white-truffle sauce; sea bass roasted in a salt crust; ravioli stuffed with crayfish; and veal kidneys in Madeira sauce. Crêpes suzette makes a spectacular finish.

3 av. des Spélugues. ✆ **93-30-70-65.** Reservations required. Main courses 21€–70€ ($27–$91). AE, MC, V. Daily 12:15–2:30pm and 7:30–11:30pm.

MODERATE

Le Texan TEX-MEX/INDIAN/MOROCCAN These incongruous specialties have entertained even the most discriminating French taste buds. Le Texan has a handful of outdoor tables, a long bar, a roughly plastered dining room with the flag of the Lone Star State, a bar whose shape was inspired by the Alamo in San Antonio, and a scattering of Mexican artifacts. You'll find it on a sloping street leading down to the harbor—a world away from the casinos and nightlife of the upper reaches. Menu items include T-bone steak, barbecued ribs, pizzas, nachos, tacos, a Dallasburger (*avec* guacamole), and the best margaritas in town. Thanks to several members of the kitchen staff who hail from India and Morocco, the restaurant also produces some great curry dishes (chicken, beef, and lamb) as well as North African–style couscous.

4 rue Suffren-Reymond. ✆ **93-30-34-54.** Reservations recommended. Main courses 13€–25€ ($17–$33). AE, DC, MC, V. Daily 11am–midnight.

INEXPENSIVE

Stars 'n' Bars *Kids* AMERICAN/PACIFIC RIM Modeled on the sports bars popular in the U.S., this place features two dining and drinking areas devoted to American-style food, as well as a bar decorated with memorabilia of notable athletes. No one will mind if you drop in just for a drink, but if you're hungry, menu items read like an homage to the American experience. Try an Indy 500, a Triathlon salad, or the Breakfast of Champions (eggs and bacon and all the fixings). For kids under 12, order the Little Leaguer's Platter or pizza.

In 2004, its owners added an all-new dining venue, **Fusion Cuisine** (same address, phone, and hours), to a space upstairs from the main dining room. Here, platters inspired by the cuisines of the Pacific Rim are featured, each within the same price range as the food served on the restaurant's street level. Examples include sushi, tempuras, rice-based dishes, and fast-wok-fried dishes of meats and seafood.

6 quai Antoine-1er. ✆ **97-97-95-95.** Reservations recommended. Dinner salads and platters 8€–24€ ($10–$31); sandwiches 9.50€–15€ ($12–$19); pizzas 9€–15€ ($12–$19). AE, DC, MC, V. June–Sept daily 11am–midnight; Oct–May Tues–Sun 11am–midnight. Bar open until 3am.

MONACO AFTER DARK

CASINOS **Sun Casino,** in the Monte Carlo Grand Hôtel, 12 av. des Spélugues (✆ **93-50-65-00**), is a huge room filled with one-armed bandits. It also features blackjack, craps, and American roulette. Additional slot machines are on the roof, with a wide view of the sea. Slot machines operate daily 11am to 4am, and gaming tables are open daily 5pm to 4am. Admission is free.

François Blanc developed the **Monte-Carlo Casino,** place du Casino (✆ **92-16-21-21**), into the most famous in the world, attracting the exiled aristocracy of Russia, Sarah Bernhardt, Mata Hari, King Farouk, and Aly Khan. The architect of Paris's Opéra Garnier, Charles Garnier, built the oldest part of the casino, and it remains an example of the 19th century's most opulent architecture. The building encompasses the casino and other areas for different kinds of entertainment, including a theater (Opéra de Monte-Carlo; see below) presenting opera and ballet. Baccarat, roulette, and chemin de fer are the most popular games, though you can play *le craps* and blackjack as well.

The casino's **Salle Américaine,** containing only slot machines, opens at 2pm Monday to Friday, noon on weekends. Doors for roulette and *trente et quarante* open at the same time. A section for roulette and chemin de fer opens at 3pm. Additional rooms open at 4pm with more roulette, craps, and blackjack. The gambling continues until very late or early, depending on the crowd. The casino classifies its "private rooms" as the more demure, nonelectronic areas without slots. To enter the casino, you must show a passport or other photo ID, and be at least 18. After 9pm, the staff will insist that men wear jackets and neckties for entrance to the private rooms.

Also on the premises is a **Cabaret,** in the Casino Gardens, where a well-rehearsed orchestra plays before the show. A performance featuring feathers, glitter, jazz dance, ballet, and Riviera-style seminudity begins at 10:30pm Wednesday to Saturday mid-September through June. For reservations, call ✆ **92-16-36-36.** Entrance to the cabaret costs 67€ ($87) and includes one drink and dinner.

The **Opéra de Monte-Carlo** is headquartered in the lavish, recently renovated Belle Epoque **Salle Garnier** of the casino. Tickets to the operas and other events scheduled inside range from 30€ to 110€ ($39–$143). Tickets to events within the Salle Garnier are available from a kiosk in the Atrium du Casino (✆ **98-06-28-28**), located within the casino; tickets can be purchased Tuesday through Saturday from 10am to 5:30pm.

The **Salle du Canton,** Les Terrasses, avenue de Fontvieille (✆ **92-16-22-99** for tickets and information), which filled in for the Salle Garnier during renovations, now hosts smaller concerts, chamber music concerts, and some ballet. At the **Grimaldi Forum,** 10 av. Princesse-Grace (✆ **99-99-30-00** for tickets and information)**, chamber music and smaller orchestral pieces are usually performed.** At both the Salle du Canton and the Grimaldi Forum, ballet tickets cost 8€ to 26€ ($10–$34); concert tickets cost 15€ to 30€ ($20–$39); and opera tickets cost 40€ to 150€ ($52–$195). If tickets are hard to come by, your best bet is to ask your hotel concierge for assistance.

DANCING & DRINKING **The Legend,** 3 av. des Spélugues (✆ **93-50-53-13**), is a favorite of the 25- to 30-year-old crowd who like a glamorous modern setting. It's open Thursday to Sunday 11:30pm to dawn. Entrance is free. The wildest night is Saturday, when it's mobbed. At **Le Living Room** (✆ **93-50-80-31**), 7 av. des Spélugues, crowds are international and dance-oriented. It's open every night from 10:30pm until dawn. Cozy and comfortable, it's a bit more formal and sedate than The Legend, attracting patrons over 35. There's no cover. Two nearly neighboring piano bars are **Le Sass-Café,** 5 av. des Spélugues (✆ **93-25-52-00**), and the **Zebra Square Café,** 10 av. des Spélugues (✆ **99-99-25-50**). Drink prices start at around 8€ ($10). Toniest of all, and under the same management as the Hôtel de Paris, is **Jimmy's,** in the Sporting d'Eté, avenue Princesse-Grace (✆ **92-16-22-77**), open nightly 11pm to 5am.

Le Karement, in the Grimaldi Forum (✆ **99-99-20-20**), is sprawling, ultracontemporary, and bigger than any nightlife venue ever before seen in Monte Carlo. It boasts two bars inside, a third bar on an outdoor terrace, a sprawling bay window that encompasses a view of the sea, and the kind of house and garage music that the young and young-at-heart clientele can really dance to. Open Thursday to Saturday year-round 10pm to 4am (often later, if business allows), its cover is 20€ ($26) and includes your first drink.

19 Roquebrune–Cap-Martin ★★

Roquebrune: 953km (592 miles) S of Paris, 7km (4½ miles) W of Menton, 58km (36 miles) NE of Cannes, 3km (1¾ miles) E of Monaco. Cap-Martin: 4km (2½ miles) W of Menton, 2.5km (1½ miles) W of Roquebrune

Roquebrune, along the Grande Corniche, is a charming mountain village with vaulted streets. It has been restored, though some critics find the restoration artificial. Artists' workshops and boutiques, with merchandise at inflated prices, line rue Moncollet.

Down the hill from Roquebrune, Cap-Martin is a satellite of the larger resort and technically part of the same town. It has been associated with the rich and famous since the empress Eugénie wintered here in the 19th century. In time, the resort was honored by the presence of Sir Winston Churchill, who came here often in his final years. Don't expect to find a wide sandy beach—you'll encounter plenty of rocks against a backdrop of pine and olive trees.

ESSENTIALS

GETTING THERE To **drive** to Roquebrune and Cap-Martin from Nice, follow N7 east for 26km (16 miles). Cap-Martin has **train** and bus connections from the other cities on the coast, including Nice and Menton. For **railway** information and schedules, call © **08-92-35-35-35,** or visit www.voyages-sncf.com. To reach Roquebrune, you'll have to take a **taxi.** There's no formal station in Roquebrune; you get off on the side of the highway. For bus information, contact the Gare Routière in Menton (© **04-93-35-93-60**).

VISITOR INFORMATION The **Office de Tourisme** is at 218 av. Aristide-Briand, Roquebrune (© **04-93-35-62-87;** fax 04-93-28-57-00; www.roquebrune-cap-martin.com). Two-hour walking tours of Roquebrune and St-Martin, each arranged with advance notice by the tourist office, cost 8€ ($10) for adults and 5€ ($6.50) for students and children under 18. Each departs from the tourist office and encompasses a running commentary, in both French and English, on the visual and historical attractions of Roquebrune and Cap-Martin.

SEEING THE SIGHTS

IN ROQUEBRUNE

Exploring Roquebrune will take about an hour. You can stroll through its colorful covered streets, which retain their authentic look even though the buildings are now devoted to handicrafts, gift and souvenir shops, and art galleries. From the parking lot at place de la République, head for place des Deux-Frères, turning left into rue Grimaldi. Then head left to **rue Moncollet.** This long, narrow street is covered with stepped passageways and filled with houses that date from the Middle Ages, most often with barred windows. Rue Moncollet leads into **rue du Château,** where you may want to explore the château.

Château de Roquebrune (© **04-93-35-07-22**) was originally a 10th-century Carolingian castle; the present structure dates in part from the 13th century. Dominated by two square towers, it houses a museum. From the towers there's a panoramic view along the coast. The interior is open in July and August daily 10am to 12:30pm and 3 to 7:30pm; April to June and September daily 10am to 12:30pm and 2 to 6:30pm; February, March, and October daily 10am to 12:30pm and 2 to 6pm; November to January daily 10am to 12:30pm and 2 to 5pm. Admission is 3.70€ ($4.80) for adults, 2.70€ ($3.50) for seniors, 1.60€ ($2.10) students and children 7 to 11, and free for children under 7.

Rue du Château leads to place William-Ingram. Cross this square to rue de la Fontaine, and take a left. This leads you to the **Olivier millénaire** (millenary olive tree), one of the oldest in the world—it's at least 1,000 years old.

On rue du Grimaldi is **Eglise Ste-Marguerite,** which hides behind a relatively common baroque facade that masks the 12th-century church. It's not entirely from that time, however, having undergone many alterations over the years. The interior is of polychrome plaster. Look for two paintings by a 17th-century local artist, Marc-Antoine Otto, who painted a Crucifixion (in the second altar) and a Pietà (above the entrance door). It's open Monday to Saturday 3 to 5pm, Sunday 10am to 5pm.

IN CAP-MARTIN

Cap-Martin is a rich town. At the center of the cape is a feudal tower that's now a telecommunications relay station. At its base you can see the ruins of the **Basilique St-Martin,** a priory constructed by the monks of the Lérins Islands in the 11th century. Privately owned, it is not open to visitors. After pirate raids in later centuries, notably around the 15th century, it was destroyed and abandoned. If you follow the road (by car) along the eastern shoreline of the cape, you'll be rewarded with a view of Menton against a backdrop of mountains. In the far distance looms the Italian Riviera, and you can see as far as the resort of Bordighera.

You can take one of the most interesting walks along the Riviera here. It lasts about 3 hours. The coastal path, **Sentier Touristique** ★, leads from Cap-Martin to Monte Carlo Beach. If you have a car, you can park it in the lot at avenue Winston-Churchill and begin your stroll. A sign labeled PROMENADE LE CORBUSIER marks the path. As you go along, you'll take in a view of Monaco set in a natural amphitheater. In the distance you'll see Cap-Ferrat and even Roquebrune. The scenic path ends at Monte Carlo Beach and takes about 2 hours.

If you have a car, you can take a **scenic 9.5km (6-mile) drive** ★. Leave the town on D23, following signs to Gorbio, a village on a hill reached by this winding road. Along the way you'll pass homes of the wealthy and view a verdant setting with pines and silvery olives. The site is wild and rocky, and the buildings were constructed to withstand pirate attacks. The most interesting street is rue Garibaldi, which leads past an old church to a panoramic belvedere.

WHERE TO STAY

Hôtel Victoria This rectangular low-rise building is behind a garden in front of the Cap-Martin beach. Built in the 1970s, it was renovated in the mid-1990s in a neoclassical style that weds tradition and modernity. It's the second choice in town for those who can't afford the Vista Palace (see below). Opening onto balconies fronting the sea, each of the midsize rooms is well furnished with contemporary furniture and has a neatly tiled bathroom with shower and tub. The casual bar and lounge sets a stylishly relaxed tone. Breakfast is the only meal served.

7 promenade du Cap, Roquebrune–Cap-Martin 06190. ✆ **04-93-35-65-90.** Fax 04-93-28-27-02. www.hotelmenton.com/hotel-victoria. 32 units. 90€–115€ $117–$150) double. AE, DC, V. Parking free outdoors, 10€ ($13) indoors. **Amenities:** Bar; room service; laundry service; dry cleaning. *In room:* A/C, TV, minibar.

Hôtel Vista Palace ★★★ This extraordinary hotel and restaurant stands above Cap-Martin on the outer ridge of the mountains running parallel to the coast, giving it a spectacular "airplane view" of Monaco. The design of the Vista Palace is just as fantastic: Three levels are cantilevered out into space so every unit seems to float. Nearly all the rooms have balconies facing the Mediterranean. You stay in luxe comfort here in grandly furnished guest rooms, with first-class bathrooms containing tubs and showers.

Grande Corniche, Roquebrune–Cap-Martin 06190. ✆ **04-92-10-40-00.** Fax 04-93-35-18-94. www.vistapalace.com. 68 units. 215€–350€ ($280–$455) double; 265€–690€ ($345–$897) suite. AE, DC, V. Parking 20€ ($26). **Amenities:** 3 restaurants; bar; outdoor pool; health club; Jacuzzi; sauna; room service; massage; babysitting; laundry service; dry cleaning; nonsmoking rooms; limited-mobility rooms. *In room:* A/C, TV, minibar, hair dryer, safe.

WHERE TO DINE

You may also like to try **Le Vistaero** at the Hôtel Vista Palace (see above).

Au Grand Inquisiteur ★ *Finds* TRADITIONAL FRENCH This 28-seat restaurant occupies a two-room vaulted cellar near the top of the medieval mountaintop village of Roquebrune. On the steep, winding road to the château, the building is made of rough-cut stone, with large oak beams. The cuisine, though not the area's most distinguished, is good, including the chef's duck special and scallops meunière. Most diners opt for one of the fresh fish choices. Other dishes include stuffed zucchini flowers with morel sauce. The wine list is exceptional—some 150 selections, most at reasonable prices.

18 rue du Château. ✆ **04-93-35-05-37**. Reservations required. Main courses 14€–27€ ($18–$35); fixed-price menu 26€–37€ ($34–$48). AE, MC, V. Wed–Sun noon–2pm; Tues–Sun 7:30–10:30pm. Closed June 27–July 4 and mid-Nov to mid-Dec.

18

Languedoc-Roussillon

Languedoc is a loosely defined area encompassing the cities of Nîmes, Toulouse, and Carcassonne. It's one of the leading wine-producing areas of the world, and it's fabled for its art treasures.

The coast of Languedoc, from Montpellier to the Spanish frontier, might be called France's "second Riviera" (after the Côte d'Azur). This land of ancient cities has an almost continuous strip of sand stretching west from the Rhône toward the Pyrénées. In the days of Charles de Gaulle, the government began a project to develop the coastline, and in July and August, the miles of sun-baking bodies along the coast attest to its success.

Ancient Roussillon is a small region of Languedoc, forming the Pyrénées Orientales *département* (mini-state). This is French Catalonia, inspired more by Barcelona than by Paris. Over its long history, it has known many rulers. Part of the French kingdom until 1258, it was surrendered to James I of Aragón. Until 1344, it was part of the kingdom of Majorca. By 1463, Roussillon had been annexed to France again. Then Ferdinand of Aragón won it back, but by 1659, France had it again. Despite local sentiment favoring reunion with Spain, France firmly controls the land.

The Camargue is a marshy delta between two arms of the Rhône. South of Arles is cattle country. Black bulls are bred here for the bullfighting arenas of Arles and Nîmes. The cattle are herded by *gardians* (French cowboys), who ride white horses said to have been brought here by the Saracens. The whitewashed houses, plaited-straw roofs, plains, sandbars, and pink flamingos in the marshes make this area exotic.

As for wine, Hérault, Aude, and Garde rank first, second, and third, respectively, in total wine production in France. Most of this is ordinary table wine. A few, however, have been granted an Appellation d'Origine Contrôlée. Some of the best are Fitou, produced in the Hautes-Corbières district near Narbonne, and Minervois, from west and northwest of Narbonne.

1 Nîmes ★★★

721km (448 miles) S of Paris, 43km (27 miles) W of Avignon

Nîmes, the ancient Nemausus, is one of the finest places in the world for wandering among Roman relics. The city grew to prominence during the reign of Caesar Augustus (27 B.C.–A.D. 14). It possesses one of the best-preserved Roman amphitheaters in the world and a near-perfect Roman temple. The city of 137,000 is more like Provence than Languedoc, in which it lies. And there's a touch of Pamplona, Spain, in the festivals of the *corridas* (bullfights) at the arena. The Spanish influence is even more apparent at night, when the bodegas fill, usually with students drinking sangria and listening to flamenco.

By 1860, the togas of Nîmes's citizenry had long given way to denim, the cloth *de Nîmes.* An Austrian immigrant to Nîmes, Levi Strauss, exported the heavy fabric to California to make into work pants for gold-rush prospectors. The rest, as they say, is history.

ESSENTIALS

GETTING THERE Nîmes has bus and train service from the rest of France and is near several autoroutes. It lies on the main **rail** line between Marseille and Bordeaux. Thirteen TGV trains arrive daily from Paris's Gare de Lyon; the one-way fare is 82€ ($107). For train information and schedules, call © **36-35** or 08-92-35-35-35 from outside France. If you're **driving,** take A7 south from Lyon to the town of Orange and connect to A9 into Nîmes.

VISITOR INFORMATION The **Office de Tourisme** is at 6 rue Auguste (© **04-66-58-38-00;** fax 04-66-58-38-01; www.ot-nimes.fr).

SPECIAL EVENTS Festivals, parties, and cultural events rule the summer nights. Once warm weather hits, all sorts of activities take place at the arena, including concerts and theater performances. Contact the Office de Tourisme for information.

Every Thursday night during July and August, many of Nîmes's squares burst with music, crowds of pedestrians, and rich troves of paintings, crafts, used objects, and sculpture. Artists, musicians, and local residents gather in observance of the city's **Les Jeudis de Nîmes.** Of special interest are place d'Assas, place de l'Horloge, place du Marché, place aux Herbes, and place de la Maison Carrée.

EXPLORING THE CITY

If you want to see all of the city's monuments and museums, consider buying a ***billet global*** (Forfait Monuments), sold at the ticket counter of any of the local attractions. It provides access for a 3-day period to Maison Carrée, les Arènes de Nîmes, and Tour Magne. For more information call **Culturespace** (© **04-66-21-82-56**). The fee is 10€ ($13) for adults, 7.40€ ($9.60) for students and children 10 to 15, and free for children under 10.

The pride of Nîmes is the **Maison Carrée** ★★★, place de la Maison Carrée (© **04-66-21-82-56**), built during the reign of Caesar Augustus. Consisting of a raised platform with tall Corinthian columns, it's one of Europe's most beautiful, best-preserved Roman temples. It inspired the builders of La Madeleine in Paris as well as Thomas Jefferson. It schedules cultural and art exhibits, presented beneath an authentically preserved roof. The temple is open daily January to February and November to December 10am to 5pm, March and October 9am to 6pm, April to May and September 9am to 7pm, and June to August 9am to 8pm.

Across the square stands its modern-day twin, the **Carré d'Art** (with one *e*), a research center and exhibition space that contains a library, newspaper kiosk, and art museum. Its understated design was inspired by (but doesn't overpower) the ancient monument. The most visible component is the **Musée d'Art Contemporain,** place de la Maison Carrée (© **04-66-76-35-70**), which often supplements its expositions with exhibits of contemporary art. It's open Tuesday to Sunday 10am to 6pm. It charges 5€ ($6.50) for adults and 3.70€ ($4.80) for students and children under 15. Entrance is free the first Sunday of each month.

Note: This building's terrace provides a panorama of most of the ancient monuments and medieval churches of Nîmes.

N20
Caussade
N88
Cordes-sur-Ciel
D964
Montauban
Albi
E72
A62
N20
D982
Toulouse
N124
Tarn
Millau
St-Affrique
N112
Lacaune
Castres
St-Pons-de-Thomières
D118
Castelnaudary
D622
Auterive
E80
N117
Garonne
St-Gaudens
Pamiers
D119
Carcassonne
N113
Limoux
D118
Foix
D618
Quillan
Ax-les-Thermes
SPAIN
0
20 mi
0
20 km
LANGUEDOC
Lodève
D35
Bédarieux
N112
Béziers
Lézignan Corbières
Narbonne
N9
Salses
D117
Perpignan
N116
ROUSSILLON
Céret
Collioure
N106
D904
Alès
Le Vigan
D7
D999
Herault
N110
N109
Montpellier
A9
E15
Séte
Rhône
Orange
N86
D981
Châteauneuf-du-Pape
Gard
N106
Avignon
N100
Nîmes
D999
Cavaillon
Arles
N572
Aigues-Mortes
Petit Rhône
D570
The Camargue
Grande Rhône
E714
Salon-de-Provence
Stes-Maries-de-la-Mer
A55
Marseille →
Golfe du Lion
Mediterranean Sea
Paris
FRANCE
Languedoc-Roussillon

Scholars call it **Amphithéâtre Romain de Nîmes** ★★★, and locals refer to it as **Les Arènes de Nîmes.** The monument at place des Arènes (✆ **04-66-76-72-77**) is a better-preserved twin of the one at Arles, and far more complete than Rome's Colosseum. It's two stories high—each floor has 60 arches—and was built of huge stones painstakingly fitted together without mortar. It once held more than 20,000 spectators who came to see gladiatorial combat and wolf or boar hunts. Today it's used for everything from ballet recitals to bullfights. Admission is 7.70€ ($10) for adults and 5.60€ ($7.30) for students and children under 16. It is open January to February and November to December daily 9:30am to 4:30pm, March and October daily 9am to 5pm, April to May and September daily 9am to 6pm, and June to August daily 9am to 7pm.

One of the most beautiful gardens in France, **Jardins de la Fontaine** ★★, at the end of quai de la Fontaine, was laid out in the 18th century using the ruins of a Roman shrine as a centerpiece. It was planted with rows of chestnuts and elms, adorned with statuary and urns, and intersected by grottoes and canals. The garden is open from April to mid-September daily 7am to 10pm; from mid-September to March, daily 7am to 6:30pm. Within the garden are the ruined **Le Temple de Diane** ★ and the remains of some Roman baths. Over the park, within a 10-minute walk north of the town center, is **Mont Cavalier,** a low, rocky hill on top of which rises the sturdy bulk of the **Tour Magne** ★, the city's oldest Roman monument. You can climb it for 2.70€ ($3.50) for adults and 2.30€ ($3) for students and children under 17. Open daily January to February and November to December 10am to 1pm and 2 to 4:30pm, March and October 9:30am to 1pm and 2 to 6pm, April to May and September 9:30 to 7pm, and June to August 9:30am to 7:30pm. It offers a panoramic view over Nîmes and its environs. For more information, call ✆ **04-66-67-65-56.**

Nîmes is home to many museums. The largest and most respected, the **Musée des Beaux-Arts,** rue Cité-Foulc (✆ **04-66-67-38-21**), contains French paintings and sculptures from the 17th to the 20th centuries as well as Flemish, Dutch, and Italian works from the 15th to the 18th centuries. Seek out one of G. B. Moroni's masterpieces, *La Calomnie d'Apelle,* and a well-preserved Gallo-Roman mosaic. The museum is open Tuesday to Sunday 10am to 6pm and until 9pm on the first Thursday of each month. Admission is 5€ ($6.50) for adults and 3.70€ ($4.80) for students and children under 17.

If time allows, visit the **Musée du Vieux-Nîmes,** place aux Herbes (✆ **04-66-76-73-70**), housed in an Episcopal palace from the 1700s. It's rich in antiques, antique porcelain, and workday objects from the 18th and 19th centuries. Admission is free. Hours are Tuesday to Sunday 10am to 6pm.

One of the city's busiest thoroughfares, **boulevard de l'Amiral-Courbet,** leads to the **Porte d'Auguste** (Porte d'Arles)—the remains of a gate built by the Romans during the reign of Augustus. About 45m (148 ft.) to the south are the **Musée de Préhistoire et d'Histoire Naturelle** (✆ **04-66-76-73-45**) and the **Musée Archéologique** ★ (✆ **04-66-76-74-80**), in the same building at 13 bis bd. l'Amiral-Courbet. Admission is free. Hours are Tuesday to Sunday 10am to 6pm.

Outside the city, 23km (14 miles) northeast, the **pont du Gard** ★ spans the Gard River; its huge stones, fitted together without mortar, stand as one of the region's most vivid reminders of the ancient glory. Consisting of three tiers of arches arranged into gracefully symmetrical patterns, it dates from about 19 B.C. Frédéric Mistral, national poet of Provence and Languedoc, recorded a legend alleging that the devil constructed

Nîmes

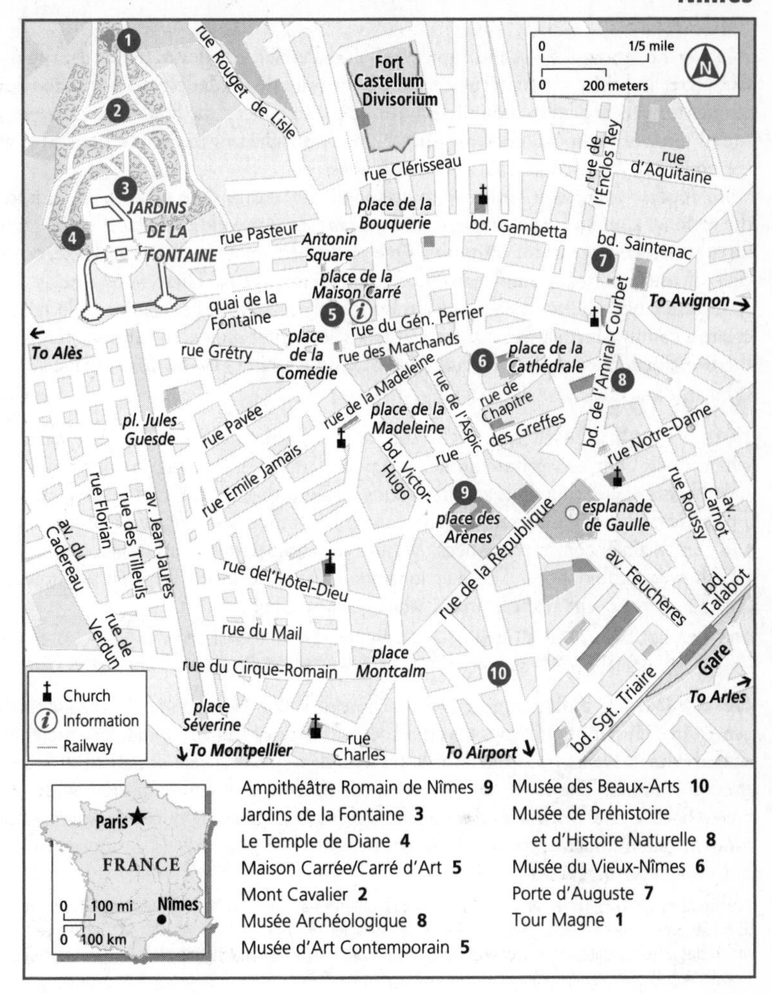

the bridge with the promise that he could claim the soul of the first person to cross it. To visit it, take highway N86 from Nîmes to a point 3km (1¾ miles) from the village of Remoulins, where signs are posted.

The pont du Gard has a museum, **La Grande Expo du Pont du Gard,** B.P. 7, 30210 Vers Pont du Gard (✆ **04-66-37-50-99**). Four exhibits detail the bridge's construction, its function throughout the Middle Ages, and insights into its role as a symbol of the architectural savvy of ancient Rome. There's also a restaurant, cafe, and gift shop. It's open daily from May to August 9:30am to 7pm (until 6pm Feb–Apr and Sept–Oct; until 5pm Nov–Jan). The exposition opens every Monday at 1:30pm and closes at the hours noted, according to the season. It is closed the first 3 weeks in January. Admission is 12€ ($16) for adults and 9€ ($12) for persons under 25 and students.

SHOPPING

Head to the center of town and **rue du Général-Perrier, rue des Marchands, rue du Chapître,** and the pedestrian **rue de l'Aspic** and **rue de la Madeleine.** A Sunday flea market runs from 8am to around 1pm in the parking lot of the **Stade des Costières,** site of most of the town's football (soccer) matches, adjacent to the southern edge of the boulevard *périphérique* that encircles Nîmes.

To appease your sweet tooth, go to just about any pastry shop in town and ask for the regional almond-based cookies called *croquants villaret* and *caladons.* They're great for a burst of energy or for souvenirs. One of the best purchases you can make, especially if you're not continuing east into Provence, is a *santon.* These wood or clay figurines are sculpted into characters from Provençal country life and can be collected to create a country-French nativity scene. For a selection of *santons* in various sizes, visit the **Boutique Provençale,** 10 place de la Maison Carré (✆ **04-66-67-81-71**).

WHERE TO STAY

Hôtel l'Amphithéâtre *Value* The core of this hotel dates from the 18th century, when it was built as a private home. A stay here involves trekking to your room up steep flights of creaking stairs and navigating a labyrinth of corridors. The small rooms are deliberately old-fashioned, usually containing antiques or antique reproductions and creaky, albeit comfortable, beds. Most of the compact tiled bathrooms come with tub/shower combinations. The staff long ago grew jaded to the fact that the hotel is less than perfect, but at these prices, who's complaining?

4 rue des Arènes, Nîmes 30000. ✆ **04-66-67-28-51.** Fax 04-66-67-07-79. 15 units. 53€–65€ ($69–$85) double. MC, V. Parking 10€ ($13). Closed Jan 2–20 and 1 week in Nov. **Amenities:** Nonsmoking rooms. *In room:* TV.

Hôtel Vatel ★ Built around 1990, this hotel lies 3km (1¾ miles) north of the town center, in a cluster of buildings that includes a university and a hospital. It's efficiently staffed with students from the local hotel school, who work here as part of their on-the-job training. The rooms are streamlined, tasteful, and contemporary, with terraces. Each comes with a midsize bathroom with a tub/shower combination. The modern establishment provides a level of comfort that older hotels, in more historic but limited settings, can't provide.

140 rue Vatel, B.P. 7128, Nîmes 30913. From the A4 autoroute, exit at NÎMES OUEST. ✆ **04-66-62-57-57.** Fax 04-66-62-57-50. www.hotelvatel.com. 46 units. 107€ ($139) double; 195€ ($254) suite. AE, DC, MC, V. Free parking. **Amenities:** 2 restaurants; bar; indoor pool; spa; sauna; room service; nonsmoking rooms; limited-mobility rooms. *In room:* A/C, TV, minibar, hair dryer, safe, Wi-Fi.

Imperator Concorde ★★ This hotel, part of the Concorde chain, is the largest and finest in town, and is adjacent to Les Jardins de la Fontaine—it's the one with the pale pink Italianate facade. In 2005, it underwent a major renovation that left it much improved. The artful and cozy good-size rooms have traditional or French furniture, with fluted or cabriole legs in one or another of the Louis styles. Each unit comes with a first-rate private bathroom with a tub/shower combination. You can order a meal in the hotel's verdant rear gardens or in the high-ceilinged dining room, L'Enclos de la Fontaine.

Quai de la Fontaine, Nîmes 30900. ✆ **04-66-21-90-30.** Fax 04-66-67-70-25. www.hotel-imperator.com. 62 units. 119€–235€ ($155–$306) double; 224€–400€ ($291–$520) suite. AE, DC, MC, V. Parking 13€ ($17). **Amenities:** Restaurant; bar; room service; babysitting; nonsmoking rooms. *In room:* A/C, TV, minibar, hair dryer, safe, Wi-Fi.

New Hôtel La Baume ★ *Finds* One of our favorite nests in Nîmes bears the name of the Marquis de la Baume, whose family built this 17th-century mansion. Its best features are the magnificent staircase that ornaments the interior courtyard and the overall sense of grandeur. During the hotel conversion, the designers carefully preserved the original architecture, and the result is a winning combination of modern and traditional. In contrast to the stately exterior, the guest rooms are hyper-contemporary, usually in tones of soft red, orange, and ocher, and the tiled bathrooms with tub/shower combos are in a postmodern style evocative of Philippe Starck's work.

21 rue Nationale, Nîmes 30000. © **04-66-76-28-42.** Fax 04-66-76-28-45. www.new-hotel.com. 34 units. 130€ ($169) double; 155€ ($202) junior suite. AE, DC, MC, V. Parking 7.60€ ($9.90). **Amenities:** Bar; room service; laundry service; dry cleaning; nonsmoking rooms; limited-mobility rooms. *In room:* A/C, TV, minibar, hair dryer, safe.

WHERE TO DINE

The dining rooms at the **New Hôtel La Baume** and the **Imperator Concorde** (see "Where to Stay," above) are good choices.

Alexandre (Michel Kayser) ★★★ TRADITIONAL FRENCH The most charming restaurant around is on the outskirts of Nîmes, 8km (5 miles) south of the center. It's the elegantly rustic domain of Michel Kayser, who adheres to classic tradition, with subtle improvements. His wife, Monique, assists him in the ultramodern dining room, which is outfitted in tones of soft red and ocher with gilded highlights. Menu items are designed to amuse as well as delight the palate: *île flottante,* a playful update of old-fashioned floating island, with truffles and velouté of cèpe mushrooms; roasted pigeon stuffed with vegetable purée and foie gras; tartare of oysters and shellfish with cardamom seeds; *brandade de Nîmes,* a regional version of *brandade* of codfish, elevated here to gourmet standards; and filet of bull from the Camargue in red-wine sauce with Camarguais herbs. Especially appealing is the selection of goat cheeses from the region and worthy cheeses from other parts of France. The dessert trolley is incredibly hard to resist.

Rte. de l'Aéroport de Garons. From town center, take rue de la République southwest to av. Jean-Jaurès; then head south and follow signs to the airport (toward Garons). © **04-66-70-08-99.** www.michelkayser.com. Reservations recommended. Main courses 39€–50€ ($51–$65); fixed-price lunch 39€ ($51); fixed-price dinner 56€–91€ ($73–$118). AE, DC, MC, V. Wed–Sun noon–1:30pm; Wed–Sat 8–9:30pm. Closed 2 weeks in Feb–Mar.

Restaurant au Chapon Fin ALSATIAN/LANGUEDOCIENNE This tavern-restaurant stands on a little square behind St. Paul's. It has beamed ceilings, small lamps, and a black-and-white stone floor. You'll have a choice of Alsatian and Languedocienne specialties. From the a la carte menu you can order foie gras with truffles, casserole of roasted lamb and eggplant, beefsteak *péllardon* (with goat-cheese sauce), and *brandade* of codfish. Other menu items include several kinds of Charolais beefsteak, a platter piled high with grilled sweetbreads and grilled veal kidneys, and several different variations of savory sauerkraut.

3 rue du Château-Fadaise. © **04-66-67-34-73.** Reservations required. Main courses 16€ ($21); fixed-price lunch 13€ ($17), fixed-price dinner 22€–45€ ($29–$59). MC, V. Mon–Fri noon–2pm; Mon–Sat 7:30–10pm (until 11pm Fri–Sat).

Wine Bar Chez Michel *Value* TRADITIONAL FRENCH This mahogany-paneled place has leather banquettes evocative of an early-1900s California saloon. Choices include an array of salads and platters. At lunch you can order a quick menu, including an appetizer, a garnished main course, and two glasses of wine. Typical dishes are magret of duckling, top-notch beefsteaks, and fresh (usually grilled) fish. You can also enjoy lunch on the terrace in the courtyard. A restaurateur extraordinaire, Michel Hermet makes his own wine at vineyards that have been associated with his family for many generations. More than 300 other varieties of wine are in stock, 15 of which are available by the glass or by the pitcher.

11 place de la Couronne. ✆ **04-66-76-19-59.** Main courses 8.50€–26€ ($11–$34); fixed-price lunch 14€–26€ ($18–$34); fixed-price dinner 18€–26€ ($23–$34). AE, MC, V. Tues–Sat noon–2pm; Mon–Sat 7pm–midnight.

NIMES AFTER DARK

Once warm weather hits, all sorts of activities take place at the arena, including open-air concerts and theater. The Office de Tourisme has a complete listing. For popular events such as football (soccer), bullfights, and rock concerts, you can contact the **Bureau de Location des Arènes,** 4 rue de la Violette (✆ **04-66-02-80-80**). Tickets for higher-brow events, such as symphonic or chamber-music concerts, theater, and opera performances, are sold through **Le Théâtre Municipal (Le Théâtre de Nîmes),** 1 place de la Calade (✆ **04-66-36-65-00;** www.theatredenimes.com).

If you like hanging out with students and soldiers, head to **Café Le Napoléon,** 46 bd. Victor-Hugo (✆ **04-66-67-20-23**). Popular with the intelligentsia is the **Haddock Cafe,** 13 rue de l'Agau (✆ **04-66-67-86-57**), which books occasional rock concerts.

The premier jazz venue in Nîmes is **Le Deep Lounge,** 41 bis rue Emile-Jamais (✆ **04-66-28-11-74**). Open nightly, except Monday, from 5:30pm until at least 2am, it offers a boozy, smoky, permissive environment where the live musicians derive from just about anywhere. Entrance is free.

Sexy, hip **La Comédie,** 28 rue Jean-Reboul (✆ **04-66-76-13-66**), is hands-down the best for dancing and attracts a pretty crowd of youthful danceaholics. A little less flashy but a lot more fun, **Lulu Club,** 10 impasse de la Curaterie (✆ **04-66-36-28-20**), is the gay and lesbian stronghold in Nîmes. Open Thursday to Saturday, it's a magnet for hip and straight folk as well. A youth-oriented contender is **Le C-Cafe,** 20 rue de l'Etoile (✆ **04-66-21-59-22**). Open Thursday to Saturday at 11pm, it rocks and rolls to music from L.A. to London, with a youthful clientele.

Streets to explore on virtually any night of the week include **place de la Maison Carrée** and **boulevard Victor-Hugo.** From June to September, locals flock to the beach to patronize the shanty restaurants and bars. Bus no. 6 will take you to the **Plage de la Corniches** for nighttime partying.

2 Aigues-Mortes ★★

750km (466 miles) SW of Paris, 63km (39 miles) NE of Séte, 40km (25 miles) E of Nîmes, 48km (30 miles) SW of Arles

South of Nîmes, you can explore much of the Camargue by car. The most rewarding place to focus on is Aigues-Mortes, the city of the "dead waters." In the middle of swamps and lagoons, Aigues-Mortes is France's most perfectly preserved walled town. Louis IX and his crusaders once set forth from Aigues-Mortes, which was then a thriving port, the first in France on the Mediterranean. Now 6.5km (4 miles) inland from the sea, it stands on four canals. The **ramparts** ★★, which still enclose the town, were constructed between 1272 and 1300. The **Tour de Constance** ★★ (✆ **04-66-53-61-55**) is a model castle of the Middle Ages. At the top, which you can reach by elevator, a panoramic view of the marshes unfolds. Admission is 6.50€ ($8.45) for adults, 4.50€ ($5.85) for ages 18 to 25, and free for children under 18. The monument is open May to August daily 10am to 7pm, September to April daily 10am to 5pm.

Aigues-Mortes's main appeal is the medieval feeling that permeates virtually every building, rampart, and cobble-covered street. The city's religious centerpiece is the **Eglise Notre-Dame des Sablons,** rue Jean-Jaurès (no phone). Constructed of wood

Moments **France's Cowboy Country: The Camargue**

The Camargue, where the cowboys of France ride the range, is an alluvial plain inhabited by wild horses, fighting black bulls, roaming Gypsies, pink flamingos, lagoons, salt marshes, wetlands, and gluttonous mosquitoes. Explore the rugged terrain by boat, bike, horse, or jeep.

With the most fragile ecosystem in France, the Camargue has been a national park since 1970. It's known for its small white horses, whose ancestors were brought here by the Arabs long ago. They roam wild in the national park, guarded by cowboys, or *gardians,* who wear large felt hats and carry long three-pronged sticks to prod the cattle. The cowboys live in thatched huts called *cabanes.* Ancestors of the *gardians* may have been the first American cowboys, who sailed on French ships to the port of New Orleans, where they rode the bayous of Louisiana and East Texas, rounding up cattle—in French, no less.

There's no more evocative sight than the proud snow-white horses running at liberty through the marshlands, with hoofs so tough that they don't need shoes. It is said that their long manes and busy tails evolved over the centuries to slap those pesky mosquitoes.

Exotic flora and fauna abound where the delta of the Rhône River empties into the Mediterranean. The bird life is the most luxuriant in Europe. The area, which resembles the Florida Everglades, is known for its colonies of pink flamingos *(Flamants roses).* They share living quarters with some 400 other bird species, including ibises, egrets, kingfishers, owls, wild ducks, swans, and ferocious birds of prey. The best place to see flamingo colonies is the area around Ginès, a hamlet on N570, 5km (3 miles) north of Camargue's capital, Stes-Maries-de-la-Mer.

Exploring the Camargue is best undertaken on the back of a Camarguais horse. The steeds can take you into the interior, which you couldn't see otherwise, fording waters to places where the black bulls graze and wild birds nest. You'll find two to three dozen stables (depending on the time of year) along the highway from Arles to Stes-Maries. Virtually all of them charge the same rate, 13€ to 16€ ($17–$21) per hour. The rides are aimed at the neophyte, not the champion equestrian. They're so easy that they're recommended even for those who have never been on a horse before.

in 1183, it was rebuilt in stone in 1246 in the ogival style. Its modern stained-glass windows were installed in 1980 as replacements for the badly damaged originals. The church is open May to September daily 8:30am to 6pm, October to April daily 9am to 5pm.

ESSENTIALS

GETTING THERE Five **trains** and four **buses** per day connect Aigues-Mortes and Nîmes. Trip time is about an hour. For information and schedules, call © **36-35** or 08-92-35-35-35 from outside France. If you're **driving** to Aigues-Mortes, take D979 south from Gallargues, or A9 from Montpellier or Nîmes.

VISITOR INFORMATION The **Office de Tourisme** is at place St. Louis (✆ **04-66-53-73-00;** fax 04-66-53-65-94; www.ot-aiguesmortes.fr).

WHERE TO STAY

The **Restaurant Les Arcades** (see "Where to Dine," below) also rents rooms.

Hostellerie des Remparts Opened about 300 years ago, this weather-worn inn lies at the foot of the Tour de Constance, adjacent to the medieval fortifications. Popular and often fully booked (especially in summer), it evokes the defensive atmosphere of the Middle Ages, albeit with charm and a sense of nostalgia. Narrow stone staircases lead to the small, simply furnished rooms. The living here is rather plain and basic. Each well-maintained unit has a small bathroom, 12 with tub and shower, the rest with showers. Breakfast is the only meal served.

6 place Anatole-France, Aigues-Mortes 30220. ✆ **04-66-53-82-77.** Fax 04-66-53-73-77. 18 units. 65€–110€ ($85–$143) double. AE, MC, V. **Amenities:** Restaurant; bar; room service; nonsmoking rooms; limited-mobility rooms. *In room:* A/C, TV.

Hôtel Les Templiers ★ The leading inn in town is a gem of peace and tranquillity. Protected by the ramparts built by St-Louis, king of France, this 17th-century residence has small to medium-size rooms decorated in Provençal style, with just enough decorative objects to lend a homelike aura. Most of the midsize bathrooms have tub/shower combinations (three have showers only). You can relax in the courtyard, where you can also enjoy breakfast. The establishment contains two restaurants, each featuring competent and traditional, if not terribly experimental, food: The less formal option is open for both lunch and dinner Wednesday to Monday; the somewhat more formal restaurant is open only for dinner Thursday to Sunday or Tuesday to Sunday in July and August.

23 rue de la République, Aigues-Mortes 30220. ✆ **04-66-53-66-56.** Fax 04-66-53-69-61. 14 units. 105€–155€ ($137–$202) double; 190€–250€ ($247–$325) suite. MC, V. **Amenities:** 2 restaurants; bar; outdoor pool; room service; limited-mobility rooms. *In room:* A/C, TV, hair dryer, Wi-Fi.

Hôtel St-Louis Even though it's not grand in any way, this is the town's second-best lodging choice. Located near place St-Louis, the inn is not as fine as the Templiers (see above) but does offer comfortably furnished rooms. They're small, with compact, shower-only bathrooms. Many locals come here to enjoy the regional meals served in the dining room.

10 rue de l'Amiral-Courbet, Aigues-Mortes 30220. ✆ **04-66-53-72-68.** Fax 04-66-53-75-92. www.lesaintlouis.fr. 22 units. 85€–110€ ($111–$143) double. AE, MC, V. Parking 12€ ($16). Closed Jan–Mar 7. **Amenities:** Restaurant; bar; room service; laundry service; dry cleaning; nonsmoking rooms. *In room:* TV, minibar.

WHERE TO DINE

Hôtel Les Templiers and **Hôtel St-Louis** (see "Where to Stay," above) are also good choices for dining.

Restaurant Les Arcades ★★ TRADITIONAL FRENCH There's no contest: This is the area's finest dining choice. This restaurant has several formal sections with beamed ceilings or stone vaults. Almost as old as the nearby fortifications, the place is especially charming on sultry days, when the thick masonry keeps the interior cool. The good, reasonably priced food is likely to include warm oysters, fish soup, fried stuffed zucchini flowers, grilled beef steak from the Camargue, roasted monkfish in red-wine sauce, and grilled duckling. A typical local dish is minced bull steak from the local salt marshes, served with regional herb sauce.

The owner also rents nine large, comfortable rooms with air-conditioning and TVs. The double rate of 98€ to 135€ ($127–$176) includes breakfast.

23 bd. Gambetta, Aigues-Mortes 30220. ✆ **04-66-53-81-13.** www.les-arcades.fr. Reservations recommended. Main courses 8€–28€ ($10–$36); fixed-price lunch 22€ ($29); fixed-price dinner 32€–42€ ($42–$55). Children's menu 12€ ($16). AE, DC, MC, V. Wed and Fri–Sun noon–2pm; Tues–Sun 7:30–10pm; daily July–Aug. Closed 2 weeks in Mar and 2 weeks in Oct.

3 Montpellier ★★

758km (471 miles) SW of Paris, 161km (100 miles) NW of Marseille, 50km (31 miles) SW of Nîmes

The capital of Mediterranean (or Lower) Languedoc, the ancient university city of Montpellier is renowned for its medical school, founded in the 13th century. Nostradamus qualified as a doctor here, and Rabelais studied at the school. Petrarch came to Montpellier in 1317 and stayed for 7 years.

Today Montpellier is a bustling metropolis with a population of 380,000, one of southern France's fastest-growing cities, thanks to an influx of new immigrants. Although some suburbs are dreary, the city has a handsome core, with tree-flanked promenades, broad avenues, and historic monuments. Students make up a quarter of the population, giving the city a lively feel. In recent years, many high-tech corporations, including IBM, have opened offices in Montpellier.

ESSENTIALS

GETTING THERE Some 12 **trains** per day arrive from Avignon (trip time: 1 hr.); 12 from Marseille (trip time: 1¾ hr.); one every 2 hours from Toulouse (trip time: 2 hr.); and 17 per day from Perpignan (trip time: 1½ hr.). Trains arriving hourly from Paris's Gare de Lyon take 8 to 10 hours, depending on the train, and usually require a change of equipment in Lyon. One TGV (very fast) train arrives daily from Paris, taking less than 3½ hours. The one-way fare starts from 75€ ($98). For rail information, call ✆ **36-35** or 08-92-35-35-35 from outside France.

If you're **driving,** Montpellier lies off A9.

VISITOR INFORMATION The **Office de Tourisme** is at 30 allée Jean de L. de Tassigny (✆ **04-67-60-60-60;** fax 04-67-60-60-61; www.ot-montpellier.fr).

SPECIAL EVENTS From June 24 to July 7, classical and modern dancers leap into town for the **Festival International Montpellier Danse.** Tickets for performances cost 6€ to 30€ ($7.80–$39) and can be purchased through the box office, **Montpellierdanse,** 18 rue Ste-Ursule (✆ **08-00-60-07-40** or 04-67-60-83-60; www.montpellier danse.com). From July 12 to July 29, the **Festival de Radio France et de Montpellier** presents orchestral music, jazz, and opera. Tickets run 6€ to 50€ ($7.80–$65); call ✆ **04-67-02-02-01** or contact the **Cité des Congrés Le Corum,** esplanade Charles de Gaulle (✆ **04-67-61-67-61**).

EXPLORING THE TOWN

Called the Oxford of France because of its burgeoning academic community, Montpellier is a city of young people. The **place de la Comédie** is the living room of Montpellier, where you can admire the theater, the 18th-century Fountain of the Three Graces, or whatever else amuses you.

Before leaving town, stroll along the 17th-century **promenade du Peyrou** ★★, a terraced park with views of the Cévennes and the Mediterranean. The broad esplanade sits at the loftiest point in Montpellier. Opposite its entrance at the end of rue Foch is the **Arc de Triomphe,** erected in 1691 and renovated in 2004 to celebrate the victories of Louis XIV. In the center of the promenade is an equestrian statue of the Sun King, and at the end is the **Château d'Eau,** a pavilion with Corinthian columns that is a monument to 18th-century classicism. Water travels here along a 15km-long (9⅓-mile) conduit and an aqueduct.

Cathédrale St-Pierre The town's spiritual centerpiece was founded in 1364. Once associated with a Benedictine monastery, the cathedral suffered badly during the religious wars of the 16th and 17th centuries. (After 1795, the medical school occupied the monastery.) Today it has a somewhat bleak western front with two towers and a canopied porch.

Place St-Pierre. ✆ **04-67-66-04-12.** Free admission. Daily 9am–noon and 2–7pm.

Jardin des Plantes Paul Valéry met André Gide in the Jardin des Plantes, the oldest such garden in France. The botanical garden, filled with exotic plants and a handful of greenhouses, opened in 1593. Check with the tourist office before visiting to make sure it's open.

163 rue Auguste-Broussonnet (enter from bd. Henri-IV). ✆ **04-67-63-43-22.** Free admission. Apr–Sept Tues–Sun noon–8pm; Oct–Mar Tues–Sun noon–6pm.

Musée Fabre ★★ One of France's great provincial art galleries occupies the former Hôtel de Massilian, where Molière once played for a season. The collection originated when Napoleon sent Montpellier an exhibition of the Royal Academy in 1803. François Fabre, a Montpellier painter, contributed its most important works in 1825. After Fabre's death, other paintings from his collection were donated to the gallery. Several were his own creations, but the more significant works were ones he had acquired—including Poussin's *Venus and Adonis* and Italian paintings such as *The Mystical Marriage of Saint Catherine.* The museum grew through other donations, notably from Valedau, who in 1836 left his collection of Rubens, Gérard Dou, and Téniers. After 2 years of renovations, the museum reopened in 2007 with an increase in its exhibition space so that more than 300 new works can now be displayed.

2 rue Montpellieret. ✆ **04-67-14-83-00.** Admission 8€ ($10) adults, 4€ ($5.20) students and ages 7–20, free for children under 7. Tues–Fri 9:30am–5:30pm; Sat–Sun 9:30am–5pm.

WHERE TO STAY

Le Jardin des Sens (see "Where to Dine," below) also rents rooms.

Best Western Hôtel Le Guilhem ★ *Finds* Two 16th-century houses make up this oasis, located on a back street. In its transformation to a hotel, the connected buildings gained all the modern conveniences, including an elevator. Each room is furnished and decorated in individual style, with more than a hint of Laura Ashley design in the striped wallpaper and flowery spreads. Although the accommodations are small, they are tastefully furnished and comfortable; each has a compact bathroom with shower. The day begins with a breakfast of freshly baked *pain au chocolat* and croissants served on a terrace overlooking the garden and the cathedral. The location is in the old town, an ideal base from which to explore the sights.

18 rue Jean-Jacques-Rousseau, Montpellier 34000. ✆ **800/528-1234** or 04-67-52-90-90. Fax 04-67-60-67-67. www.leguilhem.com. 35 units. 87€–159€ ($113–$207) double. AE, DC, MC, V. Parking 7€ ($9.10) in nearby garage. **Amenities:** Room service; laundry service; nonsmoking rooms; limited-mobility rooms. *In room:* A/C, TV, minibar, hair dryer, Wi-Fi.

Hôtel des Arceaux It's basic but still acceptable, and the price is right. A hotel has stood at this prime location, right off the promenade du Peyrou, since the late 1800s. The small rooms, renovated in 2004 and 2005, are simply but pleasantly furnished, each in a different color and each with a compact bathroom with shower. At the on-site bar, which overflows into a summer garden, simple platters are served. This is not a full-fledged restaurant; what you get is a "bar-bistro platter," a daily special including fish, meat, or poultry with vegetables.

33–35 bd. des Arceaux, Montpellier 34000. ✆ **04-67-92-03-03.** Fax 04-67-92-05-09. www.hoteldesarceaux.com. 18 units. 63€–100€ ($82–$130) double. AE, MC, V. Parking 5.50€ ($7.15) in nearby lot. **Amenities:** Bar; room service; nonsmoking rooms. *In room:* A/C in some, TV, minibar, Wi-Fi.

Hôtel du Palais ★ *Value* This hotel in the heart of a neighborhood loaded with antiques dealers is one of the best bargains in town. Built in the late 18th century, Hôtel du Palais is in the center of Montpellier, amid a labyrinth of narrow streets and monumental plazas and parks. Much of the decor dates from around 1983, when the hotel was richly restored in a style that uses lots of fabrics, big curtains, and faux marble finishes on walls of public areas. Subsequent renovations have kept the property up-to-date. The guest rooms are relatively large and appealing, thanks to thoughtful placement of antique reproductions and good maintenance. Each has a neatly tiled bathroom with shower. Breakfast is the only meal served.

3 rue du Palais, Montpellier 34000. ✆ **04-67-60-47-38.** Fax 04-67-60-40-23. 26 units. 65€–77€ ($85–$100) double. MC, V. Parking 7€ ($9.10). **Amenities:** Room service. *In room:* A/C, TV, minibar, hair dryer, Wi-Fi.

Hôtel Ulysse ★ *Value* One of the city's better bargains, built in 1993, Ulysse delivers a lot of bang for your euro. The owners have worked hard to make the simple hotel as stylish as possible. Each room is uniquely decorated. The furnishings are in an original wrought-iron design, functional but with flair. The comfortable rooms have fully equipped bathrooms with tub/shower combinations. The hotel lies within a 15-minute walk south of Montpellier's center, close to the edge of the sea.

338 av. de St-Maur, Montpellier 34000. From bd. d'Antigone, go north on av. Jean-Mermoz to rue de la Pépinière; continue right and make a left at the 1st intersection, which leads to av. de St-Maur. ✆ **04-67-02-02-30.** Fax 04-67-02-16-50. www.hotelulysse.com. 24 units. 58€–69€ ($75–$90) double. AE, DC, MC, V. Parking 5€ ($6.50). Tram: 1 (Le Mosson line). Bus: 8. **Amenities:** Room service; nonsmoking rooms; limited-mobility rooms. *In room:* TV, minibar, hair dryer, Wi-Fi.

La Maison Blanche ★★ Few other hotels in the south of France work so hard to emulate the gingerbread and French Creole ambience of old New Orleans. Suites are stylishly furnished in rattan and wicker with plenty of wood paneling, while guest rooms are outfitted with oak. Bathrooms are midsize to roomy, mostly with tub/shower combinations. Parts of the interior, especially the dining room, may remind you of Louis XIII's France more than Louisiana, but overall the setting in a verdant park (a 10-min. drive northeast of Montpellier's center) is as charming and unusual as anything else in town.

1796 av. de la Pompignane, Montpellier 34000. Take bd. d'Antigone east until you reach the intersection with av. de la Pompignane and head north until you see the hotel on your right (trip time: 5 min.). ✆ **04-99-58-20-70.** Fax 04-67-79-53-39. www.hotel-maison-blanche.com. 35 units. 76€–102€ ($99–$133) double; 140€–150€ ($182–$195) suite. AE, DC, MC, V. Free parking. **Amenities:** Restaurant; bar; outdoor pool; room service; laundry service; nonsmoking rooms; limited-mobility rooms. *In room:* A/C, TV, minibar (some rooms), hair dryer, safe (some rooms), Wi-Fi.

Sofitel Antigone ★ In the heart of Montpellier, this angular, modern, glass-sheathed hotel is the city's top hotel for comfort and first-class amenities. In summer, it does quite a trade with visitors. A particularly appealing feature is the pool, which, along with a bar and breakfast room, occupies most of the top floor. The rooms are chain format but first class. The Antigone is a winning choice, with the most efficient staff in the city, and its bar is one of the coziest hideaways in town.

1 rue des Pertuisanes, Montpellier 3400. ✆ **04-67-99-72-72.** Fax 04-67-65-17-50. www.sofitel.com. 89 units. 200€–240€ ($260–$312) double; 430€ ($559) suite. AE, DC, MC, V. Parking 3€–10€ ($3.90–$13). **Amenities:** Restaurant; bar; outdoor pool; fitness center; Jacuzzi; sauna; room service; laundry service; dry cleaning; nonsmoking rooms; limited-mobility rooms. *In room:* A/C, TV, hair dryer, safe, Wi-Fi.

WHERE TO DINE

La Compagnie des Comptoirs INTERNATIONAL Just a 5-minute walk east of the town center, lodged behind a set of massive doors that were intricately sculpted by artisans in Morocco, this restaurant manages to evoke the aesthetic and sense of internationalism of the late-19th-century French colonies in, say, India, North Africa, or Indochina. There's room inside for about 130 diners; a big outdoor terrace with flowering shrubs and a splashing fountain; and an ongoing emphasis on the kind of sunny, flavorful, and pungent cuisine you're likely to find around the edges of the Mediterranean. The best examples include a succulent version of tempura of crayfish; *accras* (beignets) of crab; grilled calamari with a confit of lemon; grilled steak from bulls from the Camargue, served with red-wine sauce; and a winning collection of desserts.

51 rue François Delmas. ✆ **04-99-58-39-29.** Reservations recommended. Main courses 17€–42€ ($22–$55). AE, DC, MC, V. Daily noon–2:30pm and 8–11:30pm.

Le Jardin des Sens ★★★ FRENCH This is one of the great restaurants of southern France, with three Michelin stars. The chefs, twins Laurent and Jacques Pourcel, have taken Montpellier by storm, and their cuisine could involve almost anything, depending on where their imaginations roam. The rich bounty of Languedoc goes through a process designed to enhance its natural flavor. A starter may be ravioli stuffed with foie gras of duckling and flap mushrooms, floating in chicken bouillon fortified with truffles, broad beans, and crispy potatoes. Main courses of note are shelled lobster, pressed flat and served with duck meat and vanilla oil; filet of dorado grilled with sesame and served with a marmalade of tomatoes, olives, and caramelized balsamic vinegar; and filet of pigeon stuffed with pistachios. A dessert specialty is gratin of limes with slices of pineapple *en confit.*

Le Jardin des Sens also rents 12 guest rooms, plus two suites, each designed in cutting-edge style by Bruno Borrione, a colleague of Philippe Starck. They cost 160€ to 270€ ($208–$351) for a double and 290€ to 470€ ($377–$611) for a suite.

11 av. St-Lazare. ✆ **04-99-58-38-38.** Fax 04-99-58-38-39. www.jardindessens.com. Reservations required. Main courses 40€–51€ ($52–$66); fixed-price lunch Tues–Fri only 50€ ($65); fixed-price dinner and Sat lunch 125€–190€ ($163–$247). AE, MC, V. Thurs–Sat noon–2pm; Tues–Sat 7:30–10pm. Closed 2 weeks in Jan.

L'Olivier ★★ *Finds* MODERN FRENCH This charming restaurant's cuisine is so satisfying that we consider it the finest in Montpellier outside the luxe Jardin des Sens. Chef Michel Breton, assisted by his charming wife, Yvette, cooks to perfection. The establishment seats only 20, in a subdued and rather bland modern space accented only by contemporary paintings. But you don't come to L'Olivier to look at the walls. You come for Breton's salmon with a tartare of oysters, warm monkfish terrine, roasted filet of lamb with sweetbread-studded macaroni, and haunch of rabbit stuffed with wild mushrooms. The welcome is warm and sincere.

12 rue Aristide-Olivier. © **04-67-92-86-28.** Reservations required. Main courses 25€–32€ ($33–$42); fixed-price menu 34€–47€ ($44–$61). AE, MC, V. Tues–Sat noon–2pm and 7:30–9:30pm. Closed Aug and holidays.

MONTPELLIER AFTER DARK

After the sun sets, head for **place Jean-Jaurès, rue de Verdun,** and **rue des Ecoles Laïques,** or walk down **rue de la Loge** and soak up its carnival atmosphere, watching talented jugglers, mimes, and musicians.

Rockstore, 20 rue de Verdun (© **04-67-06-80-00**), draws lots of students with 1950s rock memorabilia and live concerts. Up a flight of stairs is its disco, which pounds out techno and rock. There is no cover, except on concert nights. For the best jazz and blues in town, check out **JAM,** 100 rue Ferdinand-de-Lesseps (© **04-67-58-30-30**). In a noisy, smoky, and even gritty space, its regular concerts attract jazz enthusiasts from miles around. Concert tickets average 10€ to 25€ ($13–$33).

A modern, noisy, convivial disco, known throughout the region, is **Le Pacha,** route des Plages, in the hamlet of Lattes (© **04-99-52-97-06**), 4km (2½ miles) south of Montpellier. It attracts drinkers and dancers ages 23 to 40. Le Pacha is open Thursday to Saturday beginning around 11pm; on Friday and Saturday it charges a 10€-to-15€ ($13–$20) cover, which includes one drink. Gays and lesbians gather at the town's most animated bar and disco, **La Villa Rouge,** route de Palavas (© **04-67-06-50-54**), also in Lattes. Both of them lie about 5km (3 miles) south of the town center.

Le Corum (© **04-67-61-67-61**), the most up-to-date theater in town, books many plays, dance recitals, operas, and symphonic presentations. It's in the Palais des Congrès, esplanade Charles-de-Gaulle. For ticket information and schedules, contact the Corum or the **Opéra Comédie,** place de la Comédie (© **04-67-60-19-99**).

4 Narbonne ★

845km (525 miles) SW of Paris, 61km (38 miles) E of Carcassonne, 93km (58 miles) S of Montpellier

Medieval Narbonne was a port to rival the Marseille of Roman times, its "galleys laden with riches." At the time, Narbonne's size, population, and wealth were greater than those of Rome, London, and Prague. An important Jewish community existed here starting in the 6th century, and Narbonne was also the seat of an important archbishopric from the 11th century. Since then, the Mediterranean has receded from Narbonne, and the town is now 8km (5 miles) inland.

Narbonne was the first town outside Italy to be colonized by the Romans, which makes it an intriguing place. After Lyon, Narbonne was the largest town in Gaul, and even today you can see evidence of the town's former wealth. Too far from the sea to be a beach town, it attracts history buffs and others drawn to memories of its glorious past.

Some 50,000 Narbonnais live in this sleepy backwater. However, many locals are trying to raise the profile of their vineyards. Caves are open to visitors in the surrounding area (the tourist office will advise you). If you want to go to the beach, head to the nearby village of **Gruisson** and its adjoining beach, Gruisson-Plage, or to the suburb of **St-Pierre la Mer** and its adjoining beach, Narbonne-Plage. Both are 15km (9⅓ miles) south of Narbonne. Buses from the town are frequent, each marked with its destination.

ESSENTIALS

GETTING THERE Narbonne has rail, bus, and highway connections with other cities on the Mediterranean coast and with Toulouse. Rail travel is the most popular way to get here, with 14 **trains** per day arriving from Perpignan (trip time: 50 min.),

13 per day from Toulouse (trip time: 1½ hr.), and 12 per day from Montpellier (trip time: 1 hr.). Most rail passengers arriving from Paris take the TGV directly to Narbonne (trip time: 4 hr.). The one-way fare from Paris starts from 84€ ($109); from Montpellier, 14€ to 18€ ($18–$23). For rail information, call ✆ **36-35** or 08-92-35-35-35 from outside France. If you're **driving,** Narbonne is at the junction of A61 and A9, easily accessible from either Toulouse or the Riviera.

VISITOR INFORMATION The **Office de Tourisme** is on place Roger-Salengro (✆ **04-68-65-15-60;** fax 04-68-65-59-12; www.mairie-narbonne.fr).

EXPLORING THE TOWN

Few other cities in France contain such a massive medieval architectural block in their centers. Foremost among Narbonne's religious and civic buildings is the **Cathédrale St-Just** ★★, place de l'Hôtel-de-Ville, entrance on rue Gauthier (no phone). The cathedral replaced three primitive churches, the earliest of which dated from A.D. 313. Its construction began in 1272 but was never finished. Only the transept and a choir were completed; the choir is 39m (128 ft.) high, built in the bold Gothic style of northern France. At each end of the transept are 58m (190-ft.) towers from 1480. Pope Clement IV, a former archbishop of Narbonne, sent the cornerstone of the church from Rome. Inside is an impressive collection of Flemish tapestries. In 2000, the grand retable (altarpiece) of the cathedral was restored and reinaugurated with pomp and circumstance. Originally painted by unknown craftsmen in 1381, it graced a side chapel ("Axial Chapel") in the cathedral. In 1732, it was judged old-fashioned and concealed by alterations. In 1847, Viollet-le-Duc ripped out some of the 18th-century changes but never got a full understanding of the extent of the 14th-century murals in the Axial Chapel. In 1981, during the removal of a statue for an art exhibit in Paris, a glimpse of the original altarpiece emerged. A corps of volunteers, all experts in restoration, began the task of piecing together artwork that was broken into as many as 1,500 pieces. The result of their efforts is a polychromed sculpture that's celebrated in art circles throughout France. The cloisters, from the 14th and 15th centuries, connect the cathedral with the Archbishops' Palace (see below). The cathedral is open June to September daily 10am to 7pm, October through May daily 9am to noon and 2 to 6pm. Entrance is free.

The cathedral is attached to the **Palais des Archevêques** (**Archbishops' Palace,** sometimes referred to as the Palais-Vieux), place de l'Hôtel-de-Ville (✆ **04-68-90-30-30**). It was conceived as part fortress, part palace, with three military-style towers from the 13th and 14th centuries. The Old Palace on the right is from the 12th century, the so-called New Palace on the left from the 14th. It's said that the old, arthritic, and sometimes overweight archbishops were hauled up the interior's Louis XIII–style stairs on mules. Part of the complex is devoted to the neo-Gothic **Hôtel de Ville** (town hall), which was reconstructed between 1845 and 1850 by Viollet-le-Duc, a 19th-century architect involved with the refurbishment of such sites as the cathedral at Paris.

The Archbishops' Palace is the site of the Musée Archéologique, the Musée d'Art, the Horreum Romain, and the Donjon Gilles-Aycelin, all previewed below.

The **Musée Archéologique** ★ contains prehistoric artifacts, Bronze Age tools, 14th-century frescoes, and Greco-Roman amphorae. Several of the sarcophagi date from the 3rd century, and some of the mosaics are of pagan origin. The **Musée d'Art** is three floors above street level in the former private apartments of the archbishops, the rooms in which Louis XII stayed during his siege of Perpignan. Panels depicting the nine Muses enhance their coffered ceilings. A Roman mosaic floor is on display, as is a collection of antique porcelain, enamels, and a portrait bust of Louis XIV. The museum exhibits a wealth of French paintings from the 17th century. Part of the collection depicts *Arabian Nights*–style scenes with camels, palm trees, sex slaves, and lusty Saracens. In the **Horreum Romain,** 3 rue Rouget-de-l'Isle (© **04-68-32-45-30**), you'll find a labyrinth of underground passages dug by the Gallo-Romans and their successors for storage of food and supplies during times of siege. At this same site in front of the Archbishops' Palace, you can view the remains of a road constructed in 120 B.C. and not discovered until 1997.

A combination ticket (7€/$9.10 adults; 4€/$5.20 students and children under 18) admits you to all of these attractions for 6 days. If you don't visit the palace, you can pay for those attractions separately. The palace is open April through September daily 9:30am to 12:15pm and 2 to 6pm, October to March Tuesday through Sunday 10am to noon and 2 to 5pm.

If you visit between July and September, you may want to participate in one of the occasional hikes up the steep steps of the **Donjon Gilles-Aycelin,** place de l'Hôtel-de-Ville (© **04-68-90-30-30**). A watchtower and prison in the late 13th century, it has an observation platform with a view of the cathedral, the plain, and the Pyrénées. Entrance costs 2.20€ ($2.85) for adults and is free for children under 11; there's no extra charge for the hikes. The watchtower is open May to October daily 9:30am to 12:15pm and 2 to 6pm; November to April Tuesday to Sunday 10am to noon and 2 to 5pm.

A final site worth visiting is the Gothic **Basilique St-Paul-Serge,** rue de l'Hôtel-Dieu (© **04-68-32-68-98**), built on the site of a 4th-century necropolis. It has an elegant choir with fine Renaissance woodcarvings and some ancient Christian sarcophagi. The chancel, from 1229, is admirable. The north door leads to the Paleo-Christian Cemetery, part of an early Christian burial ground. The basilica is open April through September daily 9am to 7pm; October to March daily 9am to noon, Monday to Saturday 2 to 6pm.

WHERE TO STAY

Grand Hôtel du Languedoc Despite frequent modernizations, the grand stone structure of this Belle Epoque hotel still stands out from the cityscape around it. Beside the canal du Rhône, it's the site of municipal meetings and social events, with high-ceilinged public rooms and a mishmash of decors. The rooms come in a variety of shapes and sizes, usually with some of the hotel's original wood furniture and pastel color schemes. About half of the midsize bathrooms have tub/shower combinations.

22 bd. Gambetta, Narbonne 11100. © **04-68-65-14-74.** Fax 04-68-65-81-48. www.hoteldulanguedoc.com. 40 units. 56€–88€ ($73–$114) double; 96€ ($125) suite. AE, DC, MC, V. Parking 7.80€ ($10). **Amenities:** Bar/Breton-style creperie; room service; laundry service. *In room:* TV.

La Résidence ★ Our favorite hotel in Narbonne is near the Cathédrale St-Just. The 19th-century La Résidence, converted from a stately villa, is comfortable and decorated with antiques. The rooms are midsize to spacious, tastefully furnished, and very well maintained. Most of the good-size bathrooms have tub/shower combinations. The hotel doesn't have a restaurant but offers breakfast for 7.90€ ($10) and a gracious welcome.

6 rue du 1er-Mai, Narbonne 11100. © **04-68-32-19-41.** Fax 04-68-65-51-82. www.hotelresidence.fr. 25 units. 70€–96€ ($91–$125) double. AE, DC, MC, V. Parking 7€ ($9.10). Closed Jan 20–Feb 20. **Amenities:** Nonsmoking rooms. *In room:* A/C, TV, minibar, hair dryer, Wi-Fi.

WHERE TO DINE

La Table St-Crescent ★★★ FRENCH/LANGUEDOCIENNE This is one of the region's best-respected restaurants. It's just east of town, beside the road leading to Perpignan, in a complex of wine-tasting boutiques established by a local syndicate of growers. The foundations date, it's said, from the 8th century, when it functioned as an oratory (small chapel) and prayer site. Today it's outfitted with modern furniture that's little more than a foil for the cuisine. The chef delivers refined, brilliantly realized dishes, with sublime sauces and sophisticated herbs and seasonings. Menu items change four times a year based on the availability of seasonal ingredients and the inspiration of the owners. Main courses include sea bass marinated with olives, beef filet with foie gras and truffles, and lobster ravioli with oil of pistou. Especially succulent are roasted scallops floating on a bed of cream of celery soup, filet of red snapper with shellfish and almonds, ravioli stuffed with cheese-laced potatoes, and suprême of duckling with braised cabbage. Wine steward Sabrine Giraud (the chef's wife) and her assistant, Barbara, will help you select the perfect accompaniment.

In the Palais des Vins, 68 av. Général Leclerc, rte. de Perpignan. ✆ **04-68-41-37-37.** www.la-table-saint-crescent.com. Reservations recommended. Main courses 16€–41€ ($21–$53); fixed-price lunch Mon–Fri 20€ ($26); fixed-price dinner and Sun lunch 37€–79€ ($48–$103). AE, DC, MC, V. Tues–Fri and Sun noon–1:30pm; Tues–Sat 8–9:30pm.

5 Collioure ★★

929km (577 miles) SW of Paris, 28km (17 miles) SE of Perpignan

This port was established by the Greeks in 6000 B.C. and renamed "Cauco Illiberis" by the Romans. Destroyed several times by the Arabs, it was rebuilt in the 900s by the counts of Barcelona. The port later belonged to the kings of Majorca, who established a community of Knights Templar in 1344. Still later, it passed to the kings of Aragón. Ownership passed back and forth between the kings of Spain and France before General Dugommier seized it for France in 1794. In modern times, it sheltered a colony of painters including Derain, Dufy, Picasso, and Juan Gris.

You may recognize this port and its sailboats from the Fauvist paintings of Lhote and Derain. It's said to resemble St-Tropez before it was overrun; in days past, Collioure attracted Matisse, Picasso, and Dalí. It is the most alluring port of Roussillon, a gem with a vivid Spanish and Catalan flavor. Some visitors believe it's the most charming village on the Côte Vermeille (Vermilion Coast, a nickname for this area). The town's sloping narrow streets, semifortified church, lighthouse, and rich artistic culture make it worth an afternoon's stopover. While this is the ideal small-town antidote to the condominium-choked Riviera (in winter, its pop. is only 3,000), its population swells during the summer months to 15,000.

ESSENTIALS

GETTING THERE Collioure has frequent **train** and bus service, especially from Perpignan (trip time: 20 min.). For train information and schedules, call ✆ **08-92-35-35-35** from outside France. Many visitors **drive** along the coastal road (RN114) leading to the Spanish border.

VISITOR INFORMATION The **Office de Tourisme** is on place du 18-Juin (✆ **04-68-82-15-47;** fax 04-68-82-46-29; www.collioure.com).

EXPLORING THE TOWN

The two curving ports sit on either side of the heavy masonry of the 13th-century **Château Royal,** place de 8-Mai-1945 (✆ **04-68-82-06-43**). It's of interest in its own right for its medieval fortifications and overall bulk, but between the months of May and September, it's also the home to a changing series of special (temporary) exhibitions, each of which comes and goes at regular intervals. The château assesses the same entrance charge regardless of whether there's a temporary exhibition inside on the day of your visit: 4€ ($5.20) for adults, 2€ ($26) students and children ages 12 to 18, and free for children under 12. In June and September, the château is open daily 10am to 6pm; July to August daily 10am to 7pm; October to May daily 9am to 5pm.

Also try to visit the **Musée Jean-Peské,** route de Port-Vendres (✆ **04-68-82-10-19**), home to a collection of works by artists who painted here. It's open in July and August daily 10am to noon and 2 to 7pm; September to June Wednesday through Monday 10am to noon and 2 to 6pm. Admission is 2€ ($2.60) for adults, 1.50€ ($1.95) for children 12 to 16 and students, and free for children under 12.

WHERE TO STAY

Casa Pairal ★ This pleasant family-operated hotel is in a 150-year-old house a very short walk from the port and beach. In the guest rooms, charming antiques blend with more modern pieces. The best doubles have *petit salons* plus small balconies. All but five rooms have tub/shower combinations. Breakfast is the only meal served, but there are many restaurants nearby. On sunny days, guests can take a dip in the pool, which sits in the shadow of century-old trees.

Impasse des Palmiers, Collioure 66190. ✆ **04-68-82-05-81.** Fax 04-68-82-52-10. www.hotel-casa-pairal.com. 27 units. 85€–155€ ($111–$202) double; 169€–188€ ($220–$244) suite. AE, DC, MC, V. Parking 12€ ($16). Closed Nov–Mar. **Amenities:** Outdoor pool; room service; laundry service; limited-mobility rooms. *In room:* A/C, TV, minibar, hair dryer, Wi-Fi.

Les Caranques *Value* Constructed around the core of a private villa built after World War II and enlarged twice since then, this comfortably furnished hotel is one of the best bargains in town. The rooms are a bit small but neatly maintained, with shower-only bathrooms. On the perimeter of Collioure, away from the crush (and the charm) of the center, the hotel features a terrace that opens onto a view of the old port. The terrace stretches from the hotel to the sea, where guests can swim directly from the rocks.

Rte. de Port-Vendres, Collioure 66190. ✆ **04-68-82-06-68.** Fax 04-68-82-00-92. www.les-caranques.com. 22 units. 42€–76€ ($55–$99) double. AE, MC, V. Free parking. Closed Oct 15–Mar 31. **Amenities:** Room service. *In room:* TV, minibar, Wi-Fi.

Relais des 3 Mas et Restaurant La Balette ★★ This is the town's premier hotel and the restaurant of choice; the hotel was established more than 20 years ago by connecting a trio of older Provençal farmhouses. In the decor of its beautiful rooms, the hotel honors the famous artists who lived at Collioure. The rooms, which have spacious bathrooms with Jacuzzis, open onto water views. Even if you aren't a guest, you may want to have a meal in the dining room and take in its vistas of the harbor. Jose Vidal is the best chef in town. His cooking is inventive—often simple but always refined. Fixed-price menus cost 32€ to 73€ ($42–$95) and are served daily at lunch and dinner.

Rte. de Port-Vendres, Collioure 66190. ✆ **04-68-82-05-07.** Fax 04-68-82-38-08. www.relaisdes3mas.com. 23 units. 100€–280€ ($130–$364) double; 186€–450€ ($242–$585) suite. Half board 72€ ($94) per person. AE, MC, V.

Parking 12€ ($16). Closed Dec–Feb. **Amenities:** Restaurant; outdoor pool; sauna; room service; babysitting; laundry service; nonsmoking rooms. *In room:* A/C, TV, minibar, hair dryer, safe, Wi-Fi.

WHERE TO DINE

Restaurant La Balette at the Relais des 3 Mas (see "Where to Stay," above) is the best hotel dining room in town.

Neptune ★★★ FRENCH/CATALAN This is the best restaurant in Collioure, but much to the credit of its owners and staff, it's easygoing and remarkably unpretentious. You'll find it on the southeastern edge of town in a salmon-toned Provençal *mas* (farmhouse). The establishment has for many years been the domain of the talented, hardworking Mourlane family. Menu items are noteworthy for their top-quality ingredients and the respect and care with which they're handled. Our favorite starter is a platter of local anchovies marinated in herbs; you may opt for a salad of fresh wild greens garnished with chunks of lobster. Main courses change with the seasons but may include grilled Mediterranean sea wolf with oyster-flavored butter sauce; several versions of lobster; or rack of suckling lamb from the nearby salt marshes, served in orange sauce or an herb-flavored pastry crust. Equally appealing are lightly braised scallops in delicate butter, herb, and garlic sauce, and simple but succulent sole meunière.

9 rte. de Porte-Vendres. ✆ **04-68-82-02-27.** Reservations recommended. Main courses 26€–36€ ($34–$47); fixed-price lunch 30€–70€ ($39–$91); fixed-price dinner 49€–90€ ($64–$117). AE, MC, V. Thurs–Mon noon–2pm and 7:30–9pm. Closed Dec 7–24, Jan–Feb, and Mon July–Aug.

6 Perpignan ★★

905km (562 miles) SW of Paris, 369km (229 miles) NW of Marseille, 64km (40 miles) S of Narbonne

At Perpignan you may think you've crossed into Spain; this was once Catalonia's second city, after Barcelona. Earlier, it was the capital of the kingdom of Majorca. But when Roussillon—the French part of Catalonia—was partitioned off, Perpignan became French forever, under the terms of the 1659 Treaty of the Pyrénées. Catalan is still spoken here, especially among country folk.

Today Perpignan is content to rest on its former glory. Its 120,000 residents enjoy the closeness of the Côte Catalane (the coastline of Catalonia, in neighboring Spain) and the mountains to the north. The pace is relaxed. You'll have time to smell the flowers that grow here in great abundance.

This is one of the sunniest places in France, but during summer afternoons in July and August, it's a cauldron. That's when many locals catch the 9.5km (6-mile) ride to the beach resort of Canet. Bus no. 1 runs from the center of Perpignan every 15 minutes in the summer and costs 4€ ($5.20). A young scene brings energy to Perpignan, especially along the quays of the Basse River, site of impromptu nighttime concerts, beer drinking, and the devouring of tapas, a tradition adopted from nearby Barcelona.

ESSENTIALS

GETTING THERE Four **trains** per day arrive from Paris from both the Gare St. Lazare and the Gare de Nord (trip time: 6–10 hr.) after stopping at Montpellier; the one-way fare is 105€ ($137). There are also three conventional trains from Marseille via Narbonne (trip time: 4½ hr.; one-way fare: 40€/$52). For rail information and schedules, call ✆ **36-35** or 08-92-35-35-35 from outside France. If you're **driving** from the French Riviera, drive west along A9 to Perpignan.

VISITOR INFORMATION The **Office Municipal du Tourisme** is in the Palais des Congrès, place Armand-Lanoux (✆ **04-68-66-30-30;** fax 04-68-66-30-26; www.perpignantourisme.com).

SPECIAL EVENTS In the heat of July, **Les Estivales** (✆ **04-68-35-01-77;** www.estivales.com) causes the city to go a 4-week cultural binge, with music, expositions, and theater. Our favorite time to visit this area is during the **grape harvest** in September. If you visit then, you may want to drive through vineyards of the Rivesaltes district bordering the city to the west and north. Temperatures have usually dropped by then.

Perpignan is host to one of the most widely discussed celebrations of photojournalism in the industry, the **Festival International du Photojournalisme** (✆ **04-68-62-38-00;** www.visapourlimage.com). Established in the late 1980s, it's also called **Le Visa pour l'Image.** From September 2 to September 17, at least 10 sites of historical (usually medieval) interest are devoted to photojournalistic expositions from around the world. Entrance to the shows is free and an international committee awards prizes.

EXPLORING THE CITY

With its inviting pedestrian streets, Perpignan is a good town for shopping. Catalan is the style indigenous to the area, and its influence is evident in the textiles, pottery, and furniture. For one of the best selections of Catalan pieces, including pottery, furniture, carpets, and antiques, visit the **Centre Sant-Vicens,** rue Sant-Vicens (✆ **04-68-50-02-18**), where about a dozen merchants sell ceramics, pottery, and art. You'll find it 4km (2½ miles) south of the town center; follow signs pointing to Enne and Collioure. A competitor selling Catalan-inspired home-decorating items is **La Maison Quinta,** 3 rue des Grands-des-Fabriques (✆ **04-68-34-41-62**), in the town center.

A 3-hour guided **walking tour** is a good way to see the attractions in the town's historic core. On Fridays, some tour leaders even lace their commentary with English. Tours begin at 5pm daily from mid-June to mid-September. The rest of the year, they start at 2:30pm on Wednesday and 10:30am on Saturday only. They depart from in front of the tourist office and cost 5€ ($6.50) per person. For more details, contact the tourist office (see above).

Cathédrale St-Jean ★ The cathedral dates from the 14th and 15th centuries and has an admirable nave and interesting 17th-century retables (altarpieces). Leaving through the south door, you'll find on the left a chapel with the *Devost-Christ* (Devout Christ), a magnificent woodcarving depicting Jesus contorted with pain and suffering, his head, crowned with thorns, drooping on his chest. Sightseeing visits are discouraged during Sunday Mass. On Good Friday, the statue is promenaded through the streets of the town center.

Place Gambetta/rue de l'Horloge. ✆ **04-68-51-33-72.** Free admission. Daily 7:30am–7pm.

Château de Salses This fort has guarded the main road linking Spain and France since the days of the Romans. Ferdinand of Aragón erected a fort here in 1497, hoping to protect his northern frontier. Even today, the town of Salses marks the language-barrier point between Catalonia in Spain and Languedoc in France. This Spanish-style fort designed by Ferdinand is a curious example of an Iberian structure in France, but in the 17th century it was modified to look more like a château. Salses fell to Louis XIII in September 1642, and its Spanish garrison left forever. Some 2 decades later, Roussillon was incorporated into France.

Salses, 16km (10 miles) north of the center of Perpignan. From Perpignan, follow signs to Narbonne and RN9. ✆ **04-68-38-60-13.** Admission 6.50€ ($8.45) adults, 4.50€ ($5.85) ages 17–25, free for children under 17. Oct–May daily 10am–noon and 2–5pm; June–Sept daily 9:30am–7pm.

Le Castillet ★ This crenellated red-brick building is a combination gateway and fortress from the 14th century. You can climb its bulky tower for a view of the town. Also here is the **Musée des Arts et Traditions Populaires Catalans** (also known as La Casa Païral), with exhibitions of Catalan regional artifacts and folkloric items, including typical dress.

Place de Verdun. ✆ **04-68-35-42-05.** Admission 4€ ($5.20) adults, 2€ ($2.60) students and children under 18. May–Sept Wed–Mon 10am–6:30pm; Oct–Apr Wed–Mon 11am–5:30pm.

Palais des Rois de Majorque (Palace of the Kings of Majorca) ★ At the top of the town, the Spanish citadel encloses the Palace of the Kings of Majorca. The government has restored this structure, built in the 13th and 14th centuries, around a court encircled by arcades. You can see the old throne room, with its large fireplaces, and a square tower with a double gallery; from the tower there's a fine view of the Pyrénées. A free guided tour, in French only, departs four times a day if demand warrants it.

Rue des Archers. ✆ **04-68-34-48-29.** Admission 4€ ($5.20) adults, 2€ ($2.60) students, free for children under 12. June–Sept daily 10am–6pm; Oct–May daily 9am–5pm.

WHERE TO STAY

La Villa Duflot ★★★ This is the area's greatest hotel, yet its prices are reasonable for the luxury it offers. Tranquillity, style, and refinement reign supreme. Located in a suburb 4km (2½ miles) from Perpignan, La Villa Duflot is a Mediterranean-style dwelling surrounded by a park of pine, palm, and eucalyptus. You can sunbathe in the gardens surrounding the pool and order drinks from the outside bar. The good-size guest rooms surround a patio planted with century-old olive trees. All are spacious and soundproof, with marble tub/shower bathrooms and Art Deco interiors. The restaurant (reviewed below) is reason enough to stay.

Rond-Point Albert Donnezan, Perpignan 66000. From the center of Perpignan, follow signs to Perthus–Le Belou and A9, and travel 3km (1¾ miles) south. Just before you reach A9, you'll see the hotel. ✆ **04-68-56-67-67.** Fax 04-68-56-54-05. www.villa-duflot.com. 25 units. 120€–160€ ($156–$208) double. Half board 108€–128€ ($140–$166) per person double occupancy. AE, DC, MC, V. **Amenities:** Restaurant; 2 bars; outdoor pool; room service; babysitting; laundry service; nonsmoking rooms; limited-mobility rooms. *In room:* A/C, TV, minibar, hair dryer, safe, Wi-Fi.

Park Hotel ★ This five-story, mid-'60s hotel, facing the Jardins de la Ville, offers well-furnished, soundproof rooms. Although the Park is solid and reliable, it's the town's second choice, with none of the glamour of the Duflot. The midsize to spacious rooms are comfortably furnished with taste but not much flair; each comes with an average-size bathroom, and most have tub/shower combinations. The restaurant serves first-class Mediterranean cuisine. Post-nouvelle choices include roast sea scallops flavored with succulent sea urchin velouté, various lobster dishes, and penne with truffles. As an accompaniment, try one of the local wines—perhaps a Collioure or Côtes du Roussillon.

18 bd. Jean-Bourrat, Perpignan 66000. ✆ **04-68-35-14-14.** Fax 04-68-35-48-18. www.parkhotel-fr.com. 69 units. 75€–105€ ($98–$137) double; 180€–280€ ($234–$364) suite. AE, DC, MC, V. Parking 10€ ($13). **Amenities:** Restaurant; bar; room service; laundry service; nonsmoking rooms; limited-mobility rooms. *In room:* A/C, TV, minibar, hair dryer, iron, safe, Wi-Fi.

WHERE TO DINE

The **Park Hotel** (see "Where to Stay," above) has a well-recommended restaurant.

L'Assiette Catalane *Value* FRENCH/SPANISH/CATALAN Known to virtually every resident of Perpignan for its well-prepared cuisine, this restaurant resembles something you'd expect across the Pyrénées in Spain. Hand-painted ceramic plates, rugby and flamenco posters, and antique farm implements cover the thick stone walls. Even the long, lively bar is inlaid with Iberian mosaics, and copies of works by Dalí and Picasso seem to stare back at you as you dine. Menu items include four kinds of *parrilladas* (mixed grills)—one of the most appealing consists entirely of fish served on a hot slab of iron that's brought directly to your table—and zarzuelas, paella, and tapas, prepared in the Spanish style, but served as an appetizer. Chicken with crayfish is another regional specialty. It seems appropriate to follow up with a portion of flan.

9 rue de la République. ✆ **04-68-34-77-62.** Reservations recommended. Main courses 11€–17€ ($14–$22); fixed-price lunch 8€–11€ ($10–$14); fixed-price dinner 15€–25€ ($20–$33). MC, V. Mon–Sat noon–2pm; Wed–Mon 7–11pm.

La Villa Duflot ★ FRENCH Slightly removed from the city center, this *restaurant avec chambres* (see "Where to Stay," above) is the most tranquil oasis in the area. Owner André Duflot employs top-notch chefs who turn out dish after dish with remarkable skill and professionalism. Try, for example, a salad of warm squid, a platter of fresh anchovies marinated in vinegar, excellent foie gras of duckling, or lasagna of foie gras with asparagus points. A wonderful dessert is chocolate cake with saffron-flavored cream sauce. On the premises is an American-style bar.

Rond-Point Albert Donnezan, Perpignan 66000. From the center of Perpignan, follow signs to Perthus–Le Belou and A9, and travel 3km (1¾ miles) south. Just before you reach A9, you'll see the hotel. ✆ **04-68-56-67-67.** Fax 04-68-56-54-05. Reservations required. Main courses 18€–23€ ($23–$30); Sat–Sun fixed-price menu 30€ ($39). AE, DC, MC, V. Daily noon–2pm and 8–11pm.

Le Clos des Lys ★ *Value* FRENCH This well-recommended restaurant, in a stately building that sits apart from its neighbors, has an outdoor terrace overlooking a copse of cypresses and bubbling fountains. It's supervised by Jean-Claude Vila and Frank Sequret, respected chefs who have been finalists in several culinary competitions. The fixed-price menus vary widely in selection and cost. Dishes may include goat cheese in puff pastry, garnished with sesame seeds and a reduction of Banyuls dessert wine; terrine of three kinds of liver accompanied with a salad of wild greens and walnuts; foie gras of duck with passion fruit and mango chutney sauce; filets of sea wolf fried with sesame seeds and served with eggplant mousse and tomato-flavored risotto; and tournedos of beef with a layer of foie gras, creamed morels, and soufflé potatoes. The restaurant incorporates a thriving catering business that books conventions and weddings.

660 chemin de la Fauceille. From the center of Perpignan, drive 2.5km (1½ miles) west, following the rte. d'Espagne. ✆ **04-68-56-79-00.** www.closdeslys.com. Reservations recommended. Fixed-price lunch 16€–59€ ($21–$77); fixed-price dinner 22€–59€ ($29–$77). AE, DC, MC, V. Tues–Sun noon–2pm; Tues and Thurs–Sat 7–9:30pm. Closed 3 weeks in Feb.

PERPIGNAN AFTER DARK

Perpignan shows its Spanish and Catalan side at night, when a round of tapas and late-night promenades are among the activities. The streets radiating from **place de la Loge** offer a higher concentration of bars and clubs than any other part of town.

Hot and sometimes overheated Perpignan offers lots of diversions to amuse visitors during the cool of the night. An evening on the town involves a drink and a chat in one of the *bars de nuit,* followed by a visit to a disco. You may begin at **Le Habana Bodegita-Club,** 5 rue Grande-des-Fabriques (✆ **04-68-34-11-00**), where salsa and merengue play and sunset-colored cocktails flow. Suds with an Irish accent are the attraction at **Le O'Shannon Bar,** 3 rue de l'Incendie (✆ **04-68-35-12-48**), where a small community of Irish expats (and Celtic wannabes) wax nostalgic.

Discos in Perpignan open around 11pm. **Le Napoli,** 3 rue place de Catalogne (✆ **04-68-51-25-02**), a modern, mirror-sheathed space, may remind you of an airport waiting area without the chairs. (Yes, you'll have to stand up and mingle or dance, because there's almost nowhere to sit.) Another option for dancing is the **Uba-Club,** 5 bd. Mercader (✆ **04-68-34-06-70**), which has a smallish dance floor and, thankfully, some sofas and chairs.

During summer, the beachfront strip at the nearby resort of **Canet-Plage,** 12km (7½ miles) east of Perpignan's historic core, abounds with seasonal bars and dance clubs that come and go with the tourist tides.

7 Carcassonne ★★★

797km (495 miles) SW of Paris, 92km (57 miles) SE of Toulouse, 105km (65 miles) S of Albi

Evoking bold knights, fair damsels, and troubadours, the greatest fortress city of Europe rises against a background of the Pyrénées. Floodlit at night, it suggests fairy-tale magic, but in its heyday in the Middle Ages, it wasn't so romantic. Shattering the peace and quiet were battering rams, grapnels, a mobile tower (inspired by the Trojan horse), catapults, flaming arrows, and the mangonel (a type of catapult).

Today the city that once served as a backdrop for the 1991 movie *Robin Hood, Prince of Thieves* is overrun with visitors and tacky gift shops. But the elusive charm of Carcassonne emerges in the evening, when thousands of day-trippers have departed and floodlights bathe the ancient monuments.

ESSENTIALS

GETTING THERE Carcassonne is a major stop for **trains** between Toulouse and destinations south and east. There are 5 trains per day from Toulouse (trip time: 1 hr.; one-way fare: 14€/$18), 9 per day from Montpellier (trip time: 1½ hr.; 22€/$27 one-way), and 3 per day from Marseilles (trip time: 4 hr.; 40€/$52 one-way). For rail information, call ✆ **36-35** or 08-92-35-35-35 from outside France. If you're **driving,** Carcassonne is on A61 south of Toulouse.

VISITOR INFORMATION The **Office de Tourisme** has locations at 28 rue de Verdun (✆ **04-68-10-24-30;** fax 04-68-10-24-38; www.carcassonne-tourisme.com) and in the medieval town at Porte Narbonnaise (✆ **04-68-10-24-36**).

SPECIAL EVENTS The town's nightlife sparkles during its summer festivals. During the **Festival de Carcassonne** (www.festivaldecarcassonne.com) in July, concerts, modern and classical dance, operas, and theater fill the city. Tickets run 28€ to 68€ ($36–$88) and can be purchased by calling ✆ **04-68-11-59-15** or 04-68-77-74-31. On July 14, **Bastille Day,** one of the best fireworks spectacles in France lights up the skies at 10:30pm. Over 6 weeks in July and August, the merriment and raucousness of the Middle Ages overtake the city during the **Spectacles Medievaux,** in the form of jousts, parades, food fairs, and street festivals. For information, contact the **Office de Tourisme** (✆ **04-68-10-24-30**).

EXPLORING THE TOWN

Carcassonne consists of two towns: the **Bastide St-Louis** (also known as the Ville Basse or Lower City) and the medieval **Cité.** The former has little of interest, but the latter is among the major attractions in France. The fortifications consist of the inner and outer walls, a double line of ramparts. The Visigoths built the inner rampart in the 5th century. Clovis, king of the Franks, attacked it in 506 but failed to breach the fortifications. The Saracens overcame the city in 728, but Pepin the Short (father of Charlemagne) drove them out in 752.

The epic medieval poems *Chansons de Geste* tell the tale of the origin of the town's name. During a siege by Charlemagne, the populace of the city was starving and near surrender until a local noblewoman, Dame Carcas, reputedly gathered up the last of their grain, fed it to a sow, and then tossed the pig over the ramparts. The pig burst, scattering the grain. Dame Carcas then ordered the trumpets sounded for a parley and cried, *"Carcas te sonne!"* ("Carcas is calling you!"). The Franks concluded that Carcassonne must have unlimited food supplies and ended their siege.

Carcassonne's walls were further fortified by the *vicomtes* de Trencavel in the 12th century and by Louis IX and Philip the Bold during the following century. By the mid–17th century the city had lost its position as a strategic frontier, and the ramparts were left to decay. In the 19th century, the builders of the Lower Town began to remove the stone for use in new construction. But interest in the Middle Ages revived, and the government ordered Viollet-le-Duc (who restored Notre-Dame in Paris) to repair and, where necessary, rebuild the walls. Reconstruction continued until very recently. A small population lives inside the walls.

In the highest elevation of the Cité, at the uppermost terminus of rue Principale (rue Cros Mayrevielle), you'll find the **Château Comtal,** place du Château (✆ **04-68-11-70-70**), a restored 12th-century fortress that's open April to September daily 10am to 6:30pm, October to March daily 9:30am to 5pm. Entrance includes an obligatory 40-minute guided tour, in French and broken English. It's also the only way to climb onto the city's inner ramparts. The cost is 7.50€ ($9.75) for adults, 4.80€ ($6.25) for students and ages 18 to 25, and free for children under 18. The tour includes access to expositions that display the archaeological remnants discovered on-site, plus an explanation of the 19th-century restorations.

Another important monument in the fortifications is the **Basilique St-Nazaire** ★, La Cité (✆ **04-68-25-27-65**), dating from the 11th to the 14th centuries and containing some beautiful stained-glass windows and a pair of rose medallions. The nave is in the Romanesque style, and the choir and transept are Gothic. The 16th-century organ is one of the oldest in southwestern France. The 1266 tomb of Bishop Radulphe is well preserved. The cathedral is open in July and August daily 9am to 6pm, September to June daily 9am to noon and 1 to 5pm. Mass is celebrated on Sunday at 11am. Admission is free.

SHOPPING

Carcassonne has two distinct shopping areas. In the modern lower city, the major streets for shopping, particularly if you're in the market for clothing, are **rue Clemenceau** and **rue de Verdun.** In the walled medieval city, the streets are chockfull of tiny stores and boutiques; most sell gift items such as antiques and local arts and crafts.

Stores worth visiting, all in the Cité, include **Cellier des Vigneros,** 13 rue du Grand Puits (✆ **04-68-25-31-00**), where you'll find a wide selection of regional wines ranging from simple table wines to those awarded the distinction of Appellation d'Origine Contrôlée. Some antiques stores of merit are **Mme Faye-Nunez,** 4 place du Château (✆ **04-68-47-09-45**), for antique furniture; **Antiquités Safi,** 26 rue Trivalle (✆ **04-68-25-60-51**), for paintings and art objects; and **Dominique Sarraute,** 15 porte d'Aude (✆ **04-68-47-10-06**), for antique firearms.

WHERE TO STAY

IN THE CITE

Hôtel de la Cité ★★★ Originally a palace for whatever bishop or prelate happened to be in power at the time, this has been the most desirable hotel in town since 1909. It's in the actual walls of the city, adjoining the cathedral. The Orient-Express Hotel group acquired the hotel in the '90s and fluffed it up to the tune of $3 million. You enter a long Gothic corridor-gallery leading to the lounge. Many rooms open onto the ramparts and a garden, and feature antiques or reproductions. A few accommodations contain wood headboards and four-poster beds. The ideal unit is no. 308, which opens onto the most panoramic view of the city. Modern equipment has been discreetly installed throughout, including bathrooms of generous size with tub/shower combinations. The hotel is renowned for its restaurant.

Place de l'Eglise, Carcassonne 11000. ✆ **04-68-71-98-71.** Fax 04-68-71-50-15. www.hoteldelacite.com. 61 units. 325€–525€ ($423–$683) double; 400€–1,250€ ($520–$1,625) suite. AE, DC, MC, V. Parking 20€ ($26). Closed late Nov to late Dec and Feb to early Mar. **Amenities:** 3 restaurants (including La Barbacane; see "Where to Dine," below); bar; outdoor pool; room service; babysitting; laundry service; nonsmoking rooms; limited-mobility rooms. *In room:* A/C, TV, minibar, hair dryer, safe.

AT THE ENTRANCE TO THE CITE

Le Donjon et Les Remparts ★★ *Value* This little hotel is big on charm and is the best value in the moderate price range. Built in the style of the old Cité, it has a honey-colored stone exterior with iron bars on the windows. The interior is a jewel. Elaborate Louis XIII–style furniture graces the reception lounges. A newer wing contains additional rooms in medieval architectural style. Their furnishings are in a severe style that's consistent with the medieval look of the nearby ramparts. Each unit comes with a compact tiled bathroom, most with tub/shower combos. The hotel also runs the nearby Brasserie Le Donjon. In summer, the garden is the perfect breakfast spot.

2 rue du Comte-Roger, Carcassonne 11000. ✆ **800/528-1234** in the U.S. and Canada, or 04-68-11-23-00. Fax 04-68-25-06-60. www.hotel-donjon.fr. 62 units. 105€–157€ ($137–$204) double; 150€–240€ ($195–$312) suite. AE, DC, MC, V. Parking 8€ ($10). **Amenities:** Restaurant; bar; room service; laundry service; dry cleaning; nonsmoking rooms; limited-mobility rooms. *In room:* A/C, TV, minibar, hair dryer.

IN VILLE-BASSE

Hôtel Montségur ★ *Value* This stately town house with a mansard roof and dormers was built in 1887. Trees and a high wrought-iron fence screen the front garden from the street. Didier and Isabelle Faugeras have furnished the hotel with antiques, lending it a residential feel. Guest rooms vary in size, from small to spacious, and most of the small tiled bathrooms contain tub/shower combinations. Continental breakfast is available on-site, but for dinner you may wish to visit their highly recommended restaurant across the street, Le Languedoc, where Didier is the chef.

27 allée d'Iéna, Carcassonne 11000. ✆ **04-68-25-31-41.** Fax 04-68-47-13-22. www.hotelmontsegur.com. 21 units. 75€–98€ ($98–$127) double. AE, DC, MC, V. Free parking. **Amenities:** Restaurant; bar; room service; laundry service; nonsmoking rooms. *In room:* A/C, TV, hair dryer, Wi-Fi.

Trois Couronnes ★★ Reliable and dependable, though not exciting, this serviceable favorite is the best choice in Ville-Basse. It lies south of the landmark Square Gambetta, immediately west of the bridge, pont Vieux. Built in 1992, the hotel rises five stories. Rooms open onto views of the Aude River and the ramparts of the old city. A government-rated three-star hotel, "Three Crowns" has some of the best facilities in town, including an indoor pool. The rooms are functionally comfortable with tasteful furnishings. Service is top rate, and maintenance is good. A good regional cuisine is served in the on-site restaurant Le Richepin.

2 rue des Trois Couronnes, Carcassonne 11000. ✆ **04-68-25-36-10.** Fax 04-68-25-92-92. www.hotel-destroiscouronnes.com. 68 units. 74€–109€ ($96–$142) double. AE, DC, MC, V. Parking 8€ ($10). **Amenities:** Restaurant; bar; indoor pool; fitness room; sauna; car rental; room service; limited-mobility rooms. *In room:* A/C, TV, minibar, hair dryer.

WHERE TO DINE

Brasserie Donjon, run by Le Donjon et Les Remparts hotel, is a good, affordable choice for meals, especially if you're visiting the Cité at lunchtime. In Ville-Basse, the moderately priced restaurant at **Trois Couronnes** serves well-prepared regional cuisine. See "Where to Stay," above.

Au Jardin de la Tour INTERNATIONAL This restaurant and its verdant garden introduce greenery and charm into the city's medieval core. Rustic finds from local antiques fairs decorate the early-19th-century building. You can order from a large selection of salads, beef filet with morels, sushi, cassoulet, terrines of foie gras, and all kinds of grilled fish. The consistently good cooking relies on fresh ingredients deftly handled by a talented kitchen staff.

11 rue Porte-d'Aude. ✆ **04-68-25-71-24.** Reservations recommended in summer. Main courses 14€–25€ ($18–$33); fixed-price menu 22€–28€ ($29–$36). MC, V. Tues–Sat noon–2pm and 7:30–10pm. Closed Nov 1–Dec 15.

La Barbacane ★ FRENCH Named after its medieval neighborhood, this restaurant enjoys equal billing with the celebrated hotel that contains it. Its soothing-looking dining room, with green walls and lots of paneling, features the cuisine of noted chef Jérome Ryon and pastry chef Régis Chanel. Menu items are based on seasonal ingredients, with just enough zest. Examples are green ravioli perfumed with *seiche* (a species of octopus) and its own ink, crisp-fried cod with black olives, saltwater crayfish with strips of Bayonne ham, Breton lobster with artichoke hearts and caviar, and organically fed free-range guinea fowl rubbed with vanilla and stuffed with truffles. A star dessert is chestnut parfait with malt-flavored cream sauce and date-flavored ice cream.

In the Hôtel de la Cité, place de l'Eglise. ✆ **04-68-71-98-71.** Reservations recommended. Main courses 31€–80€ ($40–$104); fixed-price menu 70€–160€ ($91–$208). AE, DC, MC, V. Daily 7:30–10pm. Closed Dec–Mar.

Le Languedoc ★★ TRADITIONAL FRENCH Acclaimed chef Didier Faugeras is the creative force behind the inspired cuisine here. The high-ceilinged century-old dining room is filled with antiques; a brick fireplace contributes to the warm atmosphere. The specialty is *cassoulet au confit de canard* (the famous stew made with duck cooked in its own fat). It has been celebrated here since the early 1960s. A smooth dessert is flambéed crepes Languedoc. In summer you can dine on a patio or in the air-conditioned restaurant. Faugeras and his wife, Isabelle, own the worthy Hôtel Montségur, across the street (see "Where to Stay," above).

32 allée d'Iéna. ✆ **04-68-25-22-17.** Reservations recommended. Main courses 16€–24€ ($21–$31); fixed-price menu 24€–44€ ($31–$57). AE, DC, MC, V. July–Aug Tues–Sun noon–1:30pm, daily 7:30–9:30pm; Sept–June Tues–Sun noon–2pm, Tues–Sat 7:30–9:30pm. Closed last week of June and Dec 20–Jan 20.

WHERE TO STAY & DINE NEARBY

Château St-Martin ★ FRENCH One of Languedoc's most successful chefs operates out of this 16th-century château at Montredon, 4km (2½ miles) northeast of Carcassonne. Ringed by a wooded park, the restaurant serves the superb cuisine of co-owners Jean-Claude and Jacqueline Rodriguez. Dine inside or on the terrace. Recommended dishes are fish (according to the daily catch) with fondue of baby vegetables, sea bass with scallop mousseline, sole in tarragon, and *confit de canard carcassonnaise* (duck meat cooked in its own fat and kept in earthenware pots). Two other specialties are *cassoulet languedocienne* (made with pork, mutton, and goose or duck) and *boullinade nouvelloise* (made with an assortment of seafood that includes scallops, sole, and turbot). On the premises are 15 simple, but comfortable, hotel rooms; doubles rent for 75€ to 90€ ($98–$117). The hotel is closed November 15 to March 11. Call ✆ **04-68-47-44-41** for information on rooms.

Montredon, Carcassonne 11090. From La Cité, follow signs pointing to Stade Albert Domec 4km (2½ miles) northeast. ✆ **04-68-71-09-53.** Fax 04-68-25-46-55. www.chateausaintmartin.net. Reservations required. Main courses 17€–25€ ($22–$33); fixed-price menu 31€–55€ ($40–$72). AE, DC, MC, V. Thurs–Tues noon–1:30pm and 7:30–9:30pm (closed Sun night).

Domaine d'Auriac ★★★ The Carcassonne area's premier address for food and lodging is this moss-covered 19th-century manor house about 2.5km (1½ miles) west of the Cité. It was built around 1880 on the ruins of a medieval monastery; some of the monastery's ceiling vaults are still visible in the cellars. The cube-shaped building, a Relais & Châteaux member, has half-a-dozen stone-sided annexes, which hold many of the accommodations. Each guest room has a photo-magazine aura, with lots of flowered fabrics, a range of decorative styles, and, in many, massive sculpted ceiling beams. The first-rate tiled bathrooms contain tub/shower combinations. Anne-Marie Rigaudis is the experienced owner, assisted by her grown children, Marie-Hélène and Pierre. The hotel is one of the few in the area with its own 18-hole golf course, which affords gorgeous panoramas over the countryside (ask about combination golf/stay packages).

Part of the property's allure is the well-crafted and well-conceived meals. Fixed-price menus (60€–140€/$78–$182) change several times each season, but always demonstrate a sophisticated twist that makes local recipes more glamorous and interesting. During warmer weather, there's seating beside the pool on flowery terraces.

Rte. de Saint-Hilaire, Carcassonne 11000. ✆ **04-68-25-72-22.** Fax 04-68-47-35-54. www.domaine-d-auriac.com. 26 units. 150€–390€ ($195–$507) double; 400€–450€ ($520–$585) suite. AE, DC, MC, V. Free parking. Closed Jan, Apr 27–May 4, and Nov 15–22. Take D104 west 2.5km (1½ miles) from Carcassonne. **Amenities:** Restaurant; bar; outdoor pool; 18-hole golf course; room service; babysitting; laundry service; dry cleaning; nonsmoking rooms. *In room:* A/C, TV, minibar, hair dryer, safe, Wi-Fi.

CARCASSONNE AFTER DARK

Carcassonne nightlife centers on **rue Omer-Sarraut** in La Bastide and **place Marcou** in La Cité. **La Bulle,** 115 rue Barbacane (✆ **04-68-72-47-70**), explodes with techno and rock dance tunes for an under-30 crowd that keeps the place hopping until 5am Wednesday to Sunday. The cover charge begins at 10€ ($13) per person. Another enduringly popular disco, 4km (2½ miles) southwest of town, is **Le Black Bottom,** route de Limoux (✆ **04-68-47-37-11**), which plays every conceivable kind of dance music Thursday to Sunday beginning at 11pm. Entrance costs 10€ ($13) on Saturday only.

8 Castres ★

728km (452 miles) SW of Paris, 42km (26 miles) S of Albi

On the bank of the Agout River, Castres is the gateway for trips to the Sidobre, the mountains of Lacaune, and the Black Mountains. Castres is one of France's most important wool-producing areas; the industry's origins in the region date to the 14th century. The town, with a current population of 50,000, was once a Roman military installation. A Benedictine monastery was founded here in the 9th century, and the town fell under the *comtes* d'Albi in the 10th century. During the wars of religion, it was Protestant.

ESSENTIALS

GETTING THERE From Toulouse, there are seven **trains** per day (trip time: 1 hr., 15 min.); the one-way fare from Toulouse is 13€ ($17). For information, call ✆ **36-35** or 08-92-35-35-35 from outside France. If you're **driving,** Castres is on N126 east of Toulouse and N112 south of Albi.

VISITOR INFORMATION The **Office de Tourisme** is at 3 rue Milhau Ducommun (✆ **05-63-62-63-62;** fax 05-63-62-63-60; www.ville-castres.fr).

EXPLORING THE TOWN

Eglise St-Benoît The town's most prominent church is an outstanding example of French baroque architecture. The architect Caillau began construction in 1677 on the site of a 9th-century Benedictine abbey, but the structure was never completed according to its original plans. Gabriel Briard executed the painting above the altar in the 18th century.

Place du 8-Mai-1945. ✆ **05-63-59-05-19.** Free admission. Mon–Sat 9am–noon and 2–6pm; Sun 8:30am–noon. Closed to casual visitors Sun Oct–May, except for religious services.

Musée Goya ★ The museum is in the town hall, an archbishop's palace designed by Mansart in 1669. Some of the spacious public rooms have ceilings supported by a frieze of the archbishop's coats of arms. The collection includes 16th-century tapestries and the works of Spanish painters from the 15th to the 20th centuries. Most notable are the paintings of Francisco Goya y Lucientes, all donated to the town in 1894 by Pierre Briguiboul, son of the Castres-born artist Marcel Briguiboul. *Les Caprices* is a study of figures created in 1799 after the illness that left Goya deaf. Filling much of an entire room, the work consists of symbolic images of demons and monsters, a satire of Spanish society.

In the Jardin de l'Evêché. ✆ **05-63-71-59-30.** Admission 2.30€ ($3) adults, free for children under 18. Apr–Sept daily 10am–noon and 2–6pm; Oct–Mar Tues–Sun 10am–noon and 2–5pm.

WHERE TO STAY

Hôtel Renaissance ★ The Renaissance is the best hotel in Castres. It was built in the 17th century as a courthouse and had become a colorful but run-down hotel when it was restored in 1993. Today you'll see a dignified building with *colombages*-style half-timbering and a mixture of stone blocks and bricks. Some of the comfortable rooms, each renovated around 2001, have exposed timbers. Some rooms are in the style of Napoleon III, some are 18th-century Asiatic, some are country-comfortable with safari-themed fabrics, and others have hunting themes. Each unit contains a midsize bathroom, and all but two have tub/shower combinations.

17 rue Victor-Hugo, Castres 81100. ✆ **05-63-59-30-42.** Fax 05-63-72-11-57. www.hotel-renaissance.fr. 20 units. 60€ ($78) double; 90€ ($117) suite. AE, DC, MC, V. **Amenities:** Restaurant; bar; room service; laundry service; dry cleaning; nonsmoking rooms; limited-mobility rooms. *In room:* A/C, TV, minibar, hair dryer, Wi-Fi.

WHERE TO DINE

Brasserie de l'Europe *Value* FRENCH/PROVENÇAL This modern brasserie is a good bet for solid cuisine. The rustic decor features English-inspired furnishings with lots of well-oiled wood paneling. The expanded menu includes a selection of regional platters as well as pizzas. There are also regional sausages served with purée of apples and cheese from the foothills of the Pyrénées. Other menu items include blanquettes of veal, cassoulets, and caramelized pork filets with Provençal herbs. The service is polite, but pressed for time. Many visitors find it suitable for a simple noontime meal.

1 place Jean-Jaurès. ✆ **05-63-59-01-44.** Reservations recommended. Main courses 8€–15€ ($10–$20); fixed-price lunch 10€–19€ ($13–$25); fixed-price dinner 19€ ($25). MC, V. Mon–Sat noon–2:30pm and 7–10:30pm.

La Mandragore ★ LANGUEDOCIENNE On an easily overlooked narrow street, this restaurant, named for a legendary plant with magic powers, occupies a small section of one of the many wings of the medieval château-fort of Castres. The decor is simple, with stone walls and tones of autumn colors. The regional cuisine is among the best in town, and it's served with a smile. Among the best dishes are ravioli stuffed with braised snails and flavored with basil, rack of suckling veal with exotic mushrooms, and magret of duckling with natural Canadian maple syrup. The owners are French citizens who lived in Montreal for 15 years and worked at a famous restaurant there.

1 rue Malpas. ✆ **05-63-59-51-27.** Reservations recommended. Main courses 18€–22€ ($23–$29); fixed-price menu 12€–26€ ($16–$34). DC, MC, V. Tues–Sat noon–2pm and 7–10pm. Closed 2 weeks in Sept and 2 weeks in Mar.

9 Albi ★★★

697km (433 miles) SW of Paris, 76km (47 miles) NE of Toulouse

The "red city" (for the color of its bricks) of Albi straddles both banks of the Tarn River and is dominated by its 13th-century cathedral. Toulouse-Lautrec was born in the Hôtel Bosc in Albi; it's still a private home and not open to visitors, but there's a plaque on the wall of the building, on rue Toulouse-Lautrec in the town center. The town's major attraction is a museum with a world-class collection of the artist's work.

ESSENTIALS

GETTING THERE Fifteen **trains** per day link Toulouse with Albi (trip time: 1 hr.); the one-way fare is 13€ ($16). There's also a Paris-Albi night train. For rail information, call ✆ **36-35** or 08-92-35-35-35 from outside France. If you're **driving** from Toulouse, take N88 northeast.

VISITOR INFORMATION The **Office de Tourisme** is in the Palais de la Berbie, place Ste-Cécile (✆ **05-63-49-48-80;** fax 05-63-49-48-98; www.albi-tourisme.fr).

EXPLORING THE TOWN

Cathédrale Ste-Cécile ★★★ Fortified with ramparts and parapets and containing frescoes and paintings, this 13th-century cathedral was built by a local lord-bishop after a religious struggle with the *comte* de Toulouse (the crusade against the Cathars). Note the exceptional 16th-century rood screen with a unique suit of polychromatic statues from the Old and New Testaments. Free classical concerts take place in July and August on Wednesday at 5pm and Sunday at 4pm.

Near place du Vigan, in the medieval center of town. ✆ **05-63-43-23-43.** Cathédrale: Free admission. Treasury: 3€ ($3.90) adults, 2€ ($2.60) ages 12–25, free for children under 12. June–Sept daily 9am–6:30pm; Oct–May daily 9am–noon and 2–6:30pm.

Musée de Lapérouse Set on the opposite bank of the Tarn from the bulk of Albi's medieval core (take the Pont-Vieux to reach it), within what was originally built in the 18th century as a factory for pasta, this museum honors the achievements of Albi's native son, Jean-François de la Pérouse. Commissioned as an explorer by Louis XVI in the late 1600s, he mapped and charted the coastlines of Alaska, California, and China, bringing the French up to speed against England in its rush for colonies outside of Europe. The museum contains maps, charts, navigational instructions, and memorabilia that illustrate the progress and achievements of not only the explorer himself, but France's self-image during a period of some of its greatest glory.

Square Botany Bay. ✆ **05-63-46-01-87.** Admission 2.50€ ($3.25) adults, 1.50€ ($1.95) students and ages 12–25, free for children under 12. Mar–June and Sept–Oct Tues–Sun 9am–noon and 2–6pm; July–Aug Mon–Fri 9am–noon and 2–6pm, Sat–Sun 10am–noon and 2–7pm; Nov–Feb Tues–Sun 10am–noon and 2–5pm.

Musée Toulouse-Lautrec ★★ The Palais de la Berbie (Archbishop's Palace) is a fortified structure dating from the 13th century. This museum contains the world's most important collection of the artist's paintings, more than 600 in all. His family bequeathed the works remaining in his studio. The museum also owns paintings by Degas, Bonnard, Matisse, Utrillo, and Rouault. Late in 2005, the museum enlarged its premises with three additional display rooms, each of them a brick-lined refuge within the premises of a neighboring historic building. Within, you'll see, gathered together, some of Toulouse-Lautrec's earliest works, formulated during his earliest creative years.

Opposite the north side of the cathedral. ✆ **05-63-49-48-78.** Admission 5€ ($6.50) adults, 2.50€ ($3.25) students, free for children under 14. July–Aug daily 9am–6pm; June and Sept daily 9am–noon and 2–6pm; Apr–May daily 10am–noon and 2–6pm; Mar and Oct Wed–Mon 10am–noon and 2–5:30pm; Nov–Feb Wed–Mon 10am–noon and 2–5pm. Closed Jan 1, May 1, Nov 1, and Dec 25.

WHERE TO STAY

Hostellerie St-Antoine ★★ Some historians say this is one of the oldest continuously operated hotels in France. Originally a monastery, then a medieval hospital, the property became an inn in 1734 (when the present building was constructed). The same family has owned it for five generations; today the father-son team of Jacques and Jean-François Rieux manages it. Jacques's mother focused on Toulouse-Lautrec when designing the hotel, because her grandfather was a friend of the painter and was given a few of his paintings, sketches, and prints. Several are in the lounge, which opens onto a rear garden. The rooms have been delightfully decorated, with a sophisticated use of color, reproductions, and occasional antiques. They're generally spacious, furnished with French Provincial pieces. Most of the midsize bathrooms have tub/shower combinations. Even if you're not staying, visit the dining room. The Rieux culinary tradition is revealed in their traditional yet creative cuisine.

17 rue St-Antoine, Albi 81000. ✆ **05-63-54-04-04.** Fax 05-63-47-10-47. www.saint-antoine-albi.com. 44 units. 90€–165€ ($117–$215) double; 165€–225€ ($215–$293) suite. AE, DC, MC, V. Parking 6.50€ ($8.45). **Amenities:** Restaurant (open only to groups); bar; room service; babysitting; dry cleaning; nonsmoking rooms; limited-mobility rooms. *In room:* A/C, TV, minibar, hair dryer, Wi-Fi.

Hôtel Chiffre *Value* This hotel in the city center was built as a lodging for passengers on the mail coaches that hauled letters and people across France. The renovated building retains the original porch that sheltered carriages from the rain and sun. The rooms are artfully cozy, with upholstered walls in floral patterns; some have views of the inner courtyard. The midsize bathrooms come with tub/shower combinations or showers only. The hotel restaurant is popular among locals because of its good-value fixed-price menus. The menu priced at 20€ to 38€ ($26–$49) per person consists of choices that were compiled after Toulouse-Lautrec's death by his friends. They remembered the way he'd often prepare the dishes himself during his dinner parties. Some of his favorite dishes included radishes stuffed with braised foie gras, suprême of *sandre* (fish), and duckling roasted with garlic.

50 rue Séré-de-Rivières, Albi 81000. ✆ **05-63-48-58-48.** Fax 05-63-38-11-15. www.hotelchiffre.com. 38 units. 86€ ($112) double; 200€ ($260) suite. AE, MC, V. Parking 8€ ($10). **Amenities:** Restaurant; bar; room service. *In room:* A/C, TV, hair dryer, Wi-Fi.

La Réserve ★★★ This country-club villa in a 1.6-hectare (4-acre) park on the northern outskirts of Albi is managed by the Rieux family, who also run the Hostellerie St-Antoine. A Relais & Châteaux member, La Réserve is a Mediterranean-style villa with a pool and a fine garden in which you can dine. The rooms, well furnished and color coordinated, contain imaginative decorations (but avoid the rooms over the kitchen, which are noisy at mealtimes). The upper-story rooms have sun terraces and French doors. The modern tiled bathrooms come with deluxe toiletries and showers.

Rte. de Cordes à Fonvialane, Albi 81000. From the center of town, follow signs to Carmaux-Rodez until you cross the Tarn; then follow signs to Cordes. The hotel is adjacent to the main road leading to Cordes, 2km (1¼ miles) from Albi. ✆ **05-63-60-80-80.** Fax 05-63-47-63-60. www.relaischateaux.fr/reservealbi. 23 units. 150€–288€ ($195–$374) double; 398€ ($517) suite. AE, DC, MC, V. Closed Nov–Apr. **Amenities:** Restaurant; bar; outdoor pool; room service; babysitting; laundry service; dry cleaning; nonsmoking rooms; limited-mobility rooms. *In room:* A/C, TV, minibar, hair dryer, safe, Wi-Fi.

WHERE TO DINE

La Réserve boasts a wonderful restaurant, as does **Hostellerie St-Antoine.** Bateau Ivre at the **Hôtel Chiffre** is another worthy choice. See "Where to Stay," above.

Jardin des Quatre Saisons ★★ MODERN FRENCH The best food in Albi is served by Georges Muriel Bermond, who believes that menus, like life, should change with the seasons, which is how the restaurant got its name. In his two simple dining rooms, the service is always competent and polite. Fine-tuned menu items include delicious fricassee of snails garnished with strips of the famous hams produced in the nearby hamlet of Lacaune, and ravioli stuffed with pulverized shrimp and served with truffled cream sauce. Most delectable of all—an excuse for returning—is *pot-au-feu* of the sea, with three or four species of fish garnished with crayfish-cream sauce. The wine list is the finest in Albi.

19 bd. de Strasbourg. ✆ **05-63-60-77-76.** www.lejardindes4saisons.chez-alice.fr. Reservations recommended. Main courses 13€–20€ ($17–$26); fixed-price menu 19€–33€ ($25–$43). AE, DC, MC, V. Tues–Sun noon–2:30pm; Tues–Sat 7:30–10pm.

Le Lautrec TRADITIONAL FRENCH Part of its charm derives from its associations with Toulouse-Lautrec—the restaurant lies across the street from his birthplace and is decorated with paintings by local artists. Also appealing is the rich patina of its interior brickwork. The skillfully prepared food items include a salad of fried scallops that come with rose oil and essence of shrimp, sweetbreads with morels, and roasted rack of lamb marinated in a brewed infusion of Provençal thyme. Hearty regional dishes—beloved by local diners—are a cassoulet of codfish, savory sweetbreads (an acquired taste for some), duckling *en confit,* and rabbit stew with vegetables.

15 rue Toulouse-Lautrec. © **05-63-54-86-55.** www.restaurant-le-lautrec.com. Reservations recommended. Main courses 16€–25€ ($21–$33); fixed-price lunch Tues–Fri 14€–16€ ($18–$21); other fixed-price meals 28€–40€ ($36–$52). AE, MC, V. Tues–Sun noon–2pm; Tues–Sat 7–9:30pm. Closed Wed night Nov–Mar.

10 Cordes-sur-Ciel ★★

678km (421 miles) SW of Paris, 25km (16 miles) NW of Albi

This remarkable site is like an eagle's nest on a hilltop, opening onto the Cérou valley. In days gone by, celebrities such as Jean-Paul Sartre and Albert Camus considered this town a favorite hideaway. In low season, the population is only 1,050, but swells to 10,000 in midsummer.

Through the centuries, Cordes has been known for its textile, leather, and silk industries. Even today, it's an arts-and-crafts city, and in many of the old houses on the narrow streets, artisans—blacksmiths, enamelers, graphic artists, weavers, engravers, sculptors, and painters—ply their trades. Park outside and then pass under an arch leading to the old town.

ESSENTIALS

GETTING THERE If you're **driving,** take N88 northwest from Toulouse to Gaillac, turning north on D922 into Cordes-sur-Ciel. If you're coming by **train,** get off in Cordes-Vindrac and walk, rent a bicycle, or take a taxi the remaining 3km (1¾ miles) west of Cordes. For train information, call © **36-35** or 08-92-35-35-35. For a **minibus,** call Taxi Barrois (© **05-63-56-14-80**). The one-way fare is 4.15€ ($5.40) Monday to Saturday, rising to 6.65€ ($8.65) after 7pm and on Sunday. There's no regular bus service.

VISITOR INFORMATION The **Office de Tourisme** is in the Maison Fonpeyrouse, Grand-Rue Raymond VII (© **05-63-56-00-52;** fax 05-63-56-19-52; www.cordes-sur-ciel.org).

EXPLORING THE TOWN

Often called "the city of a hundred Gothic arches," Cordes contains numerous ***maisons gothiques*** ★★ of pink sandstone. Many of the doors and windows are fashioned of pointed (broken) arches that retain their 13th- and 14th-century grace. Some of the best-preserved ones line **Grande-Rue Raymond VII,** also called **rue Droite.**

Eglise St-Michel The church, the most important historic building in town, dates from the late 13th century and has undergone many alterations. Most of the lateral design of the side chapels probably comes from the cathedral at Albi. Before being shipped here, the organ (dating from 1830) was in Notre-Dame in Paris.

Grande-Rue Raymond VII. © **05-63-56-00-52** (tourist office). Free admission. Tours daily 10:30am–12:30pm and 3–6:30pm.

Musée d'Art et d'Histoire le Portail-Peint (Musée Charles-Portal) Small, quirky, and relatively unvisited even by residents of Cordes, this somewhat sleepy museum is named after a nearby pass-through (the Painted Gate) that pierces the fortifications surrounding the city's medieval center. It's also named for Charles-Portal, a 1920s-era (he died in 1936) archivist of the Tarn region and a local historian. In a medieval house whose foundations date from the Gallo-Roman era, it contains artifacts of the textile industry, farming implements, samples of local embroidery, a reconstruction of an old peasant home, and a scattering of medieval pieces.

Grande-Rue Raymond VII. ✆ **05-63-56-06-11.** Admission 2.30€ ($3) adults, 1.10€ ($1.45) students and ages 12–25, free for children under 12. July–Aug daily 11am–1pm and 3:30–7:30pm; May–June and Sept–Oct Sun and holidays 3–6pm. Closed Nov–Mar.

WHERE TO STAY & DINE

Hostellerie du Parc *Value* TRADITIONAL FRENCH This inn originated in the 18th century as a landowner's thick-walled home. Today, in a verdant park, the stone house holds this charming getaway *restaurant avec chambres.* It serves generous meals in a garden or paneled dining room. Specialties include homemade foie gras, duckling, *poularde* (chicken) *occitaine,* rabbit with cabbage leaves, *ballotine* of duck with foie gras, and confit of roasted rabbit with pink garlic from the nearby town of Lautrec.

The hotel offers 13 comfortable and well-furnished rooms; a double costs 60€ to 90€ ($78–$117).

Les Cabannes, Cordes 81170. From the town center, take rte. de St-Antonin (D600) for about 1km (⅔ mile) west. ✆ **05-63-56-02-59.** Fax 05-63-56-18-03. www.hostellerie-du-parc.com. Reservations recommended. Main courses 12€–28€ ($16–$36); fixed-price menu 22€–48€ ($29–$62). AE, DC, MC, V. June–Oct daily noon–2pm and 7–10pm; off season Tues–Sun noon–2pm, Tues–Sat 7–10pm. Closed Nov 15–Dec 15.

Maison du Grand Ecuyer ★★★ MODERN FRENCH The medieval monument that contains this restaurant (the 15th-c. hunting lodge of Raymond VII, *comte* de Toulouse) is a national historic treasure. Despite its glamour and undeniable charm, the restaurant remains intimate and unstuffy, although guests in recent years have included King Juan Carlos of Spain, the Emperor of Japan, and even Queen Elizabeth. Chef Yves Thuriès's platters have made his dining room an almost mandatory stop for the rich and famous. Specialties include three confits of lobster, red mullet salad with fondue of vegetables, confit of pigeon with olive oil and rosemary, and noisette of lamb in chicory sauce. The dessert selection is nearly overwhelming.

The hotel contains 12 rooms and one suite, all with antiques and modern comforts. Doubles cost 90€ to 155€ ($117–$202); the suite is 230€ ($299). The most popular room, honoring former guest Albert Camus, has a four-poster bed and a fireplace. During its annual closing, a nearby twin hotel, the **Hotel du Vieux Cordes,** 21 rue St-Michel (✆ **05-63-53-79-20**), is an alternative. This hotel is also very old (13th c.) and loaded with elegant architectural touches (marble and granite bathrooms, antiques, and high ceilings), and is under the management of Thuriès, the region's grandest and most entrepreneurial chef. Here a double ranges from 49€ to 85€ ($64–$111), with a suite costing 129€ ($168). On the premises is a terrace that's shaded with an arbor and a 300-year-old wisteria vine. The house that contains this immediately abuts the Eglise St-Michel.

Grand-Rue Raymond VIII, Haute de la Cite, Cordes 81170. ✆ **05-63-53-79-50.** Fax 05-63-53-79-51. www.thuries.fr. Reservations required. Main courses 29€–40€ ($38–$52); fixed-price menu 24€–84€ ($31–$109). AE, DC, MC, V. July–Aug Fri–Sun noon–1:30pm, daily 7–9:30pm; mid-Mar to June and Sept to mid-Oct Tues–Sun 7–9:30pm. Closed mid-Oct to mid-Mar.

11 Toulouse ★★★

705km (438 miles) SW of Paris, 245km (152 miles) SE of Bordeaux, 97km (60 miles) W of Carcassonne

The old capital of Languedoc and France's fourth-largest city, Toulouse (known as La Ville Rose) has a cosmopolitan flavor. The major city of the southwest, filled with gardens

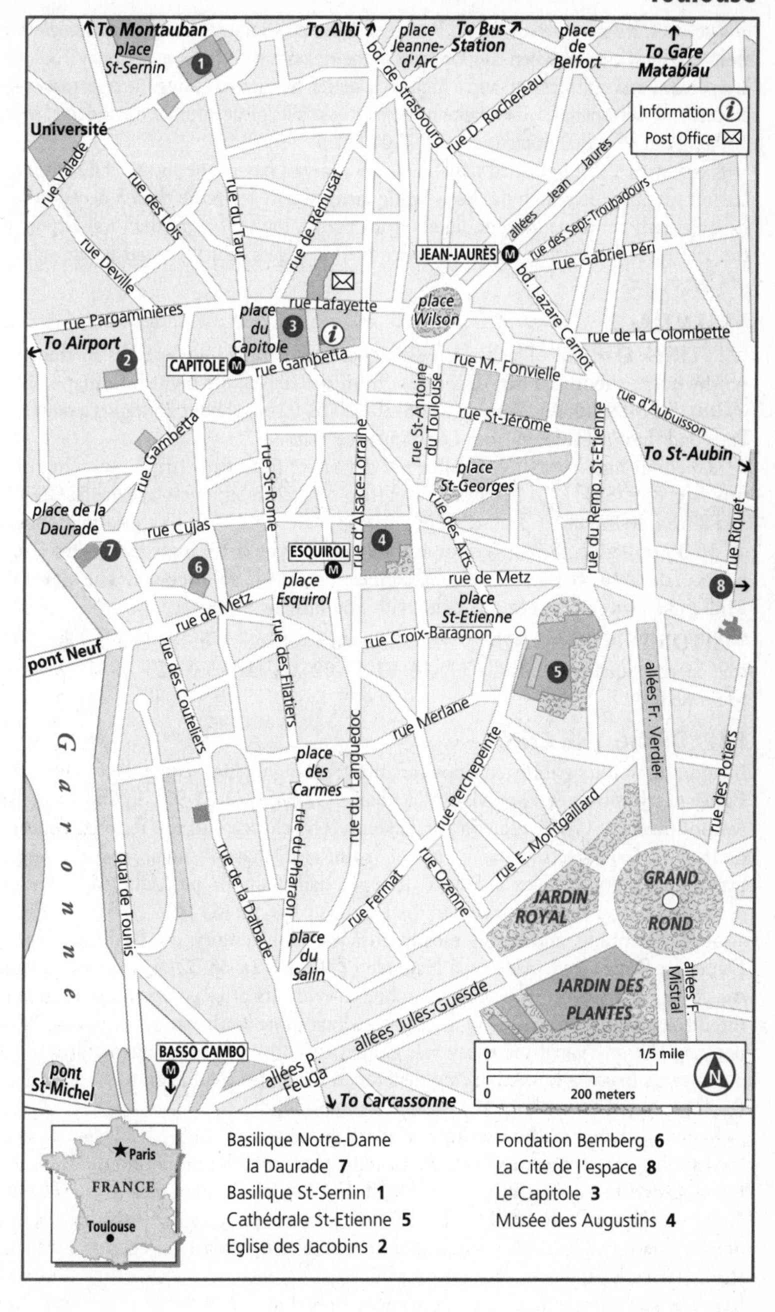
To Montauban
place St-Sernin
To Albi
place Jeanne-d'Arc
bd. de Strasbourg
To Bus Station
place de Belfort
To Gare Matabiau
Information
Post Office
Université
rue Valade
rue des Lois
rue du Taur
rue de Rémusat
rue D. Rochereau
allées Jean Jaurès
rue des Sept-Troubadours
JEAN-JAURÈS
rue Gabriel Péri
rue Deville
rue Pargaminières
place du Capitole
rue Lafayette
place Wilson
bd. Lazare Carnot
rue de la Colombette
To Airport
CAPITOLE
rue Gambetta
rue M. Fonvielle
rue St-Antoine du Toulouse
rue St-Jérôme
rue d'Aubuisson
rue Gambetta
rue St-Rome
rue d'Alsace-Lorraine
place St-Georges
rue du Remp. St-Etienne
To St-Aubin
place de la Daurade
rue Cujas
rue des Arts
rue Riquet
ESQUIROL
place Esquirol
rue de Metz
place St-Etienne
rue de Metz
pont Neuf
rue Croix-Baragnon
rue des Couteliers
rue des Filatiers
allées Fr. Verdier
rue Merlane
rue du Languedoc
rue Perchepeinte
rue des Potiers
Garonne
place des Carmes
rue E. Montgaillard
rue du Pharaon
rue de la Dalbade
quai de Tounis
rue Fermat
rue Ozenne
JARDIN ROYAL
GRAND ROND
place du Salin
JARDIN DES PLANTES
allées F. Mistral
allées Jules-Guesde
BASSO CAMBO
allées P. Feuga
pont St-Michel
To Carcassonne
0 1/5 mile
0 200 meters
N
Paris
FRANCE
Toulouse
Basilique Notre-Dame la Daurade 7
Basilique St-Sernin 1
Cathédrale St-Etienne 5
Eglise des Jacobins 2
Fondation Bemberg 6
La Cité de l'espace 8
Le Capitole 3
Musée des Augustins 4

and squares, it's the gateway to the Pyrénées. Most of Toulouse's fine old mansions date from the Renaissance, when this was one of the richest cities in Europe. Today Toulouse is an artistic and cultural hub and a high-tech center, home to two huge aircraft makers—Airbus and Aerospatiale. Also making the city tick is its great number of students: some 110,000 out of a total population of 800,000.

A city with a distinguished past, Toulouse is also a city of the future. The National Center for Space Research has been headquartered here for more than 3 decades. The first regularly scheduled airline flights from France took off from the local airport in the 1920s. Today, Airbus planes are assembled in a gargantuan hangar in the suburb of Colombiers.

ESSENTIALS

GETTING THERE The Toulouse-Blagnac international **airport** lies in the city's northwestern suburbs, 11km (6¾ miles) from the center; for flight information, call **© 08-25-38-00-00. Air France** (**© 08-20-80-28-02**) has about 25 flights a day from Paris and flies to Toulouse from London twice a day.

Some four high-speed TGV **trains** per day arrive from Paris (trip time: 6 hr.; one-way fare: 85€/$111), 14 from Bordeaux (trip time: 2–3 hr.; one-way fare: 32€/$42), and 8 from Marseille (trip time: 4½ hr.; one-way fare: 55€/$72). For information, call **© 36-35** or 08-92-35-35-35 from outside France. The **drive** from Paris takes 6 to 7 hours. Take A10 south to Bordeaux, connecting to A62 to Toulouse. The Canal du Midi links many of the region's cities with Toulouse by waterway.

VISITOR INFORMATION The **Office de Tourisme** is in the Donjon du Capitole in the Square de Gaulle (**© 05-61-11-02-22;** fax 05-61-23-74-97; www.ot-toulouse.fr).

EXPLORING THE CITY

In addition to the sights listed below, architectural highlights include the Gothic brick **Eglise des Jacobins** ★★, parvis des Jacobins (**© 05-61-22-21-92**), in Old Toulouse, west of place du Capitole along rue Lakanal. The church and the restored convent, daring in its architecture and its use of "palm tree"-shaped vaults, form the largest extant monastery complex in France. It's open daily 9am to 7pm. Admission to most of the complex is free, but a visit to the cloisters costs 3€ ($3.90).

Small, charming, and dating mostly from the 18th century, the **Basilique Notre-Dame La Daurade,** 1 place de la Daurade (**© 05-61-21-38-32**), gets its name from the gilding that covers its partially baroque exterior. Its prize possession is a statue of the Black Virgin, about 1m (3¼ ft.) tall, to which some locals attribute quasi-mystical powers. The one you'll see today was crafted in 1807 as a replacement for a much older statue that was burned during the French Revolution. Admission is free, and the Basilique Notre-Dame is open daily 8:30am to 6:30pm.

In civic architecture, **Le Capitole** ★, place du Capitole (**© 05-61-22-34-12**), is an outstanding achievement and one of the most potent symbols of Toulouse. Built in a baroque style in 1753, it houses the **Hôtel de Ville** (city hall) as well as the **Théâtre National du Capitole** (**© 05-61-22-31-31**), which presents concerts, ballets, and operas. Renovated in 1996, it's outfitted in an Italian-inspired 18th-century style with shades of scarlet and gold. Admission, which usually includes a view of the theater, is free. The Capitole complex is open Monday to Saturday 9am to 5pm, and until 7pm during holidays.

After all that sightseeing, head for **place Wilson,** a showcase 19th-century square (actually an oval) lined with fashionable cafes.

Basilique St-Sernin ★★★ Consecrated in 1096, this is the largest, finest and most pure Romanesque church in Europe. One of its most outstanding features is the Porte Miègeville, opening onto the south aisle and decorated with 12th-century sculptures. The door into the south transept is the Porte des Comtes; its capitals depict the story of Lazarus. Nearby are the tombs of the *comtes* de Toulouse. Entering by the main west door, you can see the double side aisles that give the church five naves, an unusual feature in Romanesque architecture. An upper cloister forms a passageway around the interior. Look for the Romanesque capitals surmounting the columns.

In the axis of the basilica, in the ambulatory, 11th-century bas-reliefs depict *Christ in His Majesty.* The ambulatory leads to the crypt (ask the custodian for permission to enter), which contains the relics of 128 saints, plus a thorn said to be from the Crown of Thorns. The old baroque retables (altarpieces) and shrine in the ambulatory have been reset; the relics here are those of the apostles and the first bishops of Toulouse.

Place St-Sernin. ✆ **05-61-21-70-18.** Free admission to church; combined admission to the crypt and ambulatory 3€ ($3.90). Church summer daily 8:30am–6:15pm; off season daily 8:30–11:45am and 2–5:45pm; no sightseeing during Sun morning Masses. Crypt and ambulatory summer daily 8:30am–5:45pm; off season Mon–Sat 10–11:30am, daily 2:30–5pm.

Cathédrale St-Etienne ★ Because it took so long to build (it was designed and constructed between the 11th–17th c.), some critics scorn this cathedral for its mishmash of styles. The rectangular bell tower is from the 16th century. A Gothic choir has been added to its unique ogival nave.

Place St-Etienne, at the eastern end of rue de Metz. ✆ **05-61-52-03-82.** Daily 8am–7pm.

Fondation Bemberg Opened in 1995, this quickly became one of the city's most important museums. Housed in the magnificent Hôtel Assézat (built in 1555), the museum offers an overview of 5 centuries of European art, with world-class paintings from the Renaissance to the late 19th century. The nucleus of the collection represents the lifelong work of German-French collector extraordinaire Georges Bemberg, who donated 331 works. The largest bequest was 28 paintings by Pierre Bonnard, including his *Moulin Rouge.* Bemberg also donated works by Pissarro, Matisse *(Vue d'Antibes),* and Monet, plus the Fauves. The foundation also owns Canaletto's much-reproduced *Vue de Mestre.* The mansion houses the **Académie des Jeux-Floraux,** which since 1323 has presented literary awards in the form of wrought-metal flowers to poets.

Place d'Assézat, rue de Metz. ✆ **05-61-12-06-89.** www.fondation-bemberg.fr. Admission 4.60€ ($6) adults, 3€ ($3.90) students and children 8–18, free for children under 8. Tues–Wed and Fri–Sun 10am–12:30pm and 1:30–6pm; Thurs 10am–9pm.

La Cité de l'espace ★ Kids Some half a million visitors a year come here to learn what it's like to program the launch of a satellite or how to maneuver one in space. You learn, for example, how easy it is to lose a satellite by putting on a burst of speed at the wrong point during a launch. Life-size structural models abound, including a model of an astronaut riding an exercise bike in zero gravity. On the grounds you can walk through a replica of Russia's Mir space station. The place is both a teaching tool and a lot of fun to visit. The top floor focuses on exploration of the universe, with close-ups from flybys of the moons of Jupiter.

Av. Jean Gonord. Follow N126 from the center of town to the E. Peripheral route and take Exit 17. ✆ **08-20-37-72-23.** www.cite-espace.com. Admission 21€ ($27) adults, 14€ ($18) ages 5–15, free for children under 5; family tickets (2 adults, 2 children) 102€ ($133). July–Aug daily 9:30am–7pm; Sept–June Tues–Sun 9:30am–5pm (until 6pm Sat–Sun). Closed Jan. Bus: 37 (Sat–Sun only).

Musée des Augustins ★★ The museum was established in this convent in 1793, shortly after the French Revolution, when revolutionary acts closed the institution—then one of the city's most important monasteries—and adapted it for public use. In addition to the fabulous paintings, a stroll through this place gives you the chance to view a 14th-century monastery in all its mystical splendor. This museum's 14th-century cloisters contain the world's largest and most valuable collection of Romanesque capitals. The sculptures and carvings are magnificent, and there are some fine examples of early Christian sarcophagi. On the upper floors is a large painting collection, with works by Toulouse-Lautrec, Gérard, Delacroix, and Ingres. The museum also contains several portraits by Antoine Rivalz, a local artist and major talent.

21 rue de Metz. ✆ **05-61-22-21-82.** www.augustins.org. Admission 3€ ($3.90), free for children under 12. Wed 10am–9pm; Thurs–Mon 10am–6pm. Closed Jan 1, May 1, and Dec 25.

SHOPPING

Head for **rue d'Alsace-Lorraine,** which is rich in clothing and housewares. At the well-stocked shopping mall, the **Centre Commercial St-Georges,** rue du Rempart St-Etienne, you can fill your suitcases with all kinds of glittery loot. For upscale boutiques, head to **rue Croix-Baragnon, rue des Arts,** and **rue St-Antoine du T.** The pearly gates of antiques heaven are on **rue Fermat.** More down-market antiques spread out each Sunday from 6am to 1pm during the weekly **flea market** adjacent to the Basilique St-Sernin. In addition to that, in the same spot, a *brocante* sale takes place on the first weekend (Fri–Sun) of each month from 8am to 1pm.

Violets grow in abundance in meadows on the outskirts of Toulouse. Two shops that sell everything related to violets include **Violettes & Pastels,** 10 rue St-Pantaléon (✆ **05-61-22-14-22**), and **Péniche Maison de la Violette,** 4 bd. Bonrepos (✆ **05-61-99-01-30**). Inventories include violet-scented perfume, and clothing—especially scarves—patterned with the dainty purple flower.

WHERE TO STAY

EXPENSIVE

Sofitel Toulouse Centre ★★ *Kids* Business travelers deem this hotel, built in 1989, as the best in town (though we prefer the Grand Hôtel de l'Opéra as the most tranquil retreat). Adjacent to place Wilson, this Sofitel employs a charming bilingual staff and offers suites big enough to fit an entire family or serve as an office away from the office. The rooms are furnished in chain format, and each comes with a bathroom with a tub/shower combination.

84 allée Jean-Jaurès, Toulouse 31000. ✆ **05-61-10-23-10.** Fax 05-61-10-23-20. www.sofitel.com. 119 units. 290€ ($377) double; 360€–450€ ($468–$585) suite. AE, DC, MC, V. Parking 15€ ($20). Métro: Jean-Jaurès. **Amenities:** Restaurant; bar; health club; business center; room service; babysitting; laundry service; dry cleaning; nonsmoking rooms; limited-mobility rooms. *In room:* A/C, TV, minibar, hair dryer, safe, Wi-Fi.

MODERATE

Best Western Grand Hôtel les Capitouls ★ *Value* In the heart of historic Toulouse, this chain-run hotel was carved out of what used to be a private mansion. All the midsize bedrooms are tastefully decorated with such extras as soundproofing, and the bathrooms are well maintained with modern plumbing. Near the banks of the

River Garonne, the building is what the French call a *hotel de charme.* The decor is refined and elegant both in the public rooms and the bedrooms. Directly opposite is its restaurant housed in a 16th-century vaulted cellar of red brick.

29 allée Jean-Jaurès, Toulouse 31000. ✆ **05-34-41-31-21.** Fax 05-61-63-15-17. www.bestwestern-capitouls.com. 52 units. 128€–167€ ($166–$217) double; 225€–282€ ($293–$367) suite. AE, DC, MC, V. **Amenities:** Room service; laundry service/dry cleaning. *In room:* TV, safe, Wi-Fi.

Grand Hôtel de l'Opéra ★★★ This is the most elegant oasis in Toulouse, and the owners have won several prestigious awards for transforming a 17th-century convent into a sophisticated hotel. The public rooms contain early-19th-century antiques and Napoleonic-inspired tenting over the bars. Some of the spacious and stylish guest rooms have urn-shaped balustrades overlooking formal squares, and all have high ceilings and modern amenities. The beds are elegantly attired in tasteful fabrics and soft pillows, most richly refurbished in the early millennium. Each well-maintained tiled bathroom has a tub/shower combination. The hotel restaurant, Toulousy-Les Jardins de l'Opéra, is the town's most prestigious.

1 place du Capitole, Toulouse 31000. ✆ **05-61-21-82-66.** Fax 05-61-23-41-04. www.grand-hotel-opera.com. 57 units. 180€–320€ ($234–$416) double; 380€–470€ ($494–$611) suite. AE, DC, MC, V. Parking 14€ ($18). Métro: Capitole. **Amenities:** Restaurant (see "Where to Dine," below); brasserie; bar; sauna; steam room; room service; laundry service; dry cleaning; nonsmoking rooms; limited-mobility rooms. *In room:* A/C, TV, minibar, hair dryer, safe, Wi-Fi.

INEXPENSIVE

Grand Hôtel Raymond-IV On a quiet street close to the town center and the train station, this 19th-century red-brick building contains pleasant rooms with bland but comfortable furniture and restful beds. All of the individually decorated accommodations are different—some small, others rather grand—with a vaguely Art Deco motif. Some rooms have air-conditioning. The compact bathrooms have showers. Although breakfast is the only meal served, the English-speaking staff will direct you to nearby restaurants.

16 rue Raymond-IV, Toulouse 31000. ✆ **05-61-62-89-41.** Fax 05-61-62-38-01. www.hotelraymond4-toulouse.com. 38 units. 90€–145€ ($117–$189) double. AE, MC, V. Parking 10€ ($13). Métro: Jean-Jaurès or Capitole. **Amenities:** Bar; room service; laundry service; dry cleaning; nonsmoking rooms. *In room:* A/C, TV, minibar, hair dryer, Wi-Fi.

Royal Wilson Set behind a rather formal stone facade, this historic building operates a government-rated two-star hotel in the heart of Toulouse's historic core, a 5-minute walk southwest of the heartbeat Place Wilson. Inside, some of the rooms radiate off of a glassed-over interior courtyard that contains touches of wrought-iron filigree similar to what you'll find in Spain. Bedrooms are high-ceilinged and, despite the prevalence of angular, not-particularly distinctive furniture, still retain the relatively large proportions of the building's role as a well-heeled private home. There's no restaurant or bar on the premises, but there are lots of options within the surrounding neighborhood. Staff here isn't as helpful or well-informed as that within this hotel's nearby competitor, the St-Claire Hotel, but it's nonetheless a worthy and cost-effective choice.

6 rue Labéda, Toulouse 31000. ✆ **05-61-12-41-41.** Fax 05-61-12-41-53. www.royal-wilson.com. 24 units. 46€–70€ ($60–$91) double; 85€ ($111) "family room" for 2 adults and up to 2 children. Parking 9€ ($12). AE, MC, V. Metro: Place Jean-Jaurès or Capitole. **Amenities:** Internet. *In-room:* A/C, satellite TV, hair dryer.

St-Claire Hotel Set in the heart of Toulouse's historic core, within a narrow, five-story town house whose foundations go back to the 15th century, this is a government-rated two-star hotel with few frills but a good location and a solid and comfortable presence. It was radically upgraded when its owners brought in a simple collection of furniture, most of it painted in tones of cream and white, and positioned it according to the Chinese principles of harmony and feng shui. There's no restaurant on-site, but many bars and dining outlets lie within a short walk. The staff is well-equipped to offer advice about attractions and diversions within the neighborhood.

29 place Nicolas Bachelier, Toulouse 31000. ✆ **05-34-40-58-88.** Fax 05-61-57-85-89. www.stclairehotel.fr. 16 units. 79€–89€ ($103–$116) double. Parking 5.50€ ($7.15). AE. MC, V. Metro: Place Jean-Jaurès. **Amenities:** Room service, laundry service/dry cleaning. *In room:* A/C, TV, fax, hair dryer, Wi-Fi.

WHERE TO DINE

EXPENSIVE

Chez Michel Sarran ★★★ MODERN FRENCH At the most stylish restaurant in Toulouse, you can enjoy the cuisine of master chef Michel Sarran. Sarran's wife, Françoise, oversees the three red, green, or violet dining rooms, in a building in the heart of town near the Novotel Centre. The food brings out the flavors of southern and southwestern France. Start with a warm soup of foie gras and oysters, or perhaps a cup of organic yogurt studded with black truffles from the Périgord. Move on to a succulent version of poached sea bass served with a creamy polenta and lobster sauce; or perhaps a portion of roasted wild black boar from the underpopulated Bigorre region of France, served in a stewpot with thyme and wine-roasted potatoes. Dessert may include ravioli stuffed with creamed oranges and served with an aspic of sweet white Gaillac wine.

21 bd. Armand Duportal. ✆ **05-61-12-32-32.** www.michel-sarran.com. Reservations recommended. Main courses 35€–59€ ($46–$77); fixed-price lunch 45€–120€ ($59–$156); fixed-price dinner 85€–120€ ($111–$156). AE, DC, MC, V. Mon–Fri noon–2pm and 8–9:45pm (closed Wed for lunch). Closed Aug and 1 week around Christmas. Métro: Capitole.

Le 19 ★ MODERN FRENCH This high-profile cellar restaurant is one of the city's finest. It's 19 steps down from the street, in the high-ceilinged cellar of a medieval building once used for the storage of fish and the salts to preserve them. Inside, wood panels and carpeting contrast with its terra-cotta bricks. The delicate, creative menu items change with the seasons. Among delectable dishes are a terrine of deliberately undercooked foie gras, served with figs; cream of watercress soup with warm oysters; magret of duckling served with ginger and crushed apples; roasted shoulder of rabbit served in a stewpot with polenta and baby vegetables; filet of baked red snapper with spider-crab sauce; and filet of curried duck breast with Asian-style vegetables. To end your meal, try a stir-fry of mandarin oranges flavored with balsamic vinegar, or saffron-flavored sabayon with ice cream made from unpasteurized milk.

19 descente de la Halle aux Poissons. ✆ **05-34-31-94-84.** www.restaurantle19.com. Reservations recommended. Main courses 19€–25€ ($25–$33); fixed-price lunch 15€–23€ ($20–$30); fixed-price dinner 35€ ($46). AE, DC, MC, V. Tues–Fri noon–2pm; Mon–Sat 8–10:30pm. Métro: Esquirol.

Le Pastel ★★ FRENCH One of the best restaurants in the area occupies a stone-sided manor house built around 1850. It lies 7 minutes southwest of the center by car, within the city limits. Today it's the domain of Paris-trained chef and entrepreneur Gérard Garrigues. The setting is as restful as the cuisine is superb: Terraces ringed with flowers near an outdoor pergola and dining rooms accented with paintings by local artists contribute to the placidity. Menu items change every week. During our visit, the menu featured such dishes as scallops "jubilatoire," roasted at a very high temperature (572°F/300°C) with beef marrow, garlic, and balsamic vinegar; deliberately undercooked foie gras with a confit of quince and cornmeal brioche; roebuck with wine sauce and old-fashioned vegetables; and steak of sea bass with artichoke hearts and truffled vinegar. Wine choices are sophisticated.

237 rte. de St-Simon. ✆ **05-62-87-84-30.** Reservations required. Main courses 26€–45€ ($34–$59); fixed-price lunch 27€–37€ ($35–$48); fixed-price dinner 44€–98€ ($57–$127). AE, DC, MC, V. Tues–Sat noon–2pm and 8–9:30pm. Métro: Basso-Cambo.

Toulousy-Les Jardins de l'Opéra ★★★ FRENCH The entrance to the city's best restaurant is in the 18th-century Florentine courtyard of the Grand Hôtel de l'Opéra (see "Where to Stay," above). The dining area is a series of salons, several of which face a winter garden and a reflecting pool. A long-standing staple, praised by gastronomes, is ravioli stuffed with foie gras of duckling and served with essence of truffles. Equally appealing are carpaccio of lobster served with foie gras; tartare of sturgeon, mushrooms, and oysters; and spicy breast of pigeon with a "surprise" preparation of the bird's organs decorated with rosettes of zucchini. One of the most appealing desserts is figs poached in red Banyuls wine, stuffed with homemade vanilla ice cream.

In the Grand Hôtel de l'Opéra, 1 place du Capitole. ✆ **05-61-23-07-76.** www.lejardinsdelopera.com. Reservations required. Main courses 33€–40€ ($43–$52); fixed-price lunch 35€–42€ ($46–$55); fixed-price dinner 70€–90€ ($91–$117). AE, DC, MC, V. Tues–Sat noon–2pm and 8–10pm. Closed Jan 1–17 and July 28–Aug 29. Métro: Capitole.

MODERATE

Brasserie les Beaux-Arts/La Brasserie Flo TRADITIONAL FRENCH This early-1900s brasserie has an authentic Art Nouveau interior that's been enhanced because of its connection with the Jean Bucher chain (the most successful director of Art Nouveau French brasseries in the world, some of which are classified as national historic monuments). The carefully restored decor features walnut paneling and mirrors. The cuisine emphasizes well-prepared seafood and all the typical local dishes, including cassoulet, magret of duckling, lightly smoked salmon with lentils and mussels, and confit of duckling. Try foie gras or country-style sauerkraut, accompanied by the house Riesling, served in an earthenware pitcher. During warm weather, eat on the terrace. The staff is likely to be hysterical and less than suave during peak times.

In the Hôtel des Beaux-Arts, 1 quai de la Daurade. ✆ **05-61-21-12-12.** www.flobrasseries.com. Reservations recommended. Main courses 14€–33€ ($18–$43); fixed-price menu 23€–32€ ($30–$42). AE, DC, MC, V. Daily noon–2:30pm and 7:30pm–1am. Métro: Esquirol.

Emile ★ *Finds* TOULOUSIAN In an old-fashioned house on one of Toulouse's most beautiful squares, this restaurant offers the specialties of chef Christophe Fasan. In winter, meals are served upstairs overlooking the square; in summer, seating moves to the street-level dining room and flower-filled terrace. Menu choices include cassoulet Toulousian (cooked in goose fat), magret of duckling in traditional style, a medley of Catalonian fish, and a very fresh *parillade* (mixed grill) of fish with a pungently aromatic cold sauce of sweet peppers and olive oil. The wine list is filled with intriguing surprises.

13 place St-Georges. ✆ **05-61-21-05-56.** www.restaurant-emile.com. Reservations recommended. Main courses 17€–48€ ($22–$62); fixed-price lunch 18€–30€ ($23–$39); fixed-price dinner 35€–48€ ($46–$62). AE, DC, MC, V. Mid-Oct to May Tues–Sat noon–2pm, Mon–Sat 7:30–10:30pm (mid-May to Sept also Mon 7–10:30pm). Métro: Capitole or Esquirol.

INEXPENSIVE

Eau de Folles TRADITIONAL FRENCH Low prices and the variety of the menu keep patrons coming back to this place. In a room filled with mirrors, you can choose from 10 starters, 10 main courses, and 10 desserts on the fixed-price menu. Choices vary according to the inspiration of the chef and the availability of fresh ingredients. A typical meal may include a marinade of fish, followed by strips of duck meat with green-pepper sauce, and a homemade pastry such as a tarte Tatin. Everything is very simple, served in a cramped but convivial setting.

14 allée du President Roosevelt. ✆ **05-61-23-45-50.** www.eau-de-folles.com. Reservations recommended. Fixed-price lunch 13€ ($16); fixed-price dinner 23€ ($30). MC, V. Tues–Fri noon–1:30pm; Mon-Sat 7–11pm. Métro: Wilson.

Le Bon Vivre ★ SOUTHWESTERN FRENCH One of downtown Toulouse's most appealing bistros occupies the street level of a historic 18th-century mansion immediately adjacent to the Hôtel de Ville (town hall). Established in 2004, it provides cost-conscious dining within an environment surrounded by the pink-colored bricks of antique Toulouse. Menu items feature contemporary twists upon time-tested French specialties, many of them heralded by workaday diners who appreciate the attractive ratios of value-to-quality. The best examples include an unusual version of macaroni studded with flap mushrooms, truffles, and foie gras; and a version of cassoulet (the specialty of France's southwest) that's made with both duck and pork. An appropriate starter is a braised slice of foie gras with peaches and grapes.

15 bis place Wilson. ✆ **05-61-23-07-17.** www.lebonvivre.com. Reservations recommended. Main courses 12€–22€ ($16–$29); fixed-price lunch 12€–18€ ($16–$23); fixed-price dinner 20€–35€ ($26–$46). AE, DC, MC, V. Daily 11:30am–3pm and 7–11:30pm.

WHERE TO STAY & DINE NEARBY

La Flanerie Within a large garden that slopes down to the edge of the Garonne, about 8km (5 miles) south of Toulouse, stands this dignified-looking manor house, originally built in 1799 for a local landowner. Part of its allure derives from the early 1970s, when it was the site of a hotel favored by French celebrities and international rock stars, whose names fill the guest book that the Irish-born owners, the Moloney family, have presented since their acquisition of the place late in 2004. You might be happiest interpreting this place as an informal bed-and-breakfast, where the rooms just happen to be country-elegant and the welcome particularly warm. An oddity associated with the place involves the fact that there's a free-standing garage for each of the establishment's 12 bedrooms, a quirk deriving from one of the auto-obsessed former owners. Accommodations are stylish and midsize, and although there's no restaurant on-site, the owners are well informed about dining options nearby.

7 chemin des Etroits, Vieille-Toulouse 31320. Take D4 south of Toulouse for 8km (5 miles). ✆ **05-61-73-39-12.** Fax 05-61-73-18-56. www.hotellaflanerie.com. 12 units. 86€–110€ ($112–$143) double. AE, MC, V. Free parking. Bus: R. **Amenities:** Bar; outdoor pool; limited-mobility rooms. *In room:* A/C (in some), TV, minibar, hair dryer, Wi-Fi.

TOULOUSE AFTER DARK

Toulouse's theater, dance, and opera are often on a par with those found in Paris. To stay on top of the arts scene, pick up a copy of the free monthly magazine *Toulouse Culture* from the Office de Tourisme.

The city's most notable theaters are the **Théâtre du Capitole,** place du Capitole (✆ 05-61-22-31-31), which specializes in operas, operettas, and often works from the classical French repertoire; the **Théâtre de la Digue,** 3 rue de la Digue (✆ 05-61-42-97-79), for ballets and works by local theater companies; and the **Halle aux Grains,** place Dupuy (✆ 05-61-63-13-13). The home of the Orchestre du Capitole, the Halle aux Grains is the venue for mostly classical concerts. The **Théâtre Garonne,** 1 av. du

Château d'Eau (© 05-62-48-56-56), stages everything from works by Molière to current dramas. Another important venue is the **Théâtre Zenith,** 11 av. Raymond-Badiou (© 05-62-74-49-49), which has a large stage and seating capacity. It usually schedules rock concerts, variety acts, and musical comedies from other European cities. A smaller competitor, with a roughly equivalent mix of music, theater, and entertainment, is the **Théâtre de la Cité,** 1 rue Pierre Baudis (© 05-34-45-05-00).

The liveliest squares to wander after dark are **place du Capitole, place St-Georges, place St-Pierre,** and **place Wilson.**

For bars and pubs, **La Tantina de Bourgos,** 27 rue de la Garonette (© **05-61-55-59-29**), has a Latin flair that's popular with students, and the rowdier **Chez Tonton,** 16 place St-Pierre (© **05-61-21-89-54**), has an *après-match* atmosphere, complete with the winning teams boozing it up. A popular bar that schedules both live and recorded music is **Monsieur Carnaval,** 34 rue Bayard (© **05-61-99-14-56**), where there's lots of rocking and rolling *a la française* for the under-35 crowd.

The town's trendiest and most widely sought-after disco for persons younger than 35 is **Le Purple,** 2 rue Castellane (© **05-62-73-04-67**). Set close to the Sofitel, it's the disco that has the longest lines, generates the most interest within the counterculture press, and elicits the highest level of passion within the city's A-list wannabe junkies. The busiest English-style pub in town, **Le Frog & Le Roast Beef,** 14 rue de l'Industrie (© **05-61-99-28-57**), is woodsy and Celtic-looking, and often very crowded with the city's English-speaking community. **La Pelouse interdite,** 72 av. des Etats-Unis (© **05-61-47-30-40**), offers a charming restaurant and bar behind a simple, discreetly marked green door within a venue that incorporates a garden, a restaurant, a bar, and lots of charm. If you have a car and don't mind driving about 20 minutes out of town (follow the signs pointing to Albi), a hip rendezvous point is **Le Lounge 233,** 233 rte. d'Albi (© **05-61-48-60-60**), where a complicated list of cocktails, something many young French clubbers are just getting used to, are available for around 9€ ($12) each. A somewhat less cutting-edge, but very popular, disco is **Cockpit,** 1 rue du Puits-Vert (© **05-61-21-87-53**), near Le Capitol and the nocturnally animated place Wilson. It's been around longer than Le Purple, has a strong appeal to a dance-aholic clientele, and includes all genders and sexual orientations.

Mostly heterosexuals migrate to **Disco Le Maximo,** 4 rue Gabrielle-Peri (© **05-34-41-15-65**), which starts hopping Tuesday to Saturday after 11pm, and serves a distinctly French-inspired list of tapas (foie gras on toast, perhaps). There's also a vaguely Iberian-looking establishment, **Bar La Bodega,** 2 rue Gabriel-Peri (© **05-61-63-03-63**), that's about as beer-soaked and raucous as anything else in town. It's particularly interesting in the wake of one of the region's football (soccer) games, especially if the home team has won.

The oldest and most deeply entrenched gay bar in Toulouse is **Shanghai Express,** 12 rue de la Pomme (© **05-61-23-37-80**), a man's dance domain playing the latest in techno; farther inside, it gives way to a darker and, at its best, sexy cruise-bar environment with lots of hot men on the prowl. Entrance is free and it's open every night.

19

The Basque Country

The chief area of interest in the Basque country, a land rich in folklore, is a corner of southwest France, near the Spanish border, where you can visit the Basque capital, Bayonne, and explore the resorts, Biarritz and St-Jean-de-Luz. In Bayonne's Roman arena, you can see a bullfight.

The vast Pyrénéan region is a land of glaciers, summits, thermal baths, subterranean grottoes and caverns, winter-sports centers, and trout-filled mountain streams. **Pau** is a good base for excursions to the western Pyrénées. **Lourdes** is the major religious pilgrimage center in France.

1 Lourdes ★

800km (497 miles) SW of Paris, 40km (25 miles) SE of Pau

Muslims turn to Mecca and Hindus to the Ganges, but for Catholics, Lourdes is the world's most evocative shrine. Nestled in a valley in the southwestern part of the Hautes-Pyrénées, it draws pilgrims from all over the world. If you're coming in August, the shrine's high season, book your hotel as early as possible.

Many Roman Catholics believe that on February 11, 1858, the Virgin revealed herself to a shepherd girl, Bernadette Soubirous. Eighteen such apparitions were reported. Bernadette, subject of the film *Song of Bernadette,* died in a convent in 1879. She was beatified in 1925 and canonized in 1933.

Her apparitions put Lourdes on the map. The town has attracted millions of visitors, from the illustrious to the poverty-stricken. The devout are often disappointed by the commercialism of Lourdes today. And some vacationers are disturbed by the human desperation of victims of various afflictions spending their hard-earned savings seeking a "miracle," then having to return home without a cure. However, the church has recognized many "cures" that took place after patients bathed in the springs, labeling them "true miracles."

ESSENTIALS

GETTING THERE Sixteen **trains** run from Pau (see section 2 in this chapter) daily (trip time: 30 min.; one-way fare 7€/$9.10); there are also five trains from Bayonne (trip time: 2 hr.; one-way fare: 20€/$26) and Paris (trip time: 7 hr.; 94€/$122 one-way). For train information and schedules, call ✆ **08-92-35-35-35.**

If you're **driving** from Toulouse, take N117 west until you reach Tarbes, and then take N21 south to Lourdes. From Paris, follow A10 south to Vierzon, take N20 south to Limoges, and continue on N21 south to Lourdes.

VISITOR INFORMATION The **Office de Tourisme,** place Peyramale (✆ **05-62-42-77-40;** fax 05-62-94-60-95; www.lourdes-france.com), fields questions about Lourdes. But for questions regarding the religious landscape of the city, including its shrines, grottoes, Masses, cults, ecstatic visions, and snake charmers, seek out the

The Basque Country

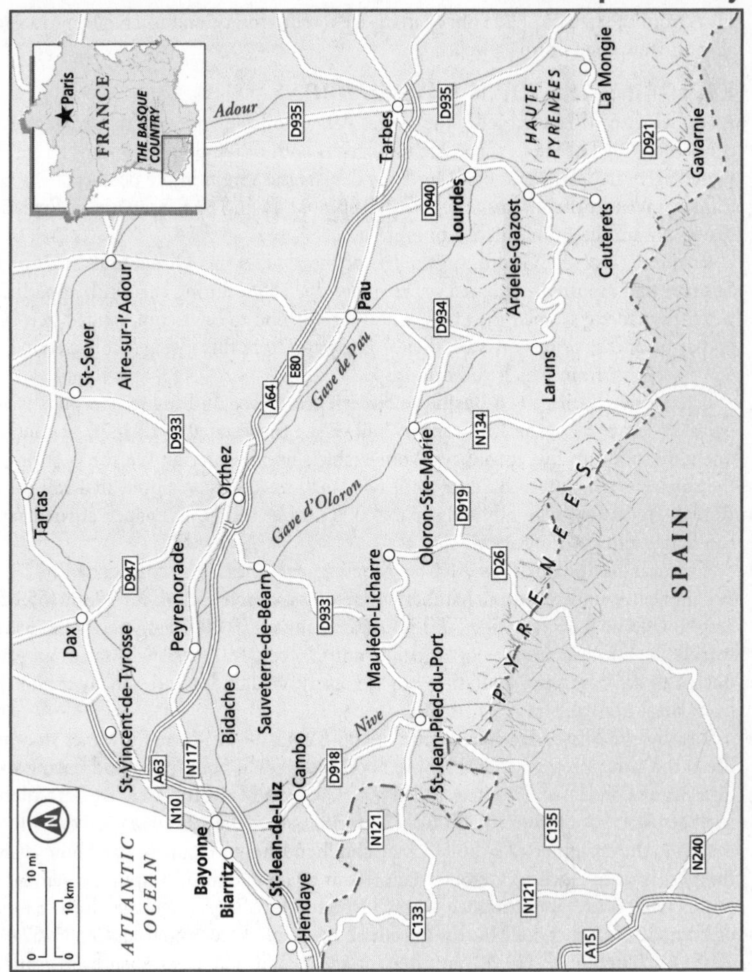

Forum Information **(Information Forum),** avenue Monseigneur Théas (© **05-62-42-78-78**). Staffed by members of the clergy and religious volunteers, it's the coordinator of everything to do with Catholicism in Lourdes.

SPECIAL EVENTS From Easter to late September, tourists and pilgrims can join the **Day Pilgrims,** or *Pélérin d'un Jour* (© **05-62-42-78-78**), a pilgrimage in English that begins at 8:30am at the statue of the Crowned Virgin with a prayer meeting in the meadow facing the Grotto. The services include following the Stations of the Cross (8:30am) and an 11:15am Mass. At 2:30pm, assembling at the same spot, pilgrims take a guided visit to the Sanctuaries, or places associated with Bernadette. In the Sanctuaries, you'll hear the story of Lourdes and Bernadette, complete with a free 30-minute slide show (also in English). At 5pm, a Procession of the Blessed Eucharist starts from the Grotto. The 9pm Marian celebration, rosary, and torchlight procession all start from the Grotto as well.

EXPLORING THE TOWN & ITS ENVIRONS

At the **Grotto of Massabielle,** the Virgin is said to have appeared to Bernadette 18 times in 1858. The site is accessible to pilgrims both day and night, and Mass is celebrated every day. The Statue of Our Lady depicts the Virgin in the posture she is said to have taken in the place she reputedly appeared, saying to Bernadette in Pyrénéan dialect, "I am the Immaculate Conception."

At the back of the Grotto, on the left of the altar, is the **Miraculous Spring (La Source)** that reportedly spouted on February 25, 1858, during the ninth apparition, when Bernadette scraped the earth. The Virgin is said to have commanded her, "Go and drink at the spring and wash there." The water from this spring is collected in several reservoirs, from which you can drink.

The **Upper Basilica (La Basilique Supérieure),** place du Rosaire, was built in the ogival style typical of the 13th century, but wasn't consecrated until 1876. It contains one nave split into five equal bays. Votive tablets line its interior. On the west side of the square is the Rosary Basilica, with two small towers. It was built in 1889 in the Roman-Byzantine style and holds up to 4,000 people. Inside, 15 chapels are dedicated to the mysteries of the rosary.

The oval **Basilica of Pius X,** 1 av. Monseigneur Théas, was consecrated in 1958. An enormous underground chamber covered by a concrete roof, it's 198m (650 ft.) long and 81m (266 ft.) wide, and holds as many as 20,000 people. It's one of the world's largest churches. It's open daily 7am to 7pm. International Masses are conducted in six languages, including English, every Wednesday and Sunday at 9:30am from April to October.

Nearby, the **Musée Ste-Bernadette** (**© 05-62-42-78-78**) contains scenes from the life of the saint; it's open daily 10am to noon and 2:30 to 5pm (call ahead during winter). Admission is free. Devotees will also seek out the **Maison Natale de Bernadette,** rue Bernadette-Soubirous (**© 05-62-42-16-36**), where the saint was born on January 7, 1844, the daughter of a miller. Her childhood home (actually the home of her mother) is open April to October daily 10am to noon and 3 to 5pm, November to March daily 3 to 5pm. Entrance is free. Just a few buildings away is the former home of Bernadette's father, **Le Moulin Lacadé,** 2 rue Bernadette-Soubirous (**© 05-62-94-22-51**). Charging 1€ ($1.30) but free for ages 9 and under, it's open from April to late October daily 9am to 12:15pm and 2:15 to 7pm. It's closed the rest of the year.

The privately owned and overly commercial wax museum, **Musée Grévin,** 87 rue de la Grotte (**© 05-62-94-33-74**), displays depictions of Bernadette's life and the life of Christ, along with a bad reproduction of Leonardo da Vinci's *Last Supper.* From April to October, it's open daily 9 to 11:40am and 1:30 to 6:30pm. During July and August, it's also open evenings 8:30 to 10pm. It's closed November to March. Admission is 6€ ($7.80) adults and 3€ ($3.90) students and children under 10.

If you want a panoramic view, take an elevator to the terrace of the **Château-Fort de Lourdes,** an example of medieval military architecture. The castle contains the **Musée Pyrénéen,** 25 rue du Fort (**© 05-62-42-37-37**), with regional handicrafts and costumes, including a collection of dolls in nuns' habits. In the courtyard are scale models of different styles of regional architecture. Admission is 5€ ($6.50) adults, 3€ ($3.90) students and children 6 to 12, and free for children under 6. From April to mid-July and mid-August to September, the château and museum are open daily 9am to noon and 1:30 to 6:30pm; mid-July to mid-August daily 9am to 6:30pm, and from October to March, daily 9am to noon and 2 to 6pm.

OUTDOOR PURSUITS Lourdes is a good base for exploring the Pyrénées. You can take tours into the snowcapped mountains across the border to Spain or go horseback riding near **Lac de Lourdes,** 3km (1¾ miles) northwest of town. Among the outstanding sites is **Bagnères-de-Bigorre,** a renowned thermal spa 23km (14 miles) east of Lourdes on D935.

Visit **Pic de Jer,** a rocky peak 933m (3,061 ft.) above sea level, high over the surrounding land formations, for a view of the surrounding countryside. To reach its summit, board the Pic de Jer funicular, which departs from the south side of esplanade des Proceswinos in the center of Lourdes. Round-trip fares are 8.50€ ($11) for adults and 6.50€ ($8.45) for students and children ages 6 to 14. At the summit, you'll see the entrance to some caves, **Les Grottes de Jer** (© **05-62-94-00-41** for both the funicular and the grottos), a sightseeing attraction that's open June to August daily 10am to 6pm, mid-March to May and September to November daily from 1:30 to 6:15pm (closed Dec to mid-Mar). Entrance to the grottos costs 3.50€ ($4.55) adults and 2.50€ ($3.25) students and children 6 to 12.

Farther afield, 23km (14 miles) southeast of Lourdes in the hamlet of Aste, you'll find even bigger and much more dramatic caves, **Les Grottes de Médous** (© **05-62-91-78-46**). An underground river formed them, along with numerous stalactites and stalagmites. Reach them by following signs to les Grottes de Médous along D26. During July and August, they're open daily 9am to noon and 2 to 6pm; May to June and September to mid-October, they're open daily 9 to 11:30am and 2 to 5pm (closed mid-Oct to Apr). Admission costs 7€ ($9.10) for adults and 3.50€ ($4.55) for children 5 to 10.

If you're in the mood for a full-fledged outing from Lourdes into the Pyrénées, drive south along D921 to a mountainous national park, **Cirque de Gavarnie (Heights of Gavarnie),** whose summits reach 1,350m (4,429 ft.). The distance from Lourdes to the center of the region is 52km (32 miles).

WHERE TO STAY

The two restaurants reviewed below (see "Where to Dine") also offer rooms.

Adriatic Hôtel Palace Built in the town center in the 1970s, this hotel offers well-maintained and uncluttered rooms. It's somewhat spartan, but comfortable. About a quarter of the rooms have minibars. Bathrooms are small to midsize and have showers. The location is close to the shrines, the home of St. Bernadette, the parish church, and the town's fortified castle.

4 rue Baron-Duprat, Lourdes 65100. © **05-62-94-31-34.** Fax 05-62-42-14-70. 87 units. 53€ ($69) double. AE, DC, MC, V. Parking 10€ ($13). Closed mid-Dec to Feb 7. Bus: 2. **Amenities:** Restaurant; bar; room service; laundry service. *In room:* TV, minibar (in some), hair dryer.

Grand Hôtel de la Grotte ★ The Grand Hôtel is an old favorite, having catered to pilgrims (and, to an increasing degree, tourists) since 1872, although it is equipped with modern amenities. It remains the best lodging choice in Lourdes. It's furnished with comfortable upper-bourgeois French decor in the style of Napoleon III. Some rooms on the upper floor open onto one of the most panoramic views in town, taking in the mountains as well as the sanctuaries and the river. Rooms on the basilica side tend to be noisy. Each modernized midsize bathroom has a tub and shower. The garden sits beside the banks of the river Gave de Pau.

66 rue de la Grotte, Lourdes 65100. ✆ **05-62-94-58-87.** Fax 05-62-94-20-50. www.hotel-grotte.com. 84 units. Summer 83€–161€ ($108–$209) double, 260€–350€ ($338–$455) junior suite; low season 75€–145€ ($98–$189) double, 235€–316€ ($306–$411) junior suite. AE, DC, MC, V. Free parking. Closed Oct–Apr. Bus: 2. **Amenities:** 2 restaurants; bar; room service; laundry service. *In room:* A/C, TV, minibar, hair dryer, safe.

Hôtel Galilée et Windsor This government-rated three-star hotel, often confused with the more comfortable, more expensive Gallia et Londres, has been a favorite since it was built after the war. Rooms are pleasant, if dull and anonymous. It is located near the Grotto and is close to the railway station. Each has a small shower-only bathroom. Because this is one of the largest hotels in Lourdes, it's a magnet for religious groups.

10 av. Peyramale, Lourdes 65100. ✆ **05-62-94-21-55.** Fax 05-62-94-53-66. www.galilee-windsor.fr. 163 units. 68€–72€ ($88–$94) double. Rates include breakfast. AE, DC, MC, V. Free street parking. Closed Nov–Mar. Bus: 2. **Amenities:** Restaurant; bar. *In room:* TV, minibar, hair dryer, safe.

Hôtel Gallia et Londres This old-fashioned choice, dating from 1880, has been completely improved and renovated with Louis XIV furnishings. The complete overhaul of the guest rooms included an upgrade in the quality of the beds. All rooms contain midsize bathrooms, and most have tubs and showers. Most guests here are parts of religious groups that tend to book en masse.

26 av. Bernadette-Soubirous, Lourdes 65100. ✆ **05-62-94-35-44.** Fax 05-62-42-24-64. www.hotelgallialondres.com. 90 units. 90€–98€ ($117–$127) double; 180€–188€ ($234–$244) suite. AE, MC, V. Parking 10€ ($13). Closed Nov–Mar. Bus: 2. **Amenities:** Restaurant; bar; free use of outdoor pool next door; business services; laundry service; dry cleaning. *In room:* A/C, TV, minibar, safe.

Hôtel Notre-Dame de France Located next to the Galilée et Windsor, this hotel is steps from the main monument (the sanctuaries associated with the visions of Bernadette). Originally built around 1928, it underwent radical rebuilding in the late 1980s that eliminated virtually every vestige of its Art Deco detailing. The owners, M. and Mme Imbert, offer simple, no-frills rooms with almost monastic furnishings, plus small bathrooms—some with shower only, some with combination tub/showers. Each bedroom has a view of the fortress of Lourdes and the nearest Pyrénées summits. Some pilgrims appreciate the emphasis here on religious activities. Overall, it's a worthy budget choice.

8 av. Peyramale, Lourdes 65100. ✆ **05-62-94-91-45.** Fax 05-62-94-57-21. www.hotelnd-france.fr. 76 units. 45€–60€ ($59–$78) double. Half board 54€–70€ ($70–$91) per person. MC, V. Parking 10€ ($13). Closed Nov–Mar. Bus: 2. **Amenities:** Restaurant; bar; laundry service; dry cleaning; nonsmoking rooms; limited-mobility rooms. *In room:* TV.

WHERE TO DINE

Relais de Saux ★ *Finds* BIGORRE This is the area's best restaurant, in an ivy-covered manor whose foundations date from the 15th century. It specializes in the cuisine of the Pyrénées, producing the authentic flavors of Southwest France. The carved-wood fireplaces complement the beamed ceilings, silk-upholstered walls, and rustic artifacts. Innkeepers Madeleine and Bernard Hères supervise meals. Begin with a selection of hot or cold hors d'oeuvres, ranging from beet flan with cheese fondue to smoked swordfish. Boneless quail and escalope of warm duck liver are especially delectable.

Upstairs are six guest rooms, some with large windows overlooking the garden. A double costs 92€ to 96€ ($120–$125).

Saux, rte. de Tarbes (N21), Lourdes 65100. Take N21 3km (1¾ miles) north of Lourdes to the village of Saux and follow signs to Tarbes. ✆ **05-62-94-29-61.** Fax 05-62-42-12-64. www.lourdes-relais.com Reservations recommended. Fixed-price menu 28€–56€ ($36–$73). MC, V. Daily 7:15–9:30pm. Closed mid-Nov to mid-Dec.

Taverne de Bigorre et Hôtel d'Albret FRENCH/BIGORRE This restaurant has some of the best food in town; tournedos with flap mushrooms are a specialty. You can order such country dishes as escalope of hot duck foie gras and duck steak kabob with green-peppercorn sauce. The trout, salmon, and monkfish are especially good. An award-winning dessert is frozen Grand Marnier soufflé with raspberry sauce and cream.

Hôtel d'Albret is one of the best budget hotels in Lourdes, with 26 comfortable rooms. A double costs 44€ ($57); for half board, add 43€ ($56) per person.

21 place du Champs-Commun, Lourdes 65100. ✆ **05-62-94-75-00.** Fax 05-62-94-78-45. www.lourdes-hotelalbret.com. Reservations recommended. Main courses 11€–35€ ($14–$46); fixed-price lunch 12€–27€ ($16–$35); fixed-price dinner 15€–27€ ($20–$35). AE, DC, MC, V. Daily noon–1:30pm and 7–9pm. Closed Jan 1–Feb 7.

2 Pau ★★★

768km (477 miles) SW of Paris, 196km (122 miles) SW of Toulouse

High above the banks of the Gave de Pau River, this year-round resort is a good place to pause in your trek through the Pyrénées. The British discovered Pau in the early 19th century, launching such practices as fox hunting, a custom that lingers. Even if you're just passing through, follow boulevard des Pyrénées, an esplanade erected on Napoleon's orders, for a famous panoramic view.

Pau is the most cosmopolitan city in the western Pyrénées, the capital of the Pyrénées-Atlantiques *département* (mini-state). It was once the capital of the Béarn region, the land of the kings of Navarre, the most famous and beloved of whom was Henri IV. Its population of approximately 81,000 still observes some English traditions, such as afternoon tea. At one time the English formed 15% of the population.

ESSENTIALS

GETTING THERE **Pau-Uzein airport** is 12km (7½ miles) north of town; call ✆ **05-59-33-33-00** for flight information. There are good **train** connections from Biarritz (six per day taking 1½ hr.); the one-way fare is 16€ ($21). For train information, call ✆ **08-92-35-35-35** from abroad. **Driving** to Pau is relatively easy because of its location along the N117 roadway, which is directly accessible from Toulouse. From Paris, take A10 south to Vierzon, changing to N20 south to Limoges, continuing on N21 south to Tarbes, and finally turning west along N117 to Pau.

VISITOR INFORMATION The **Office de Tourisme** is on place Royale (✆ **05-59-27-27-08;** fax 05-59-27-03-21; www.pau.fr).

SPECIAL EVENTS In early June there's the **Grand Prix de Pau** (✆ **05-59-27-31-89**), where race cars compete for speed records in what may remind you of a small-scale replica of the Grand Prix in Monaco.

EXPLORING THE CITY

The heart of the commercial district is **place Clemenceau,** out of which radiate at least five boulevards. At the western end of town stands the **Château de Pau** ★, 2 rue du Château (✆ **05-59-82-38-19**), dating from the 12th century and steeped in the Renaissance spirit of the bold Marguerite de Navarre, who wrote the bawdy *Heptaméron* at age 60. Marguerite commissioned the great staircase hall, and Louis XV ordered the bridge that connects the castle to the town. Around 1840, Louis-Philippe had the apartments redecorated. Inside are many souvenirs, including a crib made of a single tortoise shell for Henri de Navarre, who was born here, and a splendid array of Flemish and Gobelin tapestries. The great rectangular tower, **Tour de Gaston Phoebus,** is from the 14th century.

Another intriguing area within the château is **La Salle aux 100 Couverts,** site of some of the enormous receptions that were held here during the building's heyday. The château is open for visits as follows: mid-June to mid-September daily 9:30am to 12:15pm and 1:30 to 5:45pm; mid-September to mid-June daily 9:30 to 11:45am and 2 to 5pm. Guided tours (conducted in French and broken English, with an English-language pamphlet to supplement the tour guide), depart at 15-minute intervals during open hours. Admission is 5€ ($6.50) for adults, and 3€ ($3.90) for students 18 to 25, and free for children under 18.

The **Musée des Beaux-Arts** ★, rue Mathieu-Lalanne (✆ **05-59-27-33-02**), displays a collection of European paintings, including Spanish, Flemish, Dutch, English, and French masters such as El Greco, Zurbarán, Degas, and Boudin. It's open Wednesday to Monday 10am to noon and 2 to 6pm. Admission is 3€ ($3.90) adults, 1.50€ ($1.95) students, and free for children under 18.

SHOPPING

Pau affords ample opportunities for you to buy authentic regional specialties, such as chocolates, sweet jams, and Basque antiques. The pedestrian **rue Serviez** and **rue des Cordelières** harbor an array of boutiques and shops that carry these items, as do **rue Louis-Barthou, rue Henry-IV,** and **rue du Maréchal-Foch.**

Pau is home to some of the best antiques shops in the region, such as **Champeau Pau,** 38 av. Edouard VII (✆ **05-59-02-40-03**), which carries 18th- to 20th-century treasures for the home. You can also visit **Antiquites Delan,** 4 rue Gassion (✆ **05-59-27-45-62** or 06-08-07-82-40). The area around the château is the antiques center.

One of the best-known shops in Pau is **La Féerie Gourmande,** 48 rue du Maréchal Joffre (✆ **05-59-27-69-51**), which attracts gourmets from throughout the region. The owner, M. Francis Miot, has been voted best jam and candy maker in France several times. In addition to jams made from every Pyrénéan berry, the shop also stocks a selection of bonbons. The star and centerpiece, M. Miot's own creation, is a *coucougnette,* or jam-filled chocolate.

If you're interested in seeing where these confections are made, head for the suburbs of Pau, about 1.5km (1 mile) southeast of the center, to the residential hamlet of Uzos. Here you'll find **Musée de la Confiture** (✆ **05-59-35-05-56**), where exhibits display the history of jams from medieval times to today. It's open Monday to Saturday 10am to 5pm; admission is 4.60€ ($6) adults and 3€ ($3.90) ages 3 to 12.

WHERE TO STAY

Hôtel Continental The centrally located Continental is one of the most prominent hotels in Pau. Renovated several times since its original construction around 1900, it's one of the two best hotels in town (the Gramont is another top choice). Rooms are functionally decorated, modernized, and soundproof. About 60 have mid-size bathrooms with tub/shower combinations; the rest have showers.

2 rue du Maréchal-Foch, Pau 64000. ✆ **05-59-27-69-31**. Fax 05-59-27-99-84. www.hotel-continental-pau.com. 75 units. 69€–115€ ($90–$150) double; 150€ ($195) suite. AE, DC, DISC, MC, V. Free parking. **Amenities:** Restaurant; golf course; tennis courts; cycling; fishing; horseback riding; room service; laundry service; nonsmoking rooms; limited-mobility rooms. *In room:* TV, minibar, hair dryer, Wi-Fi.

Hôtel de Gramont In the heart of Pau, on a gracefully designed 19th-century plaza whose every architectural detail has been classified as a historic treasure, this hotel was built around 1880 in a style that complements the medievalism of the château nearby. Its management spent lots of money restoring the elegant woodwork in the street-level salons and outfitted the guest rooms with late-19th-century (mostly English) antiques. Each room has a comfortable bed and is decorated differently, but in a style that evokes grand-scale country living. Some have air-conditioning. About half of the medium-size bathrooms contain tub/shower combos; the others have showers. Many restaurants are a short walk away.

3 place Gramont, Pau 64000. ✆ **05-59-27-84-04.** Fax 05-59-27-62-23. www.hotelgramont.com. 34 units. 66€–98€ ($86–$127) double; 120€ ($156) suite. AE, DC, DISC, MC, V. Closed Dec 23–Jan 5. **Amenities:** Bar; billiard room. *In room:* A/C (some rooms), TV, minibar, Wi-Fi.

WHERE TO DINE

Au Fin Gourmet ★★ *Value* BASQUE This restaurant, on the southern periphery of Pau near the rail station, is maintained by Christian, Laurent, and Patrick, sons of the retired founder, Clément Ithurriague. The postmodern, circular dining room, with soaring windows overlooking a park, opens onto an outdoor terrace for warm-weather dining. The cuisine is based on regional ingredients. Menu items include marinated codfish with herbs from the kitchen garden and bouillon-flavored potatoes; grilled duck liver with peppers; rack of lamb flavored with herbs from the Pyrénées in a parsley-enriched crust; sliced and sautéed foie gras; and braised stuffed trout. Dessert may include four variations of caramel arranged on the same platter, or ice cream with rum.

24 av. Gaston-Lacoste. ✆ **05-59-27-47-71.** www.restaurant-aufingourmet.com. Reservations recommended. Main courses 21€–26€ ($27–$34); fixed-price lunch 18€ ($23); fixed-price dinner 35€ ($46). AE, DC, MC, V. Tues and Thurs–Sun noon–2pm; Tues–Sat 7:30–9:30pm.

Chez Pierre ★★ BEARNAISE/FRENCH Year after year, we have our finest meal in Pau at Chez Pierre, which spins regional products into creative dishes. Established in 1924, it's a 5-minute walk west of the château. One dining room resembles a salon in an English men's club, another abounds with plants like a greenhouse, and the third (upstairs) affords a sweeping view over the gardens attached to the local branch of La Banque de France. Chef Raymond Casau, who spent years apprenticing with some of the most successful chefs in France, is among the finest around. His specialties are sole braised with wine, fresh salmon braised with Jurançon (a sweet, golden Pyrénéan wine), and a Béarnaise version of cassoulet (with different sausages than the Toulouse version, with a greater emphasis on confit of goose). One of the most attractive bars in town, outfitted like the club room of a golf course, is adjacent to the dining rooms.

Rue Louis-Barthour. ✆ **05-59-27-76-86.** www.restaurant-chez-pierre.com. Reservations required. Main courses 19€–30€ ($25–$39); fixed-price menu 34€ ($44). AE, DC, MC, V. Tues–Fri noon–2pm; Mon–Sat 7–10pm. Closed 2 weeks in early Jan, 3 weeks in mid-Aug.

WHERE TO STAY & DINE NEARBY

Some of the world's most discerning people head to the town of **Eugénie-les-Bains,** about 53km (33 miles) north of Pau, in search of the marvelous domain (hotel, restaurant, and spa) of Michel Guérard. The town has no rail station, so most people drive from Pau. To get here, take N134 north to Garlin, follow the unmarked road west to the town of Geaune, and follow signs to Eugénie-les-Bains.

Les Prés d'Eugénie (Michel Guérard) ★★★ BASQUE This Relais & Châteaux property is the creation of Michel Guérard, the chef whose *cuisine minceur* started a culinary revolution in the early 1970s that emphasized presentation over portion size.

It attracts a stream of diners who appreciate the calm surroundings and the much-publicized cooking. The menu includes both *cuisine minceur,* so that calorie counters can still enjoy well-seasoned flavors and fresh ingredients, and the heartier *cuisine gourmand,* influenced by Basque and classic French recipes. Dishes are constantly evolving, usually tapping into regional sentimentality, as in the case of "bourgeois style" veal chops fried "over low flame in a corner of the fireplace." Specialties include cream of crayfish soup, freshwater crayfish roasted with limes, whiting in white-wine sauce, lamb steamed with fennel, and a variety of simply steamed fish with fresh vegetables.

Those unwilling to pay the stratospheric prices in the main restaurant sometimes book a table in a satellite restaurant operated by M. Guérard, **La Ferme aux Grives.** The cuisine focuses on rural specialties of the region, offering a single fixed-price menu for 43€ ($56). Comfortable and rustically elegant, it's open for lunch Thursday to Tuesday, dinner Thursday to Monday. A typical specialty is brochettes of free-range chicken cooked on a skewer.

In addition to the restaurants, there are a variety of accommodations. The most comfortable and expensive are the eight high-ceilinged units in an outlying annex, **Le Couvent des Herbes.** They cost 270€ to 400€ ($351–$520) for a double, 330€ to 520€ ($429–$676) for a suite. Slightly less glamorous are the 35 units in the main building, which rent for 290€ to 350€ ($377–$455), or 410€ to 520€ ($533–$676) for an apartment. Rooms are decorated in the style of a country manor house. Less expensive, and geared to the family trade, are the 30 units in **La Maison Rose,** where doubles go for 105€ to 170€ ($137–$221), and suites cost 145€ to 235€ ($189–$306). Some units contain kitchenettes.

If you're planning on truly experiencing the spa, you won't really get an insight into its methodologies unless you come for a full-immersion sojourn of a week or more. About 25% of the clientele opt for an R & R, health, and revitalization routine, the cost of which, with full board for two persons, is 4,650€ to 5,980€ ($6,045–$7,774) per week.

Eugénie-les-Bains, Beaune 40320. © **05-58-05-06-07.** Fax 05-58-51-10-10. www.michelguerard.com. Reservations recommended. Main courses 50€–85€ ($65–$111); fixed-price menu 135€–185€ ($176–$241). AE, DC, MC, V. July 15–Aug daily noon–2pm and 7:45–10pm; Sept–Dec and Apr–July 14 Sat–Sun noon–2pm, Tues–Sun 7:45–10pm. Closed Jan–Mar.

PAU AFTER DARK

Nightlife in Pau concentrates on **Le Triangle,** an area in the town center that's flanked by the rue Emile-Garet, rue Lespy, and rue Castetnau. Within its borders, you'll find our favorite bar, **Le Garage Bar and Buttery,** 49 rue Emile-Garet (© **05-59-83-75-17**), the town's most unusual watering hole. Set within the echoing premises of what was conceived in the 1930s as an auto repair shop, it retains many of its original industrial-looking fixtures, plus a collection of antique traffic lights, road signs, mopeds hanging from chains in the ceiling, and vintage auto-related nostalgia. Most people come here just for its bar facilities, but if you want food, platters cost from 6€ to 10€ ($7.80–$13) and include such items as English-style fish and chips, American-inspired burgers, and all-French versions of *bavette de boeuf* with garlic sauce and french fries. There are also fixed-price menus priced at 10€ ($13) and salads. It's open Monday to Friday noon to 2am, Saturday and Sunday 6pm and 2am. A competitor is the animated and congenial French cafe-cum-tavern, **Le Béarnais,** 3 rue Lespy (© **05-59-83-72-11**). Open at around 6:30am for the breakfast crowd, it changes its role throughout the course of the day, ultimately ending up as a hard-core drinking spot favored by mostly French-speaking long-term patrons. The town's leading and largest disco is **L'Hypnoz,** 11 place du Foirail (✆ **05-59-84-06-73**), where bright lights flash above a shadowy dance floor that's flanked with a busy bar patronized by usually attractive 20- and 30-somethings from Pau and the surrounding region. Entrance, depending on the night of the week, is free except Saturday when the cover is 11€ ($14). It's open Wednesday to Saturday nights 11pm to 5am.

3 Bayonne ★★

770km (478 miles) SW of Paris, 184km (114 miles) SW of Bordeaux

Bayonne is the leading port and pleasure-yacht basin of the Côte Basque, divided by the Nive and Adour rivers. A cathedral city and the capital of the Pays Basque, it's characterized by narrow streets, quays, and ramparts. Enlivening the scene are bullfights, *pelote* (jai alai), and street dancing at annual fiestas. You may want to buy some of Bayonne's famous chocolate at one of the arcaded shops along rue du Port-Neuf, and then enjoy coffee at a cafe along place de la Liberté, the hub of town.

ESSENTIALS

GETTING THERE Seven TGV **trains** per day link Bayonne and Paris (trip time: 5 hr.; one-way fare: 94€/$122). Nine trains per day arrive from Bordeaux (trip time: 2 hr.; 25€/$33 one-way). For train information and schedules, call ✆ **08-92-35-35-35** from abroad.

There's **bus** service from Biarritz, 15 minutes away. Bus no. 1 departs from Biarritz at 12-minute intervals throughout the daylight hours, depositing passengers on place de la Mairie in Bayonne; the one-way fare is 1.20€ ($1.55). There's also bus service between Bayonne and outlying towns and villages not serviced by train. For bus information in Bayonne, call ✆ **05-59-59-04-61.**

Bayonne is near the end of the N117 roadway, easily accessible by **car** from Toulouse and other cities in the south of France. From Paris, take A10 south to Vierzon, and then N20 south to Limoges. Continue on N21 south to Tarbes, and turn west along N117 to Bayonne.

VISITOR INFORMATION The **Office de Tourisme** is on place des Basques (✆ **05-59-46-01-46;** fax 05-59-59-37-55; www.bayonne-tourisme.com).

SPECIAL EVENTS During the 4-day **Fête de Bayonne,** the first week in August, a frenzy of outdoor concerts and dancing fills the streets. The celebration is intense. For **free concerts** on fair-weather Thursday evenings in July and August, head to the gazebo on place de-Gaulle, where styles range from jazz to traditional Basque. Contact the Office de Tourisme (see above) for more information.

EXPLORING THE TOWN

The old town, **Grand Bayonne,** is inside the ramparts, on the left bank of the Nive. The early-13th-century **Cathédrale Ste-Marie** (✆ **05-59-59-17-82**) dominates this part of town on rue d'Espagne and rue des Gouverneurs. The spiny 19th-century steeples are the best-known landmarks in Bayonne. The cathedral is worth half an hour of your time and is a good retreat on a hot day. It was begun in 1258 when Bayonne was under British control; it fell to the French in 1451. That explains the cathedral's ornamentation, mixing such elements as the English coat of arms (three leopards) with the fleur-de-lis of France. Some of the stained glass dates from the Renaissance, but the best statuary was smashed during the French Revolution. Don't miss the gorgeous 14th-century cloisters. They're like a secret garden from the Middle Ages. The cathedral is open Monday to Saturday 10am to noon and 3 to 5:45pm, Sunday 3:30 to 5:45pm.

Musée Basque ★★ Bayonne's newest museum showcases the traditions, architecture, and decorative arts (including textiles and furniture) of the Basques in a state-of-the-art format that's more advanced and sophisticated than any equivalent museum in the Basque-speaking world.

Gucir des Corsaires. ✆ **05-59-46-61-90.** www.musee-basque.com. Admission 9€ ($12) adults, 4.50€ ($5.85) students and children 6–17, free for children under 6; includes entrance to the Musée Bonnat (see below). May–Oct Tues–Sun 10:30am–6:30pm; Nov–Apr Tues–Sun 10am–12:30pm and 2–6pm.

Musée Bonnat ★★ This museum owns one of the best collections of paintings in France. It's hardly the Louvre, but it encompasses hundreds of canvases (far too many to display in its limited space). A sampling of works from some of the greatest European masters is showcased. If anybody's the star, it's Peter Paul Rubens (1577–1640), who has an entire salon devoted to his paintings. The collection's strongest point is its 19th-century art. Otherwise, it's like Art History 101, with works by David, Degas, Goya, Ingres, da Vinci, El Greco, Tiepolo, and Rembrandt—an overview of European art from the 13th to the 20th centuries. Check out the often-overlooked collection of antiquities in the basement, a museum within a museum with everything from Egyptian amulets to Greek vases.

5 rue Jacques-Lafitte. ✆ **05-59-59-08-52.** www.musee-bonnat.com. For admission, see Musée Basque above. May–Oct Wed–Mon 10am–6:30pm; Nov–Apr Wed–Mon 10am–12:30pm and 2–6pm.

SHOPPING

Most of Bayonne's specialty shops and boutiques lie inside the ramparts of the old town, Grand Bayonne. The pedestrian streets of **rue Port-Neuf** (aptly nicknamed the "street of chocolate shops"), **rue Victor-Hugo,** and **rue Salie** are major shopping destinations. For antiques, walk along the **rue des Faures** and the edges of **place Montaut,** behind the cathedral. Most of the modern shops and French chain stores are on **rue Thiers** and **quai de la Nive,** outside the old town. Visit **Maison de Jean Vier,** carrefour Cinq Cantons (✆ **05-59-59-16-18**), to get your Basque bath, kitchen, and bed linens. **Cazenave,** 19 rue Port-Neuf (✆ **05-59-59-03-16**), specializes in *chocolats de Bayonne,* which include rich, dark, strong chocolate nougats; stop in the tearoom here for warm chocolate mousse.

The accessories of one Basque tradition have become something of a fine art. In olden days, the *makila* was used as a walking stick, a cudgel, or—when equipped with a hidden blade—a knife. Today, carved *makilas* are sold as collectors' items and souvenirs. For safety's sake, they almost never come with a blade. One of the best outlets in town is **Fabrication de Makhilas,** 37 rue Vieille Boucherie (✆ **05-59-59-18-20**). Another famous product of the Basque country is its cured hams, which taste best shaved into paper-thin slices and consumed with one of the region's heady red wines and perhaps a loaf of bread and (if you prefer) a smear of butter. An establishment that prepares and sells these hams is **Saloir et Séchoire à Jambon Pierre Ibaialde,** 41 rue des Cordeliers (✆ **05-59-25-65-30**), where the hams are sold either whole or in thin slices. Also available is an impressive roster of sausages, pâtés, and terrines.

Bayonne has been known as a centerpiece for the fabrication of chocolates since the days of the Spanish Inquisition, when Spanish and Portuguese Jews were driven out of Iberia by the Catholic monarchs, bringing the craft of chocolate making with them to France. For one of the best views in the region of the complicated process of chocolate making, head for **La Fabrique du Chocolatier Puyodebat,** 66 rue d'Espagne (✆ **05-59-59-20-86**). Here, every Monday to Saturday from 9am to 7pm, you can visit the chocolate factory, as uniformed workers concoct their velvety flavors, which then move into the *salle des expositions* (showroom) for purchases.

WHERE TO STAY

Best Western Grand Hôtel ★ The best hotel in town was built in 1835 on the ruins of a medieval Carmelite convent. In 1991, it attained government-rated three-star status, a position it still admirably maintains. Rooms have modern fittings but maintain an antique feel. Each midsize bathroom has a tub and shower.

21 rue Thiers, Bayonne 64100. ✆ **800/528-1234** in the U.S. and Canada, or 05-59-59-62-00. Fax 05-59-59-62-01. www.bw-legrandhotel.com. 54 units. 70€–150€ ($91–$195) double. AE, DC, MC, V. Parking 13€ ($17). **Amenities:** Restaurant (breakfast only); bar; room service; laundry service; nonsmoking rooms; limited-mobility rooms. *In room:* TV, minibar, coffeemaker, hair dryer, safe, Wi-Fi.

Mercure Bayonne Centre The second-best choice in Bayonne, the six-story Mercure provides well-furnished rooms with views over the river Nive. Drinks are served on the terrace, which was carved out of a wooded setting beside the river, a 10-minute walk north of the cathedral. Rooms are in typical chain-hotel style, and each well-kept bathroom has a tub and shower.

Av. Jean-Rostand, Bayonne 64100. ✆ **05-59-52-84-44.** Fax 05-59-52-84-20. www.mercure.com. 109 units. 74€–140€ ($96–$182) double. AE, DC, MC, V. Free parking. **Amenities:** Restaurant; bar; outdoor pool; laundry service; dry cleaning. *In room:* A/C, TV, minibar, hair dryer.

WHERE TO DINE

François Miura ★ *Finds* FRENCH A few steps from the Eglise St-André, this restaurant occupies a late-19th-century cloister built for Visitandine nuns. The cuisine is the most eclectic and personalized in town. Menu items are sophisticated and composed with intelligence. They include flavorful, complicated dishes such as twice-cooked pigeon in regional wine stuffed with foie gras, and stuffed squid served with confit of pigs' foot flavored with squid ink and essence of crayfish. Less daring examples include warm calamari salad with two kinds of peppers, and braised rack of lamb with fresh vegetables and coriander sauce. Desserts may include a soufflé with pear liqueur.

24 rue Marengo. ✆ **05-59-59-49-89.** Reservations recommended. Main courses 14€–22€ ($18–$29); fixed-price menu 20€–31€ ($26–$40). AE, DC, MC, V. Thurs–Tues noon–2pm; Mon–Tues and Thurs–Sat 8–10pm.

Le Cheval Blanc ★★ BASQUE The finest restaurant in Bayonne occupies a half-timbered Basque-style house built in 1715 in the heart of the historic center. Menu items vary with the season, but may include slices of foie gras with caramelized endive and pine nuts, ravioli stuffed with wild boar and flavored with local red wine and confit of baby onions, and corn blinis with flap mushrooms. Dorado may be simmered in garlic and served with *crépinette de marmitako* (diced tuna with red and green peppers, bound in a pig's stomach). One of the best desserts is almond tartlet with chocolate sauce.

68 rue Bourgneuf. ✆ **05-59-59-01-33.** Reservations recommended. Main courses 18€–36€ ($23–$47); fixed-price menu 55€–65€ ($72–$85). AE, MC, V. Tues–Fri and Sun noon–3pm; Tues–Sat 7–10pm. Closed Feb 10–Mar 7, 1 week in July, 1 week in Aug.

BAYONNE AFTER DARK

Nightlife centers on the neighborhood known as Petit Bayonne, the town's historic core. **Rue des Tonneliers, rue Pannecau,** and **rue des Cordeliers** are the liveliest areas after dark. **Katie Daly's,** 3 place de la Liberté (✆ **05-59-59-09-14**), serves endless pints of Guinness; the drinkers really pile in on weekends. Expect a carefree group of rowdies and a lot of fun. For a taste of local color, try **Le Cabaret La Luna Negra,** rue des Augustins (✆ **05-59-25-78-05**), where the 6€-to-10€ ($7.80–$13) cover charge includes cabaret, jazz, or blues performances and popular French songs.

4 Biarritz ★★★

779km (484 miles) SW of Paris, 193km (120 miles) SW of Bordeaux

One of the most famous seaside resorts in the world, Biarritz was once a fishing village. Favored by Empress Eugénie, the village near the Spanish border soon attracted her husband, Napoleon III, who truly put it on the map. Later, Queen Victoria showed up often, and her son, Edward VII, visited more than once.

In the 1930s, the Prince of Wales (before he was, and then wasn't, Edward VIII) and the American divorcée he loved, Wallis Simpson, did much to make Biarritz more fashionable as they headed south with these instructions: "Chill the champagne, pack the pearls, and tune up the Bugatti." Biarritz became the pre-jet set's favorite sunning spot. Although those legendary days are long gone, the resort is still fashionable, but the unthinkable has happened: It now has surf shops, snack bars, and even some reasonably priced hotels.

ESSENTIALS

GETTING THERE Seventeen **trains** arrive daily from Bayonne (trip time: 10 min.), which has rail links with Paris and other cities in the south of France. The one-way fare is 2.25€ to 4€ ($2.95–$5.20). The rail station is 3km (1¾ miles) south of the town center, in La Négresse. For information, call ✆ **08-92-35-35-35** from outside France. Bus no. 2 carries passengers from the station to the center of Biarritz; the one-way fare is 1.20€ ($1.55). You can also take a cab for around 18€ ($23). If you're **driving,** Biarritz is at the end of the N117 roadway, the major thoroughfare for the Basque country. From Paris, take A10 south to Vierzon, and then N20 south to Limoges. Continue on N21 south to Tarbes, and then head west on N117.

VISITOR INFORMATION The **Office de Tourisme** is on square d'Ixelles (✆ **05-59-22-37-00;** fax 05-59-24-14-19; www.biarritz.fr).

SPECIAL EVENTS If you're in town in September, check out the modern dance and ballet performances during the 3-week festival of **Le Temps d'Aimer.** Cultural events take place in parks, churches, and auditoriums throughout town. Tickets cost 15€ to 35€ ($20–$46). Music is the focus at the **Les Fêtes Musicales** festival for 4 days in late April, usually at the Casino Municipal and the Théâtre Gare du Midi (which was originally a railway station). Tickets cost 10€ to 32€ ($13–$42). For reservations and ticket sales for either festival, or for tickets to events at the Théâtre Gare du Midi, contact the **Office Culturelle de Biarritz** (✆ **05-59-22-44-66**).

Biarritz is the surfing capital of France. Each year in late July, cadres of enthusiasts descend on the town for the weeklong **Biarritz Surf Festival.** You don't need to buy a ticket or show up at any particular time. The festival uses all the town's beachfronts, and a Hawaiian spirit permeates the Basque town as surfers re-create the search for

Endless Summer. Biarritz also devotes more of its landscape and energy to golf than any other city in France. Ten courses lie within a short drive of the town. A good practice setting is the **Centre d'Entraînement d'Ilbarritz-Bidart,** avenue Reine Nathalie, 64210 Bidart (✆ **05-59-43-81-30**); you can play 9 holes for 21€ to 36€ ($27–$47). Passionate golfers might consider visiting in the third week in July during the **Biarritz Cup,** a nationwide competition attended by mostly French golfers. The series of playoffs takes place at the Golf du Phare, avenue Edith-Cavell (✆ **05-59-03-71-80**). Information on both festivals is available from the tourist office.

A DAY AT THE BEACH

Along the seafront is the **Grande Plage.** During the Belle Epoque, this was where Victorian ladies promenaded under parasols and wide-brimmed veiled hats. Today's bathers don't dress up in billowing skirts. Sometimes they don't even wear tops. The beach is also popular with surfers.

Promenade du Bord de Mer, along the coast within the city limits, is still a major attraction. The paths are often carved into cliffs, and sections have been designed as rock gardens with flowers, turning the area into a public park. From here, you can head north to **Pointe St-Martin,** where you'll find more gardens and a staircase (look for the sign DESCENTE DE L'OCEAN) leading you to allée Winston-Churchill, a paved path going along **Plage Miramar.**

La Perspective de la Côte des Basques, a walk that goes up to another plateau, leads to one of the wildest beaches in France: **Plage de la Côte des Basques,** with breakers crashing at the base of the cliffs. This is where surfers head.

If you like your beaches calmer, the safest beach is the small, horseshoe-shaped **Plage du Port-Vieux,** along the path from plateau de l'Atalaye. Its tranquil waters, protected by rocks, make it a favorite with families.

EXPLORING THE TOWN

Eglise St-Martin, rue St-Martin (✆ **05-59-23-05-19**), is one of the few vestiges of the port's early boom days. In the 12th century, Biarritz grew prosperous as a whaling center. The mammals' departure from the Bay of Biscay marked a decline in the port's fortunes. The church dates from the 1100s and was restored in 1541 with a Flamboyant Gothic chancel. It's in the town center between two of Biarritz's major arteries, rue d'Espagne and avenue de Gramont. It's open daily 8am to 7:30pm. Admission is free.

Biarritz's turning point came with the arrival of the Comtesse de Montijo, who spent lazy summers here with her two daughters. One of them, Eugénie, married Napoleon III in 1853 and prevailed on him to visit Biarritz the next year. The emperor fell under its spell and ordered the construction of the **Hôtel du Palais** (see "Where to Stay," below). The hotel remains the town's most enduring landmark, though it was originally dubbed "Eugénie's Basque folly." Edward VII stayed there in 1906 and again in 1910, only days before his death. In a commanding spot on Grande Plage, the hotel is worth a visit even if you're not a guest. You can view the palatial trappings of its public rooms.

Before the Revolution of 1917, members of Russian nobility arrived: so many, in fact, that they erected the **Eglise Orthodoxe Russe,** 8 av. de l'Impératrice (✆ **05-59-24-16-74**). Across from the Hôtel du Palais, this Byzantine-Russian landmark was built in 1892 so that wintering aristocrats could worship when they weren't enjoying champagne, caviar, and Basque prostitutes. It's noted for its gilded dome, the interior of which is the color of a blue sky on a sunny day.

After you pass the Hôtel du Palais, the walkway widens into **quai de la Grande Plage,** Biarritz's principal promenade. This walkway continues to the opposite end of the resort, where a final belvedere opens onto the southernmost stretch of beach. This whole walk takes about 3 hours.

At the southern edge of Grande Plage, steps will take you to **place Ste-Eugénie,** Biarritz's most gracious old square. Lined with terraced restaurants, it's the most popular rendezvous. Right below place Ste-Eugénie is the colorful **Port des Pêcheurs** (fishers' port). Crowded with fishing boats, it has old wooden houses and shacks backed up against a cliff. Here you'll find driftwood, rope, and plenty of lobster traps along with small harborfront restaurants and cafes.

The rocky **plateau de l'Atalaye** forms one side of the Port des Pêcheurs. Carved on orders of Napoleon III, a tunnel leads through the plateau to an esplanade. Here a footbridge stretches into the sea, to a rocky islet that takes its name, **Rocher de la Vierge (Rock of the Virgin),** from the statue crowning it. Since 1865, this statue is said to have protected the sailors and fishers in the Bay of Biscay. Alexandre-Gustave Eiffel (designer of the tower) directed construction of the footbridge. The walk out onto the edge of the rock, with crashing surf on both sides, is the most dramatic in Biarritz. From the rock, you can see far to the south on a clear day, all the way to the mountains of the Spanish Basque country.

Here you can visit the **Musée de la Mer,** 14 plateau de l'Atalaye (✆ **05-59-22-33-34;** www.museedelamer.com), which houses 24 aquariums of fish native to the bay. The seals steal the show at their daily 10:30am and 5pm feedings. The museum also houses *requins* (sharks) that are fed on Tuesday and Friday at 11am and Wednesday and Sunday at 4:30pm. Admission is 7.50€ ($9.75) adults, 4.80€ ($6.25) students and children 4 to 16, and free for children under 4. It's open in July and August daily 9:30am to midnight; June and September 9:30am to 7pm; otherwise Tuesday through Sunday 9:30am to 12:30pm and 2 to 6pm; call ahead to check January open days and hours.

The only remaining building in town designed according to the tastes of the Empress Eugénie is **La Chapelle Impériale,** rue Pellot (✆ **05-59-22-37-10**). Built in 1864, it combines Romanesque-Byzantine and Hispano-Moorish styles. It's open April 15 to July 15 and September 16 to October 15, Tuesday, Thursday, and Saturday 3 to 7pm; July 16 to September 15 Monday and Saturday 3 to 7pm; and October 16 to December 31 Thursday 3 to 7pm. Admission is free.

Musée Asiatica, 1 rue Guy Petit (✆ **05-59-22-78-78;** www.museeasiatica.com), has an unusual collection, mostly from India, Nepal, Tibet, and China. The art dates from prehistory to the current age. Admission is 7€ ($9.10) for adults, 3.50€ ($4.55) for ages 13 to 25, and 2€ ($2.60) for children 8 to 12; free for children under 8. From September to June, it is open Monday to Friday 2 to 6:30pm, Saturday and Sunday 2 to 7pm. In July and August, it's open daily 10:30am to 6:30pm.

SHOPPING

The major boutiques, with all the big designer names from Paris, are on **place Clemenceau** in the heart of Biarritz. From this square, fan out to **rue Gambetta, rue Mazagran, avenue Victor-Hugo, avenue Edouard-VII, avenue du Maréchal-Foch,** and **avenue de Verdun.** Look for the exceptional Biarritz chocolates and confections, and textiles from the Basque country.

The finest chocolatiers are **Pariès,** 27 place Bellevue (✆ **05-59-22-07-52**), where you can choose from seven kinds of *tourons* (nougats) ranging from raspberry to coffee;

Daranatz, 12 av. du Maréchal-Foch (✆ **05-59-24-21-91**); and **Henriet,** place Clemenceau (✆ **05-59-24-24-15** or 05-59-24-58-80), where the house specialty is *rochers de Biarritz* (morsels of candied orange peel and roasted almonds covered in dark chocolate). The owners also run the **Musée du Chocolat,** 14–15 av. Beaurivages (✆ **05-59-41-54-64;** www.lemuseeduchocolat.com), where exhibits illustrate chocolate-making and its history. There's also a sales kiosk. During July and August, it's open daily 10am to noon and 2:30 to 7pm; the rest of the year, it's open Monday through Saturday 10am to noon and 2:30 to 6pm. Admission fees are 6€ ($7.80) adults, 5€ ($6.50) students 12 to 18, 3€ ($3.90) children 4 to 12, and free for children under 4. At the other end of the gastronomic spectrum, try **Mille et Un Fromages,** 8 rue Victor Hugo (✆ **05-59-24-67-88**), specializing in, as the name suggests, a myriad of tasty French cheeses, as well as a host of hearty wines to accompany them. Among antiques stores, your best bet is **Bakara,** 23 rue Mazagran (✆ **05-59-22-08-95**), where you'll see special porcelain dolls.

Virtually every souvenir shop and department store in the region sells **espadrilles,** the canvas-topped, rope-bottomed slippers. A simple off-the-shelf model begins at around 13€ ($17), and made-to-order versions (special sizes, special colors) rarely top 62€ ($81). Upscale espadrilles are made to order in Bidart, a hamlet between Biarritz and St-Jean-de-Luz, at **Maison Garcia,** pont de Baskutenea (✆ **05-59-26-51-27**). Opened in 1937, this is one of the last manufacturers to finish its products by hand.

WHERE TO STAY

Château de Brindos ★★ *Finds* This is one of the most architecturally and culturally unusual homes in the southwest of France, with a history entrenched in the Jazz Age. Built by American heiress Virginia Gould in 1920, it occupies 11 hectares (27 acres) of inland park and garden. With a facade inspired vaguely by the architecture of Spain, and an interior loaded with architectural remnants such as fireplaces and staircases from the Gothic age, this is the most romantic stopover on the Côte Basque. Rooms are spacious, with antique furnishings and modern fittings; bathrooms have tub/shower combinations. Fishing on the private lake can be arranged. The superb restaurant overlooks the lake.

1 allée du Château, Anglet 64600. From town center, follow AEROPORT signs; after the 2nd roundabout *(rond-point),* follow signs to château; it's about 2.5km (1½ miles) north of Biarritz. ✆ **05-59-23-89-80.** Fax 05-59-23-89-81. www.chateaudebrindos.com. 29 units. 200€–315€ ($260–$410) double; 270€–550€ ($351–$715) suite. AE, DC, MC, V. **Amenities:** Restaurant; bar; heated outdoor pool; fitness center; sauna; room service; laundry service. *In room:* TV, minibar, hair dryer.

Hôtel Atalaye For economy with a bit of style, head to this simple government-rated two-star lodging. In the heart of town on a tranquil spot overlooking the ocean, this early-20th-century hotel gets rather sleepy in winter. Rooms are well maintained and traditionally furnished; most of the small, tiled bathrooms have showers. Breakfast is provided anytime you request it. The location is right off place Ste-Eugénie near the beaches, lighthouse, and casino.

6 rue des Goelands, Plateau de L'Atalaye, Biarritz 64200. ✆ **05-59-24-06-76.** Fax 05-59-22-33-51. www.hotelatalaye.com. 25 units. 42€–72€ ($55–$94) double; 55€–89€ ($72–$116) triple or quad. MC, V. *In room:* TV.

Hôtel du Palais ★★★ *Kids* There is no finer hotel palace along the Basque coast. The Hôtel du Palais has been the grand playground for the international elite for over a century. Napoleon III built it in 1854 as a private villa for Eugénie so she wouldn't get homesick for Spain. He picked the ideal beachfront, in view of the rocks and rugged shoreline. Of course the hotel has elaborately furnished suites, but even the double rooms have period furniture and silk draperies, plus spacious private bathrooms with luxurious tubs and showers. Try to get a room facing west to enjoy the sunsets over the Basque coast.

Av. de l'Impératrice, Biarritz 64200. ✆ **800/223-6800** in the U.S. and Canada, or 05-59-41-64-00. Fax 05-59-41-67-99. www.hotel-du-palais.com. 154 units. 370€–550€ ($481–$715) double; from 600€–1,550€ ($780–$2,015) suite. AE, DC, MC, V. **Amenities:** 3 restaurants; bar; outdoor seawater pool; fitness center; spa; salon; sauna; children's program and playground; room service; laundry service; dry cleaning. *In room:* A/C, TV, minibar, hair dryer, safe.

Hôtel Plaza ★ Near the casino and beach, this hotel is a gorgeous Art Deco monument. Built in 1928, it has remained virtually unchanged, except for discreet renovations, so it's classified as a historic monument and a civic treasure. Rooms retain their original Art Deco furnishings; they tend to be large and have high ceilings, and some open onto private terraces. Each tidily kept bathroom has a tub/shower combination. Those overlooking the back and side cost less than those with seafront views. The hotel has direct access to the beach.

10 av. Edouard-VII, Biarritz 64200. ✆ **05-59-24-74-00.** Fax 05-59-22-22-01. www.groupe-segeric.com. 69 units. 115€–250€ ($150–$325) double. AE, DC, MC, V. Free parking. **Amenities:** Bar; room service; laundry service. *In room:* A/C, TV, minibar, hair dryer, Wi-Fi.

WHERE TO DINE

The restaurant at **Château de Brindos** (see "Where to Stay," above) also serves excellent Franco-Basque cuisine.

Auberge de la Négresse ★ *Finds* BASQUE Just 2.5km (1½ miles) south of Biarritz, directly adjacent to the main railway station, this restaurant is named for a 19th-century slave who escaped from an American plantation by hiding in the bottom of a French ship. Here she established an inn, which Napoleon's army used on its passage to Spain. The inn doubles as a delicatessen, and the two dining rooms serve flavorful meals. Some of the best dishes include a terrine of foie gras, along with hake, monkfish, or sea wolf prepared in the Spanish style—that is, grilled and served with a garlic-flavored parsley sauce.

10 bd. Marcel Dassault. ✆ **05-59-23-15-83.** Reservations required. Main courses 12€–22€ ($16–$29); fixed-price lunch 10€–29€ ($13–$38); fixed-price dinner 20€–29€ ($25–$38). AE, MC, V. Tues–Sun noon–2:15pm and 7–10:15pm.

Les Platanes ★★ MODERN FRENCH This stylish establishment is the restaurant in Biarritz that the world (and the world of French gastronomy in particular) most wants to experience. It's in a 19th-century town house with two vaguely Art Deco–style dining rooms strictly segregated into smoking and nonsmoking areas. The intensely creative cuisine varies with the season, the availability of raw ingredients, and the chef's inspiration. Don't expect these exact items when you dine here, but examples include such dishes as foie gras poached in consommé, served with pan-fried leeks and crisp-grilled (almost dry) mushrooms; baked sea scallops with leeks glazed in sweetened vinegar sauce; and filets of a local Atlantic whitefish, *maigre* (maiger fish), served with braised fennel.

32 av. Beau-Soleil. ✆ **05-59-23-13-68.** Reservations required. Main courses 24€–39€ ($31–$51); fixed-price lunch menu 35€ ($46); fixed-price dinner menu 63€ ($82). MC, V. July 14–Aug 21 daily noon–2pm and 8–10:30pm; Aug 22–July 13 Tues–Fri noon–2pm, Tues–Sat 8–10:30pm.

BIARRITZ AFTER DARK

Start the night with a stroll around **Port des Pécheurs,** an ideal spot for people-watching, with its sport fishers, restaurants, and fascinating crowds.

Fortunes have been made and lost at **Le Casino Municipal,** 1 av. Edouard-VII (✆ **05-59-22-37-00**), where you can easily catch gambling fever. The less formal section, containing only slot machines, is open daily 10am to 3am (until 4am Fri–Sat). Entrance is free, no ID is required, and there's no dress code. The more elegant section (for *les jeux de table,* or table games) is open Sunday through Thursday 7:30pm to 3am, Friday and Saturday 6pm to 4am. This section requires a passport or photo ID. "Correct" dress for this section means no shorts or sloppy attire—jackets aren't required.

The hippest nightclub in town is **Le Copa,** 24 av. Edouard-VII (✆ **05-59-24-65-39**), which plays Latin (particularly Cuban) salsa, and virtually every other kind of dance music. **Le Play Boy,** 15 place Clemenceau (✆ **05-59-24-38-46**), appeals to a diverse crowd ranging in age from 20 to 40. More appealing is **Disco Le Caveau,** 4 rue Gambetta (✆ **05-59-24-16-17**), where a well-dressed and attractive crowd of gay and straight people mingle with ease.

5 St-Jean-de-Luz ★★

791km (492 miles) SW of Paris, 15km (9⅓ miles) S of Biarritz

This Basque country tuna-fishing port and beach resort is ideal for a seaside vacation. St-Jean-de-Luz lies at the mouth of the Nivelle, opening onto the Bay of Biscay, with the Pyrénées in the background. Tourists have been flocking here since the 19th century, when H. G. Wells "discovered" the town.

ESSENTIALS

GETTING THERE Eight to 10 **trains** per day arrive from Biarritz (trip time: 15 min.; one-way fare: 2.80€–4.40€/$3.65–$5.70), and 10 trains per day arrive from Paris (trip time: 5½ hr.; one-way fare: 90€/$117). For train information and schedules, call ✆ **08-92-35-35-35** from outside France. **Buses** pulling into town from other parts of the Basque country arrive at the Gare Routière (✆ **05-59-26-06-99**), in front of the railway station. St-Jean-de-Luz is a short **drive** from Biarritz along N10 south.

VISITOR INFORMATION The **Office de Tourisme** is on place du Maréchal-Foch (✆ **05-59-26-03-16;** fax 05-59-26-21-47; www.saint-jean-de-luz.com).

SPECIAL EVENTS In July and August on Wednesday after 10:30pm and Sunday after 11:30pm, people pile into place Louis-XIV to take part in **Toro de Fuego,** a celebration of the bull. Revelers take to the streets to dance and watch fireworks. The highlight of the festivities is a snorting papier-mâché bull carried around place Louis-XIV. Between June 22 and June 26, the city celebrates the **Festival of St-Jean** ***(Fêtes Patronales de la Saint Jean)*** with concerts and a series of food kiosks along the harborfront. For 4 days in mid-October, a small film festival, **Festival International des Jeunes Réalisateurs** (✆ **05-59-51-65-30**), showcases the work of filmmakers from southwestern France. For information about festivals, contact the Office de Tourisme (see above).

FUN ON & OFF THE BEACH

THE BEACH The major draw here is the gracefully curving stretch of the white-sand **La Grande Plage St-Jean-de-Luz;** it's one of the best beaches in France, and consequently very crowded in July and August. The beach lies in a half-moon-shaped bay between the ocean and the source of the Nivelle River.

THE PORT TOWN Though tourism accounts for most of the revenue around here, fishing is still important. In fact, this town is the major fishing port along the Basque coast, even though it's less important than in days past. Eating seafood recently plucked from the sea is one of the reasons to visit, especially when Basque chefs transform the big catch into intriguing platters. This port's many narrow streets flanked by old houses are great for strolling.

EXPLORING THE TOWN

In the town's principal church, the 13th-century **Eglise St-Jean-Baptiste** ★★, at the corner of rue Gambetta and rue Garat (✆ **05-59-26-08-81**), Louis XIV and the Spanish Infanta, Marie-Thérèse, were married in 1660. The interior is among the handsomest of all Basque churches. Surmounting the altar is a statue-studded gilded retable (altarpiece). The interior is open to visitors Monday to Saturday 9am to noon and 2 to 6pm, and Sunday 3 to 6:30pm.

At the harbor, the Louis XIII–style **Maison de l'Infante,** quai de l'Infante (✆ **05-59-26-01-56**), sheltered the Spanish princess. The brick-and-stone historic building holds no furniture or exhibits; only two rooms are open to the public. The most noteworthy architectural feature is a monumental carved fireplace. A 1996 renovation restored the 17th-century ceiling beams to their original painted format; they're covered with mysterious symbols and themes that remain baffling even today. As visitors tour the house, a recording (in French) about the history of the building and the 1660 wedding of Louis XIV and Marie Thérèse plays aloud. To supplement the recording, the staff distributes English-language pamphlets. Admission is 4.60€ ($6) for adults and 3.80€ ($4.95) for students and children under 12. Open July and August Monday to Saturday 10:30am to 12:30pm and 2:30 to 6:30pm, Sunday 2:30 to 6:30pm. Also open September and June Monday to Saturday 10:30am to 12:30pm and 2:30 to 5:30pm, Sunday 10:30am to noon.

SHOPPING

You'll find the best shopping along pedestrian **rue Gambetta** and around the Eglise St-Jean-de-Luz. There you can find anything from clothes and leather handbags to books and chocolates to dishes and linens.

You can also ramble around the port, sip pastis in a harborfront cafe, and debate the virtues of the beret. Then scout out **Maison Adam,** 6 place Louis-XIV (✆ **05-59-26-03-54**), which has sold almond-based confections from this boutique since 1660. Specialties include sugared macaroons, *tourons* (almond-paste candies flavored with everything from chocolate to confit of berries), and *canougat* (soft caramels). The boutique is closed mid-January to mid-February and for 3 weeks in November.

A final star in a town loaded with culinary stars is **Confiserie Pariès,** 9 rue Gambetta (✆ **05-59-26-01-46**). Well known for its chocolates and its pastries, it's especially famous for its canougat, a soft and easily chewable caramel that literally melts, with explosions of flavor, in your mouth.

WHERE TO STAY

Hôtel Golf de Chantaco ★★ This mansion has enough memorabilia from its Art Deco heyday to remind you of a time when aristocrats from around Europe made it one of their preferred hotels. Surrounded by an 18-hole golf course and parklands, it's 10 minutes by car from the beach or from the center of town. It resembles the eclectically designed country château of an erudite and somewhat eccentric industrialist. Rooms are luxurious, with personalized touches. Each plush bathroom has a tub/shower combination. Breakfast is served beneath the wisteria-covered arches of an outdoor patio.

Rte. d'Ascain, St-Jean-de-Luz 64500. Take D918 1.5km (1 mile) from the town center. ✆ **05-59-26-14-76.** Fax 05-59-26-35-97. www.hotel-chantaco.com. 23 units. 150€–250€ ($195–$325) double; 250€–350€ ($325–$455) suite. AE, MC, V. Free parking. Closed Nov–Easter. **Amenities:** Salon w/bar service; outdoor pool; golf course; room service; babysitting; laundry service. *In room:* A/C, TV, minibar, hair dryer, safe.

Hôtel Hélianthal ★ *Value* Efficient, well-designed, and comfortable, this hotel dates from the early 1990s. It sits above a restaurant that has been a city monument since the 1920s. Rising above the commercial heart of town, near the beach, it earns three stars from the local tourist office and has some of the amenities you'd associate with a more expensive property. Unfortunately, none of the Art Deco–style rooms overlooks the sea, but many have terraces, bay windows, or balconies. Each room comes with an immaculately kept bathroom with tub and shower. The big-windowed restaurant, L'Atlantique, offers a terrace overlooking the sea.

Place Maurice-Ravel B.P. 469, St-Jean-de-Luz 64540. ✆ **05-59-51-51-51.** Fax 05-59-51-51-54. www.helianthal.fr. 100 units. 104€–246€ ($135–$320) double; 162€–289€ ($211–$376) 2-bedroom suite. AE, DC, MC, V. Parking 6€–12€ ($7.80–$16). **Amenities:** Restaurant; bar; pool; health club; sauna; room service; babysitting; laundry service. *In room:* A/C, TV, minibar, hair dryer, safe.

La Devinière ★★ *Value* This small establishment is the best-furnished moderately priced hotel in St-Jean-de-Luz. It occupies a former private town house, and the unsold inventories of its antiques-dealer owner helped it attain its present level of 18th-century elegance. Rooms are comfortable, well maintained, and—like the rest of the hotel—filled with attractive antiques. Each midsize bathroom has a shower and tub.

5 rue Loquin, St-Jean-de-Luz 64500. ✆ **05-59-26-05-51.** Fax 05-59-51-26-38. www.hotel-la-deviniere.com. 11 units. 120€–160€ ($156–$208) double. MC, V. Parking 8€ ($10). **Amenities:** Lounge. *In room:* TV.

Le Parc Victoria ★★ *Finds* The most secluded and tranquil hotel at the resort is a white 19th-century villa, saved from destruction and lovingly restored by its owner, M. Larralde. Surrounded by flowering beds and luxuriant trees, the house is furnished with antiques in keeping with its original style. The chandelier-lit salon of the main building, decorated in Napoleon III fashion, sets the tone. Guest rooms hold antiques and comfortable, tasteful Art Deco furnishings, and the marble-clad bathrooms are completely up-to-date. The restaurant's cuisine and wines are first class.

5 rue Cepé, St-Jean-de-Luz 64500. ✆ **05-59-26-78-78.** Fax 05-59-26-78-08. www.parcvictoria.com. 18 units. 160€–295€ ($208–$384) double; 260€–655€ ($338–$852) suite. AE, DC, MC, V. Free parking. Closed mid-Nov to mid-Mar. **Amenities:** Restaurant; bar; outdoor pool; babysitting; nonsmoking rooms; limited-mobility rooms. *In room:* A/C, TV, minibar, hair dryer, safe.

WHERE TO DINE

You may also like to check out L'Atlantique, the restaurant at the **Hôtel Hélianthal** (see "Where to Stay, above), or the reliable Basque food at the **Hôtel/Restaurant Lafayette,** 18 rue de la République (✆ **05-59-26-17-74**).

Auberge Kaïku ★ BASQUE On a narrow street off place Louis-XIV, Auberge Kaïku is the best restaurant in town outside the hotels. The structure, with hand-hewn beams and chiseled masonry, dates from 1540, and is said to be the oldest in town. Examples of the cuisine are roast suckling Pyrénéan lamb, *parillade* (mixed grill) of shellfish, fried calamari with pasta and garlic, John Dory with fresh mint, grilled shrimp, filet of beef with essence of truffles, and duckling in honey. A particularly succulent starter is *salade Kaïku,* garnished with pan-fried strips of foie gras and raspberry vinegar.

17 rue de la République. ✆ **05-59-26-13-20.** Reservations recommended. Main courses 18€–23€ ($23–$30); fixed-price menu 30€ ($39). MC, V. July–Aug daily 12:15–2pm and 7–10pm; Sept–June Thurs–Mon 12:15–2pm and 7–10pm.

Chez Maya (Petit Grill Basque) *Value* BASQUE This small auberge is highly acclaimed for quality and value, with specialties that include delectable fish soup and paella. Don't expect urban glitter. Things are too conservative and old-fashioned for that. The fixed-price menu is the best deal in town. The chefs cook as their grandparents did, preparing all the old favorites, such as squid cooked in its own ink and a local version of fish soup known as *morro.*

4 rue St-Jacques. ✆ **05-59-26-80-76.** Reservations recommended. Main courses 14€–19€ ($18–$25); fixed-price menu 20€–29€ ($26–$38). AE, DC, MC, V. Fri–Tues noon–2pm; Thurs–Tues 7–10pm. Closed Dec 19–Jan 25.

La Vieille Auberge BASQUE/LANDAISE This tavern specializes in seafood, and the owners claim that the fish soup is second to none. They offer a good-value fixed-price menu. The food, especially mussels *à la crème,* goes well with the *vin du pays* (local wine). A *parillade* of fish is particularly appealing.

22 rue Tourasse. ✆ **05-59-26-19-61.** Reservations required. Main courses 10€–15€ ($13–$20); fixed-price menu 15€–24€ ($20–$31). MC, V. July–Aug Wed–Mon noon–2pm, daily 7–10:30pm; Mar–June and Sept–Nov 11 daily noon–2:30pm, Thurs–Mon 7–11pm. Closed mid-Nov to Feb.

ST-JEAN-DE-LUZ AFTER DARK

You can start by taking a walk along the promenade to watch the sunset. Around **place Louis-XIV,** you'll find a hotbed of activity at the cafes and bars.

A fun spot in the center of town is **Pub du Corsaire,** 16 rue de la République (✆ **05-59-26-10-74**), for unpretentious merrymaking accompanied by copious amounts of alcohol and rock 'n' roll. For dancing to recorded music, many night owls head northeast of town along RN10 to the neighborhood known as A Côte.

20

Bordeaux & the Atlantic Coast

From La Rochelle to the Bordeaux wine district, the southwest of France is often a quick stopover for visitors driving from Paris to Spain. However, this area is noted for its Atlantic beaches, medieval and Renaissance ruins, Romanesque and Gothic churches, vineyards, and charming inns serving splendid regional cuisine.

On our journey through this intriguing region, we detour inland for some cognac in Cognac and for trips to nearby art cities such as Poitiers and Angoulême. If you can manage it, it's great to allow a week here—enough time to sample the wine, savor the cuisine, and see some of the sights.

1 Poitiers ★★

333km (207 miles) SW of Paris, 177km (110 miles) SE of Nantes

History fills this city, the ancient capital of Poitou, the northern part of Aquitaine. Everybody has passed through here—from Joan of Arc to Richard the Lion-Hearted.

Poitiers stands on a hill overlooking the Clain and Boivre rivers—a strategic location that tempted many conquerors. Charles Martel chased out the Muslims in A.D. 732 and altered the course of European civilization. Poitiers was the chief city of Eleanor of Aquitaine, who had her marriage to pious Louis VII annulled so she could wed England's Henry II.

For those interested in antiquity, this is one of the most fascinating towns in France. The Battle of Poitiers was fought on September 19, 1356, between the armies of Edward the Black Prince and King John of France. It was one of the three great English victories in the Hundred Years' War, distinguished by the use of the longbow in the skilled hands of English archers.

After decades of slumber, the town has really come alive, with the opening of **Futuroscope,** a cinema theme park. The thriving student population (28,000 of Poitiers's 85,000 residents are students) adds vitality as well.

ESSENTIALS

GETTING THERE **Rail** service is available from Paris, Bordeaux, and La Rochelle. Around 15 fast TGV trains arrive daily from Paris Gare Montparnasse (trip time: 2 hr.; one-way fare: 45€/$59). Another 17 (regular) trains arrive daily from Bordeaux (trip time: 2 hr.; one-way fare: 33€/$43), and 12 TGV from La Rochelle (trip time: 1¾ hr.; 20€/$26). For train information, call ✆ **36-35** or 08-92-35-35-35 from outside France. **Bus** service from Poitiers is so badly scheduled it's virtually nonexistent. If you're **driving,** Poitiers is located on the A10 highway; from Paris, follow A10 south through the cities of Orléans and Tours, on to Poitiers.

VISITOR INFORMATION The **Office de Tourisme** is at 45 place Charles-de-Gaulle (✆ **05-49-41-21-24;** fax 05-49-88-65-84; www.ot-poitiers.fr).

SPECIAL EVENTS The liveliest time to visit is from mid-June to mid-September during the **Poitiers l'Eté,** a festival of free live jazz, opera, rock, and fireworks. Colored lights illuminate the facade of Notre-Dame La Grande for 15 minutes every evening at 10:30pm; free concerts and theater pieces, both in and out of the streets, take place at various parks and churches around the city. Check with the tourist office for schedules.

For about 8 days in late September, during the **Concerts Allumés,** recitals feature the organs in some of the town's most important churches. Most performances are free. For information, contact the tourist office, or call ✆ **05-49-39-40-00.**

EXPLORING THE CITY

Baptistère St-Jean ★ From the cathedral, you can walk to the most ancient Christian monument in France. It was built as a baptistery in the early 4th century on Roman foundations and extended in the 7th century. It contains frescoes from the 11th to the 14th centuries and a collection of funerary sculpture.

Rue Jean-Jaurès. No phone. Admission 1€ ($1.30) adults, .50€ (65¢) children under 12. July–Aug daily 10:30am–12:30pm and 3–6pm; Sept–June Wed–Mon 10:30am–12:30pm and 3–6pm.

Cathédrale St-Pierre ★ In the eastern sector of Poitiers is the twin-towered Cathédrale St-Pierre, begun in 1162 by Henry II of England and Eleanor of Aquitaine on the ruins of a Roman basilica. The architecturally undistinguished cathedral was completed much later. The interior, 89m (292 ft.) long, contains some admirable 12th- and 13th-century stained glass.

Place de la Cathédrale. ✆ **05-49-41-23-76.** Free admission. Daily 8:30am–7:30pm (until 5:30pm in winter).

Eglise Notre-Dame-la-Grande ★★ This church, built in the Romanesque-Byzantine style and richly decorated, is from the late 11th century. See in particular its western front, dating from the mid–12th century. Surrounded by an open-air market, the facade, carved like an ivory casket, is characterized by pine cone-shaped towers. It was thoroughly cleaned and restored in 1996. Carvings on the doorway represent biblical scenes.

Place Charles-de-Gaulle. ✆ **05-49-41-22-56.** Free admission. Daily 8:30am–7pm.

Futuroscope ★★ Kids This science amusement park in a suburb of Poitiers is a wonderland of technology that lets you experience sounds, images, and sensations with the world's most advanced film-projection techniques and largest screens. Exhibitions include **Kinemax** (a rock crystal covered with mirrors with a 400-seat cinema); **Omnimax** (which projects films onto a gigantic dome with a special fisheye lens, putting you into the heart of the action); and **Le Tapis Magique,** a film that shows you what it's like to fly above the world's most impressive monuments and sites of natural beauty. Another part of the park is Océan Oasis, which leads you on an underwater exploration of a reef off the coast of Baja California.

Jaunay-Clan. From Poitiers, take N10 or A10 about 9km (5¾ miles) north. ✆ **05-49-49-50-06.** www.futuroscope.com. Admission 33€ ($43) adults, 24€ ($31) children 5–16, free for children under 5. Daily 10am–dusk. Bus: 9.

Musée Ste-Croix On the site of the old abbey of Ste-Croix, this museum has a fine-arts section devoted mainly to painting—especially 16th- and 17th-century Flemish art and 16th- to 18th-century Dutch pieces. Several works by Bonnard, Sisley, and Oudot are on display, along with a bronze sculpture, *The Three Graces,* by Maillol. A separate archaeological section documents the history of Poitou, from prehistoric

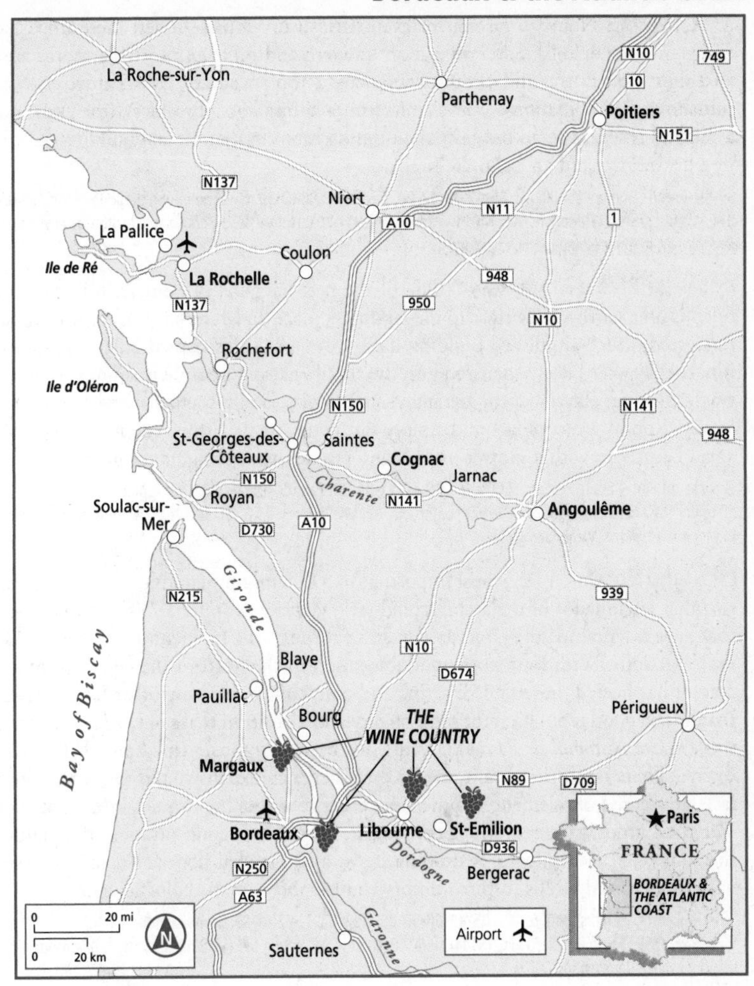

times through the Gallo-Roman era and the Renaissance, up to the end of the 19th century. Admission includes the **Musée Rupert de Chièvres,** 9 rue Victor-Hugo (same phone). You'll find a small collection of 17th- and 18th-century Italian, Flemish, and French paintings. It's in the old town of Poitiers, within a 10-minute walk of the larger and more comprehensive Musée Ste-Croix.

61 rue St. Simplicien. ✆ **05-49-41-42-21.** www.musees-poitiers.org. Admission 3.70€ ($4.80) adults, free for ages under 18. Both museums June–Sept Mon 1:15–6pm, Tues–Fri 10am–noon and 1:15–6pm, Sat–Sun 10am–noon and 2–6pm; Oct–May Mon 1:15–5pm, Tues–Fri 10am–noon and 1:15–5pm, Sat–Sun 2–6pm.

WHERE TO STAY

Hôtel de l'Europe ★ *Finds* Originally built in the 1930s, this hotel sits behind a facade of chiseled stone. The main core holds renovated high-ceilinged rooms decorated in vaguely Art Nouveau fashion or even African or Chinese styles; these units have either showers or tubs. Somewhat more modern and more comfortable rooms are in an annex built in the mid-1980s. These have a contemporary, conservative style and tub/shower combinations. Some units contain minibars. Breakfast (the only meal available) is served in an old-fashioned dining room in the original building, in front of tall windows and an elaborate fireplace.

39 rue Carnot, Poitiers 86000. ✆ **05-49-88-12-00.** Fax 05-49-88-97-30. www.hotel-europe-poitiers.com. 88 units. 56€–85€ ($73–$111) double. AE, MC, V. Parking 6€ ($7.80). **Amenities:** Room service; free Internet access. *In room:* TV, minibar (some rooms), hair dryer.

Hôtel du Plat d'Etain *Value* One of the best bargains in Poitiers, this renovated hotel is on a narrow alley close to the landmark place du Maréchal-Leclerc. The much-renovated, much-simplified building dates from 1895. It's named after the medieval inn, the "Pewter Plate," that stood on the site. (That inn became infamous for unwittingly housing Ravaillac, the deranged monk who fatally stabbed King Henri IV in 1610.) Rooms are compact and simply but comfortably furnished, and most have a small bathroom with a shower unit. Many restaurants and sights are nearby.

7–9 rue du Plat-d'Etain, Poitiers 86000. ✆ **05-49-41-04-80.** Fax 05-49-52-25-84. www.poitiers-leplatdetain.com. 20 units. 48€–66€ ($62–$86) double with bathroom. AE, MC, V. Parking 5€ ($6.50). Bus: 2A. **Amenities:** Nonsmoking rooms. *In room:* TV, minibar, Wi-Fi.

Le Grand Hotel It's the most imposing Art Deco monument in town, with an exterior that aficionados of the architectural style identify as "pure 1920s" and bedrooms that have maintained the same style in spirit through the frequent use of high-quality reproductions. With four stories and a location in the heart of the city's commercial core, it has hosted more French actors and entertainers than any other hotel in town, thanks to a good reputation for solid quality and a position that's only a few steps from the *Théâtre National de Poitiers,* a venue for both pop music and *haute* theatrics and drama. There isn't a restaurant on-site, but there's an expansive terrace, where breakfasts are served on clement summer mornings, overlooking a quiet inner courtyard. The rue Carnot, the street which contains it, has a denser concentration of restaurants than anywhere else in town. Bedrooms, depending on what floor you're on, may come with modernized 1920s-inspired decors and monochromatic color schemes.

28 rue Carnot, Poitiers 86000. ✆ **05-49-60-90-60.** Fax 05-49-62-81-89. www.grandhotelpoitiers.fr. 47 units. 76€–84€ ($99–$109) double; 111€ ($144) suite. AE, DC, MC, V. Parking 6€ ($7.80). **Amenities:** Bar; room service; laundry service/dry cleaning; Wi-Fi.

WHERE TO DINE

Maxime ★★ MODERN FRENCH Maxime is the most sophisticated restaurant in town. In a contemporary-looking dining room, Christian Rougier, the hardworking chef, offers a menu that varies with the seasons. It always includes ravioli with hot oysters and sometimes features baked back of rabbit stuffed with eggplant, mushrooms, and *fines herbes,* served with chardonnay sauce; tournedos Rossini (layered with foie gras); baby goat with green garlic; stuffed snapper with roe sauce; sautéed scallops with truffles; fried foie gras served with asparagus; and herb-laden roast rack of excellent Montmorillon lamb. Dessert may be au gratin of red berries with a champagne-based sabayon.

4 rue St-Nicolas. ✆ **05-49-41-27-37.** Reservations recommended. Main courses 18€–25€ ($23–$33); fixed-price menu 20€–71€ ($26–$92). AE, DC, MC, V. Mar–Oct Mon–Fri noon–2pm and 8–10pm; Nov–Feb also Sat 8–10:30pm. Closed July 14–Aug 15.

Poitevin *Value* FRENCH Much of Poitevin's lunch business comes from shoppers and office workers who descend on it at midday. Evening meals are less rushed. You'll have a choice of six cozy dining rooms. One room contains an 18th-century fireplace transported here from a demolished building nearby; another abounds with butterflies (on the carpets, curtains, and napery, and mounted in frames). Menu items *mouclade Charentaise* (mussels in white-wine and cream sauce); scallops with sauterne sabayon; and an unusual stewpot containing filets of eel and sole, served with lemon sauce. For dessert, try a semisoft slice of unctuously oozing chocolate cake.

76 rue Carnot. ✆ **05-49-88-35-04.** Reservations recommended. Main courses 16€–24€ ($21–$31); fixed-price menu 22€–35€ ($29–$46). AE, DC, MC, V. Daily noon–2pm; Mon–Sat 7–10pm. Closed 2 weeks at Easter, 3 weeks in late July and Aug, and 2 weeks at Christmas.

2 La Rochelle ★★★

467km (290 miles) SW of Paris, 145km (90 miles) SE of Nantes, 183km (114 miles) N of Bordeaux, 142km (88 miles) NW of Angoulême

Once known as the French Geneva, La Rochelle is a historic port and ancient sailors' city, formerly the stronghold of the Huguenots. It was founded as a fishing village in the 10th century on a rocky platform in the center of a marshland. Eleanor of Aquitaine gave La Rochelle a charter in 1199, freeing it from feudal dues. After becoming an independent city-state, the port capitalized on the wars between France and England. It was the departure point for the founders of Montreal. From the 14th to the 16th century, La Rochelle was one of France's great maritime cities. It became the principal port between France and the colony of Canada, but France's loss of Canada ruined its Atlantic trade.

As a hotbed of Protestant factions, it armed privateers to prey on Catholic vessels but was eventually besieged by Catholic troops. Two men led the fight: Cardinal Richelieu (with his Musketeers) and Jean Guiton, formerly an admiral and then mayor of the city. When Richelieu blockaded the port, La Rochelle bravely resisted, but on October 30, 1628, Richelieu entered the city. Among the 30,000 citizens of the proud city, he found only 5,000 survivors.

Today La Rochelle, a city of 140,000, is the cultural and administrative center of the Charente-Maritime *département* (mini-state). Its famous city lights have earned it the title "City of Light." While many of La Rochelle's sights are old, the city is riddled with high-rise condos and home to the largest pleasure-boat basin in Europe. In summer, the city is overrun with visitors.

ESSENTIALS

GETTING THERE The La Rochelle–Laleu **airport** (✆ **05-46-42-86-70**) is on the coast, 4km (2½ miles) north of the city. Take bus no. 7 to reach it. Rail connections from Bordeaux and Nantes are frequent. Six to eight **trains** from Bordeaux and Nantes arrive daily (trip time: 2 hr.; one-way fare: 23€/$30). There are five daily fast TGV trains from Paris's Gare Montparnasse (trip time: 3 hr.); the one-way fare is 60€ ($78). For train information, call ✆ **36-35** or 08-92-35-35-35 from outside France. **Buses** serve the Gare Routière, place de Verdun (✆ **05-46-00-95-15** for information). If you're **driving** to La Rochelle, follow A10 south from Poitiers to exit NIORT/ST-MAIXENT, and then take N11 west to the coast and La Rochelle.

VISITOR INFORMATION The **Office de Tourisme** is on place de la Petite-Sirène, Le Gabut (✆ **05-46-41-14-68;** fax 05-46-41-99-85; www.larochelle-tourisme.com).

SPECIAL EVENTS The busiest month is July; the **Festival International du Film de La Rochelle** rolls in at the beginning of the month. It attracts a huge following of fans, press, actors, directors, and, of course, paparazzi. Screenings are held around town; a pass for 10 screenings costs 45€ ($59). For information, contact the festival office in the Maison de la Culture, rue St-Jean de Perot (✆ **05-46-51-54-00** or 01-48-06-16-66; www.festival-larochelle.org). For a week in mid-July, the music festival **Les Francofolies** features big names as well as not-so-famous groups, most of them international pop musicians. The town is overrun with groupies and fans, and a party atmosphere prevails. Tickets range from 20€ to 30€ ($26–$39). Call ✆ **05-46-28-28-28** for details (www.francofolies.fr). The Office de Tourisme can also provide details on both festivals.

La Rochelle is also the site of the biggest showcase of boats and yachts in Europe, **Le Grand Pavois Salon Nautique.** It's a 5-day extravaganza in late September. The action is based in and around La Rochelle's Port de Plaisance (better known as the Bassin des Yachts, or Yacht Basin). Sellers and buyers of boats and marine hardware, as well as weekend sailors from everywhere, usually attend. For information about dates and venues, call ✆ **05-46-44-46-39** (www.grand-pavois.com).

EXPLORING THE CITY

There are two sides to La Rochelle: the old and unspoiled town inside the Vauban defenses, and the tacky modern and industrial suburbs. Its **fortifications** have a circuit of 5.5km (3⅓ miles) with a total of seven gates.

The town, with its arch-covered streets, is great for strolling. The port is a fishing harbor and one of Europe's major sailing centers. Try to schedule a visit in time to attend a fish auction. The best streets for strolling, each with a 17th-century arcade, are **rue du Palais, la Rue du Temple, rue Chaudrier,** and **rue des Merciers,** with its ancient wooden houses (seek out the ones at nos. 3, 5, 8, and 17).

Aquarium de La Rochelle ★ La Rochelle's blockbuster crowd pleaser rises from a portside position near the Port des Minimes, north of the old city. Inside are guided walkways stretching over two floors of massive and bubbling seawater tanks loaded with approximately 10,000 species of flora and fauna from the oceans of the world, living in what look like natural habitats. It's hard to miss this place: There are signs for it all over town.

Bassin des Grands Yachts, B.P. 4, Le Vieux Port. ✆ **05-46-34-00-00.** www.aquarium-larochelle.com. 13€ ($17) adults, 9.50€ ($12) students and children 3–17, free for children under 3. Use of English-language audio guide 3.50€ ($4.55). July–Aug daily 9am–11pm; Apr–June and Sept daily 9am–8pm; Oct–Mar daily 10am–8pm. Bus: 10.

Hôtel de Ville (City Hall) ★ The town's 14th-century showcase is built in Flamboyant Gothic style, with battlements. Inside you can admire the Henry II staircase with canopies and the marble desk of the heroic Jean Guiton. You must visit as part of a guided tour (in French only); advance reservations are not necessary.

Place de la Mairie, in the city center. ✆ **05-46-51-51-51.** Admission 4€ ($5.20) adults, 1.50€ ($1.95) students and children 4–18, free for children under 4. Guided tours July–Aug daily 3 and 4pm; June and Sept daily 3pm; Oct–May Sat–Sun 3pm (and some holidays at 3 and 4pm).

Musée des Beaux-Arts ★ The museum is in an Episcopal palace built in the mid–18th century. The art spans the 15th to the 19th centuries, with works by Eustache Le Sueur, Brossard de Beaulieu, Corot, and Fromentin. Twentieth-century pieces include works by Maillol and Léger.

28 rue Gargoulleau. ✆ **05-46-34-76-55.** http://perso.wanadoo.fr/musees-la-rochelle/b-arts. Admission 3.50€ ($4.55) adults, free for children under 18. Oct–Mar Mon and Wed–Fri 1:30–5pm, Sat–Sun and holidays 2:30–6pm; Apr–Sept Wed–Sat 2–6pm, Sun and bank holidays 2:30–6pm.

Musée du Nouveau-Monde ★ In an 18th-century town house rich with architectural details, this is one of the most intriguing museums in La Rochelle. It's rich with evidence of the city's prominent role in the colonization of Canada. The displays trace the port's 300-year history with the New World. Exhibits start with LaSalle's discovery of the Mississippi Delta in 1682 and end with the settling of the Louisiana territory. Other exhibits depict French settlements in the West Indies, including Guadeloupe and Martinique.

In the Hôtel Fleuriau, 10 rue Fleuriau. ✆ **05-46-41-46-50.** http://perso.wanadoo.fr/musees-la-rochelle/n-monde. Admission 4€ ($5.20) adults, free for children under 18. Oct–Mar Mon and Wed–Fri 9:30am–12:30pm and 1:30–5pm, Sat–Sun 2:30–6pm; Apr–Sept Mon and Wed–Sat 10am–12:30pm and 2–6pm, Sun 2–6pm.

Musée Orbigny-Bernon ★ The most important artifacts pertaining to the history of ceramics and of La Rochelle are in this collection, which includes painted porcelain. Established in 1917, the museum also houses a superb collection of Far Eastern art. The exhibits and photographs of La Rochelle in World War II are especially fascinating.

2 rue St-Côme. ✆ **05-46-41-18-83.** Admission 3.50€ ($4.55) adults, free for children under 18. Oct–Mar Mon and Wed–Sat 9:30am–12:30pm and 1:30–5pm, Sun 2:30–6pm; Apr–Sept Mon and Wed–Sat 9:30am–12:30pm and 2–6pm, Sun and holidays 2–6pm.

Tour de la Chaîne During the 1300s, this tower was built as an anchor piece for the large forged-iron chain that stretched across the harbor, closing it against hostile warships. The unusual exhibits focus on the history of medieval naval warfare.

Quai du Gabut. ✆ **05-46-41-74-13.** Admission 5€ ($6.50) adults, 3.50€ ($4.55) students and ages 18–25, free for children under 18. Tues–Sun 10am–12:30pm and 2–5:30pm.

Tour de la Lanterne ★ Built between 1445 and 1476, this was once a lighthouse but was used mainly as a jail as late as the 19th century. A low rampart connects the cylindrical tower to the Tour de la Chaîne. During the Wars of Religion, 13 priests were tossed from its summit. You climb 162 steps to the top hold; in clear weather, the panoramic view extends all the way to Ile d'Oléron. On the way up, you can still see graffiti scrawled by former prisoners.

Opposite Tour St-Nicolas, quai du Gabut. ✆ **05-46-41-56-04.** Admission 5€ ($6.50) adults, 3.50€ ($4.55) students and ages 18–25, free for children under 18. Tues–Sun 10am–12:30pm and 2–5:30pm.

Tour St-Nicolas ★ The oldest tower in La Rochelle, Tour St-Nicolas was built between 1371 and 1382. It originally guarded the town against surprise attacks. From its second floor you can enjoy a view of the town and harbor; from the top you can see only the old town and Ile d'Oléron.

Quai du Gabut. ✆ **05-46-41-74-13.** Admission 4.60€ ($6) adults, 3.10€ ($4.05) students and ages 18–25, free for children under 18. Tues–Sun 10am–12:30pm and 2–5:30pm.

Value Money-Saving Museum Pass

You can buy a **combination ticket** good for entrance to the Musée des Beaux-Arts, Musée Orbigny-Bernon, and Musée du Nouveau-Monde. Available at any of the museums and the tourist office, it costs 6.70€ ($8.70), a savings of 3.80€ ($4.95).

WHERE TO STAY

France-Angleterre et Champlain ★★ Close to the major parks and the old port, this is the most gracious choice in La Rochelle. It was formed by uniting two smaller hotels many years ago. It's furnished with a winning combination of antiques and art objects and has a genial staff. Rooms are tasteful and dignified; many have a nautical theme. The midsize bathrooms hold tubs or showers. One of the best aspects of the hotel is its romantic garden, brimming with flowers, shrubbery, and shade trees. Breakfast is the only meal served.

20 rue Rambaud, La Rochelle 17000. ✆ **800/528-1234** in the U.S. and Canada, or 05-46-41-23-99. Fax 05-46-41-15-19. www.france-champlain.com. 36 units. 60€–115€ ($78–$150) double; 110€–145€ ($143–$189) suite. AE, DC, MC, V. Parking 8€ ($10). **Amenities:** Room service; nonsmoking rooms. *In room:* A/C, TV, minibar, hair dryer, iron, beverage maker, Wi-Fi.

Les Brises ★ *Value* This nautically decorated seaside hotel opposite the Port des Minimes, 1.5km (1 mile) north of the old city, offers a view of a soaring 19th-century column dedicated to the Virgin. You can enjoy the view from the front balconies of the six-story building as well as the parasol-shaded patio. The immaculate rooms have cherrywood furniture, comfortable beds, and compact, neatly organized bathrooms with shower units. Breakfast is the only meal served.

Chemin de la Digue de Richelieu, La Rochelle 17000. ✆ **05-46-43-89-37.** Fax 05-46-43-27-97. www.hotellesbrises.com. 48 units. 62€–119€ ($81–$155) double. AE, DC, MC, V. Free parking. **Amenities:** Room service; laundry service; limited-mobility rooms. *In room:* A/C, TV, minibar, hair dryer, safe, Wi-Fi.

WHERE TO DINE

Bar/Bistro André *Value* SEAFOOD Seafood is an expensive item anywhere in France, but usually it's worth it. Here you can get a big meal even by choosing something from the lower end of the price scale. Traditional menu items include savory versions of fish soup; all kinds of shellfish; an unusual version of *cabillaud fumé* (home-smoked codfish) served with garlic-flavored cream sauce; curried mussels *(mouclade);* and a saltwater fish not very common in other parts of France, filet of *maîgre,* served with chive-flavored cream sauce. The restaurant is between the square overlooking the port and one of the oldest streets in town.

5 rue St-Jean/place de la Chaîne. ✆ **05-46-41-28-24.** www.bar-andre.com. Reservations recommended. Main courses 16€–29€ ($21–$38). AE, DC, MC, V. Daily noon–2:30pm and 7–10:30pm.

Comptoir des Voyages *Value* FRENCH/INTERNATIONAL This restaurant in the old town has a cost-conscious, lighthearted format that celebrates the cuisines of most of France's neighbors, the former colonies, and France itself. Surrounded by hardwood paneling and big windows, you'll have a choice of six starters, eight main courses, and six desserts. The frequently changing menu may include Martinique-style codfish fritters, lamb chops dredged in Indian spices, and buckwheat crepes stuffed with poached pears and Breton-style liqueur. Almost all the wines are from outside France.

22 rue St-Jean du Pérot. ✆ **05-46-50-62-60.** Reservations recommended. Main courses all 15€ ($20); fixed-price menu 28€ ($36). AE, DC, MC, V. Daily 12:15–2pm and 7:15–10:15pm.

Richard Coutanceau ★★★ MODERN FRENCH This is not only the most glamorous and prestigious restaurant in La Rochelle, but also one of the finest along the coast. Delectable cuisine is served in a circular concrete pavilion in a pine-filled park, with big bay windows overlooking the sea. Clearly an artist, Richard Coutanceau,

Finds Sailing the Ports of La Rochelle

La Rochelle has always earned its living from the sea and from the ships that make its harbor their home. Four distinct harbors have grown up over the centuries, each a world unto itself, rich with local nuance and lore. They include the historic **Vieux-Port,** the **Port de Plaisance** (a modern yacht marina), the **Port de Pêche** (the fishing port), and the **Port de Commerce,** which is mostly used by large container ships.

The best way to appreciate them is to visit the tourist office (see "Essentials," above), which acts as a clearinghouse for the outfitters (Croisières Inter-Iles, Navipromer, Cap à l'Ouest, and Ré Croisières) that offer tours of the harbors. Tours combine a look at the modern facilities of one of France's largest ports with a waterside view of the historic ramparts—which, despite their girth and height, did not protect the city's 18th-century Protestants from starvation and eventual annihilation.

The company with the most frequent departures is the **Croisières Inter-Iles** (✆ **08-25-13-55-00;** www.inter-iles.com). Every day from April to October, there are about a half-dozen cruises into each of the six ports. In winter, they're offered less frequently, usually only on school vacations. Tours last 70 to 180 minutes each, are conducted in French, and cost 15€ to 24€ ($20–$31) each.

Another waterborne option—but only during July and August—involves taking a ferry from the Vieux-Port of La Rochelle to Ile de Ré. The island, 26km (16 miles) off the coast of La Rochelle and ringed with 69km (43 miles) of sandy beaches, holds nature preserves crisscrossed with bike and hiking paths. Croisières Inter-Iles (see above) serves the island. If you want to get here during July or August, and if you don't have a car, we recommend taking the ferry for a round-trip fare of 19€ ($25).

You can also drive your car across the bridge that connects the Ile de Ré to the French mainland. It's accessible from a point 3km (13/4 miles) south of La Rochelle. The toll is 15€ ($20) in summer, 9€ ($12) in winter. The local bus company, **Cie. Aunis Saintonges** (✆ **05-46-09-20-15;** www.aunis-saintonge.fr), charges 2.90€ to 8€ ($3.75–$10) each way for the trip from La Rochelle to several stops along the island, with departures several times a day year-round.

the owner and genius chef, prepares "modernized" cuisine. For an appetizer, two of the most famous starters in France are combined—frogs' legs and snails roasted in parsley and garlic and served with truffle-laced creamy potatoes. The signature fish dish is line-caught sea bass cooked within its own crusty skin and served with stewed tomatoes and chorizo. Among the meat dishes, we prefer the roasted pigeon kabob with asparagus and tomato jelly, made even more alluring with truffles and a slightly bitter Choron sauce.

Plage de la Concurrence. ✆ **05-46-41-48-19.** Reservations required. Main courses 35€–52€ ($46–$68); fixed-price menu 48€–90€ ($62–$117). AE, DC, MC, V. Mon–Sat noon–2pm and 7:30–9:30pm.

LA ROCHELLE AFTER DARK

From July to September, head for **quai Duperré, cours des Dames,** and **cours des Templiers.** Once the sun starts to set, this becomes one big pedestrian zone peppered with street performers. It's a fun, almost magical area that sets the tone for the rest of the night.

3 Cognac

478km (297 miles) SW of Paris, 37km (23 miles) NW of Angoulême, 113km (70 miles) SE of La Rochelle

The world enjoys 100 million bottles a year of the nectar known as cognac, which Victor Hugo called "the drink of the gods." It's worth a detour to visit one of the château warehouses of the great bottlers. Martell, Hennessy, and Otard welcome visits from the public and even give you a free drink at the end of the tour.

ESSENTIALS

GETTING THERE Cognac's rail station is just south of the town center. Five **trains** per day arrive from Angoulême (trip time: 40 min.), and six trains pull in from Saintes (trip time: 20 min.). For train information and schedules, call © **36-35** or 08-92-35-35-35 from outside France. **Bus** travel is scarce in this part of France. For information, contact La Gare Routière (© **05-45-82-01-99**), next to the railway station. If you're **driving** to Cognac, the best route from Saintes (which lies along the major route A10) is N141 east.

VISITOR INFORMATION The **Office de Tourisme** is at 16 rue du 14-Juillet (© **05-45-82-10-71;** fax 05-45-82-34-47; www.tourism-cognac.com).

SPECIAL EVENTS Cognac grapes are among the last picked in France. Harvest time usually begins in mid-October.

The **Festival du Film Policier** (© **05-45-35-60-00;** www.festival.cognac.fr) runs for 4 days from June 20 to June 24. Screenings of crime films take place in the town's largest theater, **Théâtre de Cognac,** 1 place Robert-Schuman. The emphasis is on action and police films, with macho special effects. Entry to a single screening costs 6€ ($7.80).

EXPLORING THE TOWN

Many visitors don't realize that this unassuming town of some 22,000 people is actually a community and not just a drink. Cognac may be beautiful to drink, but it's not beautiful to make. A black fungus that lives on the vapors released by the cognac factories has turned the town's buildings an ugly gray. But while the fumes discolor the houses, they also fill the air with a sweetness.

If you'd like to visit a distillery, go to its main office during regular business hours and request a tour, or visit the tourist office for assistance. On a tour, you'll see some brandies that have aged for as long as 50 or even 100 years. You can have a free taste and then purchase a bottle or two. As far as we're concerned, **Otard** offers the most informative and insightful tours, partly because of the sheer majesty of its headquarters, in the late-medieval **Château de Cognac,** 127 bd. Denfert-Rochereau (© **05-45-36-88-88;** www.otard.com). The tour is half historical overview of the castle, half a technical explanation of cognac production. Parts of the château are appropriately baronial (King François 1er was born here), and enormous other sections hold tens of thousands of bottles of cognac. Tours last about 1 hour and cost 6.50€ ($8.45) for adults, 3.50€ ($4.55) for students 12 to 18; free for children under 12. Tours are scheduled April to June and September to October daily 11am to noon and 2 to 6pm; July to August Sunday and public holidays 11am to noon and 1:30 to 7pm; November to December Monday to Thursday 11am to 2:30pm and 3:45 to 5pm, and Friday 11am to 4pm; January to March by appointment only. Call the tourist office or the company several days in advance to check times, which rotate according to the number of visitors and availability of guides. The château lies within a 10-minute walk from the town center near the Hôtel de Ville (city hall).

Other distilleries that offer tours are **Hennessy,** 1 quai Hennessy (© **05-45-35-72-68;** www.hennessy.com); **Camus,** 29 rue Marguerite-de-Navarre (© **05-45-32-28-28;** www.camus.fr); **Martell,** place Edouard-Martell (© **05-45-36-33-33;** www.martell.com); and **Rémy-Martin,** domaine de Merpins, route de Pons (© **05-45-35-76-66;** www.remy.com). In winter, call in advance to see whether it's possible to arrange a tour.

If you're short on time, a good retail outlet is **La Cognathèque,** 8 place Jean-Monnet (© **05-45-82-43-31**), which prides itself on having the widest selection from all the distilleries, though you'll pay for the convenience of having everything under one roof.

The collections of the **Musée de Cognac,** 48 bd. Denfert-Rochereau (© **05-45-32-07-25**), include exhibits on popular arts and traditions, archaeological exhibits, and a fine-art collection (painting, sculpture, decorative arts, and furniture). An annex is devoted to the cultivation of the vines that contribute to the final product. Open November to March Wednesday to Monday 2 to 5:30pm, April to June and September to October Wednesday to Monday 11am to 6pm. In July and August it's open daily 10am to 6:30pm. The Annex has the same hours, but is closed on Mondays and open on Tuesdays. Admission is 4.50€ ($5.85) for adults, 3€ ($3.90) for students, and free for ages 17 and under.

Cognac has two beautiful parks: the **Parc François-1er** and the **Parc de l'Hôtel-de-Ville.** The Romanesque-Gothic **Eglise St-Léger,** rue de Monseigneur LaCroix (© **05-45-82-05-71**), is from the 12th century, and its bell tower is from the 15th. Admission is free; it's open daily from 8am to 7pm.

WHERE TO STAY

Domaine du Breuil ★★ This tranquil 18th-century manor house, studded with magnificent windows, is in a 7.2-hectare (18-acre) landscaped park 2 minutes from the center of Cognac. Rooms are simple but well furnished and well maintained; each compact bathroom has a combination tub/shower. Cognac aficionados and those in town to do business with the factories head here for the hospitality, the well-appointed rooms, and the excellent cuisine from the southwest of France. The food is reason enough to visit, and, naturally, you'll finish your meal with a cognac in the bar to aid digestion.

104 rue Robert-Daugas, Cognac 16100. © **05-45-35-32-06.** Fax 05-45-35-14-15. www.hotel-domaine-du-breuil.com. 24 units. 60€–97€ ($78–$126) double. AE, MC, V. Free parking. Closed Dec 23–Jan 9. **Amenities:** Restaurant; bar; outdoor pool; room service; laundry service. *In room:* TV, minibar (in some), hair dryer, safe (in some).

Hostellerie Les Pigeons Blancs ★ This stylish hotel is named after the white pigeons that nest in its moss-covered stone walls. The angular farmhouse with sloping tile roofs was built in the 17th century as a coaching inn. For many years, it was the home of the Tachet family, who transformed it into a hotel and restaurant in 1973.

It's 1.5km (1 mile) northwest of the town center and offers elegant guest rooms outfitted in styles that range from Louis XV to Directoire. The midsize-to-spacious rooms are comfortably furnished, and each average-size bathroom has a combination tub/shower. The restaurant serves modern French cuisine and is reviewed below.

110 rue Jules-Brisson, Cognac 16100. ✆ **05-45-82-16-36.** Fax 05-45-82-29-29. www.pigeons-blancs.com. 7 units. 55€–105€ ($72–$137) double. AE, MC, V. Free parking. **Amenities:** Restaurant; business center; room service; laundry service. *In room:* TV, hair dryer.

WHERE TO DINE

The restaurant at **Domaine du Breuil** (see "Where to Stay," above) serves worthwhile meals.

Hostellerie Les Pigeons Blancs ★★ MODERN FRENCH This restaurant, run by the Tachet family, has two elegant dining rooms with exposed ceiling beams and limestone fireplaces. Menu offerings depend on the availability of ingredients, but may include warm oysters with mushrooms and champagne-flavored cream sauce, lobster with champagne sauce and bay leaves, slices of warm gooseliver with pears and white wine, and particularly succulent duck steak with warm mandarin oranges and caramelized vinegar. The charming chef, Jacques Tachet, uses cognac vapors to steam many of his raw ingredients, including excellent line-caught sea bass with spices. There's also superb filet of French beef with spices, cognac, and crème fraîche; and rack of lamb with freshly grated truffles.

110 rue Jules-Brisson. ✆ **05-45-82-16-36.** Reservations recommended. Main courses 25€–32€ ($33–$42); fixed-price lunch 22€–59€ ($29–$77); fixed-price dinner 32€–59€ ($42–$77). AE, MC, V. Tues–Sun noon–2pm; Mon–Sat 7–10pm.

WHERE TO STAY & DINE NEARBY

Moulin de Cierzac ★ *Finds* This 19th-century former mill house sits beside a flowing stream at the southern periphery of a village (St-Fort-sur-le-Né) 13km (8 miles) south of Cognac. Loaded with character and charm, owner-chef Georges Renault's property is best known as a superb restaurant. Many diners do opt to spend the night, particularly after a wine-and-cognac-soaked dinner. The cuisine makes abundant use of local products, especially foie gras, vegetables, nuts, berries, lamb, and cognac. Come for dishes that include slow-cooked foie gras marinated in a mixture of cognac, sauterne, and white port, wrapped in a napkin *("au torchon")*, and poached and half-cooked in boiling water. Also appealing are slow-cooked pork-based pâté flavored with cognac; pikeperch served with a compote of cabbage; and apple crumble.

The seven quaint, charmingly decorated guest rooms overlook a park that's traversed by a stream. They have big ceiling beams and TVs; the flowery decor evokes a British country house. The double rate is 50€ to 78€ ($65–$101).

Rte. de Barbezieux, St-Fort-sur-le-Né 16130. From Cognac, drive 13km (8 miles) south of town, following the signs for Bordeaux and Barbezieux. ✆ **05-45-83-01-32.** Fax 05-45-83-03-59. www.moulindecierzac.com. Reservations recommended. Main courses 16€–34€ ($21–$44); fixed-price lunch 16€–56€ ($21–$73); fixed-price dinner 28€–56€ ($36–$73). AE, MC, V. June–Sept Tues–Sun noon–2pm, daily 7–9pm; Oct–May Tues–Sun noon–2pm, Tues–Sat 7–9pm. Closed mid-Nov to Dec 3.

4 Angoulême ★★

443km (275 miles) SW of Paris, 116km (72 miles) NE of Bordeaux

The old town of Angoulême hugs a hilltop between the Charente and Aguienne rivers. You can visit it on the same day you visit Cognac. The town was the center of the

French paper industry in the 17th century, a tradition that carries on today: Angoulême (pop. 46,000) remains the center of French comic-strip production. Rolling off the presses are the latest adventures of Tintin, Astérix, and Lucky Luke. During 3 days in January, Angoulême is the site of the **Festival de la Bande Dessinée (Festival of Cartoons),** the centerpiece of which is the **Centre National de la Bande Dessinée et de l'Image (CNBDI);** see "Exploring the Town," below. During its run, cartoon artists from around the world gather to present examples of their work and lecture about their art. For more information, contact the festival (✆ **05-45-97-86-50;** www.bdangouleme.com), CNBDI (✆ **05-45-38-65-65;** www.cnbdi.fr), or the tourist office (see below).

ESSENTIALS

GETTING THERE There are 12 regular **trains** (trip time: 1½ hr.) and 8 to 10 TGV trains (55 min.) every day from Bordeaux; the one-way fare is 22€ ($29). There are also 10 trains daily from Saintes (trip time: 1 hr.) and another five from Poitiers (trip time: 45 min.). From Paris's Montparnasse Station, there are seven TGV trains daily (trip time: 3 hr.); the one-way fare is 60€ ($78). For train information and schedules, call ✆ **36-35** or 08-92-35-35-35 from outside France. **Citram,** place du Champ de Mars, Angoulême (✆ **05-45-95-95-99;** www.citram.fr), runs eight **buses** per day between Cognac and Angoulême. The trip takes 1 hour and costs 7€ ($9.10) each way. If you're **driving** from Bordeaux, take N10 northeast to Angoulême.

VISITOR INFORMATION The **Office de Tourisme** is at place des Halles (✆ **05-45-95-16-84;** fax 05.45-95-91-76; www.angouleme.fr).

EXPLORING THE TOWN

The hub of the town is **place de l'Hôtel-de-Ville.** The town hall was erected from 1858 to 1866 on the site of the palace of the ducs d'Angoulême, where Marguerite de Navarre, sister of François I, was born. All that remains of the palace are the 15th-century Tour de Valois and 13th-century Tour de Lusignan.

Cathédrale St-Pierre ★, 4 place St-Pierre (✆ **05-45-95-44-83**), was begun in 1128 and restored in the 19th century. Flanked by towers, its facade boasts 75 statues, each in a separate niche, representing the Last Judgment. This is one of France's most startling examples of Romanesque-Byzantine style. The 19th-century architect Abadie (designer of Sacré-Coeur in Paris) tore down the north tower and then rebuilt it with the original materials in the same style. In the interior you can wander under a four-domed ceiling. It's open Monday to Saturday 9am to 7pm, Sunday 10am to 6:30pm.

Angoulême is the European capital of the cartoon industry, with strong historical and creative links to many of the pop-art and cartoon themes that are part of the French cultural experience. The art form's focal point is the **Centre National de la Bande Dessinée et de l'Image,** 121 rue de Bordeaux (✆ **05-45-38-65-65;** www.cnbdi.fr), which has a museum devoted to famous (and usually original) cartoons and their creation, a cafe, a library, a bookshop, and creative people who come here for insights into the entertainment industry. It's open in July and August Monday to Friday 10am to 7pm and Saturday and Sunday 2 to 7pm; September through June Tuesday through Friday 10am to 6pm, Saturday and Sunday 2 to 6pm. Entrance costs 5€ ($6.50) for adults, 3.50€ ($4.55) for students and children 7 to 18, and is free for children under 7.

Finally, you can walk along the panoramic **promenade des Remparts** ★, a path that flanks the site of the long-gone fortifications that once surrounded the historic core of Angoulême. The most appealing section of the 3km (1¾-mile) walkway is the 1km (⅗-mile) section that connects the cathedral with Les Halles (the covered market). Views from here stretch over the hills that flank the River Charente almost 75m (246 ft.) below.

WHERE TO STAY

Mercure Hôtel de France ★★ This 19th-century grand hotel stands in the center of the old town on extensive grounds. Rooms are generally spacious, with high ceilings and French Provincial furnishings; each comes with a fair-size bathroom. Beds are comfortably firm. A formal restaurant offers excellent food and polite service. Specialties include foie gras, sole meunière, and trout with almonds. Lunch is served Monday to Friday; dinner is offered nightly.

1 place des Halles, Angoulême 16000. ✆ **05-45-95-47-95.** Fax 05-45-92-02-70. www.mercure.com. 89 units. 103€–135€ ($134–$176) double. AE, DC, MC, V. Parking 8€ ($10). **Amenities:** Restaurant; bar; business services; room service; babysitting; laundry service; nonsmoking rooms; limited-mobility rooms. *In room:* A/C, TV, minibar, hair dryer, Wi-Fi (in some).

WHERE TO DINE

Mercure Hôtel de France (see "Where to Stay," above) serves first-rate cuisine.

La Cité FRENCH Set at the northern edge of Angoulême's medieval core, within a neighborhood devoted to the city's bureaucratic civic administration, this small and intimate restaurant is pleasantly outfitted in tones of terra cotta and pale green, offset with white napery and a hardworking staff. The best menu items include foie gras with apples; sautéed crayfish tails; and an enduring house specialty, a brochette of seafood, where crayfish, scallops, and mussels are spit-roasted and served with a creamy garlic sauce. Most of the menu is devoted to fish, but there are a handful of meat dishes on the menu, including beefsteak and magret of duckling with orange sauce.

28 rue St-Roch. ✆ **05-45-92-42-69.** Reservations recommended. Main courses 12€–15€ ($16–$20); fixed-price menus 16€–26€ ($21–$34). AE, MC, V. Tues–Sat noon–2:30pm and 7:30–9:30pm.

La Ruelle ★★ FRENCH This first-class restaurant, in the oldest part of town, is Angoulême's best. Christophe Combeau and his wife, Virginie, are the only shining lights in a dim culinary scene. Count on classic French recipes with a modern twist. The best specialties include ravioli stuffed with confit of duckling, served with vegetable bouillon with herbs; oysters in puff pastry in red-wine sauce; filet of fried red snapper with polenta and star-fruit sauce; shoulder of lamb cooked with herbs and baby vegetables; and semisoft warm chocolate cake served with coffee liqueur and essence of oranges. The space was originally part of a pair of houses separated by a narrow alleyway *(une ruelle).* Vestiges of the 17th-century structure are visible in the dining room's stonemasonry and painted ceiling beams.

6 rue Trois-Notre-Dame. ✆ **05-45-95-15-19.** www.laruelle.fr. Reservations recommended. Main courses 22€–28€ ($29–$36); fixed-price lunch 22€–53€ ($29–$69); fixed-price dinner 31€–53€ ($40–$69). AE, DC, MC, V. Tues–Sat noon–2pm and 7:30–10pm. Closed Jan–Feb and 2 weeks in Aug.

WHERE TO STAY & DINE NEARBY

Le Moulin du Maine-Brun ★★ Originally a flour mill, this Relais du Silence property (part of a chain noted for its tranquillity) is the premier place to stay and dine in this area. It's surrounded by 32 hectares (79 acres) of lowlands (including a garden, a creek, and open fields), about half of which are devoted to the production of cognac.

The maître d'hôtel's preferred brand is the one made nearby, Moulin du Domaine de Maine-Brun. These are the most luxurious accommodations around, larger than the lodgings at many competitors; each has a terrace. Rooms are individually decorated with 18th- and 19th-century French furniture. The restaurant serves splendid fare. Specialties include terrine of foie gras with cognac, and Porée charentaise, a combination of fish in a creamy Pineau wine sauce. Main courses range from 30€ to 40€ ($39–$52).

RN 141, Lieu-Dit la Vigerie, Asnières-sur-Nouère 16290. Take RN 141 7km (41/3 miles) west of Angoulême and turn right at Vigerie. ✆ **05-45-90-83-00.** Fax 05-45-96-91-14. www.hotel-maine-brun.com. 20 units. 115€–125€ ($150–$163) double; 165€ ($215) suite. AE, DC, MC, V. Hotel and restaurant closed Nov–Apr. **Amenities:** Restaurant; bar; outdoor pool; room service; laundry service. *In room:* TV, minibar, hair dryer.

5 Bordeaux ★★★

578km (359 miles) SW of Paris, 549km (341 miles) W of Lyon

On the Garonne River, the port of Bordeaux, the capital of Aquitaine, is one of the world's most important wine-producing areas. It attracts visitors to the offices of wine exporters, most of whom welcome guests. (For details of a trip through the Bordeaux wine country, see "The Wine Country," later this chapter.)

It may not exude the *joie de vivre* of Paris, but Bordeaux is a major cultural center and a transportation hub between southern France and Spain. Bordeaux is a city of warehouses, factories, mansions, suburbs, and wide quays 8km (5 miles) long. Now the fifth-largest city in France, Bordeaux belonged to the British for 300 years and even today is considered the most "un-French" of French cities.

With a population of some 650,000, much of greater Bordeaux looks seedy, but some urban-renewal projects are in the works. The early 21st century will not be the most scenic time to visit Bordeaux. The streets are mangled, thanks to the construction of a new network of aboveground trams, scheduled for completion in stages before 2009, and scaffolding covers many of the city's 18th- and 19th-century buildings. But all of this is leading to a welcome transformation of the city's historic core into one of the great urban aesthetic triumphs of western France.

ESSENTIALS

GETTING THERE The local **airport,** Bordeaux–Mérignac (✆ **05-56-34-50-50** for flight information), is served by flights from as far away as London, Dublin, Madrid, and Barcelona. It's 15km (9⅓ miles) west of Bordeaux in Mérignac. Paris is an hour's flight away. A **shuttle bus** connects the airport with the train station, departing every 45 minutes from 7:45am to 10:45pm (trip time: 40 min.) and costing 7€ ($9.10) one-way. Children ride free. A taxi (✆ **05-56-97-11-27**) between the airport and the rail depot costs about 40€ ($52).

The railway station, Gare St-Jean, is on the west bank of the river, within a 30-minute walk (or 5-min. taxi ride) of the center of the old town. Some 15 to 25 **trains** from Paris's Gare Montparnasse (trip time: 3 hr. by TGV) arrive each day. They stop, en route, at Paris Charles de Gaulle airport to pick up additional passengers. The one-way fare is 77€ ($100). For train information and schedules, call ✆ **36-35** or 08-92-35-35-35 from outside France.

Bordeaux is easy to reach by **car.** From Paris, follow A10 south through Orléans, Tours, and Poitiers into Bordeaux (trip time: about 5 hr.). Be aware that the streets of Bordeaux are fraught with hazards: narrow 18th-century alleys, massive traffic jams on the quays beside the Garonne, and simply too many cars and people. Easily available parking within the city's historic core is scarce. Whenever possible, head for one of the blue-and-white P signs that indicate public garages.

VISITOR INFORMATION The **Office de Tourisme** is at 12 cours du 30-Juillet (✆ **05-56-00-66-00;** fax 05-56-00-66-01; www.bordeaux-tourisme.com), with a branch office in the Gare St-Jean (✆ **05-56-91-64-70**).

EXPLORING BORDEAUX

Wine exporters welcome guests to sample wines and learn about the industry. In section 6, "The Wine Country," later in this chapter, we suggest a tour of the region. Plan your trip with maps, guides, and advice about local wines, available free from the **Maison du Vin (House of Wine),** 1 cours du 30-Juillet (✆ **05-56-00-22-88;** www.vins-bordeaux.fr), opposite the tourist office. To make the rounds of the vineyards, consider alternative forms of transport: bus, bicycle, or even walking.

STROLLS THROUGH TOWN The prettiest, most interesting, and most historic neighborhood in Old Bordeaux is the "golden triangle," defined by cours Clemenceau, cours de l'Intendance, and les allées de Tourny. You can traipse around the old town on your own, because it's fairly compact, or take advantage of the 2-hour **walking tour** the tourist office (see above) arranges daily at 10am (year-round) and 3pm (mid-July to mid-Aug only). Conducted in both French and English, tours take in all the most important sites and begin at the tourist office. Cost is 7.50€ ($9.75) for adults, 6.50€ ($8.45) for students, 5€ ($6.50) for children 13 to 18, and free for children under 13. We strongly recommend the tours, which correspond to the opening hours of each of the monuments listed below. Reserve in advance and call to confirm. Additionally, from April 15 to November 15, every Wednesday and Saturday at 10am, a bus tour (7.50€/$9.75) with French and English commentary departs from in front of the tourist office. The 2-hour tour includes 30 minutes of walking through narrow alleyways.

If you go it alone, your tour of Old Bordeaux can begin in the heart of this old city at **place de la Comédie,** a busy traffic hub that was once the site of a Roman temple. On this square, one of France's great theaters, **Grand Théâtre** ★★, place de la Comédie (✆ **05-56-00-85-95;** www.opera-bordeaux.com), the city's cultural symbol, was built between 1773 and 1780 as testimony to the burgeoning prosperity of Bordeaux's emerging bourgeoisie. This is one of the last remaining 18th-century theaters in the world, rivaling those of Naples, Stockholm, and Milan. A colonnade of 12 columns graces its facade. Surmounted on these are statues of goddesses and the Muses. If you'd like to visit the richly decorated interior, phone the tourist office to ask about the schedule of weekly guided tours. They cost 6€ ($7.80) for adults and 5€ ($6.50) for children.

From here you can walk north to **esplanade des Quinconces.** It was laid out between 1818 and 1828, and covers nearly 12 hectares (30 acres). A smaller but lovelier square is **place de la Bourse** ★, bounded by quays opening onto the Garonne. It was laid out between 1728 and 1755; the fountain of the Three Graces is at its center. Flanking the square are the Custom House and the Stock Exchange.

CHURCHES The largest and most ostentatious church in Bordeaux is the **Cathédrale St-André** ★★, place Pey-Berland (✆ **05-56-52-68-10**), near the southern perimeter of the old town. The sculptures on the 13th-century Porte Royale (Royal Door) are admirable; see also the 14th-century sculptures on the North Door. Separate from the rest of the church is the 47m (154-ft.) **Tour Pey-Berland** (✆ **05-56-**

Bordeaux

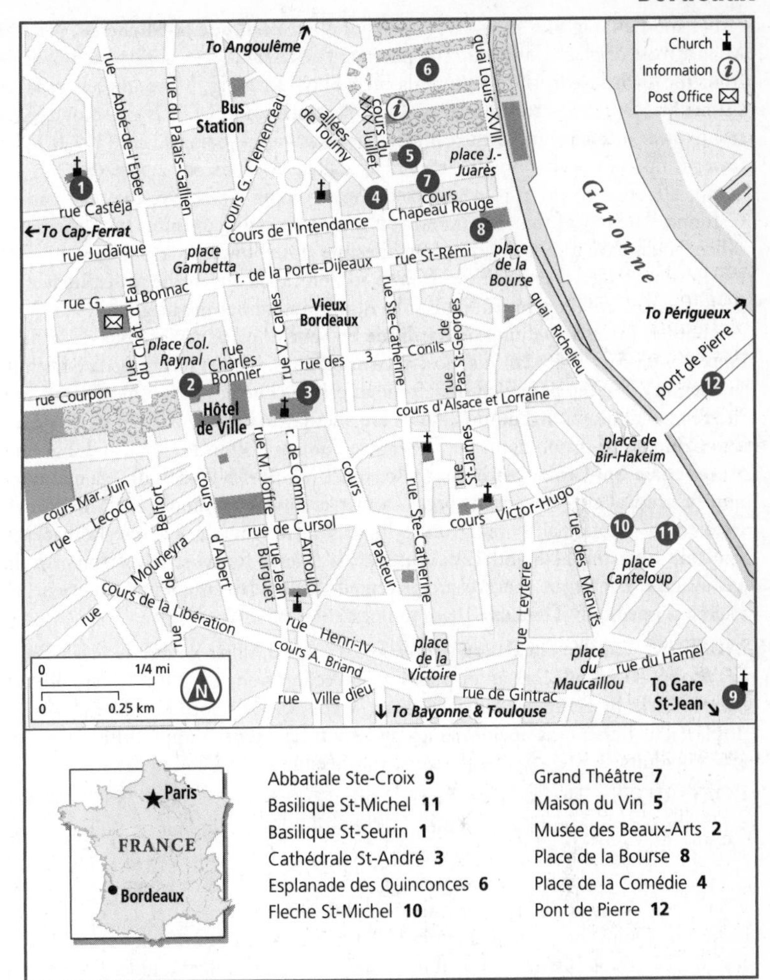

81-26-25), a belfry begun in the 15th century. Foundations date from 900 years ago. The church is open July to September daily 10 to 11:30am and 2 to 6:30pm. Off season, hours are daily 8:30 to 11:30am, Monday to Saturday 2 to 5:30pm. The tower is open daily June to September 10am to 6pm, October to May 10am to 12:30pm and 2 to 5:30pm. Tower admission is 5€ ($6.50) for adults and 3.50€ ($4.55) for those 25 and under. Organ recitals are sometimes held in July and August, usually on Thursday at 5pm. Admission is free.

Bordeaux, always a magnet for power, money, and ecclesiastical zeal, has four other important churches. For information about the churches described below, you can call the **Presbytère de l'Eglise St-Michel** (✆ **05-56-94-30-50**), but most of the people who answer speak only French. The churches' hours vary slightly but are usually Monday to Saturday 2 to 5pm.

Foremost among the "secondary" churches is the **Basilique St-Michel** ★, place St-Michel (part of place Canteloup; no phone). The church itself, constructed in stages from the 14th to the 16th century, is incredibly charming. More impressive is the **Fleche St-Michel** ★ across the street. This tower, erected in 1472, is the second-tallest stone tower in France (after the cathedral at Strasbourg), rising 112m (367 ft.). The tower is open for visits June to September, daily 2 to 7pm, for 2.50€ ($3.25). You climb 228 steps to the top, where you have sweeping views over the port and the Garonne. The rest of the year, unless you receive special permission from the tourist office, you'll have to appreciate the architecture of the tower from the ground. During July and August, every Friday from 5 to 7pm, the bells in the tower are rung as part of a free carillon concert that can be heard throughout the neighborhood.

Another interesting church is **Basilique St-Seurin,** place des Martyrs de la Résistance (✆ **05-56-93-89-28**). Its most ancient sections, such as its crypt, date from the 5th century. See the porch left over from an earlier church; it has some capitals from the Romanesque era. In summer, hours are Tuesday to Sunday 8:30 to 11:30am and 2 to 6:30pm; off-season hours are Tuesday to Sunday 7:30 to 11:30am and 2 to 5pm.

Abbatiale Ste-Croix, place Pierre-Renaudel (✆ **05-56-94-30-50**), gained attention in musical circles when its organ, a marvel built by a monk, Dom Bedos, was restored to its original working order in 1996. The church, a severe Romanesque structure from the 11th and 12th centuries, is revered for its stately dignity. In July and August, free organ concerts are presented Wednesday at 6:30pm; otherwise, the church is open only Thursday 10am to noon.

MUSEUM **Musée des Beaux-Arts** ★★, 20 cours d'Albret, Jardin du Palais-Rohan (✆ **05-56-10-20-56**), has an outstanding collection from the 15th to the 20th centuries. Works by Perugina, Titian, Rubens, Veronese, Delacroix, and Marquet are on display. The museum is open Wednesday to Sunday 11am to 6pm. Admission is 5€ ($6.50) adults, 2.50€ ($3.25) students, and free for ages 17 and under.

BOAT RIDES The **pont de Pierre,** with 17 arches, stretches 478m (1,568 ft.) across the Garonne and is one of the most beautiful bridges in France. Built on orders of Napoleon I in 1813, the bridge can be crossed on foot for a view of the quays and the port. For an even better view, we suggest a **tour of the port,** which lasts about 90 minutes and goes up the river and all around the harbor. It departs from the Embarcadère des Quinconces, on quai Louis-XVIII, in the center of town. It's available year-round. The cost is 10€ ($13) for adults and 8€ ($10) for children under 10. For exact times and a description of other cruises, call the tourist office (see "Essentials," above) or **Bateaux Ville de Bordeaux,** Embarcadère des Quinconces, 7 quai Louis XVIII (✆ **05-56-52-88-88**). Ask about the occasional floating concerts at night. Note that tours may be canceled without warning.

You may enjoy a **cruise** on one of France's mightiest (and least-visited) rivers, the Garonne. Year-round, **Alienor Loisirs,** quai Louis-XVIII (✆ **05-56-51-27-90** or 05-56-52-27-81), offers tours beginning in Bordeaux and heading upriver, touching down at such sites as Blaye, Cadillac, and Libourne. The schedule changes frequently, but usually includes cruises every Saturday and Sunday between June and September. Many begin boarding at around 11am for an 11:30am departure. A simple restaurant on board serves lunch, and departures are timed so that you can travel upriver, stretch your legs in some or all of the above-mentioned sites, and return to Bordeaux before 7pm. The cost, with lunch included, ranges from 45€ to 50€ ($59–$65), depending on the tour. There are fewer tours between October and March, and usually none during February.

Finds Buying Wine in Bordeaux

If you've come to Bordeaux to buy wine, try to choose one that carries personal significance because you've visited the vineyard, or consult the experts at the wine shops. We recommend **La Vinothèque,** 8 cours du 30-Juillet (✆ **05-56-52-32-05;** www.la-vinotheque.com), and **Badie,** 62 allées de Tourny (✆ **05-56-52-23-72**). The best red bordeaux wines come from small houses such as **Château Lesparre,** Beychac-et-Caillau, 39km (24 miles) north of Bordeaux (✆ **05-57-24-51-23**); **Château Bel Air,** Naujan-et-Postiac, 40km (25 miles) east of Bordeaux (✆ **05-57-74-62-01**); and **Château les Bouzigues,** Saintes Gemmes, 76km (47 miles) south of Bordeaux (✆ **05-56-61-80-77**).

SHOPPING

If you want antiques, concentrate your search around **rue Bouffard, rue des Remparts,** and **rue Notre-Dame,** where you'll find a market area known as **Village Notre-Dame** (✆ **05-56-52-66-13** or 05-56-79-01-95), housing all sorts of antiques shops. Another destination is the neighborhood around **Eglise St-Michel,** particularly the passage St-Michel, a narrow alleyway a few steps from the church.

For fashion, go to the couture quarter around **place des Grands Hommes** as well as the **cours Georges-Clemenceau,** with its many upscale, trendy, and classic emporiums. For the greatest concentration of shops, head to the **rue Ste-Catherine,** the longest pedestrian street in France. It has at least 100 boutiques, from the most luxurious to the cheapest. Better-known choices include the ready-to-wear boutique of the hip Bordeaux designer **Dourthe Jacqueline,** 18 rue Lafaurie-de-Monbadon (✆ **05-56-52-35-78**), for creative, not-very-expensive designs. More elegant and esoteric, and definitely worth a look, is **La Soierie (Chantal Olivier),** 54 cours Georges-Clemenceau (✆ **05-56-51-23-75**), which carries a complete line of women's inner and outer garments made mostly of fabric from the silk mills of Lyon.

Despite a fire in 2003 that destroyed some artwork, **Galerie Condillac,** 24 rue Condillac (✆ **05-56-79-04-31**), is one of the classier art houses that specializes in mostly local artists who paint with strong, vibrant colors. For a sugar rush, head over to **Cadiot Badie,** 26 allées de Tourny (✆ **05-56-44-24-22**), where the specialty for many decades has been sinfully flavorful chocolates, chocolate truffles, and pralines.

WHERE TO STAY

EXPENSIVE

Hôtel Burdigala ★★ This is the best and most appealing hotel in Bordeaux's core. Well-manicured, tasteful, and experienced at welcoming international travelers (many of them wine buyers), it rises six floors above a neighborhood that's otherwise devoted to commerce. Originally built in 1988, and frequently renovated, it feels like a modern-day grand hotel. Conservative, contemporary-looking guest rooms are relatively spacious, and the bathrooms are plush.

115 rue Georges-Bonnac, Bordeaux 33000. ✆ **05-56-90-16-16.** Fax 05-56-93-15-06. www.burdigala.com. 83 units. 180€–280€ ($234–$364) double; 400€–500€ ($520–$650) suite. AE, DC, MC, V. Parking 12€ ($16). Tram: A to Mériadeck. **Amenities:** Restaurant; bar; access to nearby health club and pool (15€/$20 per day); room service; babysitting; laundry service; dry cleaning. *In room:* TV, minibar, hair dryer, safe, Wi-Fi.

MODERATE

Mercure Bordeaux Centre Mériadeck ★ This hotel, in a sleek building facing a shopping mall in the Mériadeck business district, is a 5-minute walk from the town center. The well-furnished rooms with modern amenities and comfortable beds attract winegrowers and wine merchants from abroad as well as other business travelers and groups. The renovated accommodations are on the third and fifth through seventh floors. La Brasserie du Festival, the main restaurant, is one of Bordeaux's finest hotel grills.

5 rue Robert-Lateulade, Bordeaux 33000. ✆ **05-56-56-43-43.** Fax 05-56-96-50-59. www.mercure.com. 196 units. 123€ ($160) double; 190€ ($247) suite. AE, DC, MC, V. Overnight parking 2€ ($2.60); hourly charge for daytime parking. Bus: 7 or 8. **Amenities:** Restaurant; bar; business services; room service; laundry service; dry cleaning; limited-mobility rooms. *In room:* A/C, TV, minibar, hair dryer, Wi-Fi (in some).

Mercure Château Chartrons ★★ This is one of Bordeaux's leading hotels, located near the landmark place Tourny. The medium-size rooms are standard chain-hotel accommodations, decorated with memorabilia of the wine trade. Each comes with a midsize modern bathroom. The bar has an impressive array of local vintages available by the glass. The restaurant serves bistro-style fare.

81 cours St-Louis, Bordeaux 33300. ✆ **05-56-43-15-00.** Fax 05-56-69-15-21. www.mercure.com. 144 units. 61€–220€ ($79–$286) double; 160€ ($208) suite. AE, DC, MC, V. Parking 9€ ($12). **Amenities:** Restaurant; bar; room service; babysitting; laundry service; dry cleaning; limited-mobility rooms. *In room:* A/C, TV, minibar, hair dryer, safe, Wi-Fi.

INEXPENSIVE

Hôtel Continental ★ *Value* To get a certain class, charm, and elegance in Bordeaux at this price is a rarity. In the center of the golden triangle, on a semipedestrian mall dotted with boutiques, this 18th-century town house wins new fans every year. You'll get a warm welcome and a fine dose of Bordelaise hospitality. Rooms, although a bit small (especially the singles), are warmly decorated and furnished, each with a compact bathroom; a few have tiny balconies.

10 rue Montesquieu, Bordeaux 33000. ✆ **05-56-52-66-00.** Fax 05-56-52-77-97. www.hotel-le-continental.com. 51 units. 75€ ($98) double with shower; 81€–99€ ($105–$129) double with bathroom; 155€–190€ ($202–$247) suite. AE, DC, MC, V. Parking 2.30€ ($3). **Amenities:** Room service. *In room:* A/C, TV, minibar, Wi-Fi.

Hôtel de Sèze *Value* This boutique hotel occupies an 18th-century building in a historic neighborhood. The hotel is such a well-known value that you should make reservations as early as possible. Rooms are comfortable and well furnished; the cheapest has only a bed and bathroom. Some have air-conditioning.

7 rue Sèze, Bordeaux 33000. ✆ **05-56-52-65-54.** Fax 05-56-48-98-00. http://hotelsezemedoc.free.fr. 24 units. 59€–69€ ($77–$90) double. AE, DC, MC, V. Parking 12€ ($16). *In room:* TV, minibar.

Tulip Inn Bordeaux Le Bayonne Etche-Ona ★★ In 1997, two antique, stone-fronted town houses, Le Bayonne Hôtel and its neighbor, Hôtel Etche-Ona, were radically upgraded and joined to form this entity. The aura of the 1930s has been retained and many features added, most notably soundproofing and comfortable furnishings, along with midsize bathrooms. Rooms are medium to generous in size. Many attractions, including restaurants, the cathedral, place de la Bourse, the quays, and the Grand Théâtre, are nearby. Breakfast is the only meal served.

15 cours de l'Intendance (entrances at 4 rue Martignac and 11 rue Mautrec), Bordeaux 33000. ✆ **05-56-48-00-88.** Fax 05-56-48-41-60. www.bordeaux-hotel.com. 63 units. 84€–174€ ($109–$226) double; 250€ ($325) suite. AE, DC, MC, V. Parking 18€ ($23). **Amenities:** Bar; room service; laundry service; dry cleaning. *In room:* A/C, TV, minibar, hair dryer, trouser press, safe, Wi-Fi.

WHERE TO DINE

You can also try the restaurants at **Mercure Château Chartrons** and **Mercure Bordeaux Centre Mériadeck** (see "Where to Stay," above).

EXPENSIVE

La Tupina ★★ *Finds* TRADITIONAL FRENCH One of Bordeaux's most talented chefs runs this cozy spot with a summer terrace near quai de la Monnaie. It's been called "a tribute to country kitchens and the grandmothers who cooked in them." Jean-Pierre Xiradakis's specialty is duck, so your meal may begin with croutons spread with duck rillettes, and the kitchen often uses duck giblets, skin, and livers in salads. Other specialties are roasted shoulder of lamb *en confit* with garlic and white beans, lamprey eel à la Bordelaise, and steaks grilled and barbecued at the table. Desserts usually include pears marinated in red bordeaux wine.

6 rue de la Porte de la Monnaie. ✆ **05-56-91-56-37.** www.latupina.com. Reservations recommended. Main courses 18€–32€ ($23–$42); fixed-price lunch 16€–32€ ($21–$42); fixed-price dinner 55€ ($72). AE, DC, MC, V. Daily noon–2pm and 7–11pm.

Le Chapon-Fin ★★★ MODERN FRENCH One of the city's most prestigious restaurants occupies an early-20th-century monument that critics have referred to as "organic rococo." Designed by architect Alfred Duprat and crafted from distressed rocks into an Art Nouveau–style grotto, it soars almost 7.5m (25 ft.) to a skylight that floods the interior with light. Owner Nicolas Frion features artful renditions of fresh foie gras of duckling; lobster salad; Pauillac lamb grilled with peppers and mushrooms; sea bass with pecans, celery leaves, and cream; and succulent crayfish and scallops braised in spices and wine. The restaurant is in one of the city's upscale neighborhoods, between place Gambetta and the Marché aux Grands Hommes.

5 rue Montesquieu. ✆ **05-56-79-10-10.** www.chapon-fin.com. Reservations required. Main courses 32€–44€ ($42–$57); fixed-price lunch 30€–78€ ($39–$101); fixed-price dinner 50€–78€ ($65–$101). AE, DC, MC, V. Tues–Sat noon–1:30pm and 7:30–9:30pm.

Le Pavillon des Boulevards FRENCH Small, intimate, and charming, this is an impeccably managed restaurant where the skillful chef (Denis Franc) and the head of the dining room (his wife, Nelly Franc) provide sophisticated food for discerning customers. Menu items include a dollop of caviar from local sturgeon, served with chestnut-flavored cream sauce; grilled crayfish with grilled blood sausage and cider; Breton lobster sautéed with vanilla beans with sauterne sauce; filets of turbot with Parmesan-flavored risotto; and fried crayfish tails served with fried blood sausage and apple juice. The cuisine is attuned to the changing seasons.

120 rue Croix-de-Seguey. ✆ **05-56-81-51-02.** Reservations recommended. Main courses 30€–35€ ($39–$46); fixed-price lunch 40€ ($52); fixed price dinner 65€–100€ ($85–$130). AE, MC, V. Tues–Fri noon–1:30pm; Mon–Sat 8–9:45pm. Closed 1 week in Jan and 3 weeks in Aug. Bus: 14.

MODERATE

Le Mably ★ *Value* FRENCH In the heart of 18th-century Bordeaux, surrounded by art galleries and shops, this restaurant attracts gastronomes, hipsters, politicians, journalists, and locals interested in the fun, elegant atmosphere of a *brasserie de luxe.* Both old-fashioned rooms have late-19th-century decor. The duck-intensive menu lists salad of duck necks stuffed with pistachios, confit of duckling, magret of duckling, and, of course, duck liver. Recommendable nonduck items are veal kidneys with fresh coriander, blanquettes of veal, beef bourguignon, and several kinds of fresh fish.

Pay special attention to the comprehensive wine list, rich in esoteric burgundies. There's additional seating on an outdoor terrace during warmer weather.

12 rue Mably. ✆ **05-56-44-30-10.** Reservations recommended. Main courses 13€–30€ ($17–$39); fixed-price menu 23€–28€ ($30–$36). AE, MC, V. Tues–Sat noon–2:30pm and 7:30–11pm. Closed 3 weeks in Aug.

Le Vieux Bordeaux ★ MODERN FRENCH Nearly a neighborhood institution, this restaurant ranks among the top five in a highly competitive market. Specialties include roasted sea bass on a gratin of pulverized black olives; thin-sliced escalopes of duck foie gras with coffee-flavored sauce; and "Oriental" (sweet-and-sour) pigeon with lime sauce.

27 rue Buhan. ✆ **05-56-52-94-36.** http://le-vieux-bordeaux.com. Reservations recommended. Main courses 14€–30€ ($18–$39); fixed-price dinner menu 28€–50€ ($36–$65); fixed-price lunch 19€ ($25). AE, DC, MC, V. Tues–Sat noon–2pm and 8–10:30pm. Closed last 2 weeks in Feb and 3 weeks in Aug.

INEXPENSIVE

Le Quai Zaco FRENCH/SPANISH Its solid stone walls were originally built 200 years ago as a warehouse, and just before it became a restaurant, it functioned as a sales outlet for sporting goods. Today, it's a hardworking and conscientious restaurant with two distinctly different dining rooms, each with a decor that accents the antique masonry with jazzy artwork, molded plastic chairs, and industrial-looking tables. Cuisine derives from Southwestern France and northern Spain, and it might, on the day of your arrival, include a spicy gazpacho with ravioli stuffed with goat cheese; piccata of veal with stuffed tomatoes; sweetbreads with foie gras, endive salad, and pine nuts; a fricassee of artichoke hearts with oxtail; and stingray with caper-flavored butter. Desserts are plentiful and imaginative. How about a lemon-flavored pannacotta accented with a "carpaccio" of spiced and sliced oranges? You'll find this place about 1km (⅔ mile) north of the Gare St-Jean, immediately beside the wharves of the Garonne River.

80 quai des Chartrons. ✆ **05-57-87-67-72.** Reservations recommended. Main courses 13€–26€ ($17–$34). AE, MC, V. Daily noon–1:30pm and 7:45-11pm. Bus: 51.

L'O de l'Hâ ★ *Finds* FRENCH/INTERNATIONAL The owners got the inspiration for this fashionable restaurant during a visit to New York and the innovative French restaurant Bouley. L'O de l'Hâ is on a narrow cobbled street whose name commemorates a long-gone medieval prison. Antique masonry, roughly textured plaster, and polished concrete decorate both fashionable dining rooms. Menu items are innovative and intriguing. Examples include crabmeat lasagna with coconut flakes; *brandade* of sweet potatoes with sweet peppers; large Dover sole with spinach, walnuts, and chanterelles; and braised lamb chops with tomato marmalade. From Thursday to Saturday, a DJ spins disco from 8 until around 11pm.

5 rue de l'Hâ. ✆ **05-56-81-42-21.** www.o-de-lha.com. Reservations recommended. Main courses 14€–24€ ($18–$31); fixed-price lunch 16€ ($21). AE, DC, MC, V. Tues–Sat noon–2pm; Tues–Thurs 8–10pm; Fri–Sat 8–11:30pm. Tram: A to Musée d'Aquitaine.

BORDEAUX AFTER DARK

Pick up a copy of *Clubs et Concerts* at the Office de Tourisme or *Bordeaux Plus* at a newsstand; both detail the goings-on in and around town.

A play or an opera could make a good start to your evening. **Grand Théâtre,** place de la Comédie (✆ **05-56-00-85-20**), has a busy, diverse performance schedule.

You'll find gambling, drinking, dining, and people-watching at **Casino de Bordeaux,** in the Hôtel Sofitel Bordeaux Lac, rue Cardinal Richaud (✆ **05-56-69-49-00**).

Rooms containing slot machines operate daily 10am to 4am. There's no admission charge. To enter the more formal gaming rooms (site of the roulette and blackjack tables), you must present a passport or an identity card. They're open every night 9pm until 4am. Live entertainment of some kind usually begins around 8pm Friday. The casino has an informal brasserie on the street level, where fixed-price menus cost 20€ to 25€ ($26–$33), and a restaurant one floor up, where fixed-price menus begin at 31€ ($40).

Animated street life rules the inner core of Bordeaux by night. Head to **place de la Victoire, place St-Pierre, place du Parlement, place Camille Jullian,** and **place Gambetta;** the latter swarms with students. Night owls in Bordeaux gravitate toward quai du Paludate, where restaurants, bars, and discos remain open until the wee hours.

Two trendy, glamorous bars are **L'Absolute Lounge,** rue de la Devise (© **05-56-48-80-00**), which occasionally schedules live "electro-jazz"; and **La Casa Latina,** 59 quai Chartrons (© **05-57-87-15-80**), where merengue, salsa, and bachata might make you think that you've landed in the Dominican Republic or Brazil.

The leading gay bar, **BHV (Bar de l'Hôtel de Ville),** 4 rue de l'Hôtel de Ville (© **05-56-44-05-08**), is in the heart of town, across from the town hall. The handsomest men of Bordeaux, or so it is said, turn up here daily 6pm to 2am. Drag shows take place from September to June on Sunday at 10pm.

A good choice for dancing is **Sénéchal,** 57 bis quai de Paludate (© **05-56-85-54-80**), with its 1970s decor and just as classic 25- to 45-year-old crowd.

6 The Wine Country

The major Bordeaux wine districts are Graves, Médoc, Sauternes, Entre-deux-Mers, Libourne, Blaye, and Bourg. North of the city of Bordeaux, the Garonne River joins the Dordogne to form the Gironde, a broad estuary. More than 100,000 vineyards produce some 70 million gallons of wine a year, some of which are among the greatest reds in the world. (The white wines are less well known.)

Some of the famous vineyards welcome visitors, providing you don't arrive at the busy harvest time. However, most vineyards don't have a permanent staff to accommodate sightseers. Don't just show up—call first or check with local tourist offices about appropriate times to visit. A typical tour includes information about the winemaking process and a tour of the cellars. Most châteaux have historical artifacts on display. Tours end with a tasting, in which visitors 18 and older may participate.

VISITOR INFORMATION The best source of information about the wines of Bordeaux (and French wines in general) is the **Centre d'Information, de Documentation, et de Dégustation,** 30 rue de la Sablière, 75014 Paris (© **01-45-45-32-20;** fax 01-45-42-78-20). This independent school presents about a dozen courses yearround addressing all aspects of tasting, producing, buying, and merchandising wine. It also provides information to anyone anticipating a tour of the vineyards of France, in the region around Bordeaux or elsewhere.

Before heading out on the Wine Road, or Route des Grands-Crus, make sure you get a detailed map from the Bordeaux tourist office (see "Essentials" under the "Bordeaux" section, earlier in this chapter), because the "trail" isn't well marked. From Bordeaux, head north toward Pauillac on D2, the Wine Road.

LIBOURNE

This is a sizable market town with a railway connection. At the junction of the Dordogne and Isle rivers, Libourne is roughly the center of the St-Emilion, Pomerol, and

Fronsac wine districts. In the town, a large colonnaded square still contains some houses from the 16th century, including the **Hôtel-de-Ville** (town hall). The town hall is open Monday to Friday 8:30am to 12:30pm and 1:15 to 5pm. During that time you can enter without an appointment to see the building's two showcase rooms (if they're not in use). The **Salle des Mariages** and the **Salle des Conseils** contain some antiques from the 1400s; most of the decor and design are from the 16th to the 18th centuries. You can also explore the remains of 13th-century ramparts. In the town center is the **Office de Tourisme,** 45 allée Robert Boulin (© **05-57-51-15-04**), where you can get details on visiting the vineyards.

WHERE TO DINE

Chez Servais ★★ *Value* MODERN/TRADITIONAL FRENCH The setting for our favorite restaurant in Libourne is an antique (probably 19th-c.) house whose sculpted facade occupies a prominent position in the town center. In the dining rooms—one small and intimate, the other more convivial—a hardworking professional staff serves items from a menu that changes at least every 6 weeks. Our favorite dishes include sautéed foie gras with white grapes; roasted sea bass with herbs, butter sauce, and flap mushrooms; scallops with salsify chips; and magret of duckling with sweet-and-sour sauce concocted from red seasonal berries.

14 place Decazes. © **05-57-51-83-97.** Reservations recommended. Fixed-price menu 25€–36€ ($33–$47). AE, MC, V. Tues–Sun 12:30–2pm; Tues–Sat 7:45–9:30pm. Closed 1st week of May and 2 weeks in Aug.

MEDOC ★

The Médoc, an undulating plain covered with vineyards, is one of the most visited regions in southwestern France. Bordeaux and the Pointe de Grave mark its borders. Throughout the region are many châteaux producing grapes; only a handful of these, however, are worthy of your attention. The most visited château is that of Mouton-Rothschild, said to be second only to Lourdes among attractions in southwestern France.

EXPLORING THE AREA

Château Lafite-Rothschild This site is second in number of visitors only to the nearby Château Mouton-Rothschild. Count on spending at least an hour here. The *vinothèque* contains many vintage bottles, several dating from 1797. The Rothschilds purchased the château in 1868.

Rte. des Château, Pauillac. © **05-56-73-18-18.** www.lafite.com. Tours by appointment only; minimum 1-week notice required. Free admission. Tours Mon–Fri 2 and 3:30pm. Closed Aug–Oct.

Château Margaux Known as the Versailles of the Médoc, this Empire-style château was built in the 19th century near the village of Margaux. The estate covers more than 263 hectares (650 acres), of which 80 hectares (198 acres) produce Château Margaux and Pavillon Rouge du Château Margaux; almost 12 hectares (30 acres) are devoted to producing Pavillon Blanc du Château Margaux. To see the vat rooms and wine cellars, make an appointment by letter or phone.

On D2, south of Pauillac, Margaux 33460. © **05-57-88-83-83.** www.chateau-margaux.com. Vat rooms and wine cellars by appointment only. Mon–Fri 10am–noon and 2–4pm. Closed Aug–Oct.

Château Mouton-Rothschild ★ Thousands of tourists visit this château, 1km (⅔ mile) north of Pauillac, one of many former homes of the baron Philippe de Rothschild and his American-born wife, Pauline. Today their daughter, Philippine de Rothschild, carries on their work. The reception area is furnished with sculptures and paintings that portray wine as art. An adjoining museum, shoehorned into the former wine cellars, features 18th- and 19th-century art and objects from the Rothschild family collections, as well as a historically important 16th-century tapestry, all of which focus on the cultivation of vines. To tour the cellars, make an appointment well in advance; for a tour that does not include the cellars, call a week ahead.

Le Pouyalet, Pauillac 33250. ✆ **05-56-73-21-29.** Tours by appointment only. Tour 6€ ($7.80) without tasting, 15€ ($20) with tasting. Year-round Mon–Fri 9:30–11am; Mon–Thurs 2–4pm; Fri 2–3pm.

Société Duboscq Duboscq, a wine packager and wholesaler established in 1952, occupies the stately premises of the late-19th-century Château Haut-Marbuzet. The staff will follow your visit to the cellars with a complimentary *dégustation des vins* (wine tasting) of whichever product you request. The château is 5 minutes north of Pauillac by car.

Château Haut-Marbuzet, St-Estephe 33180. ✆ **05-56-59-30-54.** Free admission. Mon–Sat 9am–noon and 2–5pm by appointment only. Tours in English on request.

WHERE TO STAY & DINE

Cordeillan-Bages ★★ In a region obsessed with fine wine and fine food, this emerges as the most consistently celebrated restaurant and hotel. The setting is a 17th-century *chartreuse,* which the staff defines as something larger than a manor house and smaller than a château. Virtually everyone comes here for the restaurant, usually opting to spend the night after drinking wine with dinner. Fixed-price menus cost 80€ to 145€ ($104–$189). A la carte main courses go for 26€ to 45€ ($34–$59). Menu items may include a simple but elegant version of foie gras served on confit of peaches with a reduction of port wine; roasted sea bass with essence of cockles and braised, licorice-flavored leeks; and a platter of suckling lamb cooked three ways (the shoulder *en confit,* the chops grilled, the neck stuffed and baked). The establishment's most famous dessert is an eggplant crystallized in sugar and served with anise-flavored cream sauce and basil-flavored sorbet. The restaurant, but not the hotel, is closed all day Monday and at lunch on Tuesday and Saturday.

The spacious guest rooms are decorated in a style that emulates the Hôtel Ritz in Paris, with formal curtains, upholstered walls, a scattering of antiques, and—other than the bouffant-style curtains—an airy minimalism. About half are contemporary, with monochromatic color schemes; the rest are in traditional country-house style.

Rte. D2, Pauillac 33250. ✆ **05-56-59-24-24.** Fax 05-56-59-01-89. www.cordeillanbages.com. 25 units. 190€–278€ ($247–$361) double; 374€ ($486) junior suite; 492€ ($640) 2-bedroom apt for 4. AE, DC, MC, V. Closed Dec 15–Feb 14. **Amenities:** Restaurant; bar; outdoor pool; fitness room; sauna; room service; laundry service. *In room:* TV, hair dryer.

ST-EMILION ★★

Surrounded by vineyards, St-Emilion is on a limestone plateau overlooking the valley of the Dordogne; a maze of wine cellars has been dug beneath the town. The wine made in this district has been called "Wine of Honor," and British sovereigns nicknamed it "King of Wines." The town, constructed mostly of golden stone and dating from the Middle Ages, is also known for its macaroons.

St-Emilion maintains the ancient tradition of La Jurade, a society dedicated to maintaining the highest standard for the local wine and promoting and honoring it around the world. Members of this society wear silk hats and scarlet robes edged with ermine, and members of the Syndicat Viticole, which watches over the quality of wine, have been around the world to promote the wines with this appellation.

ESSENTIALS

GETTING THERE St-Emilion lies 35km (22 miles) northeast of Bordeaux between Libourne, 8km (5 miles) away, and Castillon-la-Bataille, 11km (63/4 miles) away. **Trains** from Bordeaux make the 45-minute trip to St-Emilion three times per day; the one-way fare is 7.50€ ($9.75). Trains from other parts of France usually require transfers in either Bordeaux or Libourne, a 10-minute train ride from St-Emilion. For train information in St-Emilion, call © **36-35** or 08-92-35-35-35 from outside France.

VISITOR INFORMATION The **Office de Tourisme** is on place des Créneaux (© **05-57-55-28-28;** fax 05-57-55-28-29; www.saint-emilion-tourisme.com).

EXPLORING THE TOWN

At the heart of St-Emilion is the medieval **place du Marché,** recently renamed **place de l'Eglise Monolithe,** between two hills. St-Emilion abounds with unusual monuments, some of them dug, for defensive reasons, into the limestone bedrock that adds such verve to the vineyards.

Foremost among the monuments is the **Eglise Monolithe** ★, place de l'Eglise Monolithe (© **05-57-55-28-28**), the largest underground church in Europe, carved by Benedictine monks during the 9th to 12th century. Three 14th-century bay windows mark its facade. A 14th-century sculpted portal depicts the Last Judgment and Resurrection of the Dead. The church is 11m (36 ft.) high, 20m (66 ft.) wide, and 38m (125 ft.) long. It can be visited only as part of an organized tour. Tours depart from the tourist office daily at 10am. English, German, and Spanish tours are by appointment only. Each tour includes a visit to the church, its underground Benedictine catacombs, the 13th-century Chapelle de la Trinité, and its underground grotto—a site known as the Hermitage—where St-Emilion sequestered himself during the latter part of his life. The entire complex was kept alive during the heyday of its use by underground springs, which were surrounded in the 1500s by ornate balustrades (the monks charged admission). The tour, which lasts 45 minutes, costs 5.50€ ($7.15) for adults, 3.60€ ($4.70) for students, 2.90€ ($3.75) for children 12 to 17, and is free for children under 12.

You can visit two additional monuments without an organized tour. The first is the **Bell Tower** *(clocher)* of the Eglise Monolithe (see above). It rises on place des Créneaux, near place de l'Eglise Monolithe. Built between the 1100s and the 1400s, it's the second-highest tower in the La Gironde region and for years after its construction was the only aboveground landmark that indicated the position of the underground church. You can climb the bell tower and take in the panoramic view daily between 9am and 6pm every day except Christmas and New Year's Day for a 1€ ($1.30) fee. To do this, go to the tourist office, where someone will give you a key to the tower door in exchange for an ID card. (When you return the key, you'll get your ID back.)

You may want to visit the **Château du Roi** (© **05-57-24-72-09**), founded by Henry III of the Plantagenet line during the 13th century. Don't expect a full-fledged castle. The tower was the first section built, and the construction that followed was either demolished or never completed. Until 1608, this building functioned as the town hall. From its summit, you can see as far away as the Dordogne. You can climb the tower (the procedure is the same as for visiting the Bell Tower) during daylight hours every day except Christmas and New Year's Day, 10am to 12:30pm and 2 to 6pm (to 6:30pm Apr–Sept), for 1€ ($1.30).

WHERE TO STAY & DINE

Hostellerie de Plaisance ★★ This 200-year-old stone building, on 14th-century foundations, is the best lodging and dining choice in this medieval town. The stylish rooms, some with views of stone monuments and towers, accommodate sophisticated wine tasters and buyers from all over the world. Some rooms are small, but the best doubles have terraces where you can enjoy breakfast. The cuisine served here is the best known and most praised in the area. Chef Philippe Etchebest works with the region's bountiful seasonal ingredients, especially game, usually available October through February. Otherwise, menu items include salad of grilled quail with avocados, civet of sturgeon cooked with local red wine, and filet mignon of veal with wild mushrooms. Top it all off with a warm soufflé flavored with pear liqueur and served with nougat ice cream and chocolate sauce. The fixed-price lunch menu Monday to Friday is 32€ ($42); fixed-price dinner menus (and weekend lunch) are 48€ to 85€ ($62–$111).

Place du Clocher, St-Emilion 33330. ✆ **05-57-55-07-55.** Fax 05-57-74-41-11. www.hostellerie-plaisance.com. 18 units. 140€–450€ ($182–$585) double; 350€–450€ ($455–$585) suite. Half board 70€ ($91). AE, DC, MC, V. Closed Jan. **Amenities:** Restaurant; bar; room service; laundry service. *In room:* A/C, TV, minibar (some units), hair dryer, safe.

21

The Dordogne & Périgord: Land of Prehistoric Caves, Truffles & Fine Wine

Lovers of foie gras and truffles, not to mention nature lovers, have always sought out the Dordogne and Périgord regions of France. Our first stop, Périgueux, was the capital of the old province of Périgord. After following the trail of the Cro-Magnon people to prehistoric caves, we visit Cahors, the ancient capital of Quercy, then Montauban, where the painter Ingres was born. But the towns aren't the stars—the fertile countryside holds the fascination. In some villages the Middle Ages seem to live on. It's said that no discoveries are left to be made in France, but you can disprove that by taking time to visit a region too often neglected by tourists.

1 Périgueux ★

485km (301 miles) SW of Paris, 85km (53 miles) SE of Angoulême, 113km (70 miles) NE of Bordeaux, 101km (63 miles) SW of Limoges

This is the city of foie gras and truffles. Capital of the old province of Périgord, Périgueux stands on the Isle River. In addition to its food products, the region is known for its Roman ruins and medieval churches. The city is divided into three sections: the Cité (the old Roman town), Le Puy St-Front (the medieval town) on the slope of the hill, and, to the west, the modern town.

Périgueux (pop. 35,000) is a sleepy provincial backwater. Its attractions probably won't hold your interest for more than a day, but it's a gateway to the Dordogne Valley and the cave paintings at Les Eyzies.

ESSENTIALS

GETTING THERE **Trains** run frequently from Paris, Lyon, and Toulouse, plus many regional towns. Twelve trains per day arrive from Paris from either Montparnasse or Gare d'Austerlitz (trip time: 4–6 hr.; one-way fare: 76€/$99); 12 trains from Bordeaux (trip time: 1½ hr.; one-way fare: 18€/$23); 2 trains from Lyon (trip time: 6–8 hr.; one-way fare: 50€–80€/$65–$104); and 8 from Toulouse (trip time: 4 hr.; one-way fare: 37€/$48). For train information, call ✆ **08-92-35-35-35.** There is no bus service. From Paris, take A10 south to Orléans, and then A71 south to Vierzon. Continue along A20 south to Limoges, and then pick up N21 south to Périgueux.

VISITOR INFORMATION The **Office du Tourisme** is at 26 place Francheville (✆ **05-53-53-10-63;** fax 05-53-09-02-50; www.tourisme-perigueux.fr).

The Dordogne & Périgord

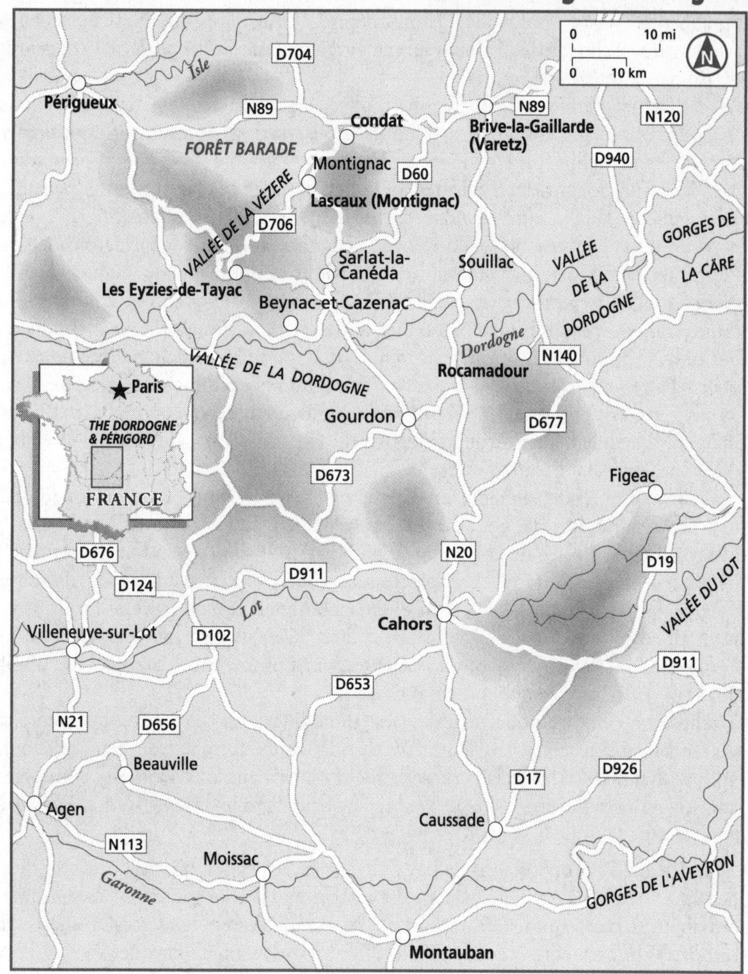

EXPLORING THE TOWN & ENVIRONS

You may want to rent a bike and explore the countryside; a map is available from the tourist office. Rent from **Cycles Cumenal,** 41 bis cours St-Georges (© **05-53-53-31-56**), which charges around 12€ ($16) per day.

Périgueux is a treasure-trove of Gallo-Roman antiquities. The most visible is the **Tour de Vésone,** a partially ruined site that stands 26m (85 ft.) tall, just southwest of town, beyond the railway station. Here you'll see the remains of a Roman temple dedicated to the goddess Vesuna, but you can't enter the site. **Jardin des Arènes,** an amphitheater that held as many as 22,000 spectators, is another reminder of Roman days. Now in ruins, the amphitheater, with a diameter of 394m (1,293 ft.), dates from the 2nd or 3rd century. This site is open May to August daily 7:30am to

9pm, September to April daily 7:30am to 6pm. Admission is free. Near the arena are the remains of the **Château Barrière,** rue Turenne, built in the 11th or 12th century on Roman foundations.

Year-round, Périgueux's tourist office offers organized walking tours of the city. Walking tours, each lasting 1½ to 2 hours, are a worthwhile means of exploring the historical and architectural nuances of Périgueux. The cost is 5€ ($6.50) for adults, 3.80€ ($4.95) for students, and free for children under 12. Between mid-September and mid-June, tours run Monday to Saturday at 2:30pm, alternating every day between tours focusing on Gallo-Roman Périgueux and tours focusing on medieval Périgueux. But during high season, from mid-June to mid-September, tours are given every Monday to Saturday at 10:30am (Gallo-Roman tours) and at 2:30 and 4pm (both of them medieval tours). Also during that period, a Sunday tour is conducted, but only at 3pm, covering whatever venues that are most demanded by the participants. The tourist office also arranges a limited number of bike tours of the city and its environs. Priced at 5€ ($6.50) per person, adult or child, and lasting 1½ to 2 hours, they are scheduled June through August Tuesday at 10am; and during September through November Saturday at 3pm.

Gastronomy reigns supreme in Périgueux, especially when it comes to smooth, melt-in-your-mouth foie gras. Stores that sell this delicacy abound. The best is **La Maison Léon,** 9 place de la Claustre (✆ **05-53-53-29-96**). Fresh foie gras, either in its natural state or in terrines and pâtés, is a specialty of Périgueux. Many of the vendors, including Maison Léon, are in the neighborhood around place St-Louis. If you want an adventure, head for a goose farm that makes its own foie gras, such as **A la Ferme de Puy Gauthier,** about 15 minutes south of town in Marsaneix (✆ **05-53-08-87-07**). To get there, follow signs to Brive.

Those who enjoy outdoor marketplaces should head for the **market** between place du Codert and place de la Claustre, Wednesday and Saturday from 9am to around 1pm. Other markets, especially those focusing on new and used clothing, housewares, and secondhand furniture, are on Wednesday from 9am to around 5pm in Esplanade du Théâtre.

Cathédrale St-Front ★ In Le Puy St-Front (the medieval quarter) rises this cathedral, the last of the Aquitanian-domed churches and one of the largest in southwestern France. Built from 1125 to 1150, it was dedicated to a local bishop. The cathedral's bell tower rises nearly 60m (195 ft.), overlooking the marketplace. With its five white domes and colonnaded turrets, St-Front evokes Constantinople. The interior is built on the plan of a Greek cross, unusual for a French cathedral. Only qualified students of art history or architecture, with special permission, are admitted to the crypt and cloisters, which date from the 9th century.

Place de la Claustre. ✆ **05-53-53-23-62.** Free admission. Daily 8am–noon and 2:30–6:30pm (closes at dusk in winter). Mass Mon–Sat 8:30am, Sun 11am and 6:30pm.

Eglise St-Etienne-de-la-Cité ★ Périgueux's other remarkable church—this one in the Cité area—was a cathedral until 1669, when it lost its position to St-Front. The church was built in the 12th century but has been much damaged since. It contains a 12th-century bishop's tomb and a carved 17th-century wooden reredos depicting the Assumption of the Madonna.

10 av. Cavaignac. ✆ **05-53-53-10-63.** Free admission. Daily 8am–7pm.

Finds Biking through the Dordogne

The Dordogne's rivers meander through countryside that's among the most verdant and historic in France. This area is underpopulated but dotted with monuments, châteaux, 12th-century villages, and charming churches.

As you bike around, the rural character of the area unfolds before you. Unlike in other regions of France, no château, hotel, or inn treats you disdainfully if you show up on two rather than four wheels. (*Au contraire,* the staff will probably offer advice on suitable bike routes.) If you're ever in doubt about where your handlebars should lead you, know that you'll rarely go wrong if your route parallels the riverbanks of the Lot, the Vézère, the Dordogne, or any of their tributaries. Architects and builders since the 11th century have added greatly to the visual allure of their watersides.

The SNCF makes it easy to transport a bike on the nation's railways. However, if you don't want to bring your own wheels on the train, there are plenty of rental shops throughout the region. (We recommend rentals in this chapter's sections on Périgueux and Les Eyzies-de-Tayac.)

Le Comité Départemental du Tourism, 25 rue du Président Wilson, Périgueux 24000 (✆ **05-53-35-50-24;** fax 05-53-09-51-41; www.dordogne-perigord-tourisme.fr), provides information about all the towns in the *département* and will help you organize bike, hiking, kayaking, and canoeing trips. Two of the best outdoors outfitters are **Canoé Loisir,** La Riviére, Vitrac 24200 (✆ **05-53-31-22-92**), and **Canoé Dordogne,** Le Bourg, La Roque Gageac 24250 (✆ **05-53-29-58-50;** www.canoe-dordogne.fr).

Musée du Périgord ★ Built on the site of an Augustinian monastery, this museum has an exceptional collection of prehistoric relics, sculptures, and medieval and Renaissance treasures. Many of the artifacts were recovered from digs in the Périgord region, which is rich in prehistoric remains.

22 cours Tourny. ✆ **05-53-06-40-70.** Admission 4€ ($5.20) adults, 2€ ($2.60) students, free for children under 18. Apr–Sept Mon and Wed–Fri 10:30am–5:30pm, Sat–Sun 1–6pm; Oct–Mar Mon and Wed–Fri 10am–5pm, Sat–Sun 1–6pm.

Musée Gallo-Romain Vesunna One of the most widely publicized museums in central France opened in July 2003 within a mostly glass shell that was designed by the well-known architect Jean Nouvel. A short walk from the center of Périgueux, it's positioned directly above excavations, which revealed an extensive, albeit ruined, ancient Roman villa, replete with mosaics and many of the workaday artifacts of everyday life in the ancient Roman provinces. Visitors are intrigued by the juxtaposition of the hyper-modern shell and the ancient artifacts within.

Rue du 26e Régiment d'Infanterie. ✆ **05-53-53-00-92.** Admission 5.50€ ($7.15) adults, 3.50€ ($4.55) students and children ages 6–12, free for children under 6. July 1–Sept 4 daily 10am–7pm; Apr 4–June 30 and Sept 5–Nov 13 Tues–Sun 10am–12:30pm and 2–6pm; Feb 2–Apr 3 and Nov 14–Dec 17 Tues–Sun 10am–12:30pm and 2–5:30pm; Dec 18–Jan 2 10am–12:30pm and 2–5pm. Closed Jan 3–Feb 1.

WHERE TO STAY

Hôtel Bristol This modern hotel, the best in the town center, is centrally located and offers recently renovated comfortable rooms, often with sleek styling. It's your best bet in a town with a limited, lackluster selection. Bathrooms are a bit small but come with a combination tub/shower. Breakfast is the only meal served, but it's only a 5-minute walk to the town's best restaurants and major points of interest.

37 rue Antoine Gadaud, Périgueux 24000. ✆ **05-53-08-75-90.** Fax 05-53-07-00-49. www.bristolfrance.com. 29 units. 70€–74€ ($91–$96) double. AE, MC, V. Closed Dec 23–Jan 10. Free parking. **Amenities:** Room service; laundry service; nonsmoking rooms. *In room:* A/C, TV, minibar, hair dryer.

WHERE TO DINE

Château des Reynats ★★ MODERN FRENCH This slate-roofed 19th-century manor has a yellow and soft-red Empire dining room in which you can enjoy the finest *cuisine du marché* in the entire region. Someone on the staff may relay stories of the role the château played during France's disastrous exit from its former department of Algeria, when it functioned as a kind of refugee center for French citizens booted off their estates. Menu items are likely to include ravioli stuffed with chunks of north Atlantic lobster; sweetbreads with truffles and confit of duckling; and a well-prepared version of sea bass with shellfish.

The château also rents 37 beautiful rooms. They run 120€ to 250€ ($156–$325) for a double and 220€ to 250€ ($286–$325) for a suite.

15 av. des Reynais, Périgueux 24650. ✆ **05-53-03-53-59.** Fax 05-53-03-44-84. www.chateau-hotel-perigord.com. Reservations recommended. Main courses 22€–40€ ($29–$52); fixed-price menus 35€–62€ ($46–$81). AE, MC, V. Tues–Fri 12:30–1:30pm; Tues–Sat 7:30–10:30pm. Closed Jan 1–Feb 6.

PERIGUEUX AFTER DARK

If the weather is good, start your evening with a walk to **place St-Silain, place St-Louis,** and **place du Marché,** where you may stumble onto a great little bar or even live music. **Disco Le Privilège,** 223 rte. d'Angoulême (✆ **05-53-53-70-18**), attracts a clientele ages 20 to around 35 that dances to reggae, R&B, merengue, salsa, house, and garage. It's open Thursday to Saturday 10pm to 5am.

If you're in the mood for a beer and a *Cheers*-type atmosphere, go to the **Gordon Pub,** 10 rue Condé (✆ **05-53-35-03-74**). A regular stop for the dance-crazed youth of town is **La Régence,** 16 rue des Chancelier-de-l'Hôpital (✆ **05-53-53-10-55**), with a booming techno-rock beat and more-than-ample supply of pheromones. If you prefer to wile the night away with good conversation over drinks, stop by **Café Le St-Louis,** place St-Louis (✆ **05-53-53-53-90**), or **Café de Paris,** 19 cours Montaigne (✆ **05-53-08-29-15**).

2 Lascaux (Montignac) ★

496km (308 miles) SW of Paris, 47km (29 miles) SE of Périgueux

The **Caves at Lascaux,** 2km (1¼ miles) from the Vézère River town of Montignac in the Dordogne region, contain the most beautiful and most famous cave paintings in the world. Unfortunately, you can't view the actual paintings (the caves have been closed to the public to prevent deterioration), but a replica gives you a clear picture of the remarkable works.

Four boys looking for a dog discovered the caves in 1940, which opened to the public in 1948, quickly becoming one of France's major attractions and drawing 125,000 visitors annually. However, the hordes of tourists caused atmospheric changes in the caves, endangering the paintings. Scientists went to work to halt the deterioration, known as "the green sickness."

ESSENTIALS

GETTING THERE The easiest way to reach Montignac is to **drive** northeast from Les Eyzies on D706 for 19km (12 miles).

Rail service is to the neighboring hamlet of Condat-Le-Lardin, 9.5km (6 miles) northeast. From there, taxis (✆ **05-53-51-80-46**), which usually wait at the railway station, take visitors to Montignac for 15€ to 21€ ($20–$27). If no taxis are waiting, a railway station employee will call one for you. There's infrequent **bus** service from Sarlat, near Les Eyzies, but no bus connections from Condat to Montignac. For train information, call ✆ **08-92-35-35-35.**

VISITOR INFORMATION The **Office de Tourisme** in Montignac is on place Bertrand-de-Born (✆ **05-53-51-82-60;** fax 05-53-50-49-72; www.bienvenue-montignac.com).

EXPLORING THE CAVES & OTHER ATTRACTIONS

Public visits to Lascaux I ceased in 1964. Permission to visit for research purposes is given only to qualified archaeologists. Apply to **Direction Régionale des Affaires Culturelles (DRAC),** Service Régional de l'Archéologie, 54 rue Magendie, 33074 Bordeaux (✆ **05-57-95-02-02**). If you want to contact the staff at the cave, call ✆ **05-53-51-95-03.** For tickets, call ✆ **05-53-51-96-23.** ***Be forewarned:*** It's not easy to get around the protocol regarding visits to the interior.

Lascaux II A short walk downhill from the real caves is Lascaux II, an impressive reproduction of the originals, duplicated in concrete and molded aboveground. The 39m-long (128-ft.) reproduction displays some 200 paintings so that you'll at least have some idea of what the "Sistine Chapel of Prehistory" looks like. You can see majestic bulls, wild boars, stags, "Chinese horses," and lifelike deer, the originals of which were painted by Stone Age hunters 15,000 to 20,000 years ago. Try to show up as close to opening time as possible—the number of visitors per day is limited to 2,000, and tickets usually sell out by 2pm. During the winter, you can buy tickets directly at Lascaux II, but from April to October, you must purchase them from a kiosk adjacent to the Montignac tourist office, place Bertran-de-Born. For information, call the number below.

2km (1¼ miles) from Montignac, off D706. ✆ **05-53-51-95-03.** Admission 8.20€ ($11) adults, 5.20€ ($6.75) children 6–12, free for children under 6. July–Aug daily 9am–8pm; mid-Apr to June and Sept–Oct 3 daily 9:30am–6:30pm; Oct 4–Nov 11 daily 10am–12:30pm and 2–6pm; early Feb to mid-Apr and Nov 12–Dec Tues–Sun 10am–12:30pm and 2–5:30pm. Closed Jan to early Feb.

Le Thot *Kids* This attraction includes a zoo with live animals, two projection rooms showing short films on the discovery of cave art at Lascaux, and exhibitions relating to prehistoric communities in the Dordogne. After your visit to Le Thot, walk out on the terrace for a view of the Vézère Valley and the Lascaux hills.

Thonac, 7km (41/3 miles) southwest of Montignac along D706 (follow the signs pointing to the hamlet of Les Eyzies). ✆ **05-53-50-70-44.** Admission 5.70€ ($7.40) adults, 3.70€ ($4.80) children 6–12, free for children under 6. Combination ticket to Le Thot and Lascaux II 11€ ($14) adults, 7.50€ ($9.75) children 6–12, free for children under 6. July–Aug daily 10am–7pm; Sept–Oct 3 daily 10am–6pm; Apr 4–June daily 10am–6:30pm; Oct 4–Nov 11 daily 10am–12:30pm and 2–6pm; Feb 10–Apr 3 and Nov 12–Dec Tues–Sun 10am–12:30pm and 2–5:30pm. Closed Jan 2–Feb 2.

Site Préhistorique de Regourdou *Kids* About 450m (1,480 ft.) uphill from Lascaux I, a minor road branches off and runs through a forest until it reaches this site, discovered in 1954 and believed to be a center for a prehistoric bear cult. Found at the site were the sepulcher and skeleton of a Neanderthal man, surrounded by the sepulcher and skeletons of several bears. Also on the site is an archaeological museum, and about 20 semiwild bears that roam around a naturalized habitat that's barricaded against humans. The only way to experience this site (including the museum) is on a guided tour, conducted in both French and English. Tours depart at frequent intervals.

✆ **05-53-51-81-23.** Admission 4.80€ ($6.25) adults, 3€ ($3.90) children 6–12, free for children under 6. July–Aug daily 9am–7pm; Sept–June daily 11am–6pm.

WHERE TO STAY & DINE

Hostellerie la Roseraie ★ *Value* In the heart of the medieval village, this little charmer is both affordable and cozy. It was converted from a comfortable home built for one of the town merchants in the 19th century on the banks of the Vézère. The midsize bedrooms have individual character and well-kept bathrooms with either a tub or shower. Adding to the charm is a rose garden in back. There is a pleasant terrace to enjoy in the summer months and the restaurant is one of the better choices in town, serving a traditional French menu. Nonresidents can also dine here, where menus cost from 22€ to 45€ ($29–$59).

11 place d'Armes, Montignac 24290. ✆ **05-53-50-53-92.** Fax 05-53-51-02-23. www.laroseraie-hotel.com. 134 units. 80€–150€ ($104–$195) double; 150€–180€ ($195–$234) suite. Rates include half board. AE, DC, MC, V. **Amenities:** Restaurant; bar; terrace; outdoor pool. *In room:* TV, hair dryer.

Hôtel Le Relais du Soleil d'Or ★ In the heart of Montignac, this place functioned as a postal relay station during the 1800s, providing food and lodging to travelers. Today, it offers traditionally furnished rooms and a landscaped garden. The larger, better-decorated accommodations with more contemporary tub/shower bathrooms lie in a modern annex built in the 1980s, a short walk from the original building. Units in the hotel's core are very comfortable, albeit a bit less stylish; each has a compact shower-only bathroom. The main restaurant serves traditional Dordogne fare such as stewed snails with garlic and magret of duckling prepared with three different flavorings: cèpes (flap mushrooms), morels, and truffles. Dessert may be a slice of walnut cake with vanilla-walnut sauce. The less formal Le Bistrot offers salads, snacks, and simple platters.

16 rue du 4-Septembre, Montignac Lascaux 24290. ✆ **05-53-51-80-22.** Fax 05-53-50-27-54. www.le-soleil-dor.com. 32 units. 75€–99€ ($98–$129) double; 126€–211€ ($164–$274) suite. AE, DC, MC, V. Closed Feb. **Amenities:** 2 restaurants; bar; outdoor pool; room service; laundry service; dry cleaning; nonsmoking rooms; limited-mobility rooms. *In room:* TV, minibar, coffeemaker, hair dryer, iron/ironing board.

3 Les Eyzies-de-Tayac ★★

533km (331 miles) SW of Paris, 45km (28 miles) SE of Périgueux

When prehistoric skeletons were unearthed here in 1868, the market town of Les Eyzies-de-Tayac (known as Les Eyzies) suddenly became an archaeologist's dream. This area in the Dordogne Valley was found to be one of the richest in the world in ancient sites and deposits. Some of the caves contain primitive drawings made 30,000 years ago. The most beautiful and most famous are at Lascaux (see above), but many caves around Les Eyzies are open to the public.

ESSENTIALS

GETTING THERE Local **trains** run from Le Buisson, 19km (12 miles) away. The several daily trains from Périgueux are more direct. For information, call ✆ **08-92-35-35-35.** To **drive** from Périgueux, start along D710 southeast to Le Bugue, and then follow the rural road east for a short distance. Look out for the road sign pointing to Les Eyzies-de-Tayac.

VISITOR INFORMATION The **Office de Tourisme** (✆ **05-53-06-97-05;** fax 05-53-06-90-79; www.leseyzies.com) is open year-round at 19 rue de la Préhistoire (place de la Mairie).

EXPLORING THE AREA

Many of the caves in this area limit the number of daily visitors they admit; you can call ahead for reservations up to a year in advance. We recommend that you do so, especially if you plan to visit in the summer.

If you want to pedal around the countryside, you can rent bicycles at the tourist office. Prices begin at 6€ ($7.80) per half-day, 9€ ($12) per full day. A 15€ ($20) deposit is required; no credit cards are accepted.

Whether you're biking or driving, the loveliest villages include Beynac-et-Cazenac, 15km (9⅓ miles) southeast of Les Eyzies, and Sarlat-la-Canéda, 7km (4⅓ miles) northeast of Beynac. Smaller villages, including Castelnaud, La Roque-Gageac, Domme, and Montfort, lie beside the road that meanders through the Dordogne Valley. Throughout the region, routes are country roads marked only with signs leading to the above-mentioned destinations.

Make a special effort to relax within the shadow of the foreboding **Château de Beynac,** Beynac 24220 (✆ **05-53-29-50-40**), a 13th-century curiosity that opened its doors to visitors in 1961. The Grosso family has been renovating the monument for almost 40 years. Once it was the gathering place for the aristocracy of Périgord; today, the view over the valley and sense of history make a visit here worthwhile. It's open March to September daily 10am to 6:30pm; October to February, daily 11am to sundown. One-hour guided tours (in French and English) begin once or twice an hour. There are no guided tours from December to February. Admission, with or without the tour, costs 7€ ($9.10); free for children under 6. There's a worthy restaurant in the nearby **Hôtel Bonnet** (✆ **05-53-29-50-01**), which occupies the site of a converted forge and blacksmith's shop in the center of Beynac.

Sarlat-la-Canéda, 9.5km (6 miles) northeast, is home to the unusual **Cathédrale St-Sacerdos** as well as the **Maison de la Boétie,** place André-Malraux, which belonged to one of France's most famous Renaissance writers, Etienne de la Boétie. One of the town's most endearing restaurants is the **Hôtel Madrigal,** 50 av. de Selves (✆ **05-53-59-21-98**).

Tips **The Scoop on Cave Tickets**

To prevent deterioration of the art, a limited number of visitors are allowed into the caves of **Les Eyzies-de-Tayac** each day (specifically Font-de-Gaume and Combarelles). Tickets are available up to a year in advance, and we advise you to reserve that far ahead if possible.

Grotte de Font-de-Gaume ★ This is one of the few authentic caves still open to visitors, though access is limited in summer. Some of the markings you see aren't from the Magdalenian (Stone) ages but from British students on a holiday in the 18th century. Here depictions of bison, reindeer, horses, and other animals reveal the skill of the prehistoric artists.

Note: Only 140 visitors per day are permitted in the caves. In midsummer, demand far exceeds the supply of tickets, so call and reserve far in advance if you're coming between April and September.

On D47, 1.5km (1 mile) outside Les Eyzies. ✆ **05-53-06-86-00.** Admission 6.50€ ($8.45) adults, 4.50€ ($5.85) students and ages 18–24, free for children under 18. May 15–Sept 15 Mon–Fri and Sun 9:30am–5:30pm; Sept 16–May 14 Mon–Fri and Sun 9:30am–12:30pm and 2-5:30pm.

Grotte des Combarelles Discovered at the turn of the 20th century, the Grotte des Combarelles, on the southeast edge of town, has many drawings of animals, including musk oxen, horses, bison, and aurochs (wild oxen). Think of it as a gallery of Magdalenian art. Advance reservations are vital—only 60 visitors per day are admitted.

On D47, 17km (11 miles) north of Bergerac. ✆ **05-53-06-86-00.** Admission 6.50€ ($8.45) adults, 4.50€ ($5.85) students and ages 18–24, free for children under 18. May 15–Sept 15 Mon–Fri and Sun 9:30am–5:30pm; Sept 16–May 14 Mon–Fri and Sun 9:30am–12:30pm and 2–5:30pm.

Grotte du Grand-Roc (Cave of the Big Rock) ★★ Geologically, this is the most fascinating cave. Upon entering, you'll come on a tunnel of stalagmites and stalactites. The cave is about 1.5km (1 mile) northwest of Les Eyzies on the left bank of the Vézère (signs point the way on D47). There are no limits to visitors at this venue.

48 av. Préhistoirie, Les Eyzies 24620. ✆ **05-53-06-92-70.** Admission 7.50€ ($9.75) adults, 4€ ($5.20) children 6–12, free for children under 6. July–Aug daily 9:30am–7pm; Sept–Oct and June Sun–Fri 10am–6pm; Nov–Dec Sun–Fri 10am–5pm. Closed Jan.

Musée National de la Préhistoire ★★★ On a cliff above the village, this $30-million museum became the major cultural event of the French world when it opened in the summer of 2004. Designed by Florentine architect Jean-Pierre Buffi, this strikingly modern museum stands next to a fortress-castle from the 16th century. This museum is hailed for its treasure-trove of Ice Age artifacts, one of the two or three greatest collections in the world. Only 18,000 objects of the five million artifacts owned by the museum are displayed at any given time. Highlights of the collection include a small **15,000-year-old bison** ★ carved in bone, its head licking its flank. Its collection of **30,000-year-old stone engravings** ★★ is among the world's most ancient objects of art. The statue of the 3.2-million-year-old "Lucy" is a fake resin composition skeleton of a 3-year-old child (aged 50,000 years), but fascinating nonetheless. Also on display are the first replicas of the first-known human footprints, dating from around 3.6 million years ago.

1 rue de Musée ✆ **05-53-06-45-45.** Admission 5€ ($6.50) adults, 3.50€ ($4.55) students and ages 18–25, free for children under 18. July–Aug daily 9:30am–6:30pm; June and Sept Wed–Mon 9:30am–6pm; Oct–May Wed–Mon 9:30am–12:30pm and 2–5:30pm.

WHERE TO STAY & DINE

Hostellerie du Passeur *Value* This is the best bet for the frugal traveler—a well-maintained hotel containing simple, cozy rooms, each with a small but tidy bathroom with shower. The family-run restaurant serves well-crafted cuisine. The fixed-price menus (starting at 29€/$38) represent some of the best bargains in town and contain such dishes as roasted rabbit with liquefied truffles and cèpes (flap mushrooms);

roasted beefsteak with wild mushrooms; and scallops also served with flap mushrooms. Dessert may be frozen walnut soufflé. During good weather, you can dine on a shaded terrace.

Place de la Mairie, Les Eyzies-de-Tayac 24620. ✆ **05-53-06-97-13.** Fax 05-53-06-91-63. www.hostellerie-du-passeur.com. 19 units. 72€–115€ ($94–$150) double. AE, DC, MC, V. Closed early Nov to early Mar. **Amenities:** Restaurant; bar; room service; laundry service. *In room:* TV, hair dryer.

Hôtel Cro-Magnon *Value* This is the second-best hotel in town after Le Centenaire and is exceedingly comfortable, with affordable prices. The hotel may be named for a primitive man, but there's nothing rustic about the ambience and the tasteful accommodations provided. Rooms are midsize to spacious, and well furnished, with modern bathrooms with tub and shower. The breakfast buffet is quite generous.

54 av. de la Préhistoire, Les Eyzies-de-Tayac 24620. ✆ **05-53-06-97-06.** Fax 05-53-06-95-45. 65€–90€ ($85–$117) double; 100€–160€ ($130–$208) suite. AE, MC, V. Free parking. **Amenities:** Restaurant; bar; outdoor pool; room service. *In room:* TV, minibar, hair dryer, safe.

Hôtel Le Centenaire ★★★ Nothing in this area equals the charms of this oasis, which is even better known for its cuisine than for its accommodations. A Relais & Châteaux member, it has undergone extensive renovations. The good-size, very comfortable rooms are conservatively modern; bathrooms have tub/shower combinations and tiled surfaces. The chef, Roland Mazère, creates light, modern French cuisine, the finest of any restaurant mentioned in this chapter. Even if you're not a guest, consider a visit to the hotel's restaurant, where fixed-price menus cost 88€ ($114), 108€ ($140), and 138€ ($179). Specialties include gooseliver pâté and goose confit terrine—both equally divine—spider crab and apricot cake with scampi fritters, and a Périgord black truffle risotto.

Rocher de la Penne, Les Eyzies-Tayac-Sireuil 24620. ✆ **05-53-06-68-68.** Fax 05-53-06-92-41. www.hotelducentenaire.fr. 24 units. 138€–230€ ($179–$299) double; 230€–305€ ($299–$397) suite. AE, DC, MC, V. Closed Nov–Mar. **Amenities:** Restaurant; bar; heated outdoor pool; health club; shopping gallery; room service; laundry service. *In room:* TV, minibar, hair dryer.

Hôtel Les Glycines ★ *Finds* We'd stay here just for the flower garden. Since 1862, this establishment has offered regional cuisine, comfortable accommodations, and charming touches such as drinks on a veranda with a grape arbor. Rooms are quaint with a regional charm and touches of designer style. Each is midsize to spacious; most of the compact bathrooms have a combination tub/shower. Restaurant specialties include macaroni laced with foie gras, cèpes (flap mushrooms), and truffles; veal roasted with cured ham and truffled polenta; *confit de canard* with truffle juice; and escalope of duck liver with lime juice. The chef is famous for desserts that include a soft-textured chocolate biscuit covered with caramel sauce.

Rte. de Périgueux (D47), 24620 Les Eyzies-Tayac-Sireuil. ✆ **05-53-06-97-07.** Fax 05-53-06-92-19. www.les-glycines-dordogne.com. 23 units. 76€–118€ ($99–$153) double; 142€–254€ ($185–$330) junior suite. AE, DC, MC, V. Closed Nov to late Mar. **Amenities:** Restaurant; bar; outdoor pool; room service; laundry. *In room:* TV, hair dryer.

4 Rocamadour ★★★

541km (336 miles) SW of Paris, 66km (41 miles) SE of Sarlat-la-Canéda, 55km (34 miles) S of Brive, 63km (39 miles) NE of Cahors

Rocamadour reached the zenith of its fame and prosperity in the 13th century. Make an effort to see it, even if it's out of your way. The setting is one of the most unusual in Europe: Towers, old buildings, and oratories rise in stages up the side of a cliff on the slope of the usually dry gorge of Alzou. The population has held steady at around 5,000 for many years.

The faithful continue to arrive today as they did more than 8 centuries ago. As a pilgrimage site, Rocamadour is billed as "the second site of France" (Mont-St-Michel ranks first). Summer visitors descend in droves, and vehicles are prohibited. Park in one of the big lots and make your way on foot.

ESSENTIALS

GETTING THERE The best way to reach Rocamadour is by **car.** From Bordeaux, travel east along N89 to Brive-la-Gaillarde, connect to N205 east into Cressensac, and continue on N140 south to Rocamadour.

Rocamadour and neighboring Padirac share a **train** station, **Gare de Rocamadour-Padirac,** that isn't really convenient to either—it's 4km (2½ miles) east of Rocamadour on N140. Trains arrive infrequently from Brive in the north and Capdenac in the south. For train information and schedules, call ✆ **08-92-35-35-35. Bus** service in and out of town is so infrequent it's almost nonexistent.

VISITOR INFORMATION The town maintains two separate **tourist offices** in the Hôtel de Ville, rue Roland-le-Preux (✆ **05-65-33-62-59**), and another well-signposted branch office within l'Hospitalet, in the old town (✆ **05-65-33-22-00;** fax 05-65-33-22-01; www.rocamadour.com).

EXPLORING THE TOWN

The **site** ★★★ of this gravity-defying village rises abruptly across the landscape. Its single street, lined with souvenir shops, runs along the side of a steep hill. It's best seen when approached from the road coming in from the tiny village of L'Hospitalet. Once in Rocamadour, you can take a flight of steps or an elevator from the lower town (Basse Ville) to the town's **Cité Réligieuse,** a cluster of chapels and churches halfway up the cliff.

To help people negotiate the town's steep inclines, the town maintains two elevators. One goes from the Basse Ville to the Cité Réligieuse, midway up the rocky heights of Rocamadour. The ride costs 2€ ($2.60) one-way, 3€ ($3.90) round-trip. The other goes from the Cité Réligieuse to the panoramic medieval ramparts *(le château)* near the hill's summit; it costs 2.50€ ($3.25) one-way, 4€ ($5.20) round-trip.

Château de Rocamadour *(le château)* perches on a rock spur above the town center. You can reach it by way of the curvy "chemin de la Croix." It was built in the 14th century and restored by the local bishops in the 19th century. Its interior is off-limits except for guests of the church officials who live and work here. You can, however, walk along its panoramic **ramparts** ★★★, which are open daily 8am to 8pm (to 6pm Oct–Apr). Admission to the ramparts costs 2€ ($2.60).

The most photogenic entrance to the Basse Ville is the **Porte du Figuier (Fig Tree Gate),** through which many of the most illustrious Europeans of the 13th century passed.

One of the oldest places of pilgrimage in France, Rocamadour became famous as a cult center of the black Madonna. Zacchaeus, who entertained Christ at Jericho, supposedly founded it. He reputedly came here with a black wooden statue of the Virgin, although some authorities have suggested that the statue was carved in the 9th century.

Basilique St-Sauveur Against the cliff, this basilica was built in the Romanesque-Gothic style from the 11th to the 13th century. It's decorated with paintings and inscriptions recalling visits of celebrated persons, including Philippe the Handsome.

In the **Chapelle Miraculeuse,** the "holy of holies," St. Amadour is said to have carved out an oratory in the rock. Hanging from the roof is one of the oldest known clocks, dating to the 8th century. The Romanesque Chapelle St-Michel is sheltered by an overhanging rock; inside are two 12th-century frescoes. The venerated **Black Madonna** ★ occupies a chapel—**Chapelle de Notre-Dame**—devoted almost exclusively to it. It was built in the 12th century, with many 19th-century additions and alterations, and lies adjacent to the Basilique St-Saveur. Above the door leading to the Chapelle Notre-Dame is an iron sword that, according to legend, belonged to Roland.

Place St-Amadour. ✆ **05-65-33-23-23.** Free admission. Daily 9am–7pm.

Cité Réligieuse This cluster of chapels and churches is the town's religious centerpiece, visited by both casual tourists and devoted pilgrims. Site of many conversions, with mystical connotations that date to the Middle Ages, it's accessible from the town on the **Grand Escalier,** a stairway of 216 steps. Even today, devout pilgrims make this journey on their knees in penance. Climbing the weathered steps will lead you to the **parvis des Eglises,** place St-Amadour, with seven chapels. Schedules of tours change frequently, based on saints' holidays and local church schedules. Three to five tours take place each day (depending on the season); times are prominently posted at the entrance.

Place de la Carreta. ✆ **05-65-33-23-23.** Free admission; donations appreciated. Suggested donation for tour 5.50€ ($7.15) adults, 3.10€ ($4.05) children 8–18.

WHERE TO STAY & DINE

Grand Hôtel Beau-Site ★ With its entrance evoking a medieval hall, this is the town's finest inn, a place with original character. The stone walls were built in the 15th century by an Order of Malta commander, Jehan de Valon (1440–1516). Today the rear terrace provides a view of the Val d'Alzou. The reception area has heavy beams and a cavernous fireplace. Rooms (23 of which are in the air-conditioned main building, the rest in a less desirable annex) are comfortable; each has a midsize bathroom, most with a combination tub/shower.

The restaurant serves regional cuisine prepared by the Menot family, who've owned the place for generations. Specialties include foie gras of duck with dark truffles, raw marinated salmon with green peppercorns, and braised and roasted duck served with truffled mashed potatoes. Dessert may be a slice of country-style fruit pie, served with caramel and whortleberry sauce, or a cake of caramelized walnuts.

Cité Médiévale, Rocamadour 46500. ✆ **800/528-1234** in the U.S. and Canada, or 05-65-33-63-08. Fax 05-65-33-65-23. www.bw-beausite.com. 38 units. 70€–120€ ($91–$156) double; 97€–129€ ($126–$168) suite. AE, DC, MC, V. Free parking. Closed mid-Nov to mid-Feb. **Amenities:** Restaurant; bar; outdoor pool; room service; laundry service. *In room:* A/C, TV, hair dryer, safe.

WHERE TO STAY & DINE NEARBY

Château de Roumégouse ★ If you prefer to be away from the tourist bustle, try this Relais & Châteaux property in Roumégouse. The 15th-century château overlooking the Causse is surrounded by 4.8 hectares (12 acres) of parkland. Each spacious room is unique in both decor and architecture, and outfitted with antique furniture and paintings. Fixed-price menus at Roumégouse range from 35€ to 45€ ($46–$59).

N140, Rignac, Gramat 46500. Take N140 to Roumégouse, 6.5km (4 miles) southeast of Rocamadour. ✆ **05-65-33-63-81.** Fax 05-65-33-71-18. www.chateauderoumegouse.com. 15 units. 140€–420€ ($182–$546) double; 300€–480€ ($390–$624) suite. AE, MC, V. Closed Jan–Apr. **Amenities:** Restaurant; bar; room service; laundry service. *In room:* A/C, TV, minibar, hair dryer.

Hôtel Domaine de La Rhue ★ *Finds* The charming owners, Christine and Eric Jooris, gutted a 19th-century stable and turned it into a series of spacious rooms, each individually decorated in superb taste. Some have terraces, some have minibars, and all are equipped with compact bathrooms, mainly with shower units. On the lower level is an inviting reception and breakfast room with a welcoming fireplace. The Joorises, who speak English, are most helpful in directing you to the best places for dinner in the center of Rocamadour, a few minutes' drive away. Christine enjoys mapping out tours of nearby villages and plotting the best direction from which to approach each town or castle to ensure a commanding view and to take advantage of afternoon sun for photographs. Eric is a pilot and takes guests for a 45-minute hot-air balloon ride over the canyon of Rocamadour for 150€ ($195). Breakfast is the only meal served.

Rocamadour 46500. Follow rte. D673, then N140 signposted RHUE for a total of 5km (3 miles) from town. ✆ **05-65-33-71-50.** Fax 05-65-33-72-48. www.domainedelarhue.com. 14 units. 70€–145€ ($91–$189) double. MC, V. Closed Oct 20–Apr. **Amenities:** Outdoor pool. *In room:* Hair dryer.

5 Cahors ★★

541km (336 miles) SW of Paris, 217km (135 miles) SE of Bordeaux, 89km (55 miles) N of Toulouse

The ancient capital of Quercy, Cahors was a thriving university city in the Middle Ages, and many antiquities from its illustrious past remain. Today, Cahors is best known for the almost-legendary red wine that's made principally from the Malbec grapes grown in vineyards around this old city. Firm but not harsh, Cahors is one of the most deeply colored fine French wines.

Since the mid-1990s, the city of Cahors has funded the redesign and replanting of at least 21 municipal gardens, most of them laid out in medieval patterns, using historically appropriate plants. The most spectacular of these gardens lie immediately adjacent to Town Hall. Overall, they function as a magnet for horticultural societies throughout France.

ESSENTIALS

GETTING THERE To **drive** to Cahors from Toulouse, follow A62 north to the junction with N20 and continue on N20 north into Cahors.

Trains serve Cahors from Toulouse, Brive, and Montauban. You may have to transfer in neighboring towns. For train information and schedules, call ✆ **08-92-35-35-35.** There's infrequent bus service from some of the outlying villages, several of which are of historical interest, but it's vastly easier to drive.

VISITOR INFORMATION The **Office de Tourisme** is on place François-Mitterrand (✆ **05-65-53-20-65;** fax 05-65-53-20-74; www.mairie-cahors.fr).

SPECIAL EVENTS The **Festival du Blues** turns this town upside down for 3 days in mid-July, when blues groups, including some from the United States, descend. Most of the performances are open-air affairs, many free, with bands playing at cafes along the boulevard Gambetta. Formal concerts are usually at the **Théâtre des Verdures,** an open-air courtyard in the heart of the medieval city. Tickets are 30€ ($39). For exact dates and information, contact the Office de Tourisme (see above). For tickets, contact **Cahors Blues Festival** (✆ **05-65-35-99-99;** www.cahorsbluesfestival.com).

EXPLORING THE AREA

The town is on a rocky **peninsula** ★ almost entirely surrounded by a loop of the Lot River. It grew near a sacred spring that still supplies the city with water. At the source

Finds **Cahors for Wine Lovers**

A robustness that mellows over time characterizes the wines of Cahors. Three wineries of exceptional merit, all within a short drive of Cahors, are Domaine de Lagrezette, in Caillac (✆ **05-65-20-07-42**); Domaine de Haute Serre, in Cieurac (✆ **05-65-20-80-20**); and Domaine de St-Didier Parnac, in Parnac (✆ **05-65-30-78-13**). Their dark wines are of consistently high quality and easily hold their own with any of the region's rich, hearty dishes. The Office de Tourisme (see above) provides detailed information and maps to these wineries.

of the spring, the **Fontaine des Chartreux** stands by the side of the **pont Valentré** ★★ (also called the pont du Diable), a bridge with a trio of towers. It's a magnificent example of medieval defensive design erected between 1308 and 1380 and restored in the 19th century. The pont, the first medieval fortified bridge in France, is the most eye-catching site in Cahors, with crenellated parapets, battlements, and seven pointed arches.

Dominating the old town, the **Cathédrale St-Etienne** ★, 30 rue de la Chanterie (✆ **05-65-35-27-80**), was begun in 1119 and reconstructed between 1285 and 1500. It was the first cathedral in the country to have cupolas, giving it a Romanesque-Byzantine look. One remarkable feature is its sculptured Romanesque north portal, carved around 1135 in the Languedoc style. It's open daily from 9am (the scheduled hour for daily Mass) to 6 or 7pm, depending on the season. Adjoining the cathedral are the remains of a Gothic cloister from the late 15th century. The cloister is open only May to October, Monday to Saturday 10am to 12:30pm. Admission to the cloister is free.

WHERE TO STAY

Hôtel de France This 1970s hotel, positioned midway between pont Valentré and the train station, provides some of the best rooms in the town center. They're well furnished and modern. Each unit comes with an average-size bathroom, most with a shower unit. Half of the rooms have air-conditioning. The room service is efficient, but breakfast is the only meal served.

252 av. Jean-Jaurès, Cahors 46000. ✆ **05-65-35-16-76.** Fax 05-65-22-01-08. www.hoteldefrance-cahors.fr. 76 units. 48€–92€ ($62–$120) double. AE, DC, MC, V. Parking 5€ ($6.50). Closed Dec 18–Jan 10. *In room:* A/C (in some), TV, minibar, Wi-Fi.

Hôtel Terminus ★ On the avenue leading from the railway station into the heart of town, this hotel oozes the turn-of-the-20th-century character of its original stone construction. Rooms are conservative yet tasteful, with floral prints, fresh flowers, and firm beds. Bathrooms are average size, most with a combination tub/shower. On the premises is Le Balandre, the town's best restaurant. It specializes in regional dishes from the surrounding Périgord-Quercy district. Even if you don't opt for a meal in its Art Deco dining room or on the outdoor terrace, you may want to stop into the 1920s-style bar for a drink.

5 av. Charles-de-Freycinet, Cahors 46000. ✆ **05-65-53-32-00.** Fax 05-65-53-32-26. www.balandre.com. 22 units. 60€–130€ ($78–$169) double; 130€–160€ ($169–$208) suite. AE, DC, MC, V. Parking free in courtyard, 8€ ($10) in garage. Closed last 2 weeks in Nov. **Amenities:** Restaurant; bar; room service; laundry service. *In room:* TV, minibar, hair dryer.

WHERE TO DINE

Le Balandre, the restaurant at **Hôtel Terminus** (see "Where to Stay," above), serves well-recommended cuisine.

Le Rendez-Vous ★ FRENCH One of the most appealing restaurants in Cahors's historic core occupies the stone-walled, ocher-colored premises of a 13th-century private house. Today, under the direction of Mme Iglesias (in the dining room) and Stéphane Brugoux (chef and owner), it turns out an array of well-prepared and reasonably priced dishes that guarantee an animated crowd. Menu items change with the season, but may include fried foie gras with spice bread; *tarte fine* (brandied tart) layered with anchovies and confit of onions; superb farm-raised veal; roasted slow-cooked lamb; scallops served with basil-flavored noodles and confit of garlic; and grilled filet of Scottish salmon with lentils.

49 rue Clément Marot. ✆ **05-65-22-65-10.** www.le-rendez-vous-cahors.com. Reservations recommended. Main courses 14€ ($18); fixed-price lunch 17€–23€ ($22–$30); fixed-price dinner 23€ ($30). MC, V. Tues–Sat noon–2pm and 7:30–10pm. Closed 2 weeks in Mar and 2 weeks in Nov.

L'O à la Bouche *Value* MODERN FRENCH One of Cahors's newest brasseries lies within a historic, 14th-century building whose two dining rooms are lined with medieval masonry and capped with massive ceiling beams. The only way meals are choreographed at this popular spot involves full fixed-price menus, each with a choice of at least four food items per category (that is, a minimum of four starters, four main courses, and four desserts). As such, you'll find a wide enough variety to please any palate. Menu items include a creamy, saffron-tinged version of mussel soup; homemade foie gras with quince jam; a changing array of fresh grilled fish, served, perhaps, with broccoli-studded risotto; and caramelized and roasted pork served with four different spices. Cheese may be substituted for any desserts on the menu, and if so, expect an esoteric type that may have derived from a small farm nearby.

134 rue St-Urcisse. ✆ **05-65-35-65-69.** Reservations recommended. Fixed-price menu 25€ ($33). MC, V. Tues–Sat noon–1:30pm and 7–9:30pm.

6 Montauban ★

644km (400 miles) SW of Paris, 72km (45 miles) NW of Albi, 50km (31 miles) N of Toulouse

This pink-brick capital of the Tarn-et-Garonne *département* is the city of the painter Ingres and the sculptor Bourdelle. Montauban, on the right bank of the Tarn, dominated by the fortified Eglise St-Jacques, is one of the most ancient of southwest France's towns. The most scenic view of Montauban is at the 14th-century brick bridge, pont Vieux, which connects the town to its satellite of Villebourbon.

Jean-Auguste-Dominique Ingres, an admirer of Raphael and a student of David, was born in 1780 in Montauban. His father, an ornamental sculptor and painter, recognized his son's artistic abilities early and encouraged him. He was noted for his nudes and historical paintings, now considered fine examples of neoclassicism. One of his first exhibitions of portraits in 1806 met with ridicule, but later generations have been more appreciative. With the exception of one work displayed in the town's cathedral, Montauban's work by Ingres is in the Musée Ingres (see below).

ESSENTIALS

GETTING THERE If you're **driving,** RN20 (Paris-Toulouse-Andorra, Spain), RN113 (Bordeaux-Marseille), and the A61 motorway run through the Tarn-et-Garonne.

Seven **trains** arrive here daily from Paris Gare d'Austerlitz (trip time: 5–6 hr.); trains arrive every hour from Toulouse (trip time: 25 min.). For train information and schedules, call ✆ **08-92-35-35-35.** For **bus** information, call ✆ **05-63-63-60-60.**

VISITOR INFORMATION The **Office de Tourisme** is at rue Prax Paris (✆ **05-63-63-60-60;** fax 05-63-63-65-12; www.montauban-tourisme.com).

SPECIAL EVENTS The major cultural happening, the **Festival Alors Chante** (✆ **05-63-63-66-77;** http://perso.wanadoo.fr/alors-chante), takes place during Ascension Week, which begins 40 days after Easter. The event showcases traditional French music and song, and offers performances by both stars and talented unknowns. Tickets cost 10€ to 35€ ($13–$46). The **Festival de Jazz à Montauban** (✆ **05-63-63-56-56;** www.jazzmontauban.com), typically held the second week of July, fills the outdoor venues with blues and jazz concerts.

EXPLORING THE AREA

Shoppers may want to pick up some foie gras at the **Conserverie Artisanale Larroque,** 1300 av. de Falguières (✆ **05-63-63-45-40**). Or visit **Pecou,** 10 rue de la République (✆ **05-63-63-06-38**), for a supply of *montauriol* (chocolate-covered cherries with a shot of Armagnac) and *boulet de Montauban* (chocolate-covered roasted hazelnuts) candies.

A specialty of the town is *pigeonniers miniatures*—models of pigeon coops that were built on local farms to attract pigeons for their "fertilizer." The **Librairie Deloche,** 21 rue de la République (✆ **05-63-63-22-66**), carries 30 models of various architectural styles and a selection of books on pigeonniers.

Head for the **Cathédrale Notre-Dame,** place Roosevelt (✆ **05-63-63-10-23**), a classical building constructed in 1692 and framed by two square towers. In the north transept is the monumental painting the church commissioned from Ingres, *Vow of Louis XIII.* It's open Monday to Saturday 9am to noon and 2 to 7pm. Masses are conducted Sunday from 9am to noon.

Musée Ingres ★★ Upon his death in 1867, the artist bequeathed to Montauban more than two dozen paintings and some 4,000 drawings (more than any other museum except the Louvre). They're on display at this 17th-century bishops' palace. One painting is *Christ and the Doctors,* a work Ingres completed at 82. The *Dream of Ossian* was intended for Napoleon's bedroom in Rome. On the ground floor are works by Antoine Bourdelle, who was influenced by Rodin. The busts Bourdelle sculpted of Ingres and of Rodin are particularly outstanding.

19 rue de l'Hôtel-de-Ville. ✆ **05-63-22-12-91.** Admission 4€ ($5.20) adults, 2€ ($2.60) seniors, free for children under 18. July–Aug daily 10am–6pm; Sept–June Tues–Sat 10am–noon, Tues–Sun 2–6pm.

WHERE TO STAY

Restaurant La Cuisine d'Alain et Hôtel Orsay (see below) also rents rooms.

Hôtel Mercure Montauban ★ In a town not known for its inns, this is a shining light. One of the most dramatic hotel renovations in the district occurred in 2001, with continuing renovations every year since then. Today, it's the most appealing modern hotel in town, with relatively large rooms and comfortable beds. All units come with midsize bathrooms, most with a combination tub/shower. The restaurant, La Brasserie Bourdelle, named after the local sculptor, serves fixed-price menus.

12 rue Notre-Dame, Montauban 82000. ✆ **05-63-63-17-23.** Fax 05-63-66-43-66. www.mercure.com. 44 units. 99€ ($129) double. AE, DC, MC, V. Parking 7€ ($9.10). **Amenities:** Restaurant; bar; room service; laundry service; nonsmoking rooms; limited-mobility rooms. *In room:* A/C, TV, minibar, hair dryer.

WHERE TO DINE

The **Hôtel Mercure Montauban** (see above) has a decent restaurant.

Les Saveurs d'Ingres ★★ FRENCH In a vaulted dining room in the center of town, Cyril Paysserand showcases his culinary wares. It's close to the Ingres Museum and makes an idyllic luncheon stopover. His cuisine uses market-fresh ingredients, and his cooking is sublime, often with imaginative touches. One of our favorite dishes is the sautéed foie gras with mango chutney and cashew nuts. You might follow with a delectable plate of sweetbreads with artichokes and truffles. In season, woodcock is a special feature.

13 rue de l'Hôtel de Ville. ✆ **05-63-91-26-42.** Reservations required. Main courses 25€–33€ ($33–$43). Fixed-price menus 25€–70€ ($33–$91). MC, V. Tues–Sat noon–1:30pm and Tues–Sat 8–9:30pm. Closed last week of Jan, 1 week in May, and 1 week in Aug.

Restaurant La Cuisine d'Alain et Hôtel Orsay ★ MODERN FRENCH This is the best restaurant in town. Chef Alain Blanc is talented and inventive. Try terrine of lentils flavored with the neck of a fattened goose *en confit,* filet of beef with foie gras and apple flan, or warm escalope of foie gras with apples. The amazing dessert trolley offers plenty of choices. Built a century ago, the well-kept Hôtel Orsay has 20 pleasantly decorated but unpretentious rooms, with doubles running 49€ to 64€ ($64–$83).

Face Gare (across from the train station). ✆ **05-63-66-06-66.** Fax 05-63-66-19-39. www.hotel-restaurant-orsay.com. Reservations recommended. Main courses 19€–34€ ($25–$44); fixed-price menu 23€–58€ ($30–$75). AE, MC, V. Tues–Fri noon–2pm; Mon–Sat 7:30–10pm. Closed 1 week in May, 2nd and 3rd weeks of Aug, and Dec 23–Jan 8.

MONTAUBAN AFTER DARK

One of the busiest and most widely visited nightclubs in Montauban is **Le Caïpirhina,** a warm and rustic-looking vaulted cellar beneath a Mexican restaurant, **Le Santa Maria,** 2 sq. Bourjade (✆ **05-63-91-99-09**), close to Musée d'Ingres. Open Thursday to Saturday, it gets busy beginning around 10pm. Entrance is usually free unless a live band is entertaining that night or if a special theme night is in effect.

22

The Massif Central

In your race south to Biarritz or through the Rhône Valley to the Riviera, you'll pass through the Massif Central, the agricultural heartland of France. Here you'll find ancient cities, lovely valleys, and wonderful provincial cuisine. With its rolling farmlands, countryside, and châteaux and manor houses (many of which you can stay and dine in), this is one of the most unspoiled parts of France—your chance to see a life too rapidly fading.

From the spa at Vichy to the volcanic *puys* of the Auvergne, the Massif Central offers much of interest and much to learn about the art of good living. We begin in George Sand country, in the province of Berry, and proceed to the Auvergne Limousin.

1 Bourges ★★★

238km (148 miles) S of Paris, 69km (43 miles) NW of Nevers, 153km (95 miles) NW of Vichy, 282km (175 miles) NW of Lyon

Once the capital of Aquitaine, Bourges lies in the heart of France; you can easily visit it from Orléans, at the eastern end of the Loire Valley (see chapter 8). The commercial and industrial center of Berry, this regional capital is still off the beaten path for most tourists, even though it boasts a rich medieval past. Its history extends far beyond the Middle Ages: In 52 B.C., Caesar called it the finest city in Gaul. Today Bourges remains a rather sleepy provincial town, awakened only by the life surrounding the Institut Universitaire de Technologie.

ESSENTIALS

GETTING THERE There are good road and rail connections from Tours and other regional cities. Five to eight **trains** arrive daily from Paris's Gare d'Austerlitz (trip time: 2 hr.; one-way fare: 31€/$40); the trip sometimes requires a transfer at nearby Vierzon. Twelve trains a day arrive from Tours, taking 1½ hours, a one-way fare costing 19€ ($25). For information and schedules, call ✆ **08-92-35-35-35.** If you're **driving** from Paris, take A10 south to Orléans and A71, and then RN 20 to Vierzon, where you pick up Route 76 east into Bourges. From Tours, head east along RN 76.

VISITOR INFORMATION The **Office de Tourisme** is at 21 rue Victor-Hugo (✆ **02-48-23-02-60;** fax 02-48-23-02-69; www.bourgestourisme.com).

SPECIAL EVENTS The energy level really picks up between April and August, thanks to several colorful music festivals. The **Festival Printemps de Bourges,** during 5 days in late April, includes dozens of concerts ranging from traditional French music to international pop and rock. Most events cost 20€ to 40€ ($26–$52), though any number of spontaneous performances pop up along the sidewalks and in the bars for everyone to enjoy at no charge. For tickets and more information, contact the **Association Printemps de Bourges,** 22 rue Henri-Sellier (✆ **02-48-27-28-29;**

www.printemps-bourges.com). At the beginning of June, a younger, high-impact music scene explodes during the **Festival Synthese,** which has attracted groups such as U2, Barry White, and some of the best performers in France. For information, call ✆ **02-48-20-41-87.** The annual event, **Un Eté à Bourges,** runs from mid-June to mid-September. During this time, the streets fill with musical performers and actors. More structured performances also take place in churches and public monuments, with free tickets (usually). For information, call ✆ **02-48-57-81-10,** or contact the tourist office.

SEEING THE SIGHTS

Cathédrale St-Etienne ★★★ On the summit of a hill dominating the town, this is one of the most beautiful Gothic cathedrals in France. Construction began at the end of the 12th century and wasn't completed until a century and a half later. Flanked by asymmetrical towers, it has five magnificent doorways, including one depicting episodes in the life of St. Stephen. The cathedral has a vaulted roof and five aisles, and is remarkably long (122m/400 ft.); it's distinguished for its stained-glass windows, best viewed with binoculars. Many were made between 1215 and 1225. One impressive scene, *A Meal in the House of Simon,* shows Jesus lecturing Simon as Mary Magdalene repents at his feet. To climb the north tower for a view of Bourges, buy a ticket from the custodian. The same ticket allows you to explore the church's 12th-century crypt, the largest in France. In the crypt is the tomb (built 1422–38) of Jean de Berry, who ruled this duchy in the 14th century. Fanatically dedicated to art, he directed a "small army" of artisans, painters, and sculptors. The recumbent figure is the only part of the original tomb that has survived.

After your visit, you may want to wander through the **Jardins de l'Archevêché,** the archbishop's gardens, credited to Le Nôtre. From these gardens you'll have a good view of the eastern side of the cathedral.

Place Etienne-Dolet. ✆ **02-48-65-49-44.** Free admission to cathedral; tower and crypt 6.50€ ($8.45) adults, 4.50€ ($5.85) ages 18–25, free for children under 18. Combination ticket to cathedral and Palais Jacques-Coeur 9€ ($12), 6€ ($7.80) ages 18–25. Cathedral Apr–Sept daily 8:30am–7:15pm; Oct–Mar daily 9am–5:45pm. Crypt closed until 1pm Sun for Mass.

Hôtel Lallemant The Renaissance Hôtel Lallemant, a 5-minute walk north of the cathedral, has been transformed into a museum of decorative art. The mansion was built for a textile merchant; today its galleries display a colorful history of Bourges. Exhibits include china, objets d'art, ceramics, and antique furniture.

6 rue Bourbonnoux. ✆ **02-48-57-81-17.** Free admission. Tues–Sat 10am–noon; Tues–Sun 2–5pm.

Musée du Berry The museum is inside the Hôtel Cujas, built about 1515. On display is a collection of Celtic and Gallo-Roman artifacts; the 280 funerary sculptures are impressive. Some rooms are devoted to finds from Egyptian archaeological digs, along with medieval masterpieces of sculpture from around 1400; some rooms on the second floor have ethnological exhibitions.

4 rue des Arènes. ✆ **02-48-57-81-15.** Free admission. Mon and Wed–Sat 10am–noon; Wed–Sun 2–6pm.

Palais Jacques-Coeur ★★ This is one of the country's greatest secular Gothic structures. Take a 1-hour guided tour—the only way to see the palace—through the four buildings surrounding a central court, constructed around 1450 by the finance minister and banker Jacques Coeur. M. Coeur never got to enjoy the palace, however. After a trial by a jury of his creditors, the wealthy financier was tossed into prison by Charles VII and died there in 1456. His furnishings no longer remain, but the decor

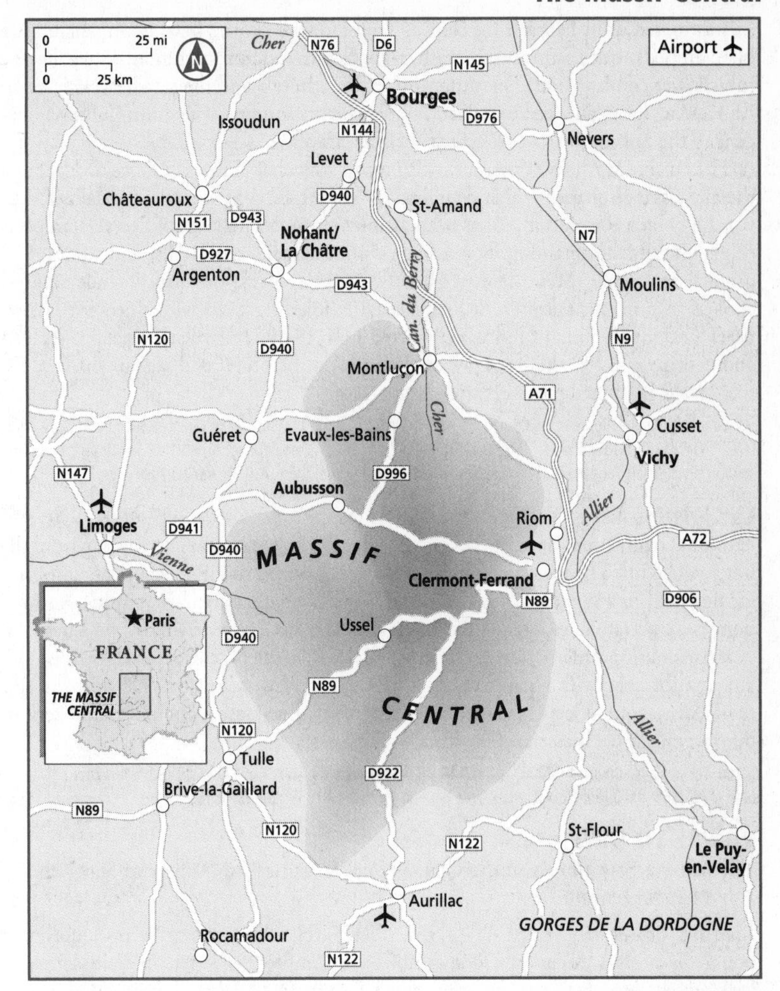

and wealth of detail inside the palace allow a remarkable view of 15th-century opulence. In the dining hall is a monumental chimney piece, and in the great hall are sculptures from the 15th and 16th centuries. The mandatory tour is in French; English speakers receive a printed translation of the commentary.

10 bis Rue Jacques-Coeur. ✆ **02-48-24-79-42.** Admission 6.50€ ($8.45) adults, 4.50€ ($5.85) ages 18–25 and over 60, free for children under 18. Combination ticket to cathedral and Palais Jacques-Coeur 9€ ($12) adults, 6€ ($7.80) students. 6 tours depart daily on a schedule that changes weekly.

WHERE TO STAY

Grand Hôtel Mercure Hôtel de Bourbon et Abbaye St-Ambroix ★★ This is the finest hotel in Bourges, and its cuisine is the best in the area. In the early 1990s, the Mercure chain converted a 17th-century abbey and a stately home into this first-class hotel. The cheerful rooms are well appointed and comfortable (except for the half-timbered units beneath the sloping mansard roof on the third floor, which are a bit cramped). Each unit comes with a small but modern bathroom; most have a tub/shower combination. The stonework of the exterior and the public areas is beautiful and artfully cadenced to reflect the site's historic origins. The setting, almost adjacent to the rail station, is convenient for train travelers.

The cuisine at Abbaye St-Ambroix is prepared by chef François Adamski. Although the Renaissance chapel, which contains the restaurant, was seriously vandalized during the French Revolution, it has been artfully restored into a simplified version of its original grandeur, retaining its massive columns, thick stone walls, and some of its original sculptures. Menu items change with the seasons, but may include scallops cooked in tarragon butter with French caviar; foie gras fried with dried fruit, fresh pears, and a reduction of red wine; roasted John Dory served with vegetable lasagna and chorizo sausage; and local pigeon cooked "on the bone" and served with a casserole of old-fashioned root vegetables and cream.

Bd. de la République, Bourges 18000. ✆ **02-48-70-70-00.** Fax 02-48-70-21-22. www.hoteldebourbon.fr. 57 units. 99€–145€ ($129–$189) double; 175€ ($228) suite. AE, DC, MC, V. Free parking. **Amenities:** Restaurant; bar; room service; dry cleaning; nonsmoking rooms; limited-mobility rooms. *In room:* A/C, TV, minibar, hair dryer.

Le Christina *Value* This is a standard but comfortable inn, built in the 1930s and renovated many times since. It rises three or five stories (depending on which part of the hotel you're in). The bigger and more recently renovated rooms have private safes and are outfitted in a vaguely Louis XVI style. Other units that are less recently renovated don't have private safes, are a bit smaller, and have decors loosely based on Louis XV or a streamlined "internationally modern" style. Regardless of their style, each is cozy and comfortable, with warm colors. The location, a few steps from the cathedral and the Palais Jacques-Coeur, is especially convenient. Breakfast is the only meal served, but several simple brasseries lie within walking distance.

5 rue de la Halle, Bourges 18000. ✆ **02-48-70-56-50.** Fax 02-48-70-58-13. www.le-christina.com. 71 units. 52€–77€ ($68–$100) double. AE, MC, V. Free parking. *In room:* A/C, TV, safe (in some).

WHERE TO DINE

The **Abbaye St-Ambroix** at the Grand Hôtel Mercure (see "Where to Stay," above) also offers fine cuisine.

Jacques-Coeur ★ TRADITIONAL FRENCH This tavern serves traditional bourgeois cuisine, though the food at Abbaye St-Ambroix is better. Specialties include veal kidneys *berrichonne,* frogs' legs sautéed with herbs, *scallops à la façon* (with a *concasse* [purée] of tomatoes, snail-flavored butter, and onion beignets), fresh filets of mackerel marinated in white wine, and chicken *en barbouille* (with a sauce made of wine and blood). The desserts are homemade and tempting, and service is efficient. The featured wines include Quincy and Menetou-Salon, two excellent but not well-known regional vintages. Of the two medieval Gothic-style dining rooms, the one on the upper floor is more interesting, with exposed beams and plaster impressions of scallop shells on its ceiling (ca. 1947).

3 place Jacques-Coeur. ✆ **02-48-26-53-01.** Reservations required. Main courses 30€ ($39); fixed-price menu 20€–60€ ($26–$78). MC, V. June–Sept daily noon–2pm and 7–10pm; Oct–May Mon–Fri and Sun noon–2pm, Mon–Sat 7:15–9:15pm.

BOURGES AFTER DARK

Most of the best clubs are in Bourges's old town. Try **Le Pub Birdland,** 4 av. Jean-Jaurès (✆ **02-48-70-66-77**), an old-fashioned establishment with a wood interior, a young crowd of heavy-duty beer drinkers, and jazz and rock. **Beau Bar,** rue des Beaux-Arts (✆ **02-48-24-40-49**), pulls in a bohemian crowd—artists, poets, songwriters, and the like. For something a little different, head to **La Soupe aux Choux,** part of the restaurant Le Guillotin, place Gordaine (✆ **02-48-65-43-66**), where you can take in an evening of *cafe-théâtre.* Shows can be anything from musical performances to stand-up comedy; tickets run 8€ to 15€ ($10–$20). Bourges' most popular, most centrally located, and most animated disco is **Le Canari,** Esplanade du Prado (✆ **02-48-65-35-67**). Attracting a clientele between 20 and 40 years of age, including lots of the recently divorced and newly available singles of the region, it's open Tuesday and Thursday to Saturday from around 9:30pm to 4am; cover is about 10€ ($13), depending on the night of the week.

2 Nohant/La Châtre

290km (180 miles) S of Paris, 31km (19 miles) S of Châteauroux

George Sand was the pen name of Amandine Lucile Aurore Dupin, baronne Dudevant, the French novelist born in 1804. Her memory is forever connected to Nohant, the little Berry hamlet near the Indre Valley.

In her early life, she wrote bucolic tales of peasants, but she also penned romantic novels in which she maintained that women were entitled to as much freedom as men. Among her 80 novels, some of the best known were *François le Champi* and *La Mare au Diable.* She was also known for her love affairs; her two most notorious were with the poet Alfred de Musset and the composer Frédéric Chopin. By the time of her death in Nohant in 1876, George Sand had become a legend.

ESSENTIALS

GETTING THERE If you're **driving,** it's a 1-hour trip from Bourges to La Châtre on D940 south. The closest **train** station is in Châteauroux, 36km (22 miles) from La Châtre; connecting bus service (no. 15) links Châteauroux to Nohant/La Châtre. Nohant and La Châtre are 6km (3¾ miles) apart. From Bourges, you can buy a combination train and bus ticket to La Châtre via Châteauroux. Five daily trains make the run to Châteauroux, where you transfer to a bus to complete the 2-hour trip. For complete train information, call ✆ **08-92-35-35-35.**

VISITOR INFORMATION The nearest **Office de Tourisme** is 134 rue Nationale (✆ **02-54-48-22-64;** fax 02-54-06-09-615; www.la-chatre.com) at avenue Nationale in La Châtre.

IN THE FOOTSTEPS OF GEORGE SAND

Le Domaine de George Sand ★ At the Château de Nohant, known today as La Maison de George Sand, the novelist learned the ways and thoughts of the peasants. During her time here, she entertained some of the intellectual and artistic elite of Europe—Flaubert, Balzac, Delacroix, Liszt, and Gautier. The building, which its guides define as a *maison bourgeoise,* is in its own park. It was constructed of stone in 1763 and purchased in 1793 by the family of George Sand. Today, it houses mementos of Sand and her admirers and friends, with testimonials to the literary conceits and eccentricities of one of France's most enduringly famous writers. The only way to visit is on a 45-minute guided tour in French (non-French speakers can follow along with a printed text). You can see the boudoir where she wrote the novel *Indiana,* published when she was 28. You can also visit her bedchamber and study. At Nohant, George

Sand staged theatricals, dramatizing several of her novels—not very successfully, according to reports. Today, over three weekends in June, *fêtes romantiques de Nohant* are sometimes staged, with an impressive list of musical performers.

36400 Nohant-Vic. ✆ **02-54-31-06-04.** Admission 6.50€ ($8.45) adults, 4.50€ ($5.85) students and ages 18–25, free for children 17 and under. July–Aug tours daily at 10am, 10:45am, 11:15am, noon, and 2pm, then every 30 min. until 6pm. Apr–June and Sept–Oct tours daily 9:30, 10:30, 11:15am, 2, 3, and 4pm. Nov–Mar tours daily 10, 11:30am, 2:30, and 3:30pm.

WHERE TO STAY & DINE

Auberge de la Petite Fadette *Value* This compound of interconnected 19th-century ivy-covered buildings abuts a château and is the focal point of one of the smallest villages in the region. Five generations of the Chapleau family have owned the renovated compound since 1890. A scattering of antiques decorates the interior. Rooms are cozy and comfortable, each outfitted with 19th-century antiques and the aura of a private home. All the compact bathrooms have showers, and about half have a tub/shower combo. The restaurant, open daily for lunch and dinner year-round, charges 18€ to 50€ ($23–$65) for its fixed-price meals.

Place du Château, Nohant 36400. ✆ **02-54-31-01-48.** Fax 02-54-31-10-19. www.aubergepetitefadette.com. 9 units. 65€–140€ ($85–$182) double. AE, MC, V. **Amenities:** Restaurant; bar; limited room service. *In room:* TV, hair dryer.

Château de la Vallée Bleue ★★ This is the area's most prestigious address. Dr. Pestel built the small, charming château in 1840 so that he could be close to his patient, George Sand. It's now a hotel and restaurant owned by Gérard Gasquet. The rooms bear the names of the doctor's guests, including Musset, Delacroix, Flaubert, Chopin, and Liszt. All rooms have dignified, sometimes antique, furniture, and six have a complete bathroom with tub/shower combination (the rest have showers). There's also a 4-hectare (10-acre) wooded park. The excellent regional specialties are characterized as *cuisine actuelle,* with an accent on presentation; they include goat cheese and carp with lentils, and chicken à la George Sand (with crayfish sauce). Fixed-price menus are 29€ ($38) and 39€ ($51). For dessert, try a delectable pear baked in pastry.

Rte. de Verneuil, St-Chartier, La Châtre 36400. ✆ **02-54-31-01-91.** Fax 02-54-31-04-48. www.chateauvalleebleue.com. 15 units. 95€–145€ ($124–$189) double; 175€–195€ ($228–$254) suite. MC, V. Hotel closed Sun. **Amenities:** Restaurant; outdoor pool; room service; laundry service. *In room:* TV, minibar, hair dryer, safe.

3 Vichy ★★★

348km (216 miles) S of Paris, 53km (33 miles) NE of Clermont-Ferrand, 174km (108 miles) NW of Lyon

This world-renowned spa on the northern edge of the Auvergne, in the heart of Bourbon country, is noted for its sparkling waters, which reputedly alleviate liver and stomach ailments. It looks much as it did a century ago, when princes and industrial barons filled its rococo casino. (The casino you'll visit today isn't the one that thrived during the spa's 19th-c. heyday. That edifice, at 5 rue du Casino, now functions as a convention hall.)

Since 1861, when Napoleon III was a frequent visitor, much has been done to add to the spa's fame. During the 1980s, the hotels and baths of Vichy underwent a modernization program to keep up with the times and the other baths of France, much to the pleasure of their clients and their ever-changing tastes.

The Perrier craze that has swept most of the world has aided the city's reputation for health and relaxation. The Perrier Company has a contract to bottle Vichy water for sale and runs the city's major attractions. Vichy is a sports and recreation center, boasting a casino, theaters, regattas, horse racing, and golf. The **Parc des Sources,** a promenade with covered walks, is the center of Vichy's fashionable life, which is at its peak from May to the end of September.

ESSENTIALS

GETTING THERE Vichy lies on the heavily traveled Paris–Clermont-Ferrand rail line. Some 20 **trains** per day arrive from Clermont-Ferrand (trip time: 35 min.). Ten trains per day arrive from Paris's Gare de Lyon (trip time: 3 hr.); the one-way fare is 44€ ($57). For train information and schedules, call ✆ **08-92-35-35-35. Bus** service into town is usually not as convenient or well orchestrated as the train. The Gare Routière (✆ **04-70-98-41-35**) lies adjacent to the rail station. If you're **driving** to Vichy from Paris, take A10 south to Orléans, and then connect to A71 south. At the Gannat/Vichy exit, follow N209 east to Vichy.

VISITOR INFORMATION The **Office de Tourisme** is at 19 rue du Parc (✆ **04-70-98-71-94;** fax 04-70-31-06-00; www.vichytourisme.com).

WHERE TO STAY

Best Western Aletti Palace Hôtel ★★ *Kids* This early-1900s hotel, the largest and, in some ways, stateliest in town, preserves the grand vistas and elegant accessories of the Belle Epoque. The high-ceilinged rooms are comfortably furnished. Many have balconies overlooking the wooded park and casino, and all come with spacious bathrooms with tub/shower combinations. If you ask, the staff will tell you about the role of this monument (under a different name, the Thermal Palace) during the tenure of the collaborationist Vichy government: It housed the headquarters of Vichy France's Ministry of War. These days, the hotel has a good restaurant and offers a bar and a terrace with a view of Vichy.

3 place Joseph-Aletti, Vichy 03200. ✆ **800/528-1234** in the U.S., or 04-70-30-20-20. Fax 04-70-98-13-82. www.bestwestern.com. 129 units. 128€–173€ ($166–$225) double; 180€–220€ ($234–$286) suite. Children under 12 stay free in parent's room. AE, DC, MC, V. **Amenities:** Restaurant; bar; outdoor heated pool; children's activities; business center; room service; babysitting; laundry service; dry cleaning; nonsmoking rooms; limited-mobility rooms. *In room:* A/C, TV, minibar, hair dryer, trouser press, iron.

Hôtel Chambord *Value* This government-rated two-star choice is one of the best bets for a spa holiday on a budget. The pleasant hotel, built near the rail station in the 1930s, has high ceilings and more space than you may find in newer buildings. Its rooms are renovated, and the rejuvenated bathrooms contain tubs and showers. The Escargot Qui Tette restaurant offers well-prepared meals in a sunny setting with reasonable prices.

82–84 rue de Paris, Vichy 03200. ✆ **04-70-30-16-30.** Fax 04-70-31-54-92. le.chambord@wanadoo.fr. 28 units. 42€–70€ ($55–$91) double. AE, DC, MC, V. **Amenities:** Restaurant; bar; laundry service. *In room:* TV.

Moments Choosing a Spa Vacation

For a sojourn at a spa and health farm, contact the **Centre Thermal des Dômes,** at the Novotel Thermalia (✆ **04-70-97-39-59**), or the **Centre des Célestins,** at the Hôtel les Célestins (✆ **04-70-30-82-00**). For questions about Vichy's spas and hydrotherapy facilities, call ✆ **04-70-97-39-59** or 0800/30-00-63 within France.

WHERE TO DINE

The restaurant in the **Hôtel Chambord** (see "Where to Stay," above), Escargot Qui Tette, serves excellent regional and French cuisine.

Brasserie du Casino TRADITIONAL FRENCH In business since 1921, with its original decor in place, this is the leading brasserie in Vichy, a preferred stop for actors and musicians visiting from Paris to perform at one of the local theaters. The restaurant, known for its sheathing of copper and Art Deco mahogany, is busy at lunch. Specialties include duck breast with a confit of figs, paupiette of rabbit with shallots, veal kidneys with fresh spinach and truffle sauce, monkfish with an essence of fennel, and veal liver with fondue of onions.

4 rue du Casino. ✆ **04-70-98-23-06.** Reservations recommended at lunch. Main courses 15€–21€ ($20–$27); fixed-price menu 15€–25€ ($20–$33). MC, V. Thurs–Mon noon–1:30pm and 7–9:15pm. Closed 2 weeks in Mar and Oct 20–Nov 20.

L'Alambic ★ MODERN FRENCH This small restaurant has only 18 seats, and because L'Alambic has some of the best food in Vichy, they fill up quickly. Since 1989, Jean-Jacques Barbot has appealed to what one food critic called "the jaded palates of Vichy." Within a pale green, warmly appointed dining room, which locals say is ideal for intimate dialogues, you can order from an array of ever-changing dishes, which may include cream of mussel and scallop soup flavored with saffron; a ravioli of sea snails served with a chicken-and-herb-flavored mousse and a lentil-flavored cream sauce; codfish stuffed with a confit of oranges, tomatoes, olives, and capers; a supreme of guinea fowl stuffed with an herb-flavored mousse; and a frozen *verveine*-flavored soufflé. Incidentally, the oil paintings that line the dining room were painted by chef Barbot's longtime companion, Marie-Ange Tupet, who supervises the service in the dining room.

8 rue Nicolas-Larbaud. ✆ **04-70-59-12-71.** Reservations required. Main courses 14€–24€ ($18–$31); fixed-price menu 26€–45€ ($34–$59). MC, V. Wed–Sun noon–1:30pm; Wed–Sat 7:30–9:30pm. Closed mid-Feb to early Mar, 3 weeks in Aug, and Dec 23–Jan 3.

VICHY AFTER DARK

If you're in the mood to meet the locals, head for the town's most animated bar, **Le Vichy,** 15 rue Burnol (✆ **04-70-97-05-70**). Here, within a mostly blue-toned setting punctuated with a long bar and a karaoke setup, you can babble and jive with a clientele aged 23 to 50, some of whom may even actually remember something about the long-ago Vichy government of World War II. The town also contains two casinos, both of them modern, contemporary-looking affairs, and both of them accessorized with dining and drinking facilities. The larger, better-accessorized, and more appealing of the two is the **Casino des Quatres-Chemin,** rue Lucas (✆ **04-70-97-93-37**). Inaugurated in 2004 within the Centre Commercial des Quatres Chemins, it replaced the grand, neoclassical casino (Casino Elysée Palace, now closed) that used to be patronized by clients who included Napoleon III in the 19th century. The new setting is glassy, glossy, and Vegas-ish. An area devoted exclusively to slot machines, with free entrance and virtually no dress code, is open daily 10am to 2am. A more formal area for blackjack and roulette (games referred to as *les grands jeux*) is open Thursday to Tuesday 8pm to 2am (until 4am Fri–Sat). To access *les grands jeux,* you must present a driver's license, ID card, or passport. Whereas *les grands jeux* are closed in February, the slot machines remain open here year-round, and there's a restaurant on-site.

Le Grand Café, 7 rue du Casino (✆ **04-70-97-16-45**), is a less impressive place to gamble, this one only with slot machines, and lies within a modern annex of the old casino. Entrance is free, and it's open daily 10am to at least 2am, and sometimes later, depending on business. A cafe-bar and restaurant are on the premises, as well as a disco, **Le Loft** (© **04-70-97-16-46**), which is modern, reverberating with pulsating electronic dance music, and noted as the town's most popular drinking and dancing joint. The disco is open Wednesday to Saturday 6:30pm until dawn, depending on the crowd. Entrance ranges from free to 12€ ($16), depending on the night of the week, the crowd, and the season.

4 Clermont-Ferrand ★★

399km (248 miles) S of Paris, 177km (110 miles) W of Lyon

This city in south-central France was the ancient capital of the Auvergne. Clermont-Ferrand has seen a long parade of history. It was created in 1731 by a merger of two towns, Clermont and Montferrand. The city is surrounded by hills, and in the distance stands one of the great attractions of the Auvergne, the volcanic mountain Puy-de-Dôme.

Today Clermont-Ferrand (commonly called Clermont) is hardly celebrated for its ancient appearance and medieval streets. Much of the town looks as if it were created in the stark 1960s and 1970s. It's not a town in which we'd choose to linger, but it's an important rail hub in this region and has a number of attractions that do bring in visitors. Its population numbers 150,000 for the city and 260,000 for the city and its surrounding region.

ESSENTIALS

GETTING THERE **Rail** lines converge on Clermont-Ferrand from all parts of France, including Marseille, Toulouse, and Paris's Gare de Lyon. The one-way fare from Paris is 48€ ($62); the trip takes 3½ hours. Trains from small towns in the Auvergne usually require a connection. For train information and schedules, call © **08-92-35-35-35.** Clermont-Ferrand is best approached by **car** from two cities. The 4-hour drive from Paris begins along A10 south to Orléans, continuing south along A71 to Clermont-Ferrand. From Lyon, take A47 west to St-Etienne, traveling northwest on A89 to Clermont-Ferrand.

Aéroport de Clermont-Aulnat (© **04-73-62-71-00**), about 4km (2½ miles) northwest of the town center, receives about 80 flights a day from all over France as well as Italy, Switzerland, and Belgium. **Air France** (© **08-20-82-08-20**) flies here from Paris round-trip. Buses meet every flight and take passengers to town, the bus station, or the rail station. The one-way fare is 4€ ($5.20). For bus information, call © **04-73-84-72-57.**

Train travel into Clermont-Ferrand is, overall, more convenient and efficient than bus service. **Buses** serve the **Gare Routière,** boulevard François-Mitterrand (© **04-73-93-13-61** for information), on the southern periphery of town.

VISITOR INFORMATION The **Office de Tourisme et des Congrès** is on place de la Victoire (© **04-73-98-65-00;** fax 04-73-90-04-11; www.clermont-fd.com). It's unique in France because it also houses an admission-free museum in its basement called the **Espace Art Roman.** An interactive presentation combines a slide show with photographs and archaeological remnants depicting the Auvergne as a rich repository of Romanesque architecture and artifacts. The short film takes 45 minutes, and it's worth spending another hour digesting all the additional information. From May to

September, the tourist office and the museum are open daily 9am to 7pm; from October to April, hours are Monday to Friday 9am to 6pm, Saturday 10am to 1pm and 2 to 6pm, and Sunday 9:30am to 12:30pm and 2 to 6pm.

SPECIAL EVENTS If you're in town at the end of January, check out one of the 40 screenings during the **Festival du Court Métrage.** Ten sites, mostly on boulevard François-Mitterrand, show works by up-and-coming directors. Tickets are 3€ ($3.90), with discounts for packages of 30 showings (56€/$73), and can be purchased through **Sauve Qui Peut le Court Métrage,** La Jetée, 6 place Michel de l'Hôpital (© **04-73-91-65-73;** www.clermont-filmfest.com).

EXPLORING THE ENVIRONS: A SPECTACULAR VOLCANIC LANDSCAPE

The region surrounding Clermont-Ferrand is one of France's most geologically distinctive. In 1977, the government designated 382,800 hectares (946,000 acres) as the **Parc Naturel Régional des Volcans d'Auvergne.** The park contains 186 villages as well as farms with herds of cows and goats that produce the Auvergne's cheeses and charcuterie. Scattered among them are at least 90 extinct volcanic cones *(puys),* which rise dramatically and eerily above the pine forests.

One of the highest and oldest of these is **Puy-de-Dôme** ★★★ (1,440m/4,724 ft. above sea level), a site used for worship since prehistoric times by the Gauls and the Romans. In 1648, Pascal used this mountaintop for his experiments that proved Torricelli's hypothesis about how altitude affects atmospheric pressure. And in 1911, one of the most dramatic events in French aviation occurred at Puy-de-Dôme when Eugène Renaux, with a passenger, flew nonstop from Paris in just over 5 hours, to land precariously on its summit and collect a prize worth 15,200€ ($19,760) in today's currency. From the summit you'll have a panoramic view—on a clear day, you can see as far east as Mont Blanc.

Shuttle buses run from the base to the summit daily 10am to 6pm in July and August; Saturday and Sunday in May, June, and September 12:30 to 6pm; the fare is 3.50€ ($4.55) round-trip. You can drive your car to the summit, but be aware that the road has many sharp curves, many steep drop-offs, and lots of potentially lethal hazards, especially when it's mobbed with visitors. If you opt to take your own car on days when the shuttle bus is operating, local authorities will let you do so only between 6pm and 10am the next day. The road and the parking lots remain open through the night. On the way up, you'll pay a toll of 4.50€ ($5.85) year-round; downhill passage is free. Frankly, unless you really want to see the summit by moonlight, it's better to take one of the shuttle buses. From November to March, the road is closed completely because of snow. Dial © **04-73-62-21-46** for more information.

The different areas of the park contain radically dissimilar features. **Les Puys** (also known as Monts Dômes) are a minichain of 112 extinct volcanoes (some capped with craters, some with rounded peaks) packed densely into an area 4km (2½ miles) wide by 31km (19 miles) long. Each dome is unique: Some were built up by slow extrusions of rock; others were the source of vast lava flows. Those with craters at their summits were the sites of violent explosions whose power contrasted with the region's peace and quiet today. The geological fury that created these hills ended between 5,000 and 6,000 years ago, but the rectangle of extinct volcanoes traces one of the most potentially unstable tectonic areas in France, the San Andreas Fault of the French mainland.

This region is relatively lightly populated, so you may not be aware of the park's boundaries during your explorations. Details about trekking and camping are available from the Parc Naturel Régional des Volcans d'Auvergne, Montlosier, 63970 Aydat (✆ **04-73-65-64-00**), 20km (12 miles) southwest of Clermont-Ferrand. A branch office is at the Château St-Etienne, 15000 Aurillac (✆ **04-71-48-68-68**). You can buy at least half a dozen guidebooks covering specific hikes and walks (2–6 hr. in duration) at either branch.

SEEING THE SIGHTS IN TOWN

Begin your tour in the center of Clermont, the bustling **place de Jaude,** where you can sample a glass of regional wine at a cafe. Later, walk north on the all-pedestrian rue du 11-Novembre, which branches off from the main plaza. This street leads to the all-pedestrian **rue des Gras,** the most historic and evocative artery of Clermont.

Most of the appealing buildings are in **Vieux-Clermont,** whose focal point is **place de la Victoire,** site of the black-lava **Cathédrale Notre-Dame de l'Assomption** ★★ (✆ **04-73-92-46-61**). One of the great churches of central France, it dates to the 13th and 14th centuries. Structural additions were made in the 19th century. Its outstanding feature is the series of stained-glass windows from the 13th and 14th centuries. Admission is free; it's open year-round Monday to Friday 7:30am to noon and 2 to 6pm; Saturday and Sunday 9:30am to noon and 3 to 7:30pm.

After leaving the cathedral, explore the buildings in this neighborhood. In particular, look for the **Maison de Savaron,** 3 rue des Chaussetiers, constructed in 1513. It's noted for the beauty of its courtyard and its Renaissance vaulting. Today it's a creperie, **Le Quinze-Treize** (✆ **04-73-92-37-46**), where you can enjoy a meal-size (savory) or dessert-style (sweet) crepe beneath the artfully crafted vaulting. It's open Monday to Friday noon to 3pm and 6:30pm to midnight, Saturday and Sunday noon to midnight.

Several blocks northeast of the cathedral is the finest example of Auvergnat Romanesque architecture, made of lava from volcanic deposits in the region, the **Eglise Notre-Dame-du-Port** ★★, rue du Port (✆ **04-73-91-32-94**). Dating from the 11th and 12th centuries, the church has four radiating chapels and a transept surmounted by an octagonal tower. The crypt holds a 17th-century black Madonna. UNESCO lists the complex as a World Heritage Site. Admission is free; it's open daily from 8am to 7pm (until 8pm June to mid-Oct).

Between the two churches stands the Renaissance **Fontaine d'Amboise,** place de la Poterne. Its pyramid supports a statue of Hercules. Nearby is **square Pascal,** commemorating the birth of mathematician Blaise Pascal in 1623 in a house on rue des Gras. Regrettably, the house was demolished in 1958, but a statue stands in honor of the native son.

Musée d'Archéologie Bargoin The collection here consists of objects excavated from Auvergnat sites founded by the Gallo-Romans and their predecessors: pottery shards, bronzes, woodcarvings, and an array of works noteworthy for anyone interested in France's prehistoric and pre-Roman origins. There's also an unusual collection of antique Oriental carpets; in the same building, the **Musée du Tapis d'Art** (✆ **04-73-90-57-48**) displays around 80 rare Middle Eastern and East Asian carpets. Each is artfully lit and suspended from walls and ceilings, and together they represent the evolution of the carpet as a prayer aid and a decorative work of art. Don't expect anything French in this place—it completely omits the carpets produced in nearby Aubusson.

45 rue de Ballainvilliers. ✆ **04-73-42-69-70.** www.ville-clermont-ferrand.fr/musees/index.asp. Joint admission 4.20€ ($5.45) adults, 2.70€ ($3.50) students and seniors, free for children under 18. Tues–Sat 10am–noon and 1–5pm; Sun 2–7pm. Closed Jan 1, May 1, Nov 1, and Dec 25.

Musée d'Art Roger Quilliot This museum is in a suburb 3km (1¾ miles) northeast of Clermont's center, in an award-winning building erected in 1992. This is the cultural showcase of the Auvergne. When it was created, multiple works of art were culled from other museums throughout the Auvergne and then reassembled into a format that displays European art and culture in chronological order. Visitors make their way in a circular pattern through rooms devoted to French, Italian, and Flemish works, progressing from the 7th to the 20th century.

Place Louis-Deteix, Montferrand. From the center of town, follow av. Michelin east until you see the signpost pointing north to Montferrand. ✆ **04-73-16-11-30.** Admission 4.20€ ($5.45). Free for students and ages 18 and under. Tues–Sun 10am–6pm. Closed Jan 1, May 1, Nov 1, and Dec 25.

WHERE TO STAY

Hôtel Le Kyriad *Value* This is not the best hotel in town, but it's still a good value. Built in unassuming 1970s style, it has well-maintained rooms that are comfortably furnished though somewhat uninspired. The small bathrooms are tidily organized; each has a shower. The hotel is a popular overnight stop for farmers and sales representatives of companies selling farm equipment, so as a casual visitor you may feel somewhat in the minority. The simple bistro offers affordable meals.

51 rue Bonnabaud, Clermont-Ferrand 63000. ✆ **04-73-93-59-69.** Fax 04-73-34-89-29. www.hotel-kyriadcentreclermont.com. 80 units. 58€–90€ ($75–$117) double. AE, MC, V. Parking 10€ ($13). **Amenities:** Bistro; bar; room service. *In room:* TV, minibar, hair dryer.

Le Mercure Centre ★ A favorite of the business traveler, this early-1970s hotel is the best of a fairly lackluster lot. It was upgraded in 1998. Its location near the Jardin Lecoq is great for jogging and strolling. Most of the well-furnished rooms are spacious. Each midsize bathroom has a tub/shower combination. Everything is functional and businesslike, not necessarily exciting. The restaurant, L'Eau à la Bouche, is a worthwhile choice.

82 bd. François-Mitterrand, Clermont-Ferrand 63000. ✆ **04-73-34-46-46.** Fax 04-73-34-46-36. www.mercure.com. 123 units. 69€–180€ ($90–$234) double. AE, DC, MC, V. Parking 11€ ($14). **Amenities:** Restaurant; bar; room service; laundry service; dry cleaning. *In room:* A/C, TV, minibar, hair dryer, Wi-Fi.

WHERE TO DINE

L'Eau à la Bouche, in the **Mercure Centre** hotel (see "Where to Stay," above), serves regional specialties and classic French cuisine.

Brasserie Danièle Bath ★ *Value* MODERN FRENCH Lots of superb flavors go into the locally inspired yet grandly creative cuisine. Begin with such delights as tarte of scallops with black truffles; rabbit, shrimp, and tomato strudel; or perhaps a small lasagna of salmon with black olives. The excellent fish changes seasonally, and you can also count on any number of savory meat dishes, including roast lamb with glazed turnips. Pigeon is another specialty, served with roasted foie gras.

Place St-Pierre. ✆ **04-73-31-23-22.** Reservations required. Main courses 13€–25€ ($17–$33); fixed-price menu 24€ ($31). AE, DC, MC, V. Tues–Sun noon–2pm and 7–10pm. Closed 3 weeks in Feb and 2 weeks in Aug.

Emmanuel Hodencq ★★★ FRENCH The namesake of this restaurant is the town's culinary king, having topped even the longtime favorite, Jean-Claude Leclerc (see below). The dynamic chef is equally at home with traditional or *moderne* cookery, and his delectable dishes almost waltz out of the kitchen and onto your table. Local "wheeler-dealers" (a reference to Michelin tires) and politicos hang out here. The menu features the best of local produce—perhaps foie gras in caramel vinegar or roasted pigeon with chanterelles. Grilled red mullet is a perfect dish, as is medallion of veal in grainy mustard sauce.

Place St-Pierre. ✆ **04-73-31-23-23.** www.hodencq.com. Reservations required. Main courses 33€–63€ ($43–$82); fixed-price menu 35€–135€ ($46–$176). AE, DC, MC, V. Tues–Sat noon–2pm; Mon–Sat 7:30–10pm.

Jean-Claude Leclerc ★★ MODERN & TRADITIONAL FRENCH One of the best-known restaurants in Clermont-Ferrand occupies a modern dining room in a late-19th-century town house in the center of Clermont's oldest neighborhood. It features ultracontemporary decor, large-scale oil paintings, and an emphasis on creative cuisine that's carefully tuned to the seasons. Our favorite dishes are roasted lobster served on rémoulade of celery and apples, truffle-studded turbot served with creamy mashed potatoes, and faux-filet of Salers beef served with gravy that's enriched with foie gras and truffles.

12 rue St-Adjutor. ✆ **04-73-36-46-30.** Reservations recommended. Main courses 25€–40€ ($33–$52); fixed-price menu 26€–80€ ($34–$104). AE, DC, MC, V. Tues–Sat noon–1:30pm and 7:30–9:30pm. Closed 3 weeks in Aug, 1st week in Jan and May.

CLERMONT-FERRAND AFTER DARK

Most French nightclubbers begin their evenings on the town by heading to the **boulevard Trudaine,** a thoroughfare in the town center that's very close to the Eglise Notre-Dame-du-Port. It's lined with at least 20 bars and restaurants catering to the young and the restless.

B. Box, La Pardieu (✆ **04-73-28-59-74;** www.bboxclub.com), is the biggest nightclub in Clermont. Expect mass consumption of alcohol and a bevy of attractive young people clubbing the night away. Cover ranges from 10€ to 14€ ($12–$17) and includes your first drink. Open Thursday to Saturday only, from 10pm to 5am. Two dance clubs are **Le Frog,** 12 rue des Petits Gras (✆ **04-73-37-99-73**), and **Le Symbol,** 11 rue de Serbie (✆ **04-73-31-01-01;** www.lesymbol.com). Both attract a crowd over 25, including lots of single, divorced, and nominally married people looking for a dance and perhaps a fling. A popular gay bar is the **Bar d'O,** place de la Victoire (✆ **04-73-91-43-14**), which tends to be busy during the late afternoon and early evening (4–9:30 or 10:30pm). After that, but only Wednesday to Saturday after 10pm, gay men and, to a lesser extent, women, head for **L'Enigme,** 32 rue Fontgieve (✆ **04-73-31-07-63;** www.l-enigme.com), the town's (and the region's) busiest and most animated gay disco. Entrance ranges from free to 10€ ($13), depending on the night of the week, and the dancing usually continues until at least 4am. You may also consider dropping into Le Frog. It's not altogether gay, but its trendiness and hipness make it an agreeable place for lots of gay patrons (along with everyone else).

5 Aubusson

380km (236 miles) S of Paris, 89km (55 miles) E of Limoges, 95km (59 miles) NW of Clermont-Ferrand

In the Creuse Valley, the little market town of Aubusson enjoys world renown for its carpets and tapestries. Aubusson abounds with clock towers, bridges, peaked roofs, and turrets—all of which inspired the painter Gromaire's widely reproduced cartoon *View of Aubusson.* Against the gray granite, rainbow-hued skeins of wool hang from windows. The craftspeople's workshops spread throughout the town; many are open to the public (just ask). The origin of the industry is unknown. Some credit the Arabs who settled here in 732. Others think the craft came from Flanders in the Middle Ages. For years, the favorite subject of the reproductions created for sale was *The Lady and the Unicorn,* the original of which was discovered in the nearby Château de Boussac. Many tapestry reproductions of the works of 18th-century painters such as Boucher and Watteau have been made. Since World War II, designs by painters such as Picasso, Matisse, and Braque have been stressed.

ESSENTIALS

GETTING THERE Aubusson has **rail** service, much of it indirect, from Clermont-Ferrand and Paris, among other cities. About 10 trains a day depart from Paris's Gare d'Austerlitz for Limoges, where passengers board an SNCF bus for the 90-minute ride on to Aubusson. Bus fare from Limoges is 13€ ($17) each way. For bus information, call ✆ **05-55-66-13-28.** Total transit time from Paris to Aubusson is about 4½ hours; the one-way fare is 55€ ($72). From Clermont-Ferrand to Aubusson, an early-afternoon train departs daily for a nearly 4-hour trip (with at least two stops and at least one change en route); the one-way fare is 24€ ($31). For information, call ✆ **08-92-35-35-35.** Most **bus** service into town originates in the area, with inconvenient connections from other parts of France. For information, call Aubusson La Gare Routière (✆ **05-55-66-13-28**). If you're **driving** from Clermont-Ferrand, take D941 west to Aubusson. The trip takes between 1 and 1½ hours.

VISITOR INFORMATION The **Office de Tourisme** is on rue Vieille (✆ **05-55-66-32-12;** fax 05-55-83-84-51; www.ot-aubusson.fr).

EXPLORING THE TOWN

Aubusson is the site of at least 15 carpet manufacturers, many of which spend their entire production year fulfilling advance orders—thereby accumulating very few inventories of unsold goods, disappointing many visitors in the process. To alleviate this, the tourist office, between March and October, maintains a carpet showroom inside its premises with about 20 carpets from different manufacturers on display and for sale. And depending on which style of carpet you like from the samples on display, the office will guide you directly to the sales staff at the manufacturer. There, if you don't mind waiting for the carpet of your dreams (it takes approximately 2 months of eye-straining labor to produce 1 square yard of completed carpet), you may eventually receive your very own Aubusson, crafted in whatever style and color palette you've indicated at the time of its original commission, at prices substantially less than what you'd have paid in a retail outlet in, say, Paris or New York.

The **Musée Départemental de la Tapisserie,** avenue des Lissiers (✆ **05-55-83-08-30;** www.cg23.fr), has exhibits related to the 600-year-old tradition of the Aubusson carpet- and tapestry-weaving industry. The displays also highlight the 20th-century rebirth of the Aubusson carpet and the art of tapestry weaving. The museum is open September to June, Wednesday through Monday 9:30am to noon and 2 to 6pm; July to August, Wednesday to Monday 10am to 6pm, Tuesday 2 to 6pm. Admission is 5€ ($6.50) for adults, 4€ ($5.20) for students, and free for ages under 18.

Maison du Tapissier, accessible directly from the tourist office, rue Vieille (✆ **05-55-66-32-12**), contains a collection of antique carpets and a replica of a carpet-weaving studio from the early 19th century. It's open in July and August daily 9am to 6:30pm, and September to June Monday to Saturday 9:30am to 12:30pm and 2 to 6pm. Admission is 5€ ($6.50) for adults and free for children under 12.

WHERE TO STAY & DINE

Hotel Le France This is the best and most appealing hotel in a town whose visitors are mostly business travelers, buyers, and decorators from other parts of Europe. It sits behind a 200-year-old facade of thick granite blocks in the heart of this "overgrown village" of 400 souls. Each of the guest rooms is different. Some rooms—especially the pricier ones—hold antiques and *baldaquin* (canopy) beds, with hanging draperies romantically positioned on all sides. Rooms are not air-conditioned, but the masonry walls tend to keep things temperate. The likable manager, M. Morel, knows a lot about the town and the surrounding region.

6 rue Deportés, Aubusson 23200. © **05-55-66-10-22.** Fax 05-55-66-88-64. 23 units. 65€–100€ ($85–$130) double. Outdoor parking free, indoor parking 8€ ($10). AE, MC, V. **Amenities:** Restaurant; bar; room service. *In room:* TV, hair dryer.

6 Limoges ★

396km (246 miles) S of Paris, 311km (193 miles) N of Toulouse, 93km (58 miles) NE of Périgueux

Limoges, the ancient capital of Limousin in west-central France, is world-famous for its exquisite porcelain and enamel works. Enamel production is a medieval industry revived in the 19th century and still going strong today. In fact, Limoges is the economic capital of western France. Occupying the Vienne's right bank, the town has historically consisted of two parts: La Cité (aka Vieux Limoges), with its narrow streets and old *maisons* on the lower slope; and La Ville Haute (aka "Le Château"), at the summit.

ESSENTIALS

GETTING THERE Limoges has good **train** service from most regional cities, with direct trains from Toulouse, Poitiers, and Paris. Fifteen trains depart daily from Paris's Gare d'Austerlitz for Limoges (trip time: 2½ hr.); the one-way fare is 45€ ($59). For complete train information, call © **08-92-35-35-35. Bus** transit in and out of the small towns and villages nearby can be arranged through the **Régie des Transports de la Haute-Vienne,** place Charentes. If you're **driving** from Aubusson, take D941 west for the 1-hour trip.

VISITOR INFORMATION The **Office de Tourisme** is at 12 bd. de Fleurus (© **05-55-34-46-87;** fax 05-55-34-19-12; www.tourismelimoges.com).

EXPLORING THE TOWN

If you'd like to see an enameler at work or an operating porcelain factory, ask at the tourist office (see above) for a list of workshops, or go directly to the famous **Pavillon de la Porcelaine** (see below).

For a sales-oriented overview of locally made porcelain, visit any of the three branches of the **Magasin Gorse,** 42 place de la Motte (© **05-55-34-26-38**), at nos. 2, 13, and 27 bd. Louis-Blanc. At nos. 13 and 27, you'll find examples of porcelain from each of the manufacturers in Limoges, including Haviland, Bernardaud, Raynaud, and Laure Japy (formerly known as Laforge). At no. 2, you'll find mostly Lalique, St. Louis, and Baccarat crystal, and silverware by Christofle and Puiforcat. Inventories shift among the three branches as new collections are released; by wandering among all three, you'll get a fast overview of what's available.

Thanks to the rich deposits of kaolin (known locally as "white gold"), found near Limoges in the 18th century, more than 30 manufacturers of porcelain have set up operations through the years. Many maintain factory outlets, sometimes offering good-quality seconds at reduced prices. For a thoroughly antique style of porcelain, visit the **Ancienne Manufacture Royale de Limoges,** 7 place Horteils, in the suburb of Aixe-sur-Vienne (✆ **05-55-70-44-98**), 5.5km (3½ miles) west of Limoges. In the center of town, you'll find **Raynaud,** 14 ancienne rte. d'Aixe (✆ **05-55-01-77-65**), and **Porcelaines Philippe Deshoulières-Lafarge,** 20 rue Armand Dutreix (✆ **05-55-50-33-43**). Largest of all, with the best publicity operation, is **Bernardaud,** 27 av. Albert-Thomas (✆ **05-55-10-55-50**), where a small-scale museum (focusing on past porcelain-related triumphs) and a tearoom adjoin the showroom.

Cathédrale St-Etienne The cathedral was begun in 1273 and took years to complete. The choir was finished in 1327, but work continued in the nave until almost 1890. The cathedral is the only one in the old province of Limousin built entirely in the Gothic style. The main entrance is through Porte St-Jean, which has carved wooden doors from the 16th century (constructed at the peak of the Flamboyant Gothic style). Inside, the nave appears so harmonious it's hard to imagine that its construction took 6 centuries. The rood screen is of particular interest, built in 1533 in the ornate style of the Italian Renaissance. The cathedral also contains some admirable bishops' tombs from the 14th to the 16th centuries.

Place de la Cathédrale. ✆ **05-55-34-53-81.** Free admission. Summer daily 10am–6pm; rest of year daily 10am–5pm.

Eglise St-Michel-des-Lions Construction of this church began in the 14th century and continued into the 15th and 16th centuries. Although the church is not as interesting as older Romanesque churches in other parts of the Auvergne, it's the headquarters of the cult of St-Martial, a Limoges hometown bishop who died in the 3rd century. The church is the home of what's reputed to be his skull, stored in an elaborately enameled reliquary. "Les Ostensions" is a religious procession, established in 994, that occurs every 7 years. The skull, "La Chasse de St-Martial"—which some adherents credit with mystical powers—is removed from storage and exhibited as part of religious ceremonies that attract as many as 100,000 devout adherents. The next such procession is scheduled for 2009.

Place St-Michel. ✆ **05-55-32-26-98.** Free admission. Mon–Sat 8am–6pm; Sun 8–11:45am and 4–6pm.

Musée Municipal de l'Evêché-de-Limoges Adjoining the cathedral in the Jardins de l'Evêché—which offer a view of the Vienne and the 13th-century pont St-Etienne—the old archbishops' palace is now the Musée Municipal. The elegant 18th-century building has an outstanding collection of Limoges enamels from the 12th century, as well as some enamel paintings by Leonard Limousin, who was born in 1505 in Limoges and went on to win world acclaim and the favor of four monarchs. Limoges was also the birthplace of Auguste Renoir, and the museum displays several of his works.

Place de la Cathédrale. ✆ **05-55-45-98-10.** Free admission. June–Sept daily 10–11:45am and 2–6pm; Oct–May Wed–Mon 10–11:45am and 2–5pm.

Musée National de la Porcelaine Adrien-Dubouché ★★ This museum, in a 19th-century building, has the largest public collection of Limoges porcelain. Its 12,000 pieces illustrate the history of glassmaking and ceramics (porcelain, earthenware, stoneware, and terra cotta) throughout the ages. In France, its porcelain collection is second in quantity only to that of Sèvres. The main gallery contains whole dinner sets of noted figures and some contemporary Limoges ware.

8 bis Place Winston-Churchill. ✆ **05-55-77-45-88.** www.musee-adriendubouche.fr. Admission 4.50€ ($5.85) adults, 3€ ($3.90) ages 18–25, free for children under 18. July–Aug Wed–Mon 10am–5:40pm; Sept–June Wed–Mon 10am–12:30pm and 2–5:40pm.

Pavillon de la Porcelaine Haviland has been exporting its porcelain to the United States and other countries since 1842, when a group of American entrepreneurs immigrated to France from Boston to found the first American-owned company ever established in Europe. Over the years, it has used the designs of artists such as Gauguin and Dalí. In the museum, you can see masterpieces as well as original pieces created for the U.S. White House. A video screening can tell you more about the manufacturing process and a large shop also sells the porcelain at factory prices.

40 av. John-Kennedy. ✆ **05-55-30-21-86.** Free admission. July–Aug daily 10am–6:30pm; Sept–June Mon–Sat 10am–1pm and 2–6:30pm.

WHERE TO STAY

Efficient, no-nonsense lodgings, favored by visiting businesspeople, can be found at the **Best Western Hotel Richelieu,** near the town center at 40 av. Baudin, Limoges 87000 (✆ **05-55-34-22-82;** fax 05-55-34-35-36; www.hotel-richelieu.com). Doubles go for 82€ to 102€ ($107–$133).

Hôtel Royal Limousin ★ This is the town's leading inn, built in the 1960s adjacent to a parking lot in the center of Limoges. The large, modern, chain-hotel-style rooms have midsize bathrooms, mostly with tub/shower combinations. Accommodations on the noisier avenue Carnot side cost less than those on the quieter place de la République. The only drawback is that a lot of tour groups stay here. There's no restaurant, but the staff refers hotel guests to the restaurant next door.

Place de la République B.P. 280, Limoges 87007. ✆ **05-55-34-65-30.** Fax 05-55-34-55-21. www.acor.com. 78 units. 92€–102€ ($120–$133) double. AE, DC, MC, V. **Amenities:** Limited room service; laundry service. *In room:* TV, minibar, hair dryer, safe.

WHERE TO DINE

Le Versailles FRENCH Set on a busy commercial boulevard near the center of town, this is a deeply entrenched staple of conservative French cuisine that's always mentioned as one of the town's most visible, most professional, and most consistent dining spots. The rooms that contain it haven't changed much (especially the wood paneling and mirrors) since it was built in 1928. Since the restaurant opened in 1932, it seems everybody in town has been here at least once. Today, the menu remains relatively conservative but with long lists of flavorful and freshly made food. The best examples include sweetbreads with morels; a cassoulet of veal kidneys with sweet red wine; a long list of grilled meats from nearby purveyors, served with your choice of béarnaise, pepper, garlic-butter, or wine sauce; a stewpot of scallops with flap mushrooms; sole meunière; and medallions of monkfish with salted ham and stewed tomatoes.

20 place d'Aine. ✆ **05-55-34-13-39.** Reservations recommended. Main courses 12€–26€ ($15–$33); set-price menus 14€ ($18; not available on Sun) and 17€–26€ ($21–$34). AE, MC, V. Daily noon–2:30pm and 7:30–11:30pm. Bus: 4 or 10.

WHERE TO STAY & DINE NEARBY

IN ST-MARTIN-DU-FAULT

La Chapelle St-Martin ★★★ This is the best place in the area if you enjoy early-1900s living and superb food in the tradition of the Relais & Châteaux group. The hotel is in a private park with two ponds. The tasteful rooms are individually decorated with a 19th-century theme, usually Directoire or Empire. The restaurant offers excellent French food, with fixed-price menus range from 39€ to 72€ ($51–$94).

87510 Nieul. Take N147 and D35 11km (6¾ miles) northeast from Limoges. ✆ **05-55-75-80-17.** Fax 05-55-75-89-50. www.chapellesaintmartin.com. 13 units. 90€–250€ ($117–$325) double; 200€–270€ ($260–$351) suite. AE, DC, MC, V. Free parking. Hotel closed Jan 1–Feb 7. Reserve well in advance. Restaurant closed Mon July–Aug. **Amenities:** Restaurant; outdoor pool; tennis court; room service; laundry service. *In room:* A/C (in some), TV, minibar, hair dryer, safe (in some).

IN NIEUIL

To get to Nieuil from Limoges, take N141 west of the town center (signposted ANGOULÊME). The town of Nieuil is signposted at the town of Suaux. Follow the signs for about 1.5km (1 mile) east of the village toward Fontafie. Nieuil lies 64km (40 miles) northwest of Limoges.

Note: Don't confuse Nieuil with La Chapelle St-Martin (see above) at Nieul, near Limoges, 55km away (34 miles), with a slightly different spelling.

Château de Nieuil ★★ This fabled old inn comes with quite a pedigree. The château, built in the 16th century as a hunting lodge for François I, became the first château-hotel in France in 1937. Restored by the *comte* de Dampierre early in the 1800s after its destruction in the Revolution, it has remained in the antique-collecting Bodinaud family since around 1900. Rooms are beautifully furnished and magnificently comfortable, with elegant bathrooms. Today, 160 hectares (395 acres) of park and forest surround a series of beautifully maintained gardens.

The restaurant, La Grange aux Oies (the Goose Farm), is in a stone-walled annex constructed in the late 19th century as stables. The cuisine focuses on classic and regional recipes. Main courses cost 18€ to 25€ ($23–$33); fixed-price menus are 25€ to 45€ ($33–$59) at lunch, 45€ ($59) at dinner. Nonguests may dine here if they call ahead.

16270 Nieuil. ✆ **05-45-71-36-38.** Fax 05-45-71-46-45. www.chateaunieuilhotel.com. 14 units. 125€–250€ ($163–$325) double; 240€–380€ ($312–$494) suite. AE, DC, MC, V. Closed Nov–Apr. **Amenities:** Restaurant; bar; outdoor pool; tennis court; room service; babysitting; laundry service; on-site art and antiques gallery. *In room:* A/C, TV, minibar, hair dryer, safe.

7 Le Puy-en-Velay ★★★

523km (325 miles) S of Paris, 129km (80 miles) SE of Clermont-Ferrand

Le Puy-en-Velay (usually shortened to Le Puy) is one of the most extraordinary sights in France. Steep volcanic spires, left over from geological activity that ended millennia ago, are capped with Romanesque churches, a cathedral, and medieval houses that rise sinuously from the plain below. The history of Le Puy centers on the cult of the Virgin Mary.

Le Puy today is a provincial city of steep cobblestone streets with lots of rather shabby buildings (many of which are being restored). Much of the population of approximately 21,000 lives off the tourist trade, and today's visitors follow in the footsteps of Charlemagne, Le Puy's "first tourist." Le Puy remains a major pilgrimage destination, although it is not as famous as Lourdes.

In France, Le Puy is defined as the capital of lentils. Lentils produced within a specific distance of Le Puy are categorized in a way that emulates the classification of the country's most prestigious wines, as A.O.C. (Appellation d'Origine Contrôlée). The town is also the point of departure for pilgrims who follow the road to Santiago de Compostela in northwest Spain. A blessing in honor of pilgrims takes place every morning at 7am in the cathedral (see below). Because of the numbers of pilgrims who have stopped at Le Puy and its cathedral, UNESCO lists the town, as well as the entire length of the chemin de St-Jacques de Compostelle, as a site of importance to the Universal Patrimony.

ESSENTIALS

GETTING THERE Passengers arriving in Le Puy from anywhere in Europe must change **trains** at St-Georges d'Aurac. From there, 10 small trains, timed for convenient connections, travel along the 28km (17-mile) spur route that connects Le Puy's railway station to the rest of the lines of the SNCF. For information, call ✆ **08-92-35-35-35. Bus** service is of use only in and out of the small villages in the Auvergne. Even buses from Clermont-Ferrand take at least 3 hours to cover the relatively short distance. For **bus** information, contact La Gare Routière at ✆ **04-71-09-25-60.** If you're **driving,** the best way to reach Le Puy is from St-Etienne, traveling southwest along N88. From Clermont-Ferrand, drive south along N88 to Lempdes, continuing southeast along N102 to Le Puy.

VISITOR INFORMATION The **Office de Tourisme** is on place du Clauzel near La Mairie (town hall; ✆ **04-71-09-38-41;** fax 04-71-05-22-62; www.ot-lepuyenvelay.fr).

SEEING THE SIGHTS

Le Puy is the historic center of the French lace industry; you'll find lace shops on every block. But to be assured of handmade authenticity, look for the words DENTELLE DU PUY. Under a 1931 local government ordinance, the display of this mark is a privilege reserved for the real thing. The best selections of local lace are at **Spécialités du Velay,** 1 bd. St-Louis (✆ **04-71-09-09-34**); **Valois Dentelles,** 28 place du Plot (✆ **04-71-09-60-69**); and **Aux Souvenirs du Puy,** 60 rue Raphaël (✆ **04-71-05-76-71**).

Cathédrale Notre-Dame ★★★ This Romanesque cathedral was conceived as a shelter and prayer site for medieval pilgrims heading to the religious shrines of Santiago de Compostela in northwestern Spain. Marked by vivid Oriental and Byzantine influences, it's worth a visit. The cloisters contain carved capitals dating from the Carolingian era. Occupying the cathedral's original treasury, and accessible from inside the cathedral, is **Le Musée d'Art Religieux.** It contains fabrics, religious icons, and gold and silver objects, including an unusual enameled chalice from the 12th century, that have been associated with the church for many centuries.

Place du For. ✆ **04-71-05-98-74.** Free admission to cathedral; to cloisters, Chapel of Relics, and museum 4.60€ ($6) adults, 3.10€ ($4.05) students and ages 18–25, free for children under 18. Cathedral Mar–Sept daily 8:30am–7:30pm; Oct–Feb daily 8:30am–6:30pm. Cloisters, Chapel of Relics, and museum Oct–Mar daily 9am–noon and 2–4:30pm; Apr–June daily 9am–12:30pm and 2–6pm; July–Sept daily 9:30am–6:30pm.

Chapelle St-Michel-d'Aiguilhe ★★ This 10th-century chapel, perched precariously atop a volcanic spur that rises abruptly from hilly terrain, is one of the city's most dramatic sights. It sits on the northwestern perimeter of Le Puy. Reaching the summit requires a long climb up rocky stairs. When you get here, you'll be struck by the Oriental influences in the floor plan, the arabesques, and the mosaics crafted from black stone. On view are some 12th-century murals and an 11th-century wooden depiction of Christ.

Atop the Rocher St-Michel. ✆ **04-71-09-50-03.** Admission 2.75€ ($3.60) adults, 2.25€ ($2.95) students, 1.25€ ($1.65) children under 14. May–Sept daily 9am–6:30pm; Apr and Oct to mid-Nov daily 9:30am–noon and 2–5:30pm; Feb–Mar daily 2–5pm. Closed mid-Nov to Jan except during occasional events.

Musée Crozatier Celebrating the history, culture, and geology of the region, this museum contains exhibits of handicrafts, especially lace, some of which date from the 16th century. It also has a collection of minerals, crystals, pottery shards, and bones from nearby archaeological excavations, architectural embellishments from the Romanesque era, and paintings from the 14th to the 20th centuries.

In the Jardin Henri-Vinay. ✆ **04-71-06-62-40.** Admission 3.20€ ($4.15) adults, 1.40€ ($1.80) students and ages 18–25, free for children under 18. June 15–Sept 15 daily 10am–noon and 2–6pm; Mar–June 14 and Sept 16–30 Wed–Mon 10am–noon and 2–6pm; Feb and Oct–Nov Mon and Wed–Sat 10am–noon and Wed–Mon 2–4pm. Closed Dec–Jan.

WHERE TO STAY

Hôtel Régina ★ In no way is this hotel grand, but it's the finest in town and well located right in the heart of town. In 1998, a radical renovation brought it into its current condition, offering simple but thoughtfully decorated rooms containing midsize bathrooms. In 2004, one entire floor received air-conditioning. The in-house brasserie offers affordable platters of food. In the afternoon, it turns into a tea salon that attracts many local retirees and shopkeepers.

34 bd. du Maréchal-Fayolle, Le Puy-en-Velay 43000. ✆ **04-71-09-14-71.** Fax 04-71-09-18-57. www.hotelrestregina.com. 25 units. 59€–85€ ($77–$111) double; 89€–104€ ($116–$135) suite. AE, MC, V. Parking 6.50€ ($8.45). **Amenities:** Restaurant; room service; laundry service. *In room:* A/C, TV, minibar, hair dryer.

WHERE TO DINE

Le Trois Paves FRENCH/AUVERGNAT In the heart of town, this lovely restaurant occupies a pair of old-fashioned dining rooms in a house whose interior is much older than its 19th-century facade. The kitchen is devoted to the traditions of the region, preparing dishes that utilize the Auvergne's robust wines, as well as lentils, which crop up in appealing and flavorful ways. Specialties include roasted local black lamb, prepared with thyme and mashed potatoes studded with morels and local whitefish *(omble chevalier)* served at least four different ways.

5 rue Portail-d'Avignon. ✆ **04-71-09-67-20.** Reservations recommended. Main courses 13€–16€ ($17–$21). MC, V. Mon–Tues and Thurs–Fri noon–2:30pm; Thurs–Sat 8–10pm.

Appendix: Useful Terms & Phrases

It's often amazing how a word or two of halting French will change your hosts' dispositions. At the very least, try to learn a few numbers, basic greetings, and—above all—the life-raft phrase, *Parlez-vous anglais?* (Do you speak English?). Many people do speak passable English and will use it liberally if you demonstrate the basic courtesy of greeting them in their language. Go out, try our glossary, and don't be bashful. *Bonne chance!* (Good luck!)

1 Basic French Vocabulary & Phrases

English	French	Pronunciation
Yes/No	**Oui/Non**	wee/nohn
Okay	**D'accord**	*dah*-core
Please	**S'il vous plaît**	seel voo play
Thank you	**Merci**	*mair*-see
You're welcome	**De rien**	duh ree-*ehn*
Hello (during daylight)	**Bonjour**	bohn-*jhoor*
Good evening	**Bonsoir**	bohn-*swahr*
Goodbye	**Au revoir**	o ruh-*vwahr*
What's your name?	**Comment vous appellez-vous?**	ko-*mahn*-voo-za-pell-ay-*voo?*
My name is	**Je m'appelle**	*jhuh* ma-pell
How are you?	**Comment allez-vous?**	kuh-mahn-tahl-ay-*voo?*
So-so	**Comme ci, comme ça**	kum-*see,* kum-*sah*
I'm sorry/excuse me	**Pardon**	pahr-*dohn*

GETTING AROUND/STREET SMARTS

English	French	Pronunciation
Do you speak English?	**Parlez-vous anglais?**	par-lay-voo-ahn-*glay?*
I don't speak French	**Je ne parle pas français**	jhuh ne parl pah frahn-*say*
I don't understand	**Je ne comprends pas**	jhuh ne kohm-*prahn* pas
Could you speak more loudly/more slowly?	**Pouvez-vous parler plus fort/plus lentement?**	Poo-*vay* voo par-lay ploo for/ploo lan-te-*ment?*
What is it?	**Qu'est-ce que c'est?**	kess-kuh-*say?*
What time is it?	**Qu'elle heure est-il?**	kel uhr eh-*teel?*
What?	**Quoi?**	kwah?
How? or What did you say?	**Comment?**	ko-*mahn?*
When?	**Quand?**	kahn?

English	French	Pronunciation
Where is?	**Où est?**	oo *eh?*
Who?	**Qui?**	kee?
Why?	**Pourquoi?**	poor-*kwah?*
here/there	**ici/là**	ee-*see*/lah
left/right	**à gauche/à droite**	a goash/a drwaht
straight ahead	**tout droit**	too-*drwah*
Fill the tank (of a car), please	**Le plein, s'il vous plaît**	luh plan, seel-voo-*play*
I want to get off at	**Je voudrais descendre à**	jhe voo-*dray* day-son drah-ah
airport	**l'aéroport**	lair-o-*por*
bank	**la banque**	lah bahnk
bridge	**le pont**	luh pohn
bus station	**la gare routière**	lah *gar* roo-tee-*air*
bus stop	**l'arrêt de bus**	lah-*ray* duh boohss
by means of a car	**en voiture**	ahn vwa-*toor*
cashier	**la caisse**	lah kess
cathedral	**le cathedral**	luh ka-tay-*dral*
church	**l'église**	lay-*gleez*
driver's license	**le permis de conduire**	luh per-*mee* duh con-*dweer*
elevator	**l'ascenseur**	lah sahn *seuhr*
entrance (to a building or a city)	**une porte**	ewn port
exit (from a building or a freeway)	**une sortie**	ewn sor-*tee*
gasoline	**du pétrol/de l'essence**	duh pay-*troll*/de lay-*sahns*
hospital	**l'hôpital**	low-pee-*tahl*
luggage storage	**la consigne**	lah kohn-*seen*-yuh
museum	**le musée**	luh mew-*zay*
no smoking	**défense de fumer**	day-*fahns* de fu-may
one-day pass	**le ticket journalier**	luh tee-*kay* jhoor-nall-ee-*ay*
one-way ticket	**l'aller simple**	lah-*lay sam*-pluh
police	**la police**	lah po-*lees*
round-trip ticket	**l'aller-retour**	lah-*lay* re-*toor*
second floor	**le premier étage**	luh prem-ee-*ehr* ay-*taj*
slow down	**ralentir**	rah-lahn-*teer*
store	**le magasin**	luh ma-ga-*zehn*
street	**la rue**	lah roo
subway/underground/ Tube	**le Métro**	le *may*-tro

English	French	Pronunciation
telephone	**le téléphone**	luh tay-lay-*phone*
ticket	**un billet**	uh *bee*-yay
toilets	**les toilettes/les WC**	lay twa-*lets*/les vay-*say*

NECESSITIES

English	French	Pronunciation
I'd like	**Je voudrais**	jhe voo-*dray*
a room	**une chambre**	ewn *shahm*-bruh
the key	**la clé (la clef)**	la clay
How much does it cost?	**C'est combien?/ Ça coûte combien?**	say comb-bee-*ehn?*/ sah coot comb-bee-*ehn?*
That's expensive	**C'est cher/chère**	say share
Do you take credit cards?	**Est-ce que vous acceptez les cartes de credit?**	es-kuh voo zaksep-*tay* lay kart duh creh-*dee?*
I'd like to buy	**Je voudrais acheter**	jhe voo-*dray* ahsh-*tay*
aspirin	**des aspirines/ des aspros**	deyz ahs-peer-*een*/ deyz ahs-*proh*
gift	**un cadeau**	uh kah-*doe*
map of the city	**un plan de ville**	uh plahn de *veel*
newspaper	**un journal**	uh zhoor-*nahl*
phone card	**une carte téléphonique**	uh cart tay-lay-fone-*eek*
postcard	**une carte postale**	ewn cart pos-*tahl*
road map	**une carte routière**	ewn cart roo-tee-*air*
stamp	**un timbre**	uh *tam*-bruh

IN YOUR HOTEL

English	French	Pronunciation
Are taxes included?	**Est-ce que les taxes sont comprises?**	ess-keh lay taks son com-*preez?*
balcony	**un balcon**	uh *bahl*-cohn
bathtub	**une baignoire**	ewn bayn-*nwar*
hot and cold water	**l'eau chaude et froide**	low showed ay fwad
Is breakfast included?	**Petit déjeuner inclus?**	peh-*tee* day-jheun-*ay* ehn-*klu?*
room	**une chambre**	ewn *shawm*-bruh
shower	**une douche**	ewn dooch
sink	**un lavabo**	uh la-va-*bow*
suite	**une suite**	ewn sweet
We're staying for . . . days	**On reste pour . . . jours**	ohn rest poor . . . jhoor

NUMBERS & ORDINALS

English	French	Pronunciation
zero	**zéro**	*zare*-oh
one	**un**	uhn
two	**deux**	duh
three	**trois**	twah
four	**quatre**	*kaht*-ruh
five	**cinq**	sank
six	**six**	seess
seven	**sept**	set
eight	**huit**	wheat
nine	**neuf**	noof
ten	**dix**	dees
twenty	**vingt**	vehn
forty	**quarante**	ka-*rahnt*
fifty	**cinquante**	sang-*kahnt*
one hundred	**cent**	sahn
one thousand	**mille**	meel

THE CALENDAR

English	French	Pronunciation
Sunday	**dimanche**	dee-*mahnsh*
Monday	**lundi**	luhn-*dee*
Tuesday	**mardi**	mahr-*dee*
Wednesday	**mercredi**	mair-kruh-*dee*
Thursday	**jeudi**	jheu-*dee*
Friday	**vendredi**	vawn-druh-*dee*
Saturday	**samedi**	sahm-*dee*

2 Food & Menu

English	French	Pronunciation
I would like to eat	**Je voudrais manger**	jhe voo-*dray* mahn-*jhay*
Please give me	**Donnez-moi, s'il vous plaît**	doe-nay-*mwah,* seel-voo-*play*
a bottle of	**une bouteille de**	ewn boo-*tay* duh
a cup of	**une tasse de**	ewn tass duh
a glass of	**un verre de**	uh vair duh
a plate of breakfast	**une assiette de le petit-déjeuner**	ewn ass-ee-*et* duh luh puh-*tee* day-zhuh-*nay*

English	French	Pronunciation
a cocktail	**un apéritif**	uh ah-pay-ree-*teef*
the check/bill	**l'addition/la note**	la-dee-see-*ohn*/la noat
dinner	**le dîner**	luh dee-*nay*
a knife	**un couteau**	uh koo-*toe*
a napkin	**une serviette**	ewn sair-vee-*et*
a spoon	**une cuillère**	ewn kwee-*air*
a fork	**une fourchette**	ewn four-shet
Cheers!	**A votre santé!**	ah vo-truh sahn-*tay!*
fixed-price menu	**un menu**	uh may-*new*
Is the tip/service included?	**Est-ce que le service est compris?**	ess-ke luh ser-*vees* eh com-*pree?*
Waiter!/Waitress!	**Monsieur!/Mademoiselle!**	muh-*syuh*/mad-mwa-*zel*
wine list	**une carte des vins**	ewn cart day *van*
appetizer	**une entrée**	ewn en-*tray*
main course	**un plat principal**	uh plah pran-see-*pahl*
tip included	**service compris**	sehr-*vees* cohm-*pree*
wide-ranging sampling of the chef's best efforts	**menu dégustation**	may-*new* day-gus-ta-see-*on*

MEATS

English	French	Pronunciation
beef stew	**du pot au feu**	dew poht o *fhe*
marinated beef braised with red wine and served with vegetables	**du boeuf à la mode**	dew bewf ah lah *mhowd*
chicken	**du poulet**	*dew poo*-lay
rolls of pounded and baked chicken, veal, or fish, often pike, usually served warm	**des quenelles**	day ke-*nelle*
chicken, stewed with mushrooms and wine	**du coq au vin**	dew cock o vhin
frogs' legs	**des cuisses de grenouilles**	day cweess duh gre-*noo*-yuh
ham	**du jambon**	dew jham-*bon*
lamb	**de l'agneau**	duh lahn-*nyo*
rabbit	**du lapin**	dew *lah*-pan
sirloin	**de l'aloyau**	duh lahl-why-*yo*
steak	**du bifteck**	dew beef-*tek*

English	French	Pronunciation
filet steak, embedded with fresh green or black peppercorns, flambéed, and served with a cognac sauce	**un steak au poivre**	uh stake o *pwah*-vruh
double tenderloin, a long muscle from which filet steaks are cut	**du chateaubriand**	dew *sha*-tow-bree-ahn
stewed meat with white sauce, enriched with cream and eggs	**de la blanquette**	duh lah blon-*kette*
veal	**du veau**	dew voh

FISH

English	French	Pronunciation
fish (freshwater)	**du poisson de rivière,** or **du poisson d'eau douce**	dew pwah-*sson* duh ree-vee-*aire,* dew pwah-sson d'o *dooss*
fish (saltwater)	**du poisson de mer**	dew pwah-*sson* duh *mehr*
Mediterranean fish soup or stew made with tomatoes, garlic, saffron, and olive oil	**de la bouillabaisse**	duh lah booh-ya-*besse*
herring	**du hareng**	dew ahr-*rahn*
lobster	**du homard**	dew oh-*mahr*
mussels	**des moules**	day moohl
mussels in herb-flavored white wine with shallots	**des moules marinières**	day moohl mar-ee-nee-*air*
oysters	**des huîtres**	dayz *hwee*-truhs
shrimp	**des crevettes**	day kreh-*vet*
smoked salmon	**du saumon fumé**	dew sow-*mohn* fu-*may*
tuna	**du thon**	dew tohn
trout	**de la truite**	duh lah tru-*eet*

SIDES/APPETIZERS

English	French	Pronunciation
butter	**du beurre**	dew bhuhr
bread	**du pain**	dew pan
gooseliver	**du foie gras**	dew fwah *grah*
potted and minced pork products, prepared as a roughly chopped pâté	**des rillettes**	day ree-*yett*
snails	**des escargots**	dayz ess-car-*goh*

FRUITS/VEGETABLES

English	French	Pronunciation
cabbage	**du choux**	dew *shoe*
eggplant	**de l'aubergine**	duh loh-ber-*jheen*
grapes	**du raisin**	dew ray-*zhan*
green beans	**des haricots verts**	day *ahr*-ee-coh *vaire*
lemon/lime	**du citron/du citron vert**	dew cee-*tron*/dew cee-tron *vaire*
potatoes	**des pommes de terre**	day puhm duh *tehr*
potatoes au gratin	**des pommes de terre dauphinois**	day puhm duh *tehr* doh-feen-*wah*
french fries	**des pommes frites**	day puhm *freet*
spinach	**des épinards**	dayz ay-pin-*ards*
strawberries	**des fraises**	day *frez*

BEVERAGES

English	French	Pronunciation
beer	**de la bière**	duh lah bee-*aire*
milk	**du lait**	dew *lay*
orange juice	**du jus d'orange**	dew joo d'or-*ahn*-jhe
water	**de l'eau**	duh *lo*
red wine	**du vin rouge**	dew vhin *rooj*
white wine	**du vin blanc**	dew vhin *blahn*
coffee (black)	**un café noir**	uh ka-fay *nwahr*
coffee (with cream)	**un café crème**	uh ka-fay *krem*
coffee (with milk)	**un café au lait**	uh ka-fay o *lay*
coffee (decaf)	**un café décaféiné** (slang: **un déca**)	un ka-fay day-kah-fay-*nay* (uh *day*-kah)
coffee (espresso)	**un café espresso (un express)**	uh ka-fay e-*sprehss-o* (un ek-*sprehss*)
tea	**du thé**	dew *tay*
herbal tea	**une tisane**	ewn tee-*zahn*

DESSERTS

English	French	Pronunciation
cake	**du gâteau**	dew *gha*-tow
cheese	**du fromage**	dew fro-*mahj*
thick custard dessert with a caramelized topping	**de la crème brûlée**	duh lah *krem* bruh-*lay*
caramelized upside-down apple pie	**une tarte Tatin**	ewn tart tah-*tihn*

English	French	Pronunciation
tart	**une tarte**	ewn tart
vanilla ice cream	**de la glace à la vanille**	duh lah *glass* a lah vah-*nee*-yuh
fruit, especially cherries, cooked in batter	**du clafoutis**	dew kla-foo-*tee*

Index

Abbatiale Ste-Croix (Bordeaux), 682
Abbaye aux Dames (Caen), 291–292
Abbaye aux Hommes (Caen), 292
Abbaye de Fontenay, 403
Abbaye de Jumièges, 276
Abbaye de St-Honorat, 530
Abbaye de St-Wandrille, 276
Abbaye d'Hautecombe (Aix-les-Bains), 441–442
Abbaye Romane de St-Martin-d'Ainay (Lyon), 411
Abbaye Royale de Fontevraud, 264–265
Abbaye St-George (St-Martin de Boscherville), 276
Accommodations, 63–67
 best, 10–12
Aéroport d'Orly (Paris), 87, 90
Aéroport Roissy-Charles de Gaulle (Paris), 87, 90
African-American travelers, 52
Aigues-Mortes, 608–611
Aiguille du Midi, 457
Airfares, 40–42
Airport security, 40
Air travel, 39–43, 47, 48, 63
Aix-en-Provence, 490–497
Aix-les-Bains, 441–443
Albertville, 463
Albi, 630–633
Alise-Ste-Reine, 402
Alsace-Lorraine, 2, 354–385
Alsace Postal History Museum (Riquewihr), 369–370
Amboise, 242–246
American cemetery (Cimetière de Belleau), 336
American Express, 46, 47, 68, 72
Amiens, 346, 348–350
Ammerschwihr, 371–372
Amnesia Café (Paris), 191
Amphitheater (Les Arènes; Arles), 482
Amphithéâtre des Trois-Gauls (Lyon), 412
Amphithéâtre Romain de Nîmes, 604
Ancien Hôtel de Ville (Les Baux), 488
Ancienne Manufacture Royale de Limoges, 724
Andlau, 367
Angers, 268–271
Angoulême, 676–679
Anna Lowe (Paris), 178
Annecy, 435–439
Antibes, 549–552
Antiques, 4
 Beaune, 395
 Biarritz, 659
 Bordeaux, 683
 Caen, 293
 Cannes, 528
 Carcassonne, 626
 Chartres, 203–204
 Colmar, 373
 Dijon, 401
 Epernay, 352
 Lyon, 413
 Marseille, 502
 Nancy, 380
 Nantes, 331
 Paris, 174
 Pau, 650
 Rouen, 278
 Tours, 251
Antiques Show (Paris), 35
Apartment rentals, 64
Apocalypse Tapestries (Angers), 269–270
Aqua Club (St-Tropez), 514
Aquarium de La Rochelle, 670
Aquarium du Val de Loire (near Amboise), 244
Arbre de la Liberté (Pérouges), 423
Arc de Triomphe
 Montpellier, 612
 Nancy, 379
 Orange, 466
 Paris, 146
Arc de Triomphe du Carrousel (Paris), 156
Archbishops' Palace (Narbonne), 616
Archbishop's Palace (Rouen), 274
Archeoscope (Mont-St-Michel), 302
Architecture, 20–26
The Ardèche, 2, 6, 429–431
Ardennes, 30, 346
Area codes, 68
Argonaute (Paris), 163
Arles, 480–486
Armistice Day, 38
Arromanches-les-Bains, 299–301
Art, 15–20
Arts et Collections d'Alsace
 Colmar, 373
 Strasbourg, 359
Atelier de Cézanne (Aix-en-Provence), 493
The Atlantic Coast, 3, 32
ATMs (automated-teller machines), 45
Au Bon Marché (Paris), 177
Aubusson, 721–723
Audio Visit (Paris), 145
Au Lapin Agile (Paris), 183
Au Nain Bleu (Paris), 176
Au Printemps (Paris), 177
Au Sauvignon (Paris), 187
Auteuil (Paris), 169
Autun, 392–394
Auxerre, 386–389
Avallon, 391–392
Avignon, 468–477
Azay-le-Rideau, 258–260
Azzedine Alaïa (Paris), 177

Baccarat (Paris), 176
Bagatelle Park (Paris), 169
Bagnères-de-Bigorre, 647
Bagnols-en-Beaujolais, 420
Baie des Fourmis (Beaulieu-sur-Mer), 582

Baiser Salé (Paris), 185
Balabus (Paris), 144–145
Ballooning, 57, 292
Balzac, Honoré de, 169, 266
Musée Balzac (Saché), 259
Rodin statue of (Paris), 94, 167, 168
Baptistère St-Jean (Poitiers), 666
Barbizon, 205–207
Bar du Crillon (Paris), 188–189
Barge cruises, 58
Bar Hemingway/Bar Vendôme (Paris), 189
Barr, 366
Barrio Latino (Paris), 189–190
Basilica of Pius X (Lourdes), 646
Basilique du Bois-Chenu (Domrémy-la-Pucelle), 383
Basilique du Sacré-Coeur (Paris), 146
Basilique Notre-Dame de Fourvière (Lyon), 410
Basilique Notre-Dame-de-la-Garde (Marseille), 500
Basilique Notre-Dame La Daurade (Toulouse), 636
Basilique St-Andoche (Saulieu), 405
Basilique St-Denis (Paris), 170
Basilique Ste-Madeleine (Vézelay), 390
Basilique St-Martin (Cap-Martin), 599
Basilique St-Michel (Bordeaux), 682
Basilique St-Nazaire (Carcassonne), 625
Basilique St-Paul-Serge (Narbonne), 617
Basilique St-Rémi (Reims), 338–339
Basilique St-Sauveur (Dinan), 315
Basilique St-Sauveur (Rocamadour), 702
Basilique St-Sernin (Toulouse), 637
Basilique St-Seurin (Bordeaux), 682
Basilique St-Victor (Marseille), 500
Basilique Supérieure (Lourdes), 646
The Basque Country, 31–32, 644–664
Bastian (Strasbourg), 359
Bastide St-Louis (Carcassonne), 625
Bastille Day, 37
Carcassonne, 624
Bateau-Lavoir (Paris), 162
Bateaux-Mouche (Paris), 145
Batofar (Paris), 186
Battle Gallery (Versailles), 196
Bayeux, 296–298
Bayonne, 653–656
Beaches
Beaulieu-sur-Mer, 582
Biarritz, 657
Cagnes-sur-Mer, 553
Cannes, 525
Carnac, 323
Concarneau, 320
Deauville, 285–286
Dinard, 311
Golfe-Juan, 544
Juan-les-Pins, 546
Le Touquet-Paris-Plage, 346
Monaco, 588
Narbonne, 615
Nice, 565, 568
St-Jean-Cap-Ferrat, 579
St-Jean-de-Luz, 662
St-Malo, 306–307
St-Tropez, 514, 516
Toulon, 508
Beaugency, 233–234
Beaujolais Country, 419–421
Beaulieu-sur-Mer, 581–584
Beaune, 394–398
Bed-and-breakfasts (B&Bs), 64
Belleau Wood (Bois de Belleau), 336
Belleville-sur-Saône, 419, 420–421
Bell Tower (St-Emilion), 690
Bergheim, 368
Biarritz, 656–661
Biarritz Cup, 657
Biarritz Surf Festival, 656–657
Bibliothèque Humaniste (Sélestat), 367–368
Biking, 4
Burgundy, 395
Cannes, 525–526
the Dordogne, 695
Loire Valley, 228
Paris, 145
Périgueux, 693
tours, 58
Wine Road, 365
Biot, 541–543
Black Madonna (Rocamadour), 703
Blois, 236–239
The Boat Fair (Paris), 39
Boating, 516, 526
Boat trips and tours
Aix-les-Bains, 441
barge cruises, 58
Bordeaux, 682
Concarneau, 320–321
Evian, 432–434
Ile de Bréhat, 313
Ile de Porquerolles, 510–511
Ile de Port-Cros, 511
Iles de Lérins, 530
La Rochelle, 673
Marseille, 500
Paris, 97, 145
St-Malo, 306
Strasbourg, 356
Bocuse, Paul, 418
Bois-Chenu, Basilique du (Domrémy-la-Pucelle), 383
Bois de Belleau (Belleau Wood), 336
Bois de Boulogne (Paris), 169
Bonpoint (Paris), 176
Bonzaï Arboretum de la Côte d'Azur (Biot), 542
Bordeaux (city), 679–687
Bordeaux (province), 665–691
wine country, 687–691
Boucher, François, 17, 160, 250, 317, 337, 380, 384, 579, 722
Bourg-en-Bresse, 424–425
Bourges, 709–713
Brancusi, l'Atelier (Paris), 147
Braque, Georges, 20, 412, 518, 722
Brasserie Lipp (Paris), 142
Brittany, 30, 305–333
***Brocante*, 467**
Bucket shops, 41
Buddha Bar (Paris), 190
Burgundy, 5, 83–86, 386–405
Business etiquette, 71
Business hours, 68
Bus Palladium (Paris), 187
Bus travel, 43
Butte de Montfaucon (Verdun), 384

Cab (Paris), 186
Cabourg, 296
Cadolle (Paris), 179
Cadre Noir de Saumur, 266
Caen, 291–296
Caen Memorial, 292–293
Café Beaubourg (Paris), 142
Café-Brasserie St-Regis (Paris), 188
Café de Flore (Paris), 143
Café de la Musique (Paris), 143
Cagnes-sur-Mer, 552–555

Cahors, 704–706
Calder, Alexander, 147, 550, 556, 558
The Camargue, 609
Camus (Cognac), 675
Canet-Plage (Perpignan), 620, 624
Cannes, 524–537
- accommodations, 530–533
- beaches, 525
- film festival, 35–36, 525
- nightlife, 536–537
- outdoor activities, 525–527
- restaurants, 534–535
- shopping, 528
- sightseeing, 529–530
- traveling to, 524
- visitor information, 524

Cannes Film Festival, 35–36, 525
Cap d'Antibes, 549–552
Carcassonne, 624–628
Carnac, 323–326
Carnac-Plage, 323
Carnaval, Nice, 35, 564
Carré d'Art (Nîmes), 602
Car rentals, 61–62
Carrousel du Louvre (Paris), 173, 179
Carte Mobilis (Paris), 96
Carte Orange (Paris), 96
Car travel, 43, 61
Casinos
- Annecy, 439
- Beaulieu-sur-Mer, 582, 584
- Biarritz, 661
- Bordeaux, 686–687
- Cannes, 536
- Chamonix-Mont Blanc, 459
- Deauville, 289
- Dinard, 314
- Evian, 435
- Juan-les-Pins, 548
- La Baule, 327
- Megève, 455
- Monaco, 596
- Nice, 576
- Reims, 345
- St-Malo, 310
- Trouville, 291
- Vals-les-Bains, 430
- Vichy, 716–717

Castres, 629–630
Cathédrale de la Major (Marseille), 500
Cathédrale d'Images (Les Baux), 488
Cathédrale Notre-Dame
- Le Puy, 727
- Montauban, 707

Cathédrale Notre-Dame d'Amiens, 9, 349
Cathédrale Notre-Dame de Chartres, 8–9, 200–202
Cathédrale Notre-Dame de Laon, 346–347
Cathédrale Notre-Dame de l'Assomption (Clermont-Ferrand), 719
Cathédrale Notre-Dame de Reims, 9, 339–340
Cathédrale Notre-Dame de Rouen, 9, 274
Cathédrale Notre-Dame des Doms (Avignon), 470
Cathédrale Notre-Dame de Senlis, 223
Cathédrale Notre-Dame de Strasbourg, 356
Cathédrale Orthodoxe Russe St-Nicolas à Nice, 566
Cathédrale St-André (Bordeaux), 680
Cathédrale St-Apollinaire (Valence), 428
Cathédrale St-Corentin (Quimper), 317
Cathédrale Ste-Cécile (Albi), 630–631
Cathédrale Ste-Croix (Orléans), 228
Cathédrale Ste-Marie (Bayonne), 653–654
Cathédrale Ste-Marie-Majeure (Toulon), 508
Cathédrale St-Etienne
- Auxerre, 387
- Bourges, 710
- Cahors, 705
- Limoges, 724
- Toulouse, 637

Cathédrale St-Front (Périgueux), 694
Cathédrale St-Gatien (Tours), 250
Cathédrale St-Jean (Perpignan), 621
Cathédrale St-Just (Narbonne), 616
Cathédrale St-Lazare (Autun), 393
Cathédrale St-Maurice
- Angers, 269
- Vienne, 426

Cathédrale St-Pierre
- Angoulême, 677
- Montpellier, 612
- Nantes, 329
- Poitiers, 666

Cathédrale St-Sacerdos (Sarlat-la-Canéda), 699
Cathédrale St-Sauveur (Aix-en-Provence), 493
Cathédrale St-Vincent (St-Malo), 306
Cathedrals, best, 8–9
Catherine (Paris), 181
Caudebec-en-Caux, 276–277
Cave art, 15, 696–700
Caveau de Morgon (Villié-Morgon), 421
Caveau des Oubliettes (Paris), 185
Cave du Musée (Colmar), 373
Caves at Lascaux (near Montignac), 696–697
Caves Plouzeau (Chinon), 261
Cellier de la Vieille Eglise (Juliénas), 421
Cellphones, 54–55
Center for Industrial Design (Paris), 147
Center for Nature Discovery, Garden in Memory of Diana, Princess of Wales (Paris), 172
Centre National de la Bande Dessinée et de l'Image (CNBDI; Angoulême), 677
Centre Pompidou (Paris), 7, 146–147
Centre Sant-Vicens (Perpignan), 621
Cézanne, Paul, 19, 157, 218, 442, 470, 491, 492
- Atelier de Cézanne (Aix-en-Provence), 493
- route de Cézanne, 492

Chagall, Marc, 20, 23, 182, 556, 560
- Musée National Message Biblique Marc Chagall (Cimiez), 567–568

Chambord, 235
Chamonix-Mont Blanc, 455–459
Champagne cellars, 340–341, 352
Champagne Country, 334–353
Chanel (Paris), 178
Channel Islands, 306
Chantilly, 219–222
Chapelle de la Miséricorde (St-Tropez), 517
Chapelle de la Vierge (Rouen), 274
Chapelle de Notre-Dame (Rocamadour), 703
Chapelle de St-Hubert (Amboise), 243

Chapelle des Bourras (Aix-en-Provence), 493
Chapelle de Trémalo (Pont-Aven), 322
Chapelle du Rosaire (Vence), 559
Chapelle Impériale (Biarritz), 658
Chapelle Miraculeuse (Rocamadour), 703
Chapelle Notre-Dame de Vie (Mougins), 538
Chapelle Penitents-gris (Aix-en-Provence), 493
Chapelle St-Jean (Avignon), 471
Chapelle St-Michel-d'Aiguilhe (Le Puy), 727–728
Chapelle St-Nicolas (Avignon), 470
Chapelle St-Pierre (Villefranche-sur-Mer), 577–578
Charles de Gaulle Airport (Roissy; Paris), 87, 90
Chartres, 199–205
Chartreuse de Champmol (Dijon), 400
Chartreuse du Val-de-Bénédiction (Villenueve-lez-Avignon), 471, 473
Château Barrière (Périgueux), 694
Château Comtal (Carcassonne), 625
Château d'Amboise, 243
Château d'Angers, 269–270
Château d'Azay-le-Rideau, 7, 258–259
Château d'Eau (Montpellier), 612
Château de Balleroy (between Bayeux and Caen), 292
Château de Beynac, 699
Château de Blois, 236, 237
Château de Bussy-Rabutin (near Grésigny), 403
Château de Caen, 293
Château de Chambord, 7, 235
Château de Chantilly/Musée Condé, 7, 220
Château de Châteaudun, 232–233
Château de Chaumont, 241
Château de Chenonceau, 7, 246–247
Château de Cheverny, 239
Château de Chinon, 261
Château de Cognac, 674–675
Château de Condé, 337–338
Château de Fontcrenne (Villié-Morgon), 421
Château de la Napoule, 522
Château de Langeais, 257
Château de Loches, 255
Château de Montrottier, 436–437
Château de Nohant, 713–714
Château de Pau, 649–650
Château de Pierrefonds (Compiègne), 225
Château de Rocamadour, 702
Château de Roquebrune, 598
Château de Rully, 394
Château de St-Malo, 306
Château de Salses (Perpignan), 621–622
Château de Saumur, 266–267
Château des Baux, 487
Château des Ducs de Bretagne (Nantes), 328, 330
Château de Valençay, 240
Château de Vauvenarges (Aix-en-Provence), 492
Château de Vaux-le-Vicomte, 210–211
Château de Versailles, 7, 195–196
Château de Villandry, 256–257
Château d'If (Marseille), 500
Château du Clos-Lucé (near Amboise), 243
Châteaudun, 232–233
Château Dunois/Le Musée des Arts et Traditions Populaires de l'Orléanais (Beaugency), 233–234
Château du Roi (St-Emilion), 690
Château d'Ussé, 264
Château et Parc Zoologique de Thoiry, 216–217
Château-Fort de Lourdes, 646–647
Château Haut-Koenigsbourg, 368
Château-Hotel de Villequier, 277
Château Lafite-Rothschild (Pauillac), 688
Château Margaux, 688
Château Mouton-Rothschild (Pauillac), 688–689
Château Musée de Dinan, 315
Château-Musée Grimaldi (Musée de l'Olivier & Musée d'Art Moderne Méditerranéen; Cagnes-sur-Mer), 553
Châteauneuf-du-Pape, 466
Château Royal (Collioure), 619
Château Royal et Parc and Musée de la Vénerie (Senlis), 223
Château Suffren (St-Tropez), 517
Château-Thierry, 336–337
Châteaux and palaces, best, 7
Chaumont-sur-Loire, 241–242
Chenonceaux, 246–248
Cheverny, 239–240
Children, 33–34, 52, 81–83
Chinese Museum (Fontainebleau), 208
Chinon, 260–264
Chocolate and chocolatiers
 Bayonne, 654–655
 Biarritz, 658–659
 Blois, 236
 Caen, 293
 Cannes, 528
 Lyon, 413
 Marseille, 501
 Nice, 568–569
 Paris, 176
 Pau, 650
 Rouen, 278
 St-Jean-de-Luz, 662
Christian (Paris), 176
Christian Dior (Paris), 178
Christmas Fairs, 38
Cimetière Américain at Romagne (Verdun), 384
Cimetière de la Madeleine (Amiens), 348
Cimetière de Montmartre (Paris), 162
Cimetière de Montparnasse (Paris), 168
Cimetière du Père-Lachaise (Paris), 169–170
Cimiez Convent (Monastère de Cimiez), 567
Cinéscénie de Puy du Fou, 36
Cirque de Gavarnie, 647
Cité de la Musique (Paris), 183
Cité des Sciences et de l'Industrie (Paris), 163
Cité Réligieuse (Rocamadour), 702, 703
Cité Royale (Loches), 255
Cityrama (Paris), 144
Claude Monet Foundation (Giverny), 218
Clermont-Ferrand, 717–723
Clock Room (Versailles), 196
Clos St-Landelin (Rouffach), 372
Coco Beach (St-Tropez), 516
Cognac, 674–676

Col de la Schlucht, 377
Col du Bonhomme, 377
Col du Galibier, 434
Colette (Paris), 177
Collection des Voitures Anciennes de S.A.S. le Prince de Monaco, 591
Collections Baron Gérard (Bayeux), 297
Collégiale de la Conversion de St-Paul (St-Paul-de-Vence), 556
Collégiale Notre-Dame (Beaune), 395
Collégiale St-Ours (Loches), 255
Colline de Fourvière (Lyon), 410
Colline St-Eutrope (Orange), 466
Collioure, 618–620
Colmar, 372–377
Colmar International Festival, 36
Colonne de Juillet (Paris), 158
Comédie-Française (Paris), 183
Comédie-Française-Théâtre du Vieux-Colombier (Paris), 183
Commonwealth Cemetery (Bayeux), 297
Compiègne, 224–226
Concarneau, 320–321
Concerts Allumés (Poitiers), 666
Conciergerie (Paris), 160
Condé-en-Brie, 337–338
Condo rentals, 64
Consolidators, 41
Consulates, 71
Context:Paris, 145
Cooking schools, 58–59
Cordeliers, Eglise des (Nancy), 380
Cordes-sur-Ciel, 633–634
Côte d'Azur. *See* The French Riviera
Côte d'Or, 6
Côte Sauvage, 325
Couly-Dutheil (Chinon), 9, 261
Courchevel 1850, 447–451
Cour d'Honneur (Paris), 164
Cours Mirabeau (Aix-en-Provence), 492
Crazy Horse Saloon (Paris), 184
Credit cards, 45
  lost or stolen, 72
Crest Road (Route des Crêtes), 6, 354, 377
Crussol, Mont (Valence), 428
Currency, 45
Customs regulations, 69–70

Dalí, Salvador, 147
  L'Espace Montmartre Salvador-Dalí (Paris), 162
Dambach, 367
Dance clubs and discos
  Amiens, 350–351
  Angers, 271
  Arles, 486
  Avignon, 477
  Beaune, 398
  Biarritz, 661
  Blois, 239
  Bordeaux, 687
  Bourges, 713
  Caen, 295–296
  Cannes, 536, 537
  Carcassonne, 628
  Carnac, 326
  Chamonix-Mont Blanc, 459
  Chartres, 205
  Clermont-Ferrand, 721
  Deauville, 289
  Grenoble, 447
  Juan-les-Pins, 549
  La Baule, 327–328
  Marseille, 507
  Monaco, 597
  Montpellier, 615
  Nancy, 382
  Nantes, 333
  Nîmes, 608
  Orléans, 232
  Paris, 186–187
  Pau, 653
  Périgueux, 696
  Perpignan, 624
  Quimper, 320
  Reims, 345
  Rouen, 281
  St-Malo, 310
  St-Tropez, 522
  Strasbourg, 364–365
  Toulouse, 643
  Tours, 254
  Vichy, 717
David, Jacques-Louis, 18, 152, 276, 470, 654
Day Pilgrims (Lourdes), 645
D-Day beaches, 4–5, 298–300
Deauville, 5, 285–289
Deep vein thrombosis, 48
Défilé des Marques (Paris), 178
Degas, Edgar, 18, 151, 162, 250, 442, 470, 631, 650, 654
Delacroix, Eugène, 18, 152, 166, 169, 220, 250, 276, 379, 638, 682, 713, 714
Deux Magots (Paris), 143
Didier Ludot (Paris), 178
Dijon, 398–404
Dinan, 314–316
Dinard, 310–314
Disabilities, travelers with, 50
Disneyland Paris, 211–216
Distillerie Cointreau (Angers), 271
Dolce & Gabbana (Paris), 177
Dolder Belfry Tower (Riquewihr), 369
Domaine de la Bressande (Château de Rully), 394
Domaine Maurice Protheau (Mercurey), 10, 393–394
Domaines Schlumberger (Guebwiller), 9, 373–374
Domrémy-la-Pucelle, 383
Donjon Gilles-Aycelin, 617
The Dordogne, 32, 692, 695–699
Driving rules, 62–63
Driving tours
  the Ardèche, 429
  best, 6
  Cap-Martin, 599
  Côte Sauvage, 325
  route de Cézanne, 492
  Route de Champagne, 345
  Route des Abbayes, 276–277
  Route des Crêtes, 377
  Route des Grandes Alpes, 434
  Route du Champagne, 341
Drugstores, 70

Economy-class syndrome, 48
Ecotourism, 53–54
Eglise Abbatiale (Mont-St-Michel), 302
Eglise de Biot, 542
Eglise de la Sorbonne (Paris), 164
Eglise de Sacré-Coeur (Beaulieu-sur-Mer), 582
Eglise de Salles Arbuissonnas, 420
Eglise des Cordeliers (Nancy), 380
Eglise des Dominicains (Colmar), 374
Eglise des Jacobins (Toulouse), 636
Eglise du Dôme (Paris), 150
Eglise Monolithe (St-Emilion), 690
Eglise Notre-Dame
  Beaugency, 234
  Bourg-en-Bresse, 424
  Villenueve-lez-Avignon, 471
Eglise Notre-Dame des Sablons (Aigues-Mortes), 608–609

Eglise Notre-Dame-du-Port (Clermont-Ferrand), 719
Eglise Notre-Dame-la-Grande (Poitiers), 666
Eglise Orthodoxe Russe (Biarritz), 657
Eglise St-Aignan (Orléans), 228–229
Eglise St-Benoît (Castres), 629
Eglise Ste-Catherine (Honfleur), 282
Eglise Ste-Foy (Sélestat), 368
Eglise Ste-Marguerite (Roquebrune), 598
Eglise St-Etienne (Beaugency), 234
Eglise St-Etienne-de-la-Cité (Périgueux), 694
Eglise St-Eustache (Paris), 156
Eglise St-George (Sélestat), 368
Eglise St-Germain-des-Prés (Paris), 165–166
Eglise St-Jean-Baptiste (St-Jean-de-Luz), 662
Eglise St-Lazare (Avallon), 391
Eglise St-Léger (Cognac), 675
Eglise St-Maclou (Rouen), 274, 281
Eglise St-Martin
  Biarritz, 657
  Colmar, 374
Eglise St-Michel (Cordes-sur-Ciel), 633
Eglise St-Michel-des-Lions (Limoges), 724
Eglise St-Ouen (Rouen), 274–275, 281
Eglise St-Paul (Lyon), 410
Eglise St-Pierre
  Paris, 162
  Vienne, 426
Eglise St-Rémi (Domrémy-la-Pucelle), 383
Eglise St-Sulpice (Paris), 166
Eglise St-Thomas (Strasbourg), 358
Eglise St-Trophime (Arles), 482–483
Eglise St-Vincent (Les Baux), 488
Egyptian obelisk (Paris), 161
Eiffel Tower (Paris), 147, 150
Electricity, 70
E-mail, 55
Embassies and consulates, 71
Emergencies, 71
English Garden (Dinan), 315
Entry requirements, 33–34
Epernay, 351
Escorted tours, 57
Espace Art Roman (Clermont-Ferrand), 717–718
Espace Culturel (Mougins), 537
Esplanade des Quinconces (Bordeaux), 680
Estivade (Dijon), 399–400
Etiquette and customs, 71
Eurailpass, 60–61
Euro, 45
Eurostar Express, 44
Eurotunnel, 44
Evian-les-Bains, 432–435
Eze, 584–586

F

Façonnable (Nice), 569
Faïencerie Carpentier Augy (Rouen), 278
Families with children, 33–34, 52, 81–83
Fat Tire Bike Tours-Paris, 145
Fauchon (Paris), 178–179
Ferries, from England, 43–44
Festival Alors Chante (Montauban), 707
Festival d'Aix-en-Provence, 37
Festival d'Automne (Paris), 38
Festival d'Avignon, 37
Festival de Carcassonne, 624
Festival de Jazz (Strasbourg), 355
Festival de Jazz à Montauban, 707
Festival de la Bande Dessinée (Angoulême), 677
Festival de Musique du Vieux-Lyon (Lyon), 408
Festival de St-Denis (Paris), 36
Festival du Court Métrage (Clermont-Ferrand), 718
Festival du Film Policier (Cognac), 674
Festival du Jazz à Vienne, 426
Festival Interceltique de Lorient, 38
Festival International de la Télévision (Monaco), 587
Festival International de Musique de Colmar, 373
Festival International des Jeunes Réalisateurs (St-Jean-de-Luz), 661
Festival International des Musiques d'Aujourd'hui (Strasbourg), 355–356
Festival International du Film (Cannes), 35–36, 525
Festival International du Film de La Rochelle, 670
Festival International du Photojournalisme (Perpignan), 621
Festival of Classical Music (Strasbourg), 355
Festival of St-Jean (Fêtes Patronales de la Saint Jean, 661
Festival Printemps de Bourges, 709
Festival Synthese (Bourges), 710
Fête Chopin (Paris), 37
Fête de Bayonne, 653
Fête de la Musique (Lyon), 408
Fête de St-Sylvestre, 39
Fête des Lumières (Lyon), 39
Fêtes des Remparts (Dinan), 314–315
Field of Megaliths (Carnac), 323
Flaubert, Gustave, Musée Flaubert et d'Histoire de la Médécine (Rouen), 276
Flavigny-sur-Ozerain, 402
Flea markets
  Avignon, 474
  Cannes, 528
  Monaco, 590
  Paris, 180
  Reims, 342
  Rouen, 278
Fleche St-Michel (Bordeaux), 682
FNAC (Paris), 180, 182
Foire à la Brocante (Isle-sur-la-Sorgue), 467
Foire de la Croix (Megève), 452
Foire du Trône (Paris), 35
Folies-Bergère (Paris), 184
Fondation Angladon-Dubrujeaud (Avignon), 470
Fondation Bemberg (Toulouse), 637
Fondation Louis Jou (Les Baux), 488–489
Fontainebleau, 207–210
Fontaine d'Amboise (Clermont-Ferrand), 719
Fontaine des Chartreux (Cahors), 705
Fontevraud-l'Abbaye, 264–265
Fontvieille (Monaco), 587, 590
Food stores and markets. *See also* Chocolate and chocolatiers
  Aix-en-Provence, 493
  Avignon, 474
  Bayonne, 654
  Biarritz, 659

Blois, 236
Cannes, 528–529
Deauville, 286
Dijon, 401
Marseille, 501, 502
Monaco, 590
Montauban, 707
Nice, 569
Nîmes, 606
Paris, 178–179
Pau, 650
Périgueux, 694
St-Jean-de-Luz, 662
St-Malo, 307
St-Rémy-de-Provence, 478
St-Tropez, 516–517
Toulon, 508
Tours, 251
Vallauris, 545
Fort de Douaumont (Verdun), 384
Fort de la Bastille (Grenoble), 443
Fort St-André (Villenueve-lez-Avignon), 473
Fort Ste-Agathe (Ile de Porquerolles), 511
Fort Vaux (Verdun), 384
Forum des Halles (Paris), 156, 179
Foundation Maeght (St-Paul-de-Vence), 8, 556–557
Fouquet's (Paris), 143
Fourvière Hill (Lyon), 410
Fragonard, Jean-Honoré, 17, 160, 276, 317, 349, 579
Villa Musée Fragonard (Mougins), 540
The French Alps, 432–463
French Open Tennis Championship (Paris), 36
The French Riviera (Côte d'Azur), 3, 31, 513–600
modern-art museums, 5
Futuroscope (Poitiers), 665, 666

Galerie Adrien Maeght (Paris), 174–175
Galerie International du Verre (Biot), 542
Galerie Jean-Claude Novaro (Biot), 542
Galeries Lafayette
Cannes, 528
Paris, 177
Galibier Pass, 434
Gallery of François I (Fontainebleau), 207–208
Gardens of Versailles, 197
Gauguin, Paul, 19, 321, 322, 444
Gay and lesbian travelers
Amiens, 351
Annecy, 439
Avignon, 477
Biarritz, 661
Bordeaux, 687
Cannes, 536
Clermont-Ferrand, 721
Grenoble, 447
information and resources, 50–51
La Baule, 328
Lyon, 419
Marseille, 507
Merville-France-Ville, 285
Montpellier, 615
Nantes, 333
Nice, 577
Nîmes, 608
Paris, 36, 187, 191
Reims, 345
Rouen, 281–282
St-Tropez, 514, 516, 521, 522
Toulon, 510
Toulouse, 643
Tours, 254
Gay Pride Parade (Paris), 36
Geneva, Lake (Lac Léman), 433
Géricault, Théodore, 18, 276
Giverny, 217–219
Global Tickets, 37
Golf
Biarritz, 657
Cannes, 526
Deauville, 286
Dinard, 311
Monaco, 588
Nice, 568
St-Tropez, 516
Talloires, 439
Golfe-Juan, 543–545
Gorges du Fier, 436
Gothic architecture, 22–23
Gothic art, 16
Goya, Francisco, 359, 489, 654
Musée Goya (Castres), 629
Grand-Ballon, 377
Grand Canyon of France, 429
Grande Plage (Biarritz), 657
Grandes Ecuries/Musée Vivant du Cheval (Chantilly), 221
Grands Appartements (Versailles), 196
Grand Théâtre (Bordeaux), 680, 686
Grand Tinel (Avignon), 471
Grand Trianon (Versailles), 197
Grasse, 539–541
Graveyard (Nice), 565
Grenoble, 443–447
Grotte de Font-de-Gaume (near Les Eyzies), 700
Grotte des Combarelles (near Bergerac), 700
Grotte du Grand-Roc (Les Eyzies), 700
Grottes de Jer (Lourdes), 647
Grottes de Médous (Lourdes), 647
Grotto of Massabielle (Lourdes), 646
Gruisson, 615

Hall of Mirrors (Versailles), 196
Harry's New York Bar (Paris), 190
HB-Henriot Faïenceries de Quimper, 318
Health concerns, 48–49
Health insurance, 48
Hédiard (Paris), 179
Hemingway, Ernest, 87, 168, 171, 175, 188–189
Hennessy (Cognac), 675
Hermès (Paris), 178
Hier, Aujourd'hui, et Demain, (Paris), 159
Hiking and walking
Annecy, 437
Beaulieu-sur-Mer, 582
Cap-Martin, 599
Fontainebleau, 208
Ile de Port-Cros, 512
Megève, 452
Narbonne, 617
Perpignan, 621
Hippodrome de Deauville Clairefontaine, 286
Hippodrome de Deauville La Touques, 286
Hohneck, 377
Holidays, 35
Honfleur, 282–284
Horreum Romain (Narbonne), 617
Horseback riding, Lourdes, 647
Horse-drawn carriages, 213, 236, 250
Horse racing, 169, 220, 286
Hospitals, 71–72
Hôtel de Beauvais (Paris), 159
Hôtel de Bethune-Sully (Paris), 159
Hôtel de Bourgtheroulde (Rouen), 275

Hôtel de la Tour du Brau (Les Baux), 487
Hôtel de Manville (Les Baux), 488
Hôtel de Rohan (Paris), 158–159
Hôtel des Ambassadeurs de Hollande (Paris), 159
Hôtel de Sens (Paris), 159
Hôtel des Invalides (Napoleon's Tomb; Paris), 150
Hôtel de Ville (city hall or town hall)
  Arles, 482
  La Rochelle, 670
  Libourne, 688
  Narbonne, 616
  Ribeauvillé, 368
  Toulon, 508
  Toulouse, 636
Hôtel du Chamarier (Lyon), 408, 410
Hôtel Groslot (Orléans), 229
Hôtel Jean-de-Brion (Les Baux), 488–489
Hôtel Lallemant (Bourges), 710
House rentals, 64
House-swapping, 66
Hugo, Victor, 155, 172, 272, 277
  Musée Victor-Hugo (Villequier), 277

Ile de Bréhat, 313
Ile de France, 27
Ile de Porquerolles, 510–511
Ile de Port-Cros, 511, 512
Ile du Grand-Bé, 306
Ile Ste-Marguerite, 530
Ile St-Honorat, 530
Iles de Lérins, 530
Iles d'Hyères, 510–512
Illiers-Combray, 202
Impressionism, 18–19
Ingres, Jean-Auguste-Dominique, 18, 220, 276, 393, 638, 654, 706
  Musée Ingres (Montauban), 8, 707
Institute for Research and Coordination of Acoustics/Music (Paris), 147
Insurance, 47–48
International Film Festival (Cannes), 35–36, 525
International Marathon of Paris, 35
International Ready-to-Wear Fashion Shows (Paris), 35
Internet access, 55–56, 72
Isle-sur-la-Sorgue, 467
Issenheim Altarpiece (Colmar), 374
Itineraries, suggested, 76–86

Jacobins, Eglise des (Toulouse), 636
Jardin Anglais (Dinan), 315
Jardin d'Acclimatation (Paris), 169
Jardin des Arènes (Périgueux), 693
Jardin des Plantes
  Montpellier, 612
  Nantes, 331
Jardin des Tuileries (Paris), 156
Jardin d'Eze, 585
Jardin du Carrousel (Paris), 156
Jardin du Luxembourg (Paris), 171
Jardin du Rosaire (Lyon), 410
Jardin Exotique (Monaco), 591
Jardins de la Fontaine (Nîmes), 604
Jardins de l'Archevêché (Bourges), 710
Jazz Pulsations (Nancy), 378
Jeanne-d'Arc. *See* Joan of Arc
Jean-Paul Gaultier (Paris), 177
Jeu de Paume (Paris), 2, 156–157
Jewish travelers, 52
Joan of Arc (Jeanne-d'Arc), 227, 260, 272, 386
  Château de Chinon, 261
  Maison Jeanne-d'Arc (Orléans), 230
  Maison Natale de Jeanne d'Arc (Domrémy-la-Pucelle), 383
  Musée Jeanne-d'Arc (Rouen), 277
  Place du Vieux-Marché (Rouen), 277
  statue of
    Compiègne, 224
    Orléans, 229
Jouarre, 334
Jour des Menetriers (Ribeauvillé), 369
Juan-les-Pins, 546–549
Juliénas, 421
July Column (Paris), 158

Kayaking, the Ardèche, 430
Kaysersberg, 370–371
Keith Prowse (Paris), 182
Kientzheim, 370
Kiosque Théâtre (Paris), 182

La Baule, 5, 326–328
La Belle Hortense (Paris), 143
La Canebière (Marseille), 498
La Casa Païral (Perpignan), 622
Lac d'Annecy, 435
La Champmeslé (Paris), 191
La Chapelle Impériale (Biarritz), 658
La Citadelle (Les Baux), 487
La Cité de l'espace (Toulouse), 637–638
Lac Léman (Lake Geneva), 433
La Cognathèque (Cognac), 675
La Condamine (Monaco), 586
La Coupole (Paris), 143
La Daille, 461
La Ferté-sous-Jouarre, 334–336
La Grande Expo du Pont du Gard (Nîmes), 605
La Grande Plage (Dinard), 311
La Grande Plage St-Jean-de-Luz, 662
La Grotte de Glace, 458
La Java (Paris), 186
Lalique (Paris), 176
La Loco (Paris), 186–187
La Maison du Chocolat (Paris), 176
La Maison du Vin (Saumur), 266
Lamastre, 431
La Merveille (Mont-St-Michel), 302
La Napoule-Plage, 522–524
L'Ancien Couvent des Bernardines (Dijon), 400
Langeais, 257–258
Language, 72
Language schools, 59
Languedoc, 3
Languedoc-Roussillon, 601–643
Laon, 345–347
La Petite France (Strasbourg), 356
La Rochelle, 669–674
La Route du Vin (Wine Road), 365–372
La Salle aux 100 Couverts (Pau), 650
Lascaux (Montignac), 696–698
Lascaux II (near Montignac), 697
La Sorbonne (University of Paris), 164
La Source (Lourdes), 646
L'Atelier Brancusi (Paris), 147
La Tuile à Loup (Paris), 176
La Turbie, 584, 585, 588
La Ville Morte (Les Baux), 487

La Villette Jazz Festival (Paris), 38
Le Bar de L'Hôtel (Paris), 190
Le Bilboquet (Paris), 185–186
Le Brévent, 457
Le Capitole (Toulouse), 636
Le Castillet (Perpignan), 622
Le Château (Nice), 565
Le Domaine de George Sand (Nohant), 713–714
Le Fornet, 461
Le Grand Pavois Salon Nautique (La Rochelle), 670
Le Grand Wazoo (Amiens), 350
Le Havre, 277
Le Legende de Buffalo Bill (Disneyland Paris), 216
Le Lieu Unique (Nantes), 332
Le Louvre des Antiquaires (Paris), 174
Le Maison du Miel (Paris), 179
Le Marais (Paris). *See* Paris, 3rd Arrondissement
Le Mémorial de Caen, 292–293
Le Montenvers, 457–458
Le Moulin Lacadé (Lourdes), 646
Le Musée d'Alésia, 402
Le Musée du quai Branly (Paris), 166–167
Le New Riverside (Paris), 187
Le Palais de l'Ile (Annecy), 437
Le Puy-en-Velay, 726–728
Le Rallye de Monte Carlo, 35
Le Relais (Nice), 576
Le Retable d'Issenheim (Colmar), 374–375
Lérins Islands, 530
Les Alignements (Carnac), 323
Le Salon Nautique de Paris, 39
Les Alyscamps (Arles), 483
Les Arènes (Amphitheater; Arles), 482
Les Arènes de Nîmes, 604
Les Bacchantes (Paris), 188
Les Bains Douches (Paris), 187
Les Baux, 6, 487–490
L'Escale Borély (Marseille), 502, 507
Les Catacombs (Paris), 171–172
Les Caves Taillevent (Paris), 181
Les Chorégies d'Orange, 36
Les Collettes (Cagnes-sur-Mer), 553
Les Egouts (The Sewers of Paris), 172–173
Les Estivales (Perpignan), 621
Les Etoiles (Paris), 187
Les Eyzies-de-Tayac, 698–701
Les Fêtes Musicales (Biarritz), 656
Les Fouilles d'Alésia, 402
Les Francofolies (La Rochelle), 670
Les Grandes Ecuries (Versailles), 197
Les Grandes Ecuries/Musée Vivant du Cheval (Chantilly), 221
Les Grands Appartements du Palais (Monaco), 591
Les Halles (Paris), 156
Les Halles et Grand Marché (Tours), 251
Les Hortillonnages (Amiens), 348
Les Mardis de la Collégiale (Colmar), 373
Les Nocturnes du Mont-St-Michel (Paris), 37
Les Nuits de Fourvière (Lyon), 408
Le Soleil (Paris), 180
L'Espace Jean Marais (Vallauris), 544
L'Espace Matisse (Vence), 559
Les Planches
  Deauville, 285
  Trouville, 290
Les Puys (Monts Dômes), 718
Les Trois Glorieuses, 38
Les 24 Heures du Mans Moto, 35
Les 24 Heures du Mans Voitures (Le Mans), 36
Le Tango (Paris), 189
Le Temple de Diane (Nîmes), 604
Le Temps d'Aimer (Biarritz), 656
Le Thot (near Montignac), 697
Le Touquet-Paris-Plage, 346
Le Visa pour l'Image (Perpignan), 621
Libourne, 687–688
Lido de Paris, 184
L'Imaginaire Jules-Verne (Amiens), 349
Limoges, 723–726
Limoges-Unic & Madronet (Paris), 176
L'Institut & Musée Lumière (Lyon), 411
Liquor laws, 72
Loches, 255–256
Logis Tiphaine (Mont-St-Michel), 302
Loire Valley, 2, 4, 27, 227–271
Longchamp (Paris), 169
Lost and found, 72–73
Lost-luggage insurance, 48
Louis Vuitton (Paris), 178
Louis XV, 164, 196, 197, 225, 265, 338, 379, 649
Louis XV Staircase (Fontainebleau), 208
Louis XVI, 156, 159, 161, 170, 196, 225, 335
Lourdes, 644–649
Louvre Museum. *See* Musée du Louvre (Paris)
Lyon, 406–419
  accommodations, 413–415
  attractions, 408–413
  nightlife, 418–419
  restaurants, 415–418
  shopping, 413
  special events, 408
  traveling to, 406
  visitor information, 408

Magasin d'Usine Les Olivades (near Arles), 484
Magasin Gorse (Limoges), 723
Mail, 73
Maison Carrée (Nîmes), 602
Maison de la Boétie (Sarlat-la-Canéda), 699
Maison de l'Infante (St-Jean-de-Luz), 662
Maison de Pommery (Reims), 340–341
Maison de Savaron (Clermont-Ferrand), 719
Maison du Tapissier (Aubusson), 722
Maison du Vin (Bordeaux), 9, 680
Maison du Vin de l'Anjou (Angers), 269
Maison et Atelier de Jean-François Millet (Barbizon), 206
Maison Jeanne-d'Arc (Orléans), 230
Maison Kiener (Riquewihr), 369
Maison Liebrich (Riquewihr), 369
Maison Natale de Bernadette (Lourdes), 646
Maison Natale de Jeanne d'Arc (Domrémy-la-Pucelle), 383
Maison Pfister (Colmar), 373
Maison Preiss-Zimmer (Riquewihr), 369
Maisons Satie (Honfleur), 283
Maison Thomassin (Lyon), 408
Maki (Paris), 181
Manet, Edouard, 18, 151, 379, 470
Man Ray (Paris), 190

Mansart, François, 24, 159, 196, 197, 237, 292, 482, 629
Maps, 63
Marché aux Fleurs
Nice, 565
Paris, 179–180
Marché aux Puces de Clignancourt (Paris), 180
Marché aux Puces de la Porte de Vanves (Paris), 180
Marché Buci (Paris), 180
Marché de Noël (Mougins), 39
Marché Forville (Cannes), 528
Marché Notre-Dame (Versailles), 197–198
Marché sur l'Eau (Marché St-Leu; Amiens), 348
Marie Antoinette, 158, 161, 169, 170, 196, 197, 225, 335, 412
Markstein, 377
Marlenheim, 365
Marseille, 497–507
accommodations, 502–505
getting around, 498
nightlife, 507
restaurants, 505–507
shopping, 501–502
sightseeing, 498–501
traveling to, 497–498
visitor information, 498
Martell (Cognac), 675
Martin Pouret (Orléans), 230
The Massif Central, 32, 709–727
Matisse, Henri, 19, 157, 444, 518, 562, 567, 631, 637, 722
Chapelle du Rosaire (Vence), 559
Musée Matisse (Cimiez), 567
Medical insurance, 48
Médoc, 688–689
Megève, 451–455
Megève Palais des Sports et des Congrès, 452
Memorial des Martyrs Français de la Déportation (Paris), 155
Mémorial de Verdun, 384
Memorial du Débarquement en Provence (Toulon), 509
Mercier (Epernay), 352
Merlin the Magician (Loches), 255
Merville-France-Ville, 285
Métro (subway; Paris), 95
Midi Plage (Cannes), 525
Miraculous Spring (Lourdes), 646
Mistral, Frédéric, 604–605
Musée de Frédéric Mistral (Maillane), 485
Museon Arlaten (Arles), 483
Mittelbergheim, 366–367
Moët et Chandon Champagne Cellars, 352
Mojito Habana (Paris), 190–191
Molsheim, 366
Monaco, 586–597
accommodations, 592–594
beaches and outdoor activities, 588–589
border crossings to, 33
nightlife, 596–597
restaurants, 594–596
shopping, 589–590
sightseeing, 591–592
special events, 587
traveling to, 587
visitor information, 587
Monaco Grand Prix de Formule, 36
Monaco-Ville, 586
Monastère de Cimiez (Cimiez Convent), 567
Monastère Royal de Brou (Bourg-en-Bresse), 424
Monastère St-Paul-de-Mausolée (St-Rémy-de-Provence), 478
Monet, Claude, 18, 151, 157, 217
Claude Monet Foundation (Giverny), 218, 272, 274, 276, 359, 444, 566, 637
Money matters, 44–47
Monoprix (Paris), 177
Montauban, 706–708
Montbard, 403
Mont Blanc, 456
Mont Blanc Tunnel, 456
Mont Cavalier (Nîmes), 604
Mont d'Arbois, 451, 452
Monte Carlo (Monaco), 586–587
Monte-Carlo Beach (Monaco), 587
Monte-Carlo Beach Club (Monaco), 588
Monte Carlo Motor Rally (Monaco), 35
Montpellier, 611–615
Mont-St-Michel, 5, 301–304
Monts Dômes (Les Puys), 718
Morabito (Paris), 179
Mougins, 537–539
Moulin Rouge (Paris), 184–185
Multicultural travelers, 52
Mumm (Reims), 341
Münster, 377
Muré (Colmar), 373
Musée Alsacien (Strasbourg), 358
Musée Archéologique
Dijon, 400
Narbonne, 616
Nîmes, 604
Musée Archéologique Municipal (Laon), 347
Musée Asiatica (Biarritz), 658
Musée Auberge Ganne (Barbizon), 206
Musée Bartholdi (Colmar), 374
Musée Basque, 654
Musée Bonnat, 654
Musée Bourdelle (Paris), 168
Musée Briard (Jouarre), 334
Musée Buffon (Montbard), 403
Musée Calvet (Avignon), 470
Musée Cantini (Marseille), 501
Musée Carnavalet-Histoire de Paris, 159
Musée Charles-Portal (Cordes-sur-Ciel), 633–634
Musée Château d'Annecy, 437
Musée Chinois (Fontainebleau), 208
Musée Condé (Chantilly), 220
Musée Crozatier (Le Puy), 728
Musée Daniel Vannier (Beaugency), 233–234
Musée d'Anthropologie Préhistorique (Monaco), 591
Musée d'Archéologie Bargoin (Clermont-Ferrand), 719–720
Musée d'Art (Narbonne), 616–617
Musée d'Art Americain Giverny, 218
Musée d'Art Contemporain (Nîmes), 602
Musée d'Art et d'Archeologie (Senlis), 223
Musée d'Art et d'Histoire de Provence (Grasse), 540
Musée d'Art et d'Histoire le Portail-Peint (Cordes-sur-Ciel), 633–634
Musée d'Art Moderne (Strasbourg), 358
Musée d'Art Religieux (Le Puy), 727
Musée d'Art Roger Quilliot (Clermont-Ferrand), 720
Musée Dauphinois (Grenoble), 444
Musée de Cire (Chenonceaux), 247
Musée de Cognac, 675
Musée de Faïence Jules Verlingue (Quimper), 318
Musée de Frédéric Mistral (Maillane), 485

Musée de Grenoble, 444–445
Musée de la Castre (Cannes), 529–530
Musée de la Céramique
  Rouen, 275–276
  Vallauris, 544–545
Musée de la Civilisation Gallo-Romaine (Lyon), 411
Musée de la Communication (Riquewihr), 369–370
Musée de la Devinière (Chinon), 261–262
Musée de la Figurine Historique (Compiègne), 225
Musée de la Marine (Toulon), 508
Musée de la Marionette (Lyon), 410
Musée de la Mer
  Biarritz, 658
  Ile Ste-Marguerite, 530
  Mont-St-Michel, 302
Musée de la Musique (Paris), 163
Musée de l'Annonciade (Musée St-Tropez), 518
Musée de la Pêche (Concarneau), 320
Musée de Lapérouse (Albi), 631
Musée de l'Arles et de la Provence Antiques, 483
Musée de la Tapisserie de Bayeux, 8, 296
Musée de la Tour des Voleurs (Riquewihr), 369
Musée de l'Automobile (Valençay), 240
Musée de l'Automobiliste (Mougins), 538
Musée de la Vénerie (Senlis), 223
Musée de la Vie Bourguignonne (Dijon), 400
Musée de l'Ecole de Nancy, 379
Musée de l'Histoire de St-Malo, 306
Musée de l'Hôtel-Dieu (Beaune), 395
Musée de l'Hôtel du Doyen (Bayeux), 297
Musée de l'Imperatrice Eugénie (Compiègne), 225
Musée de l'Imprimerie de Lyon, 411
Musée de l'Oeuvre Notre-Dame (Strasbourg), 358
Musée de l'Olivier & Musée d'Art Moderne Méditerranéen (Château-Musée Grimaldi; Cagnes-sur-Mer), 553
Musée de l'Orangerie (Paris), 2, 157
Musée de Normandie (Caen), 293
Musée Departemental Breton (Quimper), 317–318
Musée Départemental de la Tapisserie (Aubusson), 722
Musée de Picardie (Amiens), 349
Musée de Préhistoire (Carnac), 323
Musée de Préhistoire et d'Histoire Naturelle (Nîmes), 604
Musée des Arts Asiatiques (Nice), 566
Musée des Arts Décoratifs
  Paris, 1, 157
  Saumur, 266–267
Musée des Arts-Décoratifs (Lyon), 411–412
Musée des Arts et Traditions Populaires Catalans (Perpignan), 622
Musée des Augustins (Toulouse), 638
Musée des Beaux-Arts
  Bordeaux, 682
  Caen, 293
  Dijon, 400
  La Rochelle, 670–671
  Lyon, 412
  Nancy, 379–380
  Nice, 566
  Nîmes, 604
  Orléans, 230
  Pau, 650
  Quimper, 317
  Reims, 340
  Rouen, 276
  Tours, 250
Musée des Beaux-Arts de Chartres, 202–203
Musée des Beaux-Arts de Nantes, 330
Musée des Beaux-Arts et Musée Marey (Beaune), 396
Musée des Equipages (Vaux-le-Vicomte), 210
Musée des Santons (Les Baux), 488
Musée des Tapisseries (Aix-en-Provence), 493
Musée des Tissus (Lyon), 412
Musée de Toulon, 509
Musée de Vieux Montmartre (Paris), 162
Musée de Villeneuve-lez-Avignon (Musée Pierre de Luxembourg), 473
Musée d'Histoire de Marseille, 501
Musée d'Histoire de St-Paul, 556
Musée d'Histoire Locale et de Céramique Biotoise (Biot), 542
Musée Dolder (Riquewihr), 369
Musée d'Orsay (Paris), 8, 150–151
Musée du Berry (Bourges), 710
Musée du Cheval (Saumur), 267
Musée du Chocolat (Biarritz), 659
Musée du Débarquement (Arromanches), 299–300
Musée du Docteur Schweitzer (Kaysersberg), 370
Musée du Louvre (Paris), 8, 151–153. *See also* Paris, 1st Arrondissement
Musée du Nouveau-Monde (La Rochelle), 671
Musée d'Unterlinden (Colmar), 374
Musée du Palais du Prince (Souvenirs Napoléoniens et Collection d'Archives; Monaco), 591
Musée du Périgord (Périgueux), 695
Musée du Petit-Palais (Avignon), 470
Musée du Quai Branly (Paris), 1–2
Musée du Tapis d'Art (Clermont-Ferrand), 719–720
Musée du Trophée d'Auguste (La Turbie), 585
Musée du Vieux Honfleur, 283
Musée du Vieux-Nîmes, 604
Musée du Vieux-Pérouges, 423
Musée du Vin de Bourgogne (Beaune), 396
Musée Eugène-Boudin (Honfleur), 283
Musée Fabre (Montpellier), 8, 612
Musée Faure (Aix-les-Bains), 442
Musée Flaubert et d'Histoire de la Médécine (Rouen), 276
Musée Français de l'Automobile "Henri Malartre" (Lyon), 412–413
Musée François-Pompon (Saulieu), 405
Musée Gadagne (Musée Historique de Lyon), 410

Musée Gallo-Romain Vesunna (Périgueux), 695
Musée Goya (Castres), 629
Musée Grevin (Musée Historique de Mont-St-Michel), 302
Musée Grévin (Lourdes), 646
Musée Grobet-Labadié (Marseille), 501
Musée Henry-Clews (La Napoule-Plage), 522
Musée Historique de Lyon (Musée Gadagne), 410
Musée Historique Lorrain (Nancy), 8, 380
Musée Ile-de-France (Villa Ephrussi de Rothschild; St-Jean-Cap-Ferrat), 579
Musée Ingres (Montauban), 8, 707
Musée International d'Art Naïf Anatole-Jakovsky (Nice), 566
Musée Jacquemart-André (Paris), 160–161
Musée Jean-de-la-Fontaine (Château-Thierry), 336
Musée Jean Lurçat (Angers), 270
Musée Jeanne-d'Arc (Rouen), 277
Musée Jean-Peské (Collioure), 619
Musée Joseph-Déchelette (Roanne), 421
Musée Jules Verne de Nantes, 330
Musée Lambinet (Versailles), 197
Musée Lapidaire
- Avignon, 470–471
- Vienne, 426

Musée Le Secq des Tournelles (Rouen), 277
Musée Magnelli (Vallauris), 544–545
Musée Magnin (Dijon), 400
Musée Marcel Proust/Maison de Tante Léonie (Illiers-Combray), 203
Musée Matisse (Cimiez), 567
Musée Memorial de la Bataille de Normandie (Bayeux), 297
Musée Municipal (Valence), 428
Musée Municipal de l'Evêché-de-Limoges, 724
Musée Municipal de Pont-Aven, 322
Musée Municipal d'Orange, 466
Musée Napoléon III (Compiègne), 225
Musée National Auguste Rodin (Paris), 167
Musée National d'Art Moderne (Paris), 147
Musée National de la Porcelaine Adrien-Dubouché (Limoges), 724–725
Musée National de la Préhistoire (Les Eyzies), 700
Musée National de la Voiture (Compiègne), 225
Musée National de Monaco, 591
Musée National du Château de Compiègne, 224–225
Musée National du Château de Fontainebleau, 207
Musée National du Moyen Age (Thermes de Cluny; Paris), 164
Musée National Fernand-Léger (Biot), 542–543
Musée National Message Biblique Marc Chagall (Cimiez), 567–568
Musée National Picasso La Guerre et La Paix (Vallauris), 545
Musée Naval et Napoléonien (Antibes), 549–550
Musée Océanographique de Monaco, 591–592
Musée Orbigny-Bernon (La Rochelle), 671
Musée Picasso
- Antibes, 550
- Paris, 153

Musée Pierre de Luxembourg (Musée de Villeneuve-lez-Avignon), 473
Musée Pyrénéen (Lourdes), 646–647
Musée Réattu (Arles), 483
Musée Renoir & Les Collettes (Cagnes-sur-Mer), 553
Musée Rolin (Autun), 393
Musée Rupert de Chièvres (Poitiers), 667
Musée Ste-Bernadette (Lourdes), 646
Musée Ste-Croix (Poitiers), 666–667
Musée St-Tropez (Musée de l'Annonciade), 518
Musée Thomas-Dobrée (Nantes), 330
Musée Toulouse-Lautrec (Albi), 8, 631
Musée Victor-Hugo (Villequier), 277
Musée Vivant du Cheval (Chantilly), 221
Museon Arlaten (Arles), 483
Museum of Historical Figurines (Compiègne), 225
Museum of Naive Art (Nice), 566
Museums, best, 7–8
Music tours, 59

N

Nancy, 378–383
Nantes, 328–333
Napoléon, Louis (Napoléon III), 157, 161
- Musée Napoléon III (Compiègne), 225

Napoléon Bonaparte, 146, 161, 386
- Hôtel des Invalides (Napoleon's Tomb; Paris), 150
- Musée Naval et Napoléonien (Antibes), 549–550

Narbonne, 615–618
National Automobile Museum (Compiègne), 225
National Museum of Modern Art (Paris), 147
NaturoSpace (Honfleur), 283
Nautical Center (Evian), 432
Neoclassical art, 17
New Morning (Paris), 186
Newspapers and magazines, 73
New Year's Eve, 39
Nice, 562–577
- accommodations, 569–573
- exploring, 564–568
- nightlife, 575–577
- outdoor activities, 568
- restaurants, 573–575
- shopping, 568–569
- special events, 564
- traveling to, 562
- visitor information, 564

Nice Festival du Jazz, 564
Nice Jazz Festival, 37
Nice-Le Grand Tour, 564–565
Nieuil, 726
Nikki Beach (St-Tropez), 514
Nîmes, 601–608
Nohant/La Châtre, 713–714
Normandy, 2, 30
Normandy American Cemetery (Omaha Beach), 300
Notre-Dame, Cathédrale
- Le Puy, 727
- Montauban, 707
- Paris, 8, 153–155

Notre-Dame, Eglise
- Beaugency, 234
- Bourg-en-Bresse, 424
- Villenueve-lez-Avignon, 471

Notre-Dame d'Amiens, 9, 349

Notre-Dame de Bayeux, 297
Notre-Dame de Chartres, 8–9, 200–202
Notre-Dame de Fourvière, Basilique (Lyon), 410
Notre-Dame-de-la-Garde, Basilique (Marseille), 500
Notre-Dame de Laon, 346–347
Notre-Dame de l'Assomption, Cathédrale (Clermont-Ferrand), 719
Notre-Dame de Reims, 9, 339–340
Notre-Dame de Rouen, 9, 274
Notre-Dame des Doms, Cathédrale (Avignon), 470
Notre-Dame de Senlis, 223
Notre-Dame des Sablons, Eglise (Aigues-Mortes), 608–609
Notre-Dame de Strasbourg, 356
Notre-Dame-du-Port, Eglise (Clermont-Ferrand), 719
Notre-Dame La Daurade, Basilique (Toulouse), 636
Notre-Dame-la-Grande, Eglise (Poitiers), 666
Nouveau Casino (Paris), 185

Obernai, 366
Olivier millénaire (Roquebrune), 598
Olympia (Paris), 183
Omaha Beach, 300
Opéra (Versailles), 196
Opéra Bastille (Paris), 182
Opéra de Nice, 575–576
Opéra Garnier (Paris), 182
Orange, 464–468
Orchestra Kazibao (Paris), 176
Orléans, 227–232
Orléans Architectural and Historical Trail, 230
Orly Airport (Paris), 87, 90
accommodations near, 117
Ossuaire de Douaumont (Verdun), 384

Package tours, 56
Paimpol, 313
Palais de Fontainebleau, 7
Palais de l'Archevêché (Rouen), 274
Palais de Rohan (Strasbourg), 359
Palais des Archevêques (Narbonne), 616
Palais des Ducs et des Etats de Bourgogne (Dijon), 400
Palais des Papes (Avignon), 471
Palais des Rois de Majorque (Perpignan), 622
Palais du Facteur Cheval (Vienne), 426
Palais du Gouvernement (Nancy), 379
Palais du Luxembourg (Paris), 171
Palais du Tau (Reims), 340
Palais Jacques-Coeur (Bourges), 710–711
Palais Lascaris (Nice), 566–567
Palais Royal (Paris), 157–158
Panthéon (Paris), 164–165
Parc de la Tête d'Or (Lyon), 412
Parc de La Villette (Paris), 163
Parc des Expositions (near Reims), 342
Parc des Mini-Châteaux (near Amboise), 244
Parc des Sources (Vichy), 715
Parc du Pharo (Marseille), 498
Parc Monceau (Paris), 171
Parc Naturel Régional des Volcans d'Auvergne, 718, 719
Parc Zoologique (St-Jean-Cap-Ferrat), 579
Parfumerie Fragonard (Grasse), 540
Parfumerie Molinard (Grasse), 540
Parfums Caron (Paris), 181
Paris
- 1st Arrondissement (Musée du Louvre/Les Halles), 92
  - accommodations, 99–103
  - restaurants, 119–124
  - sights and attractions, 156–158
- 2nd Arrondissement (La Bourse), 92
  - restaurants, 124
- 3rd Arrondissement (Le Marais), 92
  - accommodations, 103–104
  - restaurants, 125
  - sights and attractions, 158–159
- 4th Arrondissement (Ile de la Cité/Ile St-Louis & Beaubourg), 92
  - accommodations, 104–106
  - restaurants, 125–126
  - sights and attractions, 160
- 5th Arrondissement (Latin Quarter), 92–93
  - accommodations, 110–111
  - restaurants, 134–135
  - sights and attractions, 163–165
- 6th Arrondissement (St-Germain/Luxembourg), 93
  - accommodations, 111, 114–115
  - restaurants, 137–140
  - sights and attractions, 165–166
- 7th Arrondissement (Eiffel Tower/Musée d'Orsay), 93
  - accommodations, 115–117
  - restaurants, 140–142
  - sights and attractions, 166–167
- 8th Arrondissement (Champs-Elysées/Madeleine), 93
  - accommodations, 106–108
  - restaurants, 126–130
  - sights and attractions, 160–161
- 9th Arrondissement (Opera Garnier/Pigalle), 93
  - accommodations, 104
  - restaurants, 130–131
- 10th Arrondissement (Gare du Nord/Gare de l'Est), 93
  - restaurant, 131
- 11th Arrondissement (Opéra Bastille), 94
  - restaurant, 131
- 12th Arrondissement (Bois de Vincennes/Gare de Lyon), 94
  - restaurants, 132
- 13th Arrondissement (Gare d'Austerlitz), 94
- 14th Arrondissement (Montparnasse), 94
  - restaurants, 142
  - sights and attractions, 167–168
- 15th Arrondissement (Gare Montparnasse), 94
- 16th Arrondissement (Trocadéro/Bois de Boulogne), 94
  - accommodations, 109
  - restaurants, 132–133
- 17th Arrondissement (Parc Monceau/Place Clichy), 94–95
  - restaurants, 133–134

Paris *(cont.)*
- 18th Arrondissement (Montmartre), 95, 109–110
  - restaurant, 134
  - sights and attractions, 162
- 19th Arrondissement (La Villette), 95
  - sights and attractions, 163
- accommodations, 1, 99–118
- American Express, 97
- arriving in, 87, 90–91
- average temperature and rainfall, 35
- boat trips and tours, 97
- cafes, 142–143
- currency exchange, 97–98
- discount transit passes, 96
- doctors and dentists, 98
- drugstores, 98
- emergencies, 98
- exploring, 144–173
- finding an address in, 91–92
- getting around, 95–97
- layout of, 91–92
- maps, 92
- nightlife, 181–191
- organized tours, 144–145
- police, 98
- post offices, 98
- restaurants, 118–142
- safety, 98
- shopping, 4, 173–181
- sights and attractions, 1–2
- taxis, 97
- visitor information, 91

Paris Airport Shuttle, 90
Paris Air Show, 36
Paris Art Market, 175
Paris Auto Show, 38
Paris Museum Pass, 145
Paris Quartier d'Eté, 37
Paris-Visite, 96
Passage de Retz (Paris), 159
Passe-Musée (Nancy), 378
Passports, 33–34, 73–74
Pau, 649–653
Pavillon de la Porcelaine (Limoges), 725
Pei, I. M., glass pyramid (Paris), 26, 151
Père-Lachaise cemetery (Paris), 169–170
Périgord, 32, 692
Périgueux, 692–696
Pérouges, 423–424
Perpignan, 620–624
Perpignan Jazz Festival, 38
Petite Afrique (Beaulieu-sur-Mer), 582
Petite Venise (Colmar), 373
Petits Appartements (Versailles), 196
Petit Train (Rouen), 278
Petit Train de la Bonne Mère (Marseille), 500
Petit Train de Montmartre (Paris), 162
Petit Train touristique de Cannes, 529
Petit Trianon (Versailles), 197
Picasso, Pablo, 20, 162, 412, 470, 492
- *l' Homme au Mouton* (Vallauris), 544
- Musée National Picasso La Guerre et La Paix (Vallauris), 545
- Musée Picasso (Antibes), 550
- Musée Picasso (Paris), 153

Pic de Jer, 647
Piper-Heidsieck (Reims), 341
Piscine de Trouville, 290
Piscine Olympique
- Deauville, 286
- Dinard, 311

Place Bellecour (Lyon), 408
Place de la Bastille (Paris), 158
Place de la Bourse (Bordeaux), 680
Place de la Cathédrale (Strasbourg), 364
Place de la Comédie
- Bordeaux, 680
- Montpellier, 611

Place de la Concorde (Paris), 161
Place de l'Alma (Paris), 172
Place de l'Hôtel-de-Ville (Angoulême), 677
Place des Arcades (Biot), 542
Place des Vosges (Paris), 158
Place du Forum (Arles), 482
Place du Vieux-Marché (Rouen), 277
Place Plumereau (Tours), 254
Place St-Michel (Paris), 164
Place Stanislas (Nancy), 378
Place Vendôme (Paris), 161
Plage de Bon Secours (St-Malo), 306–307
Plage de Deauville, 285
Plage de Juan-les-Pins, 546
Plage de la Bouillabaisse, 514
Plage de la Calanque (Beaulieu-sur-Mer), 582
Plage de la Croisette (Cannes), 525
Plage de la Garoupe (Juan-les-Pins), 546
Plage de Larvotto (Monaco), 588
Plage de la Salis (Juan-les-Pins), 546
Plage de l'Ecluse (Dinard), 311
Plage de Paloma (St-Jean-Cap-Ferrat), 579
Plage de Pampelonne (St-Tropez), 514
Plage de St-Enogat (Dinard), 311
Plage des Graniers (St-Tropez), 514
Plage des Jumeaux (St-Tropez), 514
Plage des Salins (St-Tropez), 514
Plage de Tahiti (St-Tropez), 516
Plage de Trouville, 290
Plage du Midi
- Cannes, 525
- Golfe-Juan, 544

Plage du Mourillon (Toulon), 508
Plage du Port-Vieux (Biarritz), 657
Plage du Prieuré (Dinard), 311
Plage du Soleil (Golfe-Juan), 544
Plage Gazagnaire (Cannes), 525
Plage Passable (St-Jean-Cap-Ferrat), 579
Plages de Cros-de-Cagnes, 553
Plateau de l'Atalaye (Biarritz), 658
Pointe du Hoc, 300
Pointe Helbronner, 457
Pointe St-Martin, 657
Poitiers, 665–669
Poitiers l'Eté, 666
Police, 74
Pont-Audemer, 282
Pont-Aven, 321–323
Pont du Gard (Nîmes), 604–605
Pont St-Bénézet (Avignon), 469–470
Port de Goulphar, 325
Port des Pêcheurs (Biarritz), 658
Porte d'Arroux (Autun), 393
Porte d'Auguste (Nîmes), 604
Porte du Figuier (Rocamadour), 702
Porte St-André (Autun), 393
Port Grimaud, 517–518
Post-Impressionism, 19
Post offices, 73
Poussin, Nicolas, 17, 152, 220, 276, 555, 612
Presbytère de l'Eglise St-Michel (Bordeaux), 681

Prieuré St-Mauritius (Senlis), 223
Primatiale St-Jean (Lyon), 408, 410
Prix de l'Arc de Triomphe (Paris), 38
Prix Diane-Hermès (Chantilly), 36
Prix du Jockey Club (Chantilly), 36
Promenade des Anglais (Nice), 565
Promenade des Remparts (Angoulême), 677–678
Promenade du Bord de Mer (Biarritz), 657
Promenade du Peyrou (Montpellier), 611
Promenade Maurice-Rouvier (Beaulieu-sur-Mer), 582
Proust, Marcel, 202–203, 432
  Cabourg, 296
Provence, 3, 31, 464–512
Public Information Library (Paris), 147
Puy-de-Dôme, 718
Pyramide du Cirque Romain (Vienne), 426

Quiberon, 325
Quimper, 317–320

Rail passes, 60–61
Réciproque (Paris), 178
Regions of France, 27–32
Reims, 338–345
Relais & Châteaux, 63–64
Rembrandt, 160, 250, 359, 489, 654
Rémy-Martin (Cognac), 675
Renaissance architecture, 23–24
Renaissance art, 16–17
Renoir, Pierre-Auguste, 18, 151, 157, 162, 359, 552, 724
  Musée Renoir & Les Collettes, 553
Restaurants, 67–68
  best, 13–14
Restrooms, 74
Revard, 441
Rhone Valley, 30–31, 406–431
Ribeauvillé, 368–369
Riquewihr, 369–370
Roanne, 421–423
Rocamadour, 701–704
Rocher de la Vierge (Biarritz), 658
Rodin, Auguste, 18–19, 168, 200, 218, 259, 384, 417, 442, 566, 707
  Musée National Auguste Rodin (Paris), 167
Rodolphe Menudier (Paris), 181
Roissy/Charles de Gaulle (Paris), 87, 90
  accommodations near, 118
Romanesque art, 15–16
Romanesque churches, 21
Romans (ruins and antiquities), 15
  Aix-en-Provence, 490–491
  Arles, 481–483
  Autun, 392
  Clermont-Ferrand, 717–718
  La Turbie, 585
  Lyon, 411
  Narbonne, 617
  Nîmes, 604
  Orange, 466
  Paris, 152, 162, 164
  Périgueux, 693–695
  St-Rémy-de-Provence, 478
  Vienne, 426
Roman Theater (Vienne), 426
Romantic art, 17–18
Roquebrune-Cap-Martin, 597–600
Rosebud (Paris), 191
Rosheim, 366
Rouen, 272–282
Rouffach, 372
Route de Champagne, 341, 345
Route de la Croix, 452
Route des Abbayes, 276
Route des Crêtes (Crest Road), 6, 354, 377
Route des Grandes Alpes, 6, 434
Route du Vin (Wine Road), 365–372
Routes du Champagne, 341
Royal Chapel (Versailles), 196
Royal Portal (Chartres), 200
Rubens, Peter Paul, 160, 171, 220, 276, 293, 317, 359, 380, 412, 612, 654, 682
Rue des Rosiers (Paris), 159
Rue du Gros-Horloge (Rouen), 278
Rue Grande (St-Paul-de-Vence), 556
Ruines de Glanum (St-Rémy-de-Provence), 478

Saché, 259
Sacré-Coeur, Eglise de (Beaulieu-sur-Mer), 582
Safety, 49, 74
St-Aignan (Orléans), 228–229
St-Andoche, Basilique (Saulieu), 405
St-André, Cathédrale (Bordeaux), 680
St-Apollinaire, Cathédrale (Valence), 428
St-Benoît, Eglise (Castres), 629
St-Corentin, Cathédrale (Quimper), 317
St-Denis (Paris), 170
Ste-Catherine, Eglise (Honfleur), 282
Ste-Cécile, Cathédrale (Albi), 630–631
Ste-Chapelle (Paris), 155
Ste-Croix, Cathédrale (Orléans), 228
Ste-Foy, Eglise (Sélestat), 368
Ste-Madeleine, Basilique (Vézelay), 390
Ste-Marguerite, Eglise (Roquebrune), 598
Ste-Marie, Cathédrale (Bayonne), 653–654
Ste-Marie-Majeure, Cathédrale (Toulon), 508
Ste-Mère-Eglise, 300
St-Emilion, 689–691
St-Etienne, Cathédrale
  Auxerre, 387
  Bourges, 710
  Cahors, 705
  Limoges, 724
  Toulouse, 637
St-Etienne, Eglise (Beaugency), 234
St-Etienne-de-la-Cité, Eglise (Périgueux), 694
St-Front, Cathédrale (Périgueux), 694
St-Gatien, Cathédrale (Tours), 250
St-George, Eglise (Sélestat), 368
St-Germain-des-Prés (Paris), 165–166
St-Guilhem Music Season, 38
St-Jean, Cathédrale (Perpignan), 621
St-Jean-Baptiste, Eglise (St-Jean-de-Luz), 662
St-Jean-Cap-Ferrat, 578–581
St-Jean-de-Luz, 661–664

St-Julien-sous-Montmelas, 419, 420
St-Just, Cathédrale (Narbonne), 616
St-Lazare, Cathédrale (Autun), 393
St-Lazare, Eglise (Avallon), 391
St-Léger, Eglise (Cognac), 675
St-Maclou, Eglise (Rouen), 274, 281
St-Malo, 305–310
St-Martin, Basilique (Cap-Martin), 599
St-Martin, Eglise
- Biarritz, 657
- Colmar, 374

St-Maurice, Cathédrale
- Angers, 269
- Vienne, 426

St-Michel, Basilique (Bordeaux), 682
St-Michel, Eglise (Cordes-sur-Ciel), 633
St-Michel-des-Lions, Eglise (Limoges), 724
St-Nazaire, Basilique (Carcassonne), 625
St-Ouen, Eglise (Rouen), 274–275, 281
St-Paul, Eglise (Lyon), 410
St-Paul-de-Vence, 555–558
St-Paul-Serge, Basilique (Narbonne), 617
St-Pierre, Cathédrale
- Angoulême, 677
- Montpellier, 612
- Nantes, 329
- Poitiers, 666

St-Pierre, Eglise (Vienne), 426
St-Pierre la Mer, 615
St-Rémi, Basilique (Reims), 338–339
St-Rémi, Eglise (Domrémy-la-Pucelle), 383
St-Rémy-de-Provence, 477–480
St-Sacerdos, Cathédrale (Sarlat-la-Canéda), 699
St-Sauveur, Basilique
- Dinan, 315
- Rocamadour, 702

St-Sauveur, Cathédrale (Aix-en-Provence), 493
St-Sernin, Basilique (Toulouse), 637
St-Seurin, Basilique (Bordeaux), 682
St-Sulpice (Paris), 166
St-Thomas, Eglise (Strasbourg), 358
St-Tropez, 6, 513–522
- accommodations, 518–520
- beaches, 514, 516
- exploring, 517–518
- nightlife, 521–522
- outdoor pursuits, 516
- restaurants, 520–521
- shopping, 516–517
- traveling to, 514
- visitor information, 514

St-Trophime, Eglise (Arles), 482–483
St-Victor, Basilique (Marseille), 500
St-Vincent, Cathédrale (St-Malo), 306
St-Vincent, Eglise (Les Baux), 488
Salle de Reddition (Reims), 340
Salle Pleyel (Paris), 182–183
Salles Arbuissonnas, Eglise de, 420
Salles-en-Beaujolais, 419, 420
Salon International de Prêt-à-Porter (Paris), 35
Sand, George, Le Domaine de (Nohant), 713
Sanz-Sans (Paris), 189
Saracen Tower (Les Baux), 488
Sarlat-la-Canéda, 699
Saulieu, 405
Saumur, 265–268
Scenic drives. *See* Driving tours
Scuba diving, 546, 568
Seasons, 34
Sélestat, 367–368
Semaines Musicales du Mont-Blanc, 456
Senior travel, 51–52
Senlis, 222–224
Sentier du Plateau St-Michel (Beaulieu-sur-Mer), 582
Sentier Touristique (Cap-Martin), 599
The Sewers of Paris (Les Egouts), 172–173
Shakespeare and Company (Paris), 175
Shipping your luggage, 42
Site Préhistorique de Regourdou, 698
Skiing, 5
- Chamonix-Mont Blanc, 455–457
- Courchevel 1850, 447
- Megève, 452
- Val d'Isère, 461

Slow Club (Paris), 186
Smoking, 74
Snowboarding, 448
Société Duboscq (St-Estephe), 689
The Sorbonne (University of Paris), 163, 164
Soufflenheim (Strasbourg), 359
Sous-Bock Tavern (Paris), 189
Spectacles Medievaux (Carcassonne), 624
Strasbourg, 354–365
- accommodations, 360–362
- exploring, 356–359
- nightlife, 364–365
- restaurants, 362–364
- shopping, 359
- special events, 355–356
- traveling to, 354–355
- visitor information, 355

Suffren, Statue de (St-Tropez), 517
Surfing, Biarritz, 656–657
Sustainable tourism, 53–54

Taittinger (Reims), 9, 341
Talloires, 5–6, 439–440
Taschen (Paris), 175
Taxes, 74
Téléphérique-Grenoble-Bastille, 444
Telephones, 54, 74
Temple d'Auguste et de Livie (Vienne), 426
Tennis
- Cannes, 527
- Monaco, 588–589
- Nice, 568
- St-Tropez, 516
- tours, 59

Terraïo (Cagnes-sur-Mer), 554
Théâtre Antique
- Arles, 482
- Orange, 466

Théâtre des Champs-Elysées (Paris), 183
Théâtre National du Capitole (Toulouse), 636, 642
Théâtre Romain (Vienne), 426
Théâtres Romains (Lyon), 411
Thermes d'Aix-les-Bains, 441
Thermes de Cluny (Musée National du Moyen Age; Paris), 164
Thermes Marins de Monte-Carlo (Monaco), 588
Tignes, 461

Time zone, 74
Tipping, 74–75
Toro de Fuego (St-Jean-de-Luz), 661
Toulon, 508–510
Toulouse, 634–643
Toulouse-Lautrec, Henri de, 19, 184, 630, 638
  Musée Toulouse-Lautrec (Albi), 8, 631
Tour de Constance (Aigues-Mortes), 608
Tour de Dolder (Riquewihr), 369
Tour de France, 37
Tour de la Chaîne (La Rochelle), 671
Tour de la Lanterne (La Rochelle), 671
Tour de l'Horloge (Dinan), 315
Tour des Bouchers (Ribeauvillé), 369
Tour des Minimes (Amboise), 243
Tour de Vésone (Périgueux), 693
Tour d'Evraud (Fontevraud-l'Abbaye), 264
Tour et Crypt de l'Abbaye de Jouarre, 334
Tour Magne (Nîmes), 604
Tour Montparnasse (Paris), 168
Tour Pey-Berland (Bordeaux), 680–681
Tour Philippe le Bel (Ville-nueve-lez-Avignon), 473
Tours, 248–254
Tour St-Fermin (Beaugency), 234
Tour St-Nicolas (La Rochelle), 671
Tour Sarrazin (Les Baux), 488
Train Touristique de Nice, 565
Train travel, 43, 59–61
Tranchée des Baïonettes (Verdun), 384
Transportation, 59–63
Traveler's checks, 45–47
Traveling to France, 39–44
Travel insurance, 47–48
Trench of Bayonets (Verdun), 384
Trésor de l'Eglise (St-Paul-de-Vence), 556
Trip-cancellation insurance, 47
Trophée des Alps (La Turbie), 585
Trouville, 289–291
Tumulus St-Michel (Carnac), 323

Un Eté à Bourges, 710
Unicorn Tapestries (Paris), 164
University of Paris (the Sorbonne), 163, 164
Upper Basilica (Lourdes), 646
Ussé, 264
Utah Beach, 300
Utrillo, Maurice, 157, 162, 183, 380, 518, 558, 631

Val d'Isère, 459–463
Valençay, 240–241
Valence, 428–429
Vallauris, 543–545
Vallée de la Tarantaise, 463
Vallée d'Isère, 463
Vallon-Pont-d'Arc, 429
Vals-les-Bains, 430–431
Van Cleef & Arpels (Paris), 179
Van Gogh, Vincent, 19, 151, 162, 470, 477, 478, 480, 482, 488
VAT (value-added tax), 74
Vaux-le-Vicomte, 210–211
Vence, 558–562
Verdun, 383–385
Verne, Jules, 348
  L'Imaginaire Jules-Verne (Amiens), 349
  Musée Jules Verne de Nantes, 330
Verrerie de Biot, 542
Versailles, 192–199
Veuve Amiot (Saumur), 266
Veuve Clicquot-Ponsardin (Reims), 341
Vézelay, 389–391
Viaduc des Arts (Paris), 175
Vichy, 714–717
Vienne, 425–427
Vieux Lyon, 408
Villa Ephrussi de Rothschild (Musée Ile-de-France; St-Jean-Cap-Ferrat), 579
Village St-Paul (Paris), 174
Village Voice Bookshop (Paris), 175
Villa Les Cèdres (St-Jean-Cap-Ferrat), 579
Villa Mauresque (St-Jean-Cap-Ferrat), 579
Villa Musée Fragonard (Grasse), 540
Villa Namouna (Beaulieu-sur-Mer), 582
Villandry, 256–257
Villas rentals, 64
Ville des Congrès (Evian), 432
Ville et Campagne (Strasbourg), 359
Villefranche-sur-Mer, 577–578
Villefranche-sur-Saône, 419, 420
Villenueve-lez-Avignon, 471, 473
Villequier, 277
Villié-Morgon, 421
Vineyards and wineries
  Beaujolais Country, 419–421
  best, 9–10
  Bordeaux, 687–691
  Burgundy, 83–86, 393–394
  Cahors, 705
  champagne cellars of Reims, 340–341
  Colmar, 373–374
  Route du Vin (Wine Road), 365–372
  Saumur, 266
Virgin Megastore (Paris), 181
Visitor information, 32–33

Wagon de l'Armistice (Wagon du Maréchal-Foch; Compiègne), 225–226
Walt Disney Studios (Disneyland Paris), 213
Wangen, 366
Water, drinking, 75
Water-skiing, Juan-les-Pins, 546
Watteau, Antoine, 17, 160, 202, 220, 337, 359, 722
Weather, 34
Websites, 33
Western Union, 72
W. H. Smith France (Paris), 175
Wi-Fi access, 55
Willi's Wine Bar (Paris), 188
Wineries and vineyards. *See* Vineyards and wineries
Wine Road (Route du Vin), 365–372
Wines and wine stores
  Angers, 271
  Beaune, 395
  Bordeaux, 683
  Caen, 293
  Chinon, 261
  Epernay, 351–352
  Orléans, 230
  Paris, 181
  Reims, 341–342
  Saumur, 266
  Vézelay, 390

Women travelers, 52
World War I
American cemetery (Cimetière de Belleau), 336
Bois de Belleau (Belleau Wood), 336
Verdun battlefields, 384
Wagon de l'Armistice (Wagon du Maréchal-Foch; Compiègne), 225–226
World War II, 157, 164
Commonwealth Cemetery (Bayeux), 297
D-Day beaches, 4–5, 298–300
Memorial des Martyrs Français de la Déportation (Paris), 155
Memorial du Débarquement en Provence (Toulon), 509
Musée Memorial de la Bataille de Normandie (Bayeux), 297
Normandy American Cemetery (Omaha Beach), 300

Yves Brayer Museum (Les Baux), 488

Zola, Emile, 1, 162, 165